The Bedford Anthology of
World Literature
The Eighteenth Century, 1650–1800

Book 4

The Bedford Anthology of
World Literature
The Eighteenth Century, 1650–1800

EDITED BY

Paul Davis
Gary Harrison
David M. Johnson
Patricia Clark Smith
John F. Crawford

THE UNIVERSITY OF NEW MEXICO

BEDFORD / ST. MARTIN'S   Boston ◆ New York

For Bedford/St. Martin's

Executive Editor: Alanya Harter
Associate Developmental Editor: Joshua Levy
Senior Production Editor: Karen S. Baart
Senior Production Supervisor: Catherine Hetmansky
Marketing Manager: Jenna Bookin Barry
Editorial Assistant: Jeffrey Voccola
Production Assistants: Courtney Jossart, Kerri Cardone
Copyeditor: Melissa Cook
Map Coordinator: Tina Samaha
Text and Cover Design: Anna George
Cover Art: The Kronos Collections, photograph by Peter Johnson; photograph © 1984, The Metropolitan Museum of Art
Composition: Stratford Publishing Services, Inc.
Printing and Binding: R. R. Donnelley & Sons Company

President: Joan E. Feinberg
Editorial Director: Denise B. Wydra
Editor in Chief: Karen S. Henry
Director of Marketing: Karen Melton
Director of Editing, Design, and Production: Marcia Cohen
Managing Editor: Elizabeth M. Schaaf

Library of Congress Control Number: 2002112262

11 10 9
i h g f

For information, write: Bedford/St. Martin's, 75 Arlington Street, Boston, MA 02116 (617-399-4000)

ISBN-10: 0–312–40263–5
ISBN-13: 978–0–312–40263–1

Acknowledgments

Matsuo Bashō, "The Narrow Road through the Backcountry." Adapted from Bashō's *Backcountry Trails* (*oku-no hosomichi*), translated by Richard Bodner and the Dragon Mountain Translation Society, with "The Narrow Road through the Backcountry," expanded notes, translator's commentary, and alternative versions of the poems, published by Land of Enchantment Poetry Theater (a division of Mapa Systems, University P. O. Box 9900, Las Vegas, NM 87701, 505-425-3430). Notes have been abridged for this anthology.

Acknowledgments and copyrights are continued at the back of the book on pages 911–12, which constitute an extension of the copyright page. It is a violation of the law to reproduce these selections by any means whatsoever without the written permission of the copyright holder.

PREFACE

∾ *The Bedford Anthology of World Literature* has a story behind it. In 1985, a group of us received a grant from the National Endowment for the Humanities. Our task: to develop and team teach a new kind of literature course—one that drew from the rich literary traditions of Asia, India, the Middle East, and the Americas as well as from the masterpieces of the Western world. We learned so much from that experience—from our students and from each other—that we applied those lessons to an anthology published in 1995, *Western Literature in a World Context.*

In that first edition of our anthology, our goal was to add works that truly represented *world* literature to the list of Western classics and to place great literary works in their historical and cultural contexts. We've kept that focus in the newly titled *Bedford Anthology*—but we've also drastically reshaped, redesigned, and reimagined it to make it the book you hold today. We talked to hundreds of instructors and students in an effort to identify and confirm what they considered challenging about the world literature course. The design and content of these pages represent our attempt to meet these challenges.

The study and teaching of world literature have changed significantly in the past twenty to thirty years. Formerly, most world literature courses consisted of masterpieces of Western literature, while the literary traditions of Asia, Africa, and Latin America were virtually ignored. The movement to broaden the canon to more accurately represent our world—and to better represent oral and marginalized traditions in the West—has greatly increased the number of texts taught in world literature courses today. Although the specifics remain controversial, nearly all teachers of literature are committed to the ongoing revaluation and expansion of the canon.

The last few decades have also seen instructors reconsidering the traditional methods of teaching world literature. In the past, most world literature courses were designed along formalistic or generic principles. But the expanded canon has complicated both of these approaches. There are no developed criteria for defining masterworks in such formerly ignored genres as letters and diaries or for unfamiliar forms from non-Western cultures, and we are frequently reminded that traditional approaches sometimes impose inappropriate Eurocentric perspectives on such works. As content and methodology for the course have been evolving, recent critical theory has reawakened interest in literature's historical and cultural contexts. All of these factors have both complicated and enriched the study of world literature. With this multivolume literature anthology, we don't claim to be presenting the definitive new canon of world literature or the last word on how to teach it. We have, however, tried to open new perspectives and possibilities for both students and teachers.

One anthology — six individual books. *The Bedford Anthology of World Literature* is now split into six separate books that correspond to the six time periods most commonly taught. These books are available in two packages: Books 1–3 and Books 4–6. Our motivation for changing the packaging is twofold and grows out of the extensive market research we did before shaping the development plan for the book. In our research, instructors from around the country confirmed that students just don't want to cart around a 2,500-page book — who would? Many also said that they focus on ancient literatures in the first semester of the course and on the twentieth

The Bedford Anthology of World Literature has been dynamically reimagined, redesigned, and restructured. We've added a second color, four hundred images, three hundred pronunciation guides, forty maps, six comparative time lines — and much more.

Portuguese Caravels Leaving to Explore the World, 1773   *The eighteenth century was a time of unprecedented global communication — political, social, economic, and literary. These painted blue tiles are found on the walls of the town of Paço de Arcos, near Lisbon, Portugal. (The Art Archive / Dagli Orti.)*

The Eighteenth Century

1650 - 1800

century in the second semester. In addition, many instructors teach an introduction to world literature that is tailored specifically to the needs of their students and their institution and thus want a text that can be adapted to *many* courses.

We believe that the extensive changes we've made to *The Bedford Anthology of World Literature*—breaking the anthology into six books rather than only two, creating a new two-color design, increasing the trim size, and adding maps, illustrations, numerous pedagogical features, an expanded instructor's manual, and a new companion Web site—will make the formidable task of teaching and taking a world literature course both manageable and pleasurable.

An expanded canon for the twenty-first century. In each of the six books of *The Bedford Anthology,* you'll find a superb collection of complete longer works, plays, prose, and poems—the best literature available in English or English translation. Five of the books are organized geographically and then by author in order of birth date. The exception to this rule is Book 6, which, reflecting our increasingly global identities, is organized by author without larger geographical groupings.

Aphra Behn's Oroonoko *is one of the texts we include in its entirety—highlighting important issues of race, gender, and slavery in the eighteenth century.*

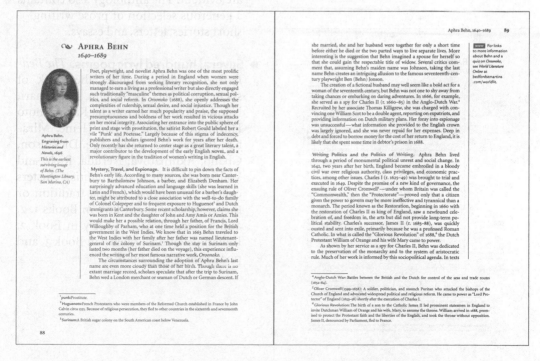

APHRA BEHN
1640–1689

Aphra Behn. Engraving from Histories and Novels, *1696. This is the earliest surviving image of Behn. (The Huntington Library, San Marino, CA)*

Poet, playwright, and novelist Aphra Behn was one of the most prolific writers of her time. During a period in England when women were strongly discouraged from seeking literary recognition, she not only managed to earn a living as a professional writer but also directly engaged such traditionally "masculine" themes as political corruption, sexual politics, and social reform. In *Oroonoko* (1688), she openly addresses the complexities of rulership, sexual desire, and social injustice. Though her talent as a writer earned her much popularity and praise, the supposed presumptuousness and boldness of her work resulted in vicious attacks on her moral integrity. Associating her entrance into the public sphere of print and stage with prostitution, the satirist Robert Gould labeled her a vile "Punk¹ and Poetesse." Largely because of this stigma of indecency, publishers and scholars ignored Behn's work for years after her death. Only recently has she returned to center stage as a great literary talent, a major contributor to the development of the early English NOVEL, and a revolutionary figure in the tradition of women's writing in English.

Mystery, Travel, and Espionage. It is difficult to pin down the facts of Behn's early life. According to many sources, she was born near Canterbury to Bartholomew Johnson, a barber, and Elizabeth Denham. Her surprisingly advanced education and language skills (she was learned in Latin and French), which would have been unusual for a barber's daughter, might be attributed to a close association with the well-to-do family of Colonel Colepeper and to frequent exposure to Huguenot² and Dutch immigrants in Canterbury. Some recent scholarship, however, claims she was born in Kent and the daughter of John and Amy Amis or Amies. This would make her a possible relation, through her father, of Francis, Lord Willoughby of Parham, who at one time held a position for the British government in the West Indies. We know that in 1663 Behn traveled to the West Indies with her family after her father was named lieutenant-general of the colony of Surinam.³ Though the stay in Surinam only lasted two months (her father died on the voyage), this experience influenced the writing of her most famous narrative work, *Oroonoko.*

The circumstances surrounding the adoption of Aphra Behn's last name are even more cloudy than those of her birth. Though there is no extant marriage record, scholars speculate that after the trip to Surinam, Behn wed a London merchant or seaman of Dutch or German descent. If

---
¹ punk: Prostitute.
² Huguenot: French Protestants who were members of the Reformed Church established in France by John Calvin circa 1555. Because of religious persecution, they fled to other countries in the sixteenth and seventeenth centuries.
³ Surinam: A British sugar colony on the South American coast below Venezuela.

88

---

she married, she and her husband were together for only a short time before either he died or the two parted ways to live separate lives. More interesting is the suggestion that Behn imagined a spouse for herself so that she could gain the respectable title of widow. Several critics comment that, assuming Behn's maiden name was Johnson, taking the last name Behn creates an intriguing allusion to the famous seventeenth-century playwright Ben (Behn) Jonson.

The creation of a fictional husband may well seem like a bold act for a woman of the seventeenth century, but Behn was not one to shy away from taking chances or embarking on daring adventures. In 1666, for example, she served as a spy for Charles II (r. 1660–85) in the Anglo-Dutch War.⁴ Recruited by her associate Thomas Killigrew, she was charged with convincing one William Scot to be a double agent, reporting on expatriots, and providing information on Dutch military plans. Her foray into espionage was unsuccessful—what information she provided to the English crown was largely ignored, and she was never repaid for her expenses. Deep in debt and forced to borrow money for the cost of her return to England, it is likely that she spent some time in debtor's prison in 1688.

Writing Politics and the Politics of Writing. Aphra Behn lived through a period of monumental political unrest and social change. In 1642, two years after her birth, England became embroiled in a bloody civil war over religious authority, class privileges, and economic practices, among other issues. Charles I (r. 1625–49) was brought to trial and executed in 1649. Despite the promise of a new kind of governance, the ensuing rule of Oliver Cromwell⁵—under whom Britain was called the "Commonwealth," then the "Protectorate"—proved only that a citizen given the power to govern may be more ineffective and tyrannical than a monarch. The period known as the Restoration, beginning in 1660 with the restoration of Charles II as king of England, saw a newfound celebration of, and freedom in, the arts but did not provide long-term political stability. Charles's successor, James II (r. 1685–88), was quickly ousted and sent into exile, primarily because he was a professed Roman Catholic. In what is called the "Glorious Revolution" of 1688,⁶ the Dutch Protestant William of Orange and his wife Mary came to power.

As shown by her service as a spy for Charles II, Behn was dedicated to the preservation of the monarchy and to the system of aristocratic rule. Much of her work is informed by this sociopolitical agenda. In texts

---
⁴ Anglo-Dutch War: Battles between the British and the Dutch for control of the seas and trade routes (1652–84).
⁵ Oliver Cromwell (1599–1658): A soldier, politician, and staunch Puritan who attacked the bishops of the Church of England and advocated widespread political and religious reform. He came to power as "Lord Protector" of England (1653–58) shortly after the execution of Charles I.
⁶ Glorious Revolution: The birth of a son to the Catholic James II led prominent statesmen in England to invite Dutchman William of Orange and his wife, Mary, to assume the throne. William arrived in 1688, promised to protect the Protestant faith and the liberties of the English, and took the throne without opposition. James II, denounced by Parliament, fled to France.

www For links to more information about Behn and a quiz on *Oroonoko,* see *World Literature Online* at bedfordstmartins.com/worldlit.

Aphra Behn, 1640–1689   89

We've tried to assemble a broad selection of the world's literatures. We've updated our selection of European texts; we have also included American writers who have had significant contact with world culture and who have influenced or defined who we are as Americans. And of course we have added many works from non-Western traditions, both frequently anthologized pieces and works unique to this anthology, including texts from Mesopotamia, Egypt, Israel, India, Persia, China, Japan, Arab countries of the Middle East, Africa, native America, Latin America, and the Caribbean.

Over thirty-five complete, longer works. These include Homer's *Odyssey* and *The Epic of Gilgamesh* in Book 1, Dante's *Inferno* and Kalidasa's *Shakuntala* in Book 2, Marlowe's *Doctor Faustus* and Shakespeare's *The Tempest* in Book 3, Bashō's *Narrow Road through the Backcountry* in Book 4, Dostoevsky's *Notes from Underground* in Book 5, and Achebe's *Things Fall Apart* in Book 6.

When a work is too long to be produced in its entirety, we've presented carefully edited selections from it; examples include the Rig Veda, *Ramayana*, *Mahabharata*, Qur'an, *The Song of Roland*, Ibn Hazm's *The Dove's Necklace*, *The Book of Margery Kempe*, Attar's *Conference of the Birds*, Cervantes's *Don Quixote*, Swift's *Gulliver's Travels*, Equiano's *Interesting Narrative*, Benjamin Franklin's *Autobiography*, Chikamatsu's *The Love Suicides at Amijima*, and Cao Xueqin's *The Story of the Stone*. In most cases the excerpts are not fragments but substantial selections wherein the structure and themes of the whole work are evident. The anthology also contains a generous selection of prose writing—short stories, letters, and essays.

Several hundred lyric poems. *The Bedford Anthology* includes the work of such fine poets as Sappho, Bhartrhari, Nezahualcoyotl, Petrarch, Kakinomoto Hitomaro, Rumi, Li Bai, Heine, Mirabai, Ramprasad, Baudelaire, Dickinson, Ghalib, Akhmatova, Neruda, Rich, and Walcott. Unique *In the Tradition* clusters collect poems that share a tradition or theme: poetry about love in Books 1, 2, and 3, Tang dynasty poetry in Book 2, Indian devotional poetry in Book 3, and poetry on war in Book 6.

∾ RAMPRASAD SEN
1718–1775

BAHK-tee

SHAHK-tee; KAH-lee
RAHM-pruh-sahd

The intensely religious village life of India produced not only storytellers—whose primary purpose was transmitting the stories of gods, goddesses, heroes, and heroines—but also poets who expressed ordinary people's spiritual longing for God. Emotional worship or surrender to God in Hinduism is called **bhakti**, a term that has its origins in the Upanishads. Bhakti became a religious movement in India during the religious reforms of the eighth, ninth, and tenth centuries. A particular version of bhakti was devoted to feminine divinity; in India there had been a long history of worshiping the greatgoddess **Shakti**[1]—also known as **Kali** and **Durga**—but a resurgence of her worship, led by the poet **Ramprasad Sen**, took place in Bengal during the eighteenth century. Like medieval Christian poets devoted to the Virgin Mother, Bengal poets of this time favored the feminine dimension of God, which seemed to invite a personal relationship, an opportunity for conversation, and expressions of sadness and longing.

Ramprasad's poems, primarily songs to Kali, were extremely popular at the end of the eighteenth century when Bengal was in a time of darkness and despair. The region had been under Muslim rule for about five hundred years when the British defeated the Mughal army in the Battle of Plassey in 1757.[3] Robber barons controlled large parts of Bengal, and Kali was their patron deity. Regional kings promoted Kali worship by supporting court poets who composed and sang songs to the goddess. The songs became part of an extremely precarious village life. Bengal is a region of extremes, feast or famine, due to unpredictable rains. Some years bring little rain or droughts, while others have heavy rain and flooding. Occasionally there are years when just the right amount of rain falls at the appropriate times; these times are thought to be blessed by Kali.

Ramprasad's simple lyricism and familiar images touched a broad range of listeners; his songs appealed to scholars and peasants alike. His poetic skills influenced succeeding generations of Indian poets. Rabindranath Tagore,[4] the most famous Bengali writer of the late nineteenth cen-

www For links to more information about Ramprasad and a quiz on his poetry, see *World Literature Online* at bedfordstmartins.com/worldlit.

[1] **Shakti:** Shakti is the collective name for the consort of Shiva who has several names. **Shakti** is the feminine dynamic energy by which God creates, preserves, and dissolves the world. **Kali** is usually portrayed as terrifying: blue-black, three-eyed, and four-armed, with a necklace of human heads and a girdle of severed hands. **Durga,** "the unfathomable one," is one of the oldest versions of the Great Mother: fair complexioned and riding a lion, she releases humans from rebirth with her touch.
[2] **Bengal:** A region in the northeast Indian peninsula, now divided between India and Bangladesh.
[3] **Battle of Plassey:** Plassey is a village in West Bengal state where the British defeated the Bengal army in 1757, leading to Britain's control of northeast India.
[4] **Rabindranath Tagore** (1861–1941): A native of Bengal anxious to preserve the cultural richness of traditional village life while at the same time bridging the philosophical and literary gap between East and West. (See Book 5.)

Literature in context. In addition to individual authors presented in chronological order, *The Bedford Anthology* features two types of cross-cultural literary groupings. In the more than thirty *In the World* clusters, five to six in each book, writings around a single theme — such as the history of religions, science, love, human rights, women's rights, colonialism, the meeting of East and West, imperialism, and existentialism — and from different countries and cultural traditions are presented side by side, helping students understand that people of every culture have had their public gods, heroes, and revolutions, their private loves, lives, and losses. Titles include "Changing Gods: From Religion to Philosophy," in Book 1; "Muslim and Christian at War," in Book 2; "Humanism, Learning, and Education" in Book 3; "Love, Marriage, and the Education of Women," in Book 4; "Emancipation," in Book 5; and "Imagining Africa," in Book 6. The second type of grouping, *In the Tradition,* presents poetry on love in Books 1, 2, and 3 and literature on war and American multiculturalism in Book 6. These clusters gather together such widely disparate writers as Hammurabi, Heraclitus, Marcus Aurelius, Ibn Battuta, Marco Polo, Sei Shonagon, Galileo, Bartolomé de las Casas, Mary Wollstonecraft, Mary Astell, Shen Fu, Karl Marx, Elizabeth Cady Stanton, Swami Vivekananda, Aimé Césaire, and Bharati Mukherjee.

In the World clusters bring together texts from different literary traditions and help students make thematic connections and comparisons.

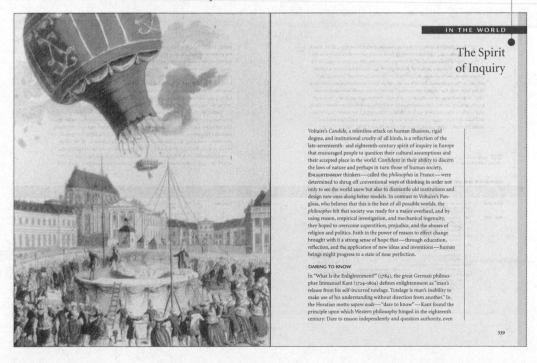

IN THE WORLD

The Spirit of Inquiry

Voltaire's *Candide*, a relentless attack on human illusions, rigid dogma, and institutional cruelty of all kinds, is a reflection of the late-seventeenth- and eighteenth-century spirit of inquiry in Europe that encouraged people to question their cultural assumptions and their accepted place in the world. Confident in their ability to discern the laws of nature and perhaps in turn those of human society, ENLIGHTENMENT thinkers — called the *philosophes* in France — were determined to shrug off conventional ways of thinking in order not only to see the world anew but also to dismantle old institutions and design new ones along better models. In contrast to Voltaire's Pangloss, who believes that this is the best of all possible worlds, the *philosophes* felt that society was ready for a major overhaul, and by using reason, empirical investigation, and mechanical ingenuity, they hoped to overcome superstition, prejudice, and the abuses of religion and politics. Faith in the power of reason to effect change brought with it a strong sense of hope that — through education, reflection, and the application of new ideas and inventions — human beings might progress to a state of near perfection.

DARING TO KNOW

In "What Is the Enlightenment?" (1784), the great German philosopher Immanuel Kant (1724–1804) defines enlightenment as "man's release from his self-incurred tutelage. Tutelage is man's inability to make use of his understanding without direction from another." In the Horatian motto *sapere aude* — "dare to know" — Kant found the principle upon which Western philosophy hinged in the eighteenth century: Dare to reason independently and question authority, even

339

Helping students and teachers navigate the wide world of literature. The hundreds of instructors we talked to before embarking on *The Bedford Anthology* shared with us their concerns about teaching an introduction to world literature course, no matter what their individual agendas were. One concern was the sheer difficulty for students of reading literature that not only spans the period from the beginning of recorded literatures to the present but also hails from vastly different cultures and historical moments. Another was the fact that no one instructor is an expert in *all* of world literature. We've put together *The Bedford Anthology of World Literature* with these factors in mind and hope that the help we offer both around and with the selected texts goes a long way toward bringing clarity to the abundance and variety of world writings.

Helping students understand the where and when of the literature in the anthology. Each book of *The Bedford Anthology* opens with an extended overview of its time period as well as with a **comparative time line** that lists what happened, where, and when in three overarching categories: history and politics; literature; and science, culture, and technology. An interactive version of each time line serves as

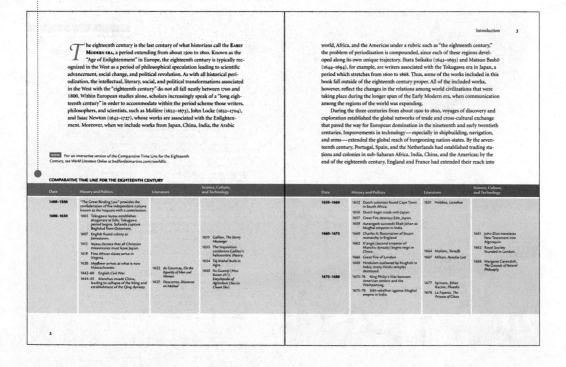

the portal to the online support offered on our Book Companion Site. In addition, **"Time and Place" boxes** in the introductions to the different geographical groupings of writers further orient students in the era and culture connected with the literature they're reading by spotlighting something interesting and specific about a certain place and time.

Maps included throughout the anthology show students where in the world various literatures came from. Besides the maps that open each geographical section and show countries in relation to the larger world at a given time in history, we've supplied maps that illustrate the shifting of national boundaries; industrial growth; the effects of conquest, conquerors, and colonialism; and the travels of Odysseus, Ibn Battuta, and Bashō.

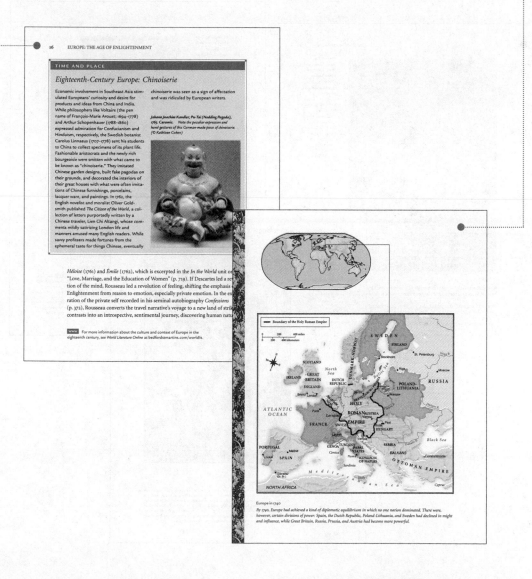

16   EUROPE: THE AGE OF ENLIGHTENMENT

TIME AND PLACE

Eighteenth-Century Europe: Chinoiserie

Economic involvement in Southeast Asia stimulated Europeans' curiosity and desire for products and ideas from China and India. While philosophers like Voltaire (the pen name of François-Marie Arouet; 1694–1778) and Arthur Schopenhauer (1788–1860) expressed admiration for Confucianism and Hinduism, respectively, the Swedish botanist Carolus Linnaeus (1707–1778) sent his students to China to collect specimens of its plant life. Fashionable aristocrats and the newly rich bourgeoisie were smitten with what came to be known as "chinoiserie." They imitated Chinese garden designs, built fake pagodas on their grounds, and decorated the interiors of their great houses with were often imitations of Chinese furnishings, porcelains, lacquer ware, and paintings. In 1762, the English novelist and moralist Oliver Goldsmith published *The Citizen of the World*, a collection of letters purportedly written by a Chinese traveler, Lien Chi Altangi, whose comments mildly satirizing London life and manners amused many English readers. While savvy profiteers made fortunes from the ephemeral taste for things Chinese, eventually

chinoiserie was seen as a sign of affectation and was ridiculed by European writers.

Johann Joachim Kandler, Pu-Tai (Nodding Pagoda), 1765. Ceramic. Note the peculiar expression and hand gestures of this German-made piece of chinoiserie. (© Kathleen Cohen)

Héloïse (1761) and *Émile* (1762), which is excerpted in the *In the World* unit on "Love, Marriage, and the Education of Women" (p. 719). If Descartes led a revolution of the mind, Rousseau led a revolution of feeling, shifting the emphasis of the Enlightenment from reason to emotion, especially private emotion. In the exploration of the private self recorded in his seminal autobiography *Confessions* (p. 372), Rousseau converts the travel narrative's voyage to a new land of striking contrasts into an introspective, sentimental journey, discovering human nature

WWW   For more information about the culture and context of Europe in the eighteenth century, see *World Literature Online* at bedfordstmartins.com/worldlit.

— Boundary of the Holy Roman Empire

Europe in 1740
By 1740, Europe had achieved a kind of diplomatic equilibrium in which no one nation dominated. There were, however, certain divisions of power: Spain, the Dutch Republic, Poland-Lithuania, and Sweden had declined in might and influence, while Great Britain, Russia, Prussia, and Austria had become more powerful.

The anthology's many illustrations — art, photographs, frontispieces, cartoons, and cultural artifacts — are meant to bring immediacy to literature that might otherwise feel spatially and temporally remote. A few examples are a photo of the Acropolis today juxtaposed with an artist's rendering of what it looked like newly built, a sketch of the first seven circles of Dante's hell, a scene from Hogarth's *Marriage à la Mode,* the ad Harriet Jacobs's owner ran for her capture and return, an editorial cartoon mocking Darwin's evolutionary theories, and a woodcut depicting Japanese boats setting out to greet Commodore Perry's warship in their harbor.

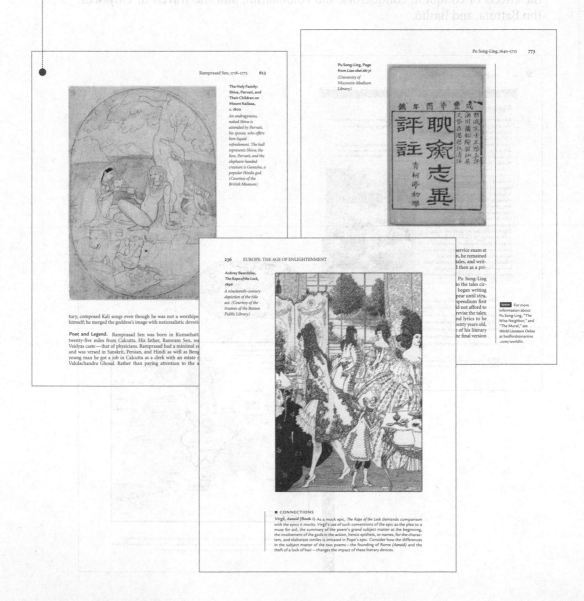

Ramprasad Sen, 1718–1775   **613**

The Holy Family: Shiva, Parvati, and Their Children on Mount Kailasa, c. 1800

An androgynous, naked Shiva is attended by Parvati, his spouse, who offers him liquid refreshment. The bull represents Shiva; the lions, Parvati; and the elephant-headed creature is Ganesha, a popular Hindu god. (Courtesy of the British Museum)

tury, composed Kali songs even though he was not a worshipe... himself; he merged the goddess's image with nationalistic devoti...

Poet and Legend. Ramprasad Sen was born in Kumarhatt... twenty-five miles from Calcutta. His father, Ramram Sen, wa... Vaidyas caste — that of physicians. Ramprasad had a minimal e... and was versed in Sanskrit, Persian, and Hindi as well as Beng... young man he got a job in Calcutta as a clerk with an estate ... Valulachandra Ghosal. Rather than paying attention to the a...

Pu Song-Ling, 1640–1715   **773**

Pu Song-Ling, Page from *Liao-zhai zhi-yi*
(University of Wisconsin–Madison Library)

service exam at ..., he remained ...tales, and writ-...d then as a pri-...

Pu Song-Ling ...to the tales cir-...began writing ...pear until 1679, ...mpendium first ...d not afford to ...evise the tales; ...nd lyrics to be ...enty years old, ...e of his literary ...he final version

www For more information about Pu Song-Ling, "The Wise Neighbor," and "The Mural," see *World Literature Online* at bedfordstmartins .com/worldlit.

236   EUROPE: THE AGE OF ENLIGHTENMENT

Aubrey Beardsley, The Rape of the Lock, 1896

A nineteenth-century depiction of the title act. (Courtesy of the trustees of the Boston Public Library)

■ CONNECTIONS

Virgil, *Aeneid* **(Book I).** As a mock epic, *The Rape of the Lock* demands comparison with the epics it mocks. Virgil's use of such conventions of the epic as the plea to a muse for aid, the summary of the poem's grand subject matter at the beginning, the involvement of the gods in the action, heroic epithets, or names, for the characters, and elaborate similes is imitated in Pope's epic. Consider how the differences in the subject matter of the two poems — the founding of Rome (*Aeneid*) and the theft of a lock of hair — changes the impact of these literary devices.

Practical and accessible editorial apparatus helps students understand what they read. Each author in the anthology is introduced by an informative and accessible literary and biographical discussion. The selections themselves are complemented with generous footnotes, marginal notes, cross-references, and critical quotations. Phonetic pronunciation guides are supplied in the margins of introductory material and before the selections for unfamiliar character and place names. Providing help with literary and historical vocabulary, bold-faced key terms throughout the text refer students to the comprehensive glossary at the end of each book.

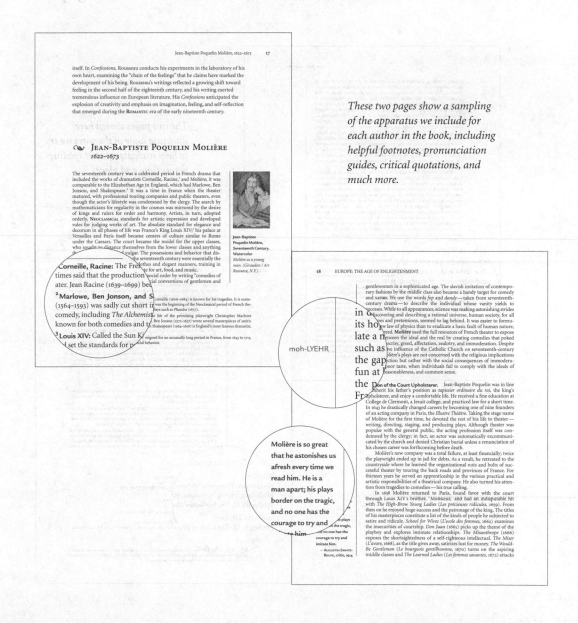

These two pages show a sampling of the apparatus we include for each author in the book, including helpful footnotes, pronunciation guides, critical quotations, and much more.

Jean-Baptiste Poquelin Molière, 1622–1673   17

itself. In *Confessions*, Rousseau conducts his experiments in the laboratory of his own heart, examining the "chain of the feelings" that he claims have marked the development of his being. Rousseau's writings reflected a growing shift toward feeling in the second half of the eighteenth century, and his writing exerted tremendous influence on European literature. His *Confessions* anticipated the explosion of creativity and emphasis on imagination, feeling, and self-reflection that emerged during the Romantic era of the early nineteenth century.

Jean-Baptiste Poquelin Molière
1622–1673

moh-LYEHR

The seventeenth century was a celebrated period in French drama that included the works of dramatists Corneille, Racine,[1] and Molière; it was comparable to the Elizabethan Age in England, which had Marlowe, Ben Jonson, and Shakespeare.[2] It was a time in France when the theater matured, with professional touring companies and public theaters, even though the actor's lifestyle was condemned by the clergy. The search by mathematicians for regularity in the cosmos was mirrored by the desire of kings and rulers for order and harmony. Artists, in turn, adopted orderly, Neoclassical standards for artistic expression and developed rules for judging works of art. The absolute standard for elegance and decorum in all phases of life was France's King Louis XIV;[3] his palace at Versailles and Paris itself became centers of culture similar to Rome under the Caesars. The court became the model for the upper classes, who sought to distance themselves from the lower classes and anything they considered vulgar. The possessions and behavior that distinguished the upper classes in the seventeenth century were essentially the prerogatives of birth: fine clothes and elegant manners, training in dancing and fencing, a taste for art, food, and music.

Jean-Baptiste Poquelin Molière, Seventeenth Century, Watercolor
Molière as a young man. (Giraudon / Art Resource, N.Y.)

Corneille, Racine: The French at times said that the production ... social order by writing "comedies of gentlemen and ...

[2] **Marlowe, Ben Jonson, and S**... Corneille (1606–1684) is known for his tragedies. It is somewhat ... (1564–1593) was sadly cut short in ... was the beginning of the Neoclassical period of French theater ... comedy, including *The Alchemist* ... life of the promising playwright Christopher Marlowe ... known for both comedies and tr... Ben Jonson (1572–1637) wrote several masterpieces of satiric ... Shakespeare (1564–1616) is England's most famous dramatist,

[3] **Louis XIV:** Called the Sun K... reigned for an unusually long period in France, from 1643 to 1715. ... and set the standards for p... ...social behavior.

18   EUROPE: THE AGE OF ENLIGHTENMENT

gentlewomen in a sophisticated age. The slavish imitation of contemporary fashions by the middle class also became a handy target for comedy and satire. We use the words *fop* and *dandy*—taken from seventeenth-century drama—to describe the individual whose vanity yields to excesses. While to all appearances, science was making astonishing strides in discovering and describing a rational universe, human society, for all its hopes and pretensions, seemed to lag behind. It was easier to formulate a new law of physics than to eradicate a basic human flaw, such as hypocrisy, greed, affectation, zealotry, and immoderation. Despite the gap between the ideal and the real by creating comedies that poked fun at hypocrisy, greed, affectation, zealotry, and immoderation. Despite the pervasive influence of the Catholic Church on seventeenth-century France, Molière's plays are not concerned with the religious implications of human action but rather with the social consequences of immoderation and poor taste, when individuals fail to comply with the ideals of reasonableness, and common sense.

Son of the Court Upholsterer.   Jean-Baptiste Poquelin was in line to inherit his father's position as *tapissier ordinaire du roi*, the king's upholsterer, and enjoy a comfortable life. He received a fine education at Collège de Clermont, a Jesuit college, and practiced law for a short time. In 1643 he drastically changed careers by becoming one of nine founders of an acting company in Paris, the *Illustre Théâtre*. Taking the stage name of Molière for the first time, he devoted the rest of his life to theater—writing, directing, staging, and producing plays. Although theater was popular with the general public, the acting profession itself was condemned by the clergy; in fact, an actor was automatically excommunicated by the church and denied Christian burial unless a renunciation of his chosen career was forthcoming before death.

Molière's new company was a total failure, at least financially; twice the playwright ended up in jail for debts. As a result, he retreated to the countryside where he learned the organizational nuts and bolts of successful theater by touring the back roads and provinces of France. For thirteen years he served an apprenticeship in the various practical and artistic responsibilities of a theatrical company. He also turned his attention from tragedies to comedies—his true calling.

In 1658 Molière returned to Paris, found favor with the court through Louis XIV's brother, "Monsieur," and had an indisputable hit with *The High-Brow Young Ladies* (*Les précieuses ridicules*, 1659). From then on he enjoyed huge success and the patronage of the king. The titles of his masterpieces constitute a list of the kinds of people he subjected to satire and ridicule. *School for Wives* (*L'école des femmes*, 1662) examines the insecurities of courtship. *Don Juan* (1665) picks up the theme of the playboy and explores intimate relationships. *The Misanthrope* (1666) exposes the shortsightedness of a self-righteous intellectual. *The Miser* (*L'avare*, 1668), as the title gives away, satirizes lust for money. *The Would-Be Gentleman* (*Le bourgeois gentilhomme*, 1670) turns on the aspiring middle classes and *The Learned Ladies* (*Les femmes savantes*, 1672) attacks

> Molière is so great that he astonishes us afresh every time we read him. He is a man apart; his plays border on the tragic, and no one has the courage to try and imitate him.
>
> — Augustin Sainte-Beuve, critic, 1914

These terms cover the generic conventions of fiction, poetry, and drama; historical forms such as epic, epigram, and myth; and relevant historical periods such as the European Enlightenment or the Edo period in Japan.

Making connections among works from different times and places. At the end of each author introduction are two catalysts for further thought and discussion. **Questions** in the Connections apparatus tie together Western and world texts, both those within a single book and selections from other centuries, making the six books more of a unit and aiding in their interplay. **Further Research bibliographies**

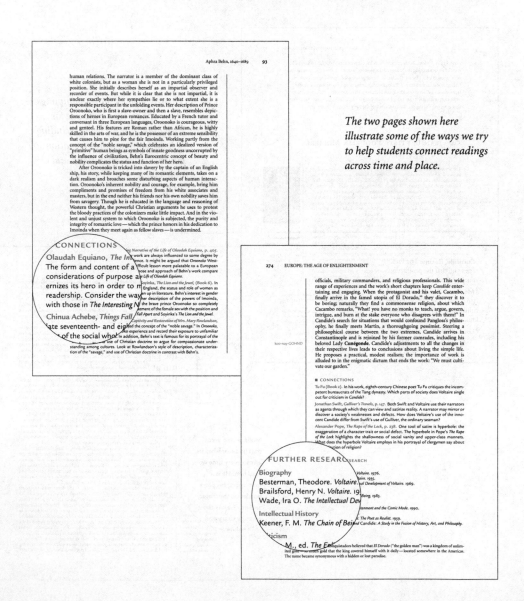

The two pages shown here illustrate some of the ways we try to help students connect readings across time and place.

provide sources for students who want to read more critical, biographical, or historical information about an author or a work.

Print and online ancillaries further support the anthology's material. Two instructor's manuals, *Resources for Teaching THE BEDFORD ANTHOLOGY OF WORLD LITERATURE,* accompany Books 1–3 and Books 4–6 (one for each package), providing additional information about the anthology's texts and the authors, suggestions for discussion and writing prompts in the classroom and beyond, and additional connections among texts in the six books.

We are especially enthusiastic about our integrated Book Companion Site, *World Literature Online,* which provides a wealth of content and information that only the interactive medium of the Web can offer. **Web links** throughout the anthology direct

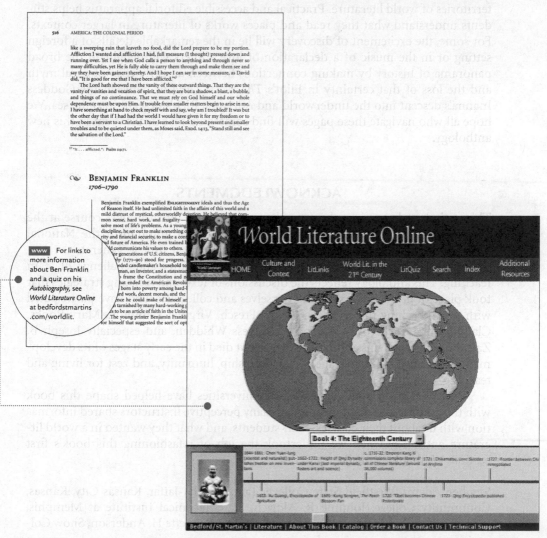

students to additional content on the Web site, where interactive illustrated time lines and maps serve as portals to more information about countries, texts, and authors. Culture and Context overviews offer additional historical background and annotated research links that students can follow to learn more on their own. Illustrated World Literature in the Twenty-First Century discussions trace the enduring presence in contemporary culture of the most frequently taught texts in world literature courses. Maps from the book are available online. Quizzes in LitQuiz offer an easy way for instructors to assess students' reading and comprehension. And LitLinks—annotated research links—provide a way for students to learn more about individual authors.

This wide variety of supplementary materials, as well as the broad spectrum of literary texts, offers teachers choices for navigating the familiar and the unfamiliar territories of world literature. Practical and accessible editorial apparatus helps students understand what they read and places works of literature in larger contexts. For some, the excitement of discovery will lie in the remarkable details of a foreign setting or in the music of a declaration of love. Others will delight in the broad panorama of history by making connections between an early cosmological myth and the loss of that certainty in Eliot's *The Waste Land* or between the Goddess Inanna's descent into the underworld and Adrienne Rich's descent into the sea. We hope all who navigate these pages will find something that thrills them in this new anthology.

ACKNOWLEDGMENTS

This anthology began in a team-taught, multicultural "great books" course at the University of New Mexico, initially developed with a grant from the National Endowment for the Humanities. The grant gave us ample time to generate the curriculum for the course, and it also supported the luxury and challenge of team teaching. This anthology reflects the discussions of texts and teaching strategies that took place over many years among ourselves and colleagues who have participated with us in teaching the course—Cheryl Fresch, Virginia Hampton, Mary Rooks, Claire Waters, Richard K. Waters, Mary Bess Whidden, and especially Joseph B. Zavadil, who began this anthology with us but died in the early stages of its development. Joe's spirit—his courage, wit, scholarship, humanity, and zest for living and teaching—endures in this book.

Reviewers from many colleges and universities have helped shape this book with their advice and suggestions. And many perceptive instructors shared information with us about their courses, their students, and what they wanted in a world literature anthology when we undertook the job of refashioning this book's first edition. We thank them all:

Stephen Adams, Westfield State College; Tamara Agha-Jaffar, Kansas City, Kansas, Community College; Johnnie R. Aldrich, State Technical Institute at Memphis; Allison Alison, Southeastern Community College; Jannette H. Anderson, Snow College; Kit Andrews, Western Oregon University; Joan Angelis, Woodbury University; Shirley Ariker, Empire State College; Sister Elena F. Arminio, College of Saint Elizabeth; Rose Lee Bancroft, Alice Lloyd College; John Bartle, Hamilton College; Amy M. Bawcom, University of Mary Hardin-Baylor; M. Susan Beck, University of Wisconsin-River Falls; Frank Beesley, Dalton State College; Peter Benson, Farleigh Dickinson University; Michael Bielmeier, Silver Lake College; Dale B. Billingsley, University of Louisville; Mark Bingham, Union University; Stephen Black, Dyersburg State Community College; Neil Blackadder, Knox College; Tyler Blake, MidAmerica Nazarene University; Gene Blanton, Jacksonville State University; James Boswell Jr., Harrisburg Area Community College; Lisa S. Bovelli, Itasca Community College; Lois Bragg, Gallaudet University; Kristin Ruth Brate, Arizona Western College; Marie Brenner, Bethel College; Linda Brown, Coastal Georgia Community College; Keith Callis, Crichton College; Charles P. Campbell, New Mexico Tech.; Zuoya Cao, Lincoln University; William Carpenter, College of ME Atlantic; May Charles, Wheeling Jesuit College; R. J. Clougherty, Tennessee Technical College; Helen Connell, Barry University; Lynn Conroy, Seton Hill College; Sue Coody, Weatherford College; Thomas A. Copeland, Youngstown State University; Peter Cortland, Quinnipiac College; R. Costomiris, Georgia Southern University; H. J. Coughlin, Eastern Connecticut State University; Marc D. Cyr, Georgia Southern University; Sarah Dangelantonio, Franklin Pierce College; James Davis, Troy State University; Barbara Dicey, Wallace College; Wilfred O. Dietrich, Blinn College; Michael Dinielli, Chaffey College; Matt Djos, Mesa State College; Marjorie Dobbin, Brewton-Parker College; Brian L. Dose, Martin Luther College; Dawn Duncan, Concordia College; Bernie Earley, Tompkins-Cortland Community College; Sarah M. Eichelman, Walters State Community College; Robert H. Ellison, East Texas Baptist University; Joshua D. Esty, Harvard University; Robert J. Ewald, University of Findlay; Shirley Felt, Southern California College; Lois Ferrer, CSU Dominguez Hills; Patricia Fite, University of the Incarnate Word; Sr. Agnes Fleck, St. Scholastica College; Robert Fliessner, Central State University; M. L. Flynn, South Dakota State University; Keith Foster, Arkansas State University; John C. Freeman, El Paso Community College; Doris Gardenshire, Trinity Valley Community College; Susan Gardner, University of North Carolina-Charlotte; Jerry D. Gibbens, Williams Baptist College; Susan Gilbert, Meredith College; Diana Glyer, Azusa Pacific University; Irene Gnarra, Kean University; R. C. Goetter, Glouster Community College; Nancy Goldfarb, Western Kentucky University; Martha Goodman, Central Virginia Community College; Lyman Grant, Austin Community College; Hazel Greenberg, San Jacinto College South; Janet Grose, Union University; Sharon Growney-Seals, Ouachita Technical College; Rachel Hadas, Rutgers University; Laura Hammons, East Central Community College; Carmen Hardin, University of Louisville; Darren Harris-Fain, Shawnee State University; Patricia B. Heaman, Wilkes University; Charles Heglan, University of South Florida; Dennis E. Hensley, Taylor University; Kathleen M. Herndon, Weber State University; Betty Higdon, Reedley College; David Hoegberg, Indiana University; Diane Long Hoeveler, Marquette University; Tyler Hoffman, Rutgers University; Lynn Hoggard, Midwestern State University; Greg Horn, Southwest VA Community College; Roger Horn, Charles County Community

College; Malinda Jay-Bartels, Gulf Coast Community College; Mell Johnson, Wallace State Community College; Kathryn Joyce, Santa Barbara City College; Steven Joyce, Ohio State University-Mansfield; Ronald A. T. Judy, University of Pittsburgh; Alan Kaufman, Bergen Community College; Tim Kelley, Northwest-Shoals Community College; Shoshanna Knapp, Virginia Technical College; Jim Knox, Roane State Community College; Mary Kraus, Bob Jones University; F. Kuzman, Bethel College; Kate Kysa, Anoka-Ramsey Community College; Linda L. Labin, Husson College; Barbara Laman, Dickinson State University; R. Scott Lamascus, GA-Southwestern State University; Sandi S. Landis, St. Johns River Community College; Ben Larson, York College; Craig Larson, Trinidad State Junior College; Linda M. Lawrence, Georgia Military College; Simon Lewis, C. of Charleston; Gary L. Litt, Moorhead State University; H. W. Lutrin, Borough of Manhattan Community College; Dennis Lynch, Elgin Community College; Donald H. Mager, Johnson C. Smith University; Barbara Manrique, California State University; W. E. Mason, Mid-Continent College; Judith Matsunobu, Atlantic Community College; Noel Mawer, Edward Waters College; Patrick McDarby, St. John's University; Judy B. McInnis, University of Delaware; Becky McLaughlin, University of Southern Alabama; Edward E. Mehok, Notre Dame College of Ohio; Patricia Menhart, Broward Community College; Arthur McA. Miller, New College of Florida; Mark James Morreale, Marist College; Toni Morris, University of Indianapolis; Philip Mosley, Penn State–Worthington; George Mower, Community College of Alleghany County; L. Carl Nadeau, University of St. Francis; Walter Nelson, Red Rocks Community College; Steven Neuwirth, Western Connecticut State University; Carol H. Oliver, St. Louis College of Pharmacy; Richard Orr, York Technical College; Geoffrey Orth, Longwood College; Ramenga M. Osotsi, James Madison University; Bonnie Pavlis, Riverside Community College; Craig Payne, Indian Hills College; Leialoha Perkins, University of Hawaii; Ralph Perrico, Mercyhurst College; Charles W. Pollard, Calvin College; Michael Popkin, Touro College; Victoria Poulakis, Northern Virginia Community College; Alan Powers, Bristol Community College; Andrew B. Preslar, Lamar University; Evan Radcliffe, Villanova University; Belle Randall, Cornish College of the Arts; Elaine Razzano, Lyndon State College; Lucia N. Robinson, Okaloosa-Walton Community College; John Rooks, Morris College; William T. Ross, University of South Florida; Andrew Rubenfeld, Stevens Institute of Technology; Elizabeth S. Ruleman, Tennessee Wesleyan College; Olena H. Saciuk, Inter-American University; Mary Lynn Saul, Worcester State College; MaryJane Schenck, University of Tampa; Kevin Schilbrack, Wesleyan College; Deborah Schlacks, University of Wisconsin; Michael Schroeder, Savannah State University; Helen Scott, Wilkes University; Asha Sen, University of Wisconsin; Mary Sheldon, Washburn University; Lisa Shoemaker, State Technical Community College; Jack Shreve, Allegany College of Maryland; Meg Simonton, Albertson College; Susan Sink, Joliet Junior College; Henry Sloss, Anne Arundel Community College; T. Sluberski, Concordia University; Betty Smith, The Criswell College; Jane Bouman Smith, Winthrop University; John Somerville, Hillsdale College; Claudia Stanger, Fullerton College; Patrick Sullivan, Manchester Community-Technical College; Joan S. Swartz, Baptist

Bible College of PA; Leah Swartz, Maryville University; Sister Renita Tadych, Silver Lake College; Janet Tarbuck, Kennebee Valley Technical College; Gina Teel, Southeast Arkansas College; Daniel Thurber, Concordia University; John Paul Vincent, Asbury College; Paul Vita, Morningside College; Tim Walsh, Otera Junior College; Julia Watson, Ohio State University; Patricia J. Webb, Maysville Community College; Lynne Weller, John Wood Community College; Roger West, Trident Technical College; Katherine Wikoff, Milwaukee School of Engineering; Evelyn M. Wilson, Tarrant County College; Carmen Wong, John Lyle Community College; Paul D. Wood, Paducah Community College; Fay Wright, North Idaho College; and finally, Pamela G. Xanthopoulos, Jackson State Community College.

We also want to thank a special group of reviewers who looked in depth at the manuscript for each book, offering us targeted advice about its strengths and weaknesses:

Cora Agatucci, Central Oregon Community College; Michael Austin, Shepherd College; Maryam Barrie, Washtenaw Community College; John Bartle, Hamilton College; Jeffry Berry, Adrian College; Lois Bragg, Gallaudet University; Ron Carter, Rappahannock Community College; Robin Clouser, Ursinus College; Eugene R. Cunnar, New Mexico State University; Karen Dahr, Ellsworth Community College; Kristine Daines, Arizona State University; Sarah Dangelantonio, Franklin Pierce College; Jim Doan, Nova SE University; Melora Giardetti, Simpson College; Audley Hall, North West Arkansas Community College; Dean Hall, Kansas State University; Wail Hassan, Illinois State University; Joris Heise, Sinclair Community College; Diane Long Hoeveler, Marquette University; Glenn Hopp, Howard Payne University; Mickey Jackson, Golden West College; Feroza Jussawalla, University of New Mexico; Linda Karch, Norwich University; David Karnos, Montana State University; William Laskowski, Jamestown College; Pat Lonchar, University of the Incarnate Word; Donald Mager, The Mott University; Judy B. McInnis, University of Delaware; Becky McLaughlin, University of South Alabama; Tony J. Morris, University of Indianapolis; Deborah Schlacks, University of Wisconsin; James Snowden, Cedarville University; David T. Stout, Luzerne County Community College; Arline Thorn, West Virginia State College; Ann Volin, University of Kansas; Mary Wack, Washington State University; Jayne A. Widmayer, Boise State University; and William Woods, Wichita State University.

No anthology of this size comes into being without critical and supportive friends and advisors. Our thanks go to the Department of English at the University of New Mexico (UNM); its chair, Scott Sanders, who encouraged and supported our work; and Margaret Shinn and the office staff, who provided administrative and technical assistance. Among our colleagues at UNM, we particularly want to thank Gail Baker, Helen Damico, Reed Dasenbrock, Patrick Gallacher, Feroza Jussawalla, Michelle LeBeau, Richard Melzer, Mary Power, Diana Robin, and Hugh Witemeyer. Several graduate students also helped with this project: Jana Giles contributed the final section on American multicultural literature; Mary Rooks wrote the sections on Aphra Behn and Wole Soyinka and served heroically as our assistant, record keeper, all-purpose editor, and consultant.

We have benefited from the knowledge and suggestions of those who have corrected our misunderstandings, illuminated topics and cultures with which we were unfamiliar, critiqued our work, and suggested ways to enrich the anthology: Paula Gunn Allen, Reynold Bean, Richard Bodner, Machiko Bomberger, Robert Dankoff, Kate Davis, Robert Hanning, Arthur Johnson, Dennis Jones, James Mischke, Harlan Nelson, Barrett Price, Clayton Rich, Julia Stein, Manjeet Tangri, William Witherup, Diane Wolkstein, and William Woods.

Resources for Teaching THE BEDFORD ANTHOLOGY OF WORLD LITERATURE was expertly developed, edited, and assembled by Mary Rooks, assisted by Julia Berrisford. Along with Mary, Shari Evans, Gabriel Gryffyn, and Rick Mott each wrote a section of the manual. The manual itself was a large and challenging endeavor; we are grateful to its authors for their enthusiasm and hard work.

A six-volume anthology is an undertaking that calls for a courageous, imaginative, and supportive publisher. Chuck Christensen, Joan Feinberg, Karen Henry, and Steve Scipione at Bedford/St. Martin's possess these qualities; we especially appreciate their confidence in our ability to carry out this task. Our editor, Alanya Harter, and her associate, Joshua Levy, have guided the project throughout, keeping us on track with a vision of the whole when we were discouraged and keeping the day-to-day work moving forward. In particular, they helped us to reconceptualize the anthology's format and content. Without their suggestions, unacknowledged contributions, and guidance, this anthology would not be what it is today. They were assisted by many others who undertook particular tasks: The brilliant design was conceived by Anna George; Genevieve Hamilton helped to manage the art program, and together with Julia Berrisford she managed the final stages of development. Martha Friedman served as photo researcher, and Tina Samaha developed the maps. Jeff Voccola acted as editorial assistant, taking on many tasks, including the onerous ones of pasting up and numbering the manuscript. Ben Fortson expertly and efficiently supplied the pronunciation guides. Harriet Wald tirelessly and imaginatively oversaw the content and production of the Web site, an enormous task; she was helped along the way by Coleen O'Hanley, Chad Crume, and Dave Batty. Jenna Bookin Barry enthusiastically developed and coordinated the marketing plan, especially challenging when six books publish over a span of six months.

We were blessed with a superb production team who took the book from manuscript to final pages. For Books 4 and 6, we owe special thanks to Senior Production Editor Karen Baart, whose dedication and eye for detail made the project better in every way. Stasia Zomkowski efficiently served as production editor for Book 5 and Ara Salibian for Book 1; they were ably assisted by Courtney Jossart and Kerri Cardone. Melissa Cook's careful and thoughtful copyediting helped to give consistency and clarity to the different voices that contributed to the manuscript. Managing Editor Elizabeth Schaaf oversaw the whole process and Senior Production Supervisor Catherine Hetmansky realized our final vision of design and content in beautifully bound and printed books.

Most of all, we thank our families, especially Mary Davis, Marlys Harrison, and Mona Johnson, for their advice, stamina, and patience during the past three years while this book has occupied so much of our time and theirs.

Paul Davis
Gary Harrison
David M. Johnson
Patricia Clark Smith
John F. Crawford

A NOTE ON TRANSLATION

Some translators of literary works into English tended to sacrifice form for literal meaning, while others subordinated literal meaning to the artistry of the original work. With the increasing number of translations of world literature available by a range of translators, it has become possible to select versions that are clear and accessible as well as literally and aesthetically faithful to the original. Thus our choice of Robert Fitzgerald's *Iliad* and *Odyssey,* Horace Gregory's poems by Catullus, Mary Barnard's poems by Sappho, Theodore Morrison's *Canterbury Tales,* Edward Seidensticker's *Tale of Genji,* and Willa and Edwin Muir's *The Metamorphosis,* among others.

There are those who question whether poetry can ever be adequately translated from one language and culture into another; our concern, however, is not with what might be lost in a translation but with what is gained. The best translations do not merely duplicate a work but re-create it in a new idiom. Coleman Barks's poems of Rumi, Stephen Mitchell's poems of Rilke, Miguel León-Portilla's translations of Nahuatl poetry, and David Hinton's poems of the Tang dynasty are in a way outstanding English poems in their own right. And William Kelly Simpson's love poems of ancient Egypt, Robert and Jean Hollander's *Inferno,* Richard Wilbur's *Tartuffe,* W. S. Merwin's poems of Ghalib, Judith Hemschemeyer's poems of Anna Akhmatova, and Robert Bly's poems of Pablo Neruda are examples of translations done by major poets whose renderings are now an important part of their own body of work.

Barbara Stoler Miller's translation of the Bhagavad Gita and Donald Keene's translation of Chikamatsu's *Love Suicides at Amijima* communicate the complexity of a literary work. Richard Bodner's contemporary translation of Bashō's *Narrow Road through the Backcountry,* especially commissioned, does justice to both the prose and the resonant haiku in that work. David Luke's excellent translation of *Death in Venice* pays tribute to Thomas Mann's original German and is at the same time very readable.

More is said about the translations in this book in the notes for individual works.

About the Editors

Paul Davis (Ph.D., University of Wisconsin), professor emeritus of English at the University of New Mexico, has been the recipient of several teaching awards and academic honors, including that of Master Teacher. He has taught courses since 1962 in composition, rhetoric, and nineteenth-century literature and has written and edited many scholarly books, including *The Penguin Dickens Companion* (1999), *Dickens A to Z* (1998), and *The Life and Times of Ebeneezer Scrooge* (1990). He has also written numerous scholarly and popular articles on solar energy and Victorian book illustration.

Gary Harrison (Ph.D., Stanford University), professor and director of undergraduate studies at the University of New Mexico, has won numerous fellowships and awards for scholarship and teaching. He has taught courses in world literature, British Romanticism, and literary theory at the University of New Mexico since 1987. Harrison's publications include a critical study on William Wordsworth, *Wordsworth's Vagrant Muse: Poetry, Poverty and Power* (1994); and many articles on the literature and culture of the early nineteenth century.

David M. Johnson (Ph.D., University of Connecticut), professor emeritus of English at the University of New Mexico, has taught courses in world literature, mythology, the Bible as literature, philosophy and literature, and creative writing since 1965. He has written, edited, and contributed to numerous scholarly books and collections of poetry, including *Fire in the Fields* (1996) and *Lord of the Dawn: The Legend of Quetzalcoatl* (1987). He has also published scholarly articles, poetry, and translations of Nahuatl myths.

Patricia Clark Smith (Ph.D., Yale University), professor emerita of English at the University of New Mexico, has taught courses in world literature, creative writing, American literature, and Native American literature since 1971. Her many publications include a collection of poetry, *Changing Your Story* (1991); the biography *As Long as the Rivers Flow* (1996); and *On the Trail of Elder Brother* (2000).

John F. Crawford (Ph.D., Columbia University), associate professor of English at the University of New Mexico–Valencia, has taught medieval, world, and other literature courses since 1965 at a number of institutions, including California Institute of Technology, Herbert Lehmann College of CUNY, and, most recently, the University of New Mexico. The publisher of West End Press, Crawford has also edited *This Is About Vision: Interviews with Southwestern Writers* (1990) and written articles on multicultural women poets of the Southwest.

Pronunciation Key

This key applies to the pronunciation guides that appear in the margins and before most selections in *The Bedford Anthology of World Literature*. The syllable receiving the main stress is CAPITALIZED.

a	mat, alabaster, laugh	MAT, AL-uh-bas-tur, LAF
ah	mama, Americana, Congo	MAH-mah, uh-meh-rih-KAH-nuh, KAHNG-goh
ar	cartoon, Harvard	kar-TOON, HAR-vurd
aw	saw, raucous	SAW, RAW-kus
ay (or a)	may, Abraham, shake	MAY, AY-bruh-ham, SHAKE
b	bet	BET
ch	church, matchstick	CHURCH, MACH-stik
d	desk	DESK
e	Edward, melted	ED-wurd, MEL-tid
ee	meet, ream, petite	MEET, REEM, puh-TEET
eh	cherub, derriere	CHEH-rub, DEH-ree-ehr
f	final	FIGH-nul
g	got, giddy	GAHT, GIH-dee
h	happenstance	HAP-un-stans
i	mit, Ipswich, impression	MIT, IP-swich, im-PRESH-un
igh (or i)	eyesore, right, Anglophile	IGH-sore, RITE, ANG-gloh-file
ih	Philippines	FIH-luh-peenz
j	judgment	JUJ-mint
k	kitten	KIT-tun
l	light, allocate	LITE, AL-oh-kate
m	ramrod	RAM-rahd
n	ran	RAN
ng	rang, thinker	RANG, THING-ker
oh (or o)	open, owned, lonesome	OH-pun, OHND, LONE-sum
ong	wrong, bonkers	RONG, BONG-kurz
oo	moot, mute, super	MOOT, MYOOT, SOO-pur
ow	loud, dowager, how	LOWD, DOW-uh-jur, HOW
oy	boy, boil, oiler	BOY, BOYL, OY-lur
p	pet	PET
r	right, wretched	RITE, RECH-id
s	see, citizen	SEE, SIH-tuh-zun
sh	shingle	SHING-gul
t	test	TEST
th	thin	THIN
th	this, whether	*TH*IS, WEH-*th*ur
u	until, sumptuous, lovely	un-TIL, SUMP-choo-us, LUV-lee
uh	about, vacation, suddenly	uh-BOWT, vuh-KAY-shun, SUH-dun-lee
ur	fur, bird, term, beggar	FUR, BURD, TURM, BEG-ur
v	vacuum	VAK-yoo-um
w	western	WES-turn
y	yesterday	YES-tur-day
z	zero, loser	ZEE-roh, LOO-zur
zh	treasure	TREH-zhur

Where a name is given two pronunciations, usually the first is the most familiar pronunciation in English and the second is a more exact rendering of the native pronunciation.

In the pronunciations of French names, nasalized vowels are indicated by adding "ng" after the vowel.

Japanese words have no strong stress accent, so the syllables marked as stressed are so given only for the convenience of English speakers.

CONTENTS

◦ CHINA: The Early Qing Dynasty   *765*

The Bedford Anthology of
World Literature
The Eighteenth Century, 1650–1800

Portuguese Caravels Leaving to Explore the World, 1775 *The eighteenth century was a time of unprecedented global communication — political, social, economic, and literary. These painted blue tiles are found on the walls of the town of Paco de Arcos, near Lisbon, Portugal. (The Art Archive / Dagli Orti.)*

The Eighteenth Century

1650 - 1800

*T*he eighteenth century is the last century of what historians call the **EARLY MODERN ERA,** a period extending from about 1500 to 1800. Known as the "Age of Enlightenment" in Europe, the eighteenth century is typically recognized in the West as a period of philosophical speculation leading to scientific advancement, social change, and political revolution. As with all historical periodization, the intellectual, literary, social, and political transformations associated in the West with the "eighteenth century" do not all fall neatly between 1700 and 1800. Within European studies alone, scholars increasingly speak of a "long eighteenth century" in order to accommodate within the period scheme those writers, philosophers, and scientists, such as Molière (1622–1673), John Locke (1632–1704), and Isaac Newton (1642–1727), whose works are associated with the Enlightenment. Moreover, when we include works from Japan, China, India, the Arabic

www For an interactive version of the Comparative Time Line for the Eighteenth Century, see *World Literature Online* at bedfordstmartins.com/worldlit.

COMPARATIVE TIME LINE FOR THE EIGHTEENTH CENTURY

Date	History and Politics	Literature	Science, Culture, and Technology
1400–1500	"The Great Binding Law" provides the confederation of five independent nations known as the Iroquois with a constitution.		
1600–1650	1603 Tokugawa Ieyasu establishes shogunate at Edo; Tokugawa period begins. Safavids capture Baghdad from Ottomans.		
	1607 English found colony at Jamestown.		1610 Galileo, *The Starry Messenger*
	1612 Ieyasu decrees that all Christian missionaries must leave Japan.		1633 The Inquisition condemns Galileo's heliocentric theory.
	1619 First African slaves arrive in Virginia.		1634 Taj Mahal built in Agra.
	1620 *Mayflower* arrives at what is now Massachusetts.	1622 de Gournay, *On the Equality of Men and Women*	1640 Xu Guanqi (Hsu Kwan-ch'i) *Encyclopedia of Agriculture* (*You Lu Chuan Shu*)
	1642–60 English Civil War	1637 Descartes, *Discourse on Method*	
	1644–45 Manchus invade China, leading to collapse of the Ming and establishment of the Qing dynasty.		

world, Africa, and the Americas under a rubric such as "the eighteenth century," the problem of periodization is compounded, since each of these regions developed along its own unique trajectory. Ihara Saikaku (1642–1693) and Matsuo Bashō (1644–1694), for example, are writers associated with the Tokugawa era in Japan, a period which stretches from 1600 to 1868. Thus, some of the works included in this book fall outside of the eighteenth century proper. All of the included works, however, reflect the changes in the relations among world civilizations that were taking place during the longer span of the Early Modern era, when communication among the regions of the world was expanding.

During the three centuries from about 1500 to 1800, voyages of discovery and exploration established the global networks of trade and cross-cultural exchange that paved the way for European domination in the nineteenth and early twentieth centuries. Improvements in technology—especially in shipbuilding, navigation, and arms—extended the global reach of burgeoning nation-states. By the seventeenth century, Portugal, Spain, and the Netherlands had established trading stations and colonies in sub-Saharan Africa, India, China, and the Americas; by the end of the eighteenth century, England and France had extended their reach into

Date	History and Politics	Literature	Science, Culture, and Technology
1650–1660	1652 Dutch colonists found Cape Town in South Africa.	1651 Hobbes, *Leviathan*	
	1656 Dutch begin trade with Japan.		
	1657 Great Fire destroys Edo, Japan.		
	1659 Aurangzeb succeeds Shah Jahan as Mughal emperor in India.		
1660–1670	1660 Charles II; Restoration of Stuart monarchy in England		1661 John Eliot translates New Testament into Algonquin.
	1662 Kangxi (second emperor of Manchu dynasty) begins reign in China.	1664 Molière, *Tartuffe*	1662 Royal Society founded in London.
	1666 Great Fire of London	1667 Milton, *Paradise Lost*	
	1669 Hinduism outlawed by Mughals in India; many Hindu temples destroyed.		1668 Margaret Cavendish, *The Grounds of Natural Philosophy*
1670–1680	1675–76 King Philip's War between American settlers and the Wampanoag	1677 Spinoza, *Ethics*; Racine, *Phaedra*	
	1675–78 Sikh rebellion against Mughal empire in India	1678 La Fayette, *The Princess of Clèves*	

those areas as well as into the newly discovered Australia. Capital, in the form of gold and silver bullion and foodstuffs such as corn from the Americas, circulated around the world and began to transform economies and social habits, not just in Europe, but also in countries that traded with the Europeans such as China, India, and Japan. The slave trade, which displaced an estimated ten million souls between the sixteenth and nineteenth centuries, had a traumatic impact on the societies of sub-Saharan Africa, and it contributed to an ethnic mix of peoples throughout the world. These dramatic changes produced a new balance of power and trade that impacted the Ottoman, Safavid, and Mughal empires in the Middle East and India. Eventually, pressures from Europe and Russia would contribute to the decline and fall of the Mughals and the Ottomans in the mid-eighteenth and nineteenth centuries, respectively. While some traditional societies remained intact in the interior of Africa and Asia, people living along the world's coasts and on islands could not ignore the troubling presence of European conquistadors, traders, missionaries, and colonizers. Thus, by the eighteenth century, as historian J. M. Roberts has put it, we had reached "the era of world history."

Date	History and Politics	Literature	Science, Culture, and Technology
1680–1690	1680 Tsunayoshi becomes shogun in Japan. Ashanti (Asante) Kingdom founded in West Africa. Pueblo Revolt in New Mexico drives out Spanish.	1682 Rowlandson, *Narrative of the Captivity and Restoration of Mrs. Mary Rowlandson*	1680 Anton van Leeuwenhoek discovers bacteria.
	1685 Louis XIV revokes Edict of Nantes; absolute monarchy in France; Kangxi opens Chinese ports to foreigners.	1686 Saikaku, *Five Women Who Loved Love*	1687 Newton, *Mathematical Principles*
	1688 Glorious Revolution in England (James II deposed; William and Mary crowned)	1688 Aphra Behn, *Oroonoko;* Genroku period in Japan; beginnings of *Kabuki* theater	
1690–1700		1694 Astell, *A Serious Proposal to the Ladies*	1690 Locke, *Two Treatises on Government* and *Essay Concerning Human Understanding*
		1699 Kong Shangren (K'ung Shan-jen), *The Peach Blossom Fan*	

GLOBAL CONTACT AND CONFLICT

As European people extended their reach to almost all parts of the world and enriched their countries with the goods and raw materials they brought back from the colonies, they fought among themselves to seize or secure precious trade routes or promising colonial holdings. The Seven Years' War (1756 to 1763)—in which Britain and Prussia joined forces against Austria, Russia, France, and Spain—is considered by some to be the first global war. Land and sea battles raged over who could finally claim ownership of British, French, and Spanish colonial holdings in India and North America. At the end of the war, France gave up its claims in India and Canada and the land east of the Mississippi River to Britain and the Louisiana territory to Spain; Spain in turn gave up Florida to Britain. At the end of the Seven Years' War, Great Britain was in a position to become the leading colonial power in the world.

INTELLECTUAL AND SOCIAL CHANGE

The Seven Years' War notwithstanding, the eighteenth century was a period of relative peace and—especially for Europe, China, and Japan—prosperity. Rapid population growth led to the increasing importance of urban life. On the heels of

Date	History and Politics	Literature	Science, Culture, and Technology
1700–1710	1701–14 War of the Spanish Succession 1703 Peter I founds St. Petersburg in Russia. 1707 Death of Mughal emperor Aurangzeb accelerates decline of Mughal empire in India. 1709 Ienobu new shogun in Japan	1702 Bashō, *The Narrow Road through the Backcountry* 1703 Chikamatsu, *The Love Suicides at Sonezaki*	1702 First daily newspaper published in London. 1704 Newton, *Opticks* 1706 Excavations of Pompeii and Herculaneum begin. 1709 Invention of the piano
1710–1720	1713 Peace of Utrecht; French domination of Europe ends. Treaty of Utrecht 1716 Yoshimune shogun in Japan	1710 Leibniz, *Theodicy* 1714 Pope, *The Rape of the Lock* 1719 Defoe, *Robinson Crusoe*	1710 Handel becomes music director to George I. 1714 Fahrenheit invents mercury thermometer.
1720–1730	1723 Collapse of Safavid empire 1726 Treaty between British colonists and the Iroquois League against France	1721 Chikamatsu, *The Love Suicides at Amijima* 1726 Swift, *Gulliver's Travels*	1720 Mammoth *History of Japan* by Tokugawa Mitsukuni completed; Yoshimune lifts restrictions on study of Western thought in Japan. 1729 Bach, *St. Matthew Passion*

increased commerce and manufacture, many parts of Europe and Japan saw the rise of an energetic and thriving middle class whose intellectual and moral values presented various challenges to the traditional social and political order. The boundaries between social groups became more permeable and the question of personal and social identity became more complex as wealthy merchant families united through marriage with the families of traditional landed aristocrats. Greater public access to education as well as cheaper methods of printing and papermaking helped to promote literacy in many parts of Europe, the United States, China, and Japan. Middle-class demand for entertainment and diversions led to the transformation of classical literary forms and the development of new ones.

In Europe—particularly in France and England—an intellectual revolution now known as the ENLIGHTENMENT shook the foundations of societies previously ruled by kings and the church. New faith in the powers of empirical science, rationalism, and philosophy to resolve social problems intensified the secularism that had taken shape during the Renaissance. In Japan, thinkers also promoted a shift from metaphysical speculation to pragmatism. NEO-CONFUCIANISTS in the seventeenth and eighteenth centuries debated the relative authority of the emperor

Date	History and Politics	Literature	Science, Culture, and Technology
1730–1740	1736–94 Literary censorship in China	1733–34 Pope, *An Essay on Man* 1733–58 Franklin, *Poor Richard's Almanack*	1735 Linnaeus, *Systema Naturae* 1739 Hume, *Treatise of Human Nature*
1740–1750	1740 Frederick the Great assumes control of Prussia; Maria Theresa head of Hapsburg empire 1745 Ieharu shogun in Japan		1748 Montesquieu, *Spirit of the Laws* 1749 Buffon, *Natural History*
1750–1760	1755 Lisbon earthquake kills 30,000 people. 1756–63 Seven Years' War; massacre of British in Black Hole of Calcutta 1757 Battle of Plassey in India; British defeat Mughal forces in Bengal.	1751–72 Diderot, *Encyclopedia* 1755 Samuel Johnson, *Dictionary* 1759 Voltaire, *Candide, or Optimism*	1751 Benjamin Franklin invents lightning rod.
1760–1770	1760 George III crowned king of England. 1762 Catherine II takes power in Russia.	1762 Rousseau, *The Social Contract* and *Émile*; Kaibara Ekken, *Greater Learning for Women*	1760s–70s Color wood block printing in Japan begins to flourish with Harunobu and Utamoro.

and shogun (the hereditary military commander in feudal Japan), spurred on empirical methods of investigation and direct observation of natural phenomena, and advocated systematic programs of education. In China, philosophers such as Huang Zong-Xi (Huang Tsung-hsi, 1610–1695) and Wang Fu-chi (Wang Fu-chih, 1619–1692) took a more rigorous, scientific approach to the study of science, politics, history, and society than had previous generations.

NEW LITERARY FORMS

The development of a literate middle class, with greater leisure time and spending power, allowed a publishing industry and new literary forms to thrive. Up to the early modern period, poetry, drama, and fiction primarily reflected the concerns of the elite—nobles and aristocrats. As the population grew and standards of living rose, the urban life of the middle classes began to dominate the attention of writers. Aristocratic models of classical tragedy and romance gave way to plays and novels exploring questions that were of particular concern to the BOURGEOISIE: social fluidity, personal identity, public morality, and private feeling. In Europe, the

Date	History and Politics	Literature	Science, Culture, and Technology
1760–1770 (cont.)	1763 End of the Seven Years' War. Britain gains colonial territories from France and Spain, including Canada, Tobago, and Florida; Spain gets Louisiana from France. 1765 The Stamp Act 1766 Ali Bey becomes ruler of Egypt, proclaims independence of Turks.	1763 Montagu, *The Turkish Letters* 1766 Pu Song-ling, *Strange Stories from a Chinese Studio*	1767–69 Bougainville sails around the world. 1769 James Watt patents steam engine.
1770–1780	1770 Captain James Cook lands at Australia. 1773 The Tea Act leads to the Boston Tea Party. 1774 British East India Company officer Warren Hastings becomes governor of India. 1775 First Maratha War in India 1775–83 American War of Independence 1776 Declaration of Independence	1771 Franklin begins *Autobiography* 1772–82 Editing of the *Complete Collection of Written Materials Divided into Four Categories* (*Siku Chuanshu*), a collection of all printed works in China 1774 Goethe, *Sorrows of Young Werther* c. 1775 Baien Miura, *Gengo* (*Deep Words*)	1770 James Hargreaves patents spinning jenny. 1771 Baien Miura, *Kagen* (*Origin of Price*) 1776 Paine, *Common Sense*; Adam Smith, *Wealth of Nations* 1777 Haydn, C Major Symphony

NOVEL developed as a realistic form that dramatized the moral and social life of ordinary people. In Japan and China, where it had a longer tradition, the novel was adapted to reflect the lives of the townspeople and to portray realistically the social life among all ranks.

Middle-class readers also looked to literature for entertainment and instruction. Poets and playwrights turned away from the highly stylized diction and formal structures associated with aristocratic culture and classical conventions and began to use more colloquial language and more popular forms. Dramatists in Japan turned to the relatively new forms of KABUKI (live theater) and JORURI (puppet theater) to reflect urban life, while those in Europe used the stage to exercise the much-valued wit of urban culture and poke fun at country life. And writers benefited from the new popularity of a variety of prose genres during this period. Readers were drawn to autobiographies, confessions, collections of letters, and conduct books—guides designed to help people improve their social status.

Date	History and Politics	Literature	Science, Culture, and Technology
1780–1790	1783 Treaty of Paris; United States recognized as an independent nation.	1781–88 Rousseau, *Confessions*	1781 Kant, *Critique of Pure Reason*
		1781 Death of Bengali writer Ramprasad Sen	
		1783 Xie Qing Gao (Hsieh Ch'ing Kao) leaves China on 14-year voyage to Europe, America, and Asia; *The Hai-lu,* an account of his travels, appears c. 1821.	1785 Charles Wilkins publishes first European (English) translation of Bhagavad Gita.
	1787 Sierra Leone founded by British colonists.		
	1789 U.S. Constitution ratified. Storming of the Bastille; Declaration of the Rights of Man and Citizen; French Revolution begins; George Washington elected first U.S. president.	1789 Equiano, *The Interesting Narrative of the Life of Olaudah Equiano*	1787–88 Mozart, *Don Giovanni* and the last three symphonies

Increased contact among peoples from diverse parts of the world—both voluntary and involuntary—also had an impact on the literature of the eighteenth century. TRAVEL NARRATIVES, recounting the adventures of visitors to foreign countries as well as fictional accounts of travels that often satirized customs of the homeland, enjoyed enormous popularity. The slave trade led to a new genre known as the SLAVE NARRATIVE, an autobiographical account of a person's captivity, education, and emancipation. In America, CAPTIVITY NARRATIVES—first-person stories of women and men captured and released by American Indians emerged as a subgenre. Literary production in the eighteenth century reflected the social, economic, and cultural shifts everywhere in the world: the expanding range of human experience, the greater status and prosperity of the middle classes, and the increasing cultural and ethnic diversity of a world continuing to grow smaller.

Date	History and Politics	Literature	Science, Culture, and Technology
1790–1800	1791 Toussaint L'Ouverture leads slave revolt in Hispaniola (Haiti), leading to first independent state in Latin America, 1804.	1791 Cao Xueqin and Gao E, *The Story of the Stone;* de Gouges, *Declaration of the Rights of Woman and the Female Citizen*	1793 Eli Whitney invents the cotton gin.
	1792 French Republic founded by National Convention; Denmark prohibits slave trade.		1796 Edward Jenner tests effectiveness of smallpox vaccination, introduced by Lady Mary Wortley Montagu after her travels in Turkey.
	1793 Lord McCartney's mission to China to increase trade; Louis XVI beheaded.	1792 Wollstonecraft, *A Vindication of the Rights of Woman*	
	1798 Napoleon invades Egypt.	1796 Diderot, *Supplement to the Voyage of Bougainville*	1799 Rosetta Stone discovered in Egypt by Napoleon's troops; provides key to translating Egyptian hieroglyphics.
	1799 Napoleon becomes first consul of France.		
1800–1810		1803 *The Travels of Mirza Abu Taleb Khan*	
		1809 Shen Fu, *Six Records from a Floating Life*	

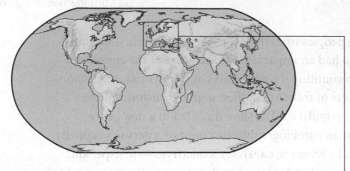

Europe in 1740

By 1740, Europe had achieved a kind of diplomatic equilibrium in which no one nation dominated. There were, however, certain divisions of power: Spain, the Dutch Republic, Poland-Lithuania, and Sweden had declined in might and influence, while Great Britain, Russia, Prussia, and Austria had become more powerful.

EUROPE
The Age of Enlightenment

❧ Throughout much of the seventeenth century, Europe was in turmoil, some
of which spilled over into the eighteenth century. The Thirty Years' War (1618–
1648) saw fighting and confusion in all of Europe and heightened religious faction-
alism. A series of attempts on the part of discontented nobles in England and
members of the Parlement of Paris in France to limit the powers of the monarch
resulted in the English Civil War (1642–1660) and the Fronde (1648–1653), respectively. These conflicts restricted royal power in England and strengthened it in
France—leading to further revolutionary struggles at the end of the eighteenth
century. Pressures for reform brought on by French intellectuals and the example
of the American Revolution led to the bloody conclusion of the French Revolution.
Beginning with the storming of the Bastille in 1789, the French people finally
brought down Louis XVI, secured a share of power for the middle classes, and
began to rebuild their society under the guiding lamp of Reason, literally idolized
as a secular god. Despite these important and costly events, during the eighteenth
century Europe as a whole experienced political and social stability. A few countries, especially England, enjoyed unprecedented prosperity.

ENLIGHTENMENT PHILOSOPHY

ENLIGHTENMENT thinkers and philosophers—known in France as the
philosophes—set out by means of reason and direct observation to discover the
fundamental laws governing nature, humanity, and society. The *philosophes*
believed that such discoveries would free the world from tyranny, violence, and
instability. If, they reasoned, universal laws such as those discovered by English scientist Isaac Newton (1642–1727) governed the natural world, surely similar laws
must govern human nature and social institutions. The delineation of such laws
was the project of David Hume's *A Treatise of Human Nature* (1739–40), in which
the Scottish philosopher attempted to "introduce the experimental method of

reasoning into moral subjects." By discovering laws governing "moral subjects"—such as knowledge, belief, the passions, justice, and goodness—human beings could learn to live together more harmoniously and perhaps experience unlimited progress. While many *philosophes* had doubts about how far such progress could go, by the end of the eighteenth century the Marquis de Condorcet's *Sketch for a Historical Picture of the Progress of the Human Mind* (1793) claimed "that the perfectibility of man is truly indefinite; and that the progress of this perfectibility . . . has no other limit than the duration of the globe upon which nature has cast us."

THE SLAVE TRADE

Ironically, the age named the Enlightenment was also an era of great blindness. Colonial expansion created a flood of new goods and materials in the trade networks, stimulating commerce and manufacturing. But since colonial trade focused mainly on labor-intensive crops such as sugar, tobacco, coffee, and cotton, many European fortunes were being built on the foundation of slavery. As we can see from the SLAVE NARRATIVE by Olaudah Equiano (1789), by the eighteenth century African traders from the kingdoms of Benin and Ife, among others, were selling Africans to Europeans in exchange for European goods. About fourteen million African men, women, and children were sold and sent to the Americas and the Caribbean, where they were put to work on plantations. When they died because of poor health or abuse, they were simply replaced by more men and women from Africa. Three times as many men, women, and children died from disease or mistreatment during the voyage from Africa to the colonies as actually arrived. Shackled together in rows so tight that they could hardly move, the captives suffered near starvation and dehydration; suicide was a powerful temptation. European empires were built in part on conflict within Africa, and resulted in political strife among and within African states and a seriously depleted population. The imposed African diaspora would have a profound impact on world history and culture over the next two centuries, introducing elements of African culture to the rest of the world as well as leading to ethnic and racial tension.

Equiano's *Interesting Narrative* records the experience of a more fortunate African slave. A unique hybrid of autobiography, moral exhortation, and TRAVEL NARRATIVE, Equiano's work served as a model for later slave narratives in Europe and America, and it played an important role in the late eighteenth- and early nineteenth-century movement to abolish the slave trade. Equiano's descriptions of the horrors of the slave ship, the brutality of slavery, and the struggle to obtain his freedom questioned slavery in the spirit of Enlightenment reform and spurred the abolitionist movements at the end of the century.

EUROPEAN LITERATURE

Eighteenth-century artists and writers in Europe, Japan, and China also began to direct their attention to the tastes and concerns of the increasingly literate and prosperous middle classes. As a result, new forms of music, art, and literature emerged. Throughout Europe the arts shifted their focus from the courts and country houses of the aristocracy to the salons and coffeehouses of the bourgeoisie.

Marcellus Laroon the Younger, *A Concert at Montagu House,* **1735. Pencil, Ink, and Wash**
This drawing portrays a gathering in an aristocratic English home. (The Courtauld Institute Gallery, Somerset House, London)

Writers during the first part of the eighteenth century—in what is known as
NEOCLASSICAL literature—imitated classical models and placed emphasis on conventional form, public purpose, and urbane wit. Neoclassical refers to the classical
tradition of Greco-Roman literature and mythology and an emphasis on classical
values of decorum and wit (decorum signifies stylistic grace and the perfect
balance between form and expression; wit denotes an inventiveness tempered by
good judgment). Pope's "An Essay on Criticism" offers the quintessential definition
of wit for the eighteenth century:

> True wit is Nature to advantage dressed,
> What oft was thought, but ne'er so well expressed;
> Something whose truth convinced at sight we find,
> That gives us back the image of our mind.

Just as Newton had discovered general laws and a grand order in the cosmos,
so the Neoclassical poet wanted to discover the general laws of art. In the works of
Augustan-age poets such as Horace and Virgil, Neoclassical writers found rules
governing art that they believed were equivalent to natural laws. In drama, these
rules were characterized by the "unities" of time, place, and action derived in part
from Aristotle's *Poetics*. In contrast to the expansive plays of Shakespeare with their
multiple subplots, Neoclassical dramatists such as Jean Racine (1639–1699) limited
their heroic tragedies to a single action, place, and time. In accordance with the
principles of decorum, writers developed an elevated and formal poetic diction
suited for serious subjects often drawn from, and almost always alluding to, classical and biblical history and mythology. The great Neoclassical writers saw these
rules as flexible rather than as prescriptions to follow to the letter. The one precept
that all Neoclassical writers agreed on was taken from Horace, who had said that all
art and literature should both please and instruct.

Cultures that value order and decorum tend to bring attention to their opposites—disorder and the grotesque—and beneath the polished surface of Neoclassical works the prince of misrule threatens to break out. There is always a rake—a
seducer without scruples—as in Pope's *The Rape of the Lock,* to threaten the pre-
ciousness of a virginal Belinda; always a Yahoo—a savage man—as in Jonathan
Swift's *Gulliver's Travels,* to disturb the all-too-perfect universe of the rational
Houyhnhnms. One of the predominant forms of European literature in the eighteenth century was SATIRE, a gentle or biting critique of morals and manners that
generally sought to instruct or to effect some kind of change in society. Satire
appeared in all major genres, including drama, poetry, and prose. Molière's play
Tartuffe (p. 22) attacks the hypocrisy of the middle classes in France, as well as their
complacent acceptance of rigid domestic roles. For Molière, his comic play aimed

to "correct men's vices," by displaying them in exaggerated form. This principle of HYPERBOLE—blowing things out of proportion—is found in the satirical fiction of the era as well, represented here by Voltaire's *Candide* (p. 275) and Jonathan Swift's *Gulliver's Travels* (p. 147). *Candide,* which follows the episodic adventures of a naive young man of the same name, exploits the possibilities of the satirical tale, and uses Candide's misadventures to attack the pieties of European society. Similarly, *Gulliver's Travels* combines the formal features of the travel narrative with those of the satirical tale to ridicule what Swift saw as the hypocritical values, self-complacency, and vicious nature of the people of Britain. At the same time, he produces an immensely entertaining fantasy that anticipates modern science fiction. In France, Denis Diderot's *Supplement to the Voyage of Bougainville* (p. 213) combined the travel narrative with philosophical dialogue to explore the essence of human nature and to attack the hypocrisy of European ideas about human sexuality. In poetry, Alexander Pope's MOCK EPIC *The Rape of the Lock* (p. 238) playfully treats the snipping of a lock of hair as an incident of Homeric proportions, mocking the participants in the family feud that results. At the same time, like Molière in *Tartuffe,* Pope appeals to common sense and good judgment as reasonable arbiters of human affairs.

By the mid eighteenth century, the conventions of reason and tradition had grown somewhat stale, if not stifling, and the critical temperament of the early Enlightenment became infused instead with a spirit of feeling. Decorum and urbane wit had to make room for a growing taste for the expressive, the meditative, and the spontaneous. Practical guides to manners flourished in the popular press, as the increasing number of middle-class readers sought to elevate themselves both economically and socially. In addition to the satirical tale, the novel, and the autobiography, the TRAVEL NARRATIVE, or travelogue, was an immensely popular form of literature in the seventeenth and eighteenth centuries. These accounts of journeys to "exotic" lands often took the form of letters, as in Lady Mary Wortley Montagu's *Turkish Letters* (p. 207). Europeans also enjoyed reading fictional accounts of their own countries presumably seen through the eyes of a foreigner; Montesquieu's *Persian Letters* (1721) and Oliver Goldsmith's *The Citizen of the World* (1762) are two important such works. On occasion, European readers could see themselves through the lens of actual travelers, such as Mirza Abu Taleb Khan, who recorded his impressions of Europeans—primarily the Irish and the English—in his *Travels* (p. 218), translated into English in 1810.

The NOVEL, focusing primarily on the morals and manners of the middle classes, stands out as the preeminent literary form of the later eighteenth century, taking the place of the satirical tale. Increasingly, the European novel concerned itself with sentiment and feeling, as in Jean-Jacques Rousseau's *Julie, or The New*

Eighteenth-Century Europe: Chinoiserie

Economic involvement in Southeast Asia stimulated Europeans' curiosity and desire for products and ideas from China and India. While philosophers like Voltaire (the pen name of François-Marie Arouet; 1694–1778) and Arthur Schopenhauer (1788–1860) expressed admiration for Confucianism and Hinduism, respectively, the Swedish botanist Carolus Linnaeus (1707–1778) sent his students to China to collect specimens of its plant life. Fashionable aristocrats and the newly rich bourgeoisie were smitten with what came to be known as "chinoiserie." They imitated Chinese garden designs, built fake pagodas on their grounds, and decorated the interiors of their great houses with what were often imitations of Chinese furnishings, porcelains, lacquer ware, and paintings. In 1762, the English novelist and moralist Oliver Goldsmith published *The Citizen of the World*, a collection of letters purportedly written by a Chinese traveler, Lien Chi Altangi, whose comments mildly satirizing London life and manners amused many English readers. While savvy profiteers made fortunes from the ephemeral taste for things Chinese, eventually chinoiserie was seen as a sign of affectation and was ridiculed by European writers.

Johann Joachim Kandler, Pu-Tai (Nodding Pagoda), 1765. Ceramic.   Note the peculiar expression and hand gestures of this German-made piece of chinoiserie. (© Kathleen Cohen)

Héloise (1761) and *Émile* (1762), which is excerpted in the *In the World* unit on "Love, Marriage, and the Education of Women" (p. 719). If Descartes led a revolution of the mind, Rousseau led a revolution of feeling, shifting the emphasis of the Enlightenment from reason to emotion, especially private emotion. In the exploration of the private self recorded in his seminal autobiography *Confessions* (p. 372), Rousseau converts the travel narrative's voyage to a new land of striking contrasts into an introspective, sentimental journey, discovering human nature

www   For more information about the culture and context of Europe in the eighteenth century, see *World Literature Online* at bedfordstmartins.com/worldlit.

itself. In *Confessions*, Rousseau conducts his experiments in the laboratory of his own heart, examining the "chain of the feelings" that he claims have marked the development of his being. Rousseau's writings reflected a growing shift toward feeling in the second half of the eighteenth century, and his writing exerted tremendous influence on European literature. His *Confessions* anticipated the explosion of creativity and emphasis on imagination, feeling, and self-reflection that emerged during the **ROMANTIC** era of the early nineteenth century.

❧ JEAN-BAPTISTE POQUELIN MOLIÈRE
1622–1673

The seventeenth century was a celebrated period in French drama that included the works of dramatists Corneille, Racine,[1] and Molière; it was comparable to the Elizabethan Age in England, which had Marlowe, Ben Jonson, and Shakespeare.[2] It was a time in France when the theater matured, with professional touring companies and public theaters, even though the actor's lifestyle was condemned by the clergy. The search by mathematicians for regularity in the cosmos was mirrored by the desire of kings and rulers for order and harmony. Artists, in turn, adopted orderly, **NEOCLASSICAL** standards for artistic expression and developed rules for judging works of art. The absolute standard for elegance and decorum in all phases of life was France's King Louis XIV;[3] his palace at Versailles and Paris itself became centers of culture similar to Rome under the Caesars. The court became the model for the upper classes, who sought to distance themselves from the lower classes and anything that could be considered vulgar. The possessions and behavior that distinguished the upper crust in the seventeenth century were essentially the same as those seen today: fine clothes and elegant manners, training in foreign languages, and a refined taste for art, food, and music.

Molière contributed to the new social order by writing "comedies of manners": plays that deal with the social conventions of gentlemen and

Jean-Baptiste Poquelin Molière, Seventeenth Century. Watercolor

Molière as a young man. (Giraudon / Art Resource, N.Y.)

---

[1] **Corneille, Racine:** The French dramatist Pierre Corneille (1606–1684) is known for his tragedies. It is sometimes said that the production of his *El Cid* in 1636 was the beginning of the Neoclassical period of French theater. Jean Racine (1639–1699) became famous for plays such as *Phaedra* (1677).

[2] **Marlowe, Ben Jonson, and Shakespeare:** The life of the promising playwright Christopher Marlowe (1564–1593) was sadly cut short in a tavern brawl. Ben Jonson (1572–1637) wrote several masterpieces of satiric comedy, including *The Alchemist* (1610). William Shakespeare (1564–1616) is England's most famous dramatist, known for both comedies and tragedies.

[3] **Louis XIV:** Called the Sun King, Louis XIV reigned for an unusually long period in France, from 1643 to 1715, and set the standards for political and social behavior.

moh-LYEHR

gentlewomen in a sophisticated age. The slavish imitation of contemporary fashions by the middle class also became a handy target for comedy and SATIRE. We use the words *fop* and *dandy*—taken from seventeenth-century drama—to describe the individual whose vanity yields to excesses. While to all appearances, science was making astonishing strides in discovering and describing a rational universe, human society, for all its hopes and pretensions, seemed to lag behind. It was easier to formulate a new law of physics than to eradicate a basic fault of human nature, such as greed. **Molière** used the full resources of French theater to expose the gap between the ideal and the real by creating comedies that poked fun at hypocrisy, greed, affectation, zealotry, and immoderation. Despite the pervasive influence of the Catholic Church on seventeenth-century France, Molière's plays are not concerned with the religious implications of imperfection but rather with the social consequences of immoderation and poor taste, when individuals fail to comply with the ideals of fairness, reasonableness, and common sense.

The Son of the Court Upholsterer.   Jean-Baptiste Poquelin was in line to inherit his father's position as *tapissier ordinaire du roi*, the king's upholsterer, and enjoy a comfortable life. He received a fine education at College de Clermont, a Jesuit college, and practiced law for a short time. In 1643 he drastically changed careers by becoming one of nine founders of an acting company in Paris, the *Illustre Théâtre*. Taking the stage name of Molière for the first time, he devoted the rest of his life to theater—writing, directing, staging, and producing plays. Although theater was popular with the general public, the acting profession itself was condemned by the clergy; in fact, an actor was automatically excommunicated by the church and denied Christian burial unless a renunciation of his chosen career was forthcoming before death.

Molière's new company was a total failure, at least financially; twice the playwright ended up in jail for debts. As a result, he retreated to the countryside where he learned the organizational nuts and bolts of successful theater by touring the back roads and provinces of France. For thirteen years he served an apprenticeship in the various practical and artistic responsibilities of a theatrical company. He also turned his attention from tragedies to comedies—his true calling.

In 1658 Molière returned to Paris, found favor with the court through Louis XIV's brother, "Monsieur," and had an indisputable hit with *The High-Brow Young Ladies* (*Les précieuses ridicules*, 1659). From then on he enjoyed huge success and the patronage of the king. The titles of his masterpieces constitute a list of the kinds of people he subjected to satire and ridicule. *School for Wives* (*L'ecole des femmes*, 1662) examines the insecurities of courtship. *Don Juan* (1665) picks up the theme of the playboy and explores intimate relationships. *The Misanthrope* (1666) exposes the shortsightedness of a self-righteous intellectual. *The Miser* (*L'avare*, 1668), as the title gives away, satirizes lust for money. *The Would-Be Gentleman* (*Le bourgeois gentilhomme*, 1670) turns on the aspiring middle classes and *The Learned Ladies* (*Les femmes savantes*, 1672) attacks

Molière is so great that he astonishes us afresh every time we read him. He is a man apart; his plays border on the tragic, and no one has the courage to try and imitate him.

– AUGUSTIN SAINTE-
BEUVE, critic, 1914

educated women. In his last play, *The Hypochondriac,* (*Le malade imagi-naire,* 1673), Molière depicts a hypochondriac at the mercy of the medical profession, a subject that grew out of his personal experiences during the last years of his life. Molière weathered the uncertainties of live theater and the maintenance of an acting company by writing a large number of plays. One of his editors, René Bray, estimates that in a fourteen-year period, 1660–73, Molière wrote thirty-one plays. In all, his company performed ninety-three Molière plays.

Molière died in 1673, a few hours after having acted the title role in *The Hypochondriac.* Priests were not allowed to bring the last rites to him, so Molière did not have the opportunity to renounce his profession. He was denied a Christian burial until his widow and friends persuaded the king to intervene with the archbishop. Only then was one of France's greatest playwrights buried, after dark, in the Saint-Joseph Cemetery on February 21. One can only wonder how Molière would have staged such a convoluted scenario. Molière understood the potential role of theater in the transformation of society. In the preface to *Tartuffe,* he explains why he chose religious hypocrisy for ridicule in that play and why the instrument of satire is so effective:

> If the function of comedy is to correct men's vices, I do not see why any should be exempt. Such a condition in our society would be much more dangerous than the thing itself; and we have seen that the theater is admirably suited to provide correction. The most forceful lines of a serious moral statement are usually less powerful than those of satire; and nothing will reform most men better than the depiction of their faults. It is a vigorous blow to vices to expose them to public laughter.

The Elements of Comedy.   Molière created his comedy by using stock characters, character types that appeared in other plays of the period: the foolish father who is an obstacle to his child's love life; the clever or impudent servant who interjects her witty opinions; the old lady with amusing eccentricities; the virtuous wife. The stock ending for a comedy is the happy marriage, which symbolizes the restoration of order to a society previously threatened by disorder. Molière uses a single character, Tartuffe, to embody the vice he wishes to ridicule — hypocrisy. The satire, as well as the humor, resides in the difference between appearance and reality, between the mask worn by Tartuffe and the man behind the mask. Tartuffe's manipulation of other characters in the play while wearing a mask represents a threat to society. The ultimate goal of the play itself is the unmasking of Tartuffe.

The character Tartuffe is a pious hypocrite who weasels his way into the household of a rather shallow, naive man named Orgon. Using religious flattery, Tartuffe eventually persuades Orgon to give him his daughter's hand, while making passes at Orgon's wife. The play becomes even more complicated and potentially damaging when Tartuffe replaces Orgon's son as the inheritor of Orgon's estate. Incredible as it seems, the church actually did place moral arbiters in people's homes to reform a

Moliere said that comedy should "correct men's errors in the course of amusing them." This marks him as a satirist, one of that ancient breed who use art forms and public forums to attack correctable human faults with the lance of ridicule.

– DAVID RICHARD JONES, Director and critic.

www   For links to more information about Molière, a quiz on *Tartuffe,* and information about the 21st-century relevance of *Tartuffe,* see *World Literature Online* at bedfordstmartins .com/worldlit.

family's practices, so Molière was cutting close to reality with his drama. Although Orgon seems decent enough, he is gullible and incapable of getting beneath the false masks worn by Tartuffe.

One of the persistent themes in this play is how private life with its passions and ambiguities can conflict with an orderly code of behavior in the public sphere. Marriage is a convenient arrangement for showing the discrepancies between public gestures and private needs, especially with the explosive power of sexuality. Although the women in the play clearly reveal the subordinate roles of women in French society of the time, two of them nevertheless have strong, intelligent roles to play. The servant Dorine not only provides humor with her outrageous tongue, she often articulates a sensible explanation for activities in the play. Orgon's wife, Elmire, is clever enough to ensnare Tartuffe in his own lust.

Underneath the laughter and wit in *Tartuffe* there is a persistent faith in common sense and the individual; with the unmasking of human foibles comes the person who, regardless of social rank, is able to sort out the excesses of human nature and pursue a path of moderation and caring companionship. It is Orgon's brother-in-law, **Cléante**, who consistently shows a common-sense point of view and an ethic of moderation; his rational commentaries reflect an **ENLIGHTENMENT** perspective, tying Molière to the conventional wisdom of his time:

klay-AHNT

> Ah, Brother, man's a strangely fashioned creature
> Who seldom is content to follow Nature,
> But recklessly pursues his inclination
> Beyond the narrow bounds of moderation,
> And often, by transgressing Reason's laws,
> Perverts a lofty aim or noble cause.

Early in the play, Orgon is incapable of appreciating the good sense behind Cléante's words, but through sad experiences and the timely intervention of the king at the end of the play, Orgon triumphs, and his daughter is promised to the appropriate suitor. Although the conclusion of the play indirectly raises questions about the patriarchal system that made Tartuffe's escapades possible, Orgon will "give **Valère**, whose love has proven so true, / The wedded happiness which is his due." Certainly the best ending for a comedy.

vah-LEHR

The attack on religious hypocrisy in *Tartuffe* (1664) ruffled the feathers of both clergy and laity, especially a secret society of Christian extremists called the Company of the Blessed Sacrament, a lay group whose task was to report private sins of the family to public authorities. The play was banned from public view by the king. In defending his play, Molière attributed the censorship to the very hypocrites he was satirizing and commented on them in the preface to the play's first printed edition (1669).

> This is a comedy about which a great deal of fuss has been made, and it has long been persecuted. The people it makes fun of have certainly shown [by keeping his play off the stage for nearly five years] that they command more influence in France than any of

those I have been concerned with before. Noblemen, pretentious women, cuckolds, and doctors have all submitted to being put on the stage and pretended to be as amused as everyone else at the way I portrayed them, but the hypocrites would not stand for a joke. . . .

Molière's defense is not completely without holes since there were those who felt that his attacks on excessive or false piety might also blemish the reputations of the truly pious. Molière had to rewrite the play twice before it met with great success in 1669.

■ CONNECTIONS

Voltaire, *Candide*, p. 275. The Enlightenment period in Europe, with its emphasis on reasonableness and moderation, criticized the extreme beliefs or actions of religious institutions. Voltaire, in particular, singled out Christian extremism for satirical treatment. What are the expressions of religious extremism in *Tartuffe* that invite Molière's criticism?

Aristotle, *Poetics* (Book One). Aristotle's doctrine of the golden mean, of "holding a middle position between two vices" is embodied by Cléante in *Tartuffe;* he represents the voice of common sense. Are there other characters in the play who take this position? Which characters are guilty of extreme actions or views?

Mary Wollstonecraft (p. 741) and Mary Astell (p. 729). In their search for equality and respect, European women of the Enlightenment argued that women were not controlled by emotions but were reasonable creatures capable of logical discourse. Both Wollstonecraft and Astell conduct their arguments with moderation and restraint. Consider Molière's portrayal of women in *Tartuffe;* does he depict women as reasonable?

■ FURTHER RESEARCH

Biography
Mantzius, Karl. *Molière.* 1908.
Scott, Virginia. *Molière: A Theatrical Life.* 2000.
Walker, Hallam. *Molière.* 1990.

Historical Background
Knutson, Harold C. *The Triumph of Wit.* 1988.

Criticism
Gossman, Lionel. *Men and Masks: A Study of Molière.* 1963.
Hubert, J. D. *Molière and the Company of Intellect.* 1962.
Lewis, D. B. Wyndham. *Molière: The Comic Mask.* 1959.
Mander, Gertrude. *Molière.* 1973.

■ PRONUNCIATION

Cléante: klay-AHNT
Damis: dah-MEES
Flipote: flee-POTE
Molière: moh-LYEHR
Valère: vah-LEHR

❧ Tartuffe

Translated by Richard Wilbur

MME. PERNELLE, *Orgon's mother*
ORGON, *Elmire's husband*
ELMIRE, *Orgon's wife*
DAMIS, *Orgon's son, Elmire's stepson*
MARIANE, *Orgon's daughter, Elmire's stepdaughter, in love with Valère*
VALÈRE, *in love with Mariane*

CLÉANTE, *Orgon's brother-in-law*
TARTUFFE, *a hypocrite*
DORINE, *Mariane's lady's-maid*
M. LOYAL, *a bailiff*
A POLICE OFFICER
FLIPOTE, *Mme. Pernelle's maid*

THE SCENE THROUGHOUT: ORGON's *house in Paris*

ACT I

Scene 1

MADAME PERNELLE:
Come, come, Flipote; it's time I left this place.

ELMIRE:
I can't keep up, you walk at such a pace.

MADAME PERNELLE:
Don't trouble, child; no need to show me out.
It's not your manners I'm concerned about.

ELMIRE:
We merely pay you the respect we owe.

Tartuffe. The first version of *Tartuffe*—the first three acts—was performed on May 12, 1664. The archbishop of Paris, Queen Mother Anne of Austria, and the Company of the Blessed Sacrament protested the play to Louis XIV; the play was banned, and Molière was censured. The extreme religious climate of the times is reflected by Pierre Roulé, vicar of St. Barthémy, who wrote that Molière was a "demon in flesh" and "should be burned at the stake as a foretaste of the fires of hell. . . ." The play was rewritten and performed on August 5, 1667, at the Palais-Royal. The president of Parliament brought in the police, and the play was stopped. The archbishop of Paris denounced this version from the pulpit and threatened spectators with excommunication. Although Molière petitioned Louis XIV for relief, the king had to steer politically between the religious zealots and Molière and his sympathizers. The third version of the play, the version we have today, was finally produced in 1669.

The failure of clerics and other public figures to live up to high standards of morality in our own day is proof of the perennial relevance of *Tartuffe*. The techniques Tartuffe uses in the play to brainwash his listeners are still used in the media today to "sell" religion. Through his play, Molière issues an invitation to take sides, to choose between the reasoned position of Cléante and the vacillating emotionalism of Orgon.

A note on the translation: The text used here is American poet Richard Wilbur's 1965 translation of the play, which captures the nuances of Molière's witty dialogue.

Jean Michel le Jeune Moreau, *Scene from Molière's* **Tartuffe**
This scene illustrates the surreptitious behavior featured in Tartuffe. *(Snark / Art Resource, N.Y.)*

But, Mother, why this hurry? Must you go?

MADAME PERNELLE:

I must. This house appalls me. No one in it
Will pay attention for a single minute.
Children, I take my leave much vexed in spirit.
10   I offer good advice, but you won't hear it.
You all break in and chatter on and on.
It's like a madhouse with the keeper gone.

DORINE:

If . . .

MADAME PERNELLE:

Girl, you talk too much, and I'm afraid
You're far too saucy for a lady's-maid.
You push in everywhere and have your say.

DAMIS:

But . . .

MADAME PERNELLE:

You, boy, grow more foolish every day.
To think my grandson should be such a dunce!
I've said a hundred times, if I've said it once,
That if you keep the course on which you've started,
20   You'll leave your worthy father broken-hearted.

MARIANE:

I think . . .

MADAME PERNELLE:

And you, his sister, seem so pure,
So shy, so innocent, and so demure.
But you know what they say about still waters.
I pity parents with secretive daughters.

ELMIRE:

Now, Mother . . .

MADAME PERNELLE:

And as for you, child, let me add
That your behavior is extremely bad,
And a poor example for these children, too.
Their dear, dead mother did far better than you.
You're much too free with money, and I'm distressed
30   To see you so elaborately dressed.
When it's one's husband that one aims to please,
One has no need of costly fripperies.

CLÉANTE:

Oh, Madame, really . . .

MADAME PERNELLE:

You are her brother, Sir,
And I respect and love you; yet if I were

My son, this lady's good and pious spouse,
I wouldn't make you welcome in my house.
You're full of worldly counsels which, I fear,
Aren't suitable for decent folk to hear.
I've spoken bluntly, Sir; but it behooves us
40   Not to mince words when righteous fervor moves us.

DAMIS:
   Your man Tartuffe is full of holy speeches . . .

MADAME PERNELLE:
   And practises precisely what he preaches.
   He's a fine man, and should be listened to.
   I will not hear him mocked by fools like you.

DAMIS:
   Good God! Do you expect me to submit
   To the tyranny of that carping hypocrite?
   Must we forgo all joys and satisfactions
   Because that bigot censures all our actions?

DORINE:
   To hear him talk—and he talks all the time—
50   There's nothing one can do that's not a crime.
   He rails at everything, your dear Tartuffe.

MADAME PERNELLE:
   Whatever he reproves deserves reproof.
   He's out to save your souls, and all of you
   Must love him, as my son would have you do.

DAMIS:
   Ah no, Grandmother, I could never take
   To such a rascal, even for my father's sake.
   That's how I feel, and I shall not dissemble.
   His every action makes me seethe and tremble
   With helpless anger, and I have no doubt
60   That he and I will shortly have it out.

DORINE:
   Surely it is a shame and a disgrace
   To see this man usurp the master's place—
   To see this beggar who, when first he came,
   Had not a shoe or shoestring to his name
   So far forget himself that he behaves
   As if the house were his, and we his slaves.

MADAME PERNELLE:
   Well, mark my words, your souls would fare far better
   If you obeyed his precepts to the letter.

DORINE:
   You see him as a saint. I'm far less awed;
70   In fact, I see right through him. He's a fraud.

MADAME PERNELLE:

Nonsense.

DORINE:

His man Laurent's the same, or worse;
I'd not trust either with a penny purse.

MADAME PERNELLE:

I can't say what his servant's morals may be;
His own great goodness I can guarantee.
You all regard him with distaste and fear
Because he tells you what you're loath to hear,
Condemns your sins, points out your moral flaws,
And humbly strives to further Heaven's cause.

DORINE:

If sin is all that bothers him, why is it
80   He's so upset when folk drop in to visit?
Is Heaven so outraged by a social call
That he must prophesy against us all?
I'll tell you what I think: if you ask me,
He's jealous of my mistress' company.

MADAME PERNELLE:

Rubbish! [*to* ELMIRE] He's not alone, child, in complaining
Of all your promiscuous entertaining.
Why, the whole neighborhood's upset, I know,
By all these carriages that come and go,
With crowds of guests parading in and out
90   And noisy servants loitering about.
In all of this, I'm sure there's nothing vicious;
But why give people cause to be suspicious?

CLÉANTE:

They need no cause; they'll talk in any case.
Madam, this world would be a joyless place
If, fearing what malicious tongues might say,
We locked our doors and turned our friends away.
And even if one did so dreary a thing,
D'you think those tongues would cease their chattering?
One can't fight slander; it's a losing battle;
100 Let us instead ignore their tittle-tattle.
Let's strive to live by conscience's clear decrees,
And let the gossips gossip as they please.

DORINE:

If there is talk against us, I know the source:
It's Daphne and her little husband, of course.
Those who have greatest cause for guilt and shame
Are quickest to besmirch a neighbor's name.
When there's a chance for libel, they never miss it;

When something can be made to seem illicit
They're off at once to spread the joyous news,
110   Adding to fact what fantasies they choose.
By talking up their neighbor's indiscretions
They seek to camouflage their own transgressions,
Hoping that others' innocent affairs
Will lend a hue of innocence to theirs,
Or that their own black guilt will come to seem
Part of a general shady color-scheme.

MADAME PERNELLE:
All that is quite irrelevant. I doubt
That anyone's more virtuous and devout
Than dear Orante; and I'm informed that she
120   Condemns your mode of life most vehemently.

DORINE:
Oh, yes, she's strict, devout, and has no taint
Of worldliness; in short, she seems a saint.
But it was time which taught her that disguise;
She's thus because she can't be otherwise.
So long as her attractions could enthrall,
She flounced and flirted and enjoyed it all,
But now that they're no longer what they were
She quits a world which fast is quitting her,
And wears a veil of virtue to conceal
130   Her bankrupt beauty and her lost appeal.
That's what becomes of old coquettes today:
Distressed when all their lovers fall away,
They see no recourse but to play the prude,
And so confer a style on solitude.
Thereafter, they're severe with everyone,
Condemning all our actions, pardoning none,
And claiming to be pure, austere, and zealous
When, if the truth were known, they're merely jealous,
And cannot bear to see another know
140   The pleasures time has forced them to forgo.

MADAME PERNELLE [*initially to* ELMIRE]:
That sort of talk is what you like to hear,
Therefore you'd have us all keep still, my dear,
While Madam rattles on the livelong day.
Nevertheless, I mean to have my say.
I tell you that you're blest to have Tartuffe
Dwelling, as my son's guest, beneath this roof;
That Heaven has sent him to forestall its wrath
By leading you, once more, to the true path;
That all he reprehends is reprehensible,

150 And that you'd better heed him, and be sensible.
These visits, balls, and parties in which you revel
Are nothing but inventions of the Devil.
One never hears a word that's edifying:
Nothing but chaff and foolishness and lying,
As well as vicious gossip in which one's neighbor
Is cut to bits with epee, foil, and saber.
People of sense are driven half-insane
At such affairs, where noise and folly reign
And reputations perish thick and fast.
160 As a wise preacher said on Sunday last,
Parties are Towers of Babylon, because
The guests all babble on with never a pause;
And then he told a story which, I think . . .
[*To* CLÉANTE] I heard that laugh, Sir, and I saw that wink!
Go find your silly friends and laugh some more!
Enough; I'm going; don't show me to the door.
I leave this household much dismayed and vexed;
I cannot say when I shall see you next.
[*Slapping* FLIPOTE] Wake up, don't stand there gaping into space!
170 I'll slap some sense into that stupid face.
Move, move, you slut.

Scene 2

CLÉANTE:
                    I think I'll stay behind;
I want no further pieces of her mind.
How that old lady . . .

DORINE:
                    Oh, what wouldn't she say
If she could hear you speak of her that way!
She'd thank you for the *lady,* but I'm sure
She'd find the *old* a little premature.

CLÉANTE:
My, what a scene she made, and what a din!
And how this man Tartuffe has taken her in!

DORINE:
Yes, but her son is even worse deceived;
10 His folly must be seen to be believed.
In the late troubles, he played an able part
And served his king with wise and loyal heart,
But he's quite lost his senses since he fell
Beneath Tartuffe's infatuating spell.

He calls him brother, and loves him as his life,
Preferring him to mother, child, or wife.
In him and him alone will he confide;
He's made him his confessor and his guide;
He pets and pampers him with love more tender
20   Than any pretty mistress could engender,
Gives him the place of honor when they dine,
Delights to see him gorging like a swine,
Stuffs him with dainties till his guts distend,
And when he belches, cries "God bless you, friend!"
In short, he's mad; he worships him; he dotes;
His deeds he marvels at, his words he quotes,
Thinking each act a miracle, each word
Oracular as those that Moses heard.
Tartuffe, much pleased to find so easy a victim,
30   Has in a hundred ways beguiled and tricked him,
Milked him of money, and with his permission
Established here a sort of Inquisition.
Even Laurent, his lackey, dares to give
Us arrogant advice on how to live;
He sermonizes us in thundering tones
And confiscates our ribbons and colognes.
Last week he tore a kerchief into pieces
Because he found it pressed in a *Life of Jesus:*
He said it was a sin to juxtapose
40   Unholy vanities and holy prose.

Scene 3

ELMIRE [*to* CLÉANTE]:
You did well not to follow; she stood in the door
And said *verbatim* all she'd said before.
I saw my husband coming. I think I'd best
Go upstairs now, and take a little rest.

CLÉANTE:
I'll wait and greet him here; then I must go.
I've really only time to say hello.

DAMIS:
Sound him about my sister's wedding, please.
I think Tartuffe's against it, and that he's
Been urging Father to withdraw his blessing.
10   As you well know, I'd find that most distressing.
Unless my sister and Valère can marry,
My hopes to wed *his* sister will miscarry,

And I'm determined . . .

DORINE:

He's coming.

Scene 4

ORGON:

Ah, Brother, good-day.

CLÉANTE:

Well, welcome back. I'm sorry I can't stay.
How was the country? Blooming, I trust, and green?

ORGON:

Excuse me, Brother; just one moment.
[*To* DORINE]   Dorine . . .
[*To* CLÉANTE] To put my mind at rest, I always learn
The household news the moment I return.
[*To* DORINE] Has all been well, these two days I've been gone?
How are the family? What's been going on?

DORINE:

Your wife, two days ago, had a bad fever,
10   And a fierce headache which refused to leave her.

ORGON:

Ah. And Tartuffe?

DORINE:

Tartuffe? Why, he's round and red,
Bursting with health, and excellently fed.

ORGON:

Poor fellow!

DORINE:

That night, the mistress was unable
To take a single bite at the dinner-table.
Her headache-pains, she said, were simply hellish.

ORGON:

Ah. And Tartuffe?

DORINE:

He ate his meal with relish,
And zealously devoured in her presence
A leg of mutton and a brace of pheasants.

ORGON:

Poor fellow!

DORINE:

Well, the pains continued strong,
20   And so she tossed and tossed the whole night long,
Now icy-cold, now burning like a flame.
We sat beside her bed till morning came.

ORGON:

    Ah. And Tartuffe?

DORINE:

              Why, having eaten, he rose

And sought his room, already in a doze,

Got into his warm bed, and snored away

In perfect peace until the break of day.

ORGON:

    Poor fellow!

DORINE:

              After much ado, we talked her

Into dispatching someone for the doctor.

He bled her, and the fever quickly fell.

ORGON:

    Ah. And Tartuffe?

DORINE:

30   He bore it very well.

To keep his cheerfulness at any cost,

And make up for the blood *Madame* had lost,

He drank, at lunch, four beakers full of port.

ORGON:

    Poor fellow!

DORINE:

             Both are doing well, in short.

I'll go and tell *Madame* that you've expressed

Keen sympathy and anxious interest.

Scene 5

CLÉANTE:

    That girl was laughing in your face, and though

I've no wish to offend you, even so

I'm bound to say that she had some excuse.

How can you possibly be such a goose?

Are you so dazed by this man's hocus-pocus

That all the world, save him, is out of focus?

You've given him clothing, shelter, food, and care;

Why must you also . . .

ORGON:

             Brother, stop right there.

You do not know the man of whom you speak.

CLÉANTE:

10   I grant you that. But my judgment's not so weak

That I can't tell, by his effect on others . . .

ORGON:

    Ah, when you meet him, you two will be like brothers!
    There's been no loftier soul since time began.
    He is a man who . . . a man who . . . an excellent man.
    To keep his precepts is to be reborn,
    And view this dunghill of a world with scorn.
    Yes, thanks to him I'm a changed man indeed.
    Under his tutelage my soul's been freed
    From earthly loves, and every human tie:

20   My mother, children, brother, and wife could die,
    And I'd not feel a single moment's pain.

CLÉANTE:

    That's a fine sentiment, Brother; most humane.

ORGON:

    Oh, had you seen Tartuffe as I first knew him,
    Your heart, like mine, would have surrendered to him.
    He used to come into our church each day
    And humbly kneel nearby, and start to pray.
    He'd draw the eyes of everybody there
    By the deep fervor of his heartfelt prayer;
    He'd sigh and weep, and sometimes with a sound

30   Of rapture he would bend and kiss the ground;
    And when I rose to go, he'd run before
    To offer me holy-water at the door.
    His serving-man, no less devout than he,
    Informed me of his master's poverty;
    I gave him gifts, but in his humbleness
    He'd beg me every time to give him less.
    "Oh, that's too much," he'd cry, "too much by twice!
    I don't deserve it. The half, Sir, would suffice."
    And when I wouldn't take it back, he'd share

40   Half of it with the poor, right then and there.
    At length, Heaven prompted me to take him in
    To dwell with us, and free our souls from sin.
    He guides our lives, and to protect my honor
    Stays by my wife, and keeps an eye upon her;
    He tells me whom she sees, and all she does,
    And seems more jealous than I ever was!
    And how austere he is! Why, he can detect
    A mortal sin where you would least suspect;
    In smallest trifles, he's extremely strict.

50   Last week, his conscience was severely pricked
    Because, while praying, he had caught a flea
    And killed it, so he felt, too wrathfully.

CLÉANTE:

Good God, man! Have you lost your common sense—
Or is this all some joke at my expense?
How can you stand there and in all sobriety . . .

ORGON:

Brother, your language savors of impiety.
Too much free-thinking's made your faith unsteady,
And as I've warned you many times already,
'Twill get you into trouble before you're through.

CLÉANTE:

60   So I've been told before by dupes like you:
Being blind, you'd have all others blind as well;
The clear-eyed man you call an infidel,
And he who sees through humbug and pretense
Is charged, by you, with want of reverence.
Spare me your warnings, Brother; I have no fear
Of speaking out, for you and Heaven to hear,
Against affected zeal and pious knavery.
There's true and false in piety, as in bravery,
And just as those whose courage shines the most
70   In battle, are the least inclined to boast,
So those whose hearts are truly pure and lowly
Don't make a flashy show of being holy.
There's a vast difference, so it seems to me,
Between true piety and hypocrisy:
How do you fail to see it, may I ask?
Is not a face quite different from a mask?
Cannot sincerity and cunning art,
Reality and semblance, be told apart?
Are scarecrows just like men, and do you hold
80   That a false coin is just as good as gold?
Ah, Brother, man's a strangely fashioned creature
Who seldom is content to follow Nature,
But recklessly pursues his inclination
Beyond the narrow bounds of moderation,
And often, by transgressing Reason's laws,
Perverts a lofty aim or noble cause.
A passing observation, but it applies.

ORGON:

I see, dear Brother, that you're profoundly wise;
You harbor all the insight of the age.
90   You are our one clear mind, our only sage,
The era's oracle, its Cato too,
And all mankind are fools compared to you.

CLÉANTE:

Brother, I don't pretend to be a sage,
Nor have I all the wisdom of the age.
There's just one insight I would dare to claim:
I know that true and false are not the same;
And just as there is nothing I more revere
Than a soul whose faith is steadfast and sincere,
Nothing that I more cherish and admire
100   Than honest zeal and true religious fire,
So there is nothing that I find more base
Than specious piety's dishonest face—
Than these bold mountebanks, these histrios
Whose impious mummeries and hollow shows
Exploit our love of Heaven, and make a jest
Of all that men think holiest and best;
These calculating souls who offer prayers
Not to their Maker, but as public wares,
And seek to buy respect and reputation
110   With lifted eyes and sighs of exaltation;
These charlatans, I say, whose pilgrim souls
Proceed, by way of Heaven, toward earthly goals,
Who weep and pray and swindle and extort,
Who preach the monkish life, but haunt the court,
Who make their zeal the partner of their vice—
Such men are vengeful, sly, and cold as ice,
And when there is an enemy to defame
They cloak their spite in fair religion's name,
Their private spleen and malice being made
120   To seem a high and virtuous crusade,
Until, to mankind's reverent applause,
They crucify their foe in Heaven's cause.
Such knaves are all too common; yet, for the wise,
True piety isn't hard to recognize,
And, happily, these present times provide us
With bright examples to instruct and guide us.
Consider Ariston and Périandre;
Look at Oronte, Alcidamas, Clitandre;
Their virtue is acknowledged; who could doubt it?
130   But you won't hear them beat the drum about it.
They're never ostentatious, never vain,
And their religion's moderate and humane;
It's not their way to criticize and chide:
They think censoriousness a mark of pride,
And therefore, letting others preach and rave,

They show, by deeds, how Christians should behave.
They think no evil of their fellow man,
But judge of him as kindly as they can.
They don't intrigue and wangle and conspire;
140   To lead a good life is their one desire;
The sinner wakes no rancorous hate in them;
It is the sin alone which they condemn;
Nor do they try to show a fiercer zeal
For Heaven's cause than Heaven itself could feel.
These men I honor, these men I advocate
As models for us all to emulate.
Your man is not their sort at all, I fear:
And, while your praise of him is quite sincere,
I think that you've been dreadfully deluded.

ORGON:

150   Now then, dear Brother, is your speech concluded?

CLÉANTE:

Why, yes.

ORGON:

        Your servant, Sir. [*He turns to go.*]

CLÉANTE:

           No, Brother; wait.
There's one more matter. You agreed of late
That young Valère might have your daughter's hand.

ORGON:

I did.

CLÉANTE:

    And set the date, I understand.

ORGON:

Quite so.

CLÉANTE:

    You've now postponed it; is that true?

ORGON:

No doubt.

CLÉANTE:

    The match no longer pleases you?

ORGON:

Who knows?

CLÉANTE:

    D'you mean to go back on your word?

ORGON:

I won't say that.

CLÉANTE:

        Has anything occurred

Which might entitle you to break your pledge?

ORGON:

   Perhaps.

CLÉANTE:

160   Why must you hem, and haw, and hedge?

   The boy asked me to sound you in this affair . . . .

ORGON:

   It's been a pleasure.

CLÉANTE:

          But what shall I tell Valère?

ORGON:

   Whatever you like.

CLÉANTE:

          But what have you decided?

   What are your plans?

ORGON:

          I plan, Sir, to be guided

   By Heaven's will.

CLÉANTE:

          Come, Brother, don't talk rot.

   You've given Valère your word; will you keep it, or not?

ORGON:

   Good day.

CLÉANTE:

          This looks like poor Valère's undoing;

   I'll go and warn him that there's trouble brewing.

ACT II

Scene 1

ORGON:

   Mariane.

MARIANE:

       Yes, Father?

ORGON:

         A word with you; come here.

MARIANE:

   What are you looking for?

ORGON [*peering into a small closet*]:

         Eavesdroppers, dear.

   I'm making sure we shan't be overheard.

   Someone in there could catch our every word.

   Ah, good, we're safe. Now, Mariane, my child,

   You're a sweet girl who's tractable and mild,

   Whom I hold dear, and think most highly of.

MARIANE:

    I'm deeply grateful, Father, for your love.

ORGON:

    That's well said, Daughter; and you can repay me

10   If, in all things, you'll cheerfully obey me.

MARIANE:

    To please you, Sir, is what delights me best.

ORGON:

    Good, good. Now, what d'you think of Tartuffe, our guest?

MARIANE:

    I, Sir?

ORGON:

        Yes. Weigh your answer; think it through.

MARIANE:

    Oh, dear. I'll say whatever you wish me to.

ORGON:

    That's wisely said, my Daughter. Say of him, then,

    That he's the very worthiest of men,

    And that you're fond of him, and would rejoice

    In being his wife, if that should be my choice.

    Well?

MARIANE:

      What?

ORGON:

        What's that?

MARIANE:

           I . . .

ORGON:

             Well?

MARIANE:

             Forgive me, pray.

ORGON:

    Did you not hear me?

MARIANE:

20   Of *whom*, Sir, must I say

    That I am fond of him, and would rejoice

    In being his wife, if that should be your choice?

ORGON:

    Why, of Tartuffe.

MARIANE:

        But, Father, that's false, you know.

    Why would you have me say what isn't so?

ORGON:

    Because I am resolved it shall be true.

    That it's my wish should be enough for you.

MARIANE:
You can't mean, Father . . .
ORGON:
         Yes, Tartuffe shall be
Allied by marriage to this family,
And he's to be your husband, is that clear?
30 It's a father's privilege . . .

Scene 2

ORGON [to DORINE]:
       What are you doing in here?
Is curiosity so fierce a passion
With you, that you must eavesdrop in this fashion?
DORINE:
There's lately been a rumor going about—
Based on some hunch or chance remark, no doubt—
That you mean Mariane to wed Tartuffe.
I've laughed it off, of course, as just a spoof.
ORGON:
You find it so incredible?
DORINE:
       Yes, I do.
I won't accept that story, even from you.
ORGON:
10 Well, you'll believe it when the thing is done.
DORINE:
Yes, yes, of course. Go on and have your fun.
ORGON:
I've never been more serious in my life.
DORINE:
Ha!
ORGON:
    Daughter, I mean it; you're to be his wife.
DORINE:
No, don't believe your father; it's all a hoax.
ORGON:
See here, young woman . . .
DORINE:
      Come, Sir, no more jokes;
You can't fool us.
ORGON:
     How dare you talk that way?
DORINE:
All right, then: we believe you, sad to say.
But how a man like you, who looks so wise

And wears a moustache of such splendid size,
Can be so foolish as to . . .

ORGON:

20   Silence, please!
My girl, you take too many liberties.
I'm master here, as you must not forget.

DORINE:

Do let's discuss this calmly; don't be upset.
You can't be serious, Sir, about this plan.
What should that bigot want with Mariane?
Praying and fasting ought to keep him busy.
And then, in terms of wealth and rank, what is he?
Why should a man of poverty like you
Pick out a beggar son-in-law?

ORGON:

                                         That will do.

30   Speak of his poverty with reverence.
His is a pure and saintly indigence
Which far transcends all worldly pride and pelf.
He lost his fortune, as he says himself,
Because he cared for Heaven alone, and so
Was careless of his interests here below.
I mean to get him out of his present straits
And help him to recover his estates—
Which, in his part of the world, have no small fame.
Poor though he is, he's a gentleman just the same.

DORINE:

40   Yes, so he tells us; and, Sir, it seems to me
Such pride goes very ill with piety.
A man whose spirit spurns this dungy earth
Ought not to brag of lands and noble birth;
Such worldly arrogance will hardly square
With meek devotion and the life of prayer.
. . . But this reproach, I see, has drawn a blank;
Let's speak, then, of his person, not his rank.
Doesn't it seem to you a trifle grim
To give a girl like her to a man like him?

50   When two are so ill-suited, can't you see
What the sad consequence is bound to be?
A young girl's virtue is imperilled, Sir,
When such a marriage is imposed on her;
For if one's bridegroom isn't to one's taste,
It's hardly an inducement to be chaste,
And many a man with horns upon his brow
Has made his wife the thing that she is now.
It's hard to be a faithful wife, in short,

To certain husbands of a certain sort,

60   And he who gives his daughter to a man she hates
Must answer for her sins at Heaven's gates.
Think, Sir, before you play so risky a role.

ORGON:

This servant-girl presumes to save my soul!

DORINE:

You would do well to ponder what I've said.

ORGON:

Daughter, we'll disregard this dunderhead.
Just trust your father's judgment. Oh, I'm aware
That I once promised you to young Valère;
But now I hear he gambles, which greatly shocks me;
What's more, I've doubts about his orthodoxy.

70   His visits to church, I note, are very few.

DORINE:

Would you have him go at the same hours as you,
And kneel nearby, to be sure of being seen?

ORGON:

I can dispense with such remarks, Dorine.
[*To* MARIANE] Tartuffe, however, is sure of Heaven's blessing,
And that's the only treasure worth possessing.
This match will bring you joys beyond all measure;
Your cup will overflow with every pleasure;
You two will interchange your faithful loves
Like two sweet cherubs, or two turtle-doves.

80   No harsh word shall be heard, no frown be seen,
And he shall make you happy as a queen.

DORINE:

And she'll make him a cuckold, just wait and see.

ORGON:

What language!

DORINE:

Oh, he's a man of destiny;
He's *made* for horns, and what the stars demand
Your daughter's virtue surely can't withstand.

ORGON:

Don't interrupt me further. Why can't you learn
That certain things are none of your concern?

DORINE:

It's for your own sake that I interfere.
[*She repeatedly interrupts* ORGON *just as he is turning to speak to his daughter.*]

ORGON:

Most kind of you. Now, hold your tongue, d'you hear?

DORINE:

If I didn't love you . . .

ORGON:

90   Spare me your affection.

DORINE:

I love you, Sir, in spite of your objection.

ORGON:

Blast!

DORINE:

      I can't bear, Sir, for your honor's sake,
To let you make this ludicrous mistake.

ORGON:

You mean to go on talking?

DORINE:

                        If I didn't protest
This sinful marriage, my conscience couldn't rest.

ORGON:

If you don't hold your tongue, you little shrew . . .

DORINE:

What, lost your temper? A pious man like you?

ORGON:

Yes! Yes! You talk and talk. I'm maddened by it.
Once and for all, I tell you to be quiet.

DORINE:

100   Well, I'll be quiet. But I'll be thinking hard.

ORGON:

Think all you like, but you had better guard
That saucy tongue of yours, or I'll . . .
[*Turning back to* MARIANE]   Now, child,
I've weighed this matter fully.

DORINE [*aside*]:

                        It drives me wild
That I can't speak.
[ORGON *turns his head, and she is silent.*]

ORGON:

                  Tartuffe is no young dandy,
But, still, his person . . .

DORINE [*aside*]:

                        Is as sweet as candy.

ORGON:

Is such that, even if you shouldn't care
For his other merits . . .
[*He turns and stands facing* DORINE, *arms crossed.*]

DORINE [*aside*]:

                  They'll make a lovely pair.
If I were she, no man would marry me
Against my inclination, and go scot-free.

110   He'd learn, before the wedding-day was over,

How readily a wife can find a lover.

ORGON [*to* DORINE]:

It seems you treat my orders as a joke.

DORINE:

Why, what's the matter? 'Twas not to you I spoke.

ORGON:

What *were* you doing?

DORINE:

Talking to myself, that's all.

ORGON:

Ah! [*aside*] One more bit of impudence and gall,
And I shall give her a good slap in the face.
[*He puts himself in position to slap her;* DORINE, *whenever he glances at her, stands immobile and silent.*]
Daughter, you shall accept, and with good grace,
The husband I've selected . . . Your wedding-day . . .
[*To* DORINE] Why don't you talk to yourself?

DORINE:

I've nothing to say.

ORGON:

Come, just one word.

DORINE:

120   No thank you, Sir. I pass.

ORGON:

Come, speak; I'm waiting.

DORINE:

I'd not be such an ass.

ORGON [*turning to* MARIANE]:

In short, dear Daughter, I mean to be obeyed,
And you must bow to the sound choice I've made.

DORINE [*moving away*]:

I'd not wed such a monster, even in jest.
[ORGON *attempts to slap her, but misses.*]

ORGON:

Daughter, that maid of yours is a thorough pest;
She makes me sinfully annoyed and nettled.
I can't speak further; my nerves are too unsettled.
She's so upset me by her insolent talk,
I'll calm myself by going for a walk.

Scene 3

DORINE [*returning*]:

Well, have you lost your tongue, girl? Must I play
Your part, and say the lines you ought to say?

Faced with a fate so hideous and absurd,
Can you not utter one dissenting word?

MARIANE:

What good would it do? A father's power is great.

DORINE:

Resist him now, or it will be too late.

MARIANE:

But . . .

DORINE:

   Tell him one cannot love at a father's whim;
That you shall marry for yourself, not him;
That since it's you who are to be the bride,
10 It's you, not he, who must be satisfied;
And that if his Tartuffe is so sublime,
He's free to marry him at any time.

MARIANE:

I've bowed so long to Father's strict control,
I couldn't oppose him now, to save my soul.

DORINE:

Come, come, Mariane. Do listen to reason, won't you?
Valère has asked your hand. Do you love him, or don't you?

MARIANE:

Oh, how unjust of you! What can you mean
By asking such a question, dear Dorine?
You know the depth of my affection for him;
20 I've told you a hundred times how I adore him.

DORINE:

I don't believe in everything I hear;
Who knows if your professions were sincere?

MARIANE:

They were, Dorine, and you do me wrong to doubt it;
Heaven knows that I've been all too frank about it.

DORINE:

You love him, then?

MARIANE:

     Oh, more than I can express.

DORINE:

And he, I take it, cares for you no less?

MARIANE:

I think so.

DORINE:

   And you both, with equal fire,
Burn to be married?

MARIANE:

     That is our one desire.

DORINE:
>What of Tartuffe, then? What of your father's plan?

MARIANE:
30>I'll kill myself, if I'm forced to wed that man.

DORINE:
>I hadn't thought of that recourse. How splendid!
>Just die, and all your troubles will be ended!
>A fine solution. Oh, it maddens me
>To hear you talk in that self-pitying key.

MARIANE:
>Dorine, how harsh you are! It's most unfair.
>You have no sympathy for my despair.

DORINE:
>I've none at all for people who talk drivel
>And, faced with difficulties, whine and snivel.

MARIANE:
>No doubt I'm timid, but it would be wrong . . .

DORINE:
40>True love requires a heart that's firm and strong.

MARIANE:
>I'm strong in my affection for Valère,
>But coping with my father is his affair.

DORINE:
>But if your father's brain has grown so cracked
>Over his dear Tartuffe that he can retract
>His blessing, though your wedding-day was named,
>It's surely not Valère who's to be blamed.

MARIANE:
>If I defied my father, as you suggest,
>Would it not seem unmaidenly, at best?
>Shall I defend my love at the expense
50>Of brazenness and disobedience?
>Shall I parade my heart's desires, and flaunt . . .

DORINE:
>No, I ask nothing of you. Clearly you want
>To be Madame Tartuffe, and I feel bound
>Not to oppose a wish so very sound.
>What right have I to criticize the match?
>Indeed, my dear, the man is a brilliant catch.
>Monsieur Tartuffe! Now, there's a man of weight!
>Yes, yes, Monsieur Tartuffe, I'm bound to state,
>Is quite a person; that's not to be denied;
60>'Twill be no little thing to be his bride.
>The world already rings with his renown;
>He's a great noble — in his native town;

His ears are red, he has a pink complexion,
And all in all, he'll suit you to perfection.

MARIANE:
　Dear God!

DORINE:
　　　　　Oh, how triumphant you will feel
At having caught a husband so ideal!

MARIANE:
　Oh, do stop teasing, and use your cleverness
To get me out of this appalling mess.
Advise me, and I'll do whatever you say.

DORINE:
70　Ah no, a dutiful daughter must obey
Her father, even if he weds her to an ape.
You've a bright future; why struggle to escape?
Tartuffe will take you back where his family lives,
To a small town aswarm with relatives—
Uncles and cousins whom you'll be charmed to meet.
You'll be received at once by the elite,
Calling upon the bailiff's wife, no less—
Even, perhaps, upon the mayoress,
Who'll sit you down in the *best* kitchen chair.
80　Then, once a year, you'll dance at the village fair
To the drone of bagpipes—two of them, in fact—
And see a puppet-show, or an animal act.
Your husband . . .

MARIANE:
　　　　　Oh, you turn my blood to ice!
Stop torturing me, and give me your advice.

DORINE [*threatening to go*]:
　Your servant, Madam.

MARIANE:
　　　　　Dorine, I beg of you . . .

DORINE:
　No, you deserve it; this marriage must go through.

MARIANE:
　Dorine!

DORINE:
　　　No.

MARIANE:
　　　　　Not Tartuffe! You know I think him . . .

DORINE:
　Tartuffe's your cup of tea, and you shall drink him.

MARIANE:
　I've always told you everything, and relied . . .

DORINE:

90   No. You deserve to be tartuffified.

MARIANE:

Well, since you mock me and refuse to care,
I'll henceforth seek my solace in despair:
Despair shall be my counsellor and friend,
And help me bring my sorrows to an end.

[*She starts to leave.*]

DORINE:

There now, come back; my anger has subsided.
You do deserve some pity, I've decided.

MARIANE:

Dorine, if Father makes me undergo
This dreadful martyrdom, I'll die, I know.

DORINE:

Don't fret; it won't be difficult to discover

100   Some plan of action . . . But here's Valère, your lover.

Scene 4

VALÈRE:

Madame, I've just received some wondrous news
Regarding which I'd like to hear your views.

MARIANE:

What news?

VALÈRE:

You're marrying Tartuffe.

MARIANE:

I find
That Father does have such a match in mind.

VALÈRE:

Your father, Madam . . .

MARIANE:

. . . has just this minute said
That it's Tartuffe he wishes me to wed.

VALÈRE:

Can he be serious?

MARIANE:

Oh, indeed he can;
He's clearly set his heart upon the plan.

VALÈRE:

And what position do you propose to take, Madam?

MARIANE:

Why—I don't know.

VALÈRE:

For heaven's sake—

10

You don't know?

MARIANE:

            No.

VALÈRE:

            Well, well!

MARIANE:

                Advise me, do.

VALÈRE:

Marry the man. That's my advice to you.

MARIANE:

That's your advice?

VALÈRE:

            Yes.

MARIANE:

              Truly?

VALÈRE:

                Oh, absolutely.
You couldn't choose more wisely, more astutely.

MARIANE:

Thanks for this counsel; I'll follow it, of course.

VALÈRE:

Do, do; I'm sure 'twill cost you no remorse.

MARIANE:

To give it didn't cause your heart to break.

VALÈRE:

I gave it, Madam, only for your sake.

MARIANE:

And it's for your sake that I take it, Sir.

DORINE [*withdrawing to the rear of the stage*]:

20 Let's see which fool will prove the stubborner.

VALÈRE:

So! I am nothing to you, and it was flat
Deception when you . . .

MARIANE:

               Please, enough of that.
You've told me plainly that I should agree
To wed the man my father's chosen for me,
And since you've designed to counsel me so wisely,
I promise, Sir, to do as you advise me.

VALÈRE:

Ah, no, 'twas not by me that you were swayed.
No, your decision was already made;
Though now, to save appearances, you protest
30 That you're betraying me at my behest.

MARIANE:

Just as you say.

VALÈRE:
> Quite so. And I now see
> That you were never truly in love with me.

MARIANE:
> Alas, you're free to think so if you choose.

VALÈRE:
> I choose to think so, and here's a bit of news:
> You've spurned my hand, but I know where to turn
> For kinder treatment, as you shall quickly learn.

MARIANE:
> I'm sure you do. Your noble qualities
> Inspire affection . . .

VALÈRE:
> Forget my qualities, please.
> They don't inspire you overmuch, I find.
40   But there's another lady I have in mind
> Whose sweet and generous nature will not scorn
> To compensate me for the loss I've borne.

MARIANE:
> I'm no great loss, and I'm sure that you'll transfer
> Your heart quite painlessly from me to her.

VALÈRE:
> I'll do my best to take it in my stride.
> The pain I feel at being cast aside
> Time and forgetfulness may put an end to.
> Or if I can't forget, I shall pretend to.
> No self-respecting person is expected
50   To go on loving once he's been rejected.

MARIANE:
> Now, that's a fine, high-minded sentiment.

VALÈRE:
> One to which any sane man would assent.
> Would you prefer it if I pined away
> In hopeless passion till my dying day?
> Am I to yield you to a rival's arms
> And not console myself with other charms?

MARIANE:
> Go then: console yourself; don't hesitate.
> I wish you to; indeed, I cannot wait.

VALÈRE:
> You wish me to?

MARIANE:
> Yes.

VALÈRE:
> That's the final straw.

60   Madam, farewell. Your wish shall be my law.
      [*He starts to leave, and then returns: this repeatedly.*]
MARIANE:
      Splendid.
VALÈRE [*coming back again*]:
                  This breach, remember, is of your making;
      It's you who've driven me to the step I'm taking.
MARIANE:
      Of course.
VALÈRE [*coming back again*]:
                  Remember, too, that I am merely
      Following your example.
MARIANE:
                        I see that clearly.
VALÈRE:
      Enough. I'll go and do your bidding, then.
MARIANE:
      Good.
VALÈRE [*coming back again*]:
              You shall never see my face again.
MARIANE:
      Excellent.
VALÈRE [*walking to the door, then turning about*]:
                  Yes?
MARIANE:
                    What?
VALÈRE:
                      What's that? What did you say?
MARIANE:
      Nothing. You're dreaming.
VALÈRE:
                      Ah. Well, I'm on my way.
      Farewell, *Madame.*
                  [*He moves slowly away.*]
MARIANE:
                    Farewell.
DORINE [*to* MARIANE]:
                      If you ask me,
70   Both of you are as mad as mad can be.
      Do stop this nonsense, now. I've only let you
      Squabble so long to see where it would get you.
      Whoa there, Monsieur Valère!
      [*She goes and seizes* VALÈRE *by the arm; he makes a great show of resistance.*]
VALÈRE:
                  What's this, Dorine?

DORINE:
> Come here.

VALÈRE:
> No, no, my heart's too full of spleen.
> Don't hold me back; her wish must be obeyed.

DORINE:
> Stop!

VALÈRE:
> It's too late now; my decision's made.

DORINE:
> Oh, pooh!

MARIANE [*aside*]:
> He hates the sight of me, that's plain.
> I'll go, and so deliver him from pain.

DORINE [*leaving* VALÈRE, *running after* MARIANE]:
> And now *you* run away! Come back.

MARIANE:
> No, no.
80 Nothing you say will keep me here. Let go!

VALÈRE [*aside*]:
> She cannot bear my presence, I perceive.
> To spare her further torment, I shall leave.

DORINE [*leaving* MARIANE, *running after* VALÈRE]:
> Again! You'll not escape, Sir; don't you try it.
> Come here, you two. Stop fussing, and be quiet.
> [*She takes* VALÈRE *by the hand, then* MARIANE, *and draws them together.*]

VALÈRE [*to* DORINE]:
> What do you want of me?

MARIANE [*to* DORINE]:
> What is the point of this?

DORINE:
> We're going to have a little armistice.
> [*To* VALÈRE] Now weren't you silly to get so overheated?

VALÈRE:
> Didn't you see how badly I was treated?

DORINE [*to* MARIANE]:
> Aren't you a simpleton, to have lost your head?

MARIANE:
90 Didn't you hear the hateful things he said?

DORINE [*to* VALÈRE]:
> You're both great fools. Her sole desire, Valère,
> Is to be yours in marriage. To that I'll swear.
> [*To* MARIANE] He loves you only, and he wants no wife
> But you, Mariane. On that I'll stake my life.

MARIANE [*to* VALÈRE]:
> Then why you advised me so, I cannot see.

VALÈRE [*to* MARIANE]:
    On such a question, why ask advice of *me*?
DORINE:
    Oh, you're impossible. Give me your hands, you two.
    [*To* VALÈRE] Yours first.
VALÈRE [*giving* DORINE *his hand*]:
                    But why?
DORINE [*to* MARIANE]:
                    And now a hand from you.
MARIANE [*also giving* DORINE *her hand*]:
    What are you doing?
DORINE:
                There: a perfect fit.
100   You suit each other better than you'll admit.
    [VALÈRE *and* MARIANE *hold hands for some time without looking at each other.*]
VALÈRE [*turning toward* MARIANE]:
    Ah, come, don't be so haughty. Give a man
    A look of kindness, won't you, Mariane?
    [MARIANE *turns toward* VALÈRE *and smiles.*]
DORINE:
    I tell you, lovers are completely mad!
VALÈRE [*to* MARIANE]:
    Now come, confess that you were very bad
    To hurt my feelings as you did just now.
    I have a just complaint, you must allow.
MARIANE:
    You must allow that you were most unpleasant . . .
DORINE:
    Let's table that discussion for the present;
    Your father has a plan which must be stopped.
MARIANE:
110   Advise us, then; what means must we adopt?
DORINE:
    We'll use all manner of means, and all at once.
    [*To* MARIANE] Your father's addled; he's acting like a dunce.
    Therefore you'd better humor the old fossil.
    Pretend to yield to him, be sweet and docile,
    And then postpone, as often as necessary,
    The day on which you have agreed to marry.
    You'll thus gain time, and time will turn the trick.
    Sometimes, for instance, you'll be taken sick,
    And that will seem good reason for delay;
120   Or some bad omen will make you change the day—
    You'll dream of muddy water, or you'll pass
    A dead man's hearse, or break a looking-glass.
    If all else fails, no man can marry you

Unless you take his ring and say "I do."
But now, let's separate. If they should find
Us talking here, our plot might be divined.
[*To* VALÈRE] Go to your friends, and tell them what's occurred,
And have them urge her father to keep his word.
Meanwhile, we'll stir her brother into action,
130   And get Elmire, as well, to join our faction.
Good-bye.

VALÈRE [*to* MARIANE]:
                        Though each of us will do his best,
It's your true heart on which my hopes shall rest.

MARIANE [*to* VALÈRE]:
Regardless of what Father may decide,
None but Valère shall claim me as his bride.

VALÈRE:
Oh, how those words content me! Come what will . . .

DORINE:
Oh, lovers, lovers! Their tongues are never still.
Be off, now.

VALÈRE [*turning to go, then turning back*]:
                        One last word . . .

DORINE:
                                          No time to chat:
You leave by this door; and *you* leave by that.
[DORINE *pushes them, by the shoulders, toward opposing doors.*]

ACT III

Scene 1

DAMIS:
May lightning strike me even as I speak,
May all men call me cowardly and weak,
If any fear or scruple holds me back
From settling things, at once, with that great quack!

DORINE:
Now, don't give way to violent emotion.
Your father's merely talked about this notion,
And words and deeds are far from being one.
Much that is talked about is left undone.

DAMIS:
No, I must stop that scoundrel's machinations;
10   I'll go and tell him off; I'm out of patience.

DORINE:
Do calm down and be practical. I had rather
My mistress dealt with him — and with your father.

She has some influence with Tartuffe, I've noted.
He hangs upon her words, seems most devoted,
And may, indeed, be smitten by her charm.
Pray Heaven it's true! 'Twould do our cause no harm.
She sent for him, just now, to sound him out
On this affair you're so incensed about;
She'll find out where he stands, and tell him, too,

20   What dreadful strife and trouble will ensue
If he lends countenance to your father's plan.
I couldn't get in to see him, but his man
Says that he's almost finished with his prayers.
Go, now. I'll catch him when he comes downstairs.

DAMIS:
   I want to hear this conference, and I will.

DORINE:
   No, they must be alone.

DAMIS:
                  Oh, I'll keep still.

DORINE:
   Not you. I know your temper. You'd start a brawl,
And shout and stamp your foot and spoil it all.
Go on.

DAMIS:
        I won't; I have a perfect right . . .

DORINE:
30   Lord, you're a nuisance! He's coming; get out of sight.
   [DAMIS *conceals himself in a closet at the rear of the stage.*]

Scene 2

TARTUFFE [*observing* DORINE, *and calling to his manservant offstage*]:
   Hang up my hair-shirt, put my scourge in place,
And pray, Laurent, for Heaven's perpetual grace.
I'm going to the prison now, to share
My last two coins with the poor wretches there.

DORINE [*aside*]:
   Dear God, what affectation! What a fake!

TARTUFFE:
   You wished to see me?

DORINE:
                  Yes . . .

TARTUFFE [*taking a handkerchief from his pocket*]:
                    For mercy's sake,
Please take this handkerchief, before you speak.

DORINE:
   What?

TARTUFFE:

       Cover that bosom, girl. The flesh is weak,
  And unclean thoughts are difficult to control.
10   Such sights as that can undermine the soul.

DORINE:

  Your soul, it seems, has very poor defenses,
  And flesh makes quite an impact on your senses.
  It's strange that you're so easily excited;
  My own desires are not so soon ignited,
  And if I saw you naked as a beast,
  Not all your hide would tempt me in the least.

TARTUFFE:

  Girl, speak more modestly; unless you do,
  I shall be forced to take my leave of you.

DORINE:

  Oh, no, it's I who must be on my way;
20 I've just one little message to convey.
  Madame is coming down, and begs you, Sir,
  To wait and have a word or two with her.

TARTUFFE:

  Gladly.

DORINE [*aside*]:

      That had a softening effect!
  I think my guess about him was correct.

TARTUFFE:

  Will she be long?

DORINE:

       No: that's her step I hear.
  Ah, here she is, and I shall disappear.

Scene 3

TARTUFFE:

  May Heaven, whose infinite goodness we adore,
  Preserve your body and soul forevermore,
  And bless your days, and answer thus the plea
  Of one who is its humblest votary.

ELMIRE:

  I thank you for that pious wish. But please,
  Do take a chair and let's be more at ease.
  [*They sit down.*]

TARTUFFE:

  I trust that you are once more well and strong?

ELMIRE:

  Oh, yes: the fever didn't last for long.

TARTUFFE:

    My prayers are too unworthy, I am sure,

10   To have gained from Heaven this most gracious cure;

    But lately, Madam, my every supplication

    Has had for object your recuperation.

ELMIRE:

    You shouldn't have troubled so. I don't deserve it.

TARTUFFE:

    Your health is priceless, Madam, and to preserve it

    I'd gladly give my own, in all sincerity.

ELMIRE:

    Sir, you outdo us all in Christian charity.

    You've been most kind. I count myself your debtor.

TARTUFFE:

    'Twas nothing, Madam. I long to serve you better.

ELMIRE:

    There's a private matter I'm anxious to discuss.

20   I'm glad there's no one here to hinder us.

TARTUFFE:

    I too am glad; it floods my heart with bliss

    To find myself alone with you like this.

    For just this chance I've prayed with all my power—

    But prayed in vain, until this happy hour.

ELMIRE:

    This won't take long, Sir, and I hope you'll be

    Entirely frank and unconstrained with me.

TARTUFFE:

    Indeed, there's nothing I had rather do

    Than bare my inmost heart and soul to you.

    First, let me say that what remarks I've made

30   About the constant visits you are paid

    Were prompted not by any mean emotion,

    But rather by a pure and deep devotion,

    A fervent zeal . . .

ELMIRE:

                 No need for explanation.

    Your sole concern, I'm sure, was my salvation.

TARTUFFE [*taking* ELMIRE's *hand and pressing her fingertips*]:

    Quite so; and such great fervor do I feel . . .

ELMIRE:

    Ooh! Please! You're pinching!

TARTUFFE:

                 'Twas from excess of zeal.

    I never meant to cause you pain, I swear.

    I'd rather . . .

[*He places his hand on* ELMIRE's *knee.*]

ELMIRE:
                        What can your hand be doing there?

TARTUFFE:
            Feeling your gown; what soft, fine-woven stuff!

ELMIRE:
40   Please, I'm extremely ticklish. That's enough.
            [*She draws her chair away;* TARTUFFE *pulls his after her.*]

TARTUFFE [*fondling the lace collar of her gown*]:
            My, my what lovely lacework on your dress!
            The workmanship's miraculous, no less.
            I've not seen anything to equal it.

ELMIRE:
            Yes, quite. But let's talk business for a bit.
            They say my husband means to break his word
            And give his daughter to you, Sir. Had you heard?

TARTUFFE:
            He did once mention it. But I confess
            I dream of quite a different happiness.
            It's elsewhere, Madam, that my eyes discern
50   The promise of that bliss for which I yearn.

ELMIRE:
            I see: you care for nothing here below.

TARTUFFE
            Ah, well — my heart's not made of stone, you know.

ELMIRE:
            All your desires mount heavenward, I'm sure,
            In scorn of all that's earthly and impure.

TARTUFFE:
            A love of heavenly beauty does not preclude
            A proper love for earthly pulchritude;
            Our senses are quite rightly captivated
            By perfect works our Maker has created.
            Some glory clings to all that Heaven has made;
60   In you, all Heaven's marvels are displayed.
            On that fair face, such beauties have been lavished,
            The eyes are dazzled and the heart is ravished;
            How could I look on you, O flawless creature,
            And not adore the Author of all Nature,
            Feeling a love both passionate and pure
            For you, his triumph of self-portraiture?
            At first, I trembled lest that love should be
            A subtle snare that Hell had laid for me;
            I vowed to flee the sight of you, eschewing

70   A rapture that might prove my soul's undoing;
    But soon, fair being, I became aware
    That my deep passion could be made to square
    With rectitude, and with my bounden duty.
    I thereupon surrendered to your beauty.
    It is, I know, presumptuous on my part
    To bring you this poor offering of my heart,
    And it is not my merit, Heaven knows,
    But your compassion on which my hopes repose.
    You are my peace, my solace, my salvation;
80   On you depends my bliss — or desolation;
    I bide your judgment and, as you think best,
    I shall be either miserable or blest.

ELMIRE:
    Your declaration is most gallant, Sir,
    But don't you think it's out of character?
    You'd have done better to restrain your passion
    And think before you spoke in such a fashion.
    It ill becomes a pious man like you . . .

TARTUFFE:
    I may be pious, but I'm human too:
    With your celestial charms before his eyes,
90   A man has not the power to be wise.
    I know such words sound strangely, coming from me,
    But I'm no angel, nor was meant to be,
    And if you blame my passion, you must needs
    Reproach as well the charms on which it feeds.
    Your loveliness I had no sooner seen
    Than you became my soul's unrivalled queen;
    Before your seraph glance, divinely sweet,
    My heart's defenses crumbled in defeat,
    And nothing fasting, prayer, or tears might do
100   Could stay my spirit from adoring you.
    My eyes, my sighs have told you in the past
    What now my lips make bold to say at last,
    And if, in your great goodness, you will deign
    To look upon your slave, and ease his pain, —
    If, in compassion for my soul's distress,
    You'll stoop to comfort my unworthiness,
    I'll raise to you, in thanks for that sweet manna,
    An endless hymn, an infinite hosanna.
    With me, of course, there need be no anxiety,
110   No fear of scandal or of notoriety.
    These young court gallants, whom all the ladies fancy,

Are vain in speech, in action rash and chancy;
When they succeed in love, the world soon knows it;
No favor's granted them but they disclose it
And by the looseness of their tongues profane
The very altar where their hearts have lain.
Men of my sort, however, love discreetly,
And one may trust our reticence completely.
My keen concern for my good name insures
120   The absolute security of yours;
In short, I offer you, my dear Elmire,
Love without scandal, pleasure without fear.

ELMIRE:

I've heard your well-turned speeches to the end,
And what you urge I clearly apprehend.
Aren't you afraid that I may take a notion
To tell my husband of your warm devotion,
And that, supposing he were duly told,
His feelings toward you might grow rather cold?

TARTUFFE:

I know, dear lady, that your exceeding charity
130   Will lead your heart to pardon my temerity;
That you'll excuse my violent affection
As human weakness, human imperfection;
And that—O fairest!—you will bear in mind
That I'm but flesh and blood, and am not blind.

ELMIRE:

Some women might do otherwise, perhaps,
But I shall be discreet about your lapse;
I'll tell my husband nothing of what's occurred
If, in return, you'll give your solemn word
To advocate as forcefully as you can
140   The marriage of Valère and Mariane,
Renouncing all desire to dispossess
Another of his rightful happiness,
And . . .

Scene 4

DAMIS [emerging from the closet where he has been hiding]:
          No! We'll not hush up this vile affair;
I heard it all inside that closet there,
Where Heaven, in order to confound the pride
Of this great rascal, prompted me to hide.
Ah, now I have my long-awaited chance
To punish his deceit and arrogance,

And give my father clear and shocking proof
Of the black character of his dear Tartuffe.

ELMIRE:

Ah no, Damis; I'll be content if he
10   Will study to deserve my leniency.
I've promised silence—don't make me break my word;
To make a scandal would be too absurd.
Good wives laugh off such trifles, and forget them;
Why should they tell their husbands, and upset them?

DAMIS:

You have your reasons for taking such a course,
And I have reasons too, of equal force.
To spare him now would be insanely wrong.
I've swallowed my just wrath for far too long
And watched this insolent bigot bringing strife
20   And bitterness into our family life.
Too long he's meddled in my father's affairs,
Thwarting my marriage-hopes, and poor Valère's.
It's high time that my father was undeceived,
And now I've proof that can't be disbelieved—
Proof that was furnished me by Heaven above.
It's too good not to take advantage of.
This is my chance, and I deserve to lose it
If, for one moment, I hesitate to use it.

ELMIRE:

Damis . . .

DAMIS:

No, I must do what I think right.
30   Madam, my heart is bursting with delight,
And, say whatever you will, I'll not consent
To lose the sweet revenge on which I'm bent.
I'll settle matters without more ado;
And here, most opportunely, is my cue.

Scene 5

DAMIS:

Father, I'm glad you've joined us. Let us advise you
Of some fresh news which doubtless will surprise you.
You've just now been repaid with interest
For all your loving-kindness to our guest.
He's proved his warm and grateful feelings toward you;
It's with a pair of horns he would reward you.
Yes, I surprised him with your wife, and heard
His whole adulterous offer, every word.

She, with her all too gentle disposition,
10   Would not have told you of his proposition;
But I shall not make terms with brazen lechery,
And feel that not to tell you would be treachery.

ELMIRE:
And I hold that one's husband's peace of mind
Should not be spoilt by tattle of this kind.
One's honor doesn't require it: to be proficient
In keeping men at bay is quite sufficient.
These are my sentiments, and I wish, Damis,
That you had heeded me and held your peace.

Scene 6

ORGON:
Can it be true, this dreadful thing I hear?

TARTUFFE:
Yes, Brother, I'm a wicked man, I fear:
A wretched sinner, all depraved and twisted,
The greatest villain that has ever existed.
My life's one heap of crimes, which grows each minute;
There's naught but foulness and corruption in it;
And I perceive that Heaven, outraged by me,
Has chosen this occasion to mortify me.
Charge me with any deed you wish to name;
10   I'll not defend myself, but take the blame.
Believe what you are told, and drive Tartuffe
Like some base criminal from beneath your roof;
Yes, drive me hence, and with a parting curse:
I shan't protest, for I deserve far worse.

ORGON [to DAMIS]:
Ah, you deceitful boy, how dare you try
To stain his purity with so foul a lie?

DAMIS:
What! Are you taken in by such a bluff?
Did you not hear . . . ?

ORGON:
                              Enough, you rogue, enough!

TARTUFFE:
Ah, Brother, let him speak: you're being unjust.
20   Believe his story; the boy deserves your trust.
Why, after all, should you have faith in me?
How can you know what I might do, or be?
Is it on my good actions that you base
Your favor? Do you trust my pious face?

Ah, no, don't be deceived by hollow shows;
I'm far, alas, from being what men suppose;
Though the world takes me for a man of worth,
I'm truly the most worthless man on earth.
[*To* DAMIS] Yes, my dear son, speak out now: call me the chief
30 Of sinners, a wretch, a murderer, a thief;
Load me with all the names men most abhor;
I'll not complain; I've earned them all, and more;
I'll kneel here while you pour them on my head
As a just punishment for the life I've led.

ORGON [*to* TARTUFFE]:
This is too much, dear Brother.
[*To* DAMIS]   Have you no heart?

DAMIS:
Are you so hoodwinked by this rascal's art . . . ?

ORGON:
Be still, you monster.
[*To* TARTUFFE]   Brother, I pray you, rise.
[*To* DAMIS] Villain!

DAMIS:
                    But . . . !

ORGON:
                              Silence!

DAMIS:
                                    Can't you realize . . . ?

ORGON:
Just one word more, and I'll tear you limb from limb.

TARTUFFE:
40 In God's name, Brother, don't be harsh with him.
I'd rather far be tortured at the stake
Than see him bear one scratch for my poor sake.

ORGON [*to* DAMIS]:
Ingrate!

TARTUFFE:
       If I must beg you, on bended knee,
To pardon him . . .

ORGON [*falling to his knees, addressing* TARTUFFE]:
                   Such goodness cannot be!
[*To* DAMIS] Now, *there's* true charity!

DAMIS:
                              What, you . . . ?

ORGON:
                                          Villain, be still!
I know your motives; I know you wish him ill:
Yes, all of you—wife, children, servants, all—

Conspire against him and desire his fall,
Employing every shameful trick you can
50   To alienate me from this saintly man.
Ah, but the more you seek to drive him away,
The more I'll do to keep him. Without delay,
I'll spite this household and confound its pride
By giving him my daughter as his bride.

DAMIS:
You're going to force her to accept his hand?

ORGON:
Yes, and this very night, d'you understand?
I shall defy you all, and make it clear
That I'm the one who gives the orders here.
Come, wretch, kneel down and clasp his blessed feet,
60   And ask his pardon for your black deceit.

DAMIS:
I ask that swindler's pardon? Why, I'd rather . . .

ORGON:
So! You insult him, and defy your father!
A stick! A stick! [to TARTUFFE] No, no — release me, do.
[To DAMIS] Out of my house this minute! Be off with you,
And never dare set foot in it again.

DAMIS:
Well, I shall go, but . . .

ORGON:
                               Well, go quickly, then.
I disinherit you; an empty purse
Is all you'll get from me — except my curse!

Scene 7

ORGON:
How he blasphemed your goodness! What a son!

TARTUFFE:
Forgive him, Lord, as I've already done.
[To ORGON] You can't know how it hurts when someone tries
To blacken me in my dear Brother's eyes.

ORGON:
Ahh!

TARTUFFE:
        The mere thought of such ingratitude
Plunges my soul into so dark a mood . . .
Such horror grips my heart . . . I gasp for breath,
And cannot speak, and feel myself near death.

ORGON [He runs, in tears, to the door through which he has just driven his son.]:

You blackguard! Why did I spare you? Why did I not
10   Break you in little pieces on the spot?
        Compose yourself, and don't be hurt, dear friend.

TARTUFFE:

        These scenes, these dreadful quarrels, have got to end.
        I've much upset your household, and I perceive
        That the best thing will be for me to leave.

ORGON:

        What are you saying!

TARTUFFE:

                                            They're all against me here;
        They'd have you think me false and insincere.

ORGON:

        Ah, what of that? Have I ceased believing in you?

TARTUFFE:

        Their adverse talk will certainly continue,
        And charges which you now repudiate
20   You may find credible at a later date.

ORGON:

        No, Brother, never.

TARTUFFE:

                                            Brother, a wife can sway
        Her husband's mind in many a subtle way.

ORGON:

        No, no.

TARTUFFE:

                        To leave at once is the solution;
        Thus only can I end their persecution.

ORGON:

        No, no, I'll not allow it; you shall remain.

TARTUFFE:

        Ah, well; 'twill mean much martyrdom and pain,
        But if you wish it . . .

ORGON:

                                            Ah!

TARTUFFE:

                                            Enough; so be it.
        But one thing must be settled, as I see it.
        For your dear honor, and for our friendship's sake,
30   There's one precaution I feel bound to take.
        I shall avoid your wife, and keep away . . .

ORGON:

        No, you shall not, whatever they may say.
        It pleases me to vex them, and for spite
        I'd have them see you with her day and night.

What's more, I'm going to drive them to despair
By making you my only son and heir;
This very day, I'll give to you alone
Clear deed and title to everything I own.
A dear, good friend and son-in-law-to-be
40   Is more than wife, or child, or kin to me.
Will you accept my offer, dearest son?

TARTUFFE:

In all things, let the will of Heaven be done.

ORGON:

Poor fellow! Come, we'll go draw up the deed.
Then let them burst with disappointed greed!

Act IV

Scene 1

CLÉANTE:

Yes, all the town's discussing it, and truly,
Their comments do not flatter you unduly.
I'm glad we've met, Sir, and I'll give my view
Of this sad matter in a word or two.
As for who's guilty, that I shan't discuss;
Let's say it was Damis who caused the fuss;
Assuming, then, that you have been ill-used
By young Damis, and groundlessly accused,
Ought not a Christian to forgive, and ought
10   He not to stifle every vengeful thought?
Should you stand by and watch a father make
His only son an exile for your sake?
Again I tell you frankly, be advised:
The whole town, high and low, is scandalized;
This quarrel must be mended, and my advice is
Not to push matters to a further crisis.
No, sacrifice your wrath to God above,
And help Damis regain his father's love.

TARTUFFE:

Alas, for my part I should take great joy
20   In doing so. I've nothing against the boy.
I pardon all, I harbor no resentment;
To serve him would afford me much contentment.
But Heaven's interest will not have it so:
If he comes back, then I shall have to go.
After his conduct—so extreme, so vicious—
Our further intercourse would look suspicious.
God knows what people would think! Why, they'd describe

My goodness to him as a sort of bribe;
They'd say that out of guilt I made pretense
30   Of loving-kindness and benevolence—
That, fearing my accuser's tongue, I strove
To buy his silence with a show of love.

CLÉANTE:

Your reasoning is badly warped and stretched,
And these excuses, Sir, are most far-fetched.
Why put yourself in charge of Heaven's cause?
Does Heaven need our help to enforce its laws?
Leave vengeance to the Lord, Sir; while we live,
Our duty's not to punish, but forgive;
And what the Lord commands, we should obey
40   Without regard to what the world may say.
What! Shall the fear of being misunderstood
Prevent our doing what is right and good?
No, no; let's simply do what Heaven ordains,
And let no other thoughts perplex our brains.

TARTUFFE:

Again, Sir, let me say that I've forgiven
Damis, and thus obeyed the laws of Heaven;
But I am not commanded by the Bible
To live with one who smears my name with libel.

CLÉANTE:

Were you commanded, Sir, to indulge the whim
50   Of poor Orgon, and to encourage him
In suddenly transferring to your name
A large estate to which you have no claim?

TARTUFFE:

'Twould never occur to those who know me best
To think I acted from self-interest.
The treasures of this world I quite despise;
Their specious glitter does not charm my eyes;
And if I have resigned myself to taking
The gift which my dear Brother insists on making,
I do so only, as he well understands,
60   Lest so much wealth fall into wicked hands,
Lest those to whom it might descend in time
Turn it to purposes of sin and crime,
And not, as I shall do, make use of it
For Heaven's glory and mankind's benefit.

CLÉANTE:

Forget these trumped-up fears. Your argument
Is one the rightful heir might well resent;
It *is* a moral burden to inherit
Such wealth, but give Damis a chance to bear it.

And would it not be worse to be accused
70   Of swindling, than to see that wealth misused?
I'm shocked that you allowed Orgon to broach
This matter, and that you feel no self-reproach;
Does true religion teach that lawful heirs
May freely be deprived of what is theirs?
And if the Lord has told you in your heart
That you and young Damis must dwell apart,
Would it not be the decent thing to beat
A generous and honorable retreat,
Rather than let the son of the house be sent,
80   For your convenience, into banishment?
Sir, if you wish to prove the honesty
Of your intentions . . .

TARTUFFE:
                    Sir, it is half-past three.
I've certain pious duties to attend to,
And hope my prompt departure won't offend you.

CLÉANTE [*alone*]:
Damn.

Scene 2

DORINE:
                    Stay, Sir, and help Mariane, for Heaven's sake!
She's suffering so, I fear her heart will break.
Her father's plan to marry her off tonight
Has put the poor child in a desperate plight.
I hear him coming. Let's stand together, now,
And see if we can't change his mind, somehow,
About this match we all deplore and fear.

Scene 3

ORGON:
                    Hah! Glad to find you all assembled here.
[*To* MARIANE] This contract, child, contains your happiness,
And what it says I think your heart can guess.

MARIANE [*falling to her knees*]:
                    Sir, by that Heaven which sees me here distressed,
And by whatever else can move your breast,
Do not employ a father's power, I pray you,
To crush my heart and force it to obey you,
Nor by your harsh commands oppress me so
That I'll begrudge the duty which I owe—
10   And do not so embitter and enslave me

That I shall hate the very life you gave me.
If my sweet hopes must perish, if you refuse
To give me to the one I've dared to choose,
Spare me at least—I beg you, I implore—
The pain of wedding one whom I abhor;
And do not, by a heartless use of force,
Drive me to contemplate some desperate course.

ORGON [*feeling himself touched by her*]:
Be firm, my soul. No human weakness, now.

MARIANE:
I don't resent your love for him. Allow
20   Your heart free rein, Sir; give him your property,
And if that's not enough, take mine from me;
He's welcome to my money; take it, do,
But don't, I pray, include my person too.
Spare me, I beg you; and let me end the tale
Of my sad days behind a convent veil.

ORGON:
A convent! Hah! When crossed in their amours,
All lovesick girls have had the same thought as yours.
Get up! The more you loathe the man, and dread him,
The more ennobling it will be to wed him.
30   Marry Tartuffe, and mortify your flesh!
Enough; don't start that whimpering afresh.

DORINE:
But why . . . ?

ORGON:
                    Be still, there. Speak when you're spoken to.
Not one more bit of impudence out of you.

CLÉANTE:
If I may offer a word of counsel here . . .

ORGON:
Brother, in counseling you have no peer;
All your advice is forceful, sound, and clever;
I don't propose to follow it, however.

ELMIRE [*to* ORGON]:
I am amazed, and don't know what to say;
Your blindness simply takes my breath away.
40   You are indeed bewitched, to take no warning
From our account of what occurred this morning.

ORGON:
Madam, I know a few plain facts, and one
Is that you're partial to my rascal son;
Hence, when he sought to make Tartuffe the victim
Of a base lie, you dared not contradict him.

Ah, but you underplayed your part, my pet;
You should have looked more angry, more upset.

ELMIRE:
When men make overtures, must we reply
With righteous anger and a battle-cry?
50   Must we turn back their amorous advances
With sharp reproaches and with fiery glances?
Myself, I find such offers merely amusing,
And make no scenes and fusses in refusing;
My taste is for good-natured rectitude,
And I dislike the savage sort of prude
Who guards her virtue with her teeth and claws,
And tears men's eyes out for the slightest cause:
The Lord preserve me from such honor as that,
Which bites and scratches like an alley-cat!
60   I've found that a polite and cool rebuff
Discourages a lover quite enough.

ORGON:
I know the facts, and I shall not be shaken.

ELMIRE:
I marvel at your power to be mistaken.
Would it, I wonder, carry weight with you
If I could *show* you that our tale was true?

ORGON:
Show me?

ELMIRE:
            Yes.

ORGON:
            Rot.

ELMIRE:
                  Come, what if I found a way
To make you see the facts as plain as day?

ORGON:
Nonsense.

ELMIRE:
            Do answer me; don't be absurd.
I'm not now asking you to trust our word.
70   Suppose that from some hiding-place in here
You learned the whole sad truth by eye and ear—
What would you say of your good friend, after that?

ORGON:
Why, I'd say . . . nothing, by Jehoshaphat!
It can't be true.

ELMIRE:
                  You've been too long deceived,

And I'm quite tired of being disbelieved.
Come now: let's put my statements to the test,
And you shall see the truth made manifest.

ORGON:
    I'll take that challenge. Now do your uttermost.
We'll see how you make good your empty boast.

ELMIRE [*to* DORINE]:
    Send him to me.

DORINE:
80   He's crafty; it may be hard
To catch the cunning scoundrel off his guard.

ELMIRE:
    No, amorous men are gullible. Their conceit
So blinds them that they're never hard to cheat.
Have him come down. [*to* CLÉANTE *and* MARIANE] Please leave us, for a bit.

Scene 4

ELMIRE:
    Pull up this table, and get under it.

ORGON:
    What?

ELMIRE:
          It's essential that you be well-hidden.

ORGON:
    Why there?

ELMIRE:
          Oh, Heavens! Just do as you are bidden.
I have my plans; we'll soon see how they fare.
Under the table, now; and once you're there,
Take care that you are neither seen nor heard.

ORGON:
    Well, I'll indulge you, since I gave my word
To see you through this infantile charade.

ELMIRE:
    Once it is over, you'll be glad we played.
[*To her husband, who is now under the table*] I'm going to act quite strangely,
10   now, and you
Must not be shocked at anything I do.
Whatever I may say, you must excuse
As part of that deceit I'm forced to use.
I shall employ sweet speeches in the task
Of making that impostor drop his mask;
I'll give encouragement to his bold desires,
And furnish fuel to his amorous fires.

Since it's for your sake, and for his destruction,
That I shall seem to yield to his seduction,
20 I'll gladly stop whenever you decide
That all your doubts are fully satisfied.
I'll count on you, as soon as you have seen
What sort of man he is, to intervene,
And not expose me to his odious lust
One moment longer than you feel you must.
Remember: you're to save me from my plight
Whenever . . . He's coming! Hush! Keep out of sight!

Scene 5

TARTUFFE:
You wish to have a word with me, I'm told.

ELMIRE:
Yes. I've a little secret to unfold.
Before I speak, however, it would be wise
To close that door, and look about for spies.
[TARTUFFE *goes to the door, closes it, and returns.*]
The very last thing that must happen now
Is a repetition of this morning's row.
I've never been so badly caught off guard.
Oh, how I feared for you! You saw how hard
I tried to make that troublesome Damis
10 Control his dreadful temper, and hold his peace.
In my confusion, I didn't have the sense
Simply to contradict his evidence;
But as it happened, that was for the best,
And all has worked out in our interest.
This storm has only bettered your position;
My husband doesn't have the least suspicion,
And now, in mockery of those who do,
He bids me be continually with you.
And that is why, quite fearless of reproof,
20 I now can be alone with my Tartuffe,
And why my heart—perhaps too quick to yield—
Feels free to let its passion be revealed.

TARTUFFE:
Madam, your words confuse me. Not long ago,
You spoke in quite a different style, you know.

ELMIRE:
Ah, Sir, if that refusal made you smart,
It's little that you know of woman's heart,
Or what that heart is trying to convey

When it resists in such a feeble way!
Always, at first, our modesty prevents
30 The frank avowal of tender sentiments;
However high the passion which inflames us,
Still, to confess its power somehow shames us.
Thus we reluct, at first, yet in a tone
Which tells you that our heart is overthrown,
That what our lips deny, our pulse confesses,
And that, in time, all noes will turn to yesses.
I fear my words are all too frank and free,
And a poor proof of woman's modesty;
But since I'm started, tell me, if you will—
40 Would I have tried to make Damis be still,
Would I have listened, calm and unoffended,
Until your lengthy offer of love was ended,
And been so very mild in my reaction,
Had your sweet words not given me satisfaction?
And when I tried to force you to undo
The marriage-plans my husband has in view,
What did my urgent pleading signify
If not that I admired you, and that I
Deplored the thought that someone else might own
50 Part of a heart I wished for mine alone?

TARTUFFE:
Madam, no happiness is so complete
As when, from lips we love, come words so sweet;
Their nectar floods my every sense, and drains
In honeyed rivulets through all my veins.
To please you is my joy, my only goal;
Your love is the restorer of my soul;
And yet I must beg leave, now, to confess
Some lingering doubts as to my happiness.
Might this not be a trick? Might not the catch
60 Be that you wish me to break off the match
With Mariane, and so have feigned to love me?
I shan't quite trust your fond opinion of me
Until the feelings you've expressed so sweetly
Are demonstrated somewhat more concretely,
And you have shown, by certain kind concessions,
That I may put my faith in your professions.

ELMIRE [*She coughs, to warn her husband.*]:
Why be in such a hurry? Must my heart
Exhaust its bounty at the very start?
To make that sweet admission cost me dear,
70 But you'll not be content, it would appear,

Unless my store of favors is disbursed
To the last farthing, and at the very first.

TARTUFFE:

The less we merit, the less we dare to hope,
And with our doubts, mere words can never cope.
We trust no promised bliss till we receive it;
Not till a joy is ours can we believe it.
I, who so little merit your esteem,
Can't credit this fulfillment of my dream,
And shan't believe it, Madam, until I savor
80   Some palpable assurance of your favor.

ELMIRE:

My, how tyrannical your love can be,
And how it flusters and perplexes me!
How furiously you take one's heart in hand,
And make your every wish a fierce command!
Come, must you hound and harry me to death?
Will you not give me time to catch my breath?
Can it be right to press me with such force,
Give me no quarter, show me no remorse,
And take advantage, by your stern insistence,
90   Of the fond feelings which weaken my resistance?

TARTUFFE:

Well, if you look with favor upon my love,
Why, then, begrudge me some clear proof thereof?

ELMIRE:

But how can I consent without offense
To Heaven, toward which you feel such reverence?

TARTUFFE:

If Heaven is all that holds you back, don't worry.
I can remove that hindrance in a hurry.
Nothing of that sort need obstruct our path.

ELMIRE:

Must one not be afraid of Heaven's wrath?

TARTUFFE:

Madam, forget such fears, and be my pupil,
100   And I shall teach you how to conquer scruple.
Some joys, it's true, are wrong in Heaven's eyes;
Yet Heaven is not averse to compromise;
There is a science, lately formulated,
Whereby one's conscience may be liberated,
And any wrongful act you care to mention
May be redeemed by purity of intention.
I'll teach you, Madam, the secrets of that science;
Meanwhile, just place on me your full reliance.

Assuage my keen desires, and feel no dread:
110   The sin, if any, shall be on my head.
       [ELMIRE *coughs, this time more loudly.*]
       You've a bad cough.

ELMIRE:

                              Yes, yes. It's bad indeed.

TARTUFFE [*producing a little paper bag*]:
       A bit of licorice may be what you need.

ELMIRE:
       No, I've a stubborn cold, it seems. I'm sure it
       Will take much more than licorice to cure it.

TARTUFFE:
       How aggravating.

ELMIRE:
                              Oh, more than I can say.

TARTUFFE:
       If you're still troubled, think of things this way:
       No one shall know our joys, save us alone,
       And there's no evil till the act is known;
       It's scandal, Madam, which makes it an offense,
120   And it's no sin to sin in confidence.

ELMIRE [*having coughed once more*]:
       Well, clearly I must do as you require,
       And yield to your importunate desire.
       It is apparent, now, that nothing less
       Will satisfy you, and so I acquiesce.
       To go so far is much against my will;
       I'm vexed that it should come to this; but still,
       Since you are so determined on it, since you
       Will not allow mere language to convince you,
       And since you ask for concrete evidence, I
130   See nothing for it, now, but to comply.
       If this is sinful, if I'm wrong to do it,
       So much the worse for him who drove me to it.
       The fault can surely not be charged to me.

TARTUFFE:
       Madam, the fault is mine, if fault there be,
       And . . .

ELMIRE:
                     Open the door a little, and peek out;
       I wouldn't want my husband poking about.

TARTUFFE:
       Why worry about that man? Each day he grows
       More gullible; one can lead him by the nose.
       To find us here would fill him with delight,

140   And if he saw the worst, he'd doubt his sight.
ELMIRE:
    Nevertheless, do step out for a minute
    Into the hall, and see that no one's in it.

Scene 6

ORGON [*coming out from under the table*]:
    That man's a perfect monster, I must admit!
    I'm simply stunned. I can't get over it.
ELMIRE:
    What, coming out so soon? How premature!
    Get back in hiding, and wait until you're sure.
    Stay till the end, and be convinced completely;
    We mustn't stop till things are proved concretely.
ORGON:
    Hell never harbored anything so vicious!
ELMIRE:
    Tut, don't be hasty. Try to be judicious.
    Wait, and be certain that there's no mistake.
10   No jumping to conclusions, for Heaven's sake!
    [*She places* ORGON *behind her, as* TARTUFFE *re-enters.*]

Scene 7

TARTUFFE [*not seeing* ORGON]:
    Madam, all things have worked out to perfection;
    I've given the neighboring rooms a full inspection;
    No one's about; and now I may at last . . .
ORGON [*intercepting him*]:
    Hold on, my passionate fellow, not so fast!
    I should advise a little more restraint.
    Well, so you thought you'd fool me, my dear saint!
    How soon you wearied of the saintly life—
    Wedding my daughter, and coveting my wife!
    I've long suspected you, and had a feeling
10   That soon I'd catch you at your double-dealing.
    Just now, you've given me evidence galore;
    It's quite enough; I have no wish for more.
ELMIRE [*to* TARTUFFE]:
    I'm sorry to have treated you so slyly,
    But circumstances forced me to be wily.
TARTUFFE:
    Brother, you can't think . . .
ORGON:
                                        No more talk from you;
    Just leave this household, without more ado.

TARTUFFE:

   What I intended . . .

ORGON:

                    That seems fairly clear.
   Spare me your falsehoods and get out of here.

TARTUFFE:

   No, I'm the master, and you're the one to go!
20   This house belongs to me, I'll have you know,
   And I shall show you that you can't hurt *me*
   By this contemptible conspiracy,
   That those who cross me know not what they do,
   And that I've means to expose and punish you,
   Avenge offended Heaven, and make you grieve
   That ever you dared order me to leave.

Scene 8

ELMIRE:

   What was the point of all that angry chatter?

ORGON:

   Dear God, I'm worried. This is no laughing matter.

ELMIRE:

   How so?

ORGON:

                    I fear I understood his drift.
   I'm much disturbed about that deed of gift.

ELMIRE:

   You gave him . . . ?

ORGON:

                    Yes, it's all been drawn and signed.
   But one thing more is weighing on my mind.

ELMIRE:

   What's that?

ORGON:

                    I'll tell you; but first let's see if there's
   A certain strong-box in his room upstairs.

ACT V

Scene 1

CLÉANTE:

   Where are you going so fast?

ORGON:

                    God knows!

CLÉANTE:

                    Then wait;

Let's have a conference, and deliberate
On how this situation's to be met.

CLÉANTE:

That strong-box has me utterly upset;
This is the worst of many, many shocks.

ORGON:

Is there some fearful mystery in that box?

CLÉANTE:

My poor friend Argas brought that box to me
With his own hands, in utmost secrecy;
'Twas on the very morning of his flight.
10   It's full of papers which, if they came to light,
Would ruin him — or such is my impression.

CLÉANTE:

Then why did you let it out of your possession?

ORGON:

Those papers vexed my conscience, and it seemed best
To ask the counsel of my pious guest.
The cunning scoundrel got me to agree
To leave the strong-box in his custody,
So that, in case of an investigation,
I could employ a slight equivocation
And swear I didn't have it, and thereby,
20   At no expense to conscience, tell a lie.

CLÉANTE:

It looks to me as if you're out on a limb.
Trusting him with that box, and offering him
That deed of gift, were actions of a kind
Which scarcely indicate a prudent mind.
With two such weapons, he has the upper hand,
And since you're vulnerable, as matters stand,
You erred once more in bringing him to bay.
You should have acted in some subtler way.

ORGON:

Just think of it: behind that fervent face,
30   A heart so wicked, and a soul so base!
I took him in, a hungry beggar, and then . . .
Enough, by God! I'm through with pious men:
Henceforth I'll hate the whole false brotherhood,
And persecute them worse than Satan could.

CLÉANTE:

Ah, there you go — extravagant as ever!
Why can you not be rational? You never
Manage to take the middle course, it seems,
But jump, instead, between absurd extremes.
You've recognized your recent grave mistake

40   In falling victim to a pious fake;
        Now, to correct that error, must you embrace
        An even greater error in its place,
        And judge our worthy neighbors as a whole
        By what you've learned of one corrupted soul?
        Come, just because one rascal made you swallow
        A show of zeal which turned out to be hollow,
        Shall you conclude that all men are deceivers,
        And that, today, there are no true believers?
        Let atheists make that foolish inference;
50   Learn to distinguish virtue from pretense,
        Be cautious in bestowing admiration,
        And cultivate a sober moderation.
        Don't humor fraud, but also don't asperse
        True piety; the latter fault is worse,
        And it is best to err, if err one must,
        As you have done, upon the side of trust.

Scene 2

DAMIS:
    Father, I hear that scoundrel's uttered threats
    Against you; that he pridefully forgets
    How, in his need, he was befriended by you,
    And means to use your gifts to crucify you.
ORGON:
    It's true, my boy. I'm too distressed for tears.
DAMIS:
    Leave it to me, Sir; let me trim his ears.
    Faced with such insolence, we must not waver.
    I shall rejoice in doing you the favor
    Of cutting short his life, and your distress.
CLÉANTE:
10   What a display of young hotheadedness!
    Do learn to moderate your fits of rage.
    In this just kingdom, this enlightened age,
    One does not settle things by violence.

Scene 3

MADAME PERNELLE:
    I hear strange tales of very strange events.
ORGON:
    Yes, strange events which these two eyes beheld.
    The man's ingratitude is unparalleled.
    I save a wretched pauper from starvation,

House him, and treat him like a blood relation,
Shower him every day with my largesse,
Give him my daughter, and all that I possess;
And meanwhile the unconscionable knave
Tries to induce my wife to misbehave;
10   And not content with such extreme rascality,
Now threatens me with my own liberality,
And aims, by taking base advantage of
The gifts I gave him out of Christian love,
To drive me from my house, a ruined man,
And make me end a pauper, as he began.

DORINE:
Poor fellow!

MADAME PERNELLE:
No, my son, I'll never bring
Myself to think him guilty of such a thing.

ORGON:
How's that?

MADAME PERNELLE:
The righteous always were maligned.

ORGON:
Speak clearly, Mother. Say what's on your mind.

MADAME PERNELLE:
20   I mean that I can smell a rat, my dear.
You know how everybody hates him, here.

ORGON:
That has no bearing on the case at all.

MADAME PERNELLE:
I told you a hundred times, when you were small,
That virtue in this world is hated ever;
Malicious men may die, but malice never.

ORGON:
No doubt that's true, but how does it apply?

MADAME PERNELLE:
They've turned you against him by a clever lie.

ORGON:
I've told you, I was there and saw it done.

MADAME PERNELLE:
Ah, slanderers will stop at nothing, Son.

ORGON:
30   Mother, I'll lose my temper . . . For the last time,
I tell you I was witness to the crime.

MADAME PERNELLE:
The tongues of spite are busy night and noon,
And to their venom no man is immune.

ORGON:

> You're talking nonsense. Can't you realize
> I saw it; saw it; saw it with my eyes?
> Saw, do you understand me? Must I shout it
> Into your ears before you'll cease to doubt it?

MADAME PERNELLE:

> Appearances can deceive, my son. Dear me,
> We cannot always judge by what we see.

ORGON:

> Drat! Drat!

MADAME PERNELLE:

40
> One often interprets things awry;
> Good can seem evil to a suspicious eye.

ORGON:

> Was I to see his pawing at Elmire
> As an act of charity?

MADAME PERNELLE:

> Till his guilt is clear,
> A man deserves the benefit of the doubt.
> You should have waited, to see how things turned out.

ORGON:

> Great God in Heaven, what more proof did I need?
> Was I to sit there, watching, until he'd . . .
> You drive me to the brink of impropriety.

MADAME PERNELLE:

> No, no, a man of such surpassing piety
50
> Could not do such a thing. You cannot shake me.
> I don't believe it, and you shall not make me.

ORGON:

> You vex me so that, if you weren't my mother,
> I'd say to you . . . some dreadful thing or other.

DORINE:

> It's your turn now, Sir, not to be listened to;
> You'd not trust us, and now she won't trust you.

CLÉANTE:

> My friends, we're wasting time which should be spent
> In facing up to our predicament.
> I fear that scoundrel's threats weren't made in sport.

DAMIS:

> Do you think he'd have the nerve to go to court?

ELMIRE:

60
> I'm sure he won't: they'd find it all too crude
> A case of swindling and ingratitude.

CLÉANTE:

> Don't be too sure. He won't be at a loss

To give his claims a high and righteous gloss;
And clever rogues with far less valid cause
Have trapped their victims in a web of laws.
I say again that to antagonize
A man so strongly armed was most unwise.

ORGON:
I know it; but the man's appalling cheek
Outraged me so, I couldn't control my pique.

CLÉANTE:
70   I wish to Heaven that we could devise
Some truce between you, or some compromise.

ELMIRE:
If I had known what cards he held, I'd not
Have roused his anger by my little plot.

ORGON [*to* DORINE, *as* M. LOYAL *enters*]:
What is that fellow looking for? Who is he?
Go talk to him—and tell him that I'm busy.

Scene 4

MONSIEUR LOYAL:
Good day, dear sister. Kindly let me see
Your master.

DORINE:
                    He's involved with company,
And cannot be disturbed just now, I fear.

MONSIEUR LOYAL:
I hate to intrude; but what has brought me here
Will not disturb your master, in any event.
Indeed, my news will make him most content.

DORINE:
Your name?

MONSIEUR LOYAL:
                    Just say that I bring greetings from
Monsieur Tartuffe, on whose behalf I've come.

DORINE [*to* ORGON]:
Sir, he's a very gracious man, and bears
10   A message from Tartuffe, which, he declares,
Will make you most content.

CLÉANTE:
                    Upon my word,
I think this man had best be seen, and heard.

ORGON:
Perhaps he has some settlement to suggest.
How shall I treat him? What manner would be best?

CLÉANTE:
> Control your anger, and if he should mention
> Some fair adjustment, give him your full attention.

MONSIEUR LOYAL:
> Good health to you, good Sir. May Heaven confound
> Your enemies, and may your joys abound.

ORGON [*aside, to* CLÉANTE]:
> A gentle salutation: it confirms
20 My guess that he is here to offer terms.

MONSIEUR LOYAL:
> I've always held your family most dear;
> I served your father, Sir, for many a year.

ORGON:
> Sir, I must ask your pardon; to my shame,
> I cannot now recall your face or name.

MONSIEUR LOYAL:
> Loyal's my name; I come from Normandy,
> And I'm a bailiff, in all modesty.
> For forty years, praise God, it's been my boast
> To serve with honor in that vital post,
> And I am here, Sir, if you will permit
30 The liberty, to serve you with this writ . . .

ORGON:
> To—*what?*

MONSIEUR LOYAL:
>   Now, please, Sir, let us have no friction:
> It's nothing but an order of eviction.
> You are to move your goods and family out
> And make way for new occupants, without
> Deferment or delay, and give the keys . . .

ORGON:
> I? Leave this house?

MONSIEUR LOYAL:
>   Why yes, Sir, if you please.
> This house, Sir, from the cellar to the roof,
> Belongs now to the good Monsieur Tartuffe,
> And he is lord and master of your estate
40 By virtue of a deed of present date,
> Drawn in due form, with clearest legal phrasing . . .

DAMIS:
> Your insolence is utterly amazing!

MONSIEUR LOYAL:
> Young man, my business here is not with you,
> But with your wise and temperate father, who,
> Like every worthy citizen, stands in awe

Of justice, and would never obstruct the law.

ORGON:
But . . .

MONSIEUR LOYAL:
Not for a million, Sir, would you rebel
Against authority; I know that well.
You'll not make trouble, Sir, or interfere
50   With the execution of my duties here.

DAMIS:
Someone may execute a smart tattoo
On that black jacket of yours, before you're through.

MONSIEUR LOYAL:
Sir, bid your son be silent. I'd much regret
Having to mention such a nasty threat
Of violence, in writing my report.

DORINE [*aside*]:
This man Loyal's a most disloyal sort!

MONSIEUR LOYAL:
I love all men of upright character,
And when I agreed to serve these papers, Sir,
It was your feelings that I had in mind.
60   I couldn't bear to see the case assigned
To someone else, who might esteem you less
And so subject you to unpleasantness.

ORGON:
What's more unpleasant than telling a man to leave
His house and home?

MONSIEUR LOYAL:
You'd like a short reprieve?
If you desire it, Sir, I shall not press you,
But wait until tomorrow to dispossess you.
Splendid. I'll come and spend the night here, then,
Most quietly, with half a score of men.
For form's sake, you might bring me, just before
70   You go to bed, the keys to the front door.
My men, I promise, will be on their best
Behavior, and will not disturb your rest.
But bright and early, Sir, you must be quick
And move out all your furniture, every stick:
The men I've chosen are both young and strong,
And with their help it shouldn't take you long.
In short, I'll make things pleasant and convenient,
And since I'm being so extremely lenient,
Please show me, Sir, a like consideration,
80   And give me your entire cooperation.

ORGON [*aside*]:

    I may be all but bankrupt, but I vow

    I'd give a hundred louis, here and now,

    Just for the pleasure of landing one good clout

    Right on the end of that complacent snout.

CLÉANTE:

    Careful; don't make things worse.

DAMIS:

                            My bootsole itches

    To give that beggar a good kick in the breeches.

DORINE:

    Monsieur Loyal, I'd love to hear the whack

    Of a stout stick across your fine broad back.

MONSIEUR LOYAL:

    Take care: a woman too may go to jail if

90   She uses threatening language to a bailiff.

CLÉANTE:

    Enough, enough, Sir. This must not go on.

    Give me that paper, please, and then begone.

MONSIEUR LOYAL:

    Well, *au revoir*. God give you all good cheer!

ORGON:

    May God confound you, and him who sent you here!

Scene 5

ORGON:

    Now, Mother, was I right or not? This writ

    Should change your notion of Tartuffe a bit.

    Do you perceive his villainy at last?

MADAME PERNELLE:

    I'm thunderstruck. I'm utterly aghast.

DORINE:

    Oh, come, be fair. You mustn't take offense

    At this new proof of his benevolence.

    He's acting out of selfless love, I know.

    Material things enslave the soul, and so

    He kindly has arranged your liberation

10   From all that might endanger your salvation.

ORGON:

    Will you not ever hold your tongue, you dunce?

CLÉANTE:

    Come, you must take some action, and at once.

ELMIRE:

    Go tell the world of the low trick he's tried.

The deed of gift is surely nullified
By such behavior, and public rage will not
Permit the wretch to carry out his plot.

Scene 6

VALÈRE:
Sir, though I hate to bring you more bad news,
Such is the danger that I cannot choose.
A friend who is extremely close to me
And knows my interest in your family
Has, for my sake, presumed to violate
The secrecy that's due to things of state,
And sends me word that you are in a plight
From which your one salvation lies in flight.
That scoundrel who's imposed upon you so
10   Denounced you to the King an hour ago
And, as supporting evidence, displayed
The strong-box of a certain renegade
Whose secret papers, so he testified,
You had disloyally agreed to hide.
I don't know just what charges may be pressed,
But there's a warrant out for your arrest;
Tartuffe has been instructed, furthermore,
To guide the arresting officer to your door.

CLÉANTE:
He's clearly done this to facilitate
20   His seizure of your house and your estate.

ORGON:
That man, I must say, is a vicious beast!

VALÈRE:
Quick, Sir; you mustn't tarry in the least.
My carriage is outside, to take you hence;
This thousand louis should cover all expense.
Let's lose no time, or you shall be undone;
The sole defense, in this case, is to run.
I shall go with you all the way, and place you
In a safe refuge to which they'll never trace you.

ORGON:
Alas, dear boy, I wish that I could show you
30   My gratitude for everything I owe you.
But now is not the time; I pray the Lord
That I may live to give you your reward.
Farewell, my dears; be careful . . .

CLÉANTE:
Brother, hurry.
We shall take care of things; you needn't worry.

Scene 7

TARTUFFE:

 Gently, Sir, gently; stay right where you are.

 No need for haste; your lodging isn't far.

 You're off to prison, by order of the Prince.

ORGON:

 This is the crowning blow, you wretch; and since

 It means my total ruin and defeat,

 Your villainy is now at last complete.

TARTUFFE:

 You needn't try to provoke me; it's no use.

 Those who serve Heaven must expect abuse.

CLÉANTE:

 You are indeed most patient, sweet, and blameless.

DORINE:

10 How he exploits the name of Heaven! It's shameless.

TARTUFFE:

 Your taunts and mockeries are all for naught;

 To do my duty is my only thought.

MARIANE:

 Your love of duty is most meritorious,

 And what you've done is little short of glorious.

TARTUFFE:

 All deeds are glorious, Madam, which obey

 The sovereign prince who sent me here today.

ORGON:

 I rescued you when you were destitute;

 Have you forgotten that, you thankless brute?

TARTUFFE:

 No, no, I well remember everything;

20 But my first duty is to serve my King.

 That obligation is so paramount

 That other claims, beside it, do not count;

 And for it I would sacrifice my wife,

 My family, my friend, or my own life.

ELMIRE:

 Hypocrite!

DORINE:

   All that we most revere, he uses

 To cloak his plots and camouflage his ruses.

CLÉANTE:

 If it is true that you are animated

 By pure and loyal zeal, as you have stated,

 Why was this zeal not roused until you'd sought

30 To make Orgon a cuckold, and been caught?

 Why weren't you moved to give your evidence

Until your outraged host had driven you hence?
I shan't say that the gift of all his treasure
Ought to have damped your zeal in any measure;
But if he is a traitor, as you declare,
How could you condescend to be his heir?

TARTUFFE [*to the* OFFICER]:
Sir, spare me all this clamor; it's growing shrill.
Please carry out your orders, if you will.

OFFICER:
Yes, I've delayed too long, Sir. Thank you kindly.
40   You're just the proper person to remind me.
Come, you are off to join the other boarders
In the King's prison, according to his orders.

TARTUFFE:
Who? I, Sir?

OFFICER:
            Yes.

TARTUFFE:
                    To prison? This can't be true!

OFFICER:
I owe an explanation, but not to you.
[*To* ORGON] Sir, all is well; rest easy, and be grateful.
We serve a Prince to whom all sham is hateful,
A Prince who sees into our inmost hearts,
And can't be fooled by any trickster's arts.
His royal soul, though generous and human,
50   Views all things with discernment and acumen;
His sovereign reason is not lightly swayed,
And all his judgments are discreetly weighed.
He honors righteous men of every kind,
And yet his zeal for virtue is not blind,
Nor does his love of piety numb his wits
And make him tolerant of hypocrites.
'Twas hardly likely that this man could cozen
A King who's foiled such liars by the dozen.
With one keen glance, the King perceived the whole
60   Perverseness and corruption of his soul,
And thus high Heaven's justice was displayed:
Betraying you, the rogue stood self-betrayed.
The King soon recognized Tartuffe as one
Notorious by another name, who'd done
So many vicious crimes that one could fill
Ten volumes with them, and be writing still.
But to be brief: our sovereign was appalled
By this man's treachery toward you, which he called
The last, worst villainy of a vile career,

70 And bade me follow the impostor here
To see how gross his impudence could be,
And force him to restore your property.
Your private papers, by the King's command,
I hereby seize and give into your hand.
The King, by royal order, invalidates
The deed which gave this rascal your estates,
And pardons, furthermore, your grave offense
In harboring an exile's documents.
By these decrees, our Prince rewards you for
80 Your loyal deeds in the late civil war,
And shows how heartfelt is his satisfaction
In recompensing any worthy action,
How much he prizes merit, and how he makes
More of men's virtues than of their mistakes.

DORINE:
　　Heaven be praised!

MADAME PERNELLE:
　　　　　　I breathe again, at last.

ELMIRE:
　　We're safe.

MARIANE:
　　　　　I can't believe the danger's past.

ORGON [*to* TARTUFFE]:
　　Well, traitor, now you see . . .

CLÉANTE:
　　　　　　　　Ah, Brother, please,
Let's not descend to such indignities.
Leave the poor wretch to his unhappy fate,
90 And don't say anything to aggravate
His present woes; but rather hope that he
Will soon embrace an honest piety,
And mend his ways, and by a true repentance
Move our just King to moderate his sentence.
Meanwhile, go kneel before your sovereign's throne
And thank him for the mercies he has shown.

ORGON:
　　Well said: let's go at once and, gladly kneeling,
Express the gratitude which all are feeling.
Then, when that first great duty has been done,
100 We'll turn with pleasure to a second one,
And give Valère, whose love has proven so true,
The wedded happiness which is his due.

∾ APHRA BEHN
1640–1689

Aphra Behn.
Engraving from
*Histories and
Novels,* 1696

*This is the earliest
surviving image
of Behn. (The
Huntington Library,
San Marino, CA)*

Poet, playwright, and novelist Aphra Behn was one of the most prolific writers of her time. During a period in England when women were strongly discouraged from seeking literary recognition, she not only managed to earn a living as a professional writer but also directly engaged such traditionally "masculine" themes as political corruption, sexual politics, and social reform. In *Oroonoko* (1688), she openly addresses the complexities of rulership, sexual desire, and social injustice. Though her talent as a writer earned her much popularity and praise, the supposed presumptuousness and boldness of her work resulted in vicious attacks on her moral integrity. Associating her entrance into the public sphere of print and stage with prostitution, the satirist Robert Gould labeled her a vile "Punk[1] and Poetesse." Largely because of this stigma of indecency, publishers and scholars ignored Behn's work for years after her death. Only recently has she returned to center stage as a great literary talent, a major contributor to the development of the early English NOVEL, and a revolutionary figure in the tradition of women's writing in English.

Mystery, Travel, and Espionage.   It is difficult to pin down the facts of Behn's early life. According to many sources, she was born near Canterbury to Bartholomew Johnson, a barber, and Elizabeth Denham. Her surprisingly advanced education and language skills (she was learned in Latin and French), which would have been unusual for a barber's daughter, might be attributed to a close association with the well-to-do family of Colonel Colepeper and to frequent exposure to Huguenot[2] and Dutch immigrants in Canterbury. Some recent scholarship, however, claims she was born in Kent and the daughter of John and Amy Amis or Amies. This would make her a possible relation, through her father, of Francis, Lord Willoughby of Parham, who at one time held a position for the British government in the West Indies. We know that in 1663 Behn traveled to the West Indies with her family after her father was named lieutenant-general of the colony of Surinam.[3] Though the stay in Surinam only lasted two months (her father died on the voyage), this experience influenced the writing of her most famous narrative work, *Oroonoko.*

The circumstances surrounding the adoption of Aphra Behn's last name are even more cloudy than those of her birth. Though there is no extant marriage record, scholars speculate that after the trip to Surinam, Behn wed a London merchant or seaman of Dutch or German descent. If

---

[1] **punk:** Prostitute.

[2] **Huguenots:** French Protestants who were members of the Reformed Church established in France by John Calvin circa 1555. Because of religious persecution, they fled to other countries in the sixteenth and seventeenth centuries.

[3] **Surinam:** A British sugar colony on the South American coast below Venezuela.

she married, she and her husband were together for only a short time before either he died or the two parted ways to live separate lives. More interesting is the suggestion that Behn imagined a spouse for herself so that she could gain the respectable title of widow. Several critics comment that, assuming Behn's maiden name was Johnson, taking the last name Behn creates an intriguing allusion to the famous seventeenth-century playwright Ben (Behn) Jonson.

The creation of a fictional husband may well seem like a bold act for a woman of the seventeenth century, but Behn was not one to shy away from taking chances or embarking on daring adventures. In 1666, for example, she served as a spy for Charles II (r. 1660–85) in the Anglo-Dutch War.[4] Recruited by her associate Thomas Killigrew, she was charged with convincing one William Scot to be a double agent, reporting on expatriots, and providing information on Dutch military plans. Her foray into espionage was unsuccessful — what information she provided to the English crown was largely ignored, and she was never repaid for her expenses. Deep in debt and forced to borrow money for the cost of her return to England, it is likely that she spent some time in debtor's prison in 1688.

Writing Politics and the Politics of Writing. Aphra Behn lived through a period of monumental political unrest and social change. In 1642, two years after her birth, England became embroiled in a bloody civil war over religious authority, class privileges, and economic practices, among other issues. Charles I (r. 1625–49) was brought to trial and executed in 1649. Despite the promise of a new kind of governance, the ensuing rule of Oliver Cromwell[5] — under whom Britain was called the "Commonwealth," then the "Protectorate" — proved only that a citizen given the power to govern may be more ineffective and tyrannical than a monarch. The period known as the Restoration, beginning in 1660 with the restoration of Charles II as king of England, saw a newfound celebration of, and freedom in, the arts but did not provide long-term political stability. Charles's successor, James II (r. 1685–88), was quickly ousted and sent into exile, primarily because he was a professed Roman Catholic. In what is called the "Glorious Revolution" of 1688,[6] the Dutch Protestant William of Orange and his wife Mary came to power.

As shown by her service as a spy for Charles II, Behn was dedicated to the preservation of the monarchy and to the system of aristocratic rule. Much of her work is informed by this sociopolitical agenda. In texts

www For links to more information about Behn and a quiz on *Oroonoko*, see *World Literature Online* at bedfordstmartins .com/worldlit.

---

[4] **Anglo-Dutch War:** Battles between the British and the Dutch for control of the seas and trade routes (1652–84).

[5] **Oliver Cromwell** (1599–1658): A soldier, politician, and staunch Puritan who attacked the bishops of the Church of England and advocated widespread political and religious reform. He came to power as "Lord Protector" of England (1653–58) shortly after the execution of Charles I.

[6] **Glorious Revolution:** The birth of a son to the Catholic James II led prominent statesmen in England to invite Dutchman William of Orange and his wife, Mary, to assume the throne. William arrived in 1688, promised to protect the Protestant faith and the liberties of the English, and took the throne without opposition. James II, denounced by Parliament, fled to France.

like *The Roundheads* (1682), *The City Heiress* (1682), and *Romulus and Hersilia* (1682), Behn uses her sharp wit and powerful pen to defend the Stuart monarchy and attack members of the opposition. In fact, her blatant and unapologetic criticism, particularly when it singled out the behavior of powerful persons, occasionally drew her into real trouble; she was probably arrested and briefly imprisoned in 1682 for satirizing the king's illegitimate son, the duke of Monmouth. The predicament of a good and just ruler undone by the machinations of those around him was another of her favorite themes, as is seen in works like *The Fair Jilt* (1688). *Oroonoko* clearly underlines the importance of noble heritage and class distinction. Behn's readers might easily have noted parallels between the noble prince Oroonoko, deprived of his rightful kingdom by the mercenary Dutch, and the situation of Charles II and James II.

The celebratory atmosphere of the Restoration rule of Charles II promoted the success of writers like Behn. Under Puritan rule, the theatres had been closed and texts were quite closely censored. Charles reopened the theatres, licensed two companies of players, and welcomed actresses onto the stage. Since public display of the female body was associated with prostitution, female roles had always been played by young boys prior to this period. The king's decision to allow women on stage, supported by a royal warrant in 1662, opened the way for female actresses to obtain fame and for playwrights to develop female characters in new ways. Behn thrived in a post-Commonwealth atmosphere that invited female participation, experimented with liberal expressions of sexuality, and celebrated the sharp wit of social satire. Her first drama, *The Forced Marriage* (1670), was followed by nearly twenty others, making her the most prolific playwright of her time after the poet laureate John Dryden.

Despite her success as a playwright, or perhaps because of it, Behn was attacked as an upstart and a prostitute. Women during the seventeenth century were expected to remain in the private sphere and, if employment was necessary, to obtain work in professions such as brewing, needlework, or housekeeping. Typically, the position of daughter, sister, wife, or possibly governess, was the prescribed height of female aspiration. Though women often did exercise their creative writing talents and shared their work with friends and relatives, very rarely did they dare to publish — and when they did, it was frequently anonymously.

In both her creative and nonfiction work, Behn condemned these contemporary expectations for women. In prefaces and other direct addresses to her audience, she insists on the right of women writers to be judged by the same standards as men. Note, for example, these lines from the preface to *The Lucky Chance* (1686):

> Had the Plays I have writ come forth under any
> Man's Name, and never known to have been mine;
> I appeal to all unbyast Judges of Sense, if
> they had not said that Person had made as many
> good Comedies, as any one Man that has writ in
> our Age; but a Devil on't the Woman damns the
> poet. . . . All I ask, is the Priviledge for my
> Masculine Part the Poet in me.

Behn's unabashed claim to the profession of writing as a means of support is widely credited with opening the door for other women who would later attempt to earn a living by the pen.

Sex, Politics, and Power.

Skilled in a variety of literary forms, including poetry, drama, narrative, and translation, Behn is probably best known for the vivacity and frankness of her wit and her open investigation of the connection between sexual politics and social power. She was fascinated with the romantic conventions of love and heroism. Addressing her friends under conventional pastoral names, like "Orinda" (the poet Katherine Philips), and assuming for herself the name "Astrea," she wrote many poems exploring the nature of love—whether it be the love of friendship shared between two women (as in "To the fair Clarinda") or the sensually charged love between a man and a woman. In "The Disappointment," one of her most popular poems, she draws parallels between the attainment of sexual gratification and of social power. A description of premature ejaculation from the female point of view, this poem wittily reverses traditional gender expectations of desire and control.

Though an accomplished poet, Behn's fame largely rests with her work as a dramatist. She used the stage as a forum to explore the problems of English society and, more importantly, to focus attention on the status and treatment of women. Works like *The Forced Marriage* (1671), *The Feign'd Courtesans* (1679), and *The Lucky Chance* (1686), take up one of her favorite themes—the ridiculousness of forcing a marriage where there is no love. Her most famous play, *The Rover* (1677–81), relates the story of a group of cavaliers exiled from England during the rule of Cromwell who find themselves in Spain during the pre-Lenten carnival. The carnival, where disguises and masks free the participants from the usual rules governing behavior according to class and gender, is the perfect setting for an analysis of social interaction and power. The treatment of the major female characters of the play, whether they be gentlewomen or prostitutes, highlights their status as property of the men in their lives and as pawns in the struggle for political power. Angellica Bianca, a courtesan who can seemingly command a high price for her services and choose among a number of suitors, finds in the end that her powers of seduction are not able to stand against social expectations.

Oroonoko, or The Royal Slave.

Addressing issues of race, gender, class, and imperialism, *Oroonoko* is one of Behn's most complex and important works. Though frequently credited as an important predecessor to the English novel, *Oroonoko* is hard to place in any one genre. Some critics identify it as one of the first attempts in English to write a historical novel, even a biography, while others categorize it as a "protonovel," TRAVEL NARRATIVE, or novella. It contains elements of the romance— idealized characters, improbable adventures, and of course a noble love story, but it also contains strong elements of realism, such as detailed accounts of the growth of a character and particular descriptions of time and place. Behn's attention to detail and the dark undertone of her text, playing against highly romantic and lighthearted elements, illustrate her

Mr. SAVIGNY *in the Character of* OROONOKO.
Oro. *I'll turn my Face away, and do it so.*
Published Nov.ʳ 23. 1776 by J. Lowndes & Partners

Frontispiece to
Oroonoko, A Tragedy,
1776
This illustration accompanied Thomas Southerne's stage adaptation of Oroonoko, *which was popular throughout the eighteenth century.*

ability to balance the demand on literature to both entertain and instruct. Although she draws her audience in with the portrayal of a noble prince and his love for a fair maiden, she also draws blood when necessary. Her frank descriptions of the horrors of the slave trade, her use of Christian rhetoric as perhaps Oroonoko's finest weapon against his oppressors, and the inescapable conclusion that superiority is finally a matter of brute domination demonstrate an amazing insightfulness for her time and Behn's great creative talent.

The tale opens with a description of the brave exploits of Prince Oroonoko — warrior, gentleman, and lover. Having fallen in love with the beautiful Imoinda, Oroonoko is driven to distraction and almost death when the king, his grandfather, is also attracted to the object of his affection. The prince and Imoinda are separated for a short while, but through a series of malevolent events, power struggles, and coincidences, Oroonoko eventually ends up as a slave on the same plantation as Imoinda.

Presented as a true story that was told to the narrator by the hero himself, the text raises questions about narrative perspective, power, and human relations. The narrator is a member of the dominant class of white colonists, but as a woman she is not in a particularly privileged position. She initially describes herself as an impartial observer and recorder of events. But while it is clear that she is not impartial, it is unclear exactly where her sympathies lie or to what extent she is a responsible participant in the unfolding events. Her description of Prince Oroonoko, who is first a slave-owner and then a slave, resembles depictions of heroes in European romances. Educated by a French tutor and conversant in three European languages, Oroonoko is courageous, witty and genteel. His features are Roman rather than African, he is highly skilled in the arts of war, and he is the possessor of an extreme sensibility that causes him to pine for the fair Imoinda. Working partly from the concept of the "noble savage," which celebrates an idealized version of "primitive" human beings as symbols of innate goodness uncorrupted by the influence of civilization, Behn's Eurocentric concept of beauty and nobility complicates the status and function of her hero.

After Oroonoko is tricked into slavery by the captain of an English ship, his story, while keeping many of its romantic elements, takes on a dark realism and broaches some disturbing aspects of human interaction. Oroonoko's inherent nobility and courage, for example, bring him compliments and promises of freedom from his white associates and masters, but in the end neither his friends nor his own nobility saves him from savagery. Though he is educated in the language and reasoning of Western thought, the powerful Christian arguments he uses to protest the bloody practices of the colonizers make little impact. And in the violent and unjust system to which Oroonoko is subjected, the purity and integrity of romantic love—which the prince honors in his dedication to Imoinda when they meet again as fellow slaves—is undermined.

■ CONNECTIONS

Olaudah Equiano, *The Interesting Narrative of the Life of Olaudah Equiano,* p. 405. The form and content of a literary work are always influenced to some degree by considerations of purpose and audience. It might be argued that *Oroonoko* Westernizes its hero in order to make a difficult lesson more palatable to a European readership. Consider the ways the purpose and approach of Behn's work compare with those in *The Interesting Narrative of the Life of Olaudah Equiano.*

Chinua Achebe, *Things Fall Apart;* Wole Soyinka, *The Lion and the Jewel,* (Book 6). In late seventeenth- and eighteenth-century England, the status and role of women as part of the social whole were subjects taken up in literature. Behn's interest in gender and sexual politics is demonstrated by her description of the powers of Imoinda, whose beauty and sensuality overcome the brave prince Oroonoko so completely that he nearly dies. Compare Behn's treatment of the female sex with the position and influence of women in Achebe's *Things Fall Apart* and Soyinka's *The Lion and the Jewel.*

Mary Rowlandson, *Narrative of the Captivity and Restoration of Mrs. Mary Rowlandson,* p. 483. Travel narratives popularized the concept of the "noble savage." In *Oroonoko,* both the narrator and Oroonoko experience and record their exposure to unfamiliar cultures and environments. In addition, Behn's text is famous for its portrayal of the "noble savage" and use of Christian doctrine to argue for compassionate understanding among cultures. Look at Rowlandson's style of description, characterization of the "savage," and use of Christian doctrine in contrast with Behn's.

■ **FURTHER RESEARCH**

Biography
Todd, Janet. *The Secret Life of Aphra Behn.* 2000.
Woodcock, George. *Aphra Behn: The English Sappho.* 1989.

Criticism
Brownley, Martine Watson. "The Narrator in *Oroonoko*." *Essays in Literature* 4 (1977): 174–81.
Ferguson, Margaret. "Juggling the Categories of Race, Class, and Gender: Aphra Behn's *Oroonoko*." *Women's Studies* 19 (1991): 159–81.
Guffey, George. "Aphra Behn's *Oroonoko*: Occasion and Accomplishment." In *Two English Novelists: Aphra Behn and Anthony Trollope: Papers Read at a Clark Library Seminar, May 11, 1974.* 1975.
Hunter, Heidi, ed. *Rereading Aphra Behn: History, Theory, and Criticism.* 1993.
Todd, Janet, ed. *Aphra Behn Studies.* 1996.

✎ Oroonoko

I do not pretend, in giving you the history of this royal slave, to entertain my reader with the adventures of a feigned hero, whose life and fortunes fancy may manage at the poet's pleasure; nor in relating the truth, design to adorn it with any accidents, but such as arrived in earnest to him. And it shall come simply into the world, recommended by its own proper merits, and natural intrigues; there being enough of reality to support it, and to render it diverting, without the addition of invention.

I was myself an eye-witness, to a great part, of what you will find here set down; and what I could not be witness of, I received from the mouth of the chief actor in

---

Oroonoko. Published in 1688, *Oroonoko* was reprinted several times in the eighteenth century, published in serial form in *Ladies Magazine,* and translated into German, Dutch, and French. In addition, it was adapted into dramatic form by Thomas Southerne in 1696. Probably based on the observations of the author during her brief stay in Surinam, the narrative follows the adventures of a royal African prince and the woman he loves, Imoinda, as they struggle with obstacles that would keep them apart and then enslaved. Even in bondage, Oroonoko's noble nature is clearly visible to his fellow slaves and many of the white colonizers. Hence, he is able to stand as a model of strength, maintain his own beliefs, and suggest to his masters the inhumanity of their actions and the hypocrisy of their Christianity. Eventually the prince experiences the cruelty of his white colonizers who bind, mutilate, and kill him but who could not take from him his innate dignity and keen sense of human rights.

The disparity between proclaimed Western values and actual Western practices as dramatized by this narrative raises important questions, including What is at the root of notions of superiority and how must dominance be maintained? and How do gender, race, and class determine or influence the exercise of power? The issue of whether *Oroonoko* takes a stand against slavery—and if so, to what degree—has likewise generated much debate.

A note on the text: This text reprints Janet Todd's edition of *Oroonoko* from *Oroonoko, The Rover, and Other Works* (Penguin, 1992). All notes are adapted from Todd's.

this history, the hero himself, who gave us the whole transactions of his youth; and though I shall omit, for brevity's sake, a thousand little accidents of his life, which, however pleasant to us, where history was scarce, and adventures very rare; yet might prove tedious and heavy to my reader, in a world where he finds diversions for every minute, new and strange. But we who were perfectly charmed with the character of this great man, were curious to gather every circumstance of his life.

The scene of the last part of his adventures lies in a colony in America, called Surinam,[1] in the West Indies.

But before I give you the story of this gallant slave, 'tis fit I tell you the manner of bringing them to these new colonies; for those they make use of there, are not natives of the place;[2] for those we live with in perfect amity, without daring to command them; but on the contrary, caress them with all the brotherly and friendly affection in the world; trading with them for their fish, venison, buffaloes, skins, and little rarities; as marmosets, a sort of monkey as big as a rat or weasel, but of a marvellous and delicate shape, and has face and hands like an human creature; and cousheries,[3] a little beast in the form and fashion of a lion, as big as a kitten; but so exactly made in all parts like that noble beast, that it is it in miniature. Then for little parakeets, great parrots, macaws, and a thousand other birds and beasts of wonderful and surprising forms, shapes, and colours. For skins of prodigious snakes, of which there are some threescore yards in length; as is the skin of one that may be seen at His Majesty's Antiquaries, where are also some rare flies,[4] of amazing forms and colours, presented to them by myself, some as big as my fist, some less; and all of various excellencies, such as art cannot imitate. Then we trade for feathers, which they order into all shapes, make themselves little short habits of them, and glorious wreaths for their heads, necks, arms and legs, whose tinctures are inconceivable. I had a set of these presented to me, and I gave them to the King's Theatre, and it was the dress of the *Indian Queen*,[5] infinitely admired by persons of quality, and were inimitable. Besides these, a thousand little knacks, and rarities in Nature, and some of art; as their baskets, weapons, aprons, etc. We dealt with them with beads of all colours, knives, axes, pins and needles; which they used only as tools to drill holes with in their ears, noses and lips, where they hang a great many little things; as long beads, bits of tin, brass, or silver, beat thin; and any shining trinket. The beads they weave into aprons about a quarter of an ell[6] long, and of the same breadth; working

---

[1] **Surinam:** The first English colonies in Surinam, later Dutch Guiana, were founded in the 1640s; in 1650 Anthony Rous and Francis, Lord Willoughby of Parham, founded further settlements.

[2] **not . . . place:** White Surinam planters tended to have large estates with many slaves, primarily brought from the Gold Coast. Black slaves were introduced into Surinam in 1650 by Lord Willoughby and soon outnumbered whites; there was considerable fear of an uprising among the settlers.

[3] **cousheries:** The local Caribee Indians spoke Galibi. Antoine Biet in *Voyage de la France équinoxiale en l'isle de Cayenne* (1654), which often gives Galibi words close to those in *Oroonoko*, calls the "couchari" a deer (*cerf*) and the "caïcouci" a tiger.

[4] **flies:** Butterflies.

[5] *Indian Queen:* Written by John Dryden and Sir Robert Howard; one of the first rhymed heroic dramas produced in London.

[6] **ell:** The English ell measured 45 inches.

them very prettily in flowers of several colours of beads; which apron they wear just before them, as Adam and Eve did the fig leaves; the men wearing a long strip of linen, which they deal with us for. They thread these beads also on long cotton threads, and make girdles to tie their aprons to, which come twenty times, or more, about the waist; and then cross, like a shoulder-belt, both ways, and round their necks, arms and legs. This adornment, with their long black hair, and the face painted in little specks or flowers here and there, makes them a wonderful figure to behold. Some of the beauties which indeed are finely shaped, as almost all are, and who have pretty features, are very charming and novel; for they have all that is called beauty, except the colour, which is a reddish yellow; or after a new oiling, which they often use to themselves, they are of the colour of a new brick, but smooth, soft and sleek. They are extreme modest and bashful, very shy, and nice[7] of being touched. And though they are all thus naked, if one lives for ever among them, there is not to be seen an indecent action, or glance; and being continually used to see one another so unadorned, so like our first parents before the Fall, it seems as if they had no wishes; there being nothing to heighten curiosity, but all you can see, you see at once, and every moment see; and where there is no novelty, there can be no curiosity.[8] Not but I have seen a handsome young Indian, dying for love of a very beautiful young Indian maid; but all his courtship was, to fold his arms, pursue her with his eyes, and sighs were all his language; while she, as if no such lover were present, or rather, as if she desired none such, carefully guarded her eyes from beholding him; and never approached him, but she looked down with all the blushing modesty I have seen in the most severe and cautious of our world. And these people represented to me an absolute idea of the first state of innocence, before man knew how to sin; and 'tis most evident and plain, that simple Nature is the most harmless, inoffensive and virtuous mistress. 'Tis she alone, if she were permitted, that better instructs the world than all the inventions of man; religion would here but destroy that tranquillity they possess by ignorance, and laws would teach them to know offence, of which now they have no notion. They once made mourning and fasting for the death of the English governor, who had given his hand to come on such a day to them, and neither came, nor sent; believing, when once a man's word was past, nothing but death could or should prevent his keeping it. And when they saw he was not dead, they asked him, what name they had for a man who promised a thing he did not do? The governor told them, such a man was a liar, which was a word of infamy to a gentleman. Then one of them replied, "Governor, you are a liar, and guilty of that infamy." They have a native justice, which knows no fraud; and they understand no vice, or cunning, but when they are taught by the white men. They have plurality of wives, which, when they grow old, they serve those that succeed them, who are young; but with a servitude easy and respected; and unless they take slaves in war, they have no other attendants.

---

[7] **nice:** Reluctant.

[8] **no curiosity:** This description of a natural lack of shame is a usual feature of Behn's depictions of a Golden Age world. It can be found in many pastoral writers and is a convention of the pastoral tradition.

Those on that continent where I was, had no king; but the oldest war captain was obeyed with great resignation.

A war captain is a man who has led them on to battle with conduct, and success; of whom I shall have occasion to speak more hereafter, and of some other of their customs and manners, as they fall in my way.

With these people, as I said, we live in perfect tranquillity, and good understanding, as it behoves us to do; they knowing all the places where to seek the best food of the country, and the means of getting it; and for very small and invaluable trifles, supply us with what 'tis impossible for us to get; for they do not only in the wood, and over the savannahs,[9] in hunting, supply the parts of hounds, by swiftly scouring through those almost impassable places, and by the mere activity of their feet, run down the nimblest deer, and other eatable beasts; but in the water, one would think they were gods of the rivers, or fellow-citizens of the deep, so rare an art they have in swimming, diving, and almost living in water, by which they command the less swift inhabitants of the floods. And then for shooting; what they cannot take, or reach with their hands, they do with arrows, and have so admirable an aim, that they will split almost a hair; and at any distance that an arrow can reach, they will shoot down oranges, and other fruit, and only touch the stalk with the darts' points, that they may not hurt the fruit. So that they being, on all occasions, very useful to us, we find it absolutely necessary to caress them as friends, and not to treat them as slaves; nor dare we do other, their numbers so far surpassing ours in that continent.

Those then whom we make use of to work in our plantations of sugar are negroes, black slaves altogether, which are transported thither in this manner.

Those who want slaves, make a bargain with a master, or captain of a ship, and contract to pay him so much apiece, a matter of twenty pound a head for as many as he agrees for, and to pay for them when they shall be delivered on such a plantation. So that when there arrives a ship laden with slaves, they who have so contracted, go aboard, and receive their number by lot; and perhaps in one lot that may be for ten, there may happen to be three or four men; the rest, women and children; or be there more or less of either sex, you are obliged to be contented with your lot.

Coramantien,[10] a country of blacks so called, was one of those places in which they found the most advantageous trading for these slaves; and thither most of our great traders in that merchandise trafficked; for that nation is very warlike and brave, and having a continual campaign, being always in hostility with one neighbouring prince or other, they had the fortune to take a great many captives; for all they took in battle, were sold as slaves, at least, those common men who could not ransom themselves. Of these slaves so taken, the general only has all the profit; and of these generals, our captains and masters of ships buy all their freights.

---

[9] **savannahs:** A large heath in the Americas.

[10] **Coramantien:** From the Dutch fort Koromantyn or Fort Amsterdam; a settlement on the west coast of Africa, a few miles east of Cape Coast in Ghana. It was an English trading post from the 1630s, and the name was used loosely for most of the area of modern Ghana. At the time it was used by the English and Dutch slave-traders as a source of supply of slaves from the Fantis, Ashantis, and interior tribes.

The king of Coramantien was himself a man of a hundred and odd years old, and had no son, though he had many beautiful black wives; for most certainly, there are beauties that can charm of that colour. In his younger years he had had many gallant men to his sons, thirteen of which died in battle, conquering when they fell; and he had only left him for his successor, one grandchild, son to one of these dead victors; who, as soon as he could bear a bow in his hand, and a quiver at his back, was sent into the field, to be trained up by one of the oldest generals, to war; where, from his natural inclination to arms, and the occasions given him, with the good conduct of the old general, he became, at the age of seventeen, one of the most expert captains, and bravest soldiers, that ever saw the field of Mars; so that he was adored as the wonder of all that world, and the darling of the soldiers. Besides, he was adorned with a native beauty so transcending all those of his gloomy race, that he struck an awe and reverence, even in those that knew not his quality; as he did in me, who beheld him with surprise and wonder, when afterwards he arrived in our world.

He had scarce arrived at his seventeenth year, when fighting by his side, the general was killed with an arrow in his eye, which the Prince Oroonoko[11] (for so was this gallant Moor called) very narrowly avoided; nor had he, if the general, who saw the arrow shot, and perceiving it aimed at the prince, had not bowed his head between, on purpose to receive it in his own body rather than it should touch that of the prince, and so saved him.

'Twas then, afflicted as Oroonoko was, that he was proclaimed general in the old man's place; and then it was, at the finishing of that war, which had continued for two years, that the prince came to court; where he had hardly been a month together, from the time of his fifth year to that of seventeen; and 'twas amazing to imagine where it was he learned so much humanity; or, to give his accomplishments a juster name, where 'twas he got that real greatness of soul, those refined notions of true honour, that absolute generosity, and that softness that was capable of the highest passions of love and gallantry, whose objects were almost continually fighting men, or those mangled, or dead; who heard no sounds, but those of war and groans. Some part of it we may attribute to the care of a Frenchman of wit and learning, who finding it turn to very good account to be a sort of royal tutor to this young Black, and perceiving him very ready, apt, and quick of apprehension, took a great pleasure to teach him morals, language and science, and was for it extremely beloved and valued by him. Another reason was, he loved, when he came from war, to see all the English gentlemen that traded thither; and did not only learn their language, but that of the Spaniards also, with whom he traded afterwards for slaves.

I have often seen and conversed with this great man, and been a witness to many of his mighty actions; and do assure my reader, the most illustrious courts could not have produced a braver man, both for greatness of courage and mind, a judgment more solid, a wit more quick, and a conversation more sweet and diverting. He knew

---

[11]**Oroonoko:** The name may be a variant of the South American river Orinoco, or perhaps a derivative from an African word such as *Oro,* a Yoruba god. Moors were commonly believed to be black or very dark, so the term was often used for Negroes as well.

almost as much as if he had read much: he had heard of, and admired the Romans; he had heard of the late Civil Wars in England, and the deplorable death of our great monarch,[12] and would discourse of it with all the sense, and abhorrence of the injustice imaginable. He had an extreme good and graceful mien, and all the civility of a well-bred great man. He had nothing of barbarity in his nature, but in all points addressed himself as if his education had been in some European court.

This great and just character of Oroonoko gave me an extreme curiosity to see him, especially when I knew he spoke French and English, and that I could talk with him. But though I had heard so much of him, I was as greatly surprised when I saw him as if I had heard nothing of him, so beyond all report I found him. He came into the room, and addressed himself to me, and some other women, with the best grace in the world. He was pretty tall, but of a shape the most exact that can be fancied; the most famous statuary[13] could not form the figure of a man more admirably turned from head to foot. His face was not of that brown, rusty black which most of that nation are, but a perfect ebony, or polished jet. His eyes were the most awful that could be seen, and very piercing; the white of them being like snow, as were his teeth. His nose was rising and Roman, instead of African and flat. His mouth, the finest shaped that could be seen; far from those great turned lips, which are so natural to the rest of the Negroes. The whole proportion and air of his face was so noble, and exactly formed, that, bating[14] his colour, there could be nothing in nature more beautiful, agreeable and handsome. There was no one grace wanting, that bears the standard of true beauty. His hair came down to his shoulders, by the aids of art; which was, by pulling it out with a quill, and keeping it combed, of which he took particular care. Nor did the perfections of his mind come short of those of his person; for his discourse was admirable upon almost any subject; and whoever had heard him speak, would have been convinced of their errors, that all fine wit is confined to the white men, especially to those of Christendom; and would have confessed that Oroonoko was as capable even of reigning well, and of governing as wisely, had as great a soul, as politic[15] maxims, and was as sensible of power as any prince civilized in the most refined schools of humanity and learning, or the most illustrious courts.

This prince, such as I have described him, whose soul and body were so admirably adorned, was (while yet he was in the court of his grandfather) as I said, as capable of love, as 'twas possible for a brave and gallant man to be; and in saying that, I have named the highest degree of love; for sure, great souls are most capable of that passion.

I have already said the old general was killed by the shot of an arrow, by the side of this prince, in battle; and that Oroonoko was made general. This old dead hero had one only daughter left of his race; a beauty that, to describe her truly, one need say only, she was female to the noble male; the beautiful black Venus, to our young

---

[12] **Civil Wars . . . great monarch:** The wars of the 1640s between Royalists and Parliamentarians, culminating in the execution of Charles I in 1649.

[13] **statuary:** Sculptor of statues.   [14] **bating:** Excepting.   [15] **politic:** Sagacious or shrewd.

Mars; as charming in her person as he, and of delicate virtues. I have seen an hundred white men sighing after her, and making a thousand vows at her feet, all vain, and unsuccessful; and she was, indeed, too great for any, but a prince of her own nation to adore.

Oroonoko coming from the wars (which were now ended) after he had made his court to his grandfather, he thought in honour he ought to make a visit to Imoinda, the daughter of his foster-father, the dead general; and to make some excuses to her, because his preservation was the occasion of her father's death; and to present her with those slaves that had been taken in this last battle, as the trophies of her father's victories. When he came, attended by all the young soldiers of any merit, he was infinitely surprised at the beauty of this fair Queen of Night, whose face and person was so exceeding all he had ever beheld; that lovely modesty with which she received him, that softness in her look, and sighs, upon the melancholy occasion of this honour that was done by so great a man as Oroonoko, and a prince of whom she had heard such admirable things; the awfulness wherewith she received him, and the sweetness of her words and behaviour while he stayed, gained a perfect conquest over his fierce heart, and made him feel the victor could be subdued. So that having made his first compliments, and presented her a hundred and fifty slaves in fetters, he told her with his eyes that he was not insensible of her charms; while Imoinda, who wished for nothing more than so glorious a conquest, was pleased to believe she understood that silent language of new-born love; and from that moment, put on all her additions to beauty.

The prince returned to court with quite another humour than before; and though he did not speak much of the fair Imoinda, he had the pleasure to hear all his followers speak of nothing but the charms of that maid; insomuch that, even in the presence of the old king, they were extolling her, and heightening, if possible, the beauties they had found in her; so that nothing else was talked of, no other sound was heard in every corner where there were whisperers, but "Imoinda! Imoinda!"

'Twill be imagined Oroonoko stayed not long before he made his second visit; nor, considering his quality, not much longer before he told her, he adored her. I have often heard him say, that he admired by what strange inspiration he came to talk things so soft, and so passionate, who never knew love, nor was used to the conversation of women; but (to use his own words) he said, most happily, some new, and till then unknown power instructed his heart and tongue in the language of love, and at the same time, in favour of him, inspired Imoinda with a sense of his passion. She was touched with what he said, and returned it all in such answers as went to his very heart, with a pleasure unknown before. Nor did he use those obligations ill that love had done him; but turned all his happy moments to the best advantage; and as he knew no vice, his flame aimed at nothing but honour, if such a distinction may be made in love; and especially in that country, where men take to themselves as many as they can maintain; and where the only crime and sin with woman is to turn her off, to abandon her to want, shame and misery. Such ill morals are only practised in Christian countries, where they prefer the bare name of religion; and, without virtue or morality, think that's sufficient. But Oroonoko was none of those professors; but as he had right notions of honour, so he made her such propositions as were not only and barely such; but, contrary to the custom of his country, he made her vows she should be the only woman he would possess while he lived; that no age or wrinkles should incline him to change, for her soul would be always fine, and always young; and he should have an eternal idea in his mind of the charms she now bore, and should look into his heart for that idea, when he could find it no longer in her face.

After a thousand assurances of his lasting flame, and her eternal empire over him, she condescended to receive him for her husband; or rather, received him, as the greatest honour the gods could do her.

There is a certain ceremony in these cases to be observed, which I forgot to ask him how performed; but 'twas concluded on both sides that, in obedience to him, the grandfather was to be first made acquainted with the design; for they pay a most absolute resignation to the monarch, especially when he is a parent also.

On the other side, the old king, who had many wives, and many concubines, wanted not court flatterers to insinuate in his heart a thousand tender thoughts for this young beauty; and who represented her to his fancy as the most charming he had ever possessed in all the long race of his numerous years. At this character his old heart, like an extinguished brand, most apt to take fire, felt new sparks of love, and began to kindle; and now grown to his second childhood, longed with impatience to behold this gay thing, with whom, alas, he could but innocently play. But how he should be confirmed she was this wonder, before he used his power to call her to court (where maidens never came, unless for the king's private use) he was next to consider; and while he was so doing, he had intelligence brought him, that Imoinda was most certainly mistress to the Prince Oroonoko. This gave him some chagrin; however, it gave him also an opportunity, one day, when the prince was a-hunting, to wait on a man of quality, as his slave and attendant, who should go and make a present to Imoinda, as from the prince; he should then, unknown, see this fair maid, and have an opportunity to hear what message she would return the prince for his present; and from thence gather the state of her heart, and degree of her inclination. This was put in execution, and the old monarch saw, and burnt; he found her all he had heard, and would not delay his happiness, but found he should have some obstacle to overcome her heart; for she expressed her sense of the present the prince had sent her, in terms so sweet, so soft and pretty, with an air of love and joy that could not be dissembled, insomuch that 'twas past doubt whether she loved Oroonoko entirely. This gave the old king some affliction, but he salved it with this, that the obedience the people pay their king, was not at all inferior to what they paid their gods, and what love would not oblige Imoinda to do, duty would compel her to.

He was therefore no sooner got to his apartment, but he sent the royal veil to Imoinda, that is, the ceremony of invitation; he sends the lady, he has a mind to honour with his bed, a veil, with which she is covered and secured for the king's use; and 'tis death to disobey; besides, held a most impious disobedience.

'Tis not to be imagined the surprise and grief that seized this lovely maid at this news and sight. However, as delays in these cases are dangerous, and pleading worse than treason, trembling, and almost fainting, she was obliged to suffer herself to be covered and led away.

They brought her thus to court; and the king, who had caused a very rich bath to be prepared, was led into it, where he sat under a canopy in state, to receive this longed for virgin; whom he having commanded should be brought to him, they (after disrobing her) led her to the bath, and making fast the doors, left her to descend. The king, without more courtship, bade her throw off her mantle and come to his arms. But Imoinda, all in tears, threw herself on the marble on the brink of the bath, and besought him to hear her. She told him, as she was a maid, how proud of the divine glory she should have been of having it in her power to oblige her king; but as by the laws he could not, and from his royal goodness would not take from any man his wedded wife, so she believed she should be the occasion of making him commit a great sin, if she did not reveal her state and condition, and tell him she was another's, and could not be so happy to be his.

The king, enraged at this delay, hastily demanded the name of the bold man that had married a woman of her degree without his consent. Imoinda, seeing his eyes fierce, and his hands tremble, whether with age or anger, I know not, but she fancied the last, almost repented she had said so much, for now she feared the storm would fall on the prince; she therefore said a thousand things to appease the raging of his flame, and to prepare him to hear who it was with calmness; but before she spoke, he imagined who she meant, but would not seem to do so, but commanded her to lay aside her mantle and suffer herself to receive his caresses; or, by his gods, he swore, that happy man whom she was going to name should die, though it were even Oroonoko himself. "Therefore," said he, "deny this marriage, and swear thyself a maid." "That," replied Imoinda, "by all our powers I do, for I am not yet known to my husband." "'Tis enough," said the king, "'tis enough to satisfy both my conscience, and my heart." And rising from his seat, he went and led her into the bath, it being in vain for her to resist.

In this time the prince, who was returned from hunting, went to visit his Imoinda, but found her gone; and not only so, but heard she had received the royal veil. This raised him to a storm, and in his madness they had much ado to save him from laying violent hands on himself. Force first prevailed, and then reason. They urged all to him that might oppose his rage; but nothing weighed so greatly with him as the king's old age, incapable of injuring him with Imoinda. He would give way to that hope, because it pleased him most, and flattered best his heart. Yet this served not altogether to make him cease his different passions, which sometimes raged within him, and sometimes softened into showers. 'Twas not enough to appease him, to tell him, his grandfather was old, and could not that way injure him, while he retained that aweful duty which the young men are used there to pay to their grave relations. He could not be convinced he had no cause to sigh and mourn for the loss of a mistress he could not with all his strength and courage retrieve. And he would often cry, "O my friends! Were she in walled cities, or confined from me in fortifications of the greatest strength; did enchantments or monsters detain her from me, I would venture through any hazard to free her. But here, in the arms of a feeble old man, my youth, my violent love, my trade in arms, and all my vast desire of glory avail me nothing. Imoinda is as irrecoverably lost to me, as if she were snatched by the cold arms of death. Oh! she is never to be retrieved. If I would wait tedious years, till fate should bow the old king to his grave, even that would not leave me Imoinda free; but still that custom that makes it so vile a crime for a son to marry his father's wives or mistress would hinder my happiness; unless I would either ignobly set an ill precedent to my successors, or abandon my country, and fly with her to some unknown world, who never heard our story."

But it was objected to him, that his case was not the same; for Imoinda being his lawful wife, by solemn contract, 'twas he was the injured man, and might, if he so pleased, take Imoinda back, the breach of the law being on his grandfather's side; and that if he could circumvent him, and redeem her from the otan,[16] which is the palace of the king's women, a sort of seraglio, it was both just and lawful for him so to do.

This reasoning had some force upon him, and he should have been entirely comforted, but for the thought that she was possessed by his grandfather. However, he loved so well that he was resolved to believe what most favoured his hope, and to endeavour to learn from Imoinda's own mouth, what only she could satisfy him in: whether she was robbed of that blessing, which was only due to his faith and love. But as it was very hard to get a sight of the women, for no men ever entered into the otan, but when the king went to entertain himself with some one of his wives or mistresses, and 'twas death at any other time for any other to go in, so he knew not how to contrive to get a sight of her.

While Oroonoko felt all the agonies of love, and suffered under a torment the most painful in the world, the old king was not exempted from his share of affliction. He was troubled for having been forced by an irresistible passion to rob his son of a treasure he knew could not but be extremely dear to him, since she was the most beautiful that ever had been seen; and had besides, all the sweetness and innocence of youth and modesty, with a charm of wit surpassing all. He found that, however she was forced to expose her lovely person to his withered arms, she could only sigh and weep there, and think of Oroonoko; and oftentimes could not forbear speaking of him, though her life were, by custom, forfeited by owning her passion. But she spoke not of a lover only, but of a prince dear to him to whom she spoke; and of the praises of a man, who, till now, filled the old man's soul with joy at every recital of his bravery, or even his name. And 'twas this dotage on our young hero that gave Imoinda a thousand privileges to speak of him without offending; and this condescension in the old king that made her take the satisfaction of speaking of him so very often.

Besides, he many times enquired how the prince bore himself; and those of whom he asked, being entirely slaves to the merits and virtues of the prince, still answered what they thought conduced best to his service; which was, to make the old king fancy that the prince had no more interest in Imoinda, and had resigned her

---

[16] **otan:** Since this section seems inspired by oriental tales and is more reminiscent of European ideas of the East than of Africa, perhaps the word derives from *oda,* the Turkish term for a room in a seraglio, or the Persian *otagh,* a tent or pavilion. Or it might be an obsolete Fanti or Ashanti word.

willingly to the pleasure of the king; that he diverted himself with his mathematicians, his fortifications, his officers, and his hunting.

This pleased the old lover, who failed not to report these things again to Imoinda, that she might, by the example of her young lover, withdraw her heart and rest better contented in his arms. But however she was forced to receive this unwelcome news, in all appearance, with unconcern, and content, her heart was bursting within, and she was only happy when she could get alone, to vent her griefs and moans with sighs and tears.

What reports of the prince's conduct were made to the king, he thought good to justify as far as possibly he could by his actions; and when he appeared in the presence of the king, he showed a face not at all betraying his heart; so that in a little time the old man, being entirely convinced that he was no longer a lover of Imoinda, he carried him with him, in his train to the otan, often to banquet with his mistress. But as soon as he entered, one day, into the apartment of Imoinda, with the king, at the first glance from her eyes, notwithstanding all his determined resolution, he was ready to sink in the place where he stood; and had certainly done so, but for the support of Aboan, a young man, who was next to him; which, with his change of countenance, had betrayed him, had the king chanced to look that way. And I have observed, 'tis a very great error in those who laugh when one says, a Negro can change colour; for I have seen them as frequently blush, and look pale, and that as visibly as ever I saw in the most beautiful white. And 'tis certain that both these changes were evident, this day, in both these lovers. And Imoinda, who saw with some joy the change in the prince's face, and found it in her own, strove to divert the king from beholding either, by a forced caress, with which she met him, which was a new wound in the heart of the poor dying prince. But as soon as the king was busied in looking on some fine thing of Imoinda's making, she had time to tell the prince with her angry, but love-darting eyes, that she resented his coldness, and bemoaned her own miserable captivity. Nor were his eyes silent, but answered hers again, as much as eyes could do, instructed by the most tender, and most passionate heart that ever loved. And they spoke so well, and so effectually, as Imoinda no longer doubted, but she was the only delight, and the darling of that soul she found pleading in them its right of love, which none was more willing to resign than she. And 'twas this powerful language alone that in an instant conveyed all the thoughts of their souls to each other, that they both found there wanted but opportunity to make them both entirely happy. But when he saw another door opened by Onahal, a former old wife of the king's who now had charge of Imoinda, and saw the prospect of a bed of state made ready with sweets and flowers for the dalliance of the king, who immediately led the trembling victim from his sight, into that prepared repose. What rage! What wild frenzies seized his heart! Which forcing to keep within bounds, and to suffer without noise, it became the more insupportable and rent his soul with ten thousand pains. He was forced to retire to vent his groans, where he fell down on a carpet, and lay struggling a long time, and only breathing now and then, "O Imoinda!" When Onahal had finished her necessary affair within, shutting the door, she came forth to wait, till the king called; and hearing some one sighing in the other room, she passed on, and found the prince in that deplorable condition which she thought needed her aid. She gave him cordials, but all in vain; till finding the nature of his disease, by his sighs, and naming Imoinda. She told him he had not so much cause as he imagined to afflict himself; for if he knew the king so well as she did, he would not lose a moment in jealousy, and that she was confident that Imoinda bore, at this minute, part in his affliction. Aboan was of the same opinion; and both together, persuaded him to reassume his courage; and all sitting down on the carpet, the prince said so many obliging things to Onahal, that he half persuaded her to be of his party. And she promised him she would thus far comply with his just desires, that she would let Imoinda know how faithful he was, what he suffered, and what he said.

This discourse lasted till the king called, which gave Oroonoko a certain satisfaction; and with the hope Onahal had made him conceive, he assumed a look as gay as 'twas possible a man in his circumstances could do; and presently after, he was called in with the rest who waited without. The king commanded music to be brought, and several of his young wives and mistresses came all together by his command, to dance before him; where Imoinda performed her part with an air and grace so passing all the rest, as her beauty was above them, and received the present, ordained as a prize. The prince was every moment more charmed with the new beauties and graces he beheld in this fair one; and while he gazed and she danced, Onahal was retired to a window with Aboan.

This Onahal, as I said, was one of the cast mistresses of the old king; and 'twas these (now past their beauty) that were made guardians, or governants to the new, and the young ones; and whose business it was, to teach them all those wanton arts of love with which they prevailed and charmed heretofore in their turn; and who now treated the triumphing happy ones with all the severity, as to liberty and freedom, that was possible, in revenge of those honours they rob them of; envying them those satisfactions, those gallantries and presents, that were once made to themselves, while youth and beauty lasted, and which they now saw pass regardless by, and paid only to the bloomings. And certainly, nothing is more afflicting to a decayed beauty than to behold in itself declining charms, that were once adored, and to find those caresses paid to new beauties to which once she laid a claim; to hear them whisper as she passes by, "That once was a delicate woman." These abandoned ladies therefore endeavour to revenge all the despites and decays of time on these flourishing happy ones. And 'twas this severity that gave Oroonoko a thousand fears he should never prevail with Onahal to see Imoinda. But, as I said, she was now retired to a window with Aboan.

This young man was not only one of the best quality, but a man extremely well made, and beautiful; and coming often to attend the king to the otan, he had subdued the heart of the antiquated Onahal, which had not forgot how pleasant it was to be in love. And though she had some decays in her face, she had none in her sense and wit; she was there agreeable still, even to Aboan's youth, so that he took pleasure in entertaining her with discourses of love. He knew also, that to make his court to these she-favourites was the way to be great; these being the persons that do all affairs and business at court. He had also observed that she had given him glances more tender and inviting than she had done to others of his quality. And now, when he saw that her favour could so absolutely oblige the prince, he failed not to sigh in her ear, and to look with eyes all soft upon her, and give her hope that she had made some impressions on his heart. He found her pleased at this, and making a thousand advances to him; but the ceremony ending, and the king departing, broke up the company for that day, and his conversation.

Aboan failed not that night to tell the prince of his success, and how advantageous the service of Onahal might be to his amour with Imoinda. The prince was overjoyed with this good news, and besought him, if it were possible, to caress her, so as to engage her entirely; which he could not fail to do, if he complied with her desires. "For then," said the prince, "her life lying at your mercy, she must grant you the request you make in my behalf." Aboan understood him, and assured him he would make love so effectually, that he would defy the most expert mistress of the art, to find out whether he dissembled it or had it really. And 'twas with impatience they waited the next opportunity of going to the otan.

The wars came on, the time of taking the field approached, and 'twas impossible for the prince to delay his going at the head of his army to encounter the enemy; so that every day seemed a tedious year, till he saw his Imoinda, for he believed he could not live, if he were forced away without being so happy. 'Twas with impatience therefore, that he expected the next visit the king would make; and, according to his wish, it was not long.

The parley of the eyes of these two lovers had not passed so secretly, but an old jealous lover could spy it; or rather, he wanted not flatterers who told him they observed it. So that the prince was hastened to the camp, and this was the last visit he found he should make to the otan; he therefore urged Aboan to make the best of this last effort, and to explain himself so to Onahal, that she, deferring her enjoyment of her young lover no longer, might make way for the prince to speak to Imoinda.

The whole affair being agreed on between the prince and Aboan, they attended the king, as the custom was, to the otan; where, while the whole company was taken up in beholding the dancing and antic[17] postures the women royal made, to divert the king, Onahal singled out Aboan, whom she found most pliable to her wish. When she had him where she believed she could not be heard, she sighed to him, and softly cried, "Ah, Aboan! When will you be sensible of my passion? I confess it with my mouth, because I would not give my eyes the lie; and you have but too much already perceived they have confessed my flame. Nor would I have you believe that because I am the abandoned mistress of a king I esteem myself altogether divested of charms. No, Aboan; I have still a rest of beauty enough engaging, and have learned to please too well, not to be desirable. I can have lovers still, but will have none but Aboan." "Madam," replied the half-feigning youth, "you have already, by my eyes, found you can still conquer; and I believe 'tis in pity of me, you condescend to this kind confession. But, Madam, words are used to be so small a part of our country courtship, that 'tis rare one can get so happy an opportunity as to tell one's heart; and those few minutes we have are forced to be snatched for more certain proofs of love than speaking and sighing; and such I languish for."

---

[17] **antic:** Grotesque.

He spoke this with such a tone, that she hoped it true, and could not forbear believing it; and being wholly transported with joy, for having subdued the finest of all the king's subjects to her desires, she took from her ears two large pearls and commanded him to wear them in his. He would have refused them, crying, "Madam, these are not the proofs of your love that I expect; 'tis opportunity, 'tis a lone hour only, that can make me happy." But forcing the pearls into his hand, she whispered softly to him, "Oh! Do not fear a woman's invention, when love sets her a-thinking." And pressing his hand, she cried, "This night you shall be happy. Come to the gate of the orange groves, behind the otan, and I will be ready, about midnight, to receive you." 'Twas thus agreed, and she left him, that no notice might be taken of their speaking together.

The ladies were still dancing, and the king, laid on a carpet, with a great deal of pleasure, was beholding them, especially Imoinda, who that day appeared more lovely than ever, being enlivened with the good tidings Onahal had brought her of the constant passion the prince had for her. The prince was laid on another carpet, at the other end of the room, with his eyes fixed on the object of his soul; and as she turned, or moved, so did they; and she alone gave his eyes and soul their motions. Nor did Imoinda employ her eyes to any other use, than in beholding with infinite pleasure the joy she produced in those of the prince. But while she was more regarding him than the steps she took, she chanced to fall, and so near him as that leaping with extreme force from the carpet, he caught her in his arms as she fell; and 'twas visible to the whole presence, the joy wherewith he received her. He clasped her close to his bosom, and quite forgot that reverence that was due to the mistress of a king, and that punishment that is the reward of a boldness of this nature; and had not the presence of mind of Imoinda (fonder of his safety, than her own) befriended him in making her spring from his arms and fall into her dance again, he had, at that instant, met his death; for the old king, jealous to the last degree, rose up in rage, broke all the diversion, and led Imoinda to her apartment, and sent out word to the prince to go immediately to the camp; and that if he were found another night in court, he should suffer the death ordained for disobedient offenders.

You may imagine how welcome this news was to Oroonoko, whose unseasonable transport and caress of Imoinda was blamed by all men that loved him; and now he perceived his fault, yet cried, that for such another moment, he would be content to die.

All the otan was in disorder about this accident; and Onahal was particularly concerned, because on the prince's stay depended her happiness, for she could no longer expect that of Aboan. So that, e'er they departed, they contrived it so that the prince and he should come both that night to the grove of the otan, which was all of oranges and citrons, and that there they should wait her orders.

They parted thus, with grief enough, till night; leaving the king in possession of the lovely maid. But nothing could appease the jealousy of the old lover. He would not be imposed on, but would have it that Imoinda made a false step on purpose to fall into Oroonoko's bosom, and that all things looked like a design on both sides, and 'twas in vain she protested her innocence. He was old and obstinate, and left her more than half assured that his fear was true.

The king going to his apartment, sent to know where the prince was, and if he intended to obey his command. The messenger returned, and told him he found the prince pensive, and altogether unpreparing for the campaign; that he lay negligently on the ground, and answered very little. This confirmed the jealousy of the king, and he commanded that they should very narrowly and privately watch his motions; and that he should not stir from his apartment, but one spy or other should be employed to watch him. So that the hour approaching, wherein he was to go to the citron grove, and taking only Aboan along with him, he leaves his apartment, and was watched to the very gate of the otan, where he was seen to enter, and where they left him, to carry back the tidings to the king.

Oroonoko and Aboan were no sooner entered but Onahal led the prince to the apartment of Imoinda, who, not knowing anything of her happiness, was laid in bed. But Onahal only left him in her chamber to make the best of his opportunity, and took her dear Aboan to her own, where he showed the height of complaisance[18] for his prince, when, to give him an opportunity, he suffered himself to be caressed in bed by Onahal.

The prince softly wakened Imoinda, who was not a little surprised with joy to find him there, and yet she trembled with a thousand fears. I believe he omitted saying nothing to this young maid, that might persuade her to suffer him to seize his own, and take the rights of love; and I believe she was not long resisting those arms where she so longed to be; and having opportunity, night and silence, youth, love and desire, he soon prevailed; and ravished in a moment what his old grandfather had been endeavouring for so many months.

'Tis not to be imagined the satisfaction of these two young lovers; nor the vows she made him, that she remained a spotless maid till that night; and that what she did with his grandfather had robbed him of no part of her virgin honour, the gods in mercy and justice having reserved that for her plighted lord, to whom of right it belonged. And 'tis impossible to express the transports he suffered, while he listened to a discourse so charming from her loved lips, and clasped that body in his arms, for whom he had so long languished; and nothing now afflicted him, but his sudden departure from her; for he told her the necessity and his commands; but should depart satisfied in this, that since the old king had hitherto not been able to deprive him of those enjoyments which only belonged to him, he believed for the future he would be less able to injure him. So that, abating the scandal of the veil, which was no otherwise so, than that she was wife to another, he believed her safe, even in the arms of the king, and innocent; yet would he have ventured at the conquest of the world, and have given it all, to have had her avoided that honour of receiving the royal veil. 'Twas thus, between a thousand caresses, that both bemoaned the hard fate of youth and beauty, so liable to that cruel promotion; 'twas a glory that could well have been spared here, though desired, and aimed at by all the young females of that kingdom.

But while they were thus fondly employed, forgetting how time ran on, and that the dawn must conduct him far away from his only happiness, they heard a great

---

[18] complaisance: Desire to please.

noise in the otan, and unusual voices of men; at which the prince, starting from the arms of the frighted Imoinda, ran to a little battle-axe he used to wear by his side; and having not so much leisure as to put on his habit, he opposed himself against some who were already opening the door; which they did with so much violence, that Oroonoko was not able to defend it, but was forced to cry out with a commanding voice, "Whoever ye are that have the boldness to attempt to approach this apartment thus rudely, know that I, the Prince Oroonoko, will revenge it with the certain death of him that first enters. Therefore stand back, and know this place is sacred to love, and me this night; tomorrow 'tis the king's."

This he spoke with a voice so resolved and assured, that they soon retired from the door, but cried, "'Tis by the king's command we are come; and being satisfied by thy voice, O Prince, as much as if we had entered, we can report to the king the truth of all his fears, and leave thee to provide for thy own safety, as thou art advised by thy friends."

At these words they departed, and left the prince to take a short and sad leave of his Imoinda; who trusting in the strength of her charms, believed she should appease the fury of a jealous king by saying she was surprised, and that it was by force of arms he got into her apartment. All her concern now was for his life, and therefore she hastened him to the camp, and with much ado, prevailed on him to go. Nor was it she alone that prevailed, Aboan and Onahal both pleaded, and both assured him of a lie that should be well enough contrived to secure Imoinda. So that, at last, with a heart sad as death, dying eyes, and sighing soul, Oroonoko departed, and took his way to the camp.

It was not long after the king in person came to the otan, where beholding Imoinda with rage in his eyes, he upbraided her wickedness and perfidy, and threatening her royal lover, she fell on her face at his feet, bedewing the floor with her tears and imploring his pardon for a fault which she had not with her will committed, as Onahal, who was also prostrate with her, could testify that, unknown to her, he had broke into her apartment, and ravished her. She spoke this much against her conscience; but to save her own life, 'twas absolutely necessary she should feign this falsity. She knew it could not injure the prince, he being fled to an army that would stand by him against any injuries that should assault him. However, this last thought of Imoinda's being ravished changed the measures of his revenge, and whereas before he designed to be himself her executioner, he now resolved she should not die. But as it is the greatest crime in nature amongst them to touch a woman, after having been possessed by a son, a father, or a brother, so now he looked on Imoinda as a polluted thing, wholly unfit for his embrace; nor would he resign her to his grandson, because she had received the royal veil. He therefore removes her from the otan, with Onahal; whom he put into safe hands, with order they should be both sold off, as slaves, to another country, either Christian, or heathen; 'twas no matter where.

This cruel sentence, worse than death, they implored might be reversed; but their prayers were vain, and it was put in execution accordingly, and that with so much secrecy, that none, either without or within the otan, knew anything of their absence, or their destiny.

The old king, nevertheless, executed this with a great deal of reluctance; but he believed he had made a very great conquest over himself when he had once resolved, and had performed what he resolved. He believed now, that his love had been unjust, and that he could not expect the gods, or Captain of the Clouds (as they call the unknown power) should suffer a better consequence from so ill a cause. He now begins to hold Oroonoko excused; and to say, he had reason for what he did; and now everybody could assure the king, how passionately Imoinda was beloved by the prince; even those confessed it now who said the contrary before his flame was abated. So that the king being old and not able to defend himself in war, and having no sons of all his race remaining alive, but only this, to maintain him on the throne; and looking on this as a man disobliged, first by the rape of his mistress, or rather, wife; and now by depriving him wholly of her, he feared, might make him desperate, and do some cruel thing, either to himself, or his old grandfather, the offender; he began to repent him extremely of the contempt he had, in his rage, put on Imoinda. Besides, he considered he ought in honour to have killed her for this offence, if it had been one. He ought to have had so much value and consideration for a maid of her quality, as to have nobly put her to death, and not to have sold her like a common slave, the greatest revenge, and the most disgraceful of any, and to which they a thousand times prefer death, and implore it as Imoinda did, but could not obtain that honour. Seeing therefore it was certain that Oroonoko would highly resent this affront, he thought good to make some excuse for his rashness to him, and to that end he sent a messenger to the camp with orders to treat with him about the matter, to gain his pardon, and to endeavour to mitigate his grief; but that by no means he should tell him she was sold, but secretly put to death; for he knew he should never obtain his pardon for the other.

When the messenger came, he found the prince upon the point of engaging with the enemy, but as soon as he heard of the arrival of the messenger he commanded him to his tent, where he embraced him, and received him with joy; which was soon abated, by the downcast looks of the messenger, who was instantly demanded the cause by Oroonoko, who, impatient of delay, asked a thousand questions in a breath; and all concerning Imoinda. But there needed little return, for he could almost answer himself of all he demanded from his sighs and eyes. At last, the messenger casting himself at the prince's feet and kissing them with all the submission of a man that had something to implore which he dreaded to utter, he besought him to hear with calmness what he had to deliver to him, and to call up all his noble and heroic courage to encounter with his words, and defend himself against the ungrateful things he must relate. Oroonoko replied, with a deep sigh, and a languishing voice, "I am armed against their worst efforts—for I know they will tell me, Imoinda is no more—and after that, you may spare the rest." Then, commanding him to rise, he laid himself on a carpet under a rich pavilion, and remained a good while silent, and was hardly heard to sigh. When he was come a little to himself, the messenger asked him leave to deliver that part of his embassy which the prince had not yet divined, and the prince cried, "I permit thee." Then he told him the affliction the old king was in for the rashness he had committed in his cruelty to Imoinda; and how he deigned to ask pardon for his offence, and to implore the prince would not suffer that loss to touch his heart too sensibly which now all the gods could not restore him, but might recompense him in glory which he begged he would pursue; and that death, that common revenger of all injuries, would soon even the account between him and a feeble old man.

Oroonoko bade him return his duty to his lord and master, and to assure him there was no account of revenge to be adjusted between them; if there were, 'twas he was the aggressor, and that death would be just, and, maugre[19] his age, would see him righted; and he was contented to leave his share of glory to youths more fortunate, and worthy of that favour from the gods. That henceforth he would never lift a weapon, or draw a bow, but abandon the small remains of his life to sighs and tears, and the continual thoughts of what his lord and grandfather had thought good to send out of the world, with all that youth, that innocence, and beauty.

After having spoken this, whatever his greatest officers, and men of the best rank could do, they could not raise him from the carpet, or persuade him to action and resolutions of life, but commanding all to retire, he shut himself into his pavilion all that day, while the enemy was ready to engage; and wondering at the delay, the whole body of the chief of the army then addressed themselves to him, and to whom they had much ado to get admittance. They fell on their faces at the foot of his carpet, where they lay, and besought him with earnest prayers and tears, to lead them forth to battle, and not let the enemy take advantages of them; and implored him to have regard to his glory, and to the world that depended on his courage and conduct. But he made no other reply to all their supplications but this, that he had now no more business for glory; and for the world, it was a trifle not worth his care. "Go," continued he, sighing, "and divide it amongst you; and reap with joy what you so vainly prize, and leave me to my more welcome destiny."

They then demanded what they should do, and whom he would constitute in his room, that the confusion of ambitious youth and power might not ruin their order, and make them a prey to the enemy. He replied, he would not give himself the trouble; but wished them to choose the bravest man amongst them, let his quality or birth be what it would, "For, O my friends!" said he, "it is not titles make men brave, or good; or birth that bestows courage and generosity, or makes the owner happy. Believe this, when you behold Oroonoko, the most wretched, and abandoned by fortune of all the creation of the gods." So turning himself about, he would make no more reply to all they could urge or implore.

The army beholding their officers return unsuccessful, with sad faces, and ominous looks, that presaged no good luck, suffered a thousand fears to take possession of their hearts, and the enemy to come even upon them, before they would provide for their safety by any defence; and though they were assured by some, who had a mind to animate them, that they should be immediately headed by the prince, and that in the meantime Aboan had orders to command as general, yet they were so dismayed for want of that great example of bravery that they could make but a very feeble resistance; and at last, downright, fled before the enemy, who pursued them to the very tents, killing them. Nor could all Aboan's courage, which that day gained

---

[19] **maugre**: In spite of.

him immortal glory, shame them into a manly defence of themselves. The guards that were left behind, about the prince's tent, seeing the soldiers flee before the enemy, and scatter themselves all over the plain, in great disorder, made such outcries as roused the prince from his amorous slumber, in which he had remained buried for two days, without permitting any sustenance to approach him. But, in spite of all his resolutions, he had not the constancy of grief to that degree as to make him insensible of the danger of his army; and in that instant he leapt from his couch, and cried, "Come, if we must die, let us meet death the noblest way; and 'twill be more like Oroonoko to encounter him at an army's head, opposing the torrent of a conquering foe, than lazily, on a couch, to wait his lingering pleasure, and die every moment by a thousand wrecking thought[s]; or be tamely taken by an enemy and led a whining, love-sick slave, to adorn the triumphs of Jamoan, that young victor, who already is entered beyond the limits I had prescribed him."

While he was speaking, he suffered his people to dress him for the field; and sallying out of his pavilion, with more life and vigour in his countenance than ever he showed, he appeared like some divine power descended to save his country from destruction; and his people had purposely put him on all things that might make him shine with most splendour, to strike a reverend awe into the beholders. He flew into the thickest of those that were pursuing his men, and being animated with despair, he fought as if he came on purpose to die, and did such things as will not be believed that human strength could perform, and such as soon inspired all the rest with new courage and new order. And now it was that they began to fight indeed, and so, as if they would not be outdone even by their adored hero, who turning the tide of the victory, changing absolutely the fate of the day, gained an entire conquest; and Oroonoko having the good fortune to single out Jamoan, he took him prisoner with his own hand, having wounded him almost to death.

This Jamoan afterwards became very dear to him, being a man very gallant and of excellent graces, and fine parts, so that he never put him amongst the rank of captives, as they used to do, without distinction, for the common sale or market, but kept him in his own court, where he retained nothing of the prisoner but the name, and returned no more into his own country, so great an affection he took for Oroonoko; and by a thousand tales and adventures of love and gallantry, flattered his disease of melancholy and languishment, which I have often heard him say had certainly killed him, but for the conversation of this prince and Aboan, [and] the French governor he had from his childhood, of whom I have spoken before, and who was a man of admirable wit, great ingenuity and learning, all which he had infused into his young pupil. This Frenchman was banished out of his own country for some heretical notions he held; and though he was a man of very little religion, he had admirable morals, and a brave soul.

After the total defeat of Jamoan's army, which all fled, or were left dead upon the place, they spent some time in the camp; Oroonoko choosing rather to remain a while there in his tents, than enter into a p[a]lace, or live in a court where he had so lately suffered so great a loss. The officers therefore, who saw and knew his cause of discontent, invented all sorts of diversions and sports to entertain their prince: so that what with those amusements abroad, and others at home, that is, within their tents, with the persuasions, arguments and care of his friends and servants that he more peculiarly prized, he wore off in time a great part of that chagrin and torture of despair which the first effects of Imoinda's death had given him; insomuch as having received a thousand kind embassies from the king, and invitations to return to court, he obeyed, though with no little reluctance; and when he did so, there was a visible change in him, and for a long time he was much more melancholy than before. But time lessens all extremes, and reduces them to mediums and unconcern; but no motives or beauties, though all endeavoured it, could engage him in any sort of amour, though he had all the invitations to it, both from his own youth and others' ambitions and designs.

Oroonoko was no sooner returned from this last conquest, and received at court with all the joy and magnificence that could be expressed to a young victor, who was not only returned triumphant, but beloved like a deity, when there arrived in the port an English ship.

This person had often before been in these countries, and was very well known to Oroonoko, with whom he had trafficked for slaves, and had used to do the same with his predecessors.

This commander was a man of a finer sort of address and conversation, better bred, and more engaging than most of that sort of men are; so that he seemed rather never to have been bred out of a court, than almost all his life at sea. This captain therefore was always better received at court, than most of the traders to those countries were; and especially by Oroonoko, who was more civilized, according to the European mode, than any other had been, and took more delight in the white nations, and, above all, men of parts and wit. To this captain he sold abundance of his slaves, and for the favour and esteem he had for him, made him many presents, and obliged him to stay at court as long as possibly he could. Which the captain seemed to take as a very great honour done him, entertaining the prince every day with globes and maps, and mathematical discourses and instruments; eating, drinking, hunting and living with him with so much familiarity, that it was not to be doubted, but he had gained very greatly upon the heart of this gallant young man. And the captain, in return of all these mighty favours, besought the prince to honour his vessel with his presence, some day or other, to dinner, before he should set sail; which he condescended to accept, and appointed his day. The captain, on his part, failed not to have all things in a readiness, in the most magnificent order he could possibly. And the day being come, the captain, in his boat, richly adorned with carpets and velvet cushions, rowed to the shore to receive the prince; with another long-boat, where was placed all his music and trumpets, with which Oroonoko was extremely delighted; who met him on the shore, attended by his French governor, Jamoan, Aboan, and about an hundred of the noblest of the youths of the court. And after they had first carried the prince on board, the boats fetched the rest off; where they found a very splendid treat, with all sorts of fine wines, and were as well entertained, as 'twas possible in such a place to be.

The prince having drunk hard of punch, and several sorts of wine, as did all the rest (for great care was taken, they should want nothing of that part of the entertainment) was very merry, and in great admiration of the ship, for he had never been in one before; so that he was curious of beholding every place, where he decently might descend. The rest, no less curious, who were not quite overcome with drinking, rambled at their pleasure fore and aft, as their fancies guided them: so that the captain, who had well laid his design before, gave the word and seized on all his guests; they clapping great irons suddenly on the prince when he was leaped down in the hold to view that part of the vessel, and locking him fast down, secured him. The same treachery was used to all the rest; and all in one instant, in several places of the ship, were lashed fast in irons and betrayed to slavery. That great design over, they set all hands to work to hoist sail; and with as treacherous and fair a wind they made from the shore with this innocent and glorious prize, who thought of nothing less than such an entertainment.

Some have commended this act, as brave in the captain; but I will spare my sense of it, and leave it to my reader to judge as he pleases.

It may be easily guessed in what manner the prince resented this indignity, who may be best resembled to a lion taken in a toil; so he raged, so he struggled for liberty, but all in vain; and they had so wisely managed his fetters, that he could not use a hand in his defence, to quit himself of a life that would by no means endure slavery; nor could he move from the place where he was tied to any solid part of the ship against which he might have beat his head, and have finished his disgrace that way; so that being deprived of all other means, he resolved to perish for want of food. And pleased at last with that thought, and toiled and tired by rage and indignation, he laid himself down, and sullenly resolved upon dying, and refused all things that were brought him.

This did not a little vex the captain, and the more so because he found almost all of them of the same humour; so that the loss of so many brave slaves, so tall and goodly to behold, would have been very considerable. He therefore ordered one to go from him (for he would not be seen himself) to Oroonoko, and to assure him he was afflicted for having rashly done so inhospitable a deed, and which could not be now remedied, since they were far from shore; but since he resented it in so high a nature, he assured him he would revoke his resolution, and set both him and his friends ashore on the next land they should touch at; and of this the messenger gave him his oath, provided he would resolve to live. And Oroonoko, whose honour was such as he never had violated a word in his life himself, much less a solemn asseveration, believed in an instant what this man said, but replied he expected for a confirmation of this to have his shameful fetters dismissed. This demand was carried to the captain, who returned him answer that the offence had been so great which he had put upon the prince, that he durst not trust him with liberty while he remained in the ship, for fear lest by a valour natural to him, and a revenge that would animate that valour, he might commit some outrage fatal to himself and the king his master, to whom his vessel did belong. To this Oroonoko replied, he would engage his honour to behave himself in all friendly order and manner, and obey the command of the captain, as he was lord of the king's vessel, and general of those men under his command.

This was delivered to the still doubting captain, who could not resolve to trust a heathen he said, upon his parole,[20] a man that had no sense or notion of the God that he worshipped. Oroonoko then replied he was very sorry to hear that the captain pretended to the knowledge and worship of any gods who had taught him no better principles, than not to credit as he would be credited; but they told him the difference of their faith occasioned that distrust: for the captain had protested to him upon the word of a Christian, and sworn in the name of a great God, which if he should violate, he would expect eternal torment in the world to come. "Is that all the obligation he has to be just to his oath?" replied Oroonoko. "Let him know I swear by my honour, which to violate, would not only render me contemptible and despised by all brave and honest men, and so give myself perpetual pain, but it would be eternally offending and diseasing all mankind, harming, betraying, circumventing and outraging all men; but punishments hereafter are suffered by oneself; and the world takes no cognizances whether this god have revenged them, or not, 'tis done so secretly, and deferred so long; while the man of no honour suffers every moment the scorn and contempt of the honester world, and dies every day ignominiously in his fame, which is more valuable than life. I speak not this to move belief, but to show you how you mistake, when you imagine that he who will violate his honour, will keep his word with his gods." So turning from him with a disdainful smile, he refused to answer him when he urged him to know what answer he should carry back to his captain; so that he departed without saying any more.

The captain pondering and consulting what to do, it was concluded that nothing but Oroonoko's liberty would encourage any of the rest to eat, except the Frenchman, whom the captain could not pretend to keep prisoner, but only told him he was secured because he might act something in favour of the prince, but that he should be freed as soon as they came to land. So that they concluded it wholly necessary to free the prince from his irons that he might show himself to the rest, that they might have an eye upon him, and that they could not fear a single man.

This being resolved, to make the obligation the greater, the captain himself went to Oroonoko; where, after many compliments, and assurances of what he had already promised, he receiving from the prince his parole, and his hand, for his good behaviour, dismissed his irons, and brought him to his own cabin; where, after having treated and reposed him a while, for he had neither eaten nor slept in four days before, he besought him to visit those obstinate people in chains, who refused all manner of sustenance; and entreated him to oblige them to eat, and assure them of their liberty the first opportunity.

Oroonoko, who was too generous not to give credit to his words, showed himself to his people, who were transported with excess of joy at the sight of their darling prince; falling at his feet, and kissing and embracing them, believing, as some divine oracle, all he assured them. But he besought them to bear their chains with that bravery that became those whom he had seen act so nobly in arms; and that they could not give him greater proofs of their love and friendship, since 'twas all the security the captain (his friend) could have against the revenge, he said, they might

---

[20] **parole:** Word or pledge.

possibly justly take, for the injuries sustained by him. And they all, with one accord, assured him they could not suffer enough when it was for his repose and safety.

After this they no longer refused to eat, but took what was brought them and were pleased with their captivity, since by it they hoped to redeem the prince, who, all the rest of the voyage, was treated with all the respect due to his birth, though nothing could divert his melancholy; and he would often sigh for Imoinda, and think this a punishment due to his misfortune, in having left that noble maid behind him that fatal night in the otan, when he fled to the camp.

Possessed with a thousand thoughts of past joys with this fair young person, and a thousand griefs for her eternal loss, he endured a tedious voyage, and at last arrived at the mouth of the river of Surinam, a colony belonging to the King of England, and where they were to deliver some part of their slaves. There the merchants and gentlemen of the country going on board to demand those lots of slaves they had already agreed on, and amongst those the overseers of those plantations where I then chanced to be, the captain, who had given the word, ordered his men to bring up those noble slaves in fetters, whom I have spoken of; and having put them, some in one, and some in other lots, with women and children (which they call pickaninnies[21]), they sold them off as slaves to several merchants and gentlemen; not putting any two in one lot, because they would separate them far from each other; not daring to trust them together, lest rage and courage should put them upon contriving some great action, to the ruin of the colony.

Oroonoko was first seized on and sold to our overseer, who had the first lot, with seventeen more of all sorts and sizes, but not one of quality with him. When he saw this, he found what they meant; for, as I said, he understood English pretty well; and being wholly unarmed and defenceless, so as it was in vain to make any resistance, he only beheld the captain with a look all fierce and disdainful, upbraiding him with eyes, that forced blushes on his guilty cheeks, he only cried in passing over the side of the ship, "Farewell, Sir! 'Tis worth my suffering to gain so true a knowledge both of you and of your gods by whom you swear." And desiring those that held him to forbear their pains, and telling them he would make no resistance, he cried, "Come, my fellow-slaves, let us descend, and see if we can meet with more honour and honesty in the next world we shall touch upon." So he nimbly leapt into the boat, and showing no more concern, suffered himself to be rowed up the river with his seventeen companions.

The gentleman that bought him was a young Cornish gentleman, whose name was Trefry;[22] a man of great wit, and fine learning, and was carried into those parts by the Lord—Governor, to manage all his affairs. He reflecting on the last words of Oroonoko to the captain, and beholding the richness of his vest, no sooner came into the boat, but he fixed his eyes on him; and finding something so extraordinary in his face, his shape and mien, a greatness of look, and haughtiness in his air, and finding he spoke English, had a great mind to be enquiring into his quality and fortune; which, though Oroonoko endeavoured to hide by only confessing he was

---

[21] pickaninnies: An early use of this word for black children.

[22] Trefry: John Treffry was Lord Willoughby's agent in his plantation of Parham.

above the rank of common slaves, Trefry soon found he was yet something greater than he confessed; and from that moment began to conceive so vast an esteem for him, that he ever after loved him as his dearest brother, and showed him all the civilities due to so great a man.

Trefry was a very good mathematician, and a linguist; could speak French and Spanish; and in the three days they remained in the boat (for so long were they going from the ship to the plantation) he entertained Oroonoko so agreeably with his art and discourse, that he was no less pleased with Trefry, than he was with the prince; and he thought himself, at least, fortunate in this, that since he was a slave, as long as he would suffer himself to remain so, he had a man of so excellent wit and parts for a master. So that before they had finished their voyage up the river, he made no scruple of declaring to Trefry all his fortunes and most part of what I have here related, and put himself wholly into the hands of his new friend, whom he found resenting all the injuries were done him, and was charmed with all the greatnesses of his actions, which were recited with that modesty and delicate sense, as wholly vanquished him, and subdued him to his interest. And he promised him on his word and honour, he would find the means to reconduct him to his own country again; assuring him, he had a perfect abhorrence of so dishonourable an action; and that he would sooner have died, than have been the author of such a perfidy. He found the prince was very much concerned to know what became of his friends, and how they took their slavery; and Trefry promised to take care about the enquiring after their condition, and that he should have an account of them.

Though, as Oroonoko afterwards said, he had little reason to credit the words of a backearary,[23] yet he knew not why, but he saw a kind of sincerity and awful truth in the face of Trefry; he saw an honesty in his eyes, and he found him wise and witty enough to understand honour; for it was one of his maxims, "A man of wit could not be a knave or villain."

In their passage up the river they put in at several houses for refreshment, and ever when they landed numbers of people would flock to behold this man; not but their eyes were daily entertained with the sight of slaves, but the fame of Oroonoko was gone before him, and all people were in admiration of his beauty. Besides, he had a rich habit on, in which he was taken, so different from the rest, and which the captain could not strip him of because he was forced to surprise his person in the minute he sold him. When he found his habit made him liable, as he thought, to be gazed at the more, he begged Trefry to give him something more befitting a slave; which he did, and took off his robes. Nevertheless, he shone through all and his osenbrigs (a sort of brown holland[24] suit he had on) could not conceal the graces of his looks and mien; and he had no less admirers than when he had his dazzling habit on. The royal youth appeared in spite of the slave, and people could not help treating him after a different manner without designing it; as soon as they approached him they venerated and esteemed him; his eyes insensibly commanded respect, and his

---

[23] **backearary:** Possibly a variant of *buckra* or *bakra* (master), the word used in Surinam by the blacks for the whites.

[24] **osenbrigs . . . holland:** Osnaburg was heavy coarse cotton or linen ("holland") fabric.

behaviour insinuated it into every soul. So that there was nothing talked of but this young and gallant slave, even by those who yet knew not that he was a prince.

I ought to tell you, that the Christians never buy any slaves but they give them some name of their own, their native ones being likely very barbarous, and hard to pronounce; so that Mr. Trefry gave Oroonoko that of Caesar, which name will live in that country as long as that (scarce more) glorious one of the great Roman, for 'tis most evident, he wanted no part of the personal courage of that Caesar,[25] and acted things as memorable, had they been done in some part of the world replenished with people and historians that might have given him his due. But his misfortune was to fall in an obscure world, that afforded only a female pen to celebrate his fame, though I doubt not but it had lived from others' endeavours, if the Dutch, who, immediately after his time, took that country, had not killed, banished, and dispersed all those that were capable of giving the world this great man's life, much better than I have done. And Mr. Trefry, who designed it, died before he began it, and bemoaned himself for not having undertook it in time.[26]

For the future therefore, I must call Oroonoko, Caesar, since by that name only he was known in our western world, and by that name he was received on shore at Parham-House,[27] where he was destined a slave. But if the king himself (God bless him) had come ashore, there could not have been greater expectations by all the whole plantation, and those neighbouring ones, than was on ours at that time; and he was received more like a governor than a slave. Notwithstanding, as the custom was, they assigned him his portion of land, his house, and his business, up in the plantation. But as it was more for form than any design to put him to his task, he endured no more of the slave but the name, and remained some days in the house, receiving all visits that were made him, without stirring towards that part of the plantation where the Negroes were.

At last, he would needs go view his land, his house, and the business assigned him. But he no sooner came to the houses of the slaves, which are like a little town by itself, the Negroes all having left work, but they all came forth to behold him, and found he was that prince who had, at several times, sold most of them to these parts; and, from a veneration they pay to great men, especially if they know them, and from the surprise and awe they had at the sight of him, they all cast themselves at his feet, crying out, in their language, "Live, O King! Long live, O King!" And kissing his feet, paid him even divine homage.

Several English gentlemen were with him; and what Mr. Trefry had told them, was here confirmed of which he himself before had no other witness than Caesar himself. But he was infinitely glad to find his grandeur confirmed by the adoration of all the slaves.

Caesar, troubled with their over-joy, and over-ceremony, besought them to rise,

---

[25] **Caesar:** It was a custom of slave-owners to give slaves Roman names.

[26] **the Dutch . . . in time:** The Dutch captured Surinam in February 1667; it was retaken by the English in October but was ceded to the Dutch at the Treaty of Breda in 1667. Treffry remained in Surinam and died there in 1674.

[27] **Parham-House:** Parham House was part of Lord Willoughby's estate of Parham Hill.

and to receive him as their fellow-slave, assuring them, he was no better. At which they set up with one accord a most terrible and hideous mourning and condoling, which he and the English had much ado to appease. But at last they prevailed with them, and they prepared all their barbarous music, and everyone killed and dressed something of his own stock (for every family has their land apart, on which, at their leisure-times, they breed all eatable things) and clubbing it together, made a most magnificent supper, inviting their grandee captain, their prince, to honour it with his presence, which he did, and several English with him, where they all waited on him, some playing, others dancing before him all the time, according to the manners of their several nations, and with unwearied industry, endeavouring to please and delight him.

While they sat at meat Mr. Trefry told Caesar, that most of these young slaves were undone in love, with a fine she slave, whom they had had about six months on their land. The prince, who never heard the name of love without a sigh, nor any mention of it without the curiosity of examining further into that tale, which of all discourses was most agreeable to him, asked, how they came to be so unhappy, as to be all undone for one fair slave? Trefry, who was naturally amorous, and loved to talk of love as well as anybody, proceeded to tell him, they had the most charming black that ever was beheld on their plantation, about fifteen or sixteen years old, as he guessed; that, for his part, he had done nothing but sigh for her ever since she came; and that all the white beauties he had seen, never charmed him so absolutely as this fine creature had done; and that no man, of any nation, ever beheld her, that did not fall in love with her; and that she had all the slaves perpetually at her feet; and the whole country resounded with the fame of Clemene, for so, said he, we have christened her. But she denies us all with such a noble disdain, that 'tis a miracle to see that she, who can give such eternal desires, should herself be all ice, and all unconcern. She is adorned with the most graceful modesty that ever beautified youth; the softest sigher—that, if she were capable of love, one would swear she languished for some absent happy man; and so retired, as if she feared a rape even from the God of Day, or that the breezes would steal kisses from her delicate mouth. Her task of work some sighing lover every day makes it his petition to perform for her, which she accepts blushing, and with reluctance, for fear he will ask her a look for a recompense, which he dares not presume to hope, so great an awe she strikes into the hearts of her admirers. "I do not wonder," replied the prince, "that Clemene should refuse slaves, being as you say so beautiful, but wonder how she escapes those who can entertain her as you can do. Or why, being your slave, you do not oblige her to yield." "I confess," said Trefry, "when I have, against her will, entertained her with love so long, as to be transported with my passion, even above decency, I have been ready to make use of those advantages of strength and force Nature has given me. But oh! she disarms me, with that modesty and weeping so tender and so moving, that I retire, and thank my stars she overcame me." The company laughed at his civility to a slave, and Caesar only applauded the nobleness of his passion and nature, since that slave might be noble, or, what was better, have true notions of honour and virtue in her. Thus passed they this night, after having received, from the slaves, all imaginable respect and obedience.

The next day Trefry asked Caesar to walk, when the heat was allayed, and designedly carried him by the cottage of the fair slave, and told him, she whom he spoke of last night lived there retired. "But," says he, "I would not wish you to approach, for, I am sure, you will be in love as soon as you behold her." Caesar assured him, he was proof against all the charms of that sex, and that if he imagined his heart could be so perfidious to love again, after Imoinda, he believed he should tear it from his bosom. They had no sooner spoke, but a little shock dog,[28] that Clemene had presented her, which she took great delight in, ran out, and she, not knowing anybody was there, ran to get it in again, and bolted out on those who were just speaking of her. When seeing them, she would have run in again, but Trefry caught her by the hand, and cried, "Clemene, however you fly a lover, you ought to pay some respect to this stranger" (pointing to Caesar). But she, as if she had resolved never to raise her eyes to the face of a man again, bent them the more to the earth, when he spoke, and gave the prince the leisure to look the more at her. There needed no long gazing, or consideration, to examine who this fair creature was. He soon saw Imoinda all over her; in a minute he saw her face, her shape, her air, her modesty, and all that called forth his soul with joy at his eyes, and left his body destitute of almost life. It stood without motion, and, for a minute, knew not that it had a being. And, I believe, he had never come to himself, so oppressed he was with overjoy, if he had not met with this allay,[29] that he perceived Imoinda fall dead in the hands of Trefry. This awakened him, and he ran to her aid, and caught her in his arms, where, by degrees, she came to herself; and 'tis needless to tell with what transports, what ecstasies of joy, they both a while beheld each other, without speaking, then snatched each other to their arms, then gaze again, as if they still doubted whether they possessed the blessing they grasped. But when they recovered their speech, 'tis not to be imagined what tender things they expressed to each other, wondering what strange fate had brought them again together. They soon informed each other of their fortunes, and equally bewailed their fate; but, at the same time, they mutually protested, that even fetters and slavery were soft and easy, and would be supported with joy and pleasure, while they could be so happy to possess each other, and to be able to make good their vows. Caesar swore he disdained the empire of the world, while he could behold his Imoinda, and she despised grandeur and pomp, those vanities of her sex, when she could gaze on Oroonoko. He adored the very cottage where she resided, and said, that little inch of the world would give him more happiness than all the universe could do, and she vowed, it was a palace, while adorned with the presence of Oroonoko.

Trefry was infinitely pleased with this novel,[30] and found this Clemene was the fair mistress of whom Caesar had before spoke; and was not a little satisfied, that Heaven was so kind to the prince, as to sweeten his misfortunes by so lucky an accident, and leaving the lovers to themselves, was impatient to come down to Parham-House (which was on the same plantation) to give me an account of what had

---

[28] **shock dog:** A poodle, or dog, with long, shaggy hair.

[29] **allay:** Abatement, diminution.   [30] **novel:** New turn in events.

happened. I was as impatient to make these lovers a visit, having already made a friendship with Caesar, and from his own mouth learned what I have related, which was confirmed by his Frenchman, who was set on shore to seek his fortunes, and of whom they could not make a slave, because a Christian, and he came daily to Parham Hill to see and pay his respects to his pupil prince. So that concerning and interesting myself in all that related to Caesar, whom I had assured of liberty as soon as the governor arrived, I hasted presently to the place where the lovers were, and was infinitely glad to find this beautiful young slave (who had already gained all our esteems, for her modesty and her extraordinary prettiness) to be the same I had heard Caesar speak so much of. One may imagine then, we paid her a treble respect; and though from her being carved in fine flowers and birds all over her body, we took her to be of quality before, yet, when we knew Clemene was Imoinda, we could not enough admire her.

I had forgot to tell you, that those who are nobly born of that country are so delicately cut and raced[31] all over the fore part of the trunk of their bodies, that it looks as if it were japanned;[32] the works being raised like high point[33] round the edges of the flowers. Some are only carved with a little flower, or bird, at the sides of the temples, as was Caesar; and those who are so carved over the body, resemble our ancient Picts, that are figured in the chronicles,[34] but these carvings are more delicate.

From that happy day Caesar took Clemene for his wife, to the general joy of all people, and there was as much magnificence as the country would afford at the celebration of this wedding. And in a very short time after she conceived with child; which made Caesar even adore her, knowing he was the last of his great race. This new accident made him more impatient of liberty, and he was every day treating with Trefry for his and Clemene's liberty; and offered either gold, or a vast quantity of slaves, which should be paid before they let him go, provided he could have any security that he should go when his ransom was paid. They fed him from day to day with promises, and delayed him, till the Lord Governor should come, so that he began to suspect them of falsehood, and that they would delay him till the time of his wife's delivery, and make a slave of that too, for all the breed is theirs to whom the parents belong. This thought made him very uneasy, and his sullenness gave them some jealousies of him, so that I was obliged, by some persons, who feared a mutiny (which is very fatal sometimes in those colonies that abound so with slaves that they exceed the whites in vast numbers),[35] to discourse with Caesar, and to give him all the satisfaction I possibly could. They knew he and Clemene were scarce an hour in a day from my lodgings, that they ate with me, and that I obliged them in all things I was capable of: I entertained him with the lives of the Romans, and great men, which

---

[31] raced: Slashed with something sharp.

[32] japanned: Varnished or lacquered with a hard black gloss.

[33] high point: A type of lace.

[34] Picts . . . chronicles: Ancient people of north Britain who were thought to paint and tattoo themselves.

[35] mutiny . . . numbers: This was a constant fear in the Caribbean and South American colonies.

charmed him to my company, and her, with teaching her all the pretty works that I was mistress of, and telling her stories of nuns, and endeavouring to bring her to the knowledge of the true God. But of all discourses Caesar liked that the worst, and would never be reconciled to our notions of the Trinity, of which he ever made a jest; it was a riddle, he said, would turn his brain to conceive, and one could not make him understand what faith was. However, these conversations failed not altogether so well to divert him, that he liked the company of us women much above the men, for he could not drink, and he is but an ill companion in that country that cannot. So that obliging him to love us very well, we had all the liberty of speech with him, especially myself, whom he called his Great Mistress; and indeed my word would go a great way with him. For these reasons, I had opportunity to take notice to him, that he was not well pleased of late, as he used to be, was more retired and thoughtful, and told him, I took it ill he should suspect we would break our words with him, and not permit both him and Clemene to return to his own kingdom, which was not so long away, but when he was once on his voyage he would quickly arrive there. He made me some answers that showed a doubt in him, which made me ask him, what advantage it would be to doubt? It would but give us a fear of him, and possibly compel us to treat him so as I should be very loth to behold: that is, it might occasion his confinement. Perhaps this was not so luckily spoke of me, for I perceived he resented that word, which I strove to soften again in vain. However, he assured me, that whatsoever resolutions he should take, he would act nothing upon the white people. And as for myself, and those upon that plantation where he was, he would sooner forfeit his eternal liberty, and life itself, than lift his hand against his greatest enemy on that place. He besought me to suffer no fears upon his account, for he could do nothing that honour should not dictate, but he accused himself for having suffered slavery so long; yet he charged that weakness on love alone, who was capable of making him neglect even glory itself, and, for which, now he reproaches himself every moment of the day. Much more to this effect he spoke, with an air impatient enough to make me know he would not be long in bondage, and though he suffered only the name of a slave, and had nothing of the toil and labour of one, yet that was sufficient to render him uneasy, and he had been too long idle, who used to be always in action, and in arms. He had a spirit all rough and fierce, and that could not be tamed to lazy rest, and though all endeavours were used to exercise himself in such actions and sports as this world afforded, as running, wrestling, pitching the bar,[36] hunting and fishing, chasing and killing tigers of a monstrous size, which this continent affords in abundance; and wonderful snakes, such as Alexander is reported to have encountered at the river of Amazons, and which Caesar took great delight to overcome; yet these were not actions great enough for his large soul, which was still panting after more renowned action.

Before I parted that day with him, I got, with much ado, a promise from him to rest yet a little longer with patience, and wait the coming of the Lord Governor, who was every day expected on our shore. He assured me he would, and this promise he

---

[36] **pitching the bar:** Throwing a heavy bar was a form of athletic exercise.

desired me to know was given perfectly in complaisance to me, in whom he had an entire confidence.

After this, I neither thought it convenient to trust him much out of our view, nor did the country who feared him; but with one accord it was advised to treat him fairly, and oblige him to remain within such a compass, and that he should be permitted, as seldom as could be, to go up to the plantations of the Negroes; or, if he did, to be accompanied by some that should be rather in appearance attendants than spies. This care was for some time taken, and Caesar looked upon it as a mark of extraordinary respect, and was glad his discontent had obliged them to be more observant to him. He received new assurance from the overseer, which was confirmed to him by the opinion of all the gentlemen of the country, who made their court to him. During this time that we had his company more frequently than hitherto we had had, it may not be unpleasant to relate to you the diversions we entertained him with, or rather he us.

My stay was to be short in that country, because my father died at sea, and never arrived to possess the honour was designed him (which was lieutenant-general of six and thirty islands, besides the continent of Surinam), nor the advantages he hoped to reap by them, so that though we were obliged to continue on our voyage, we did not intend to stay upon the place. Though, in a word, I must say thus much of it, that certainly had his late Majesty, of sacred memory, but seen and known what a vast and charming world he had been master of in that continent, he would never have parted so easily with it to the Dutch. 'Tis a continent whose vast extent was never yet known, and may contain more noble earth than all the universe besides; for, they say, it reaches from east to west, one way as far as China, and another to Peru. It affords all things both for beauty and use; 'tis there eternal Spring, always the very months of April, May and June. The shades are perpetual, the trees, bearing at once all degrees of leaves and fruit, from blooming buds to ripe Autumn, groves of oranges, lemons, citrons, figs, nutmegs, and noble aromatics, continually bearing their fragrancies. The trees appearing all like nosegays adorned with flowers of different kind; some are all white, some purple, some scarlet, some blue, some yellow; bearing, at the same time, ripe fruit and blooming young, or producing every day new. The very wood of all these trees have an intrinsic value above common timber, for they are, when cut, of different colours, glorious to behold, and bear a price considerable, to inlay withal. Besides this, they yield rich balm, and gums, so that we make our candles of such an aromatic substance, as does not only give a sufficient light, but, as they burn, they cast their perfumes all about. Cedar is the common firing, and all the houses are built with it. The very meat we eat, when set on the table, if it be native, I mean of the country, perfumes the whole room, especially a little beast called an armadillo, a thing which I can liken to nothing so well as a rhinoceros. 'Tis all in white armour so jointed, that it moves as well in it, as if it had nothing on. This beast is about the bigness of a pig of six weeks old. But it were endless to give an account of all the divers wonderful and strange things that country affords, and which we took a very great delight to go in search of, though those adventures are oftentimes fatal and at least dangerous. But while we had Caesar in our company on these designs we feared no harm, nor suffered any.

As soon as I came into the country, the best house in it was presented me, called St. John's Hill.[37] It stood on a vast rock of white marble, at the foot of which the river ran a vast depth down, and not to be descended on that side. The little waves still dashing and washing the foot of this rock, made the softest murmurs and purlings in the world, and the opposite bank was adorned with such vast quantities of different flowers eternally blowing, and every day and hour new, fenced behind them with lofty trees of a thousand rare forms and colours, that the prospect was the most rav[ish]ing that sands can create. On the edge of this white rock, towards the river, was a walk or grove of orange and lemon trees, about half the length of the Mall[38] here, whose flowery and fruity branches meet at the top, and hindered the sun, whose rays are very fierce there, from entering a beam into the grove, and the cool air that came from the river made it not only fit to entertain people in, at all the hottest hours of the day, but refreshed the sweet blossoms, and made it always sweet and charming, and sure the whole globe of the world cannot show so delightful a place as this grove was. Not all the gardens of boasted Italy can produce a shade to out-vie this, which Nature had joined with Art to render so exceeding fine. And 'tis a marvel to see how such vast trees, as big as English oaks, could take footing on so solid a rock, and in so little earth, as covered that rock, but all things by Nature there are rare, delightful and wonderful. But to our sports.

Sometimes we would go surprising, and in search of young tigers in their dens, watching when the old ones went forth to forage for prey, and oftentimes we have been in great danger, and have fled apace for our lives, when surprised by the dams. But once, above all other times, we went on this design, and Caesar was with us, who had no sooner stolen a young tiger from her nest, but going off, we encountered the dam, bearing a buttock of a cow, which he had torn off with his mighty paw, and going with it towards his den. We had only four women, Caesar, and an English gentleman, brother to Harry Martin, the great Oliverian.[39] We found there was no escaping this enraged and ravenous beast. However, we women fled as fast as we could from it, but our heels had not saved our lives, if Caesar had not laid down his cub, when he found the tiger quit her prey to make the more speed towards him, and taking Mr. Martin's sword desired him to stand aside, or follow the ladies. He obeyed him, and Caesar met this monstrous beast of might, size, and vast limbs, who came with open jaws upon him, and fixing his awful stern eyes full upon those of the beast, and putting himself into a very steady and good aiming posture of defence, ran his sword quite through his breast down to his very heart, home to the hilt of the sword. The dying beast stretched forth her paw, and going to grasp his thigh, surprised with death in that very moment, did him no other harm than fixing her long nails in his flesh very deep, feebly wounded him, but could not grasp the flesh to tear off any. When he had done this, he hollowed to us to return, which, after some

---

[37] **St. John's Hill:** A plantation belonging to Sir Robert Harley, probably sold to Willoughby in 1664.

[38] **Mall:** Presumably a reference to the walk in St. James's Park, London, where originally the game of pall-mall was played.

[39] **English . . . Oliverian:** George Marten, owner of Surinam plantations, was, according to Behn, the brother of Henry Marten, one of the regicides and supporters of Oliver Cromwell.

assurance of his victory, we did, and found him lugging out the sword from the bosom of the tiger, who was laid in her blood on the ground. He took up the cub, and with an unconcern, that had nothing of the joy or gladness of a victory, he came and laid the whelp at my feet. We all extremely wondered at his daring, and at the bigness of the beast, which was about the height of an heifer, but of mighty, great, and strong limbs.

Another time, being in the woods, he killed a tiger, which had long infested that part, and borne away abundance of sheep and oxen, and other things, that were for the support of those to whom they belonged. Abundance of people assailed this beast, some affirming they had shot her with several bullets quite through the body, at several times, and some swearing they shot her through the very heart, and they believed she was a devil rather than a mortal thing. Caesar had often said, he had a mind to encounter this monster, and spoke with several gentlemen who had attempted her, one crying, I shot her with so many poisoned arrows, another with his gun in this part of her, and another in that. So that he remarking all these places where she was shot, fancied still he should overcome her, by giving her another sort of a wound than any had yet done, and one day said (at the table) "What trophies and garlands Ladies will you make me, if I bring you home the heart of this ravenous beast, that eats up all your lambs and pigs?" We all promised he should be rewarded at all our hands. So taking a bow, which he chose out of a great many, he went up in the wood, with two gentlemen, where he imagined this devourer to be. They had not passed very far in it, but they heard her voice, growling and grumbling, as if she were pleased with something she was doing. When they came in view, they found her muzzling in the belly of a new ravished sheep, which she had torn open, and seeing herself approached, she took fast hold of her prey, with her fore paws, and set a very fierce raging look on Caesar, without offering to approach him, for fear, at the same time, of losing what she had in possession. So that Caesar remained a good while, only taking aim, and getting an opportunity to shoot her where he designed. 'Twas some time before he could accomplish it, and to wound her, and not kill her, would but have enraged her more, and endangered him. He had a quiver of arrows at his side, so that if one failed he could be supplied. At last, retiring a little, he gave her opportunity to eat, for he found she was ravenous, and fell to as soon as she saw him retire, being more eager of her prey than of doing new mischiefs. When he going softly to one side of her, and hiding his person behind certain herbage that grew high and thick, he took so good aim, that, as he intended, he shot her just into the eye, and the arrow was sent with so good a will, and so sure a hand, that it stuck in her brain, and made her caper, and become mad for a moment or two, but being seconded by another arrow, he fell dead upon the prey. Caesar cut him open with a knife, to see where those wounds were that had been reported to him, and why he did not die of them. But I shall now relate a thing that possibly will find no credit among men, because 'tis a notion commonly received with us, that nothing can receive a wound in the heart and live; but when the heart of this courageous animal was taken out, there were seven bullets of lead in it, and the wounds seamed up with great scars, and she lived with the bullets a great while, for it was long since they were shot. This heart the conqueror brought up to us, and 'twas a very great curiosity, which all the country came to see; and which gave Caesar occasion of many fine discourses, of accidents in war, and strange escapes.

At other times he would go a-fishing, and discoursing on that diversion, he found we had in that country a very strange fish, called, a numb eel[40] (an eel of which I have eaten) that while it is alive, it has a quality so cold, that those who are angling, though with a line of never so great a length, with a rod at the end of it, it shall, in the same minute the bait is touched by this eel, seize him or her that holds the rod with benumbedness, that shall deprive them of sense, for a while. And some have fallen into the water, and others dropped as dead on the banks of the rivers where they stood, as soon as this fish touches the bait. Caesar used to laugh at this, and believed it impossible a man could lose his force at the touch of a fish; and could not understand that philosophy, that a cold quality should be of that nature. However, he had a great curiosity to try whether it would have the same effect on him it had on others, and often tried, but in vain. At last, the sought for fish came to the bait, as he stood angling on the bank; and instead of throwing away the rod, or giving it a sudden twitch out of the water, whereby he might have caught both the eel, and have dismissed the rod, before it could have too much power over him for experiment sake, he grasped it but the harder, and fainting fell into the river. And being still possessed of the rod, the tide carried him senseless as he was a great way, till an Indian boat took him up, and perceived, when they touched him, a numbness seize them, and by that knew the rod was in his hand, which, with a paddle (that is, a short oar) they struck away, and snatched it into the boat, eel and all. If Caesar were almost dead, with the effect of this fish, he was more so with that of the water, where he had remained the space of going a league, and they found they had much ado to bring him back to life. But, at last, they did, and brought him home, where he was in a few hours well recovered and refreshed; and not a little ashamed to find he should be overcome by an eel, and that all the people, who heard his defiance, would laugh at him. But we cheered him up, and he, being convinced, we had the eel at supper; which was a quarter of an ell about, and most delicate meat; and was of the more value, since it cost so dear as almost the life of so gallant a man.

About this time we were in many mortal fears, about some disputes the English had with the Indians, so that we could scarce trust ourselves, without great numbers, to go to any Indian towns, or place, where they abode, for fear they should fall upon us, as they did immediately after my coming away, and that it was in the possession of the Dutch, who used them not so civilly as the English, so that they cut in pieces all they could take, getting into houses, and hanging up the mother, and all her children about her, and cut a footman, I left behind me, all in joints, and nailed him to trees.

This feud began while I was there, so that I lost half the satisfaction I proposed, in not seeing and visiting the Indian towns. But one day, bemoaning of our misfortunes upon this account, Caesar told us, we need not fear, for if we had a mind to go, he would undertake to be our guard. Some would, but most would not venture. About eighteen of us resolved, and took barge, and, after eight days, arrived near an

---

[40] **numb eel:** Electric eel.

Indian town. But approaching it, the hearts of some of our company failed, and they would not venture on shore, so we polled who would, and who would not. For my part, I said, if Caesar would, I would go. He resolved, so did my brother, and my woman, a maid of good courage. Now none of us speaking the language of the people, and imagining we should have a half diversion in gazing only and not knowing what they said, we took a fisherman that lived at the mouth of the river, who had been a long inhabitant there, and obliged him to go with us. But because he was known to the Indians, as trading among them, and being, by long living there, become a perfect Indian in colour, we, who resolved to surprise them, by making them see something they never had seen (that is, white people) resolved only myself, my brother, and woman should go. So Caesar, the fisherman, and the rest, hiding behind some thick reeds and flowers, that grew on the banks, let us pass on towards the town, which was on the bank of the river all along. A little distant from the houses, or huts, we saw some dancing, others busied in fetching and carrying of water from the river. They had no sooner spied us, but they set up a loud cry, that frighted us at first. We thought it had been for those that should kill us, but it seems it was of wonder and amazement. They were all naked, and we were dressed, so as is most commode for the hot countries, very glittering and rich, so that we appeared extremely fine. My own hair was cut short, and I had a taffeta cap, with black feathers, on my head. My brother was in a stuff suit, with silver loops and buttons, and abundance of green ribbon. This was all infinitely surprising to them, and because we saw them stand still, till we approached them, we took heart and advanced, came up to them, and offered them our hands, which they took, and looked on us round about, calling still for more company; who came swarming out, all wondering, and crying out *tepeeme*,[41] taking their hair up in their hands, and spreading it wide to those they called out to, as if they would say (as indeed it signified) "numberless wonders," or not to be recounted, no more than to number the hair of their heads. By degrees they grew more bold, and from gazing upon us round, they touched us, laying their hands upon all the features of our faces, feeling our breasts and arms, taking up one petticoat, then wondering to see another, admiring our shoes and stockings, but more our garters, which we gave them, and they tied about their legs, being laced with silver lace at the ends, for they much esteem any shining things. In fine, we suffered them to survey us as they pleased, and we thought they would never have done admiring us. When Caesar, and the rest, saw we were received with such wonder, they came up to us, and finding the Indian trader whom they knew (for 'tis by these fishermen, called Indian traders, we hold a commerce with them; for they love not to go far from home, and we never go to them), when they saw him therefore they set up a new joy, and cried, in their language, "Oh! here's our *tiguamy*, and we shall now know whether those things can speak." So advancing to him, some of them gave him their hands, and cried, "*Amora tiguamy*,"[42] which is as much as, "How do you," or "Welcome friend," and all, with one din, began to gabble to him, and

---

[41] *tepeeme:* Biet claimed the Indians said *tapouimé* for "a great number."

[42] *"Amora tiguamy":* Behn is reporting a greeting.

asked, If we had sense, and wit? If we could talk of affairs of life, and war, as they could do? If we could hunt, swim, and do a thousand things they use? He answered them, we could. Then they invited us into their houses, and dressed venison and buffalo for us; and, going out, gathered a leaf of a tree, called a sarumbo leaf, of six yards long, and spread it on the ground for a table-cloth, and cutting another in pieces instead of plates, setting us on little bow Indian stools, which they cut out of one entire piece of wood, and paint, in a sort of japan work. They serve everyone their mess on these pieces of leaves, and it was very good, but too high seasoned with pepper. When we had eaten, my brother and I took out our flutes, and played to them, which gave them new wonder, and I soon perceived, by an admiration that is natural to these people, and by the extreme ignorance and simplicity of them, it were not difficult to establish any unknown or extravagant religion among them, and to impose any notions or fictions upon them. For seeing a kinsman of mine set some paper a-fire, with a burning-glass, a trick they had never before seen, they were like to have adored him for a god, and begged he would give them the characters or figures of his name, that they might oppose it against winds and storms, which he did, and they held it up in those seasons, and fancied it had a charm to conquer them, and kept it like a holy relic. They are very superstitious, and called him the great *peeie*, that is, prophet. They showed us their Indian *peeie*, a youth of about sixteen years old, as handsome as Nature could make a man. They consecrate a beautiful youth from his infancy, and all arts are used to complete him in the finest manner, both in beauty and shape. He is bred to all the little arts and cunning they are capable of, to all the legerdemain tricks, and sleight of hand, whereby he imposes upon the rabble, and is both a doctor in physic and divinity. And by these tricks makes the sick believe he sometimes eases their pains, by drawing from the afflicted part little serpents, or odd flies, or worms, or any strange thing; and though they have besides undoubted good remedies, for almost all their diseases, they cure the patient more by fancy than by medicines, and make themselves feared, loved, and reverenced. This young *peeie* had a very young wife, who seeing my brother kiss her, came running and kissed me; after this, they kissed one another, and made it a very great jest, it being so novel, and new admiration and laughing went round the multitude, that they never will forget that ceremony, never before used or known. Caesar had a mind to see and talk with their war captains, and we were conducted to one of their houses, where we beheld several of the great captains, who had been at council. But so frightful a vision it was to see them no fancy can create; no such dreams can represent so dreadful a spectacle. For my part I took them for hobgoblins, or fiends, rather than men. But however their shapes appeared, their souls were very humane and noble, but some wanted their noses, some their lips, some both noses and lips, some their ears, and others cut through each cheek, with long slashes, through which their teeth appeared; they had several other formidable wounds and scars, or rather dismemberings. They had *comitias,* or little aprons before them, and girdles of cotton, with their knives naked, stuck in it, a bow at their backs, and a quiver of arrows on their thighs, and most had feathers on their heads of diverse colours. They cried *"Amora tigame"* to us at our entrance, and were pleased we said as much to them. They feted us, and gave us drink of the best sort, and wondered, as much as the others had done before, to see us. Caesar was marvelling as much at their faces, wondering how they should all be so wounded in war; he was impatient to know how they all came by those frightful marks of rage or malice, rather than wounds got in noble battle. They told us, by our interpreter, that when any war was waging, two men chosen out by some old captain, whose fighting was past, and who could only teach the theory of war, these two men were to stand in competition for the general-ship, or Great War Captain, and being brought before the old judges, now past labour, they are asked, what they dare do to show they are worthy to lead an army? When he, who is first asked, making no reply, cuts off his nose, and throws it contemptibly on the ground, and the other does something to himself that he thinks surpasses him, and perhaps deprives himself of lips and an eye. So they slash on till one gives out, and many have died in this debate. And 'tis by a passive valour they show and prove their activity, a sort of courage too brutal to be applauded by our black hero; nevertheless he expressed his esteem of them.

In this voyage Caesar begot so good an understanding between the Indians and the English, that there were no more fears, or heartburnings during our stay, but we had a perfect, open, and free trade with them. Many things remarkable, and worthy reciting, we met with in this short voyage, because Caesar made it his business to search out and provide for our entertainment, especially to please his dearly adored Imoinda, who was a sharer in all our adventures; we being resolved to make her chains as easy as we could, and to compliment the prince in that manner that most obliged him.

As we were coming up again, we met with some Indians of strange aspects, that is, of a larger size, and other sort of features, than those of our country. Our Indian slaves, that rowed us, asked them some questions, but they could not understand us, but showed us a long cotton string, with several knots on it, and told us, they had been coming from the mountains so many moons as there were knots. They were habited in skins of a strange beast, and brought along with them bags of gold dust, which, as well as they could give us to understand, came streaming in little small channels down the high mountains, when the rains fell, and offered to be the convoy to anybody, or persons, that would go to the mountains. We carried these men up to Parham, where they were kept till the Lord Governor came. And because all the country was mad to be going on this golden adventure, the governor, by his letters, commanded (for they sent some of the gold to him) that a guard should be set at the mouth of the river of Amazons (a river so called, almost as broad as the river of Thames), and prohibited all people from going up that river, it conducting to those mountains of gold. But we going off for England before the project was further prosecuted, and the governor being drowned in a hurricane, either the design died, or the Dutch have the advantage of it. And 'tis to be bemoaned what His Majesty lost by losing that part of America.[43]

Though this digression is a little from my story, however since it contains some proofs of the curiosity and daring of this great man, I was content to omit nothing of his character.

---

[43] **. . . America:** There had been stories of a "golden city" on the Amazon since the previous century.

It was thus, for some time we diverted him. But now Imoinda began to show she was with child, and did nothing but sigh and weep for the captivity of her lord, herself, and the infant yet unborn, and believed, if it were so hard to gain the liberty of two, 'twould be more difficult to get that for three. Her griefs were so many darts in the great heart of Caesar, and taking his opportunity one Sunday, when all the whites were overtaken in drink, as there were abundance of several trades, and slaves for four years, that inhabited among the Negro houses, and Sunday was their day of debauch (otherwise they were a sort of spies upon Caesar), he went pretending out of goodness to them, to feast amongst them, and sent all his music, and ordered a great treat for the whole gang, about three hundred Negroes. And about a hundred and fifty were able to bear arms, such as they had, which were sufficient to do execution with spirits accordingly. For the English had none but rusty swords, that no strength could draw from a scabbard, except the people of particular quality, who took care to oil them and keep them in good order. The guns also, unless here and there one, or those newly carried from England, would do no good or harm, for 'tis the nature of that county to rust and eat up iron, or any metals, but gold and silver. And they are very inexpert at the bow, which the Negroes and Indians are perfect masters of.

Caesar, having singled out these men from the women and children, made a harangue to them of the miseries, and ignominies of slavery; counting up all their toils and sufferings, under such loads, burdens, and drudgeries, as were fitter for beasts than men; senseless brutes, than human souls. He told them it was not for days, months, or years, but for eternity; there was no end to be of their misfortunes. They suffered not like men who might find a glory, and fortitude in oppression, but like dogs that loved the whip and bell,[44] and fawned the more they were beaten. That they had lost the divine quality of men, and were become insensible asses, fit only to bear. Nay worse, an ass, or dog, or horse having done his duty, could lie down in retreat, and rise to work again, and while he did his duty endured no stripes, but men, villainous, senseless men, such as they, toiled on all the tedious week till black Friday, and then, whether they worked or not, whether they were faulty or meriting, they promiscuously, the innocent with the guilty, suffered the infamous whip, the sordid stripes, from their fellow slaves till their blood trickled from all parts of their body, blood whose every drop ought to be revenged with a life of some of those tyrants that impose it. "And why," said he, "my dear friends and fellow sufferers, should we be slaves to an unknown people? Have they vanquished us nobly in fight? Have they won us in honourable battle? And are we, by the chance of war, become their slaves? This would not anger a noble heart, this would not animate a soldier's soul. No, but we are bought and sold like apes, or monkeys, to be the sport of women, fools and cowards, and the support of rogues, runagades,[45] that have abandoned their own countries, for raping, murders, thefts and villainies. Do you not hear every day how they upbraid each other with infamy of life, below the wildest

---

[44] **whip and bell:** "Something that detracts from one's comfort or pleasure" (*O.E.D.*).

[45] **runagades:** Renegades; apostates and deserters.

salvages,[46] and shall we render obedience to such a degenerate race, who have no one human virtue left, to distinguish them from the vilest creatures? Will you, I say, suffer the lash from such hands?" They all replied, with one accord, "No, no, no; Caesar has spoke like a great captain, like a great king."

After this he would have proceeded, but was interrupted by a tall Negro of some more quality than the rest. His name was Tuscan, who bowing at the feet of Caesar, cried, "My lord, we have listened with joy and attention to what you have said, and, were we only men, would follow so great a leader through the world. But oh! consider, we are husbands and parents too, and have things more dear to us than life: our wives and children unfit for travel, in these impassable woods, mountains and bogs. We have not only difficult lands to overcome, but rivers to wade, and monsters to encounter, ravenous beasts of prey—" To this, Caesar replied, that honour was the first principle in Nature that was to be obeyed; but as no man would pretend to that, without all the acts of virtue, compassion, charity, love, justice and reason, he found it not inconsistent with that, to take an equal care of their wives and children, as they would of themselves, and that he did not design, when he led them to freedom, and glorious liberty, that they should leave that better part of themselves to perish by the hand of the tyrant's whip. But if there were a woman among them so degenerate from love and virtue to choose slavery before the pursuit of her husband, and with the hazard of her life, to share with him in his fortunes, that such an one ought to be abandoned, and left as a prey to the common enemy.

To which they all agreed—and bowed. After this, he spoke of the impassable woods and rivers, and convinced them, the more danger, the more glory. He told them that he had heard of one Hannibal a great captain, had cut his way through mountains of solid rocks,[47] and should a few shrubs oppose them, which they could fire before them? No, 'twas a trifling excuse to men resolved to die, or overcome. As for bogs, they are with a little labour filled and hardened, and the rivers could be no obstacle, since they swam by nature, at least by custom, from their first hour of their birth. That when the children were weary they must carry them by turns, and the woods and their own industry would afford them food. To this they all assented with joy.

Tuscan then demanded, what he would do? He said, they would travel towards the sea; plant a new colony, and defend it by their valour; and when they could find a ship, either driven by stress of weather, or guided by providence that way, they would seize it, and make it a prize, till it had transported them to their own countries. At least, they should be made free in his kingdom, and be esteemed as his fellow sufferers, and men that had the courage, and the bravery to attempt, at least, for liberty. And if they died in the attempt it would be more brave, than to live in perpetual slavery.

---

[46] **salvages:** Savages.

[47] **cut . . . rocks:** When crossing the Alps, "in certaine places of the highest rockes, [Hannibal] was driven to make passage through, by force of fire and vinegar" (Plutarch, *The Lives of the Noble Grecians and Romanes*, North's translation, 1579 edition).

They bowed and kissed his feet at this resolution, and with one accord vowed to follow him to death. And that night was appointed to begin their march; they made it known to their wives, and directed them to tie their hamaca[48] about their shoulder, and under their arm like a scarf; and to lead their children that could go, and carry those that could not. The wives who pay an entire obedience to their husbands obeyed, and stayed for them, where they were appointed. The men stayed but to furnish themselves with what defensive arms they could get, and all met at the rendezvous, where Caesar made a new encouraging speech to them, and led them out.

But, as they could not march far that night, on Monday early, when the overseers went to call them all together, to go to work, they were extremely surprised to find not one upon the place, but all fled with what baggage they had. You may imagine this news was not only suddenly spread all over the plantation, but soon reached the neighbouring ones, and we had by noon about six hundred men, they call the militia of the county, that came to assist us in the pursuit of the fugitives. But never did one see so comical an army march forth to war. The men, of any fashion, would not concern themselves, though it were almost the common cause, for such revoltings are very ill examples, and have very fatal consequences oftentimes in many colonies. But they had a respect for Caesar, and all hands were against the Parhamites, as they called those of Parham Plantation,[49] because they did not, in the first place, love the Lord Governor, and secondly, they would have it, that Caesar was ill used, and baffled with.[50] And 'tis not impossible but some of the best in the country was of his counsel in this flight, and depriving us of all the slaves, so that they of the better sort would not meddle in the matter. The deputy governor, of whom I have had no great occasion to speak, and who was the most fawning fair-tongued fellow in the world, and one that pretended the most friendship to Caesar, was now the only violent man against him, and though he had nothing, and so need fear nothing, yet talked and looked bigger than any man. He was a fellow, whose character is not fit to be mentioned with the worst of the slaves. This fellow would lead his army forth to meet Caesar, or rather to pursue him. Most of their arms were of those sort of cruel whips they call cat with nine tails;[51] some had rusty useless guns for show; others old basket-hilts, whose blades had never seen the light in this age, and others had long staffs, and clubs. Mr. Trefry went along, rather to be a mediator than a conqueror, in such a battle; for he foresaw, and knew, if by fighting they put the Negroes into despair, they were a sort of sullen fellows, that would drown, or kill themselves, before they would yield, and he advised that fair means was best. But Byam[52] was one that abounded in his own wit, and would take his own measures.

It was not hard to find these fugitives, for as they fled they were forced to fire and cut the woods before them, so that night or day they pursued them by the light they

---

[48] **hamaca:** Hammock, from the Carib word through Spanish *hamaca.*

[49] **Parhamites . . . Plantation:** Supporters of Lord Willoughby in the faction-ridden colony.

[50] **baffled with:** Deceived and abused.

[51] **cat with nine tails:** Whip with nine knotted lashes used in the British navy and army.

[52] **Byam:** William Byam was the royalist governor of Surinam from c. 1654 and then deputy governor under Willoughby. In 1663 he became lieutenant-general, a position the narrator claims her father should have held.

made, and by the path they had cleared. But as soon as Caesar found he was pursued, he put himself in a posture of defence, placing all the women and children in the rear, and himself, with Tuscan by his side, or next to him, all promising to die or conquer. Encouraged thus, they never stood to parley, but fell on pell-mell upon the English, and killed some, and wounded a good many, they having recourse to their whips, as the best of their weapons. And as they observed no order, they perplexed the enemy so sorely, with lashing them in the eyes. And the women and children, seeing their husbands so treated, being of fearful cowardly dispositions, and hearing the English cry out, "Yield and live, yield and be pardoned," they all ran in amongst their husbands and fathers, and hung about them, crying out, "Yield, yield, and leave Caesar to their revenge," that by degrees the slaves abandoned Caesar, and left him only Tuscan and his heroic Imoinda, who, grown big as she was, did nevertheless press near her lord, having a bow, and a quiver full of poisoned arrows, which she managed with such dexterity, that she wounded several, and shot the governor into the shoulder, of which wound he had like to have died, but that an Indian woman, his mistress, sucked the wound, and cleansed it from the venom. But however, he stirred not from the place till he had parlied with Caesar, who he found was resolved to die fighting, and would not be taken; no more would Tuscan, or Imoinda. But he, more thirsting after revenge of another sort, than that of depriving him of life, now made use of all his art of talking, and dissembling, and besought Caesar to yield himself upon terms, which he himself should propose, and should be sacredly assented to and kept by him. He told him, it was not that he any longer feared him, or could believe the force of two men, and a young heroine, could overcome all them, with all the slaves now on their side also, but it was the vast esteem he had for his person, the desire he had to serve so gallant a man, and to hinder himself from the reproach hereafter, of having been the occasion of the death of a prince, whose valour and magnanimity deserved the empire of the world. He protested to him, he looked upon this action, as gallant and brave, however tending to the prejudice of his lord and master, who would by it have lost so considerable a number of slaves, that this flight of his should be looked on as a heat of youth, and rashness of a too forward courage, and an unconsidered impatience of liberty, and no more; and that he laboured in vain to accomplish that which they would effectually perform, as soon as any ship arrived that would touch on his coast. "So that if you will be pleased," continued he, "to surrender yourself, all imaginable respect shall be paid you; and yourself, your wife, and child, if it be here born, shall depart free out of our land." But Caesar would hear of no composition, though Byam urged, if he pursued, and went on in his design, he would inevitably perish, either by great snakes, wild beasts, or hunger, and he ought to have regard to his wife, whose condition required ease, and not the fatigues of tedious travel, where she could not be secured from being devoured. But Caesar told him, there was no faith in the white men, or the gods they adored, who instructed them in principles so false, that honest men could not live amongst them; though no people professed so much, none performed so little; that he knew what he had to do, when he dealt with men of honour, but with them a man ought to be eternally on his guard, and never to eat and drink with Christians without his weapon of defence in his hand, and, for his own security, never to credit one word they spoke. As for the rashness and inconsiderateness of his action he would confess the governor is in the right, and that he was ashamed of what he had done, in endeavouring to make those free, who were by nature slaves, poor wretched rogues, fit to be used as Christians' tools; dogs, treacherous and cowardly, fit for such masters, and they wanted only but to be whipped into the knowledge of the Christian gods to be the vilest of all creeping things, to learn to worship such deities as had not power to make them just, brave, or honest. In fine, after a thousand things of this nature, not fit here to be recited, he told Byam, he had rather die than live upon the same earth with such dogs. But Trefry and Byam pleaded and protested together so much, that Trefry believing the governor to mean what he said, and speaking very cordially himself, generously put himself into Caesar's hands, and took him aside, and persuaded him, even with tears, to live, by surrendering himself, and to name his conditions. Caesar was overcome by his wit and reasons, and in consideration of Imoinda, and demanding what he desired, and that it should be ratified by their hands in writing, because he had perceived that was the common way of contract between man and man, amongst the whites. All this was performed, and Tuscan's pardon was put in, and they surrender to the governor, who walked peaceably down into the plantation with them, after giving order to bury their dead. Caesar was very much toiled with the bustle of the day, for he had fought like a Fury, and what mischief was done he and Tuscan performed alone, and gave their enemies a fatal proof that they durst do anything, and feared no mortal force.

But they were no sooner arrived at the place, where all the slaves receive their punishments of whipping, but they laid hands on Caesar and Tuscan, faint with heat and toil; and, surprising them, bound them to two several stakes, and whipped them in a most deplorable and inhumane manner, rending the very flesh from their bones; especially Caesar, who was not perceived to make any moan, or to alter his face, only to roll his eyes on the faithless governor, and those he believed guilty, with fierceness and indignation. And, to complete his rage, he saw every one of those slaves, who, but a few days before, adored him as something more than mortal, now had a whip to give him some lashes, while he strove not to break his fetters, though, if he had, it were impossible. But he pronounced a woe and revenge from his eyes, that darted fire, that 'twas at once both awful and terrible to behold.[53]

When they thought they were sufficiently revenged on him, they untied him, almost fainting, with loss of blood, from a thousand wounds all over his body, from which they had rent his clothes, and led him bleeding and naked as he was, and loaded him all over with irons, and then rubbed his wounds, to complete their cruelty, with Indian pepper, which had like to have made him raving mad, and, in this condition, made him so fast to the ground that he could not stir, if his pains and wounds would have given him leave. They spared Imoinda, and did not let her see this barbarity committed towards her lord, but carried her down to Parham, and shut her up, which was not in kindness to her, but for fear she should die with the sight, or miscarry, and then they should lose a young slave, and perhaps the mother.

---

[53] . . . **terrible to behold:** Behn was contemptuous of turncoats, especially when they were disloyal to her respected James II, from whom support was slipping away during 1688.

You must know, that when the news was brought on Monday morning, that Caesar had betaken himself to the woods, and carried with him all the Negroes, we were possessed with extreme fear, which no persuasions could dissipate, that he would secure himself till night, and then, that he would come down and cut all our throats. This apprehension made all the females of us fly down the river, to be secured, and while we were away, they acted this cruelty. For I suppose I had authority and interest enough there, had I suspected any such thing, to have prevented it, but we had not gone many leagues, but the news overtook us that Caesar was taken, and whipped like a common slave. We met on the river with Colonel Martin, a man of great gallantry, wit, and goodness, and, whom I have celebrated in a character of my new comedy, by his own name, in memory of so brave a man.[54] He was wise and eloquent, and, from the fineness of his parts, bore a great sway over the hearts of all the colony. He was a friend to Caesar, and resented this false dealing with him very much. We carried him back to Parham, thinking to have made an accommodation; when we came, the first news we heard was, that the governor was dead of a wound Imoinda had given him, but it was not so well. But it seems he would have the pleasure of beholding the revenge he took on Caesar, and before the cruel ceremony was finished, he dropped down, and then they perceived the wound he had on his shoulder was by a venomed arrow, which, as I said, his Indian mistress healed, by sucking the wound.

We were no sooner arrived, but we went up to the plantation to see Caesar, whom we found in a very miserable and inexpressible condition, and I have a thousand times admired how he lived, in so much tormenting pain. We said all things to him, that trouble, pity, and good nature could suggest, protesting our innocence of the fact, and our abhorrence of such cruelties; making a thousand professions of services to him, and begging as many pardons for the offenders, till we said so much, that he believed we had no hand in his ill treatment, but told us, he could never pardon Byam. As for Trefry, he confessed he saw his grief and sorrow, for his suffering, which he could not hinder, but was like to have been beaten down by the very slaves, for speaking in his defence. But for Byam, who was their leader, their head—and should, by his justice, and honour, have been an example to them—for him, he wished to live, to take a dire revenge of him, and said, "It had been well for him, if he had sacrificed me, instead of giving me the contemptible whip." He refused to talk much, but begging us to give him our hands, he took them, and protested never to lift up his, to do us any harm. He had a great respect for Colonel Martin, and always took his counsel, like that of a parent, and assured him, he would obey him in anything, but his revenge on Byam. "Therefore," said he, "for his own safety, let him speedily dispatch me, for if I could dispatch myself, I would not, till that justice were done to my injured person, and the contempt of a soldier. No, I would not kill myself, even after a whipping, but will be content to live with that infamy, and be pointed at by every grinning slave, till I have completed my revenge; and then you shall see that Oroonoko scorns to live with the indignity that was put on Caesar." All

---

[54] **. . . so brave a man:** *The Younger Brother: or the Amorous Jilt* (1696). The Memoir of 1696 claims that Behn based the play on a true story supplied by George Marten.

we could do could get no more words from him, and we took care to have him put immediately into a healing bath, to rid him of his pepper, and ordered a chirurgeon[55] to anoint him with healing balm, which he suffered, and in some time he began to be able to walk and eat. We failed not to visit him every day, and, to that end, had him brought to an apartment at Parham.

The governor was no sooner recovered, and had heard of the menaces of Caesar, but he called his council, who (not to disgrace them, or burlesque the government there) consisted of such notorious villains as Newgate[56] never transported, and possibly originally were such, who understood neither the laws of God or man, and had no sort of principles to make them worthy the name of men. But, at the very council table, would contradict and fight with one another, and swear so bloodily that 'twas terrible to hear, and see them. (Some of them were afterwards hanged, when the Dutch took possession of the place; others sent off in chains.) But calling these special rulers of the nation together, and requiring their counsel in this weighty affair, they all concluded, that (damn them) it might be their own cases, and that Caesar ought to be made an example to all the Negroes, to fright them from daring to threaten their betters, their lords and masters, and, at this rate, no man was safe from his own slaves, and concluded, *nemine contradicente,*[57] that Caesar should be hanged.

Trefry then thought it time to use his authority, and told Byam his command did not extend to his lord's plantation, and that Parham was as much exempt from the law as Whitehall; and that they ought no more to touch the servants of the lord — (who there represented the king's person) than they could those about the king himself; and that Parham was a sanctuary, and though his lord were absent in person, his power was still in being there, which he had entrusted with him, as far as the dominions of his particular plantations reached, and all that belonged to it; the rest of the country, as Byam was lieutenant to his lord, he might exercise his tyranny upon. Trefry had others as powerful, or more, that interested themselves in Caesar's life, and absolutely said, he should be defended. So turning the governor, and his wise council, out of doors (for they sat at Parham-House) we set a guard upon our landing place, and would admit none but those we called friends to us and Caesar.

The governor having remained wounded at Parham, till his recovery was completed, Caesar did not know but he was still there, and indeed, for the most part, his time was spent there, for he was one that loved to live at other people's expense, and if he were a day absent, he was ten present there, and used to play, and walk, and hunt, and fish, with Caesar. So that Caesar did not at all doubt, if he once recovered strength, but he should find an opportunity of being revenged on him. Though, after such a revenge, he could not hope to live, for if he escaped the fury of the English mobile,[58] who perhaps would have been glad of the occasion to have killed him, he was resolved not to survive his whipping, yet he had, some tender hours, a

---

[55] **chirurgeon:** Surgeon.

[56] **Newgate:** A London prison from which many convicts were exported to work on New World plantations. For example, in 1681 Christopher Jeaffreson bought 300 convicts from the chief gaoler of Newgate to use on his plantation in Jamaica.

[57] *nemine contradicente:* Unanimously.   [58] **mobile:** Mob, rabble.

repenting softness, which he called his fits of coward, wherein he struggled with love for the victory of his heart, which took part with his charming Imoinda there, but, for the most part, his time was passed in melancholy thought, and black designs. He considered, if he should do this deed, and die either in the attempt, or after it, he left his lovely Imoinda a prey, or at best a slave, to the enraged multitude; his great heart could not endure that thought. "Perhaps," said he, "she may be first ravished by every brute, exposed first to their nasty lusts, and then a shameful death." No, he could not live a moment under that apprehension, too insupportable to be borne. These were his thoughts, and his silent arguments with his heart, as he told us afterwards, so that now resolving not only to kill Byam, but all those he thought had enraged him, pleasing his great heart with the fancied slaughter he should make over the whole face of the plantation. He first resolved on a deed, that (however horrid it at first appeared to us all) when we had heard his reasons, we thought it brave and just. Being able to walk, and, as he believed, fit for the execution of his great design, he begged Trefry to trust him into the air, believing a walk would do him good, which was granted him, and taking Imoinda with him, as he used to do in his more happy and calmer days, he led her up into a wood, where, after (with a thousand sighs, and long gazing silently on her face, while tears gushed, in spite of him, from his eyes), he told her his design first of killing her, and then his enemies, and next himself, and the impossibility of escaping, and therefore he told her the necessity of dying. He found the heroic wife faster pleading for death than he was to propose it, when she found his fixed resolution, and, on her knees, besought him, not to leave her a prey to his enemies. He (grieved to death) yet pleased at her noble resolution, took her up, and embracing her, with all the passion and languishment of a dying lover, drew his knife to kill this treasure of his soul, this pleasure of his eyes. While tears trickled down his cheeks, hers were smiling with joy she should die by so noble a hand, and be sent in her own country (for that's their notion of the next world) by him she so tenderly loved, and so truly adored in this, for wives have a respect for their husbands equal to what any other people pay a deity, and when a man finds any occasion to quit his wife, if he love her, she dies by his hand, if not, he sells her, or suffers some other to kill her. It being thus, you may believe the deed was soon resolved on, and 'tis not to be doubted, but the parting, the eternal leave-taking of two such lovers, so greatly born, so sensible, so beautiful, so young, and so fond, must be very moving, as the relation of it was to me afterwards.

All that love could say in such cases, being ended, and all the intermitting irresolutions being adjusted, the lovely, young, and adored victim lays herself down, before the sacrificer, while he, with a hand resolved, and a heart breaking within, gave the fatal stroke, first, cutting her throat, and then severing her, yet smiling, face from that delicate body, pregnant as it was with fruits of tenderest love. As soon as he had done, he laid the body decently on leaves and flowers, of which he made a bed, and concealed it under the same coverlid of Nature, only her face he left yet bare to look on. But when he found she was dead, and past all retrieve, never more to bless him with her eyes, and soft language, his grief swelled up to rage; he tore, he raved, he roared, like some monster of the wood, calling on the loved name of Imoinda. A thousand times he turned the fatal knife that did the deed, toward his own heart, with a resolution to go immediately after her, but dire revenge, which now was a thousand times more fierce in his soul than before, prevents him, and he would cry out, "No, since I have sacrificed Imoinda to my revenge, shall I lose that glory which I have purchased so dear, as at the price of the fairest, dearest, softest creature that ever Nature made? No, no!" Then, at her name, grief would get the ascendant of rage, and he would lie down by her side, and water her face with showers of tears, which never were wont to fall from those eyes. And however bent he was on his intended slaughter, he had not power to stir from the sight of this dear object, now more beloved, and more adored than ever.

He remained in this deploring condition for two days, and never rose from the ground where he had made his sad sacrifice. At last, rousing from her side, and accusing himself with living too long, now Imoinda was dead, and that the deaths of those barbarous enemies were deferred too long, he resolved now to finish the great work; but offering to rise, he found his strength so decayed, that he reeled to and fro, like boughs assailed by contrary winds, so that he was forced to lie down again, and try to summon all his courage to his aid. He found his brains turn round, and his eyes were dizzy, and objects appeared not the same to him [as] they were wont to do; his breath was short, and all his limbs surprised with a faintness he had never felt before. He had not eaten in two days, which was one occasion of this feebleness, but excess of grief was the greatest; yet still he hoped he should recover vigour to act his design, and lay expecting it yet six days longer, still mourning over the dead idol of his heart, and striving every day to rise, but could not.

In all this time you may believe we were in no little affliction for Caesar, and his wife. Some were of opinion he was escaped never to return; others thought some accident had happened to him. But however, we failed not to send out a hundred people several ways to search for him. A party, of about forty, went that way he took, among whom was Tuscan, who was perfectly reconciled to Byam. They had not gone very far into the wood, but they smelt an unusual smell, as of a dead body, for stinks must be very noisome that can be distinguished among such a quantity of natural sweets, as every inch of that land produces. So that they concluded they should find him dead, or somebody that was so. They passed on towards it, as loathsome as it was, and made such a rustling among the leaves that lie thick on the ground, by continual falling, that Caesar heard he was approached, and though he had, during the space of these eight days, endeavoured to rise, but found he wanted strength, yet looking up, and seeing his pursuers, he rose, and reeled to a neighbouring tree, against which he fixed his back. And being within a dozen yards of those that advanced, and saw him, he called out to them, and bid them approach no nearer, if they would be safe, so that they stood still, and hardly believing their eyes, that would persuade them that it was Caesar that spoke to them, so much was he altered. They asked him, what he had done with his wife? for they smelt a stink that almost struck them dead. He, pointing to the dead body, sighing, cried, "Behold her there." They put off the flowers that covered her with their sticks, and found she was killed, and cried out, "Oh monster! that hast murdered thy wife." Then asking him, why he did so cruel a deed. He replied, he had no leisure to answer impertinent questions. "You may go back," continued he, "and tell the faithless governor, he may thank Fortune that I am breathing my last, and that my arm is too feeble to obey my heart, in what it had designed him." But his tongue faltering, and trembling, he could scarce end what he was saying. The English taking advantage by his weakness, cried, "Let us take him alive by all means." He heard them; and, as if he had revived from a fainting, or a dream, he cried out, "No, gentlemen, you are deceived, you will find no more Caesars to be whipped, no more find a faith in me. Feeble as you think me, I have strength yet left to secure me from a second indignity." They swore all anew, and he only shook his head, and beheld them with scorn. Then they cried out, "Who will venture on this single man? Will nobody?" They stood all silent while Caesar replied, "Fatal will be the attempt to the first adventurer, let him assure himself," and, at that word, held up his knife in a menacing posture, "Look ye, ye faithless crew," said he, "'tis not life I seek, nor am I afraid of dying," and, at that word, cut a piece of flesh from his own throat, and threw it at them, "yet still I would live if I could, till I had perfected my revenge. But oh! it cannot be. I feel life gliding from my eyes and heart, and, if I make not haste, I shall yet fall a victim to the shameful whip." At that, he ripped up his own belly, and took his bowels and pulled them out, with what strength he could, while some, on their knees imploring, besought him to hold his hand. But when they saw him tottering, they cried out, "Will none venture on him?" A bold English cried, "Yes, if he were the Devil" (taking courage when he saw him almost dead) and swearing a horrid oath for his farewell to the world he rushed on[.] Caesar with his armed hand met him so fairly, as stuck him to the heart, and he fell dead at his feet. Tuscan seeing that, cried out, "I love thee, oh Caesar, and therefore will not let thee die, if possible." And, running to him, took him in his arms, but, at the same time, warding a blow that Caesar made at his bosom, he received it quite through his arm, and Caesar having not the strength to pluck the knife forth, though he attempted it, Tuscan neither pulled it out himself, nor suffered it to be pulled out, but came down with it sticking in his arm, and the reason he gave for it was, because the air should not get into the wound. They put their hands across, and carried Caesar between six of them, fainted as he was, and they thought dead, or just dying, and they brought him to Parham, and laid him on a couch, and had the chirurgeon immediately to him, who dressed his wounds, and sewed up his belly, and used means to bring him to life, which they effected. We ran all to see him; and, if before we thought him so beautiful a sight, he was now so altered, that his face was like a death's head blacked over, nothing but teeth, and eye-holes. For some days we suffered nobody to speak to him, but caused cordials to be poured down his throat, which sustained his life, and in six or seven days he recovered his senses. For, you must know, that wounds are almost to a miracle cured in the Indies, unless wounds in the legs, which rarely ever cure.

When he was well enough to speak, we talked to him, and asked him some questions about his wife, and the reasons why he killed her. And he then told us what I have related of that resolution, and of his parting, and he besought us, we would let him die, and was extremely afflicted to think it was possible he might live. He assured us, if we did not despatch him, he would prove very fatal to a great many. We said all we could to make him live, and gave him new assurances, but he begged we would not think so poorly of him, or of his love to Imoinda, to imagine we could flatter him to life again; but the chirurgeon assured him, he could not live, and therefore he need not fear. We were all (but Caesar) afflicted at this news; and the sight was gashly.[59] His discourse was sad; and the earthly smell about him so strong, that I was persuaded to leave the place for some time (being myself but sickly, and very apt to fall into fits of dangerous illness upon any extraordinary melancholy). The servants, and Trefry, and the chirurgeons, promised all to take what possible care they could of the life of Caesar, and I, taking boat, went with other company to Colonel Martin's, about three days' journey down the river, but I was no sooner gone, but the governor taking Trefry, about some pretended earnest business, a day's journey up the river, having communicated his design to one Banister,[60] a wild Irishman, and one of the council, a fellow of absolute barbarity, and fit to execute any villainy, but was rich. He came up to Parham, and forcibly took Caesar, and had him carried to the same post where he was whipped, and causing him to be tied to it, and a great fire made before him, he told him, he should die like a dog, as he was. Caesar replied, this was the first piece of bravery that ever Banister did, and he never spoke sense till he pronounced that word, and, if he would keep it, he would declare, in the other world, that he was the only man, of all the whites, that ever he heard speak truth. And turning to the men that bound him, he said, "My friends, am I to die, or to be whipped?" And they cried, "Whipped! no; you shall not escape so well." And then he replied, smiling, "A blessing on thee," and assured them, they need not tie him, for he would stand fixed, like a rock, and endure death so as should encourage them to die. "But if you whip me," said he, "be sure you tie me fast."

He had learned to take tobacco, and when he was assured he should die, he desired they would give him a pipe in his mouth, ready lighted, which they did, and the executioner came, and first cut off his members, and threw them into the fire. After that, with an ill-favoured knife, they cut his ears, and his nose, and burned them; he still smoked on, as if nothing had touched him. Then they hacked off one of his arms, and still he bore up, and held his pipe. But at the cutting off the other arm, his head sunk, and his pipe dropped, and he gave up the ghost, without a groan, or a reproach. My mother and sister were by him all the while, but not suffered to save him, so rude and wild were the rabble, and so inhuman were the justices, who stood by to see the execution, who after paid dearly enough for their insolence. They cut Caesar in quarters, and sent them to several of the chief plantations. One quarter was sent to Colonel Martin, who refused it, and swore, he had rather see the quarters of Banister, and the governor himself, than those of Caesar, on his plantations, and that he could govern his Negroes without terrifying and grieving them with frightful spectacles of a mangled king.

Thus died this great man, worthy of a better fate, and a more sublime wit than mine to write his praise. Yet, I hope, the reputation of my pen is considerable enough to make his glorious name to survive to all ages, with that of the brave, the beautiful, and the constant Imoinda.

---

[59] **gashly:** Ghastly.

[60] **Banister:** Major James Bannister. In 1688, after the Treaty of Breda, he negotiated with the Dutch on behalf of the remaining English settlers and was sent as a prisoner to Holland.

❧ Jonathan Swift
1667–1745

Satire was the most prominent literary genre of the European **ENLIGHT-ENMENT**, especially in France and England; its most powerful and notorious practitioner was the clergyman, political pamphleteer, poet, and prose stylist Jonathan Swift. Swift began demonstrating his genius for wit and biting satire in 1704 with the publication of *The Battle of the Books* and *A Tale of a Tub*. His masterpiece, *Gulliver's Travels* (1726), enjoyed immediate popularity and today is one of the most widely read books in the world. Modeled roughly on popular travel books and exploration narratives, *Gulliver's Travels* attacks the grossness, folly, and wickedness of human beings with stinging accuracy. The novel's realistic description of absurd events and imaginary societies anticipates science fiction and fantasy literature. Its vision of humanity, by turns hilarious, disgusting, and terrifying, has drawn charges of misanthropy and even madness. Readers who have only met *Gulliver's Travels* in abbreviated versions—as the story of a kindly traveler stranded in a Disneyesque land of miniature people and knee-high palaces—are often shocked by the actual text. Indeed, the physical and moral ugliness reflected in Swift's well-polished mirror leave no reader quite secure in his or her own virtue and dignity. Swift's satiric genius derives from his uncanny ability to provide entertainment and amusement even as he scolds and admonishes his readers.

Anglo-Irish Origins.   Jonathan Swift was born in Dublin, Ireland, in 1667, the child of English parents. He was raised by his widowed mother, his father having died before he was born. Supported by his paternal uncle, Swift was educated at Kilkenny School and then at Trinity College, Dublin. Like many Anglo-Irish seeking to avoid the troubles in Ireland just after the Glorious Revolution of 1688,[1] Swift fled to England in 1689. There he joined the household of retired diplomat Sir William Temple, who introduced his new secretary into important intellectual and political circles. While at Temple's, Swift took orders in the Anglican Church, although this initially seems to have been a practical move rather than a response to a passionate calling. In other ways, he began to discover his real tastes, talents, and vocations. He read widely in politics, philosophy, and literature; he made friends with the leading wits, poets, and intellectuals of his day, among them Alexander Pope, John Gay, and Joseph Addison. He undertook the education of Temple's steward's young daughter Esther Johnson, who became his lifelong friend, perhaps his lover or even his wife, in a relationship whose nature remained a secret. The letters and poems between Swift and his "Stella" are testaments to their lifelong playful, loving devotion to each other.

www   For links to more information about Swift, a quiz on *Gulliver's Travels,* and information about the 21st-century relevance of *Gulliver's Travels,* see *World Literature Online* at bedfordstmartins .com/worldlit.

---

[1] **Glorious Revolution of 1688:** Refers to the forced abdication in England of the Catholic king, James II, whose attempts to exercise royal authority over Parliament galvanized the largely Protestant nation against him.

141

Swift the Satirist.   In the 1690s, Swift began to come into his full powers as a writer, producing *The Battle of the Books* and *A Tale of a Tub*, both published in 1704. *The Battle of the Books* attacks corruption in educational and intellectual circles, defending classical writers against the moderns. In this satire, Swift describes the classical writers as modest bees who work earnestly to make honey and the beeswax used in candles, thus supplying civilization with both "sweetness and light." The modern writer, in contrast, is a bloated spider, utterly self-involved, spinning "nothing but dirt" out of his own entrails. *A Tale of a Tub* in part satirizes religious fanaticism from both Puritan and High Church extremes. Here, Swift depicts Christianity as a simple serviceable coat. High Church people, unable to value simplicity, decorate the garment with all sorts of gilded frippery and make faddish alterations until the garment becomes nearly unrecognizable; in their turn, rabid reformers angrily rip out the new seams and tear off all adornments, nearly destroying the fabric of the poor coat entirely. Rereading *A Tale of a Tub* as an old man, Swift exclaimed, "God, I had genius then!" It was clear from both of these early works that, like many satirists, Swift was ultimately a conservative; while he savagely critiques the status quo, he takes an equally acid view of radical attempts at reform and the waste and devastation they are likely to bring about.

Return to Ireland.   In 1699, Swift returned to Ireland as chaplain to the lord justice, although he still cherished hopes of a post back in England. Like most Anglo-Irish, Swift regarded it as a penance to live in what he called "wretched Dublin in miserable Ireland"; warmth, light, laughter, and civilization lay across the Irish Sea in England. From this point on, he seems to have become deeply committed to his double vocation as clergyman and writer. He served and defended the Anglican Church with fierce devotion and continued to write brilliant political and religious satires. In 1713 he was given the deanship at Dublin's St. Patrick's Cathedral. Once Britain's Tory government fell from power, weakening the influence of Swift's friends, he resigned himself to spending the remainder of his life in Ireland.

Despite his own feelings about living in Ireland, Swift won the enduring respect of Irish people for two brilliant satirical pieces. *The Drapier Letters* (1724) are written as if by a humble Dublin draper; the letters take aim at England's corrupt move to devalue Irish coinage when Ireland was already in a severe depression. Britain offered a reward for the name of the author of the anonymous *Letters,* but although Swift's authorship was widely known, no one betrayed him. *A Modest Proposal* (1729), a satire on the many cold-blooded or impractical "projects" devised by British outsiders to solve the woes of the Irish economy, was published five years later. In this outrageous satire, Swift's persona, a social scientist, recommends in a sweetly reasonable voice that the dual problems of Irish famine and Irish overpopulation could be solved by the simple expedient of breeding, raising, butchering, and eating Irish babies. In the end, he seems to suggest that he has been driven mad by the utter failure of the humane and rational solutions he has proposed in the past to the Irish and the English alike.

Death.   Swift apparently suffered most of his life from Ménière's syndrome, the neurological condition marked by increasing deafness, vertigo, and nausea. His life darkened toward its end as the disease worsened. Esther Johnson, his beloved friend, died in 1728. By 1732, Swift's ailments caused him to resign his duties as dean, although he remained mentally sound. Gradually, old friends deserted him, and in 1742, after he suffered a paralytic stroke that left him mute, guardians were appointed to manage his affairs. He died in 1745. The epitaph Swift composed for himself in Latin was well translated by his countryman William Butler Yeats:

> Swift has sailed into his rest.
> Savage indignation there
> Cannot lacerate his breast.
> Imitate him if you dare,
> World-besotted traveller, he
> Served human liberty.

Gulliver's Travels, **Early Voyages.**   *Travels into Several Remote Nations of the World* (1726), supposedly penned by "Lemuel Gulliver, first a surgeon and then a captain of several Ships," is Swift's greatest work, and it is one of the richest in the English language. Its surface is so simple and fascinating that children enjoy it; its depths are so complex that critics have been fighting about it ever since its appearance. Lemuel Gulliver (from *gull,* an easily duped person) is portrayed as a decent, occasionally resourceful fellow who, like Voltaire's Candide, is not terribly bright and is apt to accept uncritically what he's told. Gulliver undertakes four voyages in the course of the *Travels;* what follows here is a portion of the third trip and all of the fourth.

On Gulliver's first voyage, he is shipwrecked on the shores of the Lilliputians, who initially appear to be an enchantingly tiny and delicate people; their smallness in other regards—their overly dainty manners, their petty politics, and their narrow-mindedness—reveals itself, but only very gradually, to Gulliver, who will be accused by his Lilliputian enemies of such offenses as urinating in public (which he does in order to put out a raging fire in the palace) and of committing adultery with the six-inch-tall wife of the Lilliputian secretary of the treasury.

His second voyage lands Gulliver among the Brobdingnagians, giants whose blunt speech and physical grossness disgust him; Brobdingnagian warts and pimples appear the size of boulders to the fastidious Gulliver. But these giants prove to be as large-hearted and broad-minded as they are physically big. Gulliver finds himself in the awkward position of defending English government and European culture to their thoughtful king, who can only shake his head at the inhumane, petty, and wasteful practices he hears described.

The third voyage is largely a satire upon "projectors," or mock scientists, at the Grand Academy of Lagado, a spoof on the Royal Society of

Swift haunts me; he is always just round the next corner.

– W. B. YEATS,
Introduction,
Words upon the Window-Pane, 1934

Who that has read Dean Swift's disgusting description of the Yahoos, and insipid one of Houyhnhnm with a philosophical eye, can avoid seeing the futility of degrading the passions, or making man rest in contentment?

– MARY
WOLLSTONECRAFT,
A Vindication of the Rights of Woman, 1792

London. The theory-maddened projectors do not care that their social, linguistic, and scientific experiments are impractical or destructive; the experiment is all.

Final Voyage.   The final voyage is the most troubling. It takes Gulliver to the country of the **Houyhnhnms**, supremely rational horses, and their nasty-tempered draft-animals, the human-looking Yahoos. Houyhnhnm society is arguably in some ways an improvement over European ones. Free as it is from all dissent, shock, excess, greed, pride, and grief, it is a sort of utopia, but like ***Candide***'s Eldorado, it is not quite ideal, in that normal human beings would have a difficult time submitting to a lifetime of Houyhnhnmland's bland conformity. The upper-class equine citizens graze together in unending amiability, conversing about the virtues of friendship and benevolence. Their lives are supported by the work of their own Houyhnhnm servant-class. Those with white, sorrel, and gray coats are said to be "naturally" the inferiors of bay, black, and dapple-gray Houyhnhnms, and everyone accepts the rules; there are no rebels here. The catch is that, for good or ill, human beings are not Houyhnhnms: They possess feelings as well as reason. If a life of perfect rationalism means a life without conflict, it also means a life without joy or love, or art, or most things that seem to define for us the best of the human condition. The Houyhnhnms cannot be a symbol for moderate or well-balanced men and women, for they are devoid of all but the mildest

HWIN-ims

p. 275

ripples of emotions, and they have no imaginations. They cannot, for example, see that Gulliver is an exception to the rule, a rational Yahoo. They dwell in a middle state of being that is not really a human possibility at all.

Yahoos.   The Yahoos disturb most readers of *Gulliver's Travels.* These creatures, very likely descended from a marooned human couple, are all passion and gross sensuality. They are lazy, filthy, lustful, greedy, and aggressive. (They are, in fact, very like contemporary English notions of the Irish, who were caricatured as brawny, stupid, dirty, oversexed apes.) The Houyhnhnms claim Yahoos lack reason and the ability to learn. They scratch, bite, and lob excrement at their foes. Yahoo females flirt with males with whom they have no intention of mating. Yahoos hoard pretty rocks and fight over them; often, one Yahoo acts as go-between when two others are involved in such a dispute and makes off with the treasure himself, much like a lawyer. Yahoos, like human beings, are subject to causeless fits of melancholy and depression, and, unlike any other animals except human beings, Yahoos initially frighten or repel all other creatures in their vicinity. They are unmistakably degenerate versions of human beings, though just how corrupted Swift intended them to seem is not clear.

Some readers believe that the Yahoos are a reflection of Swift's own hatred of people. Swift admitted to hating "all nations, professions, and communities," but said that he loved individuals. What *Gulliver's Travels* would show, according to Swift, was that the being so-called "*animal rationale . . .* would only be *rationis capax*"; that is, human beings, often called the rational animal, seldom realize their capacity to reason. Nonetheless, Gulliver's contempt for others, including members of his own family and the generous Pedro de Mendez after his return home, leaves the question of Swift's own views open for discussion.

Houyhnhnms.   The Houyhnhnms cannot be read as simple allegorical figures for the good of human reason. The rigid order of their society, which includes discrimination within their own ranks as well as an utter abhorrence for and enslavement of the Yahoos, is not a model of the perfect society, as some readers may think.

Gulliver, always easily impressed, is totally won to the horses' way of life, and desperately disassociates himself from the Yahoos. His voice takes on a whinnying note and his gait is a modified trot, in imitation of his idols. Gulliver thinks of himself and the Houyhnhnms as Us, the Yahoos as Them. Exiled from the land, he embarks in a boat caulked with Yahoo tallow whose sails are fashioned from tanned Yahoo skins, and he troubles himself no more than the Houyhnhnms about Yahoo genocide. Later, he is disgusted by the very sight of the generous captain who rescues him, and once back home he is only by degrees able to bear the company of his own family, preferring to be with his carriage horses. Perhaps the final indictment is that people are capable of such mad egotism as Gulliver displays at the end, sitting smug and deluded in his darkened stable.

I have ever hated all nations, professions, and communities, and all my love is toward individuals; for instance, I hate the tribe of lawyers, but I love Counsellor Such-a-one, Judge Such-a one; for so with physicians, . . . soldiers, English, Scotch, French, and the rest. But principally I hate and detest that animal called man, although I heartily love John, Peter, Thomas, and so forth.

– JONATHAN SWIFT, Letter to Alexander Pope, 1725

■ CONNECTIONS

The Ramayana (Book 1). Because Gulliver visits marvelous places and meets creatures such as talking horses, *Gulliver's Travels* is often seen as a precursor to the popular genres of science fiction and fantasy. In *The Ramayana,* Prince Rama enters the magic world of the forest and encounters demons, monkey-kings, and bear people. Consider the way *Gulliver's Travels* approaches or represents such creatures in contrast to the way they appear in the epic. How do these texts sustain a sense of believability?

Voltaire, *Candide,* p. 275; In the World: Travel Narratives, p. 199. Both *Gulliver's Travels* and *Candide* are modeled upon travel narratives, describing the adventures of a naive protagonist who leaves his familiar surroundings and encounters new and strange places—and ends up criticizing not the foreign culture but the home culture. Consider how both writers use the conventions of the travel narrative, particularly the contact with the unfamiliar and the marvelous, as a means to launch an attack on European customs and values.

Joseph Conrad, *Heart of Darkness,* (Book 6). Like Voltaire's *Candide,* the protagonist of *Gulliver's Travels* is a picaresque hero—a relatively shallow character who, although entertaining, does not develop much from one episode to another. In the next several decades, fiction shifted its emphasis from events and action to character; static characters were discarded in favor of dynamic ones. The twentieth-century novel *Heart of Darkness,* when compared with *Gulliver's Travels* or *Candide,* shows a greater interest in psychological development and depth of character, and signals the change from an episodic to a more unified sense of plot.

■ FURTHER RESEARCH

Biography
Ehrenpreis, Irvin. *The Personality of Jonathan Swift.* 1958.
————. *Swift: The Man, His Works, and the Age.* 1962.
Nokes, David. *Jonathan Swift, A Hypocrite Reversed: A Critical Biography.* 1985.

Criticism
Bloom, Harold, ed. *Jonathan Swift's* Gulliver's Travels. 1996.
Flynn, Carol Houlihan. *The Body in Swift and Defoe.* 1990.
Palmeri, Frank, ed. *Critical Essays on Jonathan Swift.* 1993.
Rawson, Claude Julien, ed. *Swift: A Collection of Critical Essays.* 1994.
Wood, Nigel, ed. *Jonathan Swift.* 1999.
Zimmerman, Everett. *Swift's Narrative Satires: Author and Authority.* 1983.

■ PRONUNCIATION

Houyhnhnms: HWIN-ims

❧ Gulliver's Travels

FROM PART III
A VOYAGE TO LAPUTA, BALNIBARBI, GLUBBDUBDRIB, LUGGNAGG, AND JAPAN

CHAPTER 5. *The Author permitted to see the Grand Academy of* Lagado.[1] *The Academy largely described. The Arts wherein the professors employ themselves.*

This Academy is not an entire single building, but a continuation of several houses on both sides of a street, which growing waste was purchased and applied to that use.

I was received very kindly by the Warden, and went for many days to the Academy. Every room hath in it one or more projectors, and I believe I could not be in fewer than five hundred rooms.

The first man I saw was of a meagre aspect, with sooty hands and face, his hair and beard long, ragged and singed in several places. His clothes, shirt, and skin, were all of the same colour. He had been eight years upon a project for extracting sunbeams out of cucumbers, which were to be put into vials hermetically sealed, and let out to warm the air in raw inclement summers. He told me, he did not doubt, in eight years more, he should be able to supply the Governor's gardens with sunshine at a reasonable rate; but he complained that his stock was low, and entreated me to give him something as an encouragement to ingenuity, especially since this had been a very dear season for cucumbers. I made him a small present, for my lord had furnished me with money on purpose, because he knew their practice of begging from all who go to see them.

I went into another chamber, but was ready to hasten back, being almost overcome with a horrible stink. My conductor pressed me forward, conjuring me in a whisper to give no offence, which would be highly resented, and therefore I durst not

---

Gulliver's Travels. *Travels into Several Remote Nations of the World. In Four Parts, by Lemuel Gulliver,* now known as *Gulliver's Travels,* was first published in London in October 1726. Swift's name did not appear on the title page or anywhere in the book, and the anonymous version was rather aggressively edited by the publisher, Benjamin Motte, as well as one of Swift's friends, Charles Ford. In a letter of 1735 Swift complained about the alterations made to his original manuscript in the first edition. In that same year, George Faulkner, a London bookseller, published an edition of Swift's works with the original version of *Gulliver's Travels* restored. This 1735 Dublin edition forms the basis for all modern editions of the work. All notes to the portions printed here are the editors'.

At the heart of *Gulliver's Travels* lies the question, What does it mean to be a human being? Swift maintains some distance from the misanthropic Gulliver as well as from the extra-rational Houyhnhnms, and exactly where Swift would place humanity on the scale between Houyhnhnm and Yahoo is not at all clear. Readers take passionate—and very different—positions on that vexing question.

---

[1] **Grand . . . Lagado:** The account of the Academy of Lagado satirizes the Royal Society of London, founded in 1662 to advance knowledge.

so much as stop my nose. The projector of this cell was the most ancient student of the Academy; his face and beard were of a pale yellow; his hands and clothes daubed over with filth. When I was presented to him, he gave me a close embrace (a compliment I could well have excused). His employment from his first coming into the Academy, was an operation to reduce human excrement to its original food, by separating the several parts, removing the tincture which it receives from the gall, making the odour exhale, and scumming off the saliva. He had a weekly allowance from the society, of a vessel filled with human ordure, about the bigness of a Bristol barrel.

I saw another at work to calcine ice into gunpowder, who likewise showed me a treatise he had written concerning the malleability of fire, which he intended to publish.

There was a most ingenious architect who had contrived a new method for building houses, by beginning at the roof, and working downwards to the foundation, which he justified to me by the like practice of those two prudent insects, the bee and the spider.

There was a man born blind, who had several apprentices in his own condition: their employment was to mix colours for painters, which their master taught them to distinguish by feeling and smelling. It was indeed my misfortune to find them at that time not very perfect in their lessons, and the professor himself happened to be generally mistaken: this artist is much encouraged and esteemed by the whole fraternity.

In another apartment I was highly pleased with a projector, who had found a device for ploughing the ground with hogs, to save the charges of ploughs, cattle, and labour. The method is this: In an acre of ground you bury, at six inches distance and eight deep, a quantity of acorns, dates, chestnuts, and other mast or vegetables whereof these animals are fondest; then you drive six hundred or more of them into the field, where in a few days they will root up the whole ground in search of their food, and make it fit for sowing, at the same time manuring it with their dung. It is true, upon experiment they found the charge and trouble very great, and they had little or no crop. However, it is not doubted that this invention may be capable of great improvement.

I went into another room, where the walls and ceiling were all hung round with cobwebs, except a narrow passage for the artist to go in and out. At my entrance he called aloud to me not to disturb his webs. He lamented the fatal mistake the world had been so long in of using silk-worms, while we had such plenty of domestic insects, who infinitely excelled the former, because they understood how to weave as well as spin. And he proposed farther, that by employing spiders, the charge of dying silks should be wholly saved, whereof I was fully convinced when he showed me a vast number of flies most beautifully coloured, wherewith he fed his spiders, assuring us, that the webs would take a tincture from them; and as he had them in all hues, he hoped to fit everybody's fancy, as soon as he could find proper food for the flies, of certain gums, oils, and other glutinous matter to give a strength and consistence to the threads.

There was an astronomer who had undertaken to place a sun-dial upon the great weathercock on the town-house, by adjusting the annual and diurnal motions of the earth and sun, so as to answer and coincide with all accidental turnings by the wind.

I was complaining of a small fit of colic, upon which my conductor led me into a room, where a great physician resided, who was famous for curing that disease by contrary operations from the same instrument. He had a large pair of bellows with a long slender muzzle of ivory. This he conveyed eight inches up the anus, and drawing in the wind, he affirmed he could make the guts as lank as a dried bladder. But when the disease was more stubborn and violent, he let in the muzzle while the bellows were full of wind, which he discharged into the body of the patient, then withdrew the instrument to replenish it, clapping his thumb strongly against the orifice of the fundament; and this being repeated three or four times, the adventitious wind would rush out, bringing the noxious along with it (like water put into a pump), and the patient recover. I saw him try both experiments upon a dog, but could not discern any effect from the former. After the latter, the animal was ready to burst, and made so violent a discharge, as was very offensive to me and my companions. The dog died on the spot, and we left the doctor endeavouring to recover him by the same operation.

I visited many other apartments, but shall not trouble my reader with all the curiosities I observed, being studious of brevity.

I had hitherto seen only one side of the Academy, the other being appropriated to the advancers of speculative learning, of whom I shall say something when I have mentioned one illustrious person more, who is called among them *the universal artist.* He told us he had been thirty years employing his thoughts for the improvement of human life. He had two large rooms full of wonderful curiosities, and fifty men at work. Some were condensing air into a dry tangible substance, by extracting the nitre, and letting the aqueous or fluid particles percolate; others softening marble for pillows and pincushions; others petrifying the hoofs of a living horse to preserve them from foundering. The artist himself was at that time busy upon two great designs; the first, to sow land with chaff, wherein he affirmed the true seminal virtue to be contained, as he demonstrated by several experiments which I was not skilful enough to comprehend. The other was, by a certain composition of gums, minerals, and vegetables outwardly applied, to prevent the growth of wool upon two young lambs; and he hoped in a reasonable time to propagate the breed of naked sheep all over the kingdom.

We crossed a walk to the other part of the Academy, where, as I have already said, the projectors in speculative learning resided.

The first professor I saw was in a very large room, with forty pupils about him. After salutation, observing me to look earnestly upon a frame, which took up the greatest part of both the length and breadth of the room, he said perhaps I might wonder to see him employed in a project for improving speculative knowledge by practical and mechanical operations. But the world would soon be sensible of its usefulness, and he flattered himself that a more noble exalted thought never sprang in any other man's head. Every one knew how laborious the usual method is of attaining to arts and sciences; whereas, by his contrivance, the most ignorant person at a reasonable charge, and with a little bodily labour, may write books in philosophy,

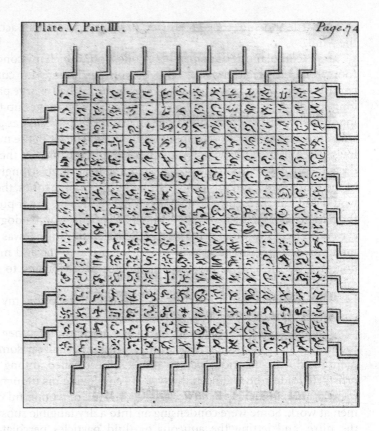

poetry, politics, law, mathematics, and theology, without the least assistance from genius or study. He then led me to the frame, about the sides whereof all his pupils stood in ranks. It was twenty foot square, placed in the middle of the room. The superficies[2] was composed of several bits of wood, about the bigness of a die, but some larger than others. They were all linked together by slender wires. These bits of wood were covered on every square with paper pasted on them, and on these papers were written all the words of their language, in their several moods, tenses, and declensions, but without any order. The professor then desired me to observe, for he was going to set his engine at work. The pupils at his command took each of them hold of an iron handle, whereof there were forty fixed round the edges of the frame, and giving them a sudden turn, the whole disposition[3] of the words was entirely changed. He then commanded six and thirty of the lads to read the several lines softly as they appeared upon the frame; and where they found three or four words together that might make part of a sentence, they dictated to the four remaining boys who were scribes. This work was repeated three or four times, and at every turn

---

[2] **superficies:** Surface.   [3] **disposition:** Arrangement.

the engine was so contrived, that the words shifted into new places, as the square bits of wood moved upside down.

Six hours a day the young students were employed in this labour, and the professor showed me several volumes in large folio already collected, of broken sentences, which he intended to piece together, and out of those rich materials to give the world a complete body of all arts and sciences; which, however, might be still improved, and much expedited, if the public would raise a fund for making and employing five hundred such frames in Lagado, and oblige the managers to contribute in common their several collections.

He assured me, that this invention had employed all his thoughts from his youth, that he had emptied the whole vocabulary into his frame, and made the strictest computation of the general proportion there is in books between the numbers of particles, nouns, and verbs, and other parts of speech.

I made my humblest acknowledgment to this illustrious person for his great communicativeness, and promised if ever I had the good fortune to return to my native country, that I would do him justice, as the sole inventor of this wonderful machine; the form and contrivance of which I desired leave to delineate upon paper, as in the figure here annexed. I told him, although it were the custom of our learned in Europe to steal inventions from each other, who had thereby at least this advantage, that it became a controversy which was the right owner, yet I would take such caution, that he should have the honour entire without a rival.

We next went to the school of languages, where three professors sat in consultation upon improving that of their own country.

The first project was to shorten discourse by cutting polysyllables into one, and leaving out verbs and participles, because in reality all things imaginable are but nouns.

The other project was a scheme for entirely abolishing all words whatsoever; and this was urged as a great advantage in point of health as well as brevity. For it is plain, that every word we speak is in some degree a diminution of our lungs by corrosion, and consequently contributes to the shortening of our lives. An expedient was therefore offered, that since words are only names for *things*, it would be more convenient for all men to carry about them such things as were necessary to express the particular business they are to discourse on. And this invention would certainly have taken place, to the great ease as well as health of the subject, if the women, in conjunction with the vulgar and illiterate, had not threatened to raise a rebellion, unless they might be allowed the liberty to speak with their tongues, after the manner of their ancestors; such constant irreconcilable enemies to science are the common people. However, many of the most learned and wise adhere to the new scheme of expressing themselves by things, which hath only this inconvenience attending it, that if a man's business be very great, and of various kinds, he must be obliged in proportion to carry a greater bundle of things upon his back, unless he can afford one or two strong servants to attend him. I have often beheld two of those sages almost sinking under the weight of their packs, like pedlars among us; who, when they met in the streets, would lay down their loads, open their sacks, and hold conversation for an hour together; then put up their implements, help each other to resume their burthens, and take their leave.

But for short conversations a man may carry implements in his pockets and under his arms, enough to supply him, and in his house he cannot be at a loss. Therefore the room where company meet who practice this art, is full of all things ready at hand, requisite to furnish matter for this kind of artificial converse.

Another great advantage proposed by this invention, was that it would serve as an universal language to be understood in all civilised nations, whose goods and utensils are generally of the same kind, or nearly resembling, so that their uses might easily be comprehended. And thus ambassadors would be qualified to treat with foreign princes or ministers of state, to whose tongues they were utter strangers.

I was at the mathematical school, where the master taught his pupils after a method scarce imaginable to us in Europe. The proposition and demonstration were fairly written on a thin wafer, with ink composed of a cephalic tincture.[4] This the student was to swallow upon a fasting stomach, and for three days following eat nothing but bread and water. As the wafer digested, the tincture mounted to his brain, bearing the proposition along with it. But the success hath not hitherto been answerable, partly by some error in the *quantum*[5] or composition, and partly by the perverseness of lads, to whom this bolus[6] is so nauseous, that they generally steal aside, and discharge it upwards before it can operate; neither have they been yet persuaded to use so long an abstinence as the prescription requires.

PART IV

A VOYAGE TO THE COUNTRY OF THE HOUYHNHNMS[7]

CHAPTER 1. *The Author sets out as Captain of a ship. His men conspire against him, confine him a long time to his cabin, set him on shore in an unknown land. He travels up into the country. The* Yahoos, *a strange sort of animal, described. The Author meets two* Houyhnhnms.

I continued at home with my wife and children about five months in a very happy condition, if I could have learned the lesson of knowing when I was well. I left my poor wife big with child, and accepted an advantageous offer made me to be Captain of the *Adventurer*, a stout merchantman of 350 tons: for I understood navigation well, and being grown weary of a surgeon's employment at sea, which however I could exercise upon occasion, I took a skilful young man of that calling, one Robert Purefoy, into my ship. We set sail from Portsmouth upon the seventh day of September, 1710; on the fourteenth we met with Captain Pocock of Bristol, at Teneriffe,[8] who was going to the bay of Campechy,[9] to cut logwood. On the sixteenth, he was parted from us by a storm; I heard since my return, that his ship foundered, and none

---

[4] cephalic tincture: A dye that is drawn toward the brain when injected.   [5] *quantum*: Amount.   [6] bolus: A pill.
[7] Houyhnhnms: The name is meant to sound like the neigh of a horse.
[8] Teneriffe: One of the Canary Islands.   [9] Campechy: In the Gulf of Mexico.

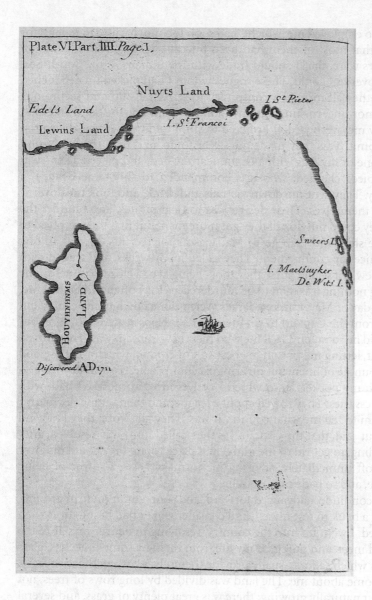

escaped but one cabin boy. He was an honest man, and a good sailor, but a little too positive in his own opinions, which was the cause of his destruction, as it hath been of several others. For if he had followed my advice, he might have been safe at home with his family at this time, as well as myself.

I had several men died in my ship of calentures,[10] so that I was forced to get recruits out of Barbadoes, and the Leeward Islands, where I touched by the direction

---

[10] **calentures:** A tropical fever.

of the merchants who employed me, which I had soon too much cause to repent: for I found afterwards that most of them had been buccaneers. I had fifty hands on board, and my orders were, that I should trade with the Indians in the South-Sea, and make what discoveries I could. These rogues whom I had picked up debauched my other men, and they all formed a conspiracy to seize the ship and secure me; which they did one morning, rushing into my cabin, and binding me hand and foot, threatening to throw me overboard, if I offered to stir. I told them, I was their prisoner, and would submit. This they made me swear to do, and then they unbound me, only fastening one of my legs with a chain near my bed, and placed a sentry at my door with his piece charged, who was commanded to shoot me dead, if I attempted my liberty. They sent me down victuals and drink, and took the government of the ship to themselves. Their design was to turn pirates, and plunder the Spaniards, which they could not do, till they got more men. But first they resolved to sell the goods in the ship, and then go to Madagascar for recruits, several among them having died since my confinement. They sailed many weeks, and traded with the Indians, but I knew not what course they took, being kept a close prisoner in my cabin, and expecting nothing less than to be murdered, as they often threatened me.

Upon the ninth day of May, 1711, one James Welch came down to my cabin; and said he had orders from the Captain to get me ashore. I expostulated with him, but in vain; neither would he so much as tell me who their new Captain was. They forced me into the longboat, letting me put on my best suit of clothes, which were as good as new, and a small bundle of linen, but no arms except my hanger; and they were so civil as not to search my pockets, into which I conveyed what money I had, with some other little necessaries. They rowed about a league, and then set me down on a strand. I desired them to tell me what country it was. They all swore, they knew no more than myself, but said, that the Captain (as they called him) was resolved, after they had sold the lading, to get rid of me in the first place where they could discover land. They pushed off immediately, advising me to make haste, for fear of being overtaken by the tide, and so bade me farewell.

In this desolate condition I advanced forward, and soon got upon firm ground, where I sat down on a bank to rest myself, and consider what I had best to do. When I was a little refreshed, I went up into the country, resolving to deliver myself to the first savages I should meet, and purchase my life from them by some bracelets, glass rings, and other toys which sailors usually provide themselves with in those voyages, and whereof I had some about me. The land was divided by long rows of trees, not regularly planted, but naturally growing; there was great plenty of grass, and several fields of oats. I walked very circumspectly for fear of being surprised, or suddenly shot with an arrow from behind or on either side. I fell into a beaten road, where I saw many tracks of human feet, and some of cows, but most of horses. At last I beheld several animals in a field, and one or two of the same kind sitting in trees. Their shape was very singular, and deformed, which a little discomposed me, so that I lay down behind a thicket to observe them better. Some of them coming forward near the place where I lay, gave me an opportunity of distinctly marking their form. Their heads and breasts were covered with a thick hair, some frizzled and others lank; they had beards like goats, and a long ridge of hair down their backs and the fore parts of their legs and feet, but the rest of their bodies were bare, so that I might see their skins, which were of a brown buff colour. They had no tails, nor any hair at all on their buttocks, except about the anus; which, I presume, nature had placed there to defend them as they sat on the ground; for this posture they used, as well as lying down, and often stood on their hind feet. They climbed high trees, as nimbly as a squirrel, for they had strong extended claws before and behind, terminating in sharp points, and hooked. They would often spring, and bound, and leap with prodigious agility. The females were not so large as the males; they had long lank hair on their heads, but none on their faces, nor any thing more than a sort of down on the rest of their bodies, except about the anus, and pudenda. Their dugs hung between their fore-feet, and often reached almost to the ground as they walked. The hair of both sexes was of several colours, brown, red, black, and yellow. Upon the whole, I never beheld in all my travels so disagreeable an animal, nor one against which I naturally conceived so strong an antipathy. So that thinking I had seen enough, full of contempt and aversion, I got up and pursued the beaten road, hoping it might direct me to the cabin of some Indian. I had not got far when I met one of these creatures full in my way, and coming up directly to me. The ugly monster, when he saw me, distorted several ways every feature of his visage, and stared as at an object he had never seen before; then approaching nearer, lifted up his fore-paw, whether out of curiosity or mischief, I could not tell. But I drew my hanger, and gave him a good blow with the flat side of it, for I durst not strike with the edge, fearing the inhabitants might be provoked against me, if they should come to know, that I had killed or maimed any of their cattle. When the beast felt the smart, he drew back, and roared so loud, that a herd of at least forty came flocking about me from the next field, howling and making odious faces; but I ran to the body of a tree, and leaning my back against it, kept them off by waving my hanger. Several of this cursed brood getting hold of the branches behind, leapt up into the tree, from whence they began to discharge their excrements on my head; however, I escaped pretty well, by sticking close to the stem of the tree, but was almost stifled with the filth, which fell about me on every side.

In the midst of this distress, I observed them all to run away on a sudden as fast as they could, at which I ventured to leave the tree, and pursue the road, wondering what it was that could put them into this fright. But looking on my left hand, I saw a horse walking softly in the field; which my persecutors having sooner discovered, was the cause of their flight. The horse started a little when he came near me, but soon recovering himself, looked full in my face with manifest tokens of wonder: he viewed my hands and feet, walking round me several times. I would have pursued my journey, but he placed himself directly in the way, yet looking with a very mild aspect, never offering the least violence. We stood gazing at each other for some time; at last I took the boldness to reach my hand towards his neck, with a design to stroke it, using the common style and whistle of jockeys when they are going to handle a strange horse. But this animal seeming to receive my civilities with disdain, shook his head, and bent his brows, softly raising up his right fore-foot to remove my hand. Then he neighed three or four times, but in so different a cadence, that I almost began to think he was speaking to himself in some language of his own.

While he and I were thus employed, another horse came up; who applying himself to the first in very formal manner, they gently struck each other's right hoof before, neighing several times by turns, and varying the sound, which seemed to be almost articulate. They went some paces off, as if it were to confer together, walking side by side, backward and forward, like persons deliberating upon some affair of weight, but often turning their eyes towards me, as it were to watch that I might not escape. I was amazed to see such actions and behaviour in brute beasts, and concluded with myself, that if the inhabitants of this country were endued with a proportionable degree of reason, they must needs be the wisest people upon earth. This thought gave me so much comfort, that I resolved to go forward until I could discover some house or village, or meet with any of the natives, leaving the two horses to discourse together as they pleased. But the first, who was a dapple gray, observing me to steal off, neighed after me in so expressive a tone, that I fancied myself to understand what he meant; whereupon I turned back, and came near him, to expect his farther commands: but concealing my fear as much as I could, for I began to be in some pain, how this adventure might terminate; and the reader will easily believe I did not much like my present situation.

The two horses came up close to me, looking with great earnestness upon my face and hands. The gray steed rubbed my hat all round with his right fore-hoof, and discomposed it so much that I was forced to adjust it better, by taking it off, and settling it again; whereat both he and his companion (who was a brown bay) appeared to be much surprised: The latter felt the lappet of my coat, and finding it to hang loose about me, they both looked with new signs of wonder. He stroked my right hand, seeming to admire the softness and colour; but he squeezed it so hard between his hoof and his pastern, that I was forced to roar; after which they both touched me with all possible tenderness. They were under great perplexity about my shoes and stockings, which they felt very often, neighing to each other, and using various gestures, not unlike those of a philosopher, when he would attempt to solve some new and difficult phenomenon.

Upon the whole, the behaviour of these animals was so orderly and rational, so acute and judicious, that I at last concluded, they must needs be magicians, who had thus metamorphosed themselves upon some design, and seeing a stranger in the way, were resolved to divert themselves with him; or perhaps were really amazed at the sight of a man so very different in habit, feature, and complexion from those who might probably live in so remote a climate. Upon the strength of this reasoning, I ventured to address them in the following manner: Gentlemen, if you be conjurers, as I have good cause to believe, you can understand any language; therefore I make bold to let your worships know, that I am a poor distressed English man, driven by his misfortunes upon your coast, and I entreat one of you, to let me ride upon his back, as if he were a real horse, to some house or village, where I can be relieved. In return of which favour, I will make you a present of this knife and bracelet (taking them out of my pocket). The two creatures stood silent while I spoke, seeming to listen with great attention; and when I had ended, they neighed frequently towards each other, as if they were engaged in serious conversation. I plainly observed, that their language expressed the passions very well, and the words might with little pains be resolved into an alphabet more easily than the Chinese.

I could frequently distinguish the word *Yahoo,* which was repeated by each of them several times; and although it was impossible for me to conjecture what it meant, yet while the two horses were busy in conversation, I endeavoured to practise this word upon my tongue; and as soon as they were silent, I boldly pronounced *Yahoo* in a loud voice, imitating, at the same time, as near as I could, the neighing of a horse; at which they were both visibly surprised, and the gray repeated the same word twice, as if he meant to teach me the right accent, wherein I spoke after him as well as I could, and found myself perceivably to improve every time, though very far from any degree of perfection. Then the bay tried me with a second word, much harder to be pronounced; but reducing it to the English orthography, may be spelt thus, *Houyhnhnm.* I did not succeed in this so well as the former, but after two or three farther trials, I had better fortune; and they both appeared amazed at my capacity.

After some further discourse, which I then conjectured might relate to me, the two friends took their leaves, with the same compliment of striking each other's hoof; and the gray made me signs that I should walk before him, wherein I thought it prudent to comply, till I could find a better director. When I offered to slacken my pace, he would cry *Hhuun, Hhuun;* I guessed his meaning, and gave him to understand, as well as I could, that I was weary, and not able to walk faster; upon which, he would stand a while to let me rest.

CHAPTER 2. *The Author conducted by a* Houyhnhnm *to his house. The house described. The Author's reception. The food of the* Houyhnhnms. *The Author in distress for want of meat, is at last relieved. His manner of feeding in this country.*

Having travelled about three miles, we came to a long kind of building, made of timber, stuck in the ground, and wattled across; the roof was low, and covered with straw. I now began to be a little comforted, and took out some toys, which travellers usually carry for presents to the savage Indians of America and other parts, in hopes the people of the house would be thereby encouraged to receive me kindly. The horse made me a sign to go in first; it was a large room with a smooth clay floor, and a rack and manger extending the whole length on one side. There were three nags, and two mares, not eating, but some of them sitting down upon their hams, which I very much wondered at; but wondered more to see the rest employed in domestic business. These seemed but ordinary cattle; however, this confirmed my first opinion, that a people who could so far civilise brute animals, must needs excel in wisdom all the nations of the world. The gray came in just after, and thereby prevented any ill treatment, which the others might have given me. He neighed to them several times in a style of authority, and received answers.

Beyond this room there were three others, reaching the length of the house, to which you passed through three doors, opposite to each other, in the manner of a vista; we went through the second room towards the third; here the gray walked in first, beckoning me to attend: I waited in the second room, and got ready my presents for the master and mistress of the house: They were two knives, three bracelets of false pearl, a small looking-glass, and a bead necklace. The horse neighed three or four times, and I waited to hear some answers in a human voice, but I heard no other returns, than in the same dialect, only one or two a little shriller than his. I began to think that this house must belong to some person of great note among them, because there appeared so much ceremony before I could gain admittance. But, that a man of quality should be served all by horses, was beyond my comprehension. I feared my brain was disturbed by my sufferings and misfortunes: I roused myself, and looked about me in the room where I was left alone; this was furnished like the first, only after a more elegant manner. I rubbed my eyes often, but the same objects still occurred. I pinched my arms and sides, to awake myself, hoping I might be in a dream. I then absolutely concluded, that all these appearances could be nothing else but necromancy and magic. But I had no time to pursue these reflections; for the gray horse came to the door, and made me a sign to follow him into the third room, where I saw a very comely mare, together with a colt and foal, sitting on their haunches, upon mats of straw, not unartfully made, and perfectly neat and clean.

The mare soon after my entrance, rose from her mat, and coming up close, after having nicely observed my hands and face, gave me a most contemptuous look; then turning to the horse, I heard the word *Yahoo* often repeated betwixt them; the meaning of which word I could not then comprehend, although it were the first I had learned to pronounce; but I was soon better informed, to my everlasting mortification: for the horse beckoning to me with his head, and repeating the word *Hhuun*, *Hhuun*, as he did upon the road, which I understood was to attend him, led me out into a kind of court, where was another building at some distance from the house. Here we entered, and I saw three of those detestable creatures, whom I first met after my landing, feeding upon roots, and the flesh of some animals, which I afterwards found to be that of asses and dogs, and now and then a cow dead by accident or disease. They were all tied by the neck with strong withes, fastened to a beam; they held their food between the claws of their fore-feet, and tore it with their teeth.

The master horse ordered a sorrel nag, one of his servants, to untie the largest of these animals, and take him into the yard. The beast and I were brought close together, and our countenances diligently compared, both by master and servant, who thereupon repeated several times the word *Yahoo*. My horror and astonishment are not to be described, when I observed, in this abominable animal, a perfect human figure: the face of it indeed was flat and broad, the nose depressed, the lips large, and the mouth wide. But these differences are common to all savage nations, where the lineaments of the countenance are distorted by the natives suffering their infants to lie grovelling on the earth, or by carrying them on their backs, nuzzling with their face against the mother's shoulders. The fore-feet of the *Yahoo* differed from my hands in nothing else but the length of the nails, the coarseness and brownness of the palms, and the hairiness on the backs. There was the same resemblance between our feet, with the same differences, which I knew very well, though the horses did not, because of my shoes and stockings; the same in every part of our bodies, except as to hairiness and colour, which I have already described.

The great difficulty that seemed to stick with the two horses, was, to see the rest of my body so very different from that of a *Yahoo,* for which I was obliged to my clothes, whereof they had no conception. The sorrel nag offered me a root, which he held (after their manner, as we shall describe in its proper place) between his hoof and pastern; I took it in my hand, and having smelt it, returned it to him again as civilly as I could. He brought out of the *Yahoo's* kennel a piece of ass's flesh, but it smelt so offensively that I turned from it with loathing: he then threw it to the *Yahoo,* by whom it was greedily devoured. He afterwards showed me a wisp of hay, and a fetlock full of oats; but I shook my head, to signify, that neither of these were food for me. And indeed, I now apprehended that I must absolutely starve, if I did not get to some of my own species; for as to those filthy *Yahoos,* although there were few greater lovers of mankind, at that time, than myself, yet I confess I never saw any sensitive being so detestable on all accounts; and the more I came near them, the more hateful they grew, while I stayed in that country. This the master horse observed by my behaviour, and therefore sent the *Yahoo* back to his kennel. He then put his fore-hoof to his mouth, at which I was much surprised, although he did it with ease, and with a motion that appeared perfectly natural, and made other signs to know what I would eat; but I could not return him such an answer as he was able to apprehend; and if he had understood me, I did not see how it was possible to contrive any way for finding myself nourishment. While we were thus engaged, I observed a cow passing by, whereupon I pointed to her, and expressed a desire to let me go and milk her. This had its effect; for he led me back into the house, and ordered a mare-servant to open a room, where a good store of milk lay in earthen and wooden vessels, after a very orderly and cleanly manner. She gave me a large bowl full, of which I drank very heartily, and found myself well refreshed.

About noon I saw coming towards the house a kind of vehicle, drawn like a sledge by four *Yahoos.* There was in it an old steed, who seemed to be of quality; he alighted with his hind-feet forward, having by accident got a hurt in his left fore-foot. He came to dine with our horse, who received him with great civility. They dined in the best room, and had oats boiled in milk for the second course, which the old horse eat warm, but the rest cold. Their mangers were placed circular in the middle of the room, and divided into several partitions, round which they sat on their haunches upon bosses of straw. In the middle was a large rack with angles answering to every partition of the manger; so that each horse and mare eat their own hay, and their own mash of oats and milk, with much decency and regularity. The behaviour of the young colt and foal appeared very modest, and that of the master and mistress extremely cheerful and complaisant to their guest. The gray ordered me to stand by him, and much discourse passed between him and his friend concerning me, as I found by the stranger's often looking on me, and the frequent repetition of the word *Yahoo.*

I happened to wear my gloves, which the master gray observing, seemed perplexed, discovering signs of wonder what I had done to my fore-feet; he put his hoof three or four times to them, as if he would signify, that I should reduce them to their former shape, which I presently did, pulling off both my gloves, and putting them into my pocket. This occasioned farther talk, and I saw the company was pleased with my behaviour, whereof I soon found the good effects. I was ordered to speak the few words I understood, and while they were at dinner, the master taught me the names for oats, milk, fire, water, and some others; which I could readily pronounce after him, having from my youth a great facility in learning languages.

When dinner was done, the master horse took me aside, and by signs and words made me understand the concern that he was in, that I had nothing to eat. Oats in their tongue are called *hlunnh*. This word I pronounced two or three times; for although I had refused them at first, yet upon second thoughts, I considered that I could contrive to make of them a kind of bread, which might be sufficient with milk to keep me alive, till I could make my escape to some other country, and to creatures of my own species. The horse immediately ordered a white mare-servant of his family to bring me a good quantity of oats in a sort of wooden tray. These I heated before the fire as well as I could, and rubbed them till the husks came off, which I made a shift to winnow from the grain; I ground and beat them between two stones, then took water, and made them into a paste or cake, which I toasted at the fire, and ate warm with milk. It was at first a very insipid diet, though common enough in many parts of Europe, but grew tolerable by time; and having been often reduced to hard fare in my life, this was not the first experiment I had made how easily nature is satisfied. And I cannot but observe, that I never had one hour's sickness, while I stayed in this island. 'Tis true, I sometimes made a shift to catch a rabbit, or bird, by springes[11] made of *Yahoos'* hairs, and I often gathered wholesome herbs, which I boiled, and eat as salads with my bread, and now and then, for a rarity, I made a little butter, and drank the whey. I was at first at a great loss for salt; but custom soon reconciled the want of it; and I am confident that the frequent use of salt among us is an effect of luxury, and was first introduced only as a provocative to drink; except where it is necessary for preserving of flesh in long voyages, or in places remote from great markets. For we observe no animal to be fond of it but man: and as to myself, when I left this country, it was a great while before I could endure the taste of it in anything that I eat.

This is enough to say upon the subject of my diet, wherewith other travellers fill their books, as if the readers were personally concerned whether we fared well or ill. However, it was necessary to mention this matter, lest the world should think it impossible that I could find sustenance for three years in such a country, and among such inhabitants.

When it grew towards evening, the master horse ordered a place for me to lodge in; it was but six yards from the house, and separated from the stable of the *Yahoos*. Here I got some straw, and covering myself with my own clothes, slept very sound. But I was in a short time better accommodated, as the reader shall know hereafter, when I come to treat more particularly about my way of living.

CHAPTER 3. *The Author studious to learn the language, the* Houyhnhnm *his master assists in teaching him. The language described. Several* Houyhnhnms *of quality come out of curiosity to see the Author. He gives his master a short account of his voyage.*

My principal endeavour was to learn the language, which my master (for so I shall henceforth call him), and his children, and every servant of his house, were desirous

---

[11]springes: Snares.

to teach me. For they looked upon it as a prodigy that a brute animal should discover such marks of a rational creature. I pointed to every thing, and enquired the name of it, which I wrote down in my journal-book when I was alone, and corrected my bad accent by desiring those of the family to pronounce it often. In this employment, a sorrel nag, one of the under servants, was very ready to assist me.

In speaking, they pronounce through the nose and throat, and their language approaches nearest to the High-Dutch, or German, of any I know in Europe; but is much more graceful and significant. The Emperor Charles V. made almost the same observation, when he said, that if he were to speak to his horse, it should be in High-Dutch.

The curiosity and impatience of my master were so great, that he spent many hours of his leisure to instruct me. He was convinced (as he afterwards told me) that I must be a *Yahoo,* but my teachableness, civility, and cleanliness, astonished him; which were qualities altogether so opposite to those animals. He was most perplexed about my clothes, reasoning sometimes with himself, whether they were a part of my body: for I never pulled them off till the family were asleep, and got them on before they waked in the morning. My master was eager to learn from whence I came, how I acquired those appearances of reason, which I discovered in all my actions, and to know my story from my own mouth, which he hoped he should soon do by the great proficiency I made in learning and pronouncing their words and sentences. To help my memory, I formed all I learned into the English alphabet, and writ the words down with the translations. This last, after some time, I ventured to do in my master's presence. It cost me much trouble to explain to him what I was doing; for the inhabitants have not the least idea of books or literature.

In about ten weeks time I was able to understand most of his questions, and in three months could give him some tolerable answers. He was extremely curious to know from what part of the country I came, and how I was taught to imitate a rational creature, because the *Yahoos* (whom he saw I exactly resembled in my head, hands, and face, that were only visible), with some appearance of cunning, and the strongest disposition to mischief, were observed to be the most unteachable of all brutes. I answered, that I came over the sea from a far place, with many others of my own kind, in a great hollow vessel made of the bodies of trees. That my companions forced me to land on this coast, and then left me to shift for myself. It was with some difficulty, and by the help of many signs, that I brought him to understand me. He replied, that I must needs be mistaken, or that I *said the thing which was not.* (For they have no word in their language to express lying or falsehood.) He knew it was impossible that there could be a country beyond the sea, or that a parcel of brutes could move a wooden vessel whither they pleased upon water. He was sure no *Houyhnhnm* alive could make such a vessel, nor would trust *Yahoos* to manage it.

The word *Houyhnhnm,* in their tongue, signifies a *horse,* and in its etymology, *the perfection of nature.* I told my master, that I was at a loss for expression, but would improve as fast as I could; and hoped in a short time I should be able to tell him wonders: he was pleased to direct his own mare, his colt and foal, and the servants of the family, to take all opportunities of instructing me, and every day for two or three hours, he was at the same pains himself. Several horses and mares of quality in the neighbourhood came often to our house upon the report spread of a wonderful *Yahoo,* that could speak like a *Houyhnhnm,* and seemed in his words and actions to discover some glimmerings of reason. These delighted to converse with me: they put many questions, and received such answers as I was able to return. By all these advantages, I made so great a progress, that in five months from my arrival I understood whatever was spoke, and could express myself tolerably well.

The *Houyhnhnms* who came to visit my master, out of a design of seeing and talking with me, could hardly believe me to be a right *Yahoo,* because my body had a different covering from others of my kind. They were astonished to observe me without the usual hair or skin, except on my head, face, and hands; but I discovered that secret to my master, upon an accident, which happened about a fortnight before.

I have already told the reader, that every night when the family were gone to bed, it was my custom to strip and cover myself with my clothes: it happened one morning early, that my master sent for me, by the sorrel nag, who was his valet; when he came, I was fast asleep, my clothes fallen off on one side, and my shirt above my waist. I awaked at the noise he made, and observed him to deliver his message in some disorder; after which he went to my master, and in a great fright gave him a very confused account of what he had seen. This I presently discovered; for going as soon as I was dressed, to pay my attendance upon his Honour, he asked me the meaning of what his servant had reported, that I was not the same thing when I slept as I appeared to be at other times; that his valet assured him, some part of me was white, some yellow, at least not so white, and some brown.

I had hitherto concealed the secret of my dress, in order to distinguish myself, as much as possible, from that cursed race of *Yahoos;* but now I found it in vain to do so any longer. Besides, I considered that my clothes and shoes would soon wear out, which already were in a declining condition, and must be supplied by some contrivance from the hides of *Yahoos* or other brutes; whereby the whole secret would be known. I therefore told my master, that in the country from whence I came, those of my kind always covered their bodies with the hairs of certain animals prepared by art, as well for decency as to avoid the inclemencies of air, both hot and cold; of which, as to my own person, I would give him immediate conviction, if he pleased to command me: only desiring his excuse, if I did not expose those parts that nature taught us to conceal. He said my discourse was all very strange, but especially the last part; for he could not understand why nature should teach us to conceal what nature had given. That neither himself nor family were ashamed of any parts of their bodies; but however I might do as I pleased. Whereupon, I first unbuttoned my coat, and pulled it off. I did the same with my waistcoat; I drew off my shoes, stockings, and breeches. I let my shirt down to my waist, and drew up the bottom, fastening it like a girdle about my middle to hide my nakedness.

My master observed the whole performance with great signs of curiosity and admiration. He took up all my clothes in his pastern, one piece after another, and examined them diligently; he then stroked my body very gently, and looked round me several times, after which he said, it was plain that I must be a perfect *Yahoo;* but that I differed very much from the rest of my species, in the softness, and whiteness, and smoothness of my skin, my want of hair in several parts of my body, the shape and shortness of my claws behind and before, and my affectation of walking continually on my two hinder feet. He desired to see no more, and gave me leave to put on my clothes again, for I was shuddering with cold.

I expressed my uneasiness at his giving me so often the appellation of *Yahoo,* an odious animal, for which I had so utter a hatred and contempt. I begged he would forbear applying that word to me, and take the same order in his family, and among his friends whom he suffered to see me. I requested likewise, that the secret of my having a false covering to my body might be known to none but himself, at least as long as my present clothing should last; for as to what the sorrel nag his valet had observed, his Honour might command him to conceal it.

All this my master very graciously consented to, and thus the secret was kept till my clothes began to wear out, which I was forced to supply by several contrivances, that shall hereafter be mentioned. In the meantime, he desired I would go on with my utmost diligence to learn their language, because he was more astonished at my capacity for speech and reason, than at the figure of my body, whether it were covered or no; adding, that he waited with some impatience to hear the wonders which I promised to tell him.

From thenceforward he doubled the pains he had been at to instruct me; he brought me into all company, and made them treat me with civility, because, as he told them, privately, this would put me into good humour, and make me more diverting.

Every day when I waited on him, beside the trouble he was at in teaching, he would ask me several questions concerning myself, which I answered as well as I could; and by these means he had already received some general ideas, though very imperfect. It would be tedious to relate the several steps by which I advanced to a more regular conversation: But the first account I gave of myself in any order and length, was to this purpose:

That I came from a very far country, as I already had attempted to tell him, with about fifty more of my own species; that we travelled upon the seas, in a great hollow vessel made of wood, and larger than his Honour's house. I described the ship to him in the best terms I could, and explained by the help of my handkerchief displayed, how it was driven forward by the wind. That upon a quarrel among us, I was set on shore on this coast, where I walked forward without knowing whither, till he delivered me from the persecution of those execrable *Yahoos.* He asked me, who made the ship, and how it was possible that the *Houyhnhnms* of my country would leave it to the management of brutes? My answer was, that I durst proceed no further in my relation, unless he would give me his word and honour that he would not be offended, and then I would tell him the wonders I had so often promised. He agreed; and I went on by assuring him, that the ship was made by creatures like myself, who in all the countries I had travelled, as well as in my own, were the only governing, rational animals; and that upon my arrival hither, I was as much astonished to see the *Houyhnhnms* act like rational beings, as he or his friends could be in finding some marks of reason in a creature he was pleased to call a *Yahoo,* to which I owned my resemblance in every part, but could not account for their degenerate and brutal nature. I said farther, that if good fortune ever restored me to my native country, to relate my travels hither, as I resolved to do, every body would believe that I *said the thing which was not;* that I invented the story out of my own head; and with all possible respect to himself, his family and friends, and under his promise of not being offended, our countrymen would hardly think it probable, that a *Houyhnhnm* should be the presiding creature of a nation, and a *Yahoo* the brute.

CHAPTER 4. *The* Houyhnhnms' *notion of truth and falsehood. The Author's discourse disapproved by his master. The Author gives a more particular account of himself, and the accidents of his voyage.*

My master heard me with great appearances of uneasiness in his countenance, because *doubting,* or *not believing,* are so little known in this country, that the inhabitants cannot tell how to behave themselves under such circumstances. And I remember in frequent discourses with my master concerning the nature of manhood, in other parts of the world, having occasion to talk of *lying* and *false representation,* it was with much difficulty that he comprehended what I meant, although he had otherwise a most acute judgment. For he argued thus: that the use of speech was to make us understand one another, and to receive information of facts; now if any one *said the thing which was not,* these ends were defeated; because I cannot properly be said to understand him; and I am so far from receiving information, that he leaves me worse than in ignorance, for I am led to believe a thing black when it is white, and short when it is long. And these were all the notions he had concerning that faculty of *lying,* so perfectly well understood, and so universally practised, among human creatures.

To return from this digression; when I asserted that the *Yahoos* were the only governing animals in my country, which my master said was altogether past his conception, he desired to know, whether we had *Houyhnhnms* among us, and what was their employment: I told him, we had great numbers, that in summer they grazed in the fields, and in winter were kept in houses, with hay and oats, where *Yahoo* servants were employed to rub their skins smooth, comb their manes, pick their feet, serve them with food, and make their beds. I understand you well, said my master, it is now very plain, from all you have spoken, that whatever share of reason the *Yahoos* pretend to, the *Houyhnhnms* are your masters; I heartily wish our *Yahoos* would be so tractable. I begged his Honour would please to excuse me from proceeding any farther, because I was very certain that the account he expected from me would be highly displeasing. But he insisted in commanding me to let him know the best and the worst: I told him, he should be obeyed. I owned, that the *Houyhnhnms* among us, whom we called horses, were the most generous and comely animals we had, that they excelled in strength and swiftness; and when they belonged to persons of quality, employed in travelling, racing, or drawing chariots, they were treated with much kindness and care, till they fell into diseases, or became foundered in the feet; and then they were sold, and used to all kind of drudgery till they died; after which their skins were stripped and sold for what they were worth, and their bodies left to be devoured by dogs and birds of prey. But the common race of horses had not so good fortune, being kept by farmers and carriers, and other mean people, who put them to greater labour, and fed them worse. I described, as well as I could, our way of riding, the shape and use of a bridle, a saddle, a spur, and a whip, of harness and wheels. I added, that we fastened plates of a certain hard substance called iron at the bottom of their feet, to preserve their hoofs from being broken by the stony ways on which we often travelled.

My master, after some expressions of great indignation, wondered how we dared to venture upon a *Houyhnhnm's* back, for he was sure, that the weakest servant in his house would be able to shake off the strongest *Yahoo*, or by lying down, and rolling on his back, squeeze the brute to death. I answered, that our horses were trained up from three or four years old to the several uses we intended them for; that if any of them proved intolerably vicious, they were employed for carriages; that they were severely beaten while they were young for any mischievous tricks; that the males, designed for common use of riding or draught, were generally castrated about two years after their birth, to take down their spirits, and make them more tame and gentle; that they were indeed sensible of rewards and punishments; but his Honour would please to consider, that they had not the least tincture of reason any more than the *Yahoos* in this country.

It put me to the pains of many circumlocutions to give my master a right idea of what I spoke; for their language doth not abound in variety of words, because their wants and passions are fewer than among us. But it is impossible to express his noble resentment at our savage treatment of the *Houyhnhnm* race, particularly after I had explained the manner and use of castrating horses among us, to hinder them from propagating their kind, and to render them more servile. He said, if it were possible there could be any country where *Yahoos* alone were endued with reason, they certainly must be the governing animal, because reason will in time always prevail against brutal strength. But, considering the frame of our bodies, and especially of mine, he thought no creature of equal bulk was so ill contrived, for employing that reason in the common offices of life; whereupon he desired to know whether those among whom I lived resembled me or the *Yahoos* of his country. I assured him, that I was as well shaped as most of my age; but the younger and the females were much more soft and tender, and the skins of the latter generally as white as milk. He said, I differed indeed from other *Yahoos*, being much more cleanly, and not altogether so deformed, but, in point of real advantage, he thought I differed for the worse. That my nails were of no use either to my fore or hinder-feet; as to my fore-feet, he could not properly call them by that name, for he never observed me to walk upon them; that they were too soft to bear the ground; that I generally went with them uncovered, neither was the covering I sometimes wore on them, of the same shape, or so strong as that on my feet behind. That I could not walk with any security, for if either of my hinder-feet slipped, I must inevitably fall. He then began to find fault with other parts of my body, the flatness of my face, the prominence of my nose, my eyes placed directly in front, so that I could not look on either side without turning my head: that I was not able to feed myself, without lifting one of my fore-feet to my mouth: and therefore nature had placed those joints to answer that necessity. He knew not what could be the use of those several clefts and divisions in my feet behind; these were too soft to bear the hardness and sharpness of stones without a covering made from the skin of some other brute; that my whole body wanted a fence against heat and cold, which I was forced to put on and off every day with tediousness and trouble. And lastly, that he observed every animal in this country naturally to abhor the *Yahoos,* whom the weaker avoided, and the stronger drove from them. So that supposing us to have the gift of reason, he could not see how it were possible to cure that natural antipathy which every creature discovered against us; nor consequently, how we could tame and render them serviceable. However, he would (as he said) debate the matter no farther, because he was more desirous to know my own story, the country where I was born, and the several actions and events of my life before I came hither.

I assured him, how extremely desirous I was that he should be satisfied on every point; but I doubted much, whether it would be possible for me to explain myself on several subjects whereof his Honour could have no conception, because I saw nothing in his country to which I could resemble them. That, however, I would do my best, and strive to express myself by similitudes, humbly desiring his assistance when I wanted proper words; which he was pleased to promise me.

I said, my birth was of honest parents in an island called England, which was remote from this country, as many days' journey as the strongest of his Honour's servants could travel in the annual course of the sun. That I was bred a surgeon, whose trade it is to cure wounds and hurts in the body, got by accident or violence; that my country was governed by a female man, whom we called a Queen. That I left it to get riches, whereby I might maintain myself and family when I should return. That, in my last voyage, I was commander of the ship, and had about fifty *Yahoos* under me, many of which died at sea, and I was forced to supply them by others picked out from several nations. That our ship was twice in danger of being sunk; the first time by a great storm, and the second, by striking against a rock. Here my master interposed, by asking me, how I could persuade strangers out of different countries to venture with me, after the losses I had sustained, and the hazards I had run. I said, they were fellows of desperate fortunes, forced to fly from the places of their birth, on account of their poverty or their crimes. Some were undone by lawsuits; others spent all they had in drinking, whoring, and gaming; others fled for treason; many for murder, theft, poisoning, robbery, perjury, forgery, coining false money, for committing rapes or sodomy, for flying from their colours, or deserting to the enemy, and most of them had broken prison; none of these durst return to their native countries for fear of being hanged, or of starving in a jail; and therefore were under the necessity of seeking a livelihood in other places.

During this discourse, my master was pleased to interrupt me several times; I had made use of many circumlocutions in describing to him the nature of the several crimes for which most of our crew had been forced to fly their country. This labour took up several days' conversation, before he was able to comprehend me. He was wholly at a loss to know what could be the use or necessity of practising those vices. To clear up which I endeavoured to give some ideas of the desire of power and riches, of the terrible effects of lust, intemperance, malice, and envy. All this I was forced to define and describe by putting of cases, and making of suppositions. After which, like one whose imagination was struck with something never seen or heard of before, he would lift up his eyes with amazement and indignation. Power, government, war, law, punishment, and a thousand other things had no terms, wherein that language could express them, which made the difficulty almost insuperable to give my master any conception of what I meant. But being of an excellent understanding, much improved by contemplation and converse, he at last arrived at a competent knowledge of what human nature in our parts of the world is capable to perform, and desired I would give him some particular account of that land which we call Europe, but especially of my own country.

CHAPTER 5. *The Author, at his master's commands, informs him of the state of* England. *The causes of war among the princes of* Europe. *The Author begins to explain the* English *constitution.*

The reader may please to observe, that the following extract of many conversations I had with my master, contains a summary of the most material points, which were discoursed at several times for above two years; his Honour often desiring fuller satisfaction as I farther improved in the *Houyhnhnm* tongue. I laid before him, as well as I could, the whole state of Europe; I discoursed of trade and manufactures, of arts and sciences; and the answers I gave to all the questions he made, as they arose upon several subjects, were a fund of conversation not to be exhausted. But I shall here only set down the substance of what passed between us concerning my own country, reducing it into order as well as I can, without any regard to time or other circumstances, while I strictly adhere to truth. My only concern is, that I shall hardly be able to do justice to my master's arguments and expressions, which must needs suffer by my want of capacity, as well as by a translation into our barbarous English.

In obedience, therefore, to his Honour's commands, I related to him the Revolution under the Prince of Orange; the long war with France entered into by the said prince, and renewed by his successor, the present Queen, wherein the greatest powers of Christendom were engaged, and which still continued: I computed at his request, that about a million of *Yahoos* might have been killed in the whole progress of it; and perhaps a hundred or more cities taken, and thrice as many ships burnt or sunk.[12]

He asked me what were the usual causes or motives that made one country go to war with another. I answered they were innumerable; but I should only mention a few of the chief. Sometimes the ambition of princes, who never think they have land or people enough to govern; sometimes the corruption of ministers, who engage their master in a war in order to stifle or divert the clamour of the subjects against their evil administration. Difference in opinions hath cost many millions of lives: for instance, whether flesh be bread, or bread be flesh; whether the juice of a certain berry be blood or wine; whether whistling be a vice or a virtue; whether it be better to kiss a post, or throw it into the fire; what is the best colour for a coat, whether

---

[12] Gulliver disingenuously describes to his master the "Glorious Revolution" of 1688 that ousted the English James II, and the War of the Spanish Succession, which occupied the decade between 1703 and 1713.

black, white, red, or gray; and whether it should be long or short, narrow or wide, dirty or clean; with many more.[13] Neither are any wars so furious and bloody, or of so long continuance, as those occasioned by difference in opinion, especially if it be in things indifferent.

Sometimes the quarrel between two princes is to decide which of them shall dispossess a third of his dominions, where neither of them pretend to any right. Sometimes one prince quarrelleth with another, for fear the other should quarrel with him. Sometimes a war is entered upon, because the enemy is too strong, and sometimes because he is too weak. Sometimes our neighbours want the things which we have, or have the things which we want; and we both fight, till they take ours or give us theirs. It is a very justifiable cause of a war to invade a country after the people have been wasted by famine, destroyed by pestilence, or embroiled by factions among themselves. It is justifiable to enter into war against our nearest ally, when one of his towns lies convenient for us, or a territory of land, that would render our dominions round and complete. If a prince sends forces into a nation, where the people are poor and ignorant, he may lawfully put half of them to death, and make slaves of the rest, in order to civilize and reduce them from their barbarous way of living. It is a very kingly, honourable, and frequent practice, when one prince desires the assistance of another to secure him against an invasion, that the assistant, when he hath driven out the invader, should seize on the dominions himself, and kill, imprison, or banish the prince he came to relieve. Alliance by blood or marriage is a frequent cause of war between princes; and the nearer the kindred is, the greater is their disposition to quarrel: Poor nations are hungry, and rich nations are proud; and pride and hunger will ever be at variance. For these reasons, the trade of a soldier is held the most honourable of all others; because a soldier is a *Yahoo* hired to kill in cold blood as many of his own species, who have never offended him, as possibly he can.

There is likewise a kind of beggarly princes in Europe, not able to make war by themselves, who hire out their troops to richer nations, for so much a day to each man; of which they keep three fourths to themselves, and it is the best part of their maintenance; such are those in Germany and other northern parts of Europe.

What you have told me (said my master), upon the subject of war, does indeed discover most admirably the effects of that reason you pretend to: however, it is happy that the shame is greater than the danger; and that nature hath left you utterly uncapable of doing much mischief.

For your mouths lying flat with your faces, you can hardly bite each other to any purpose, unless by consent. Then as to the claws upon your feet before and behind, they are so short and tender, that one of our *Yahoos* would drive a dozen of yours before him. And therefore in recounting the numbers of those who have been killed in battle, I cannot but think that you have *said the thing which is not.*

---

[13] Gulliver alludes to a number of religious doctrines and practices disputed hotly by Christians since the Reformation. He refers specifically here to transubstantiation (the Catholic belief that the bread and wine in Communion become the body and blood of Jesus Christ), to the use of crucifixes and music in worship, and to the wearing of ecclesiastical robes.

I could not forbear shaking my head, and smiling a little at his ignorance. And being no stranger to the art of war, I gave him a description of cannons, culverins, muskets, carabines, pistols, bullets, powder, swords, bayonets, battles, sieges, retreats, attacks, undermines, countermines, bombardments, sea fights; ships sunk with a thousand men, twenty thousand killed on each side; dying groans, limbs flying in the air, smoke, noise, confusion, trampling to death under horses' feet; flight, pursuit, victory; fields strewed with carcases left for food to dogs, and wolves, and birds of prey; plundering, stripping, ravishing, burning and destroying. And to set forth the valour of my own dear countrymen, I assured him, that I had seen them blow up a hundred enemies at once in a siege, and as many in a ship, and beheld the dead bodies come down in pieces from the clouds, to the great diversion of the spectators.

I was going on to more particulars, when my master commanded me silence. He said, whoever understood the nature of *Yahoos* might easily believe it possible for so vile an animal to be capable of every action I had named, if their strength and cunning equalled their malice. But as my discourse had increased his abhorrence of the whole species, so he found it gave him a disturbance in his mind, to which he was wholly a stranger before. He thought his ears being used to such abominable words, might by degrees admit them with less detestation. That although he hated the *Yahoos* of this country, yet he no more blamed them for their odious qualities, than he did a *gnnayh* (a bird of prey) for its cruelty, or a sharp stone for cutting his hoof. But when a creature pretending to reason could be capable of such enormities, he dreaded lest the corruption of that faculty might be worse than brutality itself. He seemed therefore confident, that instead of reason, we were only possessed of some quality fitted to increase our natural vices; as the reflection from a troubled stream returns the image of an ill-shapen body, not only larger, but more distorted.

He added, that he had heard too much upon the subject of war, both in this, and some former discourses. There was another point which a little perplexed him at present. I had informed him, that some of our crew left their country on account of being ruined by *Law;* that I had already explained the meaning of the word; but he was at a loss how it should come to pass, that the law which was intended for every man's preservation, should be any man's ruin. Therefore he desired to be farther satisfied what I meant by law, and the dispensers thereof, according to the present practice in my own country; because he thought nature and reason were sufficient guides for a reasonable animal, as we pretended to be, in showing us what we ought to do, and what to avoid.

I assured his Honour, that law was a science wherein I had not much conversed, further than by employing advocates, in vain, upon some injustices that had been done me; however, I would give him all the satisfaction I was able.

I said, there was a society of men among us, bred up from their youth in the art of proving by words multiplied for the purpose, that white is black, and black is white, according as they are paid. To this society all the rest of the people are slaves. For example, if my neighbour hath a mind to my cow, he hires a lawyer to prove that he ought to have my cow from me. I must then hire another to defend my right, it being against all rules of law that any man should be allowed to speak for himself. Now in this case, I, who am the right owner, lie under two great disadvantages. First, my lawyer, being practised almost from his cradle in defending falsehood, is quite out of his element when he would be an advocate for justice, which as an office unnatural, he always attempts with great awkwardness, if not with ill-will. The second disadvantage is, that my lawyer must proceed with great caution, or else he will be reprimanded by the judges, and abhorred by his brethren, as one that would lessen the practice of the law. And therefore I have but two methods to preserve my cow. The first is, to gain over my adversary's lawyer with a double fee; who will then betray his client, by insinuating that he hath justice on his side. The second way is for my lawyer to make my cause appear as unjust as he can, by allowing the cow to belong to my adversary; and this, if it be skilfully done, will certainly bespeak the favour of the bench.

Now, your Honour is to know, that these judges are persons appointed to decide all controversies of property, as well as for the trial of criminals, and picked out from the most dexterous lawyers, who are grown old or lazy, and having been biassed all their lives against truth and equity, are under such a fatal necessity of favouring fraud, perjury, and oppression, that I have known several of them refuse a large bribe from the side where justice lay, rather than injure the faculty,[14] by doing any thing unbecoming their nature or their office.

It is a maxim among these lawyers, that whatever hath been done before, may legally be done again: and therefore they take special care to record all the decisions formerly made against common justice, and the general reason of mankind. These, under the name of *precedents,* they produce as authorities, to justify the most iniquitous opinions; and the judges never fail of directing accordingly.

In pleading, they studiously avoid entering into the merits of the cause; but are loud, violent, and tedious in dwelling upon all circumstances which are not to the purpose. For instance, in the case already mentioned: they never desire to know what claim or title my adversary hath to my cow; but whether the said cow were red or black; her horns long or short; whether the field I graze her in be round or square; whether she was milked at home or abroad; what diseases she is subject to, and the like; after which they consult precedents, adjourn the cause from time to time, and in ten, twenty, or thirty years, come to an issue.

It is likewise to be observed, that this society hath a peculiar cant and jargon of their own, that no other mortal can understand, and wherein all their laws are written, which they take special care to multiply; whereby they have wholly confounded the very essence of truth and falsehood, of right and wrong; so that it will take thirty years to decide whether the field left me by my ancestors for six generations belongs to me, or to a stranger three hundred miles off.

In the trial of persons accused for crimes against the state, the method is much more short and commendable: the judge first sends to sound the disposition of those in power, after which he can easily hang or save the criminal, strictly preserving all due forms of law.

Here my master interposing, said it was a pity, that creatures endowed with such prodigious abilities of mind as these lawyers, by the description I gave of them, must

---

[14] **faculty:** Profession.

certainly be, were not rather encouraged to be instructors of others in wisdom and knowledge. In answer to which, I assured his Honour, that in all points out of their own trade, they were usually the most ignorant and stupid generation among us, the most despicable in common conversation, avowed enemies to all knowledge and learning, and equally disposed to pervert the general reason of mankind in every other subject of discourse, as in that of their own profession.

CHAPTER 6. *A continuation of the state of* England. *The character of a first or chief minister of state in* European *courts.*

My master was yet wholly at a loss to understand what motives could incite this race of lawyers to perplex, disquiet, and weary themselves, and engage in a confederacy of injustice, merely for the sake of injuring their fellow-animals; neither could he comprehend what I meant in saying they did it for hire. Whereupon I was at much pains to describe to him the use of money, the materials it was made of, and the value of the metals; that when a *Yahoo* had got a great store of this precious substance, he was able to purchase whatever he had a mind to; the finest clothing, the noblest houses, great tracts of land, the most costly meats and drinks, and have his choice of the most beautiful females. Therefore since money alone was able to perform all these feats, our *Yahoos* thought they could never have enough of it to spend or to save, as they found themselves inclined from their natural bent either to profusion or avarice. That the rich man enjoyed the fruit of the poor man's labour, and the latter were a thousand to one in proportion to the former. That the bulk of our people were forced to live miserably, by labouring every day for small wages to make a few live plentifully. I enlarged myself much on these and many other particulars to the same purpose; but his Honour was still to seek,[15] for he went upon a supposition that all animals had a title to their share in the productions of the earth, and especially those who presided over the rest. Therefore he desired I would let him know, what these costly meats were, and how any of us happened to want them. Whereupon I enumerated as many sorts as came into my head, with the various methods of dressing them, which could not be done without sending vessels by sea to every part of the world, as well for liquors to drink, as for sauces, and innumerable other conveniences. I assured him, that this whole globe of earth must be at least three times gone round, before one of our better female *Yahoos* could get her breakfast, or a cup to put it in. He said, that must needs be a miserable country which cannot furnish food for its own inhabitants. But what he chiefly wondered at, was how such vast tracts of ground as I described should be wholly without fresh water, and the people put to the necessity of sending over the sea for drink. I replied, that England (the dear place of my nativity) was computed to produce three times the quantity of food, more than its inhabitants are able to consume, as well as liquors extracted from grain, or pressed out of the fruit of certain trees, which made excellent drink, and the same proportion in every other convenience of life. But, in order to feed the luxury and intemperance of the males, and the vanity of the females, we sent away the greatest part of our necessary things to other countries, from whence in return we brought

---

[15] **still to seek:** Still did not understand.

the materials of diseases, folly, and vice, to spend among ourselves. Hence it follows of necessity, that vast numbers of our people are compelled to seek their livelihood by begging, robbing, stealing, cheating, pimping, forswearing, flattering, suborning, forging, gaming, lying, fawning, hectoring, voting, scribbling, star-gazing, poisoning, whoring, canting, libelling, free-thinking, and the like occupations: every one of which terms, I was at much pains to make him understand.

That wine was not imported among us from foreign countries, to supply the want of water or other drinks, but because it was a sort of liquid which made us merry, by putting us out of our senses; diverted all melancholy thoughts, begat wild extravagant imaginations in the brain, raised our hopes, and banished our fears, suspended every office of reason for a time, and deprived us of the use of our limbs, till we fell into a profound sleep; although it must be confessed, that we always awaked sick and dispirited, and that the use of this liquor filled us with diseases, which made our lives uncomfortable and short.

But beside all this, the bulk of our people supported themselves by furnishing the necessities or conveniences of life to the rich, and to each other. For instance, when I am at home and dressed as I ought to be, I carry on my body the workmanship of an hundred tradesmen; the building and furniture of my house employ as many more, and five times the number to adorn my wife.

I was going on to tell him of another sort of people, who get their livelihood by attending the sick, having upon some occasions informed his Honour that many of my crew had died of diseases. But here it was with the utmost difficulty, that I brought him to apprehend what I meant. He could easily conceive, that a *Houyhnhnm* grew weak and heavy a few days before his death, or by some accident might hurt a limb. But that nature, who works all things to perfection, should suffer any pains to breed in our bodies, he thought impossible, and desired to know the reason of so unaccountable an evil. I told him, we fed on a thousand things which operated contrary to each other; that we eat when we were not hungry, and drank without the provocation of thirst; that we sat whole nights drinking strong liquors without eating a bit, which disposed us to sloth, inflamed our bodies, and precipitated or prevented digestion. That prostitute female *Yahoos* acquired a certain malady, which bred rottenness in the bones of those who fell into their embraces; that this and many other diseases were propagated from father to son, so that great numbers came into the world with complicated maladies upon them; that it would be endless to give him a catalogue of all diseases incident to human bodies; for they would not be fewer than five or six hundred, spread over every limb and joint; in short, every part, external and intestine, having diseases appropriated to each. To remedy which, there was a sort of people bred up among us, in the profession or pretence of curing the sick. And because I had some skill in the faculty, I would in gratitude to his Honour, let him know the whole mystery and method by which they proceed.

Their fundamental is, that all diseases arise from repletion, from whence they conclude, that a great evacuation of the body is necessary, either through the natural passage, or upwards at the mouth. Their next business is, from herbs, minerals, gums, oils, shells, salts, juices, seaweed, excrements, barks of trees, serpents, toads, frogs, spiders, dead men's flesh and bones, birds, beasts, and fishes, to form a composition for smell and taste the most abominable, nauseous, and detestable, they can possibly contrive, which the stomach immediately rejects with loathing; and this they call a vomit; or else from the same store-house, with some other poisonous additions, they command us to take in at the orifice above or below (just as the physician then happens to be disposed) a medicine equally annoying and disgustful to the bowels; which relaxing the belly, drives down all before it, and this they call a purge, or a clyster. For nature (as the physicians allege) having intended the superior anterior orifice only for the intromission of solids and liquids, and the inferior posterior for ejection, these artists ingeniously considering that in all diseases nature is forced out of her seat, therefore to replace her in it, the body must be treated in a manner directly contrary, by interchanging the use of each orifice; forcing solids and liquids in at the anus, and making evacuations at the mouth.

But, besides real diseases, we are subject to many that are only imaginary, for which the physicians have invented imaginary cures; these have their several names, and so have the drugs that are proper for them, and with these our female *Yahoos* are always infested.

One great excellency in this tribe is their skill at prognostics, wherein they seldom fail; their predictions in real diseases, when they rise to any degree of malignity, generally portending death, which is always in their power, when recovery is not: and therefore, upon any unexpected signs of amendment, after they have pronounced their sentence, rather than be accused as false prophets, they know how to approve[16] their sagacity to the world by a seasonable dose.

They are likewise of special use to husbands and wives, who are grown weary of their mates; to eldest sons, to great ministers of state, and often to princes.

I had formerly upon occasion discoursed with my master upon the nature of government in general, and particularly of our own excellent constitution, deservedly the wonder and envy of the whole world. But having here accidentally mentioned a minister of state, he commanded me some time after to inform him, what species of *Yahoo* I particularly meant by that appellation.

I told him, that a First or Chief Minister of State, who was the person I intended to describe, was a creature wholly exempt from joy and grief, love and hatred, pity and anger; at least made use of no other passions but a violent desire of wealth, power, and titles; that he applies his words to all uses, except to the indication of his mind; that he never tells a truth, but with an intent that you should take it for a lie; nor a lie, but with a design that you should take it for a truth; that those he speaks worst of behind their backs, are in the surest way of preferment; and whenever he begins to praise you to others or to yourself, you are from that day forlorn. The worst mark you can receive is a promise, especially when it is confirmed with an oath; after which every wise man retires, and gives over all hopes.

There are three methods by which a man may rise to be chief minister: the first is, by knowing how with prudence to dispose of a wife, a daughter, or a sister: the second, by betraying or undermining his predecessor: and the third is, by a furious zeal in public assemblies against the corruptions of the court. But a wise prince

---

[16] **approve:** Prove.

would rather choose to employ those who practise the last of these methods; because such zealots prove always the most obsequious and subservient to the will and passions of their master. That these ministers having all employments at their disposal, preserve themselves in power, by bribing the majority of a senate or great council; and at last, by an expedient called an Act of Indemnity[17] (whereof I described the nature to him) they secure themselves from after-reckonings, and retire from the public, laden with the spoils of the nation.

The palace of a chief minister is a seminary to breed up others in his own trade: the pages, lackeys, and porters, by imitating their master, become ministers of state in their several districts, and learn to excel in the three principal ingredients, of insolence, lying, and bribery. Accordingly, they have a subaltern court paid to them by persons of the best rank, and sometimes by the force of dexterity and impudence, arrive through several gradations to be successors to their lord.

He is usually governed by a decayed wench, or favourite footman, who are the tunnels through which all graces are conveyed, and may properly be called, in the last resort, the governors of the kingdom.

One day in discourse my master, having heard me mention the nobility of my country, was pleased to make me a compliment which I could not pretend to deserve: that he was sure I must have been born of some noble family, because I far exceeded in shape, colour, and cleanliness, all the *Yahoos* of his nation, although I seemed to fail in strength and agility, which must be imputed to my different way of living from those other brutes; and besides, I was not only endowed with the faculty of speech, but likewise with some rudiments of reason, to a degree, that with all his acquaintance I passed for a prodigy.

He made me observe, that among the *Houyhnhnms,* the white, the sorrel, and the iron-gray, were not so exactly shaped as the bay, the dapple-gray, and the black; nor born with equal talents of the mind, or a capacity to improve them; and therefore continued always in the condition of servants, without ever aspiring to match out of their own race, which in that country would be reckoned monstrous and unnatural.

I made his Honour my most humble acknowledgments for the good opinion he was pleased to conceive of me; but assured him at the same time, that my birth was of the lower sort, having been born of plain honest parents, who were just able to give me a tolerable education; that nobility among us was altogether a different thing from the idea he had of it; that our young noblemen are bred from their childhood in idleness and luxury; that as soon as years will permit, they consume their vigour, and contract odious diseases among lewd females; and when their fortunes are almost ruined, they marry some woman of mean birth, disagreeable person, and unsound constitution, merely for the sake of money, whom they hate and despise. That the productions of such marriages are generally scrofulous, ricketty, or deformed children; by which means the family seldom continues above three generations, unless the wife takes care to provide a healthy father among her neighbours or domestics, in order to improve and continue the breed. That a weak diseased

---

[17] **Act of Indemnity:** Legislation providing immunity to statesmen who have unknowingly violated a law.

body, a meagre countenance, and sallow complexion, are the true marks of noble blood; and a healthy robust appearance is so disgraceful in a man of quality, that the world concludes his real father to have been a groom or a coachman. The imperfections of his mind run parallel with those of his body, being a composition of spleen, dullness, ignorance, caprice, sensuality, and pride.

Without the consent of this illustrious body, no law can be enacted, repealed, or altered; and these have the decision of all our possessions without appeal.

CHAPTER 7. *The Author's great love of his native country. His master's observations upon the constitution and administration of* England, *as described by the Author, with parallel cases and comparisons. His master's observations upon human nature.*

The reader may be disposed to wonder how I could prevail on myself to give so free a representation of my own species, among a race of mortals who are already too apt to conceive the vilest opinion of human kind, from that entire congruity betwixt me and their *Yahoos.* But I must freely confess, that the many virtues of those excellent quadrupeds placed in opposite view to human corruptions, had so far opened my eyes and enlarged my understanding, that I began to view the actions and passions of man in a very different light, and to think the honour of my own kind not worth managing; which, besides, it was impossible for me to do before a person of so acute a judgment as my master, who daily convinced me of a thousand faults in myself, whereof I had not the least perception before, and which with us would never be numbered even among human infirmities. I had likewise learned from his example an utter detestation of all falsehood or disguise; and truth appeared so amiable to me, that I determined upon sacrificing every thing to it.

Let me deal so candidly with the reader, as to confess, that there was yet a much stronger motive for the freedom I took in my representation of things. I had not been a year in this country, before I contracted such a love and veneration for the inhabitants, that I entered on a firm resolution never to return to human kind, but to pass the rest of my life among these admirable *Houyhnhnms* in the contemplation and practice of every virtue; where I could have no example or incitement to vice. But it was decreed by fortune, my perpetual enemy, that so great a felicity should not fall to my share. However, it is now some comfort to reflect, that in what I said of my countrymen, I extenuated their faults as much as I durst before so strict an examiner, and upon every article gave as favourable a turn as the matter would bear. For, indeed, who is there alive that will not be swayed by his bias and partiality to the place of his birth?

I have related the substance of several conversations I had with my master, during the greatest part of the time I had the honour to be in his service, but have indeed for brevity sake omitted much more than is here set down.

When I had answered all his questions, and his curiosity seemed to be fully satisfied; he sent for me one morning early, and commanding me to sit down at some distance (an honour which he had never before conferred upon me), he said, he had been very seriously considering my whole story, as far as it related both to myself and my country; that he looked upon us as a sort of animals to whose share, by what accident he could not conjecture, some small pittance of reason had fallen, whereof we made no other use than by its assistance to aggravate our natural corruptions, and to acquire new ones, which nature had not given us. That we disarmed ourselves of the few abilities she had bestowed, had been very successful in multiplying our original wants, and seemed to spend our whole lives in vain endeavours to supply them by our own inventions. That as to myself, was manifest I had neither the strength or agility of a common *Yahoo;* that I walked infirmly on my hinder feet; had found out a contrivance to make my claws of no use or defence, and to remove the hair from my chin, which was intended as a shelter from the sun and the weather. Lastly, that I could neither run with speed, nor climb trees like my brethren (as he called them) the *Yahoos* in this country.

That our institutions of government and law were plainly owing to our gross defects in reason, and by consequence, in virtue; because reason alone is sufficient to govern a rational creature; which was therefore a character we had no pretence to challenge, even from the account I had given of my own people; although he manifestly perceived, that in order to favour them, I had concealed many particulars, and often *said the thing which was not.*

He was the more confirmed in this opinion, because he observed, that as I agreed in every feature of my body with other *Yahoos,* except where it was to my real disadvantage in point of strength, speed and activity, the shortness of my claws, and some other particulars where nature had no part; so from the representation I had given him of our lives, our manners, and our actions, he found as near a resemblance in the disposition of our minds. He said the *Yahoos* were known to hate one another more than they did any different species of animals; and the reason usually assigned was the odiousness of their own shapes, which all could see in the rest, but not in themselves. He had therefore begun to think it not unwise in us to cover our bodies, and by that invention conceal many of our own deformities from each other, which would else be hardly supportable. But he now found he had been mistaken, and that the dissensions of those brutes in his country were owing to the same cause with ours, as I had described them. For if (said he), you throw among five *Yahoos* as much food as would be sufficient for fifty, they will, instead of eating peaceably, fall together by the ears, each single one impatient to have all to itself; and therefore a servant was usually employed to stand by while they were feeding abroad, and those kept at home were tied at a distance from each other: that if a cow died of age or accident, before a *Houyhnhnm* could secure it for his own *Yahoos,* those in the neighbourhood would come in herds to seize it, and then would ensue such a battle as I had described, with terrible wounds made by their claws on both sides, although they seldom were able to kill one another, for want of such convenient instruments of death as we had invented. At other times the like battles have been fought between the *Yahoos* of several neighbourhoods without any visible cause; those of one district watching all opportunities to surprise the next before they are prepared. But if they find their project hath miscarried, they return home, and, for want of enemies, engage in what I call a civil war among themselves.

That in some fields of his country, there are certain shining stones of several colours, whereof the *Yahoos* are violently fond, and when part of these stones is fixed in the earth, as it sometimes happeneth, they will dig with their claws for whole days to get them out, then carry them away, and hide them by heaps in their kennels; but still looking round with great caution, for fear their comrades should find out their treasure. My master said, he could never discover the reason of this unnatural appetite, or how these stones could be of any use to a *Yahoo;* but now he believed it might proceed from the same principle of avarice which I had ascribed to mankind: that he had once, by way of experiment, privately removed a heap of these stones from the place where one of his *Yahoos* had buried it: whereupon, the sordid animal missing his treasure, by his loud lamenting brought the whole herd to the place, there miserably howled, then fell to biting and tearing the rest, began to pine away, would neither eat, nor sleep, nor work, till he ordered a servant privately to convey the stones into the same hole, and hide them as before; which when his *Yahoo* had found, he presently recovered his spirits and good humour, but took good care to remove them to a better hiding place, and hath ever since been a very serviceable brute.

My master farther assured me, which I also observed myself, that in the fields where the shining stones abound, the fiercest and most frequent battles are fought, occasioned by perpetual inroads of the neighbouring *Yahoos.*

He said, it was common when two *Yahoos* discovered such a stone in a field, and were contending which of them should be the proprietor, a third would take the advantage, and carry it away from them both; which my master would needs contend to have some kind of resemblance with our suits at law; wherein I thought it for our credit not to undeceive him; since the decision he mentioned was much more equitable than many decrees among us; because the plaintiff and defendant there lost nothing beside the stone they contended for, whereas our courts of equity would never have dismissed the cause while either of them had any thing left.

My master continuing his discourse, said, there was nothing that rendered the *Yahoos* more odious than their undistinguishing appetite to devour every thing that came in their way, whether herbs, roots, berries, the corrupted flesh of animals, or all mingled together: and it was peculiar in their temper, that they were fonder of what they could get by rapine or stealth at a greater distance, than much better food provided for them at home. If their prey held out, they would eat till they were ready to burst, after which nature had pointed out to them a certain root that gave them a general evacuation.

There was also another kind of root very juicy, but somewhat rare and difficult to be found, which the *Yahoos* sought for with much eagerness, and would suck it with great delight; and it produced in them the same effects that wine hath upon us. It would make them sometimes hug, and sometimes tear one another; they would howl and grin, and chatter, and reel, and tumble, and then fall asleep in the mud.

I did indeed observe, that the *Yahoos* were the only animals in this country subject to any diseases; which, however, were much fewer than horses have among us, and contracted not by any ill treatment they meet with, but by the nastiness and greediness of that sordid brute. Neither has their language any more than a general appellation for those maladies, which is borrowed from the name of the beast, and called *Hnea-Yahoo,* or *Yahoo's evil,* and the cure prescribed is a mixture of their own dung and urine forcibly put down the *Yahoo's* throat. This I have since often known to have been taken with success, and do freely recommend it to my countrymen, for the public good, as an admirable specific against all diseases produced by repletion.

As to learning, government, arts, manufactures, and the like, my master confessed he could find little or no resemblance between the *Yahoos* of that country and those in ours. For he only meant to observe what parity there was in our natures. He had heard indeed some curious *Houyhnhnms* observe, that in most herds there was a sort of ruling *Yahoo* (as among us there is generally some leading or principal stag in a pack), who was always more deformed in body, and mischievous in disposition, than any of the rest. That this leader had usually a favourite as like himself as he could get, whose employment was to lick his master's feet and posteriors, and drive the female *Yahoos* to his kennel; for which he was now and then rewarded with a piece of ass's flesh. This favourite is hated by the whole herd, and therefore to protect himself, keeps always near the person of his leader. He usually continues in office till a worse can be found; but the very moment he is discarded, his successor, at the head of all the *Yahoos* in that district, young and old, male and female, come in a body, and discharge their excrements upon him from head to foot. But how far this might be applicable to our courts and favourites, and ministers of state, my master said I could best determine.

I durst make no return to this malicious insinuation, which debased human understanding below the sagacity of a common hound, who has judgment enough to distinguish and follow the cry of the ablest dog in the pack, without being ever mistaken.

My master told me, there were some qualities remarkable in the *Yahoos,* which he had not observed me to mention, or at least very slightly, in the accounts I had given him of human kind. He said, those animals, like other brutes, had their females in common; but in this they differed, that the she-*Yahoo* would admit the male while she was pregnant; and that the hes would quarrel and fight with the females as fiercely as with each other. Both which practices were such degrees of infamous brutality, that no other sensitive creature ever arrived at.

Another thing he wondered at in the *Yahoos,* was their strange disposition to nastiness and dirt, whereas there appears to be a natural love of cleanliness in all other animals. As to the two former accusations, I was glad to let them pass without any reply, because I had not a word to offer upon them in defence of my species, which otherwise I certainly had done from my own inclinations. But I could have easily vindicated human kind from the imputation of singularity upon the last article, if there had been any swine in that country (as unluckily for me there were not), which although it may be a sweeter quadruped than a *Yahoo,* cannot I humbly conceive in justice pretend to more cleanliness; and so his Honour himself must have owned, if he had seen their filthy way of feeding, and their custom of wallowing and sleeping in the mud.

My master likewise mentioned another quality which his servants had discovered in several *Yahoos,* and to him was wholly unaccountable. He said, a fancy would sometimes take a *Yahoo* to retire into a corner, to lie down and howl, and groan, and spurn away all that came near him, although he were young and fat, wanted neither food nor water; nor did the servants imagine what could possibly ail him. And the only remedy they found was to set him to hard work, after which he would infallibly come to himself. To this I was silent out of partiality to my own kind; yet here I could plainly discover the true seeds of spleen, which only seizeth on the lazy, the luxurious, and the rich; who, if they were forced to undergo the same regimen, I would undertake for the cure.

His Honour had further observed, that a female *Yahoo* would often stand behind a bank or bush, to gaze on the young males passing by, and then appear, and hide, using many antic gestures and grimaces, at which time it was observed, that she had a most offensive smell; and when any of the males advanced, would slowly retire, looking often back, and with a counterfeit show of fear, run off into some convenient place where she knew the male would follow her.

At other times if a female stranger came among them, three or four of her own sex would get about her, and stare and chatter, and grin, and smell her all over; and then turn off with gestures that seemed to express contempt and disdain.

Perhaps my master might refine a little in these speculations, which he had drawn from what he observed himself, or had been told him by others; however, I could not reflect without some amazement, and much sorrow, that the rudiments of lewdness, coquetry, censure, and scandal, should have place by instinct in womankind.

I expected every moment, that my master would accuse the *Yahoos* of those unnatural appetites in both sexes, so common among us. But nature, it seems, hath not been so expert a school-mistress; and these politer pleasures are entirely the productions of art and reason, on our side of the globe.

CHAPTER 8. *The Author relates several particulars of the* Yahoos. *The great virtues of the* Houyhnhnms. *The education and exercise of their youth. Their general assembly.*

As I ought to have understood human nature much better than I supposed it possible for my master to do, so it was easy to apply the character he gave of the *Yahoos* to myself and my countrymen; and I believed I could yet make farther discoveries from my own observation. I therefore often begged his favour to let me go among the herds of *Yahoos* in the neighbourhood, to which he always very graciously consented, being perfectly convinced that the hatred I bore those brutes would never suffer me to be corrupted by them; and his Honour ordered one of his servants, a strong sorrel nag, very honest and good-natured, to be my guard, without whose protection I durst not undertake such adventures. For I have already told the reader how much I was pestered by those odious animals upon my first arrival. And I afterwards failed very narrowly three or four times of falling into their clutches, when I happened to stray at any distance without my hanger. And I have reason to believe they had some imagination that I was of their own species, which I often assisted myself, by stripping up my sleeves, and showing my naked arms and breast in their sight, when my protector was with me. At which times they would approach as near as they durst, and imitate my actions after the manner of monkeys, but ever with great signs of hatred; as a tame jackdaw with cap and stockings is always persecuted by the wild ones, when he happens to be got among them.

They are prodigiously nimble from their infancy; however, I once caught a young male of three years old, and endeavoured by all marks of tenderness to make

it quiet; but the little imp fell a squalling, and scratching, and biting with such violence, that I was forced to let it go; and it was high time, for a whole troop of old ones
came about us at the noise, but finding the cub was safe (for away it ran), and my
sorrel nag being by, they durst not venture near us. I observed the young animal's
flesh to smell very rank, and the stink was somewhat between a weasel and a fox, but
much more disagreeable. I forgot another circumstance (and perhaps I might have
the reader's pardon if it were wholly omitted), that while I held the odious vermin in
my hands, it voided its filthy excrements of a yellow liquid substance, all over my
clothes; but by good fortune there was a small brook hard by, where I washed myself
as clean as I could; although I durst not come into my master's presence, until I were
sufficiently aired.

By what I could discover, the *Yahoos* appear to be the most unteachable of all
animals, their capacities never reaching higher than to draw or carry burdens. Yet I
am of opinion, this defect ariseth chiefly from a perverse, restive disposition. For
they are cunning, malicious, treacherous, and revengeful. They are strong and hardy,
but of a cowardly spirit, and by consequence, insolent, abject, and cruel. It is
observed, that the red-haired of both sexes are more libidinous and mischievous
than the rest, whom yet they much exceed in strength and activity.

The *Houyhnhnms* keep the *Yahoos* for present use in huts not far from the house;
but the rest are sent abroad to certain fields, where they dig up roots, eat several kinds
of herbs, and search about for carrion, or sometimes catch weasels and *luhimuhs* (a
sort of wild rat), which they greedily devour. Nature hath taught them to dig deep
holes with their nails on the side of a rising ground, wherein they lie by themselves;
only the kennels of the females are larger, sufficient to hold two or three cubs.

They swim from their infancy like frogs, and are able to continue long under
water, where they often take fish, which the females carry home to their young. And
upon this occasion, I hope the reader will pardon my relating an odd adventure.

Being one day abroad with my protector the sorrel nag, and the weather exceeding hot, I entreated him to let me bathe in a river that was near. He consented, and I
immediately stripped myself stark naked, and went down softly into the stream. It
happened that a young female *Yahoo*, standing behind a bank, saw the whole proceeding, and inflamed by desire, as the nag and I conjectured, came running with all
speed, and leaped into the water, within five yards of the place where I bathed. I was
never in my life so terribly frighted; the nag was grazing at some distance, not suspecting any harm. She embraced me after a most fulsome manner; I roared as loud
as I could, and the nag came galloping towards me, whereupon she quitted her
grasp, with the utmost reluctancy, and leaped upon the opposite bank, where she
stood gazing and howling all the time I was putting on my clothes.

This was matter of diversion to my master and his family, as well as of mortification to myself. For now I could no longer deny that I was a real *Yahoo* in every limb
and feature, since the females had a natural propensity to me, as one of their own
species. Neither was the hair of this brute of a red colour (which might have been
some excuse for an appetite a little irregular), but black as a sloe, and her countenance did not make an appearance altogether so hideous as the rest of the kind; for, I
think, she could not be above eleven years old.

Having lived three years in this country, the reader I suppose will expect, that I should, like other travellers, give him some account of the manners and customs of its inhabitants, which it was indeed my principal study to learn.

As these noble *Houyhnhnms* are endowed by nature with a general disposition to all virtues, and have no conceptions or ideas of what is evil in a rational creature, so their grand maxim is, to cultivate reason, and to be wholly governed by it. Neither is reason among them a point problematical as with us, where men can argue with plausibility on both sides of the question; but strikes you with immediate conviction; as it must needs do where it is not mingled, obscured, or discoloured by passion and interest. I remember it was with extreme difficulty that I could bring my master to understand the meaning of the word *opinion,* or how a point could be disputable; because reason taught us to affirm or deny only where we are certain; and beyond our knowledge we cannot do either. So that controversies, wranglings, disputes, and positiveness in false or dubious propositions, are evils unknown among the *Houyhnhnms.* In the like manner when I used to explain to him our several systems of natural philosophy, he would laugh that a creature pretending to reason, should value itself upon the knowledge of other people's conjectures, and in things, where that knowledge, if it were certain, could be of no use. Wherein he agreed entirely with the sentiments of Socrates, as Plato delivers them; which I mention as the highest honour I can do that prince of philosophers. I have often since reflected what destruction such a doctrine would make in the libraries of Europe; and how many paths to fame would be then shut up in the learned world.

Friendship and benevolence are the two principal virtues among the *Houyhnhnms;* and these not confined to particular objects, but universal to the whole race. For a stranger from the remotest part is equally treated with the nearest neighbour, and wherever he goes, looks upon himself as at home. They preserve decency and civility in the highest degrees, but are altogether ignorant of ceremony. They have no fondness for their colts or foals, but the care they take in educating them proceeds entirely from the dictates of reason. And I observed my master to show the same affection to his neighbour's issue that he had for his own. They will have it that nature teaches them to love the whole species, and it is reason only that maketh a distinction of persons, where there is a superior degree of virtue.

When the matron *Houyhnhnms* have produced one of each sex, they no longer accompany with their consorts, except they lose one of their issue by some casualty, which very seldom happens; but in such a case they meet again, or when the like accident befalls a person whose wife is past bearing, some other couple bestow him one of their own colts, and then go together again till the mother is pregnant. This caution is necessary to prevent the country from being overburthened with numbers. But the race of inferior *Houyhnhnms* bred up to be servants is not so strictly limited upon this article; these are allowed to produce three of each sex, to be domestics in the noble families.

In their marriages they are exactly careful to choose such colours as will not make any disagreeable mixture in the breed. Strength is chiefly valued in the male, and comeliness in the female; not upon the account of love, but to preserve the race from degenerating; for where a female happens to excel in strength, a consort is chosen with regard to comeliness. Courtship, love, presents, jointures, settlements, have no place in their thoughts; or terms whereby to express them in their language. The young couple meet and are joined, merely because it is the determination of their parents and friends: it is what they see done every day, and they look upon it as one of the necessary actions of a reasonable being. But the violation of marriage, or any other unchastity, was never heard of: and the married pair pass their lives with the same friendship, and mutual benevolence that they bear to all others of the same species, who come in their way; without jealousy, fondness, quarrelling, or discontent.

In educating the youth of both sexes, their method is admirable, and highly deserves our imitation. These are not suffered to taste a grain of oats, except upon certain days, till eighteen years old; nor milk, but very rarely; and in summer they graze two hours in the morning, and as many in the evening, which their parents likewise observe; but the servants are not allowed above half that time, and a great part of their grass is brought home, which they eat at the most convenient hours, when they can be best spared from work.

Temperance, industry, exercise, and cleanliness, are the lessons equally enjoined to the young ones of both sexes: and my master thought it monstrous in us to give the females a different kind of education from the males, except in some articles of domestic management; whereby as he truly observed, one half of our natives were good for nothing but bringing children into the world: and to trust the care of our children to such useless animals, he said, was yet a greater instance of brutality.

But the *Houyhnhnms* train up their youth to strength, speed, and hardiness, by exercising them in running races up and down steep hills, and over hard stony grounds; and when they are all in a sweat, they are ordered to leap over head and ears into a pond or a river. Four times a year the youth of a certain district meet to show their proficiency in running and leaping, and other feats of strength and agility; where the victor is rewarded with a song made in his or her praise. On this festival the servants drive a herd of *Yahoos* into the field, laden with hay, and oats, and milk, for a repast to the *Houyhnhnms;* after which, these brutes are immediately driven back again, for fear of being noisome to the assembly.

Every fourth year, at the vernal equinox, there is a representative council of the whole nation, which meets in a plain about twenty miles from our house, and continues about five or six days. Here they enquire into the state and condition of the several districts; whether they abound or be deficient in hay or oats, or cows or *Yahoos*. And wherever there is any want (which is but seldom), it is immediately supplied by unanimous consent and contribution. Here likewise the regulation of children is settled: as for instance, if a *Houyhnhnm* hath two males, he changeth one of them with another that hath two females; and when a child hath been lost by any casualty, where the mother is past breeding, it is determined what family in the district shall breed another to supply the loss.

CHAPTER 9. *A grand debate at the general assembly of the* Houyhnhnms, *and how it was determined. The learning of the* Houyhnhnms. *Their buildings. Their manner of burials. The defectiveness of their language.*

One of these grand assemblies was held in my time, about three months before my departure, whither my master went as the representative of our district. In this council was resumed their old debate, and indeed, the only debate which ever happened in that country; whereof my master after his return gave me a very particular account.

The question to be debated was, whether the *Yahoos* should be exterminated from the face of the earth. One of the members for the affirmative offered several arguments of great strength and weight, alleging, that as the *Yahoos* were the most filthy, noisome, and deformed animal which nature ever produced, so they were the most restive and indocible, mischievous and malicious: they would privately suck the teats of the *Houyhnhnms'* cows, kill and devour their cats, trample down their oats and grass, if they were not continually watched, and commit a thousand other extravagancies. He took notice of a general tradition, that *Yahoos* had not been always in that country; but, that many ages ago, two of these brutes appeared together upon a mountain; whether produced by the heat of the sun upon corrupted mud and slime, or from the ooze and froth of the sea, was never known. That these *Yahoos* engendered, and their brood in a short time grew so numerous as to over-run and infest the whole nation. That the *Houyhnhnms* to get rid of this evil, made a general hunting, and at last enclosed the whole herd; and destroying the elder, every *Houyhnhnm* kept two young ones in a kennel, and brought them to such a degree of tameness, as an animal so savage by nature can be capable of acquiring; using them for draught and carriage. That there seemed to be much truth in this tradition, and that those creatures could not be *Ylnhniamshy* (or *aborigines* of the land), because of the violent hatred the *Houyhnhnms,* as well as all other animals, bore them; which although their evil disposition sufficiently deserved, could never have arrived at so high a degree, if they had been aborigines, or else they would have long since been rooted out. That the inhabitants taking a fancy to use the service of the *Yahoos,* had very imprudently neglected to cultivate the breed of asses, which were a comely animal, easily kept, more tame and orderly, without any offensive smell, strong enough for labour, although they yield to the other in agility of body; and if their braying be no agreeable sound, it is far preferable to the horrible howlings of the *Yahoos.*

Several others declared their sentiments to the same purpose, when my master proposed an expedient to the assembly, whereof he had indeed borrowed the hint from me. He approved of the tradition mentioned by the honourable member, who spoke before, and affirmed, that the two *Yahoos* said to be first seen among them, had been driven thither over the sea; that coming to land, and being forsaken by their companions, they retired to the mountains, and degenerating by degrees, became in process of time, much more savage than those of their own species in the country from whence these two originals came. The reason of this assertion was, that he had now in his possession a certain wonderful *Yahoo* (meaning myself), which most of them had heard of, and many of them had seen. He then related to them, how he first found me; that my body was all covered with an artificial composure of the skins and hairs of other animals; that I spoke in a language of my own, and had thoroughly learned theirs: that I had related to him the accidents which brought me thither: that when he saw me without my covering, I was an exact *Yahoo* in every part, only of a whiter colour, less hairy, and with shorter claws. He added, how I had endeavoured to persuade him, that in my own and other countries the *Yahoos* acted as the governing, rational animal, and held the *Houyhnhnms* in servitude: that he observed in me all the qualities of a *Yahoo,* only a little more civilized by some tincture of reason, which however was in a degree as far inferior to the *Houyhnhnm* race, as the *Yahoos* of their country were to me: that, among other things, I mentioned a custom we had of castrating *Houyhnhnms* when they were young, in order to render them tame; that the operation was easy and safe; that it was no shame to learn wisdom from brutes, as industry is taught by the ant, and building by the swallow. (For so I translate the word *lyhannh,* although it be a much larger fowl.) That this invention might be practised upon the younger *Yahoos* here, which, besides rendering them tractable and fitter for use, would in an age put an end to the whole species without destroying life. That in the mean time the *Houyhnhnms* should be exhorted to cultivate the breed of asses, which, as they are in all respects more valuable brutes, so they have this advantage, to be fit for service at five years old, which the others are not till twelve.

This was all my master thought fit to tell me at that time, of what passed in the grand council. But he was pleased to conceal one particular, which related personally to myself, whereof I soon felt the unhappy effect, as the reader will know in its proper place, and from whence I date all the succeeding misfortunes of my life.

The *Houyhnhnms* have no letters, and consequently their knowledge is all traditional. But there happening few events of any moment among a people so well united, naturally disposed to every virtue, wholly governed by reason, and cut off from all commerce with other nations, the historical part is easily preserved without burthening their memories. I have already observed, that they are subject to no diseases, and therefore can have no need of physicians. However, they have excellent medicines composed of herbs, to cure accidental bruises and cuts in the pastern or frog of the foot by sharp stones, as well as other maims and hurts in the several parts of the body.

They calculate the year by the revolution of the sun and moon, but use no subdivision into weeks. They are well enough acquainted with the motions of those two luminaries, and understand the nature of eclipses; and this is the utmost progress of their astronomy.

In poetry they must be allowed to excel all other mortals; wherein the justness of their similes, and the minuteness, as well as exactness of their descriptions, are indeed inimitable. Their verses abound very much in both of these, and usually contain either some exalted notions of friendship and benevolence, or the praises of those who were victors in races, and other bodily exercises. Their buildings, although very rude and simple, are not inconvenient, but well contrived to defend them from all injuries of cold and heat. They have a kind of tree, which at forty years old loosens in the root, and falls with the first storm: It grows very straight, and being pointed like stakes with a sharp stone (for the *Houyhnhnms* know not the use of iron), they stick them erect in the ground about ten inches asunder, and then weave in oat-straw, or sometimes wattles betwixt them. The roof is made after the same manner, and so are the doors.

The *Houyhnhnms* use the hollow part between the pastern and the hoof of their fore-feet, as we do our hands, and this with greater dexterity than I could at first imagine. I have seen a white mare of our family thread a needle (which I lent her on purpose) with that joint. They milk their cows, reap their oats, and do all the work which requires hands, in the same manner. They have a kind of hard flints, which by grinding against other stones, they form into instruments, that serve instead of wedges, axes, and hammers. With tools made of these flints, they likewise cut their hay, and reap their oats, which there groweth naturally in several fields: The *Yahoos* draw home the sheaves in carriages, and the servants tread them in certain covered huts, to get out the grain, which is kept in stores. They make a rude kind of earthen and wooden vessels, and bake the former in the sun.

If they can avoid casualties, they die only of old age, and are buried in the obscurest places that can be found, their friends and relations expressing neither joy nor grief at their departure; nor does the dying person discover the least regret that he is leaving the world, any more than if he were upon returning home from a visit to one of his neighbours. I remember my master having once made an appointment with a friend and his family to come to his house upon some affair of importance; on the day fixed, the mistress and her two children came very late; she made two excuses, first for her husband, who, as she said, happened that very morning to *shnuwnh*. The word is strongly expressive in their language, but not easily rendered into English; it signifies, *to retire to his first mother*. Her excuse for not coming sooner was, that her husband dying late in the morning, she was a good while consulting her servants about a convenient place where his body should be laid; and I observed she behaved herself at our house as cheerfully as the rest. She died about three months after.

They live generally to seventy or seventy-five years, very seldom to fourscore: some weeks before their death they feel a gradual decay, but without pain. During this time they are much visited by their friends, because they cannot go abroad with their usual ease and satisfaction. However, about ten days before their death, which they seldom fail in computing, they return the visits that have been made them by those who are nearest in the neighbourhood, being carried in a convenient sledge drawn by *Yahoos;* which vehicle they use, not only upon this occasion, but when they grow old, upon long journeys, or when they are lamed by any accident. And therefore when the dying *Houyhnhnms* return those visits, they take a solemn leave of their friends, as if they were going to some remote part of the country, where they designed to pass the rest of their lives.

I know not whether it may be worth observing, that the *Houyhnhnms* have no word in their language to express any thing that is evil, except what they borrow from the deformities or ill qualities of the *Yahoos*. Thus they denote the folly of a servant, an omission of a child, a stone that cuts their feet, a continuance of foul or unseasonable weather, and the like, by adding to each the epithet of *Yahoo*. For instance, *Hhnm Yahoo, Whnaholm Yahoo, Ynlhmndwihlma Yahoo,* and an ill-contrived house *Ynholmhnmrohlnw Yahoo*.

I could with great pleasure enlarge further upon the manners and virtues of this excellent people; but intending in a short time to publish a volume by itself expressly upon that subject, I refer the reader thither. And in the mean time, proceed to relate my own sad catastrophe.

CHAPTER 10. *The Author's economy, and happy life among the* Houyhnhnms. *His great improvement in virtue, by conversing with them. Their conversations. The Author has notice given him by his master that he must depart from the country. He falls into a swoon for grief, but submits. He contrives and finishes a canoe, by the help of a fellow-servant, and puts to sea at a venture.*

I had settled my little economy to my own heart's content. My master had ordered a room to be made for me after their manner, about six yards from the house; the sides and floors of which I plastered with clay, and covered with rush-mats of my own contriving; I had beaten hemp, which there grows wild, and made of it a sort of ticking: this I filled with the feathers of several birds I had taken with springes made of *Yahoos'* hairs, and were excellent food. I had worked two chairs with my knife, the sorrel nag helping me in the grosser and more laborious part. When my clothes were worn to rags, I made myself others with the skins of rabbits, and a certain beautiful animal about the same size, called *nnuhnoh,* the skin of which is covered with a fine down. Of these I likewise made very tolerable stockings. I soled my shoes with wood which I cut from a tree, and fitted to the upper leather, and when this was worn out, I supplied it with the skins of *Yahoos* dried in the sun. I often got honey out of hollow trees, which I mingled with water, or eat with my bread. No man could more verify the truth of these two maxims, *That nature is very easily satisfied;* and *That necessity is the mother of invention.* I enjoyed perfect health of body, and tranquillity of mind; I did not feel the treachery of inconstancy of a friend, nor the injuries of a secret or open enemy. I had no occasion of bribing, flattering or pimping, to procure the favour of any great man or of his minion. I wanted no fence against fraud or oppression; here was neither physician to destroy my body, nor lawyer to ruin my fortune; no informer to watch my words and actions, or forge accusations against me for hire: here were no gibers, censurers, backbiters, pickpockets, highwaymen, house-breakers, attorneys, bawds, buffoons, gamesters, politicians, wits, splenetics, tedious talkers, controvertists, ravishers, murderers, robbers, virtuosos; no leaders or followers of party and faction; no encouragers to vice, by seducement or examples; no dungeon, axes, gibbets, whipping-posts, or pillories; no cheating shopkeepers or mechanics; no pride, vanity, or affectation; no fops, bullies, drunkards, strolling whores, or poxes; no ranting, lewd, expensive wives; no stupid, proud pedants; no importunate, overbearing, quarrelsome, noisy, roaring, empty, conceited, swearing companions; no scoundrels, raised from the dust for the sake of their vices, or nobility thrown into it on account of their virtues; no lords, fiddlers, judges, or dancing-masters.

I had the favour of being admitted to several *Houyhnhnms,* who came to visit or dine with my master; where his Honour graciously suffered me to wait in the room, and listen to their discourse. Both he and his company would often descend to ask me questions, and receive my answers. I had also sometimes the honour of attending my master in his visits to others. I never presumed to speak, except in answer to a question; and then I did it with inward regret, because it was a loss of so much time for improving myself: but I was infinitely delighted with the station of an humble auditor in such conversations, where nothing passed but what was useful, expressed in the fewest and most significant words; where (as I have already said) the greatest decency was observed, without the least degree of ceremony; where no person spoke without being pleased himself, and pleasing his companions; where there was no interruption, tediousness, heat, or difference of sentiments. They have a notion, that when people are met together, a short silence doth much improve conversation: this I found to be true; for during those little intermissions of talk, new ideas would arise in their thoughts, which very much enlivened the discourse. Their subjects are generally on friendship and benevolence, or order and economy; sometimes upon the visible operations of nature, or ancient traditions; upon the bounds and limits of virtue; upon the unerring rules of reason, or upon some determinations to be taken at the next great assembly; and often upon the various excellencies of poetry. I may add, without vanity, that my presence often gave them sufficient matter for discourse, because it afforded my master an occasion of letting his friends into the history of me and my country, upon which they were all pleased to descant in a manner not very advantageous to human kind; and for that reason I shall not repeat what they said: only I may be allowed to observe, that his Honour, to my great admiration, appeared to understand the nature of *Yahoos* much better than myself. He went through all our vices and follies, and discovered many which I had never mentioned to him, by only supposing what qualities a *Yahoo* of their country, with a small proportion of reason, might be capable of exerting; and concluded, with too much probability, how vile as well as miserable such a creature must be.

I freely confess, that all the little knowledge I have of any value, was acquired by the lectures I received from my master, and from hearing the discourses of him and his friends; to which I should be prouder to listen, than to dictate to the greatest and wisest assembly in Europe. I admired the strength, comeliness, and speed of the inhabitants; and such a constellation of virtues in such amiable persons produced in me the highest veneration. At first, indeed, I did not feel that natural awe which the *Yahoos* and all other animals bear towards them; but it grew upon me by degrees, much sooner than I imagined, and was mingled with a respectful love and gratitude, that they would condescend to distinguish me from the rest of my species.

When I thought of my family, my friends, my countrymen, or human race in general, I considered them as they really were, *Yahoos* in shape and disposition, perhaps a little more civilized, and qualified with the gift of speech, but making no other use of reason, than to improve and multiply those vices, whereof their brethren in this country had only the share that nature allotted them. When I happened to behold the reflection of my own form in a lake or fountain, I turned away my face in horror and detestation of myself, and could better endure the sight of a common *Yahoo,* than of my own person. By conversing with the *Houyhnhnms,* and looking upon them with delight, I fell to imitate their gait and gesture, which is now grown into a habit, and my friends often tell me in a blunt way, that *I trot like a horse;* which, however, I take for a great compliment. Neither shall I disown, that in speaking I am apt to fall into the voice and manner of the *Houyhnhnms,* and hear myself ridiculed on that account without the least mortification.

In the midst of all this happiness, and when I looked upon myself to be fully settled for life, my master sent for me one morning a little earlier than his usual hour. I observed by his countenance that he was in some perplexity, and at a loss how to begin what he had to speak. After a short silence, he told me, he did not know how I would take what he was going to say; that in the last general assembly, when the affair of the *Yahoos* was entered upon, the representatives had taken offence at his keeping a *Yahoo* (meaning myself) in his family more like a *Houyhnhnm* than a brute animal. That he was known frequently to converse with me, as if he could receive some advantage or pleasure in my company; that such a practice was not agreeable to reason or nature, or a thing ever heard of before among them. The assembly did therefore exhort him, either to employ me like the rest of my species, or command me to swim back to the place from whence I came. That the first of these expedients was utterly rejected by all the *Houyhnhnms* who had ever seen me at his house or their own: for they alleged, that because I had some rudiments of reason, added to the natural pravity of those animals, it was to be feared, I might be able to seduce them into the woody and mountainous parts of the country, and bring them in troops by night to destroy the *Houyhnhnms*' cattle, as being naturally of the ravenous kind, and averse from labour.

My master added, that he was daily pressed by the *Houyhnhnms* of the neighbourhood to have the assembly's exhortation executed, which he could not put off much longer. He doubted it would be impossible for me to swim to another country, and therefore wished I would contrive some sort of vehicle resembling those I had described to him, that might carry me on the sea; in which work I should have the assistance of his own servants, as well as those of his neighbours. He concluded, that for his own part, he could have been content to keep me in his service as long as I lived; because he found I had cured myself of some bad habits and dispositions, by endeavouring, as far as my inferior nature was capable, to imitate the *Houyhnhnms*.

I should here observe to the reader, that a decree of the general assembly in this country is expressed by the word *hnheoayn,* which signifies an exhortation, as near as I can render it; for they have no conception how a rational creature can be compelled, but only advised, or exhorted; because no person can disobey reason, without giving up his claim to be a rational creature.

I was struck with the utmost grief and despair at my master's discourse; and being unable to support the agonies I was under, I fell into a swoon at his feet; when I came to myself, he told me, that he concluded I had been dead (for these people are subject to no such imbecilities of nature). I answered, in a faint voice, that death would have been too great an happiness; that although I could not blame the assembly's exhortation, or the urgency of his friends; yet, in my weak and corrupt judgment, I thought it might consist with reason to have been less rigorous. That I could not swim a league, and probably the nearest land to theirs might be distant above an hundred: that many materials, necessary for making a small vessel to carry me off, were wholly wanting in this country, which, however, I would attempt in obedience and gratitude to his Honour, although I concluded the thing to be impossible, and therefore looked on myself as already devoted to destruction. That the certain prospect of an unnatural death was the least of my evils: for, supposing I should escape with life by some strange adventure, how could I think with temper[18] of pass-

---

[18] **with temper:** Calmly.

ing my days among *Yahoos*, and relapsing into my old corruptions, for want of examples to lead and keep me within the paths of virtue. That I knew too well upon what solid reasons all the determinations of the wise *Houyhnhnms* were founded, not to be shaken by arguments of mine, a miserable *Yahoo*; and therefore, after presenting him with my humble thanks for the offer of his servants' assistance in making a vessel, and desiring a reasonable time for so difficult a work, I told him I would endeavour to preserve a wretched being; and, if ever I returned to England, was not without hopes of being useful to my own species, by celebrating the praises of the renowned *Houyhnhnms*, and proposing their virtues to the imitation of mankind.

My master in a few words made me a very gracious reply, allowed me the space of two months to finish my boat; and ordered the sorrel nag, my fellow-servant (for so at this distance I may presume to call him) to follow my instructions, because I told my master, that his help would be sufficient, and I knew he had a tenderness for me.

In his company my first business was to go to that part of the coast where my rebellious crew had ordered me to be set on shore. I got upon a height, and looking on every side into the sea, fancied I saw a small island, towards the north-east: I took out my pocket-glass, and could then clearly distinguish it about five leagues off, as I computed; but it appeared to the sorrel nag to be only a blue cloud: for, as he had no conception of any country beside his own, so he could not be as expert in distinguishing remote objects at sea, as we who so much converse in that element.

After I had discovered this island, I considered no farther; but resolved it should, if possible, be the first place of my banishment, leaving the consequence to fortune.

I returned home, and consulting with the sorrel nag, we went into a copse at some distance, where I with my knife, and he with a sharp flint fastened very artificially,[19] after their manner, to a wooden handle, cut down several oak wattles about the thickness of a walking-staff, and some larger pieces. But I shall not trouble the reader with a particular description of my own mechanics; let it suffice to say, that in six weeks time, with the help of the sorrel nag, who performed the parts that required most labour, I finished a sort of Indian canoe, but much larger, covering it with the skins of *Yahoos* well stitched together, with hempen threads of my own making. My sail was likewise composed of the skins of the same animal; but I made use of the youngest I could get, the older being too tough and thick; and I likewise provided myself with four paddles. I laid in a stock of boiled flesh, of rabbits and fowls, and took with me two vessels, one filled with milk, and the other with water.

I tried my canoe in a large pond near my master's house, and then corrected in it what was amiss; stopping all the chinks with *Yahoos'* tallow, till I found it staunch, and able to bear me, and my freight. And when it was as complete as I could possibly make it, I had it drawn on a carriage very gently by *Yahoos* to the seaside, under the conduct of the sorrel nag, and another servant.

When all was ready, and the day came for my departure, I took leave of my master and lady, and the whole family, my eyes flowing with tears, and my heart quite sunk with grief. But his Honour, out of curiosity, and, perhaps (if I may speak it

---

[19] **artificially:** Cunningly.

without vanity) partly out of kindness, was determined to see me in my canoe, and got several of his neighbouring friends to accompany him. I was forced to wait above an hour for the tide, and then observing the wind very fortunately bearing towards the island, to which I intended to steer my course, I took a second leave of my master: but as I was going to prostrate myself to kiss his hoof, he did me the honour to raise it gently to my mouth. I am not ignorant how much I have been censured for mentioning this last particular. For my detractors are pleased to think it improbable, that so illustrious a person should descend to give so great a mark of distinction to a creature so inferior as I. Neither have I forgot, how apt some travellers are to boast of extraordinary favours they have received. But if these censurers were better acquainted with the noble and courteous disposition of the *Houyhnhnms,* they would soon change their opinion.

I paid my respects to the rest of the *Houyhnhnms* in his Honour's company; then getting into my canoe, I pushed off from shore.

CHAPTER 11. *The Author's dangerous voyage. He arrives at* New Holland, *hoping to settle there. Is wounded with an arrow by one of the natives. Is seized and carried by force into a* Portuguese *ship. The great civilities of the Captain. The Author arrives at* England.

I began this desperate voyage on February 15, 1714–15, at 9 o'clock in the morning. The wind was very favourable; however, I made use at first only of my paddles; but considering I should soon be weary, and that the wind might chop about, I ventured to set up my little sail; and thus, with the help of the tide, I went at the rate of a league and a half an hour, as near as I could guess. My master and his friends continued on the shore, till I was almost out of sight; and I often heard the sorrel nag (who always loved me) crying out, *Hnuy illa nyha majah Yahoo,* Take care of thyself, gentle *Yahoo.*

My design was, if possible, to discover some small island uninhabited, yet sufficient by my labour to furnish me with the necessaries of life, which I would have thought a greater happiness than to be first minister in the politest court of Europe; so horrible was the idea I conceived of returning to live in the society and under the government of *Yahoos.* For in such a solitude as I desired, I could at least enjoy my own thoughts, and reflect with delight on the virtues of those inimitable *Houyhnhnms,* without any opportunity of degenerating into the vices and corruptions of my own species.

The reader may remember what I related when my crew conspired against me, and confined me to my cabin. How I continued there several weeks, without knowing what course we took; and when I was put ashore in the long boat, how the sailors told me with oaths, whether true or false, that they knew not in what part of the world we were. However, I did then believe us to be about ten degrees southward of the Cape of Good Hope, or about forty-five degrees southern latitude, as I gathered from some general words I overheard among them, being I supposed to the southeast in their intended voyage to Madagascar. And although this were little better than conjecture, yet I resolved to steer my course eastward, hoping to reach the south-west coast of New Holland, and perhaps some such island as I desired, lying westward of it. The wind was full west, and by six in the evening I computed I had gone eastward at least eighteen leagues, when I spied a very small island about half a league off, which I soon reached. It was nothing but a rock with one creek,[20] naturally arched by the force of tempests. Here I put in my canoe, and climbing up a part of the rock, I could plainly discover land to the east, extending from south to north. I lay all night in my canoe; and repeating my voyage early in the morning, I arrived in seven hours to the south-east point of New Holland. This confirmed me in the opinion I have long entertained, that the maps and charts place this country at least three degrees more to the east than it really is; which thought I communicated many years ago to my worthy friend Mr. Herman Moll, and gave him my reasons for it, although he hath rather chosen to follow other authors.

I saw no inhabitants in the place where I landed, and being unarmed, I was afraid of venturing far into the country. I found some shellfish on the shore, and eat them raw, not daring to kindle a fire, for fear of being discovered by the natives. I continued three days feeding on oysters and limpets, to save my own provisions; and I fortunately found a brook of excellent water, which gave me great relief.

On the fourth day, venturing out early a little too far, I saw twenty or thirty natives upon a height, not above five hundred yards from me. They were stark naked, men, women, and children round a fire, as I could discover by the smoke. One of them spied me, and gave notice to the rest; five of them advanced towards me, leaving the women and children at the fire. I made what haste I could to the shore, and getting into my canoe, shoved off: the savages observing me retreat, ran after me; and before I could get far enough into the sea, discharged an arrow, which wounded me deeply on the inside of my left knee (I shall carry the mark to my grave). I apprehended the arrow might be poisoned, and paddling out of the reach of their darts (being a calm day), I made a shift to suck the wound, and dress it as well as I could.

I was at a loss what to do, for I durst not return to the same landing-place, but stood to the north, and was forced to paddle; for the wind, though very gentle, was against me, blowing north-west. As I was looking about for a secure landing-place, I saw a sail to the north-north-east, which appearing every minute more visible, I was in some doubt whether I should wait for them or no; but at last my detestation of the *Yahoo* race prevailed, and turning my canoe, I sailed and paddled together to the south, and got into the same creek from whence I set out in the morning, choosing rather to trust myself among these barbarians, than live with European *Yahoos*. I drew up my canoe as close as I could to the shore, and hid myself behind a stone by the little brook, which, as I have already said, was excellent water.

The ship came within half a league of this creek, and sent her long boat with vessels to take in fresh water (for the place it seems was very well known), but I did not observe it till the boat was almost on shore, and it was too late to seek another hiding-place. The seamen at their landing observed my canoe, and rummaging it all over, easily conjectured that the owner could not be far off. Four of them well armed searched every cranny and lurking-hole, till at last they found me flat on my face behind the stone. They gazed awhile in admiration at my strange uncouth dress; my

---

[20] **creek:** Bay or sheltered cove.

coat made of skins, my wooden-soled shoes, and my furred stockings; from whence, however, they concluded I was not a native of the place, who all go naked. One of the seamen in Portuguese bid me rise, and asked who I was. I understood that language very well, and getting upon my feet, said, I was a poor *Yahoo*, banished from the *Houyhnhnms*, and desired they would please to let me depart. They admired to hear me answer them in their own tongue, and saw by my complexion I must be an European; but were at a loss to know what I meant by *Yahoos* and *Houyhnhnms*, and at the same time fell a laughing at my strange tone in speaking, which resembled the neighing of a horse. I trembled all the while betwixt fear and hatred. I again desired leave to depart, and was gently moving to my canoe; but they laid hold of me, desiring to know, what country I was of? whence I came? with many other questions. I told them, I was born in England, from whence I came about five years ago, and then their country and ours were at peace. I therefore hoped they would not treat me as an enemy, since I meant them no harm, but was a poor *Yahoo*, seeking some desolate place where to pass the remainder of his unfortunate life.

When they began to talk, I thought I never heard or saw any thing so unnatural; for it appeared to me as monstrous as if a dog or a cow should speak in England, or a *Yahoo* in *Houyhnhnm-land*. The honest Portuguese were equally amazed at my strange dress, and the odd manner of delivering my words, which however they understood very well. They spoke to me with great humanity, and said they were sure their Captain would carry me *gratis* to Lisbon, from whence I might return to my own country; that two of the seamen would go back to the ship, inform the Captain of what they had seen, and receive his orders; in the mean time, unless I would give my solemn oath not to fly, they would secure me by force. I thought it best to comply with their proposal. They were very curious to know my story, but I gave them very little satisfaction; and they all conjectured that my misfortunes had impaired my reason. In two hours the boat, which went loaden with vessels of water, returned with the Captain's command to fetch me on board. I fell on my knees to preserve my liberty; but all was in vain, and the men having tied me with cords, heaved me into the boat, from whence I was taken into the ship, and from thence into the Captain's cabin.

His name was Pedro de Mendez; he was a very courteous and generous person; he entreated me to give some account of myself, and desired to know what I would eat or drink; said, I should be used as well as himself, and spoke so many obliging things, that I wondered to find such civilities from a *Yahoo*. However, I remained silent and sullen; I was ready to faint at the very smell of him and his men. At last I desired something to eat out of my own canoe; but he ordered me a chicken and some excellent wine, and then directed that I should be put to bed in a very clean cabin. I would not undress myself, but lay on the bed-clothes, and in half an hour stole out, when I thought the crew was at dinner, and getting to the side of the ship was going to leap into the sea, and swim for my life, rather than continue among *Yahoos*. But one of the seamen prevented me, and having informed the Captain, I was chained to my cabin.

After dinner Don Pedro came to me, and desired to know my reason for so desperate an attempt; assured me he only meant to do me all the service he was able;

and spoke so very movingly, that at last I descended to treat him like an animal which had some little portion of reason. I gave him a very short relation of my voyage; of the conspiracy against me by my own men; of the country where they set me on shore, and of my three years' residence there. All which he looked upon as if it were a dream or a vision; whereat I took great offence; for I had quite forgot the faculty of lying, so peculiar to *Yahoos* in all countries where they preside, and, consequently the disposition of suspecting truth in others of their own species. I asked him, whether it were the custom in his country to *say the thing that was not?* I assured him I had almost forgot what he meant by falsehood, and if I had lived a thousand years in *Houyhnhnm-land,* I should never have heard a lie from the meanest servant; that I was altogether indifferent whether he believed me or no; but however, in return for his favours, I would give so much allowance to the corruption of his nature, as to answer any objection he would please to make, and then he might easily discover the truth.

The Captain, a wise man, after many endeavours to catch me tripping in some part of my story, at last began to have a better opinion of my veracity. But he added, that since I professed so inviolable an attachment to truth, I must give him my word of honour to bear him company in this voyage, without attempting any thing against my life, or else he would continue me a prisoner till we arrived at Lisbon. I gave him the promise he required; but at the same time protested that I would suffer the greatest hardships rather than return to live among *Yahoos.*

Our voyage passed without any considerable accident. In gratitude to the Captain I sometimes sat with him at his earnest request, and strove to conceal my antipathy to human kind, although it often broke out, which he suffered to pass without observation. But the greatest part of the day, I confined myself to my cabin, to avoid seeing any of the crew. The Captain had often entreated me to strip myself of my savage dress, and offered to lend me the best suit of clothes he had. This I would not be prevailed on to accept, abhorring to cover myself with any thing that had been on the back of a *Yahoo.* I only desired he would lend me two clean shirts, which having been washed since he wore them, I believed would not so much defile me. These I changed every second day, and washed them myself.

We arrived at Lisbon, Nov. 5, 1715. At our landing the Captain forced me to cover myself with his cloak, to prevent the rabble from crowding about me. I was conveyed to his own house, and at my earnest request, he led me up to the highest room backwards.[21] I conjured him to conceal from all persons what I had told him of the *Houyhnhnms,* because the least hint of such a story would not only draw numbers of people to see me, but probably put me in danger of being imprisoned, or burnt by the Inquisition. The Captain persuaded me to accept a suit of clothes newly made; but I would not suffer the tailor to take my measure; however, Don Pedro being almost my size, they fitted me well enough. He accoutred me with other necessaries all new, which I aired for twenty-four hours before I would use them.

The Captain had no wife, nor above three servants, none of which were suffered to attend at meals, and his whole deportment was so obliging, added to very good

---

[21]**highest . . . backwards:** To the rear of the house, away from the street.

human understanding, that I really began to tolerate his company. He gained so far upon me, that I ventured to look out of the back window. By degrees I was brought into another room, from whence I peeped into the street, but drew my head back in a fright. In a week's time he seduced me down to the door. I found my terror gradually lessened, but my hatred and contempt seemed to increase. I was at last bold enough to walk the street in his company, but kept my nose well stopped with rue, or sometimes with tobacco.

In ten days, Don Pedro, to whom I had given some account of my domestic affairs, put it upon me as a matter of honour and conscience, that I ought to return to my native country, and live at home with my wife and children. He told me, there was an English ship in the port just ready to sail, and he would furnish me with all things necessary. It would be tedious to repeat his arguments, and my contradictions. He said it was altogether impossible to find such a solitary island as I desired to live in; but I might command in my own house, and pass my time in a manner as recluse as I pleased.

I complied at last, finding I could not do better. I left Lisbon the 24th day of November, in an English merchantman, but who was the master I never inquired. Don Pedro accompanied me to the ship, and lent me twenty pounds. He took kind leave of me, and embraced me at parting, which I bore as well as I could. During this last voyage I had no commerce with the master or any of his men; but pretending I was sick, kept close in my cabin. On the fifth of December, 1715, we cast anchor in the Downs about nine in the morning, and at three in the afternoon I got safe to my house at Rotherhith.

My wife and family received me with great surprise and joy, because they concluded me certainly dead; but I must freely confess the sight of them filled me only with hatred, disgust, and contempt, and the more by reflecting on the near alliance I had to them. For, although since my unfortunate exile from the *Houyhnhnm* country, I had compelled myself to tolerate the sight of *Yahoos,* and to converse with Don Pedro de Mendez; yet my memory and imagination were perpetually filled with the virtues and ideas of those exalted *Houyhnhnms.* And when I began to consider, that by copulating with one of the *Yahoo* species I had become a parent of more, it struck me with the utmost shame, confusion, and horror.

As soon as I entered the house, my wife took me in her arms, and kissed me; at which, having not been used to the touch of that odious animal for so many years, I fell in a swoon for almost an hour. At the time I am writing it is five years since my last return to England: during the first year, I could not endure my wife or children in my presence, the very smell of them was intolerable; much less could I suffer them to eat in the same room. To this hour they dare not presume to touch my bread, or drink out of the same cup, neither was I ever able to let one of them take me by the hand. The first money I laid out was to buy two young stone-horses,[22] which I keep in a good stable, and next to them the groom is my greatest favourite; for I feel my spirits revived by the smell he contracts in the stable. My horses understand me tol-

---

[22] **stone-horses:** Stallions.

erably well; I converse with them at least four hours every day. They are strangers to bridle or saddle; they live in great amity with me, and friendship to each other.

CHAPTER 12. *The Author's veracity. His design in publishing this work. His censure of those travellers who swerve from the truth. The Author clears himself from any sinister ends in writing. An objection answered. The method of planting colonies. His native country commended. The right of the Crown to those countries described by the Author, is justified. The difficulty of conquering them. The Author takes his last leave of the reader; proposeth his manner of living for the future, gives good advice, and concludes.*

Thus, gentle reader, I have given thee a faithful history of my travels for sixteen years and above seven months; wherein I have not been so studious of ornament as truth. I could perhaps like others have astonished thee with strange improbable tales; but I rather chose to relate plain matter of fact in the simplest manner and style; because my principal design was to inform, and not to amuse thee.

It is easy for us who travel into remote countries, which are seldom visited by Englishmen or other Europeans, to form descriptions of wonderful animals both at sea and land. Whereas a traveller's chief aim should be to make men wiser and better, and to improve their minds by the bad as well as good example of what they deliver concerning foreign places.

I could heartily wish a law was enacted, that every traveller, before he were permitted to publish his voyages, should be obliged to make oath before the Lord High Chancellor that all he intended to print was absolutely true to the best of his knowledge; for then the world would no longer be deceived as it usually is, while some writers, to make their works pass the better upon the public, impose the grossest falsities on the unwary reader. I have perused several books of travels with great delight in my younger days; but having since gone over most parts of the globe, and been able to contradict many fabulous accounts from my own observation, it hath given me a great disgust against this part of reading, and some indignation to see the credulity of mankind so impudently abused. Therefore since my acquaintance were pleased to think my poor endeavours might not be unacceptable to my country, I imposed on myself as a maxim, never to be swerved from, that I would *strictly adhere to truth;* neither indeed can I be ever under the least temptation to vary from it, while I retain in my mind the lectures and example of my noble master, and the other illustrious *Houyhnhnms,* of whom I had so long the honour to be an humble hearer.

> *Nec si miserum Fortuna Sinonem*
> *Finxit, vanum etiam, mendacemque improba finget.*[23]

I know very well how little reputation is to be got by writings which require neither genius nor learning, nor indeed any other talent, except a good memory, or an

---

[23] *Nec . . . finget:* Virgil, *Aeneid* 2, 79–80: ". . . fate may have made Sinon miserable, but she will never be able to make him into a liar." Sinon was the Greek who persuaded the Trojans to admit the wooden horse through their gates, and he was very much a liar; Gulliver ironically and unwittingly quotes these lines to attest to his own reliability.

exact journal. I know likewise, that writers of travels, like dictionary-makers, are sunk into oblivion by the weight and bulk of those who come after, and therefore lie uppermost. And it is highly probable, that such travellers who shall hereafter visit the countries described in this work of mine, may, by detecting my errors (if there be any), and adding many new discoveries of their own, justle me out of vogue, and stand in my place, making the world forget that I was ever an author. This indeed would be too great a mortification if I wrote for fame: But, as my sole intention was the PUBLIC GOOD, I cannot be altogether disappointed. For who can read of the virtues I have mentioned in the glorious *Houyhnhnms,* without being ashamed of his own vices, when he considers himself as the reasoning, governing animal of his country? I shall say nothing of those remote nations where *Yahoos* preside; amongst which the least corrupted are the *Brobdingnagians,* whose wise maxims in morality and government it would be our happiness to observe. But I forbear descanting farther, and rather leave the judicious reader to his own remarks and applications.

I am not a little pleased that this work of mine can possibly meet with no censurers: for what objections can be made against a writer who relates only plain facts that happened in such distant countries, where we have not the least interest with respect either to trade or negotiations? I have carefully avoided every fault with which common writers of travels are often too justly charged. Besides, I meddle not the least with any party, but write without passion, prejudice, or ill-will against any man or number of men whatsoever. I write for the noblest end, to inform and instruct mankind, over whom I may, without breach of modesty, pretend to some superiority, from the advantages I received by conversing so long among the most accomplished *Houyhnhnms.* I write without any view towards profit or praise. I never suffer a word to pass that may look like reflection, or possibly give the least offence even to those who are most ready to take it. So that I hope I may with justice pronounce myself an author perfectly blameless, against whom the tribes of answerers, considerers, observers, reflecters, detecters, remarkers, will never be able to find matter for exercising their talents.

I confess, it was whispered to me, that I was bound in duty as a subject of England, to have given in a memorial to a Secretary of State, at my first coming over; because, whatever lands are discovered by a subject, belong to the Crown. But I doubt whether our conquests in the countries I treat of, would be as easy as those of Ferdinando Cortez over the naked Americans. The *Lilliputians* I think, are hardly worth the charge of a fleet and army to reduce them; and I question whether it might be prudent or safe to attempt the *Brobdingnagians;* or whether an English army would be much at their ease with the Flying Island over their heads. The *Houyhnhnms,* indeed, appear not to be so well prepared for war, a science to which they are perfect strangers, and especially against missive weapons. However, supposing myself to be a minister of state, I could never give my advice for invading them. Their prudence, unanimity, unacquaintedness with fear, and their love of their country, would amply supply all defects in the military art. Imagine twenty thousand of them breaking into the midst of an European army, confounding the ranks, overturning the carriages, battering the warriors' faces into mummy[24] by terrible

---

[24] **into mummy:** Into powder; the modern equivalent would be "into a pulp."

yerks[25] from their hinder hoofs; for they would well deserve the character given to Augustus: *Recalcitrat undique tutus.*[26] But instead of proposals for conquering that magnanimous nation, I rather wish they were in a capacity or disposition to send a sufficient number of their inhabitants for civilizing Europe, by teaching us the first principles of honour, justice, truth, temperance, public spirit, fortitude, chastity, friendship, benevolence, and fidelity. The names of all which virtues are still retained among us in most languages and are to be met with in modern as well as ancient authors; which I am able to assert from my own small reading.

But I had another reason which made me less forward to enlarge his Majesty's dominions by my discoveries. To say the truth, I had conceived a few scruples with relation to the distributive justice of princes upon these occasions. For instance, a crew of pirates are driven by a storm they know not whither; at length a boy discovers land from the topmast; they go on shore to rob and plunder; they see an harmless people, are entertained with kindness, they give the country a new name, they take formal possession of it for their king, they set up a rotten plank or a stone for a memorial, they murder two or three dozen of the natives, bring away a couple more by force for a sample, return home, and get their pardon. Here commences a new dominion acquired with a title by *divine right*. Ships are sent with the first opportunity; the natives driven out or destroyed, their princes tortured to discover their gold; a free licence given to all acts of inhumanity and lust, the earth reeking with the blood of its inhabitants: and this execrable crew of butchers employed in so pious an expedition, is a *modern colony* sent to convert and civilize an idolatrous and barbarous people.

But this description, I confess, doth by no means affect the British nation, who may be an example to the whole world for their wisdom, care, and justice in planting colonies; their liberal endowments for the advancement of religion and learning; their choice of devout and able pastors to propagate Christianity; their caution in stocking their provinces with people of sober lives and conversations from this the mother kingdom; their strict regard to the distribution of justice, in supplying the civil administration through all their colonies with officers of the greatest abilities, utter strangers to corruption; and to crown all, by sending the most vigilant and virtuous governors, who have no other views than the happiness of the people over whom they preside, and the honour of the King their master.

But, as those countries which I have described do not appear to have any desire of being conquered, and enslaved, murdered or driven out by colonies; nor abound either in gold, silver, sugar, or tobacco; I did humbly conceive, they were by no means proper objects of our zeal, our valour, or our interest. However, if those whom it more concerns think fit to be of another opinion, I am ready to depose, when I shall be lawfully called, that no European did ever visit these countries before me. I mean, if the inhabitants ought to be believed; unless a dispute may arise about the two *Yahoos*, said to have been seen many ages ago on a mountain in *Houyhnhnm-land*.

---

[25] **yerks:** Kicks.

[26] *Recalcitrat . . . tutus:* Horace, *Satires* 2:1:20; "He kicks backward, guarding himself at every point."

But, as to the formality of taking possession in my Sovereign's name, it never came once into my thoughts; and if it had, yet as my affairs then stood, I should perhaps in point of prudence and self-preservation, have put it off to a better opportunity.

Having thus answered the only objection that can ever be raised against me as a traveller, I here take a final leave of all my courteous readers, and return to enjoy my own speculations in my little garden at Redriff, to apply those excellent lessons of virtue which I learned among the *Houyhnhnms;* to instruct the *Yahoos* of my own family as far as I shall find them docible animals; to behold my figure often in a glass, and thus if possible habituate myself by time to tolerate the sight of a human creature: to lament the brutality of *Houyhnhnms* in my own country, but always treat their persons with respect, for the sake of my noble master, his family, his friends, and the whole *Houyhnhnm* race, whom these of ours have the honour to resemble in all their lineaments, however their intellectuals came to degenerate.

I began last week to permit my wife to sit at dinner with me, at the farthest end of a long table; and to answer (but with the utmost brevity) the few questions I asked her. Yet the smell of a *Yahoo* continuing very offensive, I always keep my nose well stopped with rue, lavender, or tobacco leaves. And although it be hard for a man late in life to remove old habits, I am not altogether out of hopes in some time to suffer a neighbour *Yahoo* in my company, without the apprehensions I am yet under of his teeth or his claws.

My reconcilement to the *Yahoo*-kind in general might not be so difficult, if they would be content with those vices and follies only which nature hath entitled them to. I am not in the least provoked at the sight of a lawyer, a pickpocket, a colonel, a fool, a lord, a gamester, a politician, a whore-master, a physician, an evidence, a suborner, an attorney, a traitor, or the like; this is all according to the due course of things: but when I behold a lump of deformity, and diseases both in body and mind, smitten with *pride,* it immediately breaks all the measures of my patience; neither shall I be ever able to comprehend how such an animal and such a vice could tally together. The wise and virtuous *Houyhnhnms,* who abound in all excellencies that can adorn a rational creature, have no name for this vice in their language, which hath no terms to express any thing that is evil, except those whereby they describe the detestable qualities of their *Yahoos,* among which they were not able to distinguish this of pride, for want of thoroughly understanding human nature, as it showeth itself in other countries, where that animal presides. But I, who had more experience, could plainly observe some rudiments of it among the wild *Yahoos.*

But the *Houyhnhnms,* who live under the government of reason, are no more proud of the good qualities they possess, than I should be for not wanting a leg or an arm, which no man in his wits would boast of, although he must be miserable without them. I dwell the longer upon this subject from the desire I have to make the society of an English *Yahoo* by any means not insupportable; and therefore I here entreat those who have any tincture of this absurd vice, that they will not presume to come in my sight.

Travel Narratives

Jonathan Swift's ***Gulliver's Travels*** takes us on episodic journeys into strange lands whose unusual customs and sometimes distorted logic shed new light on the virtues and vices of European society. Swift titled his four tales about Lemuel Gulliver *Travels into Several Remote Nations of the World,* and Gulliver is said to be "First a Surgeon, and then a Captain of Several Ships," whose mishaps at sea lead to his adventures in strange lands. Thus Swift deliberately placed his work within the increasingly popular genre of the TRAVEL NARRATIVE,[1] or travelogue, and invited his readers to think of Gulliver as a world traveler, albeit a somewhat bewildered one. Indeed, Gulliver's irresistible urge to travel and his encounters with the inhabitants of Lilliput, Brobdingnag, Laputa, and Houyhnhnm-land mimic the sometimes fanciful, sometimes factual, tales that sailors, soldiers, merchants, adventurers, and tourists often told about their journeys into foreign lands in Swift's day. Piquing his reader's curiosity about these imaginary lands while mounting a full-blown satirical attack upon European folly and vice, Swift masterfully exploits the conventions of the travel narrative, which often used the unfamiliar to help define or criticize the familiar.

p. 147

TRAVEL NARRATIVES

While some travel narratives, like Swift's, were purely fictional, many were accounts recording and sometimes exaggerating the

---

[1] **travel narrative:** Accounts of exploration and adventure in newly "discovered" countries and places as well as of travels in more familiar ones.

William Hodges, *View of Part of the City of Benares*, c. 1781. Wash and Ink over Pencil
*European travelers arriving at the port of Benares, a Hindu holy city on the banks of the
Ganges in India, observed beautiful architecture far different from that of their home
countries. (Yale Center for British Art, Paul Mellon Collection)*

experience of real travelers. Many travelers were engaged in diplomatic or religious missions, colonial enterprises, or wars. Others
were tourists who took advantage of improvements in means of
transportation, expanded networks of communication, and
increased knowledge about the world to travel. Places once accessible
only to the hardiest of adventurers were beginning to open up for
the tourist, who could now find relatively safe passage to what were
once unthinkable destinations. Nonetheless, tourism was a long way
from being the industry it is today, and most people's desire to travel
had to be satisfied vicariously, through reading. Thus, like the tales
of pilgrimage and discovery from earlier centuries, the travel narrative allowed readers to venture into what was for most of them *terra
incognita*—unknown land, a place known perhaps as little more
than a name on a map or in a history book.

EUROPEAN TRAVELERS

European readers were fascinated with what they considered to be exotic cultures. Inspired early in the century by the Galland translation of *Thousand and One Nights* (1704–17),[2] the European appetite for the Orient virtually guaranteed the popularity of published accounts—genuine and invented—of travels to China, India, and the Middle East. These travel narratives appeared in many forms, from actual accounts of voyages such as those of James Cook[3] and **Louis Antoine de Bougainville**,[4] to philosophical treatises such as **Denis Diderot**'s *Supplement to the Voyage of Bougainville,* and to diaries and letters such as Lady Mary Wortley Montagu's *Turkish Letters.* In his **Supplement to the Voyage of Bougainville,** Diderot takes his reader to Tahiti—a place few Europeans in the eighteenth century would have dreamed of seeing for themselves—where he stages an imagined dialogue between a European clergyman and a native chief. Like *Gulliver's Travels,* this fictionalized tale uses an unfamiliar setting to highlight the errors of European culture governed by artificial laws and to describe a utopian society based on the laws of nature. In contrast, Lady Mary's **Turkish Letters** provide a detailed and authentic account of her stay in Turkey, a place her readers would have considered representative of the mysterious East.

loo-EE ahn-TWAHN
duh boo-gen-VEEL
duh-NEE dee-DROH

p. 213

p. 207

NON-EUROPEAN TRAVELERS

European readers were also fascinated with narratives that portrayed their own cultures through the eyes of non-European travelers, such as the imagined accounts of foreign travelers in Oliver Goldsmith's[5]

---

[2] *Thousand and One Nights:* Also known as the *Arabian Nights;* a collection of Indian, Arabic, and Persian tales dating from the ninth century C.E. (or earlier) to the fourteenth century. The stories include those of Sinbad the Sailor, Ali Baba and the Forty Thieves, and Aladdin and his magic lamp.

[3] James Cook (1728–1779): English sea captain who voyaged around the world in 1768, sailing to Australia, New Zealand, the Sandwich Islands, the West Coast of what is now the United States, and Hawaii, where he was killed.

[4] Louis Antoine de Bougainville (1729–1811): French naval officer and navigator who undertook a voyage from 1766 to 1769 that led him to the Falkland and Solomon Islands; he described this expedition in *Voyage around the World* (1771).

[5] Oliver Goldsmith (1730–1774): English poet, novelist, and editor. Author of the immensely popular novel *The Vicar of Wakefield* (1766), concerning the incidents in the life of a good-natured parson, and the pseudo-Chinese letters entitled *Citizen of the World* (1762).

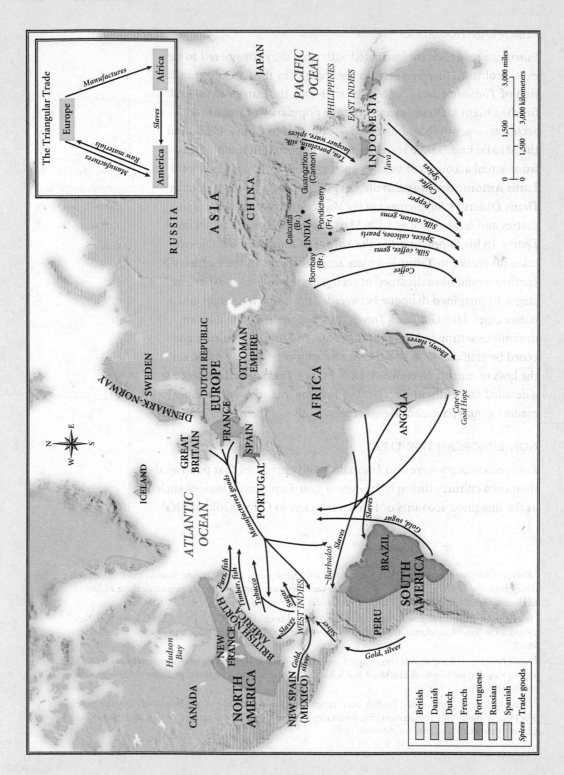

The Triangular Trade

Europe → Africa: *Manufactures*

Africa → America: *Slaves*

America → Europe: *Raw materials*

Europe → America: *Manufactures*

Citizen of the World and Montesquieu's[6] *Persian Letters.* Like Swift, Goldsmith and Montesquieu turned to the travel narrative for purposes of SATIRE; their Chinese and Persian narrators point to what they see as the absurdities and curiosities of European customs. The ***Travels of Mirza Abu Taleb Khan***, translated into English by Charles Stewart in 1810, gave European readers an opportunity to see themselves through an authentic travel narrative written by a Muslim from India for an East Indian audience. The *Travels* offer an extensive, detailed, and fascinating account of Abu Taleb's trips to Ireland, England, and France, then on through Constantinople, Baghdad, and back home to Calcutta. During his nearly three-year stay in England, **Abu Taleb** painted a picture of Europe for his Indian readers. His narrative reflects on European customs, particularly those of the English, about whom he finds much to praise and blame. **Xie Qing Gao** (Hsieh Ching Kao)'s *The Hai-lu,* which means "Ocean Record," remained unknown outside of China for almost one hundred years after it appeared in 1844. In diary form, ***The Hai-lu*** contains brief sketches of Europe, recording for a Chinese audience what its author found striking or curious in the port towns he visited.

p. 218

ah-BOO TAH-lib

shyey-ching-GOW

p. 230

READING THE TRAVEL NARRATIVE

Travel accounts raise many questions about the authenticity of the traveler-narrator, his or her ability to represent people and places accurately, as well as his or her reasons, both conscious and unconscious, for traveling and for writing. As Diderot's *Supplement to the Voyage of Bougainville* perhaps most clearly demonstrates, although travel narratives may put two cultures into dialogue, they also

---

[6] **Montesquieu:** Charles de Secondat, Baron de Montesquieu (1689–1755), French philosopher and writer. Among his many works are the *Persian Letters* (1721) and *Spirit of the Laws* (1748).

◀ **European Trade Patterns c. 1740**
Europe dominated world trade in the mid eighteenth century. As indicated by the diagram "The Triangular Trade," Europe stood at the top of the pyramid-like structure of world trade patterns, exploiting other areas of the world to increase its own wealth. Manufactures (manufactured goods) were sold to America and Africa; Africa exported slaves to America, where they were used to produce raw materials that were sent to Europe; raw materials were converted by European factories into manufactures that were then sold to Africa and America, and so on.

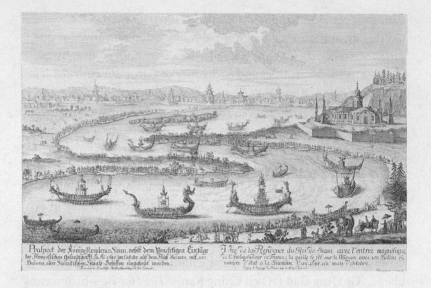

contain culturally specific assumptions made by the narrator or the
writer that sway his or her representations. Like Gulliver, the traveler
may appear completely open to the new world in which he or she is
immersed, but often he or she takes up the role of a knowledgeable
mediator between two cultures, translating the unfamiliar into the
familiar, or, depending on the effect desired, exaggerating the unfamiliar into the radically different. Renaissance travel narratives, for
example, among which we include Columbus's[7] *Diario,* recount the
adventures of explorers and colonizers whose interests in describing
potential resources for the home country often surface even in the
midst of awe before the lands or peoples they have encountered.

The imperial interests of the adventurer and conquistador differ
from the motives of the traveler, who voyages out of curiosity, restlessness, or a desire for knowledge. Yet even the traveler carries
certain culturally constructed predispositions, preferences, and often
unconscious prejudices that may distort his or her representations.
Thus, writers who actually venture into the contact zones—points
of connection between people normally separated by culture,
history, geography, or race—may unintentionally or unavoidably

---

[7] **Columbus:** Christopher Columbus (1451–1506), Italian-born explorer who reached Watling Island, in what is
now the Bahamas, in 1492, claiming the land for the Spanish monarchs Ferdinand and Isabella, who financed his
voyage; his *Diario,* or *Diary,* records the encounter between Columbus's men and the native people, the Taino.

misrepresent those they meet. These narratives are often subject to factual errors due to a failure to sympathize with the peoples or customs described. Such lapses may result in distortions and exaggerations, like those exploited satirically in Swift's *Gulliver's Travels*.

Accounts of these contact zones raise questions not only about the places and peoples described but also about the writers and their own cultural assumptions and values. As we read, we should try to distinguish between projection and observation.

■ CONNECTIONS

Voltaire, *Candide*, p. 275. Swift's *Gulliver's Travels* presents a fictionalized account of the innocent traveler encountering marvelous creatures, and the travel narratives found in this section similarly record encounters with the new and strange. Consider the ways Voltaire, too, exploits the devices of the travel narrative to launch his satire against the viciousness of the world and its effects on his naive hero, Candide.

Mary Rowlandson, *The Narrative of the Captivity and Restoration of Mrs. Mary Rowlandson*, p. 483; Olaudah Equiano, *The Interesting Narrative of the Life of Olaudah Equiano*, p. 405. Travel narratives are told from the point of view of individuals who make their journeys voluntarily. Rowlandson and Equiano recount the stories of captives who undertake journeys against their will. Consider how the point of view of the involuntary traveler alters the conventions of the travel narrative, or how that point of view changes our response to these writers' depictions of the people and places they encounter.

Matsuo Bashō, *The Narrow Road through the Backcountry*, p. 657. Although Bashō describes the physical beauty of the places he visits, his accounts primarily convey an emotional and spiritual response to his surroundings — creating a sense of place that fuses his consciousness and the physical setting. Consider whether or not the travel narratives that follow similarly evoke a sense of place.

■ PRONUNCIATION

Louis Antoine de Bougainville: loo-EE ahn-TWAHN duh boo-gen-VEEL
Denis Diderot: duh-NEE dee-DROH (DEE-duh-roh)
Abu Taleb: ah-BOO TAH-lib (AH-boo)
Xie Qing Gao: shyeh-ching-GOW

◌ LADY MARY WORTLEY MONTAGU
1689–1762

We travellers are in very hard circumstances: If we say nothing but what has been said before us, we are dull, and we have observed nothing. If we tell any thing new, we are laughed at as fabulous and romantic, not allowing for the difference of ranks, which afford difference of company, more curiosity, or the changes of customs, that happen every twenty years in every country.

– LADY MARY
WORTLEY MONTAGU,
The Turkish Letters

Among the important English travelers in the eighteenth century was Lady Mary Wortley Montagu. Lady Mary was born in 1689, the daughter of Evelyn Pierrepont, a wealthy Whig who eventually became lord of Dorchester. As a teenager Mary taught herself Latin and read widely in the classics and the popular novels of her time. Known for her keen intelligence, wit, and conversation, she moved within an elite literary circle that featured some of the greatest English writers of the day, including Alexander Pope, against whom she wrote some pointed satirical poems. In 1712 she eloped with Edward Wortley Montagu, who became ambassador to the Turkish government four years later. In January 1716 Montagu and her husband departed for Turkey, where they stayed until May 1718. While in Turkey, she learned the native language and acquired some knowledge of Turkish literature; in addition, she sought out information about inoculation for smallpox and introduced the practice to England upon her return. During her time abroad, Montagu kept notes and wrote letters describing her experiences, which she later compiled into what is known as *The Turkish Letters,* not published until 1763, a year after her death in London at the age of seventy-four. Among others, the great English historian Edward Gibbon, author of *The History of the Decline and Fall of the Roman Empire* (1776–88), praised Montagu's *Turkish Letters* for their lively style and their erudition; in his words, "What fire, what ease, what knowledge of Europe and Asia!"

Unlike the fictional constructs in Montesquieu and Goldsmith, Montagu's *Turkish Letters* attempts as nearly as possible to account for the manners and customs she witnessed directly in Turkey. The letters give us a rare opportunity to see Turkish society from a European woman's point of view, in this case relatively untainted by the prejudices common to travel narratives about the East. Remarkably, Montagu records in the letters presented here first-hand impressions of a Turkish harem and a mosque, spaces usually forbidden to Western travelers. Acknowledging her limited understanding of the Ottoman culture, Montagu often avoids romanticizing or demeaning Turkish customs, as other European writers were wont to do; instead she conveys her admiration and respect for her hosts as well as her sympathy—as in the letter included here—for some of the women she meets.

FROM

∾ The Turkish Letters

To the Countess of ———— [Mar]

Pera of Constantinople, March 10, O.S. [1718]

[. . .] I went to see the Sultana Hafiteń,[1] favourite of the late Emperor Mustapha, who, you know, (or perhaps you don't know) was deposed by his brother, the reigning Sultan Achmet, and died a few weeks after, being poisoned, as it was generally believed. This lady was, immediately after his death, saluted with an absolute order to leave the seraglio, and choose herself a husband from the great men at the Porte.[2] I suppose you may imagine her overjoyed at this proposal. Quite contrary: These women, who are called, and esteem themselves, queens, look upon this liberty as the greatest disgrace and affront that can happen to them. She threw herself at the Sultan's feet, and begged him to poignard her, rather than use his brother's widow with that contempt. She represented to him, in agonies of sorrow, that she was privileged from this misfortune, by having brought five princes into the Ottoman family; but all the boys being dead, and only one girl surviving, this excuse was not received, and she [was] compelled to make her choice. She chose Bekir Effendi, then secretary of state, and above fourscore years old, to convince the world that she firmly intended to keep the vow she had made, of never suffering a second husband to approach her bed; and since she must honour some subject so far as to be called his wife, she would choose him as a mark of her gratitude, since it was he that had presented her at the age of ten years old, to her last lord. But she has never permitted him to pay her one visit; though it is now fifteen years she has been in his house, where she passes her time in uninterrupted mourning, with a constancy very little known in Christendom, especially in a widow of twenty-one, for she is now but thirty-six. She has no black eunuchs for her guard, her husband being obliged to respect her as a queen, and not inquire at all into what is done in her apartment, where I was led into a large room with a sofa the whole length of it, adorned with white marble pillars like a *ruelle*,[3] covered with pale blue figured velvet on a silver ground, with cushions of the same, where I was desired to repose till the Sultana appeared, who had contrived this manner of reception to avoid rising up at my entrance, though she made me an inclination of her head when I rose up to her. I was very glad to observe a lady that had been distinguished by the favour of an emperor, to whom beauties were every day presented from all parts of the world. But she did not seem to me to have ever been half so beautiful as the fair Fatima I saw at Adrianople; though she had the remains of a fine face, more decayed by sorrow than time. But her dress was something so surprisingly rich, I cannot forbear describing it to you. She wore a vest

---

[1] **Sultana Hafiteń**: Widow of Sultan Mustafa II, who ruled from 1695 to 1703. She later became the wife of the Grand Vizier, the chief authority in the Ottoman empire, second only to the sultan. [All notes are the editors'.]

[2] **the Porte**: The official name of the Turkish government, taken from the high gate at the entrance to the building housing the Grand Vizier's administrative offices.   [3] *ruelle:* A passageway or lane.

called *donalma,* and which differs from a *caftán* by longer sleeves, and folding over at the bottom. It was of purple cloth, strait to her shape, and thick set, on each side, down to her feet, and round the sleeves, with pearls of the best water, of the same size as their buttons commonly are. You must not suppose I mean as large as those of my Lord————, but about the bigness of a pea; and to these buttons large loops of diamonds, in the form of those gold loops so common upon birthday coats. This habit was tied, at the waist, with two large tassels of smaller pearl, and round the arms embroidered with large diamonds: Her shift fastened at the bottom with a great diamond, shaped like a lozenge; Her girdle as broad as the broadest English ribbon, entirely covered with diamonds. Round her neck she wore three chains, which reached to her knees: one of large pearl, at the bottom of which hung a fine coloured emerald, as big as a turkey-egg; another, consisting of two hundred emeralds, close joined together, of the most lively green, perfectly matched, every one as large as a half-crown piece, and as thick as three crown pieces; and another of small emeralds, perfectly round. But her earrings eclipsed all the rest. They were two diamonds, shaped exactly like pears, as large as a big hazel-nut. Round her *talpoche*[4] she had four strings of pearl, the whitest and most perfect in the world, at least enough to make four necklaces, every one as large as the Duchess of Marlborough's, and of the same size, fastened with two roses, consisting of a large ruby for the middle stone, and round them twenty drops of clean diamonds to each. Beside this, her head-dress was covered with bodkins of emeralds and diamonds. She wore large diamond bracelets, and had five rings on her fingers, all single diamonds, (except Mr. Pitt's[5]) the largest I ever saw in my life. It is for jewellers to compute the value of these things; but, according to the common estimation of jewels in our part of the world, her whole dress must be worth above a hundred thousand pounds sterling. This I am very sure of, that no European queen has half the quantity; and the empress's jewels, though very fine, would look very mean near hers.

She gave me a dinner of fifty dishes of meat, which (after their fashion) were placed on the table but one at a time, and was extremely tedious. But the magnificence of her table answered very well to that of her dress. The knives were of gold, the hafts set with diamonds. But the piece of luxury that grieved my eyes was the tablecloth and napkins, which were all tiffany, embroidered with silks and gold, in the finest manner, in natural flowers. It was with the utmost regret that I made use of these costly napkins, as finely wrought as the finest handkerchiefs that ever came out of this country. You may be sure, that they were entirely spoiled before dinner was over. The sherbet (which is the liquor they drink at meals) was served in china bowls; but the covers and salvers massy gold. After dinner, water was brought in a gold basin, and towels of the same kind of the napkins, which I very unwillingly wiped my hands upon; and coffee was served in china, with gold *soucoupes.*[6]

The Sultana seemed in very good humour, and talked to me with the utmost civility. I did not omit this opportunity of learning all that I possibly could of the

---

[4] *talpoche:* A kind of bonnet with elongated sides.

[5] Mr. Pitt: William Pitt, Earl of Chatham (1708–1778), a powerful English statesman.

[6] *soucoupes:* Saucers.

seraglio, which is so entirely unknown among us. She assured me, that the story of the Sultan's throwing a handkerchief is altogether fabulous; and the manner upon that occasion, no other but that he sends the *kyslár agá*,[7] to signify to the lady the honour he intends her. She is immediately complimented upon it by the others, and led to the bath, where she is perfumed and dressed in the most magnificent and becoming manner. The Emperor precedes his visit by a royal present, and then comes into her apartment: neither is there any such thing as her creeping in at the bed's foot. She said, that the first he made choice of was always after the first in rank, and not the mother of the eldest son, as other writers would make us believe. Sometimes the Sultan diverts himself in the company of all his ladies, who stand in a circle round him. And she confessed that they were ready to die with jealousy and envy of the happy she that he distinguished by any appearance of preference. But this seemed to me neither better nor worse than the circles in most courts, where the glance of the monarch is watched, and every smile waited for with impatience, and envied by those who cannot obtain it.

She never mentioned the Sultan[8] without tears in her eyes, yet she seemed very fond of the discourse. "My past happiness," said she, "appears a dream to me. Yet I cannot forget that I was beloved by the greatest and most lovely of mankind. I was chosen from all the rest, to make all his campaigns with him; I would not survive him, if I was not passionately fond of the princess my daughter. Yet all my tenderness for her was hardly enough to make me preserve my life. When I lost him, I passed a whole twelvemonth without seeing the light. Time has softened my despair; yet I now pass some days every week in tears, devoted to the memory of my Sultan."

There was no affectation in these words. It was easy to see she was in a deep melancholy, though her good humour made her willing to divert me.

She asked me to walk in her garden, and one of her slaves immediately brought her a *pellice*[9] of rich brocade lined with sables. I waited on her into the garden, which had nothing in it remarkable but the fountains; and from thence she shewed me all her apartments. In her bed-chamber her toilet was displayed, consisting of two looking-glasses, the frames covered with pearls, and her night *talpoche* set with bodkins of jewels, and near it three vests of fine sables, every one of which is, at least, worth a thousand dollars (two hundred pounds English money). I don't doubt these rich habits were purposely placed in sight, but they seemed negligently thrown on the sofa. When I took my leave of her, I was complimented with perfumes, as at the Grand Vizier's, and presented with a very fine embroidered handkerchief. Her slaves were to the number of thirty, besides ten little ones, the eldest not above seven years old. These were the most beautiful girls I ever saw, all richly dressed; and I observed that the Sultana took a great deal of pleasure in these lovely children, which is a vast expense; for there is not a handsome girl of that age to be bought under a hundred pounds sterling. They wore little garlands of flowers, and their own hair, braided, which was all their head-dress; but their habits all of gold stuffs. These served her coffee, kneeling; brought water when she washed, &c. It is a great part of the business

[7] *kyslár agá:* The chief eunuch of the seraglio and key official of the court.
[8] **the Sultan:** Mustafa II, who died in 1703.   [9] *pellice:* A long cloak lined with fur.

of the older slaves to take care of these girls, to learn them to embroider, and serve them as carefully as if they were children of the family.

Now, do I fancy that you imagine I have entertained you, all this while, with a relation that has, at least, received many embellishments from my hand? This is but too like (say you) the Arabian Tales: these embroidered napkins! and a jewel as large as a turkey's egg! — You forget, dear sister, those very tales were written by an author of this country, and (excepting the enchantments) are a real representation of the manners here. We travellers are in very hard circumstances: If we say nothing but what has been said before us, we are dull, and we have observed nothing. If we tell any thing new, we are laughed at as fabulous and romantic, not allowing for the difference of ranks, which afford difference of company, more curiosity, or the changes of customs, that happen every twenty years in every country. But people judge of travellers exactly with the same candour, good nature, and impartiality, they judge of their neighbours upon all occasions. For my part, if I live to return amongst you, I am so well acquainted with the morals of all my dear friends and acquaintance, that I am resolved to tell them nothing at all, to avoid the imputation (which their charity would certainly incline them to) of my telling too much. But I depend upon your knowing me enough to believe whatever I seriously assert for truth; though I give you leave to be surprised at an account so new to you.

But what would you say if I told you, that I have been in a harém, where the winter apartment was wainscoted with inlaid work of mother-of-pearl, ivory of different colours, and olive wood, exactly like the little boxes you have seen brought out of this country; and those rooms designed for summer, the walls all crusted with japan china, the roofs gilt, and the floors spread with the finest Persian carpets? Yet there is nothing more true; such is the palace of my lovely friend, the fair Fatima, whom I was acquainted with at Adrianople. I went to visit her yesterday; and, if possible, she appeared to me handsomer than before. She met me at the door of her chamber, and, giving me her hand with the best grace in the world — "You Christian ladies," said she, with a smile that made her as handsome as an angel, "have the reputation of inconstancy, and I did not expect, whatever goodness you expressed for me at Adrianople, that I should ever see you again. But I am now convinced that I have really the happiness of pleasing you; and, if you knew how I speak of you amongst our ladies, you would be assured that you do me justice if you think me your friend." She placed me in the corner of the sofa, and I spent the afternoon in her conversation, with the greatest pleasure in the world.

The Sultana Hafiteń is, what one would naturally expect to find a Turkish lady, willing to oblige, but not knowing how to go about it; and it is easy to see in her manner, that she has lived secluded from the world. But Fatima has all the politeness and good breeding of a court; with an air that inspires, at once, respect and tenderness; and now I understand her language, I find her wit as engaging as her beauty. She is very curious after the manners of other countries, and has not that partiality for her own, so common to little minds. A Greek that I carried with me, who had never seen her before, (nor could have been admitted now, if she had not been in my train,) shewed that surprise at her beauty and manner which is unavoidable at the first sight, and said to me in Italian, "This is no Turkish lady, she is certainly some

Christian." Fatima guessed she spoke of her, and asked what she said. I would not have told, thinking she would have been no better pleased with the compliment than one of our court beauties to be told she had the air of a Turk; but the Greek lady told it her; and she smiled, saying, "It is not the first time I have heard so: My mother was a Poloneze, taken at the siege of Caminiec;[10] and my father used to rally me, saying, He believed his Christian wife had found some Christian gallant; for I had not the air of a Turkish girl." I assured her, that, if all the Turkish ladies were like her, it was absolutely necessary to confine them from public view, for the repose of mankind; and proceeded to tell her what a noise such a face as hers would make in London or Paris. "I can't believe you," replied she agreeably; "if beauty was so much valued in your country as you say, they would never have suffered you to leave it." Perhaps, dear sister, you laugh at my vanity in repeating this compliment; but I only do it as I think it very well turned, and give it you as an instance of the spirit of her conversation.

Her house was magnificently furnished, and very well fancied; her winter rooms being furnished with figured velvet on gold grounds, and those for summer with fine Indian quilting embroidered with gold. The houses of the great Turkish ladies are kept clean with as much nicety as those in Holland. This was situated in a high part of the town; and from the windows of her summer apartment we had the prospect of the sea, the islands, and the Asian mountains. [. . .]

---

[10] Camieniec: A chief town in the Russian district of Podolio, a part of the Ottoman empire since 1672; it had long been a site of fighting between Poles and Turks. Turkey lost Camieniec to Russia in 1795.

❧ DENIS DIDEROT
1713–1784

Denis Diderot was born in 1713 in the Champagne region of France and educated in Jesuit schools; eventually he moved to Paris where he completed his Masters of Arts in 1732, after which he supported himself primarily by tutoring, translating, and writing. In 1751, Diderot, along with Jean d'Alembert, began a twenty-year project to complete the *Encyclopedia,* which aimed to tabulate and catalog all that was known in philosophy, science, the arts, and the trades. Diderot also wrote novels and philosophical treatises, including *Rameau's Nephew* (not published until 1823), *The Dream of d'Alembert* (1769), and the *Supplement to The Voyage of Bougainville* (completed in 1772 but not published until more than twenty years later).

Diderot began the *Supplement* as a review of Louis Antoine de Bougainville's *Voyage around the World* (1771), describing the French explorer's voyage made between 1766 and 1769. The first Frenchman to

Whether you burn or don't burn in your country doesn't matter to me. But you will not judge the morals of Europe by those of Tahiti, nor, consequently, the morals of Tahiti by those of Europe.

– OROU TO THE ALMONER in Diderot's *Supplement to the Voyage of Bougainville*

sail around the world, Bougainville described the expulsion of the Jesuits from Paraguay in 1768, an event he witnessed, and he refuted the popular view (stemming from accounts of Magellan's[1] visit to Patagonia) that the natives of Tierra del Fuego were giants. Like other European travelers to the South Seas, Bougainville described Tahiti as a kind of terrestrial paradise. In the European imagination, the people of the South Seas were thought to live an idyllic life of ease and sexual freedom, released by nature's bounty from the necessity for labor and happily imitating natural law in their social practices.

In the *Supplement,* Diderot blends the conventions of the TRAVEL NARRATIVE with those of philosophical dialogue, as he sets up a conversation between two unidentified Frenchmen, "A" and "B." They report the testimony of a Tahitian chieftain, who predicts the demise of his people and customs, as well as a dialogue between a French priest and a Tahitian named Orou. This conversation, part of which we include here, contrasts European customs and religious mores with those of Tahiti as a means of weighing the merits of natural law, as Diderot imagines it to be practiced among the islanders. The sexual freedom of the Tahitians starkly contrasts with the taboo-ridden practices of the Europeans, represented by the Almoner, whose natural desires come into conflict with the artificial laws of civil and religious authority. These laws, Diderot suggests, lead to hypocrisy, since European men and women still secretly follow the compelling urges of that greater force—natural law. Diderot's depiction of the European as a person tormented by the struggle between natural desires and artificial moral constraints in some ways anticipates Nietzsche's[2] analysis of morality and Freud's[3] conception of the conflict between the unconscious and the conscious.

Our selection begins just after one of the speakers has described the arrival of Bougainville's vessel in Tahiti, at which time the Tahitians put on a lavish "spectacle of hospitality" for their visitors. The unnamed priest has been invited into the home of Orou, where the dramatized conflict between natural and artificial man, represented by Orou and the Almoner, begins. As their conversation proceeds, the text invites questions about how much Diderot's text plays to the curiosity of his European readers, and how much to their philosophical interests.

A note on the translation: We use the translation by Jean Stewart and Jonathan Kemp here, which faithfully reproduces the dialogue between Orou and the Almoner. All notes are the editors'.

---

[1] **Magellan:** Ferdinand Magellan (c. 1480–1521), Portuguese-born explorer and navigator who led the first voyage around the world, leaving from Spain in 1519 and reaching Patagonia, the Marianas, and the Philippines, where he was killed.

[2] **Nietzsche:** Friedrich Wilhelm Nietzsche (1844–1900), German philosopher known for his attack on the "slave morality" of Judaeo-Christian culture and his commentary on the condition of modern humanity; his works include *Thus Spake Zarathustra* (1883–91) and *Beyond Good and Evil* (1886).

[3] **Freud:** Sigmund Freud (1856–1939), Austrian psychiatrist and founder of the modern practice of psychoanalysis; his writings on dreams, the ego, the id, and the unconscious created a revolution in the understanding of human behavior.

ೞ Supplement to the Voyage of Bougainville

Translated by Jean Stewart and Jonathan Kemp

3. DISCUSSION BETWEEN THE ALMONER AND OROU

B: In the sharing of Bougainville's crew among the Tahitians, the almoner was allotted to Orou; they were about the same age, thirty-five to thirty-six. Orou had then only his wife and three daughters, called Asto, Palli, and Thia. They undressed the almoner, bathed his face, hands, and feet, and served him a wholesome and frugal meal. When he was about to go to bed, Orou, who had been absent with his family, reappeared, and presenting to him his wife and three daughters, all naked, said: "You have eaten, you are young and in good health; if you sleep alone you will sleep badly, for man needs a companion beside him at night. There is my wife, there are my daughters; choose the one who pleases you best. But if you wish to oblige me you will give preference to the youngest of my daughters, who has not yet had any children." The mother added: "Alas! But it's no good complaining about it; poor Thia! it is not her fault."

The almoner answered that his religion, his office, good morals, and decency would not allow him to accept these offers.

Orou replied: "I do not know what this thing is that you call 'religion'; but I can only think ill of it, since it prevents you from tasting an innocent pleasure to which nature, the sovereign mistress, invites us all; prevents you from giving existence to one of your own kind, from doing a service which a father, mother, and children all ask of you, from doing something for a host who has received you well, and from enriching a nation, by giving it one more citizen. I do not know what this thing is which you call your 'office' but your first duty is to be a man and to be grateful. I do not suggest that you should introduce into your country the ways of Orou, but Orou, your host and friend, begs you to lend yourself to the ways of Tahiti. Whether the ways of Tahiti are better or worse than yours is an easy question to decide. Has the land of your birth more people than it can feed? If so your ways are neither worse nor better than ours. But can it feed more than it has? Our ways are better than yours. As to the sense of decency which you offer as objection, I understand you; I agree that I was wrong, and I ask your pardon. I do not want you to injure your health; if you are tired, you must have rest; but I hope that you will not continue to sadden us. See the care you have made appear on all these faces; they fear lest you should have found blemishes on them which merit your disdain. But when it is only the pleasure of doing honour to one of my daughters, amidst her companions and sisters, and of doing a good action, won't that suffice you? Be generous!"

THE ALMONER: It's not that: they are all equally beautiful; but my religion! my office!

OROU: They are mine and I offer them to you; they are their own and they give themselves to you. Whatever may be the purity of conscience which the thing "religion" and the thing "office" prescribe, you can accept them without scruple. I am not abusing my authority at all; be sure that I know and respect the rights of the individual."

Here the truthful almoner agrees that Providence had never exposed him to such violent temptation. He was young, he became agitated and tormented; he turned his eyes away from the lovely suppliants, and then regarded them again; he raised his hands and eyes to the sky. Thia, the youngest, clasped his knees and said: "Stranger, do not distress my father and mother, do not afflict me. Honour me in the hut, among my own people; raise me to the rank of my sisters, who mock me. Asto, the eldest, already had three children; the second, Palli, has two; but Thia has none at all. Stranger, honest stranger, do not repulse me; make me a mother, make me a child that I can one day lead by the hand, by my side, here in Tahiti; who may be seen held at my breast in nine months' time; one of whom I shall be so proud and who will be part of my dowry when I go from my parents' hut to another's. I shall perhaps be more lucky with you than with our young Tahitians. If you will grant me this favour I shall never forget you; I shall bless you all my life. I shall write your name on my arm and on your son's; we shall pronounce it always with joy. And when you leave these shores, my good wishes will go with you on the seas till you reach your own land."

The candid almoner said that she clasped his knees, and gazed into his eyes so expressively and so touchingly; that she wept; that her father, mother, and sisters withdrew; that he remained alone with her, and that, still saying "my religion, my office," he found himself the next morning lying beside the young girl, who overwhelmed him with caresses, and who invited her parents and sisters, when they came to their bed in the morning, to join their gratitude to hers. Asto and Palli, who had withdrawn, returned bringing food, fruits and drink. They kissed their sister and made vows over her. They all ate together.

Then Orou, left alone with the almoner, said to him:

"I see that my daughter is well satisfied with you and I thank you. But would you teach me what is meant by this word 'religion' which you have repeated so many times and so sorrowfully?"

The almoner, after having mused a moment answered: "Who made your hut and the things which furnish it?"

OROU: I did.

THE ALMONER: Well then, we believe that this world and all that it contains is the work of a maker.

OROU: Has he feet, hands, and a head then?

THE ALMONER: No.

OROU: Where is his dwelling-place?

THE ALMONER: Everywhere.

OROU: Here too?

THE ALMONER: Here.

OROU: We have never seen him.

THE ALMONER: One doesn't see him.

OROU: That's an indifferent father, then! He must be old, for he will at least be as old as his work.

THE ALMONER: He does not age. He spoke to our ancestors, gave them laws, prescribed the manner in which he wished to be honoured; he ordered a certain behaviour as being good, and he forbade them certain other actions as being wicked.

OROU: I follow you; and one of the actions he forbade them, as wicked, was to lie with a woman or a girl? Why, then, did he make two sexes?

THE ALMONER: That they might unite; but with certain requisite conditions, after certain preliminary ceremonies in consequence of which the man belongs to the woman and only to her; and the woman belongs to the man, and only to him.

OROU: For their whole lives?

THE ALMONER: For the whole of their lives.

OROU: So that if it happened that a woman should lie with a man other than her husband, or a husband with another woman . . . but that couldn't happen. Since the maker is there and this displeases him, he will know how to prevent them doing it.

THE ALMONER: No; he lets them do it, and they sin against the law of God (for it is thus we call the great maker) against the law of the country; and they commit a crime.

OROU: I should be sorry to offend you by what I say, but if you would permit me, I would give you my opinion.

THE ALMONER: Speak.

OROU: I find these singular precepts opposed to nature and contrary to reason, made to multiply crimes and to plague at every moment this old maker, who has made everything, without help of hands, or head, or tools, who is everywhere and is not seen anywhere, who exists to-day and to-morrow and yet is not a day older, who commands and is not obeyed, who can prevent and yet does not do so. Contrary to nature because these precepts suppose that a free, thinking, and sentient being can be the property of a being like himself. On what is this law founded? Don't you see that in your country they have confused the thing which has neither consciousness nor thought, nor desire, nor will; which one picks up, puts down, keeps or exchanges, without injury to it, or without its complaining, have confused this with the thing which cannot be exchanged or acquired, which has liberty, will, desire, which can give or refuse itself for a moment or for ever, which laments and suffers, and which cannot become an article of commerce, without its character being forgotten and violence done to its nature; contrary to the general law of existence? In fact, nothing could appear to you more senseless than a precept which refuses to admit that change which is a part of us, which commands a constancy which cannot be found there and which violates the liberty of the male and female by chaining them for ever to each other; more senseless than a fidelity which limits the most capricious of enjoyments to one individual; than an oath of the immutability of two beings made of flesh; and all that in the face of a sky which never for a moment remains the same, in caverns which threaten destruction, below a rock which falls to powder, at the foot of a tree which cracks, on a stone which rocks? Believe me, you have made the condition of man worse than that of animals. I do not know what your great maker may be; but I rejoice that he has never spoken to our forefathers, and I wish that he may never speak to our children; for he might tell them the same foolishness, and they commit the folly of believing it. Yesterday, at supper, you mentioned "magistrates" and "priests," whose authority regulates your conduct; but, tell me, are they the masters of good and evil? Can they make what is just to be unjust, and unjust, just? Does it rest with them to attribute good to harmful actions, and evil to innocent or useful actions? You could not think it, for, at that rate, there would be neither true nor false, good nor bad, beautiful nor ugly; or at any rate only what pleased your great maker, your magistrates and your priests to pronounce so. And from one moment to another you would be obliged to change your ideas and your conduct. One day someone would tell you, on behalf of one of your three masters, to kill, and you would be obliged by your conscience to kill; another day, "steal," and you would have to steal; or "do not eat this fruit" and you would not dare to eat it; "I forbid you this vegetable or animal" and you would take care not to touch them. There is no good thing that could not be forbidden you, and no wickedness that you could not be ordered to do. And what would you be reduced to, if your three masters, disagreeing among themselves, should at once permit, enjoin, and forbid you the same thing, as I believe must often happen. Then, to please the priest you must become embroiled with the magistrate; to satisfy the magistrate you must displease the great maker; and to make yourself agreeable to the great maker you must renounce nature. And do you know what will happen then? You will neglect all of them, and you will be neither man, nor citizen, nor pious; you will be nothing; you will be out of favour with all the kinds of authorities, at odds even with yourself, tormented by your heart, persecuted by your enraged masters; and wretched as I saw you yesterday evening when I offered my wife and daughters to you, and you cried out, "But my religion, my office!"

Do you want to know what is good and what is bad in all times and in all places? Hold fast to the nature of things and of actions; to your relations with your fellows; to the influence of your conduct on your individual usefulness and the general good. You are mad if you believe that there is anything, high or low in the universe, which can add to or subtract from the laws of nature. Her eternal will is that good should be preferred to evil, and the general good to the individual good. You may ordain the opposite but you will not be obeyed. You will multiply the number of malefactors and the wretched by fear, punishment, and remorse. You will deprave consciences; you will corrupt minds. They will not know what to do or what to avoid. Disturbed in their state of innocence, at ease with crime, they will have lost their guiding star. [. . .]

MIRZA ABU TALEB KHAN
1752–?1806

Like the Chinese after the "Great Withdrawal" of 1433, Hindus in India were discouraged if not prohibited from traveling overseas. Unlike the Chinese, however, whose isolation resulted from a governmental edict, Hindus, especially those of the highest castes, restricted travel because they believed that contact with foreigners was unclean. Indian Muslims, however, such as Mirza Abu Taleb Khan, gave in to their desire to travel. Indeed, because all members of Islam are enjoined to undertake a pilgrimage to Mecca at least once in their lives, Muslims were accustomed to long journeys, often across strange lands.

As the British presence in and administrative control of India increased, curiosity about Britain intensified. Abu Taleb, born at Lucknow in 1752, is one of the first Indians to leave behind a narrative of his travels to England. He worked for some time as a government employee in Bengal and Oudh, and after being forced early into retirement, he joined the service of the British and moved to Calcutta. When it became clear he would not achieve the high post that he had hoped for, he accepted an invitation to travel to England.

Abu Taleb spent three years in England, where he was put on display to the king and queen and where he became a favorite with some English aristocrats who entertained him as "the Persian prince." His account of these years, *Travels of Mirza Abu Taleb Khan,* was written upon his return to Calcutta in 1803 and published in an English translation by Charles Stewart in 1810. It records what he found remarkable and different in England, gives us a sense of his attraction to life in high society, and shows his disdain of European religion and philosophy. While documenting the curious habits of the English and praising their technological advances and manufacturing abilities, he attacks their apparent greed and their want of religious feeling and humility. As he explains in his introductory remarks, he hopes that his account would both entertain his readers and provide them with some examples of useful English practices.

A note on the translation: This is the Charles Stewart translation, originally published in 1810. Thus the capitalization, punctuation, and spelling reflect those of early-nineteenth-century written English. All notes are the editors'.

> It . . . occurred to him, that if he were to write all the circumstances of his journey through Europe, to describe the curiosities and wonders which he saw, and to give some account of the manners and customs of the various nations he visited, all of which are little known to Asiatics, it would afford a gratifying banquet to his countrymen.
>
> – ABU TALEB, *Travels*

FROM

～ Travels of Mirza Abu Taleb Khan

Translated by Charles Stewart

In the Name of the Most merciful God

INTRODUCTION

Glory be to God, the Lord of all worlds, who has conferred innumerable blessings on mankind, and accomplished all the laudable desires of his creatures,. Praise be also to the Chosen of Mankind, the traveller over the whole expanse of the heavens, (Mohammed), and benedictions without end on his descendants and companions.

The wanderer over the face of the earth, Abu Taleb the son of Mohammed of Ispahan, begs leave to inform the curious in biography, that, owing to several adverse circumstances, finding it inconvenient to remain at home, he was compelled to undertake many tedious journeys; during which, he associated with men of all nations, and beheld various wonders, both by sea and by land.

It therefore occurred to him, that if he were to write all the circumstances of his journey through Europe, to describe the curiosities and wonders which he saw, and to give some account of the manners and customs of the various nations he visited, all of which are little known to Asiatics, it would afford a gratifying banquet to his countrymen.

He was also of opinion, that many of the customs, inventions, sciences, and ordinances of Europe, the good effects of which are apparent in those countries, might with great advantage [be] imitated by Mohammedans. [. . .]

A few weeks subsequent to my visit to Mr. Dundas,[1] I had the honour of being introduced to the King; and on the following day was presented to her most gracious Majesty Queen Charlotte. Both of these illustrious personages received me in the most condescending manner, and, after having honoured me with some conversation, commanded me to come frequently to court. After this introduction, I received invitations from all the Princess; and the Nobility vied with each other in their attention to me. Hospitality is one of the most esteemed virtues of the English; and I experienced it to such a degree, that I was seldom disengaged. In these parties I enjoyed every luxury my heart could desire. Their viands were delicious, and wines exquisite. The beauty of the women, and their grace in dancing, delighted my imagination; while the variety and melody of their music charmed all my senses.

I may perhaps be accused of personal vanity by saying, that my society was courted, and that my wit and repartees, with some *impromptu* applications of Oriental

---

[1] Before moving to London, Abu Taleb landed in Dublin where he spent several months among the Irish. **Henry Dundas** (1742–1811) was Member of Parliament for Midlothian and later for Edinburgh, Scotland; Dundas held various offices, including home secretary and secretary of war, in the ministry of William Pitt, then prime minister. **George III** (r. 1760–1820) was king of Great Britain; **Queen Charlotte** (1744–1818) was his wife. Abu Taleb had recently been a guest at Dundas's country estate at Wimbledon.

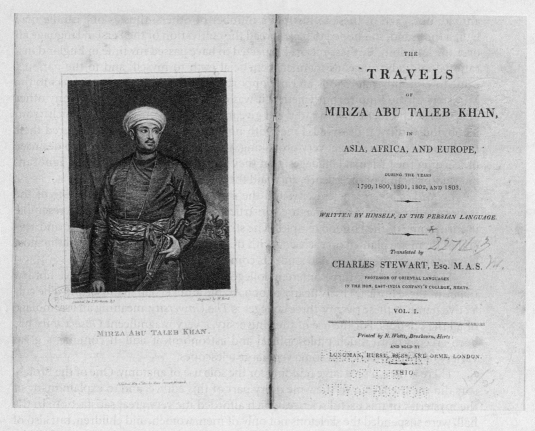

Portrait of Mirza Abu Taleb Khan and Frontispiece to *Travels of Mirza Abu Taleb Khan,* **Vol. i., 1810**

The English translation of Abu Taleb's Travels *was published in 1810, seven years after he completed his journey undertaken from 1799 to 1803. (Courtesy of the Trustees of the Boston Public Library)*

poetry, were the subject of conversation in the politest circles. I freely confess, that, during my residence in England, I was so exhilarated by the coolness of the climate and so devoid of all care, that I followed the advice of our immortal poet Hafiz,[2] and gave myself up to love and gaiety. . . .

When I first arrived in London, it had been my determination to have opened a Public Academy to be patronized by Government, for instructing such of the English as were destined to fill important situations in the East, in the Hindoostany, Persian, and Arabic languages. The plan I proposed was, that I should commence with a limited number of pupils, selected for the purpose, who were not to go

---

[2] **Hafiz;** Shams al-Din Hafiz (c. 1320–1390), a master of the *ghazal;* often considered to be the greatest lyric poet in the Persian language.

abroad; but, each of these to instruct a number of others: thus as one candle may light a thousand, so I hoped to have spread the cultivation of the Persian language all over the kingdom. By these means I expected to have passed my time in England in a rational and advantageous manner; beneficial both to myself, and to the nation I came to visit. I therefore took an early opportunity of mentioning the subject to the Ministers of the Empire: but whether it was owing to their having too many other affairs to attend to, or that they did not give my plan that consideration which, from its obvious utility, it deserved, I met with no encouragement. What rendered their indifference on this subject very provoking, was: many individuals were so desirous of learning the Oriental languages, that they attended self-taught masters, ignorant of every principle of the science, and paid them half-a-guinea a lesson. . . .

Oxford is a very ancient city, and the most celebrated *Seat of Learning* of the Empire. All the public buildings are constructed of hewn stone, and much resemble in form some of the Hindoo temples. The streets are very wide and regular, and several of them are planted on each side with trees. In this place are assembled the most learned men of the nation, and students come here from all parts.

There are twenty-three different colleges, each containing an extensive library. In *one* of these libraries I saw nearly 10,000 Arabic and Persian manuscripts. The collective name of these twenty-three colleges is *The University,* meaning an assemblage of all the sciences. For the use of the University, a very magnificent *Observatory* has been erected, with much philosophical and astronomical skill. It contains a great variety of instruments, and some very large telescopes.

There is here, also, a large building for the sole use of anatomy. One of the Professors did me the favour to shew me every part of this edifice, and to explain many of the mysteries of this useful science, which afforded me very great satisfaction. In the hall, were suspended the skeletons not only of men, women, and children, but also of all species of animals. In another apartment was as exact representation of all the veins, arteries, and muscles of the human body, filled with red and yellow wax, minutely imitating Nature. The Professor particularly pointed out to me the great nerve, which, commencing at the head, runs down the back-bone, where it divides it into four great branches, one of which extends down each arm, and leg, to the ends of the fingers and toes. In another room were, preserved in spirits, several bodies of children, who had something peculiar in their conformation. One of these *lusus Nature*[3] had two heads and four feet, but only one body. The mother having died in the act of parturition, the womb, with the children, was cut out, and preserved entire. [. . .]

CHAPTER XIX

It now becomes an unpleasant, and perhaps ungrateful, part of my duty, by complying with the positive desire of Lady Spenser[4] and several other of my friends, to mention those defects and vices which appeared to me to pervade the English character,

---

[3] *lusus Nature: Lusus Naturae* is Latin for *a freak of nature.*

[4] **Lady Spenser:** Abu Taleb most likely refers to Lady Caroline Spencer (1743–1811), wife of George Spencer, (1739–1811), Fourth Duke of Marlborough, who lived at Blenheim.

but which, perhaps, only existed in my own imagination. If the hints I shall give are not applicable, I hope they will be attributed to want of judgement, rather than to malice or ingratitude: but if my suggestions are acknowledged to be correct, I trust they (the English) will thank me for my candour, and endeavour to amend their errors.

VERSE

He is your friend, who, like a mirror, exhibits all your defects:
Not he, who, like a comb, covers them over with the hairs of flattery.

As my experience and knowledge of the common people were chiefly acquired in London, it may, and with great probability, be objected, that there are more vicious people to be found in the capital than in all the rest of the empire.

The first and greatest defect I observed in the English, is their want of faith in religion, and their great inclination to philosophy (atheism). The effects of these principles, or rather want of principle, is very conspicuous in the lower orders of people, who are totally devoid of honesty. They are, indeed, cautious how they transgress against the laws, from fear of punishment; but whenever an opportunity offers of purloining any thing without the risk of detection, they never pass it by. They are also ever on the watch to appropriate to themselves the property of the rich, who, on this account, are obliged constantly to keep their doors shut, and never to permit an unknown person to enter them. At present, owing to the vigilance of the magistrates, the severity of the laws, and the honour of the superior classes of people, no very bad consequences are to be apprehended; but if ever such nefarious practices should become prevalent, and should creep in among the higher classes, inevitable ruin must ensue.

The second defect, most conspicuous in the English character, is pride, or insolence. Puffed up with their power and good fortune for the last fifty years, they are not apprehensive of adversity, and take no pains to avert it. Thus, when the people of London, some time ago, assembled in mobs on account of the great increase of taxes and high price of provisions, and were nearly in a state of insurrection, — although the magistrates, by their vigilance in watching them, and by causing parties of soldiers to patrole the streets day and night, to disperse all persons whom they saw assembling together, succeeded in quieting the disturbance, — yet no pains were afterwards taken to eradicate the evil. Some of the men in power said, it had been merely a plan of the artificers to obtain higher wages (an attempt frequently made by the English tradesmen); others were of opinion that no remedy could be applied; therefore no further notice was taken of the affair. All this, I say, betrays a blind confidence, which, instead of meeting the danger, and endeavouring to prevent it, waits till the misfortune arrives, and then attempts to remedy it. Such was the case with the late King of France,[5] who took no step to oppose the Revolution, till it was too late. This self-confidence is to be found, more or less, in every Englishman: it however differs much from the pride of the Indians and Persians.

---

[5] **late King of France:** Louis XVI (r. 1774–1792), king of France during the French Revolution, imprisoned and guillotined on January 21, 1793.

Their third defect is a passion for acquiring money, and their attachment to worldly affairs. Although these bad qualities are not so reprehensible in them as in countries more subject to the vicissitudes of fortune, (because, in England, property is so well protected by the laws, that every person reaps the fruits of his industry, and, in his old age, enjoys the earnings or economy of his youth,) yet sordid and illiberal habits are generally found to accompany avarice and parsimony, and, consequently, render the possessor of them contemptible: on the contrary, generosity, if it does not launch into prodigality, but is guided by the hand of prudence, will render a man respected and esteemed.

The fourth of their frailities is a desire of ease, and a dislike to exertion: this, however, prevails only in a moderate degree, and bears no proportion to the apathy and indolence of the smokers of opium of Hindoostan and Constantinople; it only prevents them from perfecting themselves in science, and exerting themselves in the service of their friends, upon what they *choose* to call trivial occasions. I must, however, remark, that friendship is much oftener cemented by acts of courtesy and good-nature, than by conferring permanent obligations; the opportunities of doing which can seldom occur, whereas the former happen daily. In London, I had sometimes occasion to trouble my friends to interpret for me, in the adjustment of my accounts with my landlord and others; but, in every instance, I found that, rather than be at the trouble of stopping for five minutes longer, and saying a few words in my defence, they would yield to an unjust demand, and offer to pay the items I objected to at their own expence: at the same time, an aversion to the employment of interpreter or mediator was so conspicuous in their countenance, that, latterly, I desisted from troubling them. In this respect I found the French much more courteous; for if, in Paris, the master of an hotel attempted to impose on me, the gentlemen present always interfered, and compelled him to do me justice.

Upon a cursory observation of the conduct of gentlemen in London, you would suppose they had a vast deal of business to attend to; whereas nine out of ten, of those I was acquainted with at the west end of the town, had scarcely any thing to do. An hour or two immediately after breakfast may be allotted to business, but the rest of the day is devoted to visiting and pleasure. If a person calls on any of these gentlemen, it is more than probable he is told by the servant, his master is *not at home;* but this is merely an idle excuse, to avoid the visits of people, whose business they are either ignorant of, or do not wish to be troubled with. If the suppliant calls in the morning; and is by chance admitted to the master of the house, before he can tell half his story, he is informed, that it is now the hour of business, and a particular engagement in the city requires the gentleman's immediate attendance. If he calls later in the day, the gentleman is just going out to pay a visit of consequence, and therefore cannot be detained: but if the petitioner, unabashed by such checks, continues to relate his narrative, he is set down as a brute, and never again permitted to enter the doors. In this instance, I again say that the French are greatly superior to the English; they are always courteous, and never betray those symptoms of impatience so conspicuous and reprehensible in the English character.

Their fifth defect is nearly allied to the former, and is termed irritability of temper. This passion often leads them to quarrel with their friends and acquaintances, without any substantial cause. Of the bad effects of this quality, strangers seldom have much reason to complain; but as society can only be supported by mutual forbearance, and sometimes shutting our eyes on the frailties or ignorance of our friends, it often causes animosities and disunion between the nearest relatives, and hurries the possessor into dilemmas whence he frequently finds it difficult to extricate himself.

The sixth defect of the English is their throwing away their time, in sleeping, eating, and dressing; for, besides the necessary ablutions, they every morning shave, and dress their hair; then, to accommodate themselves to the fashion, they put on twenty-five different articles of dress: all this, except shaving, is repeated before dinner, and the whole of these clothes are again to be taken off at night: so that not less than two complete hours can be allowed on this account. One hour is expended at breakfast; three hours at dinner; and the three following hours are devoted to tea, and the company of the ladies. Nine hours are given up to sleep: so that there remain just six hours, out of the twenty-four, for visiting and business. If they are reproached with this waste of time, they reply, "How is it to be avoided?" I answer them thus: "Curtail the number of your garments; render your dress simple; wear your beards; and give up less of your time to eating, drinking, and sleeping."

Their seventh defect is a luxurious manner of living, by which their wants are increased a hundred-fold. Observe their kitchens, filled with various utensils; their rooms, fitted up with costly furniture; their side-boards, covered with plate; their tables, loaded with expensive glass and china; their cellars, stocked with wines from every quarter of the world; their parks, abounding in game of various sorts; and their ponds, stored with fish. All these expences are incurred to pamper their appetites, which, from long indulgence, have gained such absolute sway over them, that a diminution of these luxuries would be considered, by many, as a serious misfortune. How unintelligible to them is the verse of one of their own Poets:

> Man wants but little here below,
> Nor wants that little long.

It is certain, that luxurious living generates many disorders, and is productive of various other bad consequences.

If the persons above alluded to will take the trouble of reading the history of the Arabians and Tartars, they will discover that both these nations acquired their extensive conquests, not by their numbers, nor by the superiority of their arms, which were merely bows and arrows, and swords: no, it was from the paucity of their wants: they were always prepared for action, and could subsist on the coarsest food. Their chiefs were content with the fare of their soldiers, and their personal expences were a mere trifle. Thus, when they took possession of an enemy's country they ever found the current revenue of it more than requisite for their simple but effective form of government; and, instead of raising the taxes on their new subjects, they frequently alleviated one half their burthen. The approach of their armies, therefore, instead of being dreaded, was wished for by the neighbouring people, and every facility given to their conquests. To this alone must be ascribed the rapidity with which they overran great part of the globe, in so short a period. [. . .]

The eighth defect of the English is vanity, and arrogance, respecting their ac-quirements in science, and a knowledge of foreign languages, for, as soon as one of them acquires the smallest insight into the principles of any science, or the rudi-ments of any foreign language, he immediately sits down and composes a work on the subject, and, by means of the Press, circulates books which have no more intrin-sic worth than the toys bestowed on children, which serve to amuse the ignorant, but are of no use to the learned. This is not merely my own opinion, but was confirmed to me both by Greeks and Frenchmen, whose languages are cultivated in England with more ardour than any others. Such, however, is the infatuation of the English, that they give the author implicit credit for his profound knowledge, and purchase his books. Even those who are judges of the subject do not discountenance this mea-sure, but contend, that a little knowledge is better than entire ignorance, and that perfection can only be acquired by degrees. This axiom I deny; for the portion of sci-ence and truth contained in many of their books is so small, that much time is thrown away in reading them: besides, erroneous opinions and bad habits are often contracted by the perusal of such works, which are more difficult to eradicate, than it is to implant correct ideas in a mind totally uncultivated.

Far be it from me to depreciate the transcendant abilities and angelic character of Sir William Jones;[6] but his Persian Grammar, having been written when he was a young man, and previous to his having acquired any experience in Hidoostan, is, in many places, very defective; and it is much to be regretted that his public avocations, and other studies, did not permit him to revise it, after he had been some years in India. Whenever I was applied to by any person for instruction in the Persian lan-guage who had previously studied this grammar, I found it much more difficult to correct the bad pronunciation he had acquired, and the errors he had adopted, than it was to instruct a person who had never before seen the Persian alphabet. Such books are now so numerous in London, that, in a short time, it will be difficult to discriminate or separate them from works of real value.

A ninth failing prevalent among the English is selfishness. They frequently endeavour to benefit themselves, without attending to the injury it may do to others: and when they seek their own advantage, they are more humble and submissive than appears to me proper; for after they have obtained their object, they are either ashamed of their former conduct, or dislike the continuance of it so much, that they frequently break off the connection. Others, restrained by a sense of propriety, still keep up the intercourse, and endeavour to make the person they have injured, or whom they have deceived by promises, forget the circumstance, by their flattering and courteous behavior. [. . .]

The tenth vice of this nation is want of chastity; for under this head I not only include the reprehensible conduct of young women running away with their lovers, and others cohabiting with a man before marriage, but the great degree of licen-

---

[6] Sir William Jones (1746–1794): An English jurist and philologist who served for eleven years as a justice in Calcutta; with an expert knowledge of more than thirteen languages, he was one of the leading translators in England of Arabic, Persian, and Sanskrit literature, including poems from the Persian poet Hafiz and the *Shakuntula* by the Indian writer Kalidasa (fifth century C.E.).

tiousness practised by numbers of both sexes in London; evinced by the multiplicity of public-houses and bagnios in every part of the town. I was credibly informed, that in the single parish of Mary-la-bonne,[7] which is only a sixth part of London, there reside sixty thousand courtezans; besides which, there is scarcely, a street in the metropolis where they are not to be found. The conduct of these women is rendered still more blameable, by their hiring lodgings in or frequenting streets which from their names ought only to be the abode of virtue and religion; for instance, "Paradise Street," "Modest Court," "St. James's Street," "St. Martin's Lane," and "St. Paul's Churchyard." The first of these is to be the residence of the righteous; the second implies virtue; and the others are named after the holy Apostles of the Blessed Messiah. Then there is Queen Anne Street, and Charlotte Street; the one named after the greatest, the other after the best, of Queens. I however think, that persons who let the lodgings are much more reprehensible than the unfortunate women themselves.

The eleventh vice of the English is extravagance, that is, living beyond their incomes by incurring useless expences, and keeping up unnecessary establishments. Some of these I have before alluded to, under the head of luxuries; but to those are now to be added the establishments of carriages, horses, and servants, two sets of which are frequently kept, one for the husband, the other for his wife. Much money is also lavished in London, on balls, masquerades, routs etc. Sometimes the sum of £1000 is thus expended in one night's entertainment. I have known gentlemen in the receipt of six or seven thousand pounds a year, who were so straitened by such inconsiderate expences, that if asked by a friend for the loan of *ten pounds,* could not comply with this trifling request. This spirit of extravagance appears daily to increase; and being imitated by merchants and tradesmen, must have the worst of consequences; for if these people find the profits of their trade not sufficient to support their expences, they will attempt to supply the deficiency by dishonest means, and at length take to highway robbery. It also encourages dissipation and profligacy in the lower classes, which tend to the subversion of all order and good government. [. . .]

Their twelfth defect is a contempt for the customs of other nations, and the preference they give to their own; although theirs, in fact, may be much inferior. I had a striking instance of this prejudice in the conduct of my fellow-passengers on board ship. Some of these, who were otherwise respectable characters, ridiculed the idea of my wearing trowsers, and a night dress, when I went to bed; and contended, that they slept much more at their ease by going to bed nearly naked. I replied, that I slept very comfortably; that mine was certainly the most decent mode; and that, in the event of any sudden accident happening, I could run on deck instantly, and, if requisite, jump into the boat in a minute; whilst they must either lose some time in dressing, or come out of their cabins in a very immodest manner. In answer to this, they said, such sudden accidents seldom occurred, but that if it did happen, they would not hesitate to come on deck in their shirts only. This I give merely as a specimen of their obstinacy, and prejudice in favour of their own customs.

In London, I was frequently attacked on the apparent unreasonableness and childishness of some of the Mohammedan customs; but as, from my knowledge of

---

[7] **Mary-la-bonne:** Marylebone is a district in north London.

the English character, I was convinced it would be folly to argue the point philosophically with them, I contended myself with parrying the subject. Thus, when they attempted to turn into ridicule the ceremonies used by the pilgrims on their arrival at Mecca, I asked them, why they supposed the ceremony of baptism, by a clergyman, requisite for the salvation of a child, who could not possibly be sensible what he was about. When they reproached us for eating with our hands; I replied, "There is by this mode no danger of cutting yourself or your neighbours; and it is an old and a true proverb, 'The nearer the bone, the sweeter the meat': but, exclusive of these advantages, a man's own hands are surely cleaner than the *feet of a baker's boy;* for it is well known, that half the bread in London is kneaded by the feet." By this mode of argument I, completely silenced all my adversaries, and frequently turned the laugh against them, when they expected to have refuted me and made me appear ridiculous.

Many of these vices, or defects, are not natural to the English; but have been ingrafted on them by prosperity and luxury; the bad consequences of which have not yet appeared; and, for two reasons, may not be conspicuous for some time. The first of these is the strength of constitution both of individuals and of the Government: for if a person of a strong constitution swallow a dose of poison, its deleterious effects are sometimes carried off by the power of the nerves; but if a weak person should take it, he would certainly fall a victim. The second reason is, that their neighbours are not exempt from these vices; nay, possess them in a greater proportion. Our poet Sady[8] has said,

> To the inhabitants of Paradise, Purgatory would seem a Hell:
> But to Sinners in Hell, Purgatory would be a Paradise.

From what I saw and heard of the complaints and dissatisfaction of the common people in England, I am convinced, if the French had succeeded in establishing a happy and quiet government, whereby the taxes could have been abolished, and the price of provisions reduced, the English would, of themselves, have followed their example, and united with them: for, even during the height of the war, many of the English imitated the fashions, follies, and vices of the French, to an absurd degree.

Few of the English have good sense or candour enough to acknowledge the prevalence and growth of these vices, or defects, among them; but, like the smokers of *beng* (hempseed) in Turkey, when told of the virtues of their ancestors, and their own present degeneracy, make themselves ready for battle, and say, "No nation was ever exempt from vices: the people and the governments you describe as possessing such angelic virtues were not a bit better than ourselves; and so long as we are not worse than our neighbours, no danger is to be apprehended." This reasoning is, however, false; for fire still retains its inflammable nature, whether it is summer or winter; and the flame, though for a short time smothered by a heap of fuel thrown on it, breaks out in the sequel with the greatest violence. In like manner, vice will, sooner or later, cause destruction to its possessor.

---

[8] Sady: S'adi (c. 1219–1291), one of the greatest of the Persian poets, known for his *Gulistan* (The Rose Garden).

CHAPTER XX

I fear, in the foregoing Chapter, I have fatigued my readers with a long detail of the vices, or defects of the English: I shall, therefore, now give some account of their virtues; but, lest I should be accused of flattery, will endeavour to avoid prolixity on this subject.

The first of the English virtues is a high sense of honour, especially among the better classes. This is the effect of a liberal education, and of the contempt with which those who do not possess it are regarded. [. . .]

Their second good quality is a reverence for every thing or person possessing superior excellence. This mode of thinking has this great advantage—it makes them emulous of acquiring the esteem of the world, and thus renders them better men. [. . .]

The third of their perfections is a dread of offending against the rules of propriety, or the laws of the realm: they are therefore generally content with their own situations, and very seldom attempt to exalt themselves by base or nefarious practices. By these means the establishments of Church and State are supported, and the bonds of society strengthened; for when men are ambitious of raising themselves from inferior to exalted situations, they attempt to overcome all obstacles; and though a few gain their object, the greater part are disappointed, and become, ever after, unhappy and discontended.

The fourth of their virtues is a strong desire to improve the situations of the common people, and an aversion to do any thing which can injure them. It may be said, that in so doing they are not perfectly disinterested; for that the benefits of many of these institutions and inventions revert to themselves. [. . .]

Their fifth good quality is so nearly allied to weakness, that by some worldly people it has been called such: I mean, an adherence to the rules of fashion. By this arbitrary law, the rich are obliged not only to alter the shape of their clothes every year, but also to change all the furniture of their houses. It would be thought quite derogatory to a person of taste, to have his drawing room fitted up in the same manner for two successive years. The advantage of this profusion is the encouragement it gives to ingenuity and manufacturers of every kind; and it enables the middling and lower classes of people to supply their wants at a cheap rate, by purchasing the old fashioned articles.

Their sixth excellence is a passion for mechanism, and their numerous contrivances for facilitating labour and industry.

Their seventh perfection is plainness of manners: and sincerity of disposition; the former is evinced in the colours of their clothes, which are generally of a dark hue, and exempt from all tawdriness; and the latter, by their open and manly conduct.

Their other good qualities are good natural sense and soundness of judgement, which induce them to prefer things that are useful to those that are brilliant; to which may be added, their perseverance in the acquirement of science, and the attainment of wealth and honours.

Their hospitality is also very praiseworthy, and their attention to their guests can nowhere be exceeded. They have an aversion to sit down to table *alone;* and from their liberal conduct on this subject, one would suppose the following verse had been written by an Englishman:

> May the food of the misanthrope be cast to the dogs!
> May he who eats alone be shortly eaten by the worms!

It is said, that all these virtues were formerly possessed in a greater degree by the English, and that the present race owe much of their fame and celebrity to their ancestors.

The English have very peculiar opinions on the subject of *perfection*. They insist, that it is merely an ideal quality, and depends entirely upon comparison; that mankind have risen, by degrees, from the state of savages to the exalted dignity of the great philosopher NEWTON:[9] but that, so far from having yet attained *perfection,* it is possible that, in future ages, philosophers will look with as much contempt on the acquirements of Newton, as we now do on the rude state of the arts among savages. If this axiom of theirs be correct, man has yet much to learn, and all his boasted knowledge is but vanity.

---

[9] Newton: Sir Isaac Newton (1642–1727), English physicist and mathematician known for his discovery and formulation of the laws of gravity and the development of calculus; his greatest work is the *Mathematical Principles of Natural Philosophy,* or *Principia Mathematica* (1687).

❧ XIE QING GAO (HSIEH CH'ING KAO)
1765–1822

From the eleventh through the fourteenth centuries, Chinese trade by sea expanded, linking the great Chinese port towns of Chekiang, Fukien, and Kwangtung to trading centers from the Indian Ocean to Japan. During this period, travel accounts appeared—including Chao Ju-kua's *Accounts of Foreign Countries* (1225)—that, in contrast to those of the previous generations, focused on practical information useful to merchants and seafarers. In the thirteenth century, Chinese travelers such as Changchun and the Nestorian Christian Rabban Bar Sauma journeyed as far as Kabul, where Genghis Khan had his court, and Rome, the seat of the Catholic Church.

Between 1403 and 1433, the Ming emperor Yongle orchestrated seven spectacular maritime voyages under the leadership of Admiral Zheng He (Cheng Ho). Sometimes deploying a fleet of more than three hundred ships and more than twenty thousand sailors, these voyages promoted trade and impressed China's neighbors in Southeast Asia, Java, and Sumatra, and reached from Ceylon and Calicut on the west coast of India to as far as Ormuz at the entrance of the Persian Gulf and Malindi on the east African coast. After the death of Yongle, the expeditions were curtailed, as Confucian officials hostile to mercantile expansion reasserted their influence on Chinese policies and as threats from the Mongols in the north turned China's attention and its resources inward.

Despite its isolationism, China did not stop all trade with outsiders. In the next century, the arrival of the Portuguese at Macao—just south of what is today Hong Kong—opened the door to Westerners, especially Jesuit priests, including the Italian Matteo Ricci (1552–1610). The Jesuits helped spread Western ideas and scientific knowledge in China as well as interpret Chinese culture and society for Europeans, whose curiosity about this great empire was growing. By the seventeenth century, a few Chinese students and scholars accompanied Jesuit priests to Europe, where they studied in Western universities. Nonetheless, with the exception of some sketchy comments in the journals of Chinese envoys to Russia, not until the late eighteenth century do we get a descriptive account of the West from a Chinese traveler.

That traveler was Xie Qing Gao (Hsieh Ch'ing Kao), born in the Chia-ying district of Kwangtung in 1765. From 1782 to about 1795, Xie Qing Gao was a crew member on a Portuguese merchant vessel that stopped in Portugal, Spain, England, Sweden, Africa, Southeast Asia, and even the United States. In 1796, after becoming blind, he returned to China and settled in Macao. There he recounted his travels to Yang Pingnan (Yang Bing-nan), who recorded Xie Qing Gao's descriptions of foreign places for posterity. In its focus on basic facts relating to trade, resources, and places, *The Hai-lu (Ocean Record)*, differs dramatically from Abu Taleb's *Travels*, which offers a detailed analysis and critique of British and French customs and habits. Abu Taleb was a highly educated official who spent several years mingling with people of the highest ranks in the countries he describes; in contrast, Xie Qing Gao was an illiterate sailor who spent only a brief time in port towns. Moreover, according to Kenneth Ch'en, whose translation of the text follows, *The Hai-lu* is "true to the Chinese tradition of geographical writing as exemplified in the local and provincial gazetteers, which are mainly descriptive in nature" and so present factual accounts of places "without any attempt to pass moral judgment on their culture." Nonetheless, *The Hai-lu* does capture glimpses of European religion, government, and military organization, as well as mores and customs, including marriage and fashion. All notes are the editors'.

FROM

❧ # The Hai-lu

Translated by Kenneth Ch'en

[*Portugal* (called Ta-hsi-yang, or Pu-lu-chi-shih)] . . . has a climate colder than that of Fukien and Kwangtung.[1] Her chief seaport [*Lisbon*] faces the south and is protected by two forts manned by two thousand soldiers and equipped with about four or five hundred cannons. Whenever any ship calls at the port, it is first examined by officials to see whether there is any case of smallpox on board. If there is not, the ship is permitted to enter; otherwise, the ship must wait outside the harbor until all traces of the disease have disappeared. Places of importance are seven in all: Lisbon, Coimbra, Guarda, Vizeu, Villa Real, A-la-chia [?], and Chaves. All these towns are densely settled, garrisoned by heavy forces, and are connected by good land and water routes.

The people are white in color, and are fond of cleanliness. As to the dress, the men usually wear trousers and short upper clothes, both very much tight-fitting. On special occasions, another piece is worn over the shirt, short in the front and long in the back, just like the wings of a cicada. Women also wear short and tight-fitting upper clothes, but instead of trousers they wear skirts which are sometimes eight or nine folds deep. Among the poor this is made of cotton; among the rich, silk. When rich women go out they often wear a veil made of fine black silk. Both men and women wear leather shoes.

Monogamy is the prevailing practice. It is only when either the husband or wife has died that the other may remarry. The family of the prospective bridegroom takes particular pains to find out the size of the bride's dowry before marrying her. Marriages between persons of the same surname are permitted but they are prohibited between children of the same parents. All marriages must receive the sanction of the Church, and it is only after the priest has pronounced his benediction on the couple that a marriage is considered concluded. The marriage ceremonies usually take place in the church.

Religion plays a dominant part in the lives of these people. Whenever anyone would commit a crime, he would go to the priest in the church and confess his sins and repent, after which he would be absolved by the priest. The priest is strictly forbidden to tell others what he has heard; he would be hanged if he did so. When a king ascends the throne, he does not take a new reign title, but follows the Christian calendar. There are also womenfolk who withdraw from the world and live apart in convents.

The king of the country is called *li–rei*. His eldest son is called *li-fan-tieh* [*l'infante*]; his other sons, *pi-lin-hsi-pi* [*principes*]; his daughters, *pi-lin-so-shih* [*princezas*]. The Prime Minister is called *kan-tieh* [*conde*]; the commander-in-chief of the army, *ma-la-chi-tsa* [*marquesado*]. . . . These officers are usually selected from among the leading citizens of the local community. In order to assist the local officials in their administration of affairs, the home government usually sends out a military official to each region. If the possession is a large one, then three or four officials are sent. If any problem arises, a conference is held of the four local officials

---

[1] **Fukien and Kwangtung:** Two of the major port towns in China at that time.

and the two central officials from home to decide on the solution and this solution must be in conformity with local customs and habits.

[*Spain*] . . . is said to be north-northwest of Portugal and could be reached by sailing in that direction for about eight or nine days from Portugal.[2] The area of this country is larger than that of Portugal; the people are fierce and wicked. Catholicism is the main religion. Its products are gold, silver, copper, iron, wine, glass, and watches, etc. The silver dollars used in China are manufactured in this country.

[*France*] . . . is located north-northwest of Spain. The people are sincere and honest, also inquisitive and ingenious. The watches they make are superior to any other in the world. Their wine is also very excellent. In religion, customs, and habits, the country is similar to Spain. The coins used are either triangular or square, with a cross on the surface. [. . .]

[*England*] . . . is located southwest of France and could be reached by sailing north from St. Helena[3] for about two months. It is a sparsely settled island, separated from the mainland, with a large number of rich families. The dwelling houses have more than one story. Maritime commerce is one of the chief occupations of the English, and wherever there is a region in which profits could be reaped by trading, these people strive for them, with the result that their commercial vessels are to be seen on the seven seas. Commercial traders are to be found all over the country. Male inhabitants from the ages of fifteen to sixty are conscripted into the service of the king as soldiers. Moreover, a large foreign mercenary army is also maintained. Consequently, although the country is small, it has such a large military force that foreign nations are afraid of it.

Near the sea is Lun-lun [*London*], which is one of the largest cities in the country. In this city is a fine system of waterworks. From the river, which flows through the city, water is raised by means of revolving wheels, installed at three different places, and poured into pipes which carry it to all parts of the city. Anyone desirous of securing water would just have to lay a pipe between his house and the water mains, and water would be available. The water tax for each family is calculated on the number of persons in that family.

Men and women all wear white ordinarily; for mourning, however, black is used. The army wears a red uniform. Women wear long dresses that sweep the floor, with the upper part tight and the lower part loose. At the waist is a tight belt with a buckle. Whenever there is a celebration of festive occasion, then some young and beautiful girls would be asked to sing and dance to the accompaniment of music. Girls of rich and noble families start to learn these arts when they are very young.

Whenever English ships meet on the ocean a ship in dire straits, they must rescue all persons on the ill-fated ship, feed and clothe them, and then provide them with sufficient funds to take them back to their native lands. Any captains neglecting to perform such a task would be liable to punishment.

Among the minerals produced here are gold, silver, copper, tin, and iron. Manufactured articles include tin plate, cotton and woolen goods, clocks, watches, wine, and glass. [. . .]

---

[2] **eight . . . Portugal:** As in the sections on France and England, Xie's directions here are not correct. Kenneth Ch'en attributes these mistakes to a lapse of memory.

[3] **north from St. Helena:** Again, Xie's sense of the relative positions of European countries is inaccurate.

ᴥ Alexander Pope
1688–1744

By 1737, the British poet Alexander Pope, physically impaired from child-hood and nearing fifty, was already arranging and collating his poetry and his vast correspondence for final editions, as though he sensed his life were nearing its end. (He would, in fact, die at fifty-six.) In the midst of worsening physical ailments and the somber task of readying his work for posterity, Pope presented the Prince of Wales, with whom he had main-tained a wary friendship, a puppy from his Great Dane Bounce's new lit-ter, together with a collar engraved with a couplet:[1]

> I am his Highness' Dog at Kew;
> Pray tell me Sir, whose Dog are you?

Minor verse, to be sure, but in a number of ways it embodies Pope's work and times. Pope's poetry grows out of and flourishes within an intensely gossipy and self-conscious aristocratic society. The couplet is designed to be read and reacted to by people fawning over the royal puppy, their reac-tions observed by others in the know. The couplet itself is very economi-cal, small enough to fit upon a dog collar, packing into its neat repetition of the word *dog* much comment about those who fawn, those who follow, and those who are owned. Pope is matchless for his compressed subtlety, his ability to manipulate sound to convey thought. And finally, there is the darkness just beneath the surface of the playful gesture. Dogs are said to have pure hearts and to remain loyal even toward abusive owners. How many people had compromised their morality and judgment in the Prince's court in return for a good dinner or some privilege?

Avatar of a New Augustan Age.   In his own time, Pope was mocked and despised for his work, his opinions, and his body, which was cruelly misshapen and weakened by tuberculosis of the spine. But he was also regarded as *the* poet among poets, *the* heir of the spirit of Western Euro-pean poetry, *the* British writer against whom others must be measured. Physical deformities were fair game for satirists in Pope's day, and vicious caricatures of the dwarfed and hunchbacked poet showed Pope's head grotesquely topping the body of a spider or a monkey. At the same time, it became fashionable to paint and sculpt him nobly posed in the company of Homer, Virgil, Dante, Chaucer, Petrarch, and other forebears of the grand tradition of European literature.

The ancestors whose traditions Pope most consciously sought to

---

[1] **couplet:** A two-line, rhymed stanza. Pope was the master of the **heroic couplet**, an iambic-pentameter stanza which completes its thought within the closed two-line form, as in this example from *An Essay on Man:*

Through worlds unnumber'd though the God be known,
'Tis ours to trace him only in our own.

make new in his own Augustan Age[2] were Roman classical authors. Horace[3] is his model for the *Moral Essays,* where in easy, colloquial language he takes on the excesses and shortcomings of women, or landscape gardeners, or the moneyed aristocracy. Lucretius's[4] *De rerum natura* inspired Pope and his contemporaries to present complex philosophical ideas in verse, as Pope does in his *Essay on Man.* Above all, the epic poets, chiefly Homer and Virgil, echo constantly in Pope's poetry. His thorough knowledge of their poetry's scope and music becomes transmuted in his brilliant MOCK EPICS[5] *The Rape of the Lock* (1712, 1714) and *The Dunciad* (1742), where contemporary people's mundane affairs are depicted surrounded by epic panoply partly to underscore their tawdriness. The pedantic scholar Colley Cibber,[6] the principal butt of *The Dunciad,* builds a ceremonial bonfire of the writings he has been unable to sell in honor of the goddess Dulness, but just in time she stops him from burning these treasures and whisks him off to her sordid palace amid the flea-markets of London in order to proclaim him her own dear heir. Other goddesses and their favorites from classical epics come to mind—Thetis and Achilles, Athene and Odysseus, Venus and Aeneas[7]—but with a mocking difference. Pope was celebrated not only for his technical mastery of rhyme and rhythm and his ability to catch the particular satiric spirit of the times: He also gave his contemporaries confidence that this new Augustan Age was indeed an extension of a great classical tradition that valued sense, treasured knowledge, and ridiculed folly.

www For links to more information about Pope, quizzes on *The Rape of the Lock* and *An Essay on Man,* and information about the 21st-century relevance of *An Essay on Man,* see *World Literature Online* at bedfordstmartins .com/worldlit.

A Catholic Outsider.   Pope was born in 1688 into a well-do-to Catholic linen merchant's family in London, which was a fiercely anti-Catholic city. In 1711 the Pope family moved to a small farm in Windsor Forest, some thirty miles from London, where other Catholic families sought relief from persecution. Pope's passion for country scenes and gardening began here in this gentle landscape. Fragile health limited his experience of both the natural world and school; his tubercular, hunched spine halted his growth at four feet six inches, and he was racked by fierce headaches and respiratory problems all his life. But the little boy's mind

---

[2] Augustan Age: Associated with the first half of the eighteenth century and with British Neoclassicism, the Augustan Age was named after the period when Augustus (63 B.C.E.–14 C.E.) ruled the Roman empire and many of the great Latin poets, especially Horace and Virgil, flourished.

[3] Horace (65 B.C.E.–8 B.C.E.): Greatest of the Latin lyric poets of the Augustan Age in Rome.

[4] Lucretius (C. 99 B.C.E.–c. 55 B.C.E.): Latin poet who argued for a materialistic worldview in his philosophical poem *De rerum natura (On the Nature of Things).*

[5] mock epic: A form that parodies the epic by treating a trivial subject in an elevated style, employing such conventions of the form as the plea to a muse for inspiration, an extended simile, a heroic epithet, or descriptive title added to a person's name.

[6] Colley Cibber (1671–1757): English dramatist and actor-manager, appointed poet laureate of England in 1730.

[7] Thetis . . . Aeneas: The hero of the classical epic was usually supported and protected by a goddess, who was often his mother. In Homer's *Iliad,* Thetis protects her son Achilles, as Venus does her son Aeneas in Virgil's *Aeneid.* Although Athene is not Odysseus's mother, she acts as his guardian in the *Iliad* and the *Odyssey.*

In Pope I cannot read
a line
But with a sigh I wish
it mine;
When he can in one
couplet fix
More sense than I
can do in six,
It gives me such a
jealous fit,
I cry, "Pox take him
and his wit!"
– Jonathan Swift,
"Verses on the Death
of Dr. Swift," 1739

was remarkable. He avidly read English, French, and Latin poetry, and his father encouraged him to write verses of his own.

Pope's Catholicism barred him from the universities, but he was determined to venture beyond his household. In 1705 he gained a ready education by walking boldly into Will's Coffeehouse in London, where the famous writers of the older generation still gathered. Pope struck the old guard as an odd country bumpkin, but they recognized his genius, and by 1709 he had published his first poems, imitations of Virgil's *Eclogues.*

Literary Successes in London.   In 1711 the audacious newcomer brought out his *Essay on Criticism,* a long poem in which he dispensed literary criticism and wickedly satirized a number of his elders along the way. At twenty-three Pope was already famous and controversial, and in the next few years, between 1712 and 1714, he produced *The Rape of the Lock,* his brilliant mock-heroic account of a feud among society men and women. In that same year, Pope made a new set of extraordinary friends, mostly Tory and literary, whom he would keep for life, among them Jonathan Swift and John Gay.[8] Together they devised the character of a droning pedant named Martinus Scribblerus, for whom they invented a vast body of memoirs and correspondence. Swift and Pope especially spurred each other's genius, but the circle of friends, many of whom held political offices, was scattered when Queen Anne died in 1714 and the Tory government fell.

Country Life in Twickenham.   Pope next translated Homer's *Iliad* into English, a five-year project. In 1719, a year after his father's death, he and his mother moved to a villa at Twickenham, on whose five acres he would exercise his passion for landscape gardening. He built a rustic grotto and outfitted it with a system of lamps and mirrors, enabling him to project on small surfaces, in tiny "moving images," the river traffic on the Thames, much as he captured the social world of England in the miniature frame of the heroic couplet. At Twickenham he entertained company, including a number of strong and intellectual women such as Martha Blount, with whom he had an enduring friendship.

***The Dunciad* and Later Life.**   After his early and fast-paced start, the years between 1719 and 1728 were a sort of hiatus in Pope's career, largely filled with editing Shakespeare, translating the classics, and landscape gardening. But in 1728 came the *The Dunciad,* a dark mock epic in which Pope took on not merely *dunces,* his personal literary enemies, but everything that embodied for him the petty corruption, shoddy art, and slip-

---

[8]Jonathan Swift, John Gay: Jonathan Swift (1667–1745) was an English satirist and author of *Gulliver's Travels;* see p. 141. John Gay (1685–1732), the English playwright and poet, is best known for *The Beggar's Opera* (1728).

ping standards that might quietly erode an entire culture. In 1743 an edition of the revised poem, complete with full names of the dunces whom it satirized, was offered to the public. Although Pope's poetry now turned increasingly to moral and philosophical subjects such as those in *An Essay on Man,* Pope never stopped writing SATIRE; *The Dunciad,* in particular, kept appearing in ever more elaborate editions, and Pope remained a prolific writer to the end. He died of asthma on May 30, 1744, after receiving the last rites of the church.

An Essay on Man.   *An Essay on Man* (1733–34) describes a rational, hierarchical arrangement of everything in creation. Each plant, animal, and inanimate thing occupies its intended place, and everything is linked by an interdependence in this work, which builds on the concept of "the great chain of being," a Western idea seen as far back as Plato and Aristotle.

A Fashionable Mock Epic.   *The Rape of the Lock* is a more lighthearted matter, but genuine moral and social issues underlie the delightful, shimmering surface of this mock epic, a form beloved by ENLIGHTENMENT satirists. The poem's action occupies a day, as the beautiful Belinda groggily arises, forgets the warning she was given about some dire event about to happen, and dresses herself like Achilles for the particular battles that await her—not only card games and gossip, but the real dangers of predatory suitors, rivals, and a social world where the only real choices are marriage and spinsterhood, either of which may be "losing hands." Belinda travels by barge to Hampton Court, where she wins a card game but loses a lock of her hair to the scissors of the baron. Although this seems the slightest of pretexts for a full-scale war, Pope manages at once to lightly ridicule the participants and to imply something darker than a temporarily ruined hairdo. It is not thoughtlessly that he calls his work *The Rape of the Lock.* In mythology, the cutting of hair is often connected to shame and a loss of personal power, and this poem is shot through with references to virginity, one of the few "powers" young women hold in this male-dominated society, but one that becomes worthless if it is defended too well for too long. Virginity, or "honor," can be variously guarded, locked away, yielded up, lost, traded off, or forcibly taken. We may laugh at the epic seriousness used to describe an adolescent prank visited by a lovestruck beau upon a spoiled young woman, but we are conscious that at some level there has been a personal violation and that what is partly being fought over is the right to call one's body one's own. At the heart of the poem, there is an uncomfortable feeling of a social engine more sinister than any pair of scissors closing in upon Belinda. She may choose to be of "good humor" and go along with the world of courtship and marriage preordained for her, or she can be a "prude" and find herself transformed into a hysterical bottle crying piteously for a cork in the dreadful Cave of Spleen—the fate of women who deny their sexuality.

Aubrey Beardsley,
The Rape of the Lock,
1896

*A nineteenth-century
depiction of the title
act. (Courtesy of the
trustees of the Boston
Public Library)*

■ CONNECTIONS

Virgil, *Aeneid* **(Book 1).** As a mock epic, *The Rape of the Lock* demands comparison with the epics it mocks. Virgil's use of such conventions of the epic as the plea to a muse for aid, the summary of the poem's grand subject matter at the beginning, the involvement of the gods in the action, heroic epithets, or names, for the characters, and elaborate similes is imitated in Pope's epic. Consider how the differences in the subject matter of the two poems — the founding of Rome *(Aeneid)* and the theft of a lock of hair — changes the impact of these literary devices.

Milton, *Paradise Lost* (Book 3). Literature often addresses big philosophical and theological questions. In *Paradise Lost,* John Milton retells the story of Adam and Eve and the Fall to "justify the ways of God to men." Pope sets himself a similar task in *An Essay on Man* — to "vindicate the ways of God to man" — but he does it through philosophical speculation rather than storytelling. Do their different approaches lead to different conclusions? Summarize the case made by each poet.

Wang Wei, Bo Juyi (Book 2). Many poets have tried to describe and define man's relationship to nature. The poets of the Tang dynasty in China, Wang Wei and Bo Juyi, for example, define the relationship experientially and intuitively by describing personal moments in nature. Pope approaches the subject more abstractly by seeking to establish the place of human beings in the natural order. Do these differing approaches imply very different ideas about nature?

■ **FURTHER RESEARCH**

Biography
Mack, Maynard. *Alexander Pope: A Life.* 1985.

Criticism
Broich, Ulrich. *The Eighteenth-Century Mock-Heroic Poem.* 1990.
Brown, Laura. *Alexander Pope.* 1985.
Knellwolf, Christa. *A Contradiction Still: Representations of Women in the Poetry of Alexander Pope.* 1998.
Rogers, Pat. *Introduction to Pope.* 1975.
Rousseau, G. S., ed. *Twentieth-Century Interpretations of* The Rape of the Lock: *A Collection of Critical Essays.* 1969.
Solomon, Harry M. *The Rape of the Text: Reading and Misreading Pope's* Essay on Man. 1993.

The Rape of the Lock

Nolueram, Belinda, tuos violare capillos;
Sed juvat, hoc precibus me tribuisse tuis.
— MARTIAL, *EPIGRAMS XII. 84*[1]

TO MRS. ARABELLA FERMOR

Madam,

It will be in vain to deny that I have some regard for this piece, since I dedicate it to You. Yet you may bear me witness, it was intended only to divert a few young Ladies, who have good sense and good humour enough to laugh not only at their sex's little unguarded follies, but at their own. But as it was communicated with the air of a Secret, it soon found its way into the world. An imperfect copy having been offered to a Bookseller, you had the good nature for my sake to consent to the publication of one more correct: This I was forced to, before I had executed half my design, for the Machinery was entirely wanting to complete it.

The Machinery, Madam, is a term invented by the Critics, to signify that part which the Deities, Angels, or Dæmons are made to act in a Poem: For the ancient Poets are in one respect like many modern Ladies: let an action be never so trivial in itself, they always make it appear of the utmost importance. These Machines I

The Rape of the Lock. Pope's poem grew out of a real feud that started between two prominent Roman Catholic families when Robert Lord Petre sneaked up on the young beauty Arabella Fermor and cut off a lock of her hair as a trophy. Pope did not know either party, but John Caryll, a mutual friend who believed the Catholic minority in England was embattled enough without internal disputes, begged Pope to write a poem that would "laugh [the two families] together." Pope obligingly produced a short version of the current work in 1712. Two years later, he added the features for which the poem is now celebrated: the "machinery" of the attendant spirits — the sylphs and gnomes he derived from Rosicrucian belief as well as from classical gods and Miltonic angels; the delicious account of Belinda's elaborate dressing table; the long section in which the war between the sexes is recounted in terms of a game of cards called *ombre;* and the journey to the underworld that lies at the heart of most epics, here Umbriel's visit to the surreal Cave of Spleen. Later still, Pope added Clarissa's wise but disregarded words about the need for common sense and good humor. In the climactic mock-epic battle, the women apparently win, but neither side really does, for the lock, like innocence, is not restorable, nor can it be kept as a trophy of male aggression. The gods have enshrined Belinda's tresses in the skies as a new comet. Of course, it is Pope who creates this ending, immortalizing Arabella Fermor's lock and making a work of art out of a squabble. In *The Rape of the Lock,* he evokes with both irony and affection the fragile beauty of the young aristocrats whom he personally knew and the shadows he could see gathering just beyond the glitter of their charmed lives.

---

[1] *Nolueram . . . tuis:* "I did not wish, Belinda, to do violence to your locks, but I am pleased to have granted this to your prayers." This epigraph from the poet Martial implies that Arabella Fermor had asked Pope to publish the poem. [All notes are the editors'.]

determined to raise on a very new and odd foundation, the Rosicrucian doctrine of Spirits.[2]

I know how disagreeable it is to make use of hard words before a Lady; but 'tis so much the concern of a Poet to have his works understood, and particularly by your Sex, that you must give me leave to explain two or three difficult terms.

The Rosicrucians are a people I must bring you acquainted with. The best account I know of them is in a French book called *Le Comte de Gabalis*,[3] which both in its title and size is so like a Novel, that many of the Fair Sex have read it for one by mistake. According to these Gentlemen, the four Elements are inhabited by Spirits, which they call Sylphs, Gnomes, Nymphs, and Salamanders. The Gnomes or Dæmons of Earth delight in mischief; but the Sylphs, whose habitation is in the Air, are the best-conditioned creatures imaginable. For they say, any mortals may enjoy the most intimate familiarities with these gentle Spirits, upon a condition very easy to all true Adepts, an inviolate preservation of Chastity.

As to the following Cantos, all the passages of them are as fabulous as the Vision at the beginning, or the Transformation at the end; (except the loss of your Hair, which I always mention with reverence). The Human persons are as fictitious as the Airy ones; and the character of Belinda, as it is now managed, resembles you in nothing but in Beauty.

If this Poem had as many Graces as there are in your Person, or in your Mind, yet I could never hope it should pass through the world half so Uncensured as You have done. But let its fortune be what it will, mine is happy enough, to have given me this occasion of assuring you that I am, with the truest esteem,

> Madam,
> *Your most obedient, Humble Servant,*
> A. Pope

CANTO 1

What dire offence from amorous causes springs,
What mighty contests rise from trivial things,
I sing — This verse to CARYLL,[4] Muse! is due:
This, even Belinda may vouchsafe to view:
Slight is the subject, but not so the praise,
If She inspire, and He approve my lays.
    Say what strange motive, Goddess! could compel
A well-bred Lord t' assault a gentle Belle?
O say what stranger cause, yet unexplored,
10 Could make a gentle Belle reject a Lord?

---

[2] *Rosicrucian . . . Spirits:* This seventeenth-century system of mystic philosophy borrowed from a number of older occult traditions. Pope apparently learned what Rosicrucian lore he knew from a contemporary manual put out by the society.

[3] *Le . . . Gabalis:* By the Abbé de Montfauçon de Villars; the book appeared in 1670.

[4] *Caryll:* John Caryll, the unofficial leader of well-born Roman Catholic families in Pope's circle.

In tasks so bold, can little men engage,
And in soft bosoms dwells such mighty Rage?
    Sol through white curtains shot timorous ray,
And oped those eyes that must eclipse the day:
Now lap dogs give themselves the rousing shake,
And sleepless lovers, just at twelve, awake:
Thrice rung the bell, the slipper knocked the ground,
And the pressed watch returned a silver sound.[5]
Belinda still her downy pillow prest,

20 Her guardian Sᴜᴘʜ prolonged the balmy rest:
'Twas He had summoned to her silent bed
The morning dream that hovered o'er her head;
A Youth more glittering than a Birth-night[6] Beau,
(That even in slumber caused her cheek to glow)
Seemed to her ear his winning lips to lay,
And thus in whispers said, or seemed to say.
    Fairest of mortals, thou distinguished care
Of thousand bright Inhabitants of Air!
If e'er one Vision touched thy infant thought,

30 Of all the Nurse and all the Priest have taught;
Of airy Elves by moonlight shadows seen,
The silver token, and the circled green,[7]
Or virgins visited by Angel powers,
With golden crowns and wreaths of heavenly flowers;
Hear and believe! thy own importance know,
Nor bound thy narrow views to things below.
Some secret truths, from learnèd pride concealed,
To Maids alone and Children are revealed:
What though no credit doubting Wits may give?

40 The Fair and Innocent shall still believe.
Know, then, unnumbered Spirits round thee fly,
The light Militia of the lower sky:
These, though unseen, are ever on the wing,
Hang o'er the Box, and hover round the Ring.[8]
Think what an equipage thou hast in Air,
And view with scorn two Pages and a Chair.°   sedan chair

---

[5] **the slipper . . . silver sound:** Belinda thumps on the floor with her slipper to summon her maid; her watch rings the hour and the quarter when she presses its stem.

[6] **Birth-night:** On the birthday of the reigning British sovereign, people dressed elegantly.

[7] **Elves . . . green:** The "little people," spirits who go by various names, would sometimes leave a silver coin in thanks for a gift (such as a bowl of cream) or to reward an industrious servant; the fairy ring, an especially lush circle of grass, marks the places where the spirits dance.

[8] **Box . . . Ring:** Theater boxes, and the driving circle, or Ring, in Hyde Park, where the upper classes rode in their carriages to see and be seen.

As now your own, our beings were of old,
And once enclosed in Woman's beauteous mould;
Thence, by a soft transition, we repair
50 From earthly Vehicles to these of air.
Think not, when Woman's transient breath is fled,
That all her vanities at once are dead;
Succeeding vanities she still regards,
And though she plays no more, o'erlooks the cards.
Her joy in gilded Chariots, when alive,
And love of Ombre,[9] after death survive.
For when the Fair in all their pride expire,
To their first Elements[10] their Souls retire:
The Sprites of fiery Termagants in Flame
60 Mount up, and take a Salamander's name.
Soft yielding minds to Water glide away,
And sip, with Nymphs, their elemental Tea.
The graver Prude sinks downward to a Gnome,
In search of mischief still on Earth to roam.
The light Coquettes in Sylphs aloft repair,
And sport and flutter in the fields of Air.
 Know further yet; whoever fair and chaste
Rejects mankind, is by some Sylph embraced:
For Spirits, freed from mortal laws, with ease
70 Assume what sexes and what shapes they please.
What guards the purity of melting Maids,
In courtly balls, and midnight masquerades,
Safe from the treacherous friend, the daring spark,
The glance by day, the whisper in the dark,
When kind occasion prompts their warm desires,
When music softens, and when dancing fires?
'Tis but their Sylph, the wise Celestials know,
Though Honour is the word with Men below.
 Some nymphs there are, too conscious of their face,
80 For life predestined to the Gnomes' embrace.
These swell their prospects and exalt their pride,
When offers are disdained, and love denied:
Then gay Ideas° crowd the vacant brain,   flashy images
While Peers, and Dukes, and all their sweeping train,

---

[9] **Ombre:** A card game; see note 27.
[10] **Elements:** The four elements are Earth, Air, Fire, and Water. One of these elements was thought to predominate in each human being, determining personality and physical constitution. In Pope's scheme, the souls of women who have died move into spirits appropriate to their ruling element. Because salamanders—amphibians that often hide beneath loose bark—were sometimes seen escaping from blazing wood, they were believed to dwell in fire, and their name was given to a species of fire spirit.

And Garters, Stars, and Coronets[11] appear,
And in soft sounds, Your Grace salutes their ear.
'Tis these that early taint the female soul,
Instruct the eyes of young Coquettes to roll,
Teach Infant cheeks a bidden blush to know,
90   And little hearts to flutter at a Beau.
        Oft, when the world imagine women stray,
The Sylphs through mystic mazes guide their way,
Through all the giddy circle they pursue,
And old impertinence expel by new.
What tender maid but must a victim fall
To one man's treat, but for another's ball?
When Florio speaks what virgin could withstand,
If gentle Damon did not squeeze her hand?
With varying vanities, from every part,
100   They shift the moving Toyshop of their heart;
Where wigs with wigs, with sword-knots sword-knots strive,
Beaux banish beaux, and coaches coaches drive.
This erring mortals Levity may call;
Oh blind to truth! the Sylphs contrive it all.
        Of these am I, who thy protection claim,
A watchful sprite, and Ariel is my name.
Late, as I ranged the crystal wilds of air,
In the clear Mirror of thy ruling Star
I saw, alas! some dread event impend,
110   Ere to the main this morning sun descend,
But heaven reveals not what, or how, or where:
Warned by the Sylph, oh pious maid, beware!
This to disclose is all thy guardian can:
Beware of all, but most beware of Man!
        He said; when Shock,[12] who thought she slept too long,
Leaped up, and waked his mistress with his tongue.
'Twas then, Belinda, if report say true,
Thy eyes first opened on a Billet-doux;
Wounds, Charm, and Ardors were no sooner read,
120   But all the Vision vanished from thy head.
        And now, unveiled, the Toilet stands displayed,
Each silver Vase in mystic order laid.
First, robed in white, the Nymph intent adores,
With head uncovered, the Cosmetic powers.
A heavenly image in the glass appears,
To that she bends, to that her eyes she rears;

---

[11] **Garters . . . Coronets:** Symbols of the nobility.
[12] **Shock:** Belinda's dog. A "shock" was a small, long-haired poodle.

Th' inferior Priestess, at her altar's side,
Trembling, begins the sacred rites of Pride.
Unnumbered treasures ope at once, and here
130 The various offerings of the world appear;
From each she nicely culls with curious toil,
And decks the Goddess with the glittering spoil.
This casket India's glowing gems unlocks,
And all Arabia breathes from yonder box.
The Tortoise here and Elephant unite.
Transformed to combs, the speckled, and the white.[13]
Here files of pins extend their shining rows,
Puffs, Powders, Patches,[14] Bibles, Billet-doux.
Now awful Beauty puts on all its arms;
140 The fair each moment rises in her charms,
Repairs her smiles, awakens every grace,
And calls forth all the wonders of her face;
Sees by degrees a purer blush arise,
And keener lightnings quicken in her eyes.
The busy Sylphs surround their darling care,
These set the head, and those divide the hair,
Some fold the sleeve, whilst others plait the gown;
And Betty's[15] praised for labours not her own.

CANTO 2

Not with more glories, in th' etherial plain,
The Sun first rises o'er the purpled main,
Than, issuing forth, the rival of his beams
Launched on the bosom of the silver Thames.
Fair Nymphs, and well-dressed Youths around her shone,
But every eye was fixed on her alone.
On her white breast a sparkling Cross she wore,
Which Jews might kiss, and Infidels adore.
Her lively looks a sprightly mind disclose,
10 Quick as her eyes, and as unfixed as those:
Favours to none, to all she smiles extends;
Oft she rejects, but never once offends.
Bright as the sun, her eyes the gazers strike,
And, like the sun, they shine on all alike.
Yet graceful ease, and sweetness void of pride,
Might hide her faults, if Belles had faults to hide:

---

[13] **Tortoise . . . white:** Tortoiseshell and ivory were popular materials for fancy combs and brushes.

[14] **Patches:** Patches of court plaster for beauty marks, fashionable for both women and men.

[15] **Betty:** A generic name for a maid; Betty is Belinda's "inferior priestess" at the dressing-table altar.

If to her share some female errors fall,
Look on her face, and you'll forget 'em all.
    This Nymph, to the destruction of mankind,
20 Nourished two Locks, which graceful hung behind
In equal curls, and well conspired to deck
With shining ringlets the smooth ivory neck.
Love in these labyrinths his slaves detains,
And mighty hearts are held in slender chains.
With hairy springes[16] we the birds betray,
Slight lines of hair surprise the finny prey,
Fair tresses man's imperial race ensnare,
And beauty draws us with a single hair.
    Th' adventurous Baron the bright locks admired;
30 He saw, he wished, and to the prize aspired.
Resolved to win, he meditates the way,
By force to ravish, or by fraud betray;
For when success a Lover's toil attends,
Few ask, if fraud or force attained his ends.
    For this, ere Phœbus rose, he had implored
Propitious heaven, and every power adored,
But chiefly Love — to Love an Altar built,
Of twelve vast French Romances, neatly gilt.
There lay three garters, half a pair of gloves;
40 And all the trophies of his former loves;
With tender Billets-doux he lights the pyre,
And breathes three amorous sighs to raise the fire.
Then prostrate falls, and begs with ardent eyes
Soon to obtain, and long possess the prize:
The powers gave ear, and granted half his prayer,
The rest, the winds dispersed in empty air.
    But now secure the painted vessel glides,
The sunbeams trembling on the floating tides:
While melting music steals upon the sky,
50 And softened sounds along the waters die;
Smooth flow the waves, the Zephyrs gently play,
Belinda smiled, and all the world was gay.
All but the Sylph — with careful thoughts opprest,
Th' impending woe sat heavy on his breast.
He summons strait his Denizens of air;
The lucid squadrons round the sails repair:
Soft o'er the shrouds aërial whispers breathe,
That seemed but Zephyrs to the train beneath.
Some to the sun their insect wings unfold,

---

[16] **springes:** Snares to entrap birds and small animals, sometimes made of braided horsehair.

60 Waft on the breeze, or sink in clouds of gold;
    Transparent forms, too fine for mortal sight,
    Their fluid bodies half dissolved in light,
    Loose to the wind their airy garments flew,
    Thin glittering textures of the filmy dew,
    Dipped in the richest tincture of the skies,
    Where light disports in ever-mingling dyes,
    While every beam new transient colours flings,
    Colours that change whene'er they wave their wings.
    Amid the circle, on the gilded mast,
70 Superior by the head, was Ariel placed;
    His purple pinions opening to the sun,
    He raised his azure wand, and thus begun.
        Ye Sylphs and Sylphids, to your chief give ear!
    Fays, Fairies, Genii, Elves, and Dæmons, hear!
    Ye know the spheres and various tasks assigned
    By laws eternal to th' aërial kind.
    Some in the fields of purest Æther play,
    And bask and whiten in the blaze of day.
    Some guide the course of wandering orbs on high,
80 Or roll the planets through the boundless sky.
    Some less refined, beneath the moon's pale light
    Pursue the stars that shoot athwart the night,
    Or suck the mists in grosser air below,
    Or dip their pinions in the painted bow,
    Or brew fierce tempests on the wintry main,
    Or o'er the glebe[17] distil the kindly rain.
    Others on earth o'er human race preside,
    Watch all their ways, and all their actions guide:
    Of these the chief the care of Nations own,
90 And guard with Arms divine the British Throne.
        Our humbler province is to tend the Fair,
    Not a less pleasing, though less glorious care;
    To save the powder from too rude a gale,
    Nor let th' imprisoned essences exhale;[18]
    To draw fresh colours from the vernal flowers;
    To steal from rainbows e'er they drop in showers
    A brighter wash;° to curl their waving hairs,   cosmetic lotion
    Assist their blushes, and inspire their airs;
    Nay oft, in dreams, invention we bestow,
100 To change a Flounce, or add a Furbelow.
        This day, black Omens threat the brightest Fair
    That e'er deserved a watchful spirit's care;

---

[17] glebe: Field under cultivation.   [18] Nor . . . exhale: Nor allow perfume to evaporate.

Some dire disaster, or by force, or slight;
But what, or where, the fates have wrapped in night.
Whether the nymph shall break Diana's law,[19]
Or some frail China jar receive a flaw;
Or stain her honour, or her new brocade;
Forget her prayers, or miss a masquerade;
Or lose her heart, or necklace, at a ball;
110   Or whether Heaven has doomed that Shock must fall.
Haste, then, ye spirits! to your charge repair:
The fluttering fan be Zephyretta's care;
The drops to thee, Brillante, we consign;
And, Momentilla, let the watch be thine;
Do thou, Crispissa, tend her favorite Lock;[20]
Ariel himself shall be the guard of Shock.
          To fifty chosen Sylphs, of special note,
We trust th' important charge, the Petticoat:
Oft have we known that sevenfold fence to fail,
120   Though stiff with hoops, and armed with ribs of whale;
Form a strong line about the silver bound,
And guard the wide circumference around.
          Whatever spirit, careless of his charge,
His post neglects, or leaves the fair at large,
Shall feel sharp vengeance soon o'ertake his sins,
Be stopped in vials, or transfixed with pins;
Or plunged in lakes of bitter washes lie,
Or wedged whole ages in a bodkin's eye:[21]
Gums and Pomatums[22] shall his flight restrain,
130   While clogged he beats his silken wings in vain;
Or Alum styptics[23] with contracting power
Shrink his thin essence like a rivelled[24] flower:
Or, as Ixion fixed, the wretch shall feel
The giddy motion of the whirling Mill,[25]
In fumes of burning Chocolate shall glow,
And tremble at the sea that froths below!
          He spoke; the spirits from the sails descend;
Some, orb in orb, around the nymph extend;

---

[19] **Diana:** The Roman goddess of virginity and chastity.

[20] **The drops . . . Lock:** The sylphs' names are appropriate to their duties: Brillante would be in charge of drops that would dilate the pupils and make Belinda's eyes seem larger and brighter; "Crispissa" suggests curliness.

[21] **bodkin's eye:** A blunt needle used to weave ribbon through eyelets.

[22] **Pomatums:** Perfumed hair ointments.

[23] **styptics:** These contract tissue to shrink pores or check bleeding.   [24] **rivelled:** Withered.

[25] **Ixion . . . Mill:** Ixion was punished in Hades by being bound to a revolving wheel; the erring sylph will be tied to a mill for grinding coffee or cocoa beans.

140 Some thrid the mazy ringlets of her hair;
Some hang upon the pendants of her ear;
With beating hearts the dire event they wait,
Anxious, and trembling for the birth of Fate.

CANTO 3

Close by those meads, for ever crowned with flowers,
Where Thames with pride surveys his rising towers,
There stands a structure of majestic frame,
Which from the neighboring Hampton takes its name.[26]
Here Britain's statesmen oft the fall foredoom
Of foreign Tyrants, and of Nymphs at home;
Here thou, great ANNA! whom three realms obey,
Dost sometimes counsel take—and sometimes Tea.
Hither the heroes and the nymphs resort,
10 To taste awhile the pleasures of a Court;
In various talk th' instructive hours they past,
Who gave the ball, or paid the visit last;
One speaks the glory of the British Queen,
And one describes a charming Indian screen;
A third interprets motions, looks, and eyes;
At every word a reputation dies.
Snuff, or the fan, supply each pause of chat,
With singing, laughing, ogling, *and all that.*
Meanwhile, declining from the noon of day,
20 The sun obliquely shoots his burning ray;
The hungry Judges soon the sentence sign,
And wretches hang that jurymen may dine;
The merchant from th' Exchange returns in peace,
And the long labours of the Toilet cease.
Belinda now, whom thirst of fame invites,
Burns to encounter two adventurous Knights,
At Ombre[27] singly to decide their doom;
And swells her breast with conquests yet to come.
Straight the three bands prepare in arms to join,
30 Each band the number of the sacred nine.
Soon as she spreads her hand, th' aërial guard
Descend, and sit on each important card:

---

[26] **Hampton:** The royal palace, Hampton Court, situated on the Thames about fifteen miles from London.

[27] **Ombre:** A card game that originated in Spain. The player who gets the bid is called the ombre, and she names trumps. When spades are trumps in ombre, the "Matadores," the high cards, in order of descending value, are "Spadillio," the ace of spades; "Manillio," the deuce of spades; and "Basto," the ace of clubs. Belinda wins steadily until the next-to-the-last trick, which the baron takes, but she recoups on the final trick.

First Ariel perched upon a Matadore,
Then each, according to the rank they bore;
For Sylphs, yet mindful of their ancient race,
Are, as when women, wondrous fond of place.
    Behold, four Kings in majesty revered,
With hoary whiskers and a forky beard;
And four fair Queens whose hands sustain a flower,
40 Th' expressive emblem of their softer power;
Four Knaves in garbs succinct,° a trusty band,   girded up
Caps on their heads, and halberts[28] in their hand;
And particoloured troops, a shining train,
Draw forth to combat on the velvet plain.
    The skilful Nymph reviews her force with care:
Let Spades be trumps! she said, and trumps they were.
    Now move to war her sable Matadores,
In show like leaders of the swarthy Moors.
Spadillio first, unconquerable Lord!
50 Led off two captive trumps, and swept the board.
As many more Manillio forced to yield,
And marched a victor from the verdant field.
Him Basto followed, but his fate more hard
Gained but one trump and one Plebeian card.
With his broad sabre next, a chief in years,
The hoary Majesty of Spades appears,
Puts forth one manly leg, to sight revealed,
The rest, his many-coloured robe concealed.
The rebel Knave, who dares his prince engage,
60 Proves the just victim of his royal rage.
Even mighty Pam[29] that Kings and Queens o'erthrew
And mowed down armies in the fights of Lu,
Sad chance of war! now destitute of aid,
Falls undistinguished by the victor Spade!
    Thus far both armies to Belinda yield;
Now to the Baron fate inclines the field.
His warlike Amazon her host invades,
Th' imperial consort of the crown of Spades.
The Club's black Tyrant first her victim died
70 Spite of his haughty mien, and barbarous pride:
What boots the regal circle on his head,
His giant limbs, in state unwieldy spread;
That long behind he trails his pompous robe,
And, of all monarchs, only grasps the globe?

---

[28] **halberts:** A renaissance weapon combining an ax and a lance.
[29] **Pam:** The jack of clubs, the highest card in the game of loo.

The Baron now his Diamonds pours apace;
Th' embroidered King who shows but half his face,
And his refulgent Queen, with powers combined
Of broken troops an easy conquest find.
Clubs, Diamonds, Hearts, in wild disorder seen,
80 With throngs promiscuous strew the level green.
Thus when dispersed a routed army runs,
Of Asia's troops, and Afric's sable sons,
With like confusion different nations fly,
Of various habit, and of various dye,
The pierced battalions disunited fall,
In heaps on heaps; one fate o'erwhelms them all.
     The Knave of Diamonds tries his wily arts,
And wins (oh shameful chance!) the Queen of Hearts.
At this, the blood the virgin's cheek forsook,
90 A livid paleness spreads o'er all her look;
She sees, and trembles at th' approaching ill,
Just in the jaws of ruin, and Codille.[30]
And now (as oft in some distempered State)
On one nice Trick depends the general fate.
An Ace of Hearts steps forth: The King unseen
Lurked in her hand, and mourned his captive Queen:
He springs to vengeance with an eager pace,
And falls like thunder on the prostrate Ace.
The nymph exulting fills with shouts the sky;
100 The walls, the woods, and long canals reply.
     Oh thoughtless mortals! ever blind to fate,
Too soon dejected, and too soon elate.
Sudden, these honours shall be snatched away,
And cursed for ever this victorious day.
     For lo! the board with cups and spoons is crowned,
The berries crackle, and the mill turns round;[31]
On shining Altars of Japan[32] they raise
The silver lamp; the fiery spirits blaze:
From silver spouts the grateful liquors glide,
110 While China's earth receives the smoking tide:[33]
At once they gratify their scent and taste,
And frequent cups prolong the rich repast.
Strait hover round the Fair her airy band;

---

[30] Codille: Losing a hand of cards.

[31] berries . . . round: Beans are roasted and ground as the elaborate rites of preparing and drinking coffee begin.

[32] Altars of Japan: Coffee is being brewed on small lacquered tables.

[33] China's . . . tide: The coffee is poured into cups of Chinese porcelain.

Some, as she sipped, the fuming liquor fanned,
Some o'er her lap their careful plumes displayed,
Trembling, and conscious of the rich brocade.
Coffee, (which makes the politician wise,
And see through all things with his half-shut eyes)
Sent up in vapours to the Baron's brain
120 New stratagems, the radiant Lock to gain.
Ah cease, rash youth! desist ere 'tis too late,
Fear the just Gods, and think of Scylla's Fate![34]
Changed to a bird, and sent to flit in air,
She dearly pays for Nisus' injured hair!
      But when to mischief mortals bend their will,
How soon they find fit instruments of ill!
Just then, Clarissa drew with tempting grace
A two-edged weapon from her shining case:
So Ladies in Romance assist their Knight,
130 Present the spear, and arm him for the fight.
He takes the gift with reverence, and extends
The little engine on his fingers' ends;
This just behind Belinda's neck he spread,
As o'er the fragrant steams she bends her head.
Swift to the Lock a thousand Sprites repair,
A thousand wings, by turns, blow back the hair;
And thrice they twitched the diamond in her ear;
Thrice she looked back, and thrice the foe drew near.
Just in that instant, anxious Ariel sought
140 The close recesses of the Virgin's thought;
As on the nosegay in her breast reclined,
He watched th' Ideas rising in her mind,
Sudden he viewed, in spite of all her art,
An earthly Lover lurking at her heart.
Amazed, confused, he found his power expired,
Resigned to fate, and with a sigh retired.
      The Peer now spreads the glittering Forfex° wide,   *scissors*
T' enclose the Lock; now joins it, to divide.
Even then, before the fatal engine closed,
150 A wretched Sylph too fondly interposed;
Fate urged the shears, and cut the Sylph in twain,
(But airy substance soon unites again)
The meeting points the sacred hair dissever
From the fair head, for ever, and for ever!
      Then flashed the living lightning from her eyes,

---

[34] Scylla: Not the sea monster of Scylla and Charybdis; this Scylla was turned into a shore bird in punishment for cutting the lock of her father's hair that magically protected him from harm.

And screams of horror rend th' affrighted skies.
Not louder shrieks to pitying heaven are cast,
When husbands, or when lap dogs breathe their last;
Or when rich China vessels fallen from high,
160   In glittering dust, and painted fragments lie!
      Let wreaths of triumph now my temples twine,
(The Victor cried) the glorious Prize is mine!
While fish in streams, or birds delight in air,
Or in a coach and six the British Fair,
As long as Atalantis[35] shall be read,
Or the small pillow grace a Lady's bed,
While visits shall be paid on solemn days,
When numerous wax-lights in bright order blaze,
While nymphs take treats, or assignations give,
170   So long my honour, name, and praise shall live!
What Time would spare, from Steel receives its date,
And monuments, like men, submit to fate!
Steel could the labour of the Gods destroy,
And strike to dust th' imperial towers of Troy;
Steel could the works of mortal pride confound,
And hew triumphal arches to the ground.
What wonder then, fair nymph! thy hairs should feel,
The conquering force of unresisted steel?

Canto 4

But anxious cares the pensive nymph oppressed,
And secret passions laboured in her breast.
Not youthful kings in battle seized alive,
Not scornful virgins who their charms survive,
Not ardent lovers robbed of all their bliss,
Not ancient ladies when refused a kiss,
Not tyrants fierce that unrepenting die,
Not Cynthia when her manteau's° pinned awry,   negligée
E'er felt such rage, resentment, and despair,
10   As thou, sad Virgin! for thy ravished Hair.
      For, that sad moment, when the Sylphs withdrew,
And Ariel weeping from Belinda flew,
Umbriel, a dusky, melancholy sprite,
As ever sullied the fair face of light,
Down to the central earth, his proper scene,
Repaired to search the gloomy Cave of Spleen.°   ill temper
      Swift on his sooty pinions flits the Gnome,

---

[35] **Atalantis:** A 1709 novel by a Mrs. Manley that presented, in thin disguise, many current scandals.

And in a vapour reached the dismal dome.
No cheerful breeze this sullen region knows,
20 The dreaded East is all the wind that blows.
Here in a grotto, sheltered close from air,
And screened in shades from day's detested glare,
She sighs for ever on her pensive bed,
Pain at her side, and Megrim[36] at her head.
　　Two handmaids wait the throne: alike in place,
But differing far in figure and in face.
Here stood Ill Nature like an ancient maid,
Her wrinkled form in black and white arrayed;
With store of prayers, for mornings, nights, and noons,
30 Her hand is filled; her bosom with lampoons.
　　There Affectation, with a sickly mien,
Shows in her cheek the roses of eighteen,
Practised to lisp, and hang the head aside,
Faints into airs, and languishes with pride,
On the rich quilt sinks with becoming woe,
Wrapped in a gown, for sickness, and for show.
The fair ones feel such maladies as these,
When each new nightdress gives a new disease.
　　A constant Vapour[37] o'er the palace flies;
40 Strange phantoms rising as the mists arise;
Dreadful, as hermit's dreams in haunted shades,
Or bright, as visions of expiring maids.
Now glaring fiends, and snakes on rolling spires,°   coils
Pale spectres, gaping tombs, and purple fires:
Now lakes of liquid gold, Elysian scenes,
And crystal domes, and Angels in machines.[38]
　　Unnumbered throngs on every side are seen,
Of bodies changed to various forms by Spleen.
Here living Teapots stand, one arm held out,
50 One bent; the handle this, and that the spout:
A Pipkin there, like Homer's Tripod walks;[39]
Here sighs a Jar, and there a Goose Pie talks;
Men prove with child, as powerful fancy works,
And maids turned bottles, call aloud for corks.
　　Safe passed the Gnome through this fantastic band,

---

[36] **Megrim:** Migraine headache; at times, simply low spirits.

[37] **Vapour:** "The vapors" was a catchall term used to indicate hypochondria, depression, and moodiness, especially in women.

[38] **machines:** Stage machinery used to hoist aloft actors representing winged gods, angels, etc.

[39] **Homer's . . . walks:** See *Iliad* 18, 373–77, where Vulcan has created three-legged stool robots; here, the animated object is an earthen pot.

A branch of healing Spleenwort[40] in his hand.
Then thus addressed the power: "Hail, wayward Queen!
Who rule the sex to fifty from fifteen:
Parent of vapours and of female wit,
60 Who give th' hysteric, or poetic fit,
On various tempers act by various ways,
Make some take physic, others scribble plays;
Who cause the proud their visits to delay,
And send the godly in a pet to pray.
A nymph there is, that all thy power disdains,
And thousands more in equal mirth maintains.
But oh! if e'er thy Gnome could spoil a grace,
Or raise a pimple on a beauteous face,
Like Citron waters[41] matrons' cheeks inflame,
70 Or change complexions at a losing game;
If e'er with airy horns[42] I planted heads,
Or rumpled petticoats, or tumbled beds,
Or caused suspicion when no soul was rude,
Or discomposed the headdress of a Prude,
Or e'er to costive lap dog gave disease,
Which not the tears of brightest eyes could ease:
Hear me, and touch Belinda with chagrin,
That single act gives half the world the spleen."
    The Goddess with a discontented air
80 Seems to reject him, though she grants his prayer.
A wondrous Bag with both her hands she binds,
Like that where once Ulysses held the winds;[43]
There she collects the force of female lungs,
Sighs, sobs, and passions, and the war of tongues.
A Vial next she fills with fainting fears,
Soft sorrows, melting griefs, and flowing tears.
The Gnome rejoicing bears her gifts away,
Spreads his black wings, and slowly mounts to day.
    Sunk in Thalestris'[44] arms the nymph he found,
90 Her eyes dejected and her hair unbound.
Full o'er their heads the swelling bag he rent,

---

[40] **Spleenwort:** An herb that renders the bearer immune to spleen. Pope is alluding to Aeneas's golden bough that enables him to pass unharmed through the underworld in the sixth book of Virgil's *Aeneid.*

[41] **Citron waters:** Brandy in which citrus peel has been steeped.

[42] **airy horns:** Horns symbolize the cuckold whose wife has cheated on him. Umbriel is speaking of "airy"—imaginary—horns on men who wrongly suspect their wives of infidelity thanks to his mischief.

[43] **Ulysses . . . winds:** See *Odyssey* 10.19 ff., where Aeolus hands Odysseus a bag containing all the ill winds that might blow him off course.

[44] **Thalestris:** The name is taken from a queen of the Amazons.

And all the Furies issued at the vent.
Belinda burns with more than mortal ire,
And fierce Thalestris fans the rising fire.
"O wretched maid!" she spread her hands, and cried,
(While Hampton's echoes, "Wretched maid!" replied)
"Was it for this you took such constant care
The bodkin, comb, and essence to prepare?
For this your locks in paper durance bound,
100   For this with torturing irons wreathed around?
For this with fillets strained your tender head,
And bravely bore the double loads of lead?[45]
Gods! shall the ravisher display your hair,
While the Fops envy, and the Ladies stare!
Honour forbid! at whose unrivalled shrine
Ease, pleasure, virtue, all our sex resign.
Methinks already I your tears survey,
Already hear the horrid things they say,
Already see you a degraded toast,
110   And all your honour in a whisper lost!
How shall I, then, your helpless fame defend?
'Twill then be infamy to seem your friend!
And shall this prize, th' inestimable prize,
Exposed through crystal to the gazing eyes,
And heightened by the diamond's circling rays,
On that rapacious hand for ever blaze?
Sooner shall grass in Hyde Park Circus grow,
And wits take lodgings in the sound of Bow,[46]
Sooner let earth, air, sea, to Chaos fall,
120   Men, monkeys, lap dogs, parrots, perish all!"
        She said; then raging to Sir Plume repairs,°   goes
And bids her Beau demand the precious hairs:
(Sir Plume of amber snuffbox justly vain,
And the nice conduct of a clouded cane)
With earnest eyes, and round unthinking face,
He first the snuffbox opened, then the case,
And thus broke out—"My Lord, why, what the devil?
Z——ds![47] damn the lock! 'fore Gad, you must be civil!
Plague on't! 'tis past a jest—nay, prithee, pox!
130   Give her the hair"—he spoke, and rapped his box.
        "It grieves me much" (replied the Peer again)

---

[45] **double . . . lead:** The frames around which high-piled hairdos were shaped.

[46] **in . . . Bow:** Within hearing of the bells of the church of St. Mary-le-Bow in the Cockney district of London, where no fashionable person would deign to live.

[47] **Z——ds!:** Zounds; an old curse that is a contraction of "God's wounds," alluding to the passion of Christ.

"Who speaks so well should ever speak in vain.
But by this Lock, this sacred Lock I swear,
(Which never more shall join its parted hair;
Which never more its honours shall renew,
Clipped from the lovely head where late it grew)
That while my nostrils draw the vital air,
This hand, which won it, shall for ever wear."
He spoke, and speaking, in proud triumph spread
140 The long-contended honours of her head.
    But Umbriel, hateful Gnome! forbears not so;
He breaks the Vial whence the sorrows flow.
Then see! the nymph in beauteous grief appears,
Her eyes half languishing, half drowned in tears;
On her heaved bosom hung her drooping head,
Which, with a sigh, she raised; and thus she said.
    "For ever cursed be this detested day,
Which snatched my best, my favorite curl away!
Happy! ah ten times happy had I been,
150 If Hampton Court these eyes had never seen!
Yet am not I the first mistaken maid,
By love of Courts to numerous ills betrayed.
Oh had I rather unadmired remained
In some lone isle, or distant Northern land;
Where the gilt Chariot never marks the way,
Where none learn Ombre, none e'er taste Bohea![48]
There kept my charms concealed from mortal eye,
Like roses, that in deserts bloom and die.
What moved my mind with youthful Lords to roam?
160 O had I stayed, and said my prayers at home!
'Twas this, the morning omens seemed to tell,
Thrice from my trembling hand the patch box fell;[49]
The tottering China shook without a wind,
Nay, Poll° sat mute, and Shock was most unkind!   Belinda's parrot
A Sylph too warned me of the threats of fate,
In mystic visions, now believed too late!
See the poor remnants of these slighted hairs!
My hands shall rend what even thy rapine spares:
These in two sable ringlets taught to break,
170 Once gave new beauties to the snowy neck;
The sister lock now sits uncouth, alone,
And in its fellow's fate foresees its own;
Uncurled it hangs, the fatal shears demands,

---

[48] Bohea:An expensive tea.

[49] patch box:A box to contain the court plaster men and women pasted on their faces as beauty marks.

And tempts once more, thy sacrilegious hands.
Oh hadst thou, cruel! been content to seize
Hairs less in sight, or any hairs but these!"

CANTO 5

She said: the pitying audience melt in tears.
But Fate and Jove had stopped the Baron's ears.
In vain Thalestris with reproach assails,
For who can move when fair Belinda fails?
Not half so fixed the Trojan could remain,
While Anna begged and Dido raged in vain.[50]
Then grave Clarissa graceful waved her fan;
Silence ensued, and thus the nymph began.
   "Say why are Beauties praised and honoured most,
10 The wise man's passion, and the vain man's toast?
Why decked with all that land and sea afford,
Why Angels called, and Angel-like adored?
Why round our coaches crowd the white-gloved Beaux,
Why bows the side-box from its inmost rows;
How vain are all these glories, all our pains,
Unless good sense preserve what beauty gains:
That men may say, when we the front-box grace,
'Behold the first in virtue as in face!'
Oh! if to dance all night, and dress all day,
20 Charmed the smallpox, or chased old age away;
Who would not scorn what housewife's cares produce,
Or who would learn one earthly thing of use?
To patch, nay ogle, might become a Saint,
Nor could it sure be such a sin to paint.
But since, alas! frail beauty must decay,
Curled or uncurled, since Locks will turn to grey;
Since painted, or not painted, all shall fade,
And she who scorns a man, must die a maid;
What then remains but well our power to use,
30 And keep good humour still whate'er we lose?
And trust me, dear! good humour can prevail,
When airs, and flights, and screams, and scolding fail.
Beauties in vain their pretty eyes may roll;
Charms strike the sight, but merit wins the soul."
   So spoke the Dame, but no applause ensued;

---

[50] Anna . . . vain: In Virgil's *Aeneid*, Aeneas forsakes his lover Dido despite her fury and her sister Anna's attempts to intervene.

Belinda frowned, Thalestris called her Prude.
"To arms, to arms!" the fierce Virago cries,
And swift as lightning to the combat flies.
All side in parties, and begin th' attack;
40 Fans clap, silks rustle, and tough whalebones crack;
Heroes' and Heroines' shouts confusedly rise,
And bass and treble voices strike the skies.
No common weapons in their hands are found,
Like Gods they fight, nor dread a mortal wound.
　　　So when bold Homer makes the Gods engage,
And heavenly breasts with human passions rage;
'Gainst Pallas, Mars; Latona, Hermes arms;
And all Olympus rings with loud alarms:
Jove's thunder roars, heaven trembles all around,
50 Blue Neptune storms, the bellowing deeps resound:
Earth shakes her nodding towers, the ground gives way,
And the pale ghosts start at the flash of day!
　　　Triumphant Umbriel on a sconce's[51] height
Clapped his glad wings, and sat to view the fight:
Propped on their bodkin spears, the Sprites survey
The growing combat, or assist the fray.
　　　While through the press enraged Thalestris flies,
And scatters death around from both her eyes,
A Beau and Witling[52] perished in the throng,
60 One died in metaphor, and one in song.
"O cruel nymph! a living death I bear,"
Cried Dapperwit, and sunk beside his chair.
A mournful glance Sir Fopling upwards cast,
"Those eyes are made so killing"—was his last.
Thus on Mæander's flowery margin lies
Th' expiring Swan, and as he sings he dies.
　　　When bold Sir Plume had drawn Clarissa down,
Chloe stepped in, and killed him with a frown;
She smiled to see the doughty hero slain,
70 But, at her smile, the Beau revived again.
　　　Now Jove suspends his golden scales in air,
Weighs the Men's wits against the Lady's hair;
The doubtful beam long nods from side to side;
At length the wits mount up, the hairs subside.
　　　See, fierce Belinda on the Baron flies,
With more than usual lightning in her eyes:
Nor feared the Chief th' unequal fight to try,

---

[51] **sconce:** A candlestick bolted to the wall.   [52] **Witling:** One who feebly attempts to be a wit.

Who sought no more than on his foe to die.
But this bold Lord with manly strength endued,
80 She with one finger and a thumb subdued:
Just where the breath of life his nostrils drew,
A charge of Snuff the wily virgin threw;
The Gnomes direct, to every atom just,
The pungent grains of titillating dust.
Sudden with starting tears each eye o'erflows,
And the high dome re-echoes to his nose.
    Now meet thy fate, incensed Belinda cried,
And drew a deadly bodkin from her side.
(The same, his ancient personage to deck,
90 Her great great grandsire wore about his neck,
In three seal rings; which after, melted down,
Formed a vast buckle for his widow's gown:
Her infant grandame's whistle next it grew,
The bells she jingled, and the whistle blew;
Then in a bodkin graced her mother's hairs,
Which long she wore, and now Belinda wears.)
    "Boast not my fall" (he cried) "insulting foe!
Thou by some other shalt be laid as low.
Nor think, to die dejects my lofty mind:
100 All that I dread is leaving you behind!
Rather than so, ah let me still survive,
And burn in Cupid's flames—but burn alive."
    "Restore the Lock!" she cries; and all around
"Restore the Lock!" the vaulted roofs rebound.
Not fierce Othello in so loud a strain
Roared for the handkerchief that caused his pain.[53]
But see how oft ambitious aims are crossed,
And chiefs contend till all the prize is lost!
The Lock, obtained with guilt, and kept with pain,
110 In every place is sought, but sought in vain:
With such a prize no mortal must be blest,
So heaven decrees! with heaven who can contest?
    Some thought it mounted to the Lunar sphere,
Since all things lost on earth are treasured there.
There Heroes' wits are kept in ponderous vases,
And beaux' in snuffboxes and tweezer cases.
There broken vows and deathbed alms are found,

---

[53] **handkerchief . . . pain:** In Shakespeare's *Othello* 3.4, Desdemona's handkerchief is falsely produced as evidence that she has cheated on Othello.

And lovers' hearts with ends of riband bound,
The courtier's promises, and sick man's prayers,
120 The smiles of harlots, and the tears of heirs,
Cages for gnats, and chains to yoke a flea,
Dried butterflies, and tomes of casuistry.
    But trust the Muse—she saw it upward rise,
Though marked by none but quick, poetic eyes:
(So Rome's great founder to the heavens withdrew,
To Proculus alone confessed in view)[54]
A sudden Star, it shot through liquid air,
And drew behind a radiant trail of hair.
Not Berenice's Locks first rose so bright,[55]
130 The heavens bespangling with dishevelled light.
The Sylphs behold it kindling as it flies,
And pleased pursue its progress through the skies.
    This the Beau monde shall from the Mall[56] survey,
And hail with music its propitious ray.
This the blest Lover shall for Venus take,
And send up vows from Rosamonda's lake.[57]
This Partridge[58] soon shall view in cloudless skies,
When next he looks through Galileo's eyes;
And hence th' egregious wizard shall foredoom
140 The fate of Louis, and the fall of Rome.
    Then cease, bright Nymph! to mourn thy ravished hair,
Which adds new glory to the shining sphere!
Not all the tresses that fair head can boast,
Shall draw such envy as the Lock you lost.
For, after all the murders of your eye,
When, after millions slain, yourself shall die;
When those fair suns shall set, as set they must,
And all those tresses shall be laid in dust,
This Lock, the Muse shall consecrate to fame,
150 And midst the stars inscribe Belinda's name.

---

[54] **(So Rome . . . in view):** Romulus, one of the legendary founders of Rome, is said to have been transported to heaven by a storm cloud while reviewing his troops.

[55] **Berenice's Locks . . . so bright:** Berenice, the wife of Ptolemy III, sacrificed a lock of her hair to ensure her husband's safe return from battle. After it disappeared from the altar, a court astronomer found that it had been transformed into a new constellation.

[56] **the Mall:** A popular walkway for fashionable strollers in St. James's Park, London.

[57] **Rosamonda's lake:** Another feature of St. James's Park, proverbially frequented by the lovelorn.

[58] **Partridge:** A contemporary astrologer whom Pope and others enjoyed satirizing; "Galileo's eyes" means a telescope.

❧ An Essay on Man

To Henry St. John, Lord Bolingbroke

EPISTLE 1

Of the Nature and State of Man with respect to the Universe

Awake, my St. John! leave all meaner things
To low ambition, and the pride of kings.
Let us (since life can little more supply
Than just to look about us and to die)
Expatiate free° o'er all this scene of man;   *roam freely*
A mighty maze! but not without a plan;
A wild, where weeds and flowers promiscuous shoot,
Or garden, tempting with forbidden fruit.
Together let us beat this ample field,
10 Try what the open, what the covert yield;
The latent tracts, the giddy heights, explore
Of all who blindly creep, or sightless soar;
Eye Nature's walks, shoot folly as it flies,
And catch the manners living as they rise;
Laugh where we must, be candid where we can;
But vindicate the ways of God to man.

    1. Say first, of God above, or man below,
What can we reason, but from what we know?
Of man, what see we but his station here,
20 From which to reason, or to which refer?
Through worlds unnumbered though the God be known,
'Tis ours to trace him only in our own.

An Essay on Man. In *An Essay on Man* (1733–34), Pope set out to "vindicate the ways of God to man" and to prove that there were order and design in the universe. That aim was not unlike Milton's in *Paradise Lost,* but Pope, in a more secular age, sought to present his case without any explicit Christian references. The poem, which was never completed, is not so much original philosophy as it is an elegant statement of the philosophic optimism of the European Enlightenment. Though Pope derives his argument from many older sources, there is an oddly modern sounding ecological edge to it, as the poet declares that creation was not designed solely for the good of human beings and calls attention to God's care for all living things.

    Readers may recognize many of the neatly turned epigrammatic lines from the *Essay,* such as "Hope springs eternal in the human breast" and "The proper study of mankind is man." All notes are the editors'.

He, who through vast immensity can pierce,
See worlds on worlds compose one universe,
Observe how system into system runs,
What other planets circle other suns,
What varied being peoples every star,
May tell why Heaven has made us as we are.
But of this frame the bearings, and the ties,
30 The strong connections, nice dependencies,
Gradations just, has thy pervading soul
Looked through? or can a part contain the whole?
　　　Is the great chain, that draws all to agree,
And drawn supports, upheld by God, or thee?

　　　2. Presumptuous man! the reason wouldst thou find,
Why formed so weak, so little, and so blind?
First, if thou canst, the harder reason guess,
Why formed no weaker, blinder, and no less!
Ask of thy mother earth, why oaks are made
40 Taller or stronger than the weeds they shade?
Or ask of yonder argent fields above,
Why Jove's satellites are less than Jove?
　　　Of systems possible, if 'tis confessed
That Wisdom Infinite must form the best,
Where all must full or not coherent be,
And all that rises, rise in due degree;
Then, in the scale of reasoning life, 'tis plain,
There must be, somewhere, such a rank as man:
And all the question (wrangle e'er so long)
50 Is only this, if God has placed him wrong?
　　　Respecting man, whatever wrong we call,
May, must be right, as relative to all.
In human works, though labored on with pain,
A thousand movements scarce one purpose gain;
In God's, one single can its end produce;
Yet serves to second too some other use.
So man, who here seems principal alone,
Perhaps acts second to some sphere unknown,
Touches some wheel, or verges to some goal;
60 'Tis but a part we see, and not a whole.
　　　When the proud steed shall know why man restrains
His fiery course, or drives him o'er the plains;
When the dull ox, why now he breaks the clod,
Is now a victim, and now Egypt's god:
Then shall man's pride and dullness comprehend

His actions', passions', being's use and end;
Why doing, suffering, checked, impelled; and why
This hour a slave, the next a deity.
    Then say not man's imperfect, Heaven in fault;
70 Say rather, man's as perfect as he ought;
His knowledge measured to his state and place,
His time a moment, and a point his space.
If to be perfect in a certain sphere,
What matter, soon or late, or here or there?
The blest today is as completely so,
As who began a thousand years ago.

    3. Heaven from all creatures hides the book of Fate,
All but the page prescribed, their present state:
From brutes what men, from men what spirits know:
80 Or who could suffer being here below?
The lamb thy riot dooms to bleed today,
Had he thy reason, would he skip and play?
Pleased to the last, he crops the flowery food,
And licks the hand just raised to shed his blood.
O blindness to the future! kindly given,
That each may fill the circle marked by Heaven:
Who sees with equal eye, as God of all,
A hero perish, or a sparrow fall,
Atoms or systems° into ruin hurled,   °solar systems
90 And now a bubble burst, and now a world.
    Hope humbly then; with trembling pinions soar;
Wait the great teacher Death, and God adore!
What future bliss, he gives not thee to know,
But gives that hope to be thy blessing now.
Hope springs eternal in the human breast:
Man never is, but always to be blest:
The soul, uneasy and confined from home,
Rests and expatiates in a life to come.
    Lo! the poor Indian, whose untutored mind
100 Sees God in clouds, or hears him in the wind;
His soul proud Science never taught to stray
Far as the solar walk, or milky way;
Yet simple Nature to his hope has given,
Behind the cloud-topped hill, an humbler heaven;
Some safer world in depth of woods embraced,
Some happier island in the watery waste,
Where slaves once more their native land behold,
No fiends torment, no Christians thirst for gold!
To be, contents his natural desire,

110   He asks no angel's wing, no seraph's fire;
      But thinks, admitted to that equal sky,
      His faithful dog shall bear him company.

          4. Go, wiser thou! and, in thy scale of sense,
      Weigh thy opinion against Providence;
      Call imperfection what thou fancy'st such,
      Say, here he gives too little, there too much;
      Destroy all creatures for thy sport or gust,°   taste
      Yet cry, if man's unhappy, God's unjust;
      If man alone engross not Heaven's high care,
120   Alone made perfect here, immortal there:
      Snatch from his hand the balance and the rod,
      Rejudge his justice, be the God of God!
          In pride, in reasoning pride, our error lies;
      All quit their sphere, and rush into the skies.
      Pride still is aiming at the blest abodes,
      Men would be angels, angels would be gods.
      Aspiring to be gods, if angels fell,
      Aspiring to be angels, men rebel:
      And who but wishes to invert the laws
130   Of order, sins against the Eternal Cause.

          5. Ask for what end the heavenly bodies shine,
      Earth for whose use? Pride answers, "'Tis for mine:
      For me kind Nature wakes her genial power,
      Suckles each herb, and spreads out every flower;
      Annual for me, the grape, the rose renew
      The juice nectareous, and the balmy dew;
      For me, the mine a thousand treasures brings;
      For me, health gushes from a thousand springs;
      Seas roll to waft me, suns to light me rise;
140   My footstool earth, my canopy the skies."
          But errs not Nature from this gracious end,
      From burning suns when livid deaths descend,
      When earthquakes swallow, or when tempests sweep
      Towns to one grave, whole nations to the deep?
      "No," 'tis replied, "the first Almighty Cause
      Acts not by partial, but by general laws;
      The exceptions few; some change since all began,
      And what created perfect?"—Why then man?
      If the great end be human happiness,
150   Then Nature deviates; and can man do less?
      As much that end a constant course requires
      Of showers and sunshine, as of man's desires;

As much eternal springs and cloudless skies,
As men forever temperate, calm, and wise.
If plagues or earthquakes break not Heaven's design,
Why then a Borgia, or a Catiline?[1]
Who knows but he whose hand the lightning forms,
Who heaves old ocean, and who wings the storms,
Pours fierce ambition in a Caesar's mind,
160 Or turns young Ammon[2] loose to scourge mankind?
From pride, from pride, our very reasoning springs;
Account for moral, as for natural things:
Why charge we Heaven in those, in these acquit?
In both, to reason right is to submit.
        Better for us, perhaps, it might appear,
Were there all harmony, all virtue here;
That never air or ocean felt the wind;
That never passion discomposed the mind:
But ALL subsists by elemental strife;
170 And passions are the elements of life.
The general ORDER, since the whole began,
Is kept in Nature, and is kept in man.

        6. What would this man? Now upward will he soar,
And little less than angel, would be more;
Now looking downwards, just as grieved appears
To want the strength of bulls, the fur of bears.
Made for his use all creatures if he call,
Say what their use, had he the powers of all?
Nature to these, without profusion, kind,
180 The proper organs, proper powers assigned;
Each seeming want compènsated of course,
Here with degrees of swiftness, there of force;
All in exact proportion to the state;
Nothing to add, and nothing to abate.
Each beast, each insect, happy in its own;
Is Heaven unkind to man, and man alone?
Shall he alone, whom rational we call,
Be pleased with nothing, if not blessed with all?
        The bliss of man (could pride that blessing find)
190 Is not to act or think beyond mankind;
No powers of body or of soul to share,

---

[1]Borgia; Catiline:Cesare Borgia (1476–1507), son of Pope Alexander VI; Renaissance Italian prince who was, with other members of his powerful family, notorious for ruthless opportunism, greed, cruelty, and treachery. Lucius Sergius Catiline (c. 108–62 B.C.E.) was an ambitious and treacherous conspirator against the Roman state.

[2] Ammon:Alexander the Great.

But what his nature and his state can bear.
Why has not man a microscopic eye?
For this plain reason, man is not a fly.
Say what the use, were finer optics given,
To inspect a mite, not comprehend the heaven?
Or touch, if tremblingly alive all o'er,
To smart and agonize at every pore?
Or quick effluvia[3] darting through the brain,
200 Die of a rose in aromatic pain?
If nature thundered in his opening ears,
And stunned him with the music of the spheres,
How would he wish that Heaven had left him still
The whispering zephyr, and the purling rill?
Who finds not Providence all good and wise,
Alike in what it gives, and what denies?

     7. Far as creation's ample range extends,
The scale of sensual,° mental powers ascends: *sensory*
Mark how it mounts, to man's imperial race,
210 From the green myriads in the peopled grass:
What modes of sight betwixt each wide extreme,
The mole's dim curtain, and the lynx's beam:
Of smell, the headlong lioness between,
And hound sagacious on the tainted green:[4]
Of hearing, from the life that fills the flood,
To that which warbles through the vernal wood:
The spider's touch, how exquisitely fine!
Feels at each thread, and lives along the line:
In the nice° bee, what sense so subtly true   *discriminating*
220 From poisonous herbs extracts the healing dew:
How instinct varies in the groveling swine,
Compared, half-reasoning elephant, with thine!
'Twixt that, and reason, what a nice barrier,
Forever separate, yet forever near!
Remembrance and reflection how allied;
What thin partitions sense from thought divide:
And middle natures, how they long to join,
Yet never pass the insuperable line!
Without this just gradation, could they be
230 Subjected, these to those, or all to thee?

---

[3] **effluvia** Streams of particles that were thought to convey sensory impressions to the brain.

[4] **Of smell . . . green:** The lioness, who has a poor sense of smell, rushes headlong at her quarry, unlike the hound whose acute sense of smell enables it to track its prey.

The powers of all subdued by thee alone,
Is not thy reason all these powers in one?

     8. See, through this air, this ocean, and this earth,
All matter quick, and bursting into birth.
Above, how high progressive life may go!
Around, how wide! how deep extend below!
Vast Chain of Being! which from God began,
Natures ethereal, human, angel, man,
Beast, bird, fish, insect, what no eye can see,
240 No glass can reach! from Infinite to thee,
From thee to nothing. — On superior powers
Were we to press, inferior might on ours:
Or in the full creation leave a void,
Where, one step broken, the great scale's destroyed:
From Nature's chain whatever link you strike,
Tenth or ten thousandth, breaks the chain alike.
     And, if each system in gradation roll
Alike essential to the amazing whole,
The least confusion but in one, not all
250 That system only, but the whole must fall.
Let earth unbalanced from her orbit fly,
Planets and suns run lawless through the sky,
Let ruling angels from their spheres be hurled,
Being on being wrecked, and world on world,
Heaven's whole foundations to their center nod,
And Nature tremble to the throne of God:
All this dread ORDER break — for whom? for thee?
Vile worm! — oh, madness, pride, impiety!

     9. What if the foot, ordained the dust to tread,
260 Or hand, to toil, aspired to be the head?
What if the head, the eye, or ear repined
To serve mere engines to the ruling Mind?[5]
Just as absurd, to mourn the tasks or pains,
The great directing MIND of ALL ordains.
     All are but parts one stupendous whole,
Whose body Nature is, and God the soul;
That, changed through all, and yet in all the same,
Great in the earth, as in the ethereal frame,
Warms in the sun, refreshes in the breeze,
270 Glows in the stars, and blossoms in the trees,

---

[5] **What if . . . Mind:** Allusion to I Corinthians 12:14–26.

Lives through all life, extends through all extent,
Spreads undivided, operates unspent,
Breathes in our soul, informs our mortal part,
As full, as perfect, in a hair as heart;
As full, as perfect, in vile man that mourns,
As the rapt seraph that adores and burns;
To him no high, no low, no great, no small;
He fills, he bounds, connects, and equals° all.   makes equal

    10. Cease then, nor ORDER imperfection name:
280 Our proper bliss depends on what we blame.
Know thy own point: this kind, this due degree
Of blindness, weakness, Heaven bestows on thee.
Submit — In this, or any other sphere,
Secure to be as blest as thou canst bear:
Safe in the hand of one disposing Power,
Or in the natal, or the mortal hour.
All Nature is but art, unknown to thee;
All chance, direction, which thou canst not see;
All discord, harmony not understood;
290 All partial evil, universal good:
And, spite of pride, in erring reason's spite,
One truth is clear: Whatever IS, is RIGHT.

FROM EPISTLE 3

*Argument: Of the Nature and State
of Man with respect to Society*

I. The whole Universe one system of Society. Nothing made wholly for *itself,* nor yet
wholly for *another.* The happiness of *Animals* mutual. II. *Reason* or *Instinct* operate
alike to the good of each Individual. *Reason* or *Instinct* operate also to Society, in all
animals. III. How far *Society* carried by Instinct. How much farther by Reason. IV. Of
that which is called the *State of Nature.* Reason instructed by Instinct in the invention of *Arts,* and in the Forms of *Society.* V. Origin of Political Societies. Origin of
Monarchy. Patriarchal government. VI. Origin of true Religion and Government,
from the same principle, of Love. Origin of Superstition and Tyranny, from the same
principle, of Fear. The Influence of Self-love operating to the *social* and *public* Good.
Restoration of true Religion and Government on their first principle. Mixed Government. Various Forms of each, and the true end of all.

Here then we rest: "The Universal Cause
Acts to one end, but acts by various laws."
In all the madness of superfluous health,
The trim of pride, the impudence of wealth,

Let this great truth be present night and day;
But most be present, if we preach or pray.

    1. Look round our World; behold the chain of Love
Combining all below and all above.
See plastic Nature working to this end,
10 The single atoms each to other tend,
Attract, attracted to, the next in place
Formed and impelled its neighbour to embrace.
See Matter next, with various life endued,
Press to one centre still, the general Good.
See dying vegetables life sustain,
See life dissolving vegetate again:
All forms that perish other forms supply,
(By turns we catch the vital breath, and die)
Like bubbles on the sea of Matter born,
20 They rise, they break, and to that sea return.
Nothing is foreign: Parts relate to whole;
One all-extending, all-preserving Soul
Connects each being, greatest with the least;
Made Beast in aid of Man, and Man of Beast;
All served, all serving: nothing stands alone;
The chain holds on, and where it ends, unknown.
    Has God, thou fool! worked solely for thy good,
Thy joy, thy pastime, thy attire, thy food?
Who for thy table feeds the wanton fawn,
30 For him as kindly spread the flowery lawn:
Is it for thee the lark ascends and sings?
Joy tunes his voice, joy elevates his wings.
Is it for thee the linnet pours his throat?
Loves of his own and raptures swell the note.
The bounding steed you pompously bestride,
Shares with his lord the pleasure and the pride.
Is thine alone the seed that strews the plain?
The birds of heaven shall vindicate their grain.
Thine the full harvest of the golden year?
40 Part pays, and justly, the deserving steer:
The hog, that ploughs not nor obeys thy call,
Lives on the labours of this lord of all.
    Know, Nature's children all divide her care;
The fur that warms a monarch, warmed a bear.
While Man exclaims, "See all things for my use!"
"See man for mine!" replies a pampered goose:
And just as short of reason He must fall,
Who thinks all made for one, not one for all.

Ƨ FRANÇOIS-MARIE AROUET DE VOLTAIRE
1694–1778

During the French Revolution,[1] more than ten years after his death, Voltaire's bones were transported to Paris in a hearse inscribed "Poet, philosopher, historian, he gave wings to the human intelligence; he prepared us for freedom." More than any other single person of the eighteenth century, Voltaire epitomizes in the breadth of his intellectual endeavors the Age of Enlightenment, which put its faith in human reason and a rational universe, championed human rights, and believed that reason could chart a commonsense path for improving the human condition. Voltaire was not an originator of ideas, but he took hold of the liberal precepts of his time — such as John Locke's[2] theories on equality and human rights, Isaac Newton's[3] natural philosophy, and English deism — and became the propagandist for these ideas in France and eventually throughout Europe.

He wrote, he lectured, he acted in his own plays; he argued, he criticized, he satirized his intellectual and political adversaries; he was persecuted and jailed, and he fled persecution and traveled throughout Europe. For more than sixty years he was an outspoken critic of French society and for most of his life he was a refugee from his own country.

Although he gave considerable thought to the ideal conditions of human existence, Voltaire's primary efforts were directed at removing the obstacles to progress by analyzing them and holding them up to scorn or ridicule. Government and religious institutions, with their goals of dominance and control, were prime candidates for Voltaire's barbed pen. In Voltaire's Europe, the Roman Catholic Church wielded enormous power and the French government had grown top-heavy with kings and nobles who abused their privileges.

Voltaire believed in the open exchange of ideas and therefore deplored any political or religious agency that sought to shelter ignorance and superstition in order to deceive and manipulate its followers. At the end of his life, he became almost obsessed with the belief that humans needed to be freed from the authority of the church and from the centuries of theological doctrines that prevented them from acting rationally and sensibly.

The Young Rebel. The facts of Voltaire's life are a testimony to his lifelong desire to put ideas into action as well as to the power of his foes, who

Catherine Lusurier, Portrait of Voltaire, 1718. Oil on Canvas
Voltaire as a young man. (Réunion des Musées Nationaux / Art Resource, NY)

---

[1] **French Revolution:** Uprising that began in 1789, ending the thousand-year rule of kings in France. The Reign of Terror (1793–94) was ushered in with the trial and execution of King Louis XVI and Queen Marie Antoinette. Thousands of nobles and others considered to be traitors were also executed.

[2] **John Locke:** Influential English philosopher. In *Essay Concerning Human Understanding* (1690), he proposed that the human mind at birth is a *tabula rasa,* or blank slate, that experience fills up.

[3] **Isaac Newton:** Brilliant English mathematician and physicist who formulated the laws of gravity and motion, thereby describing the physical workings of the cosmos and presenting it as a finely tuned machine.

www   For links to more information about Voltaire, a quiz on *Candide,* and information about the 21st-century relevance of *Candide,* see *World Literature Online* at bedfordstmartins .com/worldlit.

tried to silence his extraordinary voice. Voltaire was born François-Marie Arouet to a prosperous bourgeois family. He was introduced at an early age to DEISM by his godfather, the Abbé de Châteauneuf. Deism was the belief that a rational deity created the world and left the running of it to natural laws, much as a watchmaker makes a watch to run on its own. Voltaire embraced deism his entire life, and it formed the basis of his unending attacks on Christianity. He was given a solid classical education at a famous Jesuit school, College Louis-le-Grand. While in his teens he steered away from his father's law profession and instead became involved with various social factions in Paris, where he wrote libelous poems for which he was briefly jailed and then exiled from France. At twenty-three he adopted the pen name of "Voltaire," the exact meaning of which is unknown. His first serious literary efforts were in the theater; his play *Oedipe* (1718)[4] was a financial success. In it the main culprit is God, who becomes responsible for the crimes of Oedipus and Jocasta. A popular epic poem, *Le Henriade,* celebrated Henry IV[5] as a champion of religious tolerance in the sixteenth century.

In 1725, Voltaire's life took a sharp turn. He was insulted by the chevalier de Rohan; Voltaire returned the insult and was beaten up by Rohan's hired thugs, in full view of aristocrats whom Voltaire had previously thought of as friends. He challenged Rohan to a duel, but on the appointed day he was arrested, jailed, and exiled to England for almost three years, from 1726 to 1729. He was so impressed by English tolerance in the areas of religion and speech that he learned to speak and read English and became friends with Alexander Pope, Jonathan Swift, and William Congreve.[6] Voltaire gained access to the English court by way of Sir Robert Walpole, an important English statesman, and Lord Bolingbroke, a friend of writers and a gentleman philosopher. Voltaire also became acquainted with the writings and ideas of Shakespeare, Bacon,[7] Locke, and Newton, and with the English parliamentary system.

Based on his experiences in England, he wrote *Philosophical Letters (Lettres philosophiques);* an English version was published in 1733 and a French edition in 1734. While complimenting English ways, it indirectly criticized the abuses of French institutions. The book was condemned in France, copies of it were burned, and a warrant was issued for Voltaire's arrest. This time, Voltaire was prepared for the attack; financially secure, he took up residence with Emilie de Breteuil, marquise du Châtelet, at the château of Cirey, situated in the independent duchy of Lorraine. At this refuge, Voltaire wrote plays and essays, experimented with physics in a

---

[4] *Oedipe:* The ancient myth of a king who killed his father and married his mother was first dramatized in ancient Greece by Sophocles (496–406 B.C.E.) in *Oedipus the King.*

[5] Henry IV: During a period of heavy religious persecution, Henry IV of France (1589–1610) issued the Edict of Nantes, which granted Protestants—especially the Huguenots—freedom of worship.

[6] Alexander Pope, Jonathan Swift, and William Congreve: Pope (1688–1744) was an English poet famous for his satires; see page 232. Swift (1667–1745), another satirist, wrote *Gulliver's Travels;* see page 141. Congreve (1670–1729) was an English dramatist.

[7] Shakespeare, Bacon: William Shakespeare (1564–1616) is England's most famous dramatist. English philosopher Francis Bacon (1561–1626) introduced empiricism—experiment and observation—to scientific thought.

laboratory, and supported the development of iron foundries. His book on the philosophy of history, *Essay on the Manners and the Spirit of Nations* (1756), stretched the domain of history to include prebiblical and Asian civilizations. He wrote a blizzard of essays and pamphlets attacking the corruption of his era and often published them under various pen names. His lucid writing style and biting wit, however, readily identified him.

Diplomatic and Religious Difficulties.

For several years, Frederick the Great of Prussia had been trying to entice Voltaire to his court in Potsdam, where he was creating a royal environment for art and ideas. Voltaire at last joined him, but this alliance of two extremely headstrong men was doomed. Voltaire was not cut from diplomatic cloth and soon was embroiled in intrigues and social power plays. The finale came when Maupertuis, the president of the Academy of Berlin, had the philosopher König dismissed from the academy. Frederick backed Maupertuis and

Jean-Honoré Fragonard, *The Love Letter,* **1770. Oil on Canvas**

This eighteenth-century portrait illustrates the vanity of French society in Voltaire's time. (The Metropolitan Museum of Art, The Jules Bache Collection, 1949. All rights reserved, the Metropolitan Museum of Art)

As for Voltaire . . . it is impossible not to look upon him as a demon of grace, wit, and very often also . . . of good sense and reason, as a blind and brilliant elemental force, which is often luminous, a meteor that cannot be controlled, rather than a human and moral being.

– CHARLES AUGUSTIN
SAINTE-BEUVE,
"Voltaire and the
Président de
Brosses," 1850

Voltaire took König's side, eventually publishing a lampoon of Maupertuis, *Diatribe of Doctor Akaia* (1752). Apparently, Voltaire obtained permission to publish this work by deceiving Frederick about the documents he was actually signing. Frederick burned the work and had Voltaire arrested.

Having been denied a residence in France, Voltaire at sixty years of age bought a country house on the border between Geneva and France. At this house called *Les Délices* (The Delights), along with his mistress, Madame Denis, and his niece, he established his own literary "court," along with a private theater where his plays were performed. Geneva, however, had a ban against theater of any kind, and again Voltaire's freedoms were threatened. He persuaded a friend, d'Alembert, to criticize Geneva's prohibition in the *Encyclopedia;* Jean-Jacques Rousseau,[8] the most famous citizen of Geneva, answered this article and Voltaire in his important *Letter to d'Alembert* (1758), which defended Geneva's ban.

Voltaire again had to move, and he bought Ferney, a large estate just inside the border of France but fronting on Lake Geneva. As the patriarch of Ferney, he experimented with a model agricultural community. During this time he also developed a stone quarry and built factories for manufacturing tiles, stockings, watches, and leather goods. He started schools and promoted fair wages and equitable taxes, and he actively defended victims of civil injustice. In one case, he rescued a young noblewoman from a convent and established her in his household, nicknaming her "Belle et Bonne" ("beautiful and good"). He eventually matched her with the marquis of Villette. And all the while he played host to the most illustrious scientists, philosophers, and artists of his time.

By 1760 his reputation as an opponent of Christianity had become almost legendary. In a letter to Voltaire, Diderot addressed him as his "sublime, honorable and dear Anti-Christ." Voltaire's *Philosophical Dictionary* (1764) was a culminating diatribe against conventional religion and a delineation of his own brand of deism. Under the heading "Religion," Voltaire discusses a deity who is a product of Copernicus and Newton, not the Bible:

> Last night I was meditating; I was absorbed in the contemplation of nature, admiring the immensity, the courses, the relations of those infinite globes, which are above the admiration of the vulgar.
> I admired still more the intelligence that presides over this vast machinery. I said to myself: A man must be blind not to be impressed by this spectacle; he must be stupid not to recognize its author; he must be mad not to adore him.

The *Philosophical Dictionary* was immediately condemned and burned by both Protestant and Catholic authorities. In February 1778, after an absence of twenty-eight years, Voltaire returned to Paris, where he was celebrated by the Académie Française, local and foreign dignitaries, and crowds of chanting Parisians. When he died ten weeks later, on May 30, he was denied burial by Christian authorities but was secretly interred at the abbey of Scellières in Champagne.

---

[8] RousseauFrench writer who produced his *Confessions* (1781–88) to illustrate the importance of the individual.

Enormous Literary Output. Voltaire's literary output amounted to more than one hundred thirty-five volumes in a modern French edition. He wrote dozens of plays and novels, and his several histories focused on important political figures. But it is his philosophical tales, especially *Zadig* (1748) and *Candide* (1759), that have brought him the greatest fame since the eighteenth century. Voltaire writes *didactic* fiction; that is, he is always interested in teaching, in using his plot and characters to develop arguments about contemporary issues. He is not concerned with creating well-rounded characters. And he is less interested in the aesthetics of fiction than in the clarity of intellectual discussion. Generally, his technique is to express his opinions through various characters from history or mythology; a character might represent a particular philosophy. His plots using Asian characters and settings are mirrors continually reflecting back on Europe or France.

Candide, whose very name suggests openness, is a naive optimist who has been educated by an impractical philosopher, Pangloss, whose name indicates a simplification of all experience. With his belief that all is for the best in the best of all possible worlds, Pangloss represents the ivory tower philosopher whose theories are radically disconnected from reality. In Chapter 5, Candide, wounded from the Lisbon earthquake, urgently begs for some wine and oil. Deaf to his request, Pangloss speculates: "This concussion of the earth is no new thing . . . the city of Lima in South America, experienced the same last year; the same cause, the same effects; there is certainly a vein of sulphur all the way underground from Lima to Lisbon." Meanwhile, Candide faints.

Voltaire's character of Pangloss suggests the philosopher Leibniz,[9] who claimed that this world is the best of all possible worlds. Because the universe was created by a God whose plans are perfect, the universe must be perfect, too, Leibniz argued. It has been suggested that Voltaire is also satirizing Christian Wolff (1679–1754), a German mathematician and philosopher who expressed the optimism and confidence of the age in a book titled *Reasonable Thoughts on God, the World, and the Soul of Man, Also on Things in General.* In fact, Voltaire is ridiculing any simplistic explanation for the complexities of experience, any universal principle that is applied unquestioningly to every situation. In particular he satirizes any religious belief that accounts for human disasters such as the Lisbon earthquake by reference to an ultimate good or a beneficent Providence. Although evil might be justified as some form of good or a mystery in God's ultimate plan, Voltaire prefers to link evil to human choice and weakness. The Lisbon earthquake of 1755 produced hardship that optimists had difficulty explaining away: The innocent suffered in hospitals, in homes, and on the streets. In all his works, Voltaire's real enemy is complacency, any attitude or theory that seems content with the present state of affairs. No particular Christian denomination, whether Protestant or Catholic, is safe from Voltaire's scorn.

In one adventure after another, Candide is exposed to the treachery and immorality, the greed and lust just below the surface of political

The friend of kings and the implacable enemy of the Roman Church and indeed, of all institutional Christianity, he was the most admired and dreaded writer of the century, and by his unforgettable and deadly mockery did more to undermine the foundations of the established order than any of its other opponents.

– ISAIAH BERLIN,
The Age of Enlightenment, 1956

---

[9] **Leibniz:** German mathematician and philosopher; see page 358.

officials, military commanders, and religious professionals. This wide range of experiences and the work's short chapters keep *Candide* entertaining and engaging. When the protagonist and his valet, Cacambo, finally arrive in the famed utopia of El Dorado,[10] they discover it to be boring; naturally they find a commonsense religion, about which Cacambo remarks, "What! you have no monks to teach, argue, govern, intrigue, and burn at the stake everyone who disagrees with them?" In Candide's search for situations that would confound Pangloss's philosophy, he finally meets Martin, a thoroughgoing pessimist. Steering a philosophical course between the two extremes, Candide arrives in Constantinople and is rejoined by his former comrades, including his beloved Lady **Cunégonde**. Candide's adjustments to all the changes in their respective lives leads to conclusions about living the simple life. He proposes a practical, modest realism; the importance of work is alluded to in the enigmatic dictum that ends the work: "We must cultivate our garden."

koo-nay-GOHND

■ CONNECTIONS

Du Fu (Book 2). In his work, eighth-century Chinese poet Du Fu critiques the incompetent bureaucrats of the Tang dynasty. Which parts of society does Voltaire single out for criticism in *Candide*?

Jonathan Swift, *Gulliver's Travels*, p. 147. Both Swift and Voltaire use their narrators as agents through which they can view and satirize reality. A narrator may mirror or discover a society's weaknesses and defects. How does Voltaire's use of the innocent Candide differ from Swift's use of Gulliver, the ordinary seaman?

Alexander Pope, *The Rape of the Lock*, p. 238. One tool of satire is hyperbole: the exaggeration of a character trait or social defect. The hyperbole in Pope's *The Rape of the Lock* highlights the shallowness of social vanity and upper-class manners. What does the hyperbole Voltaire employs in his portrayal of clergymen say about the institution of religion?

■ FURTHER RESEARCH

Biography
Besterman, Theodore. *Voltaire*. 1976.
Brailsford, Henry N. *Voltaire*. 1935.
Wade, Ira O. *The Intellectual Development of Voltaire*. 1969.

Intellectual History
Keener, F. M. *The Chain of Being*. 1983.

Criticism
Cullter, M., ed. *The Enlightenment and the Comic Mode*. 1990.
Gay, Peter. *Candide*. 1963.
————. *Voltaire's Politics: The Poet as Realist*. 1959.
Wade, Ira O. *Voltaire and Candide: A Study in the Fusion of History, Art, and Philosophy*. 1959.

---

[10] **El Dorado:** The Spanish conquistadors believed that *El Dorado* ("the golden man") was a kingdom of unlimited gold—so much gold that the king covered himself with it daily—located somewhere in the Americas. The name became synonymous with a hidden or lost paradise.

■ **PRONUNCIATION**

Cunégonde: koo-nay-GOHND
Giroflèe: zhee-roh-FLAY
Oreillons: oh-ray-YAWNG
Voltaire: vohl-TEHR

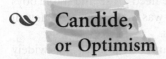

Candide,
or Optimism

Translated from the German of Dr. Ralph. With the Additions Found in the Doctor's Pocket When He Died at Minden in the Year of Our Lord 1759

Translated by Daniel Gordon

CHAPTER 1

How Candide was brought up in a fine castle, and how he was driven out of it

In the land of Westphalia,[1] in the castle of the Baron of Thunder-ten-tronckh, lived a youth endowed by nature with the gentlest of characters. His face was the mirror of

---

Candide, or Optimism. Voltaire first published *Candide* under a pseudonym in Geneva. It quickly became a best-seller, going through forty editions during his lifetime. When the book was condemned by the Geneva City Council, Voltaire denied having anything to do with what he called the "schoolboy trifling."

Candide is a picaresque narrative—a story loosely structured around a succession of episodes, focusing on a rather thinly drawn *picaro,* or hero, whose adventures allow the writer to treat society and its customs with humor and satire. Through Candide's adventures, Voltaire satirizes the follies of his own society, especially with regard to the irrationality and inhumane practices of contemporary religion.

Voltaire was not a pessimist, however. He believed that if humans could take off the blinders of traditional religion and free themselves from the influence of corrupt public officials, progress toward a better world was possible. In the meantime, he said, "we must cultivate our garden," a statement that has been much debated ever since *Candide* first appeared. Is Voltaire suggesting we retreat from involvement in the world and simply tend to our private desires and needs? Or is he saying we would do best to work on those areas of our lives that will bear fruit and abandon abstract theorizing and faddish philosophies? It is consistent with Voltaire's role as an intellectual gadfly that he would leave the resolution of personal morality and social responsibility to his readers.

All notes are the editors'.

---

[1]**Westphalia:** A region in northwestern Germany. The fictional translator, Doctor Ralph, supposedly died there at the battle of Minden during the Seven Years' War (1756–1763). "Thunder-ten-tronckh" is Voltaire's parodic name for the estate.

his soul. His judgment was quite sound, his mind simple as could be; this is the reason, I think, that he was named Candide. The old servants of the house suspected that he was the son of the Baron's sister and of a good and honorable gentleman of the region whom that lady refused to marry because he could prove only seventy-one generations[2] of noble lineage, the rest of his family tree having been lost in the shadows of time.

The Baron was one of the most powerful lords in Westphalia because his castle had a gate and windows. His reception hall was even decorated with a piece of tapestry. The barnyard dogs formed a hunting pack when the need arose; the stable boys doubled as his attendants in the chase; the village vicar was his archpriest. They all called him My Lord, and they always laughed at his jokes.

The Baroness, who weighed around three hundred and fifty pounds, was widely admired for that reason, and bestowed favors on visitors with a discretion that made her even more eminent. Her daughter Cunégonde,[3] aged seventeen, was rosy-cheeked, fresh, plump, and appetizing. The Baron's son seemed to be the equal of his father in every way. The tutor Pangloss[4] was the oracle of the household, and little Candide absorbed his lessons with all the good faith of his age and character.

Pangloss taught metaphysico-theologico-cosmolo-boobology.[5] He proved admirably that there is no effect without a cause and that, in this best of all possible worlds,[6] the Baron's castle was the finest of all castles, and his wife the best of all possible Baronesses.

"It has been proven," he used to say, "that things cannot be other than what they are, for since everything is made for an end, everything is necessarily for the best end. Observe that noses were made to wear spectacles, hence we have spectacles. Legs are patently devised to be breeched, and so we have breeches. Stones were made to be quarried and to build castles with; hence My Lord has a fine castle. The greatest Baron of the province must have the finest residence. And since pigs were made to be eaten, we eat pork all year round. Therefore, those who have affirmed that all is well talk nonsense; they ought to have said that all is for the best."[7]

Candide listened attentively and believed innocently; for he found Miss Cunégonde extremely beautiful, though he never dared to tell her so. He concluded that after the happiness of being born Baron of Thunder-ten-tronckh, the second degree of happiness was to be Miss Cunégonde, the third was to see her every day, and the

---

[2] **seventy-one generations:** The number, amounting to two thousand years of uninterrupted nobility, is meant to be ridiculously high.

[3] **Cunégonde:** From Queen Kunigunda, the wife of Holy Roman Emperor Henry II (973–1024). She proved her fidelity by walking barefoot and blindfolded over hot irons; hence, her name adds to Voltaire's irony.

[4] **Pangloss:** "All tongue" (from Greek).

[5] **cosmolo-boobology:** Voltaire uses "cosmolo-nigologie," containing the hidden French word *nigaud,* meaning simpleton; the translator uses "boob" to convey the same meaning in English.

[6] **best . . . worlds:** An allusion to the belief of the German philosopher Leibniz (1646–1716), who argued that in creating the world, God had made "the most perfect of all possible states or governments" (see p. 358).

[7] **for the best:** Voltaire here parodies the so-called argument from design, promoted by Leibniz and others, that suggests everything in the world is here for a specific purpose.

fourth was to listen to Master Pangloss, the greatest philosopher in the province and consequently in the whole world.

One day, as Cunégonde was strolling near the castle in the tiny woods they called the Park, she saw Dr. Pangloss in the bushes giving a lesson in experimental physics to her mother's maid, a very cute and obedient brunette. Now Miss Cunégonde was very intrigued by the sciences. She observed breathlessly the repeated experiments performed before her eyes. She saw clearly the doctor's sufficient reason and the action of cause and effect. And she turned back to the house all excited, all distracted, all consumed by the desire to become more instructed in science, dreaming that she might be young Candide's sufficient reason—and that he might be hers.

She met Candide on the way back to the castle. She blushed, and so did he. She said hello in a faltering voice, and Candide replied without knowing what he was saying. The next day, when they left the table after dinner, Cunégonde and Candide found themselves behind a partition. Cunégonde dropped her handkerchief, Candide picked it up. She innocently took his hand, the young man innocently kissed it with remarkable animation, emotion, and grace. Their lips met, their eyes glowed, their knees trembled, their hands wandered. The Baron of Thunder-ten-tronckh came around the partition and, seeing this cause and this effect, drove Candide out of the castle with great kicks in the behind. Cunégonde fainted. As soon as she recovered, the Baroness slapped her face, and everything was unsettled in this finest and most agreeable of all possible castles.

CHAPTER 2

What became of Candide among the Bulgars[8]

Expelled from earthly paradise, Candide walked for a long time without knowing where he was going, weeping, raising his eyes to heaven, and looking back frequently toward the finest of castles which contained the most lovely of baron's daughters. He lay down to sleep, without supper, in the furrow of a plowed field. The snow came down in large flakes. The next day, chilled to the bone, Candide dragged himself toward the nearest town, called Waldberghoff-trarbk-dikdorff. Penniless and dying of hunger and exhaustion, he came to a sad halt at the door of an inn. Two men dressed in blue[9] noticed him.

"Comrade," said one of them, "there is a well-built lad, and he is the right height too."

They approached Candide and politely invited him to dinner.

"Gentlemen," Candide answered with charming modesty, "you honor me greatly, but I lack the means to pay my share."

"But sir!" said one of the blues, "we never make people pay who have your looks and merit. Aren't you five feet ten inches tall?"

---

[8] **Bulgars:** The Prussian troops of Frederick the Great, king of Prussia from 1740 to 1786. Because it resembles in sound the French *bougre* (English "bugger"), the word suggests pederasty or sodomy.

[9] **dressed in blue:** Prussian recruiting officers wore blue and selected men for various regiments according to their size.

"Yes, gentlemen, that's my height," he said with a bow.

"Then, sir, kindly be seated. We will not only pay for your dinner, but we will never let a man like you fall short of money. Men are created only in order to help each other."

"You're right," said Candide. "That's what Dr. Pangloss always told me, and I see clearly that everything is for the best."

They urged him to accept a little money. He took it and offered to sign a promissory note, but they would not hear of it, and they all sat down to eat.

"Don't you have a tender love for your . . ."

"Oh yes!" Candide answered. "I have a tender love for Miss Cunégonde."

"No," one of the men stated, "we want to know if you have a tender love for the King of the Bulgars."

"Not at all," he said, "since I've never met him."

"What? He is the most charming of kings, and we must drink to his health."

"All right, I'll be happy to, gentlemen!" And he drank.

"That's enough," they said. "You are now the pillar, the upholder, the defender, the hero of the Bulgars: Your fortune is made, and your glory assured."

Immediately they put irons on his feet and led him to the regiment. He had to turn right, turn left, order arms, load arms, aim, fire, and do it all in double time. At the end he got thirty strokes of the rod. The next day, he did the drill a little less badly and got only twenty. The third day he got only ten, and was regarded by his comrades as a prodigy.

Candide, completely bewildered, did not yet discern very clearly how he was a hero. One fine spring day he took it into his head to go for a walk. He kept going forward, believing that humans, just like animals, had the right to use their legs as they wished.[10] He had barely gone five miles, when four other heroes, all over six feet, caught up with him, tied him, and threw him in a dungeon. In accordance with due process, he was asked which he preferred: to be thrashed thirty-six times by the entire regiment, or to receive twelve bullets in the brain all at once. He protested that human will is free and that he desired neither alternative; but he was forced to choose. Making use of the divine *liberty* that still remained to him, he elected to run the gauntlet thirty-six times. Two times he did so. The regiment was made up of two thousand men. That made four thousand strokes of the rod, which laid bare every muscle and nerve from his neck to his behind. As they were preparing for the third run, Candide, unable to go on, requested them to be kind enough to smash in his head.

The request was granted. They blindfolded him and told him to kneel. At that moment the King of the Bulgars arrived on the scene and inquired about the victim's crime. Now the King was a genius and understood from what he was told that Candide was a young metaphysician, utterly ignorant about the things of this world, and he pardoned him with a generosity that will be praised in all newspapers and in all ages. A worthy surgeon cured Candide in three weeks with the ointments prescribed

---

[10] **to use . . . they wished:** This episode alludes to the case of an actual deserter, whom Voltaire helped to free from prison. Leibniz's doctrine of free will was thought to promote desertion.

by Dioscorides.[11] He already had a little skin and was able to walk when the King of the Bulgars joined battle with the King of the Abars.[12]

Chapter 3

How Candide escaped from the Bulgars, and what became of him

Nothing was so splendid, so brisk, so brilliant, and so well-ordered as these two armies. The trumpets, fifes, oboes, drums, and cannons produced such a harmony as was never heard in hell. First the cannons laid low about six thousand men on each side; then the musketry removed from the best of worlds around nine or ten thousand scoundrels who were festering on its surface. The bayonet was also the sufficient reason for the death of several thousand men. The total must have been about thirty thousand souls. Candide, trembling like a philosopher, hid himself as best he could while this heroic butchery took place.

Finally, while each king was having his forces celebrate victory with a *Te Deum*,[13] Candide decided to theorize about causes and effects somewhere else. Making his way through heaps of the dead and dying, he came to a nearby village; it had been reduced to ashes. This was an Abar village that the Bulgars had burned in accordance with international law. Here, old men riddled with wounds looked on as life departed from their wives whose throats had been slit and whose children still clung to their blood-soaked breasts. There, young girls who had been disemboweled after they had satisfied the natural needs of various heroes, heaved their last sighs. Others, half-burned, screamed for someone to hasten their deaths. Brains were spattered over the ground amidst severed arms and legs.

Candide fled full speed to another village. This one belonged to the Bulgars, and the Abar heroes had treated it in the same manner. Forging onward through ruins and treading upon twitching limbs, Candide at last arrived outside the theater of war, carrying a few provisions in his knapsack and never forgetting Miss Cunégonde. His supplies ran out when he was in Holland; but having heard that everyone in this country was rich and that the people there were Christians, he had no doubt that he would be treated as well as he had been in the Baron's castle before he had been driven from it on account of the lovely eyes of Miss Cunégonde.

He requested alms of several grave individuals. They all replied that if he continued to beg he would be shut up in a house of correction to teach him how to behave.

Then he approached a man who had just finished giving a lecture on the topic of charity for a whole hour to a large assembly. The orator looked askance at him and said:

"What are you doing here? Are you here for the good cause?"

"There is no effect without a cause," Candide answered modestly. "Everything is linked by necessity and arranged for the best. I had to be driven from Miss

---

[11] **Dioscorides:** Greek physician from the first century C.E. who wrote a treatise on medicines.

[12] **King of the Abars:** The Abars, a semibarbaric Scythian tribe, here refers to the French who fought against the Prussians during the Seven Years' War (1756–1763).

[13] *Te Deum:* A Latin hymn celebrating victory.

Cunégonde; I had to run the gauntlet; and I have to beg for my bread until I can earn it. None of this could have been otherwise."

"My friend," said the orator, "do you believe the Pope is the Antichrist?"

"I never heard anyone say so," answered Candide, "but whether he is or not, I have no bread."

"And you do not deserve to eat any," said the other. "Go away, you scoundrel, you wretch, and never show your face here again!"

The orator's wife, having watched from a window above, and seeing a man who was not sure the Pope was the Antichrist, poured on his head a pot full of———. Oh Heavens! The zeal of pious women knows no bounds!

A man who had never been baptized, a good Anabaptist[14] named Jacques, saw the cruel and ignominious treatment inflicted on one of his fellows, a two-legged creature without feathers and with a soul. He took Candide home, washed him, gave him bread and beer, presented him with two florins, and even volunteered to teach him how to work in his Dutch factory, which specialized in the production of authentic Persian rugs. Candide was ready to kiss the man's feet and exclaimed:

"Dr. Pangloss was certainly right to tell me that all is for the best in this world. I am infinitely more touched by your extreme generosity than by the harshness of that gentleman in the black coat and his wife."

The next day, on a walk, he met a beggar all covered with sores, his eyes dull as death, the end of his nose rotting, mouth twisted, teeth black, a raspy voice, tortured by a violent cough, and spitting out a tooth with every spasm.

CHAPTER 4

How Candide met his old philosophy teacher, Dr. Pangloss, and what ensued

Candide, touched by horror and even more by compassion, gave this dreadful beggar the two florins he had received from Jacques, the worthy Anabaptist. The phantom stared at him, burst into tears, and threw his arms around his neck. Candide recoiled in terror.

"Alas," said one wretch to the other, "don't you recognize your dear Pangloss any more?"

"Can it be so? You, my dear master! You, in this horrible state! What misfortune has befallen you? Why are you no longer in the finest of castles? What has become of Miss Cunégonde, that pearl of young ladies, that masterpiece of nature?"

"I cannot go on," said Pangloss.

Candide promptly led him to the Anabaptist's stable, where he gave him a morsel of bread, and when Pangloss had recovered:

"Well," said he, "Cunégonde?"

"She is dead," replied Pangloss.

---

[14] **Anabaptist:** A number of liberal religious groups were called Anabaptists in sixteenth-century Europe. They were persecuted for their beliefs in such things as adult baptism. Holland granted Anabaptists asylum, and Voltaire respected their ideas and lifestyle. Jacques demonstrates their compassion for humans: two-footed, rational beings without feathers, according to Plato's definition.

Candide fainted at this word. His friend revived him with some old vinegar that happened to be in the stable. Candide opened his eyes.

"Cunégonde is dead! Ah, best of worlds, where are you now? But what illness did she die of? Did it stem from seeing me violently kicked out of her father's fine castle?"

"No," said Pangloss. "She was disemboweled by Bulgar soldiers after being raped until she was unconscious. They smashed in the head of the Baron when he tried to defend her; the Baroness was hacked to pieces; and my poor pupil was treated exactly the same as his sister.[15] As for the castle, not one stone was left standing upright. Not a single barn, sheep, duck, or tree is left. But we have avenged ourselves in full, for the Abars did the same thing to a nearby estate that belonged to a Bulgar lord."

At this account Candide fainted again, but after he came back to his senses and expressed his sorrow, he inquired about the cause and effect, the sufficient reason, which had reduced Pangloss to such a pitiful state.

"Alas," said he, "it is love; love, the consoler of the human race, the guardian of the universe, the soul of all sensitive beings, tender love."

"Alas," said Candide, "I have known this love, this ruler of hearts, this soul of our soul: It never got me anything except one kiss and twenty kicks in the ass. And why did this beautiful cause produce in you such a disgusting effect?"

Pangloss answered in these terms:

"Oh my dear Candide! You knew Paquette, our venerable Baron's pretty maid. In her arms I tasted the delights of paradise, which have produced the hellish torments from which I now suffer. She had the disease before me, and she may well be dead by now. Paquette received this present from a very learned Franciscan monk, who was able to trace it back to its primary source. For it came to him from an old countess, who got it from a cavalry captain, who owed it to a marquise, who had it from a page, who caught it from a Jesuit, who during his novitiate received it directly from a shipmate of Christopher Columbus.[16] As for myself, I shall not give it to anyone, for I am dying."

"Oh Pangloss!" exclaimed Candide, "What a strange genealogy! Isn't the devil at the root of it all?"

"Not at all," the great man replied. "It was an indispensable element of the best of worlds, a necessary ingredient. For had Columbus not caught this disease on an American island, this disease which poisons the source of reproduction, which often prevents reproduction entirely, and which is clearly opposed to the great purpose of nature—then we would have neither chocolate nor cochineal. It must also be noted that until now, this malady, like theological conflict, is limited to the European continent. The Turks, Indians, Persians, Chinese, Siamese, and Japanese are not yet acquainted with it. But the principle of sufficient reason will bring it to them as well, in due course of time. Meanwhile, it is making amazing progress among us, especially in those vast armies composed of decent, well-bred scholarship boys, who

---

[15] **same as his sister:** Voltaire associates homosexuality with Cunégonde's brother here and elsewhere in the text.

[16] **Christopher Columbus:** Syphilis spread to Europe from the Americas.

shape the destiny of nations. You can be sure that when thirty thousand men fight a pitched battle against an equal number of troops, there are about twenty thousand syphilitics on each side."

"Very impressive," said Candide, "but we must get you cured."

"How can I be?" said Pangloss. "I am penniless, my friend, and nowhere on earth can you be bled or get an enema for free."

This last remark made up Candide's mind. He proceeded to throw himself at the feet of his charitable Anabaptist Jacques and painted such a moving picture of his friend's condition that the good man immediately took in Dr. Pangloss and paid for his treatment. In the cure Pangloss lost only one eye and one ear. He could write well and knew arithmetic perfectly. The Anabaptist Jacques made him his bookkeeper. Two months later he was obliged to go to Lisbon on business, and he took his two philosophers with him on the boat. Pangloss explained to him how everything was for the best. Jacques was not convinced.

"Surely," he said, "humankind has corrupted its nature a little, for people were not born wolves, yet they have become wolves. God did not give them heavy cannon or bayonets, yet they have invented them to destroy each other. I could also refer to bankruptcies, and the system of justice that confiscates a bankrupt man's property just to prevent the creditors from getting it."

"All that is indispensable," replied the one-eyed doctor. "Private misfortunes work for the general good, so the more private misfortunes there are, the more all is well."

While he was theorizing, the sky clouded over, the winds rushed in from the four corners of the globe, and the ship was assailed by a terrible storm just as the port of Lisbon came into view.

CHAPTER 5

Storm, shipwreck, earthquake, and what happened to Dr. Pangloss, Candide, and Jacques the Anabaptist

Half the passengers, weakened and nearly dying from the indescribable agony that the rolling of a ship inflicts on the nerves and humors of a body shaken in different directions, were not even strong enough to recognize how great the danger was. The other half were shrieking and praying. The sails were in shreds, the masts in pieces, the hull split open. Everybody worked who could, but no one cooperated and no one commanded. The Anabaptist was trying to help on the upper deck. A panicked sailor struck him violently and laid him out flat, but his own blow threw him off balance and he fell headfirst over the side. He caught on to part of the broken mast and remained hanging there. The good Jacques got up and ran to his aid, helping him to climb back up; but in the process he was thrown into the sea, right in front of the sailor, who let him drown without even condescending to look at him. Candide rushed over and saw his benefactor appear on the surface for an instant before sinking forever into the deep. He wanted to dive into the sea after him, but the philosopher Pangloss stopped him by demonstrating that the Lisbon harbor was designed expressly for this Anabaptist to drown in. While he was perfecting his logical proof, the ship broke into two and everyone perished except for Pangloss, Candide, and that brutal sailor who had drowned the virtuous Anabaptist. The rogue swam with ease to the shore, while Pangloss and Candide drifted there on a plank.

When they had recovered, they walked toward Lisbon. They still had a little money, with which they hoped to avert hunger after escaping from the storm.

They had scarcely set foot in the city, still mourning the death of their benefactor, when they felt the ground tremble beneath them. The sea boiled up in the port and snapped the ships lying at anchor. Whirlwinds of flame and ashes bellowed through the streets and public squares. Houses crumbled. The roofs collapsed onto their foundations, and then the foundations themselves disintegrated. Thirty thousand inhabitants of every age and sex were crushed in the ruins.[17]

Swearing and whistling, the sailor remarked, "I can get something out of this."

"What can be the sufficient reason for this phenomenon?" asked Pangloss.

"It's the end of the world!" cried Candide.

The sailor jumped into the wreckage without hesitation. He defied death in the search for money, found what he was looking for, seized it, got drunk and, after sobering up a bit, coupled with the first available girl whose favors he could buy, on the ruins of destroyed houses and amid the dead and dying. Pangloss, however, began to tug on his sleeve.

"My friend," he said, "this is not good form. You are ignoring the principles of universal reason; this is not the time or the place."

"By the blood of Christ," said the other, "I am a sailor and was born in Batavia. I have trampled on the cross[18] four times to make my four voyages to Japan — you are knocking on the wrong door here with your universal reason!"

Some falling stones had wounded Candide. He lay flat on the street, covered with debris, calling out to Pangloss, "Alas! Bring me a little wine and oil; I'm dying."

"This earthquake is not a unique phenomenon," Pangloss replied. "The city of Lima in South America experienced the same shocks in South America last year. Same causes, same effects — there must be a vein of sulphur running underground from Lima to Lisbon."

"That's highly probable," said Candide, "but for God's sake, a little oil and wine."

"What do you mean, probable?" retorted the philosopher. "I maintain that the thing is a logical necessity."

Candide lost consciousness, and then Pangloss brought him some water from a nearby fountain.

The next day, as they wandered through the rubble, they found some food, which partially restored their strength. Then they fell to work with those who were aiding the survivors. Some of the citizens whom they rescued organized a dinner

---

[17] **crushed . . . ruins:** A devastating earthquake struck Lisbon on November 1, 1755, killing up to forty thousand people. Voltaire saw the earthquake as evidence that there is no benevolent design in God's providence.

[18] **Batavia . . . cross:** Batavia was the Dutch name for Djakarta, in Java, the city from which they controlled their East Asian trade. Japan had closed its ports to foreigners in 1639, exempting only the Dutch, with restrictions. Stamping on the crucifix was rumored to be required of the Dutch traders, but this was never Japanese policy.

that was as nice as could be expected in such a disaster. The meal was sad, it is true; the guests watered their bread with their tears. Pangloss, however, consoled them with his assurances that things could not be otherwise.

"For," he said, "all this is for the best, for if there is a volcano in Lisbon, it could not be anywhere else. For it is impossible that something be where it is not. For all is well."

A little dark man, a spy of the Inquisition[19] who was seated next to Pangloss, politely spoke up: "Apparently the gentleman does not believe in original sin, for if everything is for the best, then the fall of man and the punishment for sin never took place."

"I very humbly request Your Excellency's pardon," Pangloss responded even more politely. "For the fall of man and the curse that came with it were necessary components of the best of all possible worlds."

"So the gentleman does not believe in free will?" said the spy.

"Excuse me, Your Excellency," said Pangloss, "but freedom can be reconciled with absolute necessity, for it was necessary for us to be endowed with freedom; for, after all, a determined will . . ."

Pangloss was in the middle of his sentence when the spy nodded to the armed attendant who was then pouring him a glass of port wine, otherwise known as Oporto.

CHAPTER 6

How they made a fine auto-da-fé to prevent earthquakes, and how Candide was whipped

When this earthquake, which had destroyed three-quarters of Lisbon, came to an end, the wise men of the land could think of no more effective way of avoiding total ruin than to give the people a fine auto-da-fé.[20] The faculty of the University of Coimbra had concluded that the spectacle of roasting several persons over a slow fire in a ceremonious fashion is an infallible secret for preventing the earth from quaking. They had therefore seized a man from the Basque province who had been convicted of marrying the godmother of his godchild, and two Portuguese men, who when eating a chicken, had removed the bacon seasoning.[21]

After dinner, Dr. Pangloss and his disciple Candide were also arrested, the first for saying what he said, the second for listening with an air of approval. They were led separately to some extremely cool rooms in which no one was ever bothered by

---

[19] **spy of the Inquisition:** An undercover agent of the Inquisition. The Papal Inquisition of the sixteenth century, sponsored by the Roman Catholic Church, dealt with Protestantism; the Spanish Inquisition, lasting from the fifteenth through the nineteenth centuries, sought to identify and punish heretics, especially Jews and Muslims who continued to practice their beliefs, despite claiming conversion to Christianity.

[20] **auto-da-fé:** Literally, an "act of faith"; a public ceremony announcing and carrying out the judgment of the Inquisition. Such an incident had taken place in Lisbon on June 20, 1756.

[21] **Basque . . . bacon seasoning:** By marrying his child's godmother, the man from the Basque province would have broken laws against "spiritual incest"; the Portuguese are suspected of being Jews.

the sun. A week later they were both dressed in yellow robes and their heads were adorned with paper caps.[22] Candide's cap and robe were painted with inverted flames and with devils without tails or claws, whereas Pangloss's devils had claws and tails and his flames were right side up. Thus attired, they marched in procession and heard a very touching sermon, followed by charming penitential music. Candide was whipped in cadence with the chant; the man from the Basque province and the two who avoided the bacon were burned; and Pangloss was hanged, though it was not the customary form of execution. The same day the earth shook again[23] with a terrible uproar.

Stunned, stupefied, frantic, bleeding, trembling, Candide thought to himself, "If this is the best of all possible worlds, what are the others like? I can reconcile myself to this beating because I already got one from the Bulgars. But oh, my dear Pangloss! The greatest of all philosophers, was it necessary to see you hanged, without knowing why? Oh, my dear Anabaptist! The best of men, was it necessary for you to drown in the port? Oh! Miss Cunégonde, the pearl of young ladies, was it necessary that your belly be split open?"

Candide left the scene of punishment, barely able to stand, having been lectured, lacerated, absolved, and blessed. But an old woman approached and said, "My son, take courage, follow me."

Chapter 7

How an old woman took care of Candide, and how he regained what he had loved

Candide did not take courage, but he followed the old woman into a shack. She gave him a jar of ointment for his wounds and left him food and drink. She showed him to a tidy little bed, with a suit of clothing beside it.

"Eat, drink, sleep," said she, "and may Our Lady of Atocha, My Lord Saint Anthony of Padua, and My Lord Saint James of Compostela take care of you! I will return tomorrow."

Candide, still overwhelmed by all he had seen, all he had suffered, and even more by the old woman's charity, tried to kiss her hand.

"It is not my hand you should kiss," said the old woman. "I will return tomorrow. Use the ointment, eat, and sleep."

Despite his many sufferings, Candide did eat and sleep. The next morning the old woman brought him breakfast, examined his back, and treated it herself with another ointment. Afterwards she brought him lunch, and in the evening, supper. The following day she performed the same ceremonies.

"Who are you?" Candide kept asking. "Who made you so kind? How can I ever repay you?"

The good woman never answered. She came back in the evening, this time without supper.

---

[22] **yellow robes . . . caps:** A long yellow cape and a cone-shaped hat were the ceremonial dress of the Inquisition's prisoners.

[23] **earth shook again:** A second earthquake struck Lisbon on December 20, 1755.

"Come with me," she said, "and don't say a word."

She took him by the arm and they walked together into the country for a quarter mile. They arrived at an isolated house, surrounded by gardens and ponds. The old woman knocked on a small door. It opened, and she escorted Candide up a concealed staircase, into a gilded chamber, and onto a brocaded couch. Then she closed the door and disappeared. Candide thought he was hallucinating. His life, which had been a nightmare, now seemed like a pleasant dream.

The old woman soon reappeared. With great difficulty she supported a trembling young lady, with a splendid figure, sparkling with jewels, and covered by a veil.

"Remove this veil," said the old woman to Candide.

The young man stepped forward and lifted it with a timid hand. What a moment! What a surprise! He thought he perceived Miss Cunégonde—and he did, for it was she. He grew faint, speech failed him, he fell at her feet. Cunégonde collapsed on the sofa. The old woman plied them with spirits; they came to their senses and spoke to each other. First came broken words, then simultaneous questions and answers, sighs, tears, and moans. The old lady urged them to be more quiet, and left them alone.

"What! It's really you," said Candide. "You are alive! I've found you again in Portugal! Then you were not raped? They didn't slice open your belly as the philosopher Pangloss claimed?"

"It did happen," said the lovely Cunégonde, "but one doesn't always die from those two accidents."

"But your father and mother, murdered?"

"Too true," said Cunégonde crying.

"And your brother?"

"Also killed."

"And why are you in Portugal? How did you know I was here? In what mysterious way did you arrange to bring me here?"

"I will tell you everything," replied the lady, "but first you must tell me everything that has happened to you since the innocent kiss you gave me and the violent kicks you received."

Candide obeyed her with deep respect, and though he was still in shock, his voice weak and trembling, and his spine still aching, he related in simple words everything he had suffered since their parting. Cunégonde raised her eyes to heaven. She wept at the death of the good Anabaptist and of Pangloss; after which she spoke in these terms to Candide, who did not miss a word, and who consumed her with his eyes.

CHAPTER 8

Cunégonde's story

"I was sleeping soundly in my bed when heaven chose to send the Bulgars to our fine castle of Thunder-ten-tronckh. They butchered my father and brother and cut my mother to pieces. A large Bulgar, well over six feet tall, seeing that I had fainted at this spectacle, began to rape me; this brought me to and I regained my senses. I shrieked,

I struggled, I bit, I scratched, I tried to tear the eyes out of that big Bulgar—not knowing that everything happening then in my father's castle was part of military custom. The brute stabbed me in the belly on the left side, where I still have a scar."

"Alas! I hope to see that," said the simple Candide.

"You will," said Cunégonde, "but let me go on."

"Please go on," said Candide.

She took up the thread of her story: "A Bulgar captain came by. He saw me, all covered in blood, as well as the soldier who was too busy to salute him. Enraged by the brute's lack of respect for his rank, the captain killed him while he was still on top of my body. Then he had my wound dressed and took me to his quarters as a prisoner of war. I laundered the few shirts he had, I did his cooking. I have to admit, he found me attractive, and I won't deny that he was a handsome man, with soft, white skin. But he had no intellect, no philosophy; it was clear that he had not been raised by Dr. Pangloss. Three months later, he had lost all his money and grown sick of me, so he sold me to Don Issachar, a Jew who traded in Holland and Portugal and who had a passionate taste for women. This Jew took a great liking to my person, but he never conquered it. I resisted him better than I did the Bulgar soldier. A lady of honor may be raped once, but it strengthens her virtue for the future. In order to tame me, the Jew brought me to this country house. I always used to think there was nothing on earth so beautiful as the castle of Thunder-ten-tronckh. I have that illusion no longer.

"The Grand Inquisitor noticed me one day at mass. He ogled me and sent me a message that he had to speak to me about secret affairs. I was escorted to his palace, where I informed him of my high birth. He pointed out how much it was beneath my rank to belong to an Israelite. His agents suggested to Don Issachar to cede me to His Lordship. But Don Issachar, who is the court banker and a man of prestige, flatly refused. The Inquisitor threatened him with an auto-da-fé. Finally, my Jew, intimidated, made a deal whereby the house and I belong to them jointly: The Jew would get Mondays, Wednesdays, and the Sabbath, and the Inquisitor all other days of the week. The contract has lasted six months, though not without quarrels, because they have never been able to decide if the night between Saturday and Sunday belongs to the old Sabbath or the new.[24] As for me, I've resisted them both so far, and I think that's why their love for me has been so strong.

"Finally, to ward off the scourge of earthquakes and to intimidate Issachar, the Inquisitor decided to celebrate an auto-da-fé. He honored me with an invitation. I had a very good seat and they served refreshments to the ladies between the mass and the execution. I was truly gripped by horror when I saw them burn the two Jews and that upright fellow from the Basque country who had married his godchild's godmother. But imagine my surprise, my terror, my agitation, when I saw, in a yellow robe and underneath a paper cap, a form resembling Pangloss! I rubbed my eyes, I peered closely, I saw him hanged, I fainted. I had scarcely recovered my senses when I saw you, stripped down naked. This was the height of my horror, consternation, pain, and despair. I will tell you, in truth, that your skin is even whiter, and

---

[24] **old Sabbath or the new:** That is, the Hebrew Bible of the Jews, or the New Testament of the Christians.

more delightfully tinted with pink, than that of my Bulgar captain. This sight redoubled all the emotions that were crushing me, devouring me. I cried out, I tried to say, 'Stop, barbarians!' but my voice failed and my cries would have been futile. After you had been thoroughly whipped, I began to think: 'How can it be that the gentle Candide and the wise Pangloss have come to Lisbon, one to receive a hundred lashes, the other to be hanged by order of the Inquisitor whose mistress I am? Pangloss deceived me cruelly when he taught me that everything is for the best in this world.'

"Frantic and exhausted, half out of my mind and half on the verge of expiring from weakness, my head was filled with images of my murdered father, mother, and brother; of the insolence of my vile Bulgar soldier and the slashing he inflicted on me; of my servitude as a cook to my Bulgar captain; of my vile Don Issacher and my abominable Inquisitor; of the hanging of Dr. Pangloss and the solemn hymn of penitence sung while they whipped you; and above all, of the kiss I once gave you behind a partition, the day I saw you for the last time. I praised God for bringing you back to me after so many ordeals. I asked my old servant to take care of you and to bring you here as soon as she could. She has done the job well. I have tasted the indescribable pleasure of seeing you, hearing you, speaking to you again. But you must be burning with hunger. My desire is strong. Let us begin with supper."

So they sat down to table together, and after supper they installed themselves on that lovely couch that was already mentioned. There they were, when Señor Don Issachar, one of the masters of the house, arrived. It was the Sabbath day. He had come to enjoy his rights and to profess his tender love.

CHAPTER 9

What happened to Cunégonde, Candide, the Grand Inquisitor, and a Jew

This Issachar was the most hot-tempered Hebrew seen in Israel since the Babylonian captivity.

"What!" he said. "You Christian bitch, you are not satisfied with the Inquisitor? I have to share you with this scoundrel too?"

With these words he unsheathed a long dagger that he always carried with him, and supposing his adversary to be defenseless, flung himself at Candide. But our good Westphalian had gotten a fine sword from the old woman along with the suit of clothes. Though his character was gentle, he drew his sword and laid the Israelite out cold and stiff on the floor, at the feet of the beautiful Cunégonde.

"Holy Virgin!" she cried. "What are we going to do now? A man killed in my house! If the police come, we're finished."

"If Pangloss had not been hanged," said Candide, "he would offer us good advice in this emergency, for he was a great philosopher. In his absence, let's consult the old woman."

She was a prudent woman and was about to give her opinion when another little door opened. It was one o'clock in the morning, the beginning of Sunday. This day belonged to the Inquisitor. He came in and saw the whipped Candide with a sword in his hand, a dead man on the floor, Cunégonde in panic, and the old woman advising them.

This is what went on at that instant in Candide's mind, and how he theorized: "If this holy man calls for help, he will infallibly have me burned, and perhaps Cunégonde too; he has caused me to be whipped brutally; he is my rival; I have killed once already; there is no time to hesitate."

This reflection was swift and clear. Without giving the Inquisitor time to recover from his surprise, he ran his sword through his body, and cast him beside the Jew.

"You've done it again," said Cunégonde. "We're beyond salvation now; we're excommunicated, our last hour has come. How have you managed, you who are so gentle, to kill a Jew and a prelate in two minutes?"

"My fair lady," answered Candide, "when a man is in love, inflamed by jealousy, and whipped by the Inquisition, he is no longer himself."

The old woman spoke up at that moment: "There are three Andalusian horses in the stable, with saddles and bridles. Let the brave Candide prepare them. My Lady has some diamonds and gold coins. Let us mount quickly—though I can sit on only one buttock—and ride to Cadiz. The weather is ideal, and it is a great pleasure to travel in the cool of the night."

Candide immediately saddled the three horses. The three of them covered thirty miles at one stretch. While they were getting away, the officers of the Holy Brotherhood[25] arrived at the house. They buried the Inquisitor in a fine church, and threw Issachar in the public dump.

Candide, Cunégonde, and the old woman were already at an inn in the little town of Avacena in the middle of the Sierra-Morena mountains, and they spoke as follows.

CHAPTER 10

How Candide, Cunégonde, and the old woman arrived at Cadiz in distress, and how they set sail

"Who could have stolen my gold and my diamonds?" exclaimed Cunégonde, weeping. "What are we going to live on now? What are we going to do? Where can I find Inquisitors and Jews who will give me more?"

"Alas," said the old woman, "I strongly suspect a venerable Franciscan who slept at the same inn with us yesterday at Badajoz. God forgive me if my judgment is rash, but he came into our chamber twice, and he left the inn long before we did."

"Alas," said Candide, "the wise Pangloss often proved to me that the goods of the earth are common to all men, that everyone has an equal right to them. By this logic, the Franciscan should have left us enough to finish our journey. Didn't he leave you anything at all, my lovely Cunégonde?"

---

[25] **Holy Brotherhood:** A semireligious Spanish order that had police powers.

"Not a cent," said she.

"What is our plan?" Candide asked.

"We must sell one of the horses," said the old woman. "I will ride on the horse's rump behind my lady — though I can sit on only one buttock — and we will travel to Cadiz."

There was a Bendectine prior staying in the same inn. He bought the horse at a low price. Candide, Cunégonde, and the old woman passed through Lucena, Chillas, and Lebrixa, and finally reached Cadiz. A fleet was being fitted out there, and troops were being assembled to teach a lesson to the Jesuit fathers in Paraguay. The Jesuits had been accused of inciting one of the tribes near the town of Sacramento[26] to revolt against the kings of Spain and Portugal. Candide, having served in the Bulgar army, performed a Bulgar drill in front of the general of the little army with such grace, speed, skill, pride, and agility that he was put in charge of a company of infantry. He was a captain now. He embarked with Miss Cunégonde, the old woman, two valets, and the two Andalusian horses that had belonged to the Grand Inquisitor of Portugal.

Throughout the crossing, they theorized at length about the philosophy of poor Pangloss.

"We are heading for a different world," said Candide. "I am sure that over there all is well, because I have to admit that where we come from, there are grounds for complaining about how things are, both physically and morally."

"I love you with all my heart," Cunégonde told him, "but my soul is still terrified by what I have seen and endured."

"All will be well," Candide replied. "The sea of this New World is superior to the sea of our Europe; it is calmer, with steadier winds. I am certain the New World is the best of all possible universes."

"May God grant that it be so," said Cunégonde. "But my universe has been so terribly unhappy that my heart is nearly closed to the possibility of hope."

"The two of you are complaining," the old woman said to them. "Alas! You have never seen misfortunes like mine."

Cunégonde almost burst out laughing. She found it amusing that the good woman claimed to be more unhappy than herself.

"Alas!" she said. "My dear woman, unless you have been raped by two Bulgars, been stabbed in the belly twice, seen two of your castles demolished, witnessed the murder of two mothers and fathers, and watched two of your lovers being whipped in an auto-da-fé, I don't see how you can outdo me. Besides, I was born to be a baroness, with seventy-two generations of nobility, and I was forced to be a cook."

"Madame," replied the old woman, "you know nothing of my birth, and if I showed you my behind, you would speak differently and suspend your judgment."

These remarks aroused intense curiosity in the minds of Cunégonde and Candide. The old woman spoke to them in these terms.

---

[26] **Sacramento:** Colonia del Sacramento, in Paraguay. The Jesuits, who began their rebellion against Spain and Portugal in 1750, were expelled from Paraguay in 1769.

CHAPTER 11

The old woman's story

"My eyes were not always crusty and bloodshot, my nose did not always touch my chin, and I was not always a servant. I am the daughter of Pope Urban X and the Princess of Palestrina.[27] I lived until the age of fourteen in a palace so luxurious that all the castles of your German barons would not have served as stables. Any one of my dresses was worth more than all the treasures of Westphalia. I was growing in beauty, elegance, and accomplishment in the midst of pleasures, honors, and the highest hopes. I was beginning to inspire love. My bosom was forming, and what a bosom! White, firm, sculptured like the ancient statue of Venus. And what eyes! What lashes! What black brows! What flames blazed in my irises and sparkled brighter than the stars, as the local poets used to tell me. The women who dressed and undressed me fell into ecstasies when they beheld me from the front and from the rear, and any man would have desired to be in their place.

"I was betrothed to the ruling prince of Massa-Carrara. What a prince! As attractive as I, filled with sweetness and delight, with a brilliant wit and burning passion. I loved him as one always loves for the first time, with adoration and frenzy. The wedding was at hand. The pomp and splendor were unprecedented. It was an endless series of feasts, equestrian tournaments, comic operas, and all Italy honored me with sonnets of which not a single one was any good.

"I was on the verge of bliss, when an old marquise who had been my prince's mistress invited him for a cup of cocoa. He died in less than two hours, in horrible convulsions. But that was only a trifle. My mother, stricken with grief, though less than I, wished to escape from this tragic scene for a while. She had a very fine estate near Gaeta.[28] Our transport was a papal galley ship, gilded like the altar of St. Peter's in Rome. Suddenly a pirate ship from Salé swept down and boarded us. Our soldiers defended themselves like true soldiers of the Pope: They all kneeled down, threw aside their arms, and begged the pirates for absolution *in articulo mortis*.[29]

"The pirates immediately stripped them naked as monkeys, along with my mother, our ladies-in-waiting, and myself. The speed with which those gentlemen can undress people is amazing. But what surprised me even more was that they inserted their fingers in all of us, in a place where we women usually admit only the nozzle of an enema. This ceremony seemed quite bizarre to me; but that is how one sees everything foreign when one has never been abroad. I soon learned that they wished to see if we had diamonds hidden there. It is an age-old custom among the civilized people who patrol the seas. I also learned that the pious Knights of Malta always observe this ceremony when they capture Turkish men and women. It's a rule of international law that has never been broken.

---

[27] **Pope . . . Palestrina:** The following note is allegedly by Voltaire: "Note the author's extreme discretion! So far there has been no pope named Urban X; he is afraid to ascribe a bastard daughter to a known pope. What circumspection! What delicacy of conscience!" Palestrina is a town in the province of Rome, Italy.

[28] **Gaeta:** An Italian port town north of Naples.

[29] *in articulo mortis:* At the point of death.

"I will not tell you how hard it is for a young princess to be dragged off to Morocco as a slave with her mother. You can imagine everything we had to endure in the pirate ship. My mother was still beautiful; our ladies-in-waiting and even our ordinary servants had more charm than could be found in all of Africa. As for me, I was ravishing, I was beauty and grace made flesh, and I was a virgin. But not for long. The flower I had reserved for the handsome prince of Massa-Carrara was plucked by the pirate captain. He was an abominable Negro who thought he was bestowing great favors on me. The Princess of Palestrina and I certainly had to be very strong to withstand everything we went through up to our arrival in Morocco. But we can skip the details; these things are so common that they are not worth describing.

"Morocco was swimming in blood when we arrived. Fifty sons of the Emperor Muley Ismael[30] each had his own faction, which produced fifty civil wars of blacks against blacks, blacks against browns, browns against browns, mulattoes against mulattoes. There was constant slaughter throughout the empire.

"Scarcely had we landed when some blacks of a faction hostile to my pirate came on the scene to take away the booty. We were, after the diamonds and gold, his most precious possessions. The fight that took place before my eyes was worse than anything you ever see in your European climates. The peoples of the North do not have hot blood. Their lust for women is not as strong as it is in Africa. It is as if Europeans have milk in their veins, while vitriol and fire flow through the veins of the inhabitants of Mount Atlas and the countries nearby. They fought to possess us with the fury of the lions, tigers, and vipers of their land. A Moor snatched my mother by the right arm, my captain's lieutenant held her by the left. Another Moorish soldier took her by one leg, one of our pirates clung to the other. Nearly all our women were quickly pulled in this way by four soldiers. My captain shielded me behind him. Brandishing his scimitar, he killed everyone who stood up to his rage. At last I saw all our women, and then my mother, ripped and sliced and massacred by the monsters who were fighting over them. The other hostages, the pirates who had captured them, the soldiers, sailors, blacks, browns, whites, mulattoes, and finally my captain—all were killed, and I myself lay dying on a heap of corpses. As everyone knows, scenes like this were occurring for more than seven hundred and fifty miles around, without anyone failing to observe the five daily prayers prescribed by Mohammed.

"I freed myself with great difficulty from that tangled mob of bleeding cadavers and I crawled under a large orange tree on the bank of a nearby stream. There I collapsed from fear, exhaustion, horror, despair, and hunger. Soon my weary mind surrendered to an oblivion that was more of a frightful blackout than a pleasant repose. I was in that state of weakness and insensibility, between life and death, when I felt the pressure of something wriggling on my body. I opened my eyes and saw a white man with a handsome face who was moaning and whispering, *'O che sciagura d'essere senza coglioni!'*[31]

---

[30] **Muley Ismael:** A sultan of Morocco who died in 1727, leaving his kingdom in disarray.

[31] *'O che . . . coglioni!':* "O, what a misfortune to be without testicles!"

CHAPTER 12

Continuation of the old woman's story

"Astonished and delighted to hear my native tongue, and equally surprised by the words this man was uttering, I replied that there were worse misfortunes than the one he was complaining of. I gave him a brief account of my own horrors, and fainted again. He carried me to a nearby house, put me to bed, fed me, waited on me, comforted me, flattered me, and told me he had never seen anything as beautiful as I, and that he had never so much regretted the loss of what no one could ever give back to him.

"'I was born in Naples,' he told me, 'where they castrate two or three thousand children every year. Some die as a result, others acquire the ability to sing more beautifully than women, still others go on to rule states. In my case, the operation was a great success, and I became a musician in the chapel of the Princess of Palestrina.'

"'Of my mother!' I cried out.

"'Of your mother?' he exclaimed, while bursting into tears. 'Why—are you that little princess I brought up to the age of six, and who even then promised to be as gorgeous as you are now?'

"'Yes, I am. My mother is four hundred paces away, cut into four pieces, under a pile of corpses . . .'

"I told him everything that happened to me, and he in turn told me of his adventures. He had been sent to the King of Morocco by a Christian power to conclude a treaty: The King was supposed to receive gunpowder, cannons, and ships and use these to exterminate the commerce of other Christian powers.

"'My mission is accomplished,' said the worthy eunuch. 'I am setting sail to Ceuta, and I shall bring you back to Italy. But *che sciagura d'essere senza coglioni!*'

"I thanked him with tears of gratitude and pity; and instead of bringing me to Italy, he transported me to Algiers and sold me to the Dey of that province. Hardly had the sale taken place, when the plague, which was sweeping over Africa, Asia, and Europe, broke out violently in Algiers. You have seen earthquakes, but tell me, young lady, have you ever had the plague?"

"Never," replied the Baron's daughter.

"If you had been afflicted with it," the old woman went on, "you would admit that it is much worse than an earthquake. It is very widespread in Africa, and I was struck by it. Imagine the situation of a pope's daughter, only fifteen years old, who in the space of three months had undergone poverty and slavery, had been raped almost every day, had seen her mother cut in four pieces, had endured hunger and war, and now faced death from the plague in Algiers. As it turned out, I survived, but my eunuch, the Dey, and nearly the whole harem of Algiers, perished.

"When the first ravages of this ghastly plague were over, the Dey's slaves were sold off. A merchant purchased me and brought me to Tunis. He sold me to another merchant, who sold me once more in Tripoli. From Tripoli I was resold to Alexandria, from Alexandria to Smyrna, from Smyrna to Constantinople. In the end

I belonged to an Aga of the Janissaries, who was shortly sent off to defend Azov[32] against the attacking Russians.

"The Aga, a very gallant man, took his whole harem with him, and lodged us in a little fort on the shore of the Sea of Azov, guarded by two black eunuchs and twenty soldiers. Our side killed a prodigious number of Russians, but they repaid us with interest. The settlement at Azov was put to fire and sword, and neither women nor children were spared. The last place left was our little fort. The enemy tried to starve us out. The twenty Janissaries had sworn never to surrender. When they became famished, they were obliged to eat our two eunuchs, for fear of breaking their oath. A few days later they resolved to eat the women.

"We had with us a very pious and compassionate imam,[33] who preached a fine sermon, persuading them not to kill us altogether. 'Just cut off one buttock from each of these ladies,' he said, 'and you will dine well. If you need more, you can have the same fare in a few days. You will please heaven with such a charitable deed, and you will be saved from this calamity.'

"He was very eloquent and persuaded them. They performed the horrible operation on us. The imam rubbed us with the same balm that they put on children who have just been circumcised. We were all nearly dead.

"Scarcely had the Janissaries finished the meal we had furnished them, when more Russians arrived in flat-bottomed boats; not a single Janissary escaped alive. The Russians paid no attention to our condition. But there are French doctors everywhere, and one of them, who was very clever, took care of us. He cured us, and I will remember to the end of my life that when my wounds were healed, he made advances to me. Besides that, he told us all to take comfort. He assured us that such things usually happened in sieges and that it was one of the rules of war.

"As soon as my companions and I could walk, we were sent off to Moscow. I fell to the lot of a Boyar,[34] who made me his gardener and gave me twenty lashes per day. But when this noble was broken on the wheel two years later, along with thirty or so other Boyars, over a little intrigue at the royal court, I took advantage of the incident. I fled. I traversed the whole of Russia. For a long time I was a barmaid in Riga, then in Rostock, Wismar, Leipzig, Cassel, Utrecht, Leyden, the Hague, and Rotterdam. I have grown old in misery and infamy, with only half a behind, and never forgetting that I was the daughter of a Pope.

"I considered suicide a hundred times, but I still loved life. That ridiculous preference is perhaps one of our most tragic instincts. For what could be more stupid than this: to seek to carry forever a weight that we always feel like casting to the ground? To view our existence with horror, and to cling tightly to our existence? To caress the snake that devours us, until it has consumed our heart?

---

[32] **Azov:** Town near the mouth of the river Don in Crimea; it was attacked by Russian forces led by Peter the Great in 1695–96. The janissaries, "janizaries," were the elite forces of the Ottoman Turks.

[33] **imam:** A Muslim holy man.

[34] **Boyar:** A high-ranking Russian aristocrat; a group of boyars unsuccessfully tried to overthrow Peter the Great (r. 1682–1725) in 1798.

"In the countries that fate made me traverse, and in the inns where I worked, I have seen vast numbers of people who detested their own lives; but I have seen only twelve who voluntarily brought an end to their suffering — three Negroes, four Englishmen, four Genevans, and a German professor named Robek.[35] I ended up becoming a servant to the Jew, Don Issachar. He assigned me to you, my lovely Lady. I have attached myself to your destiny, and I have been more concerned with your fortune than my own. I would never have spoken about my sufferings had you not provoked me a bit, and were it not the custom on ships to pass the time with stories. In short, My Lady, I have some experience, I know the world. I propose that you amuse yourselves by asking each passenger to tell you his story, and if you find a single one who has not frequently cursed his own life, who has not often told himself that he was the unhappiest of men, then throw me into the sea headfirst."

CHAPTER 13

How Candide was forced to part from the lovely Cunégonde and the old woman

After hearing the old woman's story, the lovely Cunégonde showed her all the courtesy due to a person of her rank and merit. She accepted the old woman's proposal too, and got all the passengers, one by one, to recount their life stories. She and Candide had to admit that the old woman was right.

"It's too bad," said Candide, "that the wise Pangloss was hanged, contrary to custom, in an auto-da-fé. He would say admirable things about the physical and moral evil that cover land and sea, and I would now be independent enough to make a few respectful objections."

As each passenger was telling his story, the vessel sailed on. They landed at Buenos Aires. Cunégonde, Captain Candide, and the old woman proceeded to the home of Governor Don Fernando d'Ibaraa y Figueora y Mascarenes y Lampourdos y Souza. This lord had the pride appropriate to a man with so many names. He addressed people with the most noble disdain, tilting his nose so high in the air, raising his voice so mercilessly, adopting so imperious a tone, affecting so haughty a bearing, that everyone who met him wanted to beat him up. He loved women with a frenzy, and Cunégonde seemed to him the most beautiful creature he had ever seen. The first thing he did was to ask if she were the Captain's wife. His manner of asking the question alarmed Candide. He did not dare say she was his wife, because in fact she was not. He did not dare say she was his sister, because she was not that either; and even though this diplomatic lie was once very fashionable among the ancients[36] and can still be useful to the moderns, his soul was too pure to forsake the truth.

"Miss Cunégonde," he said, "will soon honor me by becoming my wife, and we humbly beseech Your Excellency to perform the ceremony."

Don Fernando d'Ibaraa y Figueora y Mascarenes y Lampourdos y Souza stroked his mustache, and with a spiteful smile ordered Captain Candide to go off and

---

[35] **Robek:** Johan Robeck (1678–1739) an advocate of suicide, who killed himself by drowning.

[36] **among the ancients:** Voltaire refers to the story of Abraham and Sarah in Genesis 12 and of Isaac and Rebecca in Genesis 26.

inspect his troops. Candide obeyed, while the Governor remained with Miss Cuné-gonde. He declared his passion and vowed he would marry her the next day, in the presence of the Catholic Church or in any other manner that would please her love-liness. Cunégonde requested fifteen minutes to gather her thoughts, to consult the old woman, and to make a decision.

The old woman said to Cunégonde, "My Lady, you have seventy-two genera-tions of nobility, and not a penny. You now have a chance to be the wife of a man who is the greatest lord in South America and who has a very handsome mustache. Is this a time for you to pretend to be absolutely faithful? You were raped by the Bul-gars. A Jew and an Inquisitor enjoyed your favors. Suffering bestows privileges. If I were in your place, I assure you, I would have no qualms about marrying the Gover-nor and securing the welfare of Captain Candide."

While the old woman was speaking with all the prudence that comes from age and experience, a little ship was seen entering the port carrying a Spanish magistrate and police officers. This is what happened.

The old woman had been quite right earlier when she suspected that it was a long-sleeved Franciscan who had stolen Cunégonde's gold and jewels in the town of Badajoz when she and Candide were in flight. The monk had tried to sell some of the gems to a jeweler, but the merchant recognized them as belonging to the Grand Inquisitor. The Franciscan, prior to his hanging, confessed that he had stolen them. He described the persons he had robbed and the route they were taking. It was already known that Cunégonde and Candide had fled. They were traced to Cadiz. A ship was sent to pursue them without delay. This vessel was now in the port of Buenos Aires. A rumor spread that a magistrate was coming ashore to prosecute the murderers of the Grand Inquisitor. The prudent old woman instantly recognized what had to be done.

"You cannot escape," she told Cunégonde, "but you have nothing to fear. You are not the one who killed the Inquisitor, and besides, the Governor loves you and will not tolerate anyone who mistreats you. Stay here."

She then sped off to Candide. "Run away," she said, "or you will be burned within an hour."

There was not a moment to lose—but how to part from Cunégonde, and where to hide?

Chapter 14

How Candide and Cacambo were received by the Jesuits in Paraguay

Candide had brought with him from Cadiz a valet of the kind often found on the coasts of Spain and in the colonies. He was one quarter Spanish, the child of a half-breed father in Tucuman.[37] He had been a choir boy, a sacristan, a sailor, a monk, a salesman, a soldier, and a lackey. His name was Cacambo, and he was very attached

---

[37] Tucuman: An Argentinian province northwest of Buenos Aires.

to his master because his master was a very good man. He saddled the two Andalusian horses as fast as possible.

"Let's go, Master, let's follow the old woman's advice. Let's get out of here and run for it without looking back."

Candide shed tears. "Oh, my darling Cunégonde! Why must I abandon you now, when the Governor is about to marry us? Cunégonde, so far from home, what will become of you?"

"She'll manage on her own," said Cacambo. "Women always find ways to keep themselves afloat; God sees to it; let's move."

"Where are you taking me? Where are we going? What will we do without Cunégonde?" asked Candide.

"By St. James of Compostela," said Cacambo, "you were going to make war against the Jesuits; let's go make war *for* them! I know the roads, I'll take you to their kingdom. They'll be pleased to have a captain who can move like a Bulgar. You'll become fabulously wealthy. If a man doesn't get his due in one world, he can always get it in another. It's a great pleasure to see and do new things."

"So you've been in Paraguay before?" asked Candide.

"I certainly have," said Cacambo. "I was a cook at the College of the Assumption, and I know the government of the *Padres*[38] as well as I know the streets of Cadiz. Their government is marvellous. The kingdom is already more than seven hundred and fifty miles across. It is divided into thirty provinces. The *Padres* have everything, the people nothing. It's a masterpiece of reason and justice. Personally, I can't think of anything as heavenly as the *Padres*. Over here they make war against the kings of Spain and Portugal, and in Europe they hear the confessions of the same kings. Here they kill Spaniards, and in Madrid they send them to heaven. I love it. Let's get going. You're going to be the happiest of men. What pleasure the *Padres* will feel when they learn that a Captain is coming who knows how to move like a Bulgar!"

As soon as they approached the first border post, Cacambo told the advance guards that a captain wished to speak to the Commander. Word was sent back to the rear guards, and a Paraguayan officer ran to inform the Commander. Candide and Cacambo were first disarmed, and their Andalusian horses were confiscated. The two strangers were escorted through two files of soldiers, at the end of which was the Commander, with a three-cornered hat on his head, a tucked-up gown, a sword at his side, and a short pike in his hand. He made a sign, and immediately twenty-four soldiers surrounded the two newcomers. A sergeant told them that they would have to wait, that the Commander could not speak to them and that the Reverend Provincial Father did not allow any Spaniard to parley except in his presence, or to remain in the country for more than three hours.

"And where is the Reverend Provincial Father?" asked Cacambo.

"He is inspecting the troops, after having said Mass," answered the sergeant, "and you will not be allowed to kiss his spurs until three hours from now."

"But," Cacambo said, "the Captain and I are dying of hunger, and he's not

---

[38] *Padres:* The Jesuit fathers.

Spanish at all, he's German. Couldn't we have something for breakfast while we wait for His Reverence?"

The sergeant promptly went to report this speech to the Commander.

"God be praised!" said this Lord. "Since he is a German, I can speak to him. Bring him to my arbor."

Candide was immediately led into a shady retreat adorned with a pretty colonnade in green and golden marble and with trellises containing parrots, hummingbirds of different kinds, guinea fowl, and every other sort of rare bird. An excellent meal was prepared in gold vessels, and while the Paraguayans were eating corn out of wooden bowls in the open fields, under the blazing sun, the Commander entered the arbor.

He was a very handsome young man, with a round face, fair skin, red cheeks, arched eyebrows, bright eyes, pink ears, and vermillion lips; he had a proud bearing, but it was not the pride of a Spaniard or a Jesuit. The confiscated weapons were restored to Candide and Cacambo, as were the two Andalusian horses. Cacambo fed them oats beside the arbor, keeping a close eye on them, for fear of a new assault.

Candide first kissed the hem of the Commander's robe, then they sat down to eat.

"So, you are German," said the Jesuit in that language.

"Yes, Reverend Father," said Candide.

As they uttered these words, each looked at the other with extreme surprise, and with barely controlled emotion.

"And what part of Germany are you from?" asked the Jesuit.

"From the rotten Province of Westphalia," said Candide. "I was born in the castle of Thunder-ten-tronckh."

"Oh heaven! Is it possible!" exclaimed the Commander.

"What a miracle!" cried Candide.

"Can it be you?" said the Commander.

"This is not possible," said Candide.

They both fell over backwards; they embraced; they shed streams of tears.

"What! Is it really you, my Reverend Father? You, the brother of the lovely Cunégonde! You, who were killed by the Bulgars! You, the son of My Lord the Baron! You, a Jesuit in Paraguay! I have to admit, the world is a very strange place. Oh Pangloss! Pangloss! How happy you would be if you had not been hanged!"

The Commander dismissed the Negro slaves and the Paraguayans who were serving drinks in goblets of rock crystal. He thanked God and St. Ignatius a thousand times. He clasped Candide in his arms; their faces were bathed in tears.

"You're going to be even more surprised, more moved, more beside yourself," said Candide, "when I tell you that your sister, Miss Cunégonde, whom you thought was disemboweled, is in good health."

"Where?"

"In this area, with the Governor of Buenos Aires. I was supposed to help him fight you."

Every word they spoke during their long conversation revealed a new wonder. Their souls leapt from their tongues, drew in meaning through their ears, and sparkled brilliantly in their eyes. As they were Germans, they drank for a long time while they waited for the Reverend Provincial Father; and the Commander spoke to Candide as follows.

CHAPTER 15

How Candide killed the brother of his beloved Cunégonde

"The horrible day when I saw my mother and father killed, and my sister raped, will remain in my memory forever. When the Bulgars withdrew, my adorable sister was nowhere to be found. A cart was loaded with my mother, my father, myself, two serving girls, and three little boys whose throats had been slit. We were to be buried in a Jesuit chapel five miles from the castle of my ancestors. A Jesuit sprinkled holy water on us; it was horribly salty, and a few drops of it got into my eyes. The priest noticed a slight movement of my eyelid. He placed his hand on my heart and felt it beating. I was treated, and three weeks later, I was in good shape again.

"You know, my dear Candide, I was a very pretty boy; I became even more so; and the Reverend Father Croust,[39] superior of the abbey, conceived a very tender friendship for me. He dressed me in the gown of a novice, and soon after that I was sent to Rome. The Father General needed a fresh set of young German Jesuit recruits. The rulers of Paraguay take in as few Spanish Jesuits as they can. They prefer foreigners because they think they can control them better. The Reverend Father General judged me fit to labor in this vineyard. We set out, a Pole, a Tyrolean, and I. Upon arrival, I was honored with the position of subdeacon and lieutenant. Today I am a colonel and a priest. We will give an energetic reception to the King of Spain's troops. I guarantee you they will be excommunicated and defeated. Providence has sent you here to help us. But is it true that my beloved sister Cunégonde is in the region, with the Governor of Buenos Aires?"

Candide assured him by swearing that nothing was more true. They began to shed tears all over again.

The Baron embraced Candide repeatedly, calling him his brother, his savior.

"Ah! My dear Candide," he said, "perhaps we can enter the city as conquerors and liberate my sister Cunégonde."

"I certainly hope so," said Candide, "because I was planning to marry her, and still am."

"You insolent swine!" replied the Baron. "You would have the impudence to marry my sister, who has seventy-two generations of nobility! I find it highly offensive that you dare to mention such an impossible plan to me."

Candide, petrified by this speech, answered him, "My Reverend Father, all the generations in the world make no difference. I rescued your sister from the arms of a Jew and an Inquisitor. She owes me a great deal, she wants to marry me. Dr. Pangloss always taught me that men are equal, and I am certainly going to marry her."

---

[39] **Father Croust:** A French Jesuit priest who had quarreled with Voltaire in 1754; Voltaire insinuates here that Croust is a pederast.

"We shall see about that, you scoundrel," said the Jesuit Baron Thunder-ten-tronckh, and in that instant he dealt him a great blow across the face with the flat side of his sword. Candide rapidly drew his own and thrust it into the Jesuit Baron's stomach, right up to the hilt. But when he drew out the steaming weapon, he began to weep.

"Alas, my God!" he said. "I've killed my old master, my friend, my brother-in-law. I'm the kindest man in the world, and here I've already killed three men—and two of them were priests."

Cacambo, who was standing guard at the gate to the arbor, ran in.

"There's nothing left to do but to make them pay dearly for our lives," his master told him. "They'll surely come into the arbor now; we must die with sword in hand."

Cacambo, who had seen the likes of this many times before, did not lose his head. He took the Jesuit robe that the Baron was wearing, put it on Candide, gave him the dead man's cornered hat, and had him mount his horse. All this was done in the twinkling of an eye.

"Let's gallop, Master. Everyone will take you for a Jesuit on a field mission, and we'll cross the border before they can come after us."

He was already charging ahead as he spoke, and then he cried out in Spanish, "Make way, make way for the Reverend Father Colonel!"

CHAPTER 16

What happened to the two travelers with two girls, two monkeys, and the savages called Oreillons

Candide and his valet had crossed the frontier, and still no one back at camp knew about the German Jesuit's death. The astute Cacambo had taken care to fill his saddlebag with bread, chocolate, ham, fruit, and some bottles of wine. With their Andalusian horses they plunged into an unknown land where they found no roads. Finally, a beautiful meadow, interlaced with streams, appeared before them. Our two travelers freed their horses to graze. Cacambo advised his master to eat, and he began to set the example.

"How do you expect me to eat ham," said Candide, "when I just killed the son of My Lord the Baron and find myself condemned never to see the lovely Cunégonde again? What's the use of prolonging my miserable days, if I have to endure them far away from her, in remorse and despair? And what will the *Journal de Trévoux*[40] say?"

While speaking in this way, he did not fail to eat. The sun began to set. The two wanderers heard some faint cries that seemed to proceed from women. They could not tell if these were cries of pain or joy, but they jumped to their feet with that anxiety and alarm that everything arouses in an unknown country.

The sounds came from two girls, completely nude, who were running spryly along the edge of the meadow, while two monkeys pursued them, snapping at their buttocks. Candide was moved by pity. The Bulgars had taught him how to shoot,

---

[40] *Journal de Trévoux:* A Jesuit journal that launched several attacks upon Voltaire.

and he was able to knock a nut off a bush without stirring the leaves. He raised his double-barreled musket from Spain, fired, and killed the two monkeys.

"God be praised, my dear Cacambo. I've rescued these two poor creatures from a great danger. If I committed a sin in killing an Inquisitor and a Jesuit, I've now redeemed myself by saving the lives of two girls. Perhaps these two young ladies are of noble birth, and my deed will bring us great rewards in this land."

He was going to say more, but his tongue became paralyzed when he saw the girls tenderly embrace the two monkeys, burst into tears over their bodies, and fill the air with cries of intense grief.

"I didn't expect them to be so forgiving," he said, after a long pause, to Cacambo, who replied: "That was a brilliant thing to do, Sir! You just killed the young ladies' lovers."

"Their lovers! Is that possible? You must be joking. What evidence do you have?"

"My dear Master," responded Cacambo, "you're always surprised by everything. Why do you find it so bizarre that in some countries monkeys obtain the favors of the ladies? They are a quarter human, just as I am a quarter Spanish."

"Alas!" said Candide. "I do recall hearing Dr. Pangloss say that such things used to happen, that these mixtures engendered pans, fauns, and satyrs, and that many of the heroes of ancient times saw them. But I thought that was all a fable."

"Now you should be convinced that it's the truth," said Cacambo, "and you can see how this truth is still practiced by people who have not been educated. But I'm afraid these ladies are going to make big trouble for us."

These solid reflections persuaded Candide to leave the meadow and plunge into a forest. He dined there with Cacambo, and the two of them, after cursing the Inquisitor of Portugal, the Governor of Buenos Aires, and the Baron, fell asleep on the moss. When they woke up, they noticed that they could not move; the reason was that during the night the native Oreillons,[41] to whom the two ladies had denounced them, had tied them down with cords made of bark. They were surrounded by about fifty Oreillons, completely nude, armed with arrows, clubs, and stone axes. Some were bringing a huge cauldron to boil; others were preparing spits; and all of them were chanting: "It's a Jesuit, it's a Jesuit; here's our revenge and here's a good meal; let's eat Jesuit, let's eat Jesuit."

"Dear Master, I warned you," Cacambo blurted out sadly, "that these two girls would bring us trouble."

Candide, seeing the cauldron and the spits, exclaimed, "We're definitely going to be roasted or boiled. Ah! What would Dr. Pangloss say, if he knew what the pure state of nature is really like? All is well they say; but I confess it's harsh to have lost Miss Cunégonde and to be skewered by Oreillons."

Cacambo never lost his head. "Don't give up hope yet," he said to the cheerless Candide. "I know a bit of the lingo of tribes like this; I'm going to speak to them."

---

[41] **Oreillons:** The French word Voltaire uses to translate the Spanish *Orejones,* meaning "big-eared." Voltaire got the word *orejones* from a history of Peru by Garcilaso de Vega, upon which he based much of his description of South America.

"Remember to explain to them," added Candide, "that it's the height of inhumanity to cook human beings, and that it's not very Christian either."

"Gentlemen," said Cacambo, "you intend to eat a Jesuit today; that is appropriate; nothing is more just than to treat one's enemies in this way. Indeed, natural law teaches us to kill our neighbor, and that is how everyone behaves the whole world over. If we Europeans do not exercise our right to eat others, it is because we have other ingredients for a good meal. But you do not have the same resources. It certainly makes more sense to eat your enemies than to abandon the fruits of victory to crows and ravens. But gentlemen, you do not wish to eat your friends. You think you are going to put a Jesuit on the spit, but it is your defender, the enemy of your enemies, whom you are going to roast. As for myself, I was born in your country; this gentleman whom you see is my master; and far from being a Jesuit, he just killed a Jesuit! He is wearing the plunder, and that is the source of your mistake. To verify what I am telling you, take his robe, bring it to the first outpost of the kingdom of the *Padres*. Learn for yourselves if my master has not killed a Jesuit officer. It will not take long; you can always eat us later if you find that I have lied to you. But if I have spoken the truth, you are too familiar with the principles of international justice, morality, and law not to spare our lives."

The Oreillons found this speech very reasonable. They commissioned two leaders to determine the truth with haste. The two deputies carried out their mission with precision and soon came back with the good news. The Oreillons untied their two prisoners, made all kinds of apologies, offered them girls, gave them refreshments, and escorted them up to the boundary of their state, shouting joyfully, "He's not a Jesuit, he's not a Jesuit!"

Candide could not stop admiring the cause of his deliverance. "What a people!" he kept saying. "What men! What morals! If I hadn't been lucky enough to stick a sword through the body of Miss Cunégonde's brother, I would have been eaten without mercy. But it turns out the pure state of nature is good, because I only had to show these people I wasn't a Jesuit, and they treated me with enormous kindness."

CHAPTER 17

Arrival of Candide and his valet in the country of Eldorado,[42] *and what they saw there*

When they were at the Oreillons' border, Cacambo said to Candide, "You see, this hemisphere is no better than the other. Listen, let's take the shortest route back to Europe."

"How can we?" said Candide. "And where would we go? If I go back to my country, the Bulgars and Abars are slaughtering everyone. If I return to Portugal, I'll be burned. If we stay here, we run the risk of being put on a spit. And how can I bring myself to leave the part of the world where Miss Cunégonde lives?"

---

[42] **Eldorado:** El Dorado, the legendary land or city of gold said to be somewhere in Central or South America; it was named after the fabled chieftain El Dorado, whose name means "the gilded one."

"Let's head for Cayenne," said Cacambo. "There we can find some Frenchmen who travel all over the world. They'll be able to help. Perhaps God will have pity on us."

It was not easy to get to Cayenne. They had a good idea, more or less, of the direction to take; but everywhere mountains, rivers, cliffs, bandits, and savages blocked their way. Their horses died of fatigue; their provisions were used up; they lived on wild fruits for a whole month. At last they found themselves by a little river, fringed with coconut trees, which nourished their lives and hopes.

Cacambo, whose advice was always as good as the old woman's, said to Candide: "We can't go any further, we've walked enough. I see an empty canoe on the shore. Let's fill it with coconuts, jump into this little bark, and drift with the current. A river always leads to some inhabited place. If we don't find something we like, we'll at least find something new."

"Let's go," said Candide, "and may Providence guide us."

They drifted for several miles between banks that were sometimes fertile, sometimes barren, sometimes level, sometimes steep. The river grew steadily broader, and eventually vanished under a vault of terrifying rocks that soared into the sky. The two travelers had the boldness to abandon themselves to the currents below this vault. The river narrowed at this point and carried them along with horrifying speed and noise. After twenty-four hours, they saw daylight again, but their canoe broke apart against the reefs. They had to crawl from rock to rock for three miles. Finally, they discovered a vast horizon trimmed by unscalable mountains. The lowlands were cultivated for pleasure as well as profit. Everywhere the useful was combined with the pleasing. The roads were covered, or rather embellished, with elegantly shaped carriages made from a shiny material, carrying men and women of extraordinary beauty, drawn swiftly by large red sheep that surpassed in speed the finest horses of Andalusia, Tetuan, and Mequinez.

"Here at last," said Candide, "is a country that is better than Westphalia."

He and Cacambo stepped into the first village they encountered. Some of the village children, covered with bits of golden brocade, were playing quoits near the village gate. Our two men from the other world watched them with interest. Their quoits were rather large rounded objects, yellow, red, and green, which sparkled brilliantly. Out of curiosity the travelers picked some up: gold, emeralds, rubies, of which the smallest would have been the greatest ornament of the Mogul's throne.

"No doubt about it," said Cacambo, "these youngsters playing quoits are the children of the King of this land."

Just then the village schoolteacher appeared to call the children back to school.

"There," said Candide, "is the tutor to the royal family."

The little beggars promptly stopped playing, leaving their quoits on the ground, along with their other playthings. Candide picked them up, ran after the instructor, and humbly presented them to him, using signs to tell him that the royal children had forgotten their gold and precious stones. The village schoolteacher smiled and threw them to the ground, looked briefly at Candide's face with surprise, and went on his way.

The travelers did not fail to keep the gold, rubies, and emeralds.

"Where are we?" exclaimed Candide. "The children of kings must be well educated here because they are taught to despise gold and jewels."

Cacambo was as surprised as Candide. Next they arrived at the first house in the village. It was built like a European palace. A throng of people crowded around the door, and even more were inside. A delightful music was audible, and a delicious odor of cooking filled the air. Cacambo walked up to the door and heard them speaking Peruvian. It was his mother tongue, for everyone knows that Cacambo was born in Tucuman, in a village where Peruvian was the only language.

"I'll act as your interpreter," he said to Candide. "Let's enter, this is an inn."

Two waiters and two waitresses, dressed in gold cloth, with their hair bound up in ribbons, invited them to be seated at the common dining table. They served four tureens of soup, each garnished with two parrots, a boiled condor weighing two hundred pounds, two savory roasted monkeys, three hundred round-billed hummingbirds on one platter, and six hundred straight-billed hummingbirds on another, exquisite stews, delicious pastries; and everything served on platters of a sort of rock crystal. The waiters and waitresses poured several liqueurs made from sugar cane. The guests were mostly merchants and coachmen, all extremely polite, who asked Cacambo a few questions with unintrusive discretion, and answered his own questions with the utmost clarity.

When the meal was over, Cacambo, like Candide, thought he was paying his bill amply by dropping on the table two of those large pieces of gold he had picked up. The host and hostess burst out laughing and slapped their knees for a long time. Finally, they became serious.

"Gentlemen," said the host, "we can easily see that you are foreigners; we are not accustomed to seeing any around here. Forgive us for laughing when you offered to pay us with stones from our highways. You obviously have none of our currency, but you do not need it to dine here. All inns established for the convenience of trade are paid for by the Government. You have dined poorly here because this is a poor village; but everywhere else you'll be given the reception you deserve."

Cacambo explained to Candide all of the host's remarks, and Candide heard them with the same wonder and amazement that his friend Cacambo showed in translating them.

"What is this country," they asked each other, "unknown to the rest of the world, and where the whole arrangement of Nature is so different from our own?"

"This is probably the country where all is well," Candide observed, "for it is absolutely necessary that one such country exist. And in spite of what Dr. Pangloss used to say, I often observed that everything was for the worst in Westphalia."

CHAPTER 18

What they saw in the land of Eldorado

Cacambo expressed his curiosity to his host, and the host said to him, "I am a very ignorant man, and am content to be so; but we do have an old gentleman, retired from the royal court, who is the most learned person in the kingdom, and the most communicative."

Without delay he brought Cacambo to the old man's house. Candide was merely the supporting actor now and accompanied his valet. They went into a very simple home, for the door was only silver, and the interior paneling merely gold, though designed with so much taste that the richest paneling could not surpass it. The lobby floor, it is true, was encrusted only with rubies and emeralds, but the harmonious pattern in which everything was arranged compensated for this extreme simplicity.

The old man received the two foreigners on a sofa stuffed with hummingbird feathers. He offered them liqueurs in diamond vases; after which he satisfied their curiosity in these terms.

"I am a hundred and seventy-two years old, and my late father, who was Master of the Royal Stables, told me about the astounding revolutions in Peru that he had witnessed. The kingdom we are in is the original homeland of the Incas, who unwisely left it to go out and make foreign conquests, and who ended up being destroyed by the Spanish.

"More wisdom was shown by some princes who remained here in their native land. They commanded, with the nation's consent, that no inhabitant of our little kingdom would ever leave it; and this rule has preserved our innocence and our happiness. The Spanish have some vague knowledge of this country, which they call *El Dorado,* and an English lord named Raleigh[43] even came close to it about a hundred years ago. But since we are surrounded by impassable mountains and precipices, we have so far been safe from the greed of European nations, which have an incredible passion for the stones and mud of our land and would murder every one of us to get some."

The conversation continued for a long time. It turned on the form of government, the morals, the women, the public entertainments, the arts. Finally, Candide, who always had a taste for metaphysics, inquired through Cacambo if the country had a religion.

The old man blushed slightly.

"How could you ever think we did not? Do you take us for ungrateful wretches?"

Cacambo humbly asked what the religion of Eldorado was. The old man blushed again.

"Is there more than one religion?" he said. "We have, I believe, the same religion as everyone else. We worship God from morning to night."

"Do you worship just one God?" asked Cacambo, who continued to translate Candide's uncertainties.

"I see no reason," said the old man, "to believe in two, three, or four. I must say that people from your world ask very odd questions."

Candide did not tire of interrogating the good old man through Cacambo. He wanted to know how one prayed to God in Eldorado.

---

[43] **Raleigh:** Sir Walter Raleigh (1554–1618), English explorer and writer whose *Discovery of Guiana* (1596), describing his exploration of the Orinoco River valley in 1595, helped to promote the legend of El Dorado.

"We do not pray at all," said the good and respectable sage; "we have nothing to ask him for; he has given us everything we need, and we thank him constantly."

Candide was curious to see the priests. He asked where they were. The kindly old-timer smiled.

"My friends," said he, "we are all priests. The King and all the heads of families solemnly chant the psalms of thanksgiving every morning, and five or six thousand citizens sing along with them."

"What! You have no monks who lecture, debate, govern, conspire, and burn people who don't agree with them?"

"We would be crazy if we did," said the old man. "Everyone here has the same beliefs, and we do not understand what your monks are for."

Candide was in ecstasy at these remarks, and said to himself, "This is very different from Westphalia and the Baron's chateau. If our friend Pangloss had seen Eldorado, he would have stopped asserting that the castle of Thunder-ten-tronckh was the best thing on earth. Travel is certainly instructive."

After this long conversation, the kindly old-timer had a carriage harnessed with six sheep and had twelve of his servants take the two travelers to the court.

"Forgive me," he said to them, "if my age deprives me of the honor of accompanying you. The King will give you a reception that will not disappoint you, and I am sure you will excuse us for any customs that happen to displease you."

Candide and Cacambo climbed into the carriage. The six sheep flew off, and in less than four hours they arrived at the royal palace, located on the edge of the capital city. The portal was two hundred and twenty feet high and a hundred wide. It is impossible to describe the materials it was made of, but it was obvious that it was vastly superior to those stones and sand we call gold and jewels.

Twenty beautiful girls of the palace guard met Candide and Cacambo as they descended from the carriage, escorted them to the baths, and dressed them in robes spun from hummingbird down. Then the Grand Lords and Ladies of the Crown walked them to His Majesty's apartment, passing between two lines of a thousand musicians each, as was the custom. As they approached the throne room, Cacambo asked a Grand Officer how they were supposed to show respect for His Majesty. By falling on their knees or flat on their stomachs? By putting their hands on their heads or behind their backs? By licking the dust off the floor? In short, what was the ceremony?

"The custom," said the Grand Officer, "is to embrace the King and kiss him on both cheeks."

Candide and Cacambo hugged His Majesty, who received them with the utmost grace and politely invited them to have supper with him later. In the meantime, they were shown the city: the public buildings rising to the clouds; the open markets decorated with countless columns; the fountains of clear water, the fountains of rose water, and the fountains of liqueurs made from sugar cane, which flowed continuously in great public squares that were paved with a kind of precious stone that gave off the scent of cloves and cinnamon. Candide asked to see the law courts; they told him that none existed and that trials never occurred. He inquired whether they had prisons, and the answer was no. What surprised him even more, and gave him the most pleasure, was the Palace of Science, in which he visited a gallery, two thousand paces long, filled with instruments for mathematics and physics.

After spending the whole afternoon touring about one-thousandth of the city, they returned to the Palace. Candide sat down to supper with His Majesty, his valet Cacambo, and several ladies. Never did they taste better food, and never did they encounter a more urbane host than His Majesty. Cacambo explained the King's witticisms to Candide, and they were witty even in translation. Of all the astonishing things Candide saw and heard, this was by no means the least astonishing.

They spent a month in this retreat. Candide never stopped saying to Cacambo: "It's true, my friend, and I'll repeat it: The castle where I was born doesn't compare to the land we're in now. But still, Miss Cunégonde isn't here, and you probably have a mistress yourself somewhere in Europe. If we stay here, we'll just be like everyone else, whereas if we return to our world, even with only twelve sheep loaded with stones from Eldorado, we'll be richer than all the kings put together. We won't have to be afraid of inquisitors, and we'll easily be able to rescue Miss Cunégonde."

This speech pleased Cacambo. People so much like to roam around, and then show off at home and brag about what they have seen in their travels, that the two happy men resolved to be happy no longer, and to ask His Majesty for permission to leave.

"You are doing a foolish thing," the King said to them. "I know that my country is insignificant, but when one is tolerably well off somewhere one ought to remain there. I certainly have no right to confine foreigners; such tyranny is inconsistent with our customs and with our laws. All men are free. You may leave at will, but the way out is very difficult. It is impossible to go against the swift currents which miraculously brought you here and which flow through the vaults of rock. The mountains surrounding my entire realm are ten thousand feet high and as straight as walls. Each one is more than twenty-five miles wide, and the only way down the other side is over vertical cliffs. Since you are absolutely determined to leave, however, I will order the Royal Engineers to design something that can transport you comfortably. When you have been conveyed to the other side of the mountains, no one will be able to accompany you beyond; for my subjects have sworn never to leave this retreat, and they are too wise to break their vows. But ask me for anything else you desire."

"We ask of Your Majesty," said Cacambo, "only a few sheep loaded with provisions, and some of the stones and mud of your country."

The King laughed. "I do not comprehend," he said, "the taste you Europeans have for our yellow mud; but take as much as you want, and may it bring you well-being."

He promptly gave orders to his engineers to make a machine to hoist these two extraordinary men out of the kingdom. Three thousand expert physicists worked on it; it was ready in two weeks and cost no more than twenty million pounds sterling in the local currency. Candide and Cacambo were placed in the machine. There were two large red sheep, saddled and bridled, for them to ride after they traversed the mountains, as well as twenty pack sheep loaded with provisions, thirty carrying gifts of the country's most curious items, and fifty loaded with gold, precious stones, and diamonds. The king tenderly embraced the two vagabonds.

It was a wonderful spectacle to see their departure and the ingenious way in which they and their sheep were hauled over the mountains. The physicists took leave of them after setting them down safely, and Candide's only aim and desire now was to present his sheep to Miss Cunégonde.

"We have enough to pay off the Governor of Buenos Aires," he said, "if Miss Cunégonde can be purchased. Let's head for Cayenne,[44] let's set sail, and we will see what kingdom we can buy."

Chapter 19

What happened to them in Surinam, and how Candide became acquainted with Martin

The first day was quite pleasant for our two travelers. They were encouraged by the idea that they possessed more treasure than all of Asia, Europe, and Africa combined. Candide was elated, and carved the name of Cunégonde on trees. On the second day, two of their sheep sank into a swamp and were buried with their cargo; two other sheep died of fatigue a few days after that; seven or eight perished of hunger in a desert; others fell off some cliffs a few days later. Finally, after a hundred days of travel, they had only two sheep left.

Candide said to Cacambo, "My friend, you see how the riches of this world are ephemeral; nothing is solid but virtue and the happiness of seeing Miss Cunégonde again."

"I agree," said Cacambo, "but we still have two sheep with more treasure than the King of Spain will ever have, and I see in the distance a city that I suspect is Surinam, which belongs to the Dutch. We are at the end of our troubles and the beginning of our happiness."

As they approached the town they saw a Negro stretched out on the ground, wearing only a pair of blue linen trunks that were half torn away. The poor man was missing his left leg and right hand.

"Oh my God!" Candide said to him in Dutch. "What are you doing in this horrible condition, my friend?"

"I'm waiting for my master, Mr. Vanderdendur,[45] the famous merchant," replied the Negro.

"Was it Mr. Vanderdendur," asked Candide, "who treated you this way?"

"Yes, sir," said the Negro, "it's normal. They give us one pair of linen trunks twice a year as our only clothing. When we work in the sugar mills and catch our fingers in the grinder, they cut off our hand. When we try to escape, they cut off our leg. I've had both punishments. It is at this price that you eat sugar in Europe. Yet, when my

---

[44] **Cayenne:** Small island off the coast of Guiana, colonized by the French in 1635. Surinam, where Candide goes next, was a Dutch colony in Guiana just north of Cayenne.

[45] **Mr. Vanderdendur:** Some readers suggest this name alludes to a Dutch bookseller named VanDuren who had quarreled with Voltaire.

mother sold me for ten Patagonian crowns on the coast of Guinea, she said to me, 'My dear child, pray to our charms, worship them forever, they will bring you happiness. You have the honor of becoming a slave to our Masters, the whites, and by doing so, you are making your parents rich.' Alas, I don't know if they became rich, but I certainly didn't. Dogs, monkeys, and parrots are a thousand times less miserable than we are. The Dutch sorcerers who converted me tell me every Sunday that we are all children of Adam, whites and blacks. I'm no genealogist, but if these preachers are right, we're all cousins. Now you have to admit that you can't treat your relatives more horribly than this."

"Oh Pangloss!" exclaimed Candide. "You had no idea this abomination existed. That does it; I have to renounce your optimism after all."

"What's optimism?" asked Cacambo.

"Alas!" said Candide, "it's the mania for insisting that all is well when one is suffering."

And he shed tears as he looked at the Negro. He was still crying when he entered Surinam.

The first thing he did was to inquire whether there was a ship in the harbor that could sail to Buenos Aires. The person they asked happened to be a Spanish captain who offered to make an honest deal with them and arranged to meet them later at an inn. Candide and the trusty Cacambo went to wait for him with their two sheep.

Candide, who wore his heart on his sleeve, told the Spaniard about all his adventures, and revealed that he wished to carry off Miss Cunégonde.

"The last thing I would do is take you to Buenos Aires," said the Captain. "I would be hanged, and so would you. The lovely Cunégonde is His Lordship's favorite mistress."

This was a lightning bolt for Candide. He wept for a long time. Finally, he drew Cacambo aside.

"Here's what you must do, my dear friend. Each of us has in his pockets five or six million worth of diamonds. You're more clever than I am. Go get Miss Cunégonde in Buenos Aires. If the Governor makes any trouble, give him a million. If he doesn't give in to that, offer him two. You never killed an inquisitor, they won't be suspicious of you. I'll fit out another boat and go to Venice and wait for you. It's a free country where you don't have to be afraid of Bulgars or Abars or Jews or inquisitors."

Cacambo approved of this wise resolution. He was in distress at having to separate from such a good master, who had become his intimate friend. But the pleasure of being useful to him outweighed the pain of leaving him. They embraced and shed tears. Candide urged him not to forget the old woman. Cacambo left the very next day. He was a very fine man, that Cacambo.

Candide stayed on in Surinam, waiting until another Captain could take him to Italy with the two sheep he had left. He hired servants and bought everything he needed for a long voyage. Finally, Mr. Vanderdendur, proprietor of a big ship, came to introduce himself.

"How much do you want," Candide asked this man, "to take me straight to Venice, me, my men, my baggage, and those two sheep?"

The owner suggested ten thousand piastres. Candide immediately accepted.

"Ho ho," said the prudent Vanderdendur to himself, "this foreigner gives up ten thousand piastres in a second! He must be very rich."

Then, returning a moment later, he declared that he could not embark for less than twenty thousand.

"All right, you shall be paid," said Candide.

"Hey," the merchant said under his breath, "this man gives twenty thousand piastres as easily as he gives ten."

He came back again and said that he could not transport him to Venice for less than thirty thousand piastres.

"Then you will get thirty thousand," Candide replied.

"Ah ha," the Dutch merchant said to himself again, "thirty thousand piastres mean nothing to this man. Without any doubt, the two sheep are carrying immense treasures. Let us leave it as it stands. We will collect our thirty thousand piastres first, and then we will see."

Candide sold two little diamonds, the smaller of which was worth more than all the money the merchant demanded. He paid in advance. The two sheep were loaded on board. Candide followed on a small boat in order to join the ship in the harbor. The merchant seized the moment, raised the sail, and cut loose with a favorable wind. Candide, bewildered and stupefied, soon lost sight of him.

"Alas!" he cried out. "There's a trick worthy of the Old World."

He returned to shore, sunk in misery, for after all he had lost enough to make the fortune of twenty monarchs. He rushed to the house of a Dutch judge, and since he was a bit excited, he knocked rudely on the door. He entered, related his adventure, and shouted a bit louder than was necessary. The judge began by fining him ten thousand piastres for the noise he had made. Then he listened patiently, promised to review the case as soon as the merchant returned, and charged him another ten thousand piastres for the consultation.

These measures completed Candide's despair. He had, it is true, experienced other misfortunes a thousand times more painful, but the heartless character of the judge, and of the man who robbed him, amplified his bitterness and plunged him into a black melancholy. The viciousness of men appeared to him in all its ugliness, and he fed exclusively on thoughts of gloom. Finally, when a French ship was about to leave for Bordeaux, he took a cabin at a fair price, and since he no longer had any sheep laden with diamonds to bring with him, he announced in town that he would pay the fare, board, and two thousand piastres to any honest man who wished to make the voyage with him, on condition that this man should be the most disgusted with his lot and the most miserable in the province.

A throng of applicants appeared that an entire fleet could not have held. Candide wished to select the most promising candidates; he picked out about twenty persons who seemed sociable enough and all claimed to be the most qualified. He assembled them in his inn and gave them supper, on condition that each one swear to tell his story faithfully. He would choose the one who seemed to deserve the most pity and to have the strongest claim to being unhappy with his lot; the others would receive some smaller reward.

The session lasted until four in the morning. As he listened to all their adventures, Candide remembered what the old woman had told him on the way to Buenos Aires, and the wager she had made that there was no one on board who had not experienced great misfortunes. He thought of Pangloss at each tale he heard.

"That Pangloss," he said, "would be hard put to defend his system now. I wish he were here. Obviously, if all is well, it's in Eldorado and not in the rest of the world."

Finally, he decided in favor of a poor scholar who had worked in the bookstores of Amsterdam for ten years. He came to the conclusion that there was no profession on earth with which a man could be more disgusted.

This scholar, who was in fact a decent man, had been robbed by his wife, beaten by his son, and abandoned by his daughter, who had eloped with a Portuguese. He had just been deprived of the little job that barely supported him, and the preachers of Surinam were persecuting him because they took him to be a Socinian.[46] In truth, the others were at least as unfortunate as he, but Candide hoped that the scholar would relieve his boredom during the voyage. All his other rivals thought that Candide was doing them a great injustice, but he appeased them by giving them a hundred piastres each.

CHAPTER 20

What happened to Candide and Martin at sea

The old scholar, whose name was Martin, thus set out for Bordeaux with Candide. They had both seen much, and suffered much; and even if the ship had been scheduled to sail from Surinam to Japan by the Cape of Good Hope, they would have had enough material to discuss moral and physical evil throughout the entire voyage.

Yet, Candide had one great advantage over Martin: He still hoped to see Miss Cunégonde again, while Martin had nothing to hope for. Besides, he still had some gold and diamonds. Even though he had lost a hundred big red sheep packed with the greatest treasures of the earth, and even though he was still tormented by the Dutch merchant's trickery, when he thought about what he still had in his pockets, and when he spoke of Cunégonde, especially after a good meal, he still leaned toward the system of Pangloss.

"But you, Mister Martin," said he to the scholar, "what do you think of all this? What's your conception of moral and physical evil?"

"Sir," replied Martin, "my priests accused me of being a Socinian; but the truth is that I am a Manichean."[47]

"You're joking," said Candide, "there are no more Manicheans in the world."

---

[46] **Socinian:** Socinianism was a religious movement stemming from the work of Laelius Socinus, a sixteenth-century Polish theologian, who praised the power of reason and challenged the Christian mysteries such as the Trinity and the virgin birth.

[47] **Manichean:** The Manicheans, followers of the Persian sage Mani (third century C.E.), believed that life was a struggle between the active forces of light and darkness.

"There's myself," said Martin. "I don't know what to do about it, but I can't think any other way."

"The Devil must be inside your body," said Candide.

"He's so involved in the affairs of this world," said Martin, "that he may well be in my body and everywhere else too. But I confess that when I survey this globe, or rather this tiny ball, I think that God has abandoned it all to some evil being—except of course Eldorado. Very rarely have I seen a town that did not wish for the destruction of the next town, or a family that did not seek to exterminate some other family. Everywhere the weak hate the powerful in whose presence they slither, and the strong look after the weak like sheep to be fleeced and slaughtered. A million assassins in uniform, roaming from one end of Europe to the other, murder and pillage with discipline in order to earn their daily bread, and no profession confers more honor. And in those towns that seem to enjoy peace and where the arts flourish, the jealousies, cares, and anxieties that devour men are greater than the scourges suffered by a besieged city. Secret distress is much worse than public misfortune. In short, I've seen enough, and suffered enough, to be a Manichean."

"Yet there's some good," replied Candide.

"That may be," said Martin, "but I never saw it."

In the middle of this discussion, they heard the sound of cannon growing louder at every moment. Every one reached for his spyglass and saw two ships fighting about three miles away. The wind brought them both so close to the French ship that they had the pleasure of watching the fight in comfort. Finally one of the two ships assaulted the other with a broadside so low and accurate that it sank toward the bottom. Candide and Martin clearly discerned about a hundred men on the deck of the sinking vessel; they all raised their hands to heaven and wailed in terror. A moment later they were all swallowed up.

"Well," said Martin, "that's how men treat each other."

"It's true," said Candide, "there's something diabolical in this affair."

As he uttered these words he made out something bright red swimming toward the ship. They launched a lifeboat to see what it could be: It was one of his sheep. Candide's joy at regaining his one sheep was greater than his grief when he had lost a hundred of them packed with big diamonds from Eldorado.

The French Captain soon discovered that the Captain of the attacking ship was Spanish and that the Captain of the submerged ship was a Dutch pirate; it was, in fact, the same who had robbed Candide. The immense riches stolen by that scoundrel were buried with him in the sea, and only one of the sheep survived.

"You see," Candide said to Martin, "sometimes crime is punished. That villainous Dutch merchant got the fate he deserved."

"Yes," said Martin, "but was it necessary for the ship's passengers to perish as well? God punished the deceiver, the Devil drowned the others."

Meanwhile the French and Spanish vessels continued on their way, and Candide continued his conversations with Martin. They debated for two weeks in a row, and at the end of this period they were no more advanced than on the first day. Nevertheless, they were talking, communicating ideas, and consoling one another. Candide caressed his sheep.

"Since I have found you again, I may well find Miss Cunégonde again too."

CHAPTER 21

How Candide and Martin theorized as they approached the coast of France

At last they sighted the coast of France.

"Have you been in France before, Mister Martin?" asked Candide.

"Yes," said Martin, "I have traversed many of the provinces. There are some where half the inhabitants are insane, some where the people are not to be trusted, some where they are quite gentle and rather ignorant, and others where they act like dandies all the time; and in all of them the principal occupation is lovemaking, the second is slandering, and the third is saying stupid things."

"But Mister Martin, have you ever seen Paris?"

"Yes, I have seen Paris. It has people in all of the above categories. It's a chaos, it's a mob in which everyone is seeking pleasure and in which almost no one finds it, at least so far as I could see. I did not stay there long. When I arrived I was robbed of all I had by pickpockets at the Saint Germain fair. I was arrested myself as a thief and did a week in prison, and after that I became a printer's proofreader in order to earn enough to return to Holland on foot. I met the low-life of scribblers, the low-life of conspirators, and the low-life of convulsionaries.[48] They say there are some very polite people in that city; I wish it were true."

"As for me, I'm not at all curious to see France," said Candide. "You can easily understand that when someone has spent a month in Eldorado, nothing else on earth is appealing any more, except Miss Cunégonde. I am going to wait for her in Venice. We will cross France to get to Italy. Will you join me?"

"Very gladly," Martin said. "They say that Venice is a good place only for the Venetian nobles but that they also receive foreigners well when they have a lot of money. I don't have any, but you do; I will follow you anywhere."

"By the way," said Candide, "do you think that the earth was originally a sea, as it states in that fat book[49] belonging to the ship's Captain?"

"I believe nothing of the sort," said Martin, "any more than all the other pipe dreams that people have been selling recently."

"But then for what purpose was the earth formed?" asked Candide.

"To drive us crazy," replied Martin.

"Aren't you amazed," Candide went on, "by the story I told you about those two girls who were in love with the monkeys in the land of the Oreillons?"

"Not at all," Martin said, "I see nothing bizarre in that passion. I have seen so many extraordinary things that nothing is extraordinary any more."

"Do you think," Candide asked, "that men have always massacred each other as they do today, and that they have always been liars, cheaters, traitors, ingrates, brigands, weaklings, deserters, cowards, enviers, gluttons, drunks, misers, profiteers, predators, slanderers, perverts, fanatics, hypocrites, and morons?"

---

[48] convulsionaries: The Jansenists, a conservative sect of arch-Catholics who followed the teachings of Cornelis Jansen (1585–1638), the bishop of Ypres. Their doctrines and public displays of spiritual ecstasy were denounced by the papal authorities and created much controversy in eighteenth-century France.

[49] fat book: The Bible, which describes the earth as having been covered in water (Genesis 1.6–7).

"Do you think," Martin said, "that hawks have always eaten pigeons when they found any?"

"Yes, of course," said Candide.

"Well," said Martin, "if hawks have always had the same character, why do you expect that men have changed theirs?"

"Oh!" said Candide, "that's very different, for free will . . ."

As they were theorizing, they arrived in Bordeaux.

Chapter 22

What happened to Candide and Martin in France

Candide stopped in Bordeaux only as long as it took to sell a few stones from Eldorado and to hire a fine carriage with two seats, for he could no longer do without his philosopher, Martin. He was very upset, however, that he had to leave his sheep. He left it with the Bordeaux Academy of Sciences, which organized its annual essay competition around the question of why this sheep's wool was red. The prize was awarded to a scholar from the North,[50] who proved by A plus B minus C divided by Z that the sheep had to be red, and that it would die of the sheep-pox.

Meanwhile, all the travelers Candide met in the inns along the road said to him, "We are going to Paris!" This general eagerness finally made him want to see the capital; it was not far off the route to Venice anyway.

He entered through the Faubourg Saint-Marceau[51] and thought he was in the ugliest village of Westphalia.

Scarcely was Candide in his hotel when he was struck by a mild illness caused by his fatigue. As he had an enormous diamond on his finger, and people had noticed a prodigiously heavy trunk among his belongings, he immediately had at his bedside two doctors whom he had not summoned, several intimate friends who would not leave him, and two pious women who kept his soup warm.

Martin said, "I remember being sick too during my first trip to Paris. I was a very poor man, so I had no friends, no pious ladies, no doctors, and I got better."

However, with the aid of medicines and bloodlettings, Candide's illness grew serious. A parish priest came and sweetly asked for a note payable to the bearer in the next world.[52] Candide would have nothing to do with it. The pious ladies assured him it was the latest fashion. Candide answered that he was not a fashionable man. Martin wanted to throw the priest out the window. The cleric swore that he would never grant Candide a proper burial. Martin swore that he would properly bury the cleric if he kept on bothering them. The quarrel heated up. Martin took him by the shoulders and rudely threw him out, creating a great scandal that was duly noted in a police report.

---

[50] **scholar from the North:** Maupertuis Le Lapon, a mathematician who tried to prove the existence of God with mathematical proofs.

[51] **Faubourg Saint-Marceau:** A notoriously rough-and-tumble district in Paris during Voltaire's time.

[52] **note . . . next world:** A *billet de confession,* or certificate of confession, that in Voltaire's time was needed to obtain the last rites from a priest and to be buried in consecrated ground.

Candide recovered, and throughout his convalescence he had very good company for supper. They played cards for high stakes. Candide was surprised that he never got any aces, and Martin was not surprised at all.

Among those who bestowed upon him the city's favors was a little Perigordian Abbé, one of those fellows on the move who is always alert, obliging, assertive, flattering, solicitous, and who lies in wait for foreigners passing through, offering to tell them about the town's scandals and to obtain pleasures for them at any price. This man first took Candide and Martin to the theater. They were performing a new tragedy. Candide was seated next to some highbrow critics. That did not prevent him from weeping at the perfectly acted scenes. One of the theorizers beside him said during the intermission:

"It is highly improper of you to weep. That actress is very bad, the actor playing opposite her is worse, and the play is even worse than the actors. The author does not know a word of Arabic, yet the scene takes place in Arabia. Moreover, he does not believe in innate ideas.[53] Tomorrow I will bring you twenty pamphlets against him."

"Sir, how many plays do you have in France?" Candide asked the Abbé.

"Five or six thousand," replied the Abbé.

"That's a lot," said Candide. "How many of them are good?"

"Fifteen or sixteen," answered the other.

"That's a lot," said Martin.

Candide was very pleased by an actress who played Queen Elizabeth in a rather dull tragedy[54] that is still performed from time to time.

"I like that actress a lot," he said to Martin. "She resembles Miss Cunégonde. I would like to pay her my respects."

The Perigordian Abbé volunteered to take him to her house. Candide, raised in Germany, asked what the etiquette was and how one treated the Queen of England in France.

"It depends," said the Abbé. "In the provinces you take them to a hotel. In Paris, you show them more respect if they are attractive, and then you throw them into the public dump when they are dead."[55]

"Queens in the public dump!" said Candide.

"Yes, that's how it is," said Martin. "The Abbé is right. I was in Paris when Miss Monime[56] passed, as they say, from this life to the next. They refused to give her what these people call 'the rites of burial,' in other words, the right to rot with all the beggars of the neighborhood in a sordid cemetery. Her troupe buried her all alone at the

---

[53] **innate ideas:** According to the French philosopher René Descartes (1596–1650), we are born with some ideas already in our minds. Many philosophers refuted this notion, including the English philosopher John Locke (1632–1704).

[54] **dull tragedy:** *Le Comte d'Essex (The Earl of Essex)* by Thomas Corneille (1625–1709), the younger brother of the renowned playwright Pierre Corneille (1606–1684).

[55] **public dump . . . dead:** Actors and actresses could not be buried in consecrated ground, a policy against which Voltaire argued throughout his career.

[56] **Miss Monime:** A character in the play *Mithridate* by Jean Racine (1639–1699); here, Voltaire uses the name to refer to Adrienne Lecouvreur (1690–1730), a popular actress whose death led Voltaire to write a poem protesting the church's burial policy for actors and actresses.

corner of the Rue de Bourgogne; it must have caused her extreme pain, for she always had a noble mind."

"That was very impolite," said Candide.

"What do you expect?" said Martin. "These people are made that way. Imagine every possible contradiction, every possible inconsistency; you will find it in the government, in the courts, in the churches, in the plays of this odd nation."

"Is it true that people in Paris always laugh?" asked Candide.

"Yes," said the Abbé, "but they are furious at the same time; for here people complain about everything with great bursts of laughter; they even laugh while committing the most detestable crimes."

"Who was that fat pig," asked Candide, "who said so many nasty things about the play that made me weep, and about the actors who gave me so much pleasure?"

"He is an illness in human form," replied the Abbé, "who makes a living by saying nasty things about every play and every book. He hates anyone who becomes popular, just as eunuchs hate anyone who makes love. He is one of those serpents of the literary world who feed on filth and poison; he is a folliculator."

"What do you mean by *folliculator*?" asked Candide.

"A scribbler of worthless folios, a Fréron,"[57] said the Abbé.

Candide, Martin, and the Perigordian had this discussion on the stairway, as they watched the crowd file out of the theater.

"Even though I'm very impatient to see Miss Cunégonde again," said Candide, "I would still like to have supper with Miss Clairon,[58] for she seemed admirable to me."

The Abbé was not in a position to approach Miss Clairon, who received only good company.

"She is already engaged this evening," he said, "but I will have the honor of introducing you to another lady of distinction, and there you will come to know Paris as if you had been here over four years."

Candide was naturally curious and let himself be taken to the lady's home in the middle of the Faubourg Saint-Honoré. A group was busy playing faro[59] there; twelve sad punters each had a small series of cards that plainly registered their bad luck. A deep silence reigned, the punters' faces were white, the banker's look was anxious, and the lady of the house, seated beside the pitiless banker, observed with the eyes of a lynx every doubling of the stakes, every multiple bet, which the players signified by bending their cards. She exposed cheaters strictly but politely, without anger, for fear of losing her clients. The Lady went by the name of the Marquise de Parolignac.[60] Her fifteen-year-old daughter sat with the punters and winked at her mother to reveal the tricks these poor men were playing to repair the cruelties of chance. The

---

[57] **Fréron:** A journalist who had criticized Voltaire's plays.

[58] **Miss Clairon:** Claire Leris (1723–1803), a popular actress who performed in several of Voltaire's plays.

[59] **faro:** A popular card game in the eighteenth century, in which the players, called punters, place bets against the dealer, known as the banker.

[60] **Marquise de Parolignac:** In faro, to *parole* means to double the bet, an illegal move; hence, the lady is a cardsharp.

Perigordian Abbé, Candide, and Martin entered. No one stood up, greeted them, or looked at them. Everyone was profoundly occupied with his cards.

"The Baroness of Thunder-ten-tronckh was more civil," thought Candide.

The Abbé, however, whispered in the ear of the Marquise. She stood up halfway and honored Candide with a gracious smile and Martin with a noble nod of the head. She arranged for Candide to sit and play cards. He lost fifty thousand francs in two rounds. Afterwards they had a very gay supper, and everyone was surprised that Candide was not disturbed by his loss. The lackeys said to each other, in their lackey language, "He must be some English Milord."

The supper was like most suppers in Paris: first silence; then a buzz of indistinguishable words; then jokes, insipid for the most part; inaccurate news; bad theory; a little politics, and a lot of slander. They even discussed new books.

"Has anyone seen," asked the Perigordian Abbé, "the novel by Monsieur Gauchat, Doctor of Theology?"[61]

"Yes," answered one of the guests, "but I could not finish it. We have a mass of trivial writings, but all of them put together do not match the triviality of Gauchat, Doctor of Theology. I am so nauseated by this multitude of detestable books that are swamping us that I have taken to playing faro."

"And the *Miscellaneous Essays* of Archdeacon T——,[62] what do you think of them?" asked the Abbé.

"Oh!" said Madame de Parolignac, "that deadly bore! How fervently he says what everyone already knows! How heavily he discusses what is not worth the slightest notice! How he appropriates without wit the wit of others! How he spoils what he steals! How he disgusts me! But he will disgust me no more; after reading a few pages of the Archdeacon, I am through."

Seated at the table was a man of learning and taste who supported what the Marquise said. Next they discussed tragedies. The Lady asked why tragedies that were unreadable were sometimes performed on the stage. The man of taste explained very clearly that a play could be popular and worthless at the same time. With just a few words he proved that it was not enough to bring in one or two of those situations found in novels and that always seduce the audience. Rather, the writer had to be original without being bizarre; to be sublime, and always natural; to know the human heart and make it speak; to be a great poet without letting any character in the play appear to be a poet; to know the language perfectly, speak it purely, with a flowing harmony, and make it rhyme without ever straining the sense.

"Whoever does not observe each of these rules," he added, "can write one or two tragedies that receive applause at the theater, but he will never take a place among the ranks of good writers. There are very few good tragedies. Some are merely idylls in well-written and well-rhymed dialogues; others are political theories that put you to sleep, or endless declamations that repulse you; still others are the reveries of fanatics in a barbarous style, filled with disconnected notions, long orations to the

---

[61] Gauchat . . . Theology: One of Voltaire's critics.

[62] Archdeacon T——: Trublet, another of Voltaire's critics.

gods—because the author has no idea how to communicate with men—false maxims, and pompous commonplaces."

Candide listened attentively to this speech and formed a great opinion of the speaker. Since the Marquise had taken care to seat him next to her, he leaned toward her and took the liberty of asking her who that man was who spoke so well.

"He is a scholar," said the Lady, "who does not play faro and whom the Abbé sometimes brings here for supper. He has a thorough knowledge of tragedies and books. He wrote a tragedy that was hissed in the theater and one book which no one has ever seen outside of his publisher's shop, except the copy that he presented to me."

"What a great man!" said Candide. "He is another Pangloss."

Then, turning toward him, he said, "Sir, no doubt you think that everything is for the best in the physical and moral worlds and that nothing could be otherwise than it is?"

"I, sir?" the scholar replied. "I think nothing of the sort. I find that we are wholly off course, that no one knows his station or his duties, what he is doing or should be doing, and that except during supper, when people are relatively gay and accommodating, the rest of the time is spent in trivial quarrels: Jansenists against Molinists,[63] men of parlement against men of the Church, men of letters against men of letters, courtiers against courtiers, financiers against the people, wives against their husbands, relatives against relatives: It is an eternal war."

Candide answered, "I've seen worse, but a wise man, who later had the misfortune to be hanged, taught me that such things are admirable: They are shadows in a beautiful picture."

"Your hanged teacher was mocking the world," said Martin. "Those shadows are horrible stains."

"It's men who make the stains," said Candide, "and they can't avoid it."

"Then it isn't their fault," said Martin.

Most of the card players, who grasped none of this exchange, were drinking. Martin continued to theorize with the scholars, and Candide recited part of his adventures to the Lady of the house.

After supper, the Marquise brought Candide into her boudoir and sat him down on a sofa.

"Well," she said, "are you still passionately in love with Miss Cunégonde of Thunder-ten-tronckh?"

"Yes, Madame," replied Candide.

The Marquise responded with a tender smile, "You answered me like a young man from Westphalia. A Frenchman would have said, 'It is true that I loved Miss Cunégonde, but when I see you, Madame, I fear that I am no longer in love with her.'"

"Alas! Madame," said Candide, "I will answer any way you want."

---

[63] **Molinists:** Followers of Luis de Molina (1535–1600), the Molinists were Jesuits who opposed the Jansenists (see note 48) in questions about the role of will and grace in attaining salvation.

"Your passion for her," said the Marquise, "began when you picked up her handkerchief; I want you to pick up my garter."

"With all my heart," said Candide, and he picked it up.

"But I would like you to put it back on me," and Candide did so.

"Look at what a foreigner you are," said the Lady. "I sometimes force my Parisian lovers to languish for two weeks, but I am giving myself to you on the first night, because one should always bestow the favors of one's country on a young man from Westphalia."

The beauty had observed two enormous diamonds on the fingers of her young visitor, and she praised them so unselfishly that they passed from Candide's fingers to hers.

While returning home with his Perigordian Abbé, Candide felt some remorse at having been unfaithful to Miss Cunégonde. The Abbé took part in his sorrow. He had got only a small share of the fifty thousand francs Candide had lost in the card game, and of the value of the two diamonds that had been half given away by him and half extorted from him. His scheme was to profit, as much as possible, from any advantages that his association with Candide could provide. He spoke to him a great deal about Cunégonde, and Candide told him that he would certainly ask the lovely Lady to forgive him for his infidelity when he saw her again in Venice.

The Perigordian multiplied his compliments and favors, and took a tender interest in everything Candide said, everything he did, everything he wanted to do.

"So you have a rendez-vous in Venice, sir?" he asked.

"Yes, Abbé," said Candide; "I absolutely must go find Miss Cunégonde."

Then, carried away by the pleasure of talking about his loved one, he recounted, as was his habit, part of his adventures with that illustrious Lady from Westphalia.

"I suppose," said the Abbé, "that Miss Cunégonde is highly cultivated and writes charming letters."

"I never got any from her," said Candide. "Remember that when I was driven from the castle because of my love for her, I couldn't write to her. Then soon afterward, I learned she was dead. Then I found her again. Then I lost her. And now I've sent a messenger to her, six thousand miles away, and I'm waiting for his return."

The Abbé listened attentively, and then appeared to be lost in thought. He soon took leave of the two foreigners after embracing them affectionately. The next day, when Candide awoke, he received a letter composed as follows:

"Sir, my very dear lover, for a week I have been ill in this city. I know that you are here. I would fly into your arms if I could move. I heard that you had passed through Bordeaux. I left the faithful Cacambo and the old woman there; they will soon follow me. The Governor of Buenos Aires got everything from me he wanted, but I still have your heart. Come, the sight of you will bring me back to life, or make me die of pleasure."

This charming, unexpected letter filled Candide with inexpressible joy, and the illness of his dear Cunégonde struck him with grief. Torn between these two sentiments, he took his gold and diamonds and drove with Martin to the hotel where Miss Cunégonde was staying. He went in, trembling with emotion, on the verge of sobbing, his heart pounding. He tried to draw apart the bed curtains; he wanted more light.

"You mustn't do that," said the maid. "Light will kill her," and she abruptly closed the curtain.

"My dear Cunégonde," said Candide, weeping, "how are you feeling? If you can't see me, talk to me at least."

"She cannot speak," said the maid.

But she drew out from the bed a plump hand, which Candide watered with tears for a long time, before filling it with diamonds. He also left a sack of gold on the armchair. In the midst of his raptures a police officer arrived, followed by the Perigordian Abbé and a squad of soldiers.

"Are these the foreigners under suspicion?" shouted the officer.

He immediately had them under guard, and ordered his henchmen to drag them to prison.

"This isn't the way they treated foreigners in Eldorado," said Candide.

"I'm more of a Manichean than ever," said Martin.

"But sir, where are you taking us?" said Candide.

"To a dungeon," said the officer.

Martin, who had regained his composure, figured out that the Lady claiming to be Cunégonde was a fraud, the Perigordian Abbé a fraud who had seized the chance to exploit Candide's innocence, and the police officer another fraud who could easily be bought off.

Rather than expose himself to the judicial process, Candide, enlightened by his advisor, and still eager to see the real Cunégonde, presented the officer with three little diamonds worth about three thousand pistoles each.

"Ah sir!" said the man with the ivory baton, "even if you committed every crime imaginable, you're still the best man in the world. Three diamonds! Worth three thousand pistoles each! Sir! I would rather die than take you to jail. They are arresting all foreigners now, but leave everything to me. I have a brother at Dieppe, in Normandy. I'll take you there, and if you have a little diamond for him, he'll take care of you, just like me."

"And why are they arresting all foreigners?" asked Candide.

The Perigordian Abbé spoke up and said, "It's because a beggar from the region of Atrebatum[64] fell under the influence of foolish ideas, and they were enough to inspire him to attempt a parricide, not like the one of May, 1610, but like the one of December, 1594, and like so many others attempted in other years, in other months, and by other beggars inspired by foolish ideas."

The officer then explained what it was all about.

"Oh, the monsters!" exclaimed Candide. "What! Such atrocities in a nation that dances and sings! Let me out of this country where monkeys attack tigers. I lived among bears in my country. Only in Eldorado did I live with human beings. In

---

[64] Atrebatum: Artois, a district that was home to Robert François Damiens, who tried to assassinate King Louis XV in 1757. December 1594 and May 1610 are the dates of two attempts on the life of King Henry IV (Henry of Navarre) of France; the second was successful.

the name of God, officer, take me to Venice, where I am supposed to meet Miss Cunégonde."

"I can only take you to Lower Normandy," said the enforcer.

And he immediately removed the chains, announced that he had made a mistake, dismissed his men, and brought Candide and Martin to Dieppe, where he left them in the hands of his brother. There was a little Dutch ship in the harbor. The Norman, with the help of three other diamonds, developed into the most helpful of men and conducted Candide and his retinue onto the vessel bound for Portsmouth in England. It was not en route to Venice, but Candide felt that he had escaped from hell, and he confidently expected to resume the direction to Venice at the first opportunity.

CHAPTER 23

How Candide and Martin came to the shores of England, and what they saw there

"Oh, Pangloss! Pangloss! Oh, Martin! Martin! Oh, my darling Cunégonde! What is this world we live in?" cried Candide on the Dutch ship.

"Something insane, something abominable," replied Martin.

"You've lived in England. Are they as insane there as in France?"

"It's just a different kind of insanity," said Martin. "You know that these two countries have been at war[65] over a few acres of snow in Canada, and that they are spending more on this lovely war than all of Canada is worth. As for whether there are more people in one country than another who ought to be put away, my limited intellect cannot say. I can only tell you that, in general, the people we are going to see are very melancholy."

As they were chatting, they arrived at Portsmouth. A large crowd of people covered the shore, looking out intently at a rather stout man[66] who was on his knees, blindfolded, on the deck of a naval ship. Four soldiers stationed in front of this man peacefully fired three bullets each into his brain; and the entire crowd went away extremely satisfied.

"What's this all about?" asked Candide, "and what evil demon is exercising his empire everywhere?"

He asked about the identity of the large man who was just ceremoniously murdered.

"He's an Admiral," was the answer.

"And why kill this Admiral?"

"It's because," came the answer, "he didn't kill enough people. He was engaged in a battle with a French Admiral and was later judged to have kept too great a distance from the enemy."

"But," said Candide, "the French Admiral was as far from the English Admiral as the latter was from the former."

---

[65] war:The war between France and England over Canada, which did not end until the Peace of Paris in 1763.

[66] stout man:The British admiral John Byng, who was executed on March 17, 1757, after being defeated by the French fleet; Voltaire had tried to stop the execution.

"That's incontestable," was the response. "But in this country they think it's good to kill an Admiral from time to time, to encourage the others."

Candide was so stunned and shocked by what he saw and heard that he would not even set foot on land. He made a deal with the Dutch Captain (though the Captain could have robbed him like the one in Surinam) to take him to Venice without delay.

The Captain was ready two days later. They sailed along the coast of France. They passed within sight of Lisbon, and Candide shuddered. They entered the Straits of Gibraltar and the Mediterranean. At last they landed in Venice.

"God be praised," said Candide, embracing Martin. "This is where I will see the lovely Cunégonde again. I trust Cacambo as much as myself. All is well, all goes well, all is proceeding as best as it can."

CHAPTER 24

About Paquette and Brother Giroflée

As soon as he was in Venice, he looked for Cacambo in all the inns, all the cafés, and among all the ladies of pleasure, without finding him. He sent messengers every day to investigate every arriving boat, great and small: no news of Cacambo.

"What!" he said to Martin. "I've had time to go from Surinam to Bordeaux, from Bordeaux to Paris, from Paris to Dieppe, from Dieppe to Portsmouth, to sail along the coast of Portugal and Spain, to cross the entire Mediterranean, to spend several months in Venice—and the lovely Cunégonde still hasn't arrived! All I've encountered in her place is one pretentious strumpet and one Perigordian Abbé! Cunégonde is surely dead, and there is nothing left for me to do but die. Oh! It would have been better to stay in the paradise of Eldorado than to return to this accursed Europe. How right you are, my dear Martin! All is but illusion and catastrophe."

He fell into a black melancholy and attended none of the fashionable operas and entertainments of the carnival season. None of the ladies tempted him in the least.

Martin said to him: "You are really very naive if you think a half-breed valet, with five or six million in his pocket, is going to track down your mistress at the other end of the world and bring her to you in Venice. If he finds her, he'll take her for himself. If he doesn't find her, he'll take someone else. I advise you to forget about your valet Cacambo and your mistress Cunégonde."

Martin was not very comforting. Candide's melancholy grew worse, and Martin never stopped proving to him that there was little virtue and little happiness in the world, except perhaps in Eldorado, where nobody can go.

While they were discussing this important matter and waiting for Cunégonde, Candide noticed a young Theatine[67] monk in the Piazza San Marco, arm in arm with a girl. The monk looked fresh, plump, and vigorous; his eyes were brilliant, his manner confident, his head erect, his step proud. The girl was very pretty and she

---

[67] **Theatine:** A Catholic religious order founded in 1524 by several monks, including Giovanni Pietro Carafa, who became Pope Paul IV; maintaining a strict vow of poverty, the order aimed to restore a sense of moral rigor and virtue to the church.

was singing. She gazed lovingly at him, and from time to time pinched his chubby cheeks.

"You'll at least admit," said Candide, "that those two are happy. Until now I've found nothing but miserable people throughout the inhabitable world, except Eldorado; but that girl and that monk, I'll bet they're very happy creatures."

"I'll bet they're not," said Martin.

"All we need to do is invite them to dinner," said Candide, "and we'll see if I'm wrong."

He immediately approached them, paid his respects, and invited them back to his inn to eat macaroni, Lombardy partridges, and caviar, and to drink wines from Montepulciano, Vesuvius, Cyprus, and Samos. The young lady blushed, the monk accepted the offer, and the girl followed, looking at Candide with surprised and confused eyes, which were dimmed by an occasional tear.

Scarcely had she entered Candide's room when she said, "What! Master Candide does not recognize Paquette!"

At these words, Candide, who had not looked at her closely until then, because he was preoccupied with Cunégonde, said, "Alas! my poor child, so it's you, you who put Dr. Pangloss in the fine shape in which I saw him?"

"Alas! sir, I'm the one," said Paquette. "I see you know all about it. I heard about the terrible suffering inflicted on the household of the Baroness and on the fair Cunégonde. I swear to you, my fate has been no less unhappy. I was a pure and innocent girl when you saw me last. A Franciscan who was my confessor seduced me with ease. The consequences were horrible. I was forced to leave the castle shortly after the Baron had driven you out with great kicks in the behind. If a famous doctor hadn't taken pity on me, I would have died. For some time, as an expression of gratitude, I was this doctor's mistress. His wife was insanely jealous and used to beat me every day without mercy; she was a Fury. The doctor was the ugliest man alive, and I the unhappiest of all creatures, constantly beaten on account of a man I did not love.

"You understand, Sir, how dangerous it is for a nagging woman to be a doctor's wife. One day, enraged by his wife's complaints, he gave her some medicine for a slight cold; it was so effective that she died two hours later in horrible convulsions. Her relatives started criminal proceedings; he fled, and I was the one put in prison. My innocence would never have saved me if I had not been rather pretty. The judge set me free, on condition that he become the doctor's successor. I was soon replaced by another woman, driven away without any support, and obliged to continue that shameful profession which you men think is so pleasant but which is a miserable abyss for us. I came to Venice to exercise the profession. Oh! Sir, if only you could imagine what it's like to be obliged to caress equally an old merchant, a lawyer, a monk, a gondolier, an Abbé; to be exposed to every kind of insult and outrage; to be frequently reduced to borrowing a skirt so that some disgusting man can have the pleasure of lifting it; to be robbed by one man of what you've earned from another; to be blackmailed by officers of the law; and to have no future in view except an atrocious old age, a hospital, and the public dump—if you could imagine all this, you'd conclude that I am one of the most miserable creatures on earth."

Paquette thus opened her heart to the good Candide in a private room, in the presence of Martin, who said to Candide, "You see, I've already won half the bet."

Brother Giroflée[68] had remained in the dining room and was having a drink while he waited for dinner.

"But," said Candide to Paquette, "you looked so gay, so happy, when I saw you; you were singing, you were caressing the monk with spontaneous affection; you seemed as happy then as you now claim to be miserable."

"Oh, Sir!" replied Paquette, "that's precisely one of the agonies of this profession. Yesterday I was robbed and beaten by an officer, and today I must appear to be in good spirits in order to give pleasure to a monk."

Candide did not wish to hear any more. He admitted that Martin was right. They sat down to eat with Paquette and the Theatine. The meal was quite amusing, and by the end, they were talking freely.

"Father," said Candide to the monk, "you seem to be enjoying a life that the whole world would envy. The flower of health blooms in your face; your features radiate with joy; you have a very pretty girl for recreation, and you seem content with your lot as a Theatine."

"Upon my word, Sir, I would like to see every Theatine at the bottom of the sea. A hundred times I have been tempted to set fire to the monastery and to run off and become a Turk. When I was fifteen my parents forced me to put on this detestable robe so they could leave more property to my accursed older brother, God confound him! Jealousy, discord, and rage fill the monastery. It is true that with a few bad sermons I bring in some money, half of which the Prior steals from me, half of which I use to procure women. But when I return to the monastery at night, I am ready to smash my head against the walls of the dormitory—and all the brothers feel the same."

Turning to Candide with his usual coolness, Martin said, "Well, haven't I won the whole bet?"

Candide gave two thousand piastres to Paquette and a thousand to brother Giroflée.

"I assure you," he said, "with that they will be happy."

"I know you're wrong," said Martin. "With those piastres you may even make them more unhappy than they ever were."

"Perhaps so," said Candide, "but one thing comforts me. I am learning that we often encounter people again whom we never thought we could find. It's quite possible that, having found my red sheep and Paquette again, I will also come across Cunégonde."

"If you do, I hope she makes you happy," said Martin, "but I strongly doubt she will."

"You're a hard man," said Candide.

"It's because I've lived," said Martin.

"But look at those gondoliers," said Candide. "Aren't they singing all day long?"

---

[68] Giroflée: His name means "gillyflower"; *Paquette* means "daisy."

"You don't see them at home, with their wives and bratty children," said Martin. "The Doge[69] has his troubles, the gondoliers have theirs. It's true that on the whole, the fate of a gondolier is preferable to that of a Doge, but I think the difference is so small that it's not worth examining."

"People talk," said Candide, "about a Senator Pococurante,[70] who lives in the fine palace on the Brenta and who generously receives foreigners. They claim he's a man who has never known sorrow."

"I'd like to see such a rare specimen," said Martin.

Candide promptly sent word to ask Lord Pococurante's permission to see him the next day.

Chapter 25

A visit to Lord Pococurante, nobleman of Venice

Candide and Martin took a gondola down the Brenta and arrived at the noble Pococurante's palace. The gardens were ordered harmoniously and adorned with beautiful marble statues, and the palace itself was an architectural splendor. The master of the house, a man of sixty, and very wealthy, greeted his two curious visitors politely but with very little warmth, which disappointed Candide and impressed Martin.

First, two pretty and neatly attired girls served them cocoa whipped to a froth. Candide could not resist praising their beauty, grace, and dexterity.

"They are quite amusing creatures," said Senator Pococurante. "I sometimes take them to bed with me, for I am very tired of the ladies in town, their coquetries, their jealousies, their quarrels, their moods, their pettiness, their vanity, their foolishness, as well as the sonnets you have to compose or commission for them. But now these two girls are beginning to bore me too."

After the meal, Candide strolled through a long gallery and was surprised by the beauty of the paintings. He asked which master had painted the first two.

"They are by Raphael," said the Senator. "I bought them out of vanity at a high price a few years ago. People say they are the finest in Italy, but they do not give me any pleasure. The colors are too dark, the figures are not rounded enough and do not stand out enough, the draperies do not look like real cloth at all. In short, in spite of what they say, I do not consider them to be true imitations of Nature. I only like a painting when I think I am seeing Nature itself, but there are no paintings of this kind. I possess many paintings, but I do not look at them any more."

Pococurante had a concerto performed as they waited for dinner. Candide found the music delicious.

"That noise," said Pococurante, "may be amusing for a half hour, but if it goes on longer it tires everybody, though no one dares to admit it. The music of today is

---

[69] **doge:** Chief magistrate of the republic of Venice.

[70] **Pococurante:** The name means "small care."

merely an art of performing difficult pieces, and what is merely difficult cannot be pleasing for very long.

"Perhaps I would like opera better, had they not discovered the formula for making it a revolting freak show. I have nothing against those who wish to see bad tragedies set to music, where the scenes are crudely written to introduce two or three ridiculous songs that show off an actress's windpipe. I have nothing against those who are willing or able to swoon with pleasure when a eunuch twitters the role of Caesar or Cato and struts awkwardly around the stage. But as for myself, I have long given up these trifles, which are now considered the glory of Italy, and for which Sovereigns pay so extravagantly."

Candide argued a little, but with discretion. Martin was entirely of the Senator's opinion.

They sat down to dine, and after an excellent dinner, they went into the library. Candide, seeing a superbly bound volume of Homer, complimented the most illustrious Lord on his good taste.

"Here," he said, "is a book that used to be a delight to the great Pangloss, the best philosopher in Germany."

"It has no such effect on me," said Pococurante coldly. "I was once under the delusion that reading gave me pleasure. But that endless series of battles that are all alike, those gods who are always intervening without doing anything decisive, that Helen who is the cause of the war and who hardly plays a role in the story, that Troy which is forever besieged and never captured — all of this bores me to death. I have had opportunities to ask scholars if reading it bores them as much as it does me. All the sincere ones confessed that the book puts them to sleep but added that one must always have it in one's library as a monument to antiquity, like those rusty coins that cannot be spent."

"Your Excellency doesn't have the same opinion of Virgil?" said Candide.

"I grant," said Pococurante, "that the second, fourth, and sixth books of his *Aeneid* are excellent. But as for the pious Aeneas, the strong Cloanthes, the trusty Achates, the little Ascanius, the idiotic King Latinus, the bourgeois Amata, the insipid Lavinia, I can imagine nothing more cold or unpleasant. I prefer Tasso and the fantasy stories of Ariosto."

"Dare I ask, Sir," said Candide, "if you do not take pleasure in reading Horace?"

"Some of his maxims," said Pococurante, "can be of use to a man of the world, and since they are compressed into energetic verse, they easily become engraved in the memory. But I care very little about his journey to Brundisium, or his description of a bad dinner, or the quarrel between two ruffians, one named something like Pupilus, whose words, he says, *were full of pus,* and the other whose words *were like vinegar.*[71] I can read only with extreme disgust his coarse verses against old women and witches, and I do not see what merit there can be in telling his friend Maecenas that if the latter places him in the ranks of lyric poets, he will strike the stars with his sublime forehead. Fools admire everything in an author who has a good reputation. I read only for myself; I like only what I can use."

---

[71] *pus . . . vinegar:* Voltaire here alludes to Horace's *Satires* 1.7, which Pococurante is garbling.

Candide, who had been brought up never to judge anything for himself, was astonished by what he heard. Martin found Pococurante's way of thinking quite reasonable.

"Oh, here is Cicero," said Candide. "This great man—I can't imagine that you tire of reading him?"

"I never read him," replied the Venetian. "What does it matter to me if he defended Rabirius and Cluentius? I have enough lawsuits of my own to deal with. I was more inclined to appreciate his philosophical works, but when I saw that he doubted everything, I concluded that I already knew as much as he, and that I did not need anyone's help to become ignorant."

"Ah, here are eighty volumes of the proceedings of a scientific academy," exclaimed Martin. "There may be some good things in there."

"There would be," said Pococurante, "if any of the authors of this hotchpotch had invented even a new way of producing pins. But there is nothing in these books except vain theoretical systems, and not a single useful thing."

"Look at all those plays over there!" said Candide. "In Italian, Spanish, French!"

"Yes," said the Senator, "there are three thousand, and not three dozen good ones. As for those collections of sermons, which as a whole are not worth one page of Seneca, and all those thick volumes of theology, you may be sure that neither I, nor anybody else, ever opens them."

Martin noticed some shelves loaded with English books.

"I suppose," he said, "that a republican would derive pleasure from most of these books written in defense of freedom."

"Yes," said Pococurante, "it is noble to write what one thinks; it is the privilege of humankind. Throughout Italy people write only what they do not think. The inhabitants of the land of the Caesars and Antonines do not dare to have a single idea without the permission of a Dominican. I would support the liberty that inspires English writers, if only selfishness and the spirit of faction did not corrupt all that is good in that precious freedom."

Candide, noticing a volume of Milton, asked him if he did not regard this author as a great man.

"Who?" said Pococurante. "This barbarian who writes a long commentary on the first chapter of Genesis in ten books of harsh verse? This crude imitator of the Greeks who disfigures the Creation and who, even though the Scriptures represent the Eternal Being producing the universe with His words, has the Messiah pull out a big compass from a heavenly closet in order to design His work? Am I supposed to admire a man who spoils Tasso's images of Hell and the Devil? who disguises Lucifer sometimes as a toad, sometimes as a pygmy? who has him give the same speech a hundred times and makes him argue about theology? who takes so seriously Ariosto's comical story about the invention of firearms that he makes the demons shoot cannons in Heaven? Neither I nor anyone else in Italy could draw pleasure from such pitiful absurdities. The marriage of Sin and Death, and the snakes to which Sin gives birth, make any man vomit who has the slightest sense of good taste. And his long description of a hospital can be interesting only to gravediggers. This obscure, bizarre, and disgusting poem was despised when it was published; today

I simply treat it as it was treated in the author's country by his contemporaries. Furthermore, I say what I think, and whether or not others agree matters very little to me."

Candide was distressed by these remarks. He respected Homer, and he liked Milton a bit.

"Alas!" he whispered to Martin, "I'm afraid this man may have an imperious contempt for our German poets."

"There's no harm in that," said Martin.

"Oh, what a superior man," Candide hissed. "What a great genius is this Pococurante! Nothing can please him."

After they had reviewed all the books in this manner, they went down into the garden. Candide praised the abundance of beauty.

"I know of nothing in such bad taste," said the Master. "We have nothing here but trifles; tomorrow I am going to redesign it on a nobler plan."

When the two curious travelers had taken leave of His Excellency, Candide said to Martin, "Well, you must admit that we just saw the happiest of men, for he is above everything he possesses."

"Don't you see," said Martin, "that he is disgusted with everything he possesses? Plato said a long time ago that the best stomachs are not those which refuse all food."

"But," said Candide, "isn't there joy in criticizing everything, in perceiving faults where other people think they see beauties?"

"That's to say," replied Martin, "that there is joy in having no joy?"

"Oh well!" said Candide. "So the only happy person in the world will be myself, when I see Miss Cunégonde again."

"It's always a good thing to hope," said Martin.

Yet the days flowed by, and then the weeks. Cacambo did not appear, and Candide was so immersed in his own sorrow that he did not even wonder why Paquette and Brother Giroflée had never returned to thank him.

CHAPTER 26

How Candide and Martin had supper with six foreigners, and who they were

One evening when Candide, accompanied by Martin, was about to sit down to eat with the foreigners who were lodging in the same hotel, a man whose face was the color of soot came up behind him, took him by the arm, and said, "Be ready to leave with us, do not fail."

Candide turned and saw Cacambo. Nothing but the sight of Cunégonde could have surprised and pleased him more. He nearly went mad with joy. He embraced his dear friend.

"Cunégonde must surely be here. Where is she? Take me to her, let me die of joy with her."

"Cunégonde isn't here," said Cacambo, "she's in Constantinople."

"Good heavens! In Constantinople! But even if she were in China, I'd leave in a second; let's go!"

"We'll leave after supper," replied Cacambo. "I can't tell you more. I'm a slave. My Master awaits me, I must wait on him. Don't say a word. Eat and be ready."

Candide, his heart pounding, his mind in turmoil, torn between joy and sorrow, delighted to see his faithful agent again and astonished to find him a slave, and filled with the thought of finding his mistress again, sat down with Martin, who was observing these events coolly, and with six foreigners who had come to spend the carnival season in Venice.

Cacambo, who was pouring the drinks for one of these foreigners, leaned toward his Master near the end of the meal and said, "Sire, Your Majesty may leave when he wishes; the ship is ready."

Having said these words, he walked away. The astonished guests looked at each other without uttering a single word. Then another servant approached his Master and said, "Sire, Your Majesty's carriage is in Padua and the boat is ready."

The Master gestured and the servant left. The other guests looked at each other again, and their mutual surprise redoubled. A third valet likewise approached a third foreigner and said, "Sire, I assure you, Your Majesty should not stay here any longer. I will prepare everything." And he promptly disappeared.

By now Candide and Martin were sure it was a carnival masquerade.

A fourth servant said to the fourth Master, "Your Majesty may depart when he wishes," and left like the others. The fifth valet said the same thing to a fifth Master. But the sixth valet spoke differently to the sixth foreigner, who was seated next to Candide: "I swear, Sire, they will not give any more credit to Your Majesty, or to me; we could easily be locked up tonight, you and I. I am going to take care of my own affairs. Farewell."

With all the servants gone, the six foreigners, Candide, and Martin remained in deep silence. Finally Candide broke through it.

"Gentlemen," said he, "this is a remarkable jest. Why are you all behaving like royalty? I assure you that neither I nor Martin is a King."

It was Cacambo's master who spoke up gravely, saying in Italian, "I am not jesting. My name is Achmet III.[72] I was the Grand Sultan for many years; I dethroned my brother; my nephew dethroned me; my viziers had their throats cut; I am permitted to finish out my life in my old harem; my nephew, the current Grand Sultan, Mahmoud, allows me to travel; and I have come to spend the carnival season in Venice."

The young man next to Achmet spoke next, "My name is Ivan; I was Emperor of all the Russias; I was dethroned as an infant; my mother and father were locked up; I was reared in jail; I sometimes get permission to travel, in the company of guards; and I have come to spend the carnival season in Venice."

The third said, "I am Charles Edward, King of England; my father ceded me his rights to the kingdom; I struggled to maintain them; the hearts of eight hundred of

---

[72] **Achmet III:** This ruler and the others named are all drawn from history and were either deposed early or defeated. Achmet III of Turkey lived from 1673 to 1736; Ivan VI of Russia, from 1740 to 1764; Charles Edward Stuart (Bonnie Prince Charlie) of England and Scotland, from 1720 to 1788; Augustus III of Poland, from 1697 to 1763; Stanislas Leczinski of Poland, from 1677 to 1766; and Thedore von Neuhof, briefly king of Corsica, from 1690 to 1756.

my supporters were ripped out and thrown in their faces; I was put in prison; I am going to Rome to visit the King, my father, who was dethroned like me and my grandfather; and I have come to spend the carnival season in Venice."

The fourth then spoke up: "I am the King of the Poles; the fortunes of war deprived me of my hereditary states; my father experienced the same reversal; I resign myself to Providence like Sultan Achmet, Emperor Ivan, and King Charles Edward, may they be granted long lives; and I have come to spend the carnival season in Venice."

The fifth said: "I am also King of the Poles; I lost my kingdom twice; but Providence has given me another state, where I have done more good than all of the Kings of the Sarmatians were able to do on the banks of the Vistula; I too resign myself to Providence; and I have come to spend the carnival season in Venice."

It remained for the sixth monarch to speak.

"Gentlemen," said he, "I am not as great a Master as you are, but even so, I too was once a King. I am Theodore; I was elected King of Corsica; I used to be called 'Your Majesty,' and now I am lucky if I am called 'Sir'; I used to mint new coins, and now I am penniless; I used to have two secretaries of state and now I do not even have a valet; I used to sit on a throne and I ended up lying for years on straw in a London prison. I fear I will be treated the same here, though I have come, like Your Majesties, to spend the carnival season in Venice."

The five other Kings listened to this speech with noble compassion. Each gave King Theodore twenty sequins to obtain suits and shirts. Candide presented him with a diamond worth two thousand sequins.

"Who is this ordinary citizen," said the five Kings, "who is in a position to give a hundred times more than any of us, and who voluntarily gives it?"

Just as they were leaving the table, there arrived at the same hotel four other Serene Highnesses who had also lost their states through the fortunes of war, and who had come to spend the rest of the carnival season in Venice. But Candide took no notice of these newcomers. His only concern was to go find his dear Cunégonde in Constantinople.

CHAPTER 27

Candide's voyage to Constantinople

Faithful Cacambo had convinced the Turkish captain who was taking Sultan Achmet to Constantinople to admit Candide and Martin on board. The two of them embarked after prostrating themselves before His Miserable Highness. On the way, Candide said to Martin:

"We had supper with six dethroned Kings, and I even gave alms to one of them. Perhaps there are many other Princes even more unfortunate. As for me, I've only lost a hundred sheep, and I am flying into the arms of Cunégonde. My dear Martin, once again Pangloss was right: all is well."

"I wish it were so," said Martin.

"But," said Candide, "that was an extraordinary adventure we just had in Venice.

No one before ever saw six dethroned Kings dining together in an inn or even heard of such a thing."

"It is no more extraordinary," said Martin, "than most of the things that have happened to us. It is very common for Kings to be dethroned. And as for the honor we had to dine with them, that is a trifle unworthy of our attention. What does it matter with whom you have supper, as long as you eat well?"

Scarcely was Candide on the ship than he embraced his old valet, his friend Cacambo.

"Well, what is Cunégonde doing?" he asked him. "Is she still a marvel of beauty? Does she still love me? Is she in good health? Surely you have bought a palace in Constantinople for her?"

"My dear master," answered Cacambo, "Cunégonde is scrubbing dishes on the shores of the Propontis for a Prince who has very few dishes. She's a slave in the household of a former Sovereign named Ragotski.[73] He is in exile and the Grand Turk supports him with three crowns a day. But what is even worse, she has lost her beauty and become horribly ugly."

"Ah! beautiful or ugly," said Candide, "I am an honorable man, and I am bound to love her forever. But how was she reduced to such an abject condition when I gave you five or six million?"

"All right," said Cacambo, "I had to give two million to Señor Don Fernando d'Ibaraa y Figueora y Mascarenes y Lampourdos y Souza, Governor of Buenos Aires, for permission to take back Miss Cunégonde. Then a pirate gallantly stole the rest. This pirate brought us to Cape Matapan, Melos, Nicaria, Samos, Petra, to the Dardanelles, Marmora, and Scutari. Cunégonde and the old woman are servants with that Prince I was telling you about, and I am a slave of the dethroned Sultan."

"What a horrifying series of calamities!" said Candide. "Yet, after all, I still have some diamonds. I will easily rescue Miss Cunégonde. What a pity that she's become so ugly."

Then turning toward Martin, he asked: "Which of us do you think is the most to be pitied, Emperor Achmet, Emperor Ivan, King Charles Edward, or me?"

"I have no idea," said Martin. "I would have to be inside your hearts to know."

"Ah!" said Candide. "If Pangloss were here, he would know, and he would tell us what to think."

"I don't know," said Martin, "what kind of scales your Pangloss had for weighing the miseries of humankind, and for appraising their pains. The one thing I take for granted is that there are millions of people on earth who are a hundred times more to be pitied than King Charles Edward, Emperor Ivan, and Sultan Achmet."

"That may well be true," said Candide.

In a few days they arrived in the Bosporus. Candide began by purchasing Cacambo's liberation at a high price. Then, without wasting any time, he flung himself and his companions into a galley ship to go search for Cunégonde on the shores of Propontis, however ugly she might be.

---

[73]**Ragotski:** Francis Leopold Rakoczy (1676–1735), Hungarian king of Transylvania from 1704 to 1711, who went into Turkey in exile after refusing to accept defeat at the hands of the Austrians.

Among the crew condemned to the galleys were two convicts who were rowing very badly, and upon whose bare shoulders the Levantine[74] Captain occasionally applied a few lashes of a bullwhip. Naturally intrigued, Candide looked at them more closely than the other convicts and moved toward them with pity. Some features of their disfigured faces struck him as having a slight resemblance to Pangloss and that unfortunate Jesuit, that Baron, that brother of Miss Cunégonde. This image moved and saddened him. He looked at them again more closely.

"Truly," he said to Cacambo, "if I hadn't seen the hanging of Dr. Pangloss, and if I hadn't had the misfortune of killing the Baron, I would swear that they are rowing in this galley."

At the words "Baron" and "Pangloss," the two convicts let out a loud cry, stopped rowing, and dropped their oars. The Levantine Captain rushed over with the whip and redoubled his strokes.

"Stop, stop, Sir," cried Candide. "I will give you as much money as you want."

"What! It's Candide!" cried one of the convicts.

"What! It's Candide!" cried the other.

"Is this a dream?" said Candide. "Am I awake? Am I really on this ship? Is that the Baron whom I killed? Is that Dr. Pangloss whom I saw hanged?"

"It is, it is!" they replied.

"What! Is that the great philosopher?" said Martin.

"Now, Mr. Levantine Captain," said Candide, "how much money do you want for the ransom of the gentleman from Thunder-ten-tronckh, one of the leading Barons of the Empire, and Mr. Pangloss, the most profound metaphysician of Germany?"

"Dog of a Christian," answered the Levantine captain, "since these two dogs of Christian slaves are Barons and metaphysicians, which is obviously a great honor in your country, you will give me fifty thousand sequins for them."

"You shall have them, Sir. Take me in a flash back to Constantinople, and you will be paid on the spot. No, take me first to Lady Cunégonde."

But after Candide's first offer, the Levantine Captain had already turned the prow toward the city, and the oars began to move faster than a bird's wings cleave the air.

Candide embraced the Baron and Pangloss a hundred times. "How is it that I didn't kill you, my dear Baron? And my dear Pangloss, how is it that you're alive after being hanged? And why are you both on the Turkish galleys?"

"Is it really true that my dear sister is in this country?" asked the Baron.

"Yes," replied Cacambo.

"At last I have found my dear Candide," cried Pangloss.

Candide introduced them to Martin and Cacambo. Everyone embraced, everyone spoke at the same time. The galley ship flew swiftly, and soon they were in the port. They summoned a Jew, who paid fifty thousand sequins for one of Candide's rings worth a hundred thousand, and who swore by Abraham that he could not offer more. Candide immediately paid the ransom for the Baron and Pangloss. The latter threw himself at his liberator's feet and bathed them with tears; the former thanked him with a nod and promised to pay back the money at the first opportunity.

---

[74] **Levantine:** From the Levant, the lands bordering the eastern Mediterranean Sea.

"But is it really possible that my sister is in Turkey?" he asked.

"Nothing is more possible," Cacambo answered, "because she is scrubbing dishes for a Transylvanian prince."

They promptly summoned two Jews. Candide sold two more diamonds, and they all set out in another galley ship to rescue Miss Cunégonde.

CHAPTER 28

What happened to Candide, Cunégonde, Pangloss, Martin, etc.

"Forgive me once again," said Candide to the Baron. "Forgive me, my Reverend Father, for having run you through with a thrust of my sword."

"Forget about it," said the Baron. "I was a bit too hasty, I admit. But since you want to know how fortune brought me to the galleys, I will tell you. After my wound was cured by an apothecary, who was a brother in the Jesuit college, I was captured in a Spanish raid, abducted, and imprisoned in Buenos Aires just at the time my sister left. I asked permission to return to Rome to work in the Father General's office. Instead, I was sent to Constantinople to be the chaplain in the French ambassador's office. One evening, scarcely a week after I took up my new position, I met a young, good-looking page in the Sultan's court. It was hot. The young man wished to have a bath, and I took the opportunity to have one too. I did not know that it was a capital crime for a Christian to be found naked with a young Muslim. A cadi sentenced me to be beaten a hundred times with a cane on the soles of the feet, and condemned me to the galleys. I do not think there has ever been a more horrible miscarriage of justice. But I would like to know why my sister is in the kitchen of a Transylvanian Sovereign who is in exile among the Turks."

"And you, my dear Pangloss," said Candide, "how is it that I am able to see you again?"

"It is true," said Pangloss, "that you saw me hanged. Of course, I was supposed to be burned, but you will recall that it began to rain heavily when they were preparing to cook me. The storm was so violent that they lost hope of kindling the fire. They hanged me because they could do no better. A surgeon purchased my corpse, brought me home, dissected me. First he made a cross-shaped incision from my navel up and out to my collarbones. Never had a man been hanged more poorly than I had been. The Executioner for High Affairs of the Holy Inquisition, a subdeacon, really knew how to burn people with style, but he was not accustomed to hanging them. The rope was wet and did not slip smoothly; it became knotted; in short, I was still breathing. The cross-shaped incision released such a great cry from inside me that my surgeon fell over backward. Thinking that he was dissecting the Devil, he ran out, in mortal terror, falling down the staircase as he left. His wife rushed in from a nearby room when she heard the commotion. She saw me lying on the table with my cross-shaped incision. Even more frightened than her husband, she fled and stumbled over him as she left. When they had calmed down a bit, I heard her say to him, 'My dear, whatever led you to dissect a heretic? Don't you know, the Devil is always in the bodies of those people? I am going to get a priest to exorcise him right away.'

"I shuddered at these words, and I gathered whatever strength I still had left to call out, 'Take pity on me!' Finally the Portuguese barber took courage. He sewed up my skin. His wife even took care of me. I was on my feet in two weeks. The barber found me a job as lackey to a Knight of Malta who was headed for Venice. But my Master had no money to pay me, so I began to work for a Venetian merchant, and I accompanied him to Constantinople.

"One day I had an impulse to go into a mosque. It was empty except for an old imam and a very pretty young worshipper saying her prayers. Her bosom was completely uncovered, and between her breasts was a lovely bouquet of tulips, roses, anemones, buttercups, hyacinths, and primroses. She dropped her bouquet. I picked it up and I put it back in place with meticulous care. I took so much time replacing it that the imam became angry, and when he saw that I was a Christian he called for help. They brought me before the cadi, who sentenced me to a hundred strokes with a cane on the soles of the feet, and condemned me to the galleys. I was chained up in the very same galley ship and behind the same oar as the Baron. In that galley there were also four young men from Marseilles, five Neapolitan priests, and two monks from Corfu, who told us that similar things occurred every day. The Baron claims that he has endured greater injustice than I. I argue, however, that it is more lawful to replace a bouquet of flowers on a young woman's bosom than to be naked with a young male page. We were debating the question constantly and receiving twenty lashes of the bullwhip per day, when the chain of events of this universe led you to our galley in order to ransom us."

"Well, my dear Pangloss," Candide said, "when you were being hanged, dissected, beaten black and blue, and when you were rowing in the galleys, did you still think that everything is for the best in this world?"

"I still hold to my original opinion," replied Pangloss. "For after all, I am a philosopher, and it is not appropriate for me to take back my word. Leibniz is never mistaken. Moreover, preestablished harmony is the finest aspect of the universe, along with the plenum and subtle matter."[75]

CHAPTER 29

How Candide found Cunégonde and the old woman again

While Candide, the Baron, Pangloss, Martin, and Cacambo were reciting their adventures, theorizing about contingent and noncontingent events in the universe, and having debates about cause and effect, moral and physical evil, free will and determinism, and the consolations available to a galley slave in Turkey, they landed on the shore of the Propontis and came to the house of the Transylvanian Prince. The first thing they saw was Cunégonde and the old woman hanging towels on a line to dry.

The Baron turned pale at this sight. Candide, the tender lover, seeing his beautiful Cunégonde's swarthy complexion, bloodshot eyes, withered bosom, wrinkled

---

[75] **plenum and subtle matter:** These terms come from Leibniz's theories and signify the matter that fills space (*plenum*) and the spiritual entities of the universe (subtle matter, or *materia subtilis*), including mind, soul, and spirit.

cheeks, and peeling red skin, recoiled three paces in horror, then approached her out of respect for decency. She embraced Candide and her brother. They embraced the old woman, and Candide paid the ransom for her and Cunégonde.

There was a little farm in the area. The old woman suggested to Candide that they settle into it until the destiny of the group improved. Cunégonde did not know she had become ugly; no one told her. She reminded Candide of his promise in so firm a tone that the good Candide dared not refuse her. He thus informed the Baron of their intention to marry.

"I will never accept," said the Baron, "such baseness from her, and such insolence from you. I will not allow myself to be disgraced in this way. It would prevent my sister's children from entering the noble orders in Germany.[76] No, never will my sister marry anyone but a Baron of the Empire."

Cunégonde threw herself at his feet and bathed them with tears. He was inflexible.

"You stubborn idiot," said Candide, "I rescued you from the galleys, I paid for your ransom and freed your sister. She was washing dishes here, and she's ugly. I have the generosity to make her my wife and you still protest against it. I would kill you again if I gave in to my anger."

"You may kill me again," said the Baron, "but you will never marry my sister while I am alive."

CHAPTER 30

Conclusion

In his heart, Candide had no desire to marry Cunégonde. But the Baron's extreme arrogance made him resolve to conclude the marriage, and Cunégonde pressed him so strongly that he could not take back his word. He consulted Pangloss, Martin, and the trusty Cacambo. Pangloss wrote a fine treatise in which he proved that the Baron had no legal rights over his sister and that, in accordance with all the laws of the Empire, she could marry Candide by the left hand.[77] Martin was in favor of throwing the Baron into the sea. Cacambo suggested they send him back to the Levantine Captain to serve his full term on the galleys, and then send him to the Father General in Rome on the first available ship. This idea was received very favorably. The old woman approved of it. They kept it secret from the Baron's sister. The plan was executed at a modest expense, and they had the pleasure of snaring a Jesuit and punishing the pride of a German baron at the same time.

It is quite natural to imagine that after so many disasters, Candide, now married to his mistress and living with the philosopher Pangloss, the philosopher Martin, the prudent Cacambo, and the old woman, and having also saved many diamonds from the land of the ancient Incas, must have enjoyed the most agreeable life in the world. But he was so cheated by the Jews that he soon found himself with nothing

---

[76] noble orders in Germany: Assemblies of knights.

[77] marry . . . left hand: A morganatic marriage in which the member of the lower rank gives up any rights to the rank or property of the other.

more than the little farm. His wife, growing uglier every day, became shrewish and intolerable. The old woman was infirm and even nastier than Cunégonde. Cacambo, who labored in the garden and traveled to Constantinople to sell vegetables, was worn out with toil and cursed his fate. Pangloss was in despair because he was not a star in some German university. As for Martin, fully persuaded that people are equally wretched everywhere, he bore life with patience.

Candide, Martin, and Pangloss sometimes debated metaphysical and moral issues. From the windows of the farm they often saw ships loaded with effendis, pashas, and cadis being exiled to Lemnos, Mytilene, and Erzerum. They saw other cadis, pashas, and effendis take the place of the exiles, and suffer exile in their turn. They saw heads being neatly impaled for presentation at the Sublime Port.[78] These spectacles intensified their arguments, and when they were not debating, the boredom was so excessive that the old woman dared one day to say to them:

"I'd like to know which is worse—to be raped a hundred times by Negro pirates, to have a buttock cut off, to run the gauntlet among the Bulgars, to be whipped and hanged in an auto-da-fé, to be dissected, to row on the galleys, in short, to experience every misfortune we have known—or to stay here without anything to do?"

"That's a deep question," said Candide.

These remarks gave birth to new reflections, and it was Martin who concluded that human beings are destined to live in either convulsive anxiety or lethargic boredom. Candide did not accept this, but he offered no alternative. Pangloss admitted that he had always suffered horribly, but having once affirmed that everything in the world functioned marvellously, he kept affirming it, and never believed it.

One event especially served to confirm Martin in his dreadful principles, to make Candide hesitate more than ever before, and to embarrass Pangloss. It was the arrival at their farm of Paquette and Brother Giroflée, in the most extreme misery. They had quickly wasted their three thousand piastres; they had parted; come back together; quarreled; been put in prison; escaped; and in the end Brother Giroflée had become a Turk. Paquette practiced her trade throughout, and never earned anything.

"I was right," said Martin to Candide, "that your gifts would soon be squandered and would only make them more miserable. You were rolling in millions of piastres, you and Cacambo, and you were no happier than Brother Giroflée and Paquette."

"Ah! Ah!" said Pangloss to Paquette. "Heaven has brought you back to us, my poor child! Do you realize that you cost me the tip of my nose, an eye, and an ear? Look at you! Oh! What a world!"

This new adventure led them to philosophize more than ever.

There lived in the region a very famous dervish[79] who was reputed to be the best philosopher in Turkey. They went to consult him. Pangloss spoke for everyone: "Master, we have come to ask you to tell us why such a strange animal as man was ever created."

"Why meddle in that?" said the dervish. "Is it any business of yours?"

---

[78] **Sublime Port:** The main gate of the sultan's palace.

[79] **dervish:** Member of an Islamic religious order.

"But Reverend Father," said Candide, "there is a horrible amount of evil in the world."

"What difference does it make," said the dervish, "if there is good or evil? When His Highness sends a ship to Egypt, does he worry about whether or not the mice are comfortable on board?"

"Then what is to be done?" said Pangloss.

"Keep silent," said the dervish.

"It was my humble expectation," said Pangloss, "that I could theorize a bit with you about effects and causes, the best of possible worlds, the origin of evil, the nature of the soul, and preestablished harmony."

At these words the dervish slammed the door in their faces.

During this conversation, news was spreading that the mufti and two viziers of the divan[80] had been strangled in Constantinople, and that many of their friends had been impaled. This catastrophe created a great uproar everywhere, for a few hours. Pangloss, Candide, and Martin, on their way back to the little farm, met a kindly old man, enjoying the fresh air by his door under a grove of orange trees. Pangloss, who was as curious as he was philosophical, asked him the name of the mufti who had just been strangled.

"I have no idea," replied the kindly old man, "and I have never known the name of any mufti or any vizier. I am entirely ignorant of the matter you refer to. I assume that in general those who meddle in public affairs perish, sometimes miserably, and that they deserve it. But I never think about what people are doing in Constantinople. I am content to sell them the fruits of the garden that I cultivate."

Having said these words, he invited the foreigners into his home. His two daughters and two sons served them several kinds of sherbet which they had made themselves, Turkish cream flavored with candied citron, oranges, lemons, limes, pineapples, pistachios, and mocha coffee unadulterated by the bad coffee of Batavia and the West Indies. Afterwards the kindly old Muslim's daughters sprinkled perfume on the beards of Candide, Pangloss, and Martin.

"You must possess," said Candide to the Turk, "a vast and magnificent estate?"

"I only have twenty acres," replied the Turk. "I cultivate them with my children. Work keeps away three great evils: boredom, vice, and indigence."

While returning to his farm, Candide reflected deeply on the Turk's words. He said to Pangloss and Martin, "That kindly old man seems to have made a better life than the six kings we had the honor of eating supper with."

"Power and glory," said Pangloss, "are very dangerous, as all the philosophers tell us. For indeed, Eglon, King of the Moabites, was assassinated by Ehud; Absalom was hanged by his hair and pierced with three spears; King Nadab, son of Jeroboam, was killed by Baasha; King Elah by Zimri; Ahaziah by Jehu; Athaliah by Jehoiada; Kings Jehoiakim, Jeconiah, and Zedekiah became slaves. You know how Croesus perished, and Astyages, Darius, Dionysius of Syracuse, Pyrrhus, Perseus, Hannibal, Jugurtha, Ariovistus, Caesar, Pompey, Nero, Otho, Vitellius, Domitian, Richard II of England,

---

[80] **viziers of the divan:** Advisors to the sultan; a mufti is an Islamic interpreter of the religious law.

Edward II, Henry IV, Richard III, Mary Stuart, Charles I, the three Henrys of France, the Emperor Henry IV. You know . . ."

"I know," said Candide, "that we must cultivate our garden."

"You are right," said Pangloss, "for when man was placed in the Garden of Eden, he was placed there *ut operaretur eum*,[81] in order to work on it, which proves that humankind was not made for rest."

"Let us work without theorizing," said Martin. "That is the only way to make life bearable."

The little society entered into this laudable plan. Each began to exercise his talents. The little bit of earth became productive. Cunégonde was undeniably very ugly, but she baked excellent pastries. Paquette embroidered. The old woman took care of the linen. No one failed to contribute, not even Brother Giroflée. He was a very good carpenter and even became a sociable fellow.

And sometimes Pangloss would say to Candide, "All events are linked together in the best of all possible worlds. For after all, if you had not been driven from a fine castle with great kicks in the behind for loving Miss Cunégonde, if you had not been seized by the Inquisition, if you had not crossed South America on foot, if you had not thrust a sword into the Baron, if you had not lost your sheep from the good country of Eldorado, you would not be here eating candied citrons and pistachios."

"That is well said," replied Candide, "but we must cultivate our garden."

---

[81] *ut operaretur eum:* Latin for "so that he should work it."

The Spirit of Inquiry

Voltaire's *Candide,* a relentless attack on human illusions, rigid dogma, and institutional cruelty of all kinds, is a reflection of the late-seventeenth- and eighteenth-century spirit of inquiry in Europe that encouraged people to question their cultural assumptions and their accepted place in the world. Confident in their ability to discern the laws of nature and perhaps in turn those of human society, ENLIGHTENMENT thinkers—called the *philosophes* in France—were determined to shrug off conventional ways of thinking in order not only to see the world anew but also to dismantle old institutions and design new ones along better models. In contrast to Voltaire's Pangloss, who believes that this is the best of all possible worlds, the *philosophes* felt that society was ready for a major overhaul, and by using reason, empirical investigation, and mechanical ingenuity, they hoped to overcome superstition, prejudice, and the abuses of religion and politics. Faith in the power of reason to effect change brought with it a strong sense of hope that—through education, reflection, and the application of new ideas and inventions—human beings might progress to a state of near perfection.

DARING TO KNOW

In "What Is the Enlightenment?" (1784), the great German philosopher Immanuel Kant (1724–1804) defines enlightenment as "man's release from his self-incurred tutelage. Tutelage is man's inability to make use of his understanding without direction from another." In the Horatian motto *sapere aude*— "dare to know"—Kant found the principle upon which Western philosophy hinged in the eighteenth century: Dare to reason independently and question authority, even

The Engine to Raise Water by Fire, 1747. Engraving *A diagram of Newcomen's steam engine for* Universal Magazine. *(Private collection / Bridgeman Art Library)*

if it means toppling the very foundations of culture and society, and even if it results—as it did for Voltaire, Diderot, Rousseau, and other *philosophes*—in imprisonment or exile.

This revolution in man's thinking was driven, in part, by the earlier advances of philosophers such as **René Descartes** (1596–1650) and **Gottfried Wilhelm Leibniz** (1646–1716) and astronomers and natural philosophers (scientists) such as Nicolas Copernicus (1473–1543), Galileo Galilei (1564–1642), and Sir Isaac Newton (1642–1727). Impatient with the limits, contradictions, and abstractions of conventional logic and mathematics, Descartes set out to reduce the principles of analysis to some basic laws. Similar to Baien

ruh-NAY day-KART
GAHT-freed VIL-helm
LIBE-nits

◄ Ascent of the Montgolfier Brothers' Hot-Air Balloon, 1783
This color engraving depicts the Montgolfier brothers' famous balloon flight before an audience of the royal family at Versailles. (The Bridgeman Art Library International Ltd.)

François Nicolas Martinet, *Jean-Pierre Blanchard's Flying Machine.* Eighteenth-Century Color Lithograph

Scientists of the eighteenth century became fascinated with theories of flight; some theories were more fantastic than others. (Musée de l'Air et de l'Espace, Le Bourget, France / Lautes-Giraudon-Bridgeman Art Library)

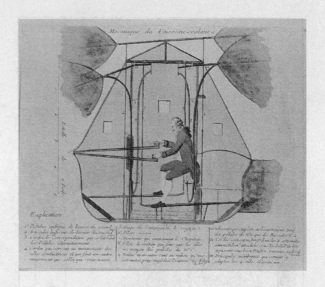

p. 348

Miura in Japan, Descartes determined in ***Discourse on Method*** (1637) that his first rule would be "to accept nothing as true which I did not clearly recognize to be so: that is to say, carefully to avoid precipitation and prejudice in judgments. . . ." From that deceptively simple premise, Descartes arrived at what is known as the *Cogito*, from *cogito ergo sum*—"I think, therefore I am." Though we cannot doubt the existence of mind *(res cogitans)*, Descartes declared, we can doubt the existence of matter *(res extensa)*; hence, the mind must be radically different from matter—a concept known as Cartesian dualism. Eventually concluding that a benevolent God does exist, Descartes's philosophy provides reasonable assurance that the material world is not an illusion and that we can be confident in our observations and sense-knowledge of it.

Descartes' "method of doubt" would become a key element of Enlightenment thinking, which was underscored by Newton's discovery of what were believed to be the fundamental laws governing motion, gravity, and light. Newton's notion that we could "derive the rest of the phenomena of Nature by . . . reasoning from mechanical principles" became another important premise for Enlightenment thinkers and bolstered the view that nature, including human nature, was a machine governed by universal principles. The idea that God was a great craftsman who had assembled the universe and set it in motion spurred empirical experimentation and intellectual

From these forces, by other propositions which are also mathematical, I deduce the motions of the planets, the comets, the moon, and the sea. I wish we could derive the rest of the phenomena of Nature by the same kind of reasoning from mechanical principles. . . .

– ISAAC NEWTON, Preface to *Mathematical Principles of Natural Philosophy*, 1686 inquiry, for it was believed that if human beings could discover the fundamental principles that kept the great machine in motion they could achieve mastery over it and take charge of their own history. Though Leibniz has been ridiculed for his notion that this world is the "best of all possible worlds," his belief in perfection was based in part upon these deistic premises. Shifting the metaphor from crafts-manship to statesmanship, Leibniz argues finally that "the kingdom of God is the most perfect of all possible states or governments"; if we cannot recognize its perfection, he reasons, it is not a flaw in the system but our failure to comprehend the totality of the design.

The works of these three philosophers, along with those of other thinkers, gave rise to the notion best expressed by Alexander Pope's ***Essay on Man***, Epistle 1, that "All Nature is but Art, unknown to thee." That is, all nature is governed by orderly and ultimately dis-cernible laws somewhat beyond the ken of ordinary perceptions and

p. 260

Guiguet, *Benjamin Franklin Conducting His Lightning Experiments*, 1752

This is a French artist's engraving of the famous story of Franklin's experiments with electricity. Franklin is said to have tied a key to a kite to see if lightning—electricity—would strike the key. (Mary Evans Picture Library) understanding. Enlightenment thinkers believed that through careful and fresh reasoning and observation, man could eventually understand the fundamental laws of nature and human nature and use that knowledge to make the world more just and humane. Hence, the spirit of inquiry in science went hand in hand with the spirit of social, political, and religious reform.

TOKUGAWAN NEO-CONFUCIANISM

In Japan, beginning in the late seventeenth century, Hayashi Razan (1583–1657), also known as Doshun, exerted a powerful influence upon neo-Confucianist doctrines in Japan. NEO-CONFUCIANISM, a blend of CONFUCIANISM, BUDDHISM, and DAOISM, stemmed from the teachings of the Chinese philosopher Zhu Xi (Chu Hsi; 1130–1200). Zhu Xi's particular blend of metaphysics, ethics, and politics as adapted by Doshun was well suited to the Tokugawa-era shoguns, who benefited from a society guided by principles that emphasized orderly participation in the world. In the study of metaphysics, Doshun, following Zhu Xi, contemplated the fundamental motive force behind all things, or *li*. Later Japanese neo-Confucians, including **Kaibara Ekken** (1630–1714), author of *Grave Doubts*, and **Baien Miura** (1723–1789), who wrote *Discourse on Metaphysics* and other treatises, transformed the study of *li* into a systematic analysis of nature, society, and economics, moving Japanese neo-Confucianism toward an empirical science. As can be seen in **Reply to Taga Bokkei** included here, Baien, best known perhaps for his work in economics, questions the widespread dependence on orthodox principles, insisting that the way to true understanding requires freeing the mind from the pieties and accepted wisdom of the past and opening up to a direct investigation of nature and humanity, much as the Enlightenment thinkers in Europe were proposing.

kigh-BAH-rah EK-ken

BAH-yen mee-OO-rah

p. 362

■ **CONNECTIONS**

Alexander Pope, *An Essay on Man*, p. 260. Many of the texts in this section are philosophical and scientific treatises that develop their ideas systematically and in an abstract, sometimes difficult style. Pope's *An Essay on Man* explores philosophical ideas in poetic form. Consider whether Pope's poetry offers a more palatable medium for philosophy. What may be gained or lost in the poetic treatment of difficult concepts?

Benjamin Franklin, *Autobiography*, p. 522 Newton, Descartes, and Leibniz, philosophers associated with the Enlightenment, argue in their various ways for a close examination of the phenomenon of the world, as does Baien Miura. Benjamin Franklin and Thomas Jefferson, among others, represented the Enlightenment in

Farming in Four Seasons: Irrigation Pump for Lifting Water, 1625–50

The Edo, or Tokugawa, period in Japan saw many technical advancements, such as the development of the irrigation pump, which allowed for speedier farming and in turn yielded more food. (Freer Gallery of Art, Smithsonian Institution, Washington, D.C.: Purchase, F1981.30) the United States. Does Franklin's pragmatic approach to life in the *Autobiography* represent a continuation of the spirit of inquiry of Newton, Descartes, or Leibniz?

Rabindranath Tagore, "Broken Ties" (Book 5). In nineteenth-century England, the emphasis on reason influenced the utilitarianism of Jeremy Bentham and John Stuart Mill, among others. Rabindranath Tagore's short story "Broken Ties" evokes the clash between European rationalism and the spiritual tradition of India. How does Tagore's story bring a new perspective to the ideals of the European Enlightenment? In Japan, Matsuo Bashō's *The Narrow Road through the Backcountry* points to a definition of and a means to enlightenment that also challenges Western rationalism. In what ways does Bashō's definition challenge that of the West? How is it similar?

■ **PRONUNCIATION**

Baien Miura: BAH-yen mee-OO-rah
René Descartes: ruh-NAY day-CART
Kaibara Ekken: kigh-BAH-rah EK-ken
Gottfried Wilhelm Leibniz: GAHT-freed VIL-helm LIBE-nits

℘ RENÉ DESCARTES
1596–1650

French philosopher, mathematician, and scientist René Descartes is, along with Francis Bacon, one of the founders of modern thought. If Bacon is the father of empiricism and experimental science, Descartes is the father of rationalism and theoretical science. He set out to create a single, mathematically based method for all the sciences and in doing so developed the systematic practice of "methodical doubt" or "Cartesian skepticism." He describes this process in his two most important philosophic treatises, *Discourse on Method* (1637) and *Meditations* (1642). The passage from *Discourse on Method* that follows is an account of the revelatory moment when Descartes discovered this method and its fundamental truth. It occurred when he was in the Bavarian army during the winter of 1619–1620; on one particularly cold day spent meditating in a warm room, he claims that he completed half his philosophy. In his meditations Descartes began by doubting the existence of all things and all the convictions he held about the world, seeking out any conviction that resisted such skepticism. He discovered that he could doubt everything except that he was doubting. By this process of elimination he arrived at his fundamental truth, *cogito ergo sum*, "I think, therefore I am."

By locating the source of truth in the mind or the self rather than in the external world or a divine being, Descartes changed the direction of Western thought. Instead of looking to past learning as a repository of truth, as his Renaissance predecessors had done, Descartes regarded works

René Descartes,
Descartes' Universe,
1668

*Descartes' drawing
shows how matter
that fills the universe
is collected in vortices,
with a star at the
center of each. Some
vortices have orbiting
planets. The path of a
comet is shown by the
wavy line beginning
at N and moving
upwards. (Copyright
Image Select / Art
Resource, NY)*

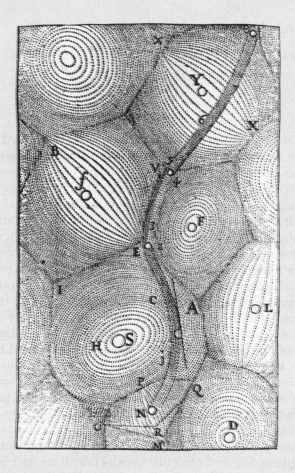

. . . I noticed that
whilst I thus wished
to think all things
false, it was
absolutely essential
that the "I" who
thought this should
be some[thing], and
remarking that this
truth *"I think, there-
fore I am"* was so
certain and so
assured . . . I came
to the conclusion
that I could receive it
without scruple as
the first principle of
the Philosophy for
which I was seeking.

– DESCARTES,
Discourse on Method,
Part 4, 1637

of the past as compilations of error. He sought truth in the mind alone. Intuition, "clear and distinct" ideas that could not be doubted, such as his *cogito ergo sum,* became the starting points from which he deduced other truths. He summarized this position in one of his twenty-one *Rules for the Direction of the Mind:* "In the subjects we propose to investigate, our inquiries should be directed, not to what others have thought, nor to what we ourselves conjecture, but to what we can clearly and perspicuously behold and with certainty deduce; for knowledge is not won in any other way." Although he began by retreating into the self and relying on his own powers of reasoning, Descartes did not end in isolation or solipsism—thinking that the self is the only reality. On the contrary, from the certainty of his individualistic starting point, he deduced the existence of God and of a material reality, and he believed that through good sense and reason others would arrive at the same conclusions.

∾ Discourse on Method

Translated by Elizabeth S. Haldane and G. R. T. Ross

FROM

PART 2

I was then in Germany, to which country I had been attracted by the wars which are not yet at an end. And as I was returning from the coronation of the Emperor to join the army, the setting in of winter detained me in a quarter where, since I found no society to divert me, while fortunately I had also no cares or passions to trouble me, I remained the whole day shut up alone in a stove-heated room, where I had complete leisure to occupy myself with my own thoughts. One of the first of the considerations that occurred to me was that there is very often less perfection in works composed of several portions, and carried out by the hands of various masters, than in those on which one individual alone has worked. Thus we see that buildings planned and carried out by one architect alone are usually more beautiful and better proportioned than those which many have tried to put in order and improve, making use of old walls which were built with other ends in view. In the same way also, those ancient cities which, originally mere villages, have become in the process of time great towns, are usually badly constructed in comparison with those which are regularly laid out on a plain by a surveyor who is free to follow his own ideas. Even though, considering their buildings each one apart, there is often as much or more display of skill in the one case than in the other, the former have large buildings and small buildings indiscriminately placed together, thus rendering the streets crooked and irregular, so that it might be said that it was chance rather than the will of men guided by reason that led to such an arrangement. And if we consider that this happens despite the fact that from all time there have been certain officials who have had the special duty of looking after the buildings of private individuals in order that they may be public ornaments, we shall understand how difficult it is to bring about much that is satisfactory in operating only upon the works of others. Thus I imagined that those people who were once half-savage, and who have become civilized only by slow degrees, merely forming their laws as the disagreeable necessities of their crimes and quarrels constrained them, could not succeed in establishing so good a system of government as those who, from the time they first came together as communities, carried into effect the constitution laid down by some prudent legislator. Thus it is quite certain that the constitution of the true Religion whose ordinances are of God alone is incomparably better regulated than any other. And, to come down to human affairs, I believe that if Sparta was very flourishing in former times, this was not because of the excellence of each and every one of its laws, seeing that many were very strange and even contrary to good morals, but because, being drawn up by one individual, they all tended towards the same end. And similarly I thought that the sciences found in books—in those at least whose reasonings are only probable and which have no demonstrations, composed as they are of the gradually accumulated opinions of many different individuals—do not approach so near to the truth as the simple reasoning which a man of common sense can quite naturally carry out respecting the things which come immediately before him. Again I thought that since we have all been children before being men, and since it has for long fallen to us to be governed by our appetites and by our teachers (who often enough contradicted one another, and none of whom perhaps counselled us always for the best), it is almost impossible that our judgments should be so excellent or solid as they should have been had we had complete use of our reason since our birth, and had we been guided by its means alone.

It is true that we do not find that all the houses in a town are rased to the ground for the sole reason that the town is to be rebuilt in another fashion, with streets made more beautiful; but at the same time we see that many people cause their own houses to be knocked down in order to rebuild them, and that sometimes they are forced so to do where there is danger of the houses falling of themselves, and when the foundations are not secure. From such examples I argued to myself that there was no plausibility in the claim of any private individual to reform a state by altering everything, and by overturning it throughout, in order to set it right again. Nor is it likewise probable that the whole body of the Sciences, or the order of teaching established by the Schools, should be reformed. But as regards all the opinions which up to this time I had embraced, I thought I could not do better than endeavour once for all to sweep them completely away, so that they might later on be replaced, either by others which were better, or by the same, when I had made them conform to the uniformity of a rational scheme. And I firmly believed that by this means I should succeed in directing my life much better than if I had only built on old foundations, and relied on principles of which I allowed myself to be in youth persuaded without having inquired into their truth. [. . .]

[. . .] My design has never extended beyond trying to reform my own opinion and to build on a foundation which is entirely my own. If my work has given me a certain satisfaction, so that I here present to you a draft of it, I do not do so because I wish to advise anybody to imitate it. Those to whom God has been most beneficent in the bestowal of His graces will perhaps form designs which are more elevated; but I fear much that this particular one will seem too venturesome for many. The simple resolve to strip oneself of all opinions and beliefs formerly received is not to be regarded as an example that each man should follow, and the world may be said to be mainly composed of two classes of minds neither of which could prudently adopt it. There are those who, believing themselves to be cleverer than they are, cannot restrain themselves from being precipitate in judgment and have not sufficient patience to arrange their thoughts in proper order; hence, once a man of this description had taken the liberty of doubting the principles he formerly accepted, and had deviated from the beaten track, he would never be able to maintain the path which must be followed to reach the appointed end more quickly, and he would hence remain wandering astray all through his life. Secondly, there are those who having reason or modesty enough to judge that they are less capable of distinguishing truth from falsehood than some others from whom instruction might be obtained, are right in contenting themselves with following the opinions of these others rather than in searching better ones for themselves. . . .

Among the different branches of Philosophy, I had in my younger days to a certain extent studied Logic; and in those of Mathematics, Geometrical Analysis, and Algebra—three arts or sciences which seemed as though they ought to contribute something to the design I had in view. But in examining them I observed in respect to Logic that the syllogisms and the greater part of the other teaching served better in explaining to others those things that one knows (or like the art of Lully, in enabling one to speak without judgment of those things of which one is ignorant) than in learning what is new. And although in reality Logic contains many precepts which are very true and very good, there are at the same time mingled with them so many others which are hurtful or superfluous, that it is almost as difficult to separate the two as to draw a Diana or a Minerva out of a block of marble which is not yet roughly hewn. And as to the Analysis of the ancients and the Algebra of the moderns, besides the fact that they embrace only matters the most abstract, such as appear to have no actual use, the former is always so restricted to the consideration of symbols that it cannot exercise the Understanding without greatly fatiguing the Imagination; and in the latter one is so subjected to certain rules and formulas that the result is the construction of an art which is confused and obscure, and which embarrasses the mind, instead of a science which contributes to its cultivation. This made me feel that some other Method must be found, which, comprising the advantages of the three, is yet exempt from their faults. And as a multiplicity of laws often furnishes excuses for evil-doing, and as a State is hence much better ruled when, having but very few laws, these are most strictly observed; so, instead of the great number of precepts of which Logic is composed, I believed that I should find the four which I shall state quite sufficient, provided that I adhered to a firm and constant resolve never on any single occasion to fail in their observance.

The first of these was to accept nothing as true which I did not clearly recognise to be so: that is to say, carefully to avoid precipitation and prejudice in judgments, and to accept in them nothing more than what was presented to my mind so clearly and distinctly that I could have no occasion to doubt it.

The second was to divide up each of the difficulties which I examined into as many parts as possible, and as seemed requisite in order that it might be resolved in the best manner possible.

The third was to carry on my reflections in due order, commencing with objects that were the most simple and easy to understand, in order to rise little by little, or by degrees, to knowledge of the most complex, assuming an order, even if a fictitious one, among those which do not follow a natural sequence relatively to one another.

The last was in all cases to make enumerations so complete and reviews so general that I should be certain of having omitted nothing. [. . .]

I can venture to say that the exact observation of the few precepts which I had chosen gave me so much facility in sifting out all the questions embraced in these two sciences [Geometry and Algebra], that in the two or three months which I employed in examining them—commencing with the most simple and general, and making each truth that I discovered a rule for helping me to find others—not only did I arrive at the solution of many questions which I had hitherto regarded as most difficult, but, towards the end, it seemed to me that I was able to determine in the case of those of which I was still ignorant, by what means, and in how far, it was possible to solve them. In this I might perhaps appear to you to be very vain if you did not remember that having but one truth to discover in respect to each matter, whoever succeeds in finding it knows in its regard as much as can be known. It is the same as with a child, for instance, who has been instructed in Arithmetic and has made an addition according to the rule prescribed; he may be sure of having found as regards the sum of figures given to him all that the human mind can know. For, in conclusion, the Method which teaches us to follow the true order and enumerate exactly every term in the matter under investigation contains everything which gives certainty to the rules of Arithmetic.

But what pleased me most in this Method was that I was certain by its means of exercising my reason in all things, if not perfectly, at least as well as was in my power. And besides this, I felt in making use of it that my mind gradually accustomed itself to conceive of its objects more accurately and distinctly; and not having restricted this Method to any particular matter, I promised myself to apply it as usefully to the difficulties of other sciences as I had done to those of Algebra. Not that on this account I dared undertake to examine just at once all those that might present themselves; for that would itself have been contrary to the order which the Method prescribes. But having noticed that the knowledge of these difficulties must be dependent on principles derived from Philosophy in which I yet found nothing to be certain, I thought that it was requisite above all to try to establish certainty in it. I considered also that since this endeavour is the most important in all the world, and that in which precipitation and prejudice were most to be feared, I should not try to grapple with it till I had attained to a much riper age than that of three and twenty, which was the age I had reached. I thought, too, that I should first of all employ much time in preparing myself for the work by eradicating from my mind all the wrong opinions which I had up to this time accepted, and accumulating a variety of experiences fitted later on to afford matter for my reasonings, and by ever exercising myself in the Method which I had prescribed, in order more and more to fortify myself in the power of using it. [. . .]

FROM

PART 4

I do not know that I ought to tell you of the first meditations there made by me, for they are so metaphysical and so unusual that they may perhaps not be acceptable to everyone. And yet at the same time, in order that one may judge whether the foundations which I have laid are sufficiently secure, I find myself constrained in some measure to refer to them. For a long time I had remarked that it is sometimes requisite in common life to follow opinions which one knows to be most uncertain, exactly as though they were indisputable, as has been said above. But because in this case I wished to give myself entirely to the search after Truth, I thought that it was necessary for me to take an apparently opposite course, and to reject as absolutely false everything as to which I could imagine the least ground of doubt, in order to see if afterwards there remained anything in my belief that was entirely certain. Thus, because our senses sometimes deceive us, I wished to suppose that nothing is just as they cause us to imagine it to be; and because there are men who deceive themselves in their reasoning and fall into paralogisms, even concerning the simplest matters of geometry, and judging that I was as subject to error as was any other, I rejected as false all the reasons formerly accepted by me as demonstrations. And since all the same thoughts and conceptions which we have while awake may also come to us in sleep, without any of them being at that time true, I resolved to assume that everything that ever entered into my mind was no more true than the illusions of my dreams. But immediately afterwards I noticed that whilst I thus wished to think all things false, it was absolutely essential that the "I" who thought this should be some[thing], and remarking that this truth *I think, therefore I am* was so certain and so assured that all the most extravagant suppositions brought forward by the sceptics were incapable of shaking it, I came to the conclusion that I could receive it without scruple as the first principle of the Philosophy for which I was seeking.

And then, examining attentively that which I was, I saw that I could conceive that I had no body, and that there was no world nor place where I might be; but yet that I could not for all that conceive that I was not. On the contrary, I saw from the very fact that I thought of doubting the truth of other things, it very evidently and certainly followed that I was; on the other hand if I had only ceased from thinking, even if all the rest of what I had ever imagined had really existed, I should have no reason for thinking that I had existed. From that I knew that I was a substance the whole essence or nature of which is to think, and that for its existence there is no need of any place, nor does it depend on any material thing; so that this "me," that is to say, the soul by which I am what I am, is entirely distinct from body, and is even more easy to know than is the latter; and even if body were not, the soul would not cease to be what it is.

After this I considered generally what in a proposition is requisite in order to be true and certain; for since I had just discovered one which I knew to be such, I thought that I ought also to know in what this certainty consisted. And having remarked that there was nothing at all in the statement *I think, therefore I am* which assures me of having thereby made a true assertion, excepting that I see very clearly that to think it is necessary to be, I came to the conclusion that I might assume, as a general rule, that the things which we conceive very clearly and distinctly are all true—remembering, however, that there is some difficulty in ascertaining which are those that we distinctly conceive.

⚓ Sir Isaac Newton
1642–1727

"Nature and Nature's Laws lay hid in Night: / God said, Let Newton be! and all was Light." In this couplet, Alexander Pope dramatized the celebrated reputation Newton held in England, where he was knighted in 1705. Born in 1642, Newton was raised by his maternal grandmother until he was eleven, at which time he returned to live with his twice-widowed mother. Encouraged by his uncle, Newton eventually left home and received a bachelor's degree from Trinity College, Cambridge University, where in 1669 he was appointed the Lucasian Professor of Mathematics. Between the summer of 1665 and the summer of 1667, the threat of plague kept Newton from Cambridge, but while staying at his family home in Woolsthorpe, Newton's genius blossomed. During these *anni mirabili*, or miracle years, Newton completed experiments in optics and mechanics, started to develop calculus, and after watching an apple fall from a tree outside his mother's home, began the serious meditations on free-falling objects that would lead to his theory of universal gravitation. Newton began to advance Descartes' theory that bodies at rest remain in a state of inertia until moved by an external force. Newton applied the notion of inertia to motion itself by suggesting that bodies in a state of uniform motion (including rest) would remain at the same velocity until moved (sped up or stopped) by an external force. This later became

William Blake,
Newton, c. 1805.
Engraving
Blake, one of the most admired poets and painters of the nineteenth century, here envisions Isaac Newton as a Greco-Roman model of physical and mental perfection. (Tate Gallery, London / Art Resource, NY)

known as Newton's First Law: "Every body continues in its state of rest, or of uniform motion in a right line, unless it is compelled to change that state by forces impressed upon it." For the rest of his life, Newton worked on the implications and details of his early discoveries and theories. His contributions to optics, mechanics, dynamics, and astronomy effected a revolution in science, and he also made contributions to the studies of alchemy, theology, and history. The selection from *Mathematical Principles of Natural Philosophy*, a work presented to the Royal Society (of which Newton was president from 1703 until his death in 1727) in 1686 and published in Latin the following year, describes the purpose and method of Newton's work. Known as the *Principia*, short for its Latin title, *Philosophiae naturalis principia mathematica*, this work develops Newton's theories of dynamics—including his three laws of motion, describes the motions of the planets and their satellites, and elaborates a theory of the tides. In the General Scholium of the *Principia*, Newton points out that although he has explained the motions of the heavens and the sea by means of gravity, he has not been able to establish the cause of gravity itself. He leaves room for the existence of a Creator whose mystery surpasses the ken of human knowledge. As he puts it, "This most beautiful system of Sun, planets, and comets, could only proceed from the counsel and dominion of an intelligent and powerful Being."

✑ Mathematical Principles of Natural Philosophy

Translated by Andrew Motte, with revisions by Florian Cajori

FROM

PREFACE TO THE FIRST EDITION

Since the Ancients (as we are told by Pappus[1]) esteemed the science of mechanics of greatest importance in the investigation of natural things, and the moderns, rejecting substantial forms and occult qualities, have endeavored to subject the phenomena of nature to the laws of mathematics, I have in this treatise cultivated mathematics as far as it relates to philosophy. . . . Geometry is founded in mechanical practice, and is nothing but that part of universal mechanics which accurately proposes and demonstrates the art of measuring. But since the manual arts are chiefly employed in the moving of bodies, it happens that geometry is commonly referred to their magnitude, and mechanics to their motion. In this sense rational mechanics will be the science of motions resulting from any forces whatsoever, and

---

[1]Pappus: Pappus of Alexandria (c. 290–c. 350 C.E.), a Greek mathematician who wrote a commentary on *Almagest*, a thirteen-volume treatise on cosmology by the Greco-Egyptian astronomer Ptolemy (fl. 2nd century C.E.), as well as a series of treatises on mathematics called *Synagoge* or *Mathematical Collection* (c. 325–40).

of the forces required to produce any motions, accurately proposed and demonstrated. This part of mechanics, as far as it extended to the five powers which relate to manual arts, was cultivated by the Ancients, who considered gravity (it not being a manual power) no otherwise than in moving weights by those powers. But I consider philosophy rather than arts and write not concerning manual but natural powers, and consider chiefly those things which relate to gravity, levity, elastic force, the resistance of fluids, and the like forces, whether attractive or impulsive; and therefore I offer this work as the mathematical principles of philosophy, for the whole burden of philosophy seems to consist in this—from the phenomena of motions to investigate the forces of nature, and then from these forces to demonstrate the other phenomena; and to this end the general propositions in the first and second Books are directed. In the third Book I give an example of this in the explication of the System of the World; for by the propositions mathematically demonstrated in the former Books, in the third I derive from the celestial phenomena the forces of gravity with which bodies tend to the sun and the several planets. Then from these forces, by other propositions which are also mathematical, I deduce the motions of the planets, the comets, the moon, and the sea. I wish we could derive the rest of the phenomena of Nature by the same kind of reasoning from mechanical principles, for I am induced by many reasons to suspect that they may all depend upon certain forces by which the particles of bodies, by some causes hitherto unknown, are either mutually impelled towards one another, and cohere in regular figures, or are repelled and recede from one another. These forces being unknown, philosophers have hitherto attempted the search of Nature in vain; but I hope the principles here laid down will afford some light either to this or some truer method of philosophy. [. . .]

Rules of Reasoning in Philosophy

RULE I. *We are to admit no more causes of natural things than such as are both true and sufficient to explain their appearances.*

To this purpose the philosophers say that Nature does nothing in vain, and more is in vain when less will serve; for Nature is pleased with simplicity, and affects not the pomp of superfluous causes.

RULE II. *Therefore to the same natural effects we must, as far as possible, assign the same causes.*

As to respiration in a man and in a beast; the descent of stone in *Europe* and in *America;* the light of our culinary fire and of the sun; the reflection of light in the earth, and in the planets.

RULE III. *The qualities of bodies, which admit neither intensification nor remission of degrees, and which are found to belong to all bodies within the reach of our experiments, are to be esteemed the universal qualities of all bodies whatsoever.*

For since the qualities of bodies are only known to us by experiments, we are to hold for universal all such as universally agree with experiments; and such as are not liable to diminution can never be quite taken away. We are certainly not to relinquish the evidence of experiments for the sake of dreams and vain fictions of our own devising; nor are we to recede from the analogy of Nature, which is wont to be simple, and always consonant to itself. We no other way know the extension of bodies than by our senses, nor do these reach it in all bodies; but because we perceive extension in all that are sensible, therefore we ascribe it universally to all others also. That abundance of bodies are hard, we learn by experience; and because the hardness of the whole arise from the hardness of the parts, we therefore justly infer the hardness of the undivided particles not only of the bodies we feel but of all others. That all bodies are impenetrable, we gather not from reason, but from sensation. The bodies which we handle we find impenetrable, and thence conclude impenetrability to be a universal property of all bodies whatsoever. That all bodies are movable, and endowed with certain powers (which we call the inertia) of persevering in their motion, or in their rest, we only infer from the like properties observed in the bodies which we have seen. The extension, hardness, impenetrability, mobility, and inertia of the whole, result from the extension, hardness, impenetrability, mobility, and inertia of the parts; and hence we conclude the least particles of all bodies to be also all extended, and hard and impenetrable, and movable, and endowed with their proper inertia. And this is the foundation of all philosophy. Moreover, that the divided but contiguous particles of bodies may be separated from one another, is matter of observation; and, in the particles that remain undivided, our minds are able to distinguish yet lesser parts, as is mathematically demonstrated. But whether the parts so distinguished, and not yet divided, may, by the powers of Nature, be actually divided and separated from one another, we cannot certainly determine. Yet, had we the proof of but one experiment that any undivided particle, in breaking a hard and solid body, suffered a division, we might by virtue of this rule conclude that the undivided as well as the divided particles may be divided and actually separated to infinity.

Lastly, if it universally appears, by experiments and astronomical observations, that all bodies about the earth gravitate towards the earth, and that in proportion to the quantity of matter which they severally contain; that the moon likewise, according to the quantity of its matter, gravitates towards the earth; that, on the other hand, our sea gravitates towards the moon; and all the planets one towards another; and the comets in like manner towards the sun; we must, in consequence of this rule, universally allow that all bodies whatsoever are endowed with a principle of mutual gravitation. For the argument from the appearances concludes with more force for the universal gravitation of all bodies than for their impenetrability; of which, among those in the celestial regions, we have no experiments, nor any manner of observation. Not that I affirm gravity to be essential to bodies; by their *vis insita* I mean nothing but their inertia. This is immutable. Their gravity is diminished as they recede from the earth.

RULE IV. *In experimental philosophy we are to look upon propositions inferred by general induction from phenomena as accurately or very nearly true, notwithstanding any contrary hypotheses that may be imagined, till such time as other phenomena occur, by which they may either be made more accurate, or liable to exceptions.*

This rule we must follow, that the argument of induction may not be evaded by hypotheses. [. . .]

(General Scholium.) The six primary planets are revolved about the sun in circles concentric with the sun, and with motions directed towards the same parts, and almost in the same plane. Ten moons are revolved about the earth, Jupiter, and Saturn, in circles concentric with them, with the same direction of motion, and nearly in the planes of the orbits of these planets; but it is not to be conceived that mere mechanical causes could give birth to so many regular motions, since the comets range over all parts of the heavens in very eccentric orbits; for by that kind of motion they pass easily through the orbs of the planets, and with great rapidity; and in their aphelions, where they move the slowest, and are detained the longest, they recede to the greatest distances from each other, and hence suffer the least disturbance from their mutual attractions. This most beautiful system of the sun, planets, and comets, could only proceed from the counsel and dominion of an intelligent and powerful Being. And if the fixed stars are the centres of other like systems, these, being formed by the like wise counsel, must be all subject to the dominion of One; especially since the light of the fixed stars is of the same nature with the light of the sun, and from every system light passes into all the other systems: and lest the systems of the fixed stars should, by their gravity, fall on each other, he hath placed those systems at immense distances from one another. [. . .]

Hitherto we have explained the phenomena of the heavens and of our sea by the power of gravity, but have not yet assigned the cause of this power. This is certain, that it must proceed from a cause that penetrates to the very centres of the sun and planets, without suffering the least diminution of its force; that operates not according to the quantity of the surfaces of the particles upon which it acts (as mechanical causes used to do), but according to the quantity of solid matter which they contain, and propagates its virtue on all sides to immense distances, decreasing always as the inverse square of the distances. Gravitation towards the sun is made up out of the gravitations towards the several particles of which the body of the sun is composed; and in receding from the sun decreases accurately as the inverse square of the distances as far as the orbit of Saturn, as evidently appears from the quiescence of the aphelion of the planets; nay, and even to the remotest aphelion of the comets, if those aphelions are also quiescent. But hitherto I have not been able to discover the cause of those properties of gravity from phenomena, and I frame no hypotheses; for whatever is not deduced from the phenomena is to be called an hypothesis; and hypotheses, whether metaphysical or physical, whether of occult qualities or mechanical, have no place in experimental philosophy. In this philosophy particular propositions are inferred from the phenomena, and afterwards rendered general by induction. Thus it was that the impenetrability, the mobility, and the impulsive forces of bodies, and the laws of motion and gravitation, were discovered. And to us it is enough that gravity does really exist, and acts according to the laws which we have explained, and abundantly serves to account for all the motions of the celestial bodies, and of our sea.

And now we might add something concerning a certain most subtle spirit which pervades and lies hid in all gross bodies; by the force and action of which spirit the particles of bodies attract one another at near distances, and cohere, if contiguous; and electric bodies operate to greater distances, as well repelling as attracting the neighboring corpuscles; and light is emitted, reflected, refracted, inflected, and heats bodies; and all sensation is excited, and the members of animal bodies move at the command of the will, namely, by the vibrations of this spirit, mutually propagated along the solid filaments of the nerves, from the outward organs of sense to the brain, and from the brain into the muscles. But these are things that cannot be explained in a few words, nor are we furnished with that sufficiency of experiments which is required to an accurate determination and demonstration of the laws by which this electric and elastic spirit operates.

❧ GOTTFRIED WILHELM LEIBNIZ
1646–1716

Although Gottfried Wilhelm Leibniz was one of the great systematic thinkers and mathematicians of his own time, he is probably best remembered in our time as the model for Voltaire's Pangloss in *Candide*. Leibniz reconciled scientific empiricism and traditional theism in a unified world view. Voltaire satirically simplifies Leibniz's philosophy, reducing it to the absurd sound bite: "This is the best of all possible worlds." But Leibniz was a many-talented man who made original contributions in multiple fields—mathematics, logic, philosophy, law, history, linguistics, and the sciences. By age twenty-six he had devised a legal reform system for the Holy Roman Empire, designed a "living bank clerk" (calculating machine), and kept Louis XIV from attacking Rhineland by encouraging him to build the Suez Canal. Clearly a man of the ENLIGHTENMENT, Leibniz published treatises on metaphysics and theology as well as advanced commentaries on John Locke and Descartes, independently developed differential calculus, and conducted practical experiments in science. His creation of calculus at the same time as Newton led to some bitter arguments over which man deserved credit for the invention.

Like Newton, Leibniz accepted the metaphor of God as clockmaker, but whereas Newton believed that God intervened in His creation like a mechanic keeping a machine in good working order, Leibniz held that such a view insulted the infinite wisdom of God. Leibniz's God stood back and let his perfect clock run without need of intervention. After all, it was *the best of all possible clocks*.

Leibniz presented considerably more complex analyses and arguments for his optimistic rationalism than the facile proofs offered by Pangloss. The son of a philosopher at the University of Leipzig and father himself to the German Enlightenment, or *Aufklärung*, Leibniz spent his working life as a government agent and diplomat. His philosophy, in its attempts to reconcile and unify opposing positions, sometimes takes on the virtues of diplomacy. Even so, as a rationalist, Leibniz sometimes went to extremes. He believed, for example, that arguments could be

I have gone even farther . . . and have even proved that this universe must be in reality better than every other possible universe.

– LEIBNIZ, Supplement to *Theodicy*

resolved if "words of vague and uncertain meanings" were replaced with mathematical "fixed symbols." Moreover, he thought that differences in ethics could be settled in the same way that mathematical issues are resolved.

The passage excerpted here, from a supplement to Leibniz's *Theodicy* (1710), treats theological issues, stating them as a series of logical deductions and then methodically addressing their premises. This systematic method might be seen as a step toward reducing complex matters to calculations. Leibniz's Panglossian conclusion is stated in the final sentence, ". . . that the kingdom of God is the most perfect of all possible states or governments, and that consequently the little evil there is, is required for the consummation of the immense good which is found there." His arguments in support of this conclusion are examples of the kind of reasoning that Voltaire satirizes in Pangloss's unremitting optimism.

FROM

◆ Supplement to *Theodicy*

Translated by George M. Duncan, with revisions by Philip P. Wiener

[A VINDICATION OF GOD'S JUSTICE]

Some intelligent persons have desired that this supplement be made [to *Theodicy*], and I have the more readily yielded to their wishes as in this way I have an opportunity again to remove certain difficulties and to make some observations which were not sufficiently emphasized in the work itself.

I. *Objection.* Whoever does not choose the best is lacking in power, or in knowledge, or in goodness.

God did not choose the best in creating this world.

Therefore, God has been lacking in power, or in knowledge, or in goodness.

Answer. I deny the minor, that is, the second premise of this syllogism; and our opponent proves it by this:

Prosyllogism. Whoever makes things in which there is evil, which could have been made without any evil, or the making of which could have been omitted, does not choose the best.

God has made a world in which there is evil; a world, I say, which could have been made without any evil, or the making of which could have been omitted altogether.

Therefore, God has not chosen the best.

Answer. I grant the minor of this prosyllogism; for it must be confessed that there is evil in this world which God has made, and that it was possible to make a world without evil, or even not to create a world at all, for its creation has depended on the free will of God; but I deny the major, that is, the first of the two premises of the prosyllogism, and I might content myself with simply demanding its proof; but in order to make the matter clearer, I have wished to justify this denial by showing that the best plan is not always that which seeks to avoid evil, since it may happen that the *evil is accompanied by a greater good.* For example, a general of an army will prefer a great victory with a slight wound to a condition without wound and without victory. We have proved this more fully in the large work by making it clear, by instances taken from mathematics and elsewhere, that an imperfection in the part may be required for a greater perfection in the whole. In this I have followed the opinion of St. Augustine,[1] who has said a hundred times, that God has permitted evil in order to bring about good, that is, a greater good; and that of Thomas Aquinas[2] (in libr. II. sent. dist. 32, qu. I, art. 1), that the permitting of evil tends to the good of the universe. I have shown that the ancients called Adam's fall *felix culpa,* a happy sin, because it had been retrieved with immense advantage by the incarnation of the Son of God, who has given to the universe something nobler than anything that ever would have been among creatures except for it. For the sake of a clearer understanding, I have added, following many good authors, that it was in accordance with order and the general good that God allowed to certain creatures the opportunity of exercising their liberty, even when he foresaw that they would turn to evil, but which he could so well rectify; because it was not fitting that, in order to hinder sin, God should always act in an extraordinary manner. To overthrow this objection, therefore, it is sufficient to show that a world with evil might be better than a world without evil; but I have gone even farther, in the work, and have even proved that this universe must be in reality better than every other possible universe.

II. *Objection.* If there is more evil than good in intelligent creatures, then there is more evil than good in the whole work of God.

Now, there is more evil than good in intelligent creatures.

Therefore, there is more evil than good in the whole work of God.

Answer. I deny the major and the minor of this conditional syllogism. As to the major, I do not admit it at all, because this pretended deduction from a part to the whole, from intelligent creatures to all creatures, supposes tacitly and without proof that creatures destitute of reason cannot enter into comparison nor into account with those which possess it. But why may it not be that the surplus of good in the non-intelligent creatures which fill the world, compensates for, and even incomparably surpasses, the surplus of evil in the rational creatures? It is true that the value of the latter is greater; but, in compensation, the others are beyond comparison the more numerous, and it may be that the proportion of number and quantity surpasses that of value and of quality.

As to the minor, that is no more to be admitted; that is, it is not at all to be admitted that there is more evil than good in the intelligent creatures. There is no need even of granting that there is more evil than good in the human race, because it is possible, and in fact very probable, that the glory and the perfection of the blessed are

---

[1] St. Augustine(354–430 C.E.): The Bishop of Hippo, who became one of the most influential theologians of the Christian church through his writings, *Confessions* (397–400) and *The City of God* (413–26), which defended Christianity against pagan religions. (See Augustine, Book 1.)

[2] Thomas Aquinas:Saint Thomas Aquinas (1225–1274), Italian theologian and author of *Summa Theologica* (1267–73), a philosophical exposition of Catholic theology famous for its synthesis of Aristotelian philosophy and Christian beliefs.

incomparably greater than the misery and the imperfection of the damned, and that here the excellence of the total good in the smaller number exceeds the total evil in the greater number. The blessed approach the Divinity, by means of a Divine Mediator, as near as may suit these creatures, and make such progress in good as is impossible for the damned to make the evil, approach as nearly as they may to the nature of demons. God is infinite, and the devil is limited; the good may and does go to infinity, while evil has its bounds. It is therefore possible, and is credible, that in the comparison of the blessed and the damned, the contrary of that which I have said might happen in the comparison of intelligent and non-intelligent creatures, takes place; namely, it is possible that in the comparison of the happy and the unhappy, the proportion of degree exceeds that of number, and that in the comparison of intelligent and non-intelligent creatures, the proportion of number is greater than that of value. I have the right to suppose that a thing is possible so long as its impossibility is not proved; and indeed that which I have here advanced is more than a supposition.

But in the second place, if I should admit that there is more evil than good in the human race, I still have good grounds for not admitting that there is more evil than good in all intelligent creatures. For there is an inconceivable number of genii, and perhaps of other rational creatures. And an opponent could not prove that in all the City of God, composed as well of genii as of rational animals without number and of an infinity of kinds, evil exceeds good. And although in order to answer an objection, there is no need of proving that a thing is, when its mere possibility suffices; yet, in this work, I have not omitted to show that it is a consequence of the supreme perfection of the Sovereign of the universe, that the kingdom of God is the most perfect of all possible states or governments, and that consequently the little evil there is, is required for the consummation of the immense good which is found there.

❧ BAIEN MIURA
1723–1789

Baien Miura was born in 1723 on Kyushu, the southernmost island of Japan. By the time he was eighteen, he had come into contact with Western science and befriended Asada Goryu (1734–1799), the greatest contemporary mathematician and astronomer in Japan. Baien, later a physician like his father, mastered the Chinese classics and eventually extended his reputation as a philosopher throughout Japanese intellectual circles. Philosopher, economist, moralist, poet, mathematician, astronomer, and physician, he exemplified the spirit of rationalism and inquiry of his time in his homeland. Like those of his European peers, Baien's studies and writings encompassed metaphysics, ethics, and economics. Indeed, his work *The Origin of Price* was known in Europe because his economic views were similar to those of Adam Smith, who

If we approach each thing with an unbiased mind, then we shall see that all these things, the rising and setting of the sun and moon, the constant changes of generation and decay, the eyes by which we see, the ears by which we hear, the limbs by which we move, the very mind itself which thinks these things, cannot have a single explanation.

– BAIEN MIURA,
"Reply to Taga Bokkei"

promoted free trade and limited government influence on the economy. And like Benjamin Franklin in America, Baien was interested in practical matters; he devised a system of cooperative savings for his village. Baien died in 1789, just a year before the Act of Prohibition outlawed opposition to NEO-CONFUCIAN orthodoxy, whose ideas Baien had pushed to the limit of acceptability.

While scholars of Japanese philosophy caution against easy comparisons between Baien and the European ENLIGHTENMENT thinkers, his philosophy, like theirs, marks a significant departure from and questioning of traditional thinking. In Japan at that time, tradition meant the Confucian system of Zhu Xi, which the Tokugawa shogunate had vigorously promoted during Baien's lifetime. In the selection that follows, from "Reply to Taga Bokkei," Baien, somewhat like Descartes, argues that we must slough off the old skin of conventional learning, free ourselves from attachments to habitual understanding, and begin to see and study phenomena objectively and with no preconceptions. Baien's opinion of book learning as a guide to truth can be seen in a letter he wrote to Asada Goryu, in which he reflects on a sunset:

> I thought of the scene that had stirred me with joy and wonder. It was made up of real things, true enough, but it was at the same time far from being real. And I thought of the sayings of those philosophers and scholars whose writings are so bulky that oxen perspire pulling them and libraries are full to overflowing with them. Are they not inspired by so many evening scenes from pavilions which aroused and delighted the sense of these philosophers?

Baien advises us to rid ourselves of our assumptions and dive into the world: "In order to know objects, man must . . . put his own interests aside and enter into the world of objects; only in that way can his intellect hope to comprehend Heaven-and-earth and understand all things." Baien hoped to inspire his contemporaries to adopt a new, empirical way of investigating life.

A note on the translation: This is the Rosemary Mercer translation of Baien's scientific work. All notes are the editors'.

FROM

 # Reply to Taga Bokkei

Translated by Rosemary Mercer

1. You ask me the meaning of "static form and dynamic flux" *(konron utsubotsu)*, and indeed, as heaven-and-earth is the house of man, scholars should make heaven-and-earth the first object of their study.

It is true that since the introduction of Western science the calendrical studies of astronomy, geography, and the motions of the heavenly bodies have been studied with more and more precision, but that is all there is to it. To my knowledge not one scholar has had a deep knowledge of the *jōri*[1] of heaven and earth. Throughout the whole wide world and the infinity of ages past, countless people have pondered over heaven and earth. Heaven and earth are not concealed, but before us day and night, so how is it that no-one has seen them clearly?

1.1   It is simply because from the moment we are born we unwittingly accustom ourselves to what we see, hear, and touch, confining ourselves by habits of thought, and we do not come to doubt or question things. These attachments are the fixations of mind that Buddhists call "*jikke*."[2] If they are not removed, the function of the mind is impeded.

Ananda[3] had received enlightenment, but because he had been a monkey in his previous life, he retained the *jikke* of a monkey. That is a good allegory, for insofar as human beings analyse and speculate about phenomena with human minds, it is difficult for us to give up our human prejudices. Past and present thinkers alike have been affected by these attachments, they have painted the manifold things of heaven and earth with their human colours. It is not easy to open our eyes wide and see with far-sightedness.

Let us consider these attachments. Because human beings walk with their feet, and grasp things with their hands, attachments of thought could lead people to believe that the motions of heaven and creations of nature also require feet and hands. It could even force them to think that snakes which have no feet, and fish which have no hands, are deficient or handicapped.

Without feet, heaven turns day and night; without hands, natural creation makes flowers bloom, provides us with children, and brings forth fish and birds. If indeed we are so confined within ourselves, celestial revolutions and natural creations should be objects of great curiosity. Although our curiosity should be aroused about certain things, no-one questions them, because we see them before us from morning to evening, passing them by with total unconcern.

When one looks at a thing as the thing it is, heaven-and-earth alone is one object, water and fire are each single objects, and plants, trees, fish, and animals, as well as human beings, are each independent objects. Ourselves and others alike are each objects.

Being human we see things in relation to ourselves, a habit that we cannot readily abandon when we look at other things. It is a human habit to think of things and see things always in human terms. Look at a children's picture book about a rat's wedding, or at a book about goblins. The rats are not treated as rats in the form that we have always known them, they are made into human beings in every detail. The bridegroom wears ceremonial robes with a pair of swords, the bride wears a gown with a long veil and rides in a palanquin borne by footmen and soldiers, all in imitation of

---

[1] *jōri:* Sometimes translated as "natural law"; it means something like the essential nature of things, or the structure of reality. In Baien's work, *jōri* often means the way we grasp reality, how it appears to us.

[2] *jikke:* A Buddhist concept of the customary habits of thought that stem from or perpetuate illusions or unexamined assumptions about the world.

[3] **Ananda:** Or *Anan* in Japanese—one of the favorite disciples of the Buddha.

a human wedding. Again, when we look at a book about goblins, we find no pictures of umbrellas changed into tea mills, or brooms changed into buckets, instead we see goblins with eyes, noses, hands, and feet, everything is changed into human form. A picture of Nirvana[4] shows the dragon lord dressed exactly in human clothes, and to indicate his dragon form a helmet is drawn on his head.

When people in such a state of mind speculate about heaven and earth they believe there to be a great lord in the heavens. Upon the solid earth they believe that there are gods of wind, thunder, and suchlike, portrayed as hideous in appearance, but moving around on feet, and working with their hands. Wind is stored in a bag, and thunder is sounded from a great drum. If there were really such a bag, how would it have come to be there in the first place? If there were really a great drum, what skin could have been stretched across it? If one were to go on like this, the heavens would not be able to turn without feet, nor could natural creation work without hands.

Furthermore, to take a simple example, animals are all male or female, but plants have no sex. It is the way of animals that they require both male and female to reproduce, and it is the way of plants that they flourish despite the absence of sexes. If we were to think of other things in terms of ourselves, how could we ever understand their *ri*?[5]

To use another allegory, it is as though fire had a mind and thought about water, wondering "How does water burn things, how does it dry them?" thinking always in terms of its own attributes, never being aware of those it lacks. Conversely, if water also had a mind, when it thought about fire it might think about fire in terms of what it lacks itself. The utmost powers of the intellect and the exertions of a lifetime could be of little benefit under such conditions.

In accordance with the maxim from *I Ching*,[6] "Strive to progress by small steps," I shall tell you a simple story.

Once upon a time there was a mikado who heard of a beautiful wisteria in Sakai and had it transplanted to his palace garden. One night a beautiful maiden appeared to him in a dream, chanting mournfully "I must return to the beloved wisteria groves of Sakai." He awoke from the dream believing that the flowers were grieving for their homeland, and had the wisteria sent back.

There are numerous such stories. Nevertheless, plants have no minds, and are not the figures that appear in dreams. It is the human heart that grieves for the

---

[4] **Nirvana:** In Buddhism and Hinduism, the state of eternal bliss that occurs when the soul is finally liberated from the cycle of death and rebirth.

[5] *ri:* In the neo-Confucian thought of twelfth-century Chinese philosopher Zhu Xi (1130–1200), *ri* (the Japanese term), the fundamental, transcendental principle, works in tandem with *ki,* the physical force that governs all things. By Baien's time, Kaibara Ekken (1630–1714) had rejected this dualistic philosophy and argued in favor of a single principle, *seiri* or *ri,* as the natural law governing the universe.

[6] *I Ching:* The *Yi Jing,* known in English as *The Book of Changes,* is essentially a manual that describes an intricate system of divination based on different combinations of hexagrams, consisting of varied patterns of broken *(yin)* and solid *(yang)* lines. The book was produced over several centuries, dating back as far as the eleventh century B.C.E., accumulating commentaries and explanations over time, up through Confucius (551–479 B.C.E.), who added his "Ten Wings" to the work.

homeland it has left, or sighs for days gone by. It is the movement of the human heart that attributes feelings to flowers, and composes lyrics about the commonplace. Wisteria flowers do not do these things. When we transfer our feelings to flowers which are innocent of them, we make flowers human too.

From ancient times, even the most outstanding thinkers have suffered such an affliction. Confined in a human world they have not been able to detach themselves from mankind, their sight has been obstructed, their thoughts have been fixed by habit and their minds have not been prepared to question things. If our minds are not ready to doubt or question, we could quite easily end our days in a state of stupor.

Nevertheless, it should not be said that there is nothing which makes people wonder. When they experience thunder or earthquakes, they all shake their heads and wonder what might be happening. But when I watch them do this, I wonder *why* they wonder about thunder and earthquakes. People wonder why the earth shakes, without enquiring how things are when it does not shake, or they marvel when it thunders, without enquiring how things are when there is no thunder. Doesn't this seem foolish? From the innocent moment of birth, it is inevitable that we should form habits of thought from what we see, hear, and touch, but people think they understand these things because they are familiar with them.

When I ask a person why a stone falls to the ground when it is released from my hand, he says "because it is heavy, everyone knows this." But he does not understand this thing he says he knows. He does not realise that he is speaking from habit, and to all intents he may as well be speaking in a drunken stupor.

For it is not strange things that should arouse our curiosity, but everyday things like the falling stone. That is what Confucius[7] means when he asks how we can expect to understand death when we do not understand life. People wonder what will happen to them when they die, yet they do not know how to conduct their present lives. As the saying goes, we cannot cross the next river before we have crossed this one. But people persist in worrying about the next crossing, ignoring the crossing straight before them. It is a mystery to me why they do this. Surely, before wondering whether a stone might speak we should wonder how it is that we ourselves should speak, before wondering whether a dead tree might flower, we should find out why it is that a living tree should flower.

If we approach each thing with an unbiased mind, then we shall see that all these things, the rising and setting of the sun and moon, the constant changes of generation and decay, the eyes by which we see, the ears by which we hear, the limbs by which we move, the very mind itself which thinks these things, cannot have a single explanation. When we ask about them, people answer simply that this is how things must be, and leave it at that: eyes "must" see, ears "must" hear, heavy objects "must" sink, light objects "must" float, these things are "common knowledge." By this token we should say simply that thunder roars because it must and earthquakes shake

---

[7] **Confucius:** Kongfuzi (c. 551–479 B.C.E.), Chinese philosopher thought to be the source of *Analects,* a collection of aphorisms and dialogues recorded by his disciples. His teachings led to the founding of Confucianism, one of the most important moral and religious systems of thought in China and Japan, particularly as it was modified by later commentators.

because they must. If a dead tree were to bloom it would be because it must bloom, if a stone were to speak it would be because it must speak.

Now someone who has read a little might tell us that thunder is the conflict of yin and yang,[8] but if we were to ask him what yin and yang are he would not know. In this respect the learned man is no better than the fool.

So when we try to understand heaven and earth, we begin by wondering about thunder or earthquakes, and heaven and earth become one vast area of doubt. A wild animal will hide when it is about to strike, a vulture will fold its wings when it is about to attack, so we ourselves should pause to reflect thoroughly before undertaking these enquiries. When a bow is drawn, the further the arrow hand is pulled back from the bow, the further the arrow will travel. He who has many doubts achieves understanding, he who has no doubts is like the man who shoots an arrow without drawing the bowstring well back.

People do not understand heaven and earth because they are confined to the familiar, they hold fast to their habits of thought. This means that if we are to see heaven and earth with insight, our first task is to query familiar everyday things, to regard everything we come across as an object of curiosity, and to acknowledge that we who are doubting and thinking are merely human, with human habits. . . .

If we were to rely entirely on books for knowledge, believing this knowledge to be thorough—as though the lords of creation themselves had spoken to us and things could not possibly be otherwise—we should still be relying on human habits of thought, there would be no escape.

Thus I may visit schools and speak to the masters, and because when I question them I find that they share my own ideas and attitudes, I call them educated and well informed. I ponder the relics of the past, and study the geography of distant lands, how far away they are to west or east, and a hundred other such things. For noting things beyond what I see and hear directly, and confirming other people's discoveries, books are indeed important. Nevertheless, heaven and earth are neither old nor new, ancient nor modern, they are always constant and unchanging. The fire in my fireplace is the same fire that is ten thousand miles away, the water in my bowl was the same water a thousand ages ago. Since this is so, if we try to understand heaven and earth, and to understand this fire and this water, we must first apply ourselves to the unchanging. When we consult the books beside us, we should reject anything contrary to our findings, and accept only what does agree. [. . .]

---

[8] yin and yang: A pair of interdynamic opposites derived from a dualistic system of ancient Chinese philosophy; symbolically representing the sun and the moon, *yang* is positive, active, and strong, while *yin* is negative, passive, and weak; an excess of one or the other in any aspect of life and consciousness is to be avoided.

❧ JEAN-JACQUES ROUSSEAU
1712–1778

In an age of philosophical skepticism and critical inquiry, an age when man searched for the universal principles that might govern human nature, and an age when the great *Encyclopedia* project was undertaken—an attempt to categorize and define everything that was known and everything that had recently been invented—it is perhaps surprising to recall that one of the **ENLIGHTENMENT**'s most important figures turned Europe's attention to the realm of human feeling. Often considered a precursor to and certainly one of the greatest influences on the European Romantic movement, Jean-Jacques Rousseau rediscovered (if not reinvented) the inner life for an era otherwise occupied with external accomplishments and achievements. While other philosophers sought to promote, through the corrosive acid of **SATIRE**, a more humane and just society that acted in accordance with the tenets of reason, Rousseau found the seat of humanity and justice in the record of his own life, in the history of the growth of his own reason and feelings. The *Confessions*, written between 1765 and 1770 but published posthumously from 1781 to 1788, records Rousseau's tortuous journey into the depths of his being, his pilgrimage to the childhood origins of the self. For Lord Byron,[1] the great English Romantic poet, Rousseau was the "apostle of affliction" who "threw / Enchantment over passion, and from woe / Wrung overwhelming eloquence" (*Childe Harold* III, Canto 77). In recording these thoughts about sentiment and feeling, Rousseau exerted an influence on Western thought that still informs our discussions of art, literature, politics, society, and human nature.

Maurice-Quentin de La Tour, Detail from *Portrait of Jean-Jacques Rousseau.* Pastel
A portrait of the philosopher as a young man. (Giraudon / Art Resource, NY)

Separation from Family.   The self-taught Rousseau was born in Geneva in 1712, the son of Isaac Rousseau, a watchmaker who was exiled when Jean-Jacques was ten years old, and Susanne Bernard, who died a few days after the boy's birth. His father introduced Jean-Jacques at a young age to the contemporary novels his mother had left behind and then to the classics, and to this reading Rousseau attributes the birth of his intensity of feeling. Upon Isaac's exile, father and son were separated, and Jean-Jacques moved in with his uncle, who set him up as an engraver's apprentice. After three unhappy years, in March 1728 the young man rather impulsively left Geneva, beginning a brief period of vagabondage through Europe, taking up jobs ranging from footman to tutor.

Citizen of Geneva.   Ending up eventually in Turin, Rousseau converted to Catholicism and moved in with thirty-year-old Madame de Warens,

www   For links to more information about Rousseau, a quiz on *Confessions*, and information about the 21st-century relevance of *Confessions*, see *World Literature Online* at bedfordstmartins .com/worldlit.

---

[1] **Lord Byron:** Celebrated English Romantic poet, known for his creation of the Byronic hero, a gloomy, self-tormented outcast whose heroic desire and defiance of authority give him a dubious freedom; author of *Childe Harold's Pilgrimage* (1812–18), *Manfred* (1817), and *Don Juan* (1819–24), among many other shorter works.

with whom he lived at Chambery and at her country house at Les Charmettes until 1742. During these years Rousseau continued his self-education, keeping extensive notes on a wide range of subjects, including science, mathematics, astronomy, and music. In 1742 Rousseau left for Paris, where he received the patronage of Madame Dupin, among others; fell in love with Thérèse Levasseur (among others), a laundress whom he would eventually marry; met Diderot and d'Alembert,[2] the editors of the *Encyclopedia;* and took up his writing in great earnest. In 1750, at the age of thirty-eight, he earned a prize from the Academy of Dijon for his *Discourse on the Sciences and Arts* and began making a name for himself as a writer of plays and operas, especially *The Village Soothsayer,* performed first in 1752. Two years later, while visiting Geneva, Rousseau converted back to Protestantism. Over the next decade, the "Citizen of Geneva," as Rousseau sometimes called himself, penned a succession of important philosophical treatises, works of criticism, and fiction, including *Discourse on Inequality* (1755), *Julie, or the New Heloise* (1761), **The Social Contract** (1762), and *Émile* (1762). In *Letter to d'Alembert on Plays* (1758), an important work that would set Rousseau apart from Voltaire and other *philosophes,* Rousseau rejected Voltaire's plan to bring a theater to Geneva. Defending the prohibition of theaters in Geneva, he argued that drama corrupts its audiences and wastes money.

p. 591
p. 735

But by 1762, Rousseau had written *Émile* and *The Social Contract,* pitting himself against the authorities. His demand in these works for individual liberties, his indictment of government and European civilization for inevitably corrupting the innate goodness of human beings, and his ideas for political reform exceeded the tolerance of those in power. On June 9, 1762, the Parlement of Paris issued a warrant for Rousseau's arrest, and ten days later the Advisory Council of Geneva banned and burned both books.

Exile.   Rousseau's flight from Paris only began a pattern of persecution and expulsion that took him across Europe — from Motiers, a territory in Prussia, to the Isle of Saint-Pierre; back to Paris, where he assumed various aliases; to England on the invitation of the philosopher David Hume; and finally back to Paris, where he was allowed to remain from 1770 until his death in 1778, even though the order for his arrest was not rescinded. In his last years he wrote the moving and troubled *Reveries of a Solitary Walker* (1782), in which he attempts to vindicate his life and work to posterity. This work records the isolation and alienation brought on by years of persecution and hostile criticism.

Society and Feeling.   *Discourse on Inequality* and *Discourse on Political Economy,* both published in 1755, as well as *The Social Contract,* published in 1762, focus on the place of the individual in society and the means by

---

[2] **Diderot and d'Alembert.** Denis Diderot (1713–1784) and Jean le Rond d'Alembert (1717–1783) were two of the leading *philosophes* of the French Enlightenment and coeditors of the massive *Encyclopedia.* (See general introduction, pp. 2–9.)

which corrupt systems of government, education, and culture erode the basic goodness of human beings. In the novels *Julie, or the New Heloise* (1761) and *Émile* (1762), Rousseau again addresses the corruption of human beings by government and civilization, emphasizing the role that nature and feeling play in the development of the self. In his novels, as in his other writings, he upholds the virtues of childhood innocence, contemplative communication with nature, and the perfectibility of society. Rousseau's ideas became a part of and some would say inaugurated European ROMANTICISM,[3] and many European writers of the early nineteenth century followed in Rousseau's footsteps, setting off along an inner path in search of a self that could transcend or escape the effects of social conditioning and acculturation.

Rousseau's *Julie* "changed the ways in which people thought and felt and acted."
– MAURICE CRANSTON, *The Noble Savage: Jean-Jacques Rousseau,* 1991

Rousseau's Critics. Nonetheless, Rousseau is not without his critics, and for good reason. As Mary Wollstonecraft[4] pointed out, Rousseau's ideals of virtue and principles of justice and egalitarianism were often compromised and contradicted in his own practices. In the words of her *Vindication of the Rights of Woman*, in which she justly attacks Rousseau for his retrograde views on the education of women, "had Rousseau mounted one step higher in his investigation [of the principles of society], or could his eye have pierced through the foggy atmosphere which he almost disdained to breathe, his active mind would have darted forward to contemplate the perfection of man in the establishment of true civilization, instead of taking his ferocious flight back to the night of sensual ignorance." Samuel Johnson[5] thought him a "bad man," and his work has been blamed for no less than the French Revolution[6] as well as for the sometimes affected "sensibility" of the late eighteenth century. Even his detractors, however, acknowledge his genius and the value of his principles.

p. 742

The *Confessions*. Rousseau attempted many times to answer the question he posed in *Reveries*, "What am I?," but nowhere more exhaustively than in the *Confessions*, where he systematically reflects upon the origins of his own subjectivity. Madame de Staël[7] may have summed up

[3] **Romanticism:** A literary and artistic movement that swept through Europe in the early nineteenth century. In its simplest form it exalted nature, the innocence of children and rustics, private emotion and experience, and the pursuit of political freedom and spiritual transcendence. (See the general introduction to Book 5.)

[4] **Mary Wollstonecraft** (1759–1797): English novelist, critic, and political philosopher whose writings include *A Vindication of the Rights of Woman* (1792), an early call for women's rights.

[5] **Samuel Johnson** (1709–1784): English novelist, poet, and critic who wrote some of the earliest biographical sketches of poets and compiled the *Dictionary* (1755), one of the earliest and most important lexicons of the English language.

[6] **French Revolution:** The first of the major revolutions in France in the late eighteenth and nineteenth centuries; it began symbolically with the storming of the Bastille in 1789 and lasted through the coup of 18th Brumaire (November 9–10, 1799), when Napoleon overthrew the revolutionary government.

[7] **Madame de Staël** (1766–1817): Genevan, née Germaine Necker; one of the most important women of letters in Europe in the early nineteenth century.

The real object of my *Confessions* is, to contribute to an accurate knowledge of my inner being in all the different situations of my life.

– ROUSSEAU,
Confessions

p. 522

Rousseau's design for the *Confessions* best in her *Letters on Rousseau* (1788), where she speculates, "I think he wrote his memoirs to shine as a historian rather than as the hero of his story. He cared about the portrait rather than the face. He observed himself and painted himself as if he had been his own model: I am convinced that his primary wish was to make himself a good likeness."

Not all critics agree with Madame de Staël regarding Rousseau's honesty or the work's verisimilitude. Indeed, it often seems that like Benjamin Franklin, Rousseau intends his portrait to draw the reader's sympathy for even his more egregious faults, of which there is no short supply. More unabashedly, consistently, and explicitly than Franklin's *Autobiography*, the *Confessions* parades before its readers a succession of errors, misfortunes, and misdeeds. Ironically, perhaps, Rousseau presents these faults to show that he is at heart a man of virtue and sensitivity, that truth and goodness are woven into the very fabric of his being. So far as the actual details of incidents in his life go, Rousseau admits to imprecision; but he argues that he cares more to present a record of his feelings than an account of events.

Although some note a certain disingenuousness in the autobiography, Rousseau's *Confessions* introduced to the Age of Enlightenment "the man of feeling," a person who attempts to bring the mind into balance with the heart through self-reflection, acts of compassion, and an appreciation of the delicate interplay of emotion involved in human relationships. Yet, like Molière, Alexander Pope, Jonathan Swift, and other Enlightenment writers who satirize the affectation and hypocrisy of their age, Rousseau distinguishes between true feeling and artificial manners. A key concept in his work is *amour propre,* or the love of social approval. Governed by *amour propre,* he says, a person loses touch with his or her true self, for his or her actions and manners are oriented toward winning the approval and respect of others. Thus, marking a transition between the Enlightenment and the age of Romanticism, Rousseau seeks in *Confessions* and other writings to achieve a kind of transparency of the self, to express the true rather than the false self. *Confessions* in particular purports to be the "artless" record of the life and feelings of a man who was essentially honest and innately good, despite the faults and errors that clutter the course of his life. In this regard, Rousseau's autobiography may be usefully compared to St. Augustine's;[8] but whereas Augustine attributes his essential goodness and salvation to the grace of God, Rousseau finds the source of his goodness in human nature itself.

■ **CONNECTIONS**

Benjamin Franklin, *Autobiography,* **p. 522.** Rousseau's *Confessions* is considered one of the great autobiographies in the European literary tradition. Like Augustine's *Confessions,* to which it deliberately alludes, Rousseau's text focuses on the narrator's

---

[8] **St. Augustine** (354–430 C.E.): The Bishop of Hippo, who became one of the most influential theologians of the Christian church through his writings, the spiritual autobiography *Confessions* (397–400) and *The City of God* (412–26). (See Augustine, Book 1.)

struggle to rise above his transgressions. In his *Autobiography*, Franklin also accounts for his sins, which he calls his "errata," but in a very different way. Name some ways in which Rousseau's and Franklin's autobiographies differ. How does Rousseau's greater candor about his personal feelings and sexuality affect your reading of his text? How might these two autobiographies demonstrate the differences in values of the American Enlightenment and European Romanticism?

Mary Rowlandson, *Narrative of the Captivity and Restoration of Mrs. Mary Rowlandson*, p. 483; Harriet Jacobs, *Incidents in the Life of a Slave Girl* (Book 5). Some see the emotional and intellectual malaise in Rousseau's *Confessions* as deriving from the narrator's inflated sense of persecution. Rowlandson and Jacobs were subjected to actual conditions of confinement and slavery and suffered much emotional distress. How does knowledge of a writer's real life affect the way we respond to the confessional elements in autobiographical works?

Shen Fu, *Six Records of a Floating Life*, p. 755. Rousseau's *Confessions* deals openly with matters of sexuality, love, and personal feelings, as does Shen Fu's autobiography. What are some of the differences and similarities between Rousseau's and Shen Fu's treatment of these subjects? What in their texts may be said to be culturally specific?

■ **FURTHER RESEARCH**

Biography

Cranston, Maurice. *The Noble Savage: Jean-Jacques Rousseau.* 1991.

———. *The Solitary Self: Jean-Jacques Rousseau in Exile and Adversity.* 1997.

Guéhenno, Jean. *Jean-Jacques.* 1948–52.

Winwar, Frances. *Jean-Jacques Rousseau: Conscience of an Era.* 1983.

Criticism

France, Peter. *Rousseau, Confessions.* 1987.

Kavanaugh, Thomas M. *Writing the Truth: Authority and Desire in the Works of Rousseau.* 1987.

Kelly, Christopher. *Rousseau's Exemplary Life: The* Confessions *as Political Philosophy.* 1987.

Shklar, Judith. *Men and Citizens: A Study of Rousseau's Social Theory.* 1969.

Starobinski, Jean. *Jean-Jacques Rousseau: Transparency and Obstruction.* 1971; trans. 1988.

Swenson, James. *On Jean-Jacques Rousseau: Considered as One of the First Authors of the Revolution.* 2000.

Williams, Huntington. *Rousseau and Romantic Autobiography.* 1983.

■ **PRONUNCIATION**

Bossey: baw-SEE
Ducommun: doo-kom-OON
Goton: goh-TOHNG
Lambercier: lahm-behr-SYAY
Madame de Staël: mah-DAHM duh STAHL
Masseron: mahs-ROHNG
Jean-Jacques Rousseau: zhawng-zhahk roo-SOH
Verrat: veh-RAH
de Vulson: duh vool-SOHNG

 # Confessions

Translator anonymous

BOOK 1

[1712–1719]

I am commencing an undertaking, hitherto without precedent, and which will never find an imitator. I desire to set before my fellows the likeness of a man in all the truth of nature, and that man will be myself.

Myself alone! I know the feelings of my heart, and I know men. I am not made like any of those I have seen; I venture to believe that I am not made like any of those who are in existence. If I am not better, at least I am different. Whether Nature has acted rightly or wrongly in destroying the mould in which she cast me, can only be decided after I have been read.

Let the trumpet of the Day of Judgment sound when it will, I will present myself before the Sovereign Judge with this book in my hand. I will say boldly: "This is what I have done, what I have thought, what I was. I have told the good and the bad with equal frankness. I have neither omitted anything bad, nor interpolated anything good. If I have occasionally made use of some immaterial embellishments, this has only been in order to fill a gap caused by lack of memory. I may have assumed the truth of that which I knew might have been true, never of that which I knew to be false. I have shown myself as I was: mean and contemptible, good, highminded and sublime, according as I was one or the other. I have unveiled my inmost self even as Thou hast seen it, O Eternal Being. Gather round me the countless host of my fellow-men; let them hear my confessions, lament for my unworthiness, and blush for my imperfections. Then let each of them in turn reveal, with the same frankness,

---

Confessions. A revolutionary work of self-reflection and self-invention, *Confessions* covers Rousseau's life through 1766, when he went to England to begin working on his autobiography in earnest. Although he completed the manuscript in 1770, *Confessions* was not published until after his death in 1778. The work appeared in two parts: Books 1 through 6 in 1781; Books 7 through 12 in 1788. This first chapter from *Confessions* is characteristic of the whole in its unabashed revelation of intimate details, its bold claims to honesty, if not accuracy, and its not always successful negotiation between narcissism and humility. This last feature of the work often presents difficulties for readers, who, unconvinced by Rousseau's claims, find him mired in self-pity and even arrogance. Full disclosure of one's personal life, however, always invites such criticism, and even Benjamin Franklin's *Autobiography,* in which Franklin avoids discussing the intimate details of his personal life, often walks a fine line between self-invention and self-revelation, vanity and sincerity. Certainly Rousseau's autobiography anticipates, perhaps even initiates, the movement toward the self-conscious display of emotion and the confessional mode of Romantic and post-Romantic European writing of the next two centuries.

A note on the translation: This anonymous translation manages to capture the spirit of Rousseau's restless inquiry into his life. All notes are the editors'.

the secrets of his heart at the foot of the Throne, and say, if he dare, '*I was better than that man!*'"

I was born at Geneva, in the year 1712, and was the son of Isaac Rousseau and Susanne Bernard, citizens. The distribution of a very moderate inheritance amongst fifteen children had reduced my father's portion almost to nothing; and his only means of livelihood was his trade of watchmaker, in which he was really very clever. My mother, a daughter of the Protestant minister Bernard, was better off. She was clever and beautiful, and my father had found difficulty in obtaining her hand. Their affection for each other had commenced almost as soon as they were born. When only eight years old, they walked every evening upon the Treille;[1] at ten, they were inseparable. Sympathy and union of soul strengthened in them the feeling produced by intimacy. Both, naturally full of tender sensibility, only waited for the moment when they should find the same disposition in another—or, rather, this moment waited for them, and each abandoned his heart to the first which opened to receive it. Destiny, which appeared to oppose their passion, only encouraged it. The young lover, unable to obtain possession of his mistress, was consumed by grief. She advised him to travel, and endeavour to forget her. He travelled, but without result, and returned more in love than ever. He found her whom he loved still faithful and true. After this trial of affection, nothing was left for them but to love each other all their lives. This they swore to do, and Heaven blessed their oath.

Gabriel Bernard, my mother's brother, fell in love with one of my father's sisters, who only consented to accept the hand of the brother, on condition that her own brother married the sister. Love arranged everything, and the two marriages took place on the same day. Thus my uncle became the husband of my aunt, and their children were doubly my first cousins. At the end of a year, a child was born to both, after which they were again obliged to separate.

My uncle Bernard was an engineer. He took service in the Empire and in Hungary, under Prince Eugène.[2] He distinguished himself at the siege and battle of Belgrade. My father, after the birth of my only brother, set out for Constantinople, whither he was summoned to undertake the post of watchmaker to the Sultan. During his absence, my mother's beauty, intellect, and talents gained for her the devotion of numerous admirers. M. de la Closure, the French Resident, was one of the most eager to offer his. His passion must have been great, for, thirty years later, I saw him greatly affected when speaking to me of her. To enable her to resist such advances, my mother had more than her virtue: she loved her husband tenderly. She pressed him to return; he left all, and returned. I was the unhappy fruit of this return. Ten months later I was born, a weak and ailing child; I cost my mother her life, and my birth was the first of my misfortunes.

I have never heard how my father bore this loss, but I know that he was inconsolable. He believed that he saw his wife again in me, without being able to forget

---

[1] **Treille:** A popular walk or promenade in Geneva.

[2] **Empire . . . Eugène:** The Austrian empire; Eugène was an Austrian general who served in the wars against Turkey.

that it was I who had robbed him of her; he never embraced me without my perceiving, by his sighs and the convulsive manner in which he clasped me to his breast, that a bitter regret was mingled with his caresses, which were on that account only the more tender. When he said to me, "Jean Jacques, let us talk of your mother," I used to answer, "Well, then, my father, we will weep!" — and this word alone was sufficient to move him to tears. "Ah!" said he, with a sigh, "give her back to me, console me for her loss, fill the void which she has left in my soul. Should I love you as I do, if you were only my son?" Forty years after he had lost her, he died in the arms of a second wife, but the name of the first was on his lips and her image at the bottom of his heart.

Such were the authors of my existence. Of all the gifts which Heaven had bestowed upon them, a sensitive heart is the only one they bequeathed to me; it had been the source of their happiness, but for me it proved the source of all the misfortunes of my life.

I was brought into the world in an almost dying condition; little hope was entertained of saving my life. I carried within me the germs of a complaint which the course of time has strengthened, and which at times allows me a respite only to make me suffer more cruelly in another manner. One of my father's sisters, an amiable and virtuous young woman, took such care of me that she saved my life. At this moment, while I am writing, she is still alive, at the age of eighty, nursing a husband younger than herself, but exhausted by excessive drinking. Dear aunt,[3] I forgive you for having preserved my life; and I deeply regret that, at the end of your days, I am unable to repay the tender care which you lavished upon me at the beginning of my own. My dear old nurse Jacqueline is also still alive, healthy and robust. The hands which opened my eyes at my birth will be able to close them for me at my death.

I felt before I thought: This is the common lot of humanity. I experienced it more than others. I do not know what I did until I was five or six years old. I do not know how I learned to read; I only remember my earliest reading, and the effect it had upon me; from that time I date my uninterrupted self-consciousness. My mother had left some romances behind her, which my father and I began to read after supper. At first it was only a question of practising me in reading by the aid of amusing books; but soon the interest became so lively, that we used to read in turns without stopping, and spent whole nights in this occupation. We were unable to leave off until the volume was finished. Sometimes, my father, hearing the swallows begin to twitter in the early morning, would say, quite ashamed, "Let us go to bed; I am more of a child than yourself."

In a short time I acquired, by this dangerous method, not only extreme facility in reading and understanding what I read, but a knowledge of the passions that was unique in a child of my age. I had no idea of things in themselves, although all the feelings of actual life were already known to me. I had conceived nothing, but felt everything. These confused emotions which I felt one after the other, certainly did not warp the reasoning powers which I did not as yet possess; but they shaped them in me of a peculiar stamp, and gave me odd and romantic notions of human life, of which experience and reflection have never been able wholly to cure me.

---

[3] **aunt:** Madame Gonçeru, to whom Rousseau paid a small stipend.

[1719–1723]

The romances came to an end in the summer of 1719. The following winter brought us something different. My mother's library being exhausted, we had recourse to the share of her father's which had fallen to us. Luckily, there were some good books in it; in fact, it could hardly have been otherwise, for the library had been collected by a minister, who was even a learned man according to the fashion of the day, and was at the same time a man of taste and intellect. The "History of the Empire and the Church," by Le Sueur; Bossuet's "Treatise upon Universal History"; Plutarch's "Lives of Famous Men"; Nani's "History of Venice"; Ovid's "Metamorphoses"; La Bruyère; Fontenelle's "Worlds"; his "Dialogues of the Dead"; and some volumes of Molière— all these were brought over into my father's room, and I read to him out of them while he worked. I conceived a taste for them that was rare and perhaps unique at my age. Plutarch, especially, became my favourite author. The pleasure I took in reading him over and over again cured me a little of my taste for romance, and I soon preferred Agesilaus, Brutus, and Aristides to Orondates, Artamenes, and Juba.[4] This interesting reading, and the conversations between my father and myself to which it gave rise, formed in me the free and republican spirit, the proud and indomitable character unable to endure slavery or servitude, which has tormented me throughout my life in situations the least fitted to afford it scope. Unceasingly occupied with thoughts of Rome and Athens, living as it were amongst their great men, myself by birth the citizen of a republic and the son of a father whose patriotism was his strongest passion, I was fired by his example; I believed myself a Greek or a Roman; I lost my identity in that of the individual whose life I was reading; the recitals of the qualities of endurance and intrepidity which arrested my attention made my eyes glisten and strengthened my voice. One day, while I was relating the history of Scaevola[5] at table, those present were alarmed to see me come forward and hold my hand over a chafing-dish, to illustrate his action.

I had a brother seven years older than myself, who was learning my father's trade. The excessive affection which was lavished upon myself caused him to be somewhat neglected, which treatment I cannot approve of. His education felt the consequences of this neglect. He took to evil courses before he was old enough to be a regular profligate. He was put with another master, from whom he was continually running away, as he had done from home. I hardly ever saw him; I can scarcely say that I knew him; but I never ceased to love him tenderly, and he loved me as much as a vagabond can love anything. I remember that, on one occasion, when my father was chastising him harshly and in anger, I threw myself impetuously between them and embraced him closely. In this manner I covered his body with mine, and received the blows which were aimed at him; I so obstinately maintained my position that at last my father was obliged to leave off, being either disarmed by my cries

---

[4] **Agesilaus . . . Juba:** Agesilaus, Brutus, and Aristides appear in Plutarch's *Lives* (c. 100 C.E.); the last three are heroes from popular romances.

[5] **Scaevola:** The legendary Roman hero; when about to be executed for attempting to kill the Etruscan chief Lars Porsena, who was attacking Rome, Scaevola (which means "left-handed") held his right hand in fire to show his determination. The chief was so impressed that he withdrew his forces from Rome.

and tears, or afraid of hurting me more than him. At last, my brother turned out so badly that he ran away and disappeared altogether. Sometime afterwards we heard that he was in Germany. He never once wrote to us. From that time nothing more has been heard of him, and thus I have remained an only son.

If this poor boy was carelessly brought up, this was not the case with his brother; the children of kings could not be more carefully looked after than I was during my early years—worshipped by all around me, and, which is far less common, treated as a beloved, never as a spoiled child. Till I left my father's house, I was never once allowed to run about the streets by myself with the other children; in my case no one ever had to satisfy or check any of those fantastic whims which are attributed to Nature, but are all in reality the result of education. I had the faults of my age: I was a chatterbox, a glutton, and, sometimes, a liar. I would have stolen fruits, bonbons, or eatables; but I have never found pleasure in doing harm or damage, in accusing others, or in tormenting poor dumb animals. I remember, however, that I once made water in a saucepan belonging to one of our neighbours, Madame Clot, while she was at church. I declare that, even now, the recollection of this makes me laugh, because Madame Clot, a good woman in other respects, was the most confirmed old grumbler I have ever known. Such is the brief and true story of all my childish offences.

How could I become wicked, when I had nothing but examples of gentleness before my eyes, and none around me but the best people in the world? My father, my aunt, my nurse, my relations, our friends, our neighbours, all who surrounded me, did not, it is true, obey me, but they loved me; and I loved them in return. My wishes were so little excited and so little opposed, that it did not occur to me to have any. I can swear that, until I served under a master, I never knew what a fancy was. Except during the time I spent in reading or writing in my father's company, or when my nurse took me for a walk, I was always with my aunt, sitting or standing by her side, watching her at her embroidery or listening to her singing; and I was content. Her cheerfulness, her gentleness, and her pleasant face have stamped so deep and lively an impression on my mind that I can still see her manner, look, and attitude; I remember her affectionate language: I could describe what clothes she wore and how her head was dressed, not forgetting the two little curls of black hair on her temples, which she wore in accordance with the fashion of the time.

I am convinced that it is to her I owe the taste, or rather passion, for music, which only became fully developed in me a long time afterwards. She knew a prodigious number of tunes and songs which she used to sing in a very thin, gentle voice. This excellent woman's cheerfulness of soul banished dreaminess and melancholy from herself and all around her. The attraction which her singing possessed for me was so great, that not only have several of her songs always remained in my memory, but even now, when I have lost her, and as I grew older, many of them, totally forgotten since the days of my childhood, return to my mind with inexpressible charm. Would anyone believe that I, an old dotard, eaten up by cares and troubles, sometimes find myself weeping like a child, when I mumble one of those little airs in a voice already broken and trembling? One of them, especially, has come back to me completely, as far as the tune is concerned; the second half of the words, however, has obstinately resisted all my efforts to recall it, although I have an indistinct recollection of the rhymes. Here is the beginning, and all that I can remember of the rest:

> Tircis, I dare not listen
> To your pipe
> Under the elm;
> For already in our village
> People have begun to talk.
>
> . . . to engage
> . . . with a shepherd
> . . . without danger
> And always the thorn is with the rose.[6]

I ask, where is the affecting charm which my heart finds in this song? it is a whim, which I am quite unable to understand; but, be that as it may, it is absolutely impossible for me to sing it through without being interrupted by my tears. I have intended, times without number, to write to Paris to make inquiries concerning the remainder of the words, in case anyone should happen to know them; but I am almost certain that the pleasure which I feel in recalling the air would partly disappear, if it should be proved that others besides my poor aunt Susan have sung it.

Such were my earliest emotions on my entry into life; thus began to form or display itself in me that heart at once so proud and tender, that character so effeminate but yet indomitable, which, ever wavering between timidity and courage, weakness and self-control, has throughout my life made me inconsistent, and has caused abstinence and enjoyment, pleasure and prudence equally to elude my grasp.

This course of education was interrupted by an accident, the consequences of which have exercised an influence upon the remainder of my life. My father had a quarrel with a captain in the French army, named Gautier, who was connected with some of the members of the Common Council. This Gautier, a cowardly and insolent fellow (whose nose happened to bleed during the affray), in order to avenge himself, accused my father of having drawn his sword within the city walls. My father, whom they wanted to send to prison, persisted that, in accordance with the law, the accuser ought to be imprisoned as well as himself. Being unable to have his way in this, he preferred to quit Geneva and expatriate himself for the rest of his life, than to give way on a point in which honour and liberty appeared to him to be compromised.

I remained under the care of my uncle Bernard, who was at the time employed upon the fortifications of Geneva. His eldest daughter was dead, but he had a son of the same age as myself. We were sent together to Bossey,[7] to board with the Protestant minister Lambercier, in order to learn, together with Latin, all the sorry trash which is included under the name of education.

Two years spent in the village in some degree softened my Roman roughness and made me a child again. At Geneva, where no tasks were imposed upon me, I

---

[6] Rousseau's text deliberately leaves out the sixth line of this popular song: "It is dangerous for a heart."

[7] **Bossey:** A village three miles from Geneva.

loved reading and study, which were almost my only amusements; at Bossey, my tasks made me love the games which formed a break in them. The country was so new to me, that my enjoyment of it never palled. I conceived so lively an affection for it, that it has never since died out. The remembrance of the happy days I have spent there filled me with regretful longing for its pleasures, at all periods of my life, until the day which has brought me back to it. M. Lambercier was a very intelligent person, who, without neglecting our education, never imposed excessive tasks upon us. The fact that, in spite of my dislike of restraint, I have never recalled my hours of study with any feeling of disgust—and also that, even if I did not learn much from him, I learnt without difficulty what I did learn and never forgot it—is sufficient proof that his system of instruction was a good one.

The simplicity of this country life was of inestimable value to me, in that it opened my heart to friendship. Up to that time I had only known lofty but imaginary sentiments. The habit of living peacefully together with my cousin Bernard drew us together in tender bonds of union. In a short time, my feelings towards him became more affectionate than those with which I had regarded my brother, and they have never been effaced. He was a tall, lanky, weakly boy, as gentle in disposition as he was feeble in body, who never abused the preference which was shown to him in the house as the son of my guardian. Our tasks, our amusements, our tastes were the same: we were alone, we were of the same age, each of us needed a companion: separation was to us, in a manner, annihilation. Although we had few opportunities of proving our mutual attachment, it was very great; not only were we unable to live an instant apart, but we did not imagine it possible that we could ever be separated. Being, both of us, ready to yield to tenderness, and docile, provided compulsion was not used, we always agreed in everything. If, in the presence of those who looked after us, he had some advantage over me in consequence of the favour with which they regarded him, when we were alone I had an advantage over him which restored the equilibrium. When we were saying our lessons, I prompted him if he hesitated; when I had finished my exercise, I helped him with his; and in our amusements, my more active mind always led the way. In short, our two characters harmonised so well, and the friendship which united us was so sincere, that, in the five years and more, during which, whether at Bossey or Geneva, we were almost inseparable, although I confess that we often fought, it was never necessary to separate us, none of our quarrels ever lasted longer than a quarter of an hour, and neither of us ever made any accusation against the other. These observations are, if you will, childish, but they furnish an example which, since the time that there have been children, is perhaps unique.

The life which I led at Bossey suited me so well that, had it only lasted longer, it would have completely decided my character. Tender, affectionate, and gentle feelings formed its foundation. I believe that no individual of our species was naturally more free from vanity than myself. I raised myself by fits and starts to lofty flights, but immediately fell down again into my natural languor. My liveliest desire was to be loved by all who came near me. I was of a gentle disposition; my cousin and our guardians were the same. During two whole years I was neither the witness nor the victim of any violent feeling. Everything nourished in my heart those tendencies which it received from Nature. I knew no higher happiness than to see all the world satisfied with me and with everything. I shall never forget how, if I happened to hesitate when saying my catechism in church, nothing troubled me more than to observe signs of restlessness and dissatisfaction on Mademoiselle Lambercier's face. That alone troubled me more than the disgrace of failing in public, which, nevertheless, affected me greatly: for, although little susceptible to praise, I felt shame keenly; and I may say here that the thought of Mademoiselle's reproaches caused me less uneasiness than the fear of offending her.

When it was necessary, however, neither she nor her brother were wanting in severity; but, since this severity was nearly always just, and never passionate, it pained me without making me insubordinate. Failure to please grieved me more than punishment, and signs of dissatisfaction hurt me more than corporal chastisement. It is somewhat embarrassing to explain myself more clearly, but, nevertheless, I must do so. How differently would one deal with youth, if one could more clearly see the remote effects of the usual method of treatment, which is employed always without discrimination, frequently without discretion! The important lesson which may be drawn from an example as common as it is fatal makes me decide to mention it.

As Mademoiselle Lambercier had the affection of a mother for us, she also exercised the authority of one, and sometimes carried it so far as to inflict upon us the punishment of children when we had deserved it. For some time she was content with threats, and this threat of a punishment that was quite new to me appeared very terrible; but, after it had been carried out, I found the reality less terrible than the expectation; and, what was still more strange, this chastisement made me still more devoted to her who had inflicted it. It needed all the strength of this devotion and all my natural docility to keep myself from doing something which would have deservedly brought upon me a repetition of it; for I had found in the pain, even in the disgrace, a mixture of sensuality which had left me less afraid than desirous of experiencing it again from the same hand. No doubt some precocious sexual instinct was mingled with this feeling, for the same chastisement inflicted by her brother would not have seemed to me at all pleasant. But, considering his disposition, there was little cause to fear the substitution; and if I kept myself from deserving punishment, it was solely for fear of displeasing Mademoiselle Lambercier; for, so great is the power exercised over me by kindness, even by that which is due to the senses, that it has always controlled the latter in my heart.

The repetition of the offence, which I avoided without being afraid of it, occurred without any fault of mine, that is to say, of my will, and I may say that I profited by it without any qualm of conscience. But this second time was also the last; for Mademoiselle Lambercier, who had no doubt noticed something which convinced her that the punishment did not have the desired effect, declared that it tired her too much, and that she would abandon it. Until then we had slept in her room, sometimes even in her bed during the winter. Two days afterwards we were put to sleep in another room, and from that time I had the honour, which I would gladly have dispensed with, of being treated by her as a big boy.

Who would believe that this childish punishment, inflicted upon me when only eight years old by a young woman of thirty, disposed of my tastes, my desires, my passions, and my own self for the remainder of my life, and that in a manner exactly contrary to that which should have been the natural result? When my feelings were once inflamed, my desires so went astray that, limited to what I had already felt, they did not trouble themselves to look for anything else. In spite of my hot blood, which has been inflamed with sensuality almost from my birth, I kept myself free from every taint until the age when the coldest and most sluggish temperaments begin to develop. In torments for a long time, without knowing why, I devoured with burning glances all the pretty women I met; my imagination unceasingly recalled them to me, only to make use of them in my own fashion, and to make of them so many Mlles. Lambercier.

Even after I had reached years of maturity, this curious taste, always abiding with me and carried to depravity and even frenzy, preserved my morality, which it might naturally have been expected to destroy. If ever a bringing-up was chaste and modest, assuredly mine was. My three aunts were not only models of propriety, but reserved to a degree which has long since been unknown amongst women. My father, a man of pleasure, but a gallant of the old school, never said a word, even in the presence of women whom he loved more than others, which would have brought a blush to a maiden's cheek; and the respect due to children has never been so much insisted upon as in my family and in my presence. In this respect I found M. Lambercier equally careful; and an excellent servant was dismissed for having used a somewhat too free expression in our presence. Until I was a young man, I not only had no distinct idea of the union of the sexes, but the confused notion which I had regarding it never presented itself to me except in a hateful and disgusting form. For common prostitutes I felt a loathing which has never been effaced: the sight of a profligate always filled me with contempt, even with affright. My horror of debauchery became thus pronounced ever since the day when, walking to Little Sacconex[8] by a hollow way, I saw on both sides holes in the ground, where I was told that these creatures carried on their intercourse. The thought of the one always brought back to my mind the copulation of dogs, and the bare recollection was sufficient to disgust me.

This tendency of my bringing-up, in itself adapted to delay the first outbreaks of an inflammable temperament, was assisted, as I have already said, by the direction which the first indications of sensuality took in my case. Only busying my imagination with what I had actually felt, in spite of most uncomfortable effervescence of blood, I only knew how to turn my desires in the direction of that kind of pleasure with which I was acquainted, without ever going as far as that which had been made hateful to me, and which, without my having the least suspicion of it, was so closely related to the other. In my foolish fancies, in my erotic frenzies, in the extravagant acts to which they sometimes led me, I had recourse in my imagination to the assistance of the other sex, without ever thinking that it was serviceable for any purpose than that for which I was burning to make use of it.

In this manner, then, in spite of an ardent, lascivious, and precocious temperament, I passed the age of puberty without desiring, even without knowing of any

---

[8] **Little Sacconex:** A village near Geneva.

other sensual pleasures than those of which Mademoiselle Lambercier had most innocently given me the idea; and when, in course of time, I became a man, that which should have destroyed me again preserved me. My old childish taste, instead of disappearing, became so associated with the other, that I could never banish it from the desires kindled by my senses; and this madness, joined to my natural shyness, has always made me very unenterprising with women, for want of courage to say all or power to do all. The kind of enjoyment, of which the other was only for me the final consummation, could neither be appropriated by him who longed for it, nor guessed by her who was able to bestow it. Thus I have spent my life in idle longing, without saying a word, in the presence of those whom I loved most. Too bashful to declare my taste, I at least satisfied it in situations which had reference to it and kept up the idea of it. To lie at the feet of an imperious mistress, to obey her commands, to ask her forgiveness—this was for me a sweet enjoyment; and, the more my lively imagination heated my blood, the more I presented the appearance of a bashful lover. It may be easily imagined that this manner of making love does not lead to very speedy results, and is not very dangerous to the virtue of those who are its object. For this reason I have rarely possessed, but have none the less enjoyed myself in my own way—that is to say, in imagination. Thus it has happened that my senses, in harmony with my timid disposition and my romantic spirit, have kept my sentiments pure and my morals blameless, owing to the very tastes which, combined with a little more impudence, might have plunged me into the most brutal sensuality.

I have taken the first and most difficult step in the dark and dirty labyrinth of my confessions. It is easier to admit that which is criminal than that which is ridiculous and makes a man feel ashamed. Henceforth I am sure of myself; after having ventured to say so much, I can shrink from nothing. One may judge what such confessions have cost me, from the fact that, during the whole course of my life, I have never dared to declare my folly to those whom I loved with the frenzy of a passion which deprived me of sight and hearing, which robbed me of my senses and caused me to tremble all over with a convulsive movement. I have never brought myself, even when on most intimate terms, to ask women to grant me the only favour of all which was wanting. This never happened to me but once—in my childhood, with a girl of my own age; even then, it was she who first proposed it.

While thus going back to the first traces of my inner life, I find elements which sometimes appear incompatible, and yet have united in order to produce with vigour a simple and uniform effect; and I find others which, although apparently the same, have formed combinations so different, owing to the co-operation of certain circumstances, that one would never imagine that these elements were in any way connected. Who, for instance, would believe that one of the most powerful movements of my soul was tempered in the same spring from which a stream of sensuality and effeminacy has entered my blood? Without leaving the subject of which I have just spoken, I shall produce by means of it a very different impression.

One day I was learning my lesson by myself in the room next to the kitchen. The servant had put Mademoiselle Lambercier's combs in front of the fire-place to dry. When she came back to fetch them, she found one with a whole row of teeth broken.

Who was to blame for the damage? No one except myself had entered the room. On being questioned, I denied that I had touched the comb. M. and Mademoiselle Lambercier both began to admonish, to press, and to threaten me; I obstinately persisted in my denial; but the evidence was too strong, and outweighed all my protestations, although it was the first time that I had been found to lie so boldly. The matter was regarded as serious, as in fact it deserved to be. The mischievousness, the falsehood, the obstinacy appeared equally deserving of punishment; but this time it was not by Mademoiselle Lambercier that chastisement was inflicted. My uncle Bernard was written to, and he came. My poor cousin was accused of another equally grave offence; we were involved in the same punishment. It was terrible. Had they wished to look for the remedy in the evil itself and to deaden for ever my depraved senses, they could not have set to work better, and for a long time my senses left me undisturbed.

They could not draw from me the desired confession. Although I was several times brought up before them and reduced to a pitiable condition, I remained unshaken. I would have endured death, and made up my mind to do so. Force was obliged to yield to the diabolical obstinacy of a child—as they called my firmness. At last I emerged from this cruel trial, utterly broken, but triumphant.

It is now nearly fifty years since this incident took place, and I have no fear of being punished again for the same thing. Well, then, I declare in the sight of heaven that I was innocent of the offence, that I neither broke nor touched the comb, that I never went near the fire-place, and had never even thought of doing so. It would be useless to ask me how the damage was done: I do not know, and I cannot understand; all that I know for certain is, that I had nothing to do with it.

Imagine a child, shy and obedient in ordinary life, but fiery, proud, and unruly in his passions: a child who had always been led by the voice of reason and always treated with gentleness, justice, and consideration, who had not even a notion of injustice, and who for the first time becomes acquainted with so terrible an example of it on the part of the very people whom he most loves and respects! What an upset of ideas! what a disturbance of feelings! what revolution in his heart, in his brain, in the whole of his little intellectual and moral being! Imagine all this, I say, if possible. As for myself, I feel incapable of disentangling and following up the least trace of what then took place within me.

I had not yet sense enough to feel how much appearances were against me, and to put myself in the place of the others. I kept to my own place, and all that I felt was the harshness of a frightful punishment for an offence which I had not committed. The bodily pain, although severe, I felt but little: all I felt was indignation, rage, despair. My cousin, whose case was almost the same, and who had been punished for an involuntary mistake as if it had been a premeditated act, following my example, flew into a rage, and worked himself up to the same pitch of excitement as myself. Both in the same bed, we embraced each other with convulsive transports: we felt suffocated; and when at length our young hearts, somewhat relieved, were able to vent their wrath, we sat upright in bed and began to shout, times without number, with all our might: *Carnifex! carnifex! carnifex!*[9]

---

[9] *Carnifex:* Executioner or torturer (Latin).

While I write these words, I feel that my pulse beats faster; those moments will always be present to me though I should live a hundred thousand years. That first feeling of violence and injustice has remained so deeply graven on my soul, that all the ideas connected with it bring back to me my first emotion; and this feeling, which, in its origin, had reference only to myself, has become so strong in itself and so completely detached from all personal interest, that, when I see or hear of any act of injustice—whoever is the victim of it, and wherever it is committed—my heart kindles with rage, as if the effect of it recoiled upon myself. When I read of the cruelties of a ferocious tyrant, the crafty atrocities of a rascally priest, I would gladly set out to plunge a dagger into the heart of such wretches, although I had to die for it a hundred times. I have often put myself in a perspiration, pursuing or stoning a cock, a cow, a dog, or any animal which I saw tormenting another merely because it felt itself the stronger. This impulse may be natural to me, and I believe that it is; but the profound impression left upon me by the first injustice I suffered was too long and too strongly connected with it, not to have greatly strengthened it.

With the above incident the tranquillity of my childish life was over. From that moment I ceased to enjoy a pure happiness, and even at the present day I feel that the recollection of the charms of my childhood ceases there. We remained a few months longer at Bossey. We were there, as the first man is represented to us—still in the earthly paradise, but we no longer enjoyed it; in appearance our condition was the same, in reality it was quite a different manner of existence. Attachment, respect, intimacy, and confidence no longer united pupils and guides: we no longer regarded them as gods, who were able to read in our hearts; we became less ashamed of doing wrong and more afraid of being accused; we began to dissemble, to be insubordinate, to lie. All the vices of our age corrupted our innocence and threw a veil of ugliness over our amusements. Even the country lost in our eyes that charm of gentleness and simplicity which goes to the heart. It appeared to us lonely and sombre: it seemed as it were covered with a veil which concealed its beauties from our eyes. We ceased to cultivate our little gardens, our plants, our flowers. We no longer scratched up the ground gently, or cried with joy when we saw the seed which we had sown beginning to sprout. We were disgusted with the life, and others were disgusted with us; my uncle took us away, and we separated from M. and Mademoiselle Lambercier, having had enough of each other, and feeling but little regret at the separation.

Nearly thirty years have passed since I left Bossey, without my recalling to mind my stay there with any connected and pleasurable recollections; but, now that I have passed the prime of life and am approaching old age, I feel these same recollections springing up again while others disappear; they stamp themselves upon my memory with features, the charm and strength of which increase daily, as if, feeling life already slipping away, I were endeavouring to grasp it again by its commencement. The most trifling incidents of that time please me, simply because they belong to that period. I remember all the details of place, persons, and time. I see the maid or the manservant busy in the room, a swallow darting through the window, a fly settling on my hand while I was saying my lesson: I see the whole arrangement of the room in which we used to live; M. Lambercier's study on the right, a copperplate engraving of all the Popes, a barometer, a large almanack hanging on the wall, the raspberry bushes which, growing in a garden situated on very high ground facing the back of the house, shaded the window and sometimes forced their way through it. I am quite aware that the reader does not want to know all this; but I am bound to tell him. Why have I not the courage to relate to him in like manner all the trifling anecdotes of that happy time, which still make me tremble with joy when I recall them? Five or six in particular — but let us make a bargain. I will let you off five, but I wish to tell you one, only one, provided that you will permit me to tell it in as much detail as possible, in order to prolong my enjoyment.

If I only had your pleasure in view, I might choose the story of Mademoiselle Lambercier's backside, which, owing to an unfortunate somersault at the bottom of the meadow, was exhibited in full view to the King of Sardinia, who happened to be passing by; but that of the walnut-tree on the terrace is more amusing for me who took an active part in it, whereas I was merely a spectator of the somersault; besides, I declare that I found absolutely nothing to laugh at in an accident which, although comic in itself, alarmed me for the safety of a person whom I loved as a mother and, perhaps, even more.

Now, O curious readers of the important history of the walnut-tree on the terrace, listen to the horrible tragedy, and keep from shuddering if you can!

Outside the gate of the court, on the left of the entrance, there was a terrace, where we often went to sit in the afternoon. As it was entirely unprotected from the sun, M. Lambercier had a walnut-tree planted there. The process of planting was carried out with the greatest solemnity. The two boarders were its godfathers; and, while the hole was being filled up, we each of us held the tree with one hand and sang songs of triumph. In order to water it, a kind of basin was made round the foot. Every day, eager spectators of this watering, my cousin and I became more strongly convinced, as was natural, that it was a finer thing to plant a tree on a terrace than a flag upon a breach, and we resolved to win this glory for ourselves without sharing it with anyone.

With this object, we proceeded to cut a slip from a young willow, and planted it on the terrace, at a distance of about eight or ten feet from the august walnut-tree. We did not forget to dig a similar trench round our tree; the difficulty was how to fill it, for the water came from some distance, and we were not allowed to run and fetch it. However, it was absolutely necessary to have some for our willow. For a few days, we had recourse to all kinds of devices to get some, and we succeeded so well that we saw it bud and put forth little leaves, the growth of which we measured every hour, convinced that, although not yet a foot high, it would soon afford us a shade.

As our tree so completely claimed our attention that we were quite incapable of attending to or learning anything else, and were in a sort of delirium: as our guardians, not knowing what was the matter with us, kept a tighter hand upon us, we saw the fatal moment approaching when we should be without water, and were inconsolable at the thought of seeing our tree perish from drought. At length necessity, the mother of invention, suggested to us how to save ourselves from grief and the tree from certain death; this was, to make a channel underground, which should secretly conduct part of the water intended for the walnut-tree to our willow. This undertaking was at first unsuccessful, in spite of the eagerness with which it was carried out. We had made the incline so clumsily that the water did not run at all. The earth fell in and stopped up the channel; the entrance was filled with mud; everything went wrong. But nothing disheartened us: *Labor omnia vincit improbus.*[10] We dug our basin deeper, in order to allow the water to run; we cut some bottoms of boxes into small narrow planks, some of which were laid flat, one after the other, and others set up on both sides of these at an angle, thus forming a triangular canal for our conduit. At the entrance we stuck small pieces of wood, some little distance apart, which, forming a kind of grating or lattice-work, kept back the mud and stones, without stopping the passage of the water. We carefully covered our work with well-trodden earth; and when all was ready, we awaited, in the greatest excitement of hope and fear, the time of watering. After centuries of waiting, the hour at length arrived; M. Lambercier came as usual to assist at the operation, during which we both kept behind him, in order to conceal our tree, to which very luckily he turned his back.

No sooner had the first pail of water been poured out, than we saw some of it running into our basin. At this sight, our prudence deserted us: we began to utter cries of joy which made M. Lambercier turn round; this was a pity, for he took great delight in seeing how good the soil of the walnut-tree was, and how greedily it absorbed the water. Astonished at seeing it distribute itself into two basins, he cried out in his turn, looked, perceived the trick, ordered a pickaxe to be brought, and, with one blow, broke off two or three pieces from our planks; then, crying loudly, "An aqueduct, an aqueduct!" he dealt merciless blows in every direction, each of which went straight to our hearts. In a moment planks, conduit, basin, willow, everything was destroyed and uprooted, without his having uttered a single word, during this terrible work of destruction, except the exclamation which he incessantly repeated. "An aqueduct!" he cried, while demolishing everything, "an aqueduct, an aqueduct!"

It will naturally be imagined that the adventure turned out badly for the little architects: that would be a mistake: it was all over. M. Lambercier never uttered a single word of reproach, or looked upon us with displeasure, and said nothing more about it; shortly afterwards, we even heard him laughing loudly with his sister, for his laughter could be heard a long way off; and what was still more astonishing, when the first fright was over, we ourselves were not much troubled about the matter. We planted another tree somewhere else, and often reminded ourselves of the disaster that overtook the first, by repeating with emphasis, "An aqueduct, an aqueduct!" Hitherto I had had intermittent attacks of pride, when I was Aristides or Brutus; then it was that I felt the first well-defined promptings of vanity. To have been able to construct an aqueduct with our own hands, to have put a cutting in competition with a large tree, appeared to me the height of glory. At ten years of age I was a better judge on this point than Cæsar at thirty.

The thought of this walnut-tree and the little history connected with it has remained so vivid in my memory, or returned to it, that one of the plans which gave

---

[10] *Labor . . . improbus:* "Tenacious work overcomes all difficulties." (Virgil, *Georgics* I)

me the greatest pleasure, on my journey to Geneva, in 1754, was to go to Bossey and revisit the memorials of my boyish amusements, above all, the dear walnut-tree, which by that time must have been a third of a century old; but I was so continually occupied, so little my own master, that I could never find the moment to afford myself this satisfaction. There is little prospect of the opportunity ever occurring again; yet the wish has not disappeared with the hope; and I am almost certain that, if ever I should return to those beloved spots and find my dear walnut-tree still alive, I should water it with my tears.

After my return to Geneva, I lived for two or three years[11] with my uncle, waiting until my friends had decided what was to be done with me. As he intended his own son to be an engineer, he made him learn a little drawing and taught him the elements of Euclid.[12] I learned these subjects together with him, and acquired a taste for them, especially for drawing. In the meantime, it was debated whether I should be a watchmaker, an attorney, or a minister. My own preference was for the last, for preaching seemed to me to be a very fine thing; but the small income from my mother's property, which had to be divided between my brother and myself, was not sufficient to allow me to prosecute my studies. As, considering my age at that time, there was no immediate need to decide, I remained for the present with my uncle, making little use of my time and, in addition, as was only fair, paying a tolerably large sum for my board. My uncle, a man of pleasure like my father, was unable, like him, to tie himself down to his duties, and troubled himself little enough about us. My aunt was somewhat of a pietist, and preferred to sing psalms rather than attend to our education. We were allowed almost absolute freedom, which we never abused. Always inseparable, we were quite contented with our own society; and, having no temptation to make companions of the street boys of our own age, we learned none of the dissolute habits into which idleness might have led us. I am even wrong in saying that we were idle, for we were never less so in our lives; and the most fortunate thing was, that all the ways of amusing ourselves, with which we successively became infatuated, kept us together busy in the house, without our being even tempted to go out into the street. We made cages, flutes, shuttlecocks, drums, houses, squirts, and cross-bows. We spoilt my good old grandfather's tools in trying to make watches as he did. We had a special taste for wasting paper, drawing, painting in water-colours, illuminating, and spoiling colours. An Italian showman, named Gamba-Corta, came to Geneva; we went to see him once and never wanted to go again. But he had a marionette-show, and we proceeded to make marionettes; his marionettes played comedies and we composed comedies for ours. For want of a squeaker, we imitated Punch's voice in our throat, in order to play the charming comedies, which our poor and kind relations had the patience to sit and listen to. But, my uncle Bernard having one day read aloud in the family circle a very fine sermon which he had composed himself, we abandoned comedy and began to write sermons. These details are not very interesting, I confess, but they show how exceedingly well-conducted our early

---

[11] **two . . . years:** Rousseau actually lived with his uncle for less than a year; this is only one of the many details in the autobiography that are inaccurate.

[12] **Euclid:** Third-century Greek mathematician, whose *Elements* established many of the principles of geometry.

education must have been, seeing that we, almost masters of our time and ourselves at so tender an age, were so little tempted to abuse our opportunities. We had so little need of making companions, that we even neglected the chances of doing so. When we went for a walk, we looked at their amusements as we passed by without the slightest desire, or even the idea of taking part in them. Our friendship so completely filled our hearts, that it was enough for us to be together to make the simplest amusements a delight.

Being thus inseparable, we began to attract attention: the more so as, my cousin being very tall while I was very short, we made an oddly-assorted couple. His long, slim figure, his little face like a boiled apple, his gentle manner, and his slovenly walk excited the children's ridicule. In the *patois* of the district he was nicknamed Barna Bredanna,[13] and, directly we went out, we heard nothing but "Barna Bredanna!" all round us. He endured it more quietly than I did: I lost my temper and wanted to fight. This was just what the little rascals desired. I fought and was beaten. My poor cousin helped me as well as he could; but he was weak, and a single blow of the fist knocked him down. Then I became furious. However, although I received blows in abundance, I was not the real object of attack, but Barna Bredanna; but my obstinate anger made matters so much worse, that, in future, we only ventured to go out during school-hours, for fear of being hooted and followed.

Behold me already a redresser of wrongs! In order to be a regular Paladin[14] I only wanted a lady; I had two. From time to time I went to see my father at Nyon, a little town in the Vaud country, where he had settled. He was very much liked, and his son felt the effects of his popularity. During the short time I stayed with him, friends vied with each other in making me welcome. A certain Madame de Vulson, especially, bestowed a thousand caresses upon me, and, to crown all, her daughter took me for her lover. It is easy to understand the meaning of a lover eleven years old for a girl of twenty-two. But all these roguish young women are so ready to put little puppets in front in order to hide larger ones, or to tempt them with the idea of an amusement which they know how to render attractive! As for myself, I saw no incongruity between us and took the matter seriously; I abandoned myself with all my heart, or rather with all my head—for it was only in that part of me that I was in love, although madly—and my transports, excitement, and frenzy produced scenes enough to make anyone split his sides with laughing.

I am acquainted with two very distinct and very real kinds of love, which have scarcely anything in common, although both are very fervent, and which both differ from tender friendship. The whole course of my life has been divided between these two kinds of love, essentially so different, and I have even felt them both at the same time; for instance, at the time of which I am speaking, while I took possession of Mademoiselle de Vulson so openly and so tyrannically that I could not endure that any man should approach her, I had several meetings, brief but lively, with a certain little Mademoiselle Goton, in which she deigned to play the schoolmistress, and that was all; but this all, which was really all for me, seemed to me the height of happiness;

---

[13] **Barna Bredanna:** A "bridled donkey."

[14] **Paladin:** A chivalric hero from the twelfth-century *Song of Roland.*

and, already feeling the value of the mystery, although I only knew how to make use of it as a child, I paid Mademoiselle de Vulson, who had scarcely any suspicion of it, in the same coin, for the assiduity with which she made use of me to conceal other amours. But, to my great regret, my secret was discovered, or not so well kept on the part of my little schoolmistress as on my own; we were soon separated; and, some time afterwards, on my return to Geneva, while passing through Coutance, I heard some little girls cry, in an undertone, "Goton tic-tac Rousseau!"[15]

This little Mademoiselle Goton was really a singular person. Without being pretty, she had a face which was not easy to forget, and which I still recall to mind, often too tenderly for an old fool. Neither her form, nor her manner, nor, above all, her eyes were in keeping with her age. She had a proud and commanding air, which suited her part admirably, and which in fact had suggested the first idea of it to us. But the oddest thing about her was a mixture of impudence and reserve which it was difficult to comprehend. She took the greatest liberties with me, but never allowed me to take any with her. She treated me just like a child, which makes me believe, either that she was no longer one herself, or that, on the contrary, she was still childish enough to see nothing but an amusement in the danger to which she exposed herself.

I belonged entirely, so to say, to each of these two persons, and so completely, that, when I was with one, I never thought of the other. In other respects, there was not the slightest similarity between the feelings with which they inspired me. I could have spent all my life with Mademoiselle de Vulson, without ever thinking of leaving her; but, when I approached her, my joy was tranquil and free from emotion. I loved her above all in fashionable society; the witty sallies, railleries, and even the petty jealousies attracted and interested me; I felt a pride and glory in the marks of preference she bestowed upon me in the presence of grown-up rivals whom she appeared to treat with disdain. I was tormented, but I loved the torment. The applause, encouragement, and laughter warmed and inspirited me. I had fits of passion and broke out into audacious sallies. In society, I was transported with love; in a *tête-à-tête* I should have been constrained, cold, perhaps wearied. However, I felt a real tenderness for her; I suffered when she was ill; I would have given my own health to restore her own, and, observe! I knew very well from experience the meaning of illness and health. When absent from her, I thought of her and missed her; when I was by her side, her caresses reached my heart—not my senses. I was intimate with her with impunity; my imagination demanded no more than she granted; yet I could not have endured to see her do even as much for others. I loved her as a brother, but I was as jealous of her as a lover.

I should have been as jealous of Mademoiselle Goton as a Turk, a madman, or a tiger, if I had once imagined that she could accord the same treatment to another as to myself; for even that was a favour which I had to ask on my knees. I approached Mademoiselle de Vulson with lively pleasure, but without emotion; whereas, if I only

---

[15] **Coutance:** A district in Geneva where Rousseau's family lived after 1718; **tic-tac:** Goton is in love with, or comes to blows with, Rousseau.

saw Mademoiselle Goton, I saw nothing else, all my senses were bewildered. With the former I was familiar without familiarity; while on the contrary, in the presence of the latter, I was as bashful as I was excited, even in the midst of our greatest familiarities. I believe that, if I had remained with her long, I should have died; the throbbings of my heart would have suffocated me. I was equally afraid of displeasing either; but I was more attentive to the one and more obedient to the other. Nothing in the world would have made me annoy Mademoiselle de Vulson; but if Mademoiselle Goton had ordered me to throw myself into the flames, I believe I should have obeyed her immediately.

My amour, or rather my meetings, with the latter, continued only for a short time—happily for both of us. Although my relations with Mademoiselle de Vulson had not the same danger, they were not without their catastrophe, after they had lasted a little longer. The end of all such connections should always be somewhat romantic, and furnish occasion for exclamations of sorrow. Although my connection with Mademoiselle de Vulson was less lively, it was perhaps closer. We never separated without tears, and it is remarkable into what an overwhelming void I felt myself plunged as soon as I had left her. I could speak and think of nothing but her; my regret was genuine and lively; but I believe that, at bottom, this heroic regret was not felt altogether for her, and that, without my perceiving it, the amusements, of which she was the centre, played their part in it. To moderate the pangs of absence, we wrote letters to each other, pathetic enough to melt the heart of a stone. At last I triumphed; she could endure it no longer, and came to Geneva to see me. This time my head was completely turned; I was drunk and mad during the two days she remained. When she left I wanted to throw myself in the water after her, and the air resounded with my screams. Eight days afterwards she sent me some bonbons and gloves, which I should have considered a great compliment, if I had not learnt at the same time that she was married, and that the visit with which she had been pleased to honour me was really made in order to buy her wedding-dress. I will not attempt to describe my fury; it may be imagined. In my noble rage I swore that I would never see the faithless one again, being unable to imagine a more terrible punishment for her. She did not, however, die of it; for, twenty years afterwards, when on a visit to my father, while rowing with him on the lake, I asked who the ladies were whom I saw in a boat not far from ours. "What!" said my father with a smile, "does not your heart tell you? it is your old love, Mademoiselle de Vulson that was, now Madame Cristin." I started at the almost forgotten name, but I told the boatmen to change their course. Although I had a fine opportunity of avenging myself at that moment, I did not think it worth while to perjure myself and to renew a quarrel, twenty years old, with a woman of forty.

[1723–1728]

Thus the most valuable time of my boyhood was wasted in follies, before my future career had been decided upon. After long deliberation as to the bent of my natural inclination, a profession was determined upon for which I had the least taste; I was put with M. Masseron, the town clerk, in order to learn, under his tuition, the useful trade of a *fee-grabber*.[16] This nickname was extremely distasteful to me; the hope of gaining a number of crowns in a somewhat sordid business by no means flattered my pride; the occupation itself appeared to me wearisome and unendurable; the constant application, the feeling of servitude completed my dislike, and I never entered the office without a feeling of horror, which daily increased in intensity. M. Masseron, on his part, was ill-satisfied with me, and treated me with contempt; he continually reproached me with my dullness and stupidity, dinning into my ears every day that my uncle had told him that I knew something, whereas, in reality, I knew nothing; that he had promised him a sharp lad, and had given him a jackass. At last I was dismissed from the office in disgrace as being utterly incapable, and M. Masseron's clerks declared that I was good for nothing except to handle a file.

My calling being thus settled, I was apprenticed, not, however, to a watchmaker, but to an engraver. The contempt with which I had been treated by M. Masseron had made me very humble, and I obeyed without a murmur. My new master, M. Ducommun, was a rough and violent young man, who in a short time succeeded in tarnishing all the brightness of my childhood, stupefying my loving and lively nature, and reducing me, in mind as well as in position, to a real state of apprenticeship. My Latin, my antiquities, my history, were all for a long time forgotten; I did not even remember that there had ever been any Romans in the world. My father, when I went to see him, no longer found in me his idol; for the ladies I was no longer the gallant Jean Jacques; and I felt so certain myself that the Lamberciers would not have recognised their pupil in me, that I was ashamed to pay them a visit, and have never seen them since. The vilest tastes, the lowest street-blackguardism took the place of my simple amusements and effaced even the remembrance of them. I must, in spite of a most upright training, have had a great propensity to degenerate; for the change took place with great rapidity, without the least trouble, and never did so precocious a Cæsar so rapidly become a Laridon.[17]

The trade in itself was not disagreeable to me; I had a decided taste for drawing; the handling of a graving-tool amused me; and as the claims upon the skill of a watchmaker's engraver were limited, I hoped to attain perfection. I should, perhaps, have done so, had not my master's brutality and excessive restraint disgusted me with my work. I stole some of my working hours to devote to similar occupations, but which had for me the charm of freedom. I engraved medals for an order of knighthood for myself and my companions. My master surprised me at this contraband occupation, and gave me a sound thrashing, declaring that I was training for a coiner, because our medals bore the arms of the Republic. I can swear that I had no idea at all of bad, and only a very faint one of good, money. I knew better how the Roman *As*[18] was made than our three-sou pieces.

My master's tyranny at length made the work, of which I should have been very fond, altogether unbearable, and filled me with vices which I should otherwise have hated, such as lying, idleness, and thieving. The recollection of the alteration produced in me by that period of my life has taught me, better than anything else, the

---

[16] **fee-grabber:** A lawyer.   [17] **Laridon:** A degenerate dog, from La Fontaine's *Fables* (1668 f.).   [18] **As:** A Roman unit of monetary measure.

difference between filial dependence and abject servitude. Naturally shy and timid, no fault was more foreign to my disposition than impudence; but I had enjoyed an honourable liberty, which hitherto had only been gradually restrained, and at length disappeared altogether. I was bold with my father, unrestrained with M. Lambercier, and modest with my uncle; I became timid with my master, and from that moment I was a lost child. Accustomed to perfect equality in my intercourse with my superiors, knowing no pleasure which was not within my reach, seeing no dish of which I could not have a share, having no desire which I could not have openly expressed, and carrying my heart upon my lips—it is easy to judge what I was bound to become, in a house in which I did not venture to open my mouth, where I was obliged to leave the table before the meal was half over, and the room as soon as I had nothing more to do there; where, incessantly fettered to my work, I saw only objects of enjoyment for others and of privation for myself; where the sight of the liberty enjoyed by my master and companions increased the weight of my servitude; where, in disputes about matters as to which I was best informed, I did not venture to open my mouth; where, in short, everything that I saw became for my heart an object of longing, simply because I was deprived of all. From that time my ease of manner, my gaiety, the happy expressions which, in former times, when I had done something wrong, had gained me immunity from punishment—all were gone. I cannot help laughing when I remember how, one evening, at my father's house, having been sent to bed without any supper for some piece of roguery, I passed through the kitchen with my melancholy piece of bread, and, seeing the joint turning on the spit, sniffed at it. All the household was standing round the hearth, and, in passing, I was obliged to say good-night to everybody. When I had gone the round, I winked at the joint, which looked so nice and smelt so good, and could not help bowing to it as well, and saying in a mournful voice, "Good-night, roast beef!" This naive sally amused them so much that they made me stop to supper. Perhaps it might have had the same effect with my master, but I am sure that it would never have occurred to me, and that I should not have had the courage, to say it in his presence.

In this manner I learnt to covet in silence, to dissemble, to lie, and, lastly, to steal—an idea which, up to that time, had never even entered my mind, and of which since then I have never been able to cure myself completely. Covetousness and weakness always lead in that direction. This explains why all servants are rogues, and why all apprentices ought to be; but the latter, in a peaceful state of equality, where all that they see is within their reach, lose, as they grow up, this disgraceful propensity. Not having had the same advantages, I have not been able to reap the same benefits.

It is nearly always good, but badly-directed principles, that make a child take the first step towards evil. In spite of continual privations and temptations, I had been more than a year with my master without being able to make up my mind to take anything, even eatables. My first theft was a matter of obliging some one else, but it opened the door to others, the motive of which was not so praiseworthy.

My master had a journeyman, named M. Verrat, whose house was in the neighbourhood, and had a garden some way off which produced very fine asparagus. M. Verrat, who was not too well supplied with money, conceived the idea of stealing some of his mother's young asparagus and selling it in order to provide himself with two or three good breakfasts. As he was unwilling to run the risk himself, and was not very active, he selected me for the expedition. After some preliminary cajoleries, which the more easily succeeded with me as I did not see their aim, he proposed it to me as an idea that had struck him on the spur of the moment. I strongly opposed it; he persisted. I have never been able to resist flattery: I gave in. I went every morning to gather a crop of the finest asparagus, and carried it to the Molard, where some good woman, who saw that I had just stolen it, told me so to my face in order to get it cheaper. In my fright I took whatever she chose to offer me, and took it to Verrat. The amount was immediately converted into a breakfast, of which I was the purveyor, and which he shared with another companion; I myself was quite satisfied with a few scraps, and never even touched their wine.

This little arrangement continued several days, without its even occurring to me to rob the robber, and to levy my tithe of the proceeds of M. Verrat's asparagus. I performed my part in the transaction with the greatest loyalty; my only motive was to please him who prompted me to carry it out. And yet, if I had been caught, what blows, abuse, and cruel treatment should I have had to endure, while the wretch, who would have been sure to give me the lie, would have been believed on his word, and I should have suffered double punishment for having had the impudence to accuse him, seeing that he was a journeyman, while I was only an apprentice! So true it is that, in every condition of life, the strong man who is guilty saves himself at the expense of the innocent who is weak.

In this manner I learned that stealing was not so terrible a thing as I had imagined, and I soon knew how to make such good use of my discovery, that nothing I desired, if it was within my reach, was safe from me. I was not absolutely ill-fed, and abstinence was only rendered difficult to me from seeing that my master observed it so ill himself. The custom of sending young people from the table when the most appetising dishes are brought on appears to me admirably adapted to make them gluttons as well as thieves. In a short time I became both the one and the other; and, as a rule, I came off very well; occasionally, when I was caught, very badly.

I shudder, and at the same time laugh, when I remember an apple-hunt which cost me dear. These apples were at the bottom of a store-room, which was lighted from the kitchen by means of a high grating. One day, when I was alone in the house, I climbed upon the kneading-trough, in order to look at the precious fruit in the garden of the Hesperides,[19] which was out of my reach. I went to fetch the spit to see if I could touch the apples; it was too short. To make it longer, I tied on to it another little spit which was used for small game, for my master was very fond of sport. I thrust several times without success; at last, to my great delight, I felt that I had secured an apple. I pulled very gently; the apple was close to the grating; I was ready to catch hold of it. But who can describe my grief, when I found that it was too large to pass through the bars? How many expedients I tried, to get it through! I had to find supports to keep the spit in its place, a knife long enough to divide the apple, a lath to hold it up. At last I managed to divide it, and hoped to be able to pull the

---

[19] **Hesperides:** In Greek mythology, the nymphs who guarded a tree of golden apples.

pieces towards me one after the other; but no sooner were they separated than they both fell into the store-room. Compassionate reader, share my affliction!

I by no means lost courage; but I had lost considerable time. I was afraid of being surprised. I put off a more lucky attempt till the following day, and returned to my work as quietly as if I had done nothing, without thinking of the two tell-tale witnesses in the store-room.

The next day, finding the opportunity favourable, I made a fresh attempt. I climbed upon my stool, lengthened the spit, adjusted it, and was ready to make a lunge . . . but, unfortunately, the dragon was not asleep; all at once the door of the store-room opened, my master came out, folded his arms, looked at me, and said, "Courage!". . . the pen falls from my hand.

In consequence of continuous ill-treatment I soon became less sensitive to it, and regarded it as a kind of compensation for theft, which gave me the right to continue the latter. Instead of looking back and considering the punishment, I looked forward and thought of revenge. I considered that, if I were beaten as a rogue, I was entitled to behave like one. I found that stealing and a flogging went together, and constituted a sort of bargain, and that, if I performed my part, I could safely leave my master to carry out his own. With this idea, I began to steal more quietly than before. I said to myself: "What will be the result? I shall be flogged. Never mind; I am made to be flogged."

I am fond of eating, but am not greedy; I am sensual, but not a gourmand; too many other tastes prevent that. I have never troubled myself about my food except when my heart has been unoccupied: and that has so seldom been the case during my life that I have scarcely had time to think about dainties. For this reason I did not long confine my thievish propensities to eatables, but soon extended them to everything which tempted me; and, if I did not become a regular thief, it was because I have never been much tempted by money. Leading out of the common workshop was a private room belonging to my master, the door of which I found means to open and shut without being noticed. There I laid under contribution his best tools, drawings, proofs—in fact, everything which attracted me and which he purposely kept out of my reach. At bottom, these thefts were quite innocent, being only committed to serve him; but I was transported with joy at having these trifles in my power; I thought that I was robbing him of his talent together with its productions. Besides, I found boxes containing gold and silver filings, little trinkets, valuables, and coins. When I had four or five sous in my pocket, I thought I was rich; and yet, far from touching anything of what I found there, I do not even remember that I ever cast longing eyes upon it. I looked upon it with more affright than pleasure. I believe that this horror of stealing money and valuables was in great part the result of my bringing-up. With it were combined secret thoughts of disgrace, prison, punishment, and the gallows, which would have made me shudder if I had been tempted; whereas my tricks only appeared to me in the light of pieces of mischief, and in fact were nothing else. They could lead to nothing but a sound flogging from my master, and I prepared myself for that beforehand.

But, I repeat, I never felt sufficient longing to need to control myself; I had nothing to contend with. A single sheet of fine drawing-paper tempted me more than money enough to buy a ream of it. This singularity is connected with one of the peculiarities of my character; it has exercised such great influence upon my conduct that it is worth while to explain it.

I am a man of very strong passions, and, while I am stirred by them, nothing can equal my impetuosity; I forget all discretion, all feelings of respect, fear, and decency; I am cynical, impudent, violent, and fearless; no feeling of shame keeps me back, no danger frightens me; with the exception of the single object which occupies my thoughts, the universe is nothing to me. But all this lasts only for a moment, and the following moment plunges me into complete annihilation. In my calmer moments I am indolence and timidity itself; everything frightens and discourages me; a fly, buzzing past, alarms me; a word which I have to say, a gesture which I have to make, terrifies my idleness; fear and shame overpower me to such an extent that I would gladly hide myself from the sight of my fellow-creatures. If I have to act, I do not know what to do; if I have to speak, I do not know what to say; if anyone looks at me, I am put out of countenance. When I am strongly moved I sometimes know how to find the right words, but in ordinary conversation I can find absolutely nothing, and my condition is unbearable for the simple reason that I am obliged to speak.

Add to this, that none of my prevailing tastes centre in things that can be bought. I want nothing but unadulterated pleasures, and money poisons all. For instance, I am fond of the pleasures of the table; but, as I cannot endure either the constraint of good society or the drunkenness of the tavern, I can only enjoy them with a friend; alone, I cannot do so, for my imagination then occupies itself with other things, and eating affords me no pleasure. If my heated blood longs for women, my excited heart longs still more for affection. Women who could be bought for money would lose for me all their charms; I even doubt whether it would be in me to make use of them. I find it the same with all pleasures within my reach; unless they cost me nothing, I find them insipid. I only love those enjoyments which belong to no one but the first man who knows how to enjoy them.

Money has never appeared to me as valuable as it is generally considered. More than that, it has never even appeared to me particularly convenient. It is good for nothing in itself; it has to be changed before it can be enjoyed; one is obliged to buy, to bargain, to be often cheated, to pay dearly, to be badly served. I should like something which is good in quality; with my money I am sure to get it bad. If I pay a high price for a fresh egg, it is stale; for a nice piece of fruit, it is unripe; for a girl, she is spoilt. I am fond of good wine, but where am I to get it? At a wine merchant's? Whatever I do, he is sure to poison me. If I really wish to be well served, what trouble and embarrassment it entails! I must have friends, correspondents, give commissions, write, go backwards and forwards, wait, and in the end be often deceived! What trouble with my money! my fear of it is greater than my fondness for good wine.

Times without number, during my apprenticeship and afterwards, I have gone out with the intention of buying some delicacy. Coming to a pastrycook's shop, I notice some women at the counter; I think I can already see them laughing amongst themselves at the little glutton. I go to a fruiterer's; I eye the fine pears; their smell tempts me. Two or three young people close by me look at me; a man who knows me is standing in front of his shop; I see a girl approaching in the distance: is it the housemaid? My short-sightedness causes all kinds of illusions. I take all the passers-by for acquaintances; everywhere I am intimidated, restrained by some obstacle; my desire increases with my shame, and at last I return home like a fool, consumed with longing, having in my pocket the means of satisfying it, and yet not having had the courage to buy anything.

I should enter into the most insipid details if, in relating how my money was spent by myself or others, I were to describe the embarrassment, the shame, the repugnance, the inconvenience, the annoyances of all kinds which I have always experienced. In proportion as the reader, following the course of my life, becomes acquainted with my real temperament, he will understand all this, without my taking the trouble to tell him.

This being understood, it will be easy to comprehend one of my apparent inconsistencies — the union of an almost sordid avarice with the greatest contempt for money. It is a piece of furniture in which I find so little convenience, that it never enters my mind to long for it when I have not got it, and that, when I have got it, I keep it for a long time without spending it, for want of knowing how to make use of it in a way to please myself; but if a convenient and agreeable opportunity presents itself, I make such good use of it that my purse is empty before I know it. Besides this, one need not expect to find in me that curious characteristic of misers — that of spending for the sake of ostentation; on the contrary, I spend in secret for the sake of enjoyment; far from glorying in my expenditure, I conceal it. I feel so strongly that money is of no use to me, that I am almost ashamed to have any, still more to make use of it. If I had ever had an income sufficient to live comfortably upon, I am certain that I should never have been tempted to be a miser. I should have spent it all, without attempting to increase it; but my precarious circumstances make me careful. I worship freedom; I abhor restraint, trouble, dependence. As long as the money in my purse lasts, it assures my independence; it relieves me of the trouble of finding expedients to replenish it, a necessity which always inspired me with dread; but the fear of seeing it exhausted makes me hoard it carefully. The money which a man possesses is the instrument of freedom; that which we eagerly pursue is the instrument of slavery. Therefore I hold fast to that which I have, and desire nothing.

My disinterestedness is, therefore, nothing but idleness; the pleasure of possession is not worth the trouble of acquisition. In like manner, my extravagance is nothing but idleness; when the opportunity of spending agreeably presents itself, it cannot be too profitably employed. Money tempts me less than things, because between money and the possession of the desired object there is always an intermediary, whereas between the thing itself and the enjoyment of it there is none. If I see the thing, it tempts me; if I only see the means of gaining possession of it, it does not. For this reason I have committed thefts, and even now I sometimes pilfer trifles which tempt me, and which I prefer to take rather than to ask for; but neither when a child nor a grown-up man do I ever remember to have robbed anyone of a farthing, except on one occasion, fifteen years ago, when I stole seven *livres* ten *sous*. The incident is worth recording, for it contains a most extraordinary mixture of folly and impudence, which I should have found difficulty in believing if it concerned anyone but myself.

It took place at Paris. I was walking with M. de Franceuil in the Palais-Royal about five o'clock. He pulled out his watch, looked at it, and said: "Let us go to the Opera." I agreed; we went. He took two tickets for the amphitheatre, gave me one, and went on in front with the other. I followed him; he went in. Entering after him, I found the door blocked. I looked, and seeing everybody standing up, thought it would be easy to lose myself in the crowd, or at any rate to make M. de Franceuil believe that I had lost myself. I went out, took back my check, then my money, and went off, without thinking that as soon as I had reached the door everybody had taken their seats, and that M. de Franceuil clearly saw that I was no longer there.

As nothing was ever more foreign to my disposition than such behaviour, I mention it in order to show that there are moments of semi-delirium during which men must not be judged by their actions. I did not exactly want to steal the money, I wanted to steal the employment of it; the less of a theft it was, the greater its disgracefulness.

I should never finish these details if I were to follow all the paths along which, during my apprenticeship, I descended from the sublimity of heroism to the depths of worthlessness. And yet, although I adopted the vices of my position, I could not altogether acquire a taste for them. I wearied of the amusements of my companions; and when excessive restraint had rendered work unendurable to me, I grew tired of everything. This renewed my taste for reading, which I had for some time lost. This reading, for which I stole time from my work, became a new offence which brought new punishment upon me. The taste for it, provoked by constraint, became a passion, and soon a regular madness. La Tribu, a well-known lender of books, provided me with all kinds of literature. Good or bad, all were alike to me; I had no choice, and read everything with equal avidity. I read at the work-table, I read on my errands, I read in the wardrobe, and forgot myself for hours together; my head became giddy with reading; I could do nothing else. My master watched me, surprised me, beat me, took away my books. How many volumes were torn, burnt, and thrown out of the window! how many works were left in odd volumes in La Tribu's stock! When I had no more money to pay her, I gave her my shirts, neckties, and clothes; my three sous of pocket-money were regularly taken to her every Sunday.

Well, then, I shall be told, money had become necessary to me. That is true; but it was not until my passion for reading had deprived me of all activity. Completely devoted to my new hobby, I did nothing but read, and no longer stole. Here again is one of my characteristic peculiarities. In the midst of a certain attachment to any manner of life, a mere trifle distracts me, alters me, rivets my attention, and finally becomes a passion. Then everything is forgotten; I no longer think of anything except the new object which engrosses my attention. My heart beat with impatience to turn over the leaves of the new book which I had in my pocket; I pulled it out as soon as I was alone, and thought no more of rummaging my master's work-room. I can hardly believe that I should have stolen even if I had had more expensive tastes. Limited to the present, it was not in my way to make preparations in this manner for the future. La Tribu gave me credit, the payments on account were small, and, as soon as I had my book in my pocket, I forgot everything else. The money which came to me honestly passed in the same manner into the hands of this woman; and, when she pressed me, nothing was easier to dispose of than my own property. It required too much foresight to steal in advance, and I was not even tempted to steal in order to pay.

In consequence of quarrels, blows, and secret and ill-chosen reading, my disposition became savage and taciturn; my mind became altogether perverted, and I lived like a misanthrope. However, if my good taste did not keep me from silly and insipid books, my good fortune preserved me from such as were filthy and licentious; not that La Tribu, a woman in all respects most accommodating, would have made any scruple about lending them to me; but, in order to increase their importance, she always mentioned them to me with an air of mystery which had just the effect of making me refuse them, as much from disgust as from shame; and chance aided my modest disposition so well, that I was more than thirty years old before I set eyes upon any of those dangerous books which a fine lady finds inconvenient because they can only be read with one hand.

In less than a year I exhausted La Tribu's little stock, and want of occupation, during my spare time, became painful to me. I had been cured of my childish and knavish propensities by my passion for reading, and even by the books I read, which, although ill-chosen and frequently bad, filled my heart with nobler sentiments than those with which my sphere of life had inspired me. Disgusted with everything that was within my reach, and feeling that everything which might have tempted me was too far removed from me, I saw nothing possible which might have flattered my heart. My excited senses had long clamoured for an enjoyment, the object of which I could not even imagine. I was as far removed from actual enjoyment as if I had been sexless; and, already fully developed and sensitive, I sometimes thought of my crazes, but saw nothing beyond them. In this strange situation, my restless imagination entered upon an occupation which saved me from myself and calmed my growing sensuality. This consisted in feeding myself upon the situations which had interested me in the course of my reading, in recalling them, in varying them, in combining them, in making them so truly my own that I became one of the persons who filled my imagination, and always saw myself in the situations most agreeable to my taste; and that, finally, the fictitious state in which I succeeded in putting myself made me forget my actual state with which I was so dissatisfied. This love of imaginary objects, and the readiness with which I occupied myself with them, ended by disgusting me with everything around me, and decided that liking for solitude which has never left me. In the sequel we shall see more than once the curious effects of this disposition, apparently so gloomy and misanthropic, but which is really due to a too affectionate, too loving, and too tender heart, which, being unable to find any in existence resembling it, is obliged to nourish itself with fancies. For the present, it is sufficient for me to have defined the origin and first cause of a propensity which has modified all my passions, and which, restraining them by means of themselves, has always made me slow to act, owing to my excessive impetuosity in desire.

In this manner I reached my sixteenth year, restless, dissatisfied with myself and everything, without any of the tastes of my condition of life, without any of the pleasures of my age, consumed by desires of the object of which I was ignorant, weeping without any cause for tears, sighing without knowing why—in short, tenderly caressing my chimeras, since I saw nothing around me which counterbalanced them. On Sundays, my fellow-apprentices came to fetch me after service to go and amuse myself with them. I would gladly have escaped from them if I had been able; but, once engaged in their amusements, I became more excited and went further than any of them; it was as difficult to set me going as to stop me. Such was always my disposition. During our walks outside the city I always went further than any of them without thinking about my return, unless others thought of it for me. Twice I was caught: the gates were shut before I could get back. The next day I was treated as may be imagined; the second time I was promised such a reception if it ever happened again, that I resolved not to run the risk of it; yet this third time, so dreaded, came to pass. My watchfulness was rendered useless by a confounded Captain Minutoli, who always shut the gate at which he was on guard half-an-hour before the others. I was returning with two companions. About half a league from the city I heard the retreat sounded: I doubled my pace: I heard the tattoo[20] beat, and ran with all my might. I arrived out of breath and bathed in perspiration; my heart beat; from a distance I saw the soldiers at their posts; I rushed up and cried out with a voice half-choked. It was too late! Twenty paces from the outposts, I saw the first bridge raised. I shuddered when I saw those terrible horns rising in the air—a sinister and fatal omen of the destiny which that moment was opening for me.

In the first violence of my grief I threw myself on the *glacis*[21] and bit the ground. My companions, laughing at their misfortune, immediately made up their minds what to do. I did the same, but my resolution was different from theirs. On the spot I swore never to return to my master; and the next morning, when they entered the city after the gates were opened, I said good-bye to them for ever, only begging them secretly to inform my cousin Bernard of the resolution I had taken, and of the place where he might be able to see me once more.

After I had entered upon my apprenticeship I saw less of him. For some time we used to meet on Sunday, but gradually each of us adopted other habits, and we saw one another less frequently. I am convinced that his mother had much to do with this change. He was a child of the upper city; I, a poor apprentice, was only a child of Saint-Gervais.[22] In spite of our relationship, there was no longer any equality between us; it was derogatory to him to associate with me. However, relations were not entirely broken off between us, and, as he was a good-natured lad, he sometimes followed the dictates of his heart instead of his mother's instructions. When he was informed of my resolution, he hastened to me, not to try and dissuade me from it or to share it, but to lessen the inconveniences of my flight by some small presents, since my own resources could not take me very far. Amongst other things he gave me a small sword, which had taken my fancy exceedingly, and which I carried as far as

---

[20] **tattoo:** A signal, sounded before taps, to call soldiers to their barracks for the night.

[21] **glacis:** The slope in front of the city walls.

[22] **He . . . Saint-Gervais:** Bernard lived in the more fashionable part of Geneva; Rousseau lived in the Saint-Gervais, the poorer part.

Turin, where necessity obliged me to dispose of it, and where, as the saying is, I passed it through my body. The more I have since reflected upon the manner in which he behaved towards me at this critical moment, the more I have felt convinced that he followed the instructions of his mother, and perhaps of his father; for it is inconceivable that, left to himself, he would not have made some effort to keep me back, or would not have been tempted to follow; but, no! he rather encouraged me in my plan than tried to dissuade me; and, when he saw me quite determined, he left me without shedding many tears. We have never corresponded or seen each other since. It is a pity: his character was essentially good; we were made to love each other.

Before I abandon myself to the fatality of my lot, allow me to turn my eyes for a moment upon the destiny which, in the nature of things, would have awaited me if I had fallen into the hands of a better master. Nothing was more suitable to my disposition or better adapted to make me happy than the quiet and obscure lot of a respectable artisan, especially of a certain class such as that of the engravers of Geneva. Such a position, sufficiently lucrative to afford a comfortable livelihood, but not sufficiently so to lead to fortune, would have limited my ambition for the rest of my days, and, leaving me an honourable leisure to cultivate modest tastes, would have confined me within my own sphere, without offering me the means of getting out of it. My imaginative powers were rich enough to beautify all callings with their chimeras, and strong enough to transport me, so to speak, at will from one to another; so it would have been immaterial to me in what position I actually found myself. It could not have been so far from the place where I was to my first castle in the air, that I could not have taken up my abode there without any difficulty. From this alone it followed that the simplest vocation, that which involved the least trouble and anxiety, that which allowed the greatest mental freedom, was the one which suited me best: and that was exactly my own. I should have passed a peaceful and quiet life, such as my disposition required, in the bosom of my religion, my country, my family, and my friends, in the monotony of a profession that suited my taste, and in a society after my own heart. I should have been a good Christian, a good citizen, a good father of a family, a good friend, a good workman, a good man in every relation of life. I should have loved my position in life, perhaps honoured it; and, having spent a life—simple, indeed, and obscure, but calm and serene—I should have died peacefully in the bosom of my family. Though, doubtless, soon forgotten, I should at least have been regretted as long as anyone remembered me.

Instead of that—what picture am I going to draw? Let us not anticipate the sorrows of my life; I shall occupy my readers more than enough with this melancholy subject.

❧ OLAUDAH EQUIANO
1745–1797

oh-LOW-dah
eh-kwee-AH-noh

About two years before the publication of the misadventures of Voltaire's ill-fated hero Candide, an eleven-year-old African was kidnapped from his home in Essaka, in what is now Nigeria. An innocent, like Candide, this young man was taken into slavery and eventually sold to traders on the Atlantic coast, where he would embark on a very real journey into misfortune, oppression, and despair. His eloquent tale of betrayal, enslavement, hardship, and finally emancipation, *The Interesting Narrative of the Life of* **Olaudah Equiano,** *or Gustavus Vassa the African,* was published in London in 1789. Although a few slaves had told their stories in print before—most notably Ignatius Sancho[1] and Ottobah Cugoano[2]— *Equiano's Travels,* as it is often called, marks a crucial moment in the development of a significant new literary genre, the SLAVE NARRATIVE. Reflecting its author's spiritual and intellectual resolution and framing the incidents of his life as a slave in a deeply felt humanitarianism, this story would inspire over the next century such works as Frederick Douglass's *Narrative of the Life of Frederick Douglass, an American Slave* (1845)[3] and Harriet Jacobs's *Incidents in the Life of a Slave Girl* (1861),[4] which are included in the nineteenth-century selections in Book 5.

EE-boh

Ibo Life. Equiano's "round unvarnished tale," as it was called in an early review, begins with a brief description of his birth in 1745. His father, he tells us, was one of the chief elders, the Embrenche, of his community, and as a child Equiano was blessed with good omens. In the first chapter of his book, Equiano describes the society, religious beliefs, and customs of the **Ibo** people with whom he spent his childhood. Within each village, a council of elders settled matters that affected the community and mediated disputes between parties. Nonetheless, a village assembly, which was open to all except the *osu* or slaves, ensured that members of the village had a voice in the decision-making process. As can be seen in Chinua Achebe's *Things Fall Apart,*[5] which describes the Ibo traditions more than

---

[1]**Ignatius Sancho** (1729–1780): Writer of the African diaspora who was born aboard a slave ship and educated in the household of the Duchess of Montagu; he became an art critic and grocer, and corresponded with several important figures in England. His *Letters of the Late Ignatius Sancho* appeared in 1782.

[2]**Ottobah Cugoano** (1757?–early nineteenth century): African writer who, like Equiano, was captured from the western coast of Africa and sold into slavery.

[3]**Frederick Douglass** (1818–1895): Author of one of the greatest American accounts of slavery, *Narrative of the Life of Frederick Douglass, an American Slave,* published in 1845. Douglass's narrative describes his quest for both freedom and identity.

[4]**Harriet Jacobs** (c. 1813–1897): Also known as Linda Brent; she was born into slavery in North Carolina and eventually escaped her master, the notorious Dr. James Norcom; her *Incidents in the Life of a Slave Girl* (1861) is one of the most important slave narratives of the nineteenth century.

Portrait of Olaudah Equiano, 1789
This engraving appeared in the first publication of The Interesting Narrative of the Life of Olaudah Equiano. *Note that Equiano is holding a Bible opened to Acts, Chapters IV and V. (Courtesy of the American Antiquarian Society, Worcester, Mass.)*

a century after Equiano's death, the Ibo also were organized along a complex system of age-group, kinship, and ritual ties. In the eighteenth century, they had an intricate network of trade among themselves and with their neighbors to the south who inhabited the city-states in the Niger delta region. Among the "commodities" traded were human beings, and when he was about eleven, Equiano was kidnapped by a raiding party and eventually taken to the Atlantic coast to be sold into slavery.

Slavery.   Equiano's story up to this point is fairly typical of the thousands of men, women, and children who were kidnapped by rival tribes or parties of raiders and exchanged for rifles, textiles, tobacco, iron, brass, and other items. Sometimes, as in Equiano's case, the captured would pass through a number of hands on their forced journey to the coastal towns along the Gold Coast or in the Niger delta, where they were held in forts until sold to European slave traders. From there they were packed into the infamous "slavers," the crowded ships that would take them to the West Indies or the United States. In his narrative, Equiano describes

www   For links to more information about Olaudah Equiano and a quiz on the *Interesting Narrative,* see *World Literature Online* at bedfordstmartins .com/worldlit.

---

[5] **Chinua Achebe** (b. 1930): Nigerian novelist, poet, and essayist; one of the most influential African writers of the twentieth century. His important novels include *Things Fall Apart* (1958), *No Longer at Ease* (1960), and *Arrow of God* (1964). (See Achebe in Book 6.)

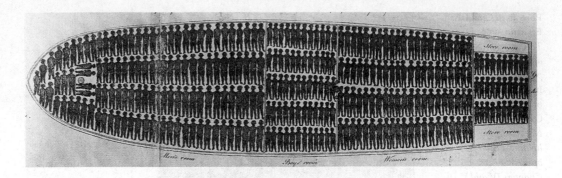

Slave Ship

Along with slave narratives, abolitionists circulated illustrations of the horrendous conditions aboard slave ships. (Courtesy of the American Antiquarian Society, Worcester, Mass.)

the horrible conditions aboard the slave ship, the anxieties and sorrows he suffered upon being moved from place to place and being separated from his sister. He was taken to Barbados, then to Virginia, and sold to a plantation owner. Within a few months he was sold again to Michael Henry Pascal, a British naval captain, with whom Equiano sailed to England, Holland, and North America, where his ship engaged in battles during the Seven Years' War. Through Pascal, Equiano learned to read and write, and he was treated with kindness and with some measure of respect by Pascal's relatives, the Guerins, in London. In 1763 Pascal sold Equiano to Captain James Doran, who took him to the West Indies, where he finally ended up the property of Robert King, a Quaker merchant.

Freedom.   Equiano notes early on that the name Olaudah means "fortunate one," and although his life would suggest the opposite, he reminds readers who haven't seen the horrors of the slave trade that, by comparison with most Africans taken into slavery, he can only consider himself "as a particular favorite of Heaven." Working for King, Equiano managed to save enough money to buy his freedom on July 11, 1766. He writes: "Before night, I, who had been a slave in the morning, trembling at the will of another, was become my own master, and completely free." Nonetheless, partly because he felt a debt of gratitude, Equiano remained in King's service as an able-bodied sailor for another year. On July 26, 1767, Equiano left for London, where he worked for a while as a hairdresser and bolstered his education before returning to the life he had come to know as a seafarer and small trader. Signing on with several ships in various capacities, Equiano traveled widely during this time throughout the Mediterranean as well as to Central America, the West Indies, and the Arctic. He traveled with Constantine John Phipps, who led a dangerous expedition by way of the Arctic in search of a northeast passage to India. That voyage had a profound influence on Equiano's life; the ships were for some time trapped in frozen waters, and Equiano once nearly drowned during an attempt to drag the boats free from the ice. The experience, he writes,

Equiano's *Narrative* is so richly structured that it became the prototype of the nineteenth-century slave narrative.

– HENRY LOUIS GATES JR., *The Classic Slave Narratives*, 1987 "made a lasting impression on my mind, and by the grace of God proved afterwards a mercy to me; it caused me to reflect deeply on my eternal state, and to seek the Lord with full purpose of heart ere it was too late."

Conversion.   Equiano's conversion marks an important turning point in his autobiography and aligns the narrative with spiritual biographies such as Augustine's *Confessions* and slave narratives such as Frederick Douglass's, texts in which conversion to Christianity is a climactic moment in the plot. Equiano's conversion experience is fraught with doubt and uncertainty, troubled dreams and feelings of guilt, leading ultimately to a vision on October 6, 1774, of Jesus on the cross. In the months leading up to his conversion and in the months it takes to unfold, Equiano studies the Bible carefully, puzzling over key passages and seeking advice from others. Often he pauses over the discrepancy between Christian teachings and slavery, shocked by the hypocrisy of those who preach the former and practice the latter. He also notes similarities between Christian and especially Hebrew practices and the customs of the Ibo.

Once convinced of the authenticity of his spiritual transformation and well studied in the Bible, Equiano joined the Methodist Church and became something of an evangelist, sparring over doctrine with a Catholic priest in Cadiz and preaching to the Mosquito Indians during his voyage to Central America in 1776. After establishing his residence in London, Equiano grew into an active leader in the abolitionist and anti-slavery movement and worked for a while as the commissary of stores and provisions for the Sierra Leone project, an effort to resettle displaced Africans in Sierra Leone. In 1787 he founded the Sons of Africa, an abolitionist group, and in 1790 he submitted a petition to Parliament advocating the abolition of slavery. In 1792, Equiano married Susanna Cullen, with whom he had two daughters, Anna Maria and Johanna. In 1796, a few months after the birth of their second daughter, Susanna died, followed by Equiano on March 31, 1797. Anna Maria survived her father by only a few months, leaving behind only Johanna, who inherited £950 from the family estate in 1816 when she turned twenty-one; after that, nothing more is known of her.

Work.   First published in 1789, *The Life of Olaudah Equiano, or Gustavus Vassa the African* was enormously popular in England and the United States, with eight English and one American edition printed by 1794. By 1797 the work had been translated into Dutch, Russian, and French. As a work of autobiography, moral exhortation, and social criticism, Equiano's book greatly enhanced the growing antislavery movement in England that eventually led to the abolition in that country of the slave trade in 1807 and the emancipation of slaves in the British colonies in 1833–34. But Equiano's narrative also came under attack, with charges of fraud raised against the text's accuracy, the author's identity, and the story's very authenticity. In the preface to a sixth edition, Equiano answers these charges, labeling them "invidious falsehoods." The authenticity of slave narratives was questioned often in England and the United States. Following Equiano's example, both Frederick Douglass and

> Surely this traffic cannot be good, which spreads like a pestilence, and taints what it touches! which violates that first natural right of mankind, equality and independency, and gives one man a dominion over his fellows which God could never intend!
>
> – OLAUDAH EQUIANO,
> *Interesting Narrative*

Harriet Jacobs added to their titles the phrase, "Written by Himself" or "Written by Herself," in anticipation of such doubts.

While important as a social text, *The Life of Olaudah Equiano* is also a significant literary achievement that exerted a powerful influence on subsequent slave narratives and generations of Anglo-African and African American writers, including some present-day authors. As critic Henry Louis Gates points out,

> Equiano's *Narrative* is so richly structured that it became the proto-type of the nineteenth-century slave narrative. From his subtitle "Written by Himself" and a signed engraving of the black author holding an open text (the Bible) in his lap . . . to the overlapping of the slave's arduous journey to freedom and his simultaneous journey from orality to literacy, Equiano's strategies of self-presentation most certainly influenced the shape of black narrative before 1865.

Gates points to a key structural feature of the slave narrative, a weaving together of plots in which the passage from slavery to emancipation follows from or is accompanied by a transition from oral culture to written culture and a surrendering to spiritual, Christian redemption. Rhetorically moving and vividly descriptive, Equiano's *Life* personalizes what for most readers are remote horrors, even as it presents Equiano himself as an exemplary figure who embodies the ENLIGHTENMENT ideals of ingenuity, stoic fortitude, and compassion for others.

As a travelogue, moral critique, and adventure story, *The Life of Olaudah Equiano* shares features with **Candide** and even with Swift's **Gulliver's Travels.** Yet in Equiano's odyssey, the hardships and oppression are not fiction but reality.

p. 275
p. 147

■ CONNECTIONS

Mary Rowlandson, *Narrative of the Captivity and Restoration of Mrs. Mary Rowlandson*, p. 483. Equiano's narrative describes a fall from innocence when the young man is captured from his home and sold into slavery. Moreover, he is terrified at the barbarism of Europeans and believes them to be demons. Eventually he meets whites who treat him with some degree of humanity. Rowlandson's account of her own captivity at the hands of the Wampanoag is strikingly similar in that she initially describes her captors as devils but gradually recognizes their fundamental humanity. How do Rowlandson and Equiano cope with their situations and what do these texts tell us about the encounter between cultures?

Jean-Jacques Rousseau, *Confessions*, p. 372. Equiano's autobiography depicts a range of personal experience that gives rise to such disparate emotions as fear, grief, confidence, and joy. Similarly, Rousseau's *Confessions* recounts its narrator's formative experiences and explores a universe of feelings. Which author do you find more sincere and what strategies does each use to gain your sympathy and respect?

Harriet Jacobs, *Incidents in the Life of a Slave Girl; In the World: Emancipation* (Book 5). Equiano's *Interesting Narrative* and Jacobs's *Incidents* are excellent companion pieces, providing points of comparison between the far-traveling Equiano and the homebound Jacobs as well as between the conventions of the slave narrative that appear in both. These narratives played a role in the emancipation movement by providing harrowing accounts of slaves' lives and by making known the forbearance, humanity, and spiritual strength of the men and women who authored them. How does each text appeal to both reason and feeling? How much does gender account for some of the differences between the two narratives?

■ **FURTHER RESEARCH**

Biography
Walvin, James. *An African's Life: The Life and Times of Olaudah Equiano, 1745–1797.* 1998.

Background
Acholonu, Catherine Obianuju. *The Igbo Roots of Olaudah Equiano.* 1989.
Davis, Charles T. and Henry Louis Gates Jr. *The Slave's Narrative.* 1985.
Edwards, Paul. *Black Writers in England, 1760–1890.* 1991.

Criticism
Allison, Robert, ed. Introduction. *The Interesting Narrative of the Life of Olaudah Equiano, Written by Himself.* 1995.
Costanzo, Angelo. *Surprising Narrative: Olaudah Equiano and the Beginnings of Black Autobiography.* 1987.
Edwards, Paul, ed. Introduction. *The Life of Olaudah Equiano.* 1988.
Gates, Henry Louis, Jr. and William L. Andrews, eds. *Pioneers of the Black Atlantic: Five Slave Narratives from the Enlightenment, 1772–1815.* 1998.
Sandiford, Keith. *Measuring the Moment: Strategies of Protest in Eighteenth-Century Afro-English Writing.* 1988.

■ **PRONUNCIATION**

Olaudah Equiano: oh-LOW-dah eh-kwee-AH-noh
Ibo: EE-boh

❧ The Interesting Narrative of the Life of Olaudah Equiano

CHAPTER 1
[Equiano's Igbo Roots]

I believe it is difficult for those who publish their own memoirs to escape the imputation of vanity; nor is this the only disadvantage under which they labor: it is also

---

The Interesting Narrative of the Life of Olaudah Equiano, or Gustavus Vassa the African, Written by Himself. First published in 1789, Equiano's autobiography quickly became one of the most important documents of the abolitionist movement in England and went through more than eight editions in six years. Equiano's moving but clear-eyed descriptions of the cruel injustices wrought upon slaves touched everyone in England, from royalty to working men and women. But Equiano's text is much more than a political tract or an abolitionist polemic. It is one of the first classic slave narratives, a work that blends the conventions of the travel narrative, the spiritual autobiography, and the sentimental novel (a novel that exploits the reader's capacity for compassion or sympathy) into a powerful form of autobiography, moral instruction, and social critique. The sections excerpted here give a sense of the progression of Equiano's story, beginning with his birth, advancing to his captivity, touching on key moments of his emancipation and his spiritual conversion, and concluding with his contributions to the abolition of slavery.

A note on the text: The text reprinted here is from Robert Allison's edition of *The Interesting Narrative* (Boston: Bedford/St. Martin's, 1995). All notes, unless otherwise indicated, are taken or adapted from those of Allison.

The Interesting Narrative of the
Life of Olaudah Equiano

GREENLAND

ENGLAND
London
Plymouth
Falmouth
Belle Isle
FRANCE
Nice   Genoa
Gulf of Lions
Barcelona
SPAIN
Malaga
Oporto
Cadiz
Gibraltar

Smyrna

Cape Breton
Louisbourg
New York
Philadelphia
UNITED STATES
Charleston
Savannah
Havana
CUBA
BAHAMA ISLANDS
Nassau
HAITI
SANTO DOMINGO
Port-au-Prince
Kingston
JAMAICA
Caribbean Sea
Montserrat
Martinique
Barbados
Cartagena
Mosquito Coast

ATLANTIC
OCEAN

MADEIRA ISLANDS
CANARY ISLANDS

DAHOMEY
ASANTE
Port Harcourt
Benin
MANDE
Niger R.
São Tomé

N
W   E
S

3,000 miles
3,000 kilometers
1,500
1,500
0

(1757–58)   ④ (1791)   ⑮
(1761)   ⑥
⑤
(1759)

(1773)   ⑫
⑤ (1759)
(1784)   ⑭
(1757)   ③
⑧ (1764)
⑨ (1767)
⑬

(1767–69)   ⑩
(1767–69)   ⑩
⑪ (1771)
⑦ (1763)
⑬ (1775)

① (1745)
② (1756)

⑩

their misfortune that what is uncommon is rarely, if ever, believed, and what is obvious we are apt to turn from with disgust, and to charge the writer with impertinence. People generally think those memoirs only worthy to be read or remembered which abound in great or striking events, those, in short, which in a high degree excite either admiration or pity; all others they consign to contempt and oblivion. It is therefore, I confess, not a little hazardous in a private and obscure individual, and a stranger too, thus to solicit the indulgent attention of the public, especially when I own I offer here the history of neither a saint, a hero, nor a tyrant. I believe there are few events in my life which have not happened to many; it is true the incidents of it are numerous, and, did I consider myself an European, I might say my sufferings were great; but when I compare my lot with that of most of my countrymen, I regard myself as a *particular favorite of heaven,* and acknowledge the mercies of Providence in every occurrence of my life. If, then, the following narrative does not appear sufficiently interesting to engage general attention, let my motive be some excuse for its publication. I am not so foolishly vain as to expect from it either immortality or

◀ **The Voyages of Olaudah Equiano**

Equiano spent ten years as a slave on trade ships that made their way back and forth across the Atlantic. His extraordinary travels continued after he gained his freedom, as he voyaged to the West Indies, continental Europe, Turkey, and Ireland.

KEY	The Voyages of Olaudah Equiano*
1. 1745	Born into Ibo tribe in Essaka, a village in what is now Nigeria.
2. 1756	Kidnapped and boarded on a slave ship; taken to Barbados, then to Virginia.
3. 1757	Bought by Michael Henry Pascal, a British naval officer, who names Equiano Gustavus Vassa and takes him to England.
4. 1757–58	Serves in British navy. Travels to Holland, Scotland, Orkneys, and the coast of France.
5. 1759	Sets out for Mediterranean and arrives at Gibraltar; sails to Barcelona through the Gulf of Lyons.
6. 1761	Nearly shipwrecked while headed toward Belle Isle.
7. 1763	Sold in England; sent to Montserrat and sold to Robert King.
8. 1764	Works on trading voyages between West Indies and mainland American colonies. Obtains freedom on July 11, 1766.
9. 1767	Shipwrecked in Bahamas. Retreats to New Providence (Nassau), then to Georgia, then back to Martinique and Montserrat.
10. 1767–69	Sails to London, continues on to Nice, Leghorn, Villa Franca, the Archipelago Islands, Turkey, and Genoa. Converts to Christianity.
11. 1771	Travels to West Indies — Madeira, Barbados, Grenada, Nevis, and Jamaica.
12. 1773	Sails for Arctic seeking a northeast passage to India; explores Greenland.
13. 1775	Admitted to Communion in Westminster Church, London. Voyages to Mosquito Coast (Nicaragua) with Dr. Irving to establish a plantation; returns to England.
14. 1784	Sails for New York.
15. 1791	Gives talks in Ireland.

*Double arrows indicate journey and return.

literary reputation. If it affords any satisfaction to my numerous friends, at whose request it has been written, or in the smallest degree promotes the interests of humanity, the ends for which it was undertaken will be fully attained, and every wish of my heart gratified. Let it therefore be remembered, that, in wishing to avoid censure, I do not aspire to praise.

That part of Africa, known by the name of Guinea, to which the trade for slaves is carried on, extends along the coast above 3400 miles, from Senegal to Angola, and includes a variety of kingdoms. Of these the most considerable is the kingdom of Benin,[1] both as to extent and wealth, the richness and cultivation of the soil, the power of its king, and the number and warlike disposition of the inhabitants. It is situated nearly under the line,[2] and extends along the coast about 170 miles, but runs back into the interior part of Africa to a distance hitherto, I believe, unexplored by any traveller, and seems only terminated at length by the empire of Abyssinia, near 1500 miles from its beginning. This kingdom is divided into many provinces or districts, in one of the most remote and fertile of which, I was born, in the year 1745, situated in a charming fruitful vale, named Essaka. The distance of this province from the capital of Benin and the sea coast must be very considerable, for I had never heard of white men or Europeans, nor of the sea; and our subjection to the king of Benin was little more than nominal, for every transaction of the government, as far as my slender observation extended, was conducted by the chief or elders of the place. The manners and government of a people who have little commerce with other countries are generally very simple, and the history of what passes in one family or village may serve as a specimen of the whole nation.

My father was one of those elders or chiefs I have spoken of, and was styled Embrenche, a term, as I remember, importing the highest distinction, and signifying in our language a *mark* of grandeur. This mark is conferred on the person entitled to it, by cutting the skin across at the top of the forehead, and drawing it down to the eyebrows; and while it is in this situation applying a warm hand, and rubbing it until it shrinks up into a thick *weal* across the lower part of the forehead.[3] Most of the judges and senators were thus marked; my father had long borne it; I had seen it conferred on one of my brothers, and I also was *destined* to receive it by my parents. Those Embrenche, or chief men, decided disputes and punished crimes, for which purpose they always assembled together. The proceedings were generally short, and in most cases the law of retaliation prevailed.

I remember a man was brought before my father, and the other judges, for kidnapping a boy; and, although he was the son of a chief or senator, he was condemned to make recompense by a man or woman slave. Adultery, however, was sometimes punished with slavery or death, a punishment which I believe is inflicted on it

---

[1] **Benin:** The kingdom of Benin, with its capital in the city of Benin, extended from the Niger delta to the city of Lagos.

[2] **the line:** The equator.

[3] **weal . . . forehead:** The Ibo phrase *igbu ichi* refers to this scarring of the face, and *mgburichi*, which Equiano renders as *Embrenche,* means "men who bear such scars." Both derive from *ichi,* "to crown." (Catherine Obianuju Acholonu, *The Igbo Roots of Olaudah Equiano: An Anthropological Research.* [Owerri, Nigeria: Afa Publications, 1989], 10–12, 29–30.)

throughout most of the nations of Africa,[4] so sacred among them is the honor of the marriage bed, and so jealous are they of the fidelity of their wives. Of this I recollect an instance—a woman was convicted before the judges of adultery, and delivered over, as the custom was, to her husband, to be punished. Accordingly he determined to put her to death; but it being found, just before her execution, that she had an infant at her breast, and no woman being prevailed on to perform the part of a nurse, she was spared on account of the child. The men, however, do not preserve the same constancy to their wives which they expect from them; for they indulge in a plurality, though seldom in more than two.

Their mode of marriage is thus—both parties are usually betrothed when young by their parents (though I have known the males to betroth themselves). On this occasion a feast is prepared, and the bride and bridegroom stand up in the midst of all their friends, who are assembled for the purpose, while he declares she is henceforth to be looked upon as his wife, and that no other person is to pay any addresses to her. This is also immediately proclaimed in the vicinity, on which the bride retires from the assembly. Some time after, she is brought home to her husband, and then another feast is made, to which the relations of both parties are invited; her parents then deliver her to the bridegroom, accompanied with a number of blessings, and at the same time they tie round her waist a cotton string of the thickness of a goose-quill, which none but married women are permitted to wear; she is now considered as completely his wife; and at this time the dowry is given to the new married pair, which generally consists of portions of land, slaves, and cattle, household goods, and implements of husbandry. These are offered by the friends of both parties; besides which the parents of the bridegroom present gifts to those of the bride, whose property she is looked upon before marriage; but after it she is esteemed the sole property of her husband. The ceremony being now ended, the festival begins, which is celebrated with bonfires and loud acclamations of joy, accompanied with music and dancing.

We are almost a nation of dancers, musicians, and poets. Thus every great event, such as a triumphant return from battle or other cause of public rejoicing, is celebrated in public dances, which are accompanied with songs and music suited to the occasion. The assembly is separated into four divisions, which dance either apart or in succession, and each with a character peculiar to itself. The first division contains the married men, who in their dances frequently exhibit feats of arms and the representation of a battle. To these succeed the married women, who dance in the second division. The young men occupy the third, and the maidens the fourth. Each represents some interesting scene of real life, such as a great achievement, domestic employment, a pathetic story, or some rural sport; and as the subject is generally founded on some recent event, it is therefore ever new. This gives our dances a spirit and variety which I have scarcely seen elsewhere.[5] We have many musical instruments,

---

[4] **nations of Africa:** See Benezet's "Account of Guinea," throughout. [Equiano's note.] Anthony Benezet (1713–1784), a Philadelphia Quaker, wrote *Some Historical Account of Guinea: Its situation, produce, and the general disposition of its inhabitants with an inquiry into the rise and progress of the Slave Trade its nature and lamentable effects* (1771) and other antislavery tracts.

[5] **spirit . . . elsewhere:** When I was in Smyrna I have frequently seen the Greeks dance after this manner. [Equiano's note.]

particularly drums of different kinds, a piece of music which resembles a guitar, and another much like a stickado. These last are chiefly used by betrothed virgins, who play on them on all grand festivals.

As our manners are simple, our luxuries are few. The dress of both sexes is nearly the same. It generally consists of a long piece of calico, or muslin, wrapped loosely round the body, somewhat in the form of a highland plaid. This is usually dyed blue, which is our favorite color. It is extracted from a berry, and is brighter and richer than any I have seen in Europe. Besides this, our women of distinction wear golden ornaments, which they dispose with some profusion on their arms and legs. When our women are not employed with the men in tillage, their usual occupation is spinning and weaving cotton, which they afterwards dye, and make into garments. They also manufacture earthen vessels, of which we have many kinds. Among the rest, tobacco pipes, made after the same fashion, and used in the same manner, as those in Turkey.[6]

Our manner of living is entirely plain; for as yet the natives are unacquainted with those refinements in cookery which debauch the taste: bullocks, goats, and poultry supply the greatest part of their food. These constitute likewise the principal wealth of the country, and the chief articles of its commerce. The flesh is usually stewed in a pan; to make it savory we sometimes use pepper, and other spices, and we have salt made of wood ashes. Our vegetables are mostly plantains, eadas,[7] yams, beans, and Indian corn. The head of the family usually eats alone; his wives and slaves have also their separate tables. Before we taste food we always wash our hands; indeed, our cleanliness on all occasions is extreme, but on this it is an indispensable ceremony. After washing, libation is made, by pouring out a small portion of the drink on the floor, and tossing a small quantity of the food in a certain place, for the spirits of departed relations, which the natives suppose to preside over their conduct and guard them from evil. They are totally unacquainted with strong or spirituous liquors; and their principal beverage is palm wine. This is got from a tree of that name, by tapping it at the top and fastening a large gourd to it; and sometimes one tree will yield three or four gallons in a night. When just drawn it is of a most delicious sweetness; but in a few days it acquires a tartish and more spirituous flavor, though I never saw anyone intoxicated by it. The same tree also produces nuts and oil. Our principal luxury is in perfumes: one sort of these is an odoriferous wood of delicious fragrance, the other a kind of earth, a small portion of which thrown into the fire diffuses a most powerful odor.[8] We beat this wood into powder, and mix it with palm oil, with which both men and women perfume themselves.[9]

---

[6] **tobacco . . . Turkey:** The bowl is earthen, curiously figured, to which a long reed is fixed as a tube. This tube is sometimes so long as to be borne by one, and frequently out of grandeur, two boys. [Equiano's note.]

[7] **eadas:** Probably eddo, or cocoa yam.

[8] **powerful odor:** When I was in Smyrna I saw the same kind of earth, and brought some of it with me to England; it resembles musk in strength, but is more delicious in scent, and is not unlike the smell of a rose. [Equiano's note.]

[9] **perfume themselves:** Camwood, or *uhie*, was ground to a powder, mixed with oil, then spread on the skin; the *uhiguihi* is a fruit resembling a piece of wood that produces a fragrance when burned. (Acholonu, *Igbo Roots*, 21)

In our buildings we study convenience rather than ornament. Each master of a family has a large square piece of ground, surrounded with a moat or fence, or enclosed with a wall made of red earth tempered, which, when dry, is as hard as brick. Within this, are his houses to accommodate his family and slaves, which, if numerous, frequently present the appearance of a village. In the middle, stands the principal building, appropriated to the sole use of the master and consisting of two apartments; in one of which he sits in the day with his family, the other is left apart for the reception of his friends. He has besides these a distinct apartment in which he sleeps, together with his male children. On each side are the apartments of his wives, who have also their separate day and night houses. The habitations of the slaves and their families are distributed throughout the rest of the enclosure. These houses never exceed one story in height; they are always built of wood, or stakes driven into the ground, crossed with wattles, and neatly plastered within and without. The roof is thatched with reeds. Our day houses are left open at the sides; but those in which we sleep are always covered, and plastered in the inside, with a composition mixed with cow-dung, to keep off the different insects which annoy us during the night. The walls and floors also of these are generally covered with mats. Our beds consist of a platform, raised three or four feet from the ground, on which are laid skins, and different parts of a spongy tree, called plaintain. Our covering is calico or muslin, the same as our dress. The usual seats are a few logs of wood; but we have benches, which are generally perfumed to accommodate strangers: these compose the greater part of our household furniture. Houses so constructed and furnished require but little skill to erect them. Every man is a sufficient architect for the purpose. The whole neighborhood afford their unanimous assistance in building them, and in return receive and expect no other recompense than a feast.

As we live in a country where nature is prodigal of her favors, our wants are few and easily supplied; of course we have few manufactures. They consist for the most part of calicoes, earthen ware, ornaments, and instruments of war and husbandry. But these make no part of our commerce, the principal articles of which, as I have observed, are provisions. In such a state, money is of little use; however, we have some small pieces of coin, if I may call them such. They are made something like an anchor, but I do not remember either their value or denomination. We have also markets, at which I have been frequently with my mother. These are sometimes visited by stout mahogany-colored men from the south-west of us: we call them *Oye-Eboe*,[10] which term signifies red men living at a distance. They generally bring us fire-arms, gun-powder, hats, beads, and dried fish. The last we esteemed a great rarity, as our waters were only brooks and springs. These articles they barter with us for odoriferous woods and earth, and our salt of wood ashes. They always carry slaves through our land; but the strictest account is exacted of their manner of procuring them before they are suffered to pass. Sometimes, indeed, we sold slaves to them, but they were only prisoners of war, or such among us as had been convicted of

---

[10] *Oye-Eboe: Oyibo* is "light-colored person." Acholonu suggests that these may have been Aro people, a mahogany-colored people from south of Isseke. Those from Arochukwu were involved in the slave trade, exchanging their captives for guns, gunpowder, and other European goods. (Acholonu, *Igbo Roots,* 14)

kidnapping, or adultery, and some other crimes, which we esteemed heinous. This practice of kidnapping induces me to think, that, notwithstanding all our strictness, their principal business among us was to trepan our people. I remember too, they carried great sacks along with them, which not long after, I had an opportunity of fatally seeing applied to that infamous purpose.

Our land is uncommonly rich and fruitful, and produces all kinds of vegetables in great abundance. We have plenty of Indian corn, and vast quantities of cotton and tobacco. Our pineapples grow without culture; they are about the size of the largest sugar-loaf, and finely flavored. We have also spices of different kinds, particularly pepper, and a variety of delicious fruits which I have never seen in Europe, together with gums of various kinds, and honey in abundance. All our industry is exerted to improve these blessings of nature. Agriculture is our chief employment; and everyone, even the children and women, are engaged in it. Thus we are all habituated to labor from our earliest years. Everyone contributes something to the common stock; and, as we are unacquainted with idleness, we have no beggars. The benefits of such a mode of living are obvious. The West India planters prefer the slaves of Benin or Eboe[11] to those of any other part of Guinea, for their hardiness, intelligence, integrity, and zeal. Those benefits are felt by us in the general healthiness of the people, and in their vigor and activity; I might have added, too, in their comeliness. Deformity is indeed unknown amongst us, I mean that of shape. Numbers of the natives of Eboe now in London might be brought in support of this assertion: for, in regard to complexion, ideas of beauty are wholly relative. I remember while in Africa to have seen three Negro children who were tawny, and another quite white, who were universally regarded by myself, and the natives in general, as far as related to their complexions, as deformed. Our women, too, were, in my eye at least, uncommonly graceful, alert, and modest to a degree of bashfulness; nor do I remember to have heard of an instance of incontinence amongst them before marriage. They are also remarkably cheerful. Indeed, cheerfulness and affability are two of the leading characteristics of our nation.

Our tillage is exercised in a large plain or common, some hour's walk from our dwellings, and all the neighbors resort thither in a body. They use no beasts of husbandry; and their only instruments are hoes, axes, shovels, and beaks, or pointed iron, to dig with. Sometimes we are visited by locusts, which come in large clouds, so as to darken the air, and destroy our harvest. This, however, happens rarely, but when it does, a famine is produced by it. I remember an instance or two wherein this happened. This common is often the theatre of war; and therefore when our people go out to till their land, they not only go in a body, but generally take their arms with them for fear of a surprise; and when they apprehend an invasion, they guard the avenues to their dwellings, by driving sticks into the ground, which are so sharp at one end as to pierce the foot, and are generally dipt in poison. From what I can recollect of these battles, they appear to have been irruptions of one little state or district on the other, to obtain prisoners or booty. Perhaps they were incited to this by those traders who brought the European goods I mentioned, amongst us. Such a mode of

---

[11] **Eboe:** Ibo or Igbo.

obtaining slaves in Africa is common; and I believe more are procured this way, and by kidnapping, than any other.[12] When a trader wants slaves, he applies to a chief for them, and tempts him with his wares. It is not extraordinary, if on this occasion he yields to the temptation with as little firmness, and accepts the price of his fellow creature's liberty, with as little reluctance as the enlightened merchant. Accordingly he falls on his neighbors, and a desperate battle ensues. If he prevails and takes prisoners, he gratifies his avarice by selling them; but, if his party be vanquished, and he falls into the hands of the enemy, he is put to death; for, as he has been known to foment their quarrels, it is thought dangerous to let him survive, and no ransom can save him, though all other prisoners may be redeemed. We have fire-arms, bows and arrows, broad two-edged swords and javelins; we have shields also which cover a man from head to foot. All are taught the use of these weapons; even our women are warriors, and march boldly out to fight along with the men. Our whole district is a kind of militia: on a certain signal given, such as the firing of a gun at night, they all rise in arms and rush upon their enemy. It is perhaps something remarkable, that when our people march to the field a red flag or banner is borne before them.

I was once a witness to a battle in our common. We had been all at work in it one day as usual, when our people were suddenly attacked. I climbed a tree at some distance, from which I beheld the fight. There were many women as well as men on both sides; among others my mother was there, and armed with a broad sword. After fighting for a considerable time with great fury, and many had been killed, our people obtained the victory, and took their enemy's Chief a prisoner. He was carried off in great triumph, and, though he offered a large ransom for his life, he was put to death. A virgin of note among our enemies had been slain in the battle, and her arm was exposed in our marketplace, where our trophies were always exhibited. The spoils were divided according to the merit of the warriors. Those prisoners which were not sold or redeemed, we kept as slaves; but how different was their condition from that of the slaves in the West Indies! With us, they do no more work than other members of the community, even their master; their food, clothing, and lodging were nearly the same as theirs (except that they were not permitted to eat with those who were free-born); and there was scarce any other difference between them, than a superior degree of importance which the head of a family possesses in our state, and that authority which, as such, he exercises over every part of his household. Some of these slaves have even slaves under them as their own property, and for their own use.

As to religion, the natives believe that there is one Creator of all things, and that he lives in the sun, and is girted round with a belt; that he may never eat or drink, but, according to some, he smokes a pipe, which is our own favorite luxury. They believe he governs events, especially our deaths or captivity; but, as for the doctrine of eternity, I do not remember to have ever heard of it; some, however, believe in the transmigration of souls in a certain degree. Those spirits which were not transmigrated, such as their dear friends or relations, they believe always attend them, and guard them from the bad spirits or their foes. For this reason they always, before

---

[12] See Benezet's "Account of Guinea," throughout. [Equiano's note.]

eating, as I have observed, put some small portion of the meat, and pour some of their drink, on the ground for them; and they often make oblations of the blood of beasts or fowls at their graves. I was very fond of my mother, and almost constantly with her. When she went to make these oblations at her mother's tomb, which was a kind of small solitary thatched house, I sometimes attended her. There she made her libations, and spent most of the night in cries and lamentations. I have been often extremely terrified on these occasions. The loneliness of the place, the darkness of the night, and the ceremony of libation, naturally awful and gloomy, were heightened by my mother's lamentations; and these concurring with the doleful cries of birds, by which these places were frequented, gave an inexpressible terror to the scene.

We compute the year from the day on which the sun crosses the line, and on its setting that evening, there is a general shout throughout the land; at least, I can speak from my own knowledge, throughout our vicinity. The people at the same time make a great noise with rattles, not unlike the basket rattles used by children here, though much larger, and hold up their hands to heaven for a blessing. It is then the greatest offerings are made; and those children whom our wise men foretell will be fortunate are then presented to different people. I remember many used to come to see me, and I was carried about to others for that purpose. They have many offerings, particularly at full moons; generally two, at harvest, before the fruits are taken out of the ground; and when any young animals are killed, sometimes they offer up part of them as a sacrifice. These offerings, when made by one of the heads of a family, serve for the whole. I remember we often had them at my father's and my uncle's, and their families have been present. Some of our offerings are eaten with bitter herbs. We had a saying among us to anyone of a cross temper, "That if they were to be eaten, they should be eaten with bitter herbs."

We practised circumcision like the Jews, and made offerings and feasts on that occasion, in the same manner as they did. Like them also, our children were named from some event, some circumstance, or fancied foreboding, at the time of their birth. I was named *Olaudah,* which in our language signifies vicissitude, or fortunate; also, one favored, and having a loud voice and well spoken.[13] I remember we never polluted the name of the object of our adoration; on the contrary, it was always mentioned with the greatest reverence; and we were totally unacquainted with swearing, and all those terms of abuse and reproach which find their way so readily and copiously into the language of more civilized people. The only expressions of that kind I remember were, "May you rot, or may you swell, or may a beast take you."

I have before remarked that the natives of this part of Africa are extremely cleanly. This necessary habit of decency was with us a part of religion, and therefore we had many purifications and washings; indeed almost as many, and used on the same occasions, if my recollection does not fail me, as the Jews. Those that touched the dead at any time were obliged to wash and purify themselves before they could enter a dwelling-house. Every woman, too, at certain times was forbidden to come

---

[13] **Olaudah:** *Ola,* or ring, is a symbol of good fortune to the Ibo. *Ude* means "pleasing sound." (Acholonu, *Igbo Roots,* 42–43)

into a dwelling-house, or touch any person, or anything we eat. I was so fond of my mother I could not keep from her, or avoid touching her at some of those periods, in consequence of which I was obliged to be kept out with her, in a little house made for that purpose, till offering was made, and then we were purified.

Though we had no places of public worship, we had priests and magicians, or wise men. I do not remember whether they had different offices, or whether they were united in the same persons, but they were held in great reverence by the people. They calculated our time, and foretold events, as their name imported, for we called them *Ah-affoe-way-cah,* which signifies calculators or yearly men, our year being called *Ah-affoe.*[14] They wore their beards, and when they died, they were succeeded by their sons. Most of their implements and things of value were interred along with them. Pipes and tobacco were also put into the grave with the corpse, which was always perfumed and ornamented, and animals were offered in sacrifice to them. None accompanied their funerals, but those of the same profession or tribe. They buried them after sunset, and always returned from the grave by a different way from that which they went.

These magicians were also our doctors or physicians. They practised bleeding by cupping, and were very successful in healing wounds and expelling poisons. They had likewise some extraordinary method of discovering jealousy, theft, poisoning, the success of which, no doubt, they derived from the unbounded influence over the credulity and superstition of the people. I do not remember what those methods were, except that as to poisoning; I recollect an instance or two, which I hope it will not be deemed impertinent here to insert, as it may serve as a kind of specimen of the rest, as is still used by the Negroes in the West Indies. A young woman had been poisoned, but it was not known by whom; the doctors ordered the corpse to be taken up by some persons, and carried to the grave. As soon as the bearers had raised it on their shoulders, they seemed seized with some sudden impulse,[15] and ran to and fro, unable to stop themselves. At last, after having passed through a number of thorns and prickly bushes unhurt, the corpse fell from them close to a house, and defaced it in the fall; and the owner being taken up, he immediately confessed the poisoning.[16]

---

[14] *Ah-affoe-way-cah . . . Ah-affoe: Ofo-nwanchi* were travelling men who calculated the years. Often dwarfs, they were sometimes called *afo-nwa-ika,* or "funny monkeys," by children in the villages they visited. Local priests were *nze nzu.* (Acholonu, *Igbo Roots,* 18–19)

[15] seized . . . impulse: See also Lieutenant Matthew's Voyage, p. 123. [Equiano's note.] John Matthews, *A Voyage to the River Sierra Leone . . . with a Letter on the . . . African Slave Trade* (London: 1788).

[16] poisoning: An instance of this kind happened at Montserrat, in the West Indies, in the year 1763. I then belonged to the *Charming Sally,* Capt. Doran. The chief mate, Mr. Mansfield, and some of the crew being one day on shore, were present at the burying of a poisoned Negro girl. Though they had often heard of the circumstance of the running in such cases, and had even seen it, they imagined it to be a trick of the corpse bearers. The mate therefore desired two of the sailors to take up the coffin, and carry it to the grave. The sailors, who were all of the same opinion, readily obeyed, but they had scarcely raised it to their shoulders before they began to run furiously about, quite unable to direct themselves, till at last, without intention, they came to the hut of him who had poisoned the girl. The coffin then immediately fell from their shoulders against the hut, and damaged part of the wall. The owner of the hut was taken into custody on this, and confessed the poisoning. I give this story as it was related by the mate and crew on their return to the ship. The credit which is due to it, I leave with the reader. [Equiano's note.]

The natives are extremely cautious about poison. When they buy any eatables, the seller kisses it all round before the buyer, to shew him it is not poisoned; and the same is done when any meat or drink is presented, particularly to a stranger. We have serpents of different kinds, some of which are esteemed ominous when they appear in our houses, and these we never molest. I remember two of those ominous snakes, each of which was as thick as the calf of a man's leg, and in color resembling a dolphin in the water, crept at different times into my mother's night house, where I always lay with her, and coiled themselves into folds, and each time they crowed like a cock. I was desired by some of our wise men to touch these, that I might be interested in the good omens, which I did, for they were quite harmless, and would tamely suffer themselves to be handled; and then they were put into a large earthen pan, and set on one side of the highway. Some of our snakes, however, were poisonous; one of them crossed the road one day as I was standing on it, and passed between my feet without offering to touch me, to the great surprise of many who saw it; and these incidents were accounted by the wise men, and likewise by my mother and the rest of the people, as remarkable omens in my favor.

Such is the imperfect sketch my memory has furnished me with, of the manners and customs of a people among whom I first drew my breath. And here I cannot forbear suggesting what has long struck me very forcibly, namely, the strong analogy which even by this sketch, imperfect as it is, appears to prevail in the manners and customs of my countrymen and those of the Jews, before they reached the land of promise, and particularly the patriarchs while they were yet in that pastoral state which is described in Genesis — an analogy, which alone would induce me to think that the one people had sprung from the other. Indeed, this is the opinion of Dr. Gill, who, in his commentary on Genesis, very ably deduces the pedigree of the Africans from Afer and Afra, the descendents of Abraham by Keturah his wife and concubine (for both these titles are applied to her). It is also conformable to the sentiments of Dr. John Clarke, formerly Dean of Sarum, in his truth of the Christian religion; both these authors concur in ascribing to us this original.[7] The reasonings of those gentlemen are still further confirmed by the scripture chronology; and if any further corroboration were required, this resemblance in so many respects, is a strong evidence in support of the opinion. Like the Israelites in their primitive state, our government was conducted by our chiefs or judges, our wise men and elders; and the head of a family with us enjoyed a similar authority over his household, with that which is ascribed to Abraham and the other patriarchs. The law of retaliation obtained almost universally with us as with them: and even their religion appeared to have shed upon us a ray of its glory, though broken and spent in its passage, or eclipsed by the cloud with which time, tradition, and ignorance might have enveloped it; for we had our circumcision (a rule, I believe, peculiar to that people), we had also our sacrifices and burnt-offerings, our washings and purifications, and on the same occasions as they did.

---

[7] **this original:** Dr. John Gill (1697–1771), a Baptist divine, published his multivolume *Exposition of the Holy Scriptures* in 1766. John Clarke's *Truth of the Christian Religion, in Six Books* (1711) is a translation of Hugo Grotius (1583–1645), *De veritatus religionis christianae* (1627).

As to the difference of color between the Eboan Africans and the modern Jews, I shall not presume to account for it. It is a subject which has engaged the pens of men of both genius and learning, and is far above my strength. The most able and Reverend Mr. T. Clarkson, however, in his much admired *Essay on the Slavery and Commerce of the Human Species,*[18] has ascertained the cause in a manner that at once solves every objection on that account, and, on my mind at least, has produced the fullest conviction. I shall therefore refer to that performance for the theory,[19] contenting myself with extracting a fact as related by Dr. Mitchel.[20] "The Spaniards, who have inhabited America, under the torrid zone, for any time, are become as dark colored as our native Indians of Virginia; of which *I myself have been a witness.*" There is also another instance[21] of a Portuguese settlement at Mitomba, a river in Sierra Leone, where the inhabitants are bred from a mixture of the first Portuguese discoverers with the natives, and are now become in their complexion, and in the woolly quality of their hair, *perfect Negroes,* retaining however a smattering of the Portuguese language.[22]

These instances, and a great many more which might be adduced, while they show how the complexions of the same persons vary in different climates, it is hoped may tend also to remove the prejudice that some conceive against the natives of Africa on account of their color. Surely the minds of the Spaniards did not change with their complexions! Are there not causes enough to which the apparent inferiority of an African may be ascribed, without limiting the goodness of God, and supposing he forebore to stamp understanding on certainly his own image, because "carved in ebony." Might it not naturally be ascribed to their situation? When they come among Europeans, they are ignorant of their language, religion, manners, and customs. Are any pains taken to teach them these? Are they treated as men? Does not slavery itself depress the mind, and extinguish all its fire and every noble sentiment? But, above all, what advantages do not a refined people possess, over those who are rude and uncultivated? Let the polished and haughty European recollect that his ancestors were once, like the Africans, uncivilized, and even barbarous. Did Nature make *them* inferior to their sons? and should *they too* have been made slaves? Every rational mind answers, No. Let such reflections as these melt the pride of their superiority into sympathy for the wants and miseries of their sable brethren, and compel them to acknowledge that understanding is not confined to feature or color. If, when they look round the world, they feel exultation, let it be tempered with benevolence

---

[18] *Essay . . . Species:* (London, 1786). Thomas Clarkson (1760–1846) wrote this essay for an academic competition at Cambridge in 1785. He won the contest and became a lifelong abolitionist. His documentation of the horrors of the slave trade became a foundation for antislavery activity. His brother John, a Royal Navy officer, helped to found the Sierra Leone colony.

[19] **the theory:** Pages 178 to 216. [Equiano's note.]

[20] **Dr. Mitchel:** Philos. Trans. No. 476, Sec. 4, cited by Mr. Clarkson, p. 205. [Equiano's note.] John Mitchell, "An Essay upon the Causes of the Different Colours of People in Different Climates," *Philosophical Transactions of the Royal Society* 43 (1746).

[21] **another instance:** Same page. [Equiano's note.]

[22] **Portuguese language:** The Portuguese established a trading post at Mitombe, Sierra Leone, in the 1460s.

to others, and gratitude to God, "who hath made of one blood all nations of men for to dwell on all the face of the earth";[23] "and whose wisdom is not our wisdom, neither are our ways his ways."

CHAPTER 2
[CAPTIVITY AND SLAVERY; THE SLAVE SHIP]

I hope the reader will not think I have trespassed on his patience in introducing myself to him with some account of the manners and customs of my country. They had been implanted in me with great care, and made an impression on my mind, which time could not erase, and which all the adversity and variety of fortune I have since experienced, served only to rivet and record: for, whether the love of one's country be real or imaginary, or a lesson of reason, or an instinct of nature, I still look back with pleasure on the first scenes of my life, though that pleasure has been for the most part mingled with sorrow.

I have already acquainted the reader with the time and place of my birth. My father, besides many slaves, had a numerous family, of which seven lived to grow up, including myself and sister, who was the only daughter. As I was the youngest of the sons, I became, of course, the greatest favorite with my mother, and was always with her; and she used to take particular pains to form my mind.[24] I was trained up from my earliest years in the art of war: my daily exercise was shooting and throwing javelins, and my mother adorned me with emblems, after the manner of our greatest warriors. In this way I grew up till I had turned the age of eleven, when an end was put to my happiness in the following manner: Generally, when the grown people in the neighborhood were gone far in the fields to labor, the children assembled together in some of the neighboring premises to play; and commonly some of us used to get up a tree to look out for any assailant, or kidnapper, that might come upon us—for they sometimes took those opportunities of our parents' absence, to attack and carry off as many as they could seize. One day as I was watching at the top of a tree in our yard, I saw one of those people come into the yard of our next neighbor but one, to kidnap, there being many stout young people in it. Immediately on this I gave the alarm of the rogue, and he was surrounded by the stoutest of them, who entangled him with cords, so that he could not escape, till some of the grown people came and secured him. But, alas! ere long it was my fate to be thus attacked, and to be carried off, when none of the grown people were nigh.

One day, when all our people were gone out to their works as usual, and only I and my dear sister were left to mind the house, two men and a woman got over our walls, and in a moment seized us both, and, without giving us time to cry out, or make resistance, they stopped our mouths, and ran off with us into the nearest wood. Here they tied our hands, and continued to carry us as far as they could, till

---

[23] **who hath . . . earth:** Acts 17:26. [Equiano's note.]

[24] **My father . . . form my mind:** Acholonu identifies Equiano's father as Ichie Ekwealuo, born about 1700, and his mother as Nwansoro, from the village of Uli. (Acholonu, *Igbo Roots*, 42–43)

night came on, when we reached a small house, where the robbers halted for refreshment, and spent the night. We were then unbound, but were unable to take any food; and, being quite overpowered by fatigue and grief, our only relief was some sleep, which allayed our misfortune for a short time. The next morning we left the house, and continued travelling all the day. For a long time we had kept the woods, but at last we came into a road which I believed I knew. I had now some hopes of being delivered; for we had advanced but a little way before I discovered some people at a distance, on which I began to cry out for their assistance; but my cries had no other effect than to make them tie me faster and stop my mouth, and then they put me into a large sack. They also stopped my sister's mouth, and tied her hands; and in this manner we proceeded till we were out of sight of these people. When we went to rest the following night, they offered us some victuals, but we refused it; and the only comfort we had was in being in one another's arms all that night, and bathing each other with our tears. But alas! we were soon deprived of even the small comfort of weeping together.

The next day proved a day of greater sorrow than I had yet experienced; for my sister and I were then separated, while we lay clasped in each other's arms. It was in vain that we besought them not to part us; she was torn from me, and immediately carried away, while I was left in a state of distraction not to be described. I cried and grieved continually; and for several days did not eat anything but what they forced into my mouth. At length, after many days' travelling, during which I had often changed masters, I got into the hands of a chieftain, in a very pleasant country. This man had two wives and some children, and they all used me extremely well, and did all they could do to comfort me; particularly the first wife, who was something like my mother. Although I was a great many days' journey from my father's house, yet these people spoke exactly the same language with us. This first master of mine, as I may call him, was a smith, and my principal employment was working his bellows, which were the same kind as I had seen in my vicinity. They were in some respects not unlike the stoves here in gentlemen's kitchens, and were covered over with leather; and in the middle of that leather a stick was fixed, and a person stood up, and worked it in the same manner as is done to pump water out of a cask with a hand pump. I believe it was gold he worked, for it was of a lovely bright yellow color, and was worn by the women on their wrists and ankles.

I was there I suppose about a month, and they at last used to trust me some little distance from the house. This liberty I used in embracing every opportunity to inquire the way to my own home; and I also sometimes, for the same purpose, went with the maidens, in the cool of the evenings, to bring pitchers of water from the springs for the use of the house. I had also remarked where the sun rose in the morning, and set in the evening, as I had travelled along; and I had observed that my father's house was towards the rising of the sun. I therefore determined to seize the first opportunity of making my escape, and to shape my course for that quarter; for I was quite oppressed and weighed down by grief after my mother and friends; and my love of liberty, ever great, was strengthened by the mortifying circumstance of not daring to eat with the free-born children, although I was mostly their companion.

While I was projecting my escape, one day an unlucky event happened, which quite disconcerted my plan, and put an end to my hopes. I used to be sometimes employed in assisting an elderly slave to cook and take care of the poultry; and one morning, while I was feeding some chickens, I happened to toss a small pebble at one of them, which hit it on the middle, and directly killed it. The old slave, having soon after missed the chicken, inquired after it; and on my relating the accident (for I told her the truth, for my mother would never suffer me to tell a lie), she flew into a violent passion, and threatened that I should suffer for it; and, my master being out, she immediately went and told her mistress what I had done. This alarmed me very much, and I expected an instant flogging, which to me was uncommonly dreadful, for I had seldom been beaten at home. I therefore resolved to fly; and accordingly I ran into a thicket that was hard by, and hid myself in the bushes. Soon afterwards my mistress and the slave returned, and, not seeing me, they searched all the house, but not finding me, and I not making answer when they called to me, they thought I had run away, and the whole neighborhood was raised in the pursuit of me.

In that part of the country, as in ours, the houses and villages were skirted with woods, or shrubberies, and the bushes were so thick that a man could readily conceal himself in them, so as to elude the strictest search. The neighbors continued the whole day looking for me, and several times many of them came within a few yards of the place where I lay hid. I expected every moment, when I heard a rustling among the trees, to be found out, and punished by my master; but they never discovered me, though they were often so near that I even heard their conjectures as they were looking about for me; and I now learned from them that any attempts to return home would be hopeless. Most of them supposed I had fled towards home; but the distance was so great, and the way so intricate, that they thought I could never reach it, and that I should be lost in the woods. When I heard this I was seized with a violent panic, and abandoned myself to despair. Night, too, began to approach, and aggravated all my fears. I had before entertained hopes of getting home, and had determined when it should be dark to make the attempt; but I was now convinced it was fruitless, and began to consider that, if possibly I could escape all other animals, I could not those of the human kind; and that, not knowing the way, I must perish in the woods. Thus was I like the hunted deer—

———Every leaf and every whisp'ring breath,
Convey'd a foe, and every foe a death.

I heard frequent rustlings among the leaves, and being pretty sure they were snakes, I expected every instant to be stung by them. This increased my anguish, and the horror of my situation became now quite insupportable. I at length quitted the thicket, very faint and hungry, for I had not eaten or drank anything all the day, and crept to my master's kitchen, from whence I set out at first, which was an open shed, and laid myself down in the ashes with an anxious wish for death, to relieve me from all my pains. I was scarcely awake in the morning, when the old woman slave, who was the first up, came to light the fire, and saw me in the fireplace. She was very much surprised to see me, and could scarcely believe her own eyes. She now promised to intercede for me, and went for her master, who soon after came, and, having slightly reprimanded me, ordered me to be taken care of, and not ill treated.

Soon after this, my master's only daughter, and child by his first wife, sickened and died, which affected him so much that for sometime he was almost frantic, and really would have killed himself, had he not been watched and prevented. However, in a short time afterwards he recovered, and I was again sold. I was now carried to the left of the sun's rising, through many dreary wastes and dismal woods, amidst the hideous roarings of wild beasts. The people I was sold to used to carry me very often, when I was tired, either on their shoulders or on their backs. I saw many convenient well-built sheds along the road, at proper distances, to accommodate the merchants and travellers, who lay in those buildings along with their wives, who often accompany them; and they always go well armed.

From the time I left my own nation, I always found somebody that understood me till I came to the sea coast. The languages of different nations did not totally differ, nor were they so copious as those of the Europeans, particularly the English. They were therefore easily learned; and, while I was journeying thus through Africa, I acquired two or three different tongues. In this manner I had been travelling for a considerable time, when, one evening, to my great surprise, whom should I see brought to the house where I was but my dear sister! As soon as she saw me, she gave a loud shriek, and ran into my arms—I was quite overpowered; neither of us could speak, but, for a considerable time, clung to each other in mutual embraces, unable to do anything but weep. Our meeting affected all who saw us; and, indeed, I must acknowledge, in honor of those sable destroyers of human rights, that I never met with any ill treatment, or saw any offered to their slaves, except tying them, when necessary, to keep them from running away.

When these people knew we were brother and sister, they indulged us to be together; and the man, to whom I supposed we belonged, lay with us, he in the middle, while she and I held one another by the hands across his breast all night; and thus for a while we forgot our misfortunes, in the joy of being together; but even this small comfort was soon to have an end; for scarcely had the fatal morning appeared when she was again torn from me forever! I was now more miserable, if possible, than before. The small relief which her presence gave me from pain, was gone, and the wretchedness of my situation was redoubled by my anxiety after her fate, and my apprehensions lest her sufferings should be greater than mine, when I could not be with her to alleviate them. Yes, thou dear partner of all my childish sports! thou sharer of my joys and sorrows! happy should I have ever esteemed myself to encounter every misery for you and to procure your freedom by the sacrifice of my own. Though you were early forced from my arms, your image has been always riveted in my heart, from which neither time nor fortune have been able to remove it; so that, while the thoughts of your sufferings have damped my prosperity, they have mingled with adversity and increased its bitterness. To that Heaven which protects the weak from the strong, I commit the care of your innocence and virtues, if they have not already received their full reward, and if your youth and delicacy have not long since fallen victims to the violence of the African trader, the pestilential stench of a Guinea ship, the seasoning in the European colonies, or the lash and lust of a brutal and unrelenting overseer.

I did not long remain after my sister. I was again sold, and carried through a number of places, till after travelling a considerable time, I came to a town called

Tinmah, in the most beautiful country I had yet seen in Africa.[25] It was extremely rich, and there were many rivulets which flowed through it, and supplied a large pond in the centre of the town, where the people washed. Here I saw for the first time cocoanuts, which I thought superior to any nuts I had ever tasted before; and the trees, which were loaded, were also interspersed among the houses, which had commodious shades adjoining, and were in the same manner as ours, the insides being neatly plastered and whitewashed. Here I also saw and tasted for the first time, sugar-cane. Their money consisted of little white shells, the size of the finger nail. I was sold here for one hundred and seventy-two of them, by a merchant who lived and brought me there.

I had been about two or three days at his house, when a wealthy widow, a neighbor of his, came there one evening, and brought with her an only son, a young gentleman about my own age and size. Here they saw me; and, having taken a fancy to me, I was bought of the merchant, and went home with them. Her house and premises were situated close to one of those rivulets I have mentioned, and were the finest I ever saw in Africa: they were very extensive, and she had a number of slaves to attend her. The next day I was washed and perfumed, and when meal time came, I was led into the presence of my mistress, and ate and drank before her with her son. This filled me with astonishment; and I could scarce help expressing my surprise that the young gentleman should suffer me, who was bound, to eat with him who was free; and not only so, but that he would not at any time either eat or drink till I had taken first, because I was the eldest, which was agreeable to our custom. Indeed, every thing here, and all their treatment of me, made me forget that I was a slave. The language of these people resembled ours so nearly, that we understood each other perfectly. They had also the very same customs as we. There were likewise slaves daily to attend us, while my young master and I, with other boys, sported with our darts and bows and arrows, as I had been used to do at home. In this resemblance to my former happy state, I passed about two months; and I now began to think I was to be adopted into the family, and was beginning to be reconciled to my situation, and to forget by degrees my misfortunes, when all at once the delusion vanished; for, without the least previous knowledge, one morning early, while my dear master and companion was still asleep, I was awakened out of my reverie to fresh sorrow, and hurried away even amongst the uncircumcised.

Thus, at the very moment I dreamed of the greatest happiness, I found myself most miserable; and it seemed as if fortune wished to give me this taste of joy only to render the reverse more poignant. The change I now experienced was as painful as it was sudden and unexpected. It was a change indeed, from a state of bliss to a scene which is inexpressible by me, as it discovered to me an element I had never before beheld, and till then had no idea of, and wherein such instances of hardship and cruelty continually occurred, as I can never reflect on but with horror.

All the nations and people I had hitherto passed through, resembled our own in their manners, customs, and language; but I came at length to a country, the inhabi-

---

[25] **Tinmah . . . Africa:** Possibly Utuma, Utu Etim, or Tinan, villages on the border between Ibo and Ibibio. (Acholonu, *Igbo Roots*, 7–9)

tants of which differed from us in all those particulars. I was very much struck with this difference, especially when I came among a people who did not circumcise, and ate without washing their hands. They cooked also in iron pots, and had European cutlasses and cross bows, which were unknown to us, and fought with their fists among themselves. Their women were not so modest as ours, for they ate, and drank, and slept with their men. But above all, I was amazed to see no sacrifices or offerings among them. In some of those places the people ornamented themselves with scars, and likewise filed their teeth very sharp. They wanted sometimes to ornament me in the same manner, but I would not suffer them; hoping that I might some time be among a people who did not thus disfigure themselves, as I thought they did. At last I came to the banks of a large river which was covered with canoes, in which the people appeared to live with their household utensils, and provisions of all kinds. I was beyond measure astonished at this, as I had never before seen any water larger than a pond or a rivulet; and my surprise was mingled with no small fear when I was put into one of these canoes, and we began to paddle and move along the river. We continued going on thus till night, and when we came to land, and made fires on the banks, each family by themselves; some dragged their canoes on shore, others stayed and cooked in theirs, and laid in them all night. Those on the land had mats, of which they made tents, some in the shape of little houses; in these we slept; and after the morning meal, we embarked again and proceeded as before. I was often very much astonished to see some of the women, as well as the men, jump into the water, dive to the bottom, come up again, and swim about.

Thus I continued to travel, sometimes by land, sometimes by water, through different countries and various nations, till, at the end of six or seven months after I had been kidnapped, I arrived at the sea coast. It would be tedious and uninteresting to relate all the incidents which befell me during this journey, and which I have not yet forgotten; of the various hands I passed through, and the manners and customs of all the different people among whom I lived—I shall therefore only observe, that in all the places where I was, the soil was exceedingly rich; the pumpkins, eadas, plantains, yams, &c. &c., were in great abundance, and of incredible size. There were also vast quantities of different gums, though not used for any purpose, and everywhere a great deal of tobacco. The cotton even grew quite wild, and there was plenty of red-wood. I saw no mechanics whatever in all the way, except such as I have mentioned. The chief employment in all these countries was agriculture, and both the males and females, as with us, were brought up to it, and trained in the arts of war.

The first object which saluted my eyes when I arrived on the coast, was the sea, and a slave ship, which was then riding at anchor, and waiting for its cargo. These filled me with astonishment, which was soon converted into terror, when I was carried on board. I was immediately handled, and tossed up to see if I were sound, by some of the crew; and I was now persuaded that I had gotten into a world of bad spirits, and that they were going to kill me. Their complexions, too, differing so much from ours, their long hair, and the language they spoke (which was very different from any I had ever heard), united to confirm me in this belief. Indeed, such were the horrors of my views and fears at the moment, that, if ten thousand worlds had been my own, I would have freely parted with them all to have exchanged my condition with that of the meanest slave in my own country. When I looked round the ship too, and saw a large furnance of copper boiling, and a multitude of black people of every description chained together, every one of their countenances expressing dejection and sorrow, I no longer doubted of my fate; and, quite overpowered with horror and anguish, I fell motionless on the deck and fainted. When I recovered a little, I found some black people about me, who I believed were some of those who had brought me on board, and had been receiving their pay; they talked to me in order to cheer me, but all in vain. I asked them if we were not to be eaten by those white men with horrible looks, red faces, and long hair. They told me I was not, and one of the crew brought me a small portion of spirituous liquor in a wine glass; but being afraid of him, I would not take it out of his hand. One of the blacks therefore took it from him and gave it to me, and I took a little down my palate, which, instead of reviving me, as they thought it would, threw me into the greatest consternation at the strange feeling it produced, having never tasted any such liquor before. Soon after this, the blacks who brought me on board went off, and left me abandoned to despair.

I now saw myself deprived of all chance of returning to my native country, or even the least glimpse of hope of gaining the shore, which I now considered as friendly; and I even wished for my former slavery in preference to my present situation, which was filled with horrors of every kind, still heightened by my ignorance of what I was to undergo. I was not long suffered to indulge my grief; I was soon put down under the decks, and there I received such a salutation in my nostrils as I had never experienced in my life: so that, with the loathsomeness of the stench, and crying together, I became so sick and low that I was not able to eat, nor had I the least desire to taste anything. I now wished for the last friend, death, to relieve me; but soon, to my grief, two of the white men offered me eatables; and, on my refusing to eat, one of them held me fast by the hands, and laid me across, I think, the windlass, and tied my feet, while the other flogged me severely. I had never experienced anything of this kind before, and, although not being used to the water, I naturally feared that element the first time I saw it, yet, nevertheless, could I have got over the nettings, I would have jumped over the side, but I could not; and besides, the crew used to watch us very closely who were not chained down to the decks, lest we should leap into the water; and I have seen some of these poor African prisoners most severely cut, for attempting to do so, and hourly whipped for not eating. This indeed was often the case with myself.

In a little time after, amongst the poor chained men, I found some of my own nation, which in a small degree gave ease to my mind. I inquired of these what was to be done with us? They gave me to understand, we were to be carried to these white people's country to work for them. I then was a little revived, and thought, if it were no worse than working, my situation was not so desperate; but still I feared I should be put to death, the white people looked and acted, as I thought, in so savage a manner; for I had never seen among any people such instances of brutal cruelty; and this not only shown towards us blacks, but also to some of the whites themselves. One white man in particular I saw, when we were permitted to be on deck, flogged so unmercifully with a large rope near the foremast, that he died in consequence of it; and they tossed him over the side as they would have done a brute. This made me fear these people the more; and I expected nothing less than to be treated in the same manner. I could not help expressing my fears and apprehensions to some of my countrymen; I asked them if these people had no country, but lived in this hollow place (the ship)? They told me they did not, but came from a distant one. "Then," said I, "how comes it in all our country we never heard of them?" They told me because they lived so very far off. I then asked where were their women? had they any like themselves? I was told they had. "And why," said I, "do we not see them?" They answered, because they were left behind. I asked how the vessel could go? They told me they could not tell; but that there was cloth put upon the masts by the help of the ropes I saw, and then the vessel went on; and the white men had some spell or magic they put in the water when they liked, in order to stop the vessel. I was exceedingly amazed at this account, and really thought they were spirits. I therefore wished much to be from amongst them, for I expected they would sacrifice me; but my wishes were vain—for we were so quartered that it was impossible for any of us to make our escape.

While we stayed on the coast I was mostly on deck; and one day, to my great astonishment, I saw one of these vessels coming in with the sails up. As soon as the whites saw it, they gave a great shout, at which we were amazed; and the more so, as the vessel appeared larger by approaching nearer. At last, she came to an anchor in my sight, and when the anchor was let go, I and my countrymen who saw it, were lost in astonishment to observe the vessel stop—and were now convinced it was done by magic. Soon after this the other ship got her boats out, and they came on board of us, and the people of both ships seemed very glad to see each other. Several of the strangers also shook hands with us black people, and made motions with their hands, signifying I suppose, we were to go to their country, but we did not understand them.

At last, when the ship we were in, had got in all her cargo, they made ready with many fearful noises, and we were all put under deck, so that we could not see how they managed the vessel. But this disappointment was the least of my sorrow. The stench of the hold while we were on the coast was so intolerably loathsome, that it was dangerous to remain there for any time, and some of us had been permitted to stay on the deck for the fresh air; but now that the whole ship's cargo were confined together, it became absolutely pestilential. The closeness of the place, and the heat of the climate, added to the number in the ship, which was so crowded that each had scarcely room to turn himself, almost suffocated us. This produced copious perspirations, so that the air soon became unfit for respiration, from a variety of loathsome smells, and brought on a sickness among the slaves, of which many died—thus falling victims to the improvident avarice, as I may call it, of their purchasers. This wretched situation was again aggravated by the galling of the chains, now became insupportable, and the filth of the necessary tubs, into which the children often fell, and were almost suffocated. The shrieks of the women, and the groans of the dying, rendered the whole a scene of horror almost inconceivable. Happily perhaps, for myself, I was soon reduced so low here that it was thought necessary to keep me almost always on deck; and from my extreme youth I was not put in fetters. In this situation I expected every hour to share the fate of my companions, some of whom were almost daily brought upon deck at the point of death, which I began to hope would soon put an end to my miseries. Often did I think many of the inhabitants of the deep much more happy than myself. I envied them the freedom they enjoyed, and as often wished I could change my condition for theirs. Every circumstance I met with, served only to render my state more painful, and heightened my apprehensions, and my opinion of the cruelty of the whites.

One day they had taken a number of fishes; and when they had killed and satisfied themselves with as many as they thought fit, to our astonishment who were on deck, rather than give any of them to us to eat, as we expected, they tossed the remaining fish into the sea again, although we begged and prayed for some as well as we could, but in vain; and some of my countrymen, being pressed by hunger, took an opportunity, when they thought no one saw them, of trying to get a little privately; but they were discovered, and the attempt procured them some very severe floggings.

One day, when we had a smooth sea and moderate wind, two of my wearied countrymen who were chained together (I was near them at the time), preferring death to such a life of misery, somehow made through the nettings and jumped into the sea; immediately, another quite dejected fellow, who, on account of his illness, was suffered to be out of irons, also followed their example; and I believe many more would very soon have done the same, if they had not been prevented by the ship's crew, who were instantly alarmed. Those of us that were the most active, were in a moment put down under the deck; and there was such a noise and confusion amongst the people of the ship as I never heard before, to stop her, and get the boat out to go after the slaves. However, two of the wretches were drowned, but they got the other, and afterwards flogged him unmercifully, for thus attempting to prefer death to slavery. In this manner we continued to undergo more hardships than I can now relate, hardships which are inseparable from this accursed trade. Many a time we were near suffocation from the want of fresh air, which we were often without for whole days together. This, and the stench of the necessary tubs, carried off many.

During our passage, I first saw flying fishes, which surprised me very much; they used frequently to fly across the ship, and many of them fell on the deck. I also now first saw the use of the quadrant; I had often with astonishment seen the mariners make observations with it, and I could not think what it meant. They at last took notice of my surprise; and one of them, willing to increase it, as well as to gratify my curiosity, made me one day look through it. The clouds appeared to me to be land, which disappeared as they passed along. This heightened my wonder; and I was now more persuaded than ever, that I was in another world, and that every thing about me was magic.

At last we came in sight of the island of Barbadoes, at which the whites on board gave a great shout, and made many signs of joy to us. We did not know what to think of this; but as the vessel drew nearer, we plainly saw the harbor, and other ships of different kinds and sizes, and we soon anchored amongst them, off Bridgetown. Many merchants and planters now came on board, though it was in the evening.

They put us in separate parcels, and examined us attentively. They also made us jump, and pointed to the land, signifying we were to go there. We thought by this, we should be eaten by these ugly men, as they appeared to us; and, when soon after we were all put down under the deck again, there was much dread and trembling among us, and nothing but bitter cries to be heard all the night from these apprehensions, insomuch, that at last the white people got some old slaves from the land to pacify us. They told us we were not to be eaten, but to work, and were soon to go on land, where we should see many of our country people. This report eased us much. And sure enough, soon after we were landed, there came to us Africans of all languages.

We were conducted immediately to the merchant's yard, where we were all pent up together, like so many sheep in a fold, without regard to sex or age. As every object was new to me, everything I saw filled me with surprise. What struck me first, was, that the houses were built with bricks and stories, and in every other respect different from those I had seen in Africa; but I was still more astonished on seeing people on horseback. I did not know what this could mean; and, indeed, I thought these people were full of nothing but magical arts. While I was in this astonishment, one of my fellow prisoners spoke to a countryman of his, about the horses, who said they were the same kind they had in their country. I understood them, though they were from a distant part of Africa; and I thought it odd I had not seen any horses there; but afterwards, when I came to converse with different Africans, I found they had many horses amongst them, and much larger than those I then saw.

We were not many days in the merchant's custody, before we were sold after their usual manner, which is this: On a signal given (as the beat of a drum), the buyers rush at once into the yard where the slaves are confined, and make choice of that parcel they like best. The noise and clamor with which this is attended, and the eagerness visible in the countenances of the buyers, serve not a little to increase the apprehension of terrified Africans, who may well be supposed to consider them as the ministers of that destruction to which they think themselves devoted. In this manner, without scruple, are relations and friends separated, most of them never to see each other again.

I remember, in the vessel in which I was brought over, in the men's apartment, there were several brothers, who, in the sale, were sold in different lots; and it was very moving on this occasion, to see and hear their cries at parting. O, ye nominal Christians! might not an African ask you—Learned you this from your God, who says unto you, Do unto all men as you would men should do unto you? Is it not enough that we are torn from our country and friends, to toil for your luxury and lust of gain? Must every tender feeling be likewise sacrificed to your avarice? Are the dearest friends and relations, now rendered more dear by their separation from their kindred, still to be parted from each other, and thus prevented from cheering the gloom of slavery, with the small comfort of being together, and mingling their sufferings and sorrows? Why are parents to lose their children, brothers their sisters, or husbands their wives? Surely, this is a new refinement in cruelty, which, while it has no advantage to atone for it, thus aggravates distress, and adds fresh horrors even to the wretchedness of slavery.

FROM CHAPTER 3

[Sold to Captain Pascal; a New Name]

I now totally lost the small remains of comfort I had enjoyed in conversing with my countrymen; the women too, who used to wash and take care of me were all gone different ways, and I never saw one of them afterwards.

I stayed in this island for a few days, I believe it could not be above a fortnight, when I, and some few more slaves that were not saleable amongst the rest, from very much fretting, were shipped off in a sloop for North America. On the passage we were better treated than when we were coming from Africa, and we had plenty of rice and fat pork. We were landed up a river a good way from the sea, about Virginia county, where we saw few or none of our native Africans, and not one soul who could talk to me. I was a few weeks weeding grass and gathering stones in a plantation; and at last all my companions were distributed different ways, and only myself was left. I was now exceedingly miserable, and thought myself worse off than any of the rest of my companions, for they could talk to each other, but I had no person to speak to that I could understand. In this state, I was constantly grieving and pining, and wishing for death rather than anything else.

While I was in this plantation, the gentleman, to whom I suppose the estate belonged, being unwell, I was one day sent for to his dwelling-house to fan him; when I came into the room where he was I was very much affrighted at some things I saw, and the more so as I had seen a black woman slave as I came through the house, who was cooking the dinner, and the poor creature was cruelly loaded with various kinds of iron machines; she had one particularly on her head, which locked her mouth so fast that she could scarcely speak; and could not eat nor drink. I was much astonished and shocked at this contrivance, which I afterwards learned was called the iron muzzle. Soon after I had a fan put in my hand, to fan the gentleman while he slept; and so I did indeed with great fear. While he was fast asleep I indulged myself a great deal in looking about the room, which to me appeared very fine and curious.

The first object that engaged my attention was a watch which hung on the chimney, and was going. I was quite surprised at the noise it made, and was afraid it would tell the gentleman anything I might do amiss; and when I immediately after observed a picture hanging in the room, which appeared constantly to look at me, I was still more affrighted, having never seen such things as these before. At one time I thought it was something relative to magic; and not seeing it move I thought it might be some way the whites had to keep their great men when they died, and offer them libations as we used to do our friendly spirits. In this state of anxiety I remained till my master awoke, when I was dismissed out of the room, to my no small satisfaction and relief; for I thought that these people were all made up of wonders.

In this place I was called Jacob; but on board the *African Snow,* I was called Michael. I had been some time in this miserable, forlorn, and much dejected state, without having anyone to talk to, which made my life a burden, when the kind and unknown hand of the Creator (who in every deed leads the blind in a way they know not) now began to appear, to my comfort; for one day the captain of a merchant ship, called the *Industrious Bee,* came on some business to my master's house. This gentleman, whose name was Michael Henry Pascal, was a lieutenant in the Royal Navy, but now commanded this trading ship, which was somewhere in the confines of the county many miles off. While he was at my master's house, it happened that he saw me, and liked me so well that he made a purchase of me. I think I have often heard him say he gave thirty or forty pounds sterling for me; but I do not remember which. However, he meant me for a present to some of his friends in England: and as I was sent accordingly from the house of my then master (one Mr. Campbell) to the place where the ship lay; I was conducted on horseback by an elderly black man (a mode of travelling which appeared very odd to me). When I arrived I was carried on board a fine large ship, loaded with tobacco, &c., and just ready to sail for England.

I now thought my condition much mended; I had sails to lie on, and plenty of good victuals to eat; and everybody on board used me very kindly, quite contrary to what I had seen of any white people before; I therefore began to think that they were not all of the same disposition. A few days after I was on board we sailed for England. I was still at a loss to conjecture my destiny. By this time, however, I could smatter a little imperfect English; and I wanted to know as well as I could where we were going. Some of the people of the ship used to tell me they were going to carry me back to my own country, and this made me very happy. I was quite rejoiced at the idea of going back, and thought if I could get home what wonders I should have to tell. But I was reserved for another fate, and was soon undeceived when we came within sight of the English coast.

While I was on board this ship, my captain and master named me *Gustavus Vassa.*[26] I at that time began to understand him a little, and refused to be called so, and told him as well as I could that I would be called Jacob; but he said I should not, and still called me Gustavus: and when I refused to answer to my new name, which I at first did, it gained me many a cuff; so at length I submitted, and by which I have been known ever since.

The ship had a very long passage; and on that account we had very short allowance of provisions. Towards the last, we had only one pound and a half of bread per week, and about the same quantity of meat, and one quart of water a day. We spoke with only one vessel the whole time we were at sea, and but once we caught a few fishes. In our extremities the captain and people told me in jest they would kill and eat me; but I thought them in earnest, and was depressed beyond measure, expecting every moment to be my last. While I was in this situation, one evening they caught, with a good deal of trouble, a large shark, and got it on board. This gladdened my poor heart exceedingly, as I thought it would serve the people to eat instead of their eating me; but very soon, to my astonishment, they cut off a small part of the tail, and tossed the rest over the side. This renewed my consternation; and I did not know what to think of these white people, though I very much feared they would kill and eat me.

---

[26] **Gustavus Vassa:** Gustavus Ericksson Vasa, a Swedish nobleman, led a successful revolt against Danish rule in the 1520s; as Gustavus I, he ruled Sweden from 1523 to 1560. At the time of Equiano's capture, Henry Brooke's *Gustavus Vasa, the Deliverer of His Country* was a popular English play.

There was on board the ship a young lad who had never been at sea before, about four or five years older than myself: his name was Richard Baker. He was a native of America, had received an excellent education, and was of a most amiable temper. Soon after I went on board, he showed me a great deal of partiality and attention, and in return I grew extremely fond of him. We at length became inseparable; and, for the space of two years, he was of very great use to me, and was my constant companion and instructor. Although this dear youth had many slaves of his own, yet he and I have gone through many sufferings together on shipboard; and we have many nights lain in each other's bosoms when we were in great distress. Thus such a friendship was cemented between us as we cherished till his death, which, to my very great sorrow, happened in the year 1759, when he was up the Archipelago, on board his Majesty's ship the *Preston*: an event which I have never ceased to regret, as I lost at once a kind interpreter, an agreeable companion, and a faithful friend; who, at the age of fifteen, discovered a mind superior to prejudice; and who was not ashamed to notice, to associate with, and to be the friend and instructor of one who was ignorant, a stranger, of a different complexion, and a slave! . . .

One morning, when I got upon deck, I saw it covered all over with the snow that fell over night. As I had never seen anything of the kind before, I thought it was salt: so I immediately ran down to the mate, and desired him, as well as I could, to come and see how somebody in the night had thrown salt all over the deck. He, knowing what it was, desired me to bring some of it down to him. Accordingly I took up a handful of it, which I found very cold indeed; and when I brought it to him he desired me to taste it. I did so, and I was surprised beyond measure. I then asked him what it was; he told me it was snow, but I could not in anywise understand him. He asked me, if we had no such thing in my country; I told him, No. I then asked him the use of it, and who made it; he told me a great man in the heavens, called God. But here again I was to all intents and purposes at a loss to understand him; and the more so, when a little after I saw the air filled with it, in a heavy shower, which fell down on the same day.

After this I went to church; and having never been at such a place before, I was again amazed at seeing and hearing the service. I asked all I could about it, and they gave me to understand it was worshipping God, who made us and all things. I was still at a great loss, and soon got into an endless field of inquiries, as well as I was able to speak and ask about things. However, my little friend Dick used to be my best interpreter; for I could make free with him, and he always instructed me with pleasure. And from what I could understand by him of this God, and in seeing these white people did not sell one another as we did, I was much pleased; and in this I thought they were much happier than we Africans. I was astonished at the wisdom of the white people in all things I saw; but was amazed at their not sacrificing, or making any offerings, and eating with unwashed hands, and touching the dead. I likewise could not help remarking the particular slenderness of their women, which I did not at first like; and I thought they were not so modest and shame-faced as the African women.

I had often seen my master and Dick employed in reading; and I had a great curiosity to talk to the books as I thought they did, and so to learn how all things had a beginning. For that purpose I have often taken up a book, and have talked to it, and then put my ears to it, when alone, in hopes it would answer me; and I have been very much concerned when I found it remained silent.

My master lodged at the house of a gentleman in Falmouth, who had a fine little daughter about six or seven years of age, and she grew prodigiously fond of me, insomuch that we used to eat together, and had servants to wait on us. I was so much caressed by this family that it often reminded me of the treatment I had received from my little noble African master. After I had been here a few days, I was sent on board of the ship; but the child cried so much after me that nothing could pacify her till I was sent for again. It is ludicrous enough, that I began to fear I should be betrothed to this young lady; and when my master asked me if I would stay there with her behind him, as he was going away with the ship, which had taken in the tobacco again, I cried immediately, and said I would not leave him. At last, by stealth, one night I was sent on board the ship again; and in a little time we sailed for Guernsey, where she was in part owned by a merchant, one Nicholas Doberry.

As I was now amongst a people who had not their faces scarred, like some of the African nation where I had been, I was very glad I did not let them ornament me in that manner when I was with them. When we arrived at Guernsey, my master placed me to board and lodge with one of his mates, who had a wife and family there; and some months afterwards he went to England, and left me in care of this mate, together with my friend Dick. This mate had a little daughter, aged about five or six years, with whom I used to be much delighted. I had often observed that when her mother washed her face it looked very rosy, but when she washed mine it did not look so. I therefore tried oftentimes myself if I could not by washing make my face of the same color as my little play-mate, Mary, but it was all in vain; and I now began to be mortified at the difference in our complexions. This woman behaved to me with great kindness and attention, and taught me everything in the same manner as she did her own child, and, indeed, in every respect, treated me as such. I remained here till the summer of the year 1757, when my master, being appointed first lieutenant of his Majesty's ship the *Roebuck*, sent for Dick and me, and his old mate. On this we all left Guernsey, and set out for England in a sloop, bound for London. [. . .]

FROM CHAPTER 4
[Baptism and the Desire for Freedom]

It was now between two and three years since I first came to England, a great part of which I had spent at sea; so that I became inured to that service, and began to consider myself as happily situated, for my master treated me always extremely well; and my attachment and gratitude to him were very great. From the various scenes I had beheld on shipboard, I soon grew a stranger to terror of every kind, and was, in that respect at least, almost an Englishman. I have often reflected with surprise that I never felt half the alarm at any of the numerous dangers I have been in, that I was filled with at the first sight of the Europeans, and at every act of theirs, even the most trifling, when I first came among them, and for some time afterwards. That fear, however, which was the effect of my ignorance, wore away as I began to know them. I could now speak English tolerably well, and I perfectly understood everything that was said. I not only felt myself quite easy with these new countrymen, but relished their society and manners. I no longer looked upon them as spirits, but as men superior to us; and therefore I had the stronger desire to resemble them, to imbibe their spirit, and imitate their manners. I therefore embraced every occasion of improvement, and every new thing that I observed I treasured up in my memory. I had long wished to be able to read and write; and for this purpose I took every opportunity to gain instruction, but had made as yet very little progress. However, when I went to London with my master, I had soon an opportunity of improving myself, which I gladly embraced. Shortly after my arrival, he sent me to wait upon the Miss Guerins, who had treated me with much kindness when I was there before; and they sent me to school.

While I was attending these ladies, their servants told me I could not go to Heaven unless I was baptized. This made me very uneasy, for I had now some faint idea of a future state: accordingly I communicated my anxiety to the eldest Miss Guerin, with whom I was become a favorite, and pressed her to have me baptized; when to my great joy, she told me I should. She had formerly asked my master to let me be baptized, but he had refused. However she now insisted on it; and he being under some obligation to her brother, complied with her request. So I was baptized in St. Margaret's church, Westminster, in February 1759, by my present name. The clergyman at the same time, gave me a book, called *A Guide to the Indians,* written by the Bishop of Sodor and Man.[27] On this occasion, Miss Guerin did me the honor to stand as god-mother, and afterwards gave me a treat.

I used to attend these ladies about the town, in which service I was extremely happy; as I had thus many opportunities of seeing London, which I desired of all things. I was sometimes, however, with my master at his rendezvous house, which was at the foot of Westminster bridge. Here I used to enjoy myself in playing about the bridge stairs, and often in the waterman's wherries,[28] with other boys. On one of these occasions there was another boy with me in a wherry, and we went out into the current of the river; while we were there, two more stout boys came to us in another wherry, and abusing us for taking the boat, desired me to get into the other wherry-boat. Accordingly, I went to get out of the wherry I was in, but just as I had got one of my feet into the other boat, the boys shoved it off, so that I fell into the Thames; and, not being able to swim, I should unavoidably have been drowned, but for the assistance of some watermen who providentially came to my relief. [. . .]

After our ship was fitted out again for service, in September she went to Guernsey, where I was very glad to see my old hostess, who was now a widow, and my former little charming companion, her daughter. I spent some time here very happily with them, till October, when we had orders to repair to Portsmouth. We parted from

---

[27] **Bishop of Sodor and Man:** Thomas Wilson (1697–1755); wrote *The Knowledge and Practice of Christianity Made Easy for the Meanest Mental Capacities; or, an Essay towards an Instruction for the Indains* in the form of a dialogue between an Indian and a Christian (London: 1740).

[28] **wherries:** Long, light rowboats.

each other with a great deal of affection; and I promised to return soon, and see them again, not knowing what all powerful fate had determined for me. Our ship having arrived at Portsmouth, we went into the harbor, and remained there till the latter end of November, when we heard great talk about a peace; and, to our very great joy, in the beginning of December we had orders to go up to London with our ship, to be paid off. We received this news with loud huzzas, and every other demonstration of gladness; and nothing but mirth was to be seen throughout every part of the ship. I too was not without my share of the general joy on this occasion.

I thought now of nothing but being freed, and working for myself, and thereby getting money to enable me to get a good education; for I always had a great desire to be able at least to read and write; and while I was on ship-board, I had endeavored to improve myself in both. While I was in the *Etna,* particularly, the captain's clerk taught me to write, and gave me a smattering of arithmetic, as far as the rule of three. There was also one Daniel Queen, about forty years of age, a man very well educated, who messed with me on board this ship, and he likewise dressed and attended the captain. Fortunately this man soon became very much attached to me, and took very great pains to instruct me in many things. He taught me to shave and dress hair a little, and also to read in the Bible, explaining many passages to me, which I did not comprehend. I was wonderfully surprised to see the laws and rules of my own country written almost exactly here; a circumstance which I believe tended to impress our manners and customs more deeply on my memory. I used to tell him of this resemblance, and many a time we have sat up the whole night together at this employment. In short, he was like a father to me, and some even used to call me after his name; they also styled me the black Christian. Indeed, I almost loved him with the affection of a son. Many things I have denied myself that he might have them; and when I used to play at marbles, or any other game, and won a few half-pence, or got any little money, which I sometimes did, for shaving anyone, I used to buy him a little sugar or tobacco, as far as my stock of money would go. He used to say, that he and I never should part; and that when our ship was paid off, as I was as free as himself, or any other man on board, he would instruct me in his business, by which I might gain a good livelihood.

This gave me new life and spirits; and my heart burned within me, while I thought the time long till I obtained my freedom. For though my master had not promised it to me, yet, besides the assurances I had received, that he had no right to detain me, he always treated me with the greatest kindness, and reposed in me an unbounded confidence; he even paid attention to my morals, and would never suffer me to deceive him, or tell lies, of which he used to tell me the consequences; and that if I did so, God would not love me. So that, from all this tenderness, I had never once supposed, in all my dreams of freedom, that he would think of detaining me any longer than I wished.

In pursuance of our orders, we sailed from Portsmouth for the Thames, and arrived at Deptford the 10th of December, where we cast anchor just as it was high water. The ship was up about half an hour, when my master ordered the barge to be manned; and all in an instant, without having before given me the least reason to suspect anything of the matter, he forced me into the barge, saying, I was going to leave him, but he would take care I should not. I was so struck with the unexpectedness of this proceeding, that for some time I did not make a reply, only I made an offer to go for my books and chest of clothes, but he swore I should not move out of his sight, and if I did, he would cut my throat, at the same time taking his hanger. I began, however, to collect myself, and plucking up courage, I told him I was free, and he could not by law serve me so. But this only enraged him the more: and he continued to swear, and said he would soon let me know whether he would or not, and at that instant sprung himself into the barge from the ship, to the astonishment and sorrow of all on board.

The tide, rather unluckily for me, had just turned downward, so that we quickly fell down the river along with it, till we came among some outward-bound West Indiamen; for he was resolved to put me on board the first vessel he could get to receive me. The boat's crew, who pulled against their will, became quite faint, different times, and would have gone ashore, but he would not let them. Some of them strove then to cheer me, and told me he could not sell me, and that they would stand by me, which revived me a little, and I still entertained hopes; for, as they pulled along, he asked some vessels to receive me, but they would not. But, just as we had got a little below Gravesend, we came alongside of a ship which was going away the next tide for the West Indies. Her name was the *Charming Sally,* Captain James Doran, and my master went on board, and agreed with him for me; and in a little time I was sent for into the cabin.

When I came there, Captain Doran asked me if I knew him. I answered that I did not. "Then," said he, "you are now my slave." I told him my master could not sell me to him, nor to anyone else. "Why," said he, "did not your master buy you?" I confessed he did. "But I have served him," said I, "many years, and he has taken all my wages and prize-money, for I had only got one six pence during the war; besides this I have been baptized, and by the laws of the land no man has a right to sell me." And I added that I had heard a lawyer and others at different times tell my master so. They both then said that those people who told me so, were not my friends; but I replied, "It was very extraordinary that other people did not know the law as well as they."

Upon this Captain Doran said I talked too much English; and if I did not behave myself well, and be quiet, he had a method on board to make me. I was too well convinced of his power over me to doubt what he said; and my former sufferings in the slave-ship presenting themselves to my mind, the recollection of them made me shudder. However, before I retired I told them that, as I could not get any right among men here, I hoped I should hereafter in Heaven; and I immediately left the cabin, filled with resentment and sorrow. The only coat I had with me my master took away with him, and said, "If your prize money had been £10,000, I had a right to it all, and would have taken it."

I had about nine guineas, which, during my long sea-faring life, I had scraped together from trifling perquisites and little ventures; and I hid it at that instant, lest my master should take that from me likewise, still hoping that by some means or other I should make my escape to the shore; and indeed some of my old shipmates told me not to despair, for they would get me back again; and that, as soon as they could get their pay, they would immediately come to Portsmouth to me, where the ship was going. But, alas! all my hopes were baffled, and the hour of my deliverance was yet far off. My master, having soon concluded his bargain with the captain, came out of the cabin, and he and his people got into the boat and put off. I followed them with aching eyes as long as I could, and when they were out of sight I threw myself on the deck, with a heart ready to burst with sorrow and anguish.

FROM CHAPTER 5

[SOLD TO ROBERT KING; THE HORRORS OF THE WEST INDIES]

However, the next morning, the 30th of December, the wind being brisk and easterly, the *Eolus* frigate, which was to escort the convoy, made a signal for sailing. All the ships then got up their anchors; and, before any of my friends had an opportunity to come off to my relief, to my inexpressible anguish, our ship had got under way. What tumultuous emotions agitated my soul when the convoy got under sail, and I a prisoner on board, now without hope! I kept my swimming eyes upon the land in a state of unutterable grief; not knowing what to do, and despairing how to help myself. While my mind was in this situation, the fleet sailed on, and in one day's time I lost sight of the wished-for land. In the first expression of my grief I reproached my fate, and wished I had never been born. I was ready to curse the tide that bore us, the gale that wafted my prison, and even the ship that conducted us; and I called on death to relieve me from the horrors I felt and dreaded, that I might be in that place

> Where slaves are free, and men oppress no more.
> Fool that I was, inur'd so long to pain,
> To trust to hope, or dream of joy again.
> . . . .
> Now dragg'd once more beyond the western main,
> To groan beneath some dastard planter's chain;
> Where my poor countrymen in bondage wait
> The long enfranchisement of a ling'ring fate.
> Hard ling'ring fate! while, ere the dawn of day,
> Rous'd by the lash they go their cheerless way;
> And as their souls with shame and anguish burn,
> Salute with groans unwelcome morn's return;
> And, chiding ev'ry hour the slow pac'd sun,
> Pursue their toils till all his race is run.
> No eye to mark their suff'rings with a tear,
> No friend to comfort, and no hope to cheer;
> Then, like the dull unpity'd brutes, repair
> To stalls as wretched, and as coarse a fare;
> Thank heaven one day of misery was o'er,
> Then sink to sleep, and wish to wake no more.[29]

---

[29] "The Dying Negro" [by Thomas Day], a poem originally published in 1773. Perhaps it may not be deemed impertinent here to add, that this elegant and pathetic little poem was occasioned, as appears by the advertisement prefixed to it, by the following incident. "A black, who, a few days before had run away from his master, and got himself christened, with intent to marry a white woman, his fellow-servant, being taken and sent on board a ship in the Thames, took an opportunity of shooting himself through the head." [Equiano's note.]

The turbulence of my emotions, however, naturally gave way to calmer thoughts, and I soon perceived what fate had decreed no mortal on earth could prevent. The convoy sailed on without any accident, with a pleasant gale and smooth sea, for six weeks, till February, when one morning the *Eolus* ran down a brig, one of the convoy, and she instantly went down, and was engulfed in the dark recesses of the ocean. The convoy was immediately thrown into great confusion till it was day-light; and the *Eolus* was illumined with lights, to prevent any further mischief. On the 13th of February, 1763, from the mast-head, we descried our destined island, Montserrat; and soon after I beheld those

> Regions of sorrow, doleful shades, where peace
> And rest can rarely dwell. Hope never comes
> That comes to all, but torture without end
> Still urges.[30]

At the sight of this land of bondage, a fresh horror ran through all my frame, and chilled me to the heart. My former slavery now rose in dreadful review to my mind, and displayed nothing but misery, stripes, and chains; and, in the first paroxysm of my grief, I called upon God's thunder, and his avenging power, to direct the stroke of death to me, rather than permit me to become a slave, and be sold from lord to lord.

In this state of my mind our ship came to anchor, and soon after discharged her cargo. I now knew what it was to work hard; I was made to help unload and load the ship. And, to comfort me in my distress in that time, two of the sailors robbed me of all my money, and ran away from the ship. I had been so long used to a European climate, that at first I felt the scorching West India sun very painful, while the dashing surf would toss the boat and the people in it, frequently above high water mark. Sometimes our limbs were broken with this, or even attended with instant death, and I was day by day mangled and torn.

About the middle of May, when the ship was got ready to sail for England, I all the time believing that fate's blackest clouds were gathering over my head, and expecting their bursting would mix me with the dead, Captain Doran sent for me ashore one morning, and I was told by the messenger that my fate was then determined. With trembling steps and fluttering heart, I came to the captain, and found with him one Mr. Robert King, a Quaker, and the first merchant in the place. The captain then told me my former master had sent me there to be sold; but that he had desired him to get me the best master he could, as he told him I was a very deserving boy, which Captain Doran said he found to be true; and if he were to stay in the West Indies, he would be glad to keep me himself; but he could not venture to take me to London, for he was very sure that when I came there I would leave him. I at that instant burst out a crying, and begged much of him to take me to England with him, but all to no purpose. He told me he had got me the very best master in the whole island, with whom I should be as happy as if I were in England, and for that reason he chose to let him have me, though he could sell me to his own brother-in-law for a great deal more money than what he got from this gentleman. Mr. King, my new master, then made a reply, and said the reason he had bought me was on account of

---

[30] **Regions . . . Still urges:** John Milton, *Paradise Lost*, 1:65–68.

my good character; and as he had not the least doubt of my good behavior, I should be very well off with him. He also told me he did not live in the West Indies, but at Philadelphia, where he was going soon; and, as I understood something of the rules of arithmetic, when we got there he would put me to school, and fit me for a clerk.

This conversation relieved my mind a little, and I left those gentlemen considerably more at ease in myself than when I came to them; and I was very thankful to Captain Doran, and even to my old master, for the character they had given me: a character which I afterwards found of infinite service to me. I went on board again, and took leave of all my ship-mates, and the next day the ship sailed. When she weighed anchor, I went to the waterside and looked at her with a very wishful and aching heart, and followed her with my eyes until she was totally out of sight. I was so bowed down with grief, that I could not hold up my head for many months; and if my new master had not been kind to me, I believe I should have died under it at last. And, indeed, I soon found that he fully deserved the good character which Captain Doran gave me of him, for he possessed a most amiable disposition and temper, and was very charitable and humane. If any of his slaves behaved amiss he did not beat or use them ill, but parted with them. This made them afraid of disobliging him; and as he treated his slaves better than any other man on the island, so he was better and more faithfully served by them in return. By this kind treatment I did at last endeavor to compose myself; and with fortitude, though moneyless, determined to face whatever fate had decreed for me. Mr. King soon asked me what I could do; and at the same time said he did not mean to treat me as a common slave. I told him I knew something of seamanship, and could shave and dress hair pretty well; and I could refine wines, which I had learned on shipboard, where I had often done it; and that I could write, and understood arithmetic tolerably well, as far as the Rule of Three. He then asked me if I knew anything of gauging, and, on my answering that I did not, he said one of his clerks should teach me to gauge.

Mr. King dealt in all manner of merchandise, and kept from one to six clerks. He loaded many vessels in a year; particularly to Philadelphia, where he was born; and was connected with a great mercantile house in that city. He had, besides, many vessels and droggers,[31] of different sizes, which used to go about the island; and others, to collect rum, sugar, and other goods. I understood pulling and managing those boats very well; and this hard work, which was the first that he set me to, in the sugar seasons used to be my constant employment. I have rowed the boat, and slaved at the oars, from one hour to sixteen in the twenty-four, during which I had fifteen pence sterling per day to live on, though sometimes only ten pence.

However, this was considerably more than was allowed to other slaves that used to work often with me, and belonged to other gentlemen on the island. Those poor souls had never more than nine pence per day, and seldom more than six pence, from their masters or owners, though they earned them three or four pistareens.[32] For it is a common practice in the West Indies for men to purchase slaves, though they have not plantations themselves, in order to let them out to planters and merchants at so much a piece by the day, and they give what allowance they choose out

---

[31] **droggers:** Droghers, or slow, clumsy boats.

[32] **pistareens:** These pistareens are of the value of a shilling. [Equiano's note.]

of this product of their daily work to their slaves for subsistence; this allowance is often very scanty. My master often gave the owners of the slaves two and a half of these pieces per day, and found the poor fellows in victuals himself, because he thought their owners did not feed them well enough according to the work they did.

The slaves used to like this very well; and, as they knew my master to be a man of feeling, they were always glad to work for him, in preference to any other gentleman; some of whom, after they had been paid for these poor people's labors, would not give them their allowance out of it. Many times have I even seen these unfortunate wretches beaten for asking for their pay; and often severely flogged by their owners if they did not bring them their daily or weekly money exactly to the time; though the poor creatures were obliged to wait on the gentlemen they had worked for, sometimes more than half the day before they could get their pay; and this generally on Sundays, when they wanted the time for themselves. In particular, I knew a countryman of mine who once did not bring the weekly money directly that it was earned; and, though he brought it the same day to his master, yet he was staked to the ground for his pretended negligence, and was just going to receive a hundred lashes, but for a gentleman who begged him off with fifty.

This poor man was very industrious; and by his frugality, had saved so much money by working on ship-board, that he had got a white man to buy him a boat, unknown to his master. Some time after he had this little estate, the governor wanted a boat to bring his sugar from different parts of the island; and, knowing this to be a Negro man's boat, he seized upon it for himself, and would not pay the owner a farthing. The man, on this, went to his master, and complained to him of this act of the governor; but the only satisfaction he received was to be damned very heartily by his master, who asked him how dared any of his Negroes to have a boat. If the justly merited ruin of the governor's fortune could be any gratification to the poor man he had thus robbed, he was not without consolation. Extortion and rapine are poor providers; and some time after this the governor died in the King's Bench[33] in England, as I was told, in great poverty. The last war favored this poor Negro man, and he found some means to escape from his Christian master. He came to England, where I saw him afterwards several times. Such treatment as this often drives these miserable wretches to despair, and they run away from their masters at the hazard of their lives. Many of them, in this place, unable to get their pay when they have earned it, and fearing to be flogged, as usual, if they return home without it, run away where they can for shelter, and a reward is often offered to bring them in dead or alive. My master used sometimes, in these cases, to agree with their owners, and to settle with them himself; and thereby he saved many of them a flogging.

Once, for a few days, I was let out to fit a vessel, and I had no victuals allowed me by either party; at last I told my master of this treatment, and he took me away from it. In many of the estates, on the different islands where I used to be sent for rum or sugar, they would not deliver it to me, or any other Negro; he was therefore obliged to send a white man along with me to those places; and then he used to pay him from six to ten pistareens a day. From being thus employed, during the time I served

---

[33] **King's Bench:** A London prison.

Mr. King, in going about the different estates on the island, I had all the opportunity I could wish for, to see the dreadful usage of the poor men; usage that reconciled me to my situation, and made me bless God for the hands into which I had fallen.

I had the good fortune to please my master in every department in which he employed me; and there was scarcely any part of his business, or household affairs, in which I was not occasionally engaged. I often supplied the place of a clerk, in receiving and delivering cargoes to the ships, in tending stores, and delivering goods. And besides this, I used to shave and dress my master when convenient, and take care of his horse; and when it was necessary, which was very often, I worked likewise on board of different vessels of his. By these means I became very useful to my master, and saved him, as he used to acknowledge, above a hundred pounds a year. Nor did he scruple to say I was of more advantage to him than any of his clerks; though their usual wages in the West Indies are from sixty to a hundred pounds current a year.

I have sometimes heard it asserted that a Negro cannot earn his master the first cost; but nothing can be further from the truth. I suppose nine-tenths of the mechanics throughout the West Indies are Negro slaves; and I well know the coopers[34] among them earn two dollars a day, the carpenters the same, and oftentimes more; as also the masons, smiths, and fishermen, &c. and I have known many slaves whose masters would not take a thousand pounds current for them. But surely this assertion refutes itself; for, if it be true, why do the planters and merchants pay such a price for slaves? And, above all, why do those who make this assertion exclaim the most loudly against the abolition of the slave trade? So much are men blinded, and to such inconsistent arguments are they driven by mistaken interest! I grant, indeed, that slaves are sometimes, by half-feeding, half-clothing, over-working, and stripes, reduced so low, that they are turned out as unfit for service, and left to perish in the woods, or expire on a dung-hill.

My master was several times offered by different gentlemen one hundred guineas for me, but he always told them he would not sell me, to my great joy. And I used to double my diligence and care, for fear of getting into the hands of those men who did not allow a valuable slave the common support of life. Many of them even used to find fault with my master for feeding his slaves so well as he did, although I often went hungry, and an Englishman might think my fare very indifferent; but he used to tell them he always would do it, because the slaves thereby looked better and did more work.

While I was thus employed by my master, I was often a witness to cruelties of every kind, which were exercised on my unhappy fellow slaves. I used frequently to have different cargoes of new Negroes in my care for sale; and it was almost a constant practice with our clerks, and other whites, to commit violent depredations on the chastity of the female slaves; and these I was, though with reluctance, obliged to submit to at all times, being unable to help them. When we have had some of these slaves on board my master's vessels, to carry them to other islands, or to America, I have known our mates to commit these acts most shamefully, to the disgrace, not of Christians only, but of men. I have even known them to gratify their brutal passion

---

[34] **coopers:** Barrel makers.

with females not ten years old; and these abominations, some of them practised to such scandalous excess, that one of our captains discharged the mate and others on that account. And yet in Montserrat I have seen a Negro man staked to the ground, and cut most shockingly, and then his ears cut off bit by bit, because he had been connected with a white woman who was a common prostitute; as if it were no crime in the whites to rob an innocent African girl of her virtue, but most heinous in a black man only to gratify a passion of nature, where the temptation was offered by one of a different color, though the most abandoned woman of her species.

One Mr. D—— told me that he had sold 41,000 Negroes, and that he once cut off a Negro man's leg for running away. I asked him if the man had died in the operation, how he, as a Christian, could answer for the horrid act before God? and he told me, answering was a thing of another world, what he thought and did were policy. I told him that the Christian doctrine taught us to do unto others as we would that others should do unto us. He then said that his scheme had the desired effect— it cured that man and some others of running away.

Another Negro man was half hanged, and then burnt, for attempting to poison a cruel overseer. Thus by repeated cruelties, are the wretched first urged to despair, and then murdered, because they still retain so much of human nature about them as to wish to put an end to their misery, and retaliate on their tyrants! These overseers are indeed for the most part persons of the worst character of any denomination of men in the West Indies. Unfortunately, many humane gentlemen, by not residing on their estates, are obliged to leave the management of them in the hands of these human butchers, who cut and mangle the slaves in a shocking manner on the most trifling occasions, and altogether treat them in every respect like brutes. They pay no regard to the situation of pregnant women, nor the least attention to the lodging of the field Negroes. Their huts, which ought to be well covered, and the place dry where they take their little repose, are often open sheds, built in damp places; so that when the poor creatures return tired from the toils of the field, they contract many disorders, from being exposed to the damp air in this uncomfortable state, while they are heated, and their pores are open. This neglect certainly conspires with many others to cause a decrease in the births as well as in the lives of the grown Negroes.

I can quote many instances of gentlemen who reside on their estates in the West Indies, and then the scene is quite changed; the Negroes are treated with lenity and proper care, by which their lives are prolonged, and their masters profited. To the honor of humanity, I knew several gentlemen who managed their estates in this manner, and they found that benevolence was their true interest. And, among many I could mention in several of the islands, I knew one in Monserrat[35] whose slaves looked remarkably well, and never needed any fresh supplies of Negroes; and there are many other estates, especially in Barbadoes, which, from such judicious treatment, need no fresh stock of Negroes at any time. I have the honor of knowing a most worthy and humane gentleman, who is a native of Barbadoes, and has estates there.[36] This gentleman has written a treatise on the usage of his own slaves. He allows them two hours of refreshment at mid-day, and many other indulgencies and

---

[35] **Monserrat:** Mr. Dubury, and many others, Montserrat. [Equiano's note.]

[36] **gentleman . . . estates there:** Sir Phillip Gibbes, Baronet, Barbadoes. [Equiano's note.]

comforts, particularly in their lodging; and, besides this, he raises more provisions on his estate than they can destroy; so that by these attentions he saves the lives of his Negroes, and keeps them healthy, and as happy as the condition of slavery can admit. I myself, as shall appear in the sequel, managed an estate, where, by those attentions, the Negroes were uncommonly cheerful and healthy, and did more work by half than by the common mode of treatment they usually do. For want, therefore, of such care and attention to the poor Negroes, and otherwise oppressed as they are, it is no wonder that the decrease should require 20,000 new Negroes annually to fill up the vacant places of the dead.

Even in Barbadoes, notwithstanding those humane exceptions which I have mentioned, and others I am acquainted with, which justly make it quoted as a place where slaves meet with the best treatment, and need fewest recruits of any in the West Indies, yet this island requires 1,000 Negroes annually to keep up the original stock, which is only 80,000. So that the whole term of a Negro's life may be said to be there but sixteen years![37] And yet the climate here in every respect is the same as that from which they are taken, except in being more wholesome. Do the British colonies decrease in this manner? And yet what prodigious difference is there between an English and West India climate?

While I was in Montserrat I knew a Negro man, named Emanuel Sankey, who endeavored to escape from his miserable bondage, by concealing himself on board of a London ship: but fate did not favor the poor oppressed man; for, being discovered when the vessel was under sail, he was delivered up again to his master. This *Christian master* immediately pinned the wretch down to the ground at each wrist and ankle, and then took some sticks of sealing wax, and lighted them, and dropped it all over his back. There was another master who was noted for cruelty; and I believe he had not a slave but what had been cut, and had pieces fairly taken out of the flesh. And after they had been punished thus, he used to make them get into a long wooden box or case he had for that purpose, in which he shut them up during pleasure. It was just about the height and breadth of a man; and the poor wretches had no room, when in the case, to move.

It was very common in several of the islands, particularly in St. Kitts, for the slaves to be branded with the initial letters of their master's name; and a load of heavy iron hooks hung about their necks. Indeed on the most trifling occasions they were loaded with chains; and often instruments of torture were added. The iron muzzle, thumb-screws, &c., are so well known as not to need a description, and were sometimes applied for the slightest faults. I have seen a Negro beaten till some of his bones were broken, for only letting a pot boil over. Is it surprising that usage like this should drive the poor creatures to despair, and make them seek a refuge in death from those evils which render their lives intolerable? — while,

> With shudd'ring horror pale, and eyes aghast,
> They view their lamentable lot, and find
> No rest![38]

---

[37] **but sixteen years!:** Benezet's "Account of Guinea," p. 16. [Equiano's note.]

[38] **With shudd'ring . . . No rest!:** John Milton, *Paradise Lost,* 2: 616–18.

This they frequently do. A Negro man, on board a vessel of my master, while I belonged to her, having been put in irons for some trifling misdemeanor, and kept in that state for some days, being weary of life, took an opportunity of jumping overboard into the sea; however, he was picked up without being drowned. Another, whose life was also a burden to him, resolved to starve himself to death, and refused to eat any victuals. This procured him a severe flogging; and he also, on the first occasion which offered, jumped overboard at Charleston, but was saved.

Nor is there any greater regard shown to the little property than there is to the persons and lives of the Negroes. I have already related an instance or two of particular oppression out of many which I have witnessed; but the following is frequent in all the islands. The wretched field slaves, after toiling all the day for an unfeeling owner, who gives them but little victuals, steal sometimes a few moments from rest or refreshment to gather some small portion of grass, according as their time will admit. This they commonly tie up in a parcel; either a bit's worth (six pence) or half a bit's worth, and bring it to town, or to the market, to sell. Nothing is more common than for the white people on this occasion to take the grass from them without paying for it; and not only so, but too often also, to my knowledge, our clerks, and many others, at the same time have committed acts of violence on the poor, wretched, and helpless females; whom I have seen for hours stand crying to no purpose, and get no redress or pay of any kind. Is not this one common and crying sin enough to bring down God's judgment on the islands? He tells us the oppressor and the oppressed are both in his hands; and if these are not the poor, the broken-hearted, the blind, the captive, the bruised, which our Saviour speaks of, who are they?

One of these depredators once, in St. Eustatius, came on board of our vessel, and bought some fowls and pigs of me; and a whole day after his departure with the things, he returned again and wanted his money back. I refused to give it, and, not seeing my captain on board, he began the common pranks with me; and swore he would even break open my chest and take my money. I therefore expected, as my captain was absent, that he would be as good as his word. And was just proceeding to strike me, when fortunately a British seaman on board, whose heart had not been debauched by a West India climate, interposed and prevented him. But had the cruel man struck me I certainly should have defended myself at the hazard of my life; for what is life to a man thus oppressed? He went away, however, swearing, and threatened that whenever he caught me on shore, he would shoot me, and pay for me afterwards.

The small account in which the life of a Negro is held in the West Indies is so universally known that it might seem impertinent to quote the following extract, if some people had not been hardy enough of late to assert that Negroes are on the same footing in that respect as Europeans. By the 329th Act, page 125, of the Assembly of Barbadoes, it is enacted "That if any Negro, or other slave, under punishment by his master, or his order, for running away, or any other crime or misdemeanor towards his said master, unfortunately shall suffer in life or member, no person whatsoever shall be liable to a fine; but if any person shall, out of *wantonness, or only of bloody-mindedness, or cruel intention, willfully kill a Negro, or other slave, of his own, he shall pay into the public treasury fifteen pounds sterling.*" And it is the same in most, if not all of the West India islands. Is not this one of the many acts of the islands which call loudly for redress? And do not the assembly which enacted it deserve the appellation of savages and brutes rather than of Christians and men? It is an act at once unmerciful, unjust, and unwise; which for cruelty would disgrace an assembly of those who are called barbarians; and for its injustice and *insanity* would shock the morality and common sense of a Samaide or Hottentot.[39]

Shocking as this and many more acts of the bloody West India code at first view appear, how is the iniquity of it heightened when we consider to whom it may be extended! Mr. James Tobin,[40] a zealous laborer in the vineyard of slavery, gives an account of a French planter of his acquaintance, in the island of Martinique, who showed him many mulattoes working in the field like beasts of burden; and he told Mr. Tobin these were all the produce of his own loins! And I myself have known similar instances. Pray, reader, are these sons and daughters of the French planter less his children by being the progeny of black women? And what must be the virtue of those legislators, and the feelings of those fathers, who estimate the lives of their sons, however begotten, at no more than fifteen pounds; though they should be murdered, as the act says, *out of wantonness and bloody-mindedness*! But is not the slave trade entirely at war with the heart of man? And surely that which is begun by breaking down the barriers of virtue, involves in its continuance destruction to every principle, and buries all sentiment in ruin!

I have often seen slaves, particularly those who were meagre, in different islands, put into scales and weighed, and then sold from three pence to six pence or nine pence a pound. My master, however, whose humanity was shocked at this mode, used to sell such by the lump. And at or after a sale, it was not uncommon to see Negroes taken from their wives, wives taken from their husbands, and children from their parents, and sent off to other islands, and wherever else their merciless lords choose; and probably never more during life see each other! Oftentimes my heart has bled at these partings, when the friends of the departed have been at the waterside, and with sighs and tears, have kept their eyes fixed on the vessel, till it went out of sight.

A poor Creole Negro, I knew well, who, after having been often thus transported from island to island, at last resided in Montserrat. This man used to tell me many melancholy tales of himself. Generally, after he had done working for his master, he used to employ his few leisure moments to go a fishing. When he had caught any fish, his master would frequently take them from him without paying him; and at other times some other white people would serve him in the same manner. One day he said to me, very movingly, "Sometimes when a white man take away my fish, I go to my maser, and he get me my right; and when my maser by strength take away my

---

[39] **Samaide or Hottentot:** Samoyeds are Mongolians in Siberia; the Hottentots live in southern Africa. Europeans regarded both as barbaric, or uncivilized.

[40] **Mr. James Tobin:** An English merchant who lived in Nevis from 1775 to 1783. A defender of slavery, his 1785 *Cursory Remarks* attacked abolitionist James Ramsay's antislavery *Essay on the Treatment and Conversion of African Slaves in the British Sugar Colonies* (London, 1784). His son James Webbe Tobin remained in Nevis and became a corresponding member of the African Institution, a British antislavery group.

fishes, what me must do? I can't go to any body to be righted; then," said the poor man, looking up above, "I must look up to God Mighty in the top for right." This artless tale moved me much, and I could not help feeling the just cause Moses had in redressing his brother against the Egyptian.[41] I exhorted the man to look up still to the God on the top, since there was no redress below. Though I little thought then that I myself should more than once experience such imposition, and need the same exhortation hereafter, in my own transactions in the islands, and that even this poor man and I should some time after suffer together in the same manner, as shall be related hereafter.

Nor was such usage as this confined to particular places or individuals, for in all the different islands in which I have been (and I have visited no less than fifteen) the treatment of the slaves was nearly the same; so nearly, indeed, that the history of an island, or even a plantation, with a few such exceptions as I have mentioned, might serve for a history of the whole. Such a tendency has the slave trade to debauch men's minds, and harden them to every feeling of humanity! For I will not suppose that the dealers in slaves are born worse than other men — No; such is the fatality of this mistaken avarice that it corrupts the milk of human kindness and turns it into gall. And, had the pursuits of those men been different, they might have been as generous, as tender-hearted and just, as they are unfeeling, rapacious, and cruel. Surely this traffic cannot be good, which spreads like a pestilence, and taints what it touches! which violates that first natural right of mankind, equality and independency, and gives one man a dominion over his fellows which God could never intend! For it raises the owner to a state as far above man as it depresses the slave below it; and, with all the presumption of human pride, sets a distinction between them, immeasurable in extent, and endless in duration! Yet how mistaken is the avarice even of the planters. Are slaves more useful by being thus humbled to the condition of brutes than they would be if suffered to enjoy the privileges of men? The freedom which diffuses health and prosperity throughout Britain answers you — No. When you make men slaves, you deprive them of half their virtue; you set them, in your own conduct, an example of fraud, rapine, and cruelty, and compel them to live with you in a state of war; and yet you complain that they are not honest or faithful! You stupify them with stripes, and think it necessary to keep them in a state of ignorance. And yet you assert that they are incapable of learning; that their minds are such a barren soil or moor that culture would be lost on them; and that they come from a climate where nature, though prodigal of her bounties in a degree unknown to yourselves, has left man alone scant and unfinished, and incapable of enjoying the treasures she has poured out for him! An assertion at once impious and absurd. Why do you use those instruments of torture? Are they fit to be applied by one rational being to another? And are ye not struck with shame and mortification, to see the partakers of your nature reduced so low? But, above all, are there no dangers attending this mode of treatment? Are you not hourly in dread of an insurrection? Nor would it be surprising; for when

---

[41] **Moses . . . Egyptian:** See Exodus 2:11–12.

> ————No peace is given
> To us enslav'd, but custody severe,
> And stripes and arbitrary punishment
> Inflicted—What peace can we return?
> But to our power, hostility and hate;
> Untam'd reluctance, and revenge, though slow.
> Yet ever plotting how the conqueror least
> May reap his conquest, and may least rejoice
> In doing what we most in suffering feel.[42]

But by changing your conduct, and treating your slaves as men, every cause of fear would be banished. They would be faithful, honest, intelligent, and vigorous; and peace, prosperity, and happiness would attend you.

FROM CHAPTER 7
[FREEDOM]

We set sail once more for Montserrat, and arrived there safe, but much out of humor with our friend the silversmith. When we had unladen the vessel, and I had sold my venture, finding myself master of about forty-seven pounds—I consulted my true friend, the captain, how I should proceed in offering my master the money for my freedom. He told me to come on a certain morning, when he and my master would be at breakfast together. Accordingly, on that morning I went, and met the captain there, as he had appointed. When I went in I made my obeisance to my master, and with my money in my hand, and many fears in my heart, I prayed him to be as good as his offer to me, when he was pleased to promise me my freedom as soon as I could purchase it. This speech seemed to confound him, he began to recoil, and my heart that instant sunk within me. "What," said he, "give you your freedom? Why, where did you get the money? Have you got forty pounds sterling?" "Yes, sir," I answered. "How did you get it?" replied he. I told him, very honestly. The captain then said he knew I got the money honestly, and with much industry, and that I was particularly careful. On which my master replied, I got money much faster than he did; and said he would not have made me the promise he did if he had thought I should have got the money so soon. "Come, come," said my worthy captain, clapping my master on the back, "Come, Robert (which was his name), I think you must let him have his freedom; you have laid your money out very well; you have received a very good interest for it all this time, and here is now the principal at last. I know Gustavus has earned you more than a hundred a year, and he will save you money, as he will not leave you. Come, Robert, take the money."

My master then said he would not be worse than his promise; and, taking the money, told me to go to the Secretary at the Register Office, and get my manumission drawn up. These words of my master were like a voice from heaven to me. In an instant all my trepidation was turned into unutterable bliss; and I most reverently

---

[42] No peace . . . feel: Milton, *Paradise Lost*, 2: 332–40.

bowed myself with gratitude, unable to express my feelings, but by the overflowing of my eyes, and a heart replete with thanks to God, while my true and worthy friend, the captain, congratulated us both with a peculiar degree of heart-felt pleasure. As soon as the first transports of my joy were over, and that I had expressed my thanks to these my worthy friends, in the best manner I was able, I rose with a heart full of affection and reverence, and left the room, in order to obey my master's joyful mandate of going to the Register Office. As I was leaving the house I called to mind the words of the Psalmist, in the 126th Psalm,[43] and like him, "I glorified God in my heart, in whom I trusted." These words had been impressed on my mind from the very day I was forced from Deptford to the present hour, and I now saw them, as I thought, fulfilled and verified. My imagination was all rapture as I flew to the Register Office; and, in this respect, like the apostle Peter[44] (whose deliverance from prison was so sudden and extraordinary that he thought he was in a vision), I could scarcely believe I was awake. Heavens! who could do justice to my feelings at this moment! Not conquering heroes themselves, in the midst of a triumph—Not the tender mother who has just regained her long lost infant, and presses it to her heart—Not the weary hungry mariner, at the sight of the desired friendly port—Not the lover, when he once more embraces his beloved mistress, after she has been ravished from his arms! All within my breast was tumult, wildness, and delirium! My feet scarcely touched the ground, for they were winged with joy; and, like Elijah, as he rose to Heaven, they "were with lightning sped as I went on." Everyone I met I told of my happiness, and blazed about the virtue of my amiable master and captain.

When I got to the office and acquainted the Register with my errand, he congratulated me on the occasion, and told me he would draw up my manumission for half price, which was a guinea. I thanked him for his kindness; and, having received it, and paid him, I hastened to my master to get him to sign it, that I might be fully released. Accordingly he signed the manumission that day; so that, before night, I, who had been a slave in the morning, trembling at the will of another, was become my own master, and completely free. I thought this was the happiest day I had ever experienced; and my joy was still heightened by the blessings and prayers of many of the sable race, particularly the aged, to whom my heart had ever been attached with reverence.

As the form of my manumission has something peculiar in it, and expresses the absolute power and dominion one man claims over his fellow, I shall beg leave to present it before my readers at full length.

MONTSERRAT.

To all men unto whom these presents shall come: I, Robert King, of the parish of St. Anthony, in the said island, merchant, send greeting: Know ye, that I the aforesaid Robert King, for and in consideration of the sum of seventy pounds current money of the said island, to me in hand paid, and to the intent that a Negro man-slave, named Gustavus Vassa, shall and may become free, having manumitted, emancipated, enfranchised, and set free, and by these presents do manumit, eman-

---

[43] 126th Psalm: "Thanksgiving for Return from Captivity."

[44] Peter: Acts 12:9. [Equiano's note.]

cipate, enfranchise, and set free, the aforesaid Negro man-slave, named Gustavus Vassa, for ever; hereby giving, granting, and releasing unto him, the said Gustavus Vassa, all right, title, dominion, sovereignty, and property, which, as lord and master over the aforesaid Gustavus Vassa, I had, or now have, or by any means whatsoever I may or can hereafter possibly have over him the aforesaid Negro, for ever. In witness whereof, I the above said Robert King have unto these presents set my hand and seal this tenth day of July, in the year of our Lord one thousand seven hundred and sixty-six.

ROBERT KING

Signed, sealed, and delivered in the presence of Terry Legay, Montserrat. Registered the within manumission at full length, this eleventh day of July 1766, in liber. D.

TERRY LEGAY, Register

In short, the fair as well as the black people immediately styled me by a new appellation, to me the most desirable in the world, which was freeman; and at the dances I gave, my Georgia super-fine blue clothes made no indifferent appearance, as I thought. Some of the sable females, who formerly stood aloof, now began to relax and appear less coy; but my heart was still fixed on London, where I hoped to be ere long. So that my worthy captain and his owner, my late master, finding that the bent of my mind was towards London, said to me, "We hope you won't leave us, but that you will still be with the vessels." Here gratitude bowed me down; and none but the generous mind can judge of my feelings, struggling between inclination and duty. However, notwithstanding my wish to be in London, I obediently answered my benefactors, that I would go in the vessel, and not leave them; and from that day I was entered on board as an able-bodied sailor, at thirty-six shillings per month, besides what perquisites I could make.

My intention was to make a voyage or two, entirely to please these my honored patrons; but I determined that the year following, if it pleased God, I would see Old England once more, and surprise my old master, Captain Pascal, who was hourly in my mind; for I still loved him, notwithstanding his usage of me, and pleased myself with thinking what he would say, when he saw what the Lord had done for me in so short a time, instead of being, as he might perhaps suppose, under the cruel yoke of some planter. With these kind of reveries I used often to entertain myself, and shorten the time till my return; and now, being as in my original free African state, I embarked on board the *Nancy,* after having got all things ready for our voyage. In this state of serenity, we sailed for St. Eustatius; and having smooth seas and calm weather, we soon arrived there. After taking our cargo on board, we proceeded to Savannah, in Georgia, in August, 1766. While we were there, as usual, I used to go for the cargo up the rivers in boats; and on this business have been frequently beset by alligators, which were very numerous on that coast; and shot many of them when they have been near getting into our boats, which we have with great difficulty sometimes prevented, and have been very much frightened at them. I have seen a young one sold in Georgia alive for six pence.

During our stay at this place, one evening, a slave belonging to Mr. Read, a merchant of Savannah, came near our vessel, and began to use me very ill. I entreated him, with all the patience I was master of, to desist, as I knew there was little or no law for a free Negro here; but the fellow, instead of taking my advice, persevered in his insults, and even struck me. At this I lost all temper, and fell on him and beat him soundly. The next morning his master came to our vessel as we lay along side the wharf, and desired me to come ashore, that he might have me flogged all round the town, for beating his Negro slave. I told him he had insulted me, and given the provocation, by first striking me. I had told my captain also the whole affair that morning, and wished him to have gone along with me to Mr. Read, to prevent bad consequences; but he said that it did not signify, and if Mr. Read said any thing, he would make matters up, and desired me to go to work, which I accordingly did. The captain being on board when Mr. Read came and applied to him to deliver me up, he said he knew nothing of the matter, I was a free man. I was astonished and frightened at this, and thought I had better keep where I was than go ashore and be flogged round the town, without judge or jury. I therefore refused to stir; and Mr. Read went away, swearing he would bring all the constables in town, for he would have me out of the vessel. When he was gone, I thought his threat might prove too true to my sorrow; and as I was confirmed in this belief, as well by the many instances I had seen of the treatment of free Negroes, as from a fact that had happened within my own knowledge here a short time before.

There was a free black man, a carpenter, that I knew, who, for asking the gentleman that he worked for, for the money he had earned, was put into jail: and afterwards this oppressed man was sent from Georgia, with false accusations, of an intention to set the gentleman's house on fire, and run away with his slaves. I was therefore much embarrassed, and very apprehensive of a flogging at least. I dreaded, of all things, the thoughts of being striped, as I never in my life had the marks of any violence of that kind. At that instant a rage seized my soul, and for a little I determined to resist the first man that should offer to lay violent hands on me, or basely use me without a trial; for I would sooner die like a free man, than suffer myself to be scourged by the hands of ruffians, and my blood drawn like a slave. The captain and others, more cautious, advised me to make haste and conceal myself; for they said Mr. Read was a very spiteful man, and he would soon come on board with constables and take me.

At first I refused this counsel, being determined to stand my ground; but at length, by the prevailing entreaties of the captain and Mr. Dixon, with whom he lodged, I went to Mr. Dixon's house, which was a little out of town, at a place called Yea-ma-chra.[45] I was but just gone, when Mr. Read, with the constables, came for me, and searched the vessel; but, not finding me there, he swore he would have me dead or alive. I was secreted about five days; however, the good character which my captain always gave me, as well as some other gentlemen who also knew me, procured me some friends. At last some of them told my captain that he did not use me well, in suffering me thus to be imposed upon, and said they would see me redressed, and get me on board some other vessel.

My captain, on this, immediately went to Mr. Read, and told him, that ever since I eloped from the vessel, his work had been neglected, and he could not go on with

---

[45] Yea-ma-chra: A Creek Indian village on the bluffs above the English settlement at Savannah.

her loading, himself and mate not being well; and, as I had managed things on board for them, my absence must retard his voyage, and consequently hurt the owner; he therefore begged of him to forgive me, as he said he never heard any complaint of me before, during the several years I had been with him. After repeated entreaties, Mr. Read said I might go to hell, and that he would not meddle with me; on which my captain came immediately to me at his lodging, and telling me how pleasantly matters had gone on, desired me to go on board.

Some of my other friends then asked him if he had got the constable's warrant from them; the captain said, No. On this I was desired by them to stay in the house; and they said they would get me on board of some other vessel before the evening. When the captain heard this, he became almost distracted. He went immediately for the warrant, and, after using every exertion in his power, he at last got it from my hunters; but I had all the expenses to pay.

After I had thanked all my friends for their kindness, I went on board again to my work, of which I had always plenty. [. . .]

We set sail for Montserrat. The captain and mate had been both complaining of sickness when we sailed, and as we proceeded on our voyage they grew worse. This was about November, and we had not been long at sea before we began to meet with strong northerly gales and rough seas; and in about seven or eight days all the bullocks were near being drowned, and four or five of them died. Our vessel, which had not been tight at first, was much less so now. And, though we were but nine in the whole, including five sailors and myself, yet we were obliged to attend to the pumps every half or three quarters of an hour. The captain and mate came on deck as often as they were able, which was now but seldom; for they declined so fast, that they were not well enough to make observations above four or five times the whole voyage. The whole care of the vessel rested therefore upon me, and I was obliged to direct her by mere dint of reason, not being able to work a traverse. The captain was now very sorry he had not taught me navigation, and protested, if ever he should get well again, he would not fail to do so; but in about seventeen days his illness increased so much, that he was obliged to keep his bed, continuing sensible, however, till the last, constantly having the owner's interest at heart; for this just and benevolent man ever appeared much concerned about the welfare of what he was intrusted with.

When this dear friend found the symptoms of death approaching, he called me by my name; and, when I came to him, he asked (with almost his last breath) if he had ever done me any harm? "God forbid I should think so," replied I, "I should then be the most ungrateful of wretches to the best of benefactors." While I was thus expressing my affection and sorrow by his bed side, he expired without saying another word; and the day following we committed his body to the deep. Every man on board loved him, and regretted his death; but I was exceedingly affected at it, and found that I did not know, till he was gone, the strength of my regard for him. Indeed, I had every reason in the world to be attached to him; for, besides that he was in general mild, affable, generous, faithful, benevolent, and just, he was to me a friend and father; and had it pleased Providence, that he had died about five months before, I verily believe I should not have obtained my freedom when I did; and it is not improbable that I might not have been able to get it at any rate afterwards.

The captain being dead, the mate came on the deck, and made such observations as he was able, but to no purpose. In the course of a few days more, the few bullocks that remained were found dead; but the turkeys I had, though on the deck, and exposed to so much wet and bad weather, did well, and I afterwards gained near three hundred per cent on the sale of them; so that in the event it proved a happy circumstance for me that I had not bought the bullocks I intended, for they must have perished with the rest; and I could not help looking on this otherwise trifling circumstance as a particular providence of God, and was thankful accordingly. The care of the vessel took up all my time, and engaged my attention entirely. As we were now out of the variable winds, I thought I should not be much puzzled to hit upon the islands. I was persuaded I steered right for Antigua, which I wished to reach, as the nearest to us; and in the course of nine or ten days we made the island, to our great joy; and the day after, we came safe to Montserrat.

Many were surprised when they heard of my conducting the sloop into the port, and I now obtained a new appellation, and was called Captain. This elated me not a little, and it was quite flattering to my vanity to be thus styled by as high a title as any freeman in this place possessed. When the death of the captain became known, he was much regretted by all who knew him, for he was a man universally respected. At the same time the sable captain lost no fame; for the success I had met with, increased the affection of my friends in no small measure.

FROM CHAPTER 9
[LONDON; SEA ADVENTURES]

I thus took a final leave of Georgia, for the treatment I had received in it disgusted me very much against the place; and when I left it and sailed for Martinique I determined never more to revisit it. My new captain conducted his vessel safer than any former one; and, after an agreeable voyage, we got safe to our intended port. While I was on this island I went about a good deal, and found it very pleasant; in particular, I admired the town of St. Pierre, which is the principal one in the island, and built more like an European town than any I had seen in the West Indies. In general also, slaves were better treated, had more holidays, and looked better than those in the English islands. After we had done our business here, I wanted my discharge, which was necessary; for it was then the month of May, and I wished much to be at Montserrat to bid farewell to Mr. King, and all my other friends there, in time to sail for Old England in the July fleet. But, alas! I had put a great stumbling block in my own way, by which I was near losing my passage that season to England.

I had lent my captain some money which I now wanted to enable me to prosecute my intentions. This I told him; but when I applied for it, though I urged the necessity of my occasion, I met with so much shuffling from him, that I began at last to be afraid of losing my money, as I could not recover it by law; for I have already mentioned that throughout the West Indies no black man's testimony is admitted, on any occasion, against any white person whatever, and therefore my own oath would have been of no use. I was obliged, therefore, to remain with him till he might be disposed to return it to me. Thus we sailed from Martinique for the Grenadas,[46] I frequently pressing the captain for my money to no purpose; and to render my condition worse, when we got there, the captain and his owners quarrelled, so that my situation became daily more irksome: for besides that, we on board had little or no victuals allowed us, and I could not get my money nor wages, as I could then have gotten my passage free to Montserrat had I been able to accept it. The worst of all was, that it was growing late in July, and the ships in the islands must sail by the 26th of that month. At last, however, with a great many entreaties, I got my money from the captain, and took the first vessel I could meet with for St. Eustatius. From thence I went in another to Basse Terre in St. Kitts, where I arrived on the 19th of July.

On the 22d, having met with a vessel bound to Montserrat, I wanted to go in her; but the captain and others would not take me on board until I should advertise myself, and give notice of my going off the island. I told them of my haste to be in Montserrat, and that the time then would not admit of advertising, it being late in the evening, and the vessel about to sail; but he insisted it was necessary, and otherwise he said he would not take me. This reduced me to great perplexity; for if I should be compelled to submit to this degrading necessity, which every black freeman is under, of advertising himself like a slave, when he leaves an island, and which I thought a gross imposition upon any freeman, I feared I should miss that opportunity of going to Montserrat, and then I could not get to England that year. The vessel was just going off, and no time could be lost; I immediately therefore set about with a heavy heart, to try who I could get to befriend me in complying with the demands of the captain. Luckily I found in a few minutes, some gentlemen of Montserrat whom I knew; and having told them my situation, I requested their friendly assistance in helping me off the island. Some of them, on this, went with me to the captain, and satisfied him of my freedom; and, to my very great joy, he desired me to go on board.

We then set sail, and the next day, 23d, I arrived at the wished-for place, after an absence of six months, in which I had more than once experienced the delivering hand of Providence, when all human means of escaping destruction seemed hopeless. I saw my friends with a gladness of heart which was increased by my absence and the dangers I had escaped, and I was received with great friendship by them all, but particularly by Mr. King, to whom I related the fate of his sloop, the *Nancy,* and the causes of her being wrecked. I now learned with extreme sorrow that his house was washed away during my absence, by the bursting of the pond at the top of a mountain that was opposite the town of Plymouth. It swept great part of the town away, and Mr. King lost a great deal of property from the inundation, and nearly his life.[47] When I told him I intended to go to London that season, and that I had come to visit him before my departure, the good man expressed a great deal of affection for me, and sorrow that I should leave him, and warmly advised me to stay there, insisting, as I was much respected by all the gentlemen in the place, that I might do very well, and in a short time have land and slaves of my own. I thanked him for this

---

[46] Grenadas: The Grenadine islands.

[47] Mr. King lost . . . life: In 1767 Fort Ghaut, a reservoir near Plymouth, Montserrat, overflowed, destroying many houses, including Robert King's, and threatening the whole town.

instance of his friendship; but, as I wished very much to be in London, I declined remaining any longer there, and begged he would excuse me. I then requested he would be kind enough to give me a certificate of my behavior while in his service, which he very readily complied with, and gave me the following:

MONTSERRAT, JULY 26, 1767.

The bearer hereof, Gustavus Vassa, was my slave for upwards of three years, during which he has always behaved himself well, and discharged his duty with honesty and assiduity.

ROBERT KING

TO ALL WHOM THIS MAY CONCERN.

Having obtained this, I parted from my kind master, after many sincere professions of gratitude and regard, and prepared for my departure for London.

I immediately agreed to go with one Capt. John Hamer, for seven guineas (the passage to London) on board a ship called the *Andromache;* and on the 24th and 25th, I had free dances, as they are called, with some of my countrymen, previous to my setting off; after which I took leave of all my friends, and on the 26th I embarked for London, exceedingly glad to see myself once more on board of a ship; and still more so, in steering the course I had long wished for. With a light heart I bade Montserrat farewell, and have never had my feet on it since; and with it I bade adieu to the sound of the cruel whip, and all other dreadful instruments of torture; adieu to the offensive sight of the violated chastity of the sable females, which has too often accosted my eyes; adieu to oppressions (although to me less severe than most of my countrymen); and adieu to the angry, howling, dashing surfs. I wished for a grateful and thankful heart to praise the Lord God on high for all his mercies! in this ecstasy, I steered the ship all night.

We had a most prosperous voyage, and, at the end of seven weeks, arrived at Cherry Garden stairs. Thus were my longing eyes once more gratified with the sight of London, after having been absent from it above four years. I immediately received my wages, and I never had earned seven guineas so quick in my life before; I had thirty-seven guineas in all, when I got cleared from the ship. I now entered upon a scene quite new to me, but full of hope. In this situation my first thoughts were to look out for some of my former friends, and amongst the first of those were the Miss Guerins. As soon, therefore, as I had regaled myself I went in quest of those kind ladies, whom I was very impatient to see; and with some difficulty and perseverance, I found them at May's-hill, Greenwich. They were most agreeably surprised to see me, and I quite overjoyed at meeting with them. I told them my history, at which they expressed great wonder, and freely acknowledged it did their cousin, Captain Pascal, no honor. He then visited there frequently; and I met him four or five days after in Greenwich park.

When he saw me he appeared a good deal surprised, and asked me how I came back? I answered, "In a ship." To which he replied dryly, "I suppose you did not walk back to London on the water." As I saw, by his manner, that he did not seem to be sorry for his behavior to me, and that I had not much reason to expect any favor from him, I told him that he had used me very ill, after I had been such a faithful servant to him for so many years; on which, without saying any more, he turned about and went away. A few days after this I met Capt. Pascal at Miss Guerin's house, and asked him for my prize money. He said there was none due to me; for, if my prize money had been £10,000 he had a right to it all. I told him I was informed otherwise: on which he bade me defiance; and in a bantering tone, desired me to commence a law-suit against him for it: "There are lawyers enough," said he, "that will take the cause in hand, and you had better try it." I told him then that I would try it, which enraged him very much; however, out of regard to the ladies, I remained still, and never made any farther demand of my right.

Some time afterwards these friendly ladies asked me what I meant to do with myself, and how they could assist me. I thanked them, and said, if they pleased, I would be their servant; but if not, I had thirty-seven guineas, which would support me for some time, I would be much obliged to them to recommend me to some person who would teach me a business whereby I might earn my living. They answered me very politely, that they were sorry it did not suit them to take me as their servant, and asked me what business I should like to learn? I said, hair dressing. They then promised to assist me in this; and soon after they recommended me to a gentleman, whom I had known before, one Capt. O'Hara, who treated me with much kindness, and procured me a master, a hair dresser, in Coventry court Haymarket, with whom he placed me. I was with this man from September till the February following. In that time we had a neighbor in the same court who taught the French horn. He used to blow it so well that I was charmed with it, and agreed with him to teach me to blow it. Accordingly he took me in hand, and began to instruct me, and I soon learned all the three parts. I took great delight in blowing on this instrument, the evenings being long; and besides that I was fond of it, I did not like to be idle, and it filled up my vacant hours innocently. At this time also I agreed with the Rev. Mr. Gregory, who lived in the same court, where he kept an academy and an evening school, to improve me in arithmetic. This he did as far as barter and alligation; so that all the time I was there I was entirely employed.

In February 1768 I hired myself to Dr. Charles Irving, in Pallmall, so celebrated for his successful experiments in making sea water fresh; and here I had plenty of hair dressing to improve my hand. This gentleman was an excellent master; he was exceedingly kind and good tempered; and allowed me in the evenings to attend my schools, which I esteemed a great blessing; therefore I thanked God and him for it, and used all my diligence to improve the opportunity. This diligence and attention recommended me to the notice and care of my three preceptors, who, on their parts, bestowed a great deal of pains in my instruction, and besides, were all very kind to me. My wages, however, which were by two-thirds less than ever I had in my life (for I had only £12 per annum), I soon found would not be sufficient to defray this extraordinary expense of masters, and my own necessary expenses; my old thirty-seven guineas had by this time worn all away to one. I thought it best, therefore, to try the sea again in quest of more money, as I had been bred to it, and had hitherto found the profession of it successful. I had also a very great desire to see Turkey, and I now determined to gratify it. Accordingly, in the month of May, 1768, I told the doctor my wish to go to sea again, to which he made no opposition; and we parted on friendly terms. [. . .]

On my return to London, I waited on my old and good master, Dr. Irving, who made me an offer of his service again. Being now tired of the sea, I gladly accepted it. I was very happy in living with this gentleman once more, during which time we were daily employed in reducing old Neptune's dominions, by purifying the briny element and making it fresh. Thus I went on till May 1773, when I was roused by the sound of fame, to seek new adventures, and find, towards the North Pole, what our Creator never intended we should, a passage to India.

An expedition was now fitting out to explore a north-east passage, conducted by the Honorable Constantine John Phipps,[48] since Lord Mulgrave, in his Majesty's sloop-of-war, the *Race Horse*. My master being anxious for the reputation of this adventure, we therefore prepared everything for our voyage, and I attended him on board the *Race Horse*, the 24th day of May, 1773. We proceeded to Sheerness, where we were joined by his Majesty's sloop, the *Carcass*, commanded by Captain Lutwidge. On the 4th of June, we sailed towards our destined place, the Pole; and on the 15th of the same month, we were off Shetland.

On this day I had a great and unexpected deliverance, from an accident which was near blowing up the ship and destroying the crew, which made me ever after, during the voyage, uncommonly cautious. The ship was so filled that there was very little room on board for anyone, which placed me in a very awkward situation. I had resolved to keep a journal of this singular and interesting voyage; and I had no other place for this purpose but a little cabin, or the doctor's store-room, where I slept. This little place was stuffed with all manner of combustibles, particularly with tow and aquafortis,[49] and many other dangerous things. Unfortunately, it happened in the evening, as I was writing my journal, that I had occasion to take the candle out of the lanthorn, and a spark having touched a single thread of the tow, all the rest caught the flame, and immediately the whole was in a blaze. I saw nothing but present death before me, and expected to be the first to perish in the flames. In a moment the alarm was spread, and many people who were near, ran to assist in putting out the fire. All this time, I was in the very midst of the flames; my shirt and the handkerchief on my neck, were burnt, and I was almost smothered with the smoke. However, through God's mercy, as I was nearly giving up all hopes, some people brought blankets and mattresses, and threw them on the flames, by which means in a short time the fire was put out. I was severely reprimanded and menaced by such of the officers who knew it, and strictly charged never more to go there with a light; and, indeed, even my own fears made me give heed to this command for a little time; but at last, not being able to write my journal in any other part of the ship, I was tempted again to venture by stealth, with a light in the same cabin, though not without considerable fear and dread on my mind.

On the 20th of June, we began to use Dr. Irving's apparatus for making salt water fresh; I used to attend the distillery: I frequently purified from twenty-six to

---

[48] **Constantine John Phipps:** In 1773 he led an expedition to the Arctic in search of a northeast passage to India; Phipps's account of that trip, *A Voyage towards the North Pole Undertaken by His Majesty's Command*, was published in 1774. [Editors' note.]

[49] **tow and aquafortis:** Rope and nitric acid.

forty gallons a day. The water thus distilled was perfectly pure, well tasted, and free from salt, and was used on various occasions on board the ship. On the 28th of June, being in latitude 78, we made Greenland, where I was surprised to see the sun did not set. The weather now became extremely cold; and as we sailed between north and east, which was our course, we saw many very high and curious mountains of ice; and also a great number of very large whales, which used to come close to our ship, and blow the water up to a very great height in the air. One morning we had vast quantities of sea horses[50] about the ship, which neighed exactly like any other horses. We fired some harpoon guns amongst them, in order to take some, but we could not get any. The 30th, the captain of a Greenland ship came on board, and told us of three ships that were lost in the ice; however, we still held on our course, till July the 11th, when we were stopt by one compact and impenetrable body of ice. We ran along it from east to west about ten degrees; and on the 27th, we got as far north as 80°37'; and in 19 or 20 degrees, east longitude from London.

On the 29th and 30th of July, we saw one continued plain of smooth, unbroken ice, bounded only by the horizon; and we fastened to a piece of ice that was eight yards eleven inches thick. We had generally sunshine, and constant daylight; which gave cheerfulness and novelty to the whole of this striking, grand, and uncommon scene; and, to heighten it still more, the reflection of the sun from the ice gave the clouds a most beautiful appearance. We killed many different animals at this time, and among the rest nine bears. Though they had nothing in their paunches but water, yet they were all very fat. We used to decoy them to the ship sometimes by burning feathers or skins. I thought them coarse eating, but some of the ship's company relished them very much. Some of our people, once in the boat, fired at and wounded a sea horse, which dived immediately, and in a little time after, brought up with it a number of others. They all joined in an attack upon the boat, and were with difficulty prevented from staving or oversetting her; but a boat from the *Carcass* having come to assist ours, and joined it, they dispersed, after having wrested an oar from one of the men. One of the ship's boats had before been attacked in the same manner, but happily no harm was done. Though we wounded several of these animals we never got but one.

We remained hereabouts until the 1st of August, when the two ships got completely fastened in the ice, occasioned by the loose ice that set in from the sea. This made our situation very dreadful and alarming; so that on the 7th day, we were in very great apprehension of having the ships squeezed to pieces. The officers now held a council to know what was best for us to do in order to save our lives; and it was determined that we should endeavor to escape by dragging our boats along the ice towards the sea, which, however, was farther off than any of us thought. This determination filled us with extreme dejection, and confounded us with despair, for we had very little prospect of escaping with life. However, we sawed some of the ice about the ships, to keep it from hurting them, and thus kept them in a kind of pond. We then began to drag the boats as well as we could towards the sea; but, after two or three days' labor, we made very little progress, so that some of our hearts totally failed us;

---

[50] **sea horses:** Walruses. The Russian word *morse* was corrupted by the sailors to "sea horse." Phipps, *Voyage*, 184.

and I really began to give up myself for lost, when I saw our surrounding calamities. While we were at this hard labor, I once fell into a pond we had made amongst some loose ice, and was very near being drowned; but providentially some people were near who gave me immediate assistance, and thereby I escaped drowning.

Our deplorable condition, which kept up the constant apprehension of our perishing in the ice, brought me gradually to think of eternity, in such a manner as I never had done before. I had the fears of death hourly upon me, and shuddered at the thoughts of meeting the grim king of terrors in the natural state I then was in, and was exceedingly doubtful of a happy eternity if I should die in it. I had no hopes of my life being prolonged for any time; for we saw that our existence could not be long on the ice after leaving the ships, which were now out of sight, and some miles from the boats. Our appearance now became truly lamentable; pale dejection seized every countenance; many, who had been before blasphemers, in this our distress, began to call on the good God of Heaven for his help; and in the time of our utter need he heard us, and against hope or human probability, delivered us! It was the eleventh day of the ships' being thus fastened, and the fourth of our drawing the boats in this manner, that the wind changed to the E. N. E. The weather immediately became mild, and the ice broke towards the sea, which was to the S. W. of us. Many of us on this got on board again, and with all our might we hove the ships into every open water we could find, and made all the sail on them in our power; and now, having a prospect of success, we made signals for the boats, and the remainder of the people.

This seemed to us like a reprieve from death, and happy was the man who could first get on board of any ship, or the first boat he could meet. We then proceeded in this manner, till we got into the open water again, which we accomplished in about thirty hours, to our infinite joy and gladness of heart. As soon as we were out of danger, we came to anchor and refitted; and on the 19th of August, we sailed from this uninhabited extremity of the world, where the inhospitable climate affords neither food nor shelter, and not a tree or a shrub of any kind grows amongst its barren rocks; but all is one desolate and expanded waste of ice, which even the constant beams of the sun for six months in the year cannot penetrate or dissolve.

The sun now being on the decline, the days shortened as we sailed to the southward; and, on the 28th, in latitude 73, it was dark by ten o'clock at night. September 10th, in latitude 58, 59, we met a very severe gale of wind and high seas, and shipped a great deal of water in the space of ten hours. This made us work exceedingly hard at all our pumps a whole day; and one sea, which struck the ship with more force than anything I ever met with of the kind before, laid her under water for some time, so that we thought she would have gone down. Two boats were washed from the booms, and the long-boat from the chucks; all other moveable things on the decks were also washed away, among which were many curious things, of different kinds, which we had brought from Greenland; and we were obliged, in order to lighten the ship, to toss some of our guns overboard. We saw a ship at the same time, in very great distress, and her masts were gone; but we were unable to assist her. We now lost sight of the *Carcass,* till the 26th, when we saw land about Orfordness, of which place she joined us. From thence we sailed for London, and on the 30th came up to Deptford.

And thus ended our Arctic voyage, to the no small joy of all on board, after having been absent four months, in which time, at the imminent hazard of our lives, we explored nearly as far towards the Pole as 81 degrees north, and 20 degrees east longitude; being much farther, by all accounts, than any navigator had ever ventured before; in which we fully proved the impracticability of finding a passage that way to India.

FROM CHAPTER 10
[CONVERSION TO CHRISTIANITY]

Our voyage to the North Pole being ended, I returned to London with Doctor Irving, with whom I continued for some time, during which I began seriously to reflect on the dangers I had escaped, particularly those of my last voyage, which made a lasting impression on my mind, and by the grace of God proved afterwards a mercy to me; it caused me to reflect deeply on my eternal state, and to seek the Lord with full purpose of heart ere it was too late. I rejoiced greatly; and heartily thanked the Lord for directing me to London, where I was determined to work out my own salvation, and in so doing procure a title to heaven; being the result of a mind blinded by ignorance and sin.

In process of time I left my master, Doctor Irving, the purifier of waters. I lodged in Coventry court, Haymarket, where I was continually oppressed and much concerned about the salvation of my soul, and was determined (in my own strength) to be a first-rate Christian. I used every means for this purpose; and, not being able to find any person amongst those with whom I was then acquainted that acquiesced with me in point of religion, or, in scripture language, that would show me any good, I was much dejected, and knew not where to seek relief; however, I first frequented the neighboring churches, St. James's and others, two or three times a day, for many weeks; still I came away dissatisfied: something was wanting that I could not obtain, and I really found more heart-felt relief in reading my Bible at home than in attending the church; and, being resolved to be saved, I pursued other methods. First I went among the Quakers, where the word of God was neither read or preached, so that I remained as much in the dark as ever. I then searched into the Roman Catholic principles, but was not in the least edified. I at length had recourse to the Jews, which availed me nothing, as the fear of eternity daily harassed my mind, and I knew not where to seek shelter from the wrath to come. However, this was my conclusion, at all events, to read the four evangelists, and whatever sect or party I found adhering thereto, such I would join.

Thus I went on heavily, without any guide to direct me the way that leadeth to eternal life. I asked different people questions about the manner of going to heaven, and was told different ways. Here I was much staggered, and could not find any at that time more righteous than myself, or indeed so much inclined to devotion. I thought we should not all be saved (this is agreeable to the holy scriptures) nor would all be damned. I found none among the circle of my acquaintance that kept wholly the Ten Commandments. So righteous was I in my own eyes, that I was convinced I excelled many of them in that point, by keeping eight out of ten; and finding those who in general termed themselves Christians not so honest or so good in their morals as the Turks, I really thought the Turks were in a safer way of salvation than my neighbors; so that between hopes and fears I went on, and the chief comforts I enjoyed were in the musical French horn, which I then practised, and also dressing of hair. Such was my situation some months, experiencing the dishonesty of many people here. I determined at last to set out for Turkey, and there to end my days.

It was now early in the spring, 1774. I sought for a master, and found a Captain John Hughes, commander of a ship called *Anglicanai*, fitting out in the river Thames, and bound to Smyrna, in Turkey. I shipped myself with him as a steward; at the same time I recommended to him a very clever black man, John Annis, as a cook. This man was on board the ship near two months doing his duty; he had formerly lived many years with Mr. William Kirkpatrick, a gentleman of the island of St. Kitts, from whom he parted by consent, though he afterwards tried many schemes to inveigle the poor man. He had applied to many captains who traded to St. Kitts to trepan him; and when all their attempts and schemes of kidnapping proved abortive, Mr. Kirkpatrick came to our ship at Union Stairs, on Easter Monday, April the fourth, with two wherry boats and six men, having learned that the man was on board, and tied, and forcibly took him away from the ship, in the presence of the crew and the chief mate, who had detained him after he had information to come away. I believe this was a combined piece of business; but, be that as it may, it certainly reflected great disgrace on the mate and captain also, who, although they had desired the oppressed man to stay on board, yet this vile act on the man who had served him, he did not in the least assist to recover or pay me a farthing of his wages, which was about five pounds.

I proved the only friend he had, who attempted to regain him his liberty if possible, having known the want of liberty myself. I sent as soon as I could to Gravesend, and got knowledge of the ship in which he was; but unluckily she had sailed the first tide after he was put on board. My intention was then immediately to apprehend Mr. Kirkpatrick, who was about setting off for Scotland; and, having obtained a habeas corpus for him and got a tipstaff[51] to go with me to St. Paul's churchyard, where he lived, he, suspecting something of this kind, set a watch to look out.

My being known to them obliged me to use the following deception: I whitened my face, that they might not know me; and this had the desired effect. He did not go out of his house that night, and next morning I contrived a well plotted stratagem, notwithstanding he had a gentleman in his house to personate him. My direction to the tipstaff, who got admittance into the house, was to conduct him to a judge, according to the writ. When he came there, his plea was, that he had not the body in custody, on which he was admitted to bail.

I proceeded immediately to that well-known philanthropist, Granville Sharp, Esq.,[52] who received me with the utmost kindness, and gave me every instruction

---

[51] **habeas corpus . . . tipstaff:** *Habeas corpus ad subjiciendum* is a writ or document questioning whether someone is being legally imprisoned or held; a tipstaff is an officer.

[52] **Granville Sharp, Esq.** (1735–1813): British abolitionist who had been rescuing blacks from being shipped to the West Indies since the 1760s.

that was needful on the occasion. I left him in full hope that I should gain the unhappy man his liberty, with the warmest sense of gratitude towards Mr. Sharp, for his kindness; but alas! my attorney proved unfaithful; he took my money, lost me many months' employ, and did not do the least good in the cause; and when the poor man arrived at St. Kitts, he was, according to custom, staked to the ground with four pins through a cord, two on his wrists, and two on his ankles, was cut and flogged most unmercifully and afterwards loaded cruelly with irons about his neck. I had two very moving letters from him, while he was in this situation, and made attempts to go after him at a great hazard, but was sadly disappointed. I also was told of it by some very respectable families now in London, who saw him in St. Kitts, in the same state, in which he remained till kind death released him out of the hands of his tyrants.

During this disagreeable business I was under strong convictions of sin, and thought that my state was worse than any man's; my mind was unaccountably disturbed; I often wished for death, though at the same time convinced I was altogether unprepared for that awful summons. Suffering much by villains in the late cause, and being much concerned about the state of my soul, these things (but particularly the latter) brought me very low, so that I became a burden to myself and viewed all things around me as emptiness and vanity, which could give no satisfaction to a troubled conscience.

I was again determined to go to Turkey, and resolved, at that time, never more to return to England. I engaged as a steward on board a Turkeyman (the *Wester Hall,* Captain Lina) but was prevented by means of my late captain, Mr. Hughes, and others. All this appeared to be against me, and the only comfort I then experienced was in reading the Holy Scriptures, where I saw that "there is no new thing under the sun" (Eccles. 1:9); and what was appointed for me I must submit to. Thus I continued to travel in much heaviness, and frequently murmured against the Almighty, particularly in his providential dealings; and, awful to think! I began to blaspheme, and wished often to be anything but a human being.

In these severe conflicts the Lord answered me by awful "visions of the night, when deep sleep falleth upon men, in slumberings upon the bed" (Job 33:15). He was pleased, in much mercy, to give me to see, and in some measure understand, the great and awful scene of the judgment day, that "no unclean person, no unholy thing, can enter into the kingdom of God" (Eph. 5:5). I would then, if it had been possible, have changed my nature with the meanest worm on the earth; and was ready to say to the mountains and rocks "fall on me" (Rev. 6:16), but all in vain. I then in the greatest agony requested the divine Creator that he would grant me a small space of time to repent of my follies and vile iniquities, which I felt were grievous. The Lord, in his manifold mercies, was pleased to grant my request, and, being yet in a state of time, the sense of God's mercies were so great on my mind when I awoke that my strength entirely failed me for many minutes, and I was exceedingly weak. This was the first spiritual mercy I ever was sensible of, and being on praying ground, as soon as I recovered a little strength, and got out of bed and dressed myself, I invoked heaven, from my inmost soul, and fervently begged that God would never again permit me to blaspheme his most holy name. The Lord, who is long-suffering and full of compassion to such poor rebels as we are, condescended to hear and answer. I felt that I was altogether unholy, and saw clearly what a bad use I had made of the faculties I was endowed with: they were given me to glorify God with; I thought, therefore, I had better want them here, and enter into life eternal, than abuse them and be cast into hell fire. I prayed to be directed, if there were any holier than those with whom I was acquainted, that the Lord would point them out to me. I appealed to the Searcher of hearts, whether I did not wish to love him more, and serve him better. Notwithstanding all this, the reader may easily discern, if a believer, that I was still in nature's darkness. At length I hated the house in which I lodged, because God's most holy name was blasphemed in it; then I saw the word of God verified, *viz.*, "Before they call, I will answer; and while they are yet speaking, I will hear."[53]

I had a great desire to read the Bible the whole day at home; but not having a convenient place for retirement, I left the house in the day, rather than stay amongst the wicked ones; and that day, as I was walking, it pleased God to direct me to a house where there was an old sea-faring man, who experienced much of the love of God shed abroad in his heart. He began to discourse with me; and, as I desired to love the Lord, his conversation rejoiced me greatly; and, indeed, I had never heard before the love of Christ to believers set forth in such a manner, and in so clear a point of view. Here I had more questions to put to the man than his time would permit him to answer; and in that memorable hour there came in a dissenting minister; he joined our discourse, and asked me some few questions; among others, where I heard the Gospel preached? I knew not what he meant by hearing the Gospel; I told him I had read the Gospel; and he asked where I went to church, or whether I went at all or not? To which I replied, "I attended St. James's, St. Martin's, and St. Ann's Soho." "So," said he, "you are a churchman?" I answered, I was. He then invited me to a love-feast at his chapel that evening. I accepted the offer, and thanked him; and soon after he went away, I had some further discourse with the old Christian, added to some profitable reading, which made me exceedingly happy. When I left him he reminded me of coming to the feast; I assured him I would be there. [. . .]

When the wished-for hour came I went, and happily the old man was there, who kindly seated me, as he belonged to the place. I was much astonished to see the place filled with people, and no signs of eating and drinking. There were many ministers in the company. At last they began by giving out hymns, and between the singing, the ministers engaged in prayer; in short, I knew not what to make of this sight, having never seen anything of the kind in my life before now. Some of the guests began to speak their experience, agreeable to what I read in the Scriptures; much was said by every speaker of the providence of God, and his unspeakable mercies, to each of them. This I knew in a great measure, and could most heartily join them. But when they spoke of a future state, they seemed to be altogether certain of their calling and election of God; and that no one could ever separate them from the love of Christ, or pluck them out of his hands. This filled me with utter consternation, intermingled with admiration.

I was so amazed as not to know what to think of the company; my heart was attracted, and my affections were enlarged. I wished to be as happy as them, and was

---

[53] **Before . . . hear:** Isaiah 65:24.

persuaded in my mind that they were different from the world "that lieth in wickedness" (I John 5:19). Their language and singing, &c., did well harmonize; I was entirely overcome, and wished to live and die thus. Lastly, some persons in the place produced some neat baskets full of buns, which they distributed about; and each person communicated with his neighbor, and sipped water out of different mugs, which they handed about to all who were present.

This kind of Christian fellowship I had never seen, nor ever thought of seeing on earth; it fully reminded me of what I had read in the Holy Scriptures, of the primitive Christians, who loved each other and broke bread, in partaking of it, even from house to house. This entertainment (which lasted about four hours) ended in singing and prayer. It was the first soul feast I ever was present at. This last twenty-four hours produced me things, spiritual and temporal, sleeping and waking, judgment and mercy, that I could not but admire the goodness of God, in directing the blind, blasphemous sinner in the path that he knew not of, even among the just; and, instead of judgment, he has shewed mercy, and will hear and answer the prayers and supplications of every returning prodigal:

> O! to grace how great a debtor
> Daily I'm constrained to be![54]

After this I was resolved to win Heaven if possible; and if I perished I thought it should be at the feet of Jesus, in praying to him for salvation. After having been an eye-witness to some of the happiness which attended those who feared God, I knew not how, with any kind of propriety, to return to my lodgings, where the name of God was continually profaned, at which I felt the greatest horror; I paused in my mind for some time, not knowing what to do; whether to hire a bed elsewhere, or go home again. At last fearing an evil report might arise, I went home, with a farewell to card playing and vain jesting, &c. I saw that time was very short, eternity long, and very near; and I viewed those persons alone blessed who were found ready at midnight call, or when the judge of all, both quick and dead, cometh.

The next day I took courage, and went to Holborn, to see my new and worthy acquaintance, the old man, Mr. C——; he, with his wife, a gracious woman, were at work, at silk weaving; they seemed mutually happy, and both quite glad to see me, and I more so to see them. I sat down and we conversed much about soul matters, &c. Their discourse was amazingly delightful, edifying, and pleasant. I knew not at last how to leave this agreeable pair, till time summoned me away. As I was going they lent me a little book, entitled *The Conversion of an Indian.* It was in questions and answers. The poor man came over the sea to London to inquire after the Christian's God, who (through rich mercy) he found and had not his journey in vain. The above book was of great use to me, and at that time was a means of strengthening my faith; however, in parting, they both invited me to call on them when I pleased.

This delighted me, and I took care to make all the improvement from it I could; and so far I thanked God for such company and desires. I prayed that the many evils I felt within might be done away, and that I might be weaned from my former carnal

---

[54] O! . . . be!: Robert Robinson (1735–1790), Hymn 686, "Come, Thou Fount of Every Blessing." *The Hymnal 1982, according to the Use of the Episcopal Church.* (New York: Church Pension Fund, 1985)

acquaintances. This was quickly heard and answered, and I was soon connected with those whom the scripture calls the excellent of the earth. I heard the gospel preached, and the thoughts of my heart and actions were laid open by the preachers, and the way of salvation by Christ alone was evidently set forth. Thus I went on happily for near two months. . . .

. . . During this time I was out of employ, nor was I likely to get a situation suitable for me, which obliged me to go once more to sea. I engaged as steward of a ship called the *Hope,* Captain Richard Strange, bound from London to Cadiz in Spain. In a short time after I was on board, I heard the name of God much blasphemed, and I feared greatly lest I should catch the horrible infection. I thought if I sinned again after having life and death set evidently before me, I should certainly go to hell. My mind was uncommonly chagrined, and I murmured much at God's providential dealings with me, and was discontented with the commandments, that I could not be saved by what I had done; I hated all things, and wished I had never been born; confusion seized me, and I wished to be annihilated.

One day I was standing on the very edge of the stern of the ship, thinking to drown myself; but this scripture was instantly impressed on my mind — "That no murderer hath eternal life abiding in him" (I John 3:15). Then I paused and thought myself the unhappiest man living. Again I was convinced that the Lord was better to me than I deserved, and I was better off in the world than many. After this I began to fear death; I fretted, mourned, and prayed, till I became a burden to others, but more so to myself. At length I concluded to beg my bread on shore rather than go again to sea amongst a people who feared not God, and I entreated the captain three different times to discharge me; he would not, but each time gave me greater and greater encouragement to continue with him, and all on board shewed me very great civility: notwithstanding all this I was unwilling to embark again. At last some of my religious friends advised me, by saying it was my lawful calling, consequently it was my duty to obey, and that God was not confined to place, &c., &c. particularly Mr. G——— S———, the governor of Tothil-fields, Bridewell, who pitied my case, and read the eleventh chapter of the Hebrews to me, with exhortations. He prayed for me, and I believed that he prevailed on my behalf, as my burden was then greatly removed, and I found a heartfelt resignation to the will of God. The good man gave me a pocket Bible and Alleine's *Alarm to the Unconverted.* We parted, and the next day I went on board again. We sailed for Spain, and I found favor with the captain. It was the fourth of the month of September when we sailed from London; we had a delightful voyage to Cadiz, where we arrived the twenty-third of the same month. The place is strong, commands a fine prospect, and is very rich. The Spanish galleons frequent that port, and some arrived whilst we were there. I had many opportunities of reading the scriptures. I wrestled hard with God in fervent prayer, who had declared in his word that he would hear the groanings and deep sighs of the poor in spirit. I found this verified to my utter astonishment and comfort in the following manner.

On the morning of the 6th of October (I pray you to attend), all that day, I thought I should either see or hear something supernatural. I had a secret impulse on my mind of something that was to take place, which drove me continually for that time to a throne of grace. It pleased God to enable me to wrestle with him, as

Jacob did: I prayed that if sudden death were to happen, and I perished, it might be at Christ's feet.

In the evening of the same day, as I was reading and meditating on the fourth chapter of Acts, twelfth verse,[55] under the solemn apprehensions of eternity, and reflecting on my past actions, I began to think I had lived a moral life, and that I had a proper ground to believe I had an interest in the divine favor; but still meditating on the subject, not knowing whether salvation was to be had partly for our own good deeds or solely as the sovereign gift of God; in this deep consternation the Lord was pleased to break in upon my soul with his bright beams of heavenly light; and in an instant, as it were, removing the veil, and letting light into a dark place, I saw clearly with an eye of faith, the crucified Saviour bleeding on the cross on mount Calvary; the scriptures became an unsealed book; I saw myself a condemned criminal under the law, which came with its full force to my conscience, and when "the commandment came sin revived, and I died." I saw the Lord Jesus Christ in his humiliation, loaded and bearing my reproach, sin, and shame. I then clearly perceived that by the deeds of the law no flesh living could be justified. I was then convinced that by the first Adam sin came, and by the second Adam (the Lord Jesus Christ) all that are saved must be made alive. It was given me at that time to know what it was to be born again (John 3:5). I saw the eighth chapter to the Romans, and the doctrines of God's decrees, verified agreeable to his eternal, everlasting, and unchangeable purposes. The word of God was sweet to my taste, yea, sweeter than honey and the honeycomb. Christ was revealed to my soul as the chiefest among ten thousand. These heavenly moments were really as life to the dead, and what John calls an earnest of the Spirit.[56] This was indeed unspeakable, and I firmly believe undeniable by many.

Now every leading providential circumstance that happened to me, from the day I was taken from my parents to that hour, was then in my view, as if it had but just then occurred. I was sensible of the invisible hand of God, which guided and protected me, when in truth I knew it not: still the Lord pursued me, although I slighted and disregarded it; this mercy melted me down. When I considered my poor wretched state I wept, seeing what a great debtor I was to sovereign free grace. Now the Ethiopian was willing to be saved by Jesus Christ, the sinner's only surety, and also to rely on none other person or thing for salvation. Self was obnoxious, and good works he had none, for it is God that worketh in us both to will and to do.

Oh! the amazing things of that hour can never be told—it was joy in the Holy Ghost! I felt an astonishing change; the burden of sin, the gaping jaws of hell, and the fears of death, that weighed me down before, now lost their horror; indeed I thought death would now be the best earthly friend I ever had. Such were my grief and joy as I believe are seldom experienced. I was bathed in tears, and said, What am I that God should thus look on me, the vilest of sinners? I felt a deep concern for my mother and friends, which occasioned me to pray with fresh ardor; and in the abyss of

---

[55] **Acts, twelfth verse:** "And there is salvation in no one else, for there is no other name under heaven given among men by which we must be saved."

[56] **earnest of the Spirit:** John 16:13, 14, &c. [Equiano's note.]

thought, I viewed the unconverted people of the world in a very awful state, being without God and without hope.

It pleased God to pour out on me the spirit of prayer and the grace of supplication, so that in loud acclamations I was enabled to praise and glorify his most holy name. When I got out of the cabin, and told some of the people what the Lord had done for me, alas! who could understand me or believe my report! None but to whom the arm of the Lord was revealed. I became a barbarian to them in talking of the love of Christ: his name was to me as ointment poured forth, indeed it was sweet to my soul, but to them a rock of offense. I thought my case singular, and every hour a day until I came to London, for I much longed to be with some to whom I could tell of the wonders of God's love towards me, and join in prayer to him whom my soul loved and thirsted after. I had uncommon commotions within, such as few can tell aught about.

Now the Bible was my only companion and comfort; I prized it much, with many thanks to God that I could read it for myself, and was not left to be tossed about or led by man's devices and notions. The worth of a soul cannot be told. May the Lord give the reader an understanding in this. Whenever I looked in the Bible I saw things new, and many texts were immediately applied to me with great comfort, for I knew that to me was the word of salvation sent. Sure I was that the Spirit which indited the word opened my heart to receive the truth of it as it is in Jesus — that the same Spirit enabled me to act in faith upon the promises that were precious to me, and enabled me to believe to the salvation of my soul. By free grace I was persuaded that I had a part in the first resurrection, and was enlightened with the "light of the living" (Job 33:30). I wished for a man of God with whom I might converse: my soul was like the chariots of Amminadib (Canticles 6:12). . . .

During this period we remained at Cadiz until our ship got laden. We sailed about the fourth of November; and, having a good passage, we arrived in London the month following, to my comfort, with heartfelt gratitude to God for his rich and unspeakable mercies. [. . .]

FROM CHAPTER 12
[PUBLIC SERVICE AND ABOLITION]

Such were the various scenes which I was a witness to, and the fortune I experienced until the year 1777. Since that period, my life has been more uniform, and the incidents of it fewer, than in any other equal number of years preceding; I therefore hasten to the conclusion of a narrative which I fear the reader may think already sufficiently tedious.

I had suffered so many impositions in my commercial transactions in different parts of the world, that I became heartily disgusted with the sea-faring life, and was determined not to return to it, at least for some time. I therefore once more engaged in service shortly after my return, and continued for the most part in this situation until 1784.

Soon after my arrival in London, I saw a remarkable circumstance relative to African complexion, which I thought so extraordinary that I beg leave just to mention it. A white Negro woman, that I had formerly seen in London and other parts, had married a white man, by whom she had three boys, and they were every one mulattoes, and yet they had fine light hair. In 1779, I served Governor Macnamara, who had been a considerable time on the coast of Africa. In the time of my service, I used to ask frequently other servants to join me in family prayer; but this only excited their mockery. However, the Governor, understanding that I was of a religious turn, wished to know what religion I was of; I told him I was a protestant of the church of England, agreeable to the thirty-nine articles of that church; and that whomsoever I found to preach according to that doctrine, those I would hear. A few days after this, we had some more discourse on the same subject; when he said he would, if I chose, as he thought I might be of service in converting my countrymen to the Gospel faith, get me sent out as missionary to Africa. I at first refused going, and told him how I had been served on a like occasion by some white people the last voyage I went to Jamaica, when I attempted (if it were the will of God) to be the means of converting the Indian prince; and said I supposed they would serve me worse than Alexander, the coppersmith, did St. Paul, if I should attempt to go amongst them in Africa.[57] He told me not to fear, for he would apply to the Bishop of London to get me ordained.[58] On these terms I consented to the Governor's proposal, to go to Africa in hope of doing good, if possible, amongst my countrymen. . . .

On my return to London in August, I was very agreeably surprised to find that the benevolence of government had adopted the plan of some philanthropic individuals, to send the Africans from hence to their native quarter; and that some vessels were then engaged to carry them to Sierra Leone, an act which redounded to the honor of all concerned in its promotion, and filled me with prayers and much rejoicing. There was then in the city a select committee of gentlemen for the black poor, to some of whom I had the honor of being known; and as soon as they heard of my arrival, they sent for me to the committee. When I came there, they informed me of the intention of government; and as they seemed to think me qualified to superintend part of the undertaking, they asked me to go with the black poor to Africa. I pointed out to them many objections to my going; and particularly I expressed some difficulties on the account of the slave dealers, as I would certainly oppose their traffic in human species by every means in my power. However, these objections were over-ruled by the gentlemen of the committee, who prevailed on me to consent to go; and recommended me to the honorable commissioners of his Majesty's Navy, as a proper person to act as commissary for government in the intended expedition; and they accordingly appointed me, in November 1786, to that office, and gave me sufficient power to act for the government, in the capacity of commissary. [. . .]

I proceeded immediately to the executing of my duty on board the vessels destined for the voyage, where I continued till the March following.

During my continuance in the employment of government, I was struck with the flagrant abuses committed by the agent, and endeavored to remedy them, but without effect. One instance, among many which I could produce, may serve as a

---

[57] **Alexander . . . in Africa:** 1 Timothy 1:18–20; 2 Timothy 4:14. Despite Paul's admonitions, Alexander the coppersmith continued to blaspheme and made "shipwreck concerning the faith."

[58] **Bishop of London:** Robert Lowth (1710–1787).

specimen. Government had ordered to be provided all necessaries (slops, as they are called, included) for 750 persons; however, not being able to muster more than 426, I was ordered to send the superfluous slops, &c., to the king's stores at Portsmouth; but, when I demanded them for that purpose from the agent, it appeared they had never been bought, though paid for by government. But that was not all; government were not the only objects of peculation; these poor people suffered infinitely more; their accommodations were most wretched, many of them wanted beds, and many more clothing and other necessaries. For the truth of this, and much more, I do not seek credit from my own assertion. I appeal to the testimony of Captain Thompson, of the *Nautilus,* who convoyed us, to whom I applied in February 1787, for a remedy, when I had remonstrated to the agent in vain, and even brought him to be a witness of the injustice and oppression I complained of. I appeal also to a letter written by these wretched people, so early as the beginning of the preceding January, and published in the *Morning Herald,* on the 4th of that month, signed by twenty of their chiefs.

I could not silently suffer government to be thus cheated, and my countrymen plundered and oppressed, and even left destitute of the necessaries for almost their existence. I therefore informed the Commissioners of the Navy of the agent's proceeding, but my dismission was soon after procured, by means of a gentleman in the city, whom the agent, conscious of his peculation, had deceived by letter, and who, moreover, empowered the same agent to receive on board, at the government expense, a number of persons as passengers, contrary to the orders I received. By this I suffered a considerable loss in my property; however the commissioners were satisfied with my conduct, and wrote to Captain Thompson, expressing their approbation of it.

Thus provided, they proceeded on their voyage; and at last, worn out by treatment, perhaps not the most mild, and wasted by sickness, brought on by want of medicine, clothes, bedding, &c., they reached Sierra Leone, just at the commencement of the rains. At that season of the year, it is impossible to cultivate the lands; their provisions therefore were exhausted before they could derive any benefit from agriculture; and it is not surprising that many, especially the Lascars, whose constitutions are very tender, and who had been cooped up in ships from October to June, and accommodated in the manner I have mentioned, should be so wasted by their confinement as not to survive it.

Thus ended my part of the long talked of expedition to Sierra Leone; an expedition which, however unfortunate in the event, was humane and politic in its design, nor was its failure owing to government; everything was done on their part; but there was evidently sufficient mismanagement attending the conduct and execution of it to defeat its success. [. . .]

I hope to have the satisfaction of seeing the renovation of liberty and justice, resting on the British government, to vindicate the honor of our common nature. These are concerns which do not perhaps belong to any particular office; but, to speak more seriously, to every man of sentiment, actions like these are the just and sure foundation of future fame; a reversion, though remote, is coveted by some noble minds as a substantial good. It is upon these grounds that I hope and expect the attention of gentlemen in power. These are designs consonant to the elevation of their rank and the dignity of their stations; they are ends suitable to the nature of a free and generous government, and, connected with views of empire and dominion, suited to the benevolence and solid merit of the legislature. It is a pursuit of substantial greatness. May the time come—at least the speculation to me is pleasing—when the sable people shall gratefully commemorate the auspicious era of extensive freedom. Then shall those persons[59] particularly be named with praise and honor who generously proposed and stood forth in the cause of humanity, liberty, and good policy, and brought to the ear of the legislature designs worthy of royal patronage and adoption. May Heaven make the British senators the dispersers of light, liberty, and science, to the uttermost parts of the earth: then will be glory to God in the highest, on earth peace, and good will to men. Glory, honor, peace, &c. to every soul of man that worketh good: to the Britons first (because to them the Gospel is preached), and also to the nations. "Those that honor their Maker have mercy on the poor." It is "righteousness exalteth a nation, but sin is a reproach to any people; destruction shall be to the workers of iniquity, and the wicked shall fall by their own wickedness." May the blessings of the Lord be upon the heads of all those who commiserated the cases of the oppressed Negroes, and the fear of God prolong their days; and may their expectations be filled with gladness! "The liberal devise liberal things, and by liberal things shall stand" (Isaiah 32:8). They can say with pious Job, "Did not I weep for him that was in trouble? Was not my soul grieved for the poor?" (Job 30:25).

As the inhuman traffic of slavery is to be taken into the consideration of the British legislature, I doubt not, if a system of commerce was established in Africa, the demand for manufactures will most rapidly augment, as the native inhabitants will sensibly adopt the British fashions, manners, customs, &c. In proportion to the civilization, so will be the consumption of British manufactures.

The wear and tear of a continent, nearly twice as large as Europe and rich in vegetable and mineral production, is much easier conceived than calculated.

A case in point. It cost the Aborigines of Britain little or nothing in clothing, &c. The difference between their forefathers and the present generation, in point of consumption, is literally infinite. The supposition is most obvious. It will be equally immense in Africa—The same cause, *viz:* civilization, will ever have the same effect.

It is trading upon safe grounds. A commercial intercourse with Africa opens an inexhaustible source of wealth to the manufacturing interest of Great Britain;[60] and to all which the slave trade is an objection.

---

[59] **those persons:** Granville Sharp, Esq., the Rev. Thomas Clarkson, the Rev. James Ramsay, our approved friends, men of virtue, are an honor to their country, ornamental to human nature, happy in themselves, and benefactors to mankind! [Equiano's note.] The Scottish-born Ramsay (1733–1789) was a doctor and sailor before becoming a parish priest on Nevis and St. Kitts, where his plans to educate slaves raised planters' opposition. He served in the British Navy during the American Revolution and in 1784 wrote *An Essay on the Treatment and Conversion of African Slaves in the British Sugar Colonies.* Ramsay was viciously attacked by slavery's defenders, and he died under the strain of abuse during the opening months of Parliament's 1789 debate on slavery.

[60] **A commercial . . . Great Britain:** In the ship *Trusty,* lately for the new Settlement of Sierra Leone, in Africa, were 1,300 pair of shoes (an article hitherto scarcely known to be exported to that country) with several others equally new, as articles of export. Thus will it not become the interest, as well as the duty, of every artificer, mechanic, and tradesman, publicly to enter their protest against this traffic of the human species? What a striking—what a beautiful contrast is here presented to view, when compared with the cargo of a slave ship! Every

If I am not misinformed, the manufacturing interest is equal, if not superior, to the landed interest, as to the value, for reasons which will soon appear. The abolition of slavery, so diabolical, will give a most rapid extension of manufactures, which is totally and diametrically opposite to what some interested people assert.

The manufactures of this country must and will, in the nature and reason of things, have a full and constant employ, by supplying the African markets.

Population, the bowels and surface of Africa, abound in valuable and useful returns; the hidden treasures of centuries will be brought to light and into circulation. Industry, enterprise, and mining will have their full scope, proportionably as they civilize. In a word, it lays open an endless field of commerce to the British manufacturers and merchant adventurer. The manufacturing interest and the general interests are synonymous. The abolition of slavery would be in reality an universal good.

Tortures, murder, and every other imaginable barbarity and iniquity, are practised upon the poor slaves with impunity. I hope the slave trade will be abolished. I pray it may be an event at hand. The great body of manufacturers, uniting in the cause, will considerably facilitate and expedite it; and as I have already stated, it is most substantially their interest and advantage, and as such the nation's at large (except those persons concerned in the manufacturing neck yokes, collars, chains, handcuffs, leg bolts, drags, thumb screws, iron muzzles, and coffins; cats, scourges, and other instruments of torture used in the slave trade). In a short time one sentiment will alone prevail, from motives of interest as well as justice and humanity. Europe contains one hundred and twenty million of inhabitants. Query: How many millions doth Africa contain? Supposing the Africans, collectively and individually, to expend £5 a head in raiment and furniture yearly when civilized, &c., an immensity beyond the reach of imagination!

This I conceive to be a theory founded upon facts, and therefore an infallible one. If the blacks were permitted to remain in their own country, they would double themselves every fifteen years. In proportion to such increase will be the demand for manufactures. Cotton and indigo grow spontaneously in most parts of Africa; a consideration this of no small consequence to the manufacturing towns of Great Britain. It opens a most immense, glorious, and happy prospect—the clothing, &c., of a continent ten thousand miles in circumference, and immensely rich in productions of every denomination in return for manufactures.

Since the first publication of my *Narrative*, I have been in a great variety of scenes in many parts of Great Britain, Ireland, and Scotland, an account of which might not improperly be added here;[61] but this would swell the volume too much, I shall only

---

feeling heart indeed sensibly participates of the joy, and with a degree of rapture reads of barrels of *flour* instead of *gunpowder*—*biscuits and bread* instead of *horse beans*—*implements of husbandry* instead of *guns* for destruction, rapine, and murder—and various articles of *usefulness* are the pleasing substitutes for the *torturing thumbscrew*, and the *galling chain*, &c. [Equiano's note.]

[61] **added here:** *Viz.* Some curious adventures beneath the earth, in a river in Manchester, and a most astonishing one under the Peak of Derbyshire—and in September 1792, I went 90 fathoms down St. Anthony's Colliery, at Newcastle, under the river Tyne some hundreds of yards on Durham side. [Equiano's note.]

observe in general, that in May 1791, I sailed from Liverpool to Dublin, where I was very kindly received, and from thence to Cork, and then travelled over many counties in Ireland. I was everywhere exceedingly well treated, by persons of all ranks. I found the people extremely hospitable, particularly in Belfast, where I took my passage on board of a vessel for Clyde, on the 29th of January, and arrived at Greenock on the 30th. Soon after I returned to London, where I found persons of note from Holland and Germany, who requested me to go there; and I was glad to hear that an edition of my *Narrative* had been printed in both places, also in New York. I remained in London till I heard the debate in the House of Commons on the slave trade, April the 2d and 3d. I then went to Soham in Cambridgeshire, and was married on the 7th of April to Miss Cullen, daughter of James and Ann Cullen, late of Ely.[62]

I have only therefore to request the reader's indulgence and conclude. I am far from the vanity of thinking there is any merit in this narrative: I hope censure will be suspended, when it is considered that it was written by one who was as unwilling as unable to adorn the plainness of truth by the coloring of imagination. My life and fortune have been extremely checkered, and my adventures various. Nay even those I have related are considerably abridged. If any incident in this little work should appear uninteresting and trifling to most readers, I can only say, as my excuse for mentioning it, that almost every event of my life made an impression on my mind, and influenced my conduct. I early accustomed myself to look at the hand of God in the minutest occurrence, and to learn from it a lesson of morality and religion; and in this light every circumstance I have related was to me of importance. After all, what makes any event important, unless by its observation we become better and wiser, and learn "to do justly, to love mercy, and to walk humbly before God"? To those who are possessed of this spirit, there is scarcely any book or incident so trifling that does not afford some profit, while to others the experience of ages seems of no use; and even to pour out to them the treasures of wisdom is throwing the jewels of instruction away.

THE END

---

[62] **married . . . Ely:** See *Gentleman's Magazine* for April 1792, *Literary and Biographical Magazine,* and *British Review* for May 1792, and the *Edinburgh Historical Register* or *Monthly Intelligencer* for April 1792. [Equiano's note.]

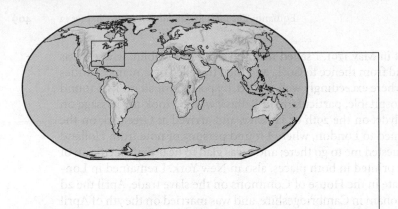

British North America, c. 1763

In 1763 Britain imposed the Proclamation Line, which prohibited white settlement to the west of the established thirteen colonies, in what was known as an Indian Reserve. Britain also decided to maintain a freestanding army to protect its interests in North America, which included Canada. These moves infuriated the American colonists, who wanted more autonomy, and helped sow the seeds of the American Revolution that began a little more than a decade later.

AMERICA
The Colonial Period

∾ By the sixteenth century, the Spanish and Portuguese had colonized parts of the Caribbean, Central America, and South America. The European settlement of the Atlantic coast of North America began in earnest a century later by the French, the English, and to a lesser degree, the Dutch. Jamestown, the first successful settlement in North America, was founded in 1607 by the London Company of Virginia, an English company that overcame initial setbacks, particularly during the "starving time" of the winter of 1609–10, to recruit more settlers who hoped to profit from feeding the tobacco craze in Europe. In 1619 the first African slaves were brought to Virginia; by 1624, Virginia's colonist population grew by some five thousand newcomers. Farther north, Samuel de Champlain and Henry Hudson had already claimed territories for France and the Netherlands, respectively, and in 1620 Pilgrims landed at Cape Cod, soon followed by Puritans. By the middle of the seventeenth century more than 20,000 English settlers lived in what was already being called New England, and at the turn of the century there were about 275,000 European- and African-born people living in the North American colonies. The stage was set for the transformation of a continent.

PILGRIMS

In 1620 a band of separatist Protestants known as Pilgrims reached Plymouth Rock after a hard sea journey on the *Mayflower*. They founded a colony and re-enacted a myth, for their story of exile in the "wilderness" and settlement in a promised land paralleled the biblical story of the Israelites' flight from Egypt. After a devastating first winter, which only half the emigrants survived, the colony began to thrive. By the end of the century, Plymouth Colony had merged with neighboring Massachusetts Bay Colony, which was settled in the 1620s and '30s by Puritans. The idea of America as the New Jerusalem permeates this country's cultural imagination.

Many Puritans, including the first governor of Massachusetts Bay Colony,

John Winthrop (1588–1649), were well-educated ministers who dreamed of founding "a city upon a hill" in the midst of a wilderness they believed to be the haunt of Satan. Like the Pilgrims, the Puritans construed their lives through the stories and teachings of the Bible: Everyday events, from the most trivial to the most traumatic, were interpreted as signs of God's work. Adapting the doctrines of the Protestant Reformation and John Calvin (1509–1564), Puritans believed in a direct, personal relationship with God as well as in original sin and predestination. All human beings were implicated in Adam's original sin against God, and for Puritans neither good works nor strong faith could alter God's will. Salvation or damnation was up to God, through whose grace certain souls were preselected for redemption. These were the "elect"; they could be recognized by their exemplary piety and, most important, by their prosperity. All were enjoined to practice rigorous self-scrutiny and to find proof of spiritual rebirth or conversion, testimony of which was required for church membership. The Puritan habit of self-questioning, coincidentally, resulted in a proliferation of diaries, journals, and spiritual autobiographies, not to mention sermons and treatises on civil, political, and religious matters. These introspective writings laid the foundations of American literature.

RELIGIOUS AND ETHNIC DIVERSITY

The America of the seventeenth century to which Puritans had immigrated was a place of religious, ethnic, and cultural diversity. People had already come to the New World from all over Europe—from England, France, Italy, Germany, Sweden, Holland, and Belgium—for a variety of reasons. Some were fleeing persecution or running from their past; others were chasing their dreams. Still others, from another continent, came in shackles.

While Boston was the center of Puritan culture, Philadelphia nurtured the Society of Friends, more commonly known as Quakers, who eschewed sacraments and ritual, turning to their "inner light" instead for spiritual guidance. Pennsylvania was also home to Mennonites, Baptists, Amish, Huguenots, and others who accepted the invitation of William Penn (1644–1718), the colony's founder, to enjoy complete religious tolerance. In New York and Maryland, Protestants settled alongside Catholics, Jews, and Anglicans; Anglicans settled throughout the colonies but particularly in the Carolinas, Maryland, and Virginia.

By the eighteenth century the increasingly heterogeneous colonies were becoming more unified by means of commerce and trade, the need for mutual protection, and the desire for cultural exchange. Moreover, population growth, manufactures, and trade had created thriving cities, such as Philadelphia and Boston, that equaled those of Europe. Colleges began to appear. Harvard was founded by Puritans in 1636. And by 1754, the College of William and Mary, Yale, and what would later be Princeton, Columbia, and the University of Pennsylvania (the first secular institution of higher learning) were established. Presses for books, newspapers, and pamphlets proliferated, also started by Puritans in the 1630s. With the circulation of newspapers, essays, and pamphlets written by and about the colonists, a sense of identity distinctive from that of the Old World began to take hold in the people of the thirteen colonies.

ENLIGHTENMENT

By the mid-eighteenth century the political ideas of European ENLIGHTENMENT philosophers such as John Locke (1632–1704) and the new science of Isaac Newton (1642–1727) had reached the colonies. In contrast to the Puritan view of the world, which emphasized the depravity of human beings and their helplessness to change history, Enlightenment thinkers sang of human beings' potential to shape their destiny through reason and practical experimentation. The ideas of progress and human perfectibility as well as the appreciation of civil rights, social justice, and equality were a dramatic departure from Puritan theocratic views and served to boost the popularity of tolerance and government-by-consensus in the colonies. No American better represents the American Enlightenment than the community leader, inventor, and statesman Benjamin Franklin (1706–1790), whose life is a model of rational inquiry, experimentation, civic virtue, and humanitarianism. Yet even Franklin's *Autobiography* reflects the Puritan call for personal accountability—not, in Franklin's case, to God, but to himself and his fellow citizens.

TOWARD REVOLUTION AND INDEPENDENCE

After the Peace of Paris treaty ended the French and Indian War in 1763, Britain acquired the entire East Coast of North America as well as Canada and the Gulf Coast, to the mouth of the Mississippi. In the same year, in response to Pontiac's Rebellion—an armed effort by Great Lakes Indians to avert further encroachments on their territory and to reclaim their traditions—England issued the Proclamation of 1763. This proclamation, which banned settlement west of the Appalachian Mountains, angered colonists eager to explore land to the west. In addition, over the next several years, England raised taxes in the colonies to support British troops and charged duties on imported goods. When the Stamp Act of 1765 imposed taxes on legal documents, newspapers, and licenses, angry Bostonians set fire to the governor's palace, and the Virginia House of Burgesses passed a resolution that said American colonists should enjoy the full rights of Englishmen. Though England quickly repealed the offending legislation, these incidents rallied the colonies around the idea of American autonomy—particularly the notion of "no taxation without representation." England continued to legislate restrictions

"The Bostonians in Distress"

After the Boston Tea Party, in which exasperated Bostonians threw English tea into Boston Harbor to protest rising taxes, England closed the port of Boston with the Boston Port Act of 1774. In this cartoon, Bostonians are incarcerated—cut off from food and supplies—and dependent on neighboring townspeople to provide for them. (The Art Archive)

and taxes, which led to more civil disturbances and culminated in the Boston Tea Party of 1773, when Americans dumped hundreds of pounds of tea into Boston Harbor. The power struggle between England and America had reached an impasse.

Approximately six months after the First Continental Congress met in Philadelphia to approve a Declaration of Rights and Grievances condemning

England's trade policies, British troops squared off against a group of Massachusetts militia known as minutemen; on the morning of April 19, 1775, a shot was fired, leading to the first casualties of the American War of Independence. As fighting fanned out through the colonies, the Second Continental Congress convened in Philadelphia, beginning on May 10, 1775; within two months, delegates to the Congress signed the Declaration of Independence. It was July 4, 1776. For the next seven years England and the American colonies were at war, which ended with the Treaty of Paris, signed on September 3, 1783.

With independence from England secured, the American colonists began to forge a nation. The new Congress called for a Constitutional Convention for the purpose of building on the 1781 Articles of Confederation, which had set forth the colonies' first principles of union. The Convention delegates, including Franklin and Thomas Jefferson (1743–1826), emerged with a signed document on September 17, 1787, and by June 1788 nine states had ratified the United States Constitution. The republican ideals of the Constitution—the division of government into branches, the independence of states, and equality—were unique to the eighteenth century. Later revolutionary movements elsewhere would use the Declaration of Independence and to some degree the Constitution as models for their own independence and governments.

EARLY AMERICAN LITERATURE

The seventeenth and eighteenth centuries in American literature might well be called an age of prose. Although American poetry and drama made some fledgling advances during this time, with poets such as Anne Bradstreet and Phyllis Wheatley at work, the great era of American poetry would not arrive until the nineteenth century. The earliest works of American literature were mainly diaries, letters, and journals describing voyages to the New World, explorations along its coasts or riverways, and journeys into its interior. During the colonial period, extensive histories appeared, such as John Smith's *The General History of Virginia* (1624) and William Bradford's *Of Plymouth Plantation* (not published until 1856), which described the land and the natives of these new places and recounted the plight of the colonists. Puritans wrote treatises and sermons on church doctrine along with philosophical reflections on religion and politics, such as John Winthrop's *A Model of Christian Charity,* a sermon delivered in 1630 on board the *Arabella* en route to America. It was at this time that the highly self-conscious meditations of Puritans were published. Known as spiritual autobiographies, these works influenced later autobiographical works, including Mary Rowlandson's *Narrative of the Captivity and Restoration of Mrs. Mary Rowlandson* (p. 483) and Benjamin Franklin's *Autobiography* (p. 522). Rowlandson's *Narrative,* one of the earliest CAPTIVITY NARRATIVES, interprets everything that happens to its

TIME AND PLACE

Eighteenth-Century America: King Philip's War

Initial contact between settlers and the Native American population tended to be cautiously friendly. But disputes over land, resources, and sovereignty led to conflict, ultimately resulting in local wars, such as the Pequot War of 1637 between Pilgrims and Algonquian-speaking Pequot and the more extensive King Philip's War (1675–1676) involving settlers and another Algonquian group, the Wampanoag. In 1643, Massachusetts, Connecticut, and Plymouth had formed a defensive alliance called the New England Confederation, which aimed in part to protect settlers encroaching on the lands of Narragansett and Wampanoag peoples. When war broke out between the Wampanoag and the Confederation in June 1675, other tribes joined Metacomet, the Wampanoag leader. Although Metacomet's forces managed to push back the frontier for a while, the Narragansett and Wampanoag were ultimately defeated and forced to concede lands to the settlers. Metacomet's wife and son were sold as slaves, and Metacomet, known as King Philip to the whites, was killed. During the raids, English women and children were sometimes seized and taken to live among Native Americans. Mary Rowlandson, a famous captive, wrote an account of her ordeal entitled *Narrative of the Captivity and Restoration of Mrs. Mary Rowlandson* (1682).

King Philip's War Rhyme.   Although King Philip (Metacomet) was the leader of the enemy, his skills as a warrior often fascinated settlers. (Courtesy of the American Antiquarian Society, Worcester, Mass.)

King Philip was a warrior bold,
Whose deeds are writ in records old;
He through New England's woods did
    roam,
And sorrow brought to many a home.

protagonist as a sign of God's judgment and grace. It is a good example of the Puritans' tendency to seek out evidence of salvation in their lives.

By the 1750s, the publication of newspapers and periodicals stimulated the writing of essays, many of which concerned politics and the increasingly complex lives of the urban middle class. Benjamin Franklin's earliest writings, for example, were satirical essays published in newspapers. Franklin also wrote, edited, and published *Poor Richard's Almanack,* one of the most enduring of the ever-popular

www   For more information about the culture and context of America in the eighteenth century, see *World Literature Online* at bedfordstmartins.com/worldlit.

almanacs — eclectic compendiums of aphorisms, astronomical predictions, weather forecasts, and entertaining tidbits. Many eighteenth-century political treatises and pamphlets, of course, were deadly serious, particularly at the dawn of the Revolution. Thomas Paine's *Common Sense* (1776), presenting the case for American independence, became an important document in the revolutionary politics of America, Britain, and France. *The Federalist Papers,* a series of essays published in newspapers between October 1787 and April 1788, aimed to persuade skeptical readers, especially in New York, of the need to ratify the Constitution. Written by Alexander Hamilton (1755–1804), James Madison (1751–1836), and John Jay (1745–1829), these essays have had a lasting influence on American politics and American literary history. Of all the political documents from this period, none ranks higher perhaps than the Declaration of Independence (p. 559), drafted by Thomas Jefferson. The Declaration exemplifies American Enlightenment thought. In a rhetorical style that embodies Jefferson's classical sense of balance and order, the Declaration presents a list of clearly articulated grievances against the Crown, while elucidating the idealistic principles of the new republic. It is one of the masterpieces of American literature as well as one of the most influential documents of the eighteenth century.

℘ MARY ROWLANDSON
C. 1635–C. 1711

Mary White **Rowlandson**'s account of her three months' captivity among the Wampanoag people[1] in 1676 was at one time entitled *The Sovereignty and Goodness of God, Together with the Faithfulness of His Promises Displayed; Being a Narrative of the Captivity and Restoration of Mrs. Mary Rowlandson.* The title clearly states the author's intention to proclaim her faith in God before her community, including her husband, minister Joseph Rowlandson. In Puritan Massachusetts, women were not expected to call attention to themselves: Rowlandson's account of the time she spent with her Native American captors was tolerated only because it was seen as serving a higher purpose. At the same time, the immense popularity of her story led to the publication of more such tales over the next two centuries. These narratives afforded readers a chance to peer into wilderness and view Native American people on their own ground, a land and a culture previously unfamiliar to white people.

ROH-lund-sun

www For links to more information about Mary Rowlandson and a quiz on *Narrative of the Captivity and Restoration of Mrs. Mary Rowlandson,* see *World Literature Online* at bedfordstmartins .com/worldlit.

---

[1]**Wampanoag:** One of several Algonquin peoples residing in New England in the seventeenth century. Their territory extended from Narragansett Bay to Cape Cod.

A

NARRATIVE

OF THE

CAPTIVITY, SUFFERINGS AND REMOVES

OF

Mrs. *Mary Rowlandson*,

Who was taken Prifoner by the INDIANS with feveral others,
and treated in the moft barbarous and cruel Manner by thofe
vile Savages : With many other remarkable Events during her
TRAVELS.

Written by her own Hand, for her private Ufe, and now made
public at the earneft Defire of fome Friends, and for the Benefit of the afflicted.

BOSTON :

Printed and Sold at JOHN BOYLE's Printing-Office, next Door
to the *Three Doves* in Marlborough-Street. 1773

1773.

Mary Rowlandson and Indians, from *A Narrative of the Captivity, Sufferings and Removes of Mrs. Mary Rowlandson,* 1773 *This illustration on the title page of an early edition shows Rowlandson armed with a gun against four of Metacomet's warriors. (Courtesy of the American Antiquarian Society, Worcester, Mass.)*

The story of Mary Rowlandson was an important early representative of this new literary genre, or type, the CAPTIVITY NARRATIVE.[2] These narratives influenced the later fictional treatment of Native Americans by American authors, including the popular nineteenth-century Leatherstocking Tales[3] of James Fenimore Cooper. Recently it has been argued that *Narrative of the Captivity and Restoration of Mrs. Mary Rowlandson*, with its strong personal voice, melodramatic adventures, and the incorruptible moral position of its female narrator, played a role in the charac-

[2] **captivity narrative:** Autobiographical accounts detailing American colonists' experiences as prisoners of Native Americans, often used to illustrate spiritual or moral growth through suffering.

[3] **Leatherstocking Tales:** These novels by James Fenimore Cooper include *The Pioneers* (1823), *The Last of the Mohicans* (1826), *The Prairie* (1827), *The Pathfinder* (1840), and *The Deerslayer* (1841). "Leatherstocking" is their protagonist's nickname.

ter of the eighteenth-century English NOVEL, beginning with Samuel Richardson's *Pamela: or, Virtue Rewarded,* published in 1740.[4]

Childhood. We know very little about Mary White Rowlandson beyond what she tells us in her narrative. The daughter of a wealthy Puritan landowner named John White, she was born about 1635 in England and probably was brought to Salem, Massachusetts, as a child. John White became one of the founders of the town of Lancaster, and around 1656 Mary married Joseph Rowlandson, the first minister of that town. We know of four children born to the couple; the death of the youngest during the events of 1676 is described in the *Narrative.* After her ransom from captivity, Mary Rowlandson moved with her husband to Wethersfield, Connecticut, where records show she was given a pension after his death in 1678. She probably lived until about 1711.

Spiritual Autobiography. Rowlandson's story belongs to the tradition of Puritan spiritual autobiography.[5] In the words of John Winthrop, the governor of Massachusetts Bay Colony, New England Puritans were about the business of founding "a City on a Hill," a Christian utopian community intended to be the New Jerusalem promised in Revelation. Like Eden and the old Jerusalem, the utopia in Massachusetts was threatened. When Puritans wrote in their journals of walking in New England forests and catching a whiff of brimstone, they were not being metaphorical; many believed that the native peoples were "imps," agents of the devil, and that the forest beyond their cleared fields was the province of the Prince of Darkness. In keeping with their sense of themselves as a chosen people under siege, Puritans practiced a rigorous self-examination of both their private lives and the histories of their communities. As already discussed, they produced vast numbers of diaries, journals, spiritual autobiographies, and histories, zealous to monitor their own conduct and to search their own stories for signs of God's providence at work—and for signs of Satan's inroads as well. Such is Rowlandson's understanding of autobiography and New England history; the sort of narrative she aimed to write was one that principally revealed God's chastising or merciful hand in events.

King Philip's War. The origins of the raids and captivities recounted in the *Narrative* predate the White and Rowlandson family presence in Massachusetts. In the 1620s, the great **Wampanoag** chief **Massasoit** had generously aided the first English colonists; Massasoit figures in sentimental First Thanksgiving pageants as the quintessential friendly Indian chief. By 1676, Massasoit and most of the original Plymouth Plantation settlers

> Today [Rowlandson's work] is considered a foundational work in American literature; it is better remembered than any other account of King Philip's War and is more widely read than any other such captivity narrative.
>
> – JILL LEPORE, *The Name of War,* 1998

wahm-puh-NOG
mass-uh-SOYT

---

[4] Samuel Richardson (1689–1761): English printer and author of pointedly moral novels. *Pamela* is the tale of a young servant who resists the advances of her master during a lengthy imprisonment. Her reward for holding on to her virtue is marriage to her former captor.

[5] spiritual autobiography: Puritan belief in personal interpretation of Scripture and predestination gave special importance to these autobiographies as means of self-examination and as guides in the search for signs of grace.

met-uh-KAHM-it

WEE-tuh-moo

were dead, and their descendants were engaged in a more hard-eyed and desperate confrontation. Massasoit's son, the young Wampanoag chief **Metacomet**, named Philip by the colonists, had come to see that it was not possible to deal with the English on equal terms. He understood that if his people lost their land base to the rapidly expanding English settlements, it would mean the end of the Wampanoag way of life. Metacomet forged an alliance among the leaders of Algonquian-speaking tribes in Massachusetts and Rhode Island, principally with his former sister-in-law **Weetamoo**, leader of the Rhode Island Pocasset tribe, the woman into whose service Mary Rowlandson would be given during her captivity. Benjamin Church, the great colonial military strategist, called Weetamoo "next after Philip in the making of this war." During the winter of 1675–1676, the Algonquian resistance movement nearly succeeded in routing the English colonists from American shores. Metacomet's forces attacked many white towns, including Lancaster, which they set afire on February 20, 1676, when Rowlandson was captured; Rowlandson gives a different date because she is using the Julian calendar.[6]

Rowlandson the Writer.   There is a conflict in the narrative between the sort of story Rowlandson believes she ought to tell and the one she feels compelled to tell. In her independent behavior during her captivity and in the act of writing for publication about her adventures, she is doing something extraordinary in her society. She is a woman giving public testimony, and she ought to be doing so only to glorify God. But she cannot contain the proud note in her voice as she recounts how she recovers from the trauma of her capture and the death of her baby and how she creates for herself an economic and social niche, which she is able to do because the Wampanoag admire her clever needlework and her resolute spirit. Rowlandson understandably thinks of her captors as instruments of Satan, but as the narrative progresses we begin to discern their humanity through her words. Even at the beginning of the trek, when she is almost mad with shock and grief at the death of her baby, we see how the Wampanoag with considerable psychological skill persuade her to leave the dead child behind and turn her attention to the necessary business of wilderness survival. Toward the end of her narrative, although she struggles to shape her adventures into the story of a Christian soul sustained by God while in the clutches of evil, she feels obligated to report that among these "savages" she has witnessed no sexual violence, and that she has seen no one, native or captive, starve among them because they share with one another whatever food they have.

Rowlandson comes genuinely to admire Metacomet, and she praises other Algonquin people for their endurance or their charity, but she cannot stand her "mistress" Weetamoo, whom she is rather loosely obligated to serve. We know from Benjamin Church's account and from Algonquian speakers' oral tradition of Weetamoo's beauty, her delight in finery, her pride of bearing, her skill at leading whole groups of children and

---

[6] **Julian calendar:** Used from the time of Julius Caesar until 1582; generally replaced by the Gregorian calendar thereafter. Rowlandson's use of the Julian calendar sets her dates off by a year.

elders stealthily through enemy lines to safety, of the loving regard in which people of many tribes held her. Rowlandson has no way to conceptualize Weetamoo's actual high status within the group as a chief in her own right; she can see Weetamoo only as a "proud hussy." Weetamoo galls Rowlandson not only because the two are temporarily set against each other as mistress and captive; Weetamoo's beauty and sexuality, her ornate dress, her air of authority, the attributes her own people value in her because they augment their collective spiritual power—all these are as alien to Rowlandson as the eating of horse hooves and acorns.

Soon after Rowlandson's release in May 1676, the Algonquin resistance reached a bloody conclusion. By late summer, both Weetamoo and Metacomet were dead, their heads impaled upon poles in the Taunton stockade. Rowlandson, restored to Puritan society, offers no further comment on the fate of her former captors. We are left with her portrait of three extraordinary people—Metacomet, Weetamoo, and herself—at

Frontispiece from
Narrative of the
Captivity and
Restoration of Mrs.
Mary Rowlandson,
1682

Note the book's full title: God is invoked and thanked before any mention of Rowlandson is made. A quote from Deuteronomy lies near the bottom of the page. (Courtesy of the Trustees of the Boston Public Library)

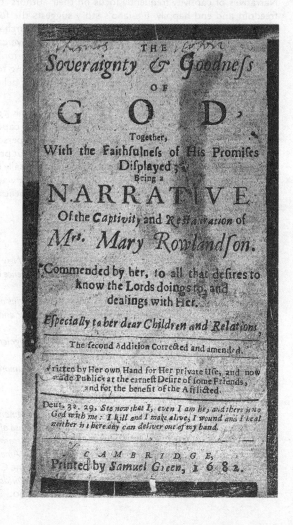

THE
Soveraignty & Goodness
OF
GOD,
Together,
With the Faithfulness of His Promises
Displayed;
Being a
NARRATIVE
Of the Captivity and Restauration of
Mrs. Mary Rowlandson.

Commended by her, to all that desires to
know the Lords doings to, and
dealings with Her.

Especially to her dear Children and Relations.

The second Addition Corrected and amended.

Written by Her own Hand for Her private Use, and now
made Publick at the earnest Desire of some Friends,
and for the benefit of the Afflicted.

Deut. 32. 29. See now that I, even I am he, and there is no
God with me: I kill and I make alive, I wound and I heal,
neither is there any can deliver out of my hand.

CAMBRIDGE,
Printed by Samuel Green, 1682.

this time of crisis in their lives. The *Narrative,* intended by its author to reveal the operations of Providence, also shows two cultures in mortal and irreconcilable conflict and the limited human relationships established under such desperate circumstances.

■ CONNECTIONS

Homer, *The Odyssey* **(Book 1).** The best stories, whether fact or fiction, appeal to our sense of adventure, contain danger and suspense, and reveal the marvelous before our eyes. Rowlandson's account of her captivity is full of life-threatening incidents through which she perseveres with bold determination. The Greek epic *The Odyssey* includes the story of the arrival of Odysseus and his crew in the land of the Cyclops and tells of the cunning of Odysseus, which results in his eventual escape from the terrible monster. Is it possible to compare the true story of Rowlandson's captivity with the fictional trials of Odysseus?

Olaudah Equiano, *The Interesting Narrative of the Life of Olaudah Equiano,* **p. 405.** Narratives of captivity frequently focus on their authors' resolution to escape to freedom and end happily. Equiano's story suggests the fortitude and courage it took him to withstand his misfortune and ends in his purchase of freedom. He does not, however, return to Africa. In her struggle to survive captivity, Rowlandson is guided by religious principles and a belief in the superiority of her civilization to that of her captors. Her "freedom" consists of returning to her own society. Can you compare Equiano and Rowlandson in light of their beliefs and the outcome of their experiences?

Harriet Jacobs, *Incidents in the Life of a Slave Girl* **(Book 5).** Part of the hardship endured by a woman captive is her vulnerability to her captors. Rowlandson, who was very fortunate to be treated with respect for her person during her captivity, eventually established a relationship with her captors that provided her some degree of dignity. Harriet Jacobs was menaced sexually and verbally during her captivity; she escaped and had to hide out for years before finding her way to freedom. Considering the hardships these two women faced, who do you believe was the stronger?

■ FURTHER RESEARCH

Historical Background

Bourne, Russell. *The Red King's Rebellion: Racial Politics in New England, 1675–1676.* 1990.

Kolodny, Annette. *The Land before Her: Fantasy and Experience of the American Frontiers, 1630–1860.* 1984.

Lepore, Jill. *The Name of War: King Philip's War and the Origins of American Identity.* 1998.

Schultz, Eric B., and Michael J. Tougais. *King Philip's War and the Origins of American Identity.* 1999.

Slotkin, Richard, and James K. Folsom. *So Dreadful a Judgment: Puritan Responses to King Philip's War, 1676–1677.* 1978.

Vaughan, Alden T., and Edward C. Clark, eds. *Puritans among the Indians: Accounts of Captivity and Redemption, 1676–1724.* 1981.

Criticism

Armstrong, Nancy, and Leonard Tennenhouse. *The Imaginary Puritan.* 1992.

Breitweiser, Mitchell R. *American Puritanism and the Defense of Mourning: Religion, Grief, and Ethnology in Mary Rowlandson's Captivity Narrative.* 1990.

Green, David L. "New Light on Mary Rowlandson." *Early American Literature* 20.1. 1985.

Lang, Amy Schrager. Introduction, "A True History of the Captivity and Restoration of Mrs. Mary Rowlandson." *Journeys in New Worlds: Early American Women's Narratives.* Ed. William Andrews, et al. 1990.

■ **PRONUNCIATION**

Massasoit: mass-uh-SOYT
matchit: MACH-it
Metacomet: met-uh-KAHM-it
Naananto: NAH-nahn-toh
Narragansett: nehr-uh-GAN-sit
Pocassets: poh-KASS-its
Quabaug: kwuh-BAWG
Quanopin: KWAN-uh-pin
Rowlandson: ROH-lund-sun
sagamore: SAG-uh-more
sannup: SAN-up
Squakeag: SKWAH-keeg
Wampanoag: wahm-puh-NOG
Weetamoo: WEE-tuh-moo
Wenimessett: weh-nee-MESS-it

ᔕ Narrative of the Captivity and Restoration of Mrs. Mary Rowlandson

On the tenth of February 1675[1] came the Indians with great numbers upon Lancaster. Their first coming was about sunrising. Hearing the noise of some guns, we looked out; several houses were burning and the smoke ascending to heaven. There were five persons taken in one house; the father and the mother and a sucking child, they knocked on the head; the other two they took and carried away alive. There were two others, who, being out of their garrison upon some occasion, were set upon; one was knocked on the head, the other escaped. Another there was who running along was shot and wounded and fell down; he begged of them his life, promising them money (as they told me), but they would not hearken to him but knocked him in [the] head, stripped him naked, and split open his bowels. Another, seeing many of the Indians about his barn, ventured and went out, but was quickly shot down. There were three others belonging to the same garrison who were killed; the Indians, getting up upon the roof of the barn, had advantage to shoot down upon

---

Narrative of the Captivity and Restoration of Mrs. Mary Rowlandson. There are two crucial structural features in Rowlandson's account: one is Rowlandson's progressive "remove" from the Puritan settlement of Lancaster, the other is her evolving installation in Wampanoag society, including the relationships she develops with her master Metacomet and her mistress Weetamoo. Although she never calls Wampanoag behavior "civilized" in the sense that it offers an alternative to Puritan society, Rowlandson does become aware of the complex social organization of the tribe, its relations with other Indian nations, and its life-or-death struggle with the Puritans, which reaches a bloody conclusion at the time she is ransomed.

---

[1] **1675:** 1676, by our present calendar.

them over their fortification. Thus these murderous wretches went on, burning and destroying before them.

At length they came and beset our own house, and quickly it was the dolefullest day that ever mine eyes saw. The house stood upon the edge of a hill. Some of the Indians got behind the hill, others into the barn, and others behind anything that could shelter them; from all which places they shot against the house so that the bullets seemed to fly like hail; and quickly they wounded one man among us, then another, and then a third. About two hours (according to my observation in that amazing time) they had been about the house before they prevailed to fire it (which they did with flax and hemp which they brought out of the barn, and there being no defense about the house, only two flankers² at two opposite corners and one of them not finished). They fired it once, and one ventured out and quenched it, but they quickly fired it again, and that took.

Now is that dreadful hour come that I have often heard of (in time of war as it was the case of others), but now mine eyes see it. Some in our house were fighting for their lives, others wallowing in their blood, the house on fire over our heads, and the bloody heathen ready to knock us on the head if we stirred out. Now might we hear mothers and children crying out for themselves and one another, "Lord, what shall we do?" Then I took my children (and one of my sisters, hers) to go forth and leave the house, but as soon as we came to the door and appeared, the Indians shot so thick that the bullets rattled against the house as if one had taken an handful of stones and threw them, so that we were fain to give back. We had six stout dogs belonging to our garrison, but none of them would stir, although another time, if any Indian had come to the door, they were ready to fly upon him and tear him down. The Lord hereby would make us the more to acknowledge His hand and to see that our help is always in Him. But out we must go, the fire increasing and coming along behind us roaring, and the Indians gaping before us with their guns, spears, and hatchets to devour us. No sooner were we out of the house, but my brother-in-law (being before wounded, in defending the house, in or near the

---

The action of the work consists of her journey deep into the interior of the Native American world followed by her return to white civilization. As Rowlandson travels, her understanding expands. She is more motivated to describe her life as a captive than as a woman restored to Puritan society. Illustrating the power of faith even in the Age of Reason, Rowlandson cites passages from the Bible that was given to her by the Indians, both to ward off despair and as a means of framing and interpreting her life.

Although the *Narrative* was not printed until 1682, Rowlandson probably composed it soon after the events it chronicles, with Mr. Rowlandson's encouragement; it was originally published with a sermon he'd written. The book was instantly popular, going through three editions in New England and a fourth in London in the course of a year.

A note on the text: Rowlandson's long preface to her narrative is not included here. Her spelling has been modernized, her use of italics normalized, and quotation marks have been introduced to identify quotes. All notes are the editors'.

---

² **flankers:** Fortifications.

throat) fell down dead; whereat the Indians scornfully shouted, hallooed, and were presently upon him, stripping off his clothes. The bullets flying thick, one went through my side, and the same (as would seem) through the bowels and hand of my dear child in my arms. One of my elder sister's children, named William, had then his leg broken, which the Indians perceiving, they knocked him on the head. Thus were we butchered by those merciless heathen, standing amazed, with the blood running down to our heels.

My eldest sister being yet in the house and seeing those woeful sights, the infidels hailing mothers one way and children another and some wallowing in their blood, and her elder son telling her that her son William was dead and myself was wounded, she said, "And, Lord, let me die with them." Which was no sooner said, but she was struck with a bullet and fell down dead over the threshold. I hope she is reaping the fruit of her good labors, being faithful to the service of God in her place. In her younger years she lay under much trouble upon spiritual accounts till it pleased God to make that precious scripture take hold of her heart, 2 Cor. 12:9, "And he said unto me, my grace is sufficient for thee." More than twenty years after I have heard her tell how sweet and comfortable that place was to her. But to return: the Indians laid hold of us, pulling me one way and the children another, and said, "Come go along with us." I told them they would kill me. They answered, if I were willing to go along with them they would not hurt me.

Oh, the doleful sight that now was to behold at this house! "Come, behold the works of the Lord, what desolation He has made in the earth."[3] Of thirty-seven persons who were in this one house, none escaped either present death or a bitter captivity save only one, who might say as he, Job 1:15, "And I only am escaped alone to tell the news." There were twelve killed, some shot, some stabbed with their spears, some knocked down with their hatchets. When we are in prosperity, oh, the little that we think of such dreadful sights, and to see our dear friends and relations lie bleeding out their heart-blood upon the ground! There was one who was chopped into the head with a hatchet and stripped naked, and yet was crawling up and down. It is a solemn sight to see so many Christians lying in their blood, some here and some there, like a company of sheep torn by wolves, all of them stripped naked by a company of hell-hounds, roaring, singing, ranting and insulting, as if they would have torn our very hearts out. Yet the Lord by his almighty power preserved a number of us from death, for there were twenty-four of us taken alive and carried captive.

I had often before this said that if the Indians should come I should choose rather to be killed by them than taken alive, but when it came to the trial, my mind changed; their glittering weapons so daunted my spirit that I chose rather to go along with those (as I may say) ravenous beasts than that moment to end my days. And that I may the better declare what happened to me during that grievous captivity, I shall particularly speak of the several removes[4] we had up and down the wilderness.

---

[3] "Come . . . earth": Psalm 46:8.

[4] **removes:** A remove is a journey; metaphorically, she means to emphasize that she is being removed farther from the center of Christianity and Euro-American civilization.

THE FIRST REMOVE

Now away we must go with those barbarous creatures with our bodies wounded and bleeding and our hearts no less than our bodies. About a mile we went that night up upon a hill within sight of the town where they intended to lodge. There was hard by a vacant house (deserted by the English before, for fear of the Indians). I asked them whether I might not lodge in the house that night, to which they answered, "What, will you love English men still?" This was the dolefullest night that ever my eyes saw. Oh, the roaring and singing and dancing and yelling of those black creatures in the night, which made the place a lively resemblance of hell. And as miserable was the waste that was there made of horses, cattle, sheep, swine, calves, lambs, roasting pigs, and fowl (which they had plundered in the town), some roasting, some lying and burning, and some boiling to feed our merciless enemies, who were joyful enough though we were disconsolate. To add to the dolefulness of the former day and the dismalness of the present night, my thoughts ran upon my losses and sad bereaved condition. All was gone: my husband gone (at least separated from me, he being in the Bay,[5] and to add to my grief, the Indians told me they would kill him as he came homeward), my children gone, my relations and friends gone, our house and home and all our comforts within door and without, all was gone except my life, and I knew not but the next moment that might go too. There remained nothing to me but one poor wounded babe, and it seemed at present worse than death that it was in such a pitiful condition bespeaking compassion, and I had no refreshing for it nor suitable things to revive it. Little do many think what is the savageness and brutishness of this barbarous enemy, ay, even those that seem to profess more than others among them when the English have fallen into their hands.

Those seven that were killed at Lancaster the summer before upon a Sabbath day and the one that was afterward killed upon a week day were slain and mangled in a barbarous manner by one-eye John and Marlborough's praying Indians[6] which Capt. Mosely brought to Boston, as the Indians told me.

THE SECOND REMOVE[7]

But now, the next morning, I must turn my back upon the town and travel with them into the vast and desolate wilderness, I knew not whither. It is not my tongue or pen can express the sorrows of my heart and bitterness of my spirit that I had at this departure, but God was with me in a wonderful manner, carrying me along and bearing up my spirit that it did not quite fail. One of the Indians carried my poor wounded babe upon a horse; it went moaning all along, "I shall die, I shall die." I went on foot after it with sorrow that cannot be expressed. At length I took it off the

---

[5] **Bay:** Boston, the capital of Massachusetts Bay Colony. Rowlandson's husband had gone there to ask for reinforcements for the defense of Lancaster.

[6] **praying Indians:** Those counted by the colonists as Christian converts. Many of them renounced the faith and joined the Native American forces during King Philip's War.

[7] **Second Remove:** To Princeton, Massachusetts.

horse and carried it in my arms till my strength failed, and I fell down with it. Then they set me upon a horse with my wounded child in my lap. And there being no furniture[8] upon the horse['s] back, as we were going down a steep hill, we both fell over the horse's head, at which they like inhuman creatures laughed and rejoiced to see it, though I thought we should there have ended our days, as overcome with so many difficulties. But the Lord renewed my strength still and carried me along that I might see more of His power; yea, so much that I could never have thought of had I not experienced it.

After this it quickly began to snow, and when night came on, they stopped. And now down I must sit in the snow by a little fire and a few boughs behind me, with my sick child in my lap and calling much for water, being now (through the wound) fallen into a violent fever. My own wound also [was] growing so stiff that I could scarce sit down or rise up; yet so it must be that I must sit all this cold winter night upon the cold, snowy ground with my sick child in my arms, looking that every hour would be the last of its life, and having no Christian friend near me either to comfort or help me. Oh, I may see the wonderful power of God that my spirit did not utterly sink under my affliction! Still the Lord upheld me with His gracious and merciful spirit, and we were both alive to see the light of the next morning.

THE THIRD REMOVE[9]

The morning being come, they prepared to go on their way. One of the Indians got up upon a horse, and they set me up behind him with my poor sick babe in my lap. A very wearisome and tedious day I had of it, what with my own wound and my child's being so exceedingly sick in a lamentable condition with her wound. It may be easily judged what a poor feeble condition we were in, there being not the least crumb of refreshing that came within either of our mouths from Wednesday night to Saturday night except only a little cold water. This day in the afternoon, about an hour by sun, we came to the place where they intended, *viz.* an Indian town called Wenimesset, nor[th]ward of Quabaug. When we were come, oh, the number of pagans (now merciless enemies) that there came about me that I may say as David, Psal. 27:13, "I had fainted, unless I had believed," etc. The next day was the Sabbath. I then remembered how careless I had been of God's holy time, how many Sabbaths I had lost and misspent and how evilly I had walked in God's sight, which lay so close unto my spirit that it was easy for me to see how righteous it was with God to cut the thread of my life and cast me out of His presence forever. Yet the Lord still showed mercy to me and upheld me, and as He wounded me with one hand, so He healed me with the other.

This day there came to me one Robert Pepper (a man belonging to Roxbury), who was taken in Captain Beers his fight and had been now a considerable time with the Indians and up with them almost as far as Albany to see King Philip, as he told

---

[8] **furniture:** Saddle.

[9] **Third Remove:** To a place near New Braintree, Massachusetts. Rowlandson was held here February 12–27.

me, and was now very lately come into these parts. Hearing, I say, that I was in this Indian town, he obtained leave to come and see me. He told me he himself was wounded in the leg at Captain Beers his fight and was not able some time to go, but, as they carried him, and as he took oaken leaves and laid to his wound, and through the blessing of God, he was able to travel again. Then I took oaken leaves and laid to my side, and, with the blessing of God, it cured me also. Yet before the cure was wrought, I may say, as it is in Psal. 38:5, 6, "My wounds stink and are corrupt, I am troubled, I am bowed down greatly, I go mourning all the day long." I sat much alone with a poor wounded child in my lap, which moaned night and day, having nothing to revive the body or cheer the spirits of her, but instead of that sometimes one Indian would come and tell me one hour that, "Your master will knock your child in the head." And then a second, and then a third, "Your master will quickly knock your child in the head."

This was the comfort I had from them. "Miserable comforters are ye all," as he said.[10] Thus nine days I sat upon my knees with my babe in my lap till my flesh was raw again; my child being even ready to depart this sorrowful world, they bade me carry it out to another wigwam (I suppose because they would not be troubled with such spectacles), whither I went with a heavy heart, and down I sat with the picture of death in my lap. About two hours in the night my sweet babe like a lamb departed this life on Feb. 18, 1675, it being about six years and five months old. It was nine days from the first wounding in this miserable condition without any refreshing of one nature or other except a little cold water. I cannot but take notice how at another time I could not bear to be in the room where any dead person was, but now the case is changed; I must and could lie down by my dead babe side by side all the night after. I have thought since of the wonderful goodness of God to me in preserving me in the use of my reason and senses in that distressed time, that I did not use wicked and violent means to end my own miserable life.

In the morning, when they understood that my child was dead, they sent for me home to my master's wigwam. (By my master in this writing must be understood Quanopin, who was a sagamore and married [to] King Philip's wife's sister,[11] not that he first took me, but I was sold to him by another Narragansett Indian, who took me when first I came out of the garrison.) I went to take up my dead child in my arms to carry it with me, but they bid me let it alone. There was no resisting, but go I must and leave it. When I had been at my master's wigwam, I took the first opportunity I could get to go look after my dead child. When I came, I asked them what they had done with it. Then they told me it was upon the hill. Then they went and showed me where it was, where I saw the ground was newly digged, and there they told me they had buried it. There I left that child in the wilderness and must commit it and myself also in this wilderness condition to Him who is above all.

---

[10] **he said:** Job, in Job 16:2.

[11] **By . . . sister:** Quanopin or Quinnapin was married to Weetamoo, Philip's sister-in-law by a previous marriage. Weetamoo was herself the respected leader of the Pocassets. *Sagamore* is the Algonquian term for a subordinate chief.

God having taken away this dear child, I went to see my daughter Mary, who was at this same Indian town at a wigwam not very far off, though we had little liberty or opportunity to see one another. She was about ten years old and taken from the door at first by a praying Indian and afterward sold for a gun. When I came in sight, she would fall a-weeping, at which they were provoked and would not let me come near her, but bade me be gone, which was a heart-cutting word to me. I had one child dead, another in the wilderness I knew not where; the third they would not let me come near to. "Me," as he said, "have ye bereaved of my children, Joseph is not, and Simeon is not, and ye will take Benjamin also, all these things are against me."[12] I could not sit still in this condition, but kept walking from one place to another. And as I was going along, my heart was even overwhelmed with the thoughts of my condition and that I should have children and a nation which I knew not ruled over them. Whereupon I earnestly entreated the Lord that He would consider my low estate and show me a token for good, and if it were His blessed will, some sign and hope of some relief.

And indeed quickly the Lord answered in some measure my poor prayers; for, as I was going up and down mourning and lamenting my condition, my son [Joseph] came to me and asked me how I did. I had not seen him before since the destruction of the town, and I knew not where he was till I was informed by himself that he was amongst a smaller parcel of Indians whose place was about six miles off. With tears in his eyes he asked me whether his sister Sarah was dead and told me he had seen his sister Mary and prayed me that I would not be troubled in reference to himself. The occasion of his coming to see me at this time was this: there was, as I said, about six miles from us a small plantation of Indians, where it seems he had been during his captivity, and at this time there were some forces of the Indians gathered out of our company and some also from them (among whom was my son's master) to go to assault and burn Medfield.[13] In this time of the absence of his master his dame brought him to see me. I took this to be some gracious answer to my earnest and unfeigned desire.

The next day, *viz.* to this, the Indians returned from Medfield (all the company, for those that belonged to the other small company came through the town that now we were at). But before they came to us, oh, the outrageous roaring and whooping that there was! They began their din about a mile before they came to us. By their noise and whooping they signified how many they had destroyed, which was at that time twenty-three. Those that were with us at home were gathered together as soon as they heard the whooping, and every time that the other went over their number, these at home gave [such] a shout that the very earth rung again. And thus they continued till those that had been upon the expedition were come up to the sagamore's wigwam. And then, oh, the hideous insulting and triumphing that there was over some Englishmen's scalps that they had taken (as their manner is) and brought with them!

I cannot but take notice of the wonderful mercy of God to me in those afflictions in sending me a Bible. One of the Indians that came from Medfield fight [who]

---

[12] **"Me . . . me.":** Genesis 42:36.   [13] **Medfield:** Attacked on February 21, 1676.

had brought some plunder came to me and asked me if I would have a Bible; he had got one in his basket. I was glad of it and asked him whether he thought the Indians would let me read. He answered, "Yes." So I took the Bible, and in that melancholy time it came into my mind to read first the 28 chapter of Deut., which I did, and when I had read it, my dark heart wrought on this manner, that there was no mercy for me, that the blessings were gone and the curses come in their room, and that I had lost my opportunity. But the Lord helped me still to go on reading till I came to chapter 30, the seven first verses, where I found there was mercy promised again if we would return to him by repentance, and, though we were scattered from one end of the earth to the other, yet the Lord would gather us together and turn all those curses upon our enemies. I do not desire to live to forget this scripture and what comfort it was to me.

Now the Indians began to talk of removing from this place, some one way and some another. There were now besides myself nine English captives in this place, all of them children except one woman. I got an opportunity to go and take my leave of them, they being to go one way and I another; I asked them whether they were earnest with God for deliverance. They told me they did as they were able, and it was some comfort to me that the Lord stirred up children to look to Him. The woman, *viz.* Goodwife[14] Joslin, told me she should never see me again and that she could find in her heart to run away; I wished her not to run away by any means, for we were near thirty miles from any English town and she very big with child and had but one week to reckon and another child in her arms, two years old, and bad rivers there were to go over, and we were feeble with our poor and coarse entertainment. I had my Bible with me; I pulled it out and asked her whether she would read. We opened the Bible and lighted on Psalm 27, in which psalm we especially took notice of that *ver. ult.,* "Wait on the Lord, be of good courage, and He shall strengthen thine heart, wait I say on the Lord."

THE FOURTH REMOVE[15]

And now I must part with that little company I had. Here I parted from my daughter Mary (whom I never saw again till I saw her in Dorchester, returned from captivity) and from four little cousins and neighbors, some of which I never saw afterward. The Lord only knows the end of them. Amongst them also was that poor woman before mentioned, who came to a sad end, as some of the company told me in my travel. She, having much grief upon her spirit about her miserable condition, being so near her time, she would be often asking the Indians to let her go home; they, not being willing to that and yet vexed with her importunity, gathered a great company together about her and stripped her naked and set her in the midst of them. And when they had sung and danced about her (in their hellish manner) as long as they pleased, they knocked her on [the] head and the child in her arms with her. When they had done that, they made a fire and put them both into it and told the other

---

[14] **Goodwife:** Analogous to the modern *Mrs.*

[15] **Fourth Remove:** To Petersham, Mass., where Rowlandson stayed from February 28 to March 3.

children that were with them that if they attempted to go home they would serve them in like manner. The children said she did not shed one tear, but prayed all the while. But to return to my own journey, we traveled about half a day or little more and came to a desolate place in the wilderness where there were no wigwams or inhabitants before; we came about the middle of the afternoon to this place, cold and wet, and snowy, and hungry, and weary, and no refreshing for man but the cold ground to sit on and our poor Indian cheer.

Heartaching thoughts here I had about my poor children, who were scattered up and down among the wild beasts of the forest. My head was light and dizzy (either through hunger or hard lodging or trouble or all together), my knees feeble, my body raw by sitting double night and day, that I cannot express to man the affliction that lay upon my spirit, but the Lord helped me at that time to express it to Himself. I opened my Bible to read, and the Lord brought that precious scripture to me, Jer. 31:16, "Thus saith the Lord, 'Refrain thy voice from weeping and thine eyes from tears, for thy work shall be rewarded, and they shall come again from the land of the enemy.'" This was a sweet cordial to me when I was ready to faint; many and many a time have I sat down and wept sweetly over this scripture. At this place we continued about four days.

The Fifth Remove[16]

The occasion (as I thought) of their moving at this time was the English army, it being near and following them. For they went as if they had gone for their lives for some considerable way, and then they made a stop and chose some of their stoutest men and sent them back to hold the English army in play whilst the rest escaped. And then, like Jehu,[17] they marched on furiously with their old and with their young; some carried their old decrepit mothers; some carried one and some another. Four of them carried a great Indian upon a bier, but, going through a thick wood with him, they were hindered and could make no haste; whereupon they took him upon their backs and carried him, one at a time, till they came to Bacquaug River. Upon a Friday a little after noon we came to this river. When all the company was come up and were gathered together, I thought to count the number of them, but they were so many and, being somewhat in motion, it was beyond my skill. In this travel, because of my wound, I was somewhat favored in my load; I carried only my knitting work and two quarts of parched meal. Being very faint, I asked my mistress to give me one spoonful of the meal, but she would not give me a taste. They quickly fell to cutting dry trees to make rafts to carry them over the river, and soon my turn came to go over. By the advantage of some brush which they had laid upon the raft to sit upon, I did not wet my foot (when many of themselves at the other end were mid-leg deep) which cannot be but acknowledged as a favor of God to my weakened body, it being a very cold time. I was not before acquainted with such kind of doings or dangers. "When thou passeth through the waters, I will be with thee, and through the rivers they shall not overflow thee," Isai. 43:2. A certain number of us got over the river that

---

[16] **Fifth Remove:** To Orange, Massachusetts, March 3–5.   [17] **like Jehu:** Jehu drove "furiously" in II Kings 9:20.

night, but it was the night after the Sabbath before all the company was got over. On the Saturday they boiled an old horse's leg which they had got, and so we drank of the broth as soon as they thought it was ready, and when it was almost all gone, they filled it up again.

The first week of my being among them I hardly ate anything; the second week, I found my stomach grow very faint for want of something; and yet it was very hard to get down their filthy trash. But the third week, though I could think how formerly my stomach would turn against this or that and I could starve and die before I could eat such things, yet they were sweet and savory to my taste. I was at this time knitting a pair of white cotton stockings for my mistress and had not yet wrought upon a Sabbath day. When the Sabbath came, they bade me go to work; I told them it was the Sabbath day and desired them to let me rest and told them I would do as much more tomorrow, to which they answered me they would break my face. And here I cannot but take notice of the strange providence of God in preserving the heathen. They were many hundreds, old and young, some sick and some lame, many had papooses at their backs. The greatest number at this time with us were squaws, and they traveled with all they had, bag and baggage, and yet they got over this river aforesaid. And on Monday they set their wigwams on fire, and away they went. On that very day came the English army after them to this river and saw the smoke of their wigwams, and yet this river put a stop to them. God did not give them courage or activity to go over after us; we were not ready for so great a mercy as victory and deliverance. If we had been, God would have found out a way for the English to have passed this river, as well as for the Indians with their squaws and children and all their luggage. "Oh that my people had hearkened to me, and Israel had walked in my ways, I should soon have subdued their enemies and turned my hand against their adversaries," Psal. 81:13, 14.

THE SIXTH REMOVE[18]

On Monday (as I said) they set their wigwams on fire and went away. It was a cold morning, and before us there was a great brook with ice on it; some waded through it up to the knees and higher, but others went till they came to a beaver dam, and I amongst them, where through the good providence of God I did not wet my foot. I went along that day mourning and lamenting, leaving farther my own country and traveling into the vast and howling wilderness, and I understood something of Lot's wife's temptation when she looked back.[19] We came that day to a great swamp by the side of which we took up our lodging that night. When I came to the brow of the hill that looked toward the swamp, I thought we had been come to a great Indian town (though there were none but our own company). The Indians were as thick as the trees: it seemed as if there had been a thousand hatchets going at once. If one looked

---

[18] **Sixth Remove:** To Northfield, Massachusetts.

[19] **Lot's . . . back:** Lot's wife was transformed into a pillar of salt when she looked back wistfully at her home as she left the wicked city of Sodom in Genesis 19:26.

before one, there was nothing but Indians, and behind one nothing but Indians, and so on either hand, I myself in the midst, and no Christian soul near me, and yet how hath the Lord preserved me in safety. Oh, the experience that I have had of the goodness of God to me and mine!

THE SEVENTH REMOVE[20]

After a restless and hungry night there, we had a wearisome time of it the next day. The swamp by which we lay was, as it were, a deep dungeon and an exceeding high and steep hill before it. Before I got to the top of the hill, I thought my heart and legs and all would have broken and failed me. . . . What through faintness and soreness of body, it was a grievous day of travel to me. As we went along, I saw a place where English cattle had been. That was comfort to me, such as it was. Quickly after that we came to an English path, which so took with me that I thought I could have freely laid down and died. That day, a little after noon, we came to Squakeag, where the Indians quickly spread themselves over the deserted English fields, gleaning what they could find; some picked up ears of wheat that were crickled[21] down; some found ears of Indian corn; some found groundnuts, and others sheaves of wheat that were frozen together in the shock, and went to threshing of them out. Myself got two ears of Indian corn, and whilst I did but turn my back, one of them was stolen from me, which much troubled me. There came an Indian to them at that time with a basket of horse liver. I asked him to give me a piece. "What," says he, "can you eat horse liver?" I told him I would try if he would give a piece, which he did, and I laid it on the coals to roast, but before it was half ready they got half of it away from me, so that I was fain to take the rest and eat it as it was with the blood about my mouth, and yet a savory bit it was to me: "For to the hungry soul every bitter thing is sweet."[22] A solemn sight methought it was to see fields of wheat and Indian corn forsaken and spoiled and the remainders of them to be food for our merciless enemies. That night we had a mess of wheat for our supper.

THE EIGHTH REMOVE[23]

On the morrow morning we must go over the river, i.e. Connecticut, to meet with King Philip. Two canoesful they had carried over; the next turn I myself was to go, but as my foot was upon the canoe to step in, there was a sudden outcry among them, and I must step back. And instead of going over the river, I must go four or five miles up the river farther northward. Some of the Indians ran one way and some another. The cause of this rout was, as I thought, their espying some English scouts who were thereabout. In this travel up the river about noon the company made a stop and sat down, some to eat and others to rest them. As I sat amongst them musing of things past, my son, Joseph, unexpectedly came to me. We asked of each

---

[20] **Seventh Remove:** Near Northfield.　　[21] **crickled:** Crushed.　　[22] **"For . . . sweet.":** Proverbs 27:7.
[23] **Eighth Remove:** To South Vernon, Vt.

other's welfare, bemoaning our doleful condition and the change that had come upon us. We had husband and father, and children, and sisters, and friends, and relations, and house, and home, and many comforts of this life, but now we may say as Job, "Naked came I out of my mother's womb, and naked shall I return. The Lord gave, and the Lord hath taken away, blessed be the name of the Lord."[24] I asked him whether he would read; he told me he earnestly desired it. I gave him my Bible, and he lighted upon that comfortable scripture, Psal. 118:17, 18, "I shall not die but live and declare the works of the Lord: the Lord hath chastened me sore, yet he hath not given me over to death." "Look here, Mother," says he, "did you read this?" And here I may take occasion to mention one principal ground of my setting forth these lines: even as the psalmist says, to declare the works of the Lord and His wonderful power in carrying us along, preserving us in the wilderness while under the enemy's hand and returning of us in safety again, and His goodness in bringing to my hand so many comfortable and suitable scriptures in my distress.

But to return, we traveled on till night, and in the morning we must go over the river to Philip's crew. When I was in the canoe, I could not but be amazed at the numerous crew of pagans that were on the bank on the other side. When I came ashore, they gathered all about me, I sitting alone in the midst. I observed they asked one another questions and laughed and rejoiced over their gains and victories. Then my heart began to fail and I fell a-weeping, which was the first time to my remembrance that I wept before them. Although I had met with so much affliction and my heart was many times ready to break, yet could I not shed one tear in their sight, but rather had been all this while in a maze and like one astonished. But now I may say as Psal. 137:1, "By the rivers of Babylon there we sat down; yea, we wept when we remembered Zion." There one of them asked me why I wept; I could hardly tell what to say, yet I answered they would kill me. "No," said he, "none will hurt you." Then came one of them and gave me two spoonfuls of meal to comfort me, and another gave me half a pint of peas, which was more worth than many bushels at another time. Then I went to see King Philip. He bade me come in and sit down and asked me whether I would smoke it (a usual compliment nowadays among saints and sinners), but this no way suited me. For though I had formerly used tobacco, yet I had left it ever since I was first taken. It seems to be a bait the devil lays to make men lose their precious time. I remember with shame how formerly when I had taken two or three pipes I was presently ready for another, such a bewitching thing it is. But I thank God He has now given me power over it; surely there are many who may be better employed than to lie sucking a stinking tobacco pipe.

Now the Indians gather their forces to go against Northampton. Overnight one went about yelling and hooting to give notice of the design, whereupon they fell to boiling of groundnuts and parching of corn (as many as had it) for their provision, and in the morning away they went. During my abode in this place Philip spoke to me to make a shirt for his boy, which I did, for which he gave me a shilling. I offered the money to my master, but he bade me keep it, and with it I bought a piece of horseflesh. Afterwards he asked me to make a cap for his boy, for which he invited

---

[24] "Naked . . . Lord": Job 1:21.

me to dinner. I went, and he gave me a pancake about as big as two fingers; it was made of parched wheat, beaten and fried in bear's grease, but I thought I never tasted pleasanter meat in my life. There was a squaw who spoke to me to make a shirt for her *sannup*[25] for which she gave me a piece of bear. Another asked me to knit a pair of stockings, for which she gave me a quart of peas. I boiled my peas and bear together and invited my master and mistress to dinner, but the proud gossip,[26] because I served them both in one dish, would eat nothing except one bit that he gave her upon the point of his knife.

Hearing that my son was come to this place, I went to see him and found him lying flat upon the ground. I asked him how he could sleep so. He answered me that he was not asleep but at prayer and lay so that they might not observe what he was doing. I pray God he may remember these things now he is returned in safety. At this place (the sun now getting higher), what with the beams and heat of the sun and the smoke of the wigwams, I thought I should have been blind. I could scarce discern one wigwam from another. There was here one Mary Thurston of Medfield, who, seeing how it was with me, lent a hat to wear; but as soon as I was gone, the squaw who owned that Mary Thurston came running after me and got it away again. Here was the squaw that gave me one spoonful of meal. I put it in my pocket to keep it safe, yet notwithstanding, somebody stole it, but put five Indian corns in the room of it,[27] which corns were the greatest provision I had in my travel for one day.

The Indians, returning from Northampton, brought with them some horses, and sheep, and other things which they had taken. I desired them that they would carry me to Albany upon one of those horses and sell me for powder, for so they had sometimes discoursed. I was utterly hopeless of getting home on foot the way that I came. I could hardly bear to think of the many weary steps I had taken to come to this place.

THE NINTH REMOVE[28]

But instead of going either to Albany or homeward, we must go five miles up the river and then go over it. Here we abode awhile. Here lived a sorry Indian who spoke to me to make him a shirt. When I had done it, he would pay me nothing. But he living by the riverside where I often went to fetch water, I would often be putting of him in mind and calling for my pay; at last he told me, if I would make another shirt for a papoose not yet born, he would give me a knife, which he did when I had done it. I carried the knife in, and my master asked me to give it him, and I was not a little glad that I had anything that they would accept of and be pleased with. When we were at this place, my master's maid came home; she had been gone three weeks into the Narragansett country to fetch corn where they had stored up some in the ground. She brought home about a peck and [a] half of corn. This was about the time that their great captain, Naananto, was killed in the Narragansett country. My

---

[25] *sannup*: Husband. [26] **gossip**: Wife. Weetamoo may be observing a menstrual taboo or other sort of taboo pertaining to wartime here. [27] **in the room of it**: In place of it. [28] **Ninth Remove**: To a camp near Keene, New Hampshire.

son being now about a mile from me, I asked liberty to go and see him; they bade me go, and away I went. But quickly [I] lost myself, traveling over hills and through swamps, and could not find the way to him. And I cannot but admire at the wonderful power and goodness of God to me in that though I was gone from home and met with all sorts of Indians, and those I had no knowledge of, and there being no Christian soul near me, yet not one of them offered the least imaginable miscarriage to me.

I turned homeward again and met with my master; he showed me the way to my son. When I came to him, I found him not well, and withall he had a boil on his side which much troubled him. We bemoaned one another awhile, as the Lord helped us, and then I returned again. When I was returned, I found myself as unsatisfied as I was before. I went up and down mourning and lamenting, and my spirit was ready to sink with the thoughts of my poor children. My son was ill, and I could not but think of his mournful looks, and no Christian friend was near him to do any office of love for him either for soul or body. And my poor girl, I know not where she was nor whether she was sick or well, or alive or dead. I repaired under these thoughts to my Bible (my great comfort in that time) and that scripture came to my hand, "Cast thy burden upon the Lord, and He shall sustain thee," Psal. 55:22.

But I was fain to go and look after something to satisfy my hunger, and going among the wigwams, I went into one and there found a squaw who showed herself very kind to me and gave me a piece of bear. I put it into my pocket and came home, but could not find an opportunity to broil it for fear they would get it from me, and there it lay all that day and night in my stinking pocket. In the morning I went to the same squaw, who had a kettle of groundnuts boiling; I asked her to let me boil my piece of bear in her kettle, which she did and gave me some groundnuts to eat with it, and I cannot but think how pleasant it was to me. I have sometime seen bear baked very handsomely among the English, and some like it, but the thoughts that it was bear made me tremble, but now that was savory to me that one would think was enough to turn the stomach of a brute creature.

One bitter cold day I could find no room to sit down before the fire. I went out and could not tell what to do, but I went into another wigwam where they were also sitting around the fire, but the squaw laid a skin for me, bid me sit down, gave me some groundnuts, bade me come again, and told me they would buy me if they were able, and yet these were strangers to me that I never saw before.

THE TENTH REMOVE

That day a small part of the company removed about three-quarters of a mile, intending further the next day. When they came to the place where they intended to lodge and had pitched their wigwams, being hungry, I went again back to the place we were before at to get something to eat, being encouraged by the squaw's kindness who bade me come again when I was there. There came an Indian to look after me, who, when he had found me, kicked me all along. I went home and found venison roasting that night, but they would not give me one bit of it. Sometimes I met with favor and sometimes with nothing but frowns.

THE ELEVENTH REMOVE[29]

The next day in the morning they took their travel, intending a day's journey up the river. I took my load at my back, and quickly we came to wade over the river and passed over tiresome and wearisome hills. One hill was so steep that I was fain to creep up upon my knees and to hold by the twigs and bushes to keep myself from falling backward. My head also was so light that I usually reeled as I went, but I hope all these wearisome steps that I have taken are but a forewarning of me to the heavenly rest. "I know, O Lord, that Thy judgments are right, and that Thou in faithfulness hast afflicted me," Psal. 119:71 [actually 75].

THE TWELFTH REMOVE

It was upon a Sabbath-day morning that they prepared for their travel. This morning I asked my master whether he would sell me to my husband; he answered me *nux*,[30] which did much rejoice my spirit. My mistress, before we went, was gone to the burial of a papoose, and, returning, she found me sitting and reading in my Bible. She snatched it hastily out of my hand and threw it out of doors; I ran out and catched it up and put it into my pocket and never let her see it afterward. Then they packed up their things to be gone and gave me my load. I complained it was too heavy, whereupon she gave me a slap in the face and bade me go. I lifted up my heart to God, hoping the redemption was not far off, and the rather because their insolency grew worse and worse.

But the thoughts of my going homeward (for so we bent our course) much cheered my spirit and made my burden seem light and almost nothing at all. But (to my amazement and great perplexity) the scale was soon turned, for when we had gone a little way, on a sudden my mistress gives out. She would go no further but turn back again and said I must go back again with her. And she called her *sannup* and would have had him gone back also, but he would not, but said he would go on and come to us again in three days. My spirit was upon this, I confess, very impatient and almost outrageous. I thought I could as well have died as went back; I cannot declare the trouble that I was in about it, but yet back again I must go. As soon as I had an opportunity, I took my Bible to read, and that quieting scripture came to my hand, Psal. 46:10, "Be still and know that I am God," which stilled my spirit for the present. But a sore time of trial, I concluded, I had to go through, my master being gone, who seemed to me the best friend that I had of an Indian both in cold and hunger, and quickly so it proved. Down I sat with my heart as full as it could hold, and yet so hungry that I could not sit neither. But, going out to see what I could find and walking among the trees, I found six acorns and two chestnuts, which were some refreshment to me. Towards night I gathered me some sticks for my own comfort that I might not lie a-cold, but when we came to lie down they bade me go out and lie somewhere else, for they had company (they said) come in more than their own. I told them I could not tell where to go; they bade me go look. I told them if I went to another wigwam they would be angry and send me home again. Then one of the company drew his sword and told me he would run me through if I did not go presently. Then was I fain to stoop to this rude fellow and to go out in the night, I knew not whither. Mine eyes have seen that fellow afterwards, walking up and down Boston under the appearance of a friend-Indian, and several others of the like cut.

I went to one wigwam, and they told me they had no room. Then I went to another, and they said the same; at last an old Indian bade me come to him, and his squaw gave me some groundnuts; she gave me also something to lay under my head, and a good fire we had. And through the good providence of God I had a comfortable lodging that night. In the morning another Indian bade me come at night, and he would give me six groundnuts, which I did. We were at this place and time about two miles from Connecticut River. We went in the morning to gather groundnuts, to the river, and went back again that night. I went with a good load at my back (for they, when they went though but a little way, would carry all their trumpery with them); I told them the skin was off my back, but I had no other comforting answer from them than this, that it would be no matter if my head were off too.

THE THIRTEENTH REMOVE[31]

Instead of going toward the Bay, which was that I desired, I must go with them five or six miles down the river into a mighty thicket of brush, where we abode almost a fortnight. Here one asked me to make a shirt for her papoose, for which she gave me a mess of broth which was thickened with meal made of the bark of a tree, and to make it the better she had put into it about a handful of peas and a few roasted groundnuts. I had not seen my son a pretty while, and here was an Indian of whom I made inquiry after him and asked him when he saw him. He answered me that such a time his master roasted him and that himself did eat a piece of him as big as his two fingers and that he was very good meat. But the Lord upheld my spirit under this discouragement, and I considered their horrible addictedness to lying and that there is not one of them that makes the least conscience of speaking of truth. In this place on a cold night as I lay by the fire, I removed a stick that kept the heat from me; a squaw moved it down again, at which I looked up, and she threw a handful of ashes in mine eyes. I thought I should have been quite blinded and have never seen more, but lying down, the water run out of my eyes and carried the dirt with it, that by the morning I recovered my sight again. Yet upon this and the like occasions I hope it is not too much to say with Job, "Have pity upon me, have pity upon me, oh, ye my friends, for the hand of the Lord has touched me."[32]

And here I cannot but remember how many times sitting in their wigwams and musing on things past I should suddenly leap up and run out as if I had been at home, forgetting where I was and what my condition was. But when I was without and saw nothing but wilderness and woods and a company of barbarous heathens, my mind quickly returned to me, which made me think of that spoken concerning

---

[31]**Thirteenth Remove:** To Hinsdale, New Hampshire.   [32]"Have . . . me.": Job 19:21.

Samson, who said, "I will go out and shake myself as at other times, but he wist not that the Lord was departed from him."[33]

About this time I began to think that all my hopes of restoration would come to nothing. I thought of the English army and hoped for their coming and being taken by them, but that failed. I hoped to be carried to Albany as the Indians had discoursed before, but that failed also. I thought of being sold to my husband, as my master spake, but instead of that my master himself was gone and I left behind, so that my spirit was now quite ready to sink. I asked them to let me go out and pick up some sticks, that I might get alone and pour out my heart unto the Lord. Then also I took my Bible to read, but I found no comfort here neither, which many times I was wont to find. So easy a thing it is with God to dry up the streams of scripture-comfort from us. Yet I can say that in all my sorrows and afflictions God did not leave me to have my impatience work towards Himself, as if His ways were unrighteous. But I knew that He laid upon me less than I deserved. Afterward, before this doleful time ended with me, I was turning the leaves of my Bible and the Lord brought to me some scriptures, which did a little revive me, as that Isai. 55:8, "'For my thoughts are not your thoughts, neither are your ways my ways,' saith the Lord." And also that Psal. 37:5, "Commit thy way unto the Lord, trust also in Him, and He shall bring it to pass."

About this time they came yelping from Hadley, where they had killed three Englishmen and brought one captive with them, *viz.* Thomas Read. They all gathered about the poor man, asking him many questions. I desired also to go and see him, and when I came he was crying bitterly, supposing they would quickly kill him. Whereupon I asked one of them whether they intended to kill him; he answered me they would not. He being a little cheered with that, I asked him about the welfare of my husband; he told me he saw him such a time in the Bay, and he was well but very melancholy. By which I certainly understood (though I suspected it before) that whatsoever the Indians told me respecting him was vanity and lies. Some of them told me he was dead, and they had killed him. Some said he was married again, and that the governor wished him to marry and told him he should have his choice, and that all persuaded [him] I was dead. So like were these barbarous creatures to him who was a liar from the beginning.[34]

As I was sitting once in the wigwam here, Philip's maid came in with the child in her arms and asked me to give her a piece of my apron to make a flap for it. I told her I would not. Then my mistress bade me give it, but still I said no. The maid told me if I would not give her a piece she would tear a piece off it. I told her I would tear her coat then; with that my mistress rises up and takes up a stick big enough to have killed me and struck me with it, but I stepped out, and she struck the stick into the mat of the wigwam. But while she was pulling of it out, I ran to the maid and gave her all my apron, and so that storm went over.

Hearing that my son was come to this place, I went to see him and told him his father was well but very melancholy. He told me he was as much grieved for his

[33] "I . . . him.": Judges 16:20.   [34] him . . . beginning: Satan.

father as for himself; I wondered at his speech, for I thought I had enough upon my spirit in reference to myself to make me mindless of my husband and everyone else, they being safe among their friends. He told me also that a while before his master, together with other Indians, were going to the French for powder, but by the way the Mohawks met with them and killed four of their company, which made the rest turn back again, for which I desire that myself and he may bless the Lord. For it might have been worse with him had he been sold to the French than it proved to be in remaining with the Indians.

I went to see an English youth in this place, one John Gilbert of Springfield. I found him lying without doors upon the ground; I asked him how he did. He told me he was very sick of a flux with eating so much blood. They had turned him out of the wigwam and with him an Indian papoose almost dead (whose parents had been killed) in a bitter cold day without fire or clothes. The young man himself had nothing on but his shirt and waistcoat. This sight was enough to melt a heart of flint. There they lay quivering in the cold, the youth [curled] round like a dog, the papoose stretched out with his eyes, nose, and mouth full of dirt and yet alive and groaning. I advised John to go and get to some fire; he told me he could not stand, but I persuaded him still, lest he should lie there and die. And with much ado I got him to a fire and went myself home. As soon as I was got home, his master's daughter came after me to know what I had done with the Englishman; I told her I had got him to a fire in such a place. Now had I need to pray Paul's prayer, 2 Thess. 3:2, "That we may be delivered from unreasonable and wicked men." For her satisfaction I went along with her and brought her to him, but before I got home again, it was noised about that I was running away and getting the English youth along with me, that as soon as I came in they began to rant and domineer, asking me where I had been, and what I had been doing, and saying they would knock him on the head. I told them I had been seeing the English youth and that I would not run away. They told me I lied, and taking up a hatchet, they came to me and said they would knock me down if I stirred out again and so confined me to the wigwam. Now may I say with David, 2 Sam. 24:14, "I am in a great strait." If I keep in, I must die with hunger, and if I go out, I must be knocked in [the] head. This distressed condition held that day and half the next. And then the Lord remembered me, whose mercies are great.

Then came an Indian to me with a pair of stockings that were too big for him, and he would have me ravel them out and knit them fit for him. I showed myself willing and bid him ask my mistress if I might go along with him a little way; she said yes, I might, but I was not a little refreshed with that news that I had my liberty again. Then I went along with him, and he gave me some roasted groundnuts, which did again revive my feeble stomach.

Being got out of her sight, I had time and liberty again to look into my Bible, which was my guide by day and my pillow by night. Now that comfortable scripture presented itself to me, Isa. 54:7, "For a small moment have I forsaken thee, but with great mercies will I gather thee." Thus the Lord carried me along from one time to another and made good to me this precious promise and many others. Then my son came to see me, and I asked his master to let him stay awhile with me that I might comb his head and look over him, for he was almost overcome with lice. He told me when I had done that he was very hungry, but I had nothing to relieve him, but bid him go into the wigwams as he went along and see if he could get anything among them, which he did. And it seems [he] tarried a little too long, for his master was angry with him and beat him, and then sold him. Then he came running to tell me he had a new master, and that he had given him some groundnuts already. Then I went along with him to his new master, who told me he loved him and he should not want. So his master carried him away, and I never saw him afterward till I saw him at Pascataqua in Portsmouth.

That night they bade me go out of the wigwam again. My mistress's papoose was sick, and it died that night, and there was one benefit in it—that there was more room. I went to a wigwam, and they bade me come in and gave me a skin to lie upon and a mess of venison and groundnuts, which was a choice dish among them. On the morrow they buried the papoose, and afterward, both morning and evening, there came a company to mourn and howl with her, though I confess I could not much condole with them. Many sorrowful days I had in this place, often getting alone; "like a crane, or a swallow, so did I chatter; I did mourn as a dove, mine eyes fail with looking upward. Oh, Lord, I am oppressed; undertake for me," Isai. 38:14. I could tell the Lord as Hezekiah, ver. 3, "Remember now, O Lord, I beseech Thee, how I have walked before Thee in truth."[35]

Now had I time to examine all my ways. My conscience did not accuse me of unrighteousness toward one or other, yet I saw how in my walk with God I had been a careless creature. As David said, "Against Thee, Thee only, have I sinned," and I might say with the poor publican, "God be merciful unto me a sinner."[36] On the Sabbath days I could look upon the sun and think how people were going to the house of God to have their souls refreshed and then home and their bodies also, but I was destitute of both and might say as the poor prodigal, "He would fain have filled his belly with the husks that the swine did eat, and no man gave unto him," Luke 15:16. For I must say with him, "Father I have sinned against heaven and in thy sight," ver. 21. I remembered how on the night before and after the Sabbath, when my family was about me and relations and neighbors with us, we could pray and sing, and then refresh our bodies with the good creatures of God, and then have a comfortable bed to lie down on. But instead of all this I had only a little swill for the body and then like a swine must lie down on the ground. I cannot express to man the sorrow that lay upon my spirit; the Lord knows it. Yet that comfortable scripture would often come to my mind, "For a small moment have I forsaken thee, but with great mercies will I gather thee."[37]

---

[35] "Remember . . . truth.": Isaiah 38:3.

[36] "Against . . . sinned."; "God . . . sinner.": Psalm 51:4; Luke 18:13.

[37] "For . . . thee": Isaiah 57:7.

THE FOURTEENTH REMOVE[38]

Now must we pack up and be gone from this thicket, bending our course toward the Bay towns, I have nothing to eat by the way this day but a few crumbs of cake that an Indian gave my girl the same day we were taken. She gave it me, and I put it in my pocket; there it lay till it was so moldy (for want of good baking) that one could not tell what it was made of; it fell all to crumbs and grew so dry and hard that it was like little flints, and this refreshed me many times when I was ready to faint. It was in my thoughts when I put it into my mouth that if ever I returned I would tell the world what a blessing the Lord gave to such mean food. As we went along, they killed a deer with a young one in her; they gave me a piece of the fawn, and it was so young and tender that one might eat the bones as well as the flesh, and yet I thought it very good. When night came on, we sat down. It rained, but they quickly got up a bark wigwam, where I lay dry that night. I looked out in the morning, and many of them had laid in the rain all night, [which] I saw by their reeking. Thus the Lord dealt mercifully with me many times, and I fared better than many of them. In the morning they took the blood of the deer and put it into the paunch and so boiled it; I could eat nothing of that, though they ate it sweetly. And yet they were so nice[39] in other things that when I had fetched water and had put the dish I dipped the water with into the kettle of water which I brought, they would say they would knock me down, for they said it was a sluttish trick.

THE FIFTEENTH REMOVE

We went on our travel. I having got one handful of groundnuts for my support that day, they gave me my load, and I went on cheerfully (with the thoughts of going homeward), having my burden more on my back than my spirit. We came to Baquaug River again that day, near which we abode a few days. Sometimes one of them would give me a pipe, another a little tobacco, another a little salt, which I would change for a little victuals. I cannot but think what a wolfish appetite persons have in a starving condition, for many times when they gave me that which was hot, I was so greedy that I should burn my mouth that it would trouble me hours after, and yet I should quickly do the same again. And after I was thoroughly hungry, I was never again satisfied. For though sometimes it fell out that I got enough and did eat till I could eat no more, yet I was as unsatisfied as I was when I began. And now could I see that scripture verified (there being many scriptures which we do not take notice of or understand till we are afflicted), Mic. 6:14, "Thou shalt eat and not be satisfied." Now might I see more than ever before the miseries that sin hath brought upon us. Many times I should be ready to run out against the heathen, but the scripture would quiet me again, Amos 3:6, "Shall there be evil in the city, and the Lord

---

[38] **Fourteenth Remove:** Removes fourteen through nineteen retrace the previous route, a total distance of about one hundred and fifty miles.

[39] **nice:** Fussy.

hath not done it?" The Lord help me to make a right improvement of His word and that I might learn that great lesson, Mic. 6:8, 9, "He hath showed thee (Oh Man) what is good, and what doth the Lord require of thee, but to do justly and love mercy and walk humbly with thy God? Hear ye the rod and who hath appointed it."

THE SIXTEENTH REMOVE

We began this remove with wading over Baquaug River; the water was up to the knees and the stream very swift and so cold that I thought it would have cut me in sunder. I was so weak and feeble that I reeled as I went along and thought there I must end my days at last after my bearing and getting through so many difficulties. The Indians stood laughing to see me staggering along, but in my distress the Lord gave me experience of the truth and goodness of that promise, Isai. 43:2, "When thou passest through the waters, I will be with thee, and through the rivers, they shall not overflow thee." Then I sat down to put on my stockings and shoes with the tears running down mine eyes and many sorrowful thoughts in my heart, but I got up to go along with them. Quickly there came up to us an Indian who informed them that I must go to Wachuset to my master, for there was a letter come from the council to the sagamores about redeeming the captives and that there would be another in fourteen days and that I must be there ready. My heart was so heavy before that I could scarce speak or go in the path and yet now so light that I could run. My strength seemed to come again and recruit my feeble knees and aching heart, yet it pleased them to go but one mile that night, and there we stayed two days. In that time came a company of Indians to us, near thirty, all on horseback. My heart skipped within me, thinking they had been Englishmen at the first sight of them, for they were dressed in English apparel, with hats, white neckcloths, and sashes about their waists, and ribbons upon their shoulders, but when they came near there was a vast difference between the lovely faces of Christians and the foul looks of those heathens which much dampened my spirit again.

THE SEVENTEENTH REMOVE

A comfortable remove it was to me because of my hopes. They gave me a pack, and along we went cheerfully, but quickly my will proved more than my strength. Having little or no refreshing, my strength failed me, and my spirits were almost quite gone. Now may I say with David, Psal. 119:22, 23, 24, "I am poor and needy, and my heart is wounded within me. I am gone like the shadow when it declineth: I am tossed up and down like the locust; my knees are weak through fasting, and my flesh faileth of fatness."

At night we came to an Indian town, and the Indians sat down by a wigwam discoursing, but I was almost spent and could scarce speak. I laid down my load and went into the wigwam, and there sat an Indian boiling of horses' feet (they being wont to eat the flesh first, and when the feet were old and dried and they had nothing else, they would cut off the feet and use them). I asked him to give me a little of his broth or water they were boiling in; he took a dish and gave me one spoonful of samp[40] and bid me take as much of the broth as I would. Then I put some of the hot water to the samp and drank it up and my spirit came again. He gave me also a piece of the rough or ridding[41] of the small guts, and I broiled it on the coals; and now may I say with Jonathan, "See, I pray you, how mine eyes have been enlightened because I tasted a little of this honey," I Sam. 14:29. Now is my spirit revived again; though means be never so inconsiderable, yet if the Lord bestow His blessing upon them, they shall refresh both soul and body.

THE EIGHTEENTH REMOVE

We took up our packs and along we went, but a wearisome day I had of it. As we went along I saw an Englishman stripped naked and lying dead upon the ground, but knew not who it was. Then we came to another Indian town where we stayed all night. In this town there were four English children, captives, and one of them my own sister's. I went to see how she did, and she was well, considering her captive condition. I would have tarried that night with her, but they that owned her would not suffer it. Then I went into another wigwam, where they were boiling corn and beans, which was a lovely sight to see, but I could not get a taste thereof. Then I went to another wigwam, where there were two of the English children. The squaw was boiling horses' feet; then she cut me off a little piece and gave one of the English children a piece also. Being very hungry, I had quickly eat up mine, but the child could not bite it, it was so tough and sinewy, but lay sucking, gnawing, chewing, and slabbering of it in the mouth and hand. Then I took it of the child and ate it myself, and savory it was to my taste. Then I may say [as] Job, chap. 6:7, "The things that my soul refused to touch are as my sorrowful meat." Thus the Lord made that pleasant and refreshing which another time would have been an abomination. Then I went home to my mistress' wigwam, and they told me I disgraced my master with begging, and if I did so anymore they would knock me in [the] head. I told them they had as good knock me in [the] head as starve me to death.

THE NINETEENTH REMOVE

They said when we went out that we must travel to Wachuset this day. But a bitter weary day I had of it, traveling now three days together without resting any day between. At last, after many weary steps, I saw Wachuset Hills, but many miles off. Then we came to a great swamp, through which we traveled up to the knees in mud and water, which was heavy going to one tired before. Being almost spent, I thought I should have sunk down at last and never got out, but I may say, as in Psal. 94:18, "When my foot slipped, Thy mercy, O Lord, held me up." Going along, having indeed my life but little spirit, Philip, who was in the company, came up and took me by the hand and said, "Two weeks more and you shall be mistress again." I asked him

---

[40] **samp:** Boiled cereal made from coarse hominy.   [41] **ridding:** Trimmed-off scrap.

if he spake true. He answered, "Yes, and quickly you shall come to your master again, who has been gone from us three weeks." After many weary steps we came to Wachuset, where he was, and glad I was to see him. He asked me when I washed me. I told him not this month. Then he fetched me some water himself and bid me wash and gave me the glass to see how I looked and bid his squaw give me something to eat. So she gave me a mess of beans and meat and a little groundnut cake. I was wonderfully revived with this favor showed me, Psal. 106:46, "He made them also to be pitied of all those that carried them captives."

My master had three squaws, living sometimes with one and sometimes with another one. This old squaw at whose wigwam I was, my master had been [with] those three weeks. Another was Weetamoo, with whom I had lived and served all this while. A severe and proud dame she was, bestowing every day in dressing herself neat as much time as any of the gentry of the land, powdering her hair and painting her face, going with necklaces, with jewels in her ears, and bracelets upon her hands. When she had dressed herself, her work was to make girdles of wampum and beads. The third squaw was a younger one, by whom he had two papooses. By that time I was refreshed by the old squaw with whom my master was, Weetamoo's maid came to call me home, at which I fell a-weeping. Then the old squaw told me, to encourage me, that if I wanted victuals I should come to her, and that I should lie there in her wigwam. Then I went with the maid and quickly came again and lodged there. The squaw laid a mat under me and a good rug over me; the first time I had any such kindness showed me. I understood that Weetamoo thought that if she should let me go and serve with the old squaw, she would be in danger to lose not only my service but the redemption pay also. And I was not a little glad to hear this, being raised in my hopes that in God's due time there would be an end of this sorrowful hour. Then came an Indian and asked me to knit him three pairs of stockings, for which I had a hat and a silk handkerchief. Then another asked me to make her a shift, for which she gave me an apron.

Then came Tom and Peter with the second letter from the council about the captives. Though they were Indians, I got them by the hand and burst out into tears; my heart was so full that I could not speak to them, but recovering myself, I asked them how my husband did and all my friends and acquaintances. They said they [were] all very well, but melancholy. They brought me two biscuits and a pound of tobacco. The tobacco I quickly gave away; when it was all gone, one asked me to give him a pipe of tobacco. I told him it was all gone. Then began he to rant and threaten. I told him when my husband came I would give some. "Hang [the] rogue," says he, "I will knock out his brains if he comes here." And then again in the same breath they would say that if there should come a hundred without guns they would do them no hurt, so unstable and like madmen they were, so that fearing the worst, I durst not send to my husband though there were some thoughts of his coming to redeem and fetch me, not knowing what might follow. For there was little more trust to them than to the master they served.

When the letter was come, the sagamores met to consult about the captives and called me to them to inquire how much my husband would give to redeem me.

When I came, I sat down among them as I was wont to do, as their manner is. Then they bade me stand up and said they were the General Court.[42] They bid me speak what I thought he would give. Now knowing that all we had was destroyed by the Indians, I was in a great strait. I thought if I should speak of but a little, it would be slighted and hinder the matter; if of a great sum, I knew not where it would be procured. Yet at a venture, I said twenty pounds, yet desired them to take less; but they would not hear of that, but sent that message to Boston that for twenty pounds I should be redeemed. It was a praying Indian that wrote their letter for them. There was another praying Indian who told me that he had a brother that would not eat horse; his conscience was so tender and scrupulous (though as large as hell for the destruction of poor Christians). Then he said he read that scripture to him, 2 Kings, 6:25, "There was a famine in Samaria, and behold they besieged it, until an ass's head was sold for fourscore pieces of silver, and the fourth part of a kab of doves' dung for five pieces of silver." He expounded this place to his brother and showed him that it was lawful to eat that in a famine which is not at another time. "And now," says he, "he will eat horse with any Indian of them all."

There was another praying Indian who, when he had done all the mischief that he could, betrayed his own father into the English hands thereby to purchase his own life. Another praying Indian was at Sudbury fight, though, as he deserved, he was afterward hanged for it. There was another praying Indian so wicked and cruel as to wear a string about his neck strung with Christians' fingers. Another praying Indian, when they went to Sudbury fight, went with them and his squaw also with him with her papoose at her back.

Before they went to that fight, they got a company together to pow-wow;[43] the manner was as followeth. There was one that kneeled upon a deerskin with the company round him in a ring, who kneeled, and striking upon the ground with their hands and with sticks, and muttering or humming with their mouths; besides him who kneeled in the ring, there also stood one with a gun in his hand. Then he on the deerskin made a speech, and all manifested assent to it, and so they did many times together. Then they bade him with the gun go out of the ring, which he did, but when he was out, they called him in again. But he seemed to make a stand; then they called the more earnestly till he returned again. Then they all sang. Then they gave him two guns, in either hand one. And so he on the deerskin began again, and at the end of every sentence in his speaking, they all assented, humming or muttering with their mouths and striking upon the ground with their hands. Then they bade him with the two guns go out of the ring again, which he did a little way. Then they called him in again, but he made a stand; so they called him with greater earnestness, but he stood reeling and wavering as if he knew not whether he should stand or fall or which way to go. Then they called him with exceeding great vehemency, all of them, one and another. After a little while he turned in, staggering as he went, with his arms stretched out, in either hand a gun. As soon as he came in, they all sang and

---

[42] **General Court:** Massachusetts Bay Colony's highest judicial and legislative body.

[43] **pow-wow:** Algonquian word for a sacred ceremony performed before a battle or hunt.

rejoiced exceedingly awhile. And then he upon the deerskin made another speech, unto which they all assented in a rejoicing manner, and so they ended their business and forthwith went to Sudbury fight.

To my thinking they went without any scruple but that they should prosper and gain the victory. And they went out not so rejoicing, but they came home with as great a victory, for they said they had killed two captains and almost an hundred men. One Englishman they brought along with them; and he said it was too true, for they had made sad work at Sudbury, as indeed it proved. Yet they came home without that rejoicing and triumphing over their victory which they were wont to show at other times but rather like dogs (as they say) which have lost their ears. Yet I could not perceive that it was for their own loss of men. They said they had not lost but above five or six, and I missed none except in one wigwam. When they went, they acted as if the devil had told them that they should gain the victory, and now they acted as if the devil had told them they should have a fall. Whither it were so or no, I cannot tell, but so it proved, for quickly they began to fall and so held on that summer till they came to utter ruin.

They came home on a Sabbath day, and the powwow[44] that kneeled upon the deerskin came home (I may say without abuse) as black as the devil. When my master came home, he came to me and bid me make a shirt for his papoose of a holland lace pillowbeer.[45] About that time there came an Indian to me and bid me come to his wigwam at night, and he would give me some pork and groundnuts, which I did. And as I was eating, another Indian said to me, "He seems to be your good friend, but he killed two Englishmen at Sudbury, and there lie their clothes behind you." I looked behind me, and there I saw bloody clothes with bullet holes in them, yet the Lord suffered not this wretch to do me any hurt. Yea, instead of that, he many times refreshed me; five or six times did he and his squaw refresh my feeble carcass. If I went to their wigwam at any time, they would always give me something, and yet they were strangers that I never saw before. Another squaw gave me a piece of fresh pork and a little salt with it and lent me her pan to fry it in, and I cannot but remember what a sweet, pleasant, and delightful relish that bit had to me to this day. So little do we prize common mercies when we have them to the full.

THE TWENTIETH REMOVE[46]

It was their usual manner to remove when they had done any mischief, lest they should be found out, and so they did at this time. We went about three or four miles, and there they built a great wigwam big enough to hold a hundred Indians, which they did in preparation to a great day of dancing. They would say now amongst themselves that the governor would be so angry for his loss at Sudbury that he would send no more about the captives, which made me grieve and tremble. My sister being not far from the place where we now were, and hearing that I was here,

---

[44] **powwow:** Medicine man who performs the pow-wow.   [45] **pillowbeer:** Pillowcase.
[46] **Twentieth Remove:** To the vicinity of Princeton, Mass., from April 28 to May 2.

desired her master to let her come and see me, and he was willing to it and would go with her. But she, being ready before him, told him she would go before and was come within a mile or two of the place. Then he overtook her and began to rant as if he had been mad and made her go back again in the rain so that I never saw her till I saw her in Charlestown. But the Lord requited many of their ill doings, for this Indian, her master, was hanged afterward at Boston.

The Indians now began to come from all quarters, against their merry dancing day. Among some of them came one Goodwife Kettle. I told her my heart was so heavy that it was ready to break. "So is mine, too," said she. But yet [she] said, "I hope we shall hear some good news shortly." I could hear how earnestly my sister desired to see me, and I as earnestly desired to see her, and yet neither of us could get an opportunity. My daughter was also now about a mile off, and I had not seen her in nine or ten weeks as I had not seen my sister since our first taking. I earnestly desired them to let me go and see them; yea, I entreated, begged, and persuaded them but to let me see my daughter, and yet so hardhearted were they that they would not suffer it. They made use of their tyrannical power whilst they had it, but through the Lord's wonderful mercy their time was now but short.

On a Sabbath day, the sun being about an hour high in the afternoon, came Mr. John Hoar (the council permitting him and his own forward spirit inclining him) together with the two forementioned Indians, Tom and Peter, with their third letter from the council. When they came near, I was abroad; though I saw them not, they presently called me in and bade me sit down and not stir. Then they catched up their guns and away they ran as if an enemy had been at hand, and the guns went off apace. I manifested some great trouble, and they asked me what was the matter. I told them I thought they had killed the Englishman (for they had in the meantime informed me that an Englishman was come). They said, "No." They shot over his horse and under, and before his horse, and they pushed him this way and that way at their pleasure, showing what they could do. Then they let them come to their wigwams. I begged of them to let me see the Englishman, but they would not; but there was I fain to sit their pleasure. When they had talked their fill with him, they suffered me to go to him. We asked each other of our welfare, and how my husband did and all my friends. He told me they were all well and would be glad to see me. Amongst other things which my husband sent me, there came a pound of tobacco, which I sold for nine shillings in money, for many of the Indians for want of tobacco smoked hemlock and ground ivy. It was a great mistake in any who thought I sent for tobacco, for through the favor of God that desire was overcome.

I now asked them whether I should go home with Mr. Hoar. They answered, "No," one and another of them. And it being night, we lay down with that answer. In the morning Mr. Hoar invited the sagamores to dinner, but when we went to get it ready, we found that they had stolen the greatest part of the provision Mr. Hoar had brought out of his bags in the night. And we may see the wonderful power of God in that one passage in that when there was such a great number of the Indians together and so greedy of a little good food and no English there but Mr. Hoar and myself, that there they did not knock us in the head and take what he had, there being not only some provision but also trading cloth, a part of the twenty pounds agreed upon. But instead of doing us any mischief, they seemed to be ashamed of the fact and said it were some *matchit*[47] Indian that did it. Oh, that we could believe that there is nothing too hard for God! God showed His power over the heathen in this as He did over the hungry lions when Daniel was cast into the den.[48] Mr. Hoar called them betime to dinner, but they ate very little, they being so busy in dressing themselves and getting ready for their dance, which was carried on by eight of them—four men and four squaws, my master and mistress being two. He was dressed in his Holland shirt with great laces sewed at the tail of it; he had his silver buttons, his white stockings, his garters were hung round with shillings, and he had girdles of wampum upon his head and shoulders. She had a kersey coat[49] and [was] covered with girdles of wampum from the loins upward; her arms from her elbows to her hands were covered with bracelets; there were handfuls of necklaces about her neck and several sorts of jewels in her ears. She had fine red stockings and white shoes, her hair powdered and face painted red that was always before black. And all the dancers were after the same manner. There were two others singing and knocking on a kettle for their music. They kept hopping up and down one after another with a kettle of water in the midst, standing warm upon some embers, to drink of when they were dry. They held on till it was almost night, throwing out wampum to the standers by.

At night I asked them again if I should go home. They all as one said no except my husband would come for me. When we were lain down, my master went out of the wigwam, and by and by sent in an Indian called James the Printer, who told Mr. Hoar that my master would let me go home tomorrow if he would let him have one pint of liquors. Then Mr. Hoar called his own Indians, Tom and Peter, and bid them go and see whether he would promise it before them three, and if he would, he should have it, which he did, and he had it. Then Philip, smelling the business, called me to him and asked me what I would give him to tell me some good news and speak a good word for me. I told him I could not tell what to give him. I would [give] anything I had and asked him what he would have. He said two coats and twenty shillings in money and half a bushel of seed corn and some tobacco. I thanked him for his love, but I knew the good news as well as the crafty fox.

My master, after he had had his drink, quickly came ranting into the wigwam again and called for Mr. Hoar, drinking to him and saying he was a good man. And then again he would say, "Hang [the] rogue." Being almost drunk, he would drink to him, and yet presently say he should be hanged. Then he called for me. I trembled to hear him, yet I was fain to go to him, and he drank to me, showing no incivility. He was the first Indian I saw drunk all the while that I was amongst them. At last his squaw ran out, and he after her round the wigwam, with his money jingling at his knees, but she escaped him. But having an old squaw, he ran to her, and so through the Lord's mercy, we were no more troubled that night.

---

[47] *matchit:* Bad.   [48] **Daniel . . . den:** Daniel 6:16–23.

[49] **kersey coat:** Wool petticoat. As war chiefs, Quinnapin and Weetamoo stage a ritual dance and a giveaway ceremony to garner power for their enterprise.

Yet I had not a comfortable night's rest, for I think I can say I did not sleep for three nights together. The night before the letter came from the council I could not rest, I was so full of fears and troubles, God many times leaving us most in the dark when deliverance is nearest. Yea, at this time I could not rest night nor day. The next night I was overjoyed, Mr. Hoar being come and that with such good tidings. The third night I was even swallowed up with the thoughts of things, *viz.* that ever I should go home again and that I must go, leaving my children behind me in the wilderness, so that sleep was now almost departed from mine eyes.

On Tuesday morning they called their General Court (as they call it) to consult and determine whether I should go home or no. And they all as one man did seemingly consent to it that I should go home, except Philip, who would not come among them.

But before I go any further, I would take leave to mention a few remarkable passages of providence which I took special notice of in my afflicted time.

1. Of the fair opportunity lost in the long march, a little after the fort fight, when our English army was so numerous, and in pursuit of the enemy, and so near as to take several and destroy them, and the enemy in such distress for food that our men might track them by their rooting in the earth for groundnuts while they were flying for their lives. I say that then our army should want provision and be forced to leave their pursuit and return homeward. And the very next week the enemy came upon our town like bears bereft of their whelps or so many ravenous wolves, rending us and our lambs to death. But what shall I say? God seemed to leave His people to themselves and order all things for His own holy ends. "Shall there be evil in the city and the Lord hath not done it? They are not grieved for the affliction of Joseph, therefore shall they go captive with the first that go captive."[50] It is the Lord's doing, and it should be marvelous in our eyes.

2. I cannot but remember how the Indians derided the slowness and dullness of the English army in its setting out. For after the desolations at Lancaster and Medfield, as I went along with them, they asked me when I thought the English would come after them. I told them I could not tell. It may be they will come in May, said they. Thus did they scoff at us, as if the English would be a quarter of a year getting ready.

3. Which also I have hinted before: when the English army with new supplies were sent forth to pursue after the enemy, and they, understanding it, fled before them till they came to Baquaug River where they forthwith went over safely, that the river should be impassable to the English. I can but admire to see the wonderful providence of God in preserving the heathen for further affliction to our poor country. They could go in great numbers over, but the English must stop. God had an overruling hand in all those things.

4. It was thought if their corn were cut down they would starve and die with hunger, and all their corn that could be found was destroyed, and they driven from that little they had in store into the woods in the midst of winter. And yet how to

---

[50] "Shall . . . captive.": Amos 3:6, 6:7.

admiration did the Lord preserve them for His holy ends and the destruction of many still amongst the English! Strangely did the Lord provide for them that I did not see (all the time I was among them) one man, woman, or child die with hunger. Though many times they would eat that that a hog or dog would hardly touch, yet by that God strengthened them to be a scourge to His people.

The chief and commonest food was groundnuts. They eat also nuts and acorns, artichokes, lily roots, groundbeans, and several other weeds and roots that I know not.

They would pick up old bones and cut them to pieces at the joints, and if they were full of worms and maggots, they would scald them over the fire to make the vermin come out and then boil them and drink up the liquor and then beat the great ends of them in a mortar and so eat them. They would eat horses' guts and ears, and all sorts of wild birds which they could catch; also bear, venison, beaver, tortoise, frogs, squirrels, dogs, skunks, rattlesnakes, yea, the very bark of trees, besides all sorts of creatures and provision which they plundered from the English. I can but stand in admiration to see the wonderful power of God in providing for such a vast number of our enemies in the wilderness, where there was nothing to be seen but from hand to mouth. Many times in a morning the generality of them would eat up all they had and yet have some further supply against what they wanted. It is said, Psal. 81:13, 14, "Oh, that My people had hearkened to Me, and Israel had walked in My ways; I should soon have subdued their enemies and turned My hand against their adversaries." But now our perverse and evil carriages in the sight of the Lord have so offended Him that instead of turning His hand against them the Lord feeds and nourishes them up to be a scourge to the whole land.

5. Another thing that I would observe is the strange providence of God in turning things about when the Indians [were] at the highest and the English at the lowest. I was with the enemy eleven weeks and five days, and not one week passed without the fury of the enemy and some desolation by fire and sword upon one place or other. They mourned (with their black faces) for their own losses, yet triumphed and rejoiced in their inhuman and many times devilish cruelty to the English. They would boast much of their victories, saying that in two hours' time they had destroyed such a captain and his company at such a place, and such a captain and his company in such a place, and such a captain and his company in such a place, and boast how many towns they had destroyed; and then scoff and say they had done them a good turn to send them to heaven so soon. Again they would say this summer that they would knock all the rogues in the head, or drive them into the sea, or make them fly the country, thinking surely Agag-like, "The bitterness of death is past."[51] Now the heathen begins to think all is their own, and the poor Christians' hopes to fail (as to man), and now their eyes are more to God, and their hearts sigh heavenward and to say in good earnest, "Help Lord, or we perish." When the Lord had brought His people to this that they saw no help in anything but Himself, then He takes the quarrel into His own hand, and though they [the Indians] had made a pit in their own imaginations as deep as hell for the Christians that summer, yet the

---

[51] "The . . . past.": I Samuel 15.

Lord hurled themselves into it. And the Lord had not so many ways before to preserve them, but now He hath as many to destroy them.

But to return again to my going home, where we may see a remarkable change of providence. At first they were all against it except my husband would come for me, but afterwards they assented to it and seemed much to rejoice in it. Some asked me to send them some bread, others some tobacco, others shaking me by the hand, offering me a hood and scarf to ride in, not one moving hand or tongue against it. Thus hath the Lord answered my poor desire and the many earnest requests of others put up unto God for me. In my travels an Indian came to me and told me if I were willing, he and his squaw would run away and go home along with me. I told him no. I was not willing to run away, but desired to wait God's time that I might go home quietly and without fear. And now God hath granted me my desire. O, the wonderful power of God that I have seen and the experience that I have had! I have been in the midst of those roaring lions and savage bears that feared neither God nor man nor the devil, by night and day, alone and in company, sleeping all sorts together, and yet not one of them ever offered me the least abuse of unchastity to me in word or action. Though some are ready to say I speak it for my own credit, I speak it in the presence of God and to His glory. God's power is as great now and as sufficient to save as when He preserved Daniel in the lion's den or the three children in the fiery furnace.[52] I may well say as his Psal. 107:12, "Oh, give thanks unto the Lord for He is good, for His mercy endureth forever." Let the redeemed of the Lord say so whom He hath redeemed from the hand of the enemy, especially that I should come away in the midst of so many hundreds of enemies quietly and peaceably and not a dog moving his tongue.

So I took my leave of them, and in coming along my heart melted into tears more than all the while I was with them, and I was almost swallowed up with the thoughts that ever I should go home again. About the sun going down, Mr. Hoar, myself, and the two Indians came to Lancaster, and a solemn sight it was to me. There had I lived many comfortable years amongst my relations and neighbors, and now not one Christian to be seen nor one house left standing. We went on to a farmhouse that was yet standing, where we lay all night, and a comfortable lodging we had, though nothing but straw to lie on. The Lord preserved us in safety that night and raised us up again in the morning and carried us along, that before noon we came to Concord. Now was I full of joy and yet not without sorrow—joy to see such a lovely sight, so many Christians together and some of them my neighbors. There I met with my brother [Josiah White] and my brother-in-law [Henry Kerley], who asked me if I knew where his wife was. Poor heart! He had helped to bury her and knew it not, she being shot down [when] the house was partly burned so that those who were at Boston at the desolation of the town and came back afterward and buried the dead did not know her. Yet I was not without sorrow to think how many were looking and longing, and my own children amongst the rest, to enjoy that deliverance that I had now received, and I did not know whether ever I should see them again.

---

[52] Daniel . . . furnace.: Daniel 3:13–30.

Being recruited with food and raiment, we went to Boston that day, where I met with my dear husband, but the thoughts of our dear children, one being dead and the others we could not tell where, abated our comfort each to other. I was not before so much hemmed in with the merciless and cruel heathen but now as much with pitiful, tenderhearted, and compassionate Christians. In that poor and distressed and beggarly condition I was received in, I was kindly entertained in several houses; so much love I received from several (some of whom I knew and others I knew not) that I am not capable to declare it. But the Lord knows them all by name. The Lord reward them sevenfold into their bosoms of His spirituals for their temporals.[53]

The twenty pounds, the price of my redemption, was raised by some Boston gentlemen and Mrs. Usher, whose bounty and religious charity I would not forget to make mention of. Then Mr. Thomas Shepard of Charlestown received us into his house, where we continued eleven weeks, and a father and mother they were to us. And many more tenderhearted friends we met with in that place. We were now in the midst of love, yet not without much and frequent heaviness of heart for our poor children and other relations who were still in affliction. The week following after my coming in, the governor and council sent forth to the Indians again, and that not without success, for they brought in my sister and Goodwife Kettle.

Their not knowing where our children were was a sore trial to us still, and yet we were not without secret hopes that we should see them again. That which was dead lay heavier upon my spirit than those which were alive and amongst the heathen, thinking how it suffered with its wounds and I was no way able to relieve it, and how it was buried by the heathen in the wilderness from among all Christians. We were hurried up and down in our thoughts; sometimes we should hear a report that they were gone this way, and sometimes that, and that they were come in in this place or that. We kept inquiring and listening to hear concerning them, but no certain news as yet. About this time the council had ordered a day of public thanksgiving, though I thought I had still cause of mourning, and, being unsettled in our minds, we thought we would ride toward the eastward to see if we could hear anything concerning our children. And as we were riding along (God is the wise disposer of all things), between Ipswich and Rowly we met with Mr. William Hubbard, who told us that our son Joseph was come in to Major Waldren's, and another with him which was my sister's son. I asked him how he knew it. He said the major himself told him so.

So along we went till we came to Newbury, and, their minister being absent, they desired my husband to preach the thanksgiving for them, but he was not willing to stay there that night but would go over to Salisbury to hear further and come again in the morning, which he did and preached there that day. At night when he had done, one came and told him that his daughter was come in at Providence. Here was mercy on both hands. Now hath God fulfilled that precious scripture which was such a comfort to me in my distressed condition. When my heart was ready to sink into the earth (my children being gone I could not tell whither), and my knees

---

[53] **temporals:** Worldly goods.

trembled under me, and I was walking through the valley of the shadow of death, then the Lord brought and now has fulfilled that reviving word unto me. Thus saith the Lord, "Refrain thy voice from weeping, and thine eyes from tears, for thy work shall be rewarded," saith the Lord, "and they shall come again from the land of the enemy."[54]

Now we were between them, the one on the east and the other on the west. Our son being nearest, we went to him first to Portsmouth, where we met with him and with the major also, who told us he had done what he could but could not redeem him under seven pounds, which the good people thereabouts were pleased to pay. The Lord reward the major and all the rest, though unknown to me, for their labor of love. My sister's son was redeemed for four pounds, which the council gave order for the payment of. Having now received one of our children, we hastened toward the other; going back through Newbury, my husband preached there on the Sabbath day, for which they rewarded him manyfold.

On Monday we came to Charlestown, where we heard that the governor of Rhode Island had sent over for our daughter to take care of her, being now within his jurisdiction, which should not pass without our acknowledgments. But she being nearer Rehoboth than Rhode Island, Mr. Newman went over and took care of her and brought her to his own house. And the goodness of God was admirable to us in our low estate in that he raised up [com]passionate friends on every side to us when we had nothing to recompense any for their love. The Indians were now gone that way, that it was apprehended dangerous to go to her; but the carts which carried provision to the English army, being guarded, brought her with them to Dorchester, where we received her safe. Blessed be the Lord for it, for great is His power, and He can do whatsoever seemeth Him good.

Her coming in was after this manner. She was traveling one day with the Indians with her basket at her back; the company of Indians were got before her and gone out of sight, all except one squaw. She followed the squaw till night, and then both of them lay down, having nothing over them but the heavens and under them but the earth. Thus she traveled three days together, not knowing whither she was going, having nothing to eat or drink but water and green hirtleberries. At last they came into Providence, where she was kindly entertained by several of that town. The Indians often said that I should never have her under twenty pounds. But now the Lord hath brought her in upon free cost and given her to me the second time. The Lord make us a blessing indeed, each to others. Now have I seen that scripture also fulfilled, Deut. 30:4, 7: "If any of thine be driven out to the outmost parts of heaven, from thence will the Lord thy God gather thee, and from thence will He fetch thee. . . . And the Lord thy God will put all these curses upon thine enemies, and on them which hate thee, which persecuted thee." Thus hath the Lord brought me and mine out of that horrible pit and hath set us in the midst of tenderhearted and compassionate Christians. It is the desire of my soul that we may walk worthy of the mercies received and which we are receiving.

---

[54] "Refrain . . . enemy.": Jeremiah 31:16.

Our family being now gathered together (those of us that were living), the South Church in Boston hired an house for us. Then we removed from Mr. Shepard's, those cordial friends, and went to Boston, where we continued about three-quarters of a year. Still the Lord went along with us and provided graciously for us. I thought it somewhat strange to set up housekeeping with bare walls, but as Solomon says, "Money answers all things,"[55] and that we had through the benevolence of Christian friends, some in this town and some in that and others, and some from England, that in a little time we might look and see the house furnished with love. The Lord hath been exceeding good to us in our low estate in that when we had neither house nor home nor other necessaries, the Lord so moved the hearts of these and those towards us that we wanted neither food nor raiment for ourselves or ours, Prov. 18:24, "There is a friend which sticketh closer than a brother." And how many such friends have we found and now living amongst! And truly such a friend have we found him to be unto us in whose house we lived, *viz.* Mr. James Whitcomb, a friend unto us near hand and afar off.

I can remember the time when I used to sleep quietly without workings in my thoughts whole nights together, but now it is other ways with me. When all are fast about me and no eye open but His who ever waketh, my thoughts are upon things past, upon the awful dispensation of the Lord toward us, upon His wonderful power and might in carrying of us through so many difficulties, in returning us in safety and suffering none to hurt us. I remember in the night season how the other day I was in the midst of thousands of enemies and nothing but death before me. It [was] then hard work to persuade myself that ever I should be satisfied with bread again. But now we are fed with the finest of the wheat, and, as I may say, with honey out of the rock. Instead of the husk, we have the fatted calf.[56] The thoughts of these things in the particulars of them, and of the love and goodness of God towards us, make it true of me what David said of himself, Psal. 6:5 [actually 6:6]. "I watered my couch with my tears." Oh, the wonderful power of God that mine eyes have seen, affording matter enough for my thoughts to run in, that when others are sleeping mine eyes are weeping!

I have seen the extreme vanity of this world. One hour I have been in health and wealth, wanting nothing, but the next hour in sickness and wounds and death, having nothing but sorrow and affliction. Before I knew what affliction meant, I was ready sometimes to wish for it. When I lived in prosperity, having the comforts of the world about me, my relations by me, my heart cheerful, and taking little care for anything, and yet seeing many whom I preferred before myself under many trials and afflictions, in sickness, weakness, poverty, losses, crosses, and cares of the world, I should be sometimes jealous lest I should have my portion in this life, and that scripture would come to mind, Heb. 12:6, "For whom the Lord loveth he chasteneth and scourgeth every son whom He receiveth." But now I see the Lord had His time to scourge and chasten me. The portion of some is to have their afflictions by drops, now one drop and then another, but the dregs of the cup, the wine of astonishment,

---

[55] "Money . . . things": Ecclesiastes 10:19.   [56] But . . . calf.: Psalm 81:16; Luke 15:23.

like a sweeping rain that leaveth no food, did the Lord prepare to be my portion. Affliction I wanted and affliction I had, full measure (I thought) pressed down and running over. Yet I see when God calls a person to anything and through never so many difficulties, yet He is fully able to carry them through and make them see and say they have been gainers thereby. And I hope I can say in some measure, as David did, "It is good for me that I have been afflicted."[57]

The Lord hath showed me the vanity of these outward things. That they are the vanity of vanities and vexation of spirit, that they are but a shadow, a blast, a bubble, and things of no continuance. That we must rely on God himself and our whole dependence must be upon Him. If trouble from smaller matters begin to arise in me, I have something at hand to check myself with and say, why am I troubled? It was but the other day that if I had had the world I would have given it for my freedom or to have been a servant to a Christian. I have learned to look beyond present and smaller troubles and to be quieted under them, as Moses said, Exod. 14:13, "Stand still and see the salvation of the Lord."

---

[57] "It . . . afflicted.": Psalm 119:71.

❧ BENJAMIN FRANKLIN
1706–1790

Benjamin Franklin exemplified ENLIGHTENMENT ideals and thus the Age of Reason itself. He had unlimited faith in the affairs of this world and a mild distrust of mystical, otherworldly devotion. He believed that common sense, hard work, and frugality—along with education—could solve most of life's problems. As a young man with a good deal of self-discipline, he set out to make something of himself and then, with maturity and financial security, to make a contribution to the common good and future of America. He even trained himself to write well so that he could communicate his values to others.

For generations of U.S. citizens, Benjamin Franklin's engaging *Autobiography* (1771–90) stood for progress. Franklin came out of a poor, overcrowded candlemaker's household to become a printer, a successful businessman, an inventor, and a statesman who toward the end of his life helped to frame the Constitution and negotiate the treaty with Great Britain that ended the American Revolution. An American boy, then, might be born into poverty among hard-hearted people, but with discipline, hard work, decent morals, and the occasional help of friends and Providence he could make of himself anything he wished. This ideal, though tarnished by many hard-working people's actual experience, continues to be an article of faith in the United States.

The young printer Benjamin Franklin wrote a witty mock epitaph for himself that suggested the sort of optimistic and secularized Chris-

www For links to more information about Ben Franklin and a quiz on his *Autobiography*, see *World Literature Online* at bedfordstmartins .com/worldlit.

tianity he subscribed to and anticipated the tone of the autobiography he would write more than forty years later:

> The Body of
> B. Franklin, Printer
> (Like the Cover of an old Book
> Its Contents torn out
> And stript of its Lettering & Gilding),
> Lies here, Food for Worms,
> But the Work shall not be lost;
> For it will, (as he believ'd) appear once more,
> In a new and more elegant Edition
> Revised and corrected
> By the Author.

Joseph Siffred Duplessis, *Portrait of Benjamin Franklin,* c. 1785
This portrait, among the more recognizable images of Franklin, was painted nine years after the end of the American Revolution. (National Portrait Gallery, Smithsonian Institution/Art Resource, NY)

Early Years.   Benjamin Franklin was born in Boston in 1706, the thirteenth of the fifteen children of Josiah and Abiah Franklin. His parents sent him to Boston Grammar School, intending to educate him for the ministry; when money ran short, he was taken out of school and put to work in the family candlemaking trade. But it was plain to see how deeply this bright boy detested cutting wicks and dipping molds, and when Benjamin was twelve, his father apprenticed him to another of his sons, Benjamin's elder half-brother James, a Boston printer and newspaper publisher. The printshop and newspaper proved a far more congenial business for Franklin, and soon, writing under the pen name of Silence Dogood, a sharp-tongued and opinionated widow, Franklin began sneaking essays into his brother's paper addressing a wide range of subjects. Speaking as Silence, the young Franklin mocked hoopskirts and other fashionable affectations, berated drunkards and religious hypocrites, and advocated the education of women. When James was briefly jailed for printing in his *New-England Courant* charges of incompetence against the government of Massachusetts, Franklin, at sixteen, managed the paper. For a time after James was freed, he was forbidden to publish the *Courant* except under government scrutiny, and young Benjamin became its nominal publisher.

Franklin's situation was not a happy one, despite all the young man was learning about printing and politics. There was a fierce rivalry between the brothers; Franklin claimed James often beat him, and the more the younger brother gained in experience, the more he longed for independence. In 1723 Franklin ran away from his apprenticeship, a criminal act in those times, and made his way to Philadelphia, arriving in October 1723. The description of him walking up Market Street eating "three great puffy rolls" purchased with his last three pennies has become emblematic of the edenic New World.[1] Quaker Philadelphia was a very different city from Puritan Boston. Philadelphia, with its Quaker emphasis on equality before God and humanitarian service, had been established as a religious refuge from persecution in England. Because the city lacked skilled artisans, Franklin immediately found work with Keimer, a

Franklin is dead. . . . He has returned to the bosom of Divinity, this genius who freed America and poured over Europe torrents of light.
    – French Revolution leader MIRABEAU, 1790

---

[1] **edenic New World:** Early immigrants often described the New World as a new Eden, a Garden of Paradise.

Like many other American works, [Franklin's *Autobiography*] is held together by a character who seems to represent the youthfulness and vibrancy of America itself. And as in such works, too, the representative character proves to have a far greater complexity and psychological depth than at first appears.

– PETER SHAW, literary critic, 1982

printer, but soon was off again, this time to England for a two-year stint in a London printing house.

Eventually, he returned to Philadelphia and prospered steadily through the very industry, temperance, and frugality he recommended to others; by the age of twenty-four he owned his own paper, and he soon began publishing the annual *Poor Richard's Almanack* (1733–1758). Almanacs were best-sellers in the American colonies; the present-day *Old Farmer's Almanac* is a continuing example of the genre. These little books were crammed full of astronomical information, jokes, mini-essays, weather predictions, tables charting the phases of the moon and the tides, and, above all, straightforward advice about how to get ahead in the world. Very soon, *Poor Richard's Almanack* was outselling all its competitors. Franklin's aphorisms, so witty and well phrased, have survived

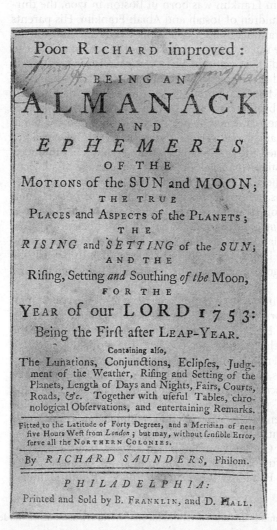

Poor RICHARD improved:

BEING AN
ALMANACK
AND
EPHEMERIS
OF THE
MOTIONS of the SUN and MOON;
THE TRUE
PLACES and ASPECTS of the PLANETS;
THE
RISING and SETTING of the SUN;
AND THE
Rifing, Setting *and* Southing *of the* Moon,
FOR THE
YEAR of our LORD 1753:
Being the Firft after LEAP-YEAR.

Containing alfo,
The Lunations, Conjunctions, Eclipfes, Judg-
ment of the Weather, Rifing and Setting of the
Planets, Length of Days and Nights, Fairs, Courts,
Roads, &c. Together with ufeful Tables, chro-
nological Obfervations, and entertaining Remarks.

Fitted to the Latitude of Forty Degrees, and a Meridian of near
five Hours Weft from *London*; but may, without fenfible Error,
ferve all the NORTHERN COLONIES.

By *RICHARD SAUNDERS*, Philom.

PHILADELPHIA:
Printed and Sold by B. FRANKLIN, and D. HALL.

Cover of *Poor Richard's Almanack*, 1753
Benjamin Franklin began publishing Poor Richard's Almanack in 1733. Almanacs were best-sellers in the American colonies, and Poor Richard's, full of witty aphorisms and soon-to-be familiar maxims, outsold all its competitors. (Courtesy of the American Antiquarian Society)

until the present day and may live forever: there are no gains without pains; to be intimate with a foolish friend is like going to bed with a razor; a penny saved is a penny earned; a small leak will sink a great ship.

Retirement and Public Service. Franklin was able to retire at the age of forty-two from the printing business thanks to the best-selling *Almanacks,* his *Pennsylvania Gazette,* and his thriving printshop, but whether officially retired or not, Franklin was always seriously busy with projects and public service. One of his most winning characteristics was his open-minded curiosity about how nature, including human nature, worked; seasick on a stormy Atlantic crossing, he passed the time noting how the mussels that were attached to the heaving hull of the ship reacted to their alternate wetting and drying. He invented the Franklin stove, the lightning rod, and bifocal spectacles, and he devised literally hair-raising experiments with kites and keys and voltaic batteries that helped prove that lightning was indeed electrical. Public libraries and volunteer fire departments, now commonplace, were his original idea. He founded the American Philosophical Society in 1743–44 and the Philadelphia Academy in 1749 (later the University of Pennsylvania), and became famous with *Experiments and Observations on Electricity* (1751–53).

Franklin served in many public posts, including Indian Commissioner of Pennsylvania in the 1750s. Through diplomatic dealings with members of the Iroquois League he came to know and admire the detailed workings of the Iroquois' Great Law of Peace.[2] In 1754, when delegates from the thirteen British colonies met at the Albany Congress to explore the possibilities of union, Franklin proposed a plan for a unified government that borrowed from the Iroquoian system; although his plan was rejected, a modified version of it was eventually incorporated into the United States Constitution.

Franklin played an indispensable part in the shaping of the young nation. He helped to frame the Declaration of Independence in 1776, and as a delegate to the Constitutional Convention of 1787 he helped draft the United States Constitution. He tirelessly carried out diplomatic missions during the Revolutionary War, and in 1783 he negotiated the Treaty of Paris, the document that recognized the United States as a sovereign nation. He died at home in Philadelphia in 1790, at the age of eighty-four, after decades spent mostly abroad in England and France.

Franklin's *Autobiography*. Like most autobiographers, Franklin simplified his life in the telling of it, and as a result it appears to follow a rational pattern of development. Concentrating on his early years, he demonstrates clearly how industry and common sense can help a young man to rise above his less disciplined peers. Seen through the mellowing distance of memory — Franklin was sixty-five when he began writing the *Autobiography* — his early years seem definitively shaped. His youth is a story

Thomas Jefferson (1743–1826) answered the question, "Is it you, sir, who replaces Dr. Franklin?" with "I succeed him, no one can replace him."

– THOMAS JEFFERSON, 1791

Of Franklin: "A philosophical Quaker full of mean and thrifty maxims."

– JOHN KEATS, 1818

---

[2] **Great Law of Peace:** A system of representative government combined with tribal sovereignty that for centuries enabled Iroquoian peoples of different tribes to work together amiably.

And sometimes, with his marvelous range, in spite of his personal tang, [Franklin] seems to have been more than any single man: a harmonious human multitude.

— CARL VAN DOREN,
   biographer, 1938

with a coherent plot line and a few "errata"—printer's jargon for misprints, a word Franklin uses to mean moral shortcomings and errors of judgment—that his printer's hand itches to correct. He ultimately presents himself as a down-to-earth and good-natured Enlightenment boy-hero, and on the whole he seems to have been just that.

St. Augustine's *Confessions,*[3] written in the fifth century C.E., was a distant model for Franklin's story, but the work was more immediately influenced by the spiritual autobiographies of the late sixteenth and seventeenth century popular among New England Puritans. Typically, they were the stories of spiritual pilgrims who survived trials and temptations through God's grace, and they read as uplifting moral paradigms. Franklin addresses the first part of *Autobiography* to his son William, intending to pass on his life lessons. He presents a picture of himself as an earnest and energetic young man tackling life as an ongoing improvement project, complete with a handy chart on which he records his progress in Order, Industry, Temperance, and other virtues of the Protestant work ethic.[4]

In the more than two centuries since Franklin wrote about his life, autobiographies have become increasingly personal and confessional. Even given the amount of reserve typical of written works of Franklin's time, it is still remarkable that Franklin's wife, Deborah Read, figures in the book as little as she does; she's presented mainly as a spectator to the poverty and adolescent awkwardness Franklin will soon overcome. While he recounts his initial courtship of Deborah and their common-law marriage, he makes almost no mention of the considerable part she played in his household and business affairs during the first half of his life. And besides William, he makes almost no mention of his other children except for the death of one child by smallpox, which he takes as an occasion to urge parents to practice immunization. Such omission seems particularly callous in the case of his favorite daughter, Sally, the only legitimate child who survived into adulthood, who served her father through much of his life as helpmate and hostess.

For many modern readers, Franklin's saving grace is a sly and self-deprecating wit. Wit, like compassion and joy and any number of other human possibilities, does not figure on Franklin's prim chart of virtues, but it marks Franklin every bit as much as his industry and his inventiveness do. This is the man who, after a long discussion of how he has increased his daily output of virtuous behavior, remarks that he has come to see that perfection invites hatred, and tells the story of the farmer who sheepishly admits he prefers a speckled ax to a brightly polished one.

---

[3] St. Augustine's *Confessions:* Augustine (354–430), a profoundly influential Catholic theologian from Hippo, North Africa, wrote *Confessions* (c. 401) to recount his conversion to Christianity.

[4] Protestant work ethic: German sociologist Max Weber (1864–1920) was the first to link Protestants to a work ethic—a belief that hard work and thrift would bring prosperity—and to the rise of capitalism. For Puritans, prosperity resulting from work was an indication of God's favor.

■ **CONNECTIONS**

Voltaire, *Candide*, p. 275. The European Enlightenment, in the hands of writers like Voltaire and Jonathan Swift, differed from the American version. Voltaire saw his task as contributing to the removal of those elements of society that stood in the way of individual human potential. Franklin's ideas grew out of the "fertile, virgin soil" of New World society and the lack of entrenched, corrupt institutions that could stand in the way of progress. How is Franklin's unbridled optimism expressed in his writing?

Bashō, *The Narrow Road through the Backcountry*, p. 657. Eighteenth-century writers commonly used autobiographies to deliver a social message. Bashō's spiritual autobiography focuses on the individual and on a personal transformation of consciousness. Franklin's rather secular version of the autobiography has a decidedly social agenda. How do Bashō's and Franklin's lives relate to their views on virtue and personal goals?

Confucius, *The Analects* (Book 1). Rather than focusing on pleasing an all-powerful deity in the heavens, social philosophers from the time of Confucius (sixth century B.C.E.) onward contemplated the kind of personal conduct that would improve society as a whole. Confucius was fond of making brief statements about how individuals might adjust their behavior in order to participate in a harmonious society. How do Franklin's attitudes about work and responsibility differ from those of Confucius?

■ **FURTHER RESEARCH**

Biography

Clark, Ronald W. *Benjamin Franklin: A Biography*. 1983.

Lopez, Claude-Anne, and Eugenia Herbert. *The Private Franklin: The Man and His Family*. 1975.

Criticism

Bushman, Richard. "On the Uses of Psychology: Conflict and Conciliation in Benjamin Franklin," *History and Theory*. 1966.

Fiering, Norman S. "Benjamin Franklin and the Ways to Virtue," *The American Quarterly*. Summer 1978.

Seavey, Ormond. *Becoming Benjamin Franklin: The Autobiography and the Life*. 1988.

❧ Autobiography

FROM

PART ONE [EARLY TRAINING]

Twyford, *at the Bishop of St. Asaph's,* 1771.

Dear son:

I have ever had pleasure in obtaining any little anecdotes of my ancestors. You may remember the inquiries I made among the remains of my relations when you were with me in England, and the journey I undertook for that purpose. Imagining it may be equally agreeable to you to know the circumstances of my life, many of which you are yet unacquainted with, and expecting the enjoyment of a week's uninterrupted leisure in my present country retirement, I sit down to write them for you. To which I have besides some other inducements. Having emerged from the poverty and obscurity in which I was born and bred, to a state of affluence and some degree of reputation in the world, and having gone so far through life with a considerable share of felicity, the conducing means I made use of, which with the blessing of God so well succeeded, my posterity may like to know, as they may find some of them suitable to their own situations, and therefore fit to be imitated.

That felicity, when I reflected on it, has induced me sometimes to say, that were it offered to my choice, I should have no objection to a repetition of the same life from its beginning, only asking the advantages authors have in a second edition to correct some faults of the first. So I might, besides correcting the faults, change some sinister accidents and events of it for others more favorable. But though this were denied, I should still accept the offer. Since such a repetition is not to be expected, the next

---

Autobiography. Franklin began his autobiography while visiting the Bishop of St. Asaph in southern England in 1771. The first part is a letter addressed to his son William Franklin (c. 1731–1813), royal governor of New Jersey, who never saw the book. Benjamin Franklin left his manuscript behind when relocated to France to serve as ambassador. An old friend, Abel James, saw the work and wrote to Franklin suggesting that he continue with it. Franklin sought the advice of Benjamin Vaughan; the letters from James and Vaughan form a bridge to part two, which was written in 1784. In 1788, Franklin resumed work on his memoirs and in the next nine months wrote part three and the seven additional pages of part four. He did not chronicle his life past 1757, although his essays and letters fill in the period until the end of his life. By the time he sent copies of the first three parts of the autobiography to friends in England and France in 1789, he had become self-conscious about the task of writing about one's life and wondered whether the manuscript should be published at all. All four parts of *Autobiography* did not appear in print until 1868.

A note on the text: This selection from Franklin's *Autobiography* comes from Peter Shaw's modernized edition, based on the transcription of Franklin's original text made by John Bigelow, who purchased the manuscript in 1867. Shaw made his corrections and additions by comparing the Yale edition of Franklin's papers and the text edited by J. A. Leo Lemay with Paul M. Zall. This modernized edition provides a readable but accurate version of Franklin's original. All notes in the following selection are the editors'.

thing most like living one's life over again seems to be a recollection of that life, and to make that recollection as durable as possible by putting it down in writing.

Hereby, too, I shall indulge the inclination so natural in old men, to be talking of themselves and their own past actions; and I shall indulge it without being tiresome to others, who, through respect to age, might conceive themselves obliged to give me a hearing, since this may be read or not as any one pleases. And, lastly (I may as well confess it, since my denial of it will be believed by nobody), perhaps I shall a good deal gratify my own *vanity*. Indeed, I scarce ever heard or saw the introductory words, *Without vanity I may say*, etc., but some vain thing immediately followed. Most people dislike vanity in others, whatever share they have of it themselves; but I give it fair quarter wherever I meet with it, being persuaded that it is often productive of good to the possessor, and to others that are within his sphere of action; and therefore, in many cases, it would not be altogether absurd if a man were to thank God for his vanity among the other comforts of life.

And now I speak of thanking God, I desire with all humility to acknowledge that I owe the mentioned happiness of my past life to His kind providence, which lead me to the means I used and gave them success. My belief of this induces me to *hope*, though I must not *presume*, that the same goodness will still be exercised toward me, in continuing that happiness, or enabling me to bear a fatal reverse, which I may experience as others have done; the complexion of my future fortune being known to Him only in whose power it is to bless to us even our afflictions. . . .

My elder brothers were all put apprentices to different trades. I was put to the grammar school at eight years of age, my father intending to devote me, as the tithe of his sons, to the service of the Church. My early readiness in learning to read (which must have been very early, as I do not remember when I could not read), and the opinion of all his friends, that I should certainly make a good scholar, encouraged him in this purpose of his. My uncle Benjamin, too, approved of it, and proposed to give me all his shorthand volumes of sermons, I suppose as a stock to set up with, if I would learn his character. I continued, however, at the grammar school not quite one year, though in that time I had risen gradually from the middle of the class of that year to be the head of it, and further was removed into the next class above it, in order to go with that into the third at the end of the year. But my father, in the meantime, from a view of the expense of a college education, which having so large a family he could not well afford, and the mean living many so educated were afterward able to obtain—reasons that he gave to his friends in my hearing—altered his first intention, took me from the grammar school, and sent me to a school for writing and arithmetic, kept by a then famous man, Mr. George Brownell, very successful in his profession generally, and that by mild, encouraging methods. Under him I acquired fair writing pretty soon, but I failed in the arithmetic, and made no progress in it. At ten years old I was taken home to assist my father in his business, which was that of a tallow chandler and soap boiler; a business he was not bred to, but had assumed on his arrival in New England, and on finding his dying trade would not maintain his family, being in little request. Accordingly, I was employed in cutting wick for the candles, filling the dipping mold and the molds for cast candles, attending the shop, going of errands, etc.

I disliked the trade, and had a strong inclination for the sea, but my father declared against it; however, living near the water, I was much in and about it, learned early to swim well, and to manage boats; and when in a boat or canoe with other boys, I was commonly allowed to govern, especially in any case of difficulty; and upon other occasions I was generally a leader among the boys, and sometimes led them into scrapes, of which I will mention one instance, as it shows an early projecting public spirit, though not then justly conducted.

There was a salt marsh that bounded part of the millpond, on the edge of which, at high water, we used to stand to fish for minnows. By much trampling, we had made it a mere quagmire. My proposal was to build a wharf there fit for us to stand upon, and I showed my comrades a large heap of stones, which were intended for a new house near the marsh, and which would very well suit our purpose. Accordingly, in the evening, when the workmen were gone, I assembled a number of my playfellows, and working with them diligently like so many emmets,[1] sometimes two or three to a stone, we brought them all away and built our little wharf. The next morning the workmen were surprised at missing the stones, which were found in our wharf. Inquiry was made after the removers; we were discovered and complained of; several of us were corrected by our fathers; and, though I pleaded the usefulness of the work, mine convinced me that nothing was useful which was not honest.

I think you may like to know something of his person and character. He had an excellent constitution of body, was of middle stature, but well set, and very strong; he was ingenious, could draw prettily, was skilled a little in music, and had a clear, pleasing voice, so that when he played psalm tunes on his violin and sung withal, as he sometimes did in an evening after the business of the day was over, it was extremely agreeable to hear. He had a mechanical genius too, and, on occasion, was very handy in the use of other tradesmen's tools; but his great excellence lay in a sound understanding and solid judgment in prudential matters, both in private and public affairs. In the latter, indeed, he was never employed, the numerous family he had to educate and the straitness of his circumstances keeping him close to his trade; but I remember well his being frequently visited by leading people, who consulted him for his opinion in affairs of the town or of the church he belonged to, and showed a good deal of respect for his judgment and advice: he was also much consulted by private persons about their affairs when any difficulty occurred, and frequently chosen an arbitrator between contending parties. At his table he liked to have, as often as he could, some sensible friend or neighbor to converse with, and always took care to start some ingenious or useful topic for discourse, which might tend to improve the minds of his children. By this means he turned our attention to what was good, just, and prudent in the conduct of life; and little or no notice was ever taken of what related to the victuals on the table, whether it was well or ill dressed, in or out of season, of good or bad flavor, preferable or inferior to this or

---

[1] emmets: Ants.

that other thing of the kind, so that I was brought up in such a perfect inattention to those matters as to be quite indifferent what kind of food was set before me, and so unobservant of it that to this day if I am asked I can scarcely tell a few hours after dinner what I dined upon. This has been a convenience to me in traveling, where my companions have been sometimes very unhappy for want of a suitable gratification of their more delicate, because better instructed, tastes and appetites.

My mother had likewise an excellent constitution: she suckled all her ten children. I never knew either my father or mother to have any sickness but that of which they died, he at eighty-nine, and she at eighty-five years of age. They lie buried together at Boston, where I some years since placed a marble over their grave, with this inscription:

Josiah Franklin,
And
Abiah his wife.
Lie here interred.
They lived lovingly together in wedlock
Fifty-five years.
Without an estate, or any gainful employment,
By constant labor and industry
With God's blessing,
They maintained a large family
Comfortably,
And brought up thirteen children
And seven grandchildren
Reputably.
From this instance, reader,
Be encouraged to diligence in thy calling,
And distrust not Providence.
He was a pious and prudent man;
She, a discreet and virtuous woman.
Their youngest son,
In filial regard to their memory,
Places this stone.
J. F. born 1655, died 1744, Ætat 89.
A. F. born 1667, died 1752, ———— 85.

By my rambling digressions I perceive myself to be grown old. I used to write more methodically. But one does not dress for private company as for a public ball. 'Tis perhaps only negligence.

To return: I continued thus employed in my father's business for two years, that is, till I was twelve years old; and my brother John, who was bred to that business, having left my father, married, and set up for himself at Rhode Island, there was all appearance that I was destined to supply his place, and become a tallow chandler. But my dislike to the trade continuing, my father was under apprehensions that if he did not find one for me more agreeable, I should break away and get to sea, as his son Josiah had done, to his great vexation. He therefore sometimes took me to walk with him, and see joiners, bricklayers, turners, braziers, etc., at their work, that he might observe my inclination, and endeavor to fix it on some trade or other on land. It has ever since been a pleasure to me to see good workmen handle their tools; and it has been useful to me, having learned so much by it as to be able to do little jobs myself in my house when a workman could not readily be got, and to construct little machines for my experiments, while the intention of making the experiment was fresh and warm in my mind. My father at last fixed upon the cutler's trade, and my uncle Benjamin's son Samuel, who was bred to that business in London, being about that time established in Boston, I was sent to be with him some time on liking. But his expectations of a fee with me displeasing my father, I was taken home again.

From a child I was fond of reading, and all the little money that came into my hands was ever laid out in books. Pleased with the *Pilgrim's Progress,* my first collection was of John Bunyan's works in separate little volumes. I afterward sold them to enable to buy R. Burton's *Historical Collections;* they were small chapmens books,[2] and cheap, forty or fifty in all. My father's little library consisted chiefly of books in polemic divinity, most of which I read, and have since often regretted that, at a time when I had such a thirst for knowledge, more proper books had not fallen in my way, since it was now resolved I should not be a clergyman. Plutarch's *Lives* there was in which I read abundantly, and I still think that time spent to great advantage. There was also a book of Defoe's, called an *Essay on Projects,* and another of Dr. Mather's, called *Essays to Do Good,* which perhaps gave me a turn of thinking that had an influence on some of the principal future events of my life.

This bookish inclination at length determined my father to make me a printer, though he had already one son (James) of that profession. In 1717 my brother James returned from England with a press and letters to set up his business in Boston. I liked it much better than that of my father, but still had a hankering for the sea. To prevent the apprehended effect of such an inclination, my father was impatient to have me bound[3] to my brother. I stood out some time, but at last was persuaded, and signed the indentures when I was yet but twelve years old. I was to serve as an apprentice till I was twenty-one years of age, only I was to be allowed journeyman's wages during the last year. In a little time I made great proficiency in the business, and became a useful hand to my brother. I now had access to better books. An acquaintance with the apprentices of booksellers enabled me sometimes to borrow a small one, which I was careful to return soon and clean. Often I sat up in my room reading the greatest part of the night, when the book was borrowed in the evening and to be returned early in the morning, lest it should be missed or wanted.

And after some time an ingenious tradesman, Mr. Matthew Adams, who had a pretty collection of books, and who frequented our printing house, took notice of me, invited me to his library, and very kindly lent me such books as I chose to read. I now took a fancy to poetry, and made some little pieces; my brother, thinking it might turn to account, encouraged me, and put me on composing occasional ballads. One was called *The Lighthouse Tragedy,* and contained an account of the

---

[2] **chapmens books:** Peddler's cheap copies.   [3] **bound:** Apprenticed.

drowning of Captain Worthilake, with his two daughters; the other was a sailor's song, on the taking of *Teach* (or Blackbeard) the pirate. They were wretched stuff, in the Grub street ballad style; and when they were printed he sent me about the town to sell them. The first sold wonderfully; the event, being recent, having made a great noise. This flattered my vanity; but my father discouraged me by ridiculing my performances, and telling me verse-makers were generally beggars. So I escaped being a poet, most probably a very bad one; but as prose writing has been of great use to me in the course of my life, and was a principal means of my advancement, I shall tell you how, in such a situation, I acquired what little ability I have in that way.

There was another bookish lad in the town, John Collins by name, with whom I was intimately acquainted. We sometimes disputed, and very fond we were of argument, and very desirous of confuting one another, which disputatious turn, by the way, is apt to become a very bad habit, making people often extremely disagreeable in company by the contradiction that is necessary to bring it into practice; and thence, besides souring and spoiling the conversation, is productive of disgusts and, perhaps, enmities where you may have occasion for friendship. I had caught it by reading my father's books of dispute about religion. Persons of good sense, I have since observed, seldom fall into it, except lawyers, university men, and men of all sorts that have been bred at Edinborough.

A question was once, somehow or other, started between Collins and me, of the propriety of educating the female sex in learning, and their abilities for study. He was of opinion that it was improper, and that they were naturally unequal to it. I took the contrary side, perhaps a little for dispute's sake. He was naturally more eloquent, had a ready plenty of words, and sometimes, as I thought, bore me down more by his fluency than by the strength of his reasons. As we parted without settling the point, and were not to see one another again for some time, I sat down to put my arguments in writing, which I copied fair and sent to him. He answered, and I replied. Three or four letters of a side had passed, when my father happened to find my papers and read them. Without entering into the discussion, he took occasion to talk to me about the manner of my writing; observed that, though I had the advantage of my antagonist in correct spelling and pointing[4] (which I owed to the printing house), I fell far short in elegance of expression, in method and in perspicuity, of which he convinced me by several instances. I saw the justice of his remarks, and thence grew more attentive to the manner in writing, and determined to endeavor at improvement.

About this time I met with an odd volume of the *Spectator.*[5] It was the third. I had never before seen any of them. I bought it, read it over and over, and was much delighted with it. I thought the writing excellent, and wished, if possible, to imitate it. With this view I took some of the papers, and, making short hints of the sentiment in each sentence, laid them by a few days, and then, without looking at the

---

[4] pointing: Punctuation.

[5] *Spectator:* An English daily paper featuring essays by Joseph Addison (1672–1719) and Richard Steele (1672–1729).

book, tried to complete the papers again, by expressing each hinted sentiment at length, and as fully as it had been expressed before, in any suitable words that should come to hand. Then I compared my *Spectator* with the original, discovered some of my faults, and corrected them. But I found I wanted a stock of words, or a readiness in recollecting and using them, which I thought I should have acquired before that time if I had gone on making verses; since the continual occasion for words of the same import, but of different length, to suit the measure, or of different sound for the rhyme, would have laid me under a constant necessity of searching for variety, and also have tended to fix that variety in my mind, and make me master of it. Therefore I took some of the tales and turned them into verse; and, after a time, when I had pretty well forgotten the prose, turned them back again. I also sometimes jumbled my collections of hints into confusion, and after some weeks endeavored to reduce them into the best order, before I began to form the full sentences and complete the paper. This was to teach me method in the arrangement of thoughts. By comparing my work afterward with the original, I discovered my faults and amended them; but I sometimes had the pleasure of fancying that, in certain particulars of small import, I had been lucky enough to improve the method or the language, and this encouraged me to think I might possibly in time come to be a tolerable English writer, of which I was extremely ambitious. My time for these exercises and for reading was at night, after work or before work began in the morning, or on Sundays, when I contrived to be in the printing house alone, evading as much as I could the common attendance on public worship which my father used to exact of me when I was under his care, and which indeed I still thought a duty, though I could not, as it seemed to me, afford time to practice it.

When about sixteen years of age I happened to meet with a book, written by one Tryon, recommending a vegetable diet. I determined to go into it. My brother, being yet unmarried, did not keep house, but boarded himself and his apprentices in another family. My refusing to eat flesh occasioned an inconvenience, and I was frequently chid for my singularity. I made myself acquainted with Tryon's manner of preparing some of his dishes, such as boiling potatoes or rice, making hasty pudding,[6] and a few others, and then proposed to my brother, that if he would give me, weekly, half the money he paid for my board, I would board myself. He instantly agreed to it, and I presently found that I could save half what he paid me. This was an additional fund for buying books. But I had another advantage in it. My brother and the rest going from the printing house to their meals, I remained there alone, and, despatching presently my light repast, which often was no more than a bisquit or a slice of bread, a handful of raisins, or a tart from the pastry cook's, and a glass of water, had the rest of the time, till their return, for study, in which I made the greater progress, from that greater clearness of head and quicker apprehension which usually attend temperance in eating and drinking.

And now it was that, being on some occasion made ashamed of my ignorance in figures, which I had twice failed in learning when at school, I took Cocker's book of arithmetic, and went through the whole by myself with great ease. I also read Seller's

---

[6] **hasty pudding:** Pudding made of sweetened cornmeal mush.

and Shermy's books of navigation, and became acquainted with the little geometry they contain; but never proceeded far in that science. And I read about this time Locke *On Human Understanding,* and the *Art of Thinking,* by Messrs. du Port Royal.

While I was intent on improving my language, I met with an English grammar (I think it was Greenwood's), at the end of which there were two little sketches of the arts of rhetoric and logic, the latter finishing with a specimen of a dispute in the Socratic method, and soon after I procured Xenophon's *Memorable Things of Socrates,* wherein there are many instances of the same method. I was charmed with it, adopted it, dropped my abrupt contradiction and positive argumentation, and put on the humble inquirer and doubter. And being then, from reading Shaftesbury and Collins,[7] become a real doubter in many points of our religious doctrine, I found this method safest for myself, and very embarrassing to those against whom I used it; therefore I took a delight in it, practiced it continually, and grew very artful and expert in drawing people, even of superior knowledge, into concessions, the consequences of which they did not foresee, entangling them in difficulties out of which they could not extricate themselves, and so obtaining victories that neither myself nor my cause always deserved. I continued this method some few years, but gradually left it, retaining only the habit of expressing myself in terms of modest diffidence, never using, when I advanced anything that may possibly be disputed, the words *certainly, undoubtedly,* or any others that give the air of positiveness to an opinion, but rather say, I conceive or apprehend a thing to be so and so; it appears to me, or *I should think it so or so,* for such and such reasons; or *I imagine it to be so;* or *it is so, if I am not mistaken.* This habit, I believe, has been of great advantage to me when I have had occasion to inculcate my opinions, and persuade men into measures that I have been from time to time engaged in promoting; and, as the chief ends of conversation are to *inform* or to be *informed,* to *please* or to *persuade,* I wish well-meaning, sensible men would not lessen their power of doing good by a positive, assuming manner, that seldom fails to disgust, tends to create opposition, and to defeat every one of those purposes for which speech was given to us—to wit, giving or receiving information or pleasure. For, if you would inform, a positive and dogmatic manner in advancing your sentiments may provoke contradiction and prevent a candid attention. If you wish information and improvement from the knowledge of others, and yet at the same time express yourself as firmly fixed in your present opinions, modest, sensible men, who do not love disputation, will probably leave you undisturbed in the possession of your error. And by such a manner, you can seldom hope to recommend yourself in *pleasing* your hearers, or to persuade those whose concurrence you desire. . . .

My brother had, in 1720 or 1721, begun to print a newspaper. It was the second that appeared in America, and was called the *New England Courant.*[8] The only one before it was the *Boston News-Letter.* I remember his being dissuaded by some of his

---

[7] **Shaftesbury and Collins:** *Characteristics of Men, Manners, Opinions, and Times* (1711), by Anthony Ashley Cooper, earl of Shaftesbury (1631–1713), and *A Discourse of Free Thinking* (1713), by Anthony Collins (1676–1729).

[8] **second . . . *Courant*:** It was actually the fifth such publication, but most earlier ones only lasted for a single issue.

friends from the undertaking, as not likely to succeed, one newspaper being, in their judgment, enough for America. At this time [1771] there are not less than five-and-twenty. He went on, however, with the undertaking, and after having worked in composing the types and printing off the sheets, I was employed to carry the papers through the streets to the customers.

He had some ingenious men among his friends, who amused themselves by writing little pieces for this paper, which gained it credit and made it more in demand, and these gentlemen often visited us. Hearing their conversations, and their accounts of the approbation their papers were received with, I was excited to try my hand among them; but, being still a boy, and suspecting that my brother would object to printing anything of mine in his paper if he knew it to be mine, I contrived to disguise my hand, and, writing an anonymous paper, I put it in at night, under the door of the printing house. It was found in the morning, and communicated to his writing friends when they called in as usual. They read it, commented on it in my hearing, and I had the exquisite pleasure of finding it met with their approbation, and that, in their different guesses at the author, none were named but men of some character among us for learning and ingenuity. I suppose now that I was rather lucky in my judges, and that perhaps they were not really so very good ones as I then esteemed them.

Encouraged, however, by this, I wrote and conveyed in the same way to the press several more papers, which were equally approved; and I kept my secret till my small fund of sense for such performances was pretty well exhausted, and then I discovered[9] it, when I began to be considered a little more by my brother's acquaintance, and in a manner that did not quite please him, as he thought, probably with reason, that it tended to make me too vain. And, perhaps, this might be one occasion of the differences that we began to have about this time. Though a brother, he considered himself as my master, and me as his apprentice, and, accordingly, expected the same services from me as he would from another, while I thought he demeaned me too much in some he required of me, who from a brother expected more indulgence. Our disputes were often brought before our father, and I fancy I was either generally in the right, or else a better pleader, because the judgment was generally in my favor. But my brother was passionate, and had often beaten me, which I took extremely amiss; and, thinking my apprenticeship very tedious, I was continually wishing for some opportunity of shortening it, which at length offered in a manner unexpected.

One of the pieces in our newspaper on some political point, which I have now forgotten, gave offense to the Assembly. He was taken up, censured, and imprisoned for a month, by the Speaker's warrant, I suppose, because he would not discover his author. I too was taken up and examined before the council; but, though I did not give them any satisfaction, they contented themselves with admonishing me, and dismissed me, considering me, perhaps, as an apprentice, who was bound to keep his master's secrets.

---

[9] **discovered:** Revealed.

During my brother's confinement, which I resented a good deal, notwithstanding our private differences, I had the management of the paper; and I made bold to give our rulers some rubs in it, which my brother took very kindly, while others began to consider me in an unfavorable light, as a young genius that had a turn for libeling and satire. My brother's discharge was accompanied with an order of the House (a very odd one), that *"James Franklin should no longer print the paper called the New England Courant."*

There was a consultation held in our printing house among his friends, what he should do in this case. Some proposed to evade the order by changing the name of the paper; but my brother, seeing inconveniences in that, it was finally concluded on as a better way, to let it be printed for the future under the name of Benjamin Franklin; and to avoid the censure of the Assembly that might fall on him as still printing it by his apprentice, the contrivance was that my old indenture should be returned to me, with a full discharge on the back of it, to be shown on occasion, but to secure to him the benefit of my service, I was to sign new indentures for the remainder of the term, which were to be kept private. A very flimsy scheme it was; however, it was immediately executed, and the paper went on accordingly, under my name for several months.

At length, a fresh difference arising between my brother and me, I took upon me to assert my freedom, presuming that he would not venture to produce the new indentures. It was not fair in me to take this advantage, and this I therefore reckon one of the first errata[10] of my life; but the unfairness of it weighed little with me, when under the impressions of resentment for the blows his passion too often urged him to bestow upon me, though he was otherwise not an ill-natured man: perhaps I was too saucy and provoking.

When he found I would leave him, he took care to prevent my getting employment in any other printing house of the town, by going round and speaking to every master, who accordingly refused to give me work. I then thought of going to New York, as the nearest place where there was a printer; and I was rather inclined to leave Boston when I reflected that I had already made myself a little obnoxious to the governing party, and, from the arbitrary proceedings of the Assembly in my brother's case, it was likely it might, if I stayed, soon bring myself into scrapes; and further, that my indiscrete disputations about religion began to make me pointed at with horror by good people as an infidel or atheist. I determined on the point, but my father now siding with my brother, I was sensible that, if I attempted to go openly, means would be used to prevent me. My friend Collins, therefore, undertook to manage a little for me. He agreed with the captain of a New York sloop for my passage, under the notion of my being a young acquaintance of his that had got a naughty girl with child, whose friends would compel me to marry her, and therefore I could not appear or come away publicly. So I sold some of my books to raise a little

---

[10] **errata:** Latin for *errors;* the word is used for mistakes in general, but in this text and in modern English it is especially used to mean printers' errors. Franklin represents himself metaphorically as the typesetter of the text of his own life, who wants to acknowledge, if not correct, the *errata* of his youth.

money, was taken on board privately, and as we had a fair wind, in three days I found myself in New York, near three hundred miles from home, a boy of but seventeen, without the least recommendation to or knowledge of, any person in the place, and with very little money in my pocket.

My inclinations for the sea were by this time worn out, or I might now have gratified them. But, having a trade, and supposing myself a pretty good workman, I offered my service to the printer in the place, old Mr. William Bradford, who had been the first printer in Pennsylvania, but removed from thence upon the quarrel of George Keith. He could give me no employment, having little to do, and help enough already; but says he: My son at Philadelphia has lately lost his principal hand, Aquila Rose, by death; if you go thither, I believe he may employ you. Philadelphia was one hundred miles farther; I set out, however, in a boat for Amboy, leaving my chest and things to follow me round by sea.

In crossing the bay, we met with a squall that tore our rotten sails to pieces, prevented our getting into the Kill[11] and drove us upon Long Island. In our way, a drunken Dutchman, who was a passenger too, fell overboard; when he was sinking, I reached through the water to his shock pate,[12] and drew him up, so that we got him in again. His ducking sobered him a little, and he went to sleep, taking first out of his pocket a book, which he desired I would dry for him. It proved to be my old favorite author, Bunyan's *Pilgrim's Progress* in Dutch, finely printed, on good paper, with copper cuts, a dress better than I had ever seen it wear in its own language. I have since found that it has been translated into most of the languages of Europe, and suppose it has been more generally read than any other book, except perhaps the Bible. Honest John was the first that I know of who mixed narration and dialogue, a method of writing very engaging to the reader, who, in the most interesting parts, finds himself, as it were, brought into the company, and present at the discourse. Defoe in his *Crusoe*, his *Moll Flanders, Religious Courtship, Family Instructor,* and other pieces, has imitated it with success, and Richardson has done the same in his *Pamela*, etc.

When we drew near the island, we found it was at a place where there could be no landing, there being a great surf on the stony beach. So we dropped anchor and swung round toward the shore. Some people came down to the water edge and hallowed to us, as we did to them, but the wind was so high, and the surf so loud that we could not hear so as to understand each other. There were canoes on the shore, and we made signs and hallowed that they should fetch us, but they either did not understand us, or thought it impracticable, so they went away, and night coming on, we had no remedy but to wait till the wind should abate; and, in the meantime, the boatman and I concluded to sleep, if we could; and so crowded into the scuttle, with the Dutchman, who was still wet, and the spray beating over the head of our boat, leaked through to us, so that we were soon almost as wet as he. In this manner we lay all night with very little rest; but, the wind abating the next day, we made a shift to

---

[11] **Kill:** The channel separating Staten Island from New Jersey.   [12] **shock pate:** A bushy outcrop of hair.

reach Amboy before night, having been thirty hours on the water, without victuals, or any drink but a bottle of filthy rum, the water we sailed on being salt.

In the evening I found myself very feverish, and went ill to bed; but, having read somewhere that cold water drank plentifully was good for a fever, I followed the prescription, sweat plentifully most of the night, my fever left me, and in the morning, crossing the ferry, I proceeded on my journey on foot, having fifty miles to Burlington, where I was told I should find boats that would carry me the rest of the way to Philadelphia.

It rained very hard all the day; I was thoroughly soaked, and by noon a good deal tired; so I stopped at a poor inn, where I stayed all night, beginning now to wish that I had never left home. I cut so miserable a figure, too, that I found, by the questions asked me, I was suspected to be some runaway servant, and in danger of being taken up on that suspicion. However, I proceeded the next day, and got in the evening to an inn, within eight or ten miles of Burlington, kept by one Dr. Brown. He entered into conversation with me while I took some refreshment, and, finding I had read a little, became very sociable and friendly. Our acquaintance continued as long as he lived. He had been, I imagine, an itinerant doctor, for there was no town in England, or country in Europe, of which he could not give a very particular account. He had some letters, and was ingenious, but much of an unbeliever, and wickedly undertook, some years after, to travesty the Bible in doggerel verse, as Cotton had done Virgil.[13] By this means he set many of the facts in a very ridiculous light, and might have hurt weak minds if his work had been published; but it never was.

At his house I lay that night, and the next morning reached Burlington, but had the mortification to find that the regular boats were gone a little before my coming, and no other expected to go before Tuesday, this being Saturday; wherefore I returned to an old woman in the town, of whom I had bought gingerbread to eat on the water, and I asked her advice. She invited me to lodge at her house till a passage by water should offer; and being tired with my foot traveling, I accepted the invitation. She understanding I was a printer, would have had me stay at that town and follow my business, being ignorant of the stock necessary to begin with. She was very hospitable, gave me a dinner of ox cheek with great goodwill, accepting only of a pot of ale in return; and I thought myself fixed till Tuesday should come. However, walking in the evening by the side of the river, a boat came by, which I found was going toward Philadelphia, with several people in her. They took me in, and, as there was no wind, we rowed all the way; and about midnight, not having yet seen the city, some of the company were confident we must have passed it, and would row no farther; the others knew not where we were; so we put toward the shore, got into a creek, landed near an old fence, with the rails of which we made a fire, the night being cold, in October, and there we remained till daylight. Then one of the company knew the place to be Cooper's Creek, a little above Philadelphia, which we saw

---

[13] **Cotton . . . Virgil:** Charles Cotton (1630–1687), an English poet, satirized the Roman poet Virgil in his *Scarronides; On the First Book of Virgil Travestied* (1664).

as soon as we got out of the creek, and arrived there about eight or nine o'clock on the Sunday morning, and landed at the Market Street wharf.

I have been the more particular in this description of my journey, and shall be so of my first entry into that city, that you may in your mind compare such unlikely beginnings with the figure I have since made there. I was in my working dress, my best clothes being to come round by sea. I was dirty from my journey; my pockets were stuffed out with shirts and stockings, and I knew no soul nor where to look for lodging. I was fatigued with traveling, rowing, and want of rest; I was very hungry; and my whole stock of cash consisted of a Dutch dollar, and about a shilling in copper. The latter I gave the people of the boat for my passage, who at first refused it, on account of my rowing; but I insisted on their taking it. A man being sometimes more generous when he has but a little money than when he has plenty, perhaps through fear of being thought to have but little.

Then I walked up the street, gazing about till near the market house I met a boy with bread. I had made many a meal on bread, and, inquiring where he got it, I went immediately to the baker's he directed me to, in Second Street, and asked for bisquit, intending such as we had in Boston; but they, it seems, were not made in Philadelphia. Then I asked for a threepenny loaf, and was told they had none such. So not considering or knowing the difference of money, and the greater cheapness nor the names of his bread, I bade him give me threepenny worth of any sort. He gave me, accordingly, three great puffy rolls. I was surprised at the quantity, but took it, and, having no room in my pockets, I walked off with a roll under each arm, and eating the other. Thus I went up Market Street as far as Fourth Street, passing by the door of Mr. Read, my future wife's father; when she, standing at the door, saw me, and thought I made, as I certainly did, a most awkward, ridiculous appearance. Then I turned and went down Chestnut Street and part of Walnut Street, eating my roll all the way, and, coming round, found myself again at Market Street wharf, near the boat I came in, to which I went for a draught of the river water; and, being filled with one of my rolls, gave the other two to a woman and her child that came down the river in the boat with us, and were waiting to go farther.

Thus refreshed, I walked again up the street, which by this time had many clean-dressed people in it, who were all walking the same way. I joined them, and thereby was led into the great meeting house of the Quakers near the market. I sat down among them, and, after looking round awhile and hearing nothing said, being very drowsy through labor and want of rest the preceding night, I fell fast asleep, and continued so till the meeting broke up, when one was kind enough to rouse me. This was, therefore, the first house I was in, or slept in, in Philadelphia.

Walking down again toward the river, and looking in the faces of people, I met a young Quaker man whose countenance I liked, and accosting him, requested he would tell me where a stranger could get lodging. We were then near the sign of the Three Mariners. Here, says he, is one place that entertains strangers, but it is not a reputable house; if thee wilt walk with me, I'll show thee a better. He brought me to the Crooked Billet in Water Street. Here I got a dinner, and, while I was eating it, several sly questions were asked me, as it seemed to be suspected, from my youth and appearance, that I might be some runaway.

After dinner, my sleepiness returned, and, being shown to a bed, I lay down without undressing, and slept till six in the evening; was called to supper, went to bed again very early, and slept soundly till next morning. Then I made myself as tidy as I could, and went to Andrew Bradford the printer's. I found in the shop the old man, his father, whom I had seen in New York, and who, traveling on horseback, had got to Philadelphia before me. He introduced me to his son, who received me civilly, gave me a breakfast, but told me he did not at present want a hand, being lately supplied with one; but there was another printer in town, lately set up, one Keimer, who, perhaps, might employ me; if not, I should be welcome to lodge at his house, and he would give me a little work to do now and then till fuller business should offer.

The old gentleman said he would go with me to the new printer; and when we found him, Neighbor, says Bradford, I have brought to see you a young man of your business; perhaps you may want such a one. He asked me a few questions, put a composing stick in my hand to see how I worked, and then said he would employ me soon, though he had just then nothing for me to do; and taking old Bradford, whom he had never seen before, to be one of the townspeople that had a good will for him, entered into a conversation on his present undertaking and prospects; while Bradford, not discovering that he was the other printer's father, on Keimer's saying he expected soon to get the greatest part of the business into his own hands, drew him on by artful questions and starting little doubts, to explain all his views, what interest he relied on, and in what manner he intended to proceed. I, who stood by and heard all, saw immediately that one of them was a crafty old sophister, and the other a mere novice. Bradford left me with Keimer, who was greatly surprised when I told him who the old man was.

Keimer's printing house, I found, consisted of an old shattered press, and one small, worn out font of English, which he was then using himself, composing an *Elegy on Aquila Rose,* before mentioned, an ingenious young man, of excellent character, much respected in the town, clerk of the Assembly, and a pretty poet. Keimer made verses too, but very indifferently. He could not be said to write them, for his manner was to compose them in the types directly out of his head. So there being no copy, but one pair of cases;[14] and the *Elegy* likely to require all the letter, no one could help him. I endeavored to put his press (which he had not yet used, and of which he understood nothing) into order fit to be worked with; and, promising to come and print off his *Elegy* as soon as he should have got it ready, I returned to Bradford's, who gave me a little job to do for the present, and there I lodged and dieted. A few days after, Keimer sent for me to print off the *Elegy.* And now he had got another pair of cases, and a pamphlet to reprint, on which he set me to work.

These two printers I found poorly qualified for their business. Bradford had not been bred to it, and was very illiterate; and Keimer, though something of a scholar, was a mere compositor, knowing nothing of presswork. He had been one of the French prophets,[15] and could act their enthusiastic agitations. At this time he did not

---

[14] **cases:** Printers' trays holding both uppercase and lowercase type.

[15] **French prophets:** French Protestant refugees who practiced a charismatic form of worship.

profess any particular religion, but something of all on occasion; was very ignorant of the world, and had, as I afterward found, a good deal of the knave in his composition. He did not like my lodging at Bradford's while I worked with him. He had a house indeed, but without furniture, so he could not lodge me; but he got me a lodging at Mr. Read's, before mentioned, who was the owner of his house; and, my chest and clothes being come by this time, I made rather a more respectable appearance in the eyes of Miss Read than I had done when she first happened to see me eating my roll in the street. . . .

FROM

Part Two [Moral Improvement]

It was about this time I conceived the bold and arduous project of arriving at moral perfection. I wished to live without committing any fault at any time; I would conquer all that either natural inclination, custom, or company might lead me into. As I knew, or thought I knew, what was right and wrong, I did not see why I might not always do the one and avoid the other. But I soon found I had undertaken a task of more difficulty than I had imagined. While my care was employed in guarding against one fault, I was often surprised by another; habit took the advantage of inattention; inclination was sometimes too strong for reason. I concluded, at length, that the mere speculative conviction that it was our interest to be completely virtuous, was not sufficient to prevent our slipping; and that the contrary habits must be broken, and good ones acquired and established, before we can have any dependence on a steady, uniform rectitude of conduct. For this purpose I therefore contrived the following method.

In the various enumerations of the moral virtues I had met with in my reading, I found the catalogue more or less numerous, as different writers included more or fewer ideas under the same name. Temperance, for example, was by some confined to eating and drinking, while by others it was extended to mean the moderating every other pleasure, appetite, inclination, or passion, bodily or mental, even to our avarice and ambition. I proposed to myself, for the sake of clearness, to use rather more names, with fewer ideas annexed to each, than a few names with more ideas; and I included under thirteen names of virtues all that at that time occurred to me as necessary or desirable, and annexed to each a short precept, which fully expressed the extent I gave to its meaning.

These names of virtues, with their precepts, were:

1. Temperance—Eat not to dullness; drink not to elevation.

2. Silence—Speak not but what may benefit others or yourself; avoid trifling conversation.

3. Order—Let all your things have their places; let each part of your business have its time.

4. Resolution—Resolve to perform what you ought; perform without fail what you resolve.

5. Frugality—Make no expense but to do good to others or yourself; i.e., waste nothing.

6. Industry—Lose no time; be always employed in something useful; cut off all unnecessary actions.

7. Sincerity—Use no hurtful deceit; think innocently and justly; and, if you speak, speak accordingly.

8. Justice—Wrong none by doing injuries, or omitting the benefits that are your duty.

9. Moderation—Avoid extremes; forbear resenting injuries so much as you think they deserve.

10. Cleanliness—Tolerate no uncleanliness in body, clothes, or habitation.

11. Tranquillity—Be not disturbed at trifles, or at accidents common or unavoidable.

12. Chastity—Rarely use venery but for health or offspring, never to dullness, weakness, or the injury of your own or another's peace or reputation.

13. Humility—Imitate Jesus and Socrates.

My intention being to acquire the *habitude* of all these virtues, I judged it would be well not to distract my attention by attempting the whole at once, but to fix it on one of them at a time; and, when I should be master of that, then proceed to another, and so on till I had gone through the thirteen; and, as the previous acquisition of some might facilitate the acquisition of certain others, I arranged them with that view, as they stand above. *Temperance* first, as it tends to procure that coolness and clearness of head, which is so necessary where constant vigilance was to be kept up, and guard maintained against the unremitting attraction of ancient habits, and the force of perpetual temptations. This being acquired and established, *Silence* would be more easy; and my desire being to gain knowledge at the same time that I improved in virtue, and considering that in conversation it was obtained rather by the use of the ears than of the tongue, and therefore wishing to break a habit I was getting into of prattling, punning, and joking, which only made me acceptable to trifling company, I gave *Silence* the second place. This and the next, *Order,* I expected would allow me more time for attending to my project and my studies. *Resolution,* once become habitual, would keep me firm in my endeavors to obtain all the subsequent virtues; *Frugality* and *Industry* freeing me from my remaining debt, and producing affluence and independence, would make more easy the practice of *Sincerity* and *Justice,* etc., etc. Conceiving, then, that, agreeably to the advice of Pythagoras in his *Golden Verses,* daily examination would be necessary, I contrived the following method for conducting that examination.

FORM OF THE PAGES

TEMPERANCE						
EAT NOT TO DULLNESS: DRINK NOT TO ELEVATION.						
	S.	M.	T.	W.	T.	F.	S.
T.							
S.	●	●		●		●	
O.	●●	●	●		●	●	●
R.			●			●	
F.		●			●		
I.			●				
S.							
J.							
M.							
C.							
T.							
C.							
H.							

I made a little book, in which I allotted a page for each of the virtues. I ruled each page with red ink, so as to have seven columns, one for each day of the week, marking each column with a letter for the day. I crossed these columns with thirteen red lines, marking the beginning of each line with the first letter of one of the virtues, on which line, and in its proper column, I might mark, by a little black spot, every fault I found upon examination to have been committed respecting that virtue upon that day.

I determined to give a week's strict attention to each of the virtues successively. Thus, in the first week, my great guard was to avoid every the least offense against *Temperance*, leaving the other virtues to their ordinary chance, only marking every evening the faults of the day. Thus, if in the first week I could keep my first line, marked T, clear of spots, I supposed the habit of that virtue so much strengthened, and its opposite weakened, that I might venture extending my attention to include the next, and for the following week keep both lines clear of spots. Proceeding thus to the last, I could go through a course complete in thirteen weeks, and four courses in a year. And like him who, having a garden to weed, does not attempt to eradicate all the bad herbs at once, which would exceed his reach and his strength, but works on one of the beds at a time, and, having accomplished the first, proceeds to a second, so I should have, I hoped, the encouraging pleasure of seeing on my pages the progress I made in virtue, by clearing successively my lines of their spots, till in the end, by a number of courses, I should be happy in viewing a clean book, after a thirteen weeks' daily examination.

This my little book had for its motto these lines from Addison's *Cato:*

Here will I hold. If there's a power above us
(And that there is, all nature cries aloud
Through all her works), He must delight in virtue;
And that which He delights in must be happy.

Another from Cicero,[16]

O vitae Philosophia dux! O virtutum indagatrix expultrixque vitiorum! Unus dies bene, et ex praeceptis tuis actus, peccanti immortalitati est anteponendus.

Another from the Proverbs of Solomon, speaking of wisdom or virtue:

Length of days is in her right hand, and in her left hand riches and honor. Her ways are ways of pleasantness, and all her paths are peace. — 3:16, 17.

And conceiving God to be the fountain of wisdom, I thought it right and necessary to solicit his assistance for obtaining it; to this end I formed the following little prayer, which was prefixed to my tables of examination, for daily use.

O powerful Goodness! bountiful Father! merciful Guide! Increase in me that wisdom which discovers my truest interest. Strengthen my resolutions to perform what that wisdom dictates. Accept my kind offices to thy other children as the only return in my power for thy continual favors to me.

I used also sometimes a little prayer which I took from Thomson's *Poems,*[17] viz.

Father of light and life, thou Good Supreme!
O teach me what is good; teach me Thyself!
Save me from folly, vanity, and vice,
From every low pursuit; and fill my soul
With knowledge, conscious peace, and virtue pure;
Sacred, substantial, never-fading bliss!

---

[16] **Cicero:** (106–43 B.C.E.) Roman philosopher and orator; the passage Franklin partially quotes from the *Tuscan Disputations* reads, "O Philosophy, guide of life! O you, who discover virtues and expel vice! . . . One day well lived according to your precepts is better than an eternity of sin."

[17] **Thomson's *Poems*:** From the long poem *The Seasons* (1726), by English poet James Thomson (1700–1748); the passage Franklin quotes is from "Winter," 218–23.

The precept of *Order* requiring that *every part of my business should have its allotted time,* one page in my little book contained the following scheme of employment for the twenty-four hours of a natural day.

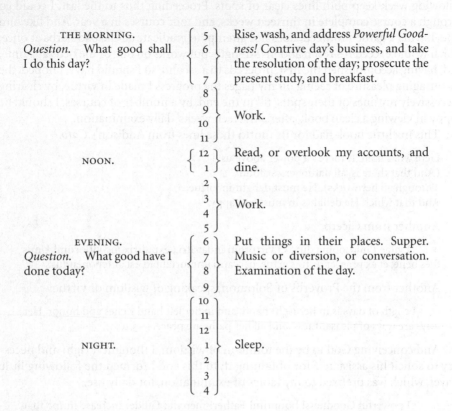

THE MORNING. *Question.* What good shall I do this day?	5 6 7	Rise, wash, and address *Powerful Goodness!* Contrive day's business, and take the resolution of the day; prosecute the present study, and breakfast.
	8 9 10 11	Work.
NOON.	12 1	Read, or overlook my accounts, and dine.
	2 3 4 5	Work.
EVENING. *Question.* What good have I done today?	6 7 8 9	Put things in their places. Supper. Music or diversion, or conversation. Examination of the day.
NIGHT.	10 11 12 1 2 3 4	Sleep.

I entered upon the execution of this plan for self-examination, and continued it with occasional intermissions for some time. I was surprised to find myself so much fuller of faults than I had imagined; but I had the satisfaction of seeing them diminish. To avoid the trouble of renewing now and then my little book, which, by scraping out the marks on the paper of old faults to make room for new ones in a new course, became full of holes, I transferred my tables and precepts to the ivory leaves of a memorandum book, on which the lines were drawn with red ink, that made a durable stain, and on those lines I marked my faults with a black lead pencil, which marks I could easily wipe out with a wet sponge. After a while I went through one course only in a year, and afterward only one in several years, till at length I omitted them entirely, being employed in voyages and business abroad, with a multiplicity of affairs that interfered; but I always carried my little book with me.

My scheme of *Order* gave me the most trouble; and I found that, though it might be practicable where a man's business was such as to leave him the disposition of his time, that of a journeyman printer, for instance, it was not possible to be exactly observed by a master who must mix with the world and often receive people of business at their own hours. *Order,* too, with regard to places for things, papers, etc., I found extremely difficult to acquire. I had not been early accustomed to it, and, having an exceeding good memory, I was not so sensible of the inconvenience attending want of method. This article, therefore cost me so much painful attention and my faults in it vexed me so much, and I made so little progress in amendment, and had such frequent relapses that I was almost ready to give up the attempt, and content myself with a faulty character in that respect, like the man who, in buying an ax from a smith, my neighbor, desired to have the whole of its surface as bright as the edge. The smith consented to grind it bright for him if he would turn the wheel; he turned while the smith pressed the broad face of the ax hard and heavily on the stone which made the turning of it very fatiguing. The man came every now and then from the wheel to see how the work went on and at length would take his ax as it was, without farther grinding. No, said the smith, turn on, turn on; we shall have it bright by and by; as yet, it is only speckled. Yes, says the man, *but I think I like a speckled ax best.* And I believe this may have been the case with many who, having, for want of some such means as I employed, found the difficulty of obtaining good and breaking bad habits in other points of vice and virtue, have given up the struggle, and concluded that *a speckled ax was best;* for something, that pretended to be reason, was every now and then suggesting to me that such extreme nicety as I exacted of myself might be a kind of foppery in morals, which, if it were known, would make me ridiculous; that a perfect character might be attended with the inconvenience of being envied and hated; and that a benevolent man should allow a few faults in himself, to keep his friends in countenance.

In truth, I found myself incorrigible with respect to *Order;* and now I am grown old and my memory bad, I feel very sensibly the want of it. But, on the whole, though I never arrived at the perfection I had been so ambitious of obtaining, but fell far short of it, yet I was, by the endeavor, a better and a happier man than I otherwise should have been if I had not attempted it; as those who aim at perfect writing by imitating the engraved copies, though they never reach the wished-for excellence of those copies, their hand is mended by the endeavor, and is tolerable while it continues fair and legible.

It may be well my posterity should be informed that to this little artifice, with the blessing of God, their ancestor owed the constant felicity of his life, down to his 79th year, in which this is written. What reverses may attend the remainder is in the hand of Providence; but, if they arrive, the reflection on past happiness enjoyed ought to help his bearing them with more resignation. To *Temperance* he ascribes his long-continued health, and what is still left to him of a good constitution; to *Industry* and *Frugality,* the early easiness of his circumstances and acquisition of his fortune, with all that knowledge that enabled him to be a useful citizen, and obtained for him some degree of reputation among the learned; to *Sincerity* and *Justice,* the confidence of his country, and the honorable employs it conferred upon him; and to the joint influence of the whole mass of virtues, even in the imperfect state he was able to acquire them, all that evenness of temper, and that cheerfulness in conversation, which makes his company still sought for and agreeable even to his younger acquaintances. I hope, therefore, that some of my descendants may follow the example and reap the benefit.

It will be remarked that, though my scheme was not wholly without religion, there was in it no mark of any of the distinguishing tenets of any particular sect. I had purposely avoided them; for, being fully persuaded of the utility and excellence of my method, and that it might be serviceable to people in all religions, and intending some time or other to publish it, I would not have any thing in it that should prejudice any one, of any sect, against it. I purposed writing a little comment on each virtue, in which I would have shown the advantages of possessing it, and the mischiefs attending its opposite vice; and I should have called my book *The Art of Virtue,* because it would have shown the means and manner of obtaining virtue, which would have distinguished it from the mere exhortation to be good, that does not instruct and indicate the means, but is like the apostle's man of verbal charity, who only, without showing to the naked and hungry how or where they might get clothes or victuals, exhorted them to be fed and clothed. — James 2:15, 16.

But it so happened that my intention of writing and publishing this comment was never fulfilled. I did, indeed, from time to time, put down short hints of the sentiments, reasonings, etc., to be made use of in it, some of which I have still by me; but the necessary close attention to private business in the earlier part of my life, and public business since, have occasioned my postponing it; for, it being connected in my mind with *a great and extensive project* that required the whole man to execute, and which an unforeseen succession of employs prevented my attending to, it has hitherto remained unfinished.

In this piece it was my design to explain and enforce this doctrine, that vicious actions are not hurtful because they are forbidden, but forbidden because they are hurtful, the nature of man alone considered; that it was, therefore, every one's interest to be virtuous who wished to be happy even in this world; and I should, from this circumstance (there being always in the world a number of rich merchants, nobility, states, and princes, who have need of honest instruments for the management of their affairs, and such being rare), have endeavored to convince young persons that no qualities were so likely to make a poor man's fortune as those of probity and integrity.

My list of virtues contained at first but twelve; but a Quaker friend having kindly informed me that I was generally thought proud; that my pride showed itself frequently in conversation; that I was not content with being in the right when discussing any point, but was overbearing, and rather insolent, of which he convinced me by mentioning several instances; I determined endeavoring to cure myself, if I could, of this vice or folly among the rest, and I added *Humility* to my list, giving an extensive meaning to the word.

I cannot boast of much success in acquiring the *reality* of this virtue, but I had a good deal with regard to the *appearance* of it. I made it a rule to forbear all direct contradiction to the sentiments of others, and all positive assertion of my own. I even forbid myself, agreeably to the old laws of our Junto, the use of every word or expression in the language that imported[18] a fixed opinion, such as *certainly,*

---

[18] **imported:** Implied.

undoubtedly, etc., and I adopted, instead of them, *I conceive, I apprehend,* or *I imagine* a thing to be so or so; or it *so appears to me at present.* When another asserted something that I thought an error, I denied myself the pleasure of contradicting him abruptly, and of showing immediately some absurdity in his proposition; and in answering I began by observing that in certain cases or circumstances his opinion would be right, but in the present case there *appeared* or *seemed* to me some difference, etc. I soon found the advantage of this change in my manner; the conversations I engaged in went on more pleasantly. The modest way in which I proposed my opinions procured them a readier reception and less contradiction; I had less mortification when I was found to be in the wrong, and I more easily prevailed with others to give up their mistakes and join with me when I happened to be in the right.

And this mode, which I at first put on with some violence to natural inclination, became at length so easy, and so habitual to me, that perhaps for these fifty years past no one has ever heard a dogmatical expression escape me. And to this habit (after my character of integrity) I think it principally owing that I had early so much weight with my fellow citizens when I proposed new institutions, or alterations in the old, and so much influence in public councils when I became a member; for I was but a bad speaker, never eloquent, subject to much hesitation in my choice of words, hardly correct in language, and yet I generally carried my points.

In reality, there is, perhaps, no one of our natural passions so hard to subdue as *Pride.* Disguise it, struggle with it, beat it down, stifle it, mortify it as much as one pleases, it is still alive, and will every now and then peep out and show itself; you will see it, perhaps, often in this history; for, even if I could conceive that I had completely overcome it, I should probably be proud of my humility.

Thus far written at Passy, 1784.

FROM

PART THREE [SOCIAL PROJECTS]

I am now about to write at home, August, 1788, but can not have the help expected from my papers, many of them being lost in the war.[19] I have, however, found the following.

Having mentioned *a great and extensive project* which I had conceived, it seems proper that some account should be here given of that project and its object. Its first rise in my mind appears in the following little paper, accidentally preserved, viz.

Observations on My Reading History in Library
May 9, 1731.

"That the great affairs of the world, the wars, revolutions, etc., are carried on and effected by parties.

"That the view of these parties is their present general interest, or what they take to be such.

---

[19] **lost . . . war:** Many of Franklin's papers left in Philadelphia were lost or destroyed.

"That the different views of these different parties occasion all confusion.

"That while a party is carrying on a general design, each man has his particular private interest in view.

"That as soon as a party has gained its general point, each member becomes intent upon his particular interest; which, thwarting others, breaks that party into divisions, and occasions more confusion.

"That few in public affairs act from a mere view of the good of their country, whatever they may pretend; and, though their actings bring real good to their country, yet men primarily considered that their own and their country's interest was united, and did not act from a principle of benevolence.

"That fewer still, in public affairs, act with a view to the good of mankind.

"There seems to me at present to be great occasion for raising a United Party for Virtue, by forming the virtuous and good men of all nations into a regular body, to be governed by suitable good and wise rules, which good and wise men may probably be more unanimous in their obedience to, than common people are to common laws.

"I at present think that whoever attempts this aright, and is well qualified, can not fail of pleasing God, and of meeting with success.   B.F."

Revolving this project in my mind, as to be undertaken hereafter, when my circumstances should afford me the necessary leisure, I put down from time to time on pieces of paper such thoughts as occurred to me respecting it. Most of these are lost; but I find one purporting to be the substance of an intended creed, containing, as I thought, the essentials of every known religion, and being free of everything that might shock the professors of any religion. It is expressed in these words, viz.,

"That there is one God, who made all things.

"That he governs the world by his providence.

"That he ought to be worshiped by adoration, prayer, and thanksgiving.

"But that the most acceptable service of God is doing good to man.

"That the soul is immortal.

"And that God will certainly reward virtue and punish vice, either here or hereafter."

My ideas at that time were, that the sect should be begun and spread at first among young and single men only; that each person to be initiated should not only declare his assent to such creed, but should have exercised himself with the thirteen weeks' examination and practice of the virtues, as in the before-mentioned model; that the existence of such a society should be kept a secret till it was become considerable, to prevent solicitations for the admission of improper persons, but that the members should each of them search among his acquaintance for ingenuous, well-disposed youths to whom with prudent caution the scheme should be gradually communicated; that the members should engage to afford their advice, assistance, and support to each other in promoting one another's interests, business, and advancement in life; that, for distinction, we should be called *The Society of the Free and Easy:* free, as being, by the general practice and habit of the virtues free from the dominion of vice; and particularly by the practice of industry and frugality, free from debt which exposes a man to confinement and a species of slavery to his creditors.

This is as much as I can now recollect of the project, except that I communicated it in part to two young men, who adopted it with some enthusiasm; but my then narrow circumstances and the necessity I was under of sticking close to my business occasioned my postponing the further prosecution of it at that time; and my multifarious occupations, public and private, induced me to continue postponing, so that it has been omitted till I have no longer strength or activity left sufficient for such an enterprise; though I am still of the opinion that it was a practicable scheme, and might have been very useful, by forming a great number of good citizens; and I was not discouraged by the seeming magnitude of the undertaking, as I have always thought that one man of tolerable abilities may work great changes, and accomplish great affairs among mankind if he first forms a good plan and, cutting off all amusements or other employments that would divert his attention, makes the execution of that same plan his sole study and business.

In 1732 I first published my Almanac, under the name of Richard Saunders; it was continued by me about twenty-five years, commonly called *Poor Richard's Almanac.* I endeavored to make it both entertaining and useful, and it accordingly came to be in such demand, that I reaped considerable profit from it, vending annually near ten thousand. And observing that it was generally read, scarce any neighborhood in the province being without it, I considered it as a proper vehicle for conveying instruction among the common people, who bought scarcely any other books; I therefore filled all the little spaces that occurred between the remarkable days in the calendar with proverbial sentences, chiefly such as inculcated industry and frugality, as the means of procuring wealth, and thereby securing virtue; it being more difficult for a man in want to act always honestly, as, to use here one of those proverbs, *it is hard for an empty sack to stand upright.*

These proverbs, which contained the wisdom of many ages and nations, I assembled and formed into a connected discourse prefixed to the Almanac of 1757, as the harangue of a wise old man to the people attending an auction. The bringing all these scattered counsels thus into a focus enabled them to make greater impression. The piece, being universally approved, was copied in all the newspapers of the continent; reprinted in Britain on a broad side, to be stuck up in houses; two translations were made of it in French, and great numbers bought by the clergy and gentry, to distribute gratis among their poor parishioners and tenants. In Pennsylvania, as it discouraged useless expense in foreign superfluities, some thought it had its share of influence in producing that growing plenty of money which was observable for several years after its publication.

I considered my newspaper, also, as another means of communicating instruction, and in that view frequently reprinted in it extracts from the *Spectator,* and other moral writers; and sometimes published little pieces of my own, which had been first composed for reading in our Junto.[20] Of these are a Socratic dialogue,[21] tending

---

[20] Junto: Group of artisans that Franklin formed in 1727, who met to discuss philosophy and social projects.

[21] Socratic dialogue: A technique of arriving at the truth about a matter through asking a series of questions.

to prove that, whatever might be his parts and abilities, a vicious man could not properly be called a man of sense; and a discourse on self-denial, showing that virtue was not secure till its practice became a habitude, and was free from the opposition of contrary inclinations. These may be found in the papers about the beginning of 1735.

In the conduct of my newspaper, I carefully excluded all libeling and personal abuse which is of late years become so disgraceful to our country. Whenever I was solicited to insert any thing of that kind, and the writers pleaded, as they generally did, the liberty of the press, and that a newspaper was like a stagecoach in which any one who would pay had a right to a place, my answer was, that I would print the piece separately if desired and the author might have as many copies as he pleased to distribute himself, but that I would not take upon me to spread his detraction; and that, having contracted with my subscribers to furnish them with what might be either useful or entertaining, I could not fill their papers with private altercation, in which they had no concern, without doing them manifest injustice. Now, many of our printers make no scruple of gratifying the malice of individuals by false accusations of the fairest characters among ourselves, augmenting animosity even to the producing of duels; and are, moreover, so indiscreet as to print scurrilous reflections on the government of neighboring states, and even on the conduct of our best national allies, which may be attended with the most pernicious consequences. These things I mention as a caution to young printers, and that they may be encouraged not to pollute their presses and disgrace their profession by such infamous practices, but refuse steadily, as they may see by my example that such a course of conduct will not, on the whole, be injurious to their interests. . . .

About the year 1734 there arrived among us from Ireland a young Presbyterian preacher, named Hemphill, who delivered with a good voice, and apparently extempore, most excellent discourses, which drew together considerable numbers of different persuasions, who joined in admiring them. Among the rest, I became one of his constant hearers, his sermons pleasing me, as they had little of the dogmatical kind, but inculcated strongly the practice of virtue or what in the religious stile are called good works. Those, however, of our congregation who considered themselves as orthodox Presbyterians disapproved his doctrine and were joined by most of the old clergy who arraigned him of heterodoxy before the synod in order to have him silenced. I became his zealous partisan and contributed all I could to raise a party in his favor, and we combated for him a while with some hopes of success. There was much scribbling pro and con upon the occasion; and finding that, though an elegant preacher, he was but a poor writer, I lent him my pen and wrote for him two or three pamphlets, and one piece in the *Gazette* of April, 1735. Those pamphlets, as is generally the case with controversial writings, though eagerly read at the time, were soon out of vogue, and I question whether a single copy of them now exists.

During the contest an unlucky occurrence hurt his cause exceedingly. One of our adversaries having heard him preach a sermon that was much admired thought he had somewhere read the sermon before, or at least a part of it. On search, he found that part quoted at length, in one of the British reviews, from a discourse of Dr. Foster's. This detection gave many of our party disgust, who accordingly abandoned his cause, and occasioned our more speedy discomfiture in the synod. I stuck by him, however, as I rather approved his giving us good sermons composed by others than bad ones of his own manufacture, though the latter was the practice of our common teachers. He afterward acknowledged to me that none of those he preached were his own; adding, that his memory was such as enabled him to retain and repeat any sermon after one reading only. On our defeat, he left us in search elsewhere of better fortune and I quitted the congregation, never joining it after, though I continued many years my subscription for the support of its ministers.

I had begun in 1732 to study languages; I soon made myself so much a master of the French as to be able to read the books with ease. I then undertook the Italian. An acquaintance, who was also learning it, used often to tempt me to play chess with him. Finding this took up too much of the time I had to spare for study, I at length refused to play any more unless on this condition, that the victor in every game should have a right to impose a task, either in parts of the grammar to be got by heart, or in translations, etc., which tasks the vanquished was to perform upon honor, before our next meeting. As we played pretty equally, we thus beat one another into that language. I afterward, with a little painstaking, acquired as much of the Spanish as to read their books also.

I have already mentioned that I had only one year's instruction in a Latin school, and that when very young after which I neglected that language entirely. But, when I had attained an acquaintance with the French, Italian, and Spanish, I was surprised to find, on looking over a Latin Testament, that I understood so much more of that language than I had imagined, which encouraged me to apply myself again to the study of it, and I met with more success, as those preceding languages had greatly smoothed my way.

From these circumstances, I have thought that there is some inconsistency in our common mode of teaching languages. We are told that it is proper to begin first with the Latin, and, having acquired that, it will be more easy to attain those modern languages which are derived from it; and yet we do not begin with the Greek, in order more easily to acquire the Latin. It is true that, if you can clamber and get to the top of the staircase without using the steps, you will more easily gain them in descending; but certainly, if you begin with the lowest you will with more ease ascend to the top; and I would therefore offer it to the consideration of those who superintend the education of our youth, whether, since many of those who begin with the Latin quit the same after spending some years without having made any great proficiency, and what they have learned becomes almost useless, so that their time has been lost, it would not have been better to have begun with the French, proceeding to the Italian, etc.; for, though, after spending the same time, they should quit the study of languages and never arrive at the Latin, they would, however, have acquired another tongue or two, that, being in modern use, might be serviceable to them in common life.

After ten years' absence from Boston, and having become easy in circumstances, I made a journey thither to visit my relations, which I could not sooner well afford. In returning, I called at Newport to see my brother, then settled there with his printing house. Our former differences were forgotten, and our meeting was very cordial and affectionate. He was fast declining in health, and requested of me that, in case of his death, which he apprehended not far distant, I would take home his son, then but ten years of age, and bring him up to the printing business. This I accordingly performed, sending him a few years to school before I took him into the office. His mother carried on the business till he was grown up, when I assisted him with an assortment of new types, those of his father being in a manner worn out. Thus it was that I made my brother ample amends for the service I had deprived him of by leaving him so early.

In 1736 I lost one of my sons, a fine boy of four years old, by the smallpox, taken in the common way. I long regretted bitterly and still regret that I had not given it to him by inoculation. This I mention for the sake of parents who omit that operation, on the supposition that they should never forgive themselves if a child died under it; my example showing that the regret may be the same either way, and that, therefore, the safer should be chosen.

Our club, the Junto, was found so useful and afforded such satisfaction to the members that several were desirous of introducing their friends, which could not well be done without exceeding what we had settled as a convenient number, viz., twelve. We had from the beginning made it a rule to keep our institution a secret, which was pretty well observed; the intention was to avoid applications of improper persons for admittance, some of whom, perhaps, we might find it difficult to refuse. I was one of those who were against any addition to our number, but, instead of it, made in writing a proposal that every member separately should endeavor to form a subordinate club, with the same rules respecting queries, etc., and without informing them of the connection with the Junto. The advantages proposed were, the improvement of so many more young citizens by the use of our institutions; our better acquaintance with the general sentiments of the inhabitants on any occasion, as the Junto member might propose what queries we should desire and was to report to the Junto what passed in his separate club; the promotion of our particular interests in business by more extensive recommendation and the increase of our influence in public affairs, and our power of doing good by spreading through the several clubs the sentiments of the Junto.

The project was approved and every member undertook to form his club, but they did not all succeed. Five or six only were completed which were called by different names as the Vine, the Union, the Band, etc. They were useful to themselves, and afforded us a good deal of amusement, information, and instruction besides answering, in some considerable degree, our views of influencing the public opinion on particular occasions, of which I shall give some instances in course of time as they happened.

My first promotion was my being chosen, in 1736, clerk of the General Assembly. The choice was made that year without opposition; but the year following, when I was again proposed (the choice, like that of the members, being annual), a new member made a long speech against me in order to favor some other candidate. I was, however, chosen, which was the more agreeable to me as, besides the pay for the immediate service as clerk, the place gave me a better opportunity of keeping up an interest among the members, which secured to me the business of printing the votes, laws, paper money, and other occasional jobs for the public that, on the whole were very profitable.

I therefore did not like the opposition of this new member who was a gentleman of fortune and education, with talents that were likely to give him, in time, great influence in the House which, indeed, afterward happened. I did not, however, aim at gaining his favor by paying any servile respect to him but, after some time, took this other method. Having heard that he had in his library a certain very scarce and curious book I wrote a note to him expressing my desire of perusing that book and requesting he would do me the favor of lending it to me for a few days. He sent it immediately and I returned it in about a week with another note expressing strongly my sense of the favor. When we next met in the House he spoke to me (which he had never done before), and with great civility; and he ever after manifested a readiness to serve me on all occasions, so that we became great friends and our friendship continued to his death. This is another instance of the truth of an old maxim I had learned, which says, *He that has once done you a kindness will be more ready to do you another than he whom you yourself have obliged.* And it shows how much more profitable it is prudently to remove, than to resent, return, and continue inimical proceedings.

In 1737, Colonel Spotswood, late governor of Virginia and then postmaster-general, being dissatisfied with the conduct of his deputy at Philadelphia respecting some negligence in rendering, and inexactitude of his accounts, took from him the commission and offered it to me. I accepted it readily and found it of great advantage; for, though the salary was small, it facilitated the correspondence that improved my newspaper, increased the number demanded, as well as the advertisements to be inserted, so that it came to afford me a considerable income. My old competitor's newspaper declined proportionably, and I was satisfied without retaliating his refusal while postmaster, to permit my papers being carried by the riders. Thus he suffered greatly from his neglect in due accounting: and I mention it as a lesson to those young men who may be employed in managing affairs for others, that they should always render accounts and make remittances with great clearness and punctuality. The character of observing such a conduct is the most powerful of all recommendations to new employments and increase of business.

I began now to turn my thoughts a little to public affairs, beginning, however, with small matters. The city watch was one of the first things that I conceived to want regulation. It was managed by the constables of the respective wards in turn; the constable warned a number of housekeepers to attend him for the night. Those who chose never to attend, paid him six shillings a year to be excused, which was supposed to be for hiring substitutes but was, in reality, much more than was necessary for that purpose and made the constableship a place of profit; and the constable, for a little drink, often got such ragamuffins about him as a watch, that respectable housekeepers did not choose to mix with. Walking the rounds, too, was often neglected and most of the nights spent in tippling. I thereupon wrote a paper to be read in Junto, representing these irregularities, but insisting more particularly on the inequality of this six-shilling tax of the constables, respecting the circumstances of those who paid it, since a poor widow housekeeper, all whose property to be guarded by the watch did not perhaps exceed the value of fifty pounds, paid as much as the wealthiest merchant who had thousands of pounds' worth of goods in his stores.

On the whole, I proposed as a more effectual watch, the hiring of proper men to serve constantly in that business; and as a more equitable way of supporting the charge, the levying a tax that should be proportioned to the property. This idea, being approved by the Junto, was communicated to the other clubs, but as arising in each of them; and though the plan was not immediately carried into execution, yet, by preparing the minds of people for the change, it paved the way for the law obtained a few years after when the members of our clubs were grown into more influence.

About this time I wrote a paper (first to be read in Junto but it was afterward published) on the different accidents and carelessnesses by which houses were set on fire, with cautions against them, and means proposed of avoiding them. This was much spoken of as a useful piece and gave rise to a project which soon followed it, of forming a company for the more ready extinguishing of fires and mutual assistance in removing and securing of goods when in danger. Associates in this scheme were presently found, amounting to thirty. Our articles of agreement obliged every member to keep always in good order and fit for use, a certain number of leather buckets with strong bags and baskets (for packing and transporting of goods), which were to be brought to every fire; and we agreed to meet once a month and spend a social evening together, in discoursing and communicating such ideas as occurred to us upon the subject of fires as might be useful in our conduct on such occasions.

The utility of this institution soon appeared, and many more desiring to be admitted than we thought convenient for one company, they were advised to form another, which was accordingly done; and this went on, one new company being formed after another till they became so numerous as to include most of the inhabitants who were men of property; and now, at the time of my writing this, though upward of fifty years since its establishment, that which I first formed, called the Union Fire Company, still subsists and flourishes, though the first members are all deceased but myself and one, who is older by a year than I am. The small fines that have been paid by members for absence at the monthly meetings have been applied to the purchase of fire engines, ladders, fire hooks, and other useful implements for each company, so that I question whether there is a city in the world better provided with the means of putting a stop to beginning conflagrations; and, in fact, since these institutions, the city has never lost by fire more than one or two houses at a time and the flames have often been extinguished before the house in which they began has been half consumed. . . .

I had, on the whole, abundant reason to be satisfied with my being established in Pennsylvania. There were, however, two things that I regretted, there being no provision for defense, nor for a complete education of youth; no militia, nor any college. I therefore, in 1743, drew up a proposal for establishing an academy, and at that time, thinking the Reverend Mr. Peters who was out of employ, a fit person to superintend such an institution, I communicated the project to him; but he, having more profitable views in the service of the proprietaries, which succeeded, declined the undertaking and, not knowing another at that time suitable for such a trust I let the scheme lie a while dormant. I succeeded better the next year, 1744, in proposing and establishing a Philosophical Society. The paper I wrote for that purpose will be found among my writings, when collected. . . .

These embarrassments that the Quakers[22] suffered from having established and published it as one of their principles that no kind of war was lawful, and which, being once published they could not afterward, however they might change their minds, easily get rid of, reminds me of what I think a more prudent conduct in another sect among us, that of the Dunkers. I was acquainted with one of its founders, Michael Welfare, soon after it appeared. He complained to me that they were grievously calumniated by the zealots of other persuasions, and charged with abominable principles and practices to which they were utter strangers. I told him this had always been the case with new sects, and that, to put a stop to such abuse I imagined it might be well to publish the articles of their belief, and the rules of their discipline. He said that it had been proposed among them, but not agreed to, for this reason: When we were first drawn together as a society, says he, it had pleased God to enlighten our minds so far as to see that some doctrines, which we once esteemed truths, were errors; and that others, which we had esteemed errors, were real truths. From time to time He has been pleased to afford us further light, and our principles have been improving, and our errors diminishing. Now we are not sure that we are arrived at the end of this progression, and at the perfection of spiritual or theological knowledge; and we fear that, if we should once print our confession of faith we should feel ourselves as if bound and confined by it and perhaps be unwilling to receive further improvement, and our successors still more so, as conceiving what we their elders and founders had done, to be something sacred, never to be departed from.

This modesty in a sect is perhaps a singular instance in the history of mankind, every other sect supposing itself in possession of all truth, and that those who differ are so far in the wrong; like a man traveling in foggy weather, those at some distance before him on the road he sees wrapped up in the fog, as well as those behind him, and also the people in the fields on each side, but near him all appears clear, though in truth he is as much in the fog as any of them. To avoid this kind of embarrassment, the Quakers have of late years been gradually declining the public service in the Assembly and in the magistracy, choosing rather to quit their power than their principle.

In order of time, I should have mentioned before, that having, in 1742, invented an open stove for the better warming of rooms, and at the same time saving fuel, as the fresh air admitted was warmed in entering, I made a present of the model to Mr. Robert Grace, one of my early friends, who, having an iron furnace found the casting

---

[22] **Quakers:** Quakers, or the Society of Friends, practiced a form of Christianity that originated in England in the 1650s. Its basic belief that the "light of God" resides in each person led to emphasizing peace, the abolition of slavery, and prison reform. William Penn (1644–1718), an English Quaker, founded Pennsylvania (named by King Charles II for Penn's father) as a "Holy Experiment" in the 1680s, a colony of religious tolerance and political freedom.

of the plates for these stoves a profitable thing, as they were growing in demand. To promote that demand, I wrote and published a pamphlet, entitled *An Account of the new-invented Pennsylvania Fireplaces; wherein their Construction and Manner of Operation is particularly explained; their Advantages above every other Method of warming Rooms demonstrated: and all Objections that have been raised against the Use of them answered and obviated,* etc. This pamphlet had a good effect. Governor Thomas was so pleased with the construction of this stove, as described in it, that he offered to give me a patent for the sole vending of them for a term of years; but I declined it from a principle which has ever weighed with me on such occasions, viz.: *that, as we enjoy great advantages from the inventions of others, we should be glad of an opportunity to serve others by any invention of ours; and this we should do freely and generously.*

An ironmonger in London, however, assuming a good deal of my pamphlet, and working it up into his own and making some small changes in the machine, which rather hurt its operation, got a patent for it there and made, as I was told, a little fortune by it. And this is not the only instance of patents taken out for my inventions by others, though not always with the same success, which I never contested, as having no desire of profiting by patents myself, and hating disputes. The use of these fireplaces in very many houses, both of this and the neighboring colonies, has been, and is, a great saving of wood to the inhabitants.

Peace being concluded, and the association business therefore at an end, I turned my thoughts again to the affair of establishing an academy. The first step I took was to associate in the design a number of active friends, of whom the Junto furnished a good part; the next was to write and publish a pamphlet, entitled *Proposals relating to the Education of Youth in Pennsylvania.* This I distributed among the principal inhabitants gratis; and as soon as I could suppose their minds a little prepared by the perusal of it, I set on foot a subscription for opening and supporting an academy: it was to be paid in quotas yearly for five years; by so dividing it, I judged the subscription might be larger and I believe it was so, amounting to no less, if I remember right, than five thousand pounds.

In the introduction to these proposals, I stated their publication, not as an act of mine, but of some *public-spirited gentlemen,* avoiding as much as I could, according to my usual rule, the presenting myself to the public as the author of any scheme for their benefit.

The subscribers, to carry the project into immediate execution, chose out of their number twenty-four trustees and appointed Mr. Francis, then attorney-general and myself to draw up constitutions for the government of the academy; which being done and signed, a house was hired, masters engaged, and the schools opened, I think, in the same year, 1749.

The scholars increasing fast, the house was soon found too small and we were looking out for a piece of ground properly situated, with intention to build, when Providence threw into our way a large house ready built which, with a few alterations, might well serve our purpose. This was the building before mentioned, erected by the hearers of Mr. Whitefield, and was obtained for us in the following manner.

It is to be noted that the contributions to this building being made by people of different sects, care was taken in the nomination of trustees, in whom the building and ground were to be vested, that a predominancy should not be given to any sect, lest in time that predominancy might be a means of appropriating the whole to the use of such sect, contrary to the original intention. It was therefore that one of each sect was appointed, viz., one Church of England man, one Presbyterian, one Baptist, one Moravian,[23] etc., those, in case of vacancy by death, were to fill it by election from among the contributors. The Moravian happened not to please his colleagues and on his death they resolved to have no other of that sect. The difficulty then was, how to avoid having two of some other sect, by means of the new choice.

Several persons were named, and for that reason not agreed to. At length one mentioned me with the observation that I was merely an honest man, and of no sect at all, which prevailed with them to choose me. The enthusiasm which existed when the house was built had long since abated, and its trustees had not been able to procure fresh contributions for paying the ground rent and discharging some other debts the building had occasioned, which embarrassed them greatly. Being now a member of both sets of trustees, that for the building and that for the academy, I had a good opportunity of negotiating with both, and brought them finally to an agreement, by which the trustees for the building were to cede it to those of the academy, the latter undertaking to discharge the debt, to keep forever open in the building a large hall for occasional preachers according to the original intention and maintain a free school for the instruction of poor children. Writings were accordingly drawn and on paying the debts, the trustees of the academy were put into possession of the premises; and by dividing the great and lofty hall into stories, and different rooms above and below for the several schools and purchasing some additional ground the whole was soon made fit for our purpose, and the scholars removed into the building. The care and trouble of agreeing with the workmen, purchasing materials, and superintending the work, fell upon me; and I went through it the more cheerfully, as it did not then interfere with my private business, having the year before taken a very able, industrious, and honest partner, Mr. David Hall with whose character I was well acquainted as he had worked for me four years. He took off my hands all care of the printing office, paying me punctually my share of the profits. This partnership continued eighteen years, successfully for us both.

The trustees of the academy, after a while, were incorporated by a charter from the governor; their funds were increased by contributions in Britain and grants of land from the proprietaries, to which the Assembly has since made considerable addition; and thus was established the present University of Philadelphia. I have been continued one of its trustees from the beginning, now near forty years, and have had the very great pleasure of seeing a number of the youth who have received their education in it, distinguished by their improved abilities, serviceable in public stations, and ornaments to their country.

---

[23] **Moravian:** Member of a Protestant denomination formally organized in eastern Germany in the 1720s; traces its doctrines to John Huss (1369?–1415), a Bohemian reformer burned as a heretic by the Roman Catholic Church.

When I disengaged myself, as above mentioned, from private business, I flattered myself that, by the sufficient though moderate fortune I had acquired, I had secured leisure during the rest of my life for philosophical studies and amusements. I purchased all Dr. Spence's apparatus, who had come from England to lecture here, and I proceeded in my electrical experiments with great alacrity; but the public, now considering me as a man of leisure, laid hold of me for their purposes; every part of our civil government, and almost at the same time, imposing some duty upon me. The governor put me into the commission of the peace, the corporation of the city chose me of the common council, and soon after an alderman, and the citizens at large chose me a burgess to represent them in Assembly. This latter station was the more agreeable to me, as I was at length tired with sitting there to hear debates, in which, as clerk, I could take no part, and which were so often unentertaining that I was induced to amuse myself with making magic squares or circles, or anything to avoid weariness; and I conceived my becoming a member would enlarge my power of doing good. I would not, however, insinuate that my ambition was not flattered by all these promotions; it certainly was; for, considering my low beginning, they were great things to me and they were still more pleasing as being so many spontaneous testimonies of the public good opinion, and by me entirely unsolicited.

The office of justice of the peace I tried a little, by attending a few courts, and sitting on the bench to hear causes, but finding that more knowledge of the common law than I possessed was necessary to act in that station with credit, I gradually withdrew from it, excusing myself by my being obliged to attend the higher duties of a legislator in the Assembly. My election to this trust was repeated every year for ten years without my ever asking any elector for his vote or signifying, either directly or indirectly, any desire of being chosen. On taking my seat in the House, my son was appointed their clerk. . . .

In 1751, Dr. Thomas Bond, a particular friend of mine, conceived the idea of establishing a hospital in Philadelphia (a very beneficent design, which has been ascribed to me, but was originally his), for the reception and cure of poor sick persons, whether inhabitants of the province or strangers. He was zealous and active in endeavoring to procure subscriptions for it, but the proposal being a novelty in America, and at first not well understood, he met with small success.

At length he came to me with the compliment that he found there was no such thing as carrying a public-spirited project through without my being concerned in it. For, says he, I am often asked by those to whom I propose subscribing, Have you consulted Franklin upon this business? And what does he think of it? And when I tell them that I have not (supposing it rather out of your line), they do not subscribe, but say they will consider of it. I enquired into the nature and probable utility of his scheme, and receiving from him a very satisfactory explanation, I not only subscribed to it myself, but engaged heartily in the design of procuring subscriptions from others. Previously, however, to the solicitation, I endeavored to prepare the minds of the people by writing on the subject in newspapers, which was my usual custom in such cases but which he had omitted.

The subscriptions afterward were more free and generous, but beginning to flag, I saw they would be insufficient without some assistance from the Assembly and therefore proposed to petition for it, which was done. The country members did not at first relish the project; they objected that it could only be serviceable to the city and therefore the citizens alone should be at the expense of it; and they doubted whether the citizens themselves generally approved of it. My allegation to the contrary, that it met with such approbation as to leave no doubt of our being able to raise two thousand pounds by voluntary donations, they considered as a most extravagant supposition, and utterly impossible.

On this I formed my plan and, asking leave to bring in a bill for incorporating the contributors according to the prayer of their petition, and granting them a blank sum of money, which leave was obtained chiefly on the consideration that the House could throw the bill out if they did not like it, I drew it so as to make the important clause a conditional one, viz.: "And be it enacted, by the authority aforesaid, that when the said contributors shall have met and chosen their managers and treasurer, *and shall have raised by their contributions a capital stock of*——*value* (the yearly interest of which is to be applied to the accommodating of the sick poor in the said hospital, free of charge for diet, attendance, advice, and medicines), *and shall make the same appear to the satisfaction of the speaker of the Assembly for the time being,* that *then* it shall and may be lawful for the said speaker, and he is hereby required, to sign an order on the provincial treasurer for the payment of two thousand pounds, in two yearly payments, to the treasurer of the said hospital, to be applied to the founding, building, and finishing of the same."

This condition carried the bill through; for the members, who had opposed the grant and now conceived they might have the credit of being charitable without the expense, agreed to its passage; and then, in soliciting subscriptions among the people, we urged the conditional promise of the law as an additional motive to give, since every man's donation would be doubled; thus the clause worked both ways. The subscriptions accordingly soon exceeded the requisite sum, and we claimed and received the public gift, which enabled us to carry the design into execution. A convenient and handsome building was soon erected; the institution has by constant experience been found useful, and flourishes to this day; and I do not remember any of my political maneuvers, the success of which gave me at the time more pleasure, or wherein, after thinking of it I more easily excused myself for having made some use of cunning.

∾ THOMAS JEFFERSON
1743–1826

Thomas Jefferson was a man of enormous intellectual ability and tremendous breadth whose interests ranged from the theoretical to the practical. At various times during his lifetime he was a scientist, an architect, a philosopher, a statesman, a farmer, a politician. Jefferson was also a product of his age; as much as any American of his time, he embodied the optimistic spirit of the ENLIGHTENMENT. He believed in the common sense of individuals and thought that citizens could best govern themselves, provided they had access to free education and support of democratic institutions. He wrote treatises on political theory, scientific agriculture, and Anglo-Saxon grammar, and he designed his beautiful home at Monticello and the halls of the University of Virginia. Jefferson is best remembered, however, for the Declaration of Independence (1776), a document of stunning rhetorical power and clarity. It was written in the tradition of the English Bill of Rights (1689), which defines the limits of the monarchy and enumerates certain inviolable political and civil rights of the English citizenry.

When Jefferson proposed an inscription for his gravestone, he wrote one that commemorated his intellectual contributions rather than his impressive record in government, which included the presidency:

HERE WAS BURIED THOMAS JEFFERSON
AUTHOR OF THE DECLARATION OF AMERICAN INDEPENDENCE
OF THE STATUTE OF VIRGINIA FOR RELIGIOUS FREEDOM
AND FATHER OF THE UNIVERSITY OF VIRGINIA

Philosopher and Politician. Born into Virginia aristocracy, Jefferson grew up quickly, especially after his father died when Thomas was fourteen, leaving him a large estate of 2,700 acres, including many slaves. After a classical education at the College of William and Mary, he practiced law and began his political career at the age of twenty-six, when he was elected to the Virginia House of Burgesses, the governing body of Virginia. This colony was already moving in the direction of revolution. By his early thirties Jefferson was recognized throughout the colonies for his intellectual and literary brilliance. His essay "A Summary View of the Rights of British America" (1774) aligned him with others weighing independence.

Jefferson became governor of Virginia in 1779 and founded the University of Virginia in 1819. Before his political career was finished he succeeded Benjamin Franklin[1] as a minister to France (1785), served as the first U.S. Secretary of State (1790–93), the second vice-president of the United States (1797–1801), and its third president (1801–09). His one book, *Notes on the State of Virginia* (1782) is a compendium of personal

www For links to more information about Thomas Jefferson and a quiz on the Declaration of Independence, see *World Literature Online* at bedfordstmartins.com/worldlit.

---

[1] **Benjamin Franklin** (1706–1790): Scientist, publisher, and inventor who served the United States as a diplomat in Great Britain and France. See page 516.

Thaddeus Kosciusko, *Portrait of Thomas Jefferson.* Aquatint Kosciusko, a Polish general who offered his services to the American Revolution, here portrays Jefferson in the style of a classical Greek philosopher, looking to the heavens and wearing a wreath on his head. The inscription below his portrait reads, "A Philosopher a Patriot and a Friend." (The Pierpont Morgan Library/Art Resource, NY)

and scientific observations about Virginia's landscape and people as well as observations on slavery, race, environment, and revolution. His wide reading and grounding in the classics contributed to his elegant, clear, and compelling writing style. He died on July 4, 1826, the fiftieth anniversary of the signing of the Declaration of Independence.

The Construction of the Declaration of Independence.

In the spring of 1776, as the war with England heated up and Thomas Paine's[2] pamphlet, *Common Sense*, was preaching the politics of independence, the Second Continental Congress appointed a committee of five to draft a formal declaration of independence. Although the committee as a whole generated the ideas and Franklin and John Adams[3] edited the work, Jefferson was largely responsible for the first version of the document.

---

[2] **Thomas Paine** (1737–1809): Libertarian English writer who worked for the American colonies during the American Revolution.

[3] **John Adams** (1735–1826): Delegate to the Second Continental Congress and member of the committee responsible for drafting the Declaration of Independence. He became the second president of the United States (1797–1801).

His attachment to
those of his friends
whom he could make
useful to himself was
thoroughgoing and
exemplary.

– JOHN QUINCY
ADAMS, Diary, 1836

It was not simply a declaration of independence; it was a succinct philosophical statement defending the principles by which such an act of separation might take place, justifying the American Revolution. The document is organized in three parts: a statement of the rational basis for having and supporting government; a detailed description of the abuses of the English government; and a logical, inevitable conclusion that independence is right and necessary.

Jefferson's acquaintance with "natural rights" philosophers like Locke (p. 586) and Rousseau[4] pitted him against Alexander Hamilton[5] and the Federalist Party, who believed that a strong central government exists to restrain man's potential for evil and to protect private property and the rights of a growing mercantile class. In Jefferson's view, the philosophical foundation for independence is "self-evident" truths about human equality and human rights to life, liberty, and the pursuit of happiness; he substituted "pursuit of happiness" for Locke's "inalienable right of property." Obviously, these principles were not "self-evident" to monarchs and other despots, or to anyone who held a pessimistic or cynical view of human nature. If equality and "unalienable" rights belong to individuals—especially in a "state of nature"—then governments are created to protect and support those rights. If a government does not adequately conform to this "social contract," then its people have a right and duty to sever relations with it. Similar ideas were later expressed in the French **Declaration of the Rights of Man and Citizen** (1789),[6] a guiding document for the French Revolution.

p. 604

The Declaration of Independence is a splendid example of a philosophical manifesto put into practice as a basis for a Constitution and new form of democratic government.

■ CONNECTIONS

Benjamin Franklin, *Autobiography,* **p. 522.** The American version of the Enlightenment stresses optimism about individual possibilities and fervent hope for the future. Franklin's regimen of moral improvement is based on a belief in the perfectibility of human nature. Is Jefferson's belief that government exists to preserve the "unalienable rights" of individuals comparable to Franklin's favorable view of human nature?

Rousseau, *Confessions,* **p. 372.** Several European and American writers and thinkers of the eighteenth century claimed that human beings were naturally good and criticized government for corrupting society. How are Rousseau's ideas about benevolent human nature as seen in *Confessions* similar to Jefferson's assumptions about human nature in the Declaration of Independence?

Aristotle, *The Doctrine of the Mean* **(Book 1).** Following the example of the Greek philosopher Aristotle, American thinkers of the Enlightenment depended upon

---

[4] Rousseau (1712–1778): French writer whose *Confessions* illustrate the importance of feelings and the individual. See page 367.

[5] Alexander Hamilton (1757–1804): One of America's founding fathers and the first secretary of the U.S. Treasury (1789–95); unlike Jefferson, who stressed a broad, free democracy, Hamilton worked for a more efficient and orderly functioning of the national government.

[6] Declaration of the Rights of Man and Citizen (1789): Declaration written by the French National Assembly, expressing Enlightenment principles; reminiscent of the American Declaration of Independence.

rational argument to persuade their audience of their opinions or theories. Aristotle uses a logical argument called a syllogism for structuring his position on ethics. What rational structure does Jefferson use and how persuasive is this structure?

■ FURTHER RESEARCH

Biography
Cunningham, Noble E., Jr. *In Pursuit of Reason: The Life of Thomas Jefferson.* 1988.
Peterson, Merrill D. *Thomas Jefferson and the New Nation: A Biography.* 1970.

Background and Criticism
Ford, P. L., ed. *The Writings of Thomas Jefferson.* 1892–99.
Koch, Adrienne. *The Philosophy of Thomas Jefferson.* 1943.
Waldenstreicher, David, ed. *Notes on the State of Virginia by Thomas Jefferson with Related Documents.* 2002.
Wills, Garry. *Inventing America.* 1978.
———. *Thomas Jefferson: Genius of Liberty.* 2000.

 # Declaration of Independence

IN CONGRESS, JULY 4, 1776

The Unanimous Declaration of the Thirteen United States of America

When in the Course of human events, it becomes necessary for one people to dissolve the political bands which have connected them with another, and to assume among the Powers of the earth, the separate and equal station to which the Laws of Nature and of Nature's God entitle them, a decent respect to the opinions of mankind requires that they should declare the causes which impel them to the separation.

Declaration of Independence. The Declaration is praised not only for its political and moral authority but also for its rhetorical genius. Its first statement is a periodic sentence: a long sentence made up of balanced phrases with a conclusion at the end. This first paragraph anticipates the conclusion of the document—separation from Great Britain—and prepares the reader for the "causes" in the body of the document that lead to this conclusion. The key to the rhetorical success of a document is the development of objective, balanced statements that inevitably lead to a desired end; the periodic sentence is a perfect vehicle for this result.

Key words like *truths* and *right* tie the phrases in the second paragraph together. This paragraph provides the moral basis for the statements that follow.

The third paragraph begins the list of causes, predicted by the last sentence of paragraph two: ". . . let Facts be submitted to a candid world." Each sentence is its own paragraph, which suggests the separate weight and seriousness of each indictment. The repetition of *He* and *For* at the beginning of the clauses is a rhetorical technique called *anaphora*. "He" is England's King George III (1738–1820); Jefferson deliberately refrains from using the king's name, since he wants to place the emphasis on the concept of the king as ruler, not on the physical person of the king of Great Britain, who had sympathizers in the American colonies. The incessant anaphora of the litany of indictments creates an insistent rhythm through twenty-seven paragraphs, like nails being pounded into a coffin. The final utterance then appears inevitable: the actual declaration of independence.

We hold these truths to be self-evident, that all men are created equal, that they are endowed by their Creator with certain unalienable Rights, that among these are Life, Liberty and the pursuit of Happiness. That to secure these rights, Governments are instituted among Men, deriving their just powers from the consent of the governed. That whenever any Form of Government becomes destructive of these ends, it is the Right of the People to alter or to abolish it, and to institute a new Government, laying its foundation on such principles and organizing its powers in such form, as to them shall seem most likely to effect their Safety and Happiness. Prudence, indeed, will dictate that Governments long established should not be changed for light and transient causes; and accordingly all experience hath shown, that mankind are more disposed to suffer, while evils are sufferable, than to right themselves by abolishing the forms to which they are accustomed. But when a long train of abuses and usurpations, pursuing invariably the same Object evinces a design to reduce them under absolute Despotism, it is their right, it is their duty, to throw off such Government, and to provide new Guards for their future security. — Such has been the patient sufferance of these Colonies; and such is now the necessity which constrains them to alter their former Systems of Government. The history of the present King of Great Britain is a history of repeated injuries and usurpations, all having in direct object the establishment of an absolute Tyranny over these States. To prove this, let Facts be submitted to a candid world.

He has refused his Assent to Laws, the most wholesome and necessary for the public good.

He has forbidden his Governors to pass Laws of immediate and pressing importance, unless suspended in their operation till his Assent should be obtained; and when so suspended, he has utterly neglected to attend to them.

He has refused to pass other laws for the accommodation of large districts of people, unless those people would relinquish the right of Representation in the Legislature, a right inestimable to them and formidable to tyrants only.

He has called together legislative bodies at places unusual, uncomfortable, and distant from the depository of their Public Records, for the sole purpose of fatiguing them into compliance with his measures.

He has dissolved Representative Houses repeatedly, for opposing with manly firmness his invasions on the rights of the people.

He has refused for a long time, after such dissolutions, to cause others to be elected; whereby the Legislative Powers, incapable of Annihilation, have returned to the People at large for their exercise; the State remaining in the mean time exposed to all the dangers of invasion from without, and convulsions within.

He has endeavoured to prevent the population of these States; for that purpose obstructing the Laws for Naturalization of Foreigners; refusing to pass others to encourage their migration hither, and raising the conditions of new Appropriations of Lands.

He has obstructed the Administration of Justice, by refusing his Assent to Laws for establishing Judiciary Powers.

He has made Judges dependent on his Will alone, for the tenure of their offices, and the amount and payment of their salaries.

William Stone, Engraving of the Declaration of Independence, 1823

(Courtesy of the National Archives)

He has erected a multitude of New Offices, and sent hither swarms of Officers to harass our People, and eat out their substance.

He has kept among us, in times of peace, Standing Armies without the Consent of our legislature.

He has affected to render the Military independent of and superior to the Civil Power.

He has combined with others to subject us to a jurisdiction foreign to our constitution, and unacknowledged by our laws; giving his Assent to their acts of pretended Legislation:

For quartering large bodies of armed troops among us:

For protecting them, by a mock Trial, from Punishment for any Murders which they should commit on the Inhabitants of these States:

For cutting off our Trade with all parts of the world:

For imposing taxes on us without our Consent:

For depriving us in many cases, of the benefits of Trial by Jury:

For transporting us beyond Seas to be tried for pretended offences:

For abolishing the free System of English Laws in a neighbouring Province, establishing therein an Arbitrary government, and enlarging its Boundaries so as to render it at once an example and fit instrument for introducing the same absolute rule into these Colonies:

For taking away our Charters, abolishing our most valuable Laws, and altering fundamentally the Forms of our Governments:

For suspending our own Legislatures, and declaring themselves invested with Power to legislate for us in all cases whatsoever.

He has abdicated Government here, by declaring us out of his Protection and waging War against us.

He has plundered our seas, ravaged our Coasts, burnt our towns, and destroyed the lives of our people.

He is at this time transporting large armies of foreign mercenaries to compleat the works of death, desolation and tyranny, already begun with circumstances of Cruelty & perfidy scarcely paralleled in the most barbarous ages, and totally unworthy the Head of a civilized nation.

He has constrained our fellow Citizens taken Captive on the High Seas to bear Arms against their Country, to become the executioners of their friends and Brethren, or to fall themselves by their Hands.

He has excited domestic insurrections amongst us, and has endeavoured to bring on the inhabitants of our frontiers, the merciless Indian Savages, whose Known rule of warfare, is an undistinguished destruction of all ages, sexes and conditions.

In every stage of these Oppressions We have Petitioned for Redress in the most humble terms: Our repeated Petitions have been answered only by repeated injury. A Prince, whose character is thus marked by every act which may define a Tyrant, is unfit to be the ruler of a free People.

Nor have We been wanting in attention to our British brethren. We have warned them from time to time of attempts by their legislature to extend an unwarrantable jurisdiction over us. We have reminded them of the circumstances of our emigration and settlement here. We have appealed to their native justice and magnanimity, and we have conjured them by the ties of our common kindred to disavow these usurpations, which, would inevitably interrupt our connections and correspondence. They too have been deaf to the voice of justice and of consanguinity. We must, therefore, acquiesce in the necessity, which denounces our Separation, and hold them, as we hold the rest of mankind, Enemies in War, in Peace Friends.

We, therefore, the Representatives of the united States of America, in General Congress, Assembled, appealing to the Supreme Judge of the world for the rectitude of our intentions, do, in the Name, and by Authority of the good People of these Colonies, solemnly publish and declare, That these United Colonies are, and of Right ought to be Free and Independent States, that they are Absolved from all Allegiance to the British Crown, and that all political connection between them and the State of Great Britain, is and ought to be totally dissolved; and that as Free and Independent States, they have full Power to levy War, conclude Peace, contract Alliances, establish Commerce, and to do all other Acts and Things which Independent States may of right do. And for the support of this Declaration, with a firm reliance on the Protection of Divine Providence, we mutually pledge to each other our Lives, our Fortunes and our sacred Honor.

Declarations of Rights and Independence

p. 559

From the time of earliest civilization, men and women have acted against forms of government they thought were unjust. Sometimes these measures took the form of violent conflict, such as peasant revolts and outright rebellion; at other times protest took the more temperate form of letters and formal petitions. In the late seventeenth and eighteenth centuries, a new genre of political protest developed out of the philosophies of just government and the natural rights of individuals. This new genre was the "declaration," a formal statement that argues against despotism and asserts the rights of citizens to life, liberty, and happiness. Thomas Jefferson's **Declaration of Independence**, like other declarations that were to follow, formally lists grievances against an offending government and draws up a list of rights claimed by the aggrieved party. In the case of the American colonists, the declaration culminated in a breach of affiliation between two parties and proclaimed the colonies an independent nation free from England's authority.

Jefferson used the structure of the English Bill of Rights (1689)[1] as a blueprint and incorporated the ideas of ENLIGHTENMENT philosophy, including those contained in John Locke's *Two Treatises on Government* (1690) and Jean-Jacques Rousseau's *The Social Contract* (1762), when shaping and composing the Declaration of Independence (1776). It in turn became a model for later documents, including the French Declaration of Rights of Man and Citizen (1789),

---

[1] English Bill of Rights: Formally known as "An Act declaring the Rights and Liberties of the Subject, and settling the Succession of the Crown," it was passed in December 1689; among other things, it extended civil rights and liberties to the people of England.

Women Marching to Versailles in 1789

This anonymous French engraving shows a crowd on its way to confront King Louis XVI. Carrying pitchforks, pikes, muskets, scythes, and other weapons, nearly six thousand women crying out "When will we have bread?" marched to the palace at Versailles to protest high grain prices. They exacted the king's promise to supply grain to Paris. After this incident, one of many popular disturbances during the summer of 1789, Louis agreed to approve the Declaration of the Rights of Man and Citizen, ending, at least in principle, all feudal entitlements in France. (Giraudon/Art Resource, NY)

which asserted citizens' freedom from absolute monarchy, and Ho Chi Minh's Declaration of Independence (1945), which, perhaps ironically, claimed Vietnam's freedom from France. Both of those texts as well as **Olympe de Gouges' Declaration of the Rights of Woman and the Female Citizen**—a feminist claim to equal treatment under the law—closely echo the language of Jefferson's

oh-LAMP duh GOOZH

p. 598

Declaration, demonstrating not only the power of that document's ideas but also its consummate rhetoric.

The selections that follow are mainly European texts written in the era of political upheaval surrounding the Glorious Revolution of 1688[2] and the French Revolution of 1789. Up until the eighteenth century, nothing like the Declaration of Independence had appeared in any language or culture. Previously, some kings and emperors were known to have sought protection for their subjects from the potential injustices of local administrators and provincial governors, and some, such as Emperors Ashoka (third century) and Akbar (1556–1605) in India, left behind decrees noted for their justice, humanity, and tolerance. But these new political writings were almost unprecedented claims for the rights of ordinary citizens. Also excerpted here is the **Iroquois** Constitution, or **"The Great Binding Law,"** an oral tradition of government that predates the eighteenth century and may have influenced Jefferson and Benjamin Franklin (1706–1790).

IH-ruh-kwoy

p. 571

THE SOCIAL CONTRACT: LOCKE AND ROUSSEAU

Following the Glorious Revolution of 1688 in England, John Locke's *Two Treatises on Government* laid the foundation for the eventual liberation of Europe's commoners from absolute monarchies. In contrast to apologists for absolutism like Thomas Hobbes[3] and defenders of the divine right of kings like Bishop Bossuet,[4] Locke argued that men had fundamental, natural rights to life, health, liberty, and property and that civil government should guarantee such rights. Under what Locke called the social contract, any ruler who failed to protect these rights could be deposed. In his *Treatises,* Locke supplied the terms for the political debate that would fuel the fires of revolution in America and France in less than a century.

---

[2] **Glorious Revolution of 1688:** The forced abdication of James II, the Catholic king of England, whose attempts to exercise royal authority over Parliament galvanized the largely Protestant nation against him. Parliament arranged for James's Protestant daughter, Mary, and her husband, William of Orange, to take over the throne, and James fled to France. Although this was largely a "bloodless revolution," some fighting between Catholics and Protestants took place in Ireland and Scotland.

[3] **Thomas Hobbes** (1588–1679): English philosopher whose *Leviathan* (1751), often denounced for its bitter and pessimistic view of society, claims that people willingly give up their freedom in order to seek protection under the absolute power of a sovereign.

[4] **Bishop Bossuet:** Jacques Bénigne Bossuet (1627–1704), churchman and political writer whose *Politics Drawn from the Very Words of Holy Scripture* (1709) argued that royal power is sacred, absolute, and established by God, who vests his power in the person of the king.

Indeed, in ***The Social Contract***, Jean-Jacques Rousseau expanded on p. 591 Locke's notion, arguing that the true sovereign in any social or political formation is the individual citizen, who voluntarily participates in the general will of the society.

RIGHTS OF MAN AND WOMAN

While Locke, Rousseau, Jefferson, and the National Assembly of France were busy advocating the rights of man—subject to qualification by virtue of property, social status, and race—they left out women. One of the earliest texts included here—Marie le Jars de Gournay's ***On the Equality of Men and Women*** (1622), defends the p. 580 rights of women and argues that if women were to have equal education, they would have equal intellectual power. In the revolutionary era that followed de Gournay's treatise, Olympe de Gouges' tract and Mary Wollstonecraft's ***A Vindication of the Rights of Woman*** p. 742 argued for the rights of citizenship to be extended to women, whose share in the social contract Locke, like the American and French revolutionaries after him, failed to acknowledge.

The transitions from monarchy to the rights of man, and from the rights of man to the rights of woman, were hotly contested throughout the century, and many European writers lamented the loss of what they believed were the two key guarantors of political and civic order: church and king. The nostalgia for what is known as benevolent paternalism is perhaps most poignantly (and revealingly) expressed in Edmund Burke's[5] *Reflections on the Revolution in France* (1790), wherein Burke acknowledges the link between Enlightenment philosophy and political revolution:

> But now all is to be changed. All the pleasing illusions, which made power gentle, and obedience liberal, which harmonized the different shades of life, and which, by a bland assimilation, incorporated into politics the sentiments which beautify and soften private society, are to be dissolved by the new conquering empire of light and reason.

Burke's *Reflections* started what became known in England as the Revolution Controversy. Mary Wollstonecraft fired the first shot in

---

[5] **Edmund Burke** (1729–1797): Anglo-Irish statesman and conservative political theorist whose most important work, *Reflections on the Revolution in France* (1790), opposed the principles and tactics of the French Revolution and anticipated some of its excesses and failures.

her *Vindication of the Rights of Woman,* followed by Thomas Paine[6] in his *Rights of Man.* Though the revolutionary fervor subsided to some degree after the executions of 1793–94 and the rise of Napoleon, who was to draw nearly all of Europe into a period of war that would result in the restoration of the old regimes, monarchy would never again enjoy the privileges it had before the revolution. At the beginning of the century, King Louis XIV declared "I am the State," but by 1798 the **Declaration of the Rights of Man and Citizen** asserted: "The nation is essentially the source of all sovereignty; nor can any individual, or any body of men, be entitled to any authority which is not expressly derived from it." The doctrine of the rights of man and woman and the notion that citizens should be able to choose their own system of governance was to inform the abolitionist and independence movements of the nineteenth and twentieth centuries.

p. 604

■ CONNECTIONS

Voltaire, *Candide,* **p. 275.** Satirists such as Molière, Voltaire, and Swift criticize their contemporaries and offer moral instruction by exaggerating human folly or wickedness, social injustice, and the abuse of power. While satire may criticize human nature, politics, and society, in order to be effective it often rests upon a common sense of what is just or right. Political writings, such as Rousseau's *Social Contract* and the various declarations of rights in this section, often strike at the heart of the shared values of a society in order to change them. How do early-eighteenth-century satires, such as *Candide* and *Gulliver's Travels,* anticipate the revolutionary politics of these texts? What common purposes do the two types of texts share, and which genre do you think is more effective as an instrument of change?

Olaudah Equiano, *The Interesting Narrative of the Life of Olaudah Equiano,* **p. 405.** The political, social, and economic conditions in eighteenth-century Europe spawned new forms of political writing, including declarations of rights and independence. Slave narratives were another new form of writing at the time, harrowing accounts of the struggle of blacks in the Americas, the West Indies, and elsewhere for emancipation, the most basic freedom of all. How does Equiano's slave narrative invoke the ideas expressed in declarations of rights and which of the two forms engages your sympathy more powerfully?

Emilia Pardo Bazán, *The Revolver;* **Kate Chopin,** *The Story of an Hour* **(Book 5); Alifa Rifaat,** *My World of the Unknown* **(Book 6).** Despite early efforts of women such as Marie le Jars de Gournay and Olympe de Gouges, women's rights made only slow gains throughout the eighteenth and nineteenth centuries. Women writers such as Emilia Pardo Bazán increasingly turned to writing short stories and novels to illus-

---

[6] **Thomas Paine** (1737–1809): American writer and political theorist; author of *Common Sense* and *The Rights of Man* (1791–92), which defended the French Revolution against Edmund Burke's *Reflections on the Revolution in France* (1790).

THE ILLUSTRIOUS PATRIOTS OF 1776 AND AUTHORS OF THE DECLARATION OF INDEPENDENCE. 1844

Edward Hicks, *The Illustrious Patriots of 1776 and Authors of the Declaration of Independence, 1844*
Prominent among the others are Thomas Jefferson (holding the document) and Benjamin Franklin (standing to Jefferson's left) in this painting of the signing of the Declaration of Independence. (Art Resource, NY)

trate the stifling conditions of women's lives. Does fiction such as Bazán's, Kate Chopin's, and Alifa Rifaat's appeal more broadly to readers' emotions and reason than political writings do, and which genre do you think might be more effective in moving readers to action?

■ PRONUNCIATION

Adodarhoh: ah-doh-DAR-hoh
Aghstawenserenthah: ahg-shtuh-wen-shuh-REN-thuh
Ayonhwhathah: ah-yone-HWAH-thuh
Cayuga: kah-YOO-guh
Dehennakrineh: deh-hen-uh-KRIN-eh
Dekanawidah: deh-kah-nuh-WEE-duh
Deyoenhegwenh: deh-yoh-en-HEG-wen
Gayanashagowa: gah-yuh-nah-shuh-GOH-wuh
Hahyonhwatha: hah-yone-HWAH-thuh
Haudenosaunee: hoh-deh-noh-SHOH-nee
Hononwiretonh: hoh-none-wih-REH-tone
Iroquois: IH-ruh-kwoy
Marie le Jars de Gournay: mah-REE luh ZHAR duh goor-NAY
Oghrenghrehgowah: oh-greng-greh-GOH-wuh
Olympe de Gouges: oh-LAMP duh GOOZH
Ongwehonweh: ong-weh-HON-weh
Onondaga: on-un-DAH-guh
Oneida: oh-NIGH-duh
Seneca: SEN-ih-kuh
Shadekariwade: shah-deh-kah-rih-WAH-deh
Sharenhowaneh: shah-ren-HOH-wuh-neh
Shoskoharowaneh: shoh-shkoh-hah-ROH-wuh-neh
Skanawatih: shkah-nah-WAH-tih
Tekarihoken: teh-kah-rih-HOH-ken

❧ IROQUOIS NATION

C. 15TH–18TH CENTURY

hoh-deh-noh-
SHOH-nee
deh-kah-nuh-
WEE-duh;
SEN-ih-kuh;
hah-yone-HWAH-thuh
on-un-DAH-guh;
oh-NIGH-duh;
kah-YOO-guh
gah-yuh-nah-shuh-
GOH-wuh

Sometime in the fourteenth or fifteenth century, the five tribal nations living in the Eastern Woodlands of the United States, primarily in what is now New York, formed a confederation known as the Confederation of **Haudenosaunee**, or, more familiarly, the Iroquois League. According to Iroquois legend, the inspiration for the confederation came from **Dekanawidah**, a Huron living among the **Seneca** who was assisted in negotiating among the independent nations by **Hahyonhwatha** (the Hiawatha of legend), a Mohawk. The five nations included the Seneca, Mohawk, **Onondaga**, **Oneida**, and **Cayuga**. Around 1715, they were joined by the Tuscarora, who joined the confederacy after leaving their homeland in what is now North Carolina. The league was bound together by "The Great Binding Law" ("**Gayanashagowa**"), a formal constitution passed down orally and recorded on wampum belts for several generations. It was eventually written down in English around 1880 by Seth Newhouse, a Mohawk, and today several versions exist with slight variations.

The constitution calls for a system of checks and balances and delineates procedures for negotiations as well as the rights and powers of each nation. This self-regulating system that could function irrespective of the particular personalities holding office may have influenced the drafters of the United States Constitution, including Benjamin Franklin, who as a publisher in Philadelphia carefully followed the treaty negotiations between the Iroquois and the colonial settlers and published accounts of them between 1736 and 1762.

"The Great Binding Law" organized the confederation on the model of the "long house," the rectangular dwelling common to the native northeastern peoples. According to this design, the Onondaga, whose lands were centrally located among the nations (near what is now Syracuse, NY), occupied the center of the confederation and as hosts of the Confederate Council meetings were appointed to be the "fire keepers." The Seneca and Mohawk, the "older brothers," were designated the keepers of the Western Door and the Eastern Door, respectively; the Cayuga and Oneida, the "younger brothers," participated fully in negotiations. As set forth in the Constitution, when a meeting of the Confederate Council was needed, each nation sent an equal number of delegates chosen by female clan leaders. Two representatives from each group had the right to speak; a third served as a sort of referee, speaking only to point out errors in protocol. The older and younger brothers began the negotiations, which were confirmed or denied by the Onondaga. As some writers have noted, this system mirrors the checks and balances built into the U.S. Constitution.

"The Great Binding Law" regulated marriage among clans and nations, spelled out the wartime responsibilities of each nation, protected the religious ceremonies of each nation, and named the rights of the five nations and those of foreign nations. These basic or fundamental rights were oriented toward collective or community rights, but they also invested individual "nephews or nieces" with the power to appeal should they believe that the laws of the Confederate Council had been violated. The excerpts reprinted here describe the confederacy, the role of women as clan leaders, and the rights of foreigners and the people of the nations.

A note on the text: Because "The Great Binding Law" was transmitted orally, there is no definitive written text. Several versions exist and are the subject of academic dispute. The portion reprinted here is a copyright-cleared text by Gerald Murphy, distributed by the Cybercasting Services Division of the National Public Telecomputing Network (NPTN). For the complete text, see www.bedfordstmartins.com/worldlit.

FROM

∾ The Great Binding Law, Gayanashagowa

1. I am Dekanawidah[1] and with the Five Nations'[2] Confederate Lords I plant the Tree of Great Peace. I plant it in your territory, Adodarhoh,[3] and the Onondaga Nation, in the territory of you who are Firekeepers.[4]

   I name the tree the Tree of the Great Long Leaves. Under the shade of this Tree of the Great Peace we spread the soft white feathery down of the globe thistle as seats for you, Adodarhoh, and your cousin Lords.

   We place you upon those seats, spread soft with the feathery down of the globe thistle, there beneath the shade of the spreading branches of the Tree of Peace. There shall you sit and watch the Council Fire of the Confederacy of the Five Nations, and all the affairs of the Five Nations shall be transacted at this place before you, Adodarhoh, and your cousin Lords, by the Confederate Lords of the Five Nations.

2. Roots have spread out from the Tree of the Great Peace, one to the north, one to the east, one to the south, and one to the west. The name of these roots is The Great White Roots and their nature is Peace and Strength.

   If any man or any nation outside the Five Nations shall obey the laws of the

---

[1] **Dekanawidah:** Legendary founder, with Hahyonhwatha (Hiawatha), of the Iroquois League. A Huron from what is now Ontario, Canada; said to have been born of a virgin. In a vision, his mother learned he should join the People of the Flint—the Mohawk—and help them establish the Great Tree of Peace.

[2] **Five Nations:** The Mohawk, Onondaga, Seneca, Oneida, and Cayuga. A sixth nation, the Tuscarora, joined the league in 1715.

[3] **Adodarhoh:** (Atotarho) According to legend, an evil sorcerer who corrupted the Onondaga people and undermined peace among the five nations before the arrival of Dekanawidah; name used to designate the chief who presided over the confederation.

[4] **Firekeepers:** The Onondaga were named the Fire Keepers, because, as the centrally located nation, they hosted the Confederate Council meetings on their lands in what is now Syracuse, NY.

Great Peace and make known their disposition to the Lords of the Confederacy, they may trace the Roots to the Tree and if their minds are clean and they are obedient and promise to obey the wishes of the Confederate Council, they shall be welcomed to take shelter beneath the Tree of the Long Leaves.

We place at the top of the Tree of the Long Leaves an Eagle who is able to see afar. If he sees in the distance any evil approaching or any danger threatening he will at once warn the people of the Confederacy.

3. To you, Adodarhoh, the Onondaga cousin Lords, I and the other Confederate Lords have entrusted the caretaking and the watching of the Five Nations Council Fire.

When there is any business to be transacted and the Confederate Council is not in session, a messenger shall be dispatched either to Adodarhoh, Hononwirehtonh, or Skanawatih, Fire Keepers, or to their War Chiefs with a full statement of the case desired to be considered. Then shall Adodarhoh call his cousin (associate) Lords together and consider whether or not the case is of sufficient importance to demand the attention of the Confederate Council. If so, Adodarhoh shall dispatch messengers to summon all the Confederate Lords to assemble beneath the Tree of the Long Leaves.

When the Lords are assembled the Council Fire shall be kindled, but not with chestnut wood, and Adodarhoh shall formally open the Council.

Then shall Adodarhoh and his cousin Lords, the Fire Keepers, announce the subject for discussion.

The Smoke of the Confederate Council Fire shall ever ascend and pierce the sky so that other nations who may be allies may see the Council Fire of the Great Peace.

Adodarhoh and his cousin Lords are entrusted with the Keeping of the Council Fire.

4. You, Adodarhoh, and your thirteen cousin Lords, shall faithfully keep the space about the Council Fire clean and you shall allow neither dust nor dirt to accumulate. I lay a Long Wing before you as a broom. As a weapon against a crawling creature I lay a staff with you so that you may thrust it away from the Council Fire. If you fail to cast it out then call the rest of the United Lords to your aid.

5. The Council of the Mohawk shall be divided into three parties as follows: Tekarihoken, Ayonhwhathah, and Shadekariwade are the first party; Sharenhowaneh, Deyoenhegwenh, and Oghrenghrehgowah are the second party, and Dehennakrineh, Aghstawenserenthah, and Shoskoharowaneh are the third party. The third party is to listen only to the discussion of the first and second parties and if an error is made or the proceeding is irregular they are to call attention to it, and when the case is right and properly decided by the two parties they shall confirm the decision of the two parties and refer the case to the Seneca Lords for their decision. When the Seneca Lords have decided in accord with the Mohawk Lords, the case or question shall be referred to the Cayuga and Oneida Lords on the opposite side of the house.

6. I, Dekanawidah, appoint the Mohawk Lords the heads and the leaders of the Five Nations Confederacy. The Mohawk Lords are the foundation of the Great Peace and it shall, therefore, be against the Great Binding Law to pass measures in the Confederate Council after the Mohawk Lords have protested against them.

   No council of the Confederate Lords shall be legal unless all the Mohawk Lords are present.

7. Whenever the Confederate Lords shall assemble for the purpose of holding a council, the Onondaga Lords shall open it by expressing their gratitude to their cousin Lords and greeting them, and they shall make an address and offer thanks to the earth where men dwell, to the streams of water, the pools, the springs and the lakes, to the maize and the fruits, to the medicinal herbs and trees, to the forest trees for their usefulness, to the animals that serve as food and give their pelts for clothing, to the great winds and the lesser winds, to the Thunders, to the Sun, the mighty warrior, to the moon, to the messengers of the Creator who reveal his wishes and to the Great Creator who dwells in the heavens above, who gives all the things useful to men, and who is the source and the ruler of health and life.

   Then shall the Onondaga Lords declare the council open.

   The council shall not sit after darkness has set in.

8. The Firekeepers shall formally open and close all councils of the Confederate Lords, and they shall pass upon all matters deliberated upon by the two sides and render their decision.

   Every Onondaga Lord (or his deputy) must be present at every Confederate Council and must agree with the majority without unwarrantable dissent, so that a unanimous decision may be rendered.

   If Adodarhoh or any of his cousin Lords are absent from a Confederate Council, any other Firekeeper may open and close the Council, but the Firekeepers present may not give any decisions, unless the matter is of small importance.

9. All the business of the Five Nations Confederate Council shall be conducted by the two combined bodies of Confederate Lords. First the question shall be passed upon by the Mohawk and Seneca Lords, then it shall be discussed and passed by the Oneida and Cayuga Lords. Their decisions shall then be referred to the Onondaga Lords, (Fire Keepers) for final judgement.

   The same process shall obtain when a question is brought before the council by an individual or a War Chief.

10. In all cases the procedure must be as follows: when the Mohawk and Seneca Lords have unanimously agreed upon a question, they shall report their decision to the Cayuga and Oneida Lords who shall deliberate upon the question and report a unanimous decision to the Mohawk Lords. The Mohawk Lords will then report the standing of the case to the Firekeepers, who shall render a decision as they see fit in case of a disagreement by the two bodies, or confirm the decisions of the two bodies if they are identical. The Fire Keepers shall then

report their decision to the Mohawk Lords who shall announce it to the open council.

11. If through any misunderstanding or obstinacy on the part of the Fire Keepers, they render a decision at variance with that of the Two Sides, the Two Sides shall reconsider the matter and if their decisions are jointly the same as before they shall report to the Fire Keepers who are then compelled to confirm their joint decision.

12. When a case comes before the Onondaga Lords (Fire Keepers) for discussion and decision, Adodarho shall introduce the matter to his comrade Lords who shall then discuss it in their two bodies. Every Onondaga Lord except Hononwiretonh shall deliberate and he shall listen only. When a unanimous decision shall have been reached by the two bodies of Fire Keepers, Adodarho shall notify Hononwiretonh of the fact when he shall confirm it. He shall refuse to confirm a decision if it is not unanimously agreed upon by both sides of the Fire Keepers.

13. No Lord shall ask a question of the body of Confederate Lords when they are discussing a case, question, or proposition. He may only deliberate in a low tone with the separate body of which he is a member.

14. When the Council of the Five Nation Lords shall convene they shall appoint a speaker for the day. He shall be a Lord of either the Mohawk, Onondaga, or Seneca Nation.

    The next day the Council shall appoint another speaker, but the first speaker may be reappointed if there is no objection, but a speaker's term shall not be regarded more than for the day.

15. No individual or foreign nation interested in a case, question, or proposition shall have any voice in the Confederate Council except to answer a question put to him or them by the speaker for the Lords.

16. If the conditions which shall arise at any future time call for an addition to or change of this law, the case shall be carefully considered and if a new beam seems necessary or beneficial, the proposed change shall be voted upon and if adopted it shall be called, "Added to the Rafters." [. . .]

CLANS AND CONSANGUINITY

42. Among the Five Nations and their posterity there shall be the following original clans: Great Name Bearer, Ancient Name Bearer, Great Bear, Ancient Bear, Turtle, Painted Turtle, Standing Rock, Large Plover, Deer, Pigeon Hawk, Eel, Ball, Opposite-Side-of-the-Hand, and Wild Potatoes. These clans distributed through their respective Nations, shall be the sole owners and holders of the soil of the country and in them is it vested as a birthright.

43. People of the Five Nations members of a certain clan shall recognize every other member of that clan, irrespective of the Nation, as relatives. Men and women, therefore, members of the same clan are forbidden to marry.

44. The lineal descent of the people of the Five Nations shall run in the female line. Women shall be considered the progenitors of the Nation. They shall own the land and the soil. Men and women shall follow the status of the mother.

45. The women heirs of the Confederated Lordship titles shall be called Royaneh (Noble) for all time to come.

46. The women of the Forty Eight (now fifty) Royaneh families shall be the heirs of the Authorized Names for all time to come.

    When an infant of the Five Nations is given an Authorized Name at the Midwinter Festival or at the Ripe Corn Festival, one in the cousinhood of which the infant is a member shall be appointed a speaker. He shall then announce to the opposite cousinhood the names of the father and the mother of the child together with the clan of the mother. Then the speaker shall announce the child's name twice. The uncle of the child shall then take the child in his arms and walking up and down the room shall sing: "My head is firm, I am of the Confederacy." As he sings the opposite cousinhood shall respond by chanting, "Hyenh, Hyenh, Hyenh, Hyenh," until the song is ended.

47. If the female heirs of a Confederate Lord's title become extinct, the title right shall be given by the Lords of the Confederacy to the sister family whom they shall elect and that family shall hold the name and transmit it to their (female) heirs, but they shall not appoint any of their sons as a candidate for a title until all the eligible men of the former family shall have died or otherwise have become ineligible.

48. If all the heirs of a Lordship title become extinct, and all the families in the clan, then the title shall be given by the Lords of the Confederacy to the family in a sister clan whom they shall elect.

49. If any of the Royaneh women, heirs of a titleship, shall wilfully withhold a Lordship or other title and refuse to bestow it, or if such heirs abandon, forsake, or despise their heritage, then shall such women be deemed buried and their family extinct. The titleship shall then revert to a sister family or clan upon application and complaint. The Lords of the Confederacy shall elect the family or clan which shall in future hold the title.

50. The Royaneh women of the Confederacy heirs of the Lordship titles shall elect two women of their family as cooks for the Lord when the people shall assemble at his house for business or other purposes.

    It is not good nor honorable for a Confederate Lord to allow his people whom he has called to go hungry.

51. When a Lord holds a conference in his home, his wife, if she wishes, may prepare the food for the Union Lords who assemble with him. This is an honorable right which she may exercise and an expression of her esteem.

52. The Royaneh women, heirs of the Lordship titles, shall, should it be necessary, correct and admonish the holders of their titles. Those only who attend the

Council may do this and those who do not shall not object to what has been said nor strive to undo the action.

53. When the Royaneh women, holders of a Lordship title, select one of their sons as a candidate, they shall select one who is trustworthy, of good character, of honest disposition, one who manages his own affairs, supports his own family, if any, and who has proven a faithful man to his Nation.

54. When a Lordship title becomes vacant through death or other cause, the Royaneh women of the clan in which the title is hereditary shall hold a council and shall choose one from among their sons to fill the office made vacant. Such a candidate shall not be the father of any Confederate Lord. If the choice is unanimous the name is referred to the men relatives of the clan. If they should disapprove it shall be their duty to select a candidate from among their own number. If then the men and women are unable to decide which of the two candidates shall be named, then the matter shall be referred to the Confederate Lords in the Clan. They shall decide which candidate shall be named. If the men and the women agree to a candidate his name shall be referred to the sister clans for confirmation. If the sister clans confirm the choice, they shall refer their action to their Confederate Lords who shall ratify the choice and present it to their cousin Lords, and if the cousin Lords confirm the name then the candidate shall be installed by the proper ceremony for the conferring of Lordship titles. [. . .]

RIGHTS OF FOREIGN NATIONS

73. The soil of the earth from one end of the land to the other is the property of the people who inhabit it. By birthright the Ongwehonweh (Original beings) are the owners of the soil which they own and occupy and none other may hold it. The same law has been held from the oldest times.

     The Great Creator has made us of the one blood and of the same soil he made us and as only different tongues constitute different nations he established different hunting grounds and territories and made boundary lines between them.

74. When any alien nation or individual is admitted into the Five Nations the admission shall be understood only to be a temporary one. Should the person or nation create loss, do wrong, or cause suffering of any kind to endanger the peace of the Confederacy, the Confederate Lords shall order one of their war chiefs to reprimand him or them and if a similar offence is again committed the offending party or parties shall be expelled from the territory of the Five United Nations.

75. When a member of an alien nation comes to the territory of the Five Nations and seeks refuge and permanent residence, the Lords of the Nation to which he comes shall extend hospitality and make him a member of the nation. Then shall he be accorded equal rights and privileges in all matters except as after mentioned.

76. No body of alien people who have been adopted temporarily shall have a vote in the council of the Lords of the Confederacy, for only they who have been invested with Lordship titles may vote in the Council. Aliens have nothing by blood to make claim to a vote and should they have it, not knowing all the traditions of the Confederacy, might go against its Great Peace. In this manner the Great Peace would be endangered and perhaps be destroyed.

77. When the Lords of the Confederacy decide to admit a foreign nation and an adoption is made, the Lords shall inform the adopted nation that its admission is only temporary. They shall also say to the nation that it must never try to control, to interfere with, or to injure the Five Nations nor disregard the Great Peace or any of its rules or customs. That in no way should they cause disturbance or injury. Then should the adopted nation disregard these injunctions, their adoption shall be annulled and they shall be expelled.

    The expulsion shall be in the following manner: The council shall appoint one of their War Chiefs to convey the message of annulment and he shall say, "You (naming the nation) listen to me while I speak. I am here to inform you again of the will of the Five Nations' Council. It was clearly made known to you at a former time. Now the Lords of the Five Nations have decided to expel you and cast you out. We disown you now and annul your adoption. Therefore you must look for a path in which to go and lead away all your people. It was you, not we, who committed wrong and caused this sentence of annulment. So then go your way and depart from the territory of the Five Nations and from the Confederacy."

78. Whenever a foreign nation enters the Confederacy or accepts the Great Peace, the Five Nations and the foreign nation shall enter into an agreement and compact by which the foreign nation shall endeavor to persuade other nations to accept the Great Peace. [. . .]

RIGHTS OF THE PEOPLE OF THE FIVE NATIONS

93. Whenever a specially important matter or a great emergency is presented before the Confederate Council and the nature of the matter affects the entire body of the Five Nations, threatening their utter ruin, then the Lords of the Confederacy must submit the matter to the decision of their people and the decision of the people shall affect the decision of the Confederate Council. This decision shall be a confirmation of the voice of the people.

94. The men of every clan of the Five Nations shall have a Council Fire ever burning in readiness for a council of the clan. When it seems necessary for a council to be held to discuss the welfare of the clans, then the men may gather about the fire. This council shall have the same rights as the council of the women.

95. The women of every clan of the Five Nations shall have a Council Fire ever burning in readiness for a council of the clan. When in their opinion it seems necessary for the interest of the people they shall hold a council and their decisions

and recommendations shall be introduced before the Council of the Lords by the War Chief for its consideration.

96. All the Clan council fires of a nation or of the Five Nations may unite into one general council fire, or delegates from all the council fires may be appointed to unite in a general council for discussing the interests of the people. The people shall have the right to make appointments and to delegate their power to others of their number. When their council shall have come to a conclusion on any matter, their decision shall be reported to the Council of the Nation or to the Confederate Council (as the case may require) by the War Chief or the War Chiefs.

97. Before the real people united their nations, each nation had its council fires. Before the Great Peace their councils were held. The five Council Fires shall continue to burn as before and they are not quenched. The Lords of each nation in future shall settle their nation's affairs at this council fire governed always by the laws and rules of the council of the Confederacy and by the Great Peace.

98. If either a nephew or a niece see an irregularity in the performance of the functions of the Great Peace and its laws, in the Confederate Council or in the conferring of Lordship titles in an improper way, through their War Chief they may demand that such actions become subject to correction and that the matter conform to the ways prescribed by the laws of the Great Peace.

Religious Ceremonies Protected

99. The rites and festivals of each nation shall remain undisturbed and shall continue as before because they were given by the people of old times as useful and necessary for the good of men.

100. It shall be the duty of the Lords of each brotherhood to confer at the approach of the time of the Midwinter Thanksgiving and to notify their people of the approaching festival. They shall hold a council over the matter and arrange its details and begin the Thanksgiving five days after the moon of Dis-ko-nah is new. The people shall assemble at the appointed place and the nephews shall notify the people of the time and place. From the beginning to the end the Lords shall preside over the Thanksgiving and address the people from time to time.

101. It shall be the duty of the appointed managers of the Thanksgiving festivals to do all that is needed for carrying out the duties of the occasions.

    The recognized festivals of Thanksgiving shall be the Midwinter Thanksgiving, the Maple or Sugar-making Thanksgiving, the Raspberry Thanksgiving, the Strawberry Thanksgiving, the Cornplanting Thanksgiving, the Corn Hoeing Thanksgiving, the Little Festival of Green Corn, the Great Festival of Ripe Corn, and the complete Thanksgiving for the Harvest.

    Each nation's festivals shall be held in their Long Houses.

102. When the Thanksgiving for the Green Corn comes the special managers, both the men and women, shall give it careful attention and do their duties properly.

103. When the Ripe Corn Thanksgiving is celebrated the Lords of the Nation must give it the same attention as they give to the Midwinter Thanksgiving.

104. Whenever any man proves himself by his good life and his knowledge of good things, naturally fitted as a teacher of good things, he shall be recognized by the Lords as a teacher of peace and religion and the people shall hear him. [. . .]

∾ MARIE LE JARS DE GOURNAY
1565?–1645

At the age of nineteen, **Marie le Jars de Gournay** began reading Montaigne's *Essays.* She was so taken by the work that when in Paris to be presented at court in 1588, she wrote to Montaigne asking him to help her escape from her family, who did not believe that women should receive an education. De Gournay did not end up leaving home, but Montaigne did pay long visits to her in Picardy, during which time the two discussed the expansion and revision of his *Essays.* De Gournay soon published a collection of her poetry, prose, and Latin translations titled *M. de Montaigne's Promenade, by his Adopted Daughter* (1594), and after Montaigne's death, at the request of his wife, she prepared the text of the 1595 edition of his works. At age thirty-four, de Gournay settled in Paris, where she wrote treatises on education, philology, and politics, translations from Latin, and a wide range of poems, dialogues, and autobiographical pieces on the condition of the woman writer. Throughout her career, de Gournay made many friends but continually drew fire for her outspoken views on political and social issues.

In *On the Equality of Men and Women,* published in 1622, de Gournay appeals to a wide range of scholarly and religious authorities to support her position that women should receive an education equal to that of men. She places particular emphasis on the noncanonical tradition surrounding Mary Magdalene, a prostitute from Galilee who became one of Jesus' followers and who was present at his crucifixion and the first to witness and report his resurrection. In the Gnostic tradition upon which de Gournay draws in her writings, Magdalene appears as the most favored of Jesus' followers, an "apostle to the Apostles" who ministered after Christ's crucifixion for some thirty years in the south of France. De Gournay claims that she will not rest her argument upon the innumerable examples of women's bravery, loyalty, intelligence, and virtue, for fear that they would be perceived as isolated incidents—mere exceptions to the rule. Instead, she says she will draw only upon those examples of

mah-REE luh
ZHAR duh goor-NAY

I . . . am content to assert that men and women are equals; in the matter of the sexes, claims of either superiority or inferiority go against nature.

– DE GOURNAY, *On the Equality of Men and Women*

women's heroism and virtue cited and sanctioned by authorities like Plato, Plutarch, and the Bible—examples that would presumably have greater validity for her readers. Although her appeal to authority does not reflect the methods of the ENLIGHTENMENT, her defense of women and appeal for equal education looks forward to the later works of Catherine Macauley and Mary Wollstonecraft.

A note on the translation: The following selection, translated and with notes by Patricia Clark Smith, renders de Gournay's text in modern English.

FROM

❧ On the Equality of Men and Women

Translated by Patricia Clark Smith

Most people who defend women against men's boasts of superiority turn right around and claim that women are really the superior sex. I, who want to avoid all such extremes, am content to assert that men and women are equals; in the matter of the sexes, claims of either superiority or inferiority go against nature.

Of course, I know that for some men it's not enough to declare they are the superior sex. They want to confine women to domesticity, and to that sphere only. But women can always console themselves with the knowledge that the men who hold such opinions are exactly those whom they themselves would least wish to emulate. If those misogynists had themselves been born women, they would justify all the spleen vomited upon our sex. They cherish the conviction that their own worth depends simply upon their maleness, because they have heard trumpeted through the streets the myth that women have neither worth nor ability, being deficient both in their minds and in the organs of their bodies. Such men wax eloquent as they preach these maxims; they can do so because for them *dignity, ability, mind, body, organs* are only empty words. These men have yet to learn that the main characteristic of an oaf is that he puts his trust in slogans, superstition, and hearsay.

You can easily see what happens when savants like these compare the two sexes: They say that at her best woman can only aspire to equal a very ordinary man. They simply cannot conceive of a great woman, were her sex to be changed, as the match of a great man, any more than they can imagine a mere mortal man elevating himself to the status of a god.

Hercules only bested twelve monsters in twelve combats, but these misogynists are more powerful than he, for with a single word they lay low half the world. And yet, how can anybody believe that people like these men, who promote themselves on the basis of others' weaknesses, are truly powerful in their own beings? Above all, these men seem to think they can absolve themselves of their shameless insulting of women simply by slathering praise on their own sex, as if their loose talk, no matter whether true or false, became more believable the more outrageous it grew. God knows, I am all too well acquainted with this race of men whose idle banter gets instantly transmuted into proverbs. They are among the men who most fiercely despise women. But there, now; if they can simply go about issuing decrees proclaiming themselves to be fine fellows, why shouldn't they turn around and degrade women by a similar fiat?

As someone who considers herself a fair judge of the worth and capability of women, I am not going to try to prove my contentions here by setting out my own reasons for valuing women, for reasons are open to debate. Nor will I cite examples of great women, even though they abound. I shall rely instead upon the authority of God himself, upon the authority of the pillars of the Church, and upon the authority of the great thinkers who have illumined the universe. But let us first turn to these last-named glorious witnesses, reserving God and the Holy Fathers, like hoarded treasure, for later.

[Socrates and Plato], to whom everyone grants divinity . . . both assign women the same rights, faculties, and functions as men, in their *Republic* and everywhere else. Moreover, they maintain that women have often surpassed the men of their country, since women actually invented some of their fine arts, and some have excelled at and taught better and more authoritatively than any man all sorts of perfections and virtues throughout the most famous cities of antiquity, including Alexandria, [which became] the greatest city of the Roman Empire after Rome herself. These two philosophers, themselves miracles of nature, believed that the most important speeches in their books took on a finer luster when spoken by Diotima and Aspasia.[1] Socrates is not afraid to name Diotima as his teacher and preceptor in the highest realms of knowledge, and he himself became the teacher and preceptor of all mankind. [. . .]

Given all Socrates' words about women's accomplishments, it is easy to see how, when he lets slip some remarks during Xenophon's[2] *Symposium* about women having less judgment than men, he is attributing that lack to the ignorance and inexperience in which women are brought up, or else to a general falling-off in society; besides, he also allows a wide margin for exceptions. But the men who make up the misogynist proverbs don't understand subtleties like that.

Perhaps women do attain excellence less often than men. But isn't it a wonder that the lack of good teaching—or, rather, the overabundance of wretched teaching— has not kept women from attaining anything at all? Is there a greater difference between a man and a woman than there is between one woman and another, taking into account each person's education and the circumstances of his or her upbringing, whether in city or hamlet, in one or another nation? And wouldn't the gap people often notice between men's and women's accomplishments be bridged if

---

[1] **Diotima:** Diotima of Mantinea, described in Plato's *Symposium,* was a priestess, real or fictional, who taught Plato about love and beauty. **Aspasia:** Aspasia of Miletus (c. 470–410 B.C.E.) was a highly educated Greek woman, orator, and rhetorician who influenced many important figures in fifth-century Athens; the mistress of Pericles, she is mentioned by Xenophon, Plato, Cicero, and Plutarch.

[2] **Xenophon** (c. 430–c. 355 B.C.E.): Greek historian and author of *Anabasis* and *Memorabilia,* among other works.

women were educated and given experience equal to men in business affairs and in arts and letters? Education is so very crucial; when even one aspect of it, such as being taught how to play a part in social affairs, is denied to Italian women, but is made easily available to their French and English sisters, the Italians are almost always outshone by the French and English. (I say *almost* always because particular Italian women have succeeded brilliantly, and we have had two Italian queens to whose prudence France owes a great deal.) Surely education could equalize the faculties of men and women. We can see from the previous example how simply through being schooled in one area — that is, in the social arts of being a hostess — the lesser have triumphed over the greater, for Italian women by nature have a more delicate air than French or English women, and they are naturally more capable of refining the spirits of those around them, as is evident when their Italian men are compared to Frenchmen and Englishmen.

In his treatise on the virtuous deeds of women, Plutarch[3] contends that virtue is identical in men and in women. Seneca[4] similarly proclaims in the *Consolations* that we must believe that nature has in no way slighted women, nor has she limited their virtues or their minds more than men's; rather, she has given women an equal measure of energy and ability to perform honest laudable deeds.

Leaving [Seneca and Plutarch], let us see what the third member of the triumvirate of human wisdom and morality has to say in his essays. [Montaigne][5] remarks that, though he isn't sure why it should be so, he has rarely seen a woman worthy to be a leader of men. But is he not thus comparing women in particular with mankind in general? And is this not in itself a confession that he is afraid of falling into error if he goes beyond generalizing about women? (Though, to be sure, he could easily enough have made excuses for his reservations on the grounds of women's scant and shameful education.) Moreover, in another part of his *Essays,* he forgets to mention that Plato gives authority to women in the *Republic,* and also omits to note that Antistines denied there was any difference between the talents and virtues of the two sexes. [. . .]

When men strip women of their right to the greatest advantages, it may be that the theft and the consequent suffering are due to the inequality of physical strength rather than to any moral lacking on the part of women, and physical strength is such a low virtue that the beasts surpass man in that regard, just as men surpass women. It is again Tacitus who tells us that where might reigns, all justice, honesty, and even modesty are attributed to the victor. What wonder, then, that ability and worth in general are accorded to men, to the exclusion of women?

Moreover, the human animal is really neither man nor woman, the sexes having been created not simply, but rather *secundum quid,* as the theologians tell us; that is

---

[3] **Plutarch** (c. 46–c. 120 c.e.): Greek writer whose *Lives of Illustrious Men,* describing the lives of important Greek and Roman figures, is one of the earliest works of biography.

[4] **Seneca:** Lucius Annaeus Seneca (4 b.c.e.–65 c.e.), Roman philosopher, orator, and dramatist, tutor to the young Nero, and one of the most important Stoic philosophers; known for his plays and moral essays; the *Consolations* are from his moral essays.

[5] **Montaigne:** Michel Eyquem de Montaigne (1533–1592), the great French humanist and essayist known for his tolerance and humane character; his *Essays* (1571–86) introduced the essay as a literary genre.

to say, only for the purpose of propagation. The only unique thing about this human animal is the human soul, and the old joke — *What is most like a tomcat on a win-dowsill?* — *A female cat on a windowsill!* — is fitting here, if we may allow ourselves a moment for laughter. Men and women are so much one creature that if a man is more than a woman, then a woman is more than a man. Man was created male and female, say the scriptures, counting the two as one. Hence, Jesus Christ is called the Son of Man, even though he is really only the son of a woman. The great Saint Basil[6] says the virtue of a man and a woman are the same, since God bestowed on both the same creation and the same honor: *masculum et feminam fecit eos.*[7] Now, those whose natures are the same must behave in the same way, and similar deeds must be accorded equal value and equal praise. Such is the testimony of Basil, that mighty pillar and venerable witness of the Church.

It is well to remember that certain ancient quibblers were so arrogant they would deny that the female sex was created in God's image; they'd have us believe that man's resemblance to God depends chiefly on his beard. Logically, it would then follow that women could not resemble men, since they don't resemble He after whom men are shaped.

God himself has given women the gift of prophesy in equal measure with man, and He has set women to be judges, teachers, and leaders of his faithful people in peace and in war. Moreover, he has caused them to triumph with him in the greatest of victories, which they have then spread to other parts of the world. [. . .]

To continue with my list of holy witnesses, though Saint Paul bans women from the ministry and bids them be silent in church, it is evident that he does so not out of contempt, but because he fears they will present a temptation by showing them-selves so brilliantly in public, as they must if they are to minister and preach, and being so much more well-endowed with beauty and grace than men. I maintain that the lack of contempt for women in the New Testament is evident, even without tak-ing into consideration Saint Peter's great respect for Saint Petronilla,[8] and without mentioning Mary Magdalene, who is named in the Church as the equal of the Apostles, *par Apostolis.* And indeed, as everyone in Provence is aware, the Church and the Apostles themselves made an exception to the rule of silence for that very woman, who preached for thirty years after Christ's death at the church of Sainte Baume near Marseille.[9] If anyone further questions the evidence that women have

---

[6] **Saint Basil** (c. 329–379 C.E.): Learned Christian scholar and prolific writer of critical, moral, and homiletic works; renowned for his personal virtue, charity, and monastic simplicity, and for his ardent defense of the Eastern Church.

[7] *masculum . . . eos:* Latin for "man and woman He created them" (Genesis 1:27).

[8] **Saint Petronilla** (fl. first century C.E.): Also known as Aurelia Petronilla and Pierrette; said to have been cured of the palsy by St. Peter, she was martyred for practicing her faith.

[9] **woman . . . Marseille:** A great deal of folklore surrounds Mary Magdalene, who was at one time venerated nearly equally with the Virgin Mary. De Gournay is drawing on the tradition that Magdalene and her sister Martha made their way to Provence, where Mary preached and Martha slew a dragon by pouring holy water on its head. At Ste. Baume ("Holy Tree"), the site of an old pagan shrine, Mary is said to have lived and preached for thirty years without touching food or drink, and her presence there reputedly ensured a good vintage for the local winemakers.

preached, one may well ask what the Sibyls were doing, if not preaching across the Universe by divine inspiration the future advent of Jesus Christ?[10] Among the ancient nations, all have agreed that women as well as men could be priests. And Christians must at least concede that women are able to administer the sacrament of baptism— but is it then fair that women are forbidden to administer the other sacraments? People say that the need to save the souls of dying infants forced the Church Fathers, however reluctantly, to permit women to baptise. But surely those men didn't think of themselves as agreeing to violate and defame a sacrament out of mere need when they consented to let women perform baptisms! It is clear they banned women from administering the other sacraments only in order to maintain more completely male authority, either because they themselves were male, or because, perversely or not, they wished to ensure peace between the two sexes by weakening and devaluing one of them. Surely Saint Jerome[11] writes wisely on this point when he says that in the matter of service to God, the spirit and the doctrine must always be considered, but not the sex, a verdict which should be extended to allow women . . . to perform all honest acts and pursue all worthwhile knowledge. Allowing women to do so would carry out the intentions of this Saint who honors and stoutly defends women. Saint John the Eagle, most beloved of the Evangelists, did not despise women, nor did Saint Peter, Saint Paul, or the two Church Fathers Basil and Jerome; Jerome addresses his epistles specifically to women. I needn't go into the infinite number of saints and Church Fathers who concur with them in their writings.

As for Judith, I should not even bother to mention what she did if hers had been an act that depended solely upon the will of the doer; I won't list here deeds of that sort, even if they are legion, and as heroic as the acts that crown the most illustrious men.[12] Here, I am trying not to record individual acts of courage by women, for fear that they will appear to be mere idiosyncratic outbursts of personal strength, rather than brave deeds that are illustrative of gifts common to all womankind. But Judith's deed does deserve to be mentioned here. Her plan grew in the heart of a young woman surrounded by many weak and fainthearted men, and, faced with the dire and difficult task of saving a city, a whole population of the faithful, Judith's act, rather than being totally voluntary, seems to me to have been divinely inspired, and divine inspiration seems a privilege especially accorded to women. The Maid of Orleans' deeds seem similar, growing out of similar desperate circumstances,

---

[10] Sibyls . . . Christ?: The Sibyl was originally an oracular spirit represented by a succession of priestesses at Cumae in Italy. By the first century B.C.E., there were said to be ten Sibyls at different locations around Europe. In the Middle Ages, the *Sibylline Books,* collections of their oracles, were doctored by Christians to make it seem as though the Sibyls foretold the coming of Christ.

[11] Saint Jerome (c. 342–420): Christian scholar and translator of the Bible, and a prolific writer of commentaries on the Bible and on theological issues; one of the early church fathers; his views on women in his *Reply to Jovinian* are attacked by Chaucer's Wife of Bath.

[12] As . . . men: The Book of Judith, one of the Apocryphal books of the Old Testament, tells the story of how a young Jewish widow saves the besieged town of Bethulia by cutting off the head of the enemy war chief Holofernes when he falls into a drunken sleep.

although Joan of Arc[13] acted for an even larger cause, the salvation of a great kingdom and its monarch:

> This noble maid, skilled in the arts of Mars,
> Mows squadrons down, and braves the heat of wars,
> With fabric stiff she binds her maiden chest:
> One rosy nipple gleams on each round breast.
> To gain laurel and glory for her crown,
> She'll face the most illustrious warriors down!

Let us add that Mary Magdalene is the only soul to whom the Redeemer spoke these words and promised this great grace: *Wherever the Gospel shall be preached, there they shall refer to you.*[14] And Jesus Christ announced his glad and glorious resurrection first to women, in order that they, according to one of the Church Fathers, might become Apostles to the Apostles themselves, with this express mission: *Go,* He said to this same Mary Magdalene, *and tell Peter and the Apostles what you have seen.* And earlier He announced His incarnation equally to women as well as to men in the person of Anna, who recognized Him at the same instant as good Saint Simon. That miraculous birth, furthermore, was predicted by the Sibyls alone among the Gentiles, a great honor for the female sex. And what an honor for women as well was the dream of Pilate's wife, a dream which was sent to a woman, bypassing all men on such an exalted occasion!

If men boast that Jesus Christ was born a member of their sex, we women may retort that He had to be incarnated as a man, for had He been born a woman He could not as a young person have mingled without scandal with the multitudes at all hours of the day and night, in the way He needed to in order to convert, succor, and save humankind; this is especially true, considering the hostility He faced from the Jewish people. And yet, if a person is so feeble-minded as to need to imagine a Male or a Female God (granted that in the French language His name does have a masculine ring) and consequently needs to elevate one sex over the other in order to honor the Incarnation of God's son, that person exposes himself as someone who is as poor a philosopher as he is a theologian. At any rate, the advantages men derive from claiming Jesus as a member of their sex . . . are compensated for by His most precious conception within the body of a woman, and by that woman's utterly perfect claim to bear the name of perfection, alone of all created beings since our first parents fell from grace, this woman set apart from others also by her Assumption into heaven.

---

[13] Joan of Arc (c. 1412–1431): Also known as the Maid of Orléans; born to a farming family, her visions led her on a divine mission to help the French prince, later Charles VII, in his battles against the English. Captured by the English, she was returned to French ecclesiastical authorities, tried for witchcraft, and eventually burned at the stake.

[14] *Wherever . . . you:* Jesus does not speak these words to Mary Magdalene in the canonical four gospels, nor does he call her "Apostle to the Apostles." De Gournay's source is uncertain, but Mary Magdalene is accorded a high degree of respect in the Gnostic tradition and in the folklore of southern France (cf. note 9).

Finally, if Scripture has declared the husband to be the head of the wife, it would be the greatest foolishness for men to take this as a seal of their nobility. The examples, authorities, and arguments chronicled in this essay prove that the favors and graces bestowed upon men and women are equal, even identical. And God Himself has spoken: *the two shall be as one;* and, further, *the man shall leave his mother and father, and cleave unto his wife.* Undoubtedly, man was designated the head of the family only because of the explicit need to promote peace within marriage. Obviously, that need required that one of the pair yield to the other, and the greater physical strength of the man meant that he would not be the one who would submit. . . .

Even if it were true, as some contend, that submission was first imposed upon women because of the sin of the apple, that leaves us still a long way from concluding that man is more noble than woman. If you should happen to believe that the Scriptures command woman to yield to man, if you believe that women are utterly unfit to stand up to men in an argument, see what absurdity follows: Woman has been found worthy of being created in God's image; worthy to take part in the most holy Eucharist; worthy of seeing visions of God, and even of being possessed by the Holy Spirit. And yet, woman is deemed unfit to receive the benefits and privileges of the human male.

Is this not the same as saying that human men are more valuable than God Himself? And do such views not elevate the human male above all Mysteries, and thus commit the greatest of blasphemies?

❧ JOHN LOCKE
1632–1704

John Locke was born in 1632 in Somerset, England. After being tutored by his father, Locke attended Westminster School for formal training and in 1652 began studies at Christ Church, Oxford. Influenced at Oxford by Robert Boyle, the leading chemist of the time, Locke gained familiarity with the experimental method, the scientific method of employing ideas, methods, or materials that have not been tried before. After graduating from Oxford in 1656, Locke served as a tutor, a physician, and a personal representative for Anthony Ashley Cooper, first earl of Shaftesbury, making contacts with scientists, physicians, and politicians in England and in France. After the death of Cooper in 1683 and fearing reprisals for his liberal views during the turbulent period before the Glorious Revolution of 1688, Locke left England for Holland, where he worked on *Essay Concerning Human Understanding* and *Two Treatises on Government.* Upon his return he continued writing and served as commissioner with the Board of Trade and Plantations from 1697 to 1700. He died on October 28, 1704.

Locke's *Two Treatises on Government,* published in 1690, was to have a profound influence on political theory in the eighteenth century and prepared the way for the acceptance of the principles at the core of the American and French Revolutions. The first *Treatise* attacked the idea of divine right, under which kings traced their authority to God's appointment. The second *Treatise,* excerpted here, laid the foundation for the theory of natural rights. In a state of nature, all men — and Locke's use of that term refers to just men, not women — are free and equal. That state of nature guarantees men the basic rights of life, liberty, health, and property, so long as a man's actions do not infringe upon the rights of another. In a state of nature, however, some people inevitably do infringe upon another's natural rights. Hence, man enters into a civil society through what Locke calls a social contract, in which he gives up some of his freedoms in order to guarantee the preservation of as many natural rights as possible. The ruler must enforce that guarantee, and the ruler must have the full consent of the people. If a ruler fails in that task, the people have the right to depose him (or her). Thus, Locke justified the deposition of the Stuarts and the bringing in, as he puts it, of "our great restorer, the present King William." Locke could not have foreseen, nor would he have approved of, the revolutions of the next century that his theories helped inspire.

A note on the text: The excerpt from Locke's *Second Treatise on Government* is based on the 1690 edition of the text. Spelling, punctuation, and capitalization have been normalized for contemporary readers.

> . . . [Man] is willing to join in society with others who are already united, or have a mind to unite for the mutual preservation of their lives, liberties, and estates, which I call by the general name — property.
>
> – JOHN LOCKE,
> *The Second Treatise on Government*

FROM

∾ The Second Treatise on Government

OF THE STATE OF NATURE

To understand political power aright and derive it from its original, we must consider what estate all men are naturally in, and that is a state of perfect freedom to order their actions, and dispose of their possessions and persons as they think fit, within the bounds of the law of nature, without asking leave or depending upon the will of any other man.

A state also of equality, wherein all the power and jurisdiction is reciprocal, no one having more than another, there being nothing more evident than that creatures of the same species and rank, promiscuously born to all the same advantages of nature and the use of the same faculties, should also be equal one amongst another, without subordination or subjection, unless the lord and master of them all should, by any manifest declaration of his will, set one above another and confer on him, by an evident and clear appointment, an undoubted right to dominion and sovereignty. . . .

But though this be a state of liberty, yet it is not a state of license; though man in that state have an uncontrollable liberty to dispose of his person or possessions, yet he has not liberty to destroy himself, or so much as any creature in his possession, but where some nobler use than its bare preservation calls for it. The state of nature has a law of nature to govern it, which obliges every one; and reason, which is that law, teaches all mankind who will but consult it, that being all equal and independent, no one ought to harm another in his life, health, liberty, or possessions. For men being all the workmanship of one omnipotent and infinitely wise Maker—all the servants of one sovereign Master, sent into the world by His order and about His business—they are His property, whose workmanship they are, made to last during His, not one another's pleasure. And, being furnished with like faculties, sharing all in one community of nature, there cannot be supposed any such subordination among us that may authorize us to destroy one another, as if we were made for one another's uses, as the inferior ranks of creatures are for ours. Every one as he is bound to preserve himself, and not to quit his station willfully, so by the like reason, when his own preservation comes not in competition, ought he as much as he can to preserve the rest of mankind, and not unless it be to do justice on an offender, take away or impair the life or what tends to be the preservation of the life, the liberty, health, limb, or goods of another. [. . .]

OF THE BEGINNINGS OF POLITICAL SOCIETIES

Men, being, as has been said, by nature all free, equal, and independent, no one can be put out of this estate and subjected to the political power of another without his own consent. The only way whereby anyone divests himself of his natural liberty and puts on the bonds of civil society is by agreeing with other men to join and unite into a community for their comfortable, safe, and peaceable living one amongst another, in a secure enjoyment of their properties, and a greater security against any that are not of it. This any number of men may do, because it injures not the freedom of the rest; they are left as they were in the liberty of the state of nature. When any number of men have so consented to make one community or government, they are thereby presently incorporated and make one body politic, wherein the majority have a right to act and conclude the rest. [. . .]

And thus every man, by consenting with others to make one body politic under one government, puts himself under an obligation to every one of that society to submit to the determination of the majority and to be concluded by it; or else this original compact whereby he with others incorporates into one society, would signify nothing. [. . .]

For if the consent of the majority shall not, in reason, be received as the act of the whole and conclude every individual, nothing but the consent of every individual can make anything to be the act of the whole: but such a consent is next to impossible ever to be had. [. . .]

OF THE ENDS OF POLITICAL SOCIETY AND GOVERNMENT

If man in the state of nature be so free as has been said, if he be absolute lord of his own person and possessions, equal to the greatest and subject to nobody, why will he part with his freedom? Why will he give up this empire and subject himself to the dominion and control of any other power? To which it is obvious to answer, that though in the state of nature he hath such a right, yet the enjoyment of it is very uncertain and constantly exposed to the invasion of others; for all being kings as much as he, every man his equal, and the greater part no strict observers of equity and justice, the enjoyment of the property he has in this state is very unsafe, very insecure. This makes him willing to quit this condition which, however free, is full of fears and continual dangers; and it is not without reason that he seeks out and is willing to join in society with others who are already united, or have a mind to unite for the mutual preservation of their lives, liberties, and estates, which I call by the general name—property.

The great and chief end, therefore, of men uniting into commonwealths, and putting themselves under government, is the preservation of their property; to which in the state of nature there are many things wanting.

First, there wants an established, settled, known law, received and allowed by common consent to be the standard of right and wrong, and the common measure to decide all controversies between them. For though the law of nature be plain and intelligible to all rational creatures, yet men, being biased by their interest, as well as ignorant for want of study of it, are not apt to allow of it as a law binding to them in the application of it to their particular cases.

Secondly, in the state of nature there wants a known and indifferent judge, with authority to determine all differences according to the established law. For every one in that state, being both judge and executioner of the law of nature, men being partial to themselves, passion and revenge is very apt to carry them too far, and with too much heat in their own cases, as well as negligence and unconcernedness, make them too remiss in other men's.

Thirdly, in the state of nature there often wants power to back and support the sentence when right and to give it due execution. They who by any injustice offend will seldom fail where they are able by force to make good their injustice. Such resistance many times makes the punishment dangerous and frequently destructive to those who attempt it.

Thus mankind, notwithstanding all the privileges of the state of nature, being but in an ill condition while they remain in it, are quickly driven into society. Hence it comes to pass that we seldom find any number of men live any time together in this state. The inconveniences that they are therein exposed to by the irregular and uncertain exercise of the power every man has of punishing the transgressions of others, make them take sanctuary under the established laws of government, and therein seek the preservation of their property. It is this makes them so willingly give up every one his single power of punishing to be exercised by such alone as shall be appointed to it amongst them, and by such rules as the community, or those authorized by them to that purpose, shall agree on. And in this we have the original right and rise of both the legislative and executive power as well as of the governments and societies themselves. [. . .]

But though men when they enter into society give up the equality, liberty, and executive power they had in the state of nature into the hands of the society, to be so far disposed of by the legislative as the good of the society shall require, yet it being only with an intention in every one the better to preserve himself, his liberty and property (for no rational creature can be supposed to change his condition with an intention to be worse), the power of the society or legislative constituted by them can never be supposed to extend farther than the common good, but is obliged to secure every one's property by providing against those three defects above mentioned that made the state of nature so unsafe and uneasy. And so, whoever has the legislative or supreme power of any commonwealth, is bound to govern by established standing laws, promulgated and known to the people, and not by extemporary decrees; by indifferent and upright judges, who are to decide controversies by those laws; and to employ the force of the community at home only in the execution of such laws, or abroad to prevent or redress foreign injuries and secure the community from inroads and invasion. And all this to be directed to no other end, but the peace, safety, and public good of the people.

∾ JEAN-JACQUES ROUSSEAU
1712–1778

In *The Social Contract* (1762) Jean-Jacques Rousseau modified and gave new impetus to John Locke's idea of the social contract. In his *Treatises,* Locke proposes that human beings live in a state of nature wherein they are personally responsible for protecting their natural rights to life, liberty, and property. Rousseau believes that in the state of nature property itself does not exist and that property itself is the first stage in the corruption of the state of nature. Whereas Locke argues that people agree to give up certain powers to enter into a civil society that protects their natural rights, Rousseau contends that people surrender all their powers when they enter into civil society. Hence, Rousseau's citizen subordinates his or her desires to the general will. Theoretically, every member of Rousseau's civil society is both sovereign and subject, ruler and ruled, because, collectively, the people themselves are the state. While submission to a sovereign authority did not appeal to many revolutionaries at the end of the century, implicit in Rousseau's theory is the idea that governments, seen as the agents of the general will, cannot act without the express consent of the people.

> Man is born free; and everywhere he is in chains.
>
> – ROUSSEAU, *The Social Contract*

A note on the translation: The translation used here for Rousseau's *Social Contract* is by G. D. H. Cole, the noted labor historian, political activist, and professor of social and political theory at Oxford University. All notes are the editors'.

FROM

❧ The Social Contract

Translated by G. D. H. Cole

CHAPTER 1
SUBJECT OF THE FIRST BOOK

Man is born free; and everywhere he is in chains. One thinks himself the master of others, and still remains a greater slave than they. How did this change come about? I do not know. What can make it legitimate? That question I think I can answer.

If I took into account only force, and the effects derived from it, I should say: "As long as a people is compelled to obey, and obeys, it does well; as soon as it can shake off the yoke, and shakes it off, it does still better; for, regaining its liberty by the same right as took it away, either it is justified in resuming it, or there was no justification for those who took it away." But the social order is a sacred right which is the basis of all other rights. Nevertheless, this right does not come from nature, and must therefore be founded on conventions. Before coming to that, I have to prove what I have just asserted.

CHAPTER 3
THE RIGHT OF THE STRONGEST

The strongest is never strong enough to be always the master, unless he transforms strength into right, and obedience into duty. Hence the right of the strongest, which, though to all seeming meant ironically, is really laid down as a fundamental principle. But are we never to have an explanation of this phrase? Force is a physical power, and I fail to see what moral effect it can have. To yield to force is an act of necessity, not of will—at the most, an act of prudence. In what sense can it be a duty?

Suppose for a moment that this so-called "right" exists. I maintain that the sole result is a mass of inexplicable nonsense. For, if force creates right, the effect changes with the cause: Every force that is greater than the first succeeds to its right. As soon as it is possible to disobey with impunity, disobedience is legitimate; and, the strongest being always in the right, the only thing that matters is to act so as to become the strongest. But what kind of right is that which perishes when force fails? If we must obey perforce, there is no need to obey because we ought; and if we are not forced to obey, we are under no obligation to do so. Clearly, the word *right* adds nothing to force: In this connection, it means absolutely nothing.

Obey the powers that be. If this means yield to force, it is a good precept, but superfluous: I can answer for its never being violated. All power comes from God, I admit; but so does all sickness: does that mean that we are forbidden to call in the doctor? A brigand surprises me at the edge of a wood: must I not merely surrender my purse on compulsion; but, even if I could withhold it, am I in conscience bound to give it up? For certainly the pistol he holds is also a power.

Let us then admit that force does not create right, and that we are obliged to obey only legitimate powers. In that case, my original question recurs.

CHAPTER 4
SLAVERY

Since no man has a natural authority over his fellow, and force creates no right, we must conclude that conventions form the basis of all legitimate authority among men.

If an individual, says Grotius,[1] can alienate his liberty and make himself the slave of a master, why could not a whole people do the same and make itself subject to a king? There are in this passage plenty of ambiguous words which would need explaining; but let us confine ourselves to the word *alienate*. To alienate is to give or to sell. Now, a man who becomes the slave of another does not give himself; he sells himself, at the least for his subsistence: but for what does a people sell itself? A king is so far from furnishing his subjects with their subsistence that he gets his own only from them; and, as Rabelais[2] says, kings do not live on nothing. Do subjects then give their persons on condition that the king takes their goods also? I fail to see what they have left to preserve.

It will be said that the despot assures his subjects civil tranquillity. Granted; but what do they gain, if the wars his ambition brings down upon them, his insatiable avidity, and the vexatious conduct of his ministers press harder on them than their own dissensions would have done? What do they gain, if the very tranquillity they enjoy is one of their miseries? Tranquillity is found also in dungeons; but is that enough to make them desirable places to live in? The Greeks imprisoned in the cave of the Cyclops lived there very tranquilly, while they were awaiting their turn to be devoured.

To say that a man gives himself freely, is to say what is absurd and inconceivable; such an act is null and illegitimate, from the mere fact that he who does it is out of his mind. To say the same of a whole people is to suppose a people of madmen; and madness creates no right.

---

[1] **Grotius:** Hugo Grotius (1583–1645), Dutch humanist and jurist, whose *Concerning the Law of War and Peace* (1625) drew on biblical sources and Roman law to prescribe principles of justice and morality among nations and people; believed that only an absolutist government could preserve order.

[2] **Rabelais:** François Rabelais (c. 1490–1553), French humanist and writer, whose *Gargantua and Pantagruel* (1532–62) is one of the great satires of the European Renaissance.

Even if each man could alienate himself, he could not alienate his children: They are born men and free; their liberty belongs to them, and no one but they has the right to dispose of it. Before they come to years of discretion, the father can, in their name, lay down conditions for their preservation and well-being, but he cannot give them irrevocably and without conditions: Such a gift is contrary to the ends of nature, and exceeds the rights of paternity. It would therefore be necessary, in order to legitimize an arbitrary government, that in every generation the people should be in a position to accept or reject it; but, were this so, the government would be no longer arbitrary.

To renounce liberty is to renounce being a man, to surrender the rights of humanity and even its duties. For him who renounces everything no indemnity is possible. Such a renunciation is incompatible with man's nature; to remove all liberty from his will is to remove all morality from his acts. Finally, it is an empty and contradictory convention that sets up, on the one side, absolute authority, and, on the other, unlimited obedience. It is not clear that we can be under no obligation to a person from whom we have the right to exact everything? Does not this condition alone, in the absence of equivalence or exchange, in itself involve the nullity of the act? For what right can my slave have against me, when all that he has belongs to me, and, his right being mine, this right of mine against myself is a phrase devoid of meaning?

Grotius and the rest find in war another origin for the so-called right of slavery. The victor having, as they hold, the right of killing the vanquished, the latter can buy back his life at the price of his liberty; and this convention is the more legitimate because it is to the advantage of both parties.

But it is clear that this supposed right to kill the conquered is by no means deducible from the state of war. Men, from the mere fact that, while they are living in their primitive independence, they have no mutual relations stable enough to constitute either the state of peace or the state of war, cannot be naturally enemies. War is constituted by a relation between things, and not between persons; and, as the state of war cannot arise out of simple personal relations, but only out of real relations, private war, or war of man with man, can exist neither in the state of nature, where there is no constant property, nor in the social state, where everything is under the authority of the laws. [...]

The right of conquest has no foundation other than the right of the strongest. If war does not give the conqueror the right to massacre the conquered peoples, the right to enslave them cannot be based upon a right which does not exist. No one has a right to kill an enemy except when he cannot make him a slave, and the right to enslave him cannot therefore be derived from the right to kill him. It is accordingly an unfair exchange to make him buy at the price of his liberty his life, over which the victor holds no right. Is it not clear that there is a vicious circle in founding the right of life and death on the right of slavery, and the right of slavery on the right of life and death?

Even if we assume this terrible right to kill everybody, I maintain that a slave made in war, or a conquered people, is under no obligation to a master, except to obey him as far as he is compelled to do so. By taking an equivalent for his life, the victor has not done him a favour; instead of killing him without profit, he has killed him usefully. So far then is he from acquiring over him any authority in addition to that of force, that the state of war continues to subsist between them: their mutual relation is the effect of it, and the usage of the right of war does not imply a treaty of peace. A convention has indeed been made; but this convention, so far from destroying the state of war, presupposes its continuance.

So, from whatever aspect we regard the question, the right of slavery is null and void, not only as being illegitimate, but also because it is absurd and meaningless. The words *slave* and *right* contradict each other, and are mutually exclusive. It will always be equally foolish for a man to say to a man or to a people: "I make with you a convention wholly at your expense and wholly to my advantage; I shall keep it as long as I like, and you will keep it as long as I like."

CHAPTER 5
That We Must Always Go Back to a First Convention

Even if I granted all that I have been refuting, the friends of despotism would be no better off. There will always be a great difference between subduing a multitude and ruling a society. Even if scattered individuals were successively enslaved by one man, however numerous they might be, I still see no more than a master and his slaves, and certainly not a people and its ruler; I see what may be termed an aggregation, but not an association; there is as yet neither public good nor body politic. The man in question, even if he has enslaved half the world, is still only an individual; his interest, apart from that of others, is still a purely private interest. If this same man comes to die, his empire, after him, remains scattered and without unity, as an oak falls and dissolves into a heap of ashes when the fire has consumed it.

A people, says Grotius, can give itself to a king. Then, according to Grotius, a people is a people before it gives itself. The gift is itself a civil act, and implies public deliberation. It would be better, before examining the act by which a people chooses a king, to examine that by which it has become a people; for this act, being necessarily prior to the other, is the true foundation of society.

Indeed, if there were no prior convention, where, unless the election were unanimous, would be the obligation on the minority to submit to the choice of the majority? How have a hundred men who wish for a master the right to vote on behalf of ten who do not? The law of majority voting is itself something established by convention, and presupposes unanimity, on one occasion at least.

CHAPTER 6
The Social Compact

I suppose men to have reached the point at which the obstacles in the way of their preservation in the state of nature show their power of resistance to be greater than the resources at the disposal of each individual for his maintenance in that state.

That primitive condition can then subsist no longer; and the human race would perish unless it changed its manner of existence.

But, as men cannot engender new forces, but only unite and direct existing ones, they have no other means of preserving themselves than the formation, by aggregation, of a sum of forces great enough to overcome the resistance. These they have to bring into play by means of a single motive power, and cause to act in concert.

This sum of forces can arise only where several persons come together: but, as the force and liberty of each man are the chief instruments of his self-preservation, how can he pledge them without harming his own interests, and neglecting the care he owes to himself? This difficulty, in its bearing on my present subject, may be stated in the following terms:

"The problem is to find a form of association which will defend and protect with the whole common force the person and goods of each associate, and in which each, while uniting himself with all, may still obey himself alone, and remain as free as before." This is the fundamental problem of which the social contract provides the solution.

The clauses of this contract are so determined by the nature of the act that the slightest modification would make them vain and ineffective; so that, although they have perhaps never been formally set forth, they are everywhere the same and everywhere tacitly admitted and recognized, until, on the violation of the social compact, each regains his original rights and resumes his natural liberty, while losing the conventional liberty in favour of which he renounced it.

These clauses, properly understood, may be reduced to one—the total alienation of each associate, together with all his rights, to the whole community; for, in the first place, as each gives himself absolutely, the conditions are the same for all; and, this being so, no one has any interest in making them burdensome to others.

Moreover, the alienation being without reserve, the union is as perfect as it can be, and no associate has anything more to demand: For, if the individuals retained certain rights, as there would be no common superior to decide between them and the public, each, being on one point his own judge, would ask to be so on all; the state of nature would thus continue, and the association would necessarily become inoperative or tyrannical.

Finally, each man, in giving himself to all, gives himself to nobody; and as there is no associate over which he does not acquire the same right as he yields others over himself, he gains an equivalent for everything he loses, and an increase of force for the preservation of what he has.

If then we discard from the social compact what is not of its essence, we shall find that it reduces itself to the following terms:

"Each of us puts his person and all his power in common under the supreme direction of the general will, and, in our corporate capacity, we receive each member as an indivisible part of the whole."

At once, in place of the individual personality of each contracting party, this act of association creates a corporate and collective body, composed of as many members as the assembly contains voters, and receiving from this act its unity, its common identity, its life, and its will. This public person, so formed by the union of all other persons, formerly took the name of *city*, and now takes that of *Republic* or *body politic*; it is called by its members *State* when passive, *Sovereign* when active, and *Power* when compared with others like itself. Those who associated in it take collectively the name of *people*, and severally are called *citizens*, as sharing in the sovereign authority, and *subjects*, as being under the laws of the State. But these terms are often confused and taken one for another: it is enough to know how to distinguish them when they are being used with precision.

CHAPTER 7

THE SOVEREIGN

This formula shows us that the act of association comprises a mutual undertaking between the public and the individuals, and that each individual, in making a contract, as we may say, with himself, is bound in a double relation; as a member of the Sovereign he is bound to the individuals, and as a member of the State to the Sovereign. But the maxim of civil right, that no one is bound by undertakings made to himself, does not apply in this case; for there is a great difference between incurring an obligation to yourself and incurring one to a whole of which you form a part.

Attention must further be called to the fact that public deliberation, while competent to bind all the subjects to the Sovereign, because of the two different capacities in which each of them may be regarded, cannot, for the opposite reason, bind the Sovereign to itself; and that it is consequently against the nature of the body politic for the Sovereign to impose on itself a law which it cannot infringe. Being able to regard itself in only one capacity, it is in the position of an individual who makes a contract with himself; and this makes it clear that there neither is nor can be any kind of fundamental law binding on the body of the people—not even the social contract itself. This does not mean that the body politic cannot enter into undertakings with others, provided the contract is not infringed by them; for in relation to the foreigner, it becomes a simple being, an individual.

But the body politic or the Sovereign, drawing its being wholly from the sanctity of the contract, can never bind itself, even to an outsider, to do anything derogatory to the original act, for instance, to alienate any part of itself, or to submit to another Sovereign. Violation of the act by which it exists would be self-annihilation; and that which is itself nothing can create nothing.

As soon as this multitude is so united in one body, it is impossible to offend against one of the members without attacking the body, and still more to offend against the body without the members resenting it. Duty and interest therefore equally oblige the two contracting parties to give each other help; and the same men should seek to combine, in their double capacity, all the advantages dependent upon that capacity.

Again, the Sovereign, being formed wholly of the individuals who compose it, neither has nor can have any interest contrary to theirs; and consequently the sovereign power need give no guarantee to its subjects, because it is impossible for the body to wish to hurt all its members. We shall also see later on that it cannot hurt any in particular. The Sovereign, merely by virtue of what it is, is always what it should be.

This, however, is not the case with the relation of the subjects to the Sovereign, which, despite the common interest, would have no security that they would fulfil their undertakings, unless it found means to assure itself of their fidelity.

In fact, each individual, as a man, may have a particular will contrary or dissimilar to the general will which he has as a citizen. His particular interest may speak to him quite differently from the common interest: his absolute and naturally independent existence may make him look upon what he owes to the common cause as a gratuitous contribution, the loss of which will do less harm to others than the payment of it is burdensome to himself; and, regarding the corporate person which constitutes the State as a *persona ficta,* because not a man, he may wish to enjoy the rights of citizenship without being ready to fulfil the duties of a subject. The continuance of such an injustice could not but prove the undoing of the body politic.

In order then that the social compact may not be an empty formula, it tacitly includes the undertaking, which alone can give force to the rest, that whoever refuses to obey the general will shall be compelled to do so by the whole body. This means nothing less than that he will be forced to be free; for this is the condition which, by giving each citizen to his country, secures him against all personal dependence. In this lies the key to the working of the political machine; this alone legitimizes civil undertakings, which, without it, would be absurd, tyrannical and liable to the most frightful abuses.

❧ OLYMPE DE GOUGES
1748–1793

Olympe de Gouges, actress, activist, and writer, hoped to ensure that women would become citizens and so participate in the new freedoms promised by the French Revolution, including the right to vote. In 1791 she wrote Declaration of the Rights of Woman and the Female Citizen, rightly accusing the French revolutionaries of ignoring women's rights and appealing to women to demand to be treated as state citizens rather than as objects of adoration. Like Mary Wollstonecraft (p. 741), de Gouges cites the need for educational reform, the restoration of moral principles, and virtue. With unequal education, women cannot live up to their full potential as human beings. Even their conventional role as mother is corrupted by the failings of the state to treat them as the intellectual equals of men. Interestingly enough, the case made against Queen Marie Antoinette by the revolutionary government was based in part on the queen's reputed failure to uphold the moral standards expected of

> Woman is born free and lives equal to man in her rights.
>
> – OLYMPE DE GOUGES, Declaration of the Rights of Woman and the Female Citizen

women and on her failure to be a good mother. Many aristocratic women were executed during the Revolution by the Jacobins—left-wing extremists—for being "unnatural" wives and mothers, and so the reform ideas of Olympe de Gouges in some ways transcended even the politics of revolution. De Gouges herself was arrested in July 1793 for attacking the policies of French Revolution leaders Robespierre and Fouquier-Tinville. Her call for a popular referendum and her open defiance of Robespierre led to her execution, by guillotine, on November 3, 1793.

A note on the translation: The excerpt reprinted here is taken from Darlene Gay Levy's translation, collected in *Women in Revolutionary Paris, 1789–1795* (Urbana: University of Illinois Press, 1979).

FROM

❧ Declaration of the Rights of Woman and the Female Citizen

Translated by Darlene Gay Levy

For the National Assembly to decree in its last sessions, or in those of the next legislature:

PREAMBLE

Mothers, daughters, sisters [and] representatives of the nation demand to be constituted into a national assembly. Believing that ignorance, omission, or scorn for the rights of woman are the only causes of public misfortunes and of the corruption of governments, [the women] have resolved to set forth in a solemn declaration the natural, inalienable, and sacred rights of woman in order that this declaration, constantly exposed before all the members of the society, will ceaselessly remind them of their rights and duties; in order that the authoritative acts of women and the authoritative acts of men may be at any moment compared with and respectful of the purpose of all political institutions; and in order that citizens' demands, henceforth based on simple and incontestable principles, will always support the constitution, good morals, and the happiness of all.

Consequently, the sex that is as superior in beauty as it is in courage during the sufferings of maternity recognizes and declares in the presence and under the auspices of the Supreme Being, the following Rights of Woman and of Female Citizens.

ARTICLE I

Woman is born free and lives equal to man in her rights. Social distinctions can be based only on the common utility.

ARTICLE II

The purpose of any political association is the conservation of the natural and imprescriptible rights of woman and man; these rights are liberty, property, security, and especially resistance to oppression.

ARTICLE III

The principle of all sovereignty rests essentially with the nation, which is nothing but the union of woman and man; no body and no individual can exercise any authority which does not come expressly from it [the nation].

ARTICLE IV

Liberty and justice consist of restoring all that belongs to others; thus, the only limits on the exercise of the natural rights of woman are perpetual male tyranny; these limits are to be reformed by the laws of nature and reason.

ARTICLE V

Laws of nature and reason proscribe all acts harmful to society; everything which is not prohibited by these wise and divine laws cannot be prevented, and no one can be constrained to do what they do not command.

ARTICLE VI

The law must be the expression of the general will; all female and male citizens must contribute either personally or through their representatives to its formation; it must be the same for all: male and female citizens, being equal in the eyes of the law, must be equally admitted to all honors, positions, and public employment according to their capacity and without other distinctions besides those of their virtues and talents.

ARTICLE VII

No woman is an exception; she is accused, arrested, and detained in cases determined by law. Women, like men, obey this rigorous law.

ARTICLE VIII

The law must establish only those penalties that are strictly and obviously necessary, and no one can be punished except by virtue of a law established and promulgated prior to the crime and legally applicable to women.

ARTICLE IX

Once any woman is declared guilty, complete rigor is [to be] exercised by the law.

ARTICLE X

No one is to be disquieted for his very basic opinions; woman has the right to mount the scaffold; she must equally have the right to mount the rostrum, provided that her demonstrations do not disturb the legally established public order.

ARTICLE XI

The free communication of thoughts and opinions is one of the most precious rights of woman, since that liberty assures the recognition of children by their fathers. Any female citizen thus may say freely, I am the mother of a child which belongs to you, without being forced by a barbarous prejudice to hide the truth; [an exception may be made] to respond to the abuse of this liberty in cases determined by the law.

ARTICLE XII

The guarantee of the rights of woman and the female citizen implies a major benefit; this guarantee must be instituted for the advantage of all, and not for the particular benefit of those to whom it is entrusted.

ARTICLE XIII

For the support of the public force and the expenses of administration, the contributions of woman and man are equal; she shares all the duties [*corvées*] and all the painful tasks; therefore, she must have the same share in the distribution of positions, employment, offices, honors, and jobs [*industrie*].

ARTICLE XIV

Female and male citizens have the right to verify, either by themselves or through their representatives, the necessity of the public contribution. This can only apply to women if they are granted an equal share, not only of wealth, but also of public administration, and in the determination of the proportion, the base, the collection, and the duration of the tax.

ARTICLE XV

The collectivity of women, joined for tax purposes to the aggregate of men, has the right to demand an accounting of his administration from any public agent.

ARTICLE XVI

No society has a constitution without the guarantee of rights and the separation of powers; the constitution is null if the majority of individuals comprising the nation have not cooperated in drafting it.

ARTICLE XVII

Property belongs to both sexes whether united or separate; for each it is an inviolable and sacred right; no one can be deprived of it, since it is the true patrimony of nature, unless the legally determined public need obviously dictates it, and then only with a just and prior indemnity.

POSTSCRIPT

Woman, wake up; the tocsin of reason is being heard throughout the whole universe; discover your rights. The powerful empire of nature is no longer surrounded by prejudice, fanaticism, superstition, and lies. The flame of truth has dispersed all the clouds of folly and usurpation. Enslaved man has multiplied his strength and needs recourse to yours to break his chains. Having become free, he has become unjust to his companion. Oh, women, women! When will you cease to be blind? What advantage have you received from the Revolution? A more pronounced scorn, a more marked disdain. In the centuries of corruption you ruled only over the weakness of men. The reclamation of your patrimony, based on the wise decrees of nature—what have you to dread from such a fine undertaking? The *bon mot* of the legislator of the marriage of Cana? Do you fear that our French legislators, correctors of that morality, long ensnared by political practices now out of date, will only say again to you: women, what is there in common between you and us? Everything, you will have to answer. If they persist in their weakness in putting this non sequitur in contradiction to their principles, courageously oppose the force of reason to the empty pretentions of superiority; unite yourselves beneath the standards of philosophy; deploy all the energy of your character, and you will soon see these haughty men, not groveling at your feet as servile adorers, but proud to share with you the treasures of the Supreme Being. Regardless of what barriers confront you, it is in your power to free yourselves; you have only to want to. Let us pass now to the shocking tableau of what you have been in society; and since national education is in question at this moment, let us see whether our wise legislators will think judiciously about the education of women.

MARQUIS DE LAFAYETTE AND THE FRENCH NATIONAL ASSEMBLY
1789

In the late eighteenth century, France was in a political, economic, and social crisis. When in 1788 Louis XVI called a meeting of the Estates General, the legislative assembly of France, the crisis began to accelerate toward revolution. France was divided into three so-called Estates: The first two, the nobles and the clergy, had fared well under the monarchy; the Third Estate, however, consisting of the upper bourgeoisie and the commoners, bore a high proportion of the tax burden and shared few of the legal rights enjoyed by the First and Second Estates. At the Estates General meeting in May, members of the Third Estate argued that they should be allowed to double their number of representatives. When Louis and his supporters refused, the Third Estate broke away and formed the National Assembly, which proclaimed itself the true representative body of the French people and set about writing a new constitution. The first two estates eventually sent members to the National Assembly, and negotiations to move France toward a constitutional monarchy began.

Meanwhile, however, high food prices and general disillusionment among the lower classes and the peasants began to outpace reforms. Though many popular disturbances erupted in the summer of 1789, the beginning of the Revolution was symbolized by the storming on July 14 of the Bastille, a prison associated in the popular mind with royal power. In that same month, the Marquis de Lafayette (1757–1834) presented a draft of what would become the Declaration of the Rights of Man and Citizen to the National Assembly. Modeled in part on the American Declaration of Independence—Thomas Jefferson, then ambassador to France, was consulted by members of the French committee—the Declaration of the Rights of Man and Citizen was passed on August 26, 1789. This declaration has been hailed for clarifying the role of citizenship in a republic and for helping to establish the principles of modern democracies: individual freedom and equality under the law and the idea that the state exists for the benefit of its citizens.

A note on the translation: The following translation of The Declaration of the Rights of Man and Citizen is by Paul H. Beik, collected in his anthology of historical and political documents *The French Revolution* (New York: Harper and Row, 1970).

> The aim of every political association is the conservation of the natural and imprescriptible rights of man; these rights are liberty, property, security, and resistance to oppression.
>
> – Declaration of the Rights of Man and Citizen

Declaration of the Rights of Man and Citizen, 1789

This painting presents the Declaration of the Rights of Man and Citizen as a secular revelation: The two tablets recall the Ten Commandments and the angel to the right suggests divine influence. The figure to the left, freed from shackles, symbolizes the freedom promised by the French Revolution. (Giraudon/Art Resource, NY)

❧ Declaration of the Rights of Man and Citizen

Translated by Paul H. Beik

The representatives of the French people, organized as a national assembly, considering that ignorance, neglect, and scorn of the rights of man are the sole causes of public misfortunes and of corruption of governments, have resolved to display in a solemn declaration the natural, inalienable, and sacred rights of man, so that this declaration, constantly in the presence of all members of society, will continually remind them of their rights and their duties, so that the acts of the legislative power and those of the executive power, being subject at any time to comparison with the purpose of any political institution, will be better respected; so that the demands of the citizens, based henceforth on simple and incontestable principles, will always contribute to the maintenance of the constitution and the happiness of all.

Consequently, the National Assembly recognizes and declares, in the presence and under the auspices of the Supreme Being, the following rights of man and citizen.

Article 1. Men are born and remain free and equal in rights; social distinctions can be established only for the common benefit.

2. The aim of every political association is the conservation of the natural and imprescriptible rights of man; these rights are liberty, property, security, and resistance to oppression.

3. The source of all sovereignty is located in essence in the nation; no body, no individual can exercise authority which does not emanate from it expressly.

4. Liberty consists in being able to do anything that does not harm another person. Thus the exercise of the natural rights of each man has no limits except those which assure to the other members of society the enjoyment of these same rights; these limits can be determined only by law.

5. The law has the right to forbid only those actions harmful to society. All that is not forbidden by the law cannot be hindered, and no one can be forced to do what it does not order.

6. The law is the expression of the general will; all citizens have the right to concur personally or through their representatives in its formation; it must be the same for all, whether it protects or punishes. All citizens being equal in its eyes are equally admissible to all honors, positions, and public employments, according to their capabilities and without other distinctions than those of their virtues and talents.

7. No man can be accused, arrested, or detained except in cases determined by the law, and according to the forms which it has prescribed. Those who solicit, draw up, execute, or have executed arbitrary orders must be punished; but any citizen summoned or seized by virtue of the law must obey instantly; he renders himself culpable by resisting.

8. The law must establish only penalties that are strictly and clearly necessary, and no one can be punished except in virtue of a law established and published prior to the offense and legally applied.

9. Every man being presumed innocent until he has been declared guilty, if it is judged indispensable to arrest him, all severity that is not necessary for making sure of his person must be severely repressed by the law.

10. No one may be disturbed because of his opinions, even religious, provided that their public demonstration does not disturb the public order established by law.

11. The free communication of thoughts and opinions is one of the most precious rights of man: every citizen can therefore freely speak, write, and print: he is answerable for abuses of this liberty in cases determined by the law.

12. The guaranteeing of the rights of man and citizen necessitates a public force; this force is therefore instituted for the advantage of all, and not for the private use of those to whom it is entrusted.

13. For the maintenance of the public force, and for the expenses of administration, a tax supported in common is indispensable; it must be assessed on all citizens in proportion to their capacities to pay.

14. Citizens have the right to determine for themselves or through their representatives the need for taxation of the public, to consent to it freely, to investigate its use, and to determine its rate, basis, collection, and duration.

15. Society has the right to demand an accounting of his administration from every public agent.

16. Any society in which guarantees of rights are not assured nor the separation of powers determined has no constitution.

17. Property being an inviolable and sacred right, no one may be deprived of it unless public necessity, legally determined, clearly requires such action, and then only on condition of a just and prior indemnity.

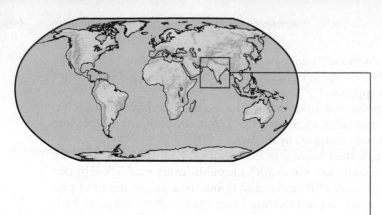

Mughal India, 1707

In the beginning of the eighteenth century, much of India was united under the Mughals, a group of Muslim rulers who had descended from the north. India flourished under Mughal rule, its splendor rivaled only by the Ottoman and Chinese empires. The Taj Mahal was constructed under Mughal rulers, and many provinces of India were unified for the first time.

THE BRITISH IN INDIA

In the eighteenth century, the Mughal empire was in decline, struggling to cope with opposition from within its own borders and threats from Europe and Persia. Already in the late seventeenth century, Hindu peasants in the Punjab and

Mathura had begun to rebel; the Mughals had also faced military opposition from a Hindu force led by Shivaji Bhonsle (1627–1680), of Maharashtra, as well as from the Sikh *khalsa,* or "army of the pure," led by guru Gobind Rai (1666–1708). While Shivaji was eventually defeated by Aurangzeb's armies, internal opposition grew and many local rulers began to reassert their autonomy at the end of Aurangzeb's reign. Taking advantage of the political chaos, Persians under the leadership of Nadir Shah sacked Delhi in 1739, killing more than thirty thousand people and absconding with more than $200 million worth of gold and jewels and the fabled peacock throne of Shah Jahan. At this time, too, the British, who had first arrived at Surat in 1608, expanded their administrative control over India.

THE BRITISH IN INDIA

When the British first reached Surat in 1608, Emperor Jahangir, advised by Portuguese ambassadors who were protecting their own interests in India, had them expelled. Persistent in their efforts, however, the British successfully negotiated a treaty in 1613 that allowed them to establish a textile factory at Surat by 1619. By the

Lady Elijah Impey, Wife of the Chief Justice of Bengal, 1782
This painting shows an eighteenth-century British drawing room in colonial India, filled with Indians tending to the wife of a British ruler. (The Art Archive)

end of the century, several British factories were operating in India, and the British had established Fort St. George, at Madras, and Fort William, in what is now Calcutta. By the middle of the eighteenth century, the British had edged out rival Dutch and French competitors, paving the way for the further expansion of their interests. When the armed forces of the British East India Company, led by Sir Robert Clive, defeated the *nawab* of Bengal at the Battle of Plassey in 1757, the British established firm control over Bengal. This turning point secured the future of British imperial power and led the way to British expansion and absolute control over India in the next several decades. Many Indians entered into the service of the British and some, such as Abu Taleb (1752–1806), an Indian Muslim from Oudh, traveled to the British Isles. Abu Taleb's *Travels,* excerpted in *In the World:* Travel Narratives (p. 218), is an example of the intercultural exchange of ideas that took off in the EARLY MODERN period.

INDIAN ARTS AND *BHAKTI* LITERATURE

As was its religion, India's arts and literature during the Mughal period were syncretic — a rich mixture of Islamic, Persian, and Hindu influences. Mughal painting, which flourished under the patronage of Akbar, for example, combines Persian and Indian elements. Indian painters even adapted the halo from European images of saints and reinterpreted it in portraits of their emperors. The architecture of the time, one of the greatest achievements of the Mughal empire, reflects this multicultural synthesis. The most outstanding example is the Taj Mahal. Built under the reign of Shah Jahan as a tribute to the memory of his wife, Mumtaz Mahal, this spectacular mausoleum, one of the world's most beautiful buildings, was designed by Persian architects and built by Indian craftsmen and laborers; it incorporates Byzantine, Persian, and Hindu elements.

One key force in Indian literature during the Mughal period was the revival of devotional literature, or *bhakti,* which played a role in India's maintaining a distinctively Indian identity. *Bhakti* was also a movement, and like the Protestant revolt against Catholicism in Europe it emphasized a personal devotion and an ecstatic union with God and was in part directed against the more rigid orthodoxy of Hinduism and its priests. While some members of the lower castes in the Mughal era turned to Islam to escape the rigid hierarchy of Hinduism, others turned to bhakti, which spread throughout India from the thirteenth to the eighteenth century. Bhakti poets wrote in the vernacular languages rather than Sanskrit, the language of Hindu classics. Poets such as Nanak (1469–1538), the founder of the Sikhs, and Tulsidas (1532–1623), the author of the great retelling of the story of Rama, *Ramcaritmanas,* wrote in Hindi; Jnanesvar (1275–1296), the author of commentaries on the Bhagavad Gita, wrote in Marathi; and Ramprasad Sen

Indian Procession

This painting illustrates the prominence of the gods in eighteenth-century Indian life.
(Courtesy of the British Musuem)

(1718–1775) wrote in Bengali (see p. 612). Bhakti writers composed hymns of
praise to the god Vishnu and, less often, the god Shiva as well as to the Mother
Goddess and Shiva's consort, or spouse, Shakti. These hymns were meant to be
sung in a kind of dance performance known as *kirtan,* whereby a worshiper would
experience an immediate communion with God. Hence these hymns typically
display a passionate intensity and employ the language of love — emotional and
sexual — to express the devotee's relation to the god or goddess, as in the poems
of Ramprasad, whose work is excerpted here. A Bengali poet and bhakti devotee
of the fearsome goddess Kali, Ramprasad represents the culmination of the
bhakti tradition.

www   For more information about the culture and context of India in the eighteenth
century, see *World Literature Online* at bedfordstmartins.com/worldlit.

Eighteenth-Century India: Kali

The Hindu goddess of death and destruction is Kali, whose Sanskrit name means "the black one." She is commonly pictured as dancing on the god Shiva's body as his consort, and though she is often portrayed as "dark," she in fact represents both the positive and negative aspects of existence. At the temple of Kalighat, in Calcutta, she is a black female with her tongue sticking out and teeth like fangs; her face is covered with blood and her hair is matted. Around her neck and waist are strings of skulls. Two of her four hands hold a sword and a severed head; the other two are extended to bestow blessings on her worshipers. In this depiction she physically represents the dark or sinister side of life. Still, as a priest decapitates the sacrificial goats at the Kali festival of Durgapuja, he chants, "In the beginning was Kali, the Life-Force."

The Mother Goddess, known by several names in India—Devi, Durga, Kali, and Parvati—originated in ancient times, when she was associated with two aspects of life. First, she gives birth, nourishes, and protects. In Hindu religious texts, her abode is Mani-dvipa (The Island of Jewels); she is red with life and all galaxies extend from her womb. Second, she is the source of death; all life returns to her. Figuratively, she is both the womb and the tomb, the light and the dark.

For a period of about a thousand years (c. 1500–500 B.C.E.), the power of the Mother Goddess was lost, outstripped by the male deities introduced by Aryan invaders. She gained prominence again in Hinduism as the consort of gods like Shiva, where she manifested the active energy of existence and became known as Shakti, from the Sanskrit for "force or energy." In fact, she is the "dynamic power" of Brahman, the Universal Being. When Being is understood as transcending all existence, then it is Brahman; when Being is physically manifested in creation, preservation, and destruction, then that force of existence is called Kali or Shakti.

The challenge for a worshiper of Kali the Mother and Kali the Life-force is to comprehend both sides of her being: the union of the creative and destructive forces in life. In her totality, Kali is called "The Ferry across the Ocean of Existence."

Kali Striding over Recumbent Shiva. *In this clay sculpture, Kali's necklace is made of severed heads, and she holds a trophy in her hand. (Courtesy of the British Museum)*

ॐ RAMPRASAD SEN
1718–1775

BAHK-tee

SHAHK-tee; KAH-lee
RAHM-pruh-sahd

The intensely religious village life of India produced not only story-tellers—whose primary purpose was transmitting the stories of gods, goddesses, heroes, and heroines—but also poets who expressed ordinary people's spiritual longing for God. Emotional worship or surrender to God in Hinduism is called **bhakti**, a term that has its origins in the Upanishads. Bhakti became a religious movement in India during the religious reforms of the eighth, ninth, and tenth centuries. A particular version of bhakti was devoted to feminine divinity; in India there had been a long history of worshiping the great goddess **Shakti**[1]—also known as **Kali** and Durga—but a resurgence of her worship, led by the poet **Ramprasad** Sen, took place in Bengal[2] during the eighteenth century. Like medieval Christian poets devoted to the Virgin Mother, Bengal poets of this time favored the feminine dimension of God, which seemed to invite a personal relationship, an opportunity for conversation, and expressions of sadness and longing.

Ramprasad's poems, primarily songs to Kali, were extremely popular at the end of the eighteenth century when Bengal was in a time of darkness and despair. The region had been under Muslim rule for about five hundred years when the British defeated the Mughal army in the Battle of Plassey in 1757.[3] Robber barons controlled large parts of Bengal, and Kali was their patron deity. Regional kings promoted Kali worship by supporting court poets who composed and sang songs to the goddess. The songs became part of an extremely precarious village life. Bengal is a region of extremes, feast or famine, due to unpredictable rains. Some years bring little rain or droughts, while others have heavy rain and flooding. Occasionally there are years when just the right amount of rain falls at the appropriate times; these times are thought to be blessed by Kali.

Ramprasad's simple lyricism and familiar images touched a broad range of listeners; his songs appealed to scholars and peasants alike. His poetic skills influenced succeeding generations of Indian poets. Rabindranath Tagore,[4] the most famous Bengali writer of the late nineteenth cen-

www For links to more information about Ramprasad and a quiz on his poetry, see *World Literature Online* at bedfordstmartins .com/worldlit.

---

[1] **Shakti:** Shakti is the collective name for the consort of Shiva who has several names. **Shakti** is the feminine dynamic energy by which God creates, preserves, and dissolves the world. **Kali** is usually portrayed as terrifying: blue-black, three-eyed, and four-armed, with a necklace of human heads and a girdle of severed hands. **Durga**, "the unfathomable one," is one of the oldest versions of the Great Mother: fair complexioned and riding a lion, she releases humans from rebirth with her touch.

[2] **Bengal:** A region in the northeast Indian peninsula, now divided between India and Bangladesh.

[3] **Battle of Plassey:** Plassey is a village in West Bengal state where the British defeated the Bengal army in 1757, leading to Britain's control of northeast India.

[4] **Rabindranath Tagore** (1861–1941): A native of Bengal anxious to preserve the cultural richness of traditional village life while at the same time bridging the philosophical and literary gap between East and West. (See Book 5.)

The Holy Family: Shiva, Parvati, and Their Children on Mount Kailasa, c. 1800

An androgynous, naked Shiva is attended by Parvati, his spouse, who offers him liquid refreshment. The bull represents Shiva; the lion, Parvati; and the elephant-headed creature is Ganesha, a popular Hindu god. (Courtesy of the British Museum)

tury, composed Kali songs even though he was not a worshiper of Kali himself; he merged the goddess's image with nationalistic devotion.

Poet and Legend.   Ramprasad Sen was born in Kumarhatta, about twenty-five miles from Calcutta. His father, Ramram Sen, was of the Vaidyas caste—that of physicians. Ramprasad had a minimal education and was versed in Sanskrit, Persian, and Hindi as well as Bengali. As a young man he got a job in Calcutta as a clerk with an estate manager, Valulachandra Ghosal. Rather than paying attention to the accounts,

These [Ramprasad's poems] have gone to the heart of a people as few poets' work has done. Such songs as the exquisite "This day will surely pass, Mother, this day will pass," I have heard from coolies on the road or workers in the paddy fields; I have heard it by broad rivers at sunset, when the parrots were flying to roost and the village folk thronging from marketing to the ferry. . . .

– critic EDWARD THOMPSON, 1923

Ramprasad wrote poetry. When his employer discovered the way Ramprasad was spending his time he was angry, until he read the lines, "I do not want this copyist's work. Give me your treasuryship, Mother." For some reason Ghosal was sympathetic to the young man's yearnings to serve Kali and provided him with a pension and an introduction to the court of the Raja of Krishnagar, where he rose to the position of "Entertainer of Poets."

Ramprasad became famous during his lifetime, and there are numerous legends about his encounters with Kali and her demands on him. His poems, which were first passed down orally, have been collected in several volumes. *Vidyasundar,* which was composed in the 1760s or 1770s, is an extended poem about how the Raja of Kanchi's son won the hand of the Raja of Burdwan's daughter. *Kalikirttan*[5] is a collection of songs or hymns to Kali. The poems in *Krishnakirttan* are devoted to Krishna.

Ramprasad died in 1775. One legend says that he died with a Kali song on his lips, beseeching her to save him, and that indeed he slipped away from the endless cycle of reincarnations into Brahman.[6] In another version, Ramprasad followed an image of Kali into the Ganges River while reciting poems to her and drowned. He was regarded a saint.

Background for Bengali Songs to Kali.   In most world religions there are at least two significant paths followed by most practitioners: the path of legalism and the path of mysticism. The first is a matter of believing certain doctrines, following prescribed rules or laws, and performing certain rituals interpreted and led by a priest, minister, rabbi, or imam. The second path is one of direct, personal experience of the sacred and involves various techniques for achieving mystical union with the divine without the mediation of a priest or institution. In the history of Hinduism, Brahmanism[7] represents the orthodox path of legalism: The Brahman priest, who masters the appropriate ceremonies or rituals, serves as an intercessor between the worshiper and god. The mystical cults in India are grouped under the name *bhakti,* a Sanskrit word meaning the path of total surrender to god as a means of achieving salvation. A guru, rather than a priest, serves as a bhakti guide. For both the orthodox and the bhakti the goal is the same: Salvation is *moksha,* the release from samsara[8] — the cycle of life, death, and rebirth — in order to be unified with God.

Since the tenth century of Indian history, Hinduism had primarily centered around the worship of two deities: Vishnu — in his manifestations, or avatars, as Rama and Krishna — and Shiva.[9] In Hinduism, wor-

---

[5] *Kalikirttan:* A processional song or hymn, in this case to Kali.

[6] Brahman: The Absolute Reality which transcends all thought, all names, and definitions. There is no equivalent concept in religions that feature a personal god.

[7] Hinduism, Brahmanism: Hinduism is a broad term used for the peoples of India who follow one of several religions that use the ancient Vedas and Upanishads for their scriptures. Brahmanism recognizes the creator Brahma and the priestly class of brahmans who administer the appropriate Hindu rituals.

[8] samsara: Refers to the endless cycle of birth, death, and rebirth. *Samsara* literally means "going round and round."

[9] Vishnu . . . Shiva: Manifestations of Brahman, the Absolute or Ultimate Being. They form a trinity with Brahma, the creator, who has little ceremonial or cult importance.

shipers are also often devoted to the consort of a deity; when the goddess is recognized as the energy or power behind existence, she is known as Shakti. Ramprasad's particular kind of bhakti worship was directed at Shiva's consort, **Shakti** or the Great Mother. An analogy can be made with Roman Catholic worship: A particular church might be devoted to the worship of Our Lady of Fatima, a manifestation of Mary. The rituals and meditative practices describing the Shakti pathway are contained in texts called Tantra;[10] Shaktism is also called Tantrism. A particular branch of tantric worship involves sexual practices that are said to lead to a mystical union with Shakti.

SHAK-tee

As a couple, Shiva represents transcendent power and Kali immanent or manifested power. Kali is usually represented as dancing or in sexual union with Shiva. Sri Ramakrishna,[11] a famous mystic from the nineteenth century, described one of his visions of Kali in a way that described her two aspects coming together. He saw a beautiful woman emerge from the Ganges and approach a grove of trees where he was meditating. The woman gave birth to a beautiful baby, and she gently nursed it. After a while she suddenly changed into a horrible monster. She took the infant in her ugly jaws and crushed it. She chewed it, swallowed it, and then returned to the Ganges and disappeared into the water. Sri Ramakrishna's vision exemplifies the idea of Kali as a totality that reconciles creation and dissolution.

Ramprasad's Kali Songs.   To somebody living in the West, writing love songs to the terrible and ferocious Kali might seem strange, yet Kali embraces many aspects of life. For Ramprasad, Kali ultimately represented release from the endless sufferings of mortality. In his poems, Ramprasad uses standard bhakti themes: Kali's neglect of her devotee, her carelessness, her preoccupation with wild dancing and her habit of standing on Shiva; the poet complains about her and threatens to give up on her. Kali's role as a goddess in the universe parallels the role she plays in Ramprasad's poetry and life.

Because Ramprasad's poems were initially passed down orally, multiple versions of the same poem arose, a challenge for any translator. Furthermore, these Kali songs were usually written in simple, colloquial Bengali, which demands a colloquial American English translation in order to communicate the voice of the poems. Kali is often addressed as "Mother" in the songs, suggesting the personal relationship of a child to its mother, or the feelings of the individual toward the greater, cosmic reality. In "It's This Hope in Hope," Ramprasad laments being lured into this world by Kali and fooled by the world's appearance of sweetness. Ordinary events are combined with spiritual yearning in "How Many Times, Mother?" wherein the poet ponders the number of incarnations

---

[10] **Tantra:** Texts describing the religious practices that surround the worship of the Mother Goddess. The Tantra are equal in importance to the Vedas, the most ancient, sacred texts of Hindus. Tantra describe complicated rituals leading to direct, mystical experience of the goddess.

[11] **Sri Ramakrishna** (1836–1886): A priest and devotee of Mother Kali in Dakshineswar, a suburb of Calcutta.

he must suffer. Ramprasad's sense of play is evident in "The Dark Mother Is Flying a Kite," although the metaphor of kite-flying ultimately takes on a serious dimension.

In "Kali, Why Are You Naked Again?" the poet evokes the popular image of Kali standing on the body of Shiva and gently chides her about her nudity. Part of the poignant attraction of a Kali song comes from the contrast between the playful tenderness of the poet and the horrifying power of the goddess. As in a personal relationship, the poet expresses disappointment, threatens to break off contact, pinpoints the mother's neglect. But in "Now Cry Kali and Take the Plunge!" the poet challenges himself to dive into the sea of consciousness and confesses his shortcomings and failures. "Why Should I Go to Kashi?" is an important statement about the bhakti spiritual path; Ramprasad makes it clear that he does not personally subscribe to the path of pilgrimage and sacrificial offerings, the brand of Hinduism associated with Brahmanism. In "What's More to Fear around This Place?" Ramprasad gives Shiva a role but concludes with an image of Kali as a tree bearing the fruits of release and immortality. With his clear, down-to-earth, accessible images, Ramprasad established a tone for Kali songs that was imitated by generations of writers after him.

■ CONNECTIONS

Rabindranath Tagore, "The Hungry Stones" (Book 5). Hoping to discover an Indian identity unique to India and not borrowed from Western Europe, modern Indian writers turned to the traditional foundation of Indian culture, the village. Tagore saw village life as a repository of values and folk wisdom. How does Ramprasad's use of earthy, rural images in his poems indicate the accessibility of Kali to ordinary consciousness and to villagers whose lives are defined by traditional folkways and rural mores?

William Blake (Book 5). Through images and metaphor, poets reveal the irony of ordinary reality—that things aren't always as they seem. In "Songs of Experience," Blake exposes the difference between appearance and reality in everyday experience. How does Ramprasad use the deceptiveness of ordinary reality to make a case for better or preferential treatment from Kali?

Adrienne Rich (Book 6). Especially after the Romantic period, poets often directed their attention to the inward journey, the descent into the realm of the psyche. Rich's "Diving into the Wreck" describes a passage into the inner world of the self; it is similar in focus to Ramprasad's "Now Cry Kali and Take the Plunge!" How are the ultimate goals of these poems both similar and radically different?

■ FURTHER RESEARCH

Cultural Background

Dutt, Romesh Chunder. *Cultural Heritage of Bengal.* 1962.

Kinsley, David R. *The Sword and the Flute: Kali and Krnsa, Dark Visions of the Terrible and the Sublime in Hindu Mythology.* 1975.

Mookerjee, Ajit. *Kali: The Feminine Force.* 1988.

Criticism

Sen, Ramprasad. *Grace and Mercy in Her Wild Hair: Selected Poems to the Mother Goddess.* 1982. (See the introduction by Leonard Nathan and Clinton Seely.)

∾ The Dark Mother Is Flying a Kite

The dark Mother
Is flying a kite
In the world's fairground.

O, Mind, see — you are up there
In the gusts of hope,
Payed out on the string of illusion,
Your frame strung together
Skeleton and pulse stuck on.

But the Maker overdid it,
10 Giving the kite too much ego
In the building,
Toughening the string with glue
And powdered glass.[1]

So Mother, if out of a thousand kites
You lose one or two,
Laugh and clap.

Prasad° says: that kite is going to take off   short for *Ramprasad*
In the southern breeze,
And on the other shore
20 Of this ocean of lives
It will dive fast to its freedom.

"The Dark Mother Is Flying a Kite." The metaphor of the kite picks up the association of play with the Mother Goddess. Ramprasad refers to his "Mind," meaning that part of him that is subject to delusion and false hope, akin to the term *psyche.* The translators add to the concept by saying "too much ego" in the third stanza, choosing a word associated with Sigmund Freud that Ramprasad would not have used.

---

[1] powdered glass: Kite strings are coated with glue and powdered glass for the purpose of cutting down another flyer's kite.

❧ Kali, Why Are You Naked Again?

Kali, why are You naked again?
Good grief, haven't You any shame?

Mother, don't You have clothes?
Where is the pride of a king's daughter?

And, Mother, is this some family duty—
This standing on the chest of Your man?

You're naked, He's naked,
You hang around the burning grounds.

O, Mother, we are dying of shame.
10 Now put on Your woman's clothes.

Mother, Your necklace gleams,
Those human heads shine at Your throat.

Prasad says: Even Shiva fears You
When You're like this.

"Kali, Why Are You Naked Again?" This poem seems almost sacrilegious in its opening lines.
Ramprasad is in a playful mood, daring to describe one of Kali's most popular postures: standing
naked on the body of Shiva. Underneath the chiding is an awareness of the power of Shiva and his
consort, who stand ready to release the individual from the mortal round of reincarnations.
"Burning grounds" refers to the places where bodies are cremated, the place where Shiva and Kali
cut away all unnecessary, egotistical elements from the human psyche.

◌ Now Cry Kali and Take the Plunge!

Now cry Kali and take the plunge!
O, my Mind, dive into this sea,
This heart which has yet to be sounded.
There are gems down there that two or three dives
Aren't going to get. Now, hold your breath
And jump! Kick down to where She sits[1]
Deep in the wise waters, a great pearl.
You can do it, all it takes
Is overwhelming love and the memory
10   Of Shiva's good words.[2]

Down there the Six Passions cruise
Like crocodiles snapping at anything
That moves, so cover yourself with knowledge
Like turmeric[3] smeared on the skin—
The odor will keep them off.
I tell you there's a world of wealth
In that water.

Ramprasad says: Dive in
And you're going to come up with a fortune.

"Now Cry Kali and Take the Plunge!"   In this poem the descent into the sea is a metaphor for
the journey into the consciousness of self, but it has also a more specific meaning for Tantrism. In
the individual, Shakti as cosmic energy resides at the base of the spinal column, in the lowest
chakra, in a serpentine form sometimes called *kundalini*. The task of the individual is to awaken
this energy and through meditative disciplines draw it upwards through the six chakras into full
spiritual expression and power. The six chakras are centers of energy stretching from the base of
the spinal column to the top of the head.

---

[1] **She sits:** A reference to Kali's residence at the bottom of consciousness or at the base of the spinal column.

[2] **Shiva's good words:** Shiva is the speaker in the tantric texts.

[3] **turmeric:** A yellow plant of the ginger family; smeared on the body, it is believed to ward off crocodiles.
Turmeric may also refer to adopting the yellow robes of the ascetic to help ward off the passions.

❧ Why Should I Go to Kashi?

Why should I go to Kashi?[1]
At Her feet you'll find it all—
Gaya,[2] the Ganges, Kashi.
Meditating in my lotus heart[3]
I float on blissful waters.
Her feet are red lotuses
Crammed with shrines
And Her name spoken
Consumes evil like a fire
10   In a pile of dry cotton.
If there is no head to worry,
You can't have a headache.

Everytime I hear about Gaya,
The offerings there, the good deeds
Recited, I laugh. I know Shiva
Has said that dying at Kashi saves.
But I know too that salvation
Always follows worship around
Like a slave, and what's this salvation
20   If it swallows the saved like water
In water? Sugar I love
But haven't the slightest desire
To merge with sugar.

Ramprasad says with amazement:
Grace and mercy in Her wild hair—
Think of that
And all good things[4] are yours.

"Why Should I Go to Kashi?" Ramprasad makes it clear in this poem that he is following the bhakti path rather than the path of traditional Hinduism with its ceremonies, pilgrimages, and offerings to the deities. For him, Kali's feet are sufficient—meaning devotion to the goddess. He uses the popular metaphor of sugar: It is one thing to taste the sweetness of the divine and quite another to be lost or absorbed in it.

---

[1] **Kashi:** Kashi is Benares, the residence of Shiva, and one of the most sacred sites along the Ganges.

[2] **Gaya:** A place of pilgrimage in northeastern India, the site of Gautama Buddha's enlightenment.

[3] **lotus heart:** The fourth chakra, the center of mystical powers.

[4] **good things:** There are four good things to get from life: 1. *(dharma)* lawful order, sacred duty, and moral virtue; 2. *(artha)* power and success; 3. *(kama)* love and pleasure; and 4. *(moksha)* release from delusion and the limitations of existence.

∾ What's More to Fear around This Place?

What's more to fear
Around this place?

My body is Tara's[1] field
In which the God of Gods
Like a good farmer
Sows His seed with a great *mantra.*[2]

Around this body, faith
Is set like a fence
With patience for posts.

10   With Shiva watching
What can the thieves of time
Hope to do?

He oversees the Six Oxen
Driving them out of the barn.

He mows the grass of sin
With the honed blade of Kali's name.

Love rains down
And Devotion night and day.

Prasad says: On Kali's tree
20   Goodness, wealth, love and release
Can be had for the picking.

"What's More to Fear around This Place?" In this poem, Ramprasad returns to a simple metaphor commonly used in other religions: The believer is a field ready for planting and cultivation by the deity. Shiva wields the blade of Kali to cut away sin; Kali is ultimately the sacred tree in the center of the garden, from which the worshiper may pick the fruits of salvation.

---

[1] **Tara:** Another name for Kali; this is not—on the surface at least—the popular Tara of Tibetan Buddhism.

[2] *mantra:* A sacred utterance, often used for meditation.

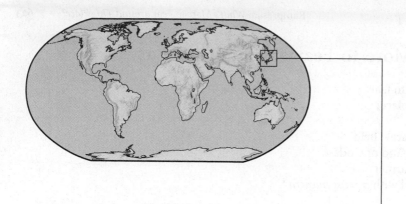

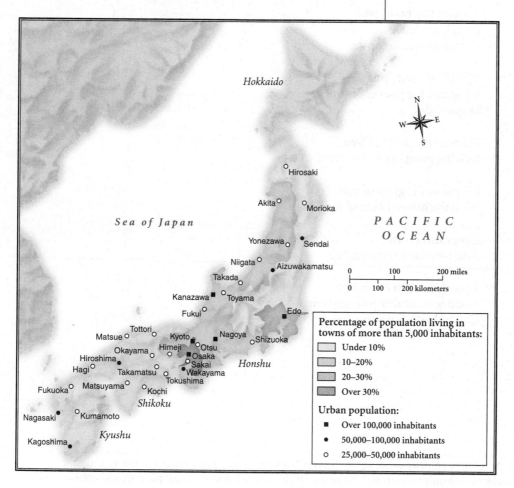

Population Density in Late Tokugawa Japan

In 1603, Tokugawa Ieyasu instituted a military government, the shogunate, which ruled Japan for the next two hundred years. This period was known as the Tokugawa or Edo period. As this map indicates, one notable change in Japanese society during this time was population growth, especially in the cities. A previously rigid social structure gave way to new trades, professions, and classes—the middle classes—and urban life changed dramatically.

JAPAN
The Tokugawa Era

❧ The period in Japan from 1603 to 1868 is known as the Tokugawa, or Edo, period, named after its first *shogun,* or military ruler, and the capital city. Like its European counterparts, Japan in the late seventeenth and early eighteenth century enjoyed a period of relative calm after a series of chaotic civil wars among rival *daimyo,* or feudal lords. Continuing the consolidation of power that had begun in the middle of the sixteenth century, in 1603 Tokugawa Ieyasu (r. 1603–1616) instituted a military government, the shogunate, which ruled Japan from the capital city Edo (now Tokyo) for the next two hundred years. Under the Tokugawa shogunate, the emperor was retained as a ceremonial figure, while the shogun and the officials of his central administration, the *bakufu,* were charged with the actual governance. Promoting neo-Confucianist doctrines that emphasized loyalty, duty, and filial piety, the Tokugawa rulers attempted to maintain a rigidly hierarchical society divided into four distinct groups—warriors *(samurai),* farmers, artisans, and merchants. Population growth, the rise of the urban middle classes, and the introduction of new trades and professions during this era, however, confounded the fourfold scheme.

EAST/WEST RELATIONS

Japan's direct trade and exchange of ideas with Westerners began when Portuguese merchants first arrived in 1543. Among other goods, the Europeans introduced gunpowder and firearms to the Japanese. Francis Xavier, a Jesuit missionary, arrived in Japan in 1549 and was followed by priests from other orders, including Franciscans, who joined in efforts to convert the Japanese to Christianity. By the time of the Tokugawa shogunate there were several hundred thousand Japanese Christians, particularly in the southern islands. Repeating similar mistakes that had been made in China, some of the missionaries, with the backing of the pope, destroyed Japanese idols and interfered with local politics. In reprisal, Tokugawa ordered the expulsion of all Christian missionaries in 1612. After a failed revolt by Christians on the island of Kyushu in 1637, Christianity was banned altogether and Japan effectively closed its doors to foreign trade. With the exception of some limited trade with Korea and China, after 1641 only the Dutch, under strict regulations, exchanged goods with Japan, operating a small trading post in Nagasaki harbor; meanwhile all Japanese were forbidden to travel outside the country. Japan was effectively isolated from the rest of the world for more than two hundred years.

GROWTH OF THE URBAN MIDDLE CLASSES

The growth of cities and the expansion of commerce and manufacturing exerted a powerful influence on society and the arts in Japan during the Tokugawa period. Edo, Kyoto, and Osaka, in particular, grew into thriving commercial centers, where *chonin,* or artisans and merchants, fostered the growth of a flourishing popular culture. One key concept associated with the social life of chonin during the Tokugawa period is *ukiyo,* or "floating world." Alluding to the transitory nature of life, ukiyo came to stand for the entertainments and diversions of the chonin, in particular their activities in the pleasure quarters, or licensed districts—areas of major cities set aside to house prostitutes and courtesans (prostitutes among the well-to-do). Originally enclosed for the purpose of regulating prostitution, pleasure quarters expanded to become cultural and social institutions that in many ways reflected the values of the chonin. Money, above all, was prized in these areas; its acquisition would allow merchants to compete with samurai, who were wealthier and enjoyed more respect. Moreover, women in the pleasure quarters achieved a level of independence and respect not possible under the strict doctrines of subordination ushered in by Tokugawa rulers. In the pleasure quarters, men enjoyed the attentions of beautiful and sometimes well-educated courtesans, who observed formal standards of etiquette.

This "floating world" of openly sexual relationships regulated by formal rituals of courtship and economic exchange was often in conflict with the world of family and social responsibility. Marriage at the time often had very little to do with romantic love. As among the upper classes in Europe, China, and India, marriages were often arranged by interested parents as a means to preserve or maintain social standing and economic power, especially among samurai and the wealthiest chonin. While some husbands and wives fell in love with each other, some did not, and a man with sufficient funds to both support his wife and finance a relationship with a courtesan had tacit license to do so. Women, however, were bound by marriage; a married woman who took a lover was subject by law to execution. As can be seen in Chikamatsu's *The Love Suicides at Amijima* (p. 691) and in Saikaku's

Torii Kiyotada, *Middle Street of the Yoshiwara*, c. 1740. Hand-Colored Woodblock Print
Many Japanese woodblock prints of the eighteenth century portrayed the "floating world," the pleasure district in Edo (Tokyo), where the newly affluent bourgeoisie enjoyed the company of courtesans, storytellers, jesters, and other entertainers. (Art Institute of Chicago)

fiction, complications stemming from a man's divided affections at home and in the floating world figures prominently in the writing of the Tokugawa era.

NEO-CONFUCIANISM

Although **BUDDHISM** and the native Shintoism played a strong role in Japanese religious life, education and social practices in the Tokugawa era were based largely on neo-Confucianist principles. A school of thought associated with the Chinese philosopher Zhu Xi (Chu Hsi, 1130–1200) and developed in Japan by Fujiwara Seika (1561–1619) and Hayashi Razan (1583–1657), **NEO-CONFUCIANISM** appealed to the ruling shoguns because it suited their aim to promote social stability and hierarchical order. For many members of Japanese society, neo-Confucianism was beneficial because it spread literacy through the classes, and even among women. Unlike most of their European peers, Japanese women studied in public or private schools, but they lost some of their previous rights to inheritance, property, and divorce under the strict Tokugawan rules of subordination. Arranged marriages were common during this time, and while men often had license to mingle with concubines (mistresses) and other sex workers in the so-called pleasure quarters, women were expected to stay at home and be virtuous.

During the Tokugawa era, neo-Confucianism began to reflect a new world-view, one oriented in its "investigation of things"—a common phrase of the time—to an empirical observation of nature. In a spirit of inquiry very much like that of their contemporaries in Europe, philosophers such as Kaibara Ekken (1630–1714) and Baien Miura (1723–1789)—whose work is excerpted in the *In the World* sections "Love, Marriage, and the Education of Women" and "The Spirit of Inquiry"—argued that in order to find our place in nature, we need to escape from convention and habit and seek to discover the principles and laws that govern nature. Kaibara in particular helped to spread neo-Confucian ideas widely, writing several treatises addressed to the newly literate classes and to women and children. Thus, the Tokugawa era witnessed a renaissance in philosophical thinking, the development of empirical studies, and the spread of education.

THE RISE OF POPULAR LITERATURE

Japanese literature and arts flourished during the seventeenth and eighteenth centuries as a result of the peace and economic stability of the Tokugawa period. Before this time, literature had been written by and for the elite—samurai and nobles. As such, it reflected the beliefs and culture of the upper classes; literature aimed at the common people was designed primarily to proclaim the values of the elite and particularly to reinforce loyalty and piety. Two phenomena of the sixteenth and seventeenth centuries began to change all that: the development of printing and the rise of the chonin. By the late sixteenth century, following the example of Jesuits who had used wood and copper type, Japan developed a relatively inexpensive form of woodblock printing. With this new method, various kinds of writing—as well as woodblock prints—could reach a wide audience. And when urban artisans and merchants began to do well in the commercial cities of Edo, Kyoto, and Osaka, they exerted a tremendous influence on the form and content of literature and the arts.

Although mass education did not produce widespread literacy until well into the eighteenth century, in the late seventeenth century chonin demand for entertainment began to affect both drama and fiction. In a portion of the Tokugawa era known as the Genroku period (1688–1704; see Time and Place box, p. 629) writers such as dramatist Chikamatsu Monzaemon (1653–1724) and fiction writer Ihara Saikaku (1642–1693) began writing plays, short stories, and novels that reflected the lives and values of the middle classes. Whereas the courtly *Nō* dramas appealed to the elite tastes of samurai and aristocrats, two new forms of drama—*KABUKI*, or

www For more information about the culture and context of Japan in the eighteenth century, see *World Literature Online* at bedfordstmartins.com/worldlit.

Eighteenth-Century Japan: Genroku Period

Between 1688 and 1704 Japan experienced a cultural renaissance in literature and the arts, brought on in part by the power and wealth of the *chonin,* or merchant classes, whose secular values inspired a new aesthetic. Known as the Genroku period, this moment of cultural creativity was centered in the cities of Edo, Japan's capital; Kyoto; and Osaka, the premier commercial city. The cultural revival was marked by a turn toward popular forms that exploited new developments in woodblock printing and that plumbed the everyday lives of the artisans, merchants, bankers, courtesans, and actors who frequented the licensed districts, or pleasure quarters. During Genroku, the transitory pleasures of the "floating world" were a dominating influence. Painters, woodblock printers, dramatists, and fiction writers were eager to satisfy the tastes and reflect the values of the thriving townspeople. In painting, Ogata Korin (1658–1716) moved away from conventional, Chinese-inspired scenes and depicted the lives of chonin, as did the woodblock printer Utamoro (1754–1806). In drama, Chikamatsu Monzaemon (1653–1724) transformed the *joruri,* or popular puppet theater, becoming one of the first writers in the world to focus on the domestic and personal tragedies of common people. His *sewamono,* or domestic plays, often dramatized actual incidents that had taken place in Kyoto or Edo; like Goethe's immensely popular novel *The Sorrows of Young Werther* (1774), which set off a series of imitation suicides in late-eighteenth-century Germany, Chikamatsu's *shinju* plays were so widely influential that the government banned their performance in order to stem the growing number of imitation suicides in Japan. Ihara Saikaku (1642–1693) became the

leading popular fiction writer of the time, using colloquial language to transform the Japanese novel into a realistic story that focused on the loves and lives of artisans and merchants. Matsuo Bashō (1644–1694) recast *haikai,* or linked verse, into personal expression, conveying a direct sense of nature and a spirit of reverie. Scholarship, too, blossomed during this time. Philosophers such as Ogyu Sorai (1666–1728) and Arai Hakuseki (1657–1725) redirected Japanese thought from metaphysics toward a more empirical study of philology, linguistics, history, ethics, and politics. Overall, the Genroku period was a reflection of the society that had emerged in the first century of the Tokugawa era, and it left a lasting mark on Japanese literature, culture, and sensibility.

H. Suzuki, **Sprigging a Plum Tree,** *c. 1755   This woodcut depicts two pleasure-seekers of the floating world of the Genroku period. (The Art Archive/Eileen Tweedy)*

live drama, and *JORURI,* or puppet theater—increasingly took for their themes the lives of courtesans, bankers, tradesmen, and artisans living in cities. In fiction, Ihara Saikaku was the first Japanese writer to create realistic portrayals of chonin, unabashedly representing their acquisitiveness and sexual desires as well as their pragmatism. From erotic stories about love and sex to tales dealing with the financial preoccupations of merchants and bankers, Saikaku's stories examined the morals and manners of the middle classes about a half century before European novelists would do the same.

In poetry, too, significant changes took place in the Tokugawa era, particularly in the case of *haikai* master Matsuo Bashō (1644–1694), whose work would revolutionize Japanese poetry and Japanese taste. Bashō's artistic sensibility evolved from his studies of the Japanese and Chinese classics, but his work is remarkable for its innovation, especially in the art of *haibun,* a mixture of linked verse and prose in which Bashō describes his sojourns through the countryside to sacred shrines and other places far from the floating world of the cities. In the sixteenth century haikai was a popular, satiric form of poetry; Bashō made it into a meditative, reflective form of personal expression.

The three writers included here represent the height of the Genroku period. The literary renaissance of the Tokugawa era declined after 1800; the next period of innovation and change in Japan was the Meiji period (1868–1912), when the country's physical and intellectual borders once again opened and the great controversy over Western influence on Japanese culture brought about another deep examination of Japan's oldest traditions.

ᔐ Ihara Saikaku
1642–1693

Along with poet Matsuo Bashō (1644–1694) and playwright Chikamatsu Monzaemon (1653–1724), Ihara Saikaku is considered one of the chief literary artists of the Tokugawa, or Edo, era.[1] In his early years Saikaku was a prolific and even ostentatious writer of *HAIKAI,* a form of Japanese linked verse written by one or more people that held a place of great importance from the sixteenth through the nineteenth centuries.

At the age of forty Saikaku turned his prodigious literary talent to the writing of popular fiction about the **chonin,** the people of the towns, especially the urban merchant classes. He was writing at a time when the fortunes of townspeople were growing and when their money and manners were beginning to take center stage not only in economic life but also in the Japanese cultural imagination. Though his first novel appeared in 1682, Saikaku's fiction is associated with the Genroku period (1688–1703).[2] Just as woodblock print artists of the **Ukiyo-e** school[3] such as **Moronobu**[4] (c. 1618–c. 1694) took up representations of city life, Saikaku turned the attention of the literary arts to the antics and desires of a class previously neglected. From the merchant class himself, Saikaku is remembered as a writer of highly imaginative stories about the loves and passions, the fortunes and failures, of the chonin. His tales vividly depict the everyday life of townspeople and realistically describe the commonplace objects of their world. Saikaku's works have gone through many editions and translations, and they have been very influential for succeeding generations of Japanese writers. Today Saikaku is regarded as one of the greatest fiction writers in Japanese literary history—according to some, second only to Lady Murasaki,[5] the author of *The Tale of Genji.*

CHOH-nin

OO-kee-yoh EH
moh-roh-NOH-boo

The Nimble Improviser of Haikai. Hirayama Togo, who would eventually take the pen name of **Ihara Saikaku**, was born into a rich merchant family in Osaka in 1642. Little is known of his early life, though it appears

ee-HAH-rah
sigh-KAH-koo

---

[1] **Tokugawa era** (1603–1868): The longest lasting of the great Japanese shogunates, founded by Tokugawa Ieyasu (1603–1616), the feudal lord or *daimyo* of Edo (now Tokyo).

[2] **Genroku period** (1688–1703): A cultural moment during the Edo era when a growing number of affluent *chonin,* or townsmen, sought diversion in the "floating world" *(ukiyo)*—city districts where theater, dance, song, courtesans, and the arts flourished. (See Time and Place box, p. 629.)

[3] *Ukiyo-e* **school:** School of Japanese woodblock printing of the Edo period that captures images of everyday life in the floating world. The greatest ukiyo-e artists include Hishikawa Moronobu (c. 1618–c. 1694), Suzuki Harunobu (1725–1770), and Ando Hiroshige (1797–1858).

[4] **Hishikawa Moronobu:** One of the earliest Japanese painters and *ukiyo-e* woodblock artists.

[5] **Lady Murasaki** (c. 978–1031): Murasaki Shikibu, among the greatest of Japanese novelists, wrote the highly acclaimed *The Tale of Genji,* one of the earliest and most celebrated works of fiction not only in Japanese but in world literature.

HIGH-kigh

that he took charge of the family's business for many years. In his early twenties and thirties, under the name of Ihara (his mother's maiden name) Kakuei, he published **haikai** verse, which he studied under the master Soin Nishiyama (1605–1682).[6] In 1673, under the name Saikaku, he collaborated with others in publishing *Ten Thousand Verses at Ikudama (Ikudama Manku),* an anthology of more than two hundred haikai poets. These poets had written in what was called the Dutch style, a new method of linking verses rejecting the traditional five-line form called the *tanka.* The two- to three-line verses, each written by a different poet, were joined by thematic association rather than by a play on words, and the poems' diction was more colloquial and less dependent on allusions to Chinese poetry than traditional poetry had been. Saikaku rather brazenly took this challenge to tradition one step further by writing linked verse by himself. In 1675 he wrote 1,000 verses in one day to commemorate his wife's death; on another day, in 1677, he produced 1,600 verses; and in 1681 he is said to have composed an astonishing 23,500 verses within a twenty-four hour period, reciting the lines so fast that the scribes could not record his words. Saikaku was turning the art of haikai into a kind of one-man road show, a pyrotechnic display of his imaginative power, much to the dismay of his former master and rival poets. He dubbed the new form *yakazu,* after archery contests. Saikaku's haikai increasingly took up themes of the floating world *(ukiyo)* and urban life, as his fiction was soon to do.

Saikaku's Turn to Fiction.   In 1675 Saikaku's wife died. He gave up his business and, like Bashō, set out on travels around Japan, soaking up new places and experiences and displaying his talent for rapid-fire poetic composition. Seven years later, he wrote his first novel, *The Life of an Amorous Man (Koshoku Ichidai Otoko,* 1682), an erotic, PICARESQUE novel[7] that follows the precocious and astounding sexual adventures of a man named Yonosuke. This landmark work changed the direction of Japanese fiction and brought the novel's potential to fruition in Japan. Divided into fifty-four chapters like Murasaki Shikibu's *The Tale of Genji,* Saikaku's tale amounts to a self-conscious rewriting of that classic novel. Here, however, the hero is not a nobleman but a merchant, and the courtly manners of Genji's world are replaced by the bourgeois manners of townspeople, explained in detail. From 1682 to 1693, Saikaku wrote as many as twenty-six books, including crime stories, love stories, collections of folktales, and even stories about samurai, who had recently fallen on hard times, their status and power usurped by the newly enriched urban populace. In 1686 Saikaku published *Five Women Who Loved Love (Koshoku Gonin Onna),* often considered his greatest work. He also pub-

[Saikaku's characters] are modeled on real people and themselves might serve as models for masterpieces of the ukiyo-e — lovely, entirely human, winning, though lacking the weight of flesh. Saikaku's style . . . is perfectly suited to sketching with swift but unerring strokes figures of enormous charm.

– DONALD KEENE, critic, *World within Walls,* 1976

---

[6] **Soin Nishiyama:** *Haikai* master and founder of the Danrin school, a revolutionary school of haikai that challenged the form's traditional syllabic structure and drew many of its themes and diction from *Nō* dramas.

[7] **picaresque novel:** A novel loosely structured around a succession of episodes, focusing on a thinly drawn *picaro,* or hero, whose adventures provide a view of society and customs that are often treated satirically by the writer. Two examples are Cervantes' *Don Quixote* and Voltaire's *Candide.*

lished the novel *The Life of an Amorous Woman (Koshoku Ichidai Onna),* which follows the sexual adventures of a courtesan whose career eventually lands her in degradation and poverty. Other works of fiction—some based on the writer's travels and experiences, others derived from contemporary drama—include *Saikaku's Tales of the Provinces (Saikaku Shokoku Hanashi,* 1685); *The Great Mirror of Manly Love (Nanshoku Okagami,* 1687), tales of homosexual love among samurai; *Tales of Samurai Duty (Buke Giri Monogatari,* 1688), a collection of tales about the responsibilities of samurai; *The Japanese Family Storehouse (Nippon Eitaigura,* 1688), stories depicting the lives of merchants; and *Reckonings that Carry Men through the World (Seken Mune Sanyo,* 1692), a series of tales about debtors who resort to extreme measures to pay their bills.

In 1690 Saikaku reappeared on the haikai scene, possibly because poor eyesight made writing fiction difficult for him. He died on September 9, 1693, leaving behind many manuscripts that were published posthumously, including *Saikaku's Parting Gift (Saikaku Okimiyage,* 1693) and *Saikaku's Parting with Friends (Saikaku Nagori no Tomo,* 1699), which were edited—sometimes with a heavy hand—and published by one of his followers, Hojo Dansui (1663–1711).

Five Women Who Loved Love.   Popular in his time as well as today, Saikaku is remembered as a prolific master of "tales of the floating world," or **ukiyo-zoshi.**[8] The five stories of his masterpiece, *Five Women Who Loved Love,* first published in 1686, were based on actual incidents—the suicide of a barrelmaker's wife found out in adultery and the execution of an almanac maker's wife and her lover, for example—that had recently occurred in the Osaka-Kyoto region and would have been familiar to his readers.

The narrative voice in each story maintains a comic distance from the characters' misfortunes and focuses the reader's attention on the abundant details of their misadventures. In "What the Seasons Brought to the Almanac Maker" (included here), these details and the sexually charged atmosphere they create exhibit a considerable interest on the part of the author in the amorous escapades of the heroines, but Saikaku stops short of celebrating their sexual bravado. As in Chikamatsu's *shinju* play ***The Love Suicides at Amijima,*** in *Five Women Who Loved Love* the struggle between *ninjo,* individual passion or desire, and *giri,* or social duty is the central conflict. The consequences of Saikaku's heroines' transgressions of social mores are severe; all but the last of the stories conclude tragically with the suicide, death, or execution of the protagonist. Although Saikaku's tales do not necessarily move the reader to pity or to feel sympathy for their heroines, they are a meditation on the moral consequences of actions and the tragedy that seems always to accompany any participation in the comedy of human errors. The stories do not impart

www   For links to more information about Saikaku and a quiz on "What the Seasons Brought the Almanac Maker," see *World Literature Online* at bedfordstmartins .com/worldlit.

OO-kee-yoh-ZOH-shee

p. 691

---

[8] *ukiyo-zoshi:* "Stories of the floating world" or "tales of the floating world"; a style of fiction associated with the period from about 1683 to 1783 whose subject matter was the everyday life of *chonin,* or townspeople, told in a colloquial voice.

moral lessons, but rather an experience of the fleeting world of temptation and desire, which Saikaku depicts with a fine hand.

"What the Seasons Brought to the Almanac Maker."   The third story of *Five Women Who Loved Love* is a fictionalized account of the 1683 execution of an adulteress and her lover. After an opening that invokes the sexually charged atmosphere of Kyoto in the spring, the story turns its focus to **Osan,** the wife of an almanac maker, and Moemon, a trusted young assistant of her father who is sent to help Osan while her husband is away on business. After Osan and Moemon fall in love, they run away together, and the story recounts their attempt to make a new life for themselves after faking a lovers' suicide. Eventually they are found out, put on trial, and executed.

While the plot is simple enough, the dramatic quality of the story, its vivid details, and the comic distance that Saikaku maintains from his protagonists are characteristics of accomplished fiction. If the story does not expose the most intimate thoughts and feelings of Osan and Moemon, it does present them convincingly as people giving in to their weaknesses and relying on their wits to extricate themselves from their errors. Saikaku draws his characters in "broad strokes," not unlike the way in which his contemporaries rendered figures in their *ukiyo-e* prints. The pacing of "What the Seasons Brought to the Almanac Maker" suits those swift strokes and captures the rapid pace and energetic acquisitiveness of city life in Saikaku's Japan.

■ CONNECTIONS

Lady Murasaki, *The Tale of Genji* (Book 2). Saikaku's *Five Women Who Loved Love,* from which the story of the almanac maker is taken, was modeled on *The Tale of Genji.* In the second chapter of Lady Murasaki's novel, Genji and some of his friends gather to discuss the traits of the ideal woman. Similarly, in the first part of "What the Seasons Brought to the Almanac Maker," four young men judge the beauty of women passing by. How is Saikaku's treatment of this subject similar to the scene in *The Tale of Genji*? How is it different? How is Saikaku's depiction of love different from Lady Murasaki's?

Molière, *Tartuffe*, p. 22. Saikaku's short story and Molière's play both involve adultery—in the potential amorous relation between the scoundrel Tartuffe and Elmire, Orgon's wife, and in the consummated love between Osan and Moemon. While sexual relationships between married men and courtesans were widely accepted in Japan during this era, women were not free to be unfaithful. What do these texts tell us about the place of married women in both seventeenth-century cultures?

James Joyce, *The Dead* (Book 6). Saikaku's stories are known for their detachment; the author wishes to present a slice of life without attempting to manipulate the reader's feelings or offering moral commentary. One of the hallmarks of European modernism is detachment; modernist authors avoided investing their fiction and poetry with their own emotion. *Dubliners,* from which the story "The Dead" is taken, is known for its objective treatment of Dublin's everyday life. Compare the way Saikaku and Joyce present their characters. Do these writers maintain an objective distance? Are they interested in different aspects of character development?

OH-sahn

Saikaku's zest for life is a fascination with the material world as it actually is — the world of concrete objects, the world of living people.

— IVAN MORRIS, translator, 1969

■ **FURTHER RESEARCH**

Hibbett, Howard. *The Floating World in Japanese Fiction.* 1959.

Keene, Donald. *World within Walls: Japanese Literature of the Pre-Modern Era, 1600–1867.*
1976.

Morris, Ivan, ed. and trans. Introduction to *The Life of an Amorous Woman and Other
Writings.* 1963.

■ **PRONUNCIATION**

chonin: CHOH-nin
haikai: HIGH-kigh
Hishikawa Moronobu: hi-shee-KAH-wah moh-roh-NOH-boo
Kyoto: KYOH-toh (kee-OH-toh)
Kyushichi: kyoo-SHI-chee
Osaka: OH-sah-kah (oh-SAH-kah)
Osan: OH-sahn
Ihara Saikaku: ee-HAH-rah sigh-KAH-koo
ukiyo-e: OO-kee-yoh EH
ukiyo-zoshi: OO-kee-yoh ZOH-shee
Zetaro: zeh-TAH-roh

ᦔ What the Seasons Brought to the Almanac Maker

Translated by William Theodore de Bary

1. The Beauty Contest

According to the calendar for the second year of Tenwa (1682), New Year's Day was to
be devoted to the practice of calligraphy.[1] Then, having started the year auspiciously,
men could start making love on January second. Since the Age of the Gods lovemaking has been taught men by the wagtail bird[2] and ever since those days it has
caused endless mischief between the sexes.

"What the Seasons Brought to the Almanac Maker." This is the third of five stories about
amorous women whose lives end tragically, which were collected in *Five Women Who Loved Love*
(*Koshoku Gonin Onna,* 1686). The story was later adapted by the playwright Chikamatsu for his
play *The Almanac Maker (Daikyoji Mukashibanashi)* in 1715. Based on an actual event that took
place in Kyoto in 1683, the story follows the flight of Osan, the wife of an almanac maker who lives
in Osaka, and Moemon, a trusted younger assistant of her father's. When the almanac maker is

---

[1] **calligraphy:** Practicing calligraphy and refraining from sexual activity on New Year's Day was a tradition
thought to bring good fortune for the upcoming year.

[2] **wagtail bird:** Literally means the "love-knowing bird"; according to the legend of *Nihonshoki* (783 c.e.), this
bird taught the ways of love to the gods Izanagi and Izanami, the parents of the Sun Goddess (Amaterasu-
Omikami). [Translator's note.]

In Kyoto lived a lady known as the Almanac-Maker's Beautiful Spouse, who stirred up a mountain of passion in the capital and figured again and again in notorious romances. Her moon-shaped eyebrows rivaled in beauty the crescent borne aloft during the Gion Festival parade;[3] her figure suggested the cherry buds, not yet blossoms, of Kiyomizu;[4] and her lovely lips looked like the topmost leaves of the maples at Takao in their full autumnal glory. She lived in Muro-machi-dori, the style center for women of discriminating taste in clothes, the most fashionable district in all Kyoto.

It was late spring; men felt gay and the wisteria hung like a cloud of purple over Yasui,[5] robbing the pines of their color. People thronged up Higashi-yama[6] and turned it into a living mountain of human figures. There was in the capital a band of four inseparable young men who were known for their handsome appearance and riotous living. Thanks to large inheritances, they could spend every day in the year seeking their own pleasure. One night, till dawn, they might amuse themselves in Shimabara[7] with Chinagirl, Fragrance, Florapoint, and Highbridge. Next day they might make love to Takenaka Kichisaburo, Karamatsu Kasen, Fujita Kichisaburo, and Mitsuse Sakon[8] in the Shijo-gawara section.[9] Night or day, girls or boys, it made no difference in their pleasure.

After the theatre one evening they were lounging around a teahouse called the Matsu-ya and one of them remarked: "I have never seen so many good-looking local girls as I did today. Do you suppose we could find others who would seem just as beautiful now?"

---

called away to Edo for business, Osan's father sends Moemon to help Osan run her household. Moemon and Osan fall in love, and they run away and go into hiding in the village of Tango. Eventually, they are found out, put on trial for adultery, and executed. The story moves at a compelling pace and gives a sense of dramatic immediacy. Although it does not present the most intimate thoughts and feelings of Osan and Moemon, it does convincingly present the adulterous wife and her lover as examples of people caught up in the accidents of the fleeting world, giving in to their weaknesses and relying upon their wits to extricate themselves from their errors. Moemon and Osan are examples of the way Saikaku draws his characters in "broad strokes," to use Ivan Morris's phrase, like the figures in the *ukiyo-e* prints of his contemporaries.

A note on the translation: This story is taken from William de Bary's translation of *Five Women Who Loved Love* (Tokyo: Charles E. Tuttle, 1956). All notes are the editors' unless otherwise indicated.

---

[3] **Gion Festival parade:** Takes place in the Sixth Moon (July); the float resembles a tower on wheels and is decorated to represent the new moon.

[4] **Kiyomizu:** A temple in Kyoto celebrated for its cherry blossoms.

[5] **Yasui:** A temple in the Eastern Hills (*Higashiyama*) renowned for its wisteria.

[6] **Higashi-yama:** A mountain to the southeast of Kyoto.

[7] **Shimabara:** The licensed district or pleasure quarters of Kyoto.

[8] **Takenaka . . . Sakon:** Kabuki actors famous for taking women's roles.

[9] **Shijo-gawara section:** Theater section of Kyoto.

They thought they might and decided to watch for pretty girls among the people who had gone to see the wisteria blossoms and were now returning to their homes. After a worldly actor in the group had been chosen as chief judge, a "beauty contest" was conducted until the twilight hours, providing a new source of amusement for the jaded gentlemen.

At first they were disappointed to see some maids riding in a carriage which hid them from sight. Then a group of girls strolled by in a rollicking mood—"not bad, not bad at all"—but none of the girls quite satisfied their exacting standards. Paper and ink had been brought to record the entries, and it was agreed that only the best should be put on their list.

Next they spied a lady of thirty-three or thirty-four with a long, graceful neck and intelligent-looking eyes, above which could be seen a natural hairline of rare beauty. Her nose, it was true, stood a little high, but that could be easily tolerated. Underneath she wore white satin; over that, light-blue satin; and outside, reddish-yellow satin. Each of these garments was luxuriously lined with the same material. On her left sleeve was a hand-painted likeness of the Yoshida monk,[10] along with this passage: "To sit alone under a lamp, and read old books . . ." Assuredly, this was a woman of exquisite taste.

Her sash was of folded taffeta bearing a tile design. Around her head she had draped a veil like that worn by court ladies; she wore stockings of pale silk and sandals with triple-braided straps. She walked noiselessly and gracefully, moving her hips with a natural rhythm.

"What a prize for some lucky fellow!" one of the young bucks exclaimed. But these words were hardly uttered when the lady, speaking to an attendant, opened her mouth and disclosed that one of her lower teeth was missing, to the complete disillusionment of her admirers.

A little behind her followed a maiden not more than fifteen or sixteen years old. On the girl's left was a woman who appeared to be her mother; on the right she was accompanied by a black-robed nun. There were also several servant women and a footman as escorts, all taking the greatest care of their charge. It seemed at first as if the girl were engaged to be married, but at second glance she proved to be married already, for her teeth were blackened and her eyebrows removed.[11] She was quite pretty, with her round face, intelligent eyes, ears delicately draped at the side of her head, and fingers, plump, thin-skinned, and white. She wore clothes with matchless elegance; underneath were purple-spotted fawns on a field of pure yellow; outside, the design of a hundred sparrows upon gray satin. Over her rainbow-colored sash she wore a breast-belt which enhanced the charm of her carriage. The tie-strings of her richly lined rainhat were made from a thousand braids of twisted

---

[10] **the Yoshida monk:** Yoshida no Kaneyoshi, known as Yoshida Kenko (1283–1352) was a court official and poet who became a Buddhist monk in 1324 and wrote *Essays in Idleness (Tsurezure-Gusa)*. [Translator's note.]

[11] **teeth . . . removed:** Married women traditionally blackened their teeth and shaved their eyebrows after the birth of their first child.

paper. They could easily see under the hat—a delight for the eyes, or so they thought until someone noticed a wide scar, three inches or more, on the side of her face. She could hardly have been born with such a deformity, and they all laughed when one of the playboys remarked: "She must really hate the nurse who is responsible for that!"

Then another girl, perhaps twenty or twenty-one, came along wearing a garment of cotton homespun, even the lining of which was so tattered and patched that the wind, blowing it out, exposed her poverty to all. The material for her sash came from an old coat and was pitifully thin. She wore socks of purple leather, apparently the only kind she could afford, and tough, rough Nara sandals. An old cloth headpiece was stuck on the top of her head. It was anybody's guess how long ago the teeth of a comb had run through her hair, which fell in sloppy disarray, relieved hardly at all by her haphazard attempts to tuck it up.

But while she made no pretensions to style or fashion, the girl, walking alone, seemed to be enjoying herself. As far as her facial features were concerned, she certainly left nothing to be desired; indeed, the men were captivated by the sight of her.

"Have you ever seen anyone with so much natural beauty?"

"If she had some fine clothes to wear, that girl would steal men's hearts away. Too bad that she should have to be born poor."

They pitied her deeply and one fellow, seeing that she was on her way home, followed hopefully to learn who she was. "She is the wife of a tobacco-cutter down at the end of Seiganji-dori," someone told him. It was disappointing—another straw of hope gone up in smoke!

Later a woman of twenty-six or twenty-seven passed that way. Her arms were covered by three layers of sleeves, all of black silk and lined in red. Her family crest was done in gold, but discreetly, on the inner lining, so as to be faintly visible through the sleeves. She had on a broad sash which tied in front and was made from dark-striped cloth woven in China. Her hair was rolled up in a bun, set further back on the head than was the case with unmarried ladies, and done up with a thick hairribbon and two combs. Covering it was a hand-painted scarf and a rainhat in the style of Kichiya,[12] also set jauntily back on her head so as not to hide the good looks in which she obviously took pride. Her figure twisted sinuously as she stepped lightly along.

"That's the one, that's the one!"

"Quiet down! Let's get a better look at her."

Sure enough, on closer inspection they found that the lady was accompanied by three servants, each carrying a baby.

"Must have had three kids in three years."

Behind her the babies kept calling out "Mama, mama," while the lady walked on, pretending not to hear them.

---

[12] **Kichiya:** Uemura Kichiya (fl. 1660–80), a Kyoto actor known for taking female roles; such actors often set the styles for lady's fashions. [Translator's note.]

"They may be her children, but she would just as soon not be seen with them. 'Charm fades with childbirth!' people say." Thus the men shouted and laughed and ridiculed her, until she almost died of chagrin.

Next, with a litter borne luxuriously beside her, came a twelve- or thirteen-year-old girl whose hair was combed out smooth, curled a bit at the ends, and tied down with a red ribbon. In front her hair was parted like a young boy's and held in place by five immaculate combs and a gold hair-ribbon. Her face was perfectly beautiful, and I shall not tire you with needless details. A black, ink-slab pattern adorned her white-satin chemise; a peacock design could be perceived in the iridescent satin of her outer garment. Over this hung lace made from Chinese thread and sleeves which were beautifully designed. A folded sash of twelve colors completed her ensemble. Her bare feet nestled in paper-strap clogs, and one of the litter-bearers carried a stylish rainhat for her.

The girl was holding a bunch of wisteria blossoms over her head, as if to attract the attention of someone who could not find her. Observed in this pose, she was clearly the most beautiful girl of all they had seen that day.

"What is the name of this fine lady?" they asked politely of an attendant.

"A girl from Muro-machi," was the reply. "She is called Modern Komachi."[13]

Yes, she had all the beauty of a flower. Only later did they learn how much devilry was hid beneath that beauty.

2. THE SLEEPER WHO SLIPPED UP

The life of a bachelor has its attractions, but nights get rather lonely for a man without a wife. So it seemed to a certain maker of almanacs[14] who had lived alone for many years. There were many elegant ladies in the capital, but his heart was set on finding a woman of exceptional beauty and distinction, and such a desire was not easily satisfied. Finally, in despair because of his solitary existence, he asked some relatives to find him a suitable mate, and it was arranged for him to meet the girl known as Modern Komachi, that delicate beauty holding wisteria blossoms over her head whom our playboys had seen during their beauty contest in the theatre section last spring.

The almanac maker was completely charmed with her. "She's the one," he told himself, and without more ado he rushed out, ludicrously enough, to arrange an immediate marriage. At the corner of Shimotachi-uri and Karasumaru[15] he found an old woman, a professional go-between who was widely known as a very fast talker. Thanks to her, the negotiations were conducted successfully. A keg of saké was

---

[13] **Komachi:**Refers to Ono no Komachi, a beautiful but cruel-hearted poet of ancient Japan. The allusion foreshadows the demise of Osan, the "Modern Komachi."

[14] **maker of almanacs:***Daikyoji*—originally an expert in the mounting of scrolls and religious paintings; a fairly respectable profession since the *daikyoji* also published the official almanac for the court and was paid by the shogun. [Translator's note.]

[15] **Shimotachi-uri and Karasumaru:**street names; Karasumaru led up to the Imperial Palace.

sent to confirm the contract and on the appointed day Osan was welcomed into her new home.

Deeply attached to his wife and absorbed in the intimacies of their life together, the almanac maker was blind to everything else—to the flower-fragrant nights of spring and to the rising of the autumn moon. Night and day for three years his wife diligently performed the many tasks which married life required of her, carefully spinning raw-silk thread by hand, supervising the weaving of cloth by her servant women, looking after her husband's personal appearance, burning as little fuel as possible for economy's sake, and keeping her expense accounts accurate and up-to-date. In fact, she was just the sort of woman any townsman would want in his home.

Their house was prospering and their companionship seemed to hold a store of endless bliss, when it became necessary for the almanac maker to travel to Edo for business reasons. The parting was sad, but there was nothing to be gained by grieving over it. When he was ready to leave, he paid a visit to Osan's father in Muromachi to tell him about the trip, and the old man was quite concerned about his daughter's welfare during the period of her husband's absence, when she would be left to manage all of his affairs. He wondered if there were not some capable person who could take over the master's business and also assist Osan in running the household. Deciding on a young man named Moemon, who had served him faithfully for many years, he sent the fellow to his son-in-law's place.

This Moemon was honest and extremely frugal, so much so that he completely neglected his personal appearance, even economizing on his coat sleeves, which measured only two and one-half inches at the wrist. His forehead was narrow, and when upon his reaching manhood his hair was allowed to grow, Moemon never bothered to buy a hat to cover it. Moreover, he went about without the protection of a short sword and slept with his abacus under his head, the better perhaps to reckon how great a fortune he could amass in a night spent dreaming of money-making.

It was fall, and a bitter storm one night set Moemon to thinking how he might fortify himself against the rigors of winter. He decided on a treatment of moxa[16] cauterizing. A maidservant named Rin, who was adept at administering the burning pills, was asked to do the job for him. She twisted several wads of the cottony herb and spread a striped bedcover over her dressing table for Moemon to lie on.

The first couple of applications were almost more than he could bear. The pain-wracked expression on his face gave great amusement to the governess, the housemistress, and all the lowly maids around him. When further doses had been applied, he could hardly wait for the final salting down which would finish the treatment. Then, accidentally, some of the burning fibers broke off and dropped down along his spine, causing his flesh to tighten and shrink a little. But out of consideration for the girl who attended him, Moemon closed his eyes, clenched his teeth, and mustered up all his patience to endure the pain.

---

[16] **moxa:** In Japanese, *mogusa*—the dried leaf of *artemisia moxa;* shaped into cones, the *moxa* was lit on fire and allowed to burn down; it was applied to the skin as a cauterizing agent and cure for many kinds of ailments. The poet Matsuo Bashō applies *moxa* to his legs in preparation for his journey to the far north (p. 657).

Rin, full of sympathy for him, extinguished the vagrant embers and began to massage his skin. How could she have known that this intimate contact with his body would arouse in her a passionate desire for Moemon, which at first she managed to conceal from others but eventually was to be whispered about and even reach her mistress's ears?

Unable to suppress her desire for Moemon, Rin hoped that somehow she might communicate with him, but as her education had only been of the most humble sort, she could not write anything, not even the crude-looking characters which Kyushichi, a fellow servant, used to scribble out as personal reminders. She asked Kyushichi if he would write a letter for her, but the knave only took advantage of her confidence by trying to make this love his own.

So, slowly, the days passed without relief, and fall came, with its long twilight of drizzling rains, the spawning season for intrigue and deception. One day, having just finished a letter to her husband in Edo, Osan playfully offered to write a love letter for Rin. With her brush she dashed off a few sweet lines of love, and then, addressing the wrapper "To Mr. Mo——, from someone who loves him," Osan gaily turned the note over to Rin.

Overjoyed, the girl kept looking for a suitable opportunity to deliver it, when all at once Moemon was heard calling from the shop for some fire with which to light his tobacco. Fortunately there was no one else in the courtyard at that time, so Rin seized the occasion to deliver her letter in person.

Considering the nature of the thing, Moemon failed to notice his mistress's handwriting and simply took Rin for a very forward girl, certainly an easy conquest. Roguishly he wrote out a reply and handed it to Rin, who was of course unable to read it and had to catch Osan in a good mood before she could learn its contents:

"In response to the unexpected note which your feelings toward me prompted you to write, I confess that, young as I am, your advances are not wholly distasteful to me. I must remind you that such trysts as you propose may produce complications involving a midwife, but if you are ready to meet all of the expenses incidental to the affair—clothes, coats, bath money, and personal toiletries—I shall be glad to oblige to the best of my ability."

"Such impudence!" Osan exclaimed when she finished reading the blunt message to Rin. "There is no dearth of men in this world, and Rin is hardly the worst-looking of all women. She can have a man like Moemon anytime she wants."

Thus aroused, Osan decided to write further importunate messages for Rin and make Moemon her loving slave. So she sent several heartbreaking appeals to him, moving Moemon to pity and then to passion. At last, to make up for his earlier impertinence, he wrote Rin an earnest note in reply. It contained a promise that on the night of May fourteenth, when it was customary to stay up and watch the full moon, he would definitely come to see her.

Mistress Osan laughed aloud when she saw this and told the assembled maids: "We shall turn his big night into a night of fun for all!"

Her plan was to take the place of Rin that night, disguise herself in cotton summer-clothes, and lie in Rin's bed. It was also arranged for the various women-servants to come running with sticks and staves and lanterns when Osan called out.

Thus all were ready and in their places when the time came, but before she knew it, Osan herself fell blissfully asleep, and the women-servants too, exhausted by all the excitement that evening, dozed off and started to snore.

Later, during the early-morning hours, Moemon stole through the darkness with his underclothes hanging half-loose around him. Impatiently he slipped naked between the bedcovers; his heart throbbed, but his lips were silent. And when his pleasure was had, Moemon sensed the faint, appealing fragrance which arose from the lady's garments. He lifted up the covers and started to tiptoe away.

"Indeed, she must know more of life than I suspected. I thought she was innocent, that she had loved no man before, that now—but someone has been here ahead of me," he concluded apprehensively. "I must pursue this no further."

When he had gone Osan awoke of her own accord. To her surprise the pillows were out of place and everything was in disorder. Her sash, missing from her waist, was nowhere at hand, her bed-tissues were a mess.

Overcome with shame at the realization of her undoing, Osan considered: "There is no way to keep this from others. From now on I may as well abandon myself to this affair, risk my life, ruin my reputation, and take Moemon as my companion on a journey to death."

She confided this resolution to Moemon, and though it was contrary to his previous decision, nevertheless, being halfway in and feeling the call to love, Moemon gave himself over to visiting her each night without a care for the reproofs of others, and spent himself in this new service as thoroughly as he had in his work. Thus, together the lovers played with life and death, the most dangerous game of all.

3. The Lake Which Took People In

It is written in *The Tale of Genji:*[17] "There is no logic to love."

When the image of Kannon[18] was put on display at the Ishiyama Temple the people of Kyoto left the cherry blossoms of Higashi-yama and flocked to see it. Travelers, on their way to and from the capital, stopped for a visit when they crossed Osaka Pass. Many among them were fashionably dressed ladies, not one of whom seemed to be making the pilgrimage with any thought of the hereafter. Each showed off her clothes and took such pride in her appearance that even Kannon must have been amused at the sight.

It happened that Osan and Moemon also made the pilgrimage together. They and the flowers they saw seemed to share a common fate: No one could tell when they might fall. Nor could anyone tell whether the lovers again might see this bay and the hills around Lake Biwa, so Moemon and Osan wanted to make it a day to remember. They rented a small boat in Seta and wished that their love would last as

---

[17] *The Tale of Genji:* One of the earliest and most celebrated works of fiction in Japanese and in world literature, written by Lady Murasaki (c. 978–1031).

[18] Kannon: Buddhist goddess of mercy; the ceremony, held on the Third Moon of 1676, took place at Ishiyama Temple, where Lady Murasaki is said to have begun writing *The Tale of Genji*.

long as the Long Bridge[19] of that town, though their pleasure might still be short lived. Floating along, the lovers made waves serve them as pillow and bed, and the disorder of Osan's hairdress testified to the nature of their delight. But there were moments, too, when the beclouded Mirror Mountain[20] seemed to reflect a more somber mood in Osan. Love for these two was as dangerous a passage as Crocodile Strait,[21] and their hearts sank when at Katada someone called the boat from shore; for a minute they feared that a courier had come after them from Kyoto.

Even though they survived this, it seemed as if their end might be told by the snows of Mt. Hiei,[22] for they were twenty years old and it is said that the snow on this Fuji-of-the-Capital always melts before twenty days have passed. So they wept and wet their sleeves and at the ancient capital of Shiga,[23] which is now just a memory of past glory, they felt sadder still, thinking of their own inevitable end. When the dragon lanterns were lit, they went to Shirahige Shrine and prayed to the gods, now even more aware of the precariousness of their fate.

"After all, we may find that longer life only brings greater grief," Osan told him. "Let us throw ourselves into the lake and consecrate our lives to Buddha in the Eternal Land."

But Moemon, though he valued his life hardly at all, was not so certain as to what would follow after death. "I think I have hit upon a way out," he said. "Let us each send letters to the capital, saying that we shall drown ourselves in the lake. We can then steal away from here, go anywhere you please, and pass the rest of our years together."

Osan was delighted. "When I left home, it was with that idea in mind. So I brought along five hundred pieces of gold in my suitcase."

That, indeed, was something with which to start life anew. "We must be careful how we do this," Moemon cautioned, as they set about writing notes to various people saying: "Driven by evil desires, we have joined in a sinful love which cannot escape Heaven's decree. Life has no place for us now; therefore today we depart forever from the Fleeting World."[24]

Osan then removed the small image of the Buddha which she had worn as a charm for bodily protection, and trimmed the edges of her black hair. Moemon took off the great sword, which he wore at his side, made by Seki Izumi-no-Kami,[25] with

---

[19] **Long Bridge:** *Seta no Nagahashi*—a famous double bridge, first built in the Nara period (781–784 C.E.). This passage marked with place names is called a *michiyuki,* wherein characters' thoughts and feelings are evoked in terms of the places they visit on a journey. The *michiyuki* is a common device in Japanese drama of the time; another example occurs at the end of Chikamatsu's *Love Suicides at Amijima* (pp. 691–718).

[20] **Mirror Mountain:** Mt. Kagami, a mountain that has many poetical associations.

[21] **Crocodile Strait:** Cape Wani; lies to the north of Katada.

[22] **Mt. Hiei:** Outside of Kyoto, where the monk Saicho (767–822 C.E.) founded a complex of Buddhist temples; once a great center of Tendai Buddhism.

[23] **Shiga:** The location of Emperor Tenchi's (661–672 C.E.) ruined palace on Lake Biwa.

[24] **Fleeting World:** The "floating world" *(Ukiyo),* denotes the transitory nature of material life as well as the transitory delights of the pleasure quarters.

[25] **Seki Izumi-no-Kami:** Member of one of the most famous families of swordmakers.

an iron guard embellished by twisting copper dragons. These things would be left behind so that people could identify them as belonging to Moemon and Osan. Then, as a final precaution, they even left their coats and sandals at the foot of a willow by the shore. And since there lived at the lakeside men with a long tradition as experts in fishing, who could leap from the rocks into the water, Moemon secretly hired two of them and explained his plan. They readily agreed to keep a rendezvous with the couple that evening.

When Moemon and Osan had prepared themselves properly, they opened the bamboo door of the inn and roused everyone by shouting: "For reasons known only to ourselves we are about to end our lives!" They then rushed away, and shortly, from the height of a craggy rock, faint voices were heard saying the Nembutsu,[26] followed by the sound of two bodies striking the water. Everyone wept and raised a great commotion over it.

But Moemon put Osan on his back and carried her around the foot of the mountain, deep into the forest to a desolate village, while the divers swam underwater and emerged on the beach undetected.

Meantime, all around beat their hands and lamented the tragedy. With help from people living along the shore they made a search, but found nothing. Then, as dawn broke, more tears fell upon the discovery of the lovers' personal effects. These were wrapped up quickly and sent back to Kyoto.

Out of concern for what people would think, the families involved privately agreed to keep the matter to themselves. But in a world full of busy ears the news was bound to leak out, and all spring long it gave people something to gossip about. There was indeed no end to the mischief these two souls created.

4. The Teahouse Which Had Not Heard of Gold Pieces

Hand in hand, Moemon and Osan trekked across the wilderness of Tamba.[27] They had to make their own road through the stubborn underbrush. At last they climbed a high peak and, looking back whence they had come, reflected on the terrors of their journey. It was, to be sure, the lot they had chosen; still, there was little pleasure in living on in the role of the dead. They were lost souls, miserably lost, on a route that was not even marked by a woodsman's footprints. Osan stumbled feebly along, so wretched that she seemed to be gasping for what might be her last breath, and her face lost all its color. Moemon tried every means to revive and sustain his beloved, even catching spring water in a leaf as it dripped from the rocks. But Osan had little

---

[26] **Nembutsu:** (*Nembutso no koe*) Very common short prayer—"Homage to Amida Buddha"—by which believers in Amida could expect to achieve salvation [translator's note]. Amida Buddha, or Buddha Amitabha, is the central figure of Pure Land Buddhism; he promised to bring salvation to all beings by granting them rebirth in the "Western Paradise."

[27] **wilderness of Tamba:** Tamba, a province north of Kyoto, was a place of exile for those who had lost their reputations or fortunes in the city.

strength left to draw on. Her pulse beat more and more faintly; any minute might be her last.

Moemon could offer nothing at all in the way of medicine. He stood by help-lessly to wait for Osan's end, then suddenly bent near and whispered in her ear: "Just a little further on we shall come to the village of some people I know. There we can forget all our misery, indulge our hearts' desire with pillows side by side, and talk again of love!"

When she heard this, Osan felt better right away. "How good that sounds! Oh, you are worth paying for with one's life!"

A pitiful woman indeed, whom lust alone could arouse, Osan was carried by Moemon pickaback into the fenced enclosure of a tiny village. Here was the highway to the capital, and a road running along the mountainside wide enough for two horses to pass each other. Here too was a teahouse thatched with straw and built up of cryptomeria branches woven together. A sign said "Finest Home-brew Here," but the rice paste was many days old and dust had deprived it of its whiteness. On a side counter were tea brushes, clay dolls, and dancing-drummer dolls—and reminiscent of Kyoto and therefore a tonic to the weary travelers, who rested there awhile.

Moemon and Osan enjoyed it so that, upon leaving, they offered the old innkeeper one piece of gold. But he scowled unappreciatively, like a cat that is shown an umbrella.[28]

"Please pay me for the tea," he demanded, and they were amused to think that less than fifteen miles from the capital there should be a village which had not yet heard of gold pieces.[29]

Thence the lovers went to a place called Kayabara, where lived an aunt of Moe-mon's whom he had not heard from for many years—who might be dead for all he knew. Calling on her, Moemon spoke of their family past, and she welcomed him as one of her own. The rest of the evening, with chin in hand and tears in her eyes, the old woman talked of nothing but his father Mosuke; but when day broke she became suddenly aware of Osan, whose beauty and refinement aroused her suspicions.

"What sort of person is she?" his aunt asked.

Moemon had not prepared himself for all the questions she might ask and found himself in an awkward spot. "My younger sister," he replied. "For many years she has served in the home of a court official, but it was a strict family and she dis-liked the fretful life of the capital. She thought there might be an opportunity to join a quiet, leisurely household—something like this—in the mountains. So she termi-nated her service and came along with me in hopes of finding housework and gar-dening to do in the village. Her expenses need be no concern; she has about two hundred gold pieces in savings."

---

[28] **a cat . . . umbrella:** Equivalent to "casting pearls before swine." [Translator's note.]

[29] **not . . . pieces:** Three kinds of currency circulated in Japan during this time: Gold, which was denominated, was used in Edo; silver, which had to be weighed in *momme* (a measure equivalent to 3.75 grams), in Kyoto and Osaka; copper coins, throughout all of Japan.

Thus he blithely concocted a story to satisfy the old woman. But it is a greedy world wherever one goes, and Moemon's aunt thought there might be something in this for her.

"Now," she exclaimed, "that is really most fortunate. My son has no wife yet and your sister is a relative, so why not have her marry him?"[30]

It was a distressing proposal. Osan sobbed quietly, cursing the fate which had led her to such a dismal prospect.

Then as evening fell the son came home. He was frightful to behold, taller than anyone she had ever seen, and his head sat like a Chinese-lion gargoyle on his squat neck. A fierce light gleamed in his big, bloodshot eyes. His beard was like a bear's, his arms and legs were as thick as pine trees, and a wisteria vine held together the rag-woven clothes he wore. In one hand he carried an old matchlock, in the other a tinder-rope. His hunting basket was full of rabbits and badgers, as much as to say: "This is how I make a living." He was called Zetaro the Rock-jumper.

In the village it was no secret that he was a mean man. But when his mother explained to him her proposal for a marriage with the lady from Kyoto, Zetaro was pleased.

"Good, let's waste no time. Tonight will do." And he reached for a hand mirror to look at his face. "Nice looking fellow," he said.

His mother prepared the wedding cup, offered them salted fish, and passed around a wine bottle which had had its neck broken off. She used floor mats as screens to enclose the room which would serve as the nuptial chamber. Two wooden pillows were also provided, two thin sleeping mats, and one striped bedcover. Split pine logs burned in the brazier. It would be a gay evening.

But Osan was as sad as could be, and Moemon was terribly depressed.

"This is the price I must pay for having spoken so impulsively. We are living on when we should have died in the waters of Omi. Heaven will not spare us now!" He drew his sword and would have killed himself had not Osan stopped and quieted him.

"Why, you are much too short-tempered. There are still ways to get out of this. At dawn we shall depart from here—leave everything to me."

That night while she was drinking the wedding cup with good grace and affability, Osan remarked to Zetaro: "Most people shun me. I was born in the year of the Fiery Horse."[31]

"I wouldn't care if you were a Fiery Cat or a Fiery Wolf. I even like blue lizards—eat 'em in fact. And you see I'm not dead yet. Twenty-seven years old, and I haven't had one case of worms. Mister Moemon should take after me! As for you—a soft creature brought up in the capital isn't what I'd like for a wife, but I'll tolerate you since you're my relative." In this generous mood he lay down and snuggled his head comfortably in her lap.

---

[30] so . . . him?: Marriage between cousins was thought to be a sign of good fortune.

[31] year . . . Horse: This year marked the coincidence of Fire, which the horse represents, with Fire in the old lunar calendar. Women born in this year were said to bully and frequently even kill their husbands. Zetaro's reply is a crude joke, for there is no year of the Fiery Wolf. [Translator's note.]

Amidst all their unhappiness Osan and Moemon found the brute somewhat amusing. Nevertheless, they could hardly wait until he went to bed, at last giving them a chance to slip away. Again they hid themselves in the depths of Tamba. Then after many days had passed they came out upon the road to Tango.

One night they slept in a chapel of the god Monju, who appeared to Osan in a dream midway through the night.

"You have committed the worst of sins. Wherever you go, you cannot escape its consequences. But that is all part of the unredeemable past; henceforth you must forsake your vain ways, shave off the hair you take such delight in, and become a nun. Once separated, the two of you can abandon your evil passion and enter upon the Way of Enlightenment. Then perhaps your lives may be saved!"

It was a worthy vision, but Osan heard herself answering: "Please don't worry about what becomes of us. We are more than glad to pay with our lives for this illicit affair. Monju may understand the love of men for men, but he knows nothing about the love of women."[32]

That instant she awoke from her dream, just as the morning breeze blew in through Hashidate's seaside pines,[33] bearing with it the dust of the world.

"Everything is dust and defilement," Osan told herself, and all hope was lost of ever saving her.

5. The Eavesdropper Whose Ears Were Burned

Men take their misfortunes to heart and keep them there. A gambler does not talk about his losses; the frequenter of brothels, who finds his favorite engaged by another, pretends to be just as well off without her; the professional street-brawler is quiet about the fights he has lost; and a merchant who speculates in goods will conceal the losses he may suffer. They are all like the "man who steps on dog dung in the dark."

But of them all the one who has a wanton, mischievous wife will feel his misfortune most, convinced that there is no more heartless creature in the world than she. To the outer world Osan's husband treated her as a closed issue: She was dead, and nothing could be said or done about her. There were times when he was reminded of their years together and would feel the greatest bitterness toward Osan, yet he would still call in a priest to hold services in her memory. Ironically enough, he offered one of her choice silk garments as an altarcloth for the local temple, where, fluttering in the fickle wind of Life and Death, it became a further source of lamentation.

Even so, there is no one bolder than a man deeply attached to the things of this world, and Moemon, who before was so prudent that he never went outdoors at night, soon lost himself in a nostalgic desire to see the capital again. Dressing in the most humble attire and pulling his hat down over his eyes, he left Osan in the care of

---

[32] **Monju . . . women:** According to a vulgar belief, Manjusri (*Monju* in Japanese) was the lover of Sakyamuni Buddha. He was therefore taken as the patron god of homosexuals. [Translator's note.]

[33] **Hashidate's . . . pines:** (*Ama-no-Hashidate*) One of the most beautiful places in Japan, Hashidate is a sandbar projecting into the Bay of Miyazu on the Japan Sea; the wind-twisted pines on the island are renowned for their unusual formations.

some villagers and made a senseless trip to Kyoto, all the while fearing more for his own safety than would a man who is about to deliver himself into the hands of an enemy.

It began to get dark when he reached the neighborhood of Hirozawa,[34] and the sight of the moon, reflected as two in the pond, made him think again of Osan, so that his sleeve became soaked with idle tears. Presently he put behind him the rapids of Narutaki, with myriad bubbles dancing over the rocks, and hurried on toward Omuro and Kitano, for he knew that way well. When he entered the city his fears were multiplied. "What's that!" he would ask himself, when he saw his own silhouette under the waning moon, and his heart would freeze with terror.

In the quarter with which he was so familiar, because his former master lived there, he took up eavesdropping to learn the state of things. He heard about the inquiry which was to be made into the overdue payment from Edo, and about the latest styles in hairdress, as discussed by a gathering of young men, who were also commenting on the style and fit of each others' clothes—the sort of silly chatter that love and lust inspire in men. When these topics of conversation were exhausted, sure enough they fell to talking about Moemon.

"That rascal Moemon, stealing a woman more beautiful than all the others! Even though he paid with his worthless life for it, he certainly got the best of the bargain—a memory worth dying with!"

But a man of more discernment upheld morality against Moemon. "He's nobody to raise up in public. He'd stink in the breeze. I can't imagine anyone worse than a man who'd cheat both his master and a husband at once."

Overhearing this, Moemon swore to himself: "That's the voice of the scoundrel Kisuke, of the Daimonji-ya. What a heartless, faithless fellow to be so outspoken against me. Why, I lent him eighty *momme* of silver on an IOU! But I'll get even for what he just said: I'll get that money back if I have to wring his neck."

Moemon gnashed his teeth and stood up in a rage. Still, there was nothing a man hiding from the world could do about the insults offered him, and while he suppressed his outraged feelings another man started to speak.

"Moemon's not dead. He's living with Mistress Osan somewhere around Ise, they say, having a wonderful time."

This shook Moemon and sent chills through his body. He left in all haste, took a room in a lodging-house along Third Avenue, and went to bed without even taking a bath. Since it was the night of the seventeenth,[35] he wrapped up twelve *mon* in a piece of paper and handed it to a beggar who would buy some candles and keep the vigil for him that night. Then he prayed that people would not discover who he was. But could he expect that even Atago-sama, the patron of lovers, would help him in his wickedness?

---

[34] **Hirozawa:** The pond in the Hirozawa district to the west of Kyoto was known for its double-reflection of the moon.

[35] **night of the seventeenth:** It was customary to spend the evenings of the 17th, 23rd, and 27th in prayer while waiting for moonrise. Often people would hire a proxy to keep the vigil for them. [Translator's note.]

In the morning, as a last memory of the capital before leaving it, he stole down Higashi-yama to the theatre section at Shijo-gawara. Someone told him that it was the opening day of a three-act Kabuki drama featuring Fujita.[36]

"I must see what it is like and tell Osan when I return."

He rented a cushion and sat far back to watch from a distance, uneasy at heart lest someone recognize him. The play was about a man whose daughter was stolen away. It made Moemon's conscience hurt. Then he looked down to the front rows. There was Osan's husband. At the sight Moemon's spirit almost left him. He felt like a man with one foot dangling over hell, and the sweat stood like pearls on his forehead. Out he rushed through an exit to return to the village of Tango, which he did not think of leaving again for Kyoto.

At that time, when the Chrysanthemum Festival[37] was almost at hand, a chestnut peddler made his annual trip to the capital. While speaking of one thing and another at the house of the almanac maker, he asked where the mistress was, but as this was an awkward subject in the household none of the servants ventured to answer.

Frowning, Osan's husband told him: "She's dead."

"That's strange," the peddler went on. "I've seen someone who looks very much like her, in fact, someone who doesn't differ from her one particle. And with her is the living image of your young man. They are near Kirito in Tango."

When the peddler had departed, Osan's husband sent someone to check up on what he had heard. Learning that Osan and Moemon were indeed alive, he gathered together a good number of his own people, who went and arrested them.

There was no room for mercy in view of their crime. When the judicial inquiry was duly concluded, the lovers, together with a maidservant named Tama[38] who had been their go-between earlier, were paraded as an example before the crowds along the way to Awada-guchi, where they died like dewdrops falling from a blade of grass.

Thus they met their end on the morning of September twenty-second, with, it should be remarked, a touching acquiescence in their fate. Their story spread everywhere, and today the name of Osan still brings to mind her beautiful figure, clothed in the pale-blue slip which she wore to her execution.

---

[36] Fujita: Fuijita Koheiji (d. 1698), a famous Kabuki actor of the time.

[37] Chrysanthemum Festival: One of the nine major festivals of the Japanese year, celebrated on the ninth day of the Ninth Month (September).

[38] Tama: The intermediary who passed notes between the actual couple upon whom this story is based; Rin is the name of the fictional maid from earlier in the story who should be named here. As an accessory to adultery, the intermediary could be subject to capital punishment. It's not clear why Saikaku gives the wrong name.

✒ MATSUO BASHŌ
1644–1694

Bashō

This portrait on a scroll depicts an elderly Bashō, weathered from his years of traveling. [Itsuo Museum, Osaka]

In the last months of his life, Matsuo Bashō handed a poem to one of his numerous students:

> Do not copy me—
> do not be like a cantaloupe
> cut into halves.

This advice was not easy to follow. Although Bashō did not invent the short poetic form known today as haiku, he mastered the form by broadening its emotional and thematic possibilities; in effect, Bashō's became the standard by which all later haiku were measured. And to serious admirers, Bashō is much more than an expert poet; long after his death, he is regarded as a sage or a religious teacher.

Published eight years after his death, Bashō's most famous work, *The Narrow Road through the Backcountry (Oku no Hosomichu)* could be classified as travel literature, but it recounts journeys that are totally different from those of Candide, Lemuel Gulliver, and Benjamin Franklin. Bashō's journeys are best characterized as pilgrimages to natural and artificial shrines, where he experiences the connections or relationships among places, their histories, previous visitors, friends, and himself. Bashō uses brief poems and carefully written prose to capture intimate moments of coalescence, when his life and the place being visited come together. These passages are like a series of photographs in which the camera points both outward and inward, bringing the two dimensions together—the poet in the place.

This kind of experience was not standard material for the European **ENLIGHTENMENT** writers included in this anthology, although writers concerned with these types of experiences existed in the West and used different poetic forms, especially during the **ROMANTIC** period[1] of the nineteenth century. Whereas Voltaire, Swift, and Franklin were public figures who broadcasted their ideas and writings to effect social and political change, Bashō led a simple, almost monastic life. Often withdrawn from society and available only to a few disciples and other poets, he earned the title "saint of haiku."

In *The Narrow Road through the Backcountry,* Bashō shows his mastery of two literary traditions, the poetic diary and **HAIKAI.** Dating from the eighth or ninth century in Japan was a tradition of using the diary or journal not only for recording events but also as an artistic form, shaped by an aesthetic purpose, and regularly containing poetry as well as prose. *The Diary of Murasaki Shikibu* (eleventh century), *The Diary of Izumi Shikibu* (eleventh century), and *The Diary of Masahiro* (fifteenth cen-

---

[1]**Romantic period:** The term *Romanticism* is used to characterize the first half of the nineteenth century in Europe when some writers and intellectuals revolted against the rationalism of the Enlightenment, favoring imagination and emotion instead. (See p. 17.)

tury) are examples of poetic diaries that artfully combined prose with poetry. Early diarists wrote poems in the *waka* or *tanka* form: five-line poems with thirty-one syllables distributed in a 5-7-5-7-7 pattern. The master of this form was Saigyo (twelfth century) who wrote *waka* about the deep connection between humans and nature.

Haikai.   Diarists gradually came to use the haikai or "linked verse" form that dates from the sixteenth century in Japan. The tradition of haikai involves alternating short three-line poems with two-line poems to form an extended sequence in a series of thirty-six or one hundred stanzas, usually written by two or more poets. The crucial opening verse, the *hokku* (5-7-5 syllables), was often composed so that it could also stand alone—the origin of what today is called haiku.

Imagine three poets sitting cross-legged together, eating and drinking. With the inspiration of several cups of saké, they decide to write a haikai. In the following example, the poet Boncho, a contemporary of Bashō, begins with a three-line hokku:

> in town
> the smells of things
> summer moon

Bashō responds:

> it's hot it's hot
> at each portal the sigh

Kyorai responds:

> not twice weeded
> and already the rice
> is earing
> — Translated by Maeda Cana

Thirty-three stanzas later, the haikai anthology was completed and was called *Summer Moon*. The skill of each poet is shown in the way in which his stanza responds or is linked to the previous stanza. The stanzas are related not by a common plot or theme but by word play, innuendo, emotion, atmosphere, and contrast.

Haikai had its source in a similar poetic form called *renga* that was developed in the thirteenth century and was characterized by seriousness and elegance, with one hundred or more stanzas. *Haikai*—with *hai* meaning "play" and *kai* meaning "friendly exchange of words"—was a liberated renga featuring popular, even vulgar, topics, and often containing fewer than one hundred stanzas. Under Bashō's influence, haikai found a middle ground between elegance and vulgarity.

Choosing a Life of Poetry.   Matsuo **Bashō** was born in 1644 in the town of **Ueno**, southeast of Kyoto. The son of a minor samurai serving the ruling Todo family, Matsuo Munefusa, later known as Bashō, seemed destined to follow his father's footsteps. When he was nine, Bashō became an attendant to the Todo family, serving primarily as a companion to Yoshitada, the eleven-year-old heir. For nearly thirteen years, Bashō and

www   For links to more information about Bashō and a quiz on *The Narrow Road through the Backcountry*, see *World Literature Online* at bedfordstmartins .com/worldlit.

RENG-gah

BAH-shoh
oo-EH-noh

Yoshitada were constant companions and friends, and as part of their training they studied linked verse under a local master. When Yoshitada died in 1666, Bashō, now twenty-three years old, broke away from his duties to the Todo family and went to Kyoto where he continued his studies of poetry, calligraphy, and the classics. When Bashō returned to his hometown of Ueno in 1671, he published an anthology of poetry entitled *The Seashell Game (Kai Oi)*. The next year he moved to Edo (Tokyo), a young, thriving city. Changing his pen name from Sobo to Tosei, Bashō became associated with Soin (1605–1682), a master poet, who taught him the importance of writing about ordinary life.

Bashō's work began to appear in numerous anthologies, and disciples gathered around him. In 1680 they built him a house and presented him with a young Japanese banana tree, a *bashō*, which provided a name for his house and eventually a new pen name. According to tradition, Bashō gained widespread recognition with this haiku written shortly after settling in his new home:

> *kare eda ni*
> *karasu no tomarikeri*
> *aki no kure*

> On a withered branch
> a crow has settled —
>   autumn nightfall.
> — Translated by Harold G. Henderson

Before Bashō, haiku were stiff and formalized, encumbered with rules. Bashō opened up new possibilities for the form, using simple images and making clear associations between the concrete and the abstract. The easy movement from object to season — from branch to autumn in the poem above — is a good example of his facility in making such connections. Bashō advised his followers: "Do not seek to follow in the footsteps of the men of old; seek what they sought."

With the priest Buccho, Bashō studied Zen Buddhism,[2] which has its roots in DAOISM as well as traditional BUDDHISM, and his perception of the world began to change. Nobuyuki Yuasa translates Bashō's description of his new awareness: "What is important is to keep our mind high in the world of true understanding, and returning to the world of our daily experience to seek therein the truth of beauty. No matter what we may be doing at a given moment, we must not forget that it has a bearing upon our everlasting self which is poetry."

The Famous Frog Haiku.   In 1684, Bashō went on his first major journey, to a region southwest of Edo; his account of it, which included prose and poetry, was published as *The Record of a Weather-Exposed Skeleton*. The combining of poetry and prose in travel diaries during the Tokugawa period (1603–1867) was called *haibun*, meaning haikai prose or haikai lit-

---

[2] **Zen Buddhism:** Originating in sixth-century China, its goals are self-realization and enlightenment. The ultimate goal is an indefinable moment of consciousness in which the contradictions caused by one's intellect are transcended in an experience of cosmic unity — a moment of enlightenment.

erature. After his return to Edo, his poems continued to be published in anthologies; his most famous poem appeared in the collection *Frog Contest (Kawazu Awase)* in 1686.

> *Furu ike ya*
> *Kawazu tobikomu*
> *Mizu no oto*

> The ancient pond
> A frog jumps in—
> Sound of water.

Although a technical definition of haiku stipulates a three-line stanza with alternating 5, 7, 5 syllables in the lines, it is not always possible to translate Japanese into English and retain the syllable count. Donald Keene's translation, above, has fewer syllables than the Japanese original, but Nobuyuki Yuasa's version, below, contains several more:

> Breaking the silence
> Of an ancient pond,
> A frog jumped into water—
> A deep resonance.

The Yuasa translation is more explanatory, making accommodations for a Western reader who is perhaps unfamiliar with the lean flashes of reality in haiku. The Japanese original is, however, a model haiku; the first line sets the scene in nature, and the last two lines suggest an instant insight or new perspective. On a first reading, the poet seems to be describing an objective scene with a simple literal meaning: One can imagine sitting by a pond in absolute quiet and then hearing the sound of a frog plopping into the water and perhaps seeing the ripples resonate outward in broad, ever-widening circles. But without stretching the situation at all, one can also easily make the connection between the pond and the poet's consciousness, and a moment when the sound of water resonates within the psyche, bringing a rich focus to the poet's attention, connecting the internal with the external. No philosophy, no psychology, just a brief look at a moment of connection.

On the Road Again.   Bashō's second major journey, in 1688, which followed the same route as his first, resulted in two works, *The Records of a Travel-Worn Satchel* and *A Visit to Sarashina Village*. Through experience, Bashō was learning how to balance prose with poetry; his message was becoming clearer, as witnessed by a passage in *The Records of a Travel-Worn Satchel:* "All who have achieved real excellence in any art, possess one thing in common, that is, a mind to obey nature, to be one with nature, throughout the four seasons of the year. Whatever such a mind sees is a flower, and whatever such a mind dreams of is the moon."

In *The Narrow Road through the Backcountry,* Bashō records his third major journey, which was begun in the spring of 1689 and lasted more than two years. Before leaving Edo at the age of forty-five, he sold his house, suggesting that he did not expect to return. More than the previous two journeys, this one was a culminating pilgrimage and reflects his mature vision of the meaning of life. Back once again in Edo, he spent

> His followers could find in him almost anything they sought—a town dandy, a youthful dreamer, a Buddhist recluse, a lonely wanderer, a nihilistic misanthrope, a happy humorist, an enlightened sage.
>
> – MAKOTO UEDA, literary historian and scholar, 1970

four years writing and revising the work, which was first published, posthumously, in 1702. In the spring of 1694, at the age of fifty, Bashō began his final journey to the south of Japan. En route, he became sick and died.

The Narrow Road through the Backcountry. In a mixture of biography and fiction, prose and poetry, Bashō describes visits to temples, historical shrines, poet friends, and intensely beautiful vistas. He passes through gates, climbs mountains, and looks at the moon. He is on a religious pilgrimage that is best described in Zen Buddhist terms. He is not looking for Christian salvation but for moments of consciousness in which he closely identifies with the scene at hand in what might be called "mystical identification" with the outside world, the flow of reality.

At the outset of the pilgrimage, Bashō is nervous, filled with anxiety. Careful preparations have to be made. Travel was difficult at that time, even dangerous, and his destination was a relatively unexplored portion of Japan—a fine symbol of the areas of consciousness that he expects to open up and engage. Each passage through a barrier gate represents another stage in Bashō's quest. The experience of the first, the Shirakawa

Bashō's Journeys, 1684–1689

Matsuo Bashō covered much of north-central Japan in his travels, which he documented in his famous haikai. This map covers his Journey to the Backcountry, 1689.

Barrier, is captured by Bashō's travel companion, Sora, who describes the change of clothes that was part of the rite of passage through the gate.

Many of the famous shrines on Bashō's itinerary, like the Islands of Matsushima, have been celebrated in other literary works, but it is characteristic of Bashō that, even at such sacred sites he often makes a direct connection with ordinary reality using ordinary, everyday objects and subjects.

> Autumn is cool now—
> Let us peel a feast with both hands,
>   Melon and eggplant.
> — TRANSLATED BY EARL MINER

In Bashō's work, a simple or seemingly insignificant thing often becomes the lightning rod for a Zen experience. At the Tada Shrine, a samurai's helmet evokes several meanings of loss associated with past dynasties and wars. But the ultimate and final loss—death itself—is evoked by the chirp of a cricket under the helmet, suggesting the living person who once wore the helmet but now is dead.

> "what a tragedy!"
> under the captain's helmet now
> . . . a cricket . . .

Making an Emotional Connection.   If Bashō can capture a moment of connection in a brief poem, then it is possible that his reader may have a similar experience reading the poem. The poem does not appeal to the intellect; it does not explain in logical terms how the world is connected. Rather the poem speaks to the intuition or the imagination, which can immediately grasp the association.

Bashō is particularly famous for invoking a quality called *sabi* to link the lines and images of verses; *sabi* is an atmosphere of sadness and loneliness from the past that colors the present, as in the following poem:

> I heard the unblown flute
> In the deep summer shadows
>   Of the Temple of Suma.
> — TRANSLATED BY R. H. BLYTH

Pilgrimages were often not simply a matter of visiting a shrine, but visiting it at the right time of year or during a full moon. Toward the end of his journey, Bashō passes through the Uguisu Barrier, crosses a mountain pass, and arrives at an inn whose host advises him to take advantage of the moonlight at the Myōjin shrine at Kei. Bashō prepares the reader for the shrine in prose: "There seemed a certain unearthly air about the place in the night silence, with moonlight through the pines turning the white sand before the stone shrine to frost." In the past, an abbot had started a tradition of carrying sand into the shrine area for the comfort of worshipers; Bashō's haiku makes this connection.

> Sand carrying pilgrims
> on the way to the sand shrine
>   moon illumined

Bashō is said to have had more than two thousand students at the time of his death. If this number is debatable, there is no question about his position: Few Japanese poets have enjoyed so high and so lasting a reputation.

— MAKOTO UEDA

The light of the moon reflecting on the sand is analogous to the poet's imagination or consciousness fully participating in the sacredness of that shrine, a kind of climax for Bashō's journey.

Bashō has had a continuing influence in Japan. Early in the twentieth century, when Japanese writers admired Western Romantics such as Wordsworth, Goethe, and Hoffmann,[3] they considered Bashō a Japanese Romantic. When French symbolist poets such as Baudelaire, Mallarmé, and Verlaine[4] became the vogue in Japan, Bashō was made a symbolist as well, with his deep appreciation for the connection of all things. Bashō and haiku were largely discovered at the turn of the century by Westerners. The exquisitely lean poem appealed particularly to British and American imagist poets such as Ezra Pound, Amy Lowell, and William Carlos Williams.[5] Today haiku is well known throughout the United States and Europe.

■ CONNECTIONS

Voltaire, *Candide*, p. 275. In the eighteenth century, travel literature was a popular medium for expressing the development or transformation of social values. Candide's travels in foreign lands reflect on aspects of French culture that Voltaire wishes to attack. How is the purpose of Candide's journey different from Bashō's? Whose travels are undertaken for personal growth and the expansion of consciousness?

Wordsworth (Book 5). Some poems are expressions of spirituality or religious meaning. In Wordsworth's poems natural settings are often the occasion for moments of transcendence. How might Bashō's visits to natural shrines famous for their luminescence be considered religious or spiritual?

Ramprasad Sen, p. 612. Religious poetry may contain objects of veneration like a deity or descriptions of a religious experience, such as ecstatic vision. Ramprasad's struggles with the goddess Kali, who cheats or challenges him, represent a religious experience for him. The struggle for Bashō is the rigor of travel itself, as he makes his way to a shrine or vista. How do Bashō's difficult journeys contribute to his experience once he arrives at his destination?

■ FURTHER RESEARCH

Biography
Yamamoto, Kenkichi. *Bashō*. 1957.
Makoto Ueda, *Matsuo Bashō*. 1970.

Historical Background
Blyth, R. H. *Zen in English Literature and Oriental Classics*. 1960.
Henderson, Harold G. *An Introduction to Haiku*. 1958.

---

[3] **Wordsworth, Goethe, and Hoffmann:** William Wordsworth (1770–1850) was an English Romantic poet who wrote intimately about nature. Goethe (1749–1832), one of the greatest of all German literary figures, wrote *Faust*, a poetic drama, and several novels, including *The Sorrows of Young Werther* (1774). E. T. A. Hoffmann (1776–1822) was a German writer and composer who described the fantastic depths of nature.

[4] **Baudelaire, Mallarmé, and Verlaine:** Charles Baudelaire (1821–1867), Stéphane Mallarmé (1842–1898), and Paul Verlaine (1844–1896) were French poets who sought exotic or eccentric moments in their poetry.

[5] **Ezra Pound, Amy Lowell, and William Carlos Williams:** Pound (1885–1972), Lowell (1874–1925), and Williams (1883–1963) were American poets who, in addition to writing longer poems, composed short, compact poems that are like photographic moments.

Kato, Shuichi. *A History of Japanese Literature.* 1997.

Keene, Donald. *Anthology of Japanese Literature.* 1955.

Miner, Earl. *Japanese Linked Poetry: An Account with Translations of Renga and Haikai Sequences.* 1979.

Suzuki, D. T. *Zen and Japanese Culture.* 1970. See especially Chapter VII, "Zen and Haiku."

Criticism

Cana, Maeda. *Monkey's Raincoat.* 1973.

Miner, Earl. *Japanese Poetic Diaries.* 1969.

Yuasa, Nobuyuki. *The Narrow Road to the Deep North and Other Travel Sketches.* 1966.

■ PRONUNCIATION

Bashō: BAH-shoh

Genroku: gen-ROH-koo

Hiraizumi: hee-righ-ZOO-mee

Iizuka: ee-ee-ZOO-kah

Muro-No-Yashima: MOO-roh noh YAH-shi-mah

Myozenji: myoh-ZEN-jee

renga: RENG-gah

Ryushakuji: ryoo-shah-KOO-jee

Saigyo: SIGH-gyoh

Tsukinowa: tski-NOH-wah (tsoo-ki-NOH-wah)

Tsutsujigaoka: tsoots-jee-gah-OH-kah (tsoo-tsoo-jee-gah-OH-kah)

Ueno: oo-EH-noh

Yanaka: yah-NAH-kah

Yoichi: yoh-EE-chee

The Narrow Road through the Backcountry

Translated by Richard Bodner

[SETTING OUT]

Sun and moon[1] are forever travelers, restless pilgrims of the days and months across endless generations. Years, too, come and go through the seasons. Life itself is a journey. And as with those who float life away on ships and those who grow bent with age before horses carrying freight from place to place, one's only final home is the open way itself, just traveling on. Some famous wayfarers even passed away on the road. At some point, who knows when, drifting clouds drew forth my own urge to wander. After roaming near seashores last fall, I'd just returned to my riverside cottage in time to sweep the old cobwebs away for the new year, when spring mists rising from ricefields woke my old longing to pass beyond the barrier-gate at Shira-

---

[1] **Sun and moon:** An old expression for "days and months," found in poems by Li Bai (Li Po) and others.

kawa into the far backcountry, and my mind would turn to nothing but beckoning trails. As if the god of wanderers possessed my soul, I mended my trousers, tied a new cord to my hat, burned *moxa*[2] to strengthen my legs, and dreamed of the full moon over Matsushima, the Pine Islands. Finally, I gave up my cottage for good, planning to stay at Sampu's guesthouse until setting out.

> my kusa grass hut
> with new dwellers may become
> . . . a house for dolls?[3]

—the opener of an eight-verse "first page" of linked poetry[4] left on a post on my way out.

Under the Seedling Sprout Moon,[5] then a pale thin thread still waning, we set out in the misty faint light of dawn, with distant Fuji summit and the blooming cherry trees of Ueno and Yanaka barely visible. Would I ever see these again, I wondered? Friends who'd gathered the night before boarded the boat to come along as far as Senju Landing. Here the great distances ahead swelled up in my heart. Such a dream of shifting images this world is, yet how attached we get, I thought, moist-eyed at leaving.

The Narrow Road through the Backcountry. In this work of poetry and prose, Bashō writes of his pilgrimages to several of Japan's spiritual sites, places where nature, history, the self, and the sacred come together. The English language sometimes seems inadequate to describe this phenomenon; the closest we can come is to call it "mystical identification" or "mystical union." The shrines that Bashō visits are typically places of extraordinary beauty or important historical significance; they are places visited by many poets and immortalized in poems. The shrines are therefore layered with meaning in somewhat the same way that Lourdes, France, the site of a Marian vision, is meaningful for Roman Catholics. With Lourdes, however, the reference is to a transcendent reality—Mary or God. But the radiance of Bashō's shrines is immanent rather than transcendent—the feeling is of something deep inside oneself rather than of something external to the self, something in the physical or spiritual world.

A note on the translation: The text reprinted here is taken from Richard Bodner's 2002 translation of Bashō's *Narrow Road through the Backcountry.* Bodner's notes have been adapted and abridged for this anthology.

---

[2] *moxa:* Still in use, *moxa* is an herbal powder shaped into little cones or nodules set on key "energy points," then lit and allowed to burn down for effects considered analogous to those from acupuncture.

[3] **house for dolls:** Bashō turned his "banana-tree hut" (*basho-an*) over to someone with daughters and grandchildren so it might well turn into "a world of dolls," especially since it was near Doll's Festival, where little girls all over the country bring their dolls out for a party. Sometimes called "Girl's" or "Peach" Festival, it falls on the third day of the third moon—then corresponding to late April, now observed March 3.

[4] **linked poetry:** Bashō is considered a great master in the art of *renga* (linked poetry), which itself includes various poetic forms—two of which (one with a hundred stanzas and one with fifty) have a first page (or front fold) of eight links. No such linked poem from Bashō's departure, or with this *hokku* (opening verse), is known.

[5] **Seedling Sprout Moon:** The year's third month in the lunar calendar Bashō used. According to the Gregorian calendar, Bashō left on May 16 (later than first planned because of bad weather). The year was 1689.

> departing spring
> birds cry — even fish eyes
> cloud with tears

— the brushed ink's first words, opening my record of the journey while lingering on the path a moment getting nowhere. Then friends watched until beyond sight, only shadows.

This year, namely "second of Genroku" (1689), I got the bug to go wandering to the far north and through the deep interior, *"under the snowy skies of another country,"* imagining frost settling in my hair and having to endure many hardships for eyes to behold places ears had heard of, and only with good luck, perhaps, returning alive. Weighed down with such thoughts, I reached the Soka post, bent under my pack like heavy-headed *kusa* grass.[6] I'd set out to travel light, with only what a body might easily carry for itself, then added a cloak for night cold, cotton kimono, rain-wear, things like brush-&-ink, plus going away gifts hard to turn down or leave behind — a traveler's burdens.

At the "Burning Birth-Room Shrine" of Muro-No-Yashima, my companion Sora said, "The deity here is the same 'Blossoming Princess' as at Fuji. This place was named after her closed birthing chamber supposedly burst into flames, and the Lord Prince Hohodemi (From Flames Come) was born out of that blaze, proof of his purely divine conception. So poetry about it usually includes smoke." Also, it's forbidden to eat *konoshiro* fish here, which smells like flesh when burned. This and other such tales are well known.[7]

On the third moon's last night, we stopped at Mt. Nikko's foot. Our inn-keeper said, "I'm called Buddha Gozaemon[8] for my honesty, so make yourself completely at ease." Had a Buddha appeared in just such a humble form to aid travelers like us through this world of dust and ashes? Observed carefully, our host did seem utterly without cleverness, just "straightforward, simpleminded, and down-to-earth," embodying old ideals with an integrity worthy of respect.

On the first day of the fourth moon, we paid our respects to Sunlit Mountain. Long ago, this mountain was called *Ni-ko*, "Twice wild." When Master Kukai started a temple here, he renamed it *Nik-ko*, slightly shifting the characters to signify "sun" and "brilliant light," as if seeing with the foresight of a thousand years to the enlightenment brightening our own horizons now — with blessings in all directions and all

---

[6] **heavy-headed *kusa* grass:** Related to the placename Soka.

[7] Bashō introduces folklore of high and low types: from a traditional story of local Shinto mythology (in which a pregnant goddess's questioned virtue is proven pure when she gives birth in the midst of divine fire) to an associated tidbit about a kind of fish said to smell like a burning corpse when cooked.

[8] **Buddha Gozaemon:** The innkeeper's nickname includes characters associated with "Buddha," "protection," and "gate," yet with a down-to-earth homely quality. The passage sheds light on the ideal man as postulated in the Confucian *Analects* — someone without pretense, embodying values of simplicity, sincerity, and integrity.

classes living in peace. Filled with such radiance, I set down my brush, with nothing more to say.[9]

> how luminous!
> green leaves, young leaves
> shining in the sun

At Blackhair Mountain (Kurokamiyama), still patched with snow and mist-drifts, Sora wrote:

> crest shorn
> Blackhair Mountain
> clothing changes, too[10]

Born Kawai Sogoro,[11] Sora lived next door to the *basho* cottage,[12] almost eave to eave, and helped with wood and water chores in the banana tree's shadow. Lured by the bright prospects of far-off places like Matsushima and Kisakata, he offered to help take on the hardships of the road. When leaving, he'd shaved his head, put on a monk's ink-black robes, and changed the *"So-go"* characters in his name slightly to read "Illuminating."[13] So the words about changing clothes go on resounding. We climbed more than a mile up the mountain to a waterfall leaping out from above a cave and plunging a hundred feet into a clear green pool ringed by countless rocks. Squeezed into the hollow behind the cascades, we peered out at Back-viewed Falls.

> stillness awhile
> in waterfall's seclusion
> —summer's practice[14]

Starting across the Nasu Moor to visit a friend in the Nasu District on our way toward a place called Blackwing (Kurobane), we tried a shortcut through fields toward a village not far off, but rain came on as dark approached, so we passed the night at a farmhouse. Setting off across the plain again in the morning, we saw a horse in a pasture with a man cutting hay nearby; still unsure of the way, we asked him for help with directions. Rough as his life seemed, he did not lack compassion.

---

[9] Bashō gives land and language equal attention here, then focuses in on the light through translucent leaves— at once down-to-earth and spiritual, humble and elegant.

[10] They arrive at Blackhair Mountain (Kurokamiyama) on the traditional day for changing into summer clothes. Sora has also shaved his head in the manner of pilgrimage monks.

[11] **Kawai Sogoro:** *Kawai* is his family name, presented first, in the traditional Japanese manner; *Sogoro* is his given name.

[12] *basho* **cottage:** The *basho* is an exotic kind of banana tree or broad-leafed plantain. One planted in Bashō's yard as a gift gave the cottage its nickname—the *basho-an* (banana-tree hut)—and its resident the pen name by which he is most known.

[13] *"So-go"* . . . **"Illuminating":** Sora's name change is homonymic, as from "bear" to "bare"; no change when spoken, but a shift in meaning from how it's written.

[14] **summer's practice:** One meaning suggests a traditional summer training period for mountain monks, with concentrated meditation practice and perhaps also so-called "ascetic practices" (e.g., dipping in icy pools or standing in waterfalls).

"Hmm, what can we do?" he replied. "These paths keep branching, with countless crosstrails, and bad luck to the traveler who doesn't know where he's heading. I'm afraid it's so easy to get lost. Better take the horse as far as he'll go. When he stops, send him back." Two children ran along awhile beside us, one a little beauty called Kasane, like the maidenflower sometimes referred to as "manifold pink."[15] This was such a rare and charming name that Sora wrote:

> pretty Kasane,
> a natural name for her
>   "petal-folded pink"

At the small village, we attached a little something for the owner to the saddle and turned the horse back.[16]

[WINDING TRAILS BEYOND]

At the castletown of Blackwing (Kurobane), we called at the home of a certain gentleman named Joboji, the Deputy Chief, who seemed pleased with our surprise appearance. We talked together day and night, and also with his younger brother, Tosui, and were then invited to his house and taken around to meet all the relatives. So days passed. One day we rambled the outskirts by the old Dog-Shooting Grounds, and then wove through Nasu's famous bamboo thicket to Foxwoman Tamamo's tomb.[17] From there we paid respects at the warrior god Hachiman's shrine. Nasu's own hero Yoichi invoked this spirit before piercing with his arrow the rising sun on a fan suspended from a ship far offshore, during the battle of Yashima Bay.[18] I was all the more moved returning to Tosui's house as dark deepened. Leaving in the morning, we passed by the nearby Shugen training school for mountain monks and were invited to the practice hall, where the founder's own worn, high-stilted wooden sandals were on display.[19]

> in summer foothills
> deep bows before the high clogs
>   on our way out

---

[15] **Kasane . . . pink":** The flower is associated with girls, though here doubled by a prefix *(yae)* added to the common name.

[16] As discussed in note 4, the first page or fold of a linked poem of fifty or one hundred verses ends following the eighth stanza.

[17] **Joboji . . . tomb:** Deputy Chief Joboji showed his visitors highlights of local history and folklore, including the stadium where an old sport of shooting dogs with blunt-tipped arrows from horseback had been practiced. Folklore claimed the sport helped train warriors how to deal with fox demons like Fox-Lady Tamamo.

[18] **Yoichi . . . Bay:** In 1185, the district's native hero Yoichi, a great archer, had hit the sun painted on a fan suspended from a pole on a moving ship, with much riding on the shot; an event in the epic struggle between Heike and Genji clans.

[19] **Leaving . . . display:** On the way out of town, the travelers stop before the high-ridged wooden clogs of a famous seventh-century wandering ascetic who'd traveled to distant parts of the country as pilgrim and teacher.

Beyond the Cloud Rock temple (Unganji), my Zen teacher Butcho[20] once lived in a mountain shelter near which, he said some time ago, he'd written on a rock with burnt pine: *"barely a few feet high and wide, my thatched hut—just in the way . . . but for the rain."* To see what was left of it, we pointed our staffs to Unganji. Joined by a merry and chattering group of youths, we reached the mountain base before we knew it. Here the path thinned out and almost disappeared above the valley, where pines and cedars clustered with shadows. Wet mosses oozed and dripped, and even the early summer air seemed chilled. At the end of Ten-Views Path, we stood a moment by the bridge, then crossed over to pass through the mountain gate. Searching for traces of Butcho's retreat, we climbed the mountainside beyond the temple and—yes, up there!—we found the small hut perched on a stone ledge before a cave, just like Myozenji's "Death's Gate Cave" or Fa Yun's "Stone Room on the Rock-top."[21] Scrambling up, I scribbled spontaneously

> even woodpeckers
> leave this hermit's hut alone
> among summer trees

—left on a post.

From Blackwing, I rode toward the "Life-snuffing Stone" at Sessoseki on a horse lent by the Deputy Chief. When the groom leading it asked for a poem, I was moved he cared.

> drawing the horse
> sideways across the field
> —a cuckoo's call![22]

The killing stone itself was in a dark little canyon in the mountain shadow, where the Nasu hotsprings flow with noxious fumes[23]—dead butterflies, moths, bees, and the like so thick the sand beneath was barely visible.

Yes! Still growing there, the wonderful trembling willow Saigyo wrote of, *"where clear spring water flows,"* by the village of Ashino, on a bank between ricefields. The

---

[20] **Butcho:** Guided Bashō in *zazen,* sitting meditation, and in other aspects of Zen practice and perspective.

[21] **"Death's . . . Rock-top":** Two famous rustic meditation retreats where seeker sages sat for long periods, contemplating fundamental reality and the nature of original being apart from the usual social distractions.

[22] Bashō offers the groom the poem brushed across a strip of "poetry-paper," made for this purpose. The original word for the bird here, *hototogisu,* represents both the bird and its call (as in calling a cooing kind of cuckoo a *"coo-coo-coo"*). In this case, its actual sound is said to be more like "hototo," made only by Asian cuckoos.

[23] **killing . . . fumes:** Folklore claims the Fox-Lady's soul, when released from its animal-human form (i.e., after she was killed), became the "breath taking" killing stone itself, or at least inhabited it and gave it its noxious, foul character.

local Cultural Secretary had repeatedly encouraged me to seek it out, and I'd long wondered about it. And here I was at last, standing in its actual shadow![24]

> a whole ricepaddy
> was planted before I left
> that willow's shade

Restless with anticipation, yet growing clearer and calmer day by day as we made our way toward it, we finally reached the Shirakawa Border Crossing, and I naturally recalled Kanemori's[25] *"if I could only / send word to the capital / to tell of it. . . ."* Shirakawa, one of the Three Great Gateways, is a favorite of poets, with many words left behind in response, so the "autumn winds" of Noin[26] whispered in my ear a line of crimson maple leaves lingering amidst the rich summer green of the actual branches, while through the pale white flowers of roadside shrubs other small white flowers[27] pressed, white on white, like the snow reported by someone passing in winter. Kiyosuke's[28] brush described a man of long ago putting on a formal black hat for the border, so Sora offered

> little white flowers
> my crown for
> the great crossing

We continued across the Abukuma River, with Aizu Peak to the left; Iwaki, Soma, and Miharu villages off to the right; mountains dividing Hitachi and Shimotsuke beyond. Under an overcast sky, we passed Mirror Pond[29]—with nothing reflected.

At the Post Town of Suka River, a fellow named Tokyu invited us to stay for four or five days, asking right off what poems Shirakawa had drawn in response. Worn out in body and mind from the efforts of traveling, and with my spirit so taken by the scene itself and with memories of what earlier poets had offered, I explained, little new of my own came forth, just

> for inspiration
> rice-planting songs
> in the backcountry

—drawn from my brush. (It would have been a shame to pass without a single poem.) But then with this for an opener, second and third verses followed from others, and before we were done, we'd made three complete linked poetry sequences together, more than a hundred stanzas.[30]

---

[24] **willow . . . shadow:** Saigyo passed about five hundred years before, yet his shadow remains, intertwined with the willow's.

[25] **Kanemori:** Poet who died in 990.   [26] **Noin:** Monk born around 987.

[27] **pale . . . flowers:** The first small white flowers seem to be Deutzia scabra (sometimes rendered as verbena or snowflowers), with the second a kind of wild briar rose.

[28] **Kiyosuke:** Died around 1175.   [29] **Mirror Pond:** Might also be translated "Shadow Lake."

[30] From Bashō's humble opening verse about backcountry planting songs, more than a hundred linked stanzas flowed. The first sequence, a *kasen* of thirty-six verses, survives.

In an out-of-the-way part of the town, a religious hermit[31] lived completely apart, in the shade of a great chestnut tree, and I thought of Saigyo's *"gathering horse chestnuts / deep in the mountains,"* suggestive of just such a life. Handed paper, I wrote: the character for "chestnut" is actually composed of two characters, "west" over "tree," with various religious associations.[32] Master Gyogi Bosatsu[33] used only chestnut for his staff and for the posts supporting his secluded abode.

> few in this world
> see . . . the chestnut flowers
>   up there, by the eaves

About five leagues from Tokyu's house, past the Hiwada Post, the Asaka Hills rise up by the road. Since it was near the famous *"katsumi* iris" time, and with much marshy meadow about, we asked and asked about the flower. "Where's the *katsumi*? Which is the *katsumi*?" But no one seemed to know anything about it, so we went on searching, with *"katsumi . . . katsumi"* on our lips till the setting sun grazed the far ridge. Then we turned right at the Twin Pines of Nihonmatsu, peering a moment into the Black Cave's mouth at Kurozuka,[34] and headed on to Fukushima for the night.

The next day, we sought out Shinobu[35] village and asked about the famous letter-rubbing stone, which we found half buried in the earth at the base of a far hill. Some local children came along and said the stone used to be near the hilltop, but that the farmers who'd gotten fed up with sightseers tearing up their green grain had shoved it over towards the valley, where it landed—and remains—face down. So it might well be true.

> pressing seedlings in
> as hands in old times pressed
>   the shinobu stone

We took the Moonarc ferry at Tsukinowa across the river to the post town of Rapids Overlook. Administrator Sato's old place was a ways further into the hills to the left. Asking as we went, we followed directions through Open Moor (Sabano) by the village of Iizuka, and finally to a place called Maruyama, Roundtop, where the castle ruins remain at the base of the hill. My eyes filled up by the old stones where the gate used to be, and overflowed again at the family graves in the nearby temple-

---

[31] **religious hermit:**Using the haikai pen name *Rissai* (chestnut), he welcomed a *renga* (linked poetry) party with Bashō.

[32] **religious associations:**Some scholars see a reference here to "Pure Land" concepts in Buddhism. Contrary to some views, however, Bashō doesn't seem to be suggesting a far-off "heaven of the west," but something more in tune with Hui Neng's "With mind pure / the Pure Land is / right here!" (Sixth Patriarch Sutra)

[33] **Gyogi Bosatsu:**Monk who helped build the Todai Temple; he died in 749 (950 years before Bashō's journey).

[34] **Black Cave . . . Kurozuka:**Supposed to house a man-eating female demon, a curse to travelers.

[35] **Shinobu:**The place name is also the name of the plant used as a dye on cloth rubbed against a rock of the same name. It suggests thinking of someone and of the past (cf. "forget-me-not"). A cloth placed on the stone, then rubbed with *shinobu* leaves, would receive the imprint of the characters from the *shinobu* stone.

grounds. I was especially moved by stories of the two young widows who had ridden home in the armor of the fallen Sato sons.[36] Accounts of the women's gallantry made my sleeves wet, and so much closer to home than the Tombstone of Tears in China![37] After tea in the temple, we learned Yoshitsune's sword and Benkei's prayer pack were among its treasures.[38]

> prayer pack and sword
> displayed high up on Boys Day
> a carp wind-sock[39]

—first day of the rice-planting moon.

We stopped that night in Iizuka and bathed in the hotsprings, then found for lodging just thin rice mats over bare dirt in a rundown place with no lamp. We bedded down by firepit light as thunder rumbled in. Then rain came on down through the leaks. With mosquitoes and fleas, and my old complaint[40] returning, I couldn't sleep. Finally, just when I thought I might pass out, the short darkness passed instead, and we were off again, mind dragging ragged shadows. With so far yet to go across the horizon, we hired horses up to the Kori Post. My recurring ailment was still a problem, and I thought how a long pilgrimage involves detachment, letting the world go, the fleeting moment, life itself transient, passing away on the roadside maybe, accepting whatever fate holds. . . . Musing so on the spirit of such yielding, my own spirits gradually revived until I found myself striding along one foot after another without a care, as if with one foot here in this world and one already in the next—and so stumbled on, crossing the Great Barrier Gate of Okido into the Da-te district.

Past the castle-towns of Abumizuri and Shirioshi, we entered the Kasashima district and asked for Fujiwara Sanekata's grave-mound. "See that village, Minowa, with straw rain-thatch in the hills far to the right? Beyond that is Kasashima itself, where the Road God's Shrine is and the memorial grass remains."[41] But the road looked bad from Fifth Moon rains, and, so washed out ourselves, we just gazed from

---

[36] **Sato sons:** Died in service to the doomed hero Yoshitsune, who was betrayed by his brother (the shogun Yoritomo). Yoshitsune died in 1189, exactly five hundred years before Bashō's journey retraces his escape route in reverse. The two Sato widows are said to have put on their fallen husbands' samurai armor for the arrival home, so the aged Sato mother might think her sons were returning victorious.

[37] **made my sleeves wet:** Idiomatic expression for shedding tears. **Tombstone of Tears in China:** It was said that all who came there wept.

[38] **Benkei's . . . pack:** The "giant monk" Benkei, loyal sidekick to Yoshitsune, died trying to protect his friend. His prayer pack is a kind of chest, stocked with religious items.

[39] **carp wind-sock:** On Boy's Day, the fifth day of the fifth moon (now celebrated May 5, but later in Bashō's time), carp wind-sock banners are flown from poles for the household sons, as prayers for their prosperity while journeying upstream through life.

[40] **my old complaint:** May have included some bowel difficulty, fever, and chills.

[41] Sanekata, a poet and battle captain, was sent to Mutsu (Oku) as governor in 996, exiled far from the mainstream for being so cantankerous and troublesome. Some folklore has him dying on the way to Mutsu though historians claim he actually served a few years before dying in 998.

afar. How well these names fit now—Minowa (Straw Raincoat) and Kasashima (Umbrella Isle).[42] So I brushed

> far Kasashima—
> Umbrella Island's where?
> down monsoon's muddy road

—and we stopped for the night at Iwanuma.

Wide eyed by Takekuma's legendary Double Pines rising just as long ago from shared roots into two great branching trunks, I naturally recalled Noin's famous poem, *"no sign now of that pine there,"* after a new governor had cut it for a bridge across the Natori River.[43] It was reported cut down and regrown time and again over a thousand years, but I can report it's in fine shape now! As we left Edo, our friend Kyohaku had offered *"late cherry blossoms / don't forget to stop at / the Takekuma's pine,"* so now I replied,

> cherry blossom time
> to now, this two-trunked pine
> —just three moons[44]

We crossed the Natori River into Sendai on the eve of the Iris Festival, the time to adorn eaves with "blue flags."[45] We found an inn for a few days and searched out an artist named Kaemon[46] for guide. Said to be a spirited poet, he'd tracked down obscure local places mentioned in old poems. With bush clovers thick on Miyagi Moor, the scenery looked promising for fall. At Tamada, Yokono, and Tsutsujigaoka (Azalea Hill), the white flowers of the horse-loco bushes[47] were at their peak. Entering the pine forest called Underwood, too thick for sunlight to penetrate, the heavy dew recalled the famous old poem beginning, *"Attendants, your master's umbrella!"*[48] As the sun declined we paid our respects at Yakushi temple, dedicated to the medicine buddha, healer of souls, and at Tenjin Shrine, which honored a famous scholar-priest, as well as at other such places. As a parting gift, Kaemon gave us sketches of

---

[42]The *kasa* (of *Kasashima*, Umbrella Isle) can be thought of equally as a rainhat or an umbrella (or an umbrella-hat).

[43]The poet monk Noin had taken the Oku Road in the eleventh century. His poem on the missing Takekuma pine asks *"Have a thousand years passed before returning?"*

[44] three moons:Another famous Takekuma pine poem says, *"If you ask of the pine, locals will talk of three moons,"* so Bashō's poem is as elegantly split as the twin pine itself, with roots of a thousand years and branches three moons back.

[45] Iris . . . flags:Celebrated with blue-flag irises and prayers for health; associated with Boy's Day.

[46] Kaemon:A carver of woodblocks who ran a haikai bookstore and was happy to show his visitors poetry-related sights, including some that had been mostly forgotten before he'd searched them out.

[47] horse-loco bushes:Said to intoxicate horses.

[48] *"Attendants, . . . umbrella!"*:The *kasa* (introduced at Kasashima) is called for at Underwood since the dew under the trees falls heavy as rain. The poem quoted is by an anonymous poet, from an eleventh-century anthology.

Matsushima and Shiogama. And then, with an eccentric artist's perfect touch, he added straw sandals with cords dyed an inspired iris-blue.

> blue cord laces
> as if irises bloomed
> on my sandals

[Narrow Paths Across]

With Kaemon's sketches to guide us, we soon found ourselves on the *Oku-no-hosomichi*[49] itself, *the* Narrow Road, that slender inland trail winding between hills and by the source of a renowned reed-straw woven into many famous poems and braided into fine mats still, the ten-strand sedge a traditional tribute to the Governor. Continuing on by old Fort Taga,[50] near Ichikawa village we came to a crossroads marking the backcountry Oku trailhead with the famous Tsubo Stone, a mossy monument over six feet high and about three feet wide, now barely readable only by fingering the grooves. Giving province border distances in four directions, the crossroad stone added: "Fortress built 1st year of Jinki [724] by General Azuma-udo of Ono, sent north as regional commander. . . . Repaired 6th year of Tempyo-hoji [762] by Lord Asakari of Emi, northeastern commander. Recorded 1st day of 12th moon." Thus from the Emperor Shomu's reign.

Most places mentioned in old poetry can never be exactly located. Mountains crumble through time, landslides change the river's course, floods wash out roads, tombstones sink into the earth, saplings replace great trees growing for generations; hardly anything remains where it was for long. Thus faced with this monument of nearly a thousand years, I felt such a powerful link with the past, so connected at the heart with men of old, I forgot the aches and pains of the journey, and, in gratitude for such a traveler's blessing, wept from joy.

After looking into the Noda region's Jewel River, at the Offshore Sunk-In-Water Stone, and other places commemorated in poetry, we reached Pine Mountain Spit (Sue-no-Matsuyama), and its temple of almost the same name—with identical characters but read in Chinese style.[51] All around between the pines were graves—so much for lovers' intimate vows to remain forever *"wings of a single bird"* or like *"twin trees eternally linked with intertwined branches,"*[52] yet come finally to this: merciless

---

[49] *Oku-no-hosomichi* (Narrow Road of Oku): This is both the name of this particular trail at the heart of the pilgrimage and the title Bashō gave his book. *Oku* is the province name, but also suggests the backcountry, the frontier, and (to some extent) the interior. The specific road named *Oku-no-hosomichi* had about a thousand years of actual history, poetry, and pilgrimage woven into it by Bashō's time, although now it is known especially for Bashō's passage.

[50] Fort Taga: Stockade outpost from the 700s; mostly forgotten before a pre-Bashō archaeological project unearthed the described stone marker.

[51] identical . . . style: *Kanji* characters [symbols representing ideas or things used in Chinese], derived from Chinese and often retaining similar meaning, may have completely unrelated oral equivalents in vernacular Japanese. In some cases, however, as Bashō points out, custom dictates a pronunciation in the Chinese manner (or at least derived from the Chinese).

[52] *"wings . . . branches"*: Poem is by the Tang era Chinese poet Po Chui (Bo Juyi).

time's deep aloneness, a vesper temple bell sounding as dusk settles on the Shiogama shore. The early summer rain-sky cleared some, and in the faint moonlight Magaki Isle seemed so close. Then little fishing boats came pulling toward shore together. And floating in after, voices of men dividing the catch seemed to deepen the feeling, suggesting lines about *"sad hands upon the net"* and *"the melancholy creak of mooring ropes."* A blind musician soulfully plucked his lute-like *biwa*-strings that night, chanting backcountry ballads of Oku, frontier airs and interior melodies. These were neither warrior tales of the Heike nor dance story tunes, but songs from beyond the border incanted in a loud backcountry style[53] — so near our pillows and so late, we couldn't sleep. Still, it was moving to find such a traditional old art being kept up in such an out-of-the-way place.

In the early morning we paid our respects to Shiogama's Myojin Shrine, its immense pillars and resplendently painted beams recently restored by a province governor. Flights of steep stone steps rise up where the road ends, and morning sun blazed on the brilliant vermillion lacquered railings with a splendid brightness! Even in this remote backcountry, such priceless national treasures are, and the practice of preserving them. Before the shrine, an old stone lantern bore on its metal lid the inscription: "in the 3rd year of Bunji (1187), given by Izumi Saburo," thus a five hundred year old image shining in our sight. Saburo was a brave soldier whose loyalty and filial devotion are respected to this day. As has been written, "Follow the way of true virtue, adapt to the path of character, stick to right principles, and honor will follow through time."[54]

The sun had nearly reached noon already when we hired a boat to Matsushima. After a crossing of more than a half mile, we landed at Ojima Beach. As often observed, the Pine Islands are one of the most beautiful places in this "land of the rising sun," easily equal to Lake Dotei's Tung-ting in Hunan and Western Lake in Hangchow, said to be the best China has to offer. Here, the mile-wide bay swells with each tide from an opening to the southeast, like the Sekko River at flood. Islands beyond counting rise from end to end, some steep with sharp heaven-pointing peaks; some low, stretched out into the wave-surge and tide-swell; some bunched in twos and threes, or layered one behind another like babes on mothers' backs; others still, as if with islands in their arms, suggest the protective embrace of parents and grandparents.

The pines there are an intense green, with sea-sprayed branches and exquisitely wind-twisted spines wound as if artfully trained, like a beautiful woman made a

---

[53] **blind . . . style:** Tales of Heike (recounting the struggle between the Genji and Taira, or Minamotos and Heike) and certain danced warrior stories were traditionally recited with *biwa*, a plaintive four-stringed lute. Bashō's blind musician plays and sings in a rarer and more rustic manner still.

[54] Izumi Saburo, Yoshitsune's loyal ally, was betrayed by his own brother in 1189 and killed at the age of twenty-two. (Yoshitsune was about thirty at his own death the same year.) The governor Masamune restored the shrine in Bashō's century.

touch more lovely still before her glass. Yet here the artist is the maker of mountains, and whose brush can equal such, earth's original divine creation?

Ojima (Male Isle), actually a peninsula connected to the mainland, curves far out into the sea. Near its tip were the remains of zen master Ungo's[55] remote retreat and his *zazen* sitting meditation rock. Among the pines, here and there, secluded rustic huts sheltered religious solitaries living silently within, with thin lines of smoke curling up from humble fires of pine-needles, cones, and fallen twigs. The serene tranquility of one such place especially touched my heart, and though I did not know who resided there, the spirit of its life drew me. As we came closer, the moon rose, shimmering in the mirror of the sea, transforming all.

Back to the inlet for lodging, we found an inn, and an upper-story room with windows wide open to the sea. Resting a night on the journey, at one with gentle wind and drifting clouds, spirits soaring with such beauty around us, Sora wrote:

> at Matsushima
> as if crane-winged
> a nightbird's[56] song

Silent and wordless, I tried to sleep, but couldn't. When I was leaving my old hut for the road, Sodo had given me a Chinese-style poem about Matsushima, and Hara Anteki a *waka*[57] *"on pine-shored isles,"* so I undid my knapsack for them, along with some verses by Sampu and Dakushi, and these were my companions that night.

On the eleventh we bowed at the Zuigan Temple, its abbot the thirty-second in succession since the Great Soul Makabe took Ch'an vows in T'ang era China, founding this temple on his return.[58] More recently, Dharma Master Ungo came and, thanks to his efforts, renewed both its spirit and structure, promoting both understanding and rebuilding. With its gold-leaf walls and gilded Buddhas shining, we might have been in "enlightened paradise" itself. Yet I wondered where the rustic temple retreat of that holy sage Kenbutsu might be.[59]

On the twelfth, we started out as if towards Hiraizumi, with places memorialized in poetry supposed to be along the way—like the Big Sister Pine of Aneha and the Cord-Cutting Bridge of Odae. But we soon found ourselves on nearly lifeless paths instead, just tracks for occasional hunters and woodcutters, not knowing

---

[55] **Ungo:** Zen master who died in 1658.

[56] **"nightbird":** The same *hototogisu* heard crossing the Nasu Moor.

[57] **waka:** A five-lined poetic form. However many descriptions there were of Matsushima's beauty before, Bashō's is the best account known now.

[58] **eleventh . . . return:** Scholars say the facts of Bashō's time frame may be off here in both the day of his visit and his accounting within the lineage. According to Sora, the visit happened on the 9th. Makabe Heishiro (also known as Hosshin) went to China in the thirteenth century. On his return he revived the temple originally founded by Master Jikaku (794–864).

[59] **rustic . . . be:** Saigyo had visited Kenbutsu here at Ojima, where Kenbutsu is said to have "given voice to many thousand holy scrolls," chanting the Lotus Sutra in particular many thousand times.

which way was which, and, having missed a turn somewhere, wound up at the harbor town of Ishi-no-Maki (Stonesroll).[60]

Far across the water, crowded with hundreds of little coastal cargo boats plying the inlet, Goldbloom Mountain (Kinkazan) rose. From its deep mine *"gold flowers blossom,"* as a poet once wrote Emperor Shomu. In the village, clustered houses jostled for space, while countless smoke-trails from cooking fires coiled up end to end. Here we were, without intending it, and, unable to find an inn with a room, we ended up in a pitiful shack for the night.

We set off again at first light, rambling awhile almost at random, it seemed, in a maze of strange paths. Later, following the bank of the Kitakami River without a break, we caught a few glimpses from afar of famous spots written about in poems—like Wet Sleeves Crossing,[61] Obuchi Meadow, and the Mano Reedflats. With spirits sinking, we slogged on around a long boggy marsh. Spending that night at a place called Toima, we finally reached Hiraizumi the next day, having come many miles.

With the splendor of three generations of Fujiwaras passed as if in the dream of a single sleep, ruins of the Great Gate of Hiraizumi stand about a third of a mile before where Hidehira's court had been, now just an overgrown field.[62] Only Goldenbird Hill, once part of the palace garden park, retained its form. Climbing up to the High Fort overlook, part of what had been Yoshitsune's last refuge, we spied the River Kitakami winding through the plains far below from the Nambu region, while the River Koromo wound by Izumi Castle[63] before joining the greater Kitakami directly beneath the overlook. Other ruins like Yasuhira's fort beyond the Koromo checkpoint had once guarded the approach south from the Ezo tribesmen of the north. But for all that—the power and loyal retainers who took refuge and fought so bravely in the stronghold here—so fleeting is such glory that of their valiant effort only so much grass remains. *"The country in ruins, yet mountains and rivers remain, and through castle rubble, spring returns grass to green again."*[64] We set down our hats and sat awhile, moist-eyed.

> of warriors' dreams
> summer grass remains
> the only trace

---

[60] In Bashō's meditation on tangled paths, the *"maki"* of *Ishi-no-maki* (the "roll" of "Stonesroll") can mean a roll of silk or scroll (as in a volume or book), as well as "coil," "roll," or "wind up."

[61] **Wet Sleeves Crossing:** *(Sode no Wateri),* a ferry crossing that suggests sleeves wet with tears.

[62] **Hidehira's court . . . field:** Hiraizumi Castle was built by Fujiwara Kiyohira in the eleventh century and maintained by the next two generations (Motohira and Hidehira); but then Hidehira's son, Yasuhira, went against his father's pledge to support Yoshitsune, a betrayal that led to Yasuhira's own double-cross and death, along with Hiraizumi's destruction in 1189.

[63] **Izumi Castle:** Home of Izumi Saburo (who had donated the lantern at the Shiogama shrine), the only Hidehira son who remained loyal to Yoshitsune.

[64] *"The country . . . to green again":* The poem Bashō recalls, from Tu Fu (Du Fu; 712–770), is one of China's most famous; Bashō's response is one of the most famous poems in Japanese.

And Sora added:

> in snowflowers
> it seems old Kanefusa's[65]
> white hair appears

Both Chuson Temple halls, whose wonders we had heard of, were open. The sutra-study hall held images of three generations of great Hiraizumi generals, their coffins in the Hikarido,[66] Hall of Splendor, along with three well-shaped Buddhas. The famous "seven gems" were absent, however, and the once-jewelled door was wind-cracked, while the once gold-leafed pillars spoke of hard times like frost and snow. The whole Great Hall of Light would be gone by now, returned to grasses and brush, but for the protection of renovated walls and a newly tiled roof able to withstand the wind and rain. So preserved, it continues as a memorial stretching a thousand years.

> weather-beaten yet
> another monsoon passed over
> "Shining Practice Hall"

With the Nambu road far off in the distance, we passed the night at Iwade village. We then went on by Little Black Point and Water Island, and from Crying Babe Hotspring to the Shitomae Checkpoint, sometimes called Passwater Crossing since it's where Yoshitsune's newborn first pee'd as they fled north across the mountains.[67] But few travellers used this route, and the border guard eyed us with suspicion at the gate, letting us through only after a long delay. With dark overtaking us as we struggled up the steep mountain path beyond, we sought shelter at another border guard's hut stumbled upon. For three days fierce winds and rain held us prisoner, attached to our bleak refuge.

> fleas and lice
> a horse passes water
> by my pillow

Our host reported there were high mountains between us and Dewa, with unclear trails, and recommended a guide to see us across, so we hired a gigantic young fellow with a great curved dagger at his belt and a bent oak staff that looked alive. I feared we were heading for disaster, in some danger at least, following after. As the man in the hut had warned, the mountains were high, beyond a single bird's song, and the forest so thick and deep we might as well have been crossing at night.

---

[65] Kanefusa: Yoshitsune's loyal old retainer, entrusted with the task of killing Yoshitsune's wife and child at the end of their valiant trail before taking his own life in the ritual manner (leaving no one for the enemy to dishonor).

[66] Hikarido: The *Kyo-do* is the sutra hall where sacred texts are kept. The *hikari-do*, "Shining Practice Hall," built in 1124, might also be rendered "Enlightenment Hall" or "Illumination Way."

[67] *Naguro* (Crying Babe Spring) is where Yoshitsune's newborn first cried, while the family fled from those seeking to kill them. *Shitomae*, for related historical reasons expressed in the text, means "urinating before."

Wind blew dust *"under ragged shadow clouds"*[68] as we pushed through bamboo thickets and *shino* brush, forded streams, and stumbled over rocks, until, sopping with cold sweat, we came to safer ground in the Mogami region at last. "Lucky to get here," the guide said before departing. "Usually it's not so easy. I've never brought people across before without some accident," hearing which set my heart racing again.

At Obanazawa, Safflower Valley, we stopped to visit a fellow named Seifu,[69] a well-off safflower merchant. From his frequent comings and goings between here and the capital, he knew what traveling was like and was sensitive to how travelers feel. With a warm welcome, he urged us to stay several days to refresh ourselves from the long hard going, offering various diversions.

> how cool!
> and at home welcomed
>   a summer's breeze . . .

> out from under
> the silkworm shed
>   a toad's voice

> safflower blooms
> eyebrow brushes
>   powder puff plants

And by Sora,

> in simple clothes
> from the old days
>   silkworm keepers

In Yamagata the Ryushakuji mountain temple, founded by abbot Jikaku,[70] remains well taken care of in a serene secluded place steeped in peace and quiet. Urged to it by many, we back-tracked a ways off the route from Obanazawa, arriving in the still light of late afternoon. Arranging space at the pilgrim's guesthouse at the foot of the mountain, we set right off up the steep slope toward the hilltop shrine. The mountain seemed to rise from heaped up boulders, one after another, with aged pines and cypresses, even more ancient earth and stones veiled with velvet smooth spots of soft green moss. At the top, we found the sanctuary doors shut tight and no sound. Skirting the steep rock edge on all fours, we made our bows to the sacred ground, our prostrations to the mountain. Calming the heart and clearing the mind, the profound stillness touched all deeply.

---

[68] *"under . . . clouds"*: Another snippet on the wind from Tu Fu (Du Fu).

[69] Seifu: In contrast to the rugged wilderness of Notched Blade Pass, the travelers are put up in luxurious ease by a wealthy safflower merchant who also happens to be a well-known haikai poet and editor of three anthologies.

[70] abbot Jikaku: Jikaku Daishi (792–862) is the same Zen master who built the Zuigan temple in Ojima. Founder of the Tendai Buddhist lineage, he brought a combination of ch'an/zen and esoteric teachings from China.

> . . . silence . . .
>   sinking in stone
>   the cicada's sound

Planning to float down the Mogami by boat, we waited for good weather at a place called Stonefield (Oishida), where we'd heard seeds of an old-style linked poetry had once been sown, taken root, and kept flowering in later generations. A heartfelt muse sang here as through rustic reed flutes. Yet locals said, "We stumble along in the dark, uncertain of the way, lost between old style and new, in need of a guide." So we sat together composing linked poetry, offering whatever inspiration brought forth. Imagine that—cultivating the haikai way even in this far field of stones!

The Mogami River begins swelling in the far north of Michinoku, beyond paths in the trackless interior. With its uppermost run here in Yamagata, it plunges through many perilous places further down, like Go-stones Rapids and the Falcon's Dive, before dropping near Mount Itajiki to join the sea at Sakata. Our small boat was swept downstream with sheer cliffs rising close up right and left. Sometimes used for rice and thus called "riceboats," ours seemed just a grain disappearing into foaming white cascades. In places the deep forest's rich foliage stretched over us. Under a green explosion of leaves, we swept past the *Sennin-do*, Hall of the Immortals, balanced over the water at the river's edge. Full of recent rains, the swift current put our speck of boat in peril time and again.

> gathering all
>   the summer rains—how swiftly
>   the Mogami flows[71]

On the third day of the sixth moon, we went up Hakuroyama (Featherblack Mountain) to visit a fellow named Zushi Sakichi. He introduced us to Master Egaku Ajari, acting abbot in charge, who welcomed us warmly, arranging board and lodging at a temple annex in Minamidani, the South Valley.

On the fourth, we gathered at the main temple hall to make linked poetry together. I expressed my appreciation in the opening verse:

> South Valley blessing
> —a summer breeze seasoned
>   with scent of snow

On the fifth, we paid our respects at Mount Hakuro's Gongen Shrine, its first temple, founded by Master Nojo at an unknown time. Though the Book of Rites[72] mentions a shrine at "Ushu's Satoyama," that may well be a scribe's mistaken copy of

---

[71]Bashō stayed three days at *Oishida* (from July 14) because of the weather (which must have added all the more force to the Mogami, considered one of the three fastest rivers in Japan). The temple passed is associated with what are sometimes called *shamanic* practices, as well as with one of Yoshitsune's loyal allies (said to have become an "immortal" for his virtue and loyalty).

[72] **Book of Rites:** (*Engi-shiki*) A collection of rules, prayers, and procedures dating from 927.

the original *Kuroyama* (*Black* Mountain), with almost the same character. Since *U-shu* is the old way of pronouncing the sign for the province name, perhaps the province indicator *shu* was dropped, and the alternatively pronounced province name *De-(h)wa* (Tribute-feather), shortened to make *H(w)a-kuro-yama* (Feather-Black-Mountain). An old geography book claims the province name "Tribute-feather" comes from the fact that feathers used to be sent from here to the court as a kind of tax or tribute.[73] Featherblack (Hakuro), Moon (Gassan), and Hotpool (Yudono) make up the so-called "*Dewa Sangan*—the Tribute-feather Pilgrimage" of the region's three sacred mountains. The Mount Hakuro temple is related to the Kanei temple in Buko, by Edo, in the Tendai lineage whose clear-moon insight-meditation energy goes on enlightening, mind shining from mountaintop to mountaintop, temple to temple. The many closely cloistered devotees here encourage each other's practice while serving the mountain with their devotions, drawing the continuing inspiration of its timeless blessings for all.[74]

On the eighth we climbed Gassan (Moon), wrapped in monk's cotton hoods and scarves, wound around with white linked paper-strips. Calling on inner strength, we followed the mountain monks up and up, through mist and cloud, with patches of snow and ice, all told maybe a few miles, as if our paths were joining with the sun's and moon's. Almost out of breath, our chilled bodies crossed through a last gateway between clouds, then there we were, at the summit, after the sun had set and moon arisen. We spread *shino* grass for beds and clumped bamboo leaves for pillows to rest the night. We rose at first light with lifting clouds, and started down toward the Yudono trail at dawn.

Downslope near the valley, we passed a famous swordsmith's forge, built on the banks of this sacred stream five hundred years ago by the blade-master Gassan. Taking his name from the mountain, he tempered himself and each sword in these magical, purifying waters, mind and body prepared for the task at hand. Thus his "moon" imprint on the blade is the sign of a true treasure. He must've drawn power from these waters as in China swordsmiths drew from the so-called Dragon Spring. The deep dedication of Kanchiang and his wife Muyeh, for example, with the famous swords they forged together, may remind us of the sincere devotion any great work requires and what profound immersion in the way might accomplish.

Reflecting thus while resting on a trailside rock, I noticed just then a small cherry tree barely three feet high, yet half in bloom, so far out of season, bringing spring back with its flowers opening out of a bed of late snow. Its fragrance seemed to persist all the more for the difficulties of such a life on the mountain, as if *"plum blossom's scent in summer's heat"* had returned or Gyoson's *"wild cherry and Zen soli-*

---

[73] Bashō offers a somewhat detailed hypothesis about how ideographic characters might have shifted through time, including his theory about a calligrapher's possible misinterpretation, changing one into another, to explain an otherwise unusual name.

[74] Two traditions flow together into a single stream at the temple. One is Tendai with its focus on insight-meditation, a transmission with many lessons brought from Ch'an Buddhist schools in China. The other is a more ancient and local *yamabushi* tradition, emphasizing the land-spirit, divine power in the heart of nature, and ascetic practices removed from secular society.

tude" had bloomed again here in what the tree had to teach. But from here the customary rule for Yodono pilgrims forbids description, so I set down my brush.[75]

Yet back at the temple hostel in South Valley, the abbot handed me paper strips for my impressions of the three mountains:[76]

> in morning chill
> a three-day moon fades above
>   Blackfeather Mountain

>   cloud peaks
> dissolved in bits into
>   the moon, the mountain

>   unable to speak
> of Hotpool Mountain—feel
>   my wet sleeve

while Sora added

>   Hotpool Mountain
> on the path of emptied pockets
>   our tears, too[77]

Leaving Hakuro, we were invited to samurai Nagayama Shigeyuki's house in the castle town of Crane Hill (Tsuregaoka), where we composed a *kasen*[78] of linked poetry together. Sakichi had come along this far and saw us off as we boarded a boat for Sakata Harbor and the home of a Dr. En'an, who writes in haikai under the pen-name Fugyoku.

> Hotspring Mountain
> to Windy Bay
>   evening cool

>   blazing red sun
> into the sea plunging
>   Mogami River, too

Our eyes had taken in such measureless beauty of rivers and mountains, land and sea, and still a small place in the heart quickened me on yet further north toward Kisa Bay. From Port Sakata we crossed a pass, then wound along a rocky shoreline,

---

[75] so I . . . brush: Passing into the unspoken-of zone, Bashō leaves words fully behind (along with distinctions of subject and object, individual mind and the great mind). He is like the solitary who "sleeps by the river to purify his ears."

[76] the abbot . . . three mountains: Ever the poet, Bashō is challenged by the abbot's request for a poem on each mountain. How can he respond to the abbot's request without breaking the rule that forbids describing the last one?

[77] Sora's tears follow a trail where pilgrims have shed coins and other currencies, emptying their pockets according to custom.

[78] kasen: A form of *haikai no renga* named for thirty-six famous hermits; playful linked poetry with thirty-six stanzas.

pressed through dunes and across sandy beaches, more than three miles. We arrived just as the sun was sinking, with sea-winds picking up bits of sand and rain gusts veiling Mount Chokai.[79] Suddenly it was so dark—rain cast a spell of gloom over all, and we groped on as if through the enchanted landscape of a fantasy, *"through shimmering veils of rain"* dreamily moving.[80] We imagined it would get better when the storm cleared, at least so we hoped, huddling in a fisherman's reed shed by the bay, waiting for the wet weather to lift.

The next morning, with clear sky and brilliant, almost blinding sun, we set off into the bay in a small boat, pointing first towards Noin's Island to pay our respects at what had been the sage Noin's refuge for three years, then across to the far shore in search of the ancient cherry tree whose reflection Saigyo had caught in a keepsake of words—*"watery blossoms rowed over by the fisherman's boat."* Now the tree reminds us of the master poet's brush.[81]

Near this shore was an imperial tomb, supposed to be the Empress Jingu's, at the Kanmanju temple, but I'd never heard of her coming or otherwise connected here, so who knows? We sat in the temple *hojo,* master's sitting room, and when the hanging bamboo screens were raised beheld the panorama unfolding before us: to the south, Chokai Mountain "holding heaven up," and its reflection in the water; to the east, a raised road-bed along the shore, stretching far-off toward Akita; to the west, Muyamuya Barrier blocking the way; to the north, the sea where it enters and leaves the sheltered harbor at Shiogoshi Inlet, the "shallows" at the tideway mouth.[82] All the way around was roughly a third of a mile, and reminiscent of Matsushima,[83] yet so different, for where Matsushima seemed to smile with cheerful beauty, Kisakata seemed to brood with a melancholy frown, the expression of a troubled spirit in its isolation, perhaps like a beautiful woman with a broken heart.

> Kisa Bay—
> in rain curled beautiful Seishi's
> mimosa silk sleep[84]

---

[79] **Mount Chokai:** Sometimes called Dewa's Fuji; has both old and new volcanoes (one of about five thousand feet, another of seven thousand feet).

[80] *"through . . . rain"*: Bashō alludes to a poem by Su-Tung-p'o (Su Dong-po; 1036–1101), about drinking rice wine by the lake as rain starts to clear, in which Lake Hsi is compared to Queen Hsi-shih (*Xi Shi* in Pinyin; *Seishi* in Japanese), a legendary beauty.

[81] Bashō crossed the bay first in search of the priestly sage Noin's hut, then to the site where Saigyo had immortalized ephemeral cherry blossom reflections in the water. The phrase "master poet's brush" echoes Bashō's own description of Matsushima, where the master maker was the original creator.

[82] With an economy of strokes, master Bashō's brush sweeps open a 360-degree panorama as the bamboo screens of the Zen master's small sitting room are raised on all four sides. (They had sought a tomb, but found this open sweep.)

[83] **reminiscent of Matsushima:** Even on the map, Kisa Bay (Kisakata) mirrors Matsushima, but with reversed orientation—on opposite coasts, even the sea openings are geographically opposite.

[84] In Bashō's exquisite-sounding poem, the bay, in rain, becomes *Seishi* again, the legendary beauty, a little dreamy in this weather, with drooping pink mimosa silk. The word used means both a silky mimosa tree and "asleep."

Shiogoshi shallows
wading cranes sprayed
with cool sea-splash

At the tideflats festival:

Kisa Bay—
what special treats to taste
in the god's honor?
— SORA

for evening air
by a fisherman's shack
an old door to sit on
— TAIJI, A MERCHANT FROM MINO

Noticing an osprey nest on a rock:

their bonds well set
on a rock above the waves,
the osprey nest[85]
— SORA

[THE ROAD SOUTH]

We hung around for days on end at Sakata, with clouds gathered over the far road inland. Hearing we were at least forty-five miles from the Kaga capital, our hearts ached across the Nizu border[86] into Echigo and on to the Ichiburi Barrier in Etchu, a hard nine-day stretch alternating heat and rain—and with my illness coming on again, mostly not able to write.

seventh moon festival[87]
even the night of the 6th
not ordinary

so wild the sea
& over Sado Island streaming
. . . heaven's river[88]

---

[85] Bashō offers a masterful sequence of linked poetry (two by him, then a chain of three he attributes to others). This five-poem sequence concludes not only the chapter but a major section of the journey and the work as a whole. (Of Taiji, only what Bashō says is known.) Meanwhile, it was to experience such places as Matsushima and Kisakata that Sora had agreed to become Bashō's road companion, sharing the burdens of traveling.

[86] **Nizu border:** The Nizu Barrier started out in 653 as a frontier outpost guarding the south against Ezo tribes, but was just a police checkpoint with a border guard's hut in Bashō's time.

[87] **seventh moon festival:** The seventh day of the seventh lunar month was celebrated as the Tanabata festival, based on a "heavenly" love story, the night when star-crossed lovers (in the astral form of Vega and Altair) meet across the "river of stars" to exchange poems "as if across a bridge of birds."

[88] **heaven's river:** A literal translation of *Ama-no-gawa*, which may also be rendered "the Milky Way" or "the galaxy."

Today we made our way by some of the most dangerous places of the journey, like "Lost Children Gorge," "Parents Gone Drop-off," a rope bridge called "Dogs Turn Back," and another place called "No-Horse Crossing."[89] Utterly exhausted, we turned to our pillows almost as soon as we reached the border-town of Ichifuri. Then we heard the whispering voices of what sounded like two young women drifting through the paper-screen walls from the next room, and mingling in, an old man's voice. From what I could gather, they seemed to be pleasure-women[90] from Nigata in Echizu on their way to the Ise Shrine.[91] The man seemed to have come along to the border, returning home tomorrow with letters they were writing and bits of spoken messages. The whispered voices floated into my sleep like dream-talk from an old geisha's poem, *"where white waves curl and break in swirls of foam, we fallen children of the floating world, fisherwomen casting our nets to every chance, inconstant lover, pay for our past sins with each new day of shame. . . ."* So words drifted in and merged with dreams as I drifted off.

But then as we were leaving the next morning, the women approached with misty eyes, and one said, "Not knowing the way, we feel lost and helpless. May we follow in your footsteps, at a discreet distance of course? By virtue of your monks' robes, please grant us compassion with the boundless grace of Buddha's blessing. . . ." "I'm very sorry, but we're not going straight anywhere," I responded on setting out. "We stop often and detour off the main road. Plenty of folks will be going your way. You can follow any, and I'm sure the goddess of boundless compassion will bring you safely across." But then I carried sorrowful thoughts of them a long while.

> at the same inn
> play-girls sleeping also
>   bush-clovers and the moon
> —SPOKEN TO SORA, WHO WROTE IT DOWN.[92]

The Kurobe River is said to have "48 flows"[93] into the sea, and we certainly crossed countless streams and watercourses on the way to the bay at Nago Creek. It wasn't *"flowering spring,"* of course, yet I wondered anyway about *"the waving wisterias of Tako"* even now in early fall, so I asked the route, and was told, "Yes, worth a look, a

---

[89] With gorges and bridges, there are places along this stretch of coast where the traveler must hug a dangerous cliff and where "sleeper waves" sometimes sweep in with a sudden rush across the road, washing the unwary off their feet and, at times, even out to sea.

[90] pleasure-women: There is no exact cultural equivalent for these "play girls" (or pleasure-women) who combine a range of associations from hostess and escort to courtesan and call girl. Bashō's are neither down-and-out prostitutes nor star geishas.

[91] Ise Shrine: Dates from 688 and is dedicated to *Amateraru-o-mi-kami.* Rebuilt ceremonially and rededicated every twenty years, it's one of the most popular pilgrimage sites in the country for all classes, and with some reputation as a place for lovers to rendezvous.

[92] Sora . . . down: Sora's own record contains no mention of either the poem or the encounter, raising speculation that Bashō may have created the story later for aesthetic reasons.

[93] "48 flows": The expression "48" is an idiomatic way of saying many or dozens.

couple miles from here along the coast, and then past that mountain over there—though you'll find only a few fishing shanties on the way, and probably not even that for lodging in." And so warned off, we continued directly on into Kaga province.

> early rice scent
> winding along beside
>   the white-capped sea

Across Snowflower Mountain (Unohana-yama) and the Kurikara valley, we reached Kanazawa in the middle of the seventh moon and met up with a writing friend named Kasho, a merchant traveling from Osaka, sharing the same inn. A young local poet named Issho, widely known for his devotion to haikai and admired even beyond this region for his contributions to linked poetry, had died the past winter. His older brother was just then holding a memorial service.

> at the grave shaking
> mournful voices wail
>   the autumn wind

Invited to a thatched hut shelter:

>   in autumn chill
> hands peeling cucumbers
>   & eggplant

And back on the way:

>   crimson on crimson:
> blazing sun unfeeling
>   uncaring autumn wind

>   aptly named "Wee Pines"
> wind sighs through
>   clover & pampas grass

In Little Pines (Komatsu), we visited the Tada Shrine and saw Sanemori's helmet and his imperial, brocade-woven armor. Presented to him as a member of the Genji clan by Lord Yoshitomo himself, it's said, they were obviously not for an ordinary soldier. The helmet was inlaid from eyebrow visor to earflaps with golden chrysanthemums interwoven with abstract scrollwork, and at the crown, a golden dragon flanked by upwardly curving gilded horns. The shrine records preserved the story of Sanemori's battle death and how Kiso Yoshinaka sent his lieutenant Higuchi Jiro with these relics and a prayer to this shrine.

>   "what a tragedy!"[94]
> under the captain's helmet now
>   . . . a cricket . . .

---

[94] **"what a tragedy!"**: Yoshinaka (1154–1184) was a rebellious general of the Genji, killed by Yoritomo's forces along with his trusted lieutenant Higuchi Jiro (one of his "four noble guardians").

At Nata, a temple dedicated to Kwannon, the spirit of compassion, is tucked in a fold of the foothills. With the White Mountains (Shirane-yama) behind us, we reached it by turning left on our way to some hotsprings in the mountains ahead. Emperor Kazan, retired from the world, made a pilgrimage to the thirty-three sacred temple sites before enshrining this image of Kwannon here as a perfect expression of mercy and caring.[95] It's said he named the place "Na-ta" from the first and last of the pilgrimage temple sites, the *Na* of Nachi and *Ta* of Tanagumi. The temple slope held many unusual rocks and a small reed-thatched retreat soulfully set on a stone ledge among old pines.

> Whitestone Mountain
> & more bleached still
> —autumn wind

We soaked in the mountain hot baths of Yamanaka, supposedly second in effect only to those at Ariake.

> mountain hotspring
> "life-flowers"[96] left unplucked
> in scented steam

The host there was a youngster named Kumenosuke, whose father had loved haikai[97] poetry. It's said that the Kyoto poet Teishitsu came by here as a novice and was so outclassed that he returned to Kyoto immediately to study with Master Teitoku, and that later, when he was well known and in demand as a poetry judge, he refused to take fees from people from here because of this early experience. This story has long been a part of Yamanakan folklore. Meanwhile, Sora developed stomach troubles, and so rushed off toward relatives in Nagashima in the Ise area, leaving with

> at the end, who knows?
> maybe just falling
> into bush clover
>   – SORA

With the pain of the one going and the emptiness of the one left behind, we were like wild ducks separating, each losing its partner in the clouds. Thus, my response:

---

[95] **Emperor . . . caring:** Emperor Kazan (968–1008), Japan's sixty-fourth emperor, went on his pilgrimage after being pushed into retirement. The *kannon-do* (practice hall of Kwannon) is dedicated to the goddess of compassion, source of mercy and grace.

[96] **"life-flowers":** The "flower of life," a kind of chrysanthemum, was reputed to have health-giving properties.

[97] **haikai:** See glossary. The haikai tradition featured popular poetry contests, for which Bashō had been a respected judge. At Yamanaka, apparently the young host's late father had so dramatically outdone an inexperienced visitor that the novice went immediately to study with a renowned master, eventually becoming famous himself, and forever after attributing his ultimate success to the impact of his "happy humiliation" here at the hands of the boy's late father, or so the story went.

> now autumn dew
> washes from my hat the words
> "here travelers two"[98]

The next night I stopped at the Zenshoji, the Zen temple at the edge of Daishoji castle town, still in Kaga country. Sora had stayed here only the night before, leaving this behind:

> all night long
> listening to autumn wind
> out back, the mountain
>   — SORA

"One night, yet as if a thousand leagues apart,"[99] came to mind in the same temple hall awake, also listening to mountain winds. Long before the sun, voices chanting sutras rose. When the gong sounded, I joined the gathering in the dininghall. Thinking I should reach the Echizen district that day, I was hurrying off when young monks rushed down the steps after me with pen and inkstone. Willows in the courtyard were just then losing their foliage, so I offered

> my thanks, sweeping
> a gust of willow leaves
> along the way

brushed quickly, my sandals already on and in motion.[100]

At the Echizen border, I crossed the Yoshizaki Inlet in a poled boat to the Shiogoshi Pines by the inlet shallows. *"All night long / storm-driven waves beat & break / on the wind-blown shore—/ moonlight in water streams / the Shiogoshi pines. . . ."* Attributed to Saigyo, this poem so perfectly expressed the spirit there that another line would be like a sixth finger, one too many.[101]

The elder priest of the Sky Dragon temple at Tenryuji was an old acquaintance, so I went there to renew the connection. Hokushi[102] had tagged along from Kanazawa. Not planning to come this far, yet reluctant to turn back, he ended up all the

---

[98] The dew is cousin to both clouds and tears. The words on Bashō's hat *(kasa)* were something like "here be travelers two," a favorite inscription for companions.

[99] *"One . . . apart"*: Bashō quotes an old Chinese poem about the pains of parting, "Clouds drift a thousand *li* . . . Who knows my heart's sorrow." While a *li* is about a third of a mile, the expression is used to suggest "far away." (See note 104.)

[100] The dining probably took place in silence. Guests customarily made some offering, along with some work service. Asked for a few words, Bashō playfully sweeps the path on the way out, his brushed offering.

[101] The poem quoted may not be Saigyo's after all, but one by Ren'nyo (1415–1499).

[102] Hokushi: Called "one of Bashō's top ten students" by scholars. He wrote down what Bashō said on haikai at Yamanaka, his record published in 1862.

way here. His keen eye had noted with fine poems many beautiful places along the way. On parting, I gave him:

> a farewell scribbled
> on my summer fan
> —& torn apart

Then I headed about three miles into the mountains to Eihei-ji, the Zen temple founded by Dogen.[103] Locating it so far into the mountains and *"a thousand leagues from the Capital"*[104] was no accident, but the inspired outcome of his deep attention.

With the castle town of Fukui only about a mile away, I set out after supper. Arriving there as darkness fell, I had no idea which way to take to find my friend Tosai's house. An old samurai who had turned to poetry, Tosai visited me once in Edo, but so long ago—maybe ten years—I thought he'd probably be quite old now or even dead. But on asking, I was told he was still going strong, and given directions. In a secluded lane a ways from the main road, I came finally to a rustic little cottage entangled in gourd vines and moonflowers,[105] even its door hidden by a cypress broom thicket and cockscomb left to run wild. This must be the place, I figured, and knocked. A humble little woman, just right for the house, appeared, asking, "And where did you come from, Holy Reverend? I'm afraid the master of the house is out at so-and-so's, but that's not too far away. So if you want him you can check there." She seemed to be his wife, quite wonderful really, as if out of an old story. I followed her directions straightaway, tracked him down, and ended up staying two nights at his house before setting off.

As I was leaving in time to catch the harvest moon at Tsuruga Bay, Tosai tucked up his kimono in a funny way to come along—as he put it "as a guidepost pointing your route where paths branch. . . ." With White Mountain disappearing, Hina Peak came into view. Then we continued across Asamuzu Bridge, and through the thickly seed-headed reeds of Tamae, past Bush Warbler Checkpoint, and over Hotspring Pass. By the Flint Castle ruins, near Mount Return, I heard the first wild geese announcing autumn on their way south.

On the evening of the fourteenth, the night before the full moon, we found lodging at an inn by Tsuruga Harbor. How bright the moon was. "Will it be like this tomorrow?" I wondered aloud, and the inn-keeper replied, "Who knows? Weather's so changeable here, there's no telling what clouds there might or might not be by then." So we drank warm saké and set off together for the Myojin shrine at Hehi, the early Emperor Chuai's memorial tomb.

---

[103] Dogen (1200–1253): The "Great Teacher" is regarded as a founder of the Soto Zen lineage.

[104] *"a . . . Capital"*: Dogen's temple is dedicated to spiritual progress, not worldly entanglements, thus it's so far from the capital (Kyoto, with its crowd of temples) and so far into the mountains. With echoes of an old poem, Bashō's expression suggests not just far away but in another world.

[105] moonflowers: *Yugao* in Japanese; the whole chapter overflows with echoes from the *"yugao"* chapter in *The Tale of Genji* (see Book 2).

There seemed a certain unearthly air about the place in the night silence, with moonlight through the pines turning the white sand before the stone shrine to frost. "Long ago," my host said, "the second abbot cut reed-grass, moved earth and rocks, drained a way through the marsh, and then hauled sand to ease access for pilgrims. His example became a custom continuing today of bringing sand to what is now sometimes called "the Sand-carrying Pilgrim's Shrine.""[106]

> sand carrying pilgrims
> on the way to the sand shrine
> moon illumined

And on the fifteenth, just as my host foretold it might, it rained.

> harvest moon?
> in backcountry weather
> nothing's for sure

On the sixteenth, the sky cleared again. Interested in collecting some small colored shells, we sailed to the Pink Beach at Iro,[107] more than two miles in all. A prosperous poet called Tenya something-or-other[108] brought along well-stocked lunch baskets, bamboo saké flasks, and helpers for the crossing. With a smart tailwind, we were there in no time. Along the shore were just a few fishermen's shacks and a small weather-beaten Hokke sect temple, where we sat, savoring green tea and hot saké in the overwhelming melancholy of the isolated shore at evening.

> lonelier
> than Suma Beach
> this autumn shore

> in each wave
> turning shells and
> bits of clover

I handed Tosai[109] the brush for a description of our time there, to leave at the temple.

My friend Rotsu joined us at the harbor with horses, coming with us to Mino and then to the walled castle town of Ogaki. Then Sora showed up from Ise, and Etsujin galloped in, and we all gathered together at Joko's house. Soon we were joined by Zensensi, plus Keiko and his sons, and other dear friends arriving day and

---

[106] Just as the "Yugao," moonflower, was a key element in the background of the Fukui section, here the critical term is *Yugyo*, pilgrimage, also used as both proper name for a particular sect of Buddhism and for the "sand-carrying masters" within that lineage.

[107] **Pink Beach at Iro:** This shore was famous for small pinkish *masuho*, shellfish that "stain the tides," according to a poem by Saigyo.

[108] **Tenya something-or-other:** Tenya Gorozaemon; apparently a shipper and haikai poet.

[109] **Tosai:** The "old samurai" whom Bashō joined up with in Fukui. His account of the visit is still in the temple there.

night. All greeted me with such joy and affection, it seemed as if I had just returned from the Great Beyond, and so in a way I had.[110]

Yet on the sixth day of the Long (9th) Moon, still not recovered from the fatigue of traveling, I was back in a boat again, setting off for the Futami shore on my way to the dedication rites at Ise.

> to the far shore bound
>   a clam torn from shells
>   parting . . . autumn, too[111]

[SCRIBE'S EPILOG, BY SORYU][112]

Immersed in this slender journey-book, we find such crisp simplicity and eloquent power, richness of beauty and wise insight that turning pages are like turns on *The Narrow Road* itself. One moment we rise up to applaud, the next stretch out, stirred to the core. Once, I even grabbed my coat, ready to take that same route, then sat back to draw yet more inspiration from these enchanting images in the mind's heart. What a treasure of spirit and deep reservoir of emotion we find here! Bashō is like that divine child Kojin, whose every knot in the woven net of creation is a precious vajra jewel, with all flowing through his, the master's, brush! What a pity that as seasons turn, he grows more ragged and weary, with frost and snow gathered in his brows. . . .

– by SORYU, the scribe, early summer, Genroku Seven (1694)

---

[110] The men rushing in to welcome Bashō are all considered "members of Bashō's school." Rotsu was a wandering poet, Etsujin a merchant, Joko an ex-samurai monk and poetry judge, Zensensi a high-ranking samurai of the local area, Keiko and his three sons government servants. Bashō arrived in Ogaki in early October. He was at the dedication of the outer shrine at Ise about two weeks later (the 13th day of the ninth month).

[111] Bashō seems to have intended an unusual stagger for this last poem. The poem itself is one of the hardest to translate. In it, the term *futami* has both geographical reference (to Futami Bay, an inlet famous for its clams) and various shades of its own meaning (e.g., shell-bodied or bound flesh, a jewel-inlaid lid, two views . . .). The essence of the poem has to do with parting, going separate ways: Bashō and his friends, the opening clam shells, the flesh from the shell—and autumn, too.

[112] Not every translation includes Soryu's epilog, yet it so perfectly caps the "clean copy" prepared at Bashō's request (and probably under his supervision). It also brings the final context of the work into the 1694 of its final composition, beyond the 1689 of the original journey. Bashō died that fall (on or about October 12, 1694), just a few months after the last draft was completed.

❧ CHIKAMATSU MONZAEMON
1653–1724

Often considered Japan's greatest playwright, **Chikamatsu Monzaemon** is sometimes compared to Shakespeare because of his breadth of vision and his extensive influence on theater in his culture. The comparison can be misleading, however; the Japanese theater, especially *ningyo* JORURI[1] puppet theater, now called *bunraku,* for which Chikamatsu wrote, differs fundamentally in its theatrical effects, music, stage, and performance from traditional Western theater. Relying on the combined effects of spectacle, the rhythmic pacing of the *samisen,*[2] and the varied intonation and voicing of the master chanter, the puppet plays may be compared to the earliest Greek dramas, in which a single speaker retold an incident from the Homeric tales or from familiar myths. In joruri plays, similarly, a single master chanter gives voice to all the puppets, which are manipulated by three puppet masters veiled in black costumes who remain utterly expressionless to focus attention on the nearly life-sized puppets, which seem to come alive during the performance. Like the *Nō* dramas[3] from which they evolved, joruri plays sometimes are based on great stories from classic tales, like *The Tale of Genji* or *The Tale of the Heike.*[4] Although his dramas contain numerous allusions to these works, in many of his plays Chikamatsu turned to historical characters as well as to contemporary incidents involving ordinary people. Such stories were also portrayed in the KABUKI[5] theater and in some novels. Tanizaki Junichuro's novel *Some Prefer Nettles* (1929)[6] details with fine sensitivity the importance of the puppet theater in Japanese culture and turns especially on the play selected here, *The Love Suicides at Amijima.*

chee-kah-MAH-tsoo
mawn-ZAH-eh-mawn

---

[1] *ningyo joruri:* Puppet plays developed in Japan in the seventeenth and eighteenth centuries wherein expert puppeteers manipulate lifelike dolls while a master chanter, accompanied by the samisen, sings and chants the story, speaks for the characters, and describes the scenes.

[2] *samisen:* A three-stringed instrument with a long, fretless neck and a nearly square sound box introduced in Japan in the late sixteenth century; it became the preferred instrument for accompanying the narration of joruri.

[3] *Nō dramas:* The highly elaborate and ritualistic classical theater of Japan, known for its minimalist approach to plot, scenery, and stage effects and its emphasis on the stately performance and Zen-like mastery of its actors; *Nō* means "talent" or "accomplishment."

[4] *The Tale of Genji* (*Genji Monogatari,* c. 1001–13): This novel of more than one thousand pages, recounting the adventures of the shining prince Genji, was written by Murasaki Shikibu (c. 978–1031), one of the great Japanese novelists. *The Tale of the Heike:* (*Heike Monogatari,* 1371) Recounts events of the Minamoto-Tairo (Heike) wars, which took place in the middle of the twelfth century. (See Book 2.)

[5] *Kabuki:* A form of popular Japanese drama using live, male actors that is primarily aimed at the middle classes.

[6] *Tanizaki Junichiro* (1886–1965): One of modern Japan's most prolific and acclaimed writers; the author of many short stories and novels, including the novel *Some Prefer Nettles* (1929), whose main character, Kaname, attempts to find spiritual renewal in the classical puppet theater. (See Tanizaki, Book 6.)

Fascination with the Puppet Theater.   Sugimore Nobumori, who later took the pen name Chikamatsu Monzaemon, was born in 1653 in Echizen (now Fukui prefecture), Japan. Sometime between 1664 and 1670, when Chikamatsu was in his teens, his father gave up his duties as a samurai and moved the family to Kyoto where Chikamatsu served as an attendant to an aristocratic family. In 1671 some of his poems appeared in a family album collected by the poet Yamaoka Genrin (1631–1672), with whom Chikamatsu studied HAIKAI and the Japanese classics. In Kyoto, Chikamatsu may have met the master chanter Uji Kaganojo, for whose puppet theater he wrote his first acclaimed play, *The Soga Heir* (*Yotsugi Soga*, 1683). While some scholars believe Chikamatsu had written earlier plays for the *ningyo joruri*, or puppet theater, *The Soga Heir* was his first major achievement in this genre, breaking out of the traditional plot lines of previous joruri written about the Soga family. Chikamatsu's play was so popular that in 1684 the master chanter Takemoto Gidayu (1651–1714) chose it for the opening debut of his theater in Osaka. With *Kagekiyo Victorious* (*Shusse Kagekiyo*, 1686), a play relatively neglected in its own time, Chikamatsu continued to innovate, abandoning the conventional language of earlier plays and giving characters more psychological depth.

The Kabuki Era.   In 1684 Chikamatsu wrote a play for live theater, or Kabuki, entitled *The Seventh Anniversary of Yugiri's Death* (*Yugir Shyichinen Ki*). In the years that followed he wrote many more Kabuki plays, especially for Sakata Tojuro (1647–1709), one of the great Kabuki actors. From about 1688 to 1703 Chikamatsu wrote primarily for the Kabuki theater, becoming in 1695 the official playwright of Tojuro's theater in Kyoto. In 1703, while visiting Osaka, Chikamatsu heard about the double suicide of two lovers, a shopkeeper's assistant and a courtesan. Within three weeks his dramatized version of the story was performed as a joruri play, the first *shinju*[7] or suicide play of that genre ever performed. *The Love Suicides at Sonezaki* (*Sonezaki Shinju*, 1703) would eventually establish Chikamatsu as one of the world's great dramatists and was the first of many shinju plays he wrote. Like his contemporary Ihara Saikaku, Chikamatsu transformed the lives of townspeople, the *chonin*, into art and gave everyday events a dramatic character that elevated the ordinary to the tragic.

The Playwright in Osaka.   When Tojuro, Chikamatsu's favored actor, retired in about 1706, Chikamatsu returned to the Takemoto theater in Osaka, then under the direction of Takeda Izumo (d. 1747), and focused his considerable energies on joruri plays. Contributing to the introduction of more elaborate stage machinery, more spectacular sets, and more intricate manipulation of the puppets, Chikamatsu continued writing joruri for the rest of his life, producing more than one hundred plays in all three genres: the *jidaimono*, or history play, with work such as *The Battles of Coxinga* (*Kokusenya Kassen*, 1715); the *sewamono*, or play of contemporary domestic life, with dramas such as *The Uprooted Pine* (*Nebiki no Kado-*

---

[7] *shinju:* One of the three major types of joruri plays; in this case a play culminating in suicide.

Nishikawa Sukeyuki, *Activities of Twelve Months of the Year*
Kabuki theater was a mainstay of Tokugawa public life. Outdoor theaters and performances were quite common. (Freer Gallery of Art, Smithsonian Institution, Washington, D.C. Gift of Victor and Takako Hauge, F1991.53)

matsu, 1718); and shinju, or suicide plays, such as his masterpiece, *The Love Suicides at Amijima* (*Shinju Ten no Amijima,* 1721). On November 22, 1724, Chikamatsu, Japan's greatest master of the joruri, died in Osaka.

Joruri and Kabuki Theater.   With the rise of the chonin, theater flourished during Chikamatsu's lifetime. Addressing the interests and tastes of the Japanese middle classes, Chikamatsu was one of the first dramatists in world literature to take up the lives of ordinary men and women as material worthy of formal treatment in tragedies. He wrote plays in both of the popular dramatic forms of the Tokugawa era: the Kabuki and the ningyo joruri. Whereas live actors perform on stage in Kabuki, joruri uses puppets. While classical and formal *Nō* plays were still being performed in exclusive venues such as the Imperial Court, widespread enthusiasm in the seventeenth century for Kabuki and joruri led to the opening of public theaters in Edo, Kyoto, and, especially, the commercial city of Osaka; many of these theaters were located in the pleasure districts. Both Kabuki and joruri plays drew upon the domestic life of the chonin for their stories and backgrounds. Though they borrowed some elements from the courtly *Nō* dramas, the language, manners, and characters of these new plays reflected the taste and spirit of shopkeepers, traders, artisans, accountants, prostitutes, and actors, whose prosperity and activity transformed all aspects of Japanese culture during the Tokugawa era. Kabuki audiences were primarily from the chonin, but joruri was popular among all classes.

www   For links to more information about Monzaemon and a quiz on *The Love Suicides at Amijima,* see *World Literature Online* at bedfordstmartins .com/worldlit.

The live performances of Kabuki depended on the charm and talent as well as the sex appeal of the actors. Like moviegoers today, theater audiences cultivated a kind of hero worship for Kabuki actors, in spite of the official condemnation of the theater. Moreover, because actors and actresses were associated early on with sexual misconduct, after 1629 Japanese women were not allowed to perform on stage, as was the case in English theater during Shakespeare's time. Many male actors won high acclaim for their impersonation of female characters, a phenomenon touched on in the opening pages of Saikaku's **"What the Seasons Brought to the Almanac Maker."** In the performance of a joruri play, a chanter, accompanied by a musician playing the samisen, voiced all the roles, narrated the events, and described the scenery as puppet masters manipulated elaborately carved and decorated puppets. Given the parallels between Kabuki and joruri, some puppets were actually modeled in ways that exaggerated striking features of famous live actors. Conversely, Kabuki actors would sometimes imitate the stiff movements of puppets. This exchange between the puppets and the real actors reflects the subtle play between fiction and reality in joruri itself. Chikamatsu exploited the possibilities of the puppet theater, brilliantly negotiating what he called "the slender margin between the real and the unreal." The high and exaggerated artifice of the puppets gratified the audience's demand for theatricality, while the illusion of realism fulfilled their expectations for plausible action. In describing his work, Chikamatsu observed that "one attempts first to describe facts as they really are, but in so doing one writes things which are not true, in the interest of art."

The Love Suicides at Amijima.   This story of a man, his wife, and a courtesan exemplifies relationships that were fairly common among the chonin in Chikamatsu's day, partly because marriages were arranged by parents and because society condoned relationships outside of marriage so long as they were limited to courtesans. The courtesans, like **Koharu**, were not just sexual partners but often well educated and culturally sophisticated women who offered middle-class men polite conversation, partnership, and a sense of class that they would not necessarily find in their everyday routines or in their marriages.

In a few cases a townsman and his courtesan would fall in love; such is the case with Chikamatsu's Jihei and Koharu. Nonetheless, even those who fell in love and hoped to redeem a courtesan from her employer and make her his concubine, or mistress, were expected to maintain their families in good standing. **Jihei**, caught in the net of passion, has neglected and nearly bankrupted both his household and his business in order to pay for his visits to Koharu. Although his wife seems to accept Jihei's behavior, her father, **Gozaemon**, is outraged and threatens to break up the marriage. In the meantime, a rival, **Tahei**, threatens to buy out Koharu's contract and make her his concubine, thus ending the relationship between the courtesan and Jihei. Because Jihei cannot afford to challenge Tahei and claim Koharu for his own concubine, he and Koharu turn to suicide as the only means to resolve their dilemma and preserve their relationship in the afterlife.

p. 635

koh-HAH-roo

JEE-hay

goh-ZAH-eh-mawn
TAH-hay

Duty and Desire.   Jihei faces a classic dilemma of tragedy known in both the East and West: the conflicting pulls of duty and personal desire. The Japanese define this opposition as one between *giri,* duty and social responsibility, and *ninjo,* human feelings and passion. Koharu, too, is bound by *giri,* which would demand that she give up Jihei to his wife. Thus, in the final scenes of Act III, Jihei and Koharu undertake the *michi-yuki,*[8] the symbolic journey from Osaka to **Amijima**, where they commit *shinju,* ritual love suicide, with the belief that they will be reborn in the Pure Land of the Amida Buddha, where they can renew their bonds. Critic Donald Shively explains that Chikamatsu "made the most of the tradition of popular Buddhism, derived from the Lotus Sutra,[9] that lovers who died together would be reborn on the same lotus calyx on the lake before Amida's throne in the Western Paradise." As Koharu says in Act III, "What have we to grieve about? Though in this world we could not stay together, in the next and through each successive world to come until the end of time we shall be husband and wife." Yet even in their preparations for death, the lovers consider their *giri* to Osan and so determine to die apart to minimize their offense to her.

ah-mee-JEE-mah

The play is steeped in literary allusions and Buddhist symbolism that many Western readers will miss, even with heavy annotations. In Act III, as the lovers make their *michiyuki,* or farewell journey, they pass over six bridges, each symbolizing the threshold into a new world. The journey involves a symbolic passage into the Buddhist underworld, a descent that must take place before the lovers can cross the Onari bridge (a bridge whose name suggests "to become Buddha") onto the "other shore" (nirvana) of Amijima, where they will die. *Ami* ("net") in the play's title alludes to two doctrines: the karmic "Heaven's net" of Chapter 73 of the Dao De Jing (Tao Te Ching)[10] ("Heaven's net is wide; coarse are the meshes, yet nothing slips through") and the net of redemption offered by Amida Nyorai — the Amida Buddha. Thus, the suffering that results from Jihei's and Koharu's actions leaves open the possibility for an eventual life of bliss in the next world.

> Chikamatsu's plays offer . . . a vivid picture of a unique age in Japan, and have a special importance among the dramas of the world in that they constitute the first mature tragedies written about the common man.
>
> – Critic DONALD KEENE, 1961

■ CONNECTIONS

Dante, *The Divine Comedy* (Book 3).   *The Love Suicides at Amijima* dramatizes a love triangle involving Jihei, his lover Koharu, and Jihei's wife, Osan. To transcend their worldly responsibilities, Jihei and Koharu perform a ritual love suicide, *shinju,* in the belief that they will be forever united in the Western Paradise under the grace of Amidha Buddha. Though graphically violent, the love suicide is treated as a digni-

---

[8] *michiyuki:* A convention in Japanese literature wherein the places characters travel suggest spiritual transformation by means of symbolism and allusion.

[9] Lotus Sutra: One of the key texts of Mahayana or "Great Wheel" Buddhism; it uses parables and poetic examples to illustrate the major doctrines of Mahayana Buddhism, including the belief in individual salvation and the Buddha-essence of all sentient beings.

[10] Dao De Jing (Tao Te Ching) (third century B.C.E.): One of the founding texts of Daoism, often attributed to Laozi (Lao-Tze). Daoism is a Chinese religious philosophy that seeks withdrawal from the world and unity with nature; the dao, or Way, suggests harmonizing human and natural forces and processes. (See Book 1.)

fied act. In Canto 5 of Dante's *Inferno*, Dante comes across Paulo and Francesca, whose adulterous love affair has tragically condemned them to the second circle of Hell; in Canto 6 those who have taken their own lives are condemned to punishment in the Wood of Suicides in circle seven, one of the deepest circles of Hell. Compare Dante's view of adultery and suicide with Chikamatsu's in the context of their respective cultures and religions.

Ihara Saikaku, "What the Seasons Brought to the Almanac Maker," p. 635. Chikamatsu's play, like Saikaku's short story, invokes the floating world of the officially sanctioned pleasure districts and their networks of romantic intrigue. Both "What the Seasons Brought to the Almanac Maker" and *The Love Suicides at Amijima* were based on true stories about married men who fell in love with courtesans. In both, the lovers vow to break their ties to family and be together; in the first case, concealing their identities after faking *shinju*, and in the second, actually committing *shinju*. How is Chikamatsu's treatment of adultery and shinju different from Saikaku's and which story more successfully engages your sympathy?

Mori Ogai, "The Dancing Girl" (Book 5). Many dramas involve a love triangle. Between Jihei and Koharu, whose love for each other becomes quite strong, stands Osan, who, along with her father, represents the world of economic and domestic responsibilities. In Ogai's "The Dancing Girl," Ota falls in love with a German dancer, Elise, only to be pulled away from her by Count Amataka, who similarly stands for responsibility, in this case loyalty to country. Despite these parallels, the two dramas end quite differently, one with the promise of salvation and the other with a kind of resignation. Consider the different outcomes of these two tales. Might Ogai's conclusion be linked to the cultural and historical changes that took place in nineteenth-century Japan?

■ FURTHER RESEARCH

Cultural Background
Adachi, Barbara. *Voices and Hands of Bunraku.* 1978.
Keene, Donald. *Bunraku, the Art of the Japanese Puppet Theater.* 1965.
————. *Worlds within Walls: Japanese Literature of the Pre-Modern Era, 1600–1867.* 1976.

Criticism
Gerstle, C. Andrew. *Circles of Fantasy: Convention in the Plays of Chikamatsu.* 1986.
Keene, Donald, ed. Introduction to *Major Plays of Chikamatsu.* 1961.
Shively, Donald H. *The Love Suicides at Amijima: A Study of a Japanese Domestic Tragedy.* 1953.

■ PRONUNCIATION

Amijima: ah-mee-JEE-mah
Chikamatsu Monzaemon: chee-kah-MAH-tsoo mawn-ZAH-eh-mawn
Dembei: DEM-bay
Gozaemon: goh-ZAH-eh-mawn
Kamiya Jihei: KAH-mee-yah JEE-hay
Kantarō: kahn-TAH-roh
Koharu: koh-HAH-roo
Konaya Magoemon: koh-NAH-yah mah-GOH-eh-mawn
Osue: oh-SOO-eh
Sangorō: sahng-GOH-roh
Sugi: SOO-gee
Tahei: TAH-hay
Tama: TAH-mah

✺ The Love Suicides at Amijima

Translated by Donald Keene

CAST OF CHARACTERS

KAMIYA JIHEI, *aged 28, a paper merchant*
KONAYA MAGOEMON, *his brother, a flour merchant*
GOZAEMON, *Jihei's father-in-law*
TAHEI, *a rival for Koharu*
DEMBEI, *proprietor of the Yamato House*
SANGORŌ, *Jihei's servant*
KANTARŌ, *aged 6, Jihei's son*
A MINSTREL PRIEST
PORTERS, FISHERMEN, PERSONS OF THE QUARTER

KOHARU, *aged 19, a courtesan at the Kinokuni House in Sonezaki*
OSAN, *Jihei's wife*
OSAN'S MOTHER (*who is also Jihei's aunt*), *aged 56*
OSUE, *aged 4, Jihei's daughter*
PROPRIETRESS *at Kawachi House*
KIYO, *a receptionist*
TAMA, *Osan's servant*
SUGI, *Koharu's maid*
MAIDS, PROSTITUTES, SERVANTS

ACT I

Scene 1

A street in Sonezaki New Quarter, Osaka.
TIME: *November 4, 1720.*

NARRATOR:

> *Sanjō bakkara fungoro nokkoro*
> *Chokkoro fungoro de*
> *Mate tokkoro wakkara yukkuru*
> *Wakkara yukkuru ta ga*
> *Kasa wo wanga ranga ra su*
> *Sora ga kunguru kunguru mo*
> *Renge rengere bakkara fungoro.*[1]

The love of a prostitute is deep beyond measure; it's a bottomless sea of affection that cannot be emptied or dried. By Shell River,[2] love songs in every

---

The Love Suicides at Amijima. This *shinju*, or suicide play, was written during Chikamatsu's late period, which ran from 1715, the date of the great history play *The Battles of Coxinga*, to 1724, when the playwright died. It tells the story of Kamiya Jihei, a paper merchant caught in a love triangle between Koharu, a young indentured courtesan whom he has met in the Sonezaki pleasure quarters of Osaka, and Osan, his wife. Focusing on Jihei's conflict between his duty to his family and business and his love for Koharu, *The Love Suicides at Amijima* presents a familiar struggle between two contradictory value systems—that of the individual and that of society. Although the play resolves itself tragically in a joint suicide, the promise of Buddhist salvation suggests that the outcome may actually be positive; the lovers believe they will be reunited in the Western Paradise that awaits them after death.

A note on the translation: The following text was translated by the renowned Donald Keene, translator, scholar, and historian of Japanese literature. All notes are adapted from the translator's.

---

[1] *Sanjō . . . fungoro:* Scholars have been unable to discover the meaning of these rhythmic lines.
[2] **Shell River:** The Shijimi River bordering Sonezaki Quarter.

mood fill the air, and hearts stop short at the barrier of doorway lanterns. Men roam the streets in high spirits, humming snatches of puppet plays, mimicking the actors, or singing bawdy ballads as they pass; others are drawn into the houses by samisens played in upstairs rooms. But here is a visitor who hides his face, avoiding the gift day.[3] See how he creeps along, afraid to be forced into spending too much!

Kiyo, the receptionist, notices him.

KIYO: Who's this trying to avoid me?

NARRATOR: She snatches again and again at his hood-flap; he dodges her twice or thrice, but this is a valuable customer, and she refuses to let him escape. At last she pounces on him with the cry:

KIYO: No more of your nonsense! Come along!

NARRATOR: And the customer, caught flap and cap, is trapped into folly by this female Kagekiyo.

Among the flowers on display—even the bridges are called Plum and Cherry Blossom[4]—here is Koharu of the Kinokuni House, now graduated from the smock of a bath attendant in the South to the garments of love in the New Quarter.[5] Is her name "Second Spring" a sign that she is fated to leave behind a fleeting name in November?

"Who has sent for me tonight?" she wonders, uncertain as a dove in the uncertain light of a standing lantern. A prostitute passes her, then turns back.

PROSTITUTE: Is that you, Koharu? Where have you been keeping yourself? We don't get invited to the same parties anymore, and I never see you or hear a word from you. Have you been sick? Your face looks thinner. Somebody was telling me that the master at your place now gives all your customers a thorough examination and hardly lets you out of the house, all on account of your Kamiji.[6] But I've also heard that you're to be ransomed by Tahei and go live with him in the country—in Itami, was it? Is it true?

KOHARU: I'd be much obliged if you'd please stop talking about Itami! The relations between Jihei and myself, I'm sorry to say, are not as close as people suppose. It's that loud-mouthed Tahei who's started the rumors and spread them everywhere, until every last customer has deserted me. The master blames Kamiya Jihei, and he's done everything to keep us from meeting. Why, I'm not even allowed to receive letters from Jihei. Tonight, strangely enough, I've been sent to Kawashō. My customer's a samurai, I'm told. But I keep worrying that I might meet that dreadful Tahei on the way. I feel exactly as if I had some mortal enemy. Do you suppose he might be over there?

PROSTITUTE: If you feel that way about Tahei, you'd better hide quickly. Look—coming out of the first block—there's one of those street minstrels, singing his

---

[3] **gift day:** Days when customers in the Pleasure Quarters gave presents to proprietors of the teahouses.

[4] **Plum . . . Blossom:** Umeda and Sakura Bridges over the Shijimi.

[5] **South . . . Quarter:** The Shimanouchi and Sonezaki Quarters, respectively.

[6] **Kamiji:** That is, Kamiya Jihei.

nonsense hymns. I can see in the crowd round him a dissolute-looking fellow with his hair tricked up in some funny style—the stuck-up swell! I'm sure it's Tahei. Oh—they're heading this way!

NARRATOR: A moment later the defrocked priest, in a flat cap and ink-black robes with the sleeves tucked back, comes bumbling along, surrounded by a crowd of idlers. He bangs at random on his bell, mixing his nonsense with the burden of a hymn.

MINSTREL:

> *"Fan Kuai's[7] style was no great shakes—*
> *See how Asahina of Japan used to break down gates!"*
> *He rips through the gate bars and tangle of felled trees,*
> *Slays Uryōko and Saryōko and passes the barrier, As time passes by.*
> *Namamida Namaida Namamida Namaida.*
> *Ei Ei Ei Ei Ei.*
> *"Though I wander all over,*
> *The sad world holds no one*
> *Who looks like my dear Matsuyama!"*
> *—He weeps, he howls, only to burst into laughs.*
> *"How wretched that I must end my life in madness!"*
> *He falls prostrate, the grass for his pallet,*
> *A sight too sad for the eyes to behold.*
> *Namamida Namaida Namamida Namaida.*
> *Ei Ei Ei Ei Ei.*
> *Tokubei of the dyer's shop,*
> *Since he first fell in love with Fusa,*
> *Has yielded to passion that absorbs his fortune,*
> *A love stained so deep lye itself cannot cleanse it.*
> *Namamida Namaida Namamida Namaida*
> *Namamida Namaida.*

SUGI: Excuse me, priest.

MINSTREL: What is it?

SUGI: It's bad luck to sing those songs, just when stories about love suicides in the Quarter have at last quieted down. Why don't you give us instead a *nembutsu* song on the journey from *The Battles of Coxinga*?[8]

NARRATOR: Sugi offers him some coins from her sleeve.

MINSTREL:

> For a mere one or two coppers
> You can't expect to travel all the way,

---

[7] The characters the minstrel refers to in his song are historical and fictional figures who play important roles in Chikamatsu's earlier plays.

[8] *The Battles of Coxinga:* Chikamatsu's most popular play, a history play first performed in 1715.

Three thousand leagues to the Land of Great Ming!
It doesn't pay, it doesn't pray Amida Buddha.[9]
NARRATOR: Grumbling in this strain, he moves on.

Scene 2

The Kawachi House, a Sonezaki teahouse.

NARRATOR: Koharu slips away, under cover of the crowd, and hurries into the Kawachi House.

PROPRIETRESS: Well, well, I hadn't expected you so soon. — It's been ages even since I've heard your name mentioned. What a rare visitor you are, Koharu! And what a long time it's been!

NARRATOR: The proprietress greets Koharu cheerfully.

KOHARU: Oh — you can be heard as far as the gate. Please don't call me Koharu in such a loud voice. That horrible Ri Tōten[10] is out there. I beg you, keep your voice down.

NARRATOR: Were her words overheard? In bursts a party of three men.

TAHEI: I must thank you first of all, dear Koharu, for bestowing a new name on me, Ri Tōten. I never was called *that* before. Well, friends, this is the Koharu I've confided to you about — the good-hearted, good-natured, good-in-bed Koharu. Step up and meet the whore who's started all the rivalry! Will I soon be the lucky man and get Koharu for my wife? Or will Kamiya Jihei ransom her?

NARRATOR: He swaggers up.

KOHARU: I don't want to hear another word. If you think it's such an achievement to start unfounded rumors about someone you don't even know, throw yourself into it, say what you please. But I don't want to hear.

NARRATOR: She steps away suddenly, but he sidles up again.

TAHEI: You may not want to hear me, but the clink of my gold coins will make you listen! What a lucky girl you are! Just think — of all the many men in Temma and the rest of Osaka, you chose Jihei the paper dealer, the father of two children, with his cousin for his wife and his uncle for his father-in-law! A man whose business is so tight he's at his wits' ends every sixty days merely to pay the wholesalers' bills! Do you think he'll be able to fork over nearly ten *kamme*[11] to ransom you? That reminds me of the mantis who picked a fight with an oncoming vehicle! But look at me — I haven't a wife, a father-in-law, a father, or even an uncle, for that matter. Tahei the Lone Wolf — that's the name I'm known by. I admit that I'm no match for Jihei when it comes to bragging about myself in the

---

[9] **the Land of Great Ming:** China. **Amida Buddha:** The Buddha of Infinite Life and Light; the central deity of Pure Land or Jōdo Buddhism, which maintains that invoking the name of Buddha leads to rebirth in the Western Paradise.

[10] **Ri Tōten:** The antagonist in *The Battles of Coxinga*.

[11] *kamme:* Worth 1,000 *momme* of silver; one *momme* was worth 3.75 grams of silver. As the play indicates, ten *kamme* was considered to be a lot of money.

Quarter, but when it comes to money, I'm an easy winner. If I pushed with all the strength of my money, who knows what I might conquer?—How about it, men?—Your customer tonight, I'm sure, is none other than Jihei, but I'm taking over. The Lone Wolf's taking over. Hostess! Bring on the saké! On with the saké!

PROPRIETRESS: What are you saying? Her customer tonight is a samurai, and he'll be here any moment. Please amuse yourself elsewhere.

NARRATOR: But Tahei's look is playful.

TAHEI: A customer's a customer, whether he's a samurai or a townsman. The only difference is that one wears swords and the other doesn't. But even if this samurai wears his swords he won't have five or six—there'll only be two, the broadsword and dirk. I'll take care of the samurai and borrow Koharu afterwards. [*To* KOHARU.] You may try to avoid me all you please, but some special connection from a former life must have brought us together. I owe everything to that ballad-singing priest—what a wonderful thing the power of prayer is! I think I'll recite a prayer of my own. Here, this ashtray will be my bell, and my pipe the hammer. This is fun.

> Chan Chan Cha Chan Chan.
> Ei Ei Ei Ei Ei.
> *Jihei the paper dealer—*
> *Too much love for Koharu*
> *Has made him a foolscap,*
> *He wastepapers sheets of gold*
> *Till his fortune's shredded to confetti*
> *And Jihei himself is like scrap paper*
> *You can't even blow your nose on!*
> *Hail, Hail Amida Buddha!*
> Namaida Namaida Namaida.

NARRATOR: As he prances wildly, roaring his song, a man appears at the gate, so anxious not to be recognized that he wears, even at night, a wicker hat.

TAHEI: Well, Toilet paper's showed up! That's quite a disguise! Why don't you come in, Toilet paper? If my prayer's frightened you, say a Hail Amida! Here, I'll take off your hat!

NARRATOR: He drags the man in and examines him: It is the genuine article, a two-sworded samurai, somber in dress and expression, who glares at Tahei through his woven hat, his eyeballs round as gongs. Tahei, unable to utter either a Hail or an Amida, gasps "Haaa!" in dismay, but his face is unflinching.

TAHEI: Koharu, I'm a townsman. I've never worn a sword, but I've lots of New Silver[12] at my place, and I think that the glint could twist a mere couple of swords out of joint. Imagine that wretch from the toilet paper shop, with a capital as thin as tissue, trying to compete with the Lone Wolf! That's the height of impertinence! I'll

---

[12] New Silver: Coins of high value.

wander down now from Sakura Bridge to Middle Street, and if I meet that Wastepaper along the way, I'll trample him under foot. Come on, men.

NARRATOR: Their gestures, at least, have a cavalier assurance as they swagger off, taking up the whole street.

      The samurai customer patiently endures the fool, indifferent to his remarks because of the surroundings, but every word of gossip about Jihei, whether for good or ill, affects Koharu. She is so depressed that she stands there blankly, unable even to greet her guest. Sugi, the maid from the Kinokuni House, runs up from home, looking annoyed.

SUGI: When I left you here a while ago, Miss Koharu, your guest hadn't appeared yet, and they gave me a terrible scolding when I got back for not having checked on him. I'm very sorry, sir, but please excuse me a minute.

NARRATOR: She lifts the woven hat and examines the face.

SUGI: Oh—it's not him! There's nothing to worry about, Koharu. Ask your guest to keep you for the whole night, and show him how sweet you can be. Give him a barrelful of nectar! Good-by, madam, I'll see you later, honey.

NARRATOR: She takes her leave with a cloying stream of puns. The extremely hard-baked samurai is furious.

SAMURAI: What's the meaning of this? You'd think from the way she appraised my face that I was a tea canister or a porcelain cup! I didn't come here to be trifled with. It's difficult enough for me to leave the Residence even by day, and in order to spend the night away I had to ask the senior officer's permission and sign the register. You can see how complicated the regulations make things. But I'm in love, miss, just from hearing about you, and I wanted very badly to spend a night with you. I came here a while ago without an escort and made the arrangements with the teahouse. I had been looking forward to your kind reception, a memory to last me a lifetime, but you haven't so much as smiled at me or said a word of greeting. You keep your head down, as if you were counting money in your lap. Aren't you afraid of getting a stiff neck? Madam—I've never heard the like. Here I come to a teahouse, and I must play the part of night nurse in a maternity room!

PROPRIETRESS: You're quite right, sir. Your surprise is entirely justified, considering that you don't know the reasons. This girl is deeply in love with a customer named Kamiji. It's been Kamiji today and Kamiji tomorrow, with nobody else allowed a chance at her. Her other customers have scattered in every direction, like leaves in a storm. When two people get so carried away with each other, it often leads to trouble, for both the customer and the girl. In the first place, it interferes with business, and the owner, whoever he may be, is bound to prevent it. That's why all her guests are examined. Koharu is naturally depressed—it's only to be expected. You are annoyed, which is equally to be expected. But, speaking as the proprietress here, it seems to me that the essential thing is for you to meet each other halfway and cheer up. Come, have a drink.—Act a little more lively, Koharu.

NARRATOR: Koharu, without answering, lifts her tear-stained face.

KOHARU: Tell me, samurai, they say that, if you're going to kill yourself anyway, people who die during the Ten Nights[13] are sure to become Buddhas. Is that really true?

SAMURAI: How should I know? Ask the priest at your family temple.

KOHARU: Yes, that's right. But there's something I'd like to ask a samurai. If you're committing suicide, it'd be a lot more painful, wouldn't it, to cut your throat rather than hang yourself?

SAMURAI: I've never tried cutting my throat to see whether or not it hurt. Please ask more sensible questions. — What an unpleasant girl!

NARRATOR: Samurai though he is, he looks nonplussed.

PROPRIETRESS: Koharu, that's a shocking way to treat a guest the first time you meet him. I'll go and get my husband. We'll have some saké together. That ought to liven things a bit.

NARRATOR: The gate she leaves is illumined by the evening moon low in the sky; the clouds and the passers in the street have thinned.

For long years there has lived in Temma, the seat of the mighty god,[14] though not a god himself, Kamiji, a name often bruited by the gongs of worldly gossip, so deeply, hopelessly, is he tied to Koharu by the ropes of an ill-starred love. Now is the tenth moon, the month when no gods will unite them;[15] they are thwarted in their love, unable to meet. They swore in the last letters they exchanged that if only they could meet, that day would be their last. Night after night Jihei, ready for death, trudges to the Quarter, distractedly, as though his soul had left a body consumed by the fires of love.

At a roadside eating stand he hears people gossiping about Koharu. "She's at Kawashō with a samurai customer," someone says, and immediately Jihei decides, "It will be tonight!"

He peers through the latticework window and sees a guest in the inside room, his face obscured by a hood. Only the moving chin is visible, and Jihei cannot hear what is said.

JIHEI: Poor Koharu! How thin her face is! She keeps it averted from the lamp. In her heart she's thinking only of me. I'll signal her that I'm here, and we'll run off together. Then which will it be — Umeda or Kitano?[16] Oh — I want to tell her I'm here. I want to call her.

NARRATOR: He beckons with his heart, his spirit flies to her, but his body, like a cicada's cast-off shell, clings to the latticework. He weeps with impatience.

The guest in the inside room gives a great yawn.

---

[13] **Ten Nights:** A period from the sixth to the fifteenth of the tenth month during which Pure Land ceremonies were held; a popular saying suggested that those who died during this time would attain immediate salvation.

[14] **Temma . . . god:** Tenjin Shrine was located in Temma, one of the three major districts of Osaka; Temma Tenjin was one of the guardian deities of Osaka.

[15] **Now . . . them:** In the tenth month all the gods assembled at Izumo, leaving the god of marriage absent from Osaka.

[16] **Umeda or Kitano:** Places north and east of Sonezaki with well-known cemeteries; both names are associated with the god Temma Tenjin.

SAMURAI: What a bore, playing nursemaid to a prostitute with worries on her mind! —
The street seems quiet now. Let's go to the end room. We can at least distract
ourselves by looking at the lanterns. Come with me.

NARRATOR: They go together to the outer room. Jihei, alarmed, squeezes into the
patch of shadow under the lattice window. Inside they do not realize that anyone eavesdrops.

SAMURAI: I've been noticing your behavior and the little things you've said this
evening. It's plain to me that you intend a love suicide with Kamiji, or whatever
his name is—the man the hostess mentioned. I'm sure I'm right. I realize that
no amount of advice or reasoning is likely to penetrate the ears of somebody
bewitched by the god of death, but I must say that you're exceedingly foolish.
The boy's family won't blame him for his recklessness, but they will blame and
hate you. You'll be shamed by the public exposure of your body. Your parents
may be dead, for all I know, but if they're alive, you'll be punished in hell as a
wicked daughter. Do you suppose that you'll become a Buddha? You and your
lover won't even be able to fall smoothly into hell together! What a pity—and
what a tragedy! This is only our first meeting but, as a samurai, I can't let you die
without trying to save you. No doubt money's the problem. I'd like to help, if
five or ten *ryō*[17] would be of service. I swear by the god Hachiman[18] and by my
good fortune as a samurai that I will never reveal to anyone what you tell me.
Open your heart without fear.

NARRATOR: He whispers these words. She joins her hands and bows.

KOHARU: I'm extremely grateful. Thank you for your kind words and for swearing an
oath to me, someone you've never had for a lover or even a friend. I'm so grateful that I'm crying. — Yes, it's as they say, when you've something on your mind
it shows on your face. You were right. I have promised Kamiji to die with him.
But we've been completely prevented from meeting by my master, and Jihei, for
various reasons, can't ransom me at once. My contracts with my former master
and my present one still have five years to run. If somebody else claimed me
during that time, it would be a blow to me, of course, but a worse disgrace to
Jihei's honor. He suggested that it would be better if we killed ourselves, and I
agreed. I was caught by obligations from which I could not withdraw, and I
promised him before I knew what I was doing. I said, "We'll watch for a chance,
and I'll slip out when you give the signal." "Yes," he said, "slip out somehow."
Ever since then I've been leading a life of uncertainty, never knowing from one
day to the next when my last hour will come.

I have a mother living in a back alley south of here. She has no one but me
to depend on, and she does piecework to eke out a living. I keep thinking that
after I'm dead she'll become a beggar or an outcast, and maybe she'll die of starvation. That's the only sad part about dying. I have just this one life. I'm
ashamed that you may think me a coldhearted woman, but I must endure the
shame. The most important thing is that I don't want to die. I beg you, please
help me to stay alive.

---

[17] *ryō:* Gold pieces.   [18] Hachiman: A god of war and protector of warriors.

NARRATOR: As she speaks the samurai nods thoughtfully. Jihei, crouching outside, hears her words with astonishment; they are so unexpected to his manly heart that he feels like a monkey who has tumbled from a tree. He is frantic with agitation.

JIHEI [*to himself*]: Then was everything a lie? Ahhh—I'm furious! For two whole years I've been bewitched by that rotten she-fox! Shall I break in and kill her with one blow of my sword? Or shall I satisfy my anger by shaming her to her face?

NARRATOR: He gnashes his teeth and weeps in chagrin. Inside the house Koharu speaks through her tears.

KOHARU: It's a curious thing to ask, but would you please show the kindness of a samurai and become my customer for the rest of this year and into next spring? Whenever Jihei comes, intent on death, please interfere and force him to postpone and postpone his plan. In this way our relations can be broken quite naturally. He won't have to kill himself, and my life will also be saved.—What evil connection from a former existence made us promise to die? How I regret it now!

NARRATOR: She weeps, leaning on the samurai's knee.

SAMURAI: Very well, I'll do as you ask. I think I can help you.—But there's a draft blowing. Somebody may be watching.

NARRATOR: He slams shut the latticework *shōji*.[19] Jihei, listening outside, is in a frenzy.

JIHEI: Exactly what you'd expect from a whore, a cheap whore! I misjudged her foul nature. She robbed the soul from my body, the thieving harlot! Shall I slash her down or run her through? What am I to do?

NARRATOR: The shadows of two profiles fall on the *shōji*.

JIHEI: I'd like to give her a taste of my fist and trample her.—What are they chattering about? See how they nod to each other! Now she's bowing to him, whispering and sniveling. I've tried to control myself—I've pressed my chest, I've stroked it—but I can't stand any more. This is too much to endure!

NARRATOR: His heart pounds wildly as he unsheathes his dirk, a Magoroku of Seki. "Koharu's side must be here," he judges, and stabs through an opening in the latticework. But Koharu is too far away for his thrust, and though she cries out in terror, she remains unharmed. Her guest instantly leaps at Jihei, grabs his hands, and jerks them through the latticework. With his sword knot he quickly and securely fastens Jihei's hands to the window upright.

SAMURAI: Don't make any outcry, Koharu. You are not to look at him.

NARRATOR: At this moment the proprietor and his wife return. They exclaim in alarm.

SAMURAI: This needn't concern you. Some ruffian ran his sword through the *shōji*, and I've tied his arms to the latticework. I have my own way of dealing with him. Don't untie the cord. If you attract a crowd, the place is sure to be thrown in an uproar. Let's all go inside. Come with me, Koharu. We'll go to bed.

NARRATOR: Koharu answers, "Yes," but she recognizes the handle of the dirk, and the memory—if not the blade—transfixes her breast.

---

[19] *shōji*: A window or door sash covered with thin paper.

KOHARU: There're always people doing crazy things in the Quarter when they've had too much to drink. Why don't you let him go without making any trouble? I think that's best, don't you, Kawashō?

SAMURAI: Out of the question. Do as I say—inside, all of you. Koharu, come along.

NARRATOR: Jihei can still see their shadows even after they enter the inner room, but he is bound to the spot, his hands held in fetters which grip him the tighter as he struggles, his body beset by suffering as he tastes a living shame worse than a dog's. More determined than ever to die, he sheds tears of blood, a pitiful sight. Tahei the Lone Wolf returns from his carousing.

TAHEI: That's Jihei standing by Kawashō's window. I'll give him a tossing.

NARRATOR: He catches Jihei by the collar and starts to lift him over his back.

JIHEI: Owww!

TAHEI: Owww? What kind of weakling are you? Oh, I see—you're tied here. You must've been pulling off a robbery. You dirty pickpocket! You rotten pickpocket!

NARRATOR: He drubs Jihei mercilessly.

TAHEI: You burglar! You convict!

NARRATOR: He kicks him wildly.

TAHEI: Kamiya Jihei's been caught burgling, and they've tied him up!

NARRATOR: Passersby and people of the neighborhood, attracted by his shouts, quickly gather. The samurai rushes from the house.

SAMURAI: Who's calling him a burglar? You? Tell what Jihei's stolen! Out with it!

NARRATOR: He seizes Tahei and forces him into the dirt. Tahei rises to his feet only for the samurai to kick him down again and again. He grips Tahei.

SAMURAI: Jihei! Trample him to your heart's content!

NARRATOR: He pushes Tahei under Jihei's feet. Bound though he is, Jihei stamps furiously over Tahei's face. Tahei, thoroughly trampled and covered with mire, gets to his feet and glares around him.

TAHEI [*to bystander*]: How could you fools stand there calmly and let him step on me? I've memorized every one of your faces, and I intend to pay you back. Remember that!

NARRATOR: He makes his escape, still determined to have the last word. The spectators burst out laughing.

VOICES: Listen to him brag, even after he's been trampled on! Let's throw him from the bridge and give him a drink of water! Don't let him get away!

NARRATOR: They chase after him. When the crowd has dispersed, the samurai approaches Jihei and unfastens the knots. He shows his face with his hood removed.

JIHEI: Magoemon! My brother! How shaming!

NARRATOR: He sinks to the ground and weeps, prostrating himself in the dirt.

KOHARU: Are you his brother, sir?

NARRATOR: Koharu runs to them. Jihei, catching her by the front of the kimono, forces her to the ground.

JIHEI: Beast! She-fox! I'd sooner trample on you than on Tahei!

NARRATOR: He raises his foot, but Magoemon calls out.

MAGOEMON: That's the kind of foolishness responsible for all your trouble. A prostitute's business is to deceive men. Have you just now waked up to that? I've seen to the bottom of her heart the very first time I met her, but you're so scatter-brained that in over two years of intimacy with the woman you never discovered what she was thinking. Instead of stamping on Koharu, why don't you use your feet on your own misguided disposition?—It's deplorable. You're my younger brother, but you're almost thirty, and you've got a six-year-old boy and a four-year-old girl, Kantarō and Osue. You run a shop with a thirty-six-foot frontage, but you don't seem to realize that your whole fortune's collapsing. You shouldn't have to be lectured to by your brother. Your father-in-law is your aunt's husband, and your mother-in-law is your aunt. They've always been like real parents to you. Your wife Osan is my cousin too. The ties of marriage are multiplied by those of blood. But when the family has a reunion the only subject of discussion is our mortification over your incessant visits to Sonezaki. I feel sorry for our poor aunt. You know what a stiff-necked gentleman of the old school her husband Gozaemon is. He's forever flying into a rage and saying, "We've been tricked by your nephew. He's deserted our daughter. I'll take Osan back and ruin Jihei's reputation throughout Temma." Our aunt, with all the heartache to bear herself, sometimes sides with him and sometimes with you. She's worried herself sick. What an ingrate, not to appreciate how she's defended you in your shame! This one offense is enough to make you the target for Heaven's future punishment!

I realized that your marriage couldn't last much longer at this rate. I decided, in the hopes of relieving our aunt's worries, that I'd see with my own eyes what kind of woman Koharu was, and work out some sort of solution afterwards. I consulted the proprietor here, then came myself to investigate the cause of your sickness. I see now how natural it was that you should desert your wife and children. What a faithful prostitute you discovered! I congratulate you!

And here I am, Magoemon the Miller, known far and wide for my paragon of a brother, dressed up like a masquerader at a festival or maybe a lunatic! I put on swords for the first time in my life, and announced myself, like a bit player in a costume piece, as an officer at a residence. I feel like an absolute idiot with these swords, but there's nowhere I can dispose of them now.—It's so infuriating—and ridiculous—that it's given me a pain in the chest.

NARRATOR: He gnashes his teeth and grimaces, attempting to hide his tears. Koharu, choking the while with emotion, can only say:

KOHARU: Yes, you're entirely right.

NARRATOR: The rest is lost in tears. Jihei pounds the earth with his fist.

JIHEI: I was wrong. Forgive me, Magoemon. For three years I've been possessed by that witch. I've neglected my parents, relatives—even my wife and children—and wrecked my fortune, all because I was deceived by Koharu, that sneak thief! I'm utterly mortified. But I'm through with her now, and I'll never set foot here again. Weasel! Vixen! Sneak thief! Here's proof that I've broken with her!

NARRATOR: He pulls out the amulet bag which has rested next to his skin.

JIHEI: Here are the written oaths we've exchanged, one at the beginning of each month, twenty-nine in all. I return them. This means our love and affection are over. Take them.

NARRATOR: He flings the notes at her.

JIHEI: Magoemon, collect from her my pledges. Please make sure you get them all. Then burn them with your own hands. [*To* KOHARU.] Hand them to my brother.

KOHARU: As you wish.

NARRATOR: In tears, she surrenders the amulet bag. Magoemon opens it.

MAGOEMON: One, two, three, four . . . ten . . . twenty-nine. They're all here. There's also a letter from a woman. What's this?

NARRATOR: He starts to unfold it.

KOHARU: That's an important letter. I can't let you see it.

NARRATOR: She clings to Magoemon's arm, but he pushes her away. He holds the letter to the lamplight and examines the address, "To Miss Koharu from Kamiya Osan." As soon as he reads the words, he casually thrusts the letter into his kimono.

MAGOEMON: Koharu. A while ago I swore by my good fortune as a samurai, but now Magoemon the Miller swears by his good fortune as a businessman that he will show this letter to no one, not even his wife. I alone will read it, then burn it with the oaths. You can trust me. I will not break this oath.

KOHARU: Thank you. You save my honor.

NARRATOR: She bursts into tears again.

JIHEI [*laughs contemptuously*]: Save your honor! You talk like a human being! [*To* MAGOEMON.] I don't want to see her cursed face another minute. Let's go. No— I can't hold so much resentment and bitterness! I'll kick her one in the face, a memory to treasure for the rest of my life. Excuse me, please.

NARRATOR: He strides up to Koharu and stamps on the ground.

JIHEI: For three years I've loved you, delighted in you, longed for you, adored you, but today my foot will say my only farewells.

NARRATOR: He kicks her sharply on the forehead and bursts into tears. The brothers leave, forlorn figures. Koharu, unhappy woman, raises her voice in lament as she watches them go. Is she faithful or unfaithful? Her true feelings are hidden in the words penned by Jihei's wife, a letter no one has seen. Jihei goes his separate way without learning the truth.

ACT II

SCENE: *The house and shop of Kamiya Jihei.*

TIME: *Ten days later.*

NARRATOR: The busy street that runs straight to Tenjin Bridge named for the god of Temma, bringer of good fortune, is known as the Street Before the Kami,[20] and here a paper shop does business under the name Kamiya Jihei. The paper is honestly sold, the shop well situated; it is a long-established firm, and customers come thick as raindrops.

Outside crowds pass in the street, on their way to the Ten Nights service, while inside the husband dozes in the *kotatsu*,[21] shielded from draughts by a

---

[20] Kami: Means both "god" and "paper."   [21] *kotatsu:* A coal-burning fireplace or brazier constructed of a wooden frame covered by a quilt and usually located in the center of a room.

screen at his pillow. His wife Osan keeps solitary, anxious watch over shop and house.

OSAN: The days are so short—it's dinnertime already, but Tama still hasn't returned from her errand to Ichinokawa.[22] I wonder what can be keeping her. That scamp Sangorō isn't back either. The wind is freezing. I'm sure the children will both be cold. He doesn't even realize that it's time for Osue to be nursed. Heaven preserve me from ever becoming such a fool! What an infuriating creature!

NARRATOR: She speaks to herself.

KANTARŌ: Mama, I've come back all by myself.

NARRATOR: Her son, the older child, runs up to the house.

OSAN: Kantarō—is that you? What happened to Osue and Sangorō?

KANTARŌ: They're playing by the shrine. Osue wanted her milk and she was bawling her head off.

OSAN: I was sure she would. Oh—your hands and feet are frozen stiff as nails! Go and warm yourself at the *kotatsu*. Your father's sleeping there.—What am I to do with that idiot?

NARRATOR: She runs out impatiently to the shop just as Sangorō shuffles back, alone.

OSAN: Come here, you fool! Where have you left Osue?

SANGORŌ: You know, I must've lost her somewhere. Maybe somebody's picked her up. Should I go back for her?

OSAN: How could you? If any harm has come to my precious child, I'll beat you to death!

NARRATOR: But even as she screams at him, the maid Tama returns with Osue on her back.

TAMA: The poor child—I found her in tears at the corner. Sangorō, when you're supposed to look after the child, do it properly.

OSAN: You poor dear. You must want your milk.

NARRATOR: She joins the others by the *kotatsu* and suckles the child.

OSAN: Tama—give that fool a taste of something that he'll remember!

NARRATOR: Sangorō shakes his head.

SANGORŌ: No, thanks. I gave each of the children two tangerines just a while ago at the shrine, and I tasted five myself.

NARRATOR: Fool though he is, bad puns come from him nimbly enough, and the others can only smile despite themselves.

TAMA: Oh—I've become so involved with this half-wit that I almost forgot to tell you, ma'am, that Mr. Magoemon and his aunt are on their way here from the west.

OSAN: Oh dear! I'll have to wake Jihei in that case. [*To* JIHEI.] Please get up. Mother and Magoemon are coming. They'll be upset again if you let them see you, a businessman, sleeping in the afternoon, with the day so short as it is.

JIHEI: All right.

NARRATOR: He struggles to a sitting position and, with his abacus in one hand, pulls his account book to him with the other.

---

[22] Ichinokawa: A vegetable market at the north end of Tenjin Bridge in the Temma district.

JIHEI: Two into ten goes five, three into nine goes three, three into six goes two, seven times eight is fifty-six.

NARRATOR: His fifty-six-year-old aunt enters with Magoemon.

JIHEI: Magoemon, aunt. How good of you. Please come in. I was in the midst of some urgent calculations. Four nines makes thirty-six *momme*. Three sixes make eighteen *fun*. That's two *momme* less two *fun*.[23] Kantarō! Osue! Granny and Uncle have come! Bring the tobacco tray! One times three makes three. Osan, serve the tea!

NARRATOR: He jabbers away.

AUNT: We haven't come for tea or tobacco. Osan, you're young I know, but you're the mother of two children, and your excessive forbearance does you no credit. A man's dissipation can always be traced to his wife's carelessness. Remember, it's not only the man who's disgraced when he goes bankrupt and his marriage breaks up. You'd do well to take notice of what's going on and assert yourself a bit more.

MAGOEMON: It's foolish to hope for any results, aunt. The scoundrel even deceives me, his elder brother. Why should he take to heart criticism from his wife? Jihei—you played me for a fool. After showing me how you returned Koharu's pledges, here you are, not ten days later, redeeming her! What does this mean? I suppose your urgent calculations are of Koharu's debts! I've had enough!

NARRATOR: He snatches away the abacus and flings it clattering into the hallway.

JIHEI: You're making an enormous fuss without any cause. I haven't crossed the threshold since the last time I saw you except to go twice to the wholesalers in Imabashi and once to the Tenjin Shrine. I haven't even thought of Koharu, much less redeemed her.

AUNT: None of your evasions! Last evening at the Ten Nights service I heard the people in the congregation gossiping. Everybody was talking about the great patron from Temma who'd fallen in love with a prostitute named Koharu from the Kinokuni House in Sonezaki. They said he'd driven away her other guests and was going to ransom her in the next couple of days. There was all kinds of gossip about the abundance of money and fools even in these days of high prices.

My husband Gozaemon has been hearing about Koharu constantly, and he's sure that her great patron from Temma must be you, Jihei. He told me, "He's your nephew, but for me he's a stranger, and my daughter's happiness is my chief concern. Once he ransoms the prostitute he'll no doubt sell his wife to a brothel. I intend to take her back before he starts selling her clothes."

He was halfway out of the house before I could restrain him. "Don't get so excited. We can settle this calmly. First we must make sure whether or not the rumors are true."

That's why Magoemon and I are here now. He was telling me a while ago that the Jihei of today was not the Jihei of yesterday—that you'd broken all con-

---

[23] Twenty *fun* made two *momme;* see note 11.

nections with Sonezaki and completely reformed. But now I hear that you've had a relapse. What disease can this be?

Your father was my brother. When the poor man was on his deathbed, he lifted his head from the pillow and begged me to look after you, as my son-in-law and nephew. I've never forgotten those last words, but your perversity has made a mockery of his request!

NARRATOR: She collapses in tears of resentment. Jihei claps his hands in sudden recognition.

JIHEI: I have it! The Koharu everybody's gossiping about is the same Koharu, but the great patron who's to redeem her is a different man. The other day, as my brother can tell you, Tahei—they call him the Lone Wolf because he hasn't any family or relations—started a fight and was trampled on. He gets all the money he needs from his home town, and he's been trying for a long time to redeem Koharu. I've always prevented him, but I'm sure he's decided that now is his chance. I have nothing to do with it.

NARRATOR: Osan brightens at his words.

OSAN: No matter how forbearing I might be—even if I were an angel—you don't suppose I'd encourage my husband to redeem a prostitute! In this instance at any rate there's not a word of untruth in what my husband has said. I'll be a witness to that, Mother.

NARRATOR: Husband's and wife's words tally perfectly.

AUNT: Then it's true?

NARRATOR: The aunt and nephew clap their hands with relief.

MAGOEMON: Well, I'm happy it's over, anyway. To make us feel doubly reassured, will you write an affidavit which will dispel any doubts your stubborn uncle may have?

JIHEI: Certainly. I'll write a thousand if you like.

MAGOEMON: Splendid! I happen to have bought this on the way here.

NARRATOR: Magoemon takes from the fold of his kimono a sheet of oath-paper[24] from Kumano, the sacred characters formed by flocks of crows. Instead of vows of eternal love, Jihei now signs under penalty of Heaven's wrath an oath that he will sever all ties and affections with Koharu. "If I should die, may Bonten and Taishaku above, and the Four Great Kings below afflict me!"[25] So the text runs, and to it is appended the names of many Buddhas and gods. He signs his name, Kamiya Jihei, in bold characters, imprints the oath with a seal of blood, and proffers it.

OSAN: It's a great relief to me, too. Mother, I have you and Magoemon to thank. Jihei and I have had two children, but this is his firmest pledge of affection. I hope you share my joy.

---

[24] **oath-paper:** The Shinto shrine at Kumano issued such paper with crow-shaped characters on the face and the obverse side blank for writing oaths.

[25] **"If . . . me!":** Bonten and Taishaku are the Japanese version of the Hindu gods Brahma, ruler of the world, and Sakra (Indra), god of battle; the four kings are the Deva kings who served Sakra.

AUNT: Indeed we do. I'm sure that Jihei will settle down and his business will improve, now that he's in this frame of mind. It's been entirely for his sake and for love of the grandchildren that we've intervened. Come, Magoemon, let's be on our way. I'm anxious to set my husband's mind at ease. — It's become chilly here. See that the children don't catch cold. — This too we owe to the Buddha of the Ten Nights. I'll say a prayer of thanks before I go. Hail, Amida Buddha!

NARRATOR: She leaves, her heart innocent as Buddha's. Jihei is perfunctory even about seeing them to the door. Hardly have they crossed the threshold than he slumps down again at the *kotatsu*. He pulls the checked quilting over his head.

OSAN: You still haven't forgotten Sonezaki, have you?

NARRATOR: She goes up to him in disgust and tears away the quilting. He is weeping; a waterfall of tears streams along the pillow, deep enough to bear him afloat. She tugs him upright and props his body against the *kotatsu* frame. She stares into his face.

OSAN: You're acting outrageously, Jihei. You shouldn't have signed that oath if you felt so reluctant to leave her. The year before last, on the middle day of the Boar of the tenth moon, we lit the first fire in the *kotatsu* and celebrated by sleeping here together, pillow to pillow. Ever since then — did some demon or snake creep into my bosom that night? — for two whole years I've been condemned to keep watch over an empty nest. I thought that tonight at least, thanks to Mother and Magoemon, we'd share sweet words in bed as husbands and wives do, but my pleasure didn't last long. How cruel of you, how utterly heartless! Go ahead, cry your eyes out, if you're so attached to her. Your tears will flow into Shijimi River and Koharu, no doubt, will ladle them out and drink them! You're ignoble, inhuman.

NARRATOR: She embraces his knees and throws herself over him, moaning in supplication. Jihei wipes his eyes.

JIHEI: If tears of grief flowed from the eyes and tears of anger from the ears, I could show my heart without saying a word. But my tears all pour in the same way from my eyes, and there's no difference in their color. It's not surprising that you can't tell what's in my heart. I have not a shred of attachment left for that vampire in human skin, but I bear a grudge against Tahei. He has all the money he wants, no wife or children. He's schemed again and again to redeem her, but Koharu refused to give in, at least until I broke with her. She told me time and again, "You have nothing to worry about. I'll never let myself be redeemed by Tahei, not even if my ties with you are ended and I can no longer stay by your side. If my master is induced by Tahei's money to deliver me to him, I'll kill myself in a way that'll do you credit!" But think — not ten days have passed since I broke with her, and she's to be redeemed by Tahei! That rotten whore! That animal! No, I haven't a trace of affection left for her, but I can just hear how Tahei will be boasting. He'll spread the word around Osaka that my business has come to a standstill and I'm hard pressed for money. I'll meet with contemptuous stares from the wholesalers. I'll be dishonored. My heart is broken and my body burns with shame. What a disgrace! How maddening! I've passed the stage of shedding hot tears, tears of blood, sticky tears — my tears now are of molten iron!

NARRATOR: He collapses with weeping. Osan pales with alarm.

OSAN: If that's the situation, poor Koharu will surely kill herself.

JIHEI: You're too well bred, despite your intelligence, to understand her likes! What makes you suppose that faithless creature would kill herself? Far from it—she's probably taking moxa treatments and medicine to prolong her life!

OSAN: No, that's not true. I was determined never to tell you so long as I lived, but I'm afraid of the crime I'd be committing if I concealed the facts and let her die with my knowledge. I will reveal my great secret. There is not a grain of deceit in Koharu. It was I who schemed to end the relations between you. I could see signs that you were drifting towards suicide. I felt so unhappy that I wrote a letter, begging her as one woman to another to break with you, though I knew how painful it would be. I asked her to save your life. The letter must have moved her. She answered that she would give you up, though you were more precious than life itself, because she could not shirk her duty to me. I've kept her letter with me ever since—it's been like a protective charm. Could such a noble-hearted woman violate her promise and brazenly marry Tahei? When a woman—I no less than another—has given herself completely to a man, she does not change. I'm sure she'll kill herself. I'm sure of it. Ahhh—what a dreadful thing to have happened! Save her, please.

NARRATOR: Her voice rises in agitation. Her husband is thrown into a turmoil.

JIHEI: There was a letter in an unknown woman's hand among the written oaths she surrendered to my brother. It must have been from you. If that's the case, Koharu will surely commit suicide.

OSAN: Alas! I'd be failing in the obligations I owe her as another woman if I allowed her to die. Please go to her at once. Don't let her kill herself.

NARRATOR: Clinging to her husband, she melts in tears.

JIHEI: But what can I possibly do? It'd take half the amount of her ransom in earnest money merely to keep her out of Tahei's clutches. I can't save Koharu's life without administering a dose of 750 *momme* in New Silver. How could I raise that much money in my present financial straits? Even if I crush my body to powder, where will the money come from?

OSAN: Don't exaggerate the difficulties. If that's all you need, it's simple enough.

NARRATOR: She goes to the wardrobe, and opening a small drawer takes out a bag fastened with cords of twisted silk. She unhesitantly tears it open and throws down a packet which Jihei retrieves.

JIHEI: What's this? Money? Four hundred *momme* in New Silver? How in the world—

NARRATOR: He stares astonished at this money he never put there.

OSAN: I'll tell you later where this money came from. I've scraped it together to pay the bill for Iwakuni paper that falls due the day after tomorrow. We'll have to ask Magoemon to help us keep the business from betraying its insolvency. But Koharu comes first. The packet contains 400 *momme*. That leaves 350 *momme* to raise.

NARRATOR: She unlocks a large drawer. From the wardrobe lightly fly kite-colored Hachijō silks; a Kyoto crepe kimono lined in pale brown, insubstantial as her husband's life which flickers today and may vanish tomorrow; a padded kimono of Osue's, a flaming scarlet inside and out—Osan flushes with pain to part with it; Kantarō's sleeveless, unlined jacket—if she pawns this, he'll be cold this winter. Next comes a garment of striped Gunnai silk lined in pale blue and never worn, and then her best formal costume—heavy black silk dyed with her family crest, an ivy leaf in a ring. They say that those joined by marriage ties can even go naked at home, though outside the house clothes make the man: She snatches up even her husband's finery, a silken cloak, making fifteen articles in all.

OSAN: The very least the pawnshop can offer is 30 *momme* in New Silver.

NARRATOR: Her face glows as though she already held the money she needs; she hides in the one bundle her husband's shame and her own obligation, and puts her love in besides.

OSAN: It doesn't matter if the children and I have nothing to wear. My husband's reputation concerns me more. Ransom Koharu. Save her. Assert your honor before Tahei.

NARRATOR: But Jihei's eyes remain downcast all the while, and he is silently weeping.

JIHEI: Yes, I can pay the earnest money and keep her out of Tahei's hands. But once I've redeemed her, I'll either have to maintain her in a separate establishment or bring her here. Then what will become of you?

NARRATOR: Osan is at a loss to answer.

OSAN: Yes, what shall I do? Shall I become your children's nurse or the cook? Or perhaps the retired mistress of the house?

NARRATOR: She falls to the floor with a cry of woe.

JIHEI: That would be too selfish. I'd be afraid to accept such generosity. Even if the punishment for my crimes against my parents, against Heaven, against the gods and the Buddhas fails to strike me, the punishment for my crimes against my wife alone will be sufficient to destroy all hope for the future life. Forgive me, I beg you.

NARRATOR: He joins his hands in tearful entreaty.

OSAN: Why should you bow before me? I don't deserve it. I'd be glad to rip the nails from my fingers and toes, to do anything which might serve my husband. I've been pawning my clothes for some time in order to scrape together the money for the paper wholesalers' bills. My wardrobe is empty, but I don't regret it in the least. But it's too late now to talk of such things. Hurry, change your cloak and go to her with a smile.

NARRATOR: He puts on an under kimono of Gunnai silk, a robe of heavy black silk, and a striped cloak. His sash of figured damask holds a dirk of middle length worked in gold: Buddha surely knows that tonight it will be stained with Koharu's blood.

JIHEI: Sangorō! Come here!

NARRATOR: Jihei loads the bundle on the servant's back, intending to take him along. Then he firmly thrusts the wallet next to his skin and starts towards the gate.

VOICE: Is Jihei at home?

NARRATOR: A man enters, removing his fur cap. They see — good heavens! — that it is Gozaemon.

OSAN *AND* JIHEI: Ahhh — how fortunate that you should come at this moment!

NARRATOR: Husband and wife are upset and confused. Gozaemon snatches away Sangorō's bundle and sits heavily. His voice is sharp.

GOZAEMON: Stay where you are, harlot! — My esteemed son-in-law, what a rare pleasure to see you dressed in your finest attire, with a dirk and a silken cloak! Ahhh — that's how a gentleman of means spends his money! No one would take you for a paper dealer. Are you perchance on your way to the New Quarter? What commendable perseverance! You have no need for your wife, I take it. — Give her a divorce. I've come to take her home with me.

NARRATOR: He speaks needles and his voice is bitter. Jihei has not a word to reply.

OSAN: How kind of you, Father, to walk here on such a cold day. Do have a cup of tea.

NARRATOR: Offering the teacup serves as an excuse for edging closer.

OSAN: Mother and Magoemon came here a while ago, and they told my husband how much they disapproved of his visits to the New Quarter. Jihei was in tears and he wrote out an oath swearing he had reformed. He gave it to Mother. Haven't you seen it yet?

GOZAEMON: His written oath? Do you mean this?

NARRATOR: He takes the paper from his kimono.

GOZAEMON: Libertines scatter vows and oaths wherever they go, as if they were monthly statements of accounts. I thought there was something peculiar about this oath, and now that I am here I can see I was right. Do you still swear to Bonten and Taishaku? Instead of such nonsense, write out a bill of divorcement!

NARRATOR: He rips the oath to shreds and throws down the pieces. Husband and wife exchange looks of alarm, stunned into silence. Jihei touches his hands to the floor and bows his head.

JIHEI: Your anger is justified. If I were still my former self, I would try to offer explanations, but today I appeal entirely to your generosity. Please let me stay with Osan. I promise that even if I become a beggar or an outcast and must sustain life with the scraps that fall from other people's chopsticks, I will hold Osan in high honor and protect her from every harsh and bitter experience. I feel so deeply indebted to Osan that I cannot divorce her. You will understand that this is true as time passes and I show you how I apply myself to my work and restore my fortune. Until then please shut your eyes and allow us to remain together.

NARRATOR: Tears of blood stream from his eyes and his face is pressed to the matting in contrition.

GOZAEMON: The wife of an outcast! That's all the worse. Write the bill of divorcement at once! I will verify and seal the furniture and clothes Osan brought in her dowry.

NARRATOR: He goes to the wardrobe. Osan is alarmed.

OSAN: My clothes are all here. There's no need to examine them.

NARRATOR: She runs up to forestall him, but Gozaemon pushes her aside and jerks open a drawer.

GOZAEMON: What does this mean?

NARRATOR: He opens another drawer: It too is empty. He pulls out every last drawer, but not so much as a foot of patchwork cloth is to be seen. He tears open the wicker hampers, long boxes, and clothes chests.

GOZAEMON: Stripped bare, are they?

NARRATOR: His eyes set in fury. Jihei and Osan huddle under the striped *kotatsu* quilts, ready to sink into the fire with humiliation.

GOZAEMON: This bundle looks suspicious.

NARRATOR: He unties the knots and dumps out the contents.

GOZAEMON: As I thought! You were sending these to the pawnshop, I take it. Jihei—you'd strip the skin from your wife's and your children's bodies to squander the money on your whore! Dirty thief! You're my wife's nephew, but an utter stranger to me, and I'm under no obligation to suffer for your sake. I'll explain to Magoemon what has happened and ask him to make good whatever inroads you've already made on Osan's belongings. But first, the bill of divorcement!

NARRATOR: Even if Jihei could escape through seven padlocked doors, eight thicknesses of chains, and a hundred girdling walls, he could not evade so stringent a demand.

JIHEI: I won't use a brush to write the bill of divorcement. Here's what I'll do instead! Good-by, Osan.

NARRATOR: He lays his hand on his dirk, but Osan clings to him.

OSAN: Father—Jihei admits that he's done wrong and he's apologized in every way. You press your advantage too hard. Jihei may be a stranger, but his children are your grandchildren. Have you no affection for them? I will not accept a bill of divorcement.

NARRATOR: She embraces her husband and raises her voice in tears.

GOZAEMON: Very well. I won't insist on it. Come with me, woman.

NARRATOR: He pulls her to her feet.

OSAN: No, I won't go. What bitterness makes you expose to such shame a man and wife who still love each other? I will not suffer it.

NARRATOR: She pleads with him, weeping, but he pays her no heed.

GOZAEMON: Is there some greater shame? I'll shout it through the town!

NARRATOR: He pulls her up, but she shakes free. Caught by the wrist she totters forward when—alas!—her toes brush against her sleeping children. They open their eyes.

CHILDREN: Mother dear, why is Grandfather, the bad man, taking you away? Whom will we sleep beside now?

NARRATOR: They call out after her.

OSAN: My poor dears! You've never spent a night away from Mother's side since you were born. Sleep tonight beside your father. [*To* JIHEI.] Please don't forget to give the children their tonic before breakfast.—Oh, my heart is broken!

NARRATOR: These are her parting words. She leaves her children behind, abandoned as in the woods; the twin-trunked bamboo of conjugal love is sundered forever.

Act III

Scene 1

Sonezaki New Quarter, in front of the Yamato House.
TIME: *That night.*

NARRATOR: This is Shijimi River, the haunt of love and affection. Its flowing water and the feet of passersby are stilled now at two in the morning, and the full moon shines clear in the sky. Here in the street a dim doorway lantern is marked "Yamatoya Dembei" in a single scrawl. The night watchman's clappers take on a sleepy cadence as he totters by on uncertain legs. The very thickness of his voice crying, "Beware of fire! Beware of fire!" tells how far advanced the night is. A serving woman from the upper town comes along, followed by a palanquin. "It's terribly late," she remarks to the bearers as she clatters open the side door of the Yamato House and steps inside.

SERVANT: I've come to take back Koharu of the Kinokuni House.

NARRATOR: Her voice is faintly heard outside. A few moments later, after hardly time enough to exchange three or four words of greeting, she emerges.

SERVANT: Koharu is spending the night. Bearers, you may leave now and get some rest. [*To proprietress, inside the doorway.*] Oh, I forgot to tell you, madam. Please keep an eye on Koharu. Now that the ransom to Tahei has been arranged and the money's been accepted, we're merely her custodians. Please don't let her drink too much saké.

NARRATOR: She leaves, having scattered at the doorway the seeds that before morning will turn Jihei and Koharu to dust.

At night between two and four even the teahouse kettle rests; the flame flickering in the low candle stand narrows; and the frost spreads in the cold river-wind of the deepening night. The master's voice breaks the stillness.

DEMBEI [*to* JIHEI]: It's still the middle of the night. I'll send somebody with you. [*To servants.*] Mr. Jihei is leaving. Wake Koharu. Call her here.

NARRATOR: Jihei slides open the side door.

JIHEI: No, Dembei, not a word to Koharu. I'll be trapped here till dawn if she hears I'm leaving. That's why I'm letting her sleep and slipping off this way. Wake her up after sunrise and send her back then. I'm returning home now and will leave for Kyoto immediately on business. I have so many engagements that I may not be able to return in time for the interim payment. Please use the money I gave you earlier this evening to clear my account. I'd like you also to send 150 *me* of Old Silver to Kawashō for the moon-viewing party last month. Please get a receipt. Give Saietsubō from Fukushima[26] one piece of silver as a contribution to the Buddhist altar he's bought, and tell him to use it for a memorial service. Wasn't there something else? Oh yes—give Isoichi a tip of four silver coins.

---

[26] **Saietsubō from Fukushima:** Perhaps a priest who presided over entertainment in the Gay Quarters, or a male entertainer; Fukushima bordered Sonezaki to the west.

That's the lot. Now you can close up and get to bed. Good-by. I'll see you when I return from Kyoto.

NARRATOR: Hardly has he taken two or three steps than he turns back.

JIHEI: I forgot my dirk. Fetch it for me, won't you? — Yes, Dembei, this is one respect in which it's easier being a townsman. If I were a samurai and forgot my sword, I'd probably commit suicide on the spot!

DEMBEI: I completely forgot that I was keeping it for you. Yes, here's the knife with it.

NARRATOR: He gives the dirk to Jihei, who fastens it firmly into his sash.

JIHEI: I feel secure as long as I have this. Good night!

NARRATOR: He goes off.

DEMBEI: Please come back to Osaka soon! Thank you for your patronage!

NARRATOR: With this hasty farewell Dembei rattles the door bolt shut; then not another sound is heard as the silence deepens. Jihei pretends to leave, only to creep back again with stealthy steps. He clings to the door of the Yamato House. As he peeps within he is startled by shadows moving towards him. He takes cover at the house across the way until the figures pass.

Magoemon the Miller, his heart pulverized with anxiety over his younger brother, comes first, followed by the apprentice Sangorō with Jihei's son Kantarō on his back. They hurry along until they spy the lantern of the Yamato House. Magoemon pounds on the door.

MAGOEMON: Excuse me. Kamiya Jihei's here, isn't he? I'd like to see him a moment.

NARRATOR: Jihei thinks, "It's my brother!" but dares not stir from his place of concealment. From inside a man's sleep-laden voice is heard.

DEMBEI: Jihei left a while ago saying he was going up to Kyoto. He's not here.

NARRATOR: Not another sound is heard. Magoemon's tears fall unchecked.

MAGOEMON [*to himself*]: I ought to have met him on the way if he'd been going home. I can't understand what takes him to Kyoto. Ahhh—I'm trembling all over with worry. I wonder if he didn't take Koharu with him.

NARRATOR: The thought pierces his heart; unable to bear the pain, he pounds again on the door.

DEMBEI: Who is it, so late at night? We've gone to bed.

MAGOEMON: I'm sorry to disturb you, but I'd like to ask one more thing. Has Koharu of the Kinokuni House left? I was wondering if she mightn't have gone with Jihei.

DEMBEI: What's that? Koharu's upstairs, fast asleep.

MAGOEMON: That's a relief, anyway. There's no fear of a lovers' suicide. But where is he hiding himself causing me all this anxiety? He can't imagine the agony of suspense that the whole family is going through on his account. I'm afraid that bitterness towards his father-in-law may make him forget himself and do something rash. I brought Kantarō along, hoping he would help to dissuade Jihei, but the gesture was in vain. I wonder why I failed to meet him?

NARRATOR: He murmurs to himself, his eyes moist with tears. Jihei's hiding place is close enough for him to hear every word. He chokes with emotion, but can only swallow his tears.

MAGOEMON: Sangorō! Where does the fool go night after night? Don't you know anywhere else?

NARRATOR: Sangorō imagines that he himself is the fool referred to.

SANGORŌ: I know a couple of places, but I'm too embarrassed to mention them.

MAGOEMON: You know them? Where are they? Tell me.

SANGORŌ: Please don't scold me when you've heard. Every night I wander down below the warehouses by the market.

MAGOEMON: Imbecile! Who's asking about that? Come on, let's search the back streets. Don't let Kantarō catch a chill. The poor kid's having a cold time of it, thanks to that useless father of his. Still, if the worst the boy experiences is the cold I won't complain. I'm afraid that Jihei may cause him much greater pain. The scoundrel!

NARRATOR: But beneath the rancor in his heart of hearts is profound pity.

MAGOEMON: Let's look at the back street!

NARRATOR: They pass on. As soon as their figures have gone off a distance Jihei runs from his hiding place. Standing on tiptoes he gazes with yearning after them and cries out in his heart.

JIHEI: He cannot leave me to my death, though I am the worst of sinners! I remain to the last a burden to him! I'm unworthy of such kindness!

NARRATOR: He joins his hands and kneels in prayer.

JIHEI: If I may make one further request of your mercy, look after my children!

NARRATOR: These are his only words; for a while he chokes with tears.

JIHEI: At any rate, our decision's been made. Koharu must be waiting.

NARRATOR: He peers through a crack in the side door of the Yamato House and glimpses a figure.

JIHEI: That's Koharu, isn't it? I'll let her know I'm here.

NARRATOR: He clears his throat, their signal. "Ahem, ahem"—the sound blends with the clack of wooden clappers as the watchman comes from the upper street, coughing in the night wind. He hurries on his round of fire warning, "Take care! Beware!" Even this cry has a dismal sound to one in hiding. Jihei, concealing himself like the god of Katsuragi[27] lets the watchman pass. He sees his chance and rushes to the side door, which softly opens from within.

JIHEI: Koharu?

KOHARU: Were you waiting? Jihei—I want to leave quickly.

NARRATOR: She is all impatience, but the more hastily they open the door, the more likely people will be to hear the casters turning. They lift the door; it gives a moaning that thunders in their ears and in their hearts. Jihei lends a hand from the outside, but his fingertips tremble with the trembling of his heart. The door opens a quarter of an inch, a half, an inch—an inch ahead are the tortures of hell, but more than hell itself they fear the guardian-demon's eyes. At last the

---

[27] **god of Katsuragi:** A god associated with Mount Katsuragi; he was so ugly that he only came out at night to work on a bridge he was building between Mt. Katsuragi and Mt. Kimpu.

door opens, and with the joy of New Year's morn Koharu slips out. They catch each other's hands. Shall they go north or south, west or east? Their pounding hearts urge them on, though they know not to what destination: Turning their backs on the moon reflected in Shijimi River, they hurry eastward as fast as their legs will carry them.

Scene 2

The farewell journey of many bridges.

NARRATOR:
The running hand in texts of Nō is always Konoe style;[28]
An actor in a woman's part is sure to wear a purple hat.
Does some teaching of the Buddha as rigidly decree
That men who spend their days in evil haunts must end like this?

 Poor creatures, though they would discover today their destiny in the Sutra of Cause and Effect,[29] tomorrow the gossip of the world will scatter like blossoms the scandal of Kamiya Jihei's love suicide, and, carved in cherry wood, his story to the last detail will be printed in illustrated sheets.

 Jihei, led on by the spirit of death—if such there be among the gods—is resigned to this punishment for neglect of his trade. But at times—who could blame him?—his heart is drawn to those he has left behind, and it is hard to keep walking on. Even in the full moon's light, this fifteenth night of the tenth moon, he cannot see his way ahead—a sign perhaps of the darkness in his heart? The frost now falling will melt by dawn but, even more quickly than this symbol of human frailty, the lovers themselves will melt away. What will become of the fragrance that lingered when he held her tenderly at night in their bed-chamber?

 This bridge, Tenjin Bridge, he has crossed every day, morning and night, gazing at Shijimi River to the west. Long ago, when Tenjin, then called Michi-zane, was exiled to Tsukushi, his plum tree, following its master, flew in one bound to Dazaifu, and here is Plum-field Bridge. Green Bridge recalls the aged pine that followed later, and Cherry Bridge[30] the tree that withered away in grief over parting. Such are the tales still told, bespeaking the power of a single poem.

JIHEI: Though born the parishioner of so holy and mighty a god, I shall kill you and then myself. If you ask the cause, it was that I lacked even the wisdom that might fill a tiny Shell Bridge. Our stay in this world has been short as an autumn day. This evening will be the last of your nineteen, of my twenty-eight years. The time has come to cast away our lives. We promised we'd remain together faith-fully, till you were an old woman and I an old man, but before we knew each

---

[28] **Konoe style:** A style of calligraphy dating from the sixteenth century, used for printing texts of Nō plays.

[29] **Sutra . . . Effect:** The Karma Sutra, a sacred Buddhist scripture, that relates action in a chain of cause and effect.

[30] **Tenjin Bridge . . . Cherry Bridge:** The bridges named here are those the lovers cross on their journey east from Sonezaki to Amijima.

other three full years, we have met this disaster. Look, there is Ōe Bridge. We follow the river from Little Naniwa Bridge to Funairi Bridge. The farther we journey, the closer we approach the road to death.

NARRATOR: He laments. She clings to him.

KOHARU: Is this already the road to death?

NARRATOR: Falling tears obscure from each the other's face and threaten to immerse even the Horikawa bridges.

JIHEI: A few steps north and I could glimpse my house, but I will not turn back. I will bury in my breast all thoughts of my children's future, all pity for my wife. We cross southward over the river. Why did they call a place with as many buildings as a bridge has piers "Eight Houses"? Hurry, we want to arrive before the downriver boat from Fushimi comes — with what happy couples sleeping aboard!

Next is Temma Bridge, a frightening name for us about to depart this world. Here the two streams Yodo and Yamato join in one great river, as fish with water, and as Koharu and I, dying on one blade will cross together the River of Three Fords.[31] I would like this water for our tomb offering!

KOHARU: What have we to grieve about? Though in this world we could not stay together, in the next and through each successive world to come until the end of time we shall be husband and wife. Every summer for my devotions I have copied the All Compassionate and All Merciful Chapter of the Lotus Sutra,[32] in the hope that we may be reborn on one lotus.

NARRATOR: They cross over Kyō Bridge and reach the opposite shore.

KOHARU: If I can save living creatures at will when once I mount a lotus calyx in Paradise and become a Buddha, I want to protect women of my profession, so that never again will there be love suicides.

NARRATOR: This unattainable prayer stems from worldly attachment, but it touchingly reveals her heart.

They cross Onari Bridge. The waters of Noda Creek[33] are shrouded with morning haze; the mountain tips show faintly white.

JIHEI: Listen — the voices of the temple bells begin to boom. How much farther can we go on this way? We are not fated to live any longer — let us make an end quickly. Come this way.

NARRATOR: Tears are strung with the 108 beads of the rosaries in their hands. They have come now to Amijima, to the Daichō Temple;[34] the overflowing sluice gate of a little stream beside a bamboo thicket will be their place of death.

---

[31] **River . . . Fords:** *Mitsuse-gawa*, the river in the Buddhist underworld that one must cross to reach the land of the dead; Jihei hopes that people will use water from the Yodo and Yamato as offerings to the gods in their prayers to himself and Koharu.

[32] **All Compassionate . . . Sutra:** This section of the Buddhist scripture tells the story of the Goddess of Mercy.

[33] **Noda Creek:** A small river northwest of Amijima.

[34] **the 108 beads:** Represent the 108 passions or ties to the world that the teller of the beads attempts to subdue; **Daichō Temple:** A Jōdo or Pure Land temple in the Amijima section of Osaka.

Scene 3

Amijima.

JIHEI: No matter how far we walk, there'll never be a spot marked "For Suicides." Let
    us kill ourselves here.

NARRATOR: He takes her hand and sits on the ground.

KOHARU: Yes, that's true. One place is as good as another to die. But I've been think-
    ing on the way that if they find our dead bodies together people will say that
    Koharu and Jihei committed a lovers' suicide. Osan will think then that I treated
    as mere scrap paper the letter I sent promising her, when she asked me not to kill
    you, that I would not, and vowing to break all relations. She will be sure that I
    lured her precious husband into a lovers' suicide. She will despise me as a one-
    night prostitute, a false woman with no sense of decency. I fear her contempt
    more than the slander of a thousand or ten thousand strangers. I can imagine
    how she will resent and envy me. That is the greatest obstacle to my salvation.
    Kill me here, then choose another spot, far away, for yourself.

NARRATOR: She leans against him. Jihei joins in her tears of pleading.

JIHEI: What foolish worries! Osan has been taken back by my father-in-law. I've
    divorced her. She and I are strangers now. Why should you feel obliged to a
    divorced woman? You were saying on the way that you and I will be husband
    and wife through each successive world until the end of time. Who can criticize
    us, who can be jealous if we die side by side?

KOHARU: But who is responsible for your divorce? You're even less reasonable than I.
    Do you suppose that our bodies will accompany us to the afterworld? We may
    die in different places, our bodies may be pecked by kites and crows, but what
    does it matter as long as our souls are twined together? Take me with you to
    heaven or to hell!

NARRATOR: She sinks again in tears.

JIHEI: You're right. Our bodies are made of earth, water, fire, and wind, and when we
    die they revert to emptiness. But our souls will not decay, no matter how often
    reborn. And here's a guarantee that our souls will be married and never part!

NARRATOR: He whips out his dirk and slashes off his black locks at the base of the top
    knot.

JIHEI: Look, Koharu. As long as I had this hair I was Kamiya Jihei, Osan's husband,
    but cutting it has made me a monk. I have fled the burning house of the three
    worlds of delusion; I am a priest, unencumbered by wife, children, or worldly
    possessions. Now that I no longer have a wife named Osan, you owe her no obli-
    gations either.

NARRATOR: In tears he flings away the hair.

KOHARU: I am happy.

NARRATOR: Koharu takes up the dirk and ruthlessly, unhesitantly, slices through her
    flowing Shimada coiffure. She casts aside the tresses she has so often washed and
    combed and stroked. How heartbreaking to see their locks tangled with the
    weeds and midnight frost of this desolate field!

JIHEI: We have escaped the inconstant world, a nun and a priest. Our duties as hus-
    band and wife belong to our profane past. It would be best to choose quite sepa-

rate places for our deaths, a mountain for one, the river for the other. We will pretend that the ground above this sluice gate is a mountain. You will die there. I shall hang myself by this stream. The time of our deaths will be the same, but the method and place will differ. In this way we can honor to the end our duty to Osan. Give me your under sash.

NARRATOR: Its fresh violet color and fragrance will be lost in the winds of impermanence; the crinkled silk long enough to wind twice round her body will bind two worlds, this and the next. He firmly fastens one end to the crosspiece of the sluice, then twists the other into a noose for his neck. He will hang for love of his wife like the "pheasant in the hunting grounds."[35]

Koharu watches Jihei prepare for his death. Her eyes swim with tears, her mind is distraught.

KOHARU: Is that how you're going to kill yourself?—If we are to die apart, I have only a little while longer by your side. Come near me.

NARRATOR: They take each other's hands.

KOHARU: It's over in a moment with a sword, but I'm sure you'll suffer. My poor darling!

NARRATOR: She cannot stop the silent tears.

JIHEI: Can suicide ever be pleasant, whether by hanging or cutting the throat? You mustn't let worries over trifles disturb the prayers of your last moments. Keep your eyes on the westward-moving moon, and worship it as Amida himself.[36] Concentrate your thoughts on the Western Paradise. If you have any regrets about leaving the world, tell me now, then die.

KOHARU: I have none at all, none at all. But I'm sure you must be worried about your children.

JIHEI: You make me cry all over again by mentioning them. I can almost see their faces, sleeping peacefully, unaware, poor dears, that their father is about to kill himself. They're the one thing I can't forget.

NARRATOR: He droops to the ground with weeping. The voices of the crows leaving their nests at dawn rival his sobs. Are the crows mourning his fate? The thought brings more tears.

JIHEI: Listen to them. The crows have come to guide us to the world of the dead. There's an old saying that every time somebody writes an oath on the back of a Kumano charm, three crows of Kumano die on the holy mountain. The first words we've written each New Year have been vows of love, and how often we've inscribed oaths at the beginning of the month! If each oath has killed three crows, what a multitude must have perished! Their cries have always sounded like "beloved, beloved," but hatred for our crime of taking life makes their voices ring tonight "revenge, revenge!" Whose fault is it they demand revenge? Because of me you will die a painful death. Forgive me!

NARRATOR: He takes her in his arms.

KOHARU: No, it's my fault!

---

[35] **"pheasant . . . grounds":** An allusion to a poem by Otomo no Yakamochi (718–785); the pheasant calling to its mate attracts the attention of the hunters.

[36] **westward-moving . . . himself:** Amida Buddha's paradise, the Pure Land, was in the west.

NARRATOR: They cling to each other, face pressed to face; their sidelocks, drenched with tears, freeze in the winds blowing over the fields. Behind them echoes the voice of the Daichō Temple.

JIHEI: Even the long winter night seems short as our lives.

NARRATOR: Dawn is already breaking, and matins can be heard. He draws her to him.

JIHEI: The moment has come for our glorious end. Let there be no tears on your face when they find you later.

KOHARU: There won't be any.

NARRATOR: She smiles. His hands, numbed by the frost, tremble before the pale vision of her face, and his eyes are first to cloud. He is weeping so profusely that he cannot control the blade.

KOHARU: Compose yourself—but be quick!

NARRATOR: Her encouragement lends him strength; the invocations to Amida carried by the wind urge a final prayer. *Namu Amida Butsu.*[37] He thrusts in the saving sword. Stabbed, she falls backwards, despite his staying hand, and struggles in terrible pain. The point of the blade has missed her windpipe, and these are the final tortures before she can die. He writhes with her in agony, then painfully summons his strength again. He draws her to him, and plunges his dirk to the hilt. He twists the blade in the wound, and her life fades away like an unfinished dream at dawning.

He arranges her corpse head to the north, face to the west, lying on her right side,[38] and throws his cloak over her. He turns away at last, unable to exhaust with tears his grief over parting. He pulls the sash to him and fastens the noose around his neck. The service in the temple has reached the closing section, the prayers for the dead. "Believers and unbelievers will equally share in the divine grace,"[39] the voices proclaim, and at the final words Jihei jumps from the sluice gate.

JIHEI: May we be reborn on one lotus! Hail Amida Buddha!

NARRATOR: For a few moments he writhes like a gourd swinging in the wind, but gradually the passage of his breath is blocked as the stream is dammed by the sluice gate, where his ties with this life are snapped.

Fishermen out for the morning catch find the body in their net.

FISHERMEN: A dead man! Look, a dead man! Come here, everybody!

NARRATOR: The tale is spread from mouth to mouth. People say that they who were caught in the net of Buddha's vow[40] immediately gained salvation and deliverance, and all who hear the tale of the Love Suicides at Amijima are moved to tears.

---

[37] *Namu Amida Butsu:* The traditional prayer or invocation of Amida's name; it roughly means "Adoration for the Buddha of Infinite Light and Life."

[38] head . . . side: Imitating the position of the dying Sakyamuni Buddha.

[39] "Believers . . . grace": The final refrain of a Pure Land memorial prayer.

[40] Buddha's vow: In contrast to the fishermen who find only the body in their net, the souls of Koharu and Jihei have been caught in the net *(ami)* of Buddha and so will be freed from the cycle of rebirth.

Love, Marriage, and the Education of Women

While love may be a universal human emotion, the conventions of love, sexual behavior, courtship, and marriage vary widely. Nonetheless, certain common themes emerge across cultures, including the struggle between private desires and community values. As in Chikamatsu's **Love Suicides at Amijima,** love sometimes leads to conflict between the lovers and the customs and expectations of their families and community. Jihei is torn between duty and desire, just as the two lovers in Shakespeare's *Romeo and Juliet* are torn between family loyalties and the desires of their hearts.

p. 691

Within particular societies conventions vary according to class, religion, ethnicity, and age. Marriage, a key ritual of most cultures, is important because it brings together public and private life as well as secular and religious values. Although it may be seen as a personal relationship between a man and a woman sanctioned by the community, it is also an institution by which societies regulate desire and the circulation of hereditary property and social status. In some cultures marriage may mark the culmination of love between two people; in others it may not involve love at all. When it does, marriage becomes an institution in which familial, social, and religious concerns intersect with personal desire. Rituals of courtship and marriage, as sources of personal and social conflict as well as harmony, have long been generative themes in literature.

KAIBARA EKKEN'S *GREATER LEARNING FOR WOMEN*

Writers around the globe explored the subjects of love and marriage during the eighteenth century. Kaibara Ekken (1630–1714), one of the most important NEO-CONFUCIAN thinkers of the early Tokugawa era,

Vilaval Ragini, *The Toilet of the Princess,* c. 1720
This painting portrays an Indian princess, center, being catered to by her servants. (The Art Archive/Marco Polo Gallery Paris/Dagli Orti [A])

p. 726

wrote several popular treatises of CONFUCIAN moralism, including ***Greater Learning for Women,*** a conduct book addressed to young women. Like Rousseau's *Émile,* Ekken's text emphasizes the importance of a woman's loyalty and subordination to her husband and his family. Following the Confucian principles of subordination, Ekken recommends the separation of the male and female spheres and prescribes only limited education for girls, since they will not be called upon to participate in higher civic or intellectual pursuits. A woman's charge is the domestic world, the household of her husband, which, according to Ekken, she may rule over to ensure proper order. The philosophical grounds of his ideas are quite different from Rousseau's, but Ekken's advocacy of female subordination bears striking similarities to the role of women advocated in *Émile.*

p. 735

WOMEN, EDUCATION, AND MARRIAGE IN EUROPE

The contest between love and social convention—a conflict love does not always win—appears everywhere in the plays, novels, poetry, essays, and letters of eighteenth-century European writers. The treatment of love in these texts ranges from the satirical in Molière's play *Tartuffe,* first performed in 1664, to the sentimental in p. 22 Jean-Jacques Rousseau's popular novels *Julie, or the New Heloise* and *Émile,* to the critical in Mary Astell's essay *Some Reflections upon* p. 732 *Marriage* and Mary Wollstonecraft's treatise *A Vindication of the* p. 742 *Rights of Woman.* Whether comic or serious, these works reflect the ongoing debate about the conventions and laws governing marriage,

William Hogarth, *Marriage à la Mode (Shortly after Marriage),* 1742–44
From a series of six satirical paintings, this one shows boredom setting in—shortly after a fashionable wedding. (Erich Lessing/Art Resource, NY)

which was often seen as a contractual arrangement in which the bride, who gave up all her rights and property to her husband, was little more than an object of exchange. Moreover, these texts directly address the part education plays in preparing men and women, particularly women, for their role in marriage.

MARY ASTELL: REFLECTIONS UPON MARRIAGE

In *Some Reflections upon Marriage,* Astell attacks the commodification of the bride, saying it both dehumanizes the woman and encourages the worst appetite in men — the love of money. Marriages that result from base desires — the love of money, beauty, and even wit — are doomed, Astell claims, to end unhappily for both partners. Laying the foundation for arguments that Wollstonecraft would pursue in *A Vindication of the Rights of Woman,* Astell further maintains that women's education should go beyond simply preparing them to be docile and entertaining marriage partners for men. Women must develop their reason, acquire knowledge, and enlarge their souls. Once prepared to exercise rational judgment, women will make better, more equal marriage partners, rising above vanity and passion. Further, reason may not only save women from bad marriages but also lead them to reject marriage altogether.

ROUSSEAU VERSUS WOLLSTONECRAFT

Wollstonecraft's *A Vindication of the Rights of Woman* takes up these issues, launching a vigorous attack on the double standards in education and the subordination of women that Rousseau presents in *Émile.* A novelistic treatise on education, *Émile* advocates a graduated approach to book learning for men, beginning with history and biography then moving to religion and philosophy, so as to cultivate first the heart, then the mind. This course of education serves Rousseau's male protagonist Émile; but when it comes to the education of Sophy, Rousseau's ideal woman and Émile's wife-to-be, the author proposes an education that would make her into a docile object at the mercy of her husband's whims and demands. The passages from Rousseau's novel and Wollstonecraft's counterargument in *A Vindication* are the beginnings of the "nature and nurture" debate about the role of socialization and education in the shaping of gender roles. For Wollstonecraft, Rousseau's Sophy is nothing more than a plaything for men, the result of a misguided educational program that thwarts her intellect and denies her a fair share of the world's knowledge and experience. She is thus kept from being a full partner in the family and, as a citizen, in the state.

SIX RECORDS OF A FLOATING LIFE

The final selection is not so much about the politics of gender as it is a moving account of a married couple in China, who struggle with family jealousies, illness, financial troubles, and ultimately death. Shen Fu's *Six Records of a Floating Life* recounts the first years of the writer's married life with Chen Yün, who early in the marriage bungles an attempt to get a concubine for her father-in-law, thus alienating herself from the family. As in Chikamatsu's *The Love Suicides at Amijima,* Shen Fu's life becomes more complicated when he and his wife meet Han-yüan, a beautiful young woman whom Yün hopes to bring into the house as her husband's concubine. In contrast to Chikamatsu's characters, however, Shen Fu's concubine and his wife get along handsomely, and when the arrangement falls through because of Shen Fu's poverty, his wife is so deeply disappointed that she becomes fatally ill. Shen Fu's frank account of his love for his wife and the misfortunes they endure together offers a glimpse into the private life of a low-level official in the Qing era and shows how parental meddling and the expectations of society may lead to tragic consequences.

p. 755

A Party Arranging Flowers, c. 1790. **Gouache on Paper** *This work showcases the clear-cut gender roles in Qing China. The women are relegated to the task of arranging flowers as the men direct their actions. (Claydon House, Buckinghamshire, UK/National Trust Photographic Library/John Hammond/ Bridgeman Art Library)*

■ CONNECTIONS

Alexander Pope, *The Rape of the Lock*, p. 238. The selections here suggest that the subordination of women was common in Japan, China, and Europe. Women did not enjoy the same opportunities and freedoms that were granted to men. Wollstonecraft proposes that women were formed only to be "alluring objects" and discardable playthings for men. Pope's *The Rape of the Lock* satirizes the game-playing between men and women in high society during the early eighteenth century, and according to some readers trivializes the issue of rape in the process. How might the writers of the texts in this section respond to Pope's portrayal of woman in his poem?

Denis Diderot, *Supplement to the Voyage of Bougainville*, p. 213. The selections here offer various views on the position of women in society, the important role education plays in reinforcing women's roles, and the relationship between women and men. Diderot's *Supplement* raises questions about love and marriage in the debate between the Tahitian Orou and the French Almoner. How might Mary Astell or Mary Wollstonecraft respond to Diderot's critique of European hypocrisy in matters of sexuality and marriage? Are Diderot's views compatible with those of Kaibara Ekken?

Rokeya Sakhawat Hossain, "Sultana's Dream" (Book 6). As the texts here show, in the eighteenth century, education for women was inseparable from the issues of women's rights and their role in society. "Sultana's Dream," by twentieth-century Indian writer Rokeya Hossain, makes the same connection: The story is a vision of a utopian society wherein women receive the benefits of education and govern the country with ecologically enlightened policies, while men are isolated in a reverse form of purdah. Compare Hossain's vision of a feminist utopia with Mary Astell's "Monastery" for women. How do cultural and historical differences account for some of the qualities of each woman's ideal?

∾ KAIBARA EKKEN
1630–1714

Kaibara Ekken was one of the most important NEO-CONFUCIAN thinkers of the Tokugawa era. Born in 1630 into a SAMURAI family on the island of Kyushu, Kaibara, who lost his mother when he was five, was a precocious student and an enthusiastic reader. Taught primarily by his father and older brother, Kaibara developed a strong interest in medicine, the Confucian classics, and the neo-Confucian doctrines of Zhu Xi (Chu Hsi; 1130–1200). Kaibara eventually studied medicine at Nagasaki and entered into the service of a *daimyo* in Fukuoka, who sent him to Kyoto to continue his studies, which included the natural sciences and philosophy. After returning to Fukuoka, Kaibara married and began a life of teaching and writing.

Eventually, Kaibara effected a sort of revolution in neo-Confucian thinking. He wrote treatises on health care and education, government and politics, calligraphy and literature, and botany and topography as well as philosophical treatises and commentaries on the works of Zhu Xi. In a gesture reminiscent of the natural philosopher Francis Bacon in

England, who thought that through science, humans could master the universe, Kaibara urged his readers to observe nature directly for a better understanding of human behavior and society. He also advocated a kind of ecological principle, believing that family loyalty and duty to nature were essentially the same. Throughout his work, Kaibara emphasized the importance of practical knowledge, the cultivation of one's own understanding, and the need to work for the benefit of others.

Kaibara's empirical bent and his desire to make Confucian ideas more accessible led him to write several works specifically for women and children, audiences hitherto largely neglected by philosophers. To this end he wrote *Precepts for Daily Life in Japan (Yamanto Zokkun), Precepts for Children (Shogaku-kun),* and *Greater Learning for Women (Onna daigaku).* Like Rousseau's *Émile, Greater Learning for Women* serves as a book of conduct for women, describing their duties. Following the Confucian ideal of strict hierarchical relationships and obligatory responsibility, Kaibara's treatise advises the woman to be passively obedient to the male, enjoins her to be chaste and loyal, and urges her to prepare herself for service to her husband. Like Astell and Wollstonecraft, however, Kaibara maintains that women must exercise their judgment and reason in order to conduct themselves in a dignified manner. Unlike them, he

p. 735

Woman Reading

This woodblock shows a woman at ease with a book in her hand. Many elite women in eighteenth-century Japan learned to read and write at home, though they saw a decline in their social status. (The Japan Ukiyoe Museum)

A woman has no particular lord. She must look to her husband as her lord, and must serve him with all worship and reverence, not despising or thinking lightly of him. The great lifelong duty of a woman is obedience.

– KAIBARA EKKEN,
Greater Learning for Women

does not urge women to challenge the present order of things nor to exercise independent judgment to protect or pursue their own interests. Kaibara died in 1714; *Greater Learning for Women* was influential throughout the eighteenth and nineteenth centuries in Japan.

FROM

∾ Greater Learning for Women

Translated by Basil Hall Chamberlain   ·

I
GIRL'S INSTRUCTION

Seeing that it is a girl's destiny, on reaching womanhood, to go to a new home, and live in submission to her father-in-law, it is even more incumbent upon her than it is on a boy to receive with all reverence her parents' instructions. Should her parents, through her tenderness, allow her to grow up self-willed, she will infallibly show herself capricious in her husband's house, and thus alienate his affection; while, if her father-in-law be a man of correct principles, the girl will find the yoke of these principles intolerable. She will hate and decry her father-in-law, and the end of these domestic dissensions will be her dismissal from her husband's house and the covering of herself with ignominy. Her parents, forgetting the faulty education they gave her, may, indeed, lay all the blame on the father-in-law. But they will be in error; for the whole disaster should rightly be attributed to the faulty education the girl received from her parents.

More precious in a woman is a virtuous heart than a face of beauty. The vicious woman's heart is ever excited; she glares wildly around her, she vents her anger on others, her words are harsh and her accent vulgar. When she speaks, it is to set herself above others, to upbraid others, to envy others, to be puffed up with individual pride, to jeer at others, to outdo others—all things at variance with the way in which a woman should walk. The only qualities that befit a woman are gentle obedience, chastity, mercy, and quietness.

II
DEMARCATION BETWEEN THE SEXES

From her earliest youth a girl should observe the line of demarcation separating women from men, and never, even for an instant, should she be allowed to see or hear the least impropriety. The customs of antiquity did not allow men and women to sit in the same apartment, to keep their wearing apparel in the same place, to bathe in the same place, or to transmit to each other anything directly from hand to hand. A woman going abroad at night must in all cases carry a lighted lamp; and (not to speak of strangers) she must observe a certain distance in her relations even with her husband and with her brothers. In our days the women of lower classes, ignoring all rules of this nature, behave themselves disorderly; they contaminate their reputations, bring down reproach upon the head of their parents and brothers, and spend their whole lives in an unprofitable manner. Is not this truly lamentable? [. . .]

III
"SEVEN REASONS FOR DIVORCE"

In China marriage is called "returning," for the reason that a woman must consider her husband's home as her own, and that, when she marries, she is therefore returning to her own home. However low and needy her husband's position may be, she must find no fault with him, but consider the poverty of the household which it has pleased Heaven to give her as the ordering of an unpropitious fate. The sage of old taught that, once married, she must never leave her husband's house. Should she forsake the "way" and be divorced, shame shall cover her till her latest hour. [. . .]

It is the chief duty of a girl living in the parental house to practise filial piety towards her father and mother. But after marriage her duty is to honour her father-in-law and mother-in-law, to honour them beyond her father and mother, to love and reverence them with all ardour, and to tend them with practise of every filial piety. While thou honourest thine own parents, think not lightly of thy father-in-law! Never should a woman fail, night and morning, to pay her respects to her father-in-law and mother-in-law. Never should she be remiss in performing any tasks they may require of her. With all reverence must she carry out, and never rebel against, her father-in-law's commands. On every point must she inquire of her father-in-law and mother-in-law, and abandon herself to their direction. Even if thy father-in-law and mother-in-law be pleased to hate and vilify thee, be not angry with them, and murmur not. If thou carry piety towards them to its utmost limits, and minister to them in all sincerity, it cannot be but that they will end by becoming friendly to thee.

IV
THE WIFE'S MISCELLANEOUS DUTIES

A woman has no particular lord. She must look to her husband as her lord, and must serve him with all worship and reverence, not despising or thinking lightly of him. The great lifelong duty of a woman is obedience. In her dealings with her husband, both the expression of her countenance and style of her address should be courteous, humble, and conciliatory, never peevish and intractable, never rude and arrogant—that should be a woman's first and chiefest care. When the husband issues his instructions, the wife must never disobey them. In doubtful case she should inquire of her husband, and obediently follow his commands. If ever her husband should inquire of her, she should answer to the point—to answer in a careless fashion were a mark of rudeness. Should her husband be roused at any time to anger, she must obey him with fear and trembling, and not set herself up against him in anger and forwardness. A woman should look on her husband as if he were Heaven itself, and never weary of thinking how she may yield to her husband and thus escape celestial castigation. [. . .]

Let her never even dream of jealousy. If her husband be dissolute, she must expostulate with him, but never either nurse or vent her anger. If her jealousy be extreme, it will render her countenance frightful and her accent repulsive, and can only result in completely alienating her husband from her, and making her intolerable to his eyes. Should her husband act ill and unreasonably, she must compose her countenance and soften her voice to remonstrate with him; and if he be angry and listen not to the remonstrance, she must wait over a season, and then expostulate with him again when his heart is softened. Never set thyself up against thy husband with harsh features and a boisterous voice. [. . .]

A woman must be ever on the alert, and keep a strict watch over her own conduct. In the morning she must rise early, and at night go late to rest. Instead of sleeping in the middle of the day, she must be intent on the duties of her household, and must not weary of weaving, sewing, and spinning. Of tea and wine she must not drink overmuch, nor must she feed her eyes and ears with theatrical performances, ditties, and ballads. [. . .]

In her capacity of wife, she must keep her husband's household in proper order. If the wife be evil and profligate, the house is ruined. In everything she must avoid extravagance, and both with regard to food and raiment must act according to her station in life, and never give way to luxury and pride.

While young, she must avoid the intimacy and familiarity of her husband's kinsmen, comrades, and retainers, ever strictly adhering to the rule of separation between the sexes; and on no account whatever should she enter into correspondence with a young man. Her personal adornments and the colour and pattern of her garments should be unobtrusive. It suffices for her to be neat and cleanly in her person and in her wearing apparel. It is wrong in her, by an excess of care, to obtrude herself on other people's notice. Only that which is suitable should be practised.

She must not selfishly think first of her own parents and only secondly of her husband's relations. At New Year, on Five Festivals, and on other like occasions she should pay her first respect to those of her husband's house, and then to her own parents. Without her husband's permission, she must go nowhere, neither should she make any gift on her own responsibility.

As a woman rears up posterity not to her own parents, but to her father-in-law and mother-in-law, she must value the latter even more than the former, and tend them filial piety. Her visits, also, to the paternal house should be rare after marriage. Much more then with regard to other friends should it generally suffice for her to send a message to inquire after their health. Again, she must not be filled with pride at the recollection of the splendour of her parental house, and must not make it the subject of her conversations.

❧ MARY ASTELL
1666–1731

Mary Astell was born in 1666 to a middle-class family in Newcastle, England, where a clergyman uncle taught her philosophy and the logic that she was to wield so skillfully in her own writing. In 1688 she moved to Chelsea, just outside of London; she earned a reputation as the defender of the Church of England and lived on the patronage of clergy and minor nobility. Yet Astell was also a defender of women's causes, advocating celibacy for women and the foundation of a women's monastery in *A Serious Proposal to the Ladies* (1694) and cataloging the injustices that married women endured in *Some Reflections upon Marriage* (1700). Though she argued for women's equality outside of marriage, she nonetheless believed that, by the laws of God, marriage required the subordination of women to men. Only a single woman could hope to enjoy the intellectual and spiritual refreshment of the "delicious gardens" of Astell's utopian monastery, where English women could worship God,

> . . . one great end of this institution shall be, to expel that cloud of ignorance which custom has involved us in, to furnish our minds with a stock of solid and useful knowledge, that the souls of women may no longer be the only unadorned and neglected things.
>
> – MARY ASTELL, *A Serious Proposal to the Ladies*

Joseph Highmore, *Pamela Tells a Nursery Tale*, c. 1744
This painting illustrates a scene from the Samuel Richardson novel Pamela. *There was a great gap between the classes in the eighteenth century in terms of rights, privileges, and education. (Photograph © copyright Fitzwilliam Museum, University of Cambridge)*

p. 742

educate themselves, and rejoice in one another's friendship. In the selection from *Some Reflections upon Marriage,* Astell repudiates the conventions and laws that treated women as mere chattel in marriage and cautions against following the passions. Anticipating Mary Wollstonecraft's discussion of marriage in **A Vindication of the Rights of Woman**, Astell argues that women must cultivate their reason, educate themselves on a par with men, and then exercise their rational judgment when making choices about whom to marry—or whether to marry at all.

A note on the text: The texts from Mary Astell have been edited to modernize spelling and punctuation; some of her italics have been kept for emphasis. All notes are the editors'.

FROM

❧ A Serious Proposal to the Ladies

Now as to the proposal, it is to erect a *Monastery,* or if you will (to avoid giving offense to the scrupulous and injudicious, by names which though innocent in themselves, have been abused by superstitious practices), we will call it a *Religious Retirement,* and such as shall have a double aspect, being not only a retreat from the world for those who desire that advantage, but likewise, an institution and previous discipline, to fit us to do the greatest good in it; such an institution as this (if I do not mightily deceive myself) would be the most probable method to amend the present and improve the future age. For here those who are convinced of the emptiness of earthly enjoyments, who are sick of the vanity of the world and its impertinencies, may find more substantial and satisfying entertainments, and need not be confined to what they justly loathe. Those who are desirous to know and fortify their weak side, first do good to themselves, that hereafter they may be capable of doing more good to others; or for their greater security are willing to avoid temptation, may get out of that danger which a continual stay in view of the enemy, and the familiarity and unwearied application of the temptation may expose them to; and gain an opportunity to look into themselves, to be acquainted at home and no longer the greatest strangers to their own hearts. Such as are willing in a more peculiar and undisturbed manner to attend the great business they came into the world about, the service of God and improvement of their own minds, may find a convenient and blissful recess from the noise and hurry of the world. A world so cumbersome, so infectious, that although through the grace of God and their own strict watchfulness, they are kept from sinking down into its corruptions, 'twill however damp their flight to Heaven, hinder them from attaining any eminent pitch of virtue.

You are therefore, ladies, invited into a place where you shall suffer no other confinement but to be kept out of the road of sin: You shall not be deprived of your grandeur but only exchange the vain pomps and pageantry of the world, empty titles and forms of state, for the true and solid greatness of being able to despise them. You will not only quit the chat of insignificant people for an ingenious conversation; the froth of flashy wit for real wisdom; idle tales for instructive discourses. The deceitful flatteries of those who, under pretense of loving and admiring you, really served their own base ends, for the seasonable reproofs and wholesome counsels of your hearty well-wishers and affectionate friends, which will procure you those perfections your feigned lovers pretended you had, and kept you from obtaining. No uneasy task will be enjoined you, all your labor being only to prepare for the highest degrees of that glory, the very lowest of which is more than at present you are able to conceive, and the prospect of it sufficient to outweigh all the pains of religion, were there any in it, as really there are none. All that is required of you, is only to be as happy as possibly you can, and to make sure of a felicity that will fill all the capacities of your souls! [. . .]

For since God has given women as well as men intelligent souls, why should they be forbidden to improve them? Since he has not denied us the faculty of thinking, why should we not (at least in gratitude to him) employ our thoughts on himself, their noblest object, and not unworthily bestow them on trifles and gaieties and secular affairs? Being the soul was created for the contemplation of truth as well as for the fruition of good, is it not as cruel and unjust to exclude women from the knowledge of the one as from the enjoyment of the other? Especially since the will is blind, and cannot choose but by the direction of the understanding; or to speak more properly, since the soul always wills according as she understands, so that if she understands amiss, she wills amiss. And as exercise enlarges and exalts any faculty, so through want of using it becomes cramped and lessened; if therefore we make little or no use of our understandings, we shall shortly have none to use; and the more contracted and unemployed the deliberating and directive power is, the more liable is the elective to unworthy and mischievous choices. What is it but the want of an ingenious education that renders the generality of feminine conversations so insipid and foolish and their solitude so insupportable? Learning is therefore necessary to render them more agreeable and useful in company, and to furnish them with becoming entertainments when alone, that so they may not be driven to those miserable shifts, which too many make use of to put off their time, that precious talent that never lies on the hands of a judicious person. . . .

The ladies, I'm sure, have no reason to dislike this proposal, but I know not how the men will resent it to have their enclosure broke down, and women invited to taste of that tree of knowledge they have so long unjustly monopolized. But they must excuse me if I be as partial to my own sex as they are to theirs, and think women as capable of learning as men are, and that it becomes them as well. For I cannot imagine wherein the hurt lies, if instead of doing mischief to one another, by an uncharitable and vain conversation, women be enabled to inform and instruct those of their own sex at least; the Holy Ghost having left it on record, that Priscilla[1] as well as her husband, catechized the eloquent Apollos and the great Apostle found

---

[1] **Priscilla:** An early Roman Christian of humble background; she spoke up in public and corrected a learned male convert on points of Jesus' teachings and so has figured as a hero to Christian feminists. See Acts 18:24–26.

no fault with her. It will therefore be very proper for our ladies to spend part of their time in this retirement in adorning their minds with useful knowledge.

FROM

☙ Some Reflections upon Marriage

[. . .] If marriage be such a blessed state, how comes it, may you say, that there are so few happy marriages? Now in answer to this, it is not to be wondered that so few succeed, we should rather be surprised to find so many do considering how imprudently men engage, the motives they act by, and the very strange conduct they observe throughout.

For pray, what do men propose to themselves in marriage? What qualifications do they look after in a spouse? What will she bring is the first enquiry? How many acres? Or how much ready coin? Not that this is altogether an unnecessary question, for marriage without a competency,[1] that is, not only a bare subsistence, but even a handsome and plentiful provision, according to the quality and circumstances of the parties, is no very comfortable condition. They who marry for love as they call it, find time enough to repent their rash folly, and are not long in being convinced, that whatever fine speeches might be made in the heat of passion, there could be no *real kindness* between those who can agree to make each other miserable. But as an estate is to be considered, so it should not be the *main,* much less the *only* consideration, for happiness does not depend on wealth. [. . .]

But suppose a man does not marry for money, though for one that does not, perhaps there are thousands that do; let him marry for love, an heroic action, which makes a mighty noise in the world, partly because of its rarity, and partly in regard of its extravagancy, and what does his marrying for love amount to? There's no great odds between his marrying for the love of money, or for the love of beauty; the man does not act according to reason in either case, but is governed by irregular appetites. But he loves her wit[2] perhaps, and this you'll say is more spiritual, more refined; not at all if you examine it to the bottom. For what is that which nowadays passes under the name of wit? A bitter and ill-natured raillery, a pert repartee, or a confident talking at all, and in such a multitude of words, it's odds if something or other does not pass that is surprising, though everything that surprises does not please; some things being wondered at for their ugliness, as well as others for their beauty. True wit, durst one venture to describe it, is quite another thing; it consists in such a sprightliness of imagination, such a reach and turn of thought, so properly expressed, as strikes and

---

[1] **competency:** Income sufficient to support a wife and family in a manner appropriate to their social station.

[2] **wit:** In eighteenth-century England, wit signified general intellectual capacity and creativity as well as the facility to turn a clever phrase.

pleases a judicious taste. For though as one says of beauty, *'tis in no face but in the lover's mind,* so it may be said of some sort of wit, it is not in him that speaks, but in the imagination of his hearer. Yet doubtless there is a true standard-wit, which must be allowed for such by everyone who understands the terms; I don't say that they shall *equally* like it; and it is this standard-wit that always pleases, the spurious does so only for a season. [. . .]

Thus, whether it be wit or beauty that a man's in love with, there's no great hopes of a lasting happiness; beauty with all the helps of art is of no long date, the more it is helped the sooner it decays, and he who only or chiefly chose for beauty, will in a little time find the same reason for another choice. Nor is that sort of wit which he prefers of a more sure tenure, or allowing it to last, it will not always please. For that which has not a real excellency and value in itself, entertains no longer than the giddy humour which recommended it to us holds; and when we can like on no just, or on very little ground, tis certain a dislike will arise, as lightly and as unaccountably. And it is not improbable that such a husband may in a little time by ill usage provoke such a wife to exercise her wit, that is, her spleen on him, and then it is not hard to guess how very agreeable it will be to him.

In a word, when we have reckoned up how many look no further than the making of their fortune, as they call it; who don't so much as propose to themselves any satisfaction in the woman to whom they plight their faith, seeking only to be masters of her estate, that so they may have money enough to indulge all their irregular appetites; who think they are as good as can be expected, if they are but according to the fashionable term, *Civil Husbands;* when we have taken the number of your giddy lovers, who are not more violent in their passion than they are certain to repent of it; when to these you have added such as marry without any thought at all, further than that it is the custom of the world, what others have done before them, that the family must be kept up, the ancient race preserved, and therefore their kind parents and guardians choose as they think convenient, without ever consulting the young ones' inclinations, who must be satisfied or pretend so at least, upon pain of their displeasure, and that heavy consequence of it, forfeiture of their estate: These set aside, I fear there will be but a small remainder to marry out of better considerations, and even amongst the few that do, not one in a hundred takes care to deserve his choice. [. . .]

And as men have little reason to expect happiness when they marry only for the love of money, wit, or beauty, as has been already shown, so much less can a woman expect a tolerable life, when she goes upon these considerations. Let the business be carried as prudently as it can be on the woman's side, a reasonable man can't deny that she has by much the harder bargain. Because she puts herself entirely into her husband's power, and if the matrimonial yoke be grievous, neither law nor custom afford her that redress which a man obtains. He who has sovereign power does not value the provocations of a rebellious subject, but knows how to subdue him with ease, and will make himself obeyed; but patience and submission are the only comforts that are left to a poor people, who groan under tyranny, unless they are strong enough to break the yoke, to depose and abdicate, which I doubt would not be allowed of here. For whatever may be said against passive-obedience in another case,

I suppose there's no man but likes it very well in this; how much soever arbitrary power may be disliked on a throne, not *Milton*[3] himself would cry up liberty to poor *Female Slaves,* or plead for the lawfulness of resisting a private tyranny. . . .

Again, it may be said, if a wife's case be as it is here represented, it is not good for a woman to marry, and so there's an end of [the] human race. But this is no fair consequence, for all that can justly be inferred from hence is that a woman has no mighty obligations to the man who makes love to her, she has no reason to be fond of being a wife, or to reckon it a piece of preferment when she is taken to be a man's upper-servant; it is no advantage to her in this world, if rightly managed it may prove one as to the next. For she who marries purely to do good, to educate souls for heaven, who can be so truly mortified as to lay aside her own will and desires, to pay such as entire submission for life, to one whom she cannot be sure will always deserve it, does certainly perform a more heroic action than all the famous masculine heroes can boast of; she suffers a continual martyrdom to bring glory to God and benefit to mankind, which consideration indeed may carry her through all difficulties, I know not what else can, and engage her to love him who proves perhaps so much worse than a brute, as to make this condition yet more grievous than it needed to be. She has need of a strong reason, of a truly Christian and well-tempered spirit, of all the assistance the best education can give her, and ought to have some good assurance of her own firmness and virtue, who ventures on such a trial; and for this reason it is less to be wondered at that women marry off in haste, for perhaps if they took time to consider and reflect upon it, they seldom would marry. [. . .]

---

[3] **Milton:** John Milton (1608–1674), English poet and humanist whose greatest work is the epic poem *Paradise Lost.* Astell alludes to Milton's reputation as a liberal thinker and advocate of freedom, derived in part from *The Doctrine and Discipline of Divorce* (1643), which defends divorce on the grounds that marriage involves a mental and spiritual accordance between husband and wife, in addition to mutual physical attraction.

∾ JEAN-JACQUES ROUSSEAU
1712–1778

As mentioned in this book's introduction to *Confessions,* Rousseau revolutionized the status of feeling in late-eighteenth-century Europe. In *The New Heloise* (1761), Rousseau writes about the love between a sentimental young tutor, Saint-Preux, and his student, Julie D'Étange. In this novel, Rousseau suggests that while true love may excuse indiscretions on the part of a single woman, marriage requires strict fidelity. Presenting its heroine as a model of virtue and sanctioning the bond between husband and wife, *The New Heloise* reaffirms marriage as a foundation for civil society. In *Émile* (1762), a novelized treatise on education, Rousseau elaborates on the role of men and women and on the education and training needed to prepare both for their place in society. In the selection from *Émile* that follows, Rousseau describes the character of Sophy, a representative of all women, whose education should make her a submissive and docile marital companion. Rousseau also defines the marriage relationship as he understands it and criticizes the deceit and cunning that turn women against their husbands. As indicated by Mary Wollstonecraft's counterargument, also included here, those who championed women's rights in Europe found Rousseau an impediment to their cause.

A note on the translation: The translation of Rousseau's text is by Barbara Foxley. All notes are the editors'.

> If you would guard against these abuses, and secure happy marriages, you must stifle your prejudices, forget human institutions, and consult nature.
>
> – JEAN-JACQUES ROUSSEAU, *Émile*

 # Émile

Translated by Barbara Foxley

FROM BOOK V

We have reached the last act of youth's drama; we are approaching its closing scene.

It is not good that man should be alone. Émile is now a man, and we must give him his promised helpmeet. That helpmeet is Sophy. Where is her dwelling-place, where shall she be found? We must know beforehand what she is, and then we can decide where to look for her. And when she is found, our task is not ended. "Since our young gentleman," says Locke,[1] "is about to marry, it is time to leave him with his mistress." And with these words he ends his book. As I have not the honour of educating "A young gentleman," I shall take care not to follow his example.

Sophy, or Woman

Sophy should be as truly a woman as Émile is a man, *i.e.*, she must possess all those characters of her sex which are required to enable her to play her part in the physical and moral order. Let us inquire to begin with in what respects her sex differs from our own.

But for her sex, a woman is a man; she has the same organs, the same needs, the same faculties. The machine is the same in its construction; its parts, its working, and its appearance are similar. Regard it as you will the difference is only in degree.

Yet where sex is concerned man and woman are unlike; each is the complement of the other; the difficulty in comparing them lies in our inability to decide, in either case, what is a matter of sex, and what is not. General differences present themselves to the comparative anatomist and even to the superficial observer; they seem not to

---

[1] Locke John Locke (1632–1704), English philosopher and author of *Essay Concerning Human Understanding* (1690) and *Two Treatises on Government* (1690). (See Locke, *In the World: Declarations of Rights and Independence*, p. 586.)

be a matter of sex; yet they are really sex differences, though the connection eludes our observation. How far such differences may extend we cannot tell; all we know for certain is that where man and woman are alike we have to do with the characteristics of the species; where they are unlike, we have to do with the characteristics of sex. Considered from these two standpoints, we find so many instances of likeness and unlikeness that it is perhaps one of the greatest of marvels how nature has contrived to make two beings so like and yet so different.

These resemblances and differences must have an influence on the moral nature; this inference is obvious, and it is confirmed by experience; it shows the vanity of the disputes as to the superiority or the equality of the sexes; as if each sex, pursuing the path marked out for it by nature, were not more perfect in that very divergence than if it more closely resembled the other. A perfect man and a perfect woman should no more be alike in mind than in face, and perfection admits of neither less nor more.

In the union of the sexes each alike contributes to the common end, but in different ways. From this diversity springs the first difference which may be observed between man and woman in their moral relations. The man should be strong and active; the woman should be weak and passive; the one must have both the power and the will; it is enough that the other should offer little resistance.

When this principle is admitted, it follows that woman is specially made for man's delight. If man in his turn ought to be pleasing in her eyes, the necessity is less urgent, his virtue is in his strength, he pleases because he is strong. I grant you this is not the law of love, but it is the law of nature, which is older than love itself.

If woman is made to please and to be in subjection to man, she ought to make herself pleasing in his eyes and not provoke him to anger; her strength is in her charms, by their means she should compel him to discover and use his strength. The surest way of arousing this strength is to make it necessary by resistance. Thus pride comes to the help of desire and each exults in the other's victory. This is the origin of attack and defence, of the boldness of one sex and the timidity of the other, and even of the shame and modesty with which nature has armed the weak for the conquest of the strong. [. . .]

Women so easily stir a man's senses and fan the ashes of a dying passion, that if philosophy ever succeeded in introducing this custom into any unlucky country, especially if it were a warm country where more women are born than men, the men, tyrannised over by the women, would at last become their victims, and would be dragged to their death without the least chance of escape.

Female animals are without this sense of shame, but what of that? Are their desires as boundless as those of women, which are curbed by this shame? The desires of the animals are the result of necessity, and when the need is satisfied, the desire ceases; they no longer make a feint of repulsing the male, they do it in earnest. Their seasons of complaisance are short and soon over. Impulse and restraint are alike the work of nature. But what would take the place of this negative instinct in women if you rob them of their modesty?

The Most High has deigned to do honour to mankind; he has endowed man with boundless passions, together with a law to guide them, so that man may be alike free and self-controlled; though swayed by these passions man is endowed with reason by which to control them. Woman is also endowed with boundless passions; God has given her modesty to restrain them. Moreover, he has given to both a present reward for the right use of their powers, in the delight which springs from that right use of them, *i.e.,* the taste for right conduct established as the law of our behaviour. To my mind this is far higher than the instinct of the beasts. . . .

Thus the different constitution of the two sexes leads us to a third conclusion, that the stronger party seems to be master, but is as a matter of fact dependent on the weaker, and that, not by any foolish custom of gallantry, nor yet by the magnanimity of the protector, but by an inexorable law of nature. For nature has endowed woman with a power of stimulating man's passions in excess of man's power of satisfying those passions, and has thus made him dependent on her goodwill, and compelled him in his turn to endeavour to please her, so that she may be willing to yield to his superior strength. Is it weakness which yields to force, or is it voluntary self-surrender? This uncertainty constitutes the chief charm of the man's victory, and the woman is usually cunning enough to leave him in doubt. In this respect the woman's mind exactly resembles her body; far from being ashamed of her weakness, she is proud of it; her soft muscles offer no resistance, she professes that she cannot lift the lightest weight; she would be ashamed to be strong. And why? Not only to gain an appearance of refinement; she is too clever for that; she is providing herself beforehand with excuses, with the right to be weak if she chooses. [. . .]

Although equality of rank is not essential in marriage, yet this equality along with other kinds of suitability increases their value; it is not to be weighed against any one of them, but, other things being equal, it turns the scale.

A man, unless he is a king, cannot seek a wife in any and every class; if he himself is free from prejudices, he will find them in others; and this girl or that might perhaps suit him and yet she would be beyond his reach. A wise father will therefore restrict his inquiries within the bounds of prudence. He should not wish to marry his pupil into a family above his own, for that is not within his power. If he could do so he ought not desire it; for what difference does rank make to a young man, at least to my pupil? Yet, if he rises he is exposed to all sorts of real evils which he will feel all his life long. I even say that he should not try to adjust the balance between different gifts, such as rank and money; for each of these adds less to the value of the other than the amount deducted from its own value in the process of adjustment; moreover, we can never agree as to a common denominator; and finally the preference, which each feels for his own surroundings, paves the way for discord between the two families and often to difficulties between husband and wife.

It makes a considerable difference as to the suitability of a marriage whether a man marries above or beneath him. The former case is quite contrary to reason, the latter is more in conformity with reason. As the family is only connected with society through its head, it is the rank of that head which decides that of the family as a whole. When he marries into a lower rank, a man does not lower himself, he raises his wife; if, on the other hand, he marries above his position, he lowers his wife and does not raise himself. Thus there is in the first case good unmixed with evil, in the other evil unmixed with good. Moreover, the law of nature bids the woman obey the man. If he takes a wife from a lower class, natural and civil law are in accordance and all goes well. When he marries a woman of higher rank it is just the opposite case; the man must choose between diminished rights or imperfect gratitude; he must be ungrateful or despised. Then the wife, laying claim to authority, makes herself a tyrant over her lawful head; and the master, who has become a slave, is the most ridiculous and miserable of creatures. Such are the unhappy favourites whom the sovereigns of Asia honour and torment with their alliance; people tell us that if they desire to sleep with their wife they must enter by the foot of the bed.

I expect that many of my readers will remember that I think women have a natural gift for managing men, and will accuse me of contradicting myself; yet they are mistaken. There is a vast difference between claiming the right to command, and managing him who commands. Woman's reign is a reign of gentleness, tact, and kindness; her commands are caresses, her threats are tears. She should reign in the home as a minister reigns in the state, by contriving to be ordered to do what she wants. In this sense, I grant you, that the best managed homes are those where the wife has most power. But when she despises the voice of her head, when she desires to usurp his rights and take the command upon herself, this inversion of the proper order of things leads only to misery, scandal, and dishonour.

There remains the choice between our equals and our inferiors; and I think we ought also to make certain restrictions with regard to the latter; for it is hard to find in the lowest stratum of society a woman who is able to make a good man happy; not that the lower classes are more vicious than the higher, but because they have so little idea of what is good and beautiful, and because the injustice of other classes makes its very vices seem right in the eyes of this class.

By nature man thinks but seldom. He learns to think as he acquires the other arts, but with even greater difficulty. In both sexes alike I am only aware of two really distinct classes, those who think and those who do not; and this difference is almost entirely one of education. A man who thinks should not ally himself with a woman who does not think, for he loses the chief delight of social life if he has a wife who cannot share his thoughts. People who spend their whole life in working for a living have no ideas beyond their work and their own interests, and their mind seems to reside in their arms. This ignorance is not necessarily unfavourable either to their honesty or their morals; it is often favourable; we often content ourselves with thinking about our duties, and in the end we substitute words for things. Conscience is the most enlightened philosopher; to be an honest man we need not read Cicero's[2] *De Officiis,* and the most virtuous woman in the world is probably she who knows least about virtue. But it is none the less true that a cultivated mind alone makes intercourse pleasant, and it is a sad thing for a father of a family, who delights in his home, to be forced to shut himself up in himself and to be unable to make himself understood.

Moreover, if a woman is quite unaccustomed to think, how can she bring up her children? How will she know what is good for them? How can she incline them to

---

[2] Cicero Marcus Tullius Cicero (106 B.C.E.–43 B.C.E.), Roman orator, statesman, and philosopher, known as one of the greatest Latin prose stylists.

virtues of which she is ignorant, to merit of which she has no conception? She can only flatter or threaten, she can only make them insolent or timid; she will make them performing monkeys or noisy little rascals; she will never make them intelligent or pleasing children.

Therefore it is not fitting that a man of education should choose a wife who has none, or take her from a class where she cannot be expected to have any education. But I would a thousand times rather have a homely girl, simply brought up, than a learned lady and a wit who would make a literary circle of my house and install herself as its president. A female wit is a scourge to her husband, her children, her friends, her servants, to everybody. From the lofty height of her genius she scorns every womanly duty, and she is always trying to make a man of herself after the fashion of Mlle. de L'Enclos.[3] Outside her home she always makes herself ridiculous and she is very rightly a butt for criticism, as we always are when we try to escape from our own position into one for which we are unfitted. These highly talented women only get a hold over fools. We can always tell what artist or friend holds the pen or pencil when they are at work; we know what discreet man of letters dictates their oracles in private. This trickery is unworthy of a decent woman. If she really had talents, her pretentiousness would degrade them. Her honour is to be unknown; her glory is the respect of her husband; her joys the happiness of her family. I appeal to my readers to give me an honest answer; when you enter a woman's room what makes you think more highly of her, what makes you address her with more respect—to see her busy with feminine occupations, with her household duties, with her children's clothes about her, or to find her writing verses at her toilet table surrounded with pamphlets of every kind and with notes on tinted paper? If there were none but wise men upon earth such a woman would die an old maid.

> Quæris cur nolim te ducere, galla? diserta es.
> — MARTIAL, *XI. 20*.[4]

Looks must next be considered; they are the first thing that strikes us and they ought to be the last, still they should not count for nothing. I think that great beauty is rather to be shunned than sought after in marriage. Possession soon exhausts our appreciation of beauty; in six weeks' time we think no more about it, but its dangers endure as long as life itself. Unless a beautiful woman is an angel, her husband is the most miserable of men; and even if she were an angel he would still be the centre of a hostile crowd and she could not prevent it. If extreme ugliness were not repulsive I should prefer it to extreme beauty; for before very long the husband would cease to notice either, but beauty would still have its disadvantages and ugliness its

---

[3] **Mlle. de L'Enclos:** Ninon de L'Enclos (1620–1705), French courtesan and woman of letters, author of *Letters to the Marquis de Sévigné*. Said to be the most beautiful woman in France, keeping her beauty preserved into her old age. As a critical gesture, in order to claim the privileges of men, she declared herself to be a man; hence Rousseau's comment.

[4] **Martial:** Marcus Valerius Martialis (c. 40–c. 104), Roman poet, author of *Liber Spectaculorum* (80 C.E.) and several books of epigrammatic poems now known as *Epigrams*. The quote, from Epigram 19 of Book XI, has been interpreted as an attack on well-educated women of high social standing. The lines roughly translate as "You ask why I won't marry you, Galla? You are eloquent, / and my penis often makes a solecism."

advantages. But ugliness which is actually repulsive is the worst misfortune; repulsion increases rather than diminishes, and it turns to hatred. Such a union is a hell upon earth; better death than such a marriage.

Desire mediocrity in all things, even in beauty. A pleasant attractive countenance, which inspires kindly feelings rather than love, is what we should prefer; the husband runs no risk, and the advantages are common to husband and wife; charm is less perishable than beauty; it is a living thing, which constantly renews itself, and after thirty years of married life, the charms of a good woman delight her husband even as they did on the wedding-day.

Such are the considerations which decided my choice of Sophy. Brought up, like Émile, by Nature, she is better suited to him than any other; she will be his true mate. She is his equal in birth and character, his inferior in fortune. She makes no great impression at first sight, but day by day reveals fresh charms. Her chief influence only takes effect gradually, it is only discovered in friendly intercourse; and her husband will feel it more than any one. Her education is neither showy nor neglected; she has taste without deep study, talent without art, judgment without learning. Her mind knows little, but it is trained to learn; it is well-tilled soil ready for the sower. She has read no book but *Barème* and *Telemachus*[5] which happened to fall into her hands; but no girl who can feel so passionately towards Telemachus can have a heart without feeling or a mind without discernment. What charming ignorance! Happy is he who is destined to be her tutor. She will not be her husband's teacher but his scholar; far from seeking to control his tastes, she will share them. She will suit him far better than a blue-stocking and he will have the pleasure of teaching her everything. It is time they made acquaintance; let us try to plan a meeting. [. . .]

---

[5] **Telemachus:** Sophy has been reading *The Adventures of Telemachus* (1699), a utopian fantasy about Odysseus's son by François Fénélon (1651–1715), French archbishop and man of letters who also wrote a treatise on the education of young women. Sophy has fallen in love with the romantic image of Telemachus created in the story, a point Rousseau makes to speak out against women reading such tales.

❧ MARY WOLLSTONECRAFT
1759–1797

Mary Wollstonecraft was born in 1759 in London, where she received a formal education and was called on to help support her family, whose modest fortunes her father had lost. After nursing her dying mother, at the age of nineteen Wollstonecraft founded a school for girls in Islington and then another in Newington Green, where Dr. Richard Price encouraged the inquisitive and intelligent woman to read the works of the ENLIGHTENMENT philosophers. After unhappy relationships with the painter Henry Fuseli and the American entrepreneur and gambler Gilbert Imlay, Wollstonecraft eventually married William Godwin, the most respected radical philosopher of the time and author of the important *Enquiry Concerning Political Justice* (1793). In addition to treatises on women's rights, Wollstonecraft wrote books on the French Revolution, education, and travel as well as two novels. She died in September 1797, about ten days after giving birth to Mary Wollstonecraft Godwin, later Mary Shelley, the author of *Frankenstein*.

A Vindication of the Rights of Woman elicited a strong reaction from many conservative writers, who responded with virulent attacks on Wollstonecraft's character and free thinking. After her untimely death, her husband added fuel to this fire by publishing, rather naively, a completely candid biography of her life, *Memoirs of the Author of "A Vindication of the Rights of Woman."* Despite the disapproval of many contemporaries, Wollstonecraft found sympathetic readers among the budding feminist writers of her age, including the English writers Mary Hays and Mary Ann Evans (George Eliot), and the American feminists Lucretia Mott and Elizabeth Cady Stanton, who organized the first women's rights convention in Seneca Falls, New York, in 1848; moreover, *A Vindication* was available in American, French, and German editions throughout the nineteenth century. The standing of her work took a positive turn in the twentieth century, finally receiving the respect it deserved. Emma Goldman eloquently sums up Wollstonecraft's life and work in a brief tribute to her: "The treasure of her soul, the wisdom of her life's philosophy, the depth of her World of thought, the intensity of her battle for human emancipation and especially her indomitable struggle for the liberation of her own sex, are even today so far ahead of the average grasp that we may indeed claim for her the rare exception which nature has created once in a century."

Wollstonecraft's first work, *Thoughts on the Education of Daughters* (1786), promoting an enlightened view of education for women, paved the way for *A Vindication of the Rights of Woman* (1792), a full-blown critique of education for women and a defense of women's rights. Although the way had been partially prepared in England by Mary Astell's **Some Reflections upon Marriage** (1700) and Catherine Macaulay's *Letters on Education* (1790), Wollstonecraft's treatise pointed more directly to the blatant injustice of the present "false system of education"

> Let woman share the rights and she will emulate the virtues of man; for she must grow more perfect when emancipated, or justify the authority that chains such a weak being to her duty.
>
> – MARY WOLLSTONECRAFT, *A Vindication of the Rights of Woman*

p. 732

p. 735

for women, particularly the kind of education advocated in Rousseau's *Émile*. Throughout *A Vindication,* Wollstonecraft attacks Rousseau's ideal woman, Sophy, arguing that she is a model for no more than a man's plaything—trained in superficial conversation, shallow thinking, and frivolous accomplishments. For Wollstonecraft, Sophy is the quintessence of all that is wrong with women under the current state of society and the customary system of education, which enables women to become only "alluring objects for the moment"—toys for the amusement and titillation of men. Thus, like Sophy, women not only become subordinate to and dependent on men for their economic and social standing, but they are prevented from developing into capable and contributing citizens. Cultivated as ornamental objects, women cannot form rational friendships with or earn the respect of their husbands, who, as a result, turn to affairs with younger women when their wives lose their "charms." Since friendship is a higher form of bond than those affections based on money, beauty, and wit, to use Mary Astell's terms, Wollstonecraft asserts that women must receive an education that will prepare them to build marriages based not on subordination and passion, as Rousseau would have it, but on equal partnership and levelheaded friendship with men.

A note on the text: Wollstonecraft's spelling and punctuation have been modernized. All notes are the editors' unless otherwise indicated.

❧ A Vindication of the Rights of Woman

Introduction to the First Edition

After considering the historic page, and viewing the living world with anxious solicitude, the most melancholy emotions of sorrowful indignation have depressed my spirits, and I have sighed when obliged to confess, that either nature has made a great difference between man and man, or that the civilization which has hitherto taken place in the world has been very partial. I have turned over various books written on the subject of education, and patiently observed the conduct of parents and the management of schools; but what has been the result?—a profound conviction that the neglected education of my fellow-creatures is the grand source of the misery I deplore; and that women, in particular, are rendered weak and wretched by a variety of concurring causes, originating from one hasty conclusion. The conduct and manners of women, in fact, evidently prove that their minds are not in a healthy state; for, like the flowers which are planted in too rich a soil, strength and usefulness are sacrificed to beauty; and the flaunting leaves, after having pleased a fastidious eye, fade, disregarded on the stalk, long before the season when they ought to have arrived at maturity. One cause of this barren blooming I attribute to a false system of education, gathered from the books written on this subject by men who, considering females rather as women than human creatures, have been more anxious to make them alluring mistresses than affectionate wives and rational mothers; and the understanding of the sex has been so bubbled by this specious homage, that the civilized women of the present century, with a few exceptions, are only anxious to inspire love, when they ought to cherish a nobler ambition, and by their abilities and virtues exact respect.

In a treatise, therefore, on female rights and manners, the works which have been particularly written for their improvement must not be overlooked; especially when it is asserted, in direct terms, that the minds of women are enfeebled by false refinement; that the books of instruction, written by men of genius, have had the same tendency as more frivolous productions; and that, in the true style of Mahometanism, they are treated as a kind of subordinate beings, and not as a part of the human species, when improveable reason is allowed to be the dignified distinction which raises men above the brute creation, and puts a natural sceptre in a feeble hand.

Yet, because I am a woman, I would not lead my readers to suppose that I mean violently to agitate the contested question respecting the quality or inferiority of the sex; but as the subject lies in my way, and I cannot pass it over without subjecting the main tendency of my reasoning to misconstruction, I shall stop a moment to deliver, in a few words, my opinion. In the government of the physical world it is observable that the female in point of strength is, in general, inferior to the male. This is the law of nature; and it does not appear to be suspended or abrogated in favour of woman. A degree of physical superiority cannot, therefore, be denied—and it is a noble prerogative! But not content with this natural pre-eminence, men endeavour to sink us still lower, merely to render us alluring objects for a moment; and women, intoxicated by the adoration which men, under the influence of their senses, pay them, do not seek to obtain a durable interest in their hearts, or to become the friends of the fellow creatures who find amusement in their society.

I am aware of an obvious inference:—from every quarter have I heard exclamations against masculine women; but where are they to be found? If by this appellation men mean to inveigh against their ardour in hunting, shooting, and gaming, I shall most cordially join in the cry; but if it be against the imitation of manly virtues, or, more properly speaking, the attainment of those talents and virtues, the exercise of which ennobles the human character, and which raise females in the scale of animal being, when they are comprehensively termed mankind;—all those who view them with a philosophic eye must, I should think, wish with me, that they may every day grow more and more masculine.

This discussion naturally divides the subject. I shall first consider women in the grand light of human creatures, who, in common with men, are placed on this earth to unfold their faculties; and afterwards I shall more particularly point out their peculiar designation.

I wish also to steer clear of an error which many respectable writers have fallen into; for the instruction which has hitherto been addressed to women, has rather been applicable to *ladies,* if the little indirect advice, that is scattered through Sandford and Merton,[1] be excepted; but, addressing my sex in a firmer tone, I pay

---

[1]**Sandford and Merton:**   *The History of Sandford and Merton* (1783–89), a popular children's book by Thomas Day.

particular attention to those in the middle class, because they appear to be in the most natural state. Perhaps the seeds of false refinement, immorality, and vanity, have ever been shed by the great. Weak, artificial beings, raised above the common wants and affections of their race, in a premature unnatural manner, undermine the very foundation of virtue, and spread corruption through the whole mass of society! As a class of mankind they have the strongest claim to pity; the education of the rich tends to render them vain and helpless, and the unfolding mind is not strengthened by the practice of those duties which dignify the human character. They only live to amuse themselves, and by the same law which in nature invariably produces certain effects, they soon only afford barren amusement.

But as I purpose taking a separate view of the different ranks of society, and of the moral character of women, in each, this hint is, for the present, sufficient; and I have only alluded to the subject, because it appears to me to be the very essence of an introduction to give a cursory account of the contents of the work it introduces.

My own sex, I hope, will excuse me, if I treat them like rational creatures, instead of flattering their *fascinating* graces, and viewing them as if they were in a state of perpetual childhood, unable to stand alone. I earnestly wish to point out in what true dignity and human happiness consists—I wish to persuade women to endeavour to acquire strength, both of mind and body, and to convince them that the soft phrases, susceptibility of heart, delicacy of sentiment, and refinement of taste, are almost synonymous with epithets of weakness, and that those beings who are only the objects of pity and that kind of love, which has been termed its sister, will soon become objects of contempt.

Dismissing, then, those pretty feminine phrases, which the men condescendingly use to soften our slavish dependence, and despising that weak elegancy of mind, exquisite sensibility, and sweet docility of manners, supposed to be the sexual characteristics of the weaker vessel, I wish to show that elegance is inferior to virtue, that the first object of laudable ambition is to obtain a character as a human being, regardless of the distinction of sex; and that secondary views should be brought to this simple touchstone.

This is a rough sketch of my plan; and should I express my conviction with the energetic emotions that I feel whenever I think of the subject, the dictates of experience and reflection will be felt by some of my readers. Animated by this important object, I shall disdain to cull my phrases or polish my style;—I aim at being useful, and sincerity will render me unaffected; for, wishing rather to persuade by the force of my arguments, than dazzle by the elegance of my language, I shall not waste my time in rounding periods, or in fabricating the turgid bombast of artificial feelings, which, coming from the head, never reach the heart. I shall be employed about things, not words! and, anxious to render my sex more respectable members of society, I shall try to avoid that flowery diction which has slided from essays into novels, and from novels into familiar letters and conversation.

These pretty superlatives, dropping glibly from the tongue, vitiate the taste, and create a kind of sickly delicacy that turns away from simple unadorned truth; and a deluge of false sentiments and overstretched feelings, stifling the natural emotions of the heart, render the domestic pleasures insipid, that ought to sweeten the exercise of those severe duties, which educate a rational and immortal being for a nobler field of action.

The education of women has, of late, been more attended to than formerly; yet they are still reckoned a frivolous sex, and ridiculed or pitied by the writers who endeavour by satire or instruction to improve them. It is acknowledged that they spend many of the first years of their lives in acquiring a smattering of accomplishments; meanwhile strength of body and mind are sacrificed to libertine notions of beauty, to the desire of establishing themselves, — the only way women can rise in the world, — by marriage. And this desire making mere animals of them, when they marry they act as such children may be expected to act: — they dress; they paint, and nickname God's creatures. Surely these weak beings are only fit for a seraglio! — Can they be expected to govern a family with judgment, or take care of the poor babes whom they bring into the world?

If then it can be fairly deduced from the present conduct of the sex, from the prevalent fondness for pleasure which takes place of ambition and those nobler passions that open and enlarge the soul; that the instruction which women have hitherto received has only tended with the constitution of civil society, to render them insignificant objects of desire—mere propagators of fools! — if it can be proved that in aiming to accomplish them, without cultivating their understandings, they are taken out of their sphere of duties, and made ridiculous and useless when the short-lived bloom of beauty is over,[2] I presume that *rational* men will excuse me for endeavouring to persuade them to become more masculine and respectable.

Indeed the word *masculine* is only a bugbear: there is little reason to fear that women will acquire too much courage or fortitude; for their apparent inferiority with respect to bodily strength, must render them, in some degree, dependent on men in the various relations of life; but why should it be increased by prejudices that give a sex to virtue, and confound simple truths with sensual reveries?

Women are, in fact, so much degraded by mistaken notions of female excellence, that I do not mean to add a paradox when I assert, that this artificial weakness produces a propensity to tyrranize, and gives birth to cunning, the natural opponent of strength, which leads them to play off those contemptible infantine airs that undermine esteem even whilst they excite desire. Let men become more chaste and modest, and if women do not grow wiser in the same ratio, it will be clear that they have weaker understandings. It seems scarcely necessary to say, that I now speak of the sex in general. Many individuals have more sense than their male relatives; and, as nothing preponderates where there is a constant struggle for an equilibrium, without it has naturally more gravity, some women govern their husbands without degrading themselves, because intellect will always govern.

---

[2] A lively writer, I cannot recollect his name, asks what business women turned of forty have to do in the world? [Wollstonecraft's note.]

FROM CHAPTER 2

The Prevailing Opinion of a Sexual Character Discussed

To account for, and excuse the tyranny of man, many ingenious arguments have been brought forward to prove that the two sexes, in the acquirement of virtue, ought to aim at attaining a very different character; or, to speak explicitly, women are not allowed to have sufficient strength of mind to acquire what really deserves the name of virtue. Yet it should seem, allowing them to have souls, that there is but one way appointed by Providence to lead mankind to either virtue or happiness.

If then women are not a swarm of ephemeron triflers, why should they be kept in ignorance under the specious name of innocence? Men complain, and with reason, of the follies and caprices of our sex, when they do not keenly satirize our headstrong passions and grovelling vices. Behold, I should answer, the natural effect of ignorance! The mind will ever be unstable that has only prejudices to rest on, and the current will run with destructive fury when there are no barriers to break its force. Women are told from their infancy, and taught by the example of their mothers, that a little knowledge of human weakness, justly termed cunning, softness of temper, outward obedience, and a scrupulous attention to a puerile kind of propriety will obtain for them the protection of man; and should they be beautiful, everything else is needless, for at least twenty years of their lives.

John Opie, *Mary Wollstonecraft*, c. 1790–91

This portrait was painted when Wollstonecraft was thirty-one or thirty-two years old. (Tate Gallery, London/ Art Resource)

Thus Milton[3] describes our first frail mother; though when he tells us that women are formed for softness and sweet attractive grace, I cannot comprehend his meaning, unless, in the true Mahometan strain, he meant to deprive us of souls[4] and insinuate that we were beings only designed by sweet attractive grace and docile blind obedience, to gratify the senses of man when he can no longer soar on the wing of contemplation.

How grossly do they insult us who thus advise us only to render ourselves gentle, domestic brutes! For instance, the winning softness, so warmly and frequently recommended, that governs by obeying. What childish expressions, and how insignificant is the being—can it be an immortal one? who will condescend to govern by such sinister methods! "Certainly," says Lord Bacon,[5] "man is of kin to the beasts by his body; and if he be not of kin to God by his spirit, he is a base and ignoble creature!" Men, indeed, appear to me to act in a very unphilosophical manner when they try to secure the good conduct of women by attempting to keep them always in a state of childhood. Rousseau was more consistent when he wished to stop the progress of reason in both sexes, for if men eat of the tree of knowledge, women will come in for a taste; but, from the imperfect cultivation which their understandings now receive, they only attain a knowledge of evil. [. . .]

I may be accused of arrogance; still I must declare what I firmly believe, that all the writers who have written on the subject of female education and manners, from Rousseau to Dr. Gregory,[6] have contributed to render women more artificial, weak characters, than they would otherwise have been; and consequently, more useless members of society. I might have expressed this conviction in a lower key; but I am afraid it would have been the whine of affectation, and not the faithful expression of my feelings, of the clear result which experience and reflection have led me to draw. When I come to that division of the subject, I shall advert to the passages that I more particularly disapprove of in the works of the authors I have just alluded to; but it is first necessary to observe, that my objection extends to the whole purport of those books, which tend, in my opinion, to degrade one half of the human species and render women pleasing at the expense of every solid virtue.

Though, to reason on Rousseau's ground, if man did attain a degree of perfection of mind when his body arrived at maturity, it might be proper, in order to make a man and his wife one, that she should rely entirely on his understanding; and the graceful ivy, clasping the oak that supported it, would form a whole in which strength and beauty would be equally conspicuous. But, alas! husbands, as well as their helpmates, are often only overgrown children; nay, thanks to early debauchery,

---

[3] **Milton:** John Milton (1608–1674) describes Adam and Eve in *Paradise Lost* IV.297–99: "For contemplation he and valor form'd, / For softness she and sweet attractive grade; / He for God only, she for God in him."

[4] **deprive us of souls:** Wollstonecraft here voices the common error that Islam, the religion founded upon the teachings and prophecies of Muhammad, did not grant women souls.

[5] **Lord Bacon:** Sir Francis Bacon (1561–1626), English philosopher and scientist; the quote is from his essay, "Of Atheism."

[6] **Dr. Gregory:** Dr. John Gregory (1724–1773), Scottish physician who wrote *A Father's Legacy to His Daughters* (1774), a popular and influential conduct book concerning the education of young women.

scarcely men in their outward form—and if the blind lead the blind, one need not come from heaven to tell us the consequence.

Many are the causes that, in the present corrupt state of society, contribute to enslave women by cramping their understandings and sharpening their senses. One, perhaps, that silently does more mischief than all the rest, is their disregard of order.

To do everything in an orderly manner is a most important precept, which women, who, generally speaking, receive only a disorderly kind of education, seldom attend to with that degree of exactness that men, who from their infancy are broken into method, observe. This negligent kind of guess-work, for what other epithet can be used to point out the random exertions of a sort of instinctive common sense, never brought to the test of reason? prevents their generalizing matters of fact—so they do to-day, what they did yesterday, merely because they did it yesterday.

This contempt of the understanding in early life has more baneful consequences than is commonly supposed; for the little knowledge which women of strong minds attain, is, from various circumstances, of a more desultory kind than the knowledge of men, and it is acquired more by sheer observations on real life, than from comparing what has been individually observed with the results of experience generalized by speculation. Led by their dependent situation and domestic employments more into society, what they learn is rather by snatches; and as learning is with them, in general, only a secondary thing, they do not pursue any one branch with that persevering ardour necessary to give vigour to the faculties, and clearness to the judgment. In the present state of society, a little learning is required to support the character of a gentleman; and boys are obliged to submit to a few years of discipline. But in the education of women, the cultivation of the understanding is always subordinate to the acquirement of some corporeal accomplishment; even while enervated by confinement and false notions of modesty, the body is prevented from attaining that grace and beauty which relaxed half-formed limbs never exhibit. Besides, in youth their faculties are not brought forward by emulation; and having no serious scientific study, if they have natural sagacity it is turned too soon on life and manners. They dwell on effects, and modifications, without tracing them back to causes; and complicated rules to adjust behaviour are a weak substitute for simple principles.

As a proof that education gives this appearance of weakness to females, we may instance the example of military men, who are, like them, sent into the world before their minds have been stored with knowledge or fortified by principles. The consequences are similar; soldiers acquire a little superficial knowledge, snatched from the muddy current of conversation, and, from continually mixing with society, they gain what is termed a knowledge of the world; and this acquaintance with manners and customs has frequently been confounded with a knowledge of the human heart. But can the crude fruit of casual observation, never brought to the test of judgment, formed by comparing speculation and experience, deserve such a distinction? Soldiers, as well as women, practice the minor virtues with punctilious politeness. Where is then the sexual difference, when the education has been the same? All the difference that I can discern, arises from the superior advantage of liberty, which enables the former to see more of life. . . .

[. . .] Strengthen the female mind by enlarging it, and there will be an end to blind obedience; but, as blind obedience is ever sought for by power, tyrants and sensualists are in the right when they endeavour to keep women in the dark, because the former only want slaves, and the latter a plaything. The sensualist, indeed, has been the most dangerous of tyrants, and women have been duped by their lovers, as princes by their ministers, whilst dreaming that they reigned over them.

I now principally allude to Rousseau, for his character of Sophia is, undoubtedly, a captivating one, though it appears to me grossly unnatural; however it is not the superstructure, but the foundation of her character, the principles on which her education was built, that I mean to attack; nay, warmly as I admire the genius of that able writer, whose opinions I shall often have occasion to cite, indignation always takes place of admiration, and the rigid frown of insulted virtue effaces the smile of complacency, which his eloquent periods are wont to raise, when I read his voluptuous reveries. Is this the man, who, in his ardour for virtue, would banish all the soft arts of peace, and almost carry us back to Spartan discipline? Is this the man who delights to paint the useful struggles of passion, the triumphs of good dispositions, and the heroic flights which carry the glowing soul out of itself?—How are these mighty sentiments lowered when he describes the pretty foot and enticing airs of his little favourite! But, for the present, I waive the subject, and instead of severely reprehending the transient effusions of overweening sensibility, I shall only observe that whoever has cast a benevolent eye on society must often have been gratified by the sight of humble mutual love, not dignified by sentiment or strengthened by a union in intellectual pursuits. The domestic trifles of the day have afforded matters for cheerful converse, and innocent caresses have softened toils which did not require great exercise of mind or stretch of thought: yet, has not the sight of this moderate felicity excited more tenderness than respect? An emotion similar to what we feel when children are playing, or animals sporting,[7] whilst the contemplation of the noble struggles of suffering merit has raised admiration, and carried our thoughts to that world where sensation will give place to reason.

Women are, therefore, to be considered either as moral beings, or so weak that they must be entirely subjected to the superior faculties of men.

Let us examine this question. Rousseau declares that a woman should never, for a moment, feel herself independent, that she should be governed by fear to exercise her natural cunning, and made a coquettish slave in order to render her a more alluring object of desire, a sweeter companion to man, whenever he chooses to relax himself. He carries the arguments, which he pretends to draw from the indications of nature, still further, and insinuates that truth and fortitude, the cornerstones of all human virtue, should be cultivated with certain restrictions, because, with respect to

---

[7] **animals sporting:** Similar feelings has Milton's pleasing picture of paradisiacal happiness ever raised in my mind: Yet, instead of envying the lovely pair, I have, with conscious dignity, or Satanic pride, turned to hell for sublimer objects. In the same style, when viewing some noble monument of human art, I have traced the emanation of the Deity in the order I admired, till, descending from that giddy height, I have caught myself contemplating the grandest of all human sights;—for fancy quickly placed, in some solitary recess, an outcast of fortune, rising superior to passion and discontent. [Wollstonecraft's note.]

the female character, obedience is the grand lesson which ought to be impressed with unrelenting rigour.

What nonsense! When will a great man arise with sufficient strength of mind to puff away the fumes which pride and sensuality have thus spread over the subject! If women are by nature inferior to men, their virtues must be the same in quality, if not in degree, or virtue is a relative idea; consequently, their conduct should be founded on the same principles, and have the same aim. . . .

To speak disrespectfully of love is, I know, high treason against sentiment and fine feelings; but I wish to speak the simple language of truth, and rather to address the head than the heart. To endeavour to reason love out of the world, would be to out-Quixote Cervantes,[8] and equally offend against common sense; but an endeavour to restrain this tumultuous passion, and to prove that it should not be allowed to dethrone superior powers, or to usurp the sceptre which the understanding should ever coolly wield, appears less wild.

Youth is the season for love in both sexes; but in those days of thoughtless enjoyment provision should be made for the more important years of life, when reflection takes place of sensation. But Rousseau, and most of the male writers who have followed his steps, have warmly inculcated that the whole tendency of female education ought to be directed to one point: — to render them pleasing.

Let me reason with the supporters of this opinion who have any knowledge of human nature, do they imagine that marriage can eradicate the habitude of life? The woman who has only been taught to please will soon find that her charms are oblique sunbeams, and that they cannot have much effect on her husband's heart when they are seen every day, when the summer is passed and gone. Will she then have sufficient native energy to look into herself for comfort, and cultivate her dormant faculties? Or, is it not more rational to expect that she will try to please other men; and, in the emotions raised by the expectation of new conquests, endeavour to forget the mortification her love or pride has received? When the husband ceases to be a lover — and the time will inevitably come, — her desire of pleasing will then grow languid, or become a spring of bitterness; and love, perhaps, the most evanescent of all passions, gives place to jealousy or vanity.

I now speak of women who are restrained by principle or prejudice; such women, though they would shrink from an intrigue with real abhorrence, yet, nevertheless, wish to be convinced by the homage of gallantry that they are cruelly neglected by their husbands; or, days and weeks are spent in dreaming of the happiness enjoyed by congenial souls till their health is undermined and their spirits broken by discontent. How then can the great art of pleasing be such a necessary study? It is only useful to a mistress; the chaste wife and serious mother should only consider her power to please as the polish of her virtues, and the affection of her husband as one of the comforts that render her talk less difficult and her life happier. But, whether she be loved or neglected, her first wish should be to make herself respectable, and not to rely for all her happiness on a being subject to like infirmities with herself. . . .

---

[8] **out-Quixote Cervantes:** Miguel de Cervantes Saavedra (1547–1616), author of *Don Quixote* (1605, 1615), whose bumbling, idealistic protagonist has become a symbol of innocent and good-intentioned folly.

Love, the common passion, in which chance and sensation take place of choice and reason, is, in some degree, felt by the mass of mankind; for it is not necessary to speak, at present, of the emotions that rise above or sink below love. This passion, naturally increased by suspense and difficulties, draws the mind out of its accustomed state, and exalts the affections; but the security of marriage, allowing the fever of love to subside, a healthy temperature is thought insipid only by those who have not sufficient intellect to substitute the calm tenderness of friendship, the confidence of respect, instead of blind admiration, and the sensual emotions of fondness.

This is, must be, the course of nature—friendship or indifference inevitably succeeds love. And this constitution seems perfectly to harmonize with the system of government which prevails in the moral world. Passions are spurs to action and open the mind; but they sink into mere appetites, become a personal and momentary gratification, when the object is gained, and the satisfied mind rests in enjoyment. The man who had some virtue whilst he was struggling for a crown, often becomes a voluptuous tyrant when it graces his brow; and when the lover is not lost in the husband, the dotard, a prey to childish caprices and fond jealousies, neglects the serious duties of life, and the caresses which should excite confidence in his children are lavished on the overgrown child, his wife. [. . .]

FROM CHAPTER 4

Observations on the State of Degradation to Which Woman Is Reduced by Various Causes

. . . Love, considered as an animal appetite, cannot long feed on itself without expiring. And this extinction in its own flame, may be termed the violent death of love. But the wife who has thus been rendered licentious, will probably endeavour to fill the void left by the loss of her husband's attentions, for she cannot contentedly become merely an upper servant after having been treated like a goddess. She is still handsome, and, instead of transferring her fondness to her children, she only dreams of enjoying the sunshine of life. Besides, there are many husbands so devoid of sense and parental affection that during the first effervescence of voluptuous fondness they refuse to let their wives suckle their children. They are only to dress and live to please them: and love—even innocent love, soon sinks into lasciviousness when the exercise of a duty is sacrificed to its indulgence.

Personal attachment is a very happy foundation for friendship; yet, when even two virtuous young people marry, it would, perhaps, be happy if some circumstances checked their passion, if the recollection of some prior attachment, or disappointed affection, made it on one side, at least, rather a match founded on esteem. In that case they would look beyond the present moment and try to render the whole of life respectable, by forming a plan to regulate a friendship which only death ought to dissolve.

Friendship is a serious affection; the most sublime of all affections, because it is founded on principle, and cemented by time. The very reverse may be said of love. In a great degree, love and friendship cannot subsist in the same bosom; even when inspired by different objects they weaken or destroy each other, and for the same object can only be felt in succession. The vain fears and fond jealousies, the winds which fan the flame of love, when judiciously or artfully tempered, are both incompatible with the tender confidence and sincere respect of friendship. [. . .]

FROM CHAPTER 5

Animadversions on Some of the Writers Who Have Rendered Women Objects of Pity, Bordering on Contempt

. . . Sophia, says Rousseau, should be as perfect a woman as Emilius is a man, and to render her so, it is necessary to examine the character which nature has given to the sex.

He then proceeds to prove that woman ought to be weak and passive, because she has less bodily strength than man; and hence infers that she was formed to please and to be subject to him; and that it is her duty to render herself *agreeable* to her master—this being the grand end of her existence. Still, however, to give a little mock dignity to lust, he insists that man should not exert his strength, but depend on the will of the woman when he seeks for pleasure with her. [. . .]

Supposing woman to have been formed only to please, and be subject to man, the conclusion is just, she ought to sacrifice every other consideration to render herself agreeable to him: and let this brutal desire of self-preservation be the grand spring of all her actions, when it is proved to be the iron bed of fate,[9] to fit which her character should be stretched or contracted, regardless of all moral or physical distinctions. But if, as I think may be demonstrated, the purposes of even this life, viewing the whole, be subverted by practical rules built upon this ignoble base, I may be allowed to doubt whether woman were created for man; and, though the cry of irreligion or even atheism be raised against me, I will simply declare, that were an angel from heaven to tell me that Moses' beautiful, poetical cosmogony, and the account of the fall of man, were literally true, I could not believe what my reason told me was derogatory to the character of the Supreme Being: and, having no fear of the devil before mine eyes, I venture to call this a suggestion of reason, instead of resting my weakness on the broad shoulders of the first seducer of my frail sex. . . .

FROM CHAPTER 13

Some Instances of the Folly Which the Ignorance of Women Generates; with Concluding Reflections on the Moral Improvement That a Revolution in Female Manners Might Naturally Be Expected to Produce

. . . It is not necessary to inform the sagacious reader, now I enter on my concluding reflections, that the discussion of this subject merely consists in opening a few simple principles and clearing away the rubbish which obscured them. But as all readers are

---

[9] **iron bed of fate:** Alludes to the Greek legend of Procrustes, who would place his guests on an iron bed and either stretch them if they were too short or chop them down if they were too tall to fit.

not sagacious, I must be allowed to add some explanatory remarks to bring the subject home to reason—to that sluggish reason which supinely takes opinions on trust, and obstinately supports them to spare itself the labour of thinking.

Moralists have unanimously agreed that unless virtue be nursed by liberty it will never attain due strength—and what they say of man I extend to mankind, insisting that in all cases morals must be fixed on immutable principles; and that the being cannot be termed rational or virtuous who obeys any authority but that of reason.

To render women truly useful members of society, I argue that they should be led, by having their understandings cultivated on a large scale, to acquire a rational affection for their country, founded on knowledge, because it is obvious that we are little interested about what we do not understand. And to render this general knowledge of due importance, I have endeavoured to show that private duties are never properly fulfilled unless the understanding enlarges the heart; and that public virtue is only an aggregate of private. . . .

That women at present are by ignorance rendered foolish or vicious, is, I think, not to be disputed; and that the most salutary effects tending to improve mankind might be expected from a REVOLUTION in female manners appears, at least with a face of probability, to rise out of the observation. For as marriage has been termed the parent of those endearing charities which draw man from the brutal herd, the corrupting intercourse that wealth, idleness, and folly produce between the sexes is more universally injurious to morality than all the other vices of mankind collectively considered. To adulterous lust the most sacred duties are sacrificed, because before marriage, men, by a promiscuous intimacy with women, learned to consider love as a selfish gratification—learned to separate it not only from esteem, but from the affection merely built on habit, which mixes a little humanity with it. Justice and friendship are also set at defiance, and that purity of taste is vitiated which would naturally lead a man to relish an artless display of affection rather than affected airs. But that noble simplicity of affection which dares to appear unadorned has few attractions for the libertine, though it be the charm which, by cementing the matrimonial tie, secures to the pledges of a warmer passion the necessary parental attention; for children will never be properly educated till friendship subsists between parents. Virtue flies from a house divided against itself—and a whole legion of devils take up their residence there.

The affection of husbands and wives cannot be pure when they have so few sentiments in common, and when so little confidence is established at home, as must be the case when their pursuits are so different. That intimacy from which tenderness should flow, will not, cannot subsist between the vicious.

Contending, therefore, that the sexual distinction which men have so warmly insisted upon is arbitrary, I have dwelt on an observation that several sensible men, with whom I have conversed on the subject, allowed to be well founded; and it is simply this, that the little chastity to be found amongst men, and consequent disregard of modesty, tend to degrade both sexes; and further, that the modesty of women, characterized as such, will often be only the artful veil of wantonness instead of being the natural reflection of purity, till modesty be universally respected.

From the tyranny of man, I firmly believe, the greater number of female follies proceed; and the cunning, which I allow makes at present a part of their character, I likewise have repeatedly endeavoured to prove, is produced by oppression. . . .

Let women share the rights and she will emulate the virtues of man; for she must grow more perfect when emancipated, or justify the authority that chains such a weak being to her duty.—If the latter, it will be expedient to open a fresh trade with Russia for whips: a present which a father should always make to his son-in-law on his wedding day, that a husband may keep his whole family in order by the same means; and without any violation of justice reign, wielding this sceptre, sole master of his house, because he is the only being in it who has reason:—the divine, indefeasible earthly sovereignty breathed into man by the Master of the universe. Allowing this position, women have not any inherent rights to claim, and by the same rule their duties vanish, for rights and duties are inseparable.

Be just then, O ye men of understanding! and mark not more severely what women do amiss, than the vicious tricks of the horse or the ass for whom ye provide provender—and allow her the privileges of ignorance, to whom ye deny the rights of reason, or ye will be worse than Egyptian task-masters, expecting virtue where nature has not given understanding!

❧ SHEN FU
1763–?

Born in 1763, Shen Fu went on to become a government clerk, an amateur painter, and a sometime businessman. When he was in his forties, Shen Fu wrote his autobiography, *Six Records of a Floating Life*. Chinese marriages at the time were prearranged by parents. As a boy, Shen Fu was engaged to Chin Sha-yu, a girl who died when she was eight years old, so in 1775, after Shen Fu met Yün for the first time, his mother arranged for him to marry her. He studied for a while in Hangchou, and then at age seventeen Shen Fu married Yün, who bore him two children, Ching-chün (b. 1786) and Fen-sen (b. 1788). As he tells us in his autobiography, Shen Fu and Yün often struggled to keep out of debt, and Shen Fu, whose first position was that of a government clerk, drifted in and out of several occupations. Just two years after Yün's inept attempt to obtain a concubine for her father-in-law, she and Shen Fu were banished from the family over a misunderstanding about a loan. Though later reconciled with his father, Shen Fu endured more such disruptions in his life. Most important, Shen Fu recounts what he came to call the "curse of Han-yüan," the beautiful young courtesan who seemed to be the answer to Yün's wish to find a concubine for her husband. Shen Fu's poverty, however, proved too great an obstacle, and Han-Yüan was, in Shen Fu's words, "snatched away by an influential man who paid a thousand golds for her. . . ." When Yün learned of this misfortune, she had a relapse of her chronic illness, and she gradually weakened and died in 1803. Her death adds a sense of tragedy to Shen Fu's memoir, which depicts poverty, family strife, illness, and anxiety of the sort that must have been familiar to many ordinary people in the Qing dynasty.

Though the following selection has been edited to focus on the love between husband and wife, the *Six Records* goes on to describe his wife's death, Shen Fu's travels with his friend Hsia Yi-shan, his move to Szechuan, the death of his son, and his move to Beijing (Peking) in 1807. After 1809, when Shen Fu was writing the autobiography, the manuscript was lost until the 1870s. This intimate portrayal of an ordinary man's life up through his forties survived, but nothing is known about Shen Fu's life after 1809 or about his death.

A note on the translation: Shen Fu's text is translated by Leonard Pratt and Chiang Su-hui. Unless otherwise indicated, the notes are the translators'.

❧ Six Records of a Floating Life

Translated by Leonard Pratt and Chiang Su-hui

FROM PART 1
THE JOYS OF THE WEDDING CHAMBER

I was born in the winter of the twenty-seventh year of the reign of the Emperor Chien Lung,[1] on the second and twentieth day of the eleventh month. Heaven blessed me, and life then could not have been more full. It was a time of great peace and plenty, and my family was an official one that lived next to the Pavilion of the Waves in Soochow. As the poet Su Tung-po wrote, "All things are like spring dreams, passing with no trace." If I did not make a record of that time, I should be ungrateful for the blessings of heaven.

The very first of the three hundred chapters of the *Book of Odes*[2] concerns husbands and wives, so I too will write of other matters in their turn. Unfortunately I never completed my studies, so my writing is not very skilful. But here my purpose is merely to record true feelings and actual events. Criticism of my writing will be like the shining of a bright light into a dirty mirror.

When I was young I was engaged to Chin Sha-yu, but she died when she was eight years old. Eventually I married Chen Yün, the daughter of my uncle, Mr. Chen Hsin-yü. Her literary name was Shu-chen.

---

[1] **twenty-seventh year . . . Lung:** 1763.

[2] ***Book of Odes:*** The *Shi-jing*, also translated as the *Book of Songs* or the *Classic of Poetry,* is an anthology of poems from the twelfth to the seventh century B.C.E. edited by Confucius; it is one of the classics of the Confucian school. [Editors' note.]

Even while small, she was very clever. While she was learning to talk she was taught the poem *The Mandolin Song*[3] and could repeat it almost immediately.

Yün's father died when she was four years old, leaving her mother, whose family name was Chin, and her younger brother, Ko-chang. At first they had virtually nothing, but as Yün grew older she became very adept at needlework, and the labour of her ten fingers came to provide for all three of them. Thanks to her work, they were always able to afford to pay the tuition for her brother's teachers.

One day Yün found a copy of *The Mandolin Song* in her brother's book-box and, remembering her lessons as a child, was able to pick out the characters one by one. That is how she began learning to read. In her spare moments she gradually learned how to write poetry, one line of which was, "We grow thin in the shadows of autumn, but chrysanthemums grow fat with the dew."

When I was thirteen, my mother took me along on a visit to her relatives. That was the first time I met my cousin Yün, and we two children got on well together. I had a chance to see her poems that day, and though I sighed at her brilliance I privately feared she was too sensitive to be completely happy in life. Still, I could not forget her, and I remember saying to my mother, "If you are going to choose a wife for me, I will marry no other than Yün."

Mother also loved her gentleness, so she was quick to arrange our engagement, sealing the match by giving Yün a gold ring from her own finger. This was in the thirty-ninth year of the reign of the Emperor Chien Lung,[4] on the sixteenth day of the seventh month.

That winter mother took me to their home once again, for the marriage of Yün's cousin. Yün and I were born in the same year, but because she was ten months older than I, I had always called her "elder sister," while she called me "younger brother." We continued to call one another by these names even after we were engaged.

At her cousin's wedding the room was full of beautifully dressed people. Yün alone wore a plain dress; only her shoes were new. I noticed they were skilfully embroidered, and when she told me she had done them herself I began to appreciate that her cleverness lay not only in her writing.

Yün had delicate shoulders and a stately neck, and her figure was slim. Her brows arched over beautiful, lively eyes. Her only blemish was two slightly protruding front teeth, the sign of a lack of good fortune. But her manner was altogether charming, and she captivated all who saw her.

I asked to see more of her poems that day, and found some had only one line, others three or four, and most were unfinished. I asked her why.

"I have done them without a teacher," she replied, laughing. "I hope you, my best friend, can be my teacher now and help me finish them." Then as a joke I wrote on her book, "The Embroidered Bag of Beautiful Verses." I did not then realize that the origin of her early death already lay in that book.

---

[3] *The Mandolin Song: P'i-p'a Husing*, a Tang dynasty poem by Bo Juyi (772–864). It tells of the meeting between an official exiled to the distant south and a former courtesan from the capital who has been abandoned there by her merchant husband.

[4] **thirty-ninth year . . . Lung:** 1775.

That night after the wedding I escorted my relatives out of the city, and it was midnight by the time I returned. I was terribly hungry and asked for something to eat. A servant brought me some dried plums, but they were too sweet for me. So Yün secretly took me to her room, where she had hidden some warm rice porridge and some small dishes of food. I delightedly picked up my chopsticks, but suddenly heard Yün's cousin Yu-heng call, "Yün, come quickly!"

Yün hurriedly shut the door and called back, "I'm very tired. I was just going to sleep." But Yu-heng pushed open the door and came in anyway.

He saw me just about to begin eating the rice porridge, and chuckled, looking out of the corner of his eye at Yün. "When I asked you for some rice porridge just now, you said there wasn't any more! But I see you were just hiding it in here and saving it for your 'husband'!"

Yün was terribly embarrassed, and ran out. The whole household broke into laughter. I was also embarrassed and angry, roused my servant, and left early.

Every time I returned after that, Yün would hide. I knew she was afraid that everyone would laugh at her.

On the night of the twenty-second day of the first month in the forty-fourth year of the reign of the Emperor Chien Lung[5] I saw by the light of our wedding candles that Yün's figure was as slim as before. When her veil was lifted we smiled at each other. After we had shared the ceremonial cup of wine and sat down together for the wedding banquet, I secretly took her small hand under the table. It was warm and it was soft, and my heart beat uncontrollably.

I asked her to begin eating, but it turned out to be a day on which she did not eat meat, a Buddhist practice which she had followed for several years. I thought to myself that she had begun this practice at the very time I had begun to break out with acne, and I asked her, "Since my skin is now clear and healthy, couldn't you give up this custom?" Her eyes smiled amusement, and her head nodded agreement.

That same night of the twenty-second there was a wedding-eve party for my elder sister. She was to be married on the twenty-fourth, but the twenty-third was a day of national mourning on which all entertaining was forbidden and the holding of the wedding-eve party would have been impossible. Yün attended the dinner, but I spent the time in our bedroom drinking with my sister's maid of honour. We played a drinking game which I lost frequently, and I wound up getting very drunk and falling asleep. By the time I woke up the next morning, Yün was already putting on her make-up.

During the day a constant stream of relatives and friends came to congratulate Yün and me on our marriage. In the evening there were some musical performances in honour of the wedding, after the lamps had been lit.

At midnight I escorted my sister to her new husband's home, and it was almost three in the morning when I returned. The candles had burned low and the house was silent. I stole quietly into our room to find my wife's servant dozing beside the bed and Yün herself with her make-up off but not yet asleep. A candle burned brightly beside her; she was bent intently over a book, but I could not tell what it was

---

[5] **forty-fourth year . . . Lung:** 1780.

that she was reading with such concentration. I went up to her, rubbed her shoulder, and said, "You've been so busy these past few days, why are you reading so late?"

Yün turned and stood up. "I was just thinking of going to sleep, but I opened the bookcase and found this book, *The Romance of the Western Chamber*.[6] Once I had started reading it, I forgot how tired I was. I had often heard it spoken of, but this was the first time I had had a chance to read it. The author really is as talented as people say, but I do think his tale is too explicitly told."

I laughed and said, "Only a talented writer could be so explicit."

Yün's servant then urged us to go to sleep, but we told her she should go to sleep first, and to shut the door to our room. We sat up making jokes, like two close friends meeting after a long separation. I playfully felt her breast and found her heart was beating as fast as mine. I pulled her to me and whispered in her ear, "Why is your heart beating so fast?" She answered with a bewitching smile that made me feel a love so endless it shook my soul. I held her close as I parted the curtains and led her into bed. We never noticed what time the sun rose in the morning.

As a new bride, Yün was very quiet. She never got angry, and when anyone spoke to her she always replied with a smile. She was respectful to her elders and amiable to everyone else. Everything she did was orderly, and was done properly. Each morning when she saw the first rays of the sun touch the top of the window, she would dress quickly and hurry out of bed, as if someone were calling her. I once laughed at her about it; "This is not like that time with the rice porridge! Why are you still afraid of someone laughing at you?"

"True," she answered, "my hiding the rice porridge for you that time has become a joke. But I'm not worried about people laughing at me now. I am afraid your parents will think I'm lazy."

While I would have liked it if she could have slept more, I had to agree that she was right. So every morning I got up early with her, and from that time on we were inseparable, like a man and his shadow. Words could not describe our love. [. . .]

On the evening of the seventh day of the seventh month that year, Yün lit candles and set out fruit on the altar by the Pavilion of My Desire, and we worshipped Tien Sun[7] together. I had had two matching seals engraved with the inscription, "May we remain husband and wife in all our lives to come"; on mine the characters were raised and on hers they were incised. We used them to sign the letters we wrote one another. That night the moonlight was very lovely, and as it was reflected in the stream it turned the ripples of the water as white as silk. We sat together near the water wearing light robes and fanned ourselves gently as we looked up at the clouds flying across the sky and changing into ten thousand shapes.

---

[6] *The Romance of the Western Chamber:* A Yüan dynasty play by Wang Shih-fu and Kuan Han-ch'ing that concludes with a young woman giving in to the desires of a student. [Adapted from translators' note.]

[7] **Tien Sun:** The Weaver's Star. The legend tells that the weaver and the cowherd were so much in love they neglected both cloth and cows. Thus they were banished to separate stars and could come together in the sky only once a year, on the seventh day of the seventh month of the lunar calendar. It is a day for lovers and for young women in search of a husband.

Yün said, "The world is so vast, but still everyone looks up at the same moon. I wonder if there is another couple in the world as much in love as we are."

"Naturally there are people everywhere who like to enjoy the night air and gaze at the moon," I said, "and there are more than a few women who enjoy discussing the sunset. But when a man and wife look at it together, I don't think it is the sunset they will wind up talking about." The candles soon burned out, and the moon set. We took the fruit inside and went to bed.

The fifteenth day of the seventh month, when the moon is full, is the day called the Ghost Festival. Yün had prepared some small dishes, and we had planned to invite the moon to drink with us. But when night came, clouds suddenly darkened the sky.

Yün grew melancholy and said, "If I am to grow old together with you, the moon must come out."

I also felt depressed. On the opposite bank I could see will-o'-the-wisps winking on and off like ten thousand fireflies, as their light threaded through the high grass and willow trees that grew on the small island in the stream. To get ourselves into a better mood Yün and I began composing a poem out loud, with me offering the first couplet, her the second, and so on. After the first two couplets we gradually became less and less restrained and more and more excited, until we were saying anything that came into our heads. Yün was soon laughing so hard that she cried, and had to lean up against me, unable to speak a word. The heavy scent of jasmine in her hair assailed my nostrils, so to stop her laughing I patted her on the back and changed the subject, saying, "I thought women of ancient times put jasmine flowers in their hair because they resembled pearls. I never realized that the jasmine is so attractive when mixed with the scent of women's make-up, much more attractive than the lime."

Yün stopped laughing. "Lime is the gentleman of perfumes," she said, "and you notice its scent unconsciously. But the jasmine is a commoner that has to rely on a woman's make-up for its effect. It's suggestive, like a wicked smile."

"So why are you avoiding the gentleman and taking up with the commoner?"

"I'm only making fun of gentlemen who love commoners," she replied.

Just as we were speaking, the water clock showed midnight. The wind gradually began to sweep the clouds away, and the full moon finally came out. We were delighted, and drank some wine leaning against the windowsill. But before we had finished three cups we heard a loud noise from under the bridge, as if someone had fallen into the water. We leaned out of the window and looked around carefully. The surface of the stream was as bright as a mirror, but we saw not a thing. We only heard the sound of a duck running quickly along the river bank. I knew that the ghosts of people who had drowned often appeared by the river near the Pavilion of the Waves, but I was worried that Yün would be afraid and so I did not dare tell her.

"Yi!" she said, none the less frightened for my silence. "Where did that sound come from?"

We could not keep ourselves from trembling. I closed the window and we took the wine into the bedroom. The flame in the lamp was as small as a bean, and the curtains around the bed cast shadows that writhed like snakes. We were still frightened.

I turned up the lamp and we got into bed, but Yün was already suffering hot and cold attacks from the shock. I caught the same fever, and we were ill for twenty days. It is true what people say, that happiness carried to an extreme turns into sadness. The events of that day were another omen that we were not to grow old together. [. . .]

About half a *li* from my house, on Vinegar Warehouse Lane, was the Tungting Temple, which we usually called the Narcissus Temple.[8] Inside there were winding covered paths and a small park with pavilions. Every year on the god's birthday the members of each family association would gather in their corner of the temple, hang up a special glass lantern, and erect a throne below it. Beside the throne they would set out vases filled with flowers, in a competition to see whose decorations were most beautiful. During the day operas were performed, and at night candles of different lengths were set out among the vases and the flowers. This was called the "lighting of the flowers." The colours of the flowers, the shadows of the lamps, and the fragrant smoke floating up from the incense urns, made it all seem like a night banquet at the palace of the Dragon King himself. The heads of the family associations would play the flute and sing, or brew fine tea and chat with one another. Townspeople gathered like ants to watch this spectacle, and a fence had to be put up under the eaves of the temple to keep them out.

One year some friends of mine invited me to go and help to arrange their flowers, so I had a chance to see the festival myself. I went home and told Yün how beautiful it was.

"What a shame that I cannot go just because I am not a man," said Yün.

"If you wore one of my hats and some of my clothes, you could look like a man."

Yün thereupon braided her hair into a plait and made up her eyebrows. She put on my hat, and though her hair showed a little around her ears it was easy to conceal. When she put on my robe we found it was an inch and a half too long, but she took it up around the waist and put on a riding jacket over it.

"What about my feet?" Yün asked.

"In the street they sell 'butterfly shoes'," I said, "in all sizes. They're easy to buy, and afterwards you can wear them around the house. Wouldn't they do?"

Yün was delighted, and when she had put on my clothes after dinner she practised for a long time, putting her hands into her sleeves and taking large steps like a man.

But suddenly she changed her mind. "I am not going! It would be awful if someone found out. If your parents knew, they would never allow us to go."

I still encouraged her to go, however. "Everyone at the temple knows me. Even if they find out, they will only take it as a joke. Mother is at ninth sister's house, so if we come and go secretly no one will ever know."

Yün looked at herself in the mirror and laughed endlessly. I pulled her along, and we left quietly. We walked all around inside the temple, with no one realizing she

---

[8] **Narcissus Temple:** To the Dragon King of Tung-t'ing Lake, a popular deity in central China, generally in charge of watering the crops. Among his more spectacular accomplishments was coercing a mortal to marry his daughter during the Tang dynasty.

was a woman. If someone asked who she was, I would tell them she was my cousin. They would only fold their hands and bow to her.

At the last place we came to, young women and girls were sitting behind the throne that had been erected there. They were the family of a Mr. Yang, one of the organizers of the festival. Without thinking, Yün walked over and began to chat with them as a woman quite naturally might, and as she bent over to do so she inadvertently laid her hand on the shoulder of one of the young ladies.

One of the maids angrily jumped up and shouted, "What kind of a rogue are you, to behave like that!" I went over to try to explain, but Yün, seeing how embarrassing the situation could become, quickly took off her hat and kicked up her foot, saying, "See, I am a woman too!"

At first they all stared at Yün in surprise, but then their anger turned to laughter. We stayed to have some tea and refreshments with them, and then called sedan chairs and went home. . . .

In the seventh month of the Chiayen year of the reign of the Emperor Chien Lung[9] I returned from Yüehtung with my friend Hsü Hsiu-feng, who was my cousin's husband. He brought a new concubine back with him, raving about her beauty to everyone, and one day he invited Yün to go and see her. Afterwards Yün said to Hsiu-feng, "She certainly is beautiful, but she is not the least bit charming."

"If your husband were to take a concubine," Hsiu-feng asked, "would she have to be charming as well as beautiful?"

"Naturally," said Yün.

From then on, Yün was obsessed with the idea of finding me a concubine, even though we had nowhere near enough money for such an ambition.

There was a courtesan from Chekiang named Wen Leng-hsiang then living in Soochow. She was something of a poet, and had written four stanzas on the theme of willow catkins that had taken the city by storm, many talented writers composing couplets in response to her originals. My friend from Wuchiang, Chang Hsien-han, had long admired Leng-hsiang, and asked us to help him write some verses to accompany hers. Yün thought little of her and so declined, but I longed to write, and thus composed some verses to her rhyme. One couplet that Yün liked very much was, "They arouse my springtime wistfulness, and ensnare her wandering fancy."

A year later, on the fifth day of the eighth month, mother was planning to take Yün on a visit to Tiger Hill,[10] when my friend Hsien-han suddenly arrived at our house. "I am going to Tiger Hill too," he said, "and today I came especially to invite you to go with me and admire some flowers[11] along the way."

I then asked mother to go on ahead, and said I would meet her at Pantang near Tiger Hill. Hsien-han took me to Leng-hsiang's home, where I discovered that she was already middle-aged.

---

[9] Chiayen year . . . Lung1794.

[10] Tiger Hill: A collection of temples and pagodas northwest of Soochow. It takes its name from a tiger that is said to have appeared there to guard the grave of an ancient king.

[11] admire some flowers: A euphemism for spending time with courtesans.

However, she had a daughter named Han-yüan, who, though not yet fully mature, was as beautiful as a piece of jade. Her eyes were as lovely as the surface of an autumn pond, and while they entertained us it became obvious that her literary knowledge was extensive. She had a younger sister named Wen-yüan who was still quite small.

At first I had no wild ideas and wanted only to have a cup of wine and chat with them. I well knew that a poor scholar like myself could not afford this sort of thing, and once inside I began to feel quite nervous. While I did not show my unease in my conversation, I did quietly say to Hsien-han "I'm only a poor fellow. How can you invite these girls to entertain me?"

Hsien-han laughed. "It's not that way at all. A friend of mine had invited me to come and be entertained by Han-yüan today, but then he was called away by an important visitor. He asked me to be the host and invite someone else. Don't worry about it."

At that, I began to relax. Later, when our boat reached Pantang, I told Han-yüan to go aboard my mother's boat and pay her respects. That was when Yün met Han-yüan and, as happy as old friends at a reunion, they soon set off hand in hand to climb the hill in search of all the scenic spots it offered. Yün especially liked the height and vista of Thousand Clouds, and they sat there enjoying the view for some time. When we returned to Yehfangpin, we moored the boats side by side and drank long and happily.

As the boats were being unmoored, Yün asked me if Han-yüan could return aboard hers, while I went back with Hsien-han. To this, I agreed. When we returned to the Tuting Bridge we went back aboard our own boats and took leave of one another. By the time we arrived home it was already the third night watch.

"Today I have met someone who is both beautiful and charming," said Yün. "I have just invited Han-yüan to come and see me tomorrow, so I can try to arrange things for you."

"But we're not a rich family," I said, worried. "We cannot afford to keep someone like that. How could people as poor as ourselves dare think of such a thing? And we are so happily married, why should we look for someone else?"

"But I love her too," Yün said, laughing. "You just let me take care of everything."

The next day at noon, Han-yüan actually came. Yün entertained her warmly, and during the meal we played a game—the winner would read a poem, while the loser had to drink a cup of wine. By the end of the meal still not a word had been said about our obtaining Han-yüan.

As soon as she left, Yün said to me, "I have just made a secret agreement with her. She will come here on the eighteenth, and we will pledge ourselves as sisters. You will have to prepare animals for the sacrifice."

Then, laughing and pointing to the jade bracelet on her arm, she said, "If you see this bracelet on Han-yüan's arm then, it will mean she has agreed to our proposal. I have just told her my idea, but I am still not very sure what she thinks about it all."

I only listened to what she said, making no reply.

It rained very hard on the eighteenth, but Han-yüan came all the same. She and Yün went into another room and were alone there for some time. They were holding hands when they emerged, and Han-yüan looked at me shyly. She was wearing the jade bracelet!

We had intended, after the incense was burned and they had become sisters, that we should carry on drinking. As it turned out, however, Han-yüan had promised to go on a trip to Stone Lake, so she left as soon as the ceremony was over.

"She has agreed," Yün told me happily. "Now, how will you reward your go-between?" I asked her the details of the arrangement.

"Just now I spoke to her privately because I was afraid she might have another attachment. When she said she did not, I asked her, 'Do you know why we have invited you here today, little sister?'

"'The respect of an honourable lady like yourself makes me feel like a small weed leaning up against a great tree,' she replied, 'but my mother has high hopes for me, and I'm afraid I cannot agree without consulting her. I do hope, though, that you and I can think of a way to work things out.'

"When I took off the bracelet and put it on her arm I said to her, 'The jade of this bracelet is hard and represents the constancy of our pledge; and like our pledge, the circle of the bracelet has no end. Wear it as the first token of our understanding.' To which she replied, 'The power to unite us rests entirely with you.' So it seems as if we have already won over Han-yüan. The difficult part will be convincing her mother, but I will think of a plan for that."

I laughed, and asked her, "Are you trying to imitate Li-weng's *Pitying the Fragrant Companion*?"[12]

"Yes," she replied.

From that time on there was not a day that Yün did not talk about Han-yüan. But later Han-yüan was taken off by a powerful man, and all the plans came to nothing. In fact, it was because of this that Yün died.

---

[12] *Pitying the Fragrant Companion:* A play by Li Yü (1611–c. 1680), whose pen name was Li-weng, about a married woman who falls in love with a girl whom she procures as a concubine for her husband so that she can be with her. [Adapted from translators' note.]

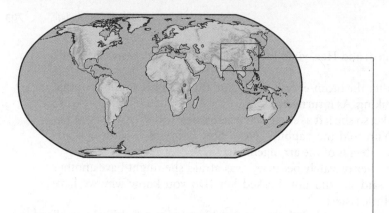

Manchu expansion

- Manchu homeland
- Expansion before 1644
- Expansion 1644–59
- New territories from 1660
- — Border of Qing China, 1760

1755–57 Ili Protectorate

1697 Outer Mongolia

1629–30 Khorchin

Mukden

Tarim Basin 1759–60

Eastern Turkestan

KUNLUN MTS.

1635 Inner Mongolia

Peking

1644 Chihli

KOREA

1724 Tsinghai

1644–45 Shansi

1645 Shantung

1649 Kansu

Yellow R.

Tibet Protectorate establibed 1750

Lhasa

1645–46 Shensi

1644–45 Honan

1645 Kiangsu

NEPAL

1646 Szechwan

1645 Hupeh

1645 Anhwei

East China Sea

BHUTAN

Yangtze R.

1646 Chekiang

INDIA

1647–50 Hunan

1649–52 Kiangsi

1658 Kweichow

1646 Fukien

1659 Yunnan

1650–52 Kwangsi

1650–55 Kwangtung

Canton

TAIWAN

BURMA

TONKIN

LAOS

South China Sea

SIAM

0   500   1,000 miles

0   500   1,000 kilometers

ALTAI MTS.

RUSSIA

Amur R.

Manchuria

HIMALAYAS

Qing China, c. 1760

The Qing dynasty grew very powerful and expanded geographically in the seventeenth and eighteenth centuries. There were two phases of imperial expansion. Phase one began with a move southward from the Manchu homeland (Qing rulers were from Manchuria, in the north) into Inner Mongolia and the southern provinces. Phase two consisted of a westward expansion into Tibet, Eastern Turkestan, Tarim Basin, and other western provinces. China during this time experienced an unprecedented rise in wealth and power to become one of the most impressive empires in the world.

CHINA
The Early Qing Dynasty

Like Europe and Japan, China experienced a period of relative peace in the eighteenth century that had been preceded by a time of civil unrest. At the end of the Ming dynasty (1368–1644), general dissatisfaction among the people culminated in a revolt led by Li Zicheng (1604–1651), whose rebel army took the capital of Beijing (Peking) in 1644. Seizing the opportunity to intervene and take control of China themselves, the MANCHU, a people from what is now Manchuria, enlisted the help of some disgruntled Ming generals and set themselves up as rulers in Beijing. By 1683, when Emperor Kangxi (r. 1661–1722) seized Taiwan, Manchu rule had engulfed both north and south China. Thus was born the Qing (Ch'ing) or Manchu dynasty that endured until the October Revolution of 1911.

THE QING DYNASTY

After more than fifty years of severe repression at the onset of their reign, the Manchu eased their policies and replaced terror with strategic accommodation. Adopting the Chinese system of bureaucratic government, the Manchu inaugurated a period of peace and prosperity in China. Manchu soldiers, known as Bannermen, enforced Manchu policies and helped stabilize China's many miles of border while extending its boundaries. The Qing emperors increased trade with Europe and Russia and brokered a system of shared governance that enabled the Manchu to maintain the chief authority while including some Chinese, even in the highest ranks of government, and benefitting from the administrative expertise of the Chinese intelligentsia. In addition, the Manchu eventually won the favor of small farmers by promoting agriculture and keeping taxes low, at least through the mid eighteenth century. The Manchu embraced the traditional CONFUCIAN principles of order, revived the Chinese system of civil service examinations, and patronized the arts, letters, and scholarship.

CONFUCIANISM AND LITERACY

The Confucian doctrines espoused by Qing emperors emphasized hierarchy, filial piety, and loyalty. Like the so-called enlightened despots of Europe, Kangxi was not only an effective politician and leader but also a cultured individual—an amateur musician, a poet, and a calligrapher who displayed a keen interest in traditional Chinese history and culture. His respect for that culture and his desire to discourage potential dissent led him to push for rote memorization of the Confucian classics and imitation of classical poetic and aesthetic forms. As illustrated by the meritocratic examination system (see Time and Place box, p. 771), Kangxi and later Manchu emperors promoted a high degree of literacy, some of which trickled down to the larger population. During this time, along with their training in etiquette, calligraphy, and poetry, some women received at least an introduction to the Confucianist texts, which their brothers and male cousins studied intensively in order to pass the civil service examinations. The Manchu sponsored a number of extensive writing projects, including the translation of Chinese texts into Manchu, the writing of a detailed history of the Ming dynasty, and the production of a massive illustrated encyclopedia that covered astronomy, mathematics, geography, history, zoology, philosophy, literature, law, politics, and more. But above all these works stood *The Complete Collection of Written Materials Divided into Four Categories*, completed in 1782 after ten years by a group of 360 scholars and 15,000 copyists; this treatise on and compilation of all known materials in print or manuscript contained nearly 80,000 volumes, grouped into four categories: canonical, historical, philosophical, and literary. While this work was a valuable bibliographical resource, it was also used by Emperor Qianlong (r. 1736–96) to censor and destroy any texts that he believed were hostile to the Manchu.

EAST-WEST CONTACT

By the eighteenth century China had had a long, if discontinuous, history of trading with the West. Often that trade was conducted through middlemen—Arabs, Turks, and Mongols—who controlled the lands linking the western Chinese border to the port towns of the Mediterranean. From at least the thirteenth century, expeditions like those of Marco Polo had reached China directly via land routes, and by 1514 the Portuguese had come by sea and set up limited trade with Canton. The Dutch arrived in 1624, establishing a trading center on the island of Taiwan (then called Formosa), and the English set up trade at Canton in 1699. The Chinese strictly regulated the activities of these European traders, who did a heavy business in Chinese silks, porcelain, and tea. In exchange the Chinese wanted only gold or silver, for they had no desire for European goods. When the British emissary Lord Macartney

tried to increase Britain's access to China in 1793, Emperor Qianlong made clear the Chinese position: ". . . the virtue of the Celestial dynasty having spread far and wide, the kings of myriad nations come by land and sea with all sorts of precious things. Consequently there is nothing we lack, as your principal envoy and others have themselves observed. We have never set much store on strange or ingenious objects, nor do we need any more of your country's manufactures. . . ."

The Chinese were interested, however, in Western science, astronomy, and mathematics, so that scholars such as the Italian Jesuit Matteo Ricci (1552–1610)

Scholar and Attendant. Porcelain
During the Qing dynasty, scholars were once again revered members of society. People of literary accomplishment were portrayed in art with an air of tranquility and nobility. (Laurie Platt Winfrey)

were not only tolerated but respected. The Jesuits helped the Chinese in cartography, translated treatises (for example, Galileo's writings on astronomy), and improved the design of firearms. These missionaries converted some two to three hundred thousand Chinese to Christianity by the eighteenth century. Dominican and Franciscan missionaries, however, condemned Confucianism and tried to force strict Catholic ritual on already converted Christians. As a result, the Manchu expelled all foreign missionaries in 1742. After 1757, when an imperial decree limited all foreign trade to Canton, the Qing dynasty, like the neighboring Tokugawa government in Japan, maintained a policy of isolation and exclusion until the British forced China to open its ports to foreigners in the nineteenth century.

By the end of the eighteenth century, the expense of maintaining China's long inland border had begun to sap the imperial budgetary reserves. This led to an increase in taxes on agriculture and peasants, precipitating the White Lotus Rebellion (1796–1804). Although this rebellion was eventually suppressed, the Qing dynasty was beginning to weaken in the face of governmental corruption, overspending, increased population, and, eventually, the aggressive actions of the British that culminated in the Opium War (1839–42). That war opened Chinese ports to the British and ultimately to large-scale foreign trade. Staving off foreign intervention and struggling with internal problems, the Qing dynasty managed to endure through the nineteenth century, finally collapsing with the October Revolution of 1911, led by followers of Sun Yat-sen, founder of the first Chinese republic and often called the father of modern China.

CHINESE LITERATURE

As in Europe and Japan, China during the late Ming (1368–1644) and early Qing (1644–1911) dynasties witnessed a burgeoning of popular, or vernacular, literature (literature written in the spoken dialect rather than in the classical literary style), due in part to rising urban populations and the spread of literacy. Those who had previously relied on oral storytellers and classical plays for their entertainment were drawn to literary forms like the short story, the novel, and popular theater. Like their European and Japanese counterparts, Chinese writers moved toward realistic depictions of everyday life and therefore used a more colloquial style of writing. Some writers also left behind autobiographical writings or "records," such as Shen Fu's *Six Records of a Floating Life* (p. 755), a touching memoir written in 1809 excerpted in *In the World: Love, Marriage, and the Education of Women.*

While drama had always been popular in China and took many forms, ranging from variety plays to musical performances, in the late seventeenth century a new, highly elaborate drama emerged that was aimed primarily at elite, literate audiences. These so-called southern-style Chinese plays, unlike the short, four-act plays of the northern-style, or Yuan, play, sometimes comprised more than fifty scenes and are difficult to excerpt. Two of the most important are *The Peony Pavilion (Mu-dan ting)* by Tang Xian-zu and *The Peach Blossom Fan* by Kong Shang-ren. Also during the seventeenth and eighteenth centuries, some of China's greatest novels appeared, including *The Journey to the West,* also known as *Monkey (Xi-you ji,* 1592); *The Golden Lotus (Jin Ping Mei);* *The Scholars (Ru-lin wai-shi,* 1803); and above all *The Story of the Stone (Shitouji),* also known as *The Dream of the Red Chamber (Hung lou meng). The Golden Lotus* and *The Scholars* are satirical novels, the former exposing the decadence of the late Ming dynasty, the latter launching a trenchant attack on the hypocrisy and corruption among high Chinese officials and on the institution of the civil service examinations.

The Story of the Stone (p. 789), by Cao Xueqin and Gao E, is considered China's greatest novel, equivalent to Cervantes' *Don Quixote* and Tolstoy's *War and Peace* (1863–69). It presents a panoramic view of Chinese society in the early Qing dynasty. Centered on the declining fortunes of the affluent Jia clan, the novel recounts the complicated relationship between Jia Bao-yu, the protagonist, and his two cousins, Lin Dai-yu (Black Jade) and Xue Bao-ch'ai (Precious Clasp). In meticulous detail, this novel with more than 430 characters describes everyday life with its political and domestic intrigues, in particular the education of Bao-yu and his cousins and their tragic love affair.

Short fiction also flourished during this time, particularly VERNACULAR FICTION — stories that came from folklore and oral traditions. Three writers who devoted their lives to collecting and rewriting popular stories and folklore, and in some cases composing new works, were Feng Meng-long (1574–1646), Ling Meng-chu (1574–1646), and Pu Song-Ling (P'u Sung Ling; 1640–1715). Many of the collected stories are realistic tales of merchants and people living in the cities, though ghost stories and stories about court life were still popular. Pu Song-Ling's *Strange Stories from a Chinese Studio (Liao-zhai zhi-yi,* 1766) were written in the classical rather than vernacular style. They portray everyday life but often contain elements of the supernatural as well. "The Wise Neighbor" and "The Mural," included in this book (pp. 776 and 780), emphasize both aspects of Pu Song-Ling's fiction.

As the Qing dynasty advanced, the morality implicit in Confucianist doctrines was strictly interpreted and enforced. From 1774 to 1794 a literary inquisition took place under the rule of Qianlong. Early works were censored and many writers were arrested for portraying the Manchus in an unflattering light. Overall more than ten thousand books were prohibited and over two thousand works destroyed. This massive censorship was just one of many signs of the government's weakness

www   For more information about the culture and context of China in the eighteenth century, see *World Literature Online* at bedfordstmartins.com/worldlit.

Eighteenth-Century China: The Civil Service Examinations

China's system of selecting government officials by means of a civil service examination dates back to the Han dynasty (202 B.C.E.–220 C.E.). Although at first candidates for the exam came only from well-born and influential families, the Han introduced a principle of advancement based on merit and talent that came to characterize the Chinese bureaucratic system, up through the nineteenth century. During the great Tang dynasty (618–907), academies were established at the capital cities of Chang'an and Luoyuang to train candidates for the rigorous tests, but the Song dynasty (960–1279) formalized the system that was in effect during the late seventeenth and early eighteenth centuries. District and provincial schools were established and their doors were open to students from a broad but by no means universal spectrum of society. Only men were admitted to these training schools, and women and the poor tended to be excluded from taking the civil service exams. The Ming dynasty government set up schools in the country and even provided scholarships for promising students, thus implementing a more universal meritocracy. And Qing emperors introduced quotas for different ethnic groups in China for the schools, but they also allowed wealthy families to purchase degrees.

Somewhat like graduate exams in universities today, the civil service examinations had three levels. The first, a qualifying examination, was administered once a year at the provincial capital and allowed the successful candidate to move to the second level or to work in the local bureaucracy. The second permitted the successful candidate to apply for an official position in the imperial government or to go on to the final examination. Passing the third-level examination enabled someone to work in the central bureaucracy or as a district magistrate.

Preparation for these exams was based entirely on the Confucian classics, as part of a political effort to unify the culture and reinforce the values of loyalty, order, and filial piety. Candidates had to memorize long passages from The Four Books and The Five Scriptures. The Four Books, a compilation of Confucian texts, consist of *The Analects, The Doctrine of the Mean, The Great Learning,* and *The Mencius,* commentaries on Confucian ideas by the philosopher Mencius (fourth century B.C.E.). The Five Scriptures comprise *The Book of Songs, The Book of History, The Book of Changes, The Book of Rites,* and *The Spring and Autumn Annals.* During the Ming dynasty (1368–1644), the *ba-gu wen,* or "eight-legged essay"—a difficult and highly formal essay of eight parts on a Confucian theme—was also required of all candidates.

Examination of Country Magistrates, early eighteenth century. This painting illustrates the rigid nature of Qing-era Chinese education. The official at the pinnacle of the composition looms over the heads of the students, indicative of the authoritative world of the civil service examinations. (The Art Archive)

in the late eighteenth century, setting the stage for the final collapse of the Qing dynasty in the twentieth century. By the nineteenth century, China was on the verge of a European onslaught that would utterly transform its society. Writers would look back on the late Ming and early Qing period as one of the greatest cultural and literary eras since the Tang dynasty (618–907), which had basked in the light of poets such as Li Bai (701–762) and Du Fu (712–770).

∾ Pu Song-Ling (P'u Sung Ling)
1640–1715

poo-song-LING

Pu Song-Ling's short stories are as well known in China as are those of E. T. A. Hoffmann[1] in Germany and Edgar Allan Poe[2] in the United States. Like Hoffmann and Poe, Pu Song-Ling wrote about the strange and the fantastic; his stories concern ordinary people whose lives somehow come into contact with the supernatural in the form of ghosts, fox spirits, genii, and other uncanny beings. Moreover, like his European and American counterparts, Pu Song-Ling transformed the supernatural tale into a sophisticated art form. His classic collection of 431 tales, *Strange Stories from a Chinese Studio* (*Liao-zhai zhi-yi*, 1766), influenced the revival of the classical-language story in China and delighted readers. Though their elevated prose style makes them difficult even for Chinese readers, Pu Song-Ling's stories continue to be praised as classics and—reproduced in other forms and translated into modern Chinese and other languages—to appeal to a wide audience.

ching

"Chill and Desolate as a Monastery."   Pu Song-Ling was born in 1640 in Shan-dong (Shantung) province. He lived during the early years of the **Qing** (Ch'ing) dynasty (1644–1911), a time of transition when many families of the gentry, including Pu Song-Ling's own, were disenfranchised, as power shifted hands to the new Manchu rulers. In a brief autobiographical record, Pu Song-Ling describes himself as thin and of poor health and says that his father's home was "chill and desolate as a monastery." Although he received a solid classical education and passed the first stage of

---

[1] E. T. A. Hoffmann (1776–1822): German Romantic writer of supernatural and fantastic tales such as "The Sandman" and "The Mines of Falun," published in the early nineteenth century. (See E. T. A. Hoffmann, Book 5.)

[2] Edgar Allan Poe (1809–1849): This nineteenth-century American writer produced classic suspense tales such as "The Fall of the House of Usher" and "The Telltale Heart."

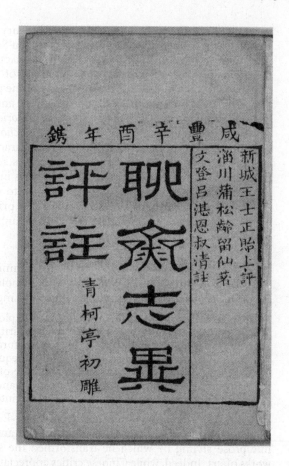

his examinations, Pu Song-Ling failed the provincial civil service exam at least twice. Unable to gain access to a government position, he remained in his native province of Shan-dong, teaching, collecting tales, and writing. He worked for some time as a personal secretary and then as a private tutor to a prominent family, from 1672 to 1710.

An ardent collector of classical and popular stories, Pu Song-Ling might be considered a folklorist who listened attentively to the tales circulating among the people of Shan-dong. Apparently he began writing early in life, but the first version of *Strange Tales* did not appear until 1679, when Pu Song-Ling was almost forty years old. The compendium first circulated in manuscript form only, for Pu Song-Ling could not afford to have it printed. Over the years he continued to add to and revise the tales; in the meantime he wrote a novel, three plays, poetry, and lyrics to be sung to popular tunes. In 1710, when Pu Song-Ling was seventy years old, he was given an official post as a senior licentiate because of his literary reputation. Pu Song-Ling died a short time later, in 1715; the final version of *Strange Tales* was published posthumously in 1766.

www   For links to more information about Pu Song-Ling and quizzes on "The Wise Neighbor" and "The Mural," see *World Literature Online* at bedfordstmartins .com/worldlit.

One striking differ-
ence between many
of Pu Song-Ling's lit-
erary ghost stories
and their Western
counterparts is the
frequent undercur-
rent of whimsy and
humor, found pre-
cisely in the conjunc-
tion of the ordinary
and the supernatu-
ral, the domestic and
demonic.

– STEPHEN OWEN, *An
Anthology of Chinese
Literature: Beginnings
to 1911, 1996*

Short Fiction in the Early Qing.

The final century of the Ming dynasty[3] and the early years of the Qing dynasty, when Pu Song-Ling lived, coincided with an increase in the production of VERNACULAR FICTION. As with the rise of the European NOVEL, the popularity of vernacular fiction in China was partly the result of the prosperity of the urban middle classes, who were drawn to the short story, the novel, and popular theater as forms of diversion and entertainment. *Strange Stories from a Chinese Studio* (also translated as *Uncanny Stories from a Scholar's Studio*) are portraits of everyday life, but ones in which the characters inevitably brush up against the supernatural in the form of ghosts, fox spirits, immortals, and other beings. Pu Song-Ling wrote his stories in a refined, "old style" prose that imitated classical styles dating back to the Western Han era (206 B.C.E.–8 C.E.). When his collection was first printed, classical supernatural stories were accompanied by extensive annotations and critical commentaries.

Strange Stories from a Chinese Studio.

After committing overheard popular stories to memory, Pu Song-Ling would polish them into a new form. Of his own storytelling abilities, Pu Song-Ling wrote,

> My talents are not those of Kan Pao, elegant explorer of the records of the Gods; I am rather animated by the spirit of Su Tung-p'o,[4] who loved to hear men speak of the supernatural. I get people to commit what they tell me to writing, and subsequently I dress it up in the form of a story; and thus, in the lapse of time my friends from all quarters have supplied me with quantities of material, which, from my habit of collecting, has grown into a vast pile.

His self-assessment notwithstanding, Pu Song-Ling's reputation as a great writer rests not on his abilities as a listener and collector but on his fine prose styling by which he transformed the stories he heard into works of art. Indeed, while Chinese critics appreciate the wit and irony of Pu Song-Ling's stories, they single out for praise their elevated style. Pu Song-Ling was a meticulous artist who honed and polished his stories until they met all the formal requirements of classic Chinese prose style — simplicity, invention, innovation, and density of allusions. Unfortunately, the apparent simplicity of these tales in translation doesn't do justice to Pu Song-Ling's perfection of this complex prose form.

"The Wise Neighbor."

p. 776

Whereas earlier Chinese tales of the supernatural take for granted a belief in spirits and magical powers, Pu Song-Ling's stories demonstrate a somewhat unique treatment of the otherworldly. In **"The Wise Neighbor,"** spirits embody human attributes and interact with human characters in ways more "natural" than supernatural. Moreover, as Stephen Owen has noted, unlike Poe and Hoffmann, who rely on

---

[3] Ming dynasty (1368–1644): A blossoming of Chinese culture, the restoration of Confucianism, and an elevation of the arts, including porcelain, architecture, drama, and the novel, are characteristic of this period.

[4] Kan Pao: Fourth-century author of a thirty-volume work called *Supernatural Researches.* Su Tung-p'o: Poet and essayist from the tenth century.

more grotesque imagery, in Pu Song-Ling's stories there is often an "undercurrent of whimsy and humor" when the ordinary characters recognize the appearance of the supernatural in their world. As Owen puts it, "At the very moment that the supernatural reveals itself in the ordinary world, . . . the strange has become ordinary." Thus, in "The Wise Neighbor" the friendship between Mrs. Chu and Mrs. Hêng seems quite normal, and there is nothing uncanny about the advice Mrs. Hêng, a fox spirit, offers.

"The Mural."   Such is not the case in **"The Mural,"** the second of Pu Song-Ling's stories included here. Rather more like the stories of E. T. A. Hoffmann, which blur the boundaries between the ordinary world and the supernatural, "The Mural" takes its readers into a kind of dreamscape that confounds the divide between illusion and reality. Here Chu, the master of letters, gazes into a mural depicting heavenly maidens scattering flowers and becomes so mesmerized by one of the figures that he is transported into another world. Chu's journey might well be compared to that of Elis Froebom in Hoffmann's "The Mines of Falun," for both Chu and Froebom encounter a female apparition whose existence may be illusory. Both characters seem to be physically present in, or incorporated into, the world of their "illusions," further confusing the boundary between reality and imagination.

p. 780

■ CONNECTIONS

Chikamatsu Monzaemon, *The Love Suicides at Amijima*, p. 691; Shen Fu, *Six Records of a Floating Life*, p. 755. The plot of "The Wise Neighbor" revolves around a love triangle, in this case among husband, wife, and concubine. Chikamatsu's play and Shen Fu's autobiography are a Japanese and another Chinese rendering of this same type of love triangle that show to what extent the officially sanctioned amours of the floating world became entangled, sometimes tragically, with the domestic life of the family in Japan and China. Consider how these tales are variations on the love triangle. How are Chikamatsu's and Shen Fu's tone different from Pu Song-Ling's? Which texts more effectively elicit sympathy or compassion from the reader?

E. T. A. Hoffmann, "The Mines of Falun" (Book 5); Alifa Rifaat, "My World of the Unknown" (Book 6). Pu Song-Ling is well known for his stories involving the supernatural. "The Mural" tells the story of a young man who falls in love with an image of a young girl and then is drawn into a dreamlike world where he consummates his love for her. At least, that's what seems to happen. The short stories of German writer E. T. A. Hoffmann and Egyptian writer Alifa Rifaat similarly describe a man and a woman, respectively, who are lured into mysterious worlds beyond the ken of ordinary consciousness by avatars, or incarnations. How does the monk's statement from "The Mural," "Illusion is born in the mind," apply to these stories? Does the blurring of dream and reality suggest something universal about the creative imagination? What makes each of these stories culturally unique?

Samuel Taylor Coleridge, *The Rime of the Ancient Mariner* (Book 5). In order to draw the reader into their fictional worlds, stories of the supernatural and the fantastic strive to create plausibility. The English poet Coleridge claimed that in some of his works he aimed to make the supernatural seem ordinary in order to sustain the "willing suspension of disbelief" of the reader. Compare Coleridge's poem with Pu Song-Ling's stories and describe the strategies each writer uses to create a believable world.

■ **FURTHER RESEARCH**

Biography

Giles, Herbert A. *A History of Chinese Literature*. 1901; rpt. 1967.

———, trans. *Strange Stories from a Chinese Studio*. 1925.

Criticism

Chang, Chun-shu. *Redefining History: Ghosts, Spirits, and Human Society in Pёu Sung-ling's World, 1640–1715*. 1998.

Owen, Stephen, ed. Introduction to Pu Song-ling in *An Anthology of Chinese Literature: Beginnings to 1911*. 1996.

Zeitlin, Judith T. *Pu Songling and the Chinese Classical Tale*. 1993.

■ **PRONUNCIATION**

Hsi-shih (Xi Shi): shee-SHUR
Hung Ta-yeh: hong-dah-YEH
Pao-chih: bow-JUR
Pao-tai: bow-TIGH
Pu Song-Ling: poo-song-LING
Qing: ching

❧ The Wise Neighbor

Translated by Christopher Levenson

Hung Ta-yeh was a man of the capital who was married to a girl whose maiden name was Chu, an exceptionally charming and pretty woman, whom he loved as much as she him. After some time Hung took a girl by the name of Pao-tai as his second wife and, although she was not nearly as beautiful as Mrs. Chu, the husband preferred the concubine to the wife. This upset Mrs. Chu and led to matrimonial quarrels between them. Although Hung did not dare to spend all his nights openly in the concubine's rooms, he nevertheless favoured her in every respect and neglected his wife.

Later Hung moved to another house and thereby became the neighbor of a textile merchant by the name of Ti. Ti's wife, Mrs. Hêng by name, of her own accord paid a call on Mrs. Chu. Mrs. Hêng must have been more than thirty years old by then and was scarcely of even average beauty, but her conversation was so amusing

---

"The Wise Neighbor." Mrs. Chu's husband is devoting more time to his concubine, Pao-tai, whom he has taken as a second wife, than to Mrs. Chu. When the family moves to a new neighborhood, Mrs. Chu meets Mrs. Hêng, who seems wise beyond her thirty years in the ways of love. Mrs. Hêng, who turns out to be a fox spirit, teaches Mrs. Chu how to win back her husband's affection and then disappears. The tale offers its readers insight into one of the recurrent themes of Chinese literature: the complex relations involved in polygamous marriages and the rivalries among wives or between wives and concubines. The strategies neglected partners might use to renew their beloved's respect and desire transcend the historical and cultural context of the Qing dynasty.

The translation of "The Wise Neighbor" is by Christopher Levenson; the notes are the editors'.

and quick-witted that Mrs. Chu at once took a liking to her and paid her a return visit the following day. In doing so she found that Mr. Ti also had a younger concubine who was as pretty as she was lovable. But even after Hung had lived with his family for almost half a year next to Mr. Ti they never noticed any sign of quarrels or discord in their household. Mr. Ti esteemed and loved only his wife Hêng, while the concubine in her "side chamber" was nothing more than mere decoration.

One day Hung's wife visited her neighbor and asked her: "I always used to think that my husband loved a secondary wife simply because she was a secondary wife, and I wished I could exchange the title of wife for that of secondary wife. But now I know that that cannot be the explanation. How have you managed this? If you would be so kind as to reveal your secret methods, I should like to be your humble pupil."

"Well then, you must simply withdraw into yourself, and repulse your husband for a change. You should keep him waiting the whole day with trivial chit-chat. In the twinkling of an eye, the separation from you will arouse his desires, but you must leave it all to him. Only, when he comes back to you of his own accord, you should not let him have his will. In a month's time I will see what further advice I can give you."

Mrs. Chu obeyed these instructions and adorned the girl Pao-tai even more beautifully and even let her husband spend whole nights with her. Likewise she arranged for Mr. Hung to take all his meals with the concubine. But as soon as he so much as approached his wife in a friendly way she repulsed him as hard as she could. Mr. Hung therefore praised his principal wife everywhere as virtuous. When this had gone on for more than a month Mrs. Chu went to call on Mrs. Hêng again.

"Well done," said her neighbor. "Now as soon as you get home you must make yourself ugly. Don't wear any more beautiful clothes and don't take any more trouble with your complexion; go among your maids with a dirty face and worn-out shoes, and do housework. After a month you can come to me again."

Mrs. Chu followed this advice also, put on threadbare, patched clothes, and deliberately did not keep herself clean any longer. Moreover, she devoted all her time to spinning, without demanding anything more. Thereupon Mr. Hung began to take pity on her and instructed Pao-tai to help his wife in her work. Mrs. Chu, however, refused all offers of help and scolded the girl and sent her packing.

After a month she paid another visit to Mrs. Hêng and received new instructions: "You are really a diligent pupil! In a few days' time it will be the Spring Festival. I will then invite you to admire the beauty of the blossoms in our garden. On this occasion, take off your old clothes and put on the most beautiful and newest gown, shoes, and stockings that you possess and come first to me."

Mrs. Chu promised to do this and, when the day of the Festival had come, seated herself in front of her mirror and made herself up most beautifully, just as Mrs. Hêng had advised her. When she had finished her toilette she went across to Mrs. Hêng, who exclaimed joyfully: "That is just right!" Then her neighbor put her phoenix hair style in order with her own hands, so that you could see your reflection in the gleaming black hair. Moreover, as the cut of the gown was not in the very latest fashion, she opened the seams and altered the gown. She felt too that the shoes were of inelegant shape and fetched from her own wardrobe a pair of not quite finished shoes that the two women then finished together with embroideries. When Mrs. Chu had put on the shoes, Mrs. Hêng offered her guest a glass of wine before she took her leave and impressed upon her: "Go home now and when your husband has seen you, lock yourself into your room early and retire to bed. If he knocks at your door, pay no attention to it at first. When he has called you three times, you may at most let him in once, and when he seeks your tongue with his mouth, when his hands strive towards your feet, be sparing of your favours. Then after half a month, you must come to me again."

On arriving home, Mrs. Chu showed herself in all the glory of her outfit to her husband, who did not tire of looking her up and down and laughed and joked with her as he had never done before. But Mrs. Chu said little during the Festival and walked around looking at the garden, with her head propped on her hand and with an expression of indifference on her face. And even before sunset she withdrew to her bedroom, barred the door, and lay down to sleep. Sure enough, Mr. Hung came along shortly afterwards and knocked on the door, but Mrs. Chu remained lying where she was and did not even rise from the bed, so that Hung had to go away again. The next day exactly the same thing occurred and only on the third day, when Hung began to insist politely, did Mrs. Chu say: "As a matter of fact, I've got used to sleeping by myself and don't feel I can put up with such interference again." As the sun sank down towards the west, Mr. Hung went into the bedroom where his wife was already seated waiting for him. The lamps were extinguished and both of them climbed into bed. Hung felt as if he were with a young married woman and found the greatest of pleasure in their embraces. He wanted to make an arrangement with her for the following evening also but Mrs. Chu said that it was impossible and as a special favour gave him permission to come to her every third day.

A fortnight later she again visited Mrs. Hêng. The neighbor locked the door behind her guest and said to her: "From now on, you have the upper hand in the bedroom. But however beautiful you may be, you are not seductive. If your attractiveness were as great as your beauty, you would enjoy favour among men at least equal to that of the famous Hsi-shih."[1]

Then she got Mrs. Chu to practise casting glances and said: "Quite wrong! The fault lies in the far corner of your eye." Then Mrs. Chu had to practise smiling, but to this too her neighbor said: "Wrong again! Your left cheek is not right yet." Then Mrs. Hêng herself cast a few glances that radiated the seductiveness of the damp autumn wave, smiling so winsomely that her regular white teeth were slightly visible. Mrs. Chu had to imitate all this a few dozen times before she had approximately caught the knack of it. Then Mrs. Hêng said: "Now go home and practise everything exactly with a mirror in your hand. I can't teach you anything more in the way of tactics. As for how you behave in bed, act as the occasion demands and surrender yourself in the way that he likes best. I can't teach you that with mere words."

---

[1] **Hsi-shih:** Xi Shi (fifth century B.C.E.) was a legendary beauty of ancient China; like Helen of Troy in Greek legend, Xi Shi caused the downfall of a state: She distracted the prince of Wu from his political responsibilities, enabling the king of Yue to invade Wu.

Mrs. Chu went home and acted in every point in accordance with her neighbor's advice. Mr. Hung was beside himself with joy and fell heart and soul in love with his wife, so that he feared only one thing—to be repulsed by her. As day was declining he used to smile at her in a friendly way and his steps no longer made their way towards the other woman's chamber. So it went on, day by day, and finally he could no longer be induced to go to the secondary wife. But Mrs. Chu treated Pao-tai ever better, and whenever she prepared a supper in her bedroom Pao-tai had to sit with her on the same bed. Mr. Hung, however, began to find Pao-tai uglier and uglier and usually sent her away before the end of the meal. On such occasions Mrs. Chu played the trick on her husband of going to Pao-tai's room herself and locking herself in there so that the whole night through Hung could find no place where he could satisfy his desires. To add to it all, Pao-tai began to grow resentful of Mr. Hung and to grumble about him in front of other people so that Hung got more and more tired of her, lost his temper with her, and even began to beat her. From sorrow at this Pao-tai neglected her toilette and began to go about with poor clothes on, with dirty shoes and tousled hair, so that she hardly looked human any more.

"How have my arts worked?" Mrs. Chu's neighbor asked her one day.

"Your method is really wonderful, but although I follow it as your pupil, I don't quite see how it all comes about."

"Have you never heard how it is with such matters? In love, you value whatever is new and find what is old depressing; you throw yourself wholeheartedly into difficult things and despise what is easy. If a husband loves his concubine, it's not because she just happens to be beautiful. It is rather that he finds it delicious to possess her through some unexpected adventure and is happy when he can get together with her only under difficulties. Let someone gorge as he pleases, and he will soon grow sick of the most costly foods—and all the more so when he is just offered groats."

"But why make yourself ugly first before shining out in radiant beauty?"

"If you arrange things so that you attract no glances at all, it's just as good as a long separation. If your husband then sees you again suddenly in all your seductive charm, it's as good as if you were coming to him for the first time. If a poor man is suddenly given meat and millet to eat, he finds that coarse hulled rice is no longer tasty. And if a wife does not casually allow her husband to have everything, the result is that the other woman grows old for him while the wife herself is new, the other woman easy to get while she herself is obtained with difficulty. That, you see, is my method: to become, instead of your husband's main wife, his concubine."

Mrs. Chu was extremely pleased and remained subsequently for a number of years her neighbor's intimate friend. One day Mrs. Hêng said: "We two like each other as much as if we had but the one body, and I don't want shadows to be cast across your life on my account. For a long time I have often wanted to talk openly to you but I feared that you would mistrust me. Now, however, our ways must part, so I may dare to tell you the truth. You see, I am a fox spirit.[2] In my youth I was unlucky

---

[2] **fox spirit:** Some people were said to be possessed by the spirits of foxes, which could foresee the future and influence people's lives through magic powers; fox spirits could also turn themselves into humans in order to intervene in human affairs.

enough to have a stepmother who sold me at the capital. But because my husband treated me so well, I could not bring myself to leave him and our love has lasted up to the present day. But tomorrow my old father will give up his corporeal existence and I must therefore go back to my family and will not return."

Mrs. Chu gripped her hands and took her leave sobbing. When she went over again next morning, the whole family next door was in a great commotion, for Mrs. Hêng had vanished without a trace.

ꙮ The Mural

Translated by Denis C. Mair and Victor H. Mair

While staying in the capital, Meng Lung-t'an of Kiangsi and Master of Letters Chu once happened upon a monastery. Neither the shrine-hall nor the meditation room was very spacious, and only one old monk was found putting up within. Seeing the guests enter, the monk straightened up his clothes, went to greet them, and showed them around the place. An image of Zen Master Pao-chih[1] stood in the shrine-hall. On either side-wall were painted fine murals with lifelike human figures. The east wall depicted the Buddhist legend of "Heavenly Maidens Scattering Flowers." Among the figures was a young girl with flowing hair with a flower in her hand and a faint smile on her face. Her cherry-red lips were on the verge of moving, and the

---

"**The Mural.**" Master Chu and his friend Meng Lung-t'an come upon a monastery in their travels to the capital. Fascinated by the mural "Heavenly Maidens Scattering Flowers," Master Chu becomes entranced with the figure of innocence, a "young girl with flowing hair." Seemingly drawn up into the world of the immortals depicted in the mural, Chu imagines—or does it happen?—that he makes love to this young woman, who is then subject to the humiliation and punishment ministered by a shadowy officer dressed in armor. Chu seems literally to have become part of the mural in his passage between the two worlds, and his friend Meng Lung-t'an trembles in fear when he sees the image of Chu on the wall. Did they both imagine this experience? Was Chu's lust, as the Chronicler of the Tales suggests, strong enough to implicate Meng in his forbidden fantasy? The young woman's hair, no longer flowing but bound up in the chignon (bun) of married women, casts a palpable sense of doubt over both Chu and Meng, who leave the monastery in confusion, apparently no more enlightened than before. As the translators Denis C. Mair and Victor H. Mair note, the comments at the end of the tale are modeled on those that conclude the chapters of the influential dynastic history *Records of the Grand Historian* (*Shih chi*), by Ssu-ma Ch'ien (145–90? B.C.E.); such comments often offer a new, sometimes critical, perspective on a story, without, as the Mairs note, "being overtly and offensively didactic."

The translation of "The Mural" is by Denis C. Mair and Victor H. Mair; the footnotes are the editors'.

---

[1]**Pao-chih:** Pao zhi; a legendary monk from the era of the Northern (386–581) and Southern (420–589) dynasties.

liquid pools of her eyes seemed to stir with wavelike glances. After gazing intently for some time, Chu's self-possession began to waver, and his thoughts grew so abstracted that he fell into a trance. His body went adrift as if floating on mist; suddenly he was inside the mural. Peak upon peak of palaces and pavilions made him feel as if he was beyond this earth. An old monk was preaching the Dharma[2] on a dais, around which stood a large crowd of viewers in robes with their right shoulders bared out of respect. Chu mingled in among them.

Before long, he felt someone tugging furtively at his sleeve. He turned to look, and there was the girl with flowing hair giving him a dazzling smile. She tripped abruptly away, and he lost no time following her along a winding walkway into a small chamber. Once there, he hesitated to approach any farther. When she turned her head and raised the flower with a beckoning motion, he went across to her in the quiet, deserted chamber. Swiftly he embraced her and, as she did not put up much resistance, they grew intimate. When it was over she told him not to make a sound and left, closing the door behind her. That night she came again. After two days of this, the girl's companions realized what was happening and searched together until they found the scholar.

"A little gentleman is already growing in your belly, but still you wear those flowing tresses, pretending to be a maiden," they said teasingly. Holding out hairpins and earrings, they pressured her to put her hair up in the coiled knot of a married woman, which she did in silent embarrassment. One of the girls said, "Sisters, let's not outstay our welcome." At this the group left all in a titter.

Looking at the soft, cloudlike chignon piled atop her head and her phoenix ringlets curved low before her ears, the scholar was more struck by her charms than when she had worn her hair long. Seeing that no one was around, he began to make free with her. His heart throbbed at her musky fragrance but, before they had quite finished their pleasure, the heavy tread of leather boots was heard. A clanking of chains and manacles was followed by clamorous, arguing voices. The girl got up in alarm. Peering out, they saw an officer dressed in armor, his face black as lacquer, with chains in one hand and a mace in the other. Standing around him were all the maidens. "Is this all of you?" asked the officer. "We're all here," they answered. "Report if any of you are concealing a man from the lower world. Don't bring trouble on yourselves." "We aren't," said the maidens in unison. The officer turned around and looked malevolently in the direction of the chamber, giving every appearance of an intention to search it. The girl's face turned pale as ashes in fear. "Quick, hide under the bed," she told Chu in panic. She opened a little door in the wall and was gone in an instant. Chu lay prostrate, hardly daring to take a little breath. Soon he heard the sound of boots stumping into, then back out of, the room. Before long, the din of voices gradually receded. He regained some composure, though the sound of passersby discussing the matter could be heard frequently outside the door. After cringing there for quite some time, he heard ringing in his ears and felt a burning ache in his eyes. Though the intensity of these sensations threatened to overwhelm

---

[2] **Dharma:** In Buddhism, the truth that reflects the moral law of the universe.

him, there was no choice but to listen quietly for the girl's return. He was reduced to the point that he no longer recalled where he had been before coming here.

Just then his friend Meng Lung-t'an, who had been standing in the shrine-hall, found that Chu had disappeared in the blink of an eye. Perplexed, he asked the monk what had happened. "He has gone to hear a sermon on the Dharma," said the monk laughingly. "Where?" asked Meng. "Not far," was the answer. After a moment, the monk tapped on the wall with his finger and called, "Why do you tarry so long, my good patron?" Presently there appeared on the wall an image of Chu standing motionless with his head cocked to one side as if listening to something. "You have kept your traveling companion waiting a long time," called the monk again. Thereupon he drifted out of the mural and down to the floor. He stood woodenly, his mind like burned-out ashes, with eyes staring straight ahead and legs wobbling. Meng was terribly frightened, but in time calmed down enough to ask what had happened. It turned out that Chu had been hiding under the bed when he heard a thunderous knocking, so he came out of the room to listen for the source of the sound.

They looked at the girl holding the flower and saw, instead of flowing hair, a high coiled chignon on her head. Chu bowed down to the old monk in amazement and asked the reason for this. "Illusion is born in the mind. How can a poor mendicant like myself explain it?" laughed the monk. Chu was dispirited and cast down; Meng was shaken and confused. Together they walked down the shrine-hall steps and left.

The Chronicler of the Tales comments: "'Illusion is born in the mind.' These sound like the words of one who has found the truth. A wanton mind gives rise to visions of lustfulness. The mind dominated by lust gives rise to a state of fear. The Bodhisattva made it possible for ignorant persons to attain realization for themselves. All the myriad transformations of illusion are nothing but the movements of the human mind itself. The old monk spoke in earnest solicitude, but regrettably there is no sign that the youth found enlightenment in his words and entered the mountains with hair unbound to seek the truth."

Cao Xueqin
c. 1715–1763

Gao E
c. 1740–1815

In the late Ming (1368–1644) and early Qing (1644–1911) dynasties, the Chinese NOVEL reached a point of high perfection with the appearance of two premier works of the genre: Wu Jing Zi's *The Scholars* (*Ju-lin wai-shih,* 1750) and Cao Xueqin's *The Story of the Stone* (*Shitouji,* 1791), also known as the *Dream of the Red Chamber* (*Hong lou meng*). Considered the most important Chinese popular novel by most scholars as well as one of the great works of world literature, *The Story of the Stone* provides a panoramic view of Chinese culture and society during the early Qing era. A sweeping narrative involving more than 420 characters, *The Story of the Stone* follows the decline of the aristocratic Jia clan, an extended family with strong connections to the MANCHU.[1] Remarkable for its realistic and meticulous description of the daily life of the Chinese elite, this novel is also a BILDUNGSROMAN—a work that recounts the intellectual, emotional, and spiritual growth of one of its main characters, Jia Bao-yu. From a philosophical viewpoint, *The Story of the Stone* can be seen as a depiction of the Chinese effort to juggle the contrasting ideals of CONFUCIANISM, DAOISM, and BUDDHISM, weighing the balance between Bao-yu's worldy entanglements and his spiritual quest.

Cao Xueqin. The first eighty chapters of *The Story of the Stone* were completed in about 1750 by **Cao Xueqin** (Ts'ao Hsueh-ch'in), the talented son of a wealthy family whose misfortunes are reflected in the plot of the novel; the last forty chapters were added by Gao E (Kao E), who produced the first printed version of the novel in 1791. Cao Xueqin's ancestors had been Bannermen to the Manchu emperors. Bannermen, who ranked among the top three tiers of aristocracy in China, served as leaders of the elite Banner army, a sort of royal guard. They offered their services in exchange for lucrative political appointments, special privileges, and gifts of land and goods. The Cao clan's post was Commissioner of the Imperial Textile Mills at Nanking, an office the family held from 1663 to 1728. Cao Yin, who may have been Cao Xueqin's grandfather or his granduncle, was himself a poet, playwright, and patron of letters as well as a favorite of Emperor Kangxi (K'ang-hsi; 1661–1722). After Cao Yin's death in 1712, the commission and privileges fell to his heirs, but after Kangxi's death in 1722, problems began to arise. In 1728 the new emperor

tsow-shweh-CHIN

www For links to more information about Cao Xueqin and Gao E, and three quizzes on *The Story of the Stone,* see *World Literature Online* at bedfordstmartins .com/worldlit.

---

[1]**Manchu:** Also known as the Jurchen, the Manchu lived northeast of the Great Wall, in the area now known as Manchuria; when civil disturbances weakened the authority of the last Ming emperor, the Manchu, assisted by some inside China, took over Beijing and founded a new empire. Their dynasty, known as the Qing (Ch'ing) or Manchu dynasty, lasted from 1644 to 1911.

Yongzheng (Yung-cheng; 1722–1736) effectively stripped the family of its commission and confiscated much of its property. Cao Xueqin was about thirteen years old at the time, and it is not clear how his family managed after this misfortune, but we do know they took up residence in Beijing (Peking). Later in life, Cao Xueqin eked out a living as a seller of rock paintings and part-time tutor. In the last years of his life, Cao Xueqin moved to the "Western Hills" outside of Beijing, where he died in 1763.

The fall of the once prosperous Jia clan at the hands of the imperial government depicted in *The Story of the Stone* appears to be Cao Xueqin's thinly veiled version of the plight of his own family. He probably began the novel around 1740, while living in Beijing. From manuscript copies found by scholars it is clear that the first eighty chapters were circulating among Cao Xueqin's friends before his death. The last forty chapters of the complete novel published in 1792 were written by another hand, Gao E's, who along with the publisher, Cheng Weiyuan (Ch'eng Wei-yuan), saw the book into print.

Gao E.   Born sometime around 1740 to a family that appears to have been from Tieling, in what is now the province Liaoning, **Gao E** was a Bannerman who worked as a tutor before passing his civil service examinations in 1788 and 1795, when he became a minor bureaucrat in Beijing. He eventually attained the post of Junior Metropolitan Censor in 1812. A talented writer of the "eight-legged essay"[2] as well as a minor poet, Gao E circulated among and sometimes collaborated with other Bannerman literary figures and artists, including Cheng Weiyuan, the artist and publisher who invited Gao E to prepare *The Story of the Stone* for publication. In 1781, Gao E lost his father and his wife; a second marriage in 1785 ended abruptly when his wife died only two years later. Adding to his misfortunes, Gao E's mother, whom he cared for after the death of his father, forced him to separate from his concubine. It was during this period of successive difficulties that Gao E edited *The Story of the Stone* for publication. While varying versions of the first eighty chapters of the novel had been circulating among private collectors for more than thirty years, the last forty chapters had been lost. In a preface to the first printed version, Cheng Weiyuan and Gao E state that they have merely edited the novel, including the final forty chapters, bits and pieces of which Cheng claimed he had acquired from several sources, including rare book collectors and a peddler. Some scholars believe that Gao E actually wrote several if not all of the final forty chapters of *The Story of the Stone*. Whatever his role, Gao E completed his work on the novel in December 1791 (the date of his preface). The novel was an immediate success, with a second edition going to press just a few months after the first. Gao E died sometime around 1815, having lived in relative comfort as a government official and a man of letters.

gow-UH

[The] *Story of the Stone* is an extraordinarily rich novel in the physical and cultural details of life in eighteenth-century China; it is no less rich in the complexity of its vision of the society, with moments of everyday pettiness and tenderness framed in a larger and dangerous world of men and political power.

– STEPHEN OWEN, *An Anthology of Chinese Literature, Beginnings to 1911, 1996*

---

[2] **"eight-legged essay":** *Ba-gu wen*, an essay of eight parts written on a Confucian theme; developed during the Ming dynasty (1368–1644) as a requirement on civil service examinations.

The Fall of the Jia Family.   When Cao Xueqin began writing *The Story of the Stone*, his once wealthy family had fallen into disfavor and poverty, circumstances the novel takes up in its realistic and detailed portrayal of the Jia clan. The book traces the lives of the clan's two main branches, from the height of imperial favor and luxury to decline into near ruin through mismanagement of their affairs. The two family branches reside in the capital city of Beijing in adjacent compounds, Ning-guo and Rong-guo. At the center of both branches is the great ancestress, Grandmother Jia. Over the course of the novel, the two houses unite their fortunes, a union symbolized by the Prospect Garden that now links their estates. The combined houses fall under the management of Weng Xifeng, the wife of Jia Lian and the niece of Lady Wang, who loses control of the family's affairs and squanders its fortunes. This thread of the plot demonstrates how family fortunes can become entangled with affairs of the state and how personal ambition and greed can devastate even the most secure household. More important, the rise and fall of the Jias' fortunes points to the illusory nature of things in the material world, a truth underscored by the story of the book's main protagonist, Bao-yu, the son of Jia Zheng.

The Stone and the Crimson Flower.   The excerpt that follows focuses on **Jia Bao-yu**, the son of the patriarch of Rong-guo mansion, Jia Zheng. It follows Bao-yu's life from his playful childhood and problematic adolescence, when he rebels against his father, to young adulthood, when he finds disappointment in marriage and gives up the world for spiritual salvation. For much of his life, he is involved in a troubled triangular relationship with his two beautiful but very different cousins, **Lin Dai-yu** (Black Jade) and **Xue Bao-chai** (Precious Clasp). Born mysteriously with a jade stone in his mouth, Bao-yu is considered the earthly embodiment of the magical stone. He is brought into the world in order to experience desire and suffering so that he can achieve enlightenment. Lin Dai-yu, his sensitive and frail cousin, is the earthly embodiment of the Crimson Pearl Flower, which grows near the Rock of Rebirth mentioned in Chapter 1. In his supernatural life as the stone, Bao-yu watered this flower with his tears, bringing it to life as a fairy. The intimacy of Bao-yu and Lin Dai-yu thus has been prefigured in the narrative as one of mutual obligation: In return for the stone giving her life, Crimson Pearl Flower owes him a "debt of tears." In the realm of the Red Dust — that is, on earth — Bao-yu and Lin Dai-yu are endowed with similar literary talent, emotional sensitivity, and a certain predisposition toward melancholy.

The Love Triangle.   Their relationship becomes complicated when Xue Bao-chai arrives at Rong-guo. Less refined but happier and physically more fit than Dai-yu, Bao-chai competes for Bao-yu's attention and wins the favor of the matriarch. Because Bao-yu and Bao-chai have matching inscriptions — on his jade stone and her gold necklace — they too seem destined for a close relationship, if not marriage. Bao-chai's dallying with Bao-yu sends Dai-yu into fits of jealousy and self-pity that eventually sap

jyah-bow-YOO

lin-digh-YOO
shweh-bow-CHIGH

her strength. In the sometimes playful, sometimes serious fighting of the three cousins, the novel presents a realistic account of the everyday life of the Qing-era elite. In a particularly cruel turn in the novel, Grandmother Jia, who favors Bao-chai over Dai-yu, tricks Bao-yu into marrying Bao-chai. Realizing what has happened, Dai-yu languishes, partly from consumption, partly from grief, and she dies on the night of Bao-yu's marriage to her cousin. After initially taking ill at the news that he has been deceived into marrying the wrong cousin and grieving over the death of Dai-yu, Bao-yu eventually recovers, accepts his world responsibilities, has a son with Bao-chai, and goes on to take his examinations, which have been a subject of dispute between him and his father, **Jia Zheng**.

jyah-JUNG

The Culture of Learning.

The Story of the Stone is a window on the Chinese aristocracy, or *shen-shih,* who rose to positions of power by passing the rigorous and highly prestigious civil service examinations, which play an important role in the novel. The examinations symbolize the world of work and civic responsibility, the CONFUCIAN element in Bao-yu's story. Bao-yu, the somewhat self-indulgent hero of the novel, succeeds in deferring the exams, which loom nonetheless as a reminder of his obligation to his father and the state and as a symbol of his earthly destiny. When he finally does take the examinations, his exceptional performance earns him not only his father's praise but also the attention of the Imperial Lord himself. His success helps to restore his fallen family to its former position of rank and honor; the same is not known to have happened for the novel's author.

Of supreme importance to the relatively small and elite population of *shen-shih* was the cultivation of *wen,* or refinement and good taste in all aspects of life. Confucianism, with its emphasis on respect for tradition, ritual, and above all, order, provided the philosophical foundations for mastering wen. In *The Story of the Stone,* Jia Zheng exemplifies the man leading a life governed by wen. By means of birth, training, and the observation of ritual ceremony, Jia Zheng has earned the respect and honor of his superiors, his peers, and his family. Because Bao-yu tends to shirk his responsibilities, neglect his lessons, and spend his time in the company of girls, Jia Zheng often loses patience with him.

. . . [Bao-yu]'s meaningless life unconsciously evolves slowly toward illumination. He is a Taoist saint who doesn't know he is one and doesn't want to be one. Like Prince Genji [from Lady Murasaki's *The Tale of Genji*], he is indifferent to and ignorant of his cosmic role.

– KENNETH REXROTH,
Classics Revisited,
1969

Enlightenment.

Although the early Qing dynasty is best characterized by its Confucianist tendencies, Buddhism and Daoism (Taoism) also had their place and did influence the thought and everyday life of Chinese from all walks of life. The appearance at three crucial moments in Bao-yu's life of a Buddhist priest and a Daoist monk who guide his destiny show the novel's Daoist and Buddhist leanings. Indeed, Bao-yu's favorite authors are Laozi (Lao Tzu) and Zhuangzi (Chuang Tzu),[3] whose

---

[3] **Laozi** (Lao Tzu; third century B.C.E.?): Considered one of the founders of Daoist (Taoist) thought in China: *Laozi* in Chinese means "old philosopher" or simply "old man," and some scholars doubt whether a man of

teachings profoundly inform his decision to renounce the world and seek spiritual enlightenment. From the first chapter—a kind of mythic overture that introduces the book's important themes and anticipates its plot—the reader is alerted to the spiritual and moral meaning of the story, as the divergent Confucian, Daoist, and Buddhist doctrines are brought to bear on the issue of balancing public responsibility and private salvation. This conflict is most poignantly dramatized in the relationship between the somewhat dreamy Bao-yu and his pragmatic father, Jia Zheng. Toward the end of the novel, Bao-yu seems to have moved beyond the carefree spirit of his childhood and adolescence and to have finally accepted his family duties and worldly responsibilities. Yet, shortly after he honors his filial duty and passes his civil service examinations with high honors, he disappears. Influenced by the Daoist teachings and angered and saddened by his fraudulent marriage and the death of his cousin, Bao-yu forsakes the world of torment, passion, and desire. He abandons Confucian responsibilities and his attachment to the world of illusion and finds spiritual enlightenment by following the way of personal salvation. In the final chapter, Bao-yu reappears as a Buddhist immortal before his father. His trial on earth completed, Bao-yu returns to the "Great Unity." In the words of the final chapter, "From the moment the Stone's worldly karma was complete, its substance had returned to the Great Unity. . . . Thus its precious nature, its magical power, its capacity for spiritual transformation, these were made manifest, and all could know that it was no ordinary stone of this world."

The Jia household is restored to order and Bao-yu's son by Bao-chai will inherit Rong-guo. Bao-yu's sainthood and the writings he leaves behind earn him the respect of both his father and the emperor, and the novel concludes with the fortunes of the Jia family once again on the rise. Some critics interpret Bao-yu's adherence to spiritual enlightenment as a subtle criticism of the Manchu rulers of the Qing dynasty, who clung to the practical, worldly values of Confucianism. Like all great novels, *The Story of the Stone* supports myriad, sometimes conflicting readings.

> As a panorama of Chinese social life, in which almost every imaginable feature is submitted in turn to the reader, the *Hong lou meng* [*Dream of the Red Chamber*] is altogether without a rival.
>
> – HERBERT A. GILES, *A History of Chinese Literature*, 1901

■ CONNECTIONS

Lady Murasaki, *The Tale of Genji* **(Book 2).** Bao-yu, the hero of *The Story of the Stone*, grows up preferring the company of girls and women to that of men, to the great disappointment of his father. Bao-yu cultivates a strong aesthetic sensibility and intense feeling. Genji, the hero of Lady Murasaki's novel, also possesses a refined sensibility, and though he has devoted male friends like To No Chujo, he too seeks out the company of women. Compare these two characters: How does each author develop their psychological complexity? What makes these two protagonists different?

---

such a name existed at all. The Dao De Jing (Tao Te Ching), a collection of poems emphasizing the value of entering into harmony with the Dao, or the Way of nature, is attributed to him. **Zuangzi** (Chuang Tzu; c. 369–c. 286 B.C.E.): One of the founders of Daoism, whose parables and fables set forth the idea that in order to achieve salvation human beings must become one with the Dao (Tao), the underlying principle of unity that governs the universe.

Molière, *Tartuffe*, p. 22; Alexander Pope, *The Rape of the Lock,* p. 238. Through the lens of *The Story of the Stone,* we get a glimpse of life among the well-to-do in eighteenth-century China. Despite the serious nature of the historical plot—the collapse of a family—there are many playful moments in the text. Although in a vein of satire and play quite different from Cao Xueqin's, both Molière's *Tartuffe* and Alexander Pope's *The Rape of the Lock* mirror high-society life in France and England during the Enlightenment. Which behaviors and manners depicted in these works are culturally distinctive and which defy cultural boundaries?

Anton Chekhov, *The Cherry Orchard* (Book 5); Chinua Achebe, *Things Fall Apart* (Book 6). A novel of epic proportions, *The Story of the Stone* chronicles the fall of a dynastic family in an era of political and social change in China. *The Cherry Orchard,* by Russian playwright Chekhov, and *Things Fall Apart,* by Nigerian novelist Achebe, also depict the collapse of social and political order. How do these writers solicit sympathy for their main characters? In what ways do these authors reveal their own political perspectives?

■ FURTHER RESEARCH

Literary Context
Hsia, C. T. *The Classic Chinese Novel.* 1968.
Plaks, Andrew. *Chinese Narrative.* 1977.
Smith, Richard J. *China's Cultural Heritage: The Ch'ing Dynasty.* 1983.

Criticism
Hsia, C. T. "Love and Compassion in *Dream of the Red Chamber.*" *Criticism* (summer 1963): 261–71.
Knoerle, Jeanne. The Story of the Stone, *A Critical Study.* 1972.
Levy, Dore J. *Ideal and Actual in* The Story of the Stone. 1999.
McMahon, Keith. "Polygyny, Crossing of Gender, and the Superiority of Women in *Honglou Meng.*" In *Misers, Shrews and Polygamists: Sexuality and Male-Female Relations in Eighteenth-Century Chinese Fiction.* 1995.
Miller, Lucien. *Masks of Fiction in* Dream of the Red Chamber. 1975.
Plaks, Andrew. *Archetype and Allegory in the* Dream of the Red Chamber. 1976.
Wang, Jing. *The Story of Stone: Intertexuality, Ancient Chinese Stone Lore and the Stone Symbolism in* Dream of the Red Chamber. 1992.
Wu Shih-ch'ang. *On the* Red Chamber Dream: *A Critical Study of Two Annotated Manuscripts of the XVIIIth Century.* 1961.
Yu, Anthony C. *Rereading the Stone: Desire and the Making of Fiction in* Dream of the Red Chamber. 1997.

■ PRONUNCIATION

Cao Xueqin: tsow-shweh-CHIN
Feng-shi: fung-SHUR
Gao E: gow-UH
Jia Bao-yu: jyah-bow-YOO
Jia Zheng: jyah-JUNG
Lin Dai-yu: lin-digh-YOO
Qin-shi: chin-SHUR
Qin Zhong: chin-JONG
Xue Bao-chai: shweh-bow-CHIGH
Zhen Shi-yin: jun-shur-YIN

❧ The Story of the Stone

Translated by David Hawkes and John Minford

FROM CHAPTER 1

[The Origin of the Stone]

GENTLE READER,

What, you may ask, was the origin of this book?

Though the answer to this question may at first seem to border on the absurd, reflection will show that there is a good deal more in it than meets the eye.

Long ago, when the goddess Nü-wa was repairing the sky, she melted down a great quantity of rock and, on the Incredible Crags of the Great Fable Mountains, moulded the amalgam into thirty-six thousand, five hundred and one large building blocks, each measuring seventy-two feet by a hundred and forty-four feet square. She used thirty-six thousand five hundred of these blocks in the course of her building operations, leaving a single odd block unused, which lay, all on its own, at the foot of Greensickness Peak in the aforementioned mountains.

Now this block of stone, having undergone the melting and moulding of a goddess, possessed magic powers. It could move about at will and could grow or shrink to any size it wanted. Observing that all the other blocks had been used for celestial repairs and that it was the only one to have been rejected as unworthy, it became filled with shame and resentment and passed its days in sorrow and lamentation.

One day, in the midst of its lamentings, it saw a monk and a Taoist approaching from a great distance, each of them remarkable for certain eccentricities of manner and appearance. When they arrived at the foot of Greensickness Peak, they sat down on the ground and began to talk. The monk, catching sight of a lustrous, translucent stone—it was in fact the rejected building block which had now shrunk itself to the

---

The Story of the Stone. The composition and publication of *The Story of the Stone* are complicated matters and remain the subject of scholarly debate by specialists in what has come to be known as Redology, after the alternate title of the novel, *Dream of the Red Chamber*. While most agree that sometime between 1740 and 1761 Cao Xueqin wrote the first eighty chapters of the novel, Gao E's role in the completion of the final forty chapters is less clear. David Hawkes and John Minford, the translators of the following selection, have weighed the evidence and suggest that, as he claims in his preface, Gao E probably edited the text based on copies of the first eighty chapters and manuscript fragments of the final forty chapters, which most likely were written by someone close to Cao Xueqin—possibly a family member. The 120-chapter novel published by Cheng Weiyuan and Gao E in January 1792 (some give 1791 as the publication year) has been accepted by readers in China and throughout the world as a complete work and one of the last millennium's greatest works of fiction.

   A note on the translation: David Hawkes is the translator of Volumes 1 through 3 of *The Story of the Stone* (Chapters 1 through 80), and John Minford is the translator of Volumes 4 and 5 (Chapters 81 through 120). The notes are the editors'.

size of a fan-pendant and looked very attractive in its new shape—took it up on the palm of his hand and addressed it with a smile:

"Ha, I see you have magical properties! But nothing to recommend you. I shall have to cut a few words on you so that anyone seeing you will know at once that you are something special. After that I shall take you to a certain

brilliant
successful
poetical
cultivated
aristocratic
elegant
delectable
luxurious
opulent
locality on a little trip."

The stone was delighted.

"What words will you cut? Where is this place you will take me to? I beg to be enlightened."

"Do not ask," replied the monk with a laugh. "You will know soon enough when the time comes."

And with that he slipped the stone into his sleeve and set off at a great pace with the Taoist. But where they both went to I have no idea.

Countless aeons went by and a certain Taoist called Vanitas in quest of the secret of immortality chanced to be passing below that same Greensickness Peak in the Incredible Crags of the Great Fable Mountains when he caught sight of a large stone standing there, on which the characters of a long inscription were clearly discernible.

Vanitas read the inscription through from beginning to end and learned that this was a once lifeless stone block which had been found unworthy to repair the sky, but which had magically transformed its shape and been taken down by the Buddhist mahāsattva[1] Impervioso and the Taoist illuminate Mysterioso into the world of mortals, where it had lived out the life of a man before finally attaining nirvana[2] and returning to the other shore. The inscription named the country where it had been born, and went into considerable detail about its domestic life, youthful amours, and even the verses, mottoes, and riddles it had written. All it lacked was the authentication of a dynasty and date. On the back of the stone was inscribed the following quatrain:

Found unfit to repair the azure sky
Long years a foolish mortal man was I.
My life in both worlds on this stone is writ:
Pray who will copy out and publish it?

---

[1] **mahāsattva:** Wise man.

[2] **nirvana:** State of enlightenment that releases the soul from the cycle of rebirth.

From his reading of the inscription Vanitas realized that this was a stone of some consequence. Accordingly he addressed himself to it in the following manner:

"Brother Stone, according to what you yourself seem to imply in these verses, this story of yours contains matter of sufficient interest to merit publication and has been carved here with that end in view. But as far as I can see (a) it has no discoverable dynastic period, and (b) it contains no examples of moral grandeur among its characters—no statesmanship, no social message of any kind. All I can find in it, in fact, are a number of females, conspicuous, if at all, only for their passion or folly or for some trifling talent or insignificant virtue. Even if I were to copy all this out, I cannot see that it would make a very remarkable book."

"Come, your reverence," said the stone (for Vanitas had been correct in assuming that it could speak) "must you be so obtuse? All the romances ever written have an artificial period setting—Han or Tang for the most part. In refusing to make use of that stale old convention and telling my *Story of the Stone* exactly as it occurred, it seems to me that, far from *depriving* it of anything, I have given it a freshness these other books do not have.

"Your so-called 'historical romances,' consisting, as they do, of scandalous anecdotes about statesmen and emperors of bygone days and scabrous attacks on the reputations of long-dead gentlewomen, contain more wickedness and immorality than I care to mention. Still worse is the 'erotic novel,' by whose filthy obscenities our young folk are all too easily corrupted. And the 'boudoir romances,' those dreary stereotypes with their volume after volume all pitched on the same note and their different characters undistinguishable except by name (all those ideally beautiful young ladies and ideally eligible young bachelors)—even they seem unable to avoid descending sooner or later into indecency.

"The trouble with this last kind of romance is that it only gets written in the first place because the author requires a framework in which to show off his love-poems. He goes about constructing this framework quite mechanically, beginning with the names of his pair of young lovers and invariably adding a third character, a servant or the like, to make mischief between them, like the *chou*[3] in a comedy.

"What makes these romances even more detestable is the stilted, bombastic language—inanities dressed in pompous rhetoric, remote alike from nature and common sense and teeming with the grossest absurdities.

"Surely my 'number of females,' whom I spent half a lifetime studying with my own eyes and ears, are preferable to this kind of stuff? I do not claim that they are better people than the ones who appear in books written before my time; I am only saying that the contemplation of their actions and motives may prove a more effective antidote to boredom and melancholy. And even the inelegant verses with which my story is interlarded could serve to entertain and amuse on those convivial occasions when rhymes and riddles are in demand.

"All that my story narrates, the meetings and partings, the joys and sorrows, the ups and downs of fortune, are recorded exactly as they happened. I have not dared to add the tiniest bit of touching-up, for fear of losing the true picture.

---

[3] *chou:* The clown, a stock character in Chinese drama.

"My only wish is that men in the world below may sometimes pick up this tale when they are recovering from sleep or drunkenness, or when they wish to escape from business worries or a fit of the dumps, and in doing so find not only mental refreshment but even perhaps, if they will heed its lesson and abandon their vain and frivolous pursuits, some small arrest in the deterioration of their vital forces. What does your reverence say to that?"

For a long time Vanitas stood lost in thought, pondering this speech. He then subjected the *Story of the Stone* to a careful second reading. He could see that its main theme was love; that it consisted quite simply of a true record of real events; and that it was entirely free from any tendency to deprave and corrupt. He therefore copied it all out from beginning to end and took it back with him to look for a publisher.

As a consequence of all this, Vanitas, starting off in the Void (which is Truth) came to the contemplation of Form (which is Illusion); and from Form engendered Passion; and by communicating Passion, entered again into Form; and from Form awoke to the Void (which is Truth). He therefore changed his name from Vanitas to Brother Amor, or the Passionate Monk, (because he had approached Truth by way of Passion), and changed the title of the book from *The Story of the Stone* to *The Tale of Brother Amor*.

Old Kong Mei-xi from the homeland of Confucius called the book *A Mirror for the Romantic*. Wu Yu-feng called it *A Dream of Golden Days*. Cao Xueqin in his Nostalgia Studio worked on it for ten years, in the course of which he rewrote it no less than five times, dividing it into chapters, composing chapter headings, renaming it *The Twelve Beauties of Jinling*, and adding an introductory quatrain. Red Inkstone restored the original title when he recopied the book and added his second set of annotations to it.

This, then, is a true account of how *The Story of the Stone* came to be written.

> Pages full of idle words
> Penned with hot and bitter tears:
> All men call the author fool;
> None his secret message hears.

The origin of *The Story of the Stone* has now been made clear. The same cannot, however, be said of the characters and events which it recorded. Gentle reader, have patience! This is how the inscription began:

Long, long ago the world was tilted downwards towards the south-east; and in that lower-lying south-easterly part of the earth there is a city called Soochow; and in Soochow the district around the Chang-men Gate is reckoned one of the two or three wealthiest and most fashionable quarters in the world of men. Outside the Chang-men Gate is a wide thoroughfare called Worldly Way; and somewhere off Worldly Way is an area called Carnal Lane. There is an old temple in the Carnal Lane area which, because of the way it is bottled up inside a narrow *cul-de-sac*, is referred to locally as Bottle-gourd Temple. Next door to Bottle-gourd Temple lived a gentleman of private means called Zhen Shi-yin and his wife Feng-shi, a kind, good woman with a profound sense of decency and decorum. The household was not a particularly wealthy one, but they were nevertheless looked up to by all and sundry as the leading family in the neighbourhood.

Zhen Shi-yin himself was by nature a quiet and totally unambitious person. He devoted his time to his garden and to the pleasures of wine and poetry. Except for a single flaw, his existence could, indeed, have been described as an idyllic one. The flaw was that, although already past fifty, he had no son, only a little girl, just two years old, whose name was Ying-lian.

Once, during the tedium of a burning summer's day, Shi-yin was sitting idly in his study. The book had slipped from his nerveless grasp and his head had nodded down onto the desk in a doze. While in this drowsy state he seemed to drift off to some place he could not identify, where he became aware of a monk and a Taoist walking along and talking as they went.

"Where do you intend to take that thing you are carrying?" the Taoist was asking.

"Don't you worry about him!" replied the monk with a laugh. "There is a batch of lovesick souls awaiting incarnation in the world below whose fate is due to be decided this very day. I intend to take advantage of this opportunity to slip our little friend in amongst them and let him have a taste of human life along with the rest."

"Well, well, so another lot of these amorous wretches is about to enter the vale of tears," said the Taoist. "How did all this begin? And where are the souls to be reborn?"

"You will laugh when I tell you," said the monk. "When this stone was left unused by the goddess, he found himself at a loose end and took to wandering about all over the place for want of better to do, until one day his wanderings took him to the place where the fairy Disenchantment lives.

"Now Disenchantment could tell that there was something unusual about this stone, so she kept him there in her Sunset Glow Palace and gave him the honorary title of Divine Luminescent Stone-in-Waiting in the Court of Sunset Glow.

"But most of his time he spent west of Sunset Glow exploring the banks of the Magic River. There, by the Rock of Rebirth, he found the beautiful Crimson Pearl Flower, for which he conceived such a fancy that he took to watering her every day with sweet dew, thereby conferring on her the gift of life.

"Crimson Pearl's substance was composed of the purest cosmic essences, so she was already half-divine; and now, thanks to the vitalizing effect of the sweet dew, she was able to shed her vegetable shape and assume the form of a girl.

"This fairy girl wandered about outside the Realm of Separation, eating the Secret Passion Fruit when she was hungry and drinking from the Pool of Sadness when she was thirsty. The consciousness that she owed the stone something for his kindness in watering her began to prey on her mind and ended by becoming an obsession.

" 'I have no sweet dew here that I can repay him with,' she would say to herself. 'The only way in which I could perhaps repay him would be with the tears shed during the whole of a mortal lifetime if he and I were ever to be reborn as humans in the world below.'

"Because of this strange affair, Disenchantment has got together a group of amorous young souls, of which Crimson Pearl is one, and intends to send them down into the world to take part in the great illusion of human life. And as today happens to be the day on which this stone is fated to go into the world too, I am taking him with me to Disenchantment's tribunal for the purpose of getting him registered and sent down to earth with the rest of these romantic creatures."

"How very amusing!" said the Taoist. "I have certainly never heard of a debt of tears before. Why shouldn't the two of us take advantage of this opportunity to go down into the world ourselves and save a few souls? It would be a work of merit."

"That is exactly what I was thinking," said the monk. "Come with me to Disenchantment's palace to get this absurd creature cleared. Then, when this last batch of romantic idiots goes down, you and I can go down with them. At present about half have already been born. They await this last batch to make up the number."

"Very good, I will go with you then," said the Taoist. Shi-yin heard all this conversation quite clearly, and curiosity impelled him to go forward and greet the two reverend gentlemen. They returned his greeting and asked him what he wanted.

"It is not often that one has the opportunity of listening to a discussion of the operations of *karma*[4] such as the one I have just been privileged to overhear," said Shi-yin. "Unfortunately I am a man of very limited understanding and have not been able to derive the full benefit from your conversation. If you would have the very great kindness to enlighten my benighted understanding with a somewhat fuller account of what you were discussing, I can promise you the most devout attention. I feel sure that your teaching would have a salutary effect on me and— who knows—might save me from the pains of hell."

The reverend gentlemen laughed. "These are heavenly mysteries and may not be divulged. But if you wish to escape from the fiery pit, you have only to remember us when the time comes, and all will be well."

Shi-yin saw that it would be useless to press them. "Heavenly mysteries must not, of course, be revealed. But might one perhaps inquire what the 'absurd creature' is that you were talking about? Is it possible that I might be allowed to see it?"

"Oh, as for that," said the monk: "I think it is on the cards for you to have a look at *him*," and he took the object from his sleeve and handed it to Shi-yin.

Shi-yin took the object from him and saw that it was a clear, beautiful jade on one side of which were carved the words "Magic Jade." There were several columns of smaller characters on the back, which Shi-yin was just going to examine more closely when the monk, with a cry of "Here we are, at the frontier of Illusion," snatched the stone from him and disappeared, with the Taoist, through a big stone archway above which

THE LAND OF ILLUSION

was written in large characters. A couplet in smaller characters was inscribed vertically on either side of the arch:

---

[4] *karma:* The law of action whereby what one does determines one's future destiny; it may refer to the store of good and bad actions that over many lives either frees the soul or traps it in the world of illusion.

Truth becomes fiction when the fiction's true;
Real becomes not-real where the unreal's real.

Shi-yin was on the point of following them through the archway when suddenly a great clap of thunder seemed to shake the earth to its very foundations, making him cry out in alarm.

And there he was sitting in his study, the contents of his dream already half forgotten, with the sun still blazing on the ever-rustling plantains outside, and the wet-nurse at the door with his little daughter Ying-lian in her arms. Her delicate little pink-and-white face seemed dearer to him than ever at that moment, and he stretched out his arms to take her and hugged her to him. [. . .]

FROM CHAPTER 3

[Lin Dai-yu Arrives in the Jia Household]

. . . On the day of her arrival in the capital, Dai-yu stepped ashore to find covered chairs from the Rong mansion for her and her women and a cart for the luggage ready waiting on the quay.

She had often heard her mother say that her Grandmother Jia's home was not like other people's houses. The servants she had been in contact with during the past few days were comparatively low-ranking ones in the domestic hierarchy, yet the food they ate, the clothes they wore, and everything about them was quite out of the ordinary. Dai-yu tried to imagine what the people who employed these superior beings must be like. When she arrived at their house she would have to watch every step she took and weigh every word she said, for if she put a foot wrong they would surely laugh her to scorn.

Dai-yu got into her chair and was soon carried through the city walls. Peeping through the gauze panel which served as a window, she could see streets and buildings more rich and elegant and throngs of people more lively and numerous than she had ever seen in her life before. After being carried for what seemed a very great length of time, she saw, on the north front of the east-west street through which they were passing, two great stone lions crouched one on each side of a triple gateway whose doors were embellished with animal-heads. In front of the gateway ten or so splendidly dressed flunkeys sat in a row. The centre of the three gates was closed, but people were going in and out of the two side ones. There was a board above the centre gate on which were written in large characters the words:

NING-GUO HOUSE
Founded and Constructed by
    Imperial Command

Dai-yu realized that this must be where the elder branch of her grandmother's family lived. The chair proceeded some distance more down the street and presently there was another triple gate, this time with the legend

RONG-GUO HOUSE

above it.

Ignoring the central gate, her bearers went in by the western entrance and after traversing the distance of a bowshot inside, half turned a corner and set the chair down. The chairs of her female attendants which were following behind were set down simultaneously and the old women got out. The places of Dai-yu's bearers were taken by four handsome, fresh-faced pages of seventeen or eighteen. They shouldered her chair and, with the old women now following on foot, carried it as far as an ornamental inner gate. There they set it down again and then retired in respectful silence. The old women came forward to the front of the chair, held up the curtain, and helped Dai-yu to get out.

Each hand resting on the outstretched hand of an elderly attendant, Dai-yu passed through the ornamental gate into a courtyard which had balustraded loggias running along its sides and a covered passage-way through the centre. The foreground of the courtyard beyond was partially hidden by a screen of polished marble set in an elaborate red sandalwood frame. Passing round the screen and through a small reception hall beyond it, they entered the large courtyard of the mansion's principal apartments. These were housed in an imposing five-frame building resplendent with carved and painted beams and rafters which faced them across the courtyard. Running along either side of the courtyard were galleries hung with cages containing a variety of different-coloured parrots, cockatoos, white-eyes, and other birds. Some gaily-dressed maids were sitting on the steps of the main building opposite. At the appearance of the visitors they rose to their feet and came forward with smiling faces to welcome them.

"You've come just at the right time! Lady Jia was only this moment asking about you."

Three or four of them ran to lift up the door-curtain, while another of them announced in loud tones,

"Miss Lin is here!"

As Dai-yu entered the room she saw a silver-haired old lady advancing to meet her, supported on either side by a servant. She knew that this must be her Grandmother Jia and would have fallen on her knees and made her kowtow, but before she could do so her grandmother had caught her in her arms and pressing her to her bosom with cries of "My pet!" and "My poor lamb!" burst into loud sobs, while all those present wept in sympathy, and Dai-yu felt herself crying as though she would never stop. It was some time before those present succeeded in calming them both down and Dai-yu was at last able to make her kowtow.

Grandmother Jia now introduced those present.

"This is your elder uncle's wife, Aunt Xing. This is your Uncle Zheng's wife, Aunt Wang. This is Li Wan, the wife of your Cousin Zhu, who died."

Dai-yu kowtowed to each of them in turn.

"Call the girls!" said Grandmother Jia. "Tell them that we have a very special visitor and that they need not do their lessons today."

There was a cry of "Yes ma'am" from the assembled maids, and two of them went off to do her bidding.

Presently three girls arrived, attended by three nurses and five or six maids.

The first girl was of medium height and slightly plumpish, with cheeks as white and firm as a fresh lychee and a nose as white and shiny as soap made from the whitest goose-fat. She had a gentle, sweet, reserved manner. To look at her was to love her.

The second girl was rather tall, with sloping shoulders and a slender waist. She had an oval face under whose well-formed brows large, expressive eyes shot out glances that sparkled with animation. To look at her was to forget all that was mean or vulgar.

The third girl was undersized and her looks were still somewhat babyish and unformed.

All three were dressed in identical skirts and dresses and wore identical sets of bracelets and hair ornaments.

Dai-yu rose to meet them and exchanged curtseys and introductions. When she was seated once more, a maid served tea, and a conversation began on the subject of her mother: how her illness had started, what doctors had been called in, what medicines prescribed, what arrangements had been made for the funeral, and how the mourning had been observed. This conversation had the foreseeable effect of upsetting the old lady all over again.

"Of all my girls your mother was the one I loved the best," she said, "and now she's been the first to go, and without my even being able to see her again before the end. I can't help being upset!" And holding fast to Dai-yu's hand, she once more burst into tears. The rest of the company did their best to comfort her, until at last she had more or less recovered.

Everyone's attention now centred on Dai-yu. They observed that although she was still young, her speech and manner already showed unusual refinement. They also noticed the frail body which seemed scarcely strong enough to bear the weight of its clothes, but which yet had an inexpressible grace about it, and realizing that she must be suffering from some deficiency, asked her what medicine she took for it and why it was still not better.

"I have always been like this," said Dai-yu. "I have been taking medicine ever since I could eat and been looked at by ever so many well-known doctors, but it has never done me any good. Once, when I was only three, I can remember a scabby-headed old monk came and said he wanted to take me away and have me brought up as a nun; but of course, Mother and Father wouldn't hear of it. So he said, 'Since you are not prepared to give her up, I am afraid her illness will never get better as long as she lives. The only way it might get better would be if she were never to hear the sound of weeping from this day onwards and never to see any relations other than her own mother and father. Only in those conditions could she get through her life without trouble.' Of course, he was quite crazy, and no one took any notice of the things he said. I'm still taking Ginseng Tonic Pills."

"Well, that's handy," said Grandmother Jia. "I take the Pills myself. We can easily tell them to make up a few more each time."

She had scarcely finished speaking when someone could be heard talking and laughing in a very loud voice in the inner courtyard behind them.

"Oh dear! I'm late," said the voice. "I've missed the arrival of our guest."

"Everyone else around here seems to go about with bated breath," thought Dai-yu. "Who can this new arrival be who is so brash and unmannerly?"

Even as she wondered, a beautiful young woman entered from the room behind the one they were sitting in, surrounded by a bevy of serving women and maids. She was dressed quite differently from the others present, gleaming like some fairy princess with sparkling jewels and gay embroideries.

Her chignon was enclosed in a circlet of gold filigree and clustered pearls. It was fastened with a pin embellished with flying phoenixes, from whose beaks pearls were suspended on tiny chains.

Her necklet was of red gold in the form of a coiling dragon.

Her dress had a fitted bodice and was made of dark red silk damask with a pattern of flowers and butterflies in raised gold thread.

Her jacket was lined with ermine. It was of a slate-blue stuff with woven insets in coloured silks.

Her under-skirt was of a turquoise-coloured imported silk crêpe embroidered with flowers.

She had, moreover,
eyes like a painted phoenix,
eyebrows like willow-leaves,
a slender form,
seductive grace;
the ever-smiling summer face
of hidden thunders showed no trace;
the ever-bubbling laughter started
almost before the lips were parted.

"You don't know her," said Grandmother Jia merrily. "She's a holy terror this one. What we used to call in Nanking a 'peppercorn.' You just call her 'Peppercorn Feng.' She'll know who you mean!"

Dai-yu was at a loss to know how she was to address this Peppercorn Feng until one of the cousins whispered that it was "Cousin Lian's wife," and she remembered having heard her mother say that her elder uncle, Uncle She, had a son called Jia Lian who was married to the niece of her Uncle Zheng's wife, Lady Wang. She had been brought up from earliest childhood just like a boy, and had acquired in the schoolroom the somewhat boyish-sounding name of Wang Xi-feng. Dai-yu accordingly smiled and curtseyed, greeting her by her correct name as she did so.

Xi-feng took Dai-yu by the hand and for a few moments scrutinized her carefully from top to toe before conducting her back to her seat beside Grandmother Jia.

"She's a beauty, Grannie dear! If I hadn't set eyes on her today, I shouldn't have believed that such a beautiful creature could exist! And everything about her so *distingué*! She doesn't take after your side of the family, Grannie. She's more like a Jia. I don't blame you for having gone on so about her during the past few days—but poor little thing! What a cruel fate to have lost Auntie like that!" and she dabbed at her eyes with a handkerchief.

"I've only just recovered," laughed Grandmother Jia. "Don't you go trying to start me off again! Besides, your little cousin is not very strong, and we've only just managed to get *her* cheered up. So let's have no more of this!"

In obedience to the command Xi-feng at once exchanged her grief for merriment.

"Yes, of course. It was just that seeing my little cousin here put everything else out of my mind. It made me want to laugh and cry all at the same time. I'm afraid I quite forgot about you, Grannie dear. I deserve to be spanked, don't I?"

She grabbed Dai-yu by the hand.

"How old are you dear? Have you begun school yet? You mustn't feel homesick here. If there's anything you want to eat or anything you want to play with, just come and tell me. And you must tell me if any of the maids or the old nannies are nasty to you."

Dai-yu made appropriate responses to all of these questions and injunctions.

Xi-feng turned to the servants.

"Have Miss Lin's things been brought in yet? How many people did she bring with her? You'd better hurry up and get a couple of rooms swept out for them to rest in."

While Xi-feng was speaking, the servants brought in tea and various plates of food, the distribution of which she proceeded to supervise in person.

Dai-yu noticed her Aunt Wang questioning Xi-feng on the side:

"Have this month's allowances been paid out yet?"

"Yes. By the way, just now I went with some of the women to the upstairs store-room at the back to look for that satin. We looked and looked, but we couldn't find any like the one you described yesterday. Perhaps you misremembered."

"Oh well, if you can't find it, it doesn't really matter," said Lady Wang. Then, after a moment's reflection, "You'd better pick out a couple of lengths presently to have made up into clothes for your little cousin here. If you think of it, send some-one round in the evening to fetch them!"

"It's already been seen to. I knew she was going to arrive within a day or two, so I had some brought out in readiness. They are waiting back at your place for your approval. If you think they are all right, they can be sent over straight away."

Lady Wang merely smiled and nodded her head without saying anything.

The tea things and dishes were now cleared away, and Grandmother Jia ordered two old nurses to take Dai-yu round to see her uncles; but Uncle She's wife, Lady Xing, hurriedly rose to her feet and suggested that it would be more convenient if she were to take her niece round herself.

"Very well," said Grandmother Jia. "You go now, then. There is no need for you to come back afterwards."

So having, together with Lady Wang, who was also returning to her quarters, taken leave of the old lady, Lady Xing went off with Dai-yu, attended across the courtyard as far as the covered way by the rest of the company.

A carriage painted dark blue and hung with kingfisher-blue curtains had been drawn up in front of the ornamental gateway by some pages. Into this Aunt Xing ascended hand in hand with Dai-yu. The old women pulled down the carriage blind and ordered the pages to take up the shafts, the pages drew the carriage into an open space and harnessed mules to it, and Dai-yu and her aunt were driven out of the west gate, eastwards past the main gate of the Rong mansion, in again through a big black-lacquered gate, and up to an inner gate, where they were set down again.

Holding Dai-yu by the hand, Aunt Xing led her into a courtyard in the middle of what she imagined must once have been part of the mansion's gardens. This impression was strengthened when they passed through a third gateway into the quarters occupied by her uncle and aunt; for here the smaller scale and quiet elegance of the halls, galleries, and loggias were quite unlike the heavy magnificence and imposing grandeur they had just come from, and ornamental trees and artificial rock formations, all in exquisite taste, were to be seen on every hand.

As they entered the main reception hall, a number of heavily made-up and expensively dressed maids and concubines, who had been waiting in readiness, came forward to greet them.

Aunt Xing asked Dai-yu to be seated while she sent a servant to call Uncle She. After a considerable wait the servant returned with the following message:

"The Master says he hasn't been well these last few days, and as it would only upset them both if he were to see Miss Lin now, he doesn't feel up to it for the time being. He says, tell Miss Lin not to grieve and not to feel homesick. She must think of her grandmother and her aunts as her own family now. He says that her cousins may not be very clever girls, but at least they should be company for her and help to take her mind off things. If she finds anything at all here to distress her, she is to speak up at once. She mustn't feel like an outsider. She is to make herself completely at home."

Dai-yu stood up throughout this recital and murmured polite assent whenever assent seemed indicated. She then sat for about another quarter of an hour before rising to take her leave. Her Aunt Xing was very pressing that she should have a meal with her before she went, but Dai-yu smilingly replied that though it was very kind of her aunt to offer, and though she ought really not to refuse, nevertheless she still had to pay her respects to her Uncle Zheng, and feared that it would be disrespectful if she were to arrive late. She hoped that she might accept on another occasion and begged her aunt to excuse her.

"In that case, never mind," said Lady Xing, and instructed the old nurses to see her to her Uncle Zheng's in the same carriage she had come by. Dai-yu formally took her leave, and Lady Xing saw her as far as the inner gate, where she issued a few more instructions to the servants and watched her niece's carriage out of sight before returning to her rooms.

Presently they re-entered the Rong mansion proper and Dai-yu got down from the carriage. There was a raised stone walk running all the way up to the main gate, along which the old nurses now conducted her. Turning right, they led her down a roofed passage-way along the back of a south-facing hall, then through an inner gate into a large courtyard.

The big building at the head of the courtyard was connected at each end to galleries running through the length of the side buildings by means of "stag's head" roofing over the corners. The whole formed an architectural unit of greater sumptuousness and magnificence than anything Dai-yu had yet seen that day, from which she concluded that this must be the main inner hall of the whole mansion.

High overhead on the wall facing her as she entered the hall was a great blue board framed in gilded dragons, on which was written in large gold characters

THE HALL OF EXALTED FELICITY

with a column of smaller characters at the side giving a date and the words ". . . written for Our beloved Subject, Jia Yuan, Duke of Rong-guo," followed by the Emperor's private seal, a device containing the words "kingly cares" and "royal brush" in archaic seal-script.

A long, high table of carved red sandalwood, ornamented with dragons, stood against the wall underneath. In the centre of this was a huge antique bronze *ding*,[5] fully a yard high, covered with a green patina. On the wall above the *ding* hung a long vertical scroll with an ink-painting of a dragon emerging from clouds and waves, of the kind often presented to high court officials in token of their office. The *ding* was flanked on one side by a smaller antique bronze vessel with a pattern of gold inlay and on the other by a crystal bowl. At each side of the table stood a row of eight yellow cedar-wood armchairs with their backs to the wall; and above the chairs hung, one on each side, a pair of vertical ebony boards inlaid with a couplet in characters of gold:

(on the right-hand one)

May the jewel of learning shine in this house more effulgently than the sun and moon.

(on the left-hand one)

May the insignia of honour glitter in these halls more brilliantly than the starry sky.

This was followed by a colophon in smaller characters:

With the Respectful Compliments of your Fellow-Student, Mu Shi, Hereditary Prince of Dong-an.

Lady Wang did not, however, normally spend her leisure hours in this main reception hall, but in a smaller room on the east side of the same building. Accordingly the nurses conducted Dai-yu through the door into this side apartment.

Here there was a large *kang*[6] underneath the window, covered with a scarlet Kashmir rug. In the middle of the kang was a dark-red bolster[7] with a pattern of medallions in the form of tiny dragons, and a long russet-green seating strip in the same pattern. A low rose-shaped table of coloured lacquer-work stood at each side. On the left-hand one was a small, square, four-legged *ding*, together with a bronze ladle, metal chopsticks, and an incense container. On the right-hand one was a narrow-waisted Ru-ware imitation *gu*[8] with a spray of freshly cut flowers in it.

---

[5] *ding:* Or *ting,* a bronze or glazed porcelain cooking vessel or bowl elevated on a tripodlike stand.

[6] *kang:* Elevated platform for sitting or sleeping that can be heated for winter use.

[7] bolster: Long, narrow cushion.

[8] *gu:* Or *ku,* a trumpet-shaped vessel made of bronze, originally from the Shang dynasty (eighteenth to twelfth century B.C.E.).

In the part of the room below the kang there was a row of four big chairs against the east wall. All had footstools in front of them and chair-backs and seat-covers in old rose brocade sprigged with flowers. There were also narrow side-tables on which tea things and vases of flowers were arranged, besides other furnishings which it would be superfluous to enumerate.

The old nurses invited Dai-yu to get up on the kang; but guessing that the brocade cushions arranged one on each side near the edge of it must be her uncle's and aunt's places, she deemed it more proper to sit on one of the chairs against the wall below. The maids in charge of the apartment served tea, and as she sipped it Dai-yu observed that their clothing, makeup, and deportment were quite different from those of the maids she had seen so far in other parts of the mansion.

Before she had time to finish her tea, a smiling maid came in wearing a dress of red damask and a black silk sleeveless jacket which had scalloped borders of some coloured material.

"The Mistress says will Miss Lin come over to the other side, please."

The old nurses now led Dai-yu down the east gallery to a reception room at the side of the courtyard. This too had a kang. It was bisected by a long, low table piled with books and tea things. A much-used black satin back-rest was pushed up against the east wall. Lady Wang was seated on a black satin cushion and leaning against another comfortable-looking back-rest of black satin somewhat farther forward on the opposite side.

Seeing her niece enter, she motioned her to sit opposite her on the kang, but Dai-yu felt sure that this must be her Uncle Zheng's place. So, having observed a row of three chairs near the kang with covers of flower-sprigged brocade which looked as though they were in fairly constant use, she sat upon one of those instead. Only after much further pressing from her aunt would she get up on the kang, and even then she would only sit beside her and not in the position of honour opposite.

"Your uncle is in retreat today," said Lady Wang. "He will see you another time. There is, however, something I have got to talk to you about. The three girls are very well-behaved children, and in future, when you are studying or sewing together, even if once in a while they may grow a bit high-spirited, I can depend on them not to go too far. There is only one thing that worries me. I have a little monster of a son who tyrannizes over all the rest of this household. He has gone off to the temple today in fulfilment of a vow and is not yet back; but you will see what I mean this evening. The thing to do is never to take any notice of him. None of your cousins dare provoke him."

Dai-yu had long ago been told by her mother that she had a boy cousin who was born with a piece of jade in his mouth and who was exceptionally wild and naughty. He hated study and liked to spend all his time in the women's apartments with the girls; but because Grandmother Jia doted on him so much, no one ever dared to correct him. She realized that it must be this cousin her aunt was now referring to.

"Do you mean the boy born with the jade, Aunt?" she asked. "Mother often told me about him at home. She told me that he was one year older than me and that his name was Bao-yu. But she said that though he was very wilful, he always behaved very nicely to girls. Now that I am here, I suppose I shall be spending all my time with my girl cousins and not in the same part of the house as the boys. Surely there will be no danger of *my* provoking him?"

Lady Wang gave a rueful smile. "You little know how things are here! Bao-yu is a law unto himself. Because your grandmother is so fond of him she has thoroughly spoiled him. When he was little he lived with the girls, so with the girls he remains now. As long as they take no notice of him, things run quietly enough. But if they give him the least encouragement, he at once becomes excitable, and then there is no end to the mischief he may get up to. That is why I counsel you to ignore him. He can be all honey-sweet words one minute and ranting and raving like a lunatic the next. So don't believe anything he says."

Dai-yu promised to follow her aunt's advice.

Just then a maid came in with a message that "Lady Jia said it was time for dinner," whereupon Lady Wang took Dai-yu by the hand and hurried her out through a back door. Passing along a verandah which ran beneath the rear eaves of the hall they came to a corner gate through which they passed into an alley-way running north and south. At the south end it was traversed by a narrow little building with a short passage-way running through its middle. At the north end was a white-painted screen wall masking a medium-sized gateway leading to a small courtyard in which stood a very little house.

"That," said Lady Wang, pointing to the little house, "is where your Cousin Lian's wife, Wang Xi-feng, lives, in case you want to see her later on. She is the person to talk to if there is anything you need."

There were a few young pages at the gate of the courtyard who, when they saw Lady Wang coming, all stood to attention with their hands at their sides.

Lady Wang now led Dai-yu along a gallery, running from east to west, which brought them out into the courtyard behind Grandmother Jia's apartments. Entering these by a back entrance, they found a number of servants waiting there who, as soon as they saw Lady Wang, began to arrange the table and chairs for dinner. The ladies of the house themselves took part in the service. Li Wan brought in the cups, Xi-feng laid out the chopsticks, and Lady Wang brought in the soup.

The table at which Grandmother Jia presided, seated alone on a couch, had two empty chairs on either side. Xi-feng tried to seat Dai-yu in the one on the left nearer to her grandmother—an honour which she strenuously resisted until her grandmother explained that her aunt and her elder cousins' wives would not be eating with them, so that, since she was a guest, the place was properly hers. Only then did she ask permission to sit, as etiquette prescribed. Grandmother Jia then ordered Lady Wang to be seated. This was the cue for the three girls to ask permission to sit. Ying-chun sat in the first place on the right opposite Dai-yu, Tan-chun sat second on the left, and Xi-chun sat second on the right.

While Li Wan and Xi-feng stood by the table helping to distribute food from the dishes, maids holding fly-whisks, spittoons, and napkins ranged themselves on either side. In addition to these, there were numerous other maids and serving-women in attendance in the outer room, yet not so much as a cough was heard throughout the whole of the meal.

When they had finished eating, a maid served each diner with tea on a little tray. Dai-yu's parents had brought their daughter up to believe that good health was founded on careful habits, and in pursuance of this principle, had always insisted that after a meal one should allow a certain interval to elapse before taking tea in order to avoid indigestion. However, she could see that many of the rules in this household were different from the ones she had been used to at home; so, being anxious to conform as much as possible, she accepted the tea. But as she did so, another maid proffered a spittoon, from which she inferred that the tea was for rinsing her mouth with. And it was not, in fact, until they had all rinsed out their mouths and washed their hands that another lot of tea was served, this time for drinking.

Grandmother Jia now dismissed her lady servers, observing that she wished to enjoy a little chat with her young grandchildren without the restraint of their grown-up presence.

Lady Wang obediently rose to her feet and, after exchanging a few pleasantries, went out, taking Li Wan and Wang Xi-feng with her.

Grandmother Jia asked Dai-yu what books she was studying.

"The Four Books,"[9] said Dai-yu, and inquired in turn what books her cousins were currently engaged on.

"Gracious, child, they don't study books," said her grandmother; "they can barely read and write!"

While they were speaking, a flurry of footsteps could be heard outside and a maid came in to say that Bao-yu was back.

"I wonder," thought Dai-yu, "just what sort of graceless creature this Bao-yu is going to be!"

The young gentleman who entered in answer to her unspoken question had a small jewel-encrusted gold coronet on the top of his head and a golden headband low down over his brow in the form of two dragons playing with a large pearl.

He was wearing a narrow-sleeved, full-skirted robe of dark red material with a pattern of flowers and butterflies in two shades of gold. It was confined at the waist with a court girdle of coloured silks braided at regular intervals into elaborate clusters of knotwork and terminating in long tassels.

Over the upper part of his robe he wore a jacket of slate-blue Japanese silk damask with a raised pattern of eight large medallions on the front and with tasselled borders.

On his feet he had half-length dress boots of black satin with thick white soles.

As to his person, he had:

a face like the moon of Mid-Autumn,
a complexion like flowers at dawn,
a hairline straight as a knife-cut,

---

[9] **The Four Books:** The Confucianist classics that formed the basis for the civil service examinations were collectively known as The Four Books and The Five Scriptures. The Four Books comprise *The Analects, The Doctrine of the Mean, The Great Learning,* and *The Mencius,* commentaries on Confucius by the philosopher Mencius (fourth century B.C.E.); The Five Scriptures consist of *The Book of Songs, The Book of History, The Book of Changes, The Book of Rites,* and *The Spring and Autumn Annals.*

eyebrows that might have been painted by an artist's brush,
a shapely nose, and
eyes clear as limpid pools,
that even in anger seemed to smile,
and, as they glared, beamed tenderness the while.

Around his neck he wore a golden torque in the likeness of a dragon and a woven cord of coloured silks to which the famous jade was attached.

Dai-yu looked at him with astonishment. How strange! How very strange! It was as though she had seen him somewhere before, he was so extraordinarily familiar. Bao-yu went straight past her and saluted his grandmother, who told him to come after he had seen his mother, whereupon he turned round and walked straight out again.

Quite soon he was back once more, this time dressed in a completely different outfit.

The crown and circlet had gone. She could now see that his side hair was dressed in a number of small braids plaited with red silk, which were drawn round to join the long hair at the back in a single large queue of glistening jet black, fastened at intervals from the nape downwards with four enormous pearls and ending in a jewelled gold clasp. He had changed his robe and jacket for a rather more worn-looking rose-coloured gown, sprigged with flowers. He wore the gold torque and his jade as before, and she observed that the collection of objects round his neck had been further augmented by a padlock-shaped amulet and a lucky charm. A pair of ivy-coloured embroidered silk trousers were partially visible beneath his gown, thrust into black and white socks trimmed with brocade. In place of the formal boots he was wearing thick-soled crimson slippers.

She was even more struck than before by his fresh complexion. The cheeks might have been brushed with powder and the lips touched with rouge, so bright was their natural colour.

His glance was soulful,
yet from his lips the laughter often leaped;
a world of charm upon that brow was heaped;
a world of feeling from those dark eyes peeped.

In short, his outward appearance was very fine. But appearances can be misleading. A perceptive poet has supplied two sets of verses, to be sung to the tune of *Moon on West River,* which contain a more accurate appraisal of our hero than the foregoing descriptions.

1

Oft-times he sought out what would make him sad;
Sometimes an idiot seemed and sometimes mad.
Though outwardly a handsome sausage-skin,
He proved to have but sorry meat within.
A harum-scarum, to all duty blind,
A doltish mule, to study disinclined;
His acts outlandish and his nature queer;
Yet not a whit cared he how folk might jeer!

2

Prosperous, he could not play his part with grace,
Nor, poor, bear hardship with a smiling face.
So shamefully the precious hours he'd waste
That both indoors and out he was disgraced.
For uselessness the world's prize he might bear;
His gracelessness in history has no peer.
Let gilded youths who every dainty sample
Not imitate this rascal's dire example!

"Fancy changing your clothes before you have welcomed the visitor!" Grandmother Jia chided indulgently on seeing Bao-yu back again. "Aren't you going to pay your respects to your cousin?"

Bao-yu had already caught sight of a slender, delicate girl whom he surmised to be his Aunt Lin's daughter and quickly went over to greet her. Then, returning to his place and taking a seat, he studied her attentively. How different she seemed from the other girls he knew!

Her mist-wreathed brows at first seemed to frown, yet were not frowning;
Her passionate eyes at first seemed to smile, yet were not merry.
Habit had given a melancholy cast to her tender face;
Nature had bestowed a sickly constitution on her delicate frame.
Often the eyes swam with glistening tears;
Often the breath came in gentle gasps.
In stillness she made one think of a graceful flower reflected in the water;
In motion she called to mind tender willow shoots caressed by the wind.
She had more chambers in her heart than the martyred Bi Gan;
And suffered a tithe more pain in it than the beautiful Xi Shi.[10]
Having completed his survey, Bao-yu gave a laugh.

"I have seen this cousin before."

"Nonsense!" said Grandmother Jia. "How could you possibly have done?"

"Well, perhaps not," said Bao-yu, "but her face seems so familiar that I have the impression of meeting her again after a long separation."

"All the better," said Grandmother Jia. "That means that you should get on well together."

Bao-yu moved over again and, drawing a chair up beside Dai-yu, recommenced his scrutiny.

Presently: "Do you study books yet, cousin?"

"No," said Dai-yu. "I have only been taking lessons for a year or so. I can barely read and write."

"What's your name?"

Dai-yu told him.

---

[10] Xi Shi (fifth century B.C.E.): Legendary beauty of ancient China. Like Helen of Troy in Greek legend, Xi Shi caused the downfall of a state: She distracted the prince of Wu from his political responsibilities, enabling the king of Yue to invade Wu.

"What's your school-name?"

"I haven't got one."

Bao-yu laughed. "I'll give you one, cousin. I think 'Frowner' would suit you perfectly."

"Where's your reference?" said Tan-chun.

"In the *Encyclopedia of Men and Objects Ancient and Modern* it says that somewhere in the West there is a mineral called 'dai' which can be used instead of eyeblack for painting the eyebrows with. She has this 'dai' in her name and she knits her brows together in a little frown. I think it's a splendid name for her!"

"I expect you made it up," said Tan-chun scornfully.

"What if I did?" said Bao-yu. "There are lots of made-up things in books—apart from the Four Books, of course."

He returned to his interrogation of Dai-yu.

"Have you got a jade?"

The rest of the company were puzzled, but Dai-yu at once divined that he was asking her if she too had a jade like the one he was born with.

"No," said Dai-yu. "That jade of yours is a very rare object. You can't expect everybody to have one."

This sent Bao-yu off instantly into one of his mad fits. Snatching the jade from his neck he hurled it violently on the floor as if to smash it and began abusing it passionately.

"Rare object! Rare object! What's so lucky about a stone that can't even tell which people are better than others? Beastly thing! I don't want it!"

The maids all seemed terrified and rushed forward to pick it up, while Grandmother Jia clung to Bao-yu in alarm.

"Naughty, naughty boy! Shout at someone or strike them if you like when you are in a nasty temper, but why go smashing that precious thing that your very life depends on?"

"None of the girls has got one," said Bao-yu, his face streaming with tears and sobbing hysterically. "Only I have got one. It always upsets me. And now this new cousin comes here who is as beautiful as an angel and she hasn't got one either, so I *know* it can't be any good."

"Your cousin did have a jade once," said Grandmother Jia, coaxing him like a little child, "but because when Auntie died she couldn't bear to leave her little girl behind, they had to let her take the jade with her instead. In that way your cousin could show her mamma how much she loved her by letting the jade be buried with her; and at the same time, whenever Auntie's spirit looked at the jade, it would be just like looking at her own little girl again.

"So when your cousin said she hadn't got one, it was only because she didn't want to boast about the good, kind thing she did when she gave it to her mamma. Now you put yours on again like a good boy, and mind your mother doesn't find out how naughty you have been."

So saying, she took the jade from the hands of one of the maids and hung it round his neck for him. And Bao-yu, after reflecting for a moment or two on what she had said, offered no further resistance.

At this point some of the older women came to inquire what room Dai-yu was to sleep in.

"Move Bao-yu into the closet-bed with me," said Grandmother Jia, "and put Miss Lin for the time being in the green muslin summer-bed. We had better wait until spring when the last of the cold weather is over before seeing about the rooms for them and getting them settled permanently."

"Dearest Grannie," said Bao-yu pleadingly, "I should be perfectly all right next to the summer-bed. There's no need to move me into your room. I should only keep you awake."

Grandmother Jia, after a moment's reflection, gave her consent. She further gave instructions that Dai-yu and Bao-yu were each to have one nurse and one maid to sleep with them. The rest of their servants were to do night duty by rota in the adjoining room. Xi-feng had already sent across some lilac-coloured hangings, brocade quilts, satin coverlets, and the like for Dai-yu's bedding.

Dai-yu had brought only two of her own people with her from home. One was her old wet-nurse Nannie Wang, the other was a little ten-year-old maid called Snowgoose. Considering Snowgoose too young and irresponsible and Nannie Wang too old and decrepit to be of much real service, Grandmother Jia gave Dai-yu one of her own maids, a body-servant of the second grade called Nightingale. She also gave orders that Dai-yu and Bao-yu were to be attended in other respects exactly like the three girls: That is to say, apart from the one wet-nurse, each was to have four other nurses to act as chaperones, two maids as body-servants to attend to their washing, dressing, and so forth, and four or five maids for dusting and cleaning, running errands, and general duties.

These arrangements completed, Nannie Wang and Nightingale accompanied Dai-yu to bed inside the tent-like summer-bed, while Bao-yu's wet-nurse Nannie Li and his chief maid Aroma settled him down for the night in a big bed on the other side of the canopy.

Like Nightingale, Aroma had previously been one of Grandmother Jia's own maids. Her real name was Pearl. Bao-yu's grandmother, fearful that the maids who already waited on her darling boy could not be trusted to look after him properly, had picked out Pearl as a girl of tried and conspicuous fidelity and put her in charge over them. It was Bao-yu who was responsible for the curious name "Aroma." Discovering that Pearl's surname was Hua, which means "Flowers," and having recently come across the line

The flowers' aroma breathes of hotter days

in a book of poems, he told his grandmother that he wanted to call his new maid "Aroma," so "Aroma" her name thenceforth became.

Aroma had a certain dogged streak in her nature which had made her utterly devoted to Grandmother Jia as long as she was Grandmother Jia's servant, but which caused her to become just as exclusively and single-mindedly devoted to Bao-yu when her services were transferred to him. Since she found his character strange and incomprehensible, her simple devotion frequently impelled her to remonstrate with him, and when, as invariably happened, he took not the least notice of what she said, she was worried and hurt.

That night, when Bao-yu and Nannie Li were already asleep, Aroma could hear that Dai-yu and Nightingale on their side of the canopy had still not settled down, so, when she had finished taking down her hair and making herself ready for bed, she tiptoed through the muslin curtains and in a friendly way inquired what was the matter. Dai-yu invited her to sit down, and when she had seated herself on the edge of the bed, Nightingale proceeded to tell her what was troubling her new mistress.

"Miss Lin is all upset. She has just been crying her eyes out because she says she only just arrived here today, and yet already she has started young hopeful off on one of his turns. She says if that jade had been really smashed, it would have been all her fault. That's what she's so upset about. I've had no end of a job trying to comfort her."

"You mustn't take on so, Miss," said Aroma. "You'll see him do much stranger things than that before he's finished. If you allow yourself to feel hurt every time he carries on like that, he will always be hurting you. Try not to be so sensitive, Miss!"

Dai-yu thanked her and promised to bear in mind what she had said, and after talking a little longer, they all settled down and went to sleep.

Rising early next day, they visited Grandmother Jia to wish her a good morning and then went over to Lady Wang's. They found her closeted with Wang Xi-feng, deep in discussion of a letter which had just arrived from Nanking, and attended by two women who had come with a message from Lady Wang's elder brother and sister-in-law. Tan-chun and the girls told Dai-yu, who knew nothing of the matter under discussion, that they were talking about Xue Pan, the son of their Aunt Xue who lived in Nanking.

It seemed that Xue Pan, relying on wealth and family pull to protect him from the consequences, had taken another man's life. The case was at present under investigation by the Ying-tian-fu yamen. Their uncle Wang Zi-teng had been informed of it, and had sent these messengers to the members of the family in the Rong mansion to suggest that they should invite Xue Pan to the capital.

But the outcome of this discussion will be dealt with in the following chapter.

FROM CHAPTER 4

[Xue Bao-chai Arrives in the Jia Household]

[. . .] Lady Wang had just breathed a sigh of relief on learning that the affair of Xue Pan's manslaughter charge had been retrieved through the good offices of Jia Yu-cun, when the news that her elder brother had been promoted to a frontier post plunged her once more in gloom at the prospect of losing her main source of contact with the members of her own family. Several days passed in despondency, and then suddenly the servants announced that her sister, bringing her son and daughter and all her household with her, had arrived in the capital and was at that very moment outside the gate dismounting from her carriage.

Delightedly she hurried with her women to the entrance of the main reception hall and conducted Aunt Xue and her party inside. The sudden reunion of the two sisters was, it goes without saying, an affecting one in which joy and sorrow mingled. After an exchange of information about the years of separation, and after they had been taken to see Grandmother Jia and made their reverence to her, and after the gifts of Nanking produce had been presented and everyone had been introduced to everyone else, there was a family party to welcome the new arrivals.

Xue Pan, meanwhile, had paid his respects to Jia Zheng and Jia Lian and been taken to see Jia She and Cousin Zhen. Jia Zheng now sent a servant round to Lady Wang with the following message:

"Your sister is getting on in years and our nephew is very young and seems rather inexperienced and, I fear, quite capable of getting into a scrape again if they are going to live outside. Pear Tree Court in the north-east corner of our property is lying completely unoccupied at the moment and has quite a sizeable amount of room in it. Why not invite your sister and her children to move in there?"

Lady Wang had wanted all along to ask her sister to stay. Grandmother Jia had sent someone round to tell her that she should "ask Mrs. Xue to stay with us here, so that we can all be close to one another." And Aunt Xue for her own part had been wanting to stay so that some sort of check could be kept on her son. She was sure that if they were to be on their own somewhere else in the city his unbridled nature would precipitate some fresh calamity. She therefore accepted the invitation with alacrity, privately adding the proviso that she could only contemplate a long stay if it was on the understanding that they were themselves to be responsible for all their expenses. Lady Wang knew that money was no problem to them, so she readily consented, and Aunt Xue and her children proceeded there and then to move into Pear Tree Court.

This Pear Tree Court had been the Duke of Rong-guo's retreat during the last years of his life. Its buildings totalled not much more than ten frames; but though small and charming, it was complete in every respect, with a little reception room in the front and all the usual rooms and offices behind. It had its own outer door on to the street, through which Xue Pan and the menservants could come and go, and another gate in the south-west corner giving on to a passage-way which led into the courtyard east of Lady Wang's compound.

Through this passage-way Aunt Xue would now daily repair, either after dinner or in the evening, to gossip with Grandmother Jia or reminisce with her sister, Lady Wang. Bao-chai for her part spent her time each day in great contentment, reading or playing Go or sewing with Dai-yu and the three girls.

The only dissatisfied member of the party—to begin with, at any rate—was Xue Pan. He had not wanted to stay in the Jia household, fearing that his uncle's control would prevent him from enjoying himself, but what with his mother's obstinacy and the insistence of the Jias themselves, he was obliged to acquiesce in settling there for the time being, contenting himself with sending some of his people to clean up one of their houses outside so that he would be able to move there later on.

But, to his pleasant surprise, he discovered that the young males of the Jia establishment, half of whom he was already on familiar terms with before he had been there a month, were of the same idle, extravagant persuasion as himself and thought him a capital fellow and boon companion. And so he found himself meeting them for a drinking-party one day, for theatregoing the next, on a third day perhaps gambling with them or visiting brothels. For there were no limits to the depravity of their pleasures, and Xue Pan, who was bad enough to start with, soon became ten times worse under their expert guidance.

It was not that Jia Zheng was a slack disciplinarian, incapable of keeping his house in order; but the clan was so numerous that he simply could not keep an eye on everyone at once. And in any case the nominal head of the family was not Jia Zheng but Cousin Zhen who, as eldest grandson of the senior, Ning-guo branch, had inherited the founder's office and emoluments and was therefore officially in charge of all the clan's affairs.

Besides, Jia Zheng was kept busy with public and private business of his own and, being by nature a quiet, retiring man who attached little importance to mundane affairs, tended to use whatever leisure time he had for reading and playing Go.

Then again, the Pear Tree Court was two courtyards away from Jia Zheng's compound and had its own private door onto the street by which Xue Pan could come and go as he pleased, so that he and his young cronies could enjoy themselves to their heart's content with no one being any the wiser.

Under these agreeable circumstances Xue Pan gradually abandoned all thought of moving out.

But as to the outcome of these capers: That will be told in a later chapter.

CHAPTER 5

Jia Bao-yu Visits the Land of Illusion
And the Fairy Disenchantment Performs the
"Dream of Golden Days"

From the moment Lin Dai-yu entered the Rong mansion, Grandmother Jia's solicitude for her had manifested itself in a hundred different ways. The arrangements made for her meals and accommodation were exactly the same as for Bao-yu. The other three granddaughters, Ying-chun, Tan-chun, and Xi-chun, were relegated to a secondary place in the old lady's affections, and the objects of her partiality themselves began to feel an affection for each other which far exceeded what they felt for any of the rest. Sharing each other's company every minute of the day and sleeping in the same room at night, they developed an understanding so intense that it was almost as if they had grown into a single person.

And now suddenly this Xue Bao-chai had appeared on the scene — a young lady who, though very little older than Dai-yu, possessed a grown-up beauty and aplomb in which all agreed Dai-yu was her inferior. Moreover, in contrast to Dai-yu with her air of lofty self-sufficiency and total obliviousness to all who did not move on the same exalted level as herself, Bao-chai had a generous, accommodating disposition which greatly endeared her to subordinates, so that even the tiniest maid looked on Miss Bao-chai as a familiar friend. Dai-yu could not but feel somewhat put out by this — a fact of which Bao-chai herself, however, was totally unaware.

As for Bao-yu, he was still only a child—a child, moreover, whom nature had endowed with the eccentric obtuseness of a simpleton. Brothers, sisters, cousins, were all one to him. In his relationships with people he made no distinction between one person and another. If his relationship with Dai-yu was exceptional, it was because greater proximity—since she was living with him in his grandmother's quarters—made her more familiar to him than the rest; and greater familiarity bred greater intimacy.

And of course, with greater intimacy came the occasional tiffs and misunderstandings that are usual with people who have a great deal to do with each other.

One day the two of them had fallen out over something or other and the argument had ended with Dai-yu crying alone in her room and Bao-yu feeling remorsefully that perhaps he had spoken too roughly. Presently he went in to make his peace with her and gradually, very gradually, Dai-yu's equanimity was restored.

The winter plum in the gardens of the Ning Mansion was now at its best, and this particular day Cousin Zhen's wife, You-shi, had some wine taken into the gardens and came over in person, bringing her son Jia Rong and his young wife with her, to invite Grandmother Jia, Lady Xing, and Lady Wang to a flower-viewing party.

Grandmother Jia and the rest went round as soon as they had finished their breakfast. The party was in the All-scents Garden. It began with tea and continued with wine, and as it was a family gathering confined to the ladies of the Ning and Rong households, nothing particularly worth recording took place.

At one point in the party Bao-yu was overcome with tiredness and heaviness and expressed a desire to take an afternoon nap. Grandmother Jia ordered some of the servants to go back to the house with him and get him comfortably settled, adding that they might return with him later when he was rested; but Qin-shi, the little wife of Jia Rong, smilingly proposed an alternative.

"We have got just the room here for Uncle Bao. Leave him to me, Grannie dear! He will be quite safe in my hands."

She turned to address the nurses and maidservants who were in attendance on Bao-yu.

"Come, my dears! Tell Uncle Bao to follow me."

Grandmother Jia had always had a high opinion of Qin-shi's trustworthiness—she was such a charming, delightful little creature, the favourite among her great-granddaughters-in-law—and was quite content to leave the arrangements to her.

Qin-shi conducted Bao-yu and his little knot of attendants to an inner room in the main building. As they entered, Bao-yu glanced up and saw a painting hanging above them on the opposite wall. The figures in it were very finely executed. They represented Scholarly Diligence in the person of the Han philosopher Liu Xiang[11] at his book, obligingly illuminated for him by a supernatural being holding a large flaming torch. Bao-yu found the painting—or rather its subject—distasteful. But the pair of mottoes which flanked it proved the last straw:

---

[11]**Liu Xiang** (?79 B.C.E.–?8 C.E.): Important philosopher, bibliographer, and scholar from the Han dynasty (202 B.C.E.–221 C.E.); author of *Biographies of Exemplary Women*, the first Chinese work to focus solely on the lives of women.

True learning implies a clear insight into human activities.

Genuine culture involves the skilful manipulation of human relationships.

In vain the elegant beauty and splendid furnishings of the room! Qin-shi was given to understand in no uncertain terms that her uncle Bao-yu wished to be out of it *at once*.

"If this is not good enough for you," said Qin-shi with a laugh, "where *are* we going to put you? — unless you would like to have your rest in my bedroom."

A little smile played over Bao-yu's face and he nodded. The nurses were shocked.

"An uncle sleep in the bedroom of his nephew's wife! Who ever heard of such a thing!"

Qin-shi laughed again.

"He won't misbehave. Good gracious, he's only a little boy! We don't have to worry about that sort of thing yet! You know my little brother who came last month: he's the same age as Uncle Bao, but if you stood them side by side I shouldn't be a bit surprised if he wasn't the taller of the two."

"Why haven't I seen your brother yet?" Bao-yu demanded. "Bring him in and let me have a look at him!"

The servants all laughed.

"Bring him in? Why, he's ten or twenty miles away! But I expect you'll meet him one of these days."

In the course of this exchange the party had made its way to Qin-shi's bedroom. As Bao-yu entered, a subtle whiff of the most delicious perfume assailed his nostrils, making a sweet stickiness inside his drooping eyelids and causing all the joints in his body to dissolve.

"What a lovely smell!"

He repeated the words several times over.

Inside the room there was a painting by Tang Yin[12] entitled "Spring Slumber" depicting a beautiful woman asleep under a crab-apple tree, whose buds had not yet opened. The painting was flanked on either side by a pair of calligraphic scrolls inscribed with a couplet from the brush of the Song poet Qin Guan:[13]

(on one side)

The coldness of spring has imprisoned the soft buds in a wintry dream;

(on the other side)

The fragrance of wine has intoxicated the beholder with imagined flower-scents.

On a table stood an antique mirror that had once graced the tiring-room of the lascivious empress Wu Ze-tian. Beside it stood the golden platter on which Flying Swallow once danced for her emperor's delight. And on the platter was that very quince which the villainous An Lu-shan threw at beautiful Yang Gui-fei, bruising her plump

---

[12] **Tang Yin** (c. 1470–1524): The style name of Bo Hu, a famous painter of the Ming dynasty (1368–1644).

[13] **Qin Guan** (1049–1100): Song dynasty (960–1279) poet famous for his poems about parting.

white breast. At the far end of the room stood the priceless bed on which Princess Shou-yang was sleeping out of doors under the eaves of the Han-zhang Palace when the plum-flower lighted on her forehead and set a new fashion for coloured patches. Over it hung a canopy commissioned by Princess Tong-chang[14] entirely fashioned out of ropes of pearls.

"I like it here," said Bao-yu happily.

"My room," said Qin-shi with a proud smile, "is fit for an immortal to sleep in." And she unfolded a quilted coverlet, whose silk had been laundered by the fabulous Xi Shi, and arranged the double head-rest that Hong-niang once carried for her amorous mistress.

The nurses now helped Bao-yu into bed and then tiptoed out, leaving him attended only by his four young maids: Aroma, Skybright, Musk, and Ripple. Qin-shi told them to go outside and stop the cats from fighting on the eaves.

As soon as Bao-yu closed his eyes he sank into a confused sleep in which Qin-shi was still there yet at the same time seemed to be drifting along weightlessly in front of him. He followed her until they came to a place of marble terraces and vermilion balustrades where there were green trees and crystal streams. Everything in this place was so clean and so pure that it seemed as if no human foot could ever have trodden there or floating speck of dust ever blown into it. Bao-yu's dreaming self rejoiced. "What a delightful place!" he thought. "If only I could spend all my life here! How much nicer it would be than living under the daily restraint of my parents and teachers!"

These idle reflections were interrupted by someone singing a song on the other side of a hill:

> Spring's dream-time will like drifting clouds disperse,
> Its flowers snatched by a flood none can reverse,
> Then tell each nymph and swain
> 'Tis folly to invite love's pain!

It was the voice of a girl. Before its last echoes had died away, a beautiful woman appeared in the quarter from which the voice had come, approaching him with a floating, fluttering motion. She was quite unlike any earthly lady, as the following poem will make clear:

> She has left her willow-tree house, from her blossoming bower stepped out;
> For the birds betray where she walks through the trees that cluster about,
> And a shadow athwart the winding walk announces that she is near,
> And a fragrance of musk and orchid from fluttering fairy sleeves,
> And a tinkle of girdle-gems that falls on the ear
> At each movement of her dress of lotus leaves.

---

[14] **Wu Ze-tian . . . Princess Tong-chang:** Legendary female lovers from Chinese history and literature. Wu Ze-tian (624–705), the concubine of two emperors, used the power of the Buddhist church to become China's only woman emperor, founding the Chou dynasty (690–705) in the Tang period. An Lu-shan (d. 757) was a Chinese general during the Tang dynasty (618–907), who was said to have had an affair with Yang Gui-fei, the concubine of Emperor Xuan Zong.

A peach-tree blossoms in her dimpling cheek;
Her cloud-coiled tresses are halcyon-sleek;
And she reveals, through parted cherry lips,
Teeth like pomegranate pips.
Her slim waist's sinuous swaying calls to mind
The dance of snowflakes with the waltzing wind;
Hair ornaments of pearl and halcyon blue
Outshine her painted forehead's golden hue.
Her face, through blossoms fleetingly disclosed,
To mirth or ire seems equally disposed;
And as by the waterside she goes,
Hovering on light-stepping toes,
A half-incipient look of pique
Says she would speak, yet would not speak;
While her feet, with the same irresolution,
Would halt, yet would not interrupt their motion.
I contemplate her rare complexion,
Ice-pure and jade-like in perfection;
I marvel at her glittering dress,
Where art lends grace to sumptuousness;
I wonder at her fine-cut features—
Marble, which fragrance marks as one with living creatures;
And I admire her queenly gait,
Like stately dance of simurgh with his mate.
Her purity I can best show
In plum-trees flowering in the snow;
Her chastity I shall recall
In orchids white at first frost-fall;
Her tranquil nature will prevail,
Constant as lone pine in an empty vale;
Her loveliness as dazzled make
As sunset gilding a pellucid lake;
Her glittering elegance I can compare
With dragons in an ornamental mere;
Her dreamy soulfulness most seems
Like wintry waters in the moon's cold beams.
The beauties of days gone by by her beauty are all abashed.
Where was she born, and from whence descended?
Immortal I judge her, fresh come from fairy feastings by the Jasper Pool,
Or from fluting in starry halls, some heavenly concert ended.

Observing delightedly that the lady was a fairy, Bao-yu hurried forward and saluted her with a smile.

"Madam Fairy, I don't know where you have come from or where you are going to, but as I am quite lost in this place, will you please take me with you and be my guide?"

"I am the fairy Disenchantment," the fairy woman replied. "I live beyond the Realm of Separation, in the Sea of Sadness. There is a Mountain of Spring Awakening which rises from the midst of that sea, and on that mountain is the Paradise of the Full-blown Flower, and in that paradise is the Land of Illusion, which is my home. My business is with the romantic passions, love-debts, girlish heartbreaks, and male philanderings of your dust-stained, human world. The reason I have come here today is that recently there has been a heavy concentration of love-*karma* in this area, and I hope to be able to find an opportunity of distributing a quantity of amorous thoughts by implanting them in the appropriate breasts. My meeting you here today is no accident but a part of the same project.

"This place where we are now is not so very far from my home. I have not much to offer you, but would you like to come back with me and let me try to entertain you? I have some fairy tea, which I picked myself. You could have a cup of that. And I have a few jars of choice new wine of my own brewing. I have also been rehearsing a fairy choir and a troupe of fairy dancers in a twelve-part suite which I recently composed called 'A Dream of Golden Days.' I could get them to perform it for you. What do you think?"

Bao-yu was so excited by this invitation that he quite forgot to wonder what had become of Qin-shi in his eagerness to accompany the fairy. As he followed her, a big stone archway suddenly loomed up in front of them on which

THE LAND OF ILLUSION

was written in large characters. A couplet in smaller characters was inscribed on either side of the arch:

Truth becomes fiction when the fiction's true;
Real becomes not-real when the unreal's real.

Having negotiated the archway, they presently came to the gateway of a palace. The following words were inscribed horizontally above the lintel:

SEAS OF PAIN AND SKIES OF PASSION

whilst the following words were inscribed vertically on the two sides:

Ancient earth and sky
   Marvel that love's passion should outlast all time.
Star-crossed men and maids
   Groan that love's debts should be so hard to pay.

"I see," said Bao-yu to himself. "I wonder what the meaning of 'passion that outlasts all time' can be. And what are 'love's debts'? From now on I must make an effort to understand these things."

He could not, of course, have known it, but merely by thinking this he had invited the attentions of the demon Lust, and at that very moment a little of the demon's evil poison had entered Bao-yu's body and lodged itself in the innermost recesses of his heart.

Wholly unconscious of his mortal peril, Bao-yu continued to follow the fairy woman. They passed through a second gateway, and Bao-yu saw a range of palace buildings ahead of them on either hand. The entrance to each building had a board above it proclaiming its name, and there were couplets on either side of the doorways. Bao-yu did not have time to read all of the names, but he managed to make out a few, viz:

DEPARTMENT OF FOND INFATUATION
DEPARTMENT OF CRUEL REJECTION
DEPARTMENT OF EARLY MORNING WEEPING
DEPARTMENT OF LATE NIGHT SOBBING
DEPARTMENT OF SPRING FEVER
DEPARTMENT OF AUTUMN GRIEF

"Madam Fairy," said Bao-yu, whose interest had been whetted by what he had managed to read, "couldn't you take me inside these offices to have a look around?"

"In these offices," said the fairy woman, "are kept registers in which are recorded the past, present, and future of girls from all over the world. It is not permitted that your earthly eyes should look on things that are yet to come."

Bao-yu was most unwilling to accept this answer, and begged and pleaded so persistently that at last Disenchantment gave in.

"Very well. You may make a very brief inspection of this office here."

Delighted beyond measure, Bao-yu raised his head and read the notice above the doorway:

DEPARTMENT OF THE ILL-FATED FAIR

The couplet inscribed vertically on either side of the doorway was as follows:

Spring griefs and autumn sorrows were by yourselves provoked.
Flower faces, moonlike beauty were to what end disclosed?

Bao-yu grasped enough of the meaning to be affected by its melancholy.

Passing inside, he saw a dozen or more large cupboards with paper strips pasted on their doors on which were written the names of different provinces. He was careful to look out for the one belonging to his own area and presently found one on which the paper strip said "Jinling, Twelve Beauties of, Main Register." Bao-yu asked Disenchantment what this meant, and she explained that it was a register of the twelve most outstanding girls of his home province.

"People all say what a big place Jinling[15] is," said Bao-yu. "Surely there should be more than just twelve names? Why, even in my own home, if you count the servants, there must be altogether several hundred girls."

"Certainly there are a great many girls in the whole province," said Disenchantment with a smile, "but only the most important ones have been selected for recording in this register. The registers in the cupboards on either side contain two other selections from the same area. But of the host of ordinary girls outside those three dozen we keep no records."

---

[15]**Jinling:** Jinling, or Nanking, raises a question, for it implies that Bao-yu's hometown is Nanking, whereas the rest of the text suggests that he lives near the Imperial Palace at Beijing. Cao Xueqin's family lived in Nanking. The translator, David Hawkes, suggests that the author may have inserted a chapter here based primarily on an autobiographical detail that is inconsistent with other place references in the novel.

Bao-yu glanced at the other two cupboards referred to by Disenchantment. One was labelled "Jinling, Twelve Beauties of, Supplementary Register No. 1"; the other was labelled "Jinling, Twelve Beauties of, Supplementary Register No. 2." Stretching out his hand he opened the door of the second one, took out Supplementary Register No. 2, which was like a large album, and opened it at the first page.

It was a picture, but not of a person or a view. The whole page was covered with dark ink washes representing stormclouds or fog, followed on the next page by a few lines of verse:

> Seldom the moon shines in a cloudless sky,
> And days of brightness all too soon pass by.
> A noble and aspiring mind
> In a base-born frame confined,
> Your charm and wit did only hatred gain,
> And in the end you were by slanders slain,
> Your gentle lord's solicitude in vain.

Bao-yu could not make much sense of this, and turned to the next page. It was another picture, this time of a bunch of fresh flowers and a worn-out mat, again followed by a few lines of verse.

> What price your kindness and compliance,
> Of sweetest flower the rich perfume?
> You chose the player fortune favoured,
> Unmindful of your master's doom.

Bao-yu was even more mystified by this than by the first page, and laying the album aside, opened the door of the cupboard marked "Supplementary Register No. 1" and took out the album from that.

As in the previous album, the first page was a picture. It represented a branch of cassia with a pool underneath. The water in the pool had dried up and the mud in the bottom was dry and cracked. Growing from it was a withered and broken lotus plant. The picture was followed by these lines:

> Your stem grew from a noble lotus root,
> Yet your life passed, poor flower, in low repute.
> The day two earths shall bear a single tree,
> Your soul must fly home to its own country.

Once more failing to make any sense of what he saw, Bao-yu picked up the Main Register to look at. In this album the picture on the first page represented two dead trees with a jade belt hanging in their branches and on the ground beneath them a pile of snow in which a golden hairpin lay half-buried. This was followed by a quatrain:

> One was a pattern of female virtue,
> One a wit who made other wits seem slow.
> The jade belt in the greenwood hangs,
> The gold pin is buried beneath the snow.

Still Bao-yu was unable to understand the meaning. He would have liked to ask, but he knew that Disenchantment would be unwilling to divulge the secrets of her immortal world. Yet though he could make no sense of the book, for some reason he found himself unable this time to lay it down, and continued to look through it to the end.

The picture that followed was of a bow with a citron hanging from it, followed by what looked like the words of a song:

> You shall, when twenty years in life's hard school are done,
> In pomegranate-time to palace halls ascend.
> Though three springs never could with your first spring compare,
> When hare meets tiger your great dream shall end.

Next was a picture of two people flying a kite. There was also a large expanse of sea with a boat in it and a girl in the boat who had buried her face in her hands and appeared to be crying. This was followed by a quatrain:

> Blessed with a shrewd mind and a noble heart,
> Yet born in time of twilight and decay,
> In spring through tears at river's bank you gaze,
> Borne by the wind a thousand miles away.

The next picture showed some scudding wisps of cloud and a stretch of running water followed by these words:

> What shall avail you rank and riches,
> Orphaned while yet in swaddling bands you lay?
> Soon you must mourn your bright sun's early setting.
> The Xiang flows and the Chu clouds sail away.

Next was a picture showing a beautiful jade which had fallen into the mud, followed by words of judgement:

> For all your would-be spotlessness
> And vaunted otherworldliness,
> You that look down on common flesh and blood,
> Yourself impure, shall end up in the mud.

Next was a striking picture of a savage wolf pursuing a beautiful girl. He had just seized her with his jaws and appeared to be about to eat her. Underneath it was written:

> Paired with a brute like the wolf in the old fable,
> Who on his saviour turned when he was able,
> To cruelty not used, your gentle heart
> Shall, in a twelvemonth only, break apart.

After this was an old temple with a beautiful girl sitting all on her own inside it reading a Buddhist sūtra.[16] The words said:

> When you see through the spring scene's transient state,
> A nun's black habit shall replace your own.

---

[16] **sūtra:** A Buddhist spiritual text, especially one recounting a sermon of the Buddha.

Alas, that daughter of so great a house
By Buddha's altar lamp should sleep alone!

Next was an iceberg with a hen phoenix perched on the top of it, and these words:

This phoenix in a bad time came;
All praised her great ability.
"Two" makes my riddle with a man and tree:
Returning south in tears she met calamity.

Next was a cottage in a deserted village inside which a beautiful girl sat spinning, followed by these words:

When power is lost, rank matters not a jot;
When families fall, kinship must be forgot.
Through a chance kindness to a country wife
Deliverance came for your afflicted life.

This was followed by a picture of a vigorously growing orchid in a pot, beside which stood a lady in full court dress. The words said:

The plum-tree bore her fruit after the rest,
Yet, when all's done, her Orchid was the best.
Against your ice-pure nature all in vain
The tongues of envy wagged; you felt no pain.

The picture after that showed an upper room in a tall building in which a beautiful girl was hanging by her neck from a beam, having apparently taken her own life. The words said:

Love was her sea, her sky; in such excess
Love, meeting with its like, breeds wantonness.
Say not our troubles all from Rong's side came;
For their beginning Ning must take the blame.

Bao-yu would have liked to see some more, but the fairy woman, knowing how intelligent and sharp-witted he was, began to fear that she was in danger of becoming responsible for a leakage of celestial secrets, and so, snapping the album shut, she said with a laugh, "Come with me and we will do some more sight-seeing. Why stay here puzzling your head over these silly riddles?"

Next moment, without quite knowing how it happened, Bao-yu found that he had left the place of registers behind him and was following Disenchantment through the rear parts of the palace. Everywhere there were buildings with ornately carved and painted eaves and rafters, their doorways curtained with strings of pearls and their interiors draped with embroidered hangings. The courtyards outside them were full of deliciously fragrant fairy blooms and rare aromatic herbs.

Gleam of gold pavement flashed on scarlet doors,
And in jade walls jewelled casements snow white shone.

"Hurry, hurry! Come out and welcome the honoured guest!" he heard Disenchantment calling to someone inside, and almost at once a bevy of fairy maidens came running from the palace, lotus-sleeves fluttering and feather-skirts billowing, each as enchantingly beautiful as the flowers of spring or the autumn moon. Seeing Bao-yu, they began to reproach Disenchantment angrily.

"So this is your 'honoured guest'! What do you mean by making us hurry out to meet *him*? You told us that today at this very hour the dream-soul of our darling Crimson Pearl was coming to play with us, and we have been waiting I don't know how long for her arrival. And now, instead, you have brought this disgusting creature to pollute our pure, maidenly precincts. What's the idea?"

At these words Bao-yu was suddenly overwhelmed with a sense of the uncleanness and impurity of his own body and sought in vain for somewhere to escape to; but Disenchantment held him by the hand and advanced towards the fairy maidens with a conciliatory smile.

"Let me tell you the reason for my change of plan. It is true that I set off for the Rong mansion with the intention of fetching Crimson Pearl, but as I was passing through the Ning mansion on my way, I happened to run into the Duke of Ning-guo and his brother the Duke of Rong-guo and they laid a solemn charge on me which I found it hard to refuse.

"'In the hundred years since the foundation of the present dynasty,' they said, 'several generations of our house have distinguished themselves by their services to the Throne and have covered themselves with riches and honours; but now its stock of good fortune has run out, and nothing can be done to replenish it. And though our descendants are many, not one of them is worthy to carry on the line. The only possible exception, our great-grandson Bao-yu, has inherited a perverse, intractable nature and is eccentric and emotionally unstable; and although his natural brightness and intelligence augur well, we fear that owing to the fated eclipse of our family's fortunes there will be no one at hand to give the lad proper guidance and to start him off along the right lines.

"'May we profit from the fortunate accident of this encounter, Madam, to entreat you to take the boy in hand for us? Could you perhaps initiate him in the pleasures of the flesh and all that sort of thing in such a way as to shock the silliness out of him? In that way he might stand a chance of escaping some of the traps that people fall into and be able to devote himself single-mindedly to the serious things of life. It would be such a kindness if you would do this for us.'

"Hearing the old gentlemen so earnest in their entreaty, I was moved to compassion and agreed to bring the boy here. I began by letting him have a good look at the records of the three grades of girls belonging to his own household; but the experience did not bring any awareness; and so I have brought him to this place for another attempt. It is my hope that a full exposure to the illusions of feasting, drinking, music, and dancing may succeed in bringing about an awakening in him some time in the future."

Having concluded her explanation, she led Bao-yu indoors. At once he became aware of a faint, subtle scent, the source of which he was quite unable to identify and about which he felt impelled to question Disenchantment.

"How could you possibly know what it was," said Disenchantment with a somewhat scornful smile, "since this perfume is not to be found anywhere in your mortal world? It is made from the essences of rare plants found on famous mountains and other places of great natural beauty, culled when they are new-grown and blended with gums from the pearl-laden trees that grow in the jewelled groves of paradise. It is called *'Belles Se Fanent.'* "[17]

Bao-yu expressed his admiration.

The company now seated themselves, and some little maids served them with tea. Bao-yu found its fragrance fresh and clean and its flavour delicious, totally unlike those of any earthly blend he knew. He asked Disenchantment for the name.

"The leaves are picked in the Paradise of the Full-blown Flower on the Mountain of Spring Awakening," Disenchantment informed him. "It is infused in water collected from the dew that lies on fairy flowers and leaves. The name is 'Maiden's Tears.' "

Bao-yu nodded attentively and commended the tea.

Looking around the room he noticed various musical instruments, antique bronzes, paintings by old masters, poems by new poets, and other hallmarks of gracious living. He was particularly delighted to observe some rouge-stained pieces of cotton-wool lying on the window-sill—evidently the aftermath of some fairy-woman's toilet. A pair of calligraphic scrolls hung on the wall, making up the following couplet:

> Earth's choicest spirits in the dark lie hid:
> Heaven ineluctably enforced their fate.

After reading the scrolls, Bao-yu asked to be introduced to the fairy maidens. They had a strange assortment of names. One was called Dream-of-bliss, another was called Loving-heart, a third Ask-for-trouble, a fourth Past-regrets, and the rest all had names that were equally bizarre.

Presently the little maids came in again and proceeded to arrange some chairs around a table and to lay it with food and wine for a feast. In the words of the poet,

> Celestial nectar filled the crystal cup,
> And liquid gold in amber goblets glowed.

The wine's bouquet was delectable, and once again Bao-yu could not resist asking about it.

"This wine," said Disenchantment, "is made from the petals of hundreds of different kinds of flowers and extracts from thousands of different sorts of trees. These are blended and fermented with kylin's marrow and phoenix milk. Hence its name, *'Lachrymae Rerum.'* "[18]

Bao-yu praised it enthusiastically.

As they sat drinking wine, a troupe of twelve dancers entered and inquired what pieces they should perform for the company's entertainment.

---

[17] ***Belles Se Fanent:*** French for "fading beauties."

[18] ***Lachrymae Rerum:*** Latin for "the tears of things"; the translator has borrowed a famous phrase from Virgil's *Aeneid* to characterize melancholia and loss.

"You can do the twelve songs of my new song-and-dance suite 'A Dream of Golden Days,' " said Disenchantment.

At once the sandalwood clappers began, very softly, to beat out a rhythm, accompanied by the sedate twang of the *zheng*'s[19] silver strings and by the voice of a singer.

When first the world from chaos rose . . .

The singer had got no further than the first line of the first song when Disenchantment interrupted.

"This suite," she told Bao-yu, "is not like the music-dramas of your earthly composers in which there are always the fixed parts of *sheng, dan, jing, mo,* and so on, and set tunes in the various Northern and Southern modes. In my suite each song is an elegy on a single person or event and the tunes are original compositions which we have orchestrated ourselves. You need to know what the songs are about in order to appreciate them properly. I should not imagine you are very familiar with this sort of entertainment; so unless you read the libretto of the songs first before listening to them, I fear you may find them rather insipid."

Turning to one of the maids, she ordered her to fetch the manuscript of her libretto of "A Dream of Golden Days" and gave it to Bao-yu to read, so that he could listen to the songs with one eye on the text. These were the words in Disenchantment's manuscript:

PRELUDE: *A Dream of Golden Days*

When first the world from chaos rose,
Tell me, how did love begin?
The wind and moonlight first did love compose.
Now woebegone
And quite cast down
In low estate
I would my foolish heart expose,
And so perform
This *Dream of Golden Days,*
And all my grief for my lost loves disclose.

FIRST SONG: *The Mistaken Marriage*

Let others all
Commend the marriage rites of gold and jade;
I still recall
The bond of old by stone and flower made;
And while my vacant eyes behold
Crystalline snows of beauty pure and cold,
From my mind can not be banished
That fairy wood forlorn that from the world has vanished.
How true I find
That every good some imperfection holds!

---

[19] ***zheng:*** A Chinese zither, a plucked string instrument with thirteen to twenty-one strings.

Even a wife so courteous and so kind
No comfort brings to my afflicted mind.

SECOND SONG: *Hope Betrayed*

One was a flower from paradise,
One a pure jade without spot or stain.
If each for the other one was not intended,
Then why in this life did they meet again?
And yet if fate had meant them for each other,
Why was their earthly meeting all in vain?
In vain were all her sighs and tears,
In vain were all his anxious fears:
All, insubstantial, doomed to pass,
As moonlight mirrored in the water
Or flowers reflected in a glass.
How many tears from those poor eyes could flow,
Which every season rained upon her woe?

THIRD SONG: *Mutability*

In the full flower of her prosperity
Once more came mortal mutability,
Bidding her, with both eyes wide,
All earthly things to cast aside,
And her sweet soul upon the airs to glide.
So far the road back home did seem
That to her parents in a dream
Thus she her final duty paid:
"I that now am but a shade,
Parents dear,
For your happiness I fear:
Do not tempt the hand of fate!
Draw back, draw back, before it is too late!"

FOURTH SONG: *From Dear Ones Parted*

Sail, boat, a thousand miles through rain and wind,
Leaving my home and dear ones far behind.
I fear that my remaining years
Will waste away in homesick tears.
Father dear and mother mild,
Be not troubled for your child!
From of old our rising, falling
Was ordained; so now this parting.
Each in another land must be;
Each for himself must fend as best he may;
Now I am gone, oh do not weep for me!

FIFTH SONG: *Grief Amidst Gladness*

While you still in cradle lay,
Both your parents passed away.

Though born to silken luxury,
No warmth or kind indulgence came your way.
Yet yours was a generous, open-hearted nature,
And never could be snared or soured
By childish piques and envious passions—
You were a crystal house by wind and moonlight scoured.
Matched to a perfect, gentle husband,
Security of bliss at last it seemed,
And all your childish miseries redeemed.
But soon alas! the clouds of Gao-tang faded,
The waters of the Xian ran dry.
In our grey world so are things always ordered:
What then avails it to lament and sigh?

SIXTH SONG: *All at Odds*

Heaven made you like a flower,
With grace and wit to match the gods,
Adding a strange, contrary nature
That set you with the rest at odds.
Nauseous to you the world's rank diet,
Vulgar its fashion's gaudy dress:
But the world envies the superior
And hates a too precious daintiness.
Sad it seemed that your life should in dim-lit shrines be wasted,
All the sweets of spring untasted:
Yet, at the last,
Down into mud and shame your hopes were cast,
Like a white, flawless jade dropped in the muck,
Where only wealthy rakes might bless their luck.

SEVENTH SONG: *Husband and Enemy*

Zhong-shan wolf,
Inhuman sot,
Who for past kindnesses cared not a jot!
Bully and spendthrift, reckless in debauch,
For riot or for whoring always hot!
A delicate young wife of gentle stock
To you was no more than a lifeless block,
And bore, when you would rant and rave,
Treatment far worse than any slave;
So that her delicate, sweet soul
In just a twelvemonth from its body stole.

EIGHTH SONG: *The Vanity of Spring*

When triple spring as vanity was seen,
What use the blushing flowers, the willows green?
From youth's extravagance you sought release
To win chaste quietness and heavenly peace.
The hymeneal peach-blooms in the sky,

The flowering almond's blossoms seen on high
Dismiss, since none, for sure,
Can autumn's blighting frost endure.
Amidst sad aspens mourners sob and sigh,
In maple woods the poor ghosts thinly cry,
And under the dead grasslands lost graves lie.
Now poor, now rich, men's lives in toil are passed
To be, like summer's pride, cut down at last.
The doors of life and death all must go through.
Yet this I know is true:
In Paradise there grows a precious tree
Which bears the fruit of immortality.

NINTH SONG: *Caught by Her Own Cunning*

Too shrewd by half, with such finesse you wrought
That your own life in your own toils was caught;
But long before you died your heart was slain,
And when you died your spirit walked in vain.
Fall'n the great house once so secure in wealth,
Each scattered member shifting for himself;
And half a life-time's anxious schemes
Proved no more than the stuff of dreams.
Like a great building's tottering crash,
Like flickering lampwick burned to ash,
Your scene of happiness concludes in grief:
For worldly bliss is always insecure and brief.

TENTH SONG: *The Survivor*

Some good remained,
Some good remained:
The daughter found a friend in need
Through her mother's one good deed.
So let all men the poor and meek sustain,
And from the example of her cruel kin refrain,
Who kinship scorned and only thought of gain.
For far above the constellations
One watches all and makes just calculations.

ELEVENTH SONG: *Splendour Come Late*

Favour, a shadow in the glass;
Fame, a dream that soon would pass:
The blissful flowering-time of youth soon fled,
Soon, too, the pleasures of the bridal bed.
A pearl-encrusted crown and robes of state
Could not for death untimely compensate;
And though each man desires
Old age from want made free,
True blessedness requires

A clutch of young heirs at the knee.
Proudly upright
The head with cap and bands of office on,
And gleaming bright
Upon his breast the gold insignia shone.
An awesome sight
To see him so exalted stand!—
Yet the black night
Of death's dark frontier lay close at hand.
All those whom history calls great
Left only empty names for us to venerate.

TWELFTH SONG: *The Good Things Have an End*

Perfumed was the dust that fell
From painted beams where springtime ended.
Her sportive heart
And amorous looks
The ruin of a mighty house portended.
The weakness in the line began with Jing;
The blame for the decline lay first in Ning;
But retribution all was of Love's fashioning.

EPILOGUE: *The Birds into the Wood Have Flown*

The office jack's career is blighted,
The rich man's fortune now all vanished,
The kind with life have been requited,
The cruel exemplarily punished;
The one who owed a life is dead,
The tears one owed have all been shed.
Wrongs suffered have the wrongs done expiated;
The couplings and the sunderings were fated.
Untimely death sin in some past life shows,
But only luck a blest old age bestows.
The disillusioned to their convents fly,
The still deluded miserably die.
Like birds who, having fed, to the woods repair,
They leave the landscape desolate and bare.

Having reached the end of this suite, the singers showed signs of embarking on another one. Disenchantment observed with a sigh that Bao-yu was dreadfully bored.

"Silly boy! You still don't understand, do you?"

Bao-yu hurriedly stopped the girls and told them that they need not sing any more. He felt dizzy and his head was spinning. He explained to Disenchantment that he had drunk too much and would like to lie down.

At once she ordered the remains of the feast to be removed and conducted Bao-yu to a dainty bedroom. The furnishings and hangings of the bed were more sumptuous and beautiful than anything he had ever seen. To his intense surprise there was a fairy girl sitting in the middle of it. Her rose-fresh beauty reminded him strongly of Bao-chai, but there was also something about her of Dai-yu's delicate charm. As he was pondering the meaning of this apparition, he suddenly became aware that Disenchantment was addressing him.

"In the rich and noble households of your mortal world, too many of those bowers and boudoirs where innocent tenderness and sweet girlish fantasy should reign are injuriously defiled by coarse young voluptuaries and loose, wanton girls. And what is even more detestable, there are always any number of worthless philanderers to protest that it is woman's beauty alone that inspires them, or loving feelings alone, unsullied by any taint of lust. They lie in their teeth! To be moved by woman's beauty is itself a kind of lust. To experience loving feelings is, even more assuredly, a kind of lust. Every act of love, every carnal congress of the sexes is brought about precisely because sensual delight in beauty has kindled the feeling of love.

"The reason I like you so much is because you are full of lust. You are the most lustful person I have ever known in the whole world!"

Bao-yu was scared by the vehemence of her words.

"Madam Fairy, you are wrong! Because I am lazy over my lessons, Mother and Father still have to scold me quite often; but surely that doesn't make me *lustful*? I'm still too young to know what they do, the people they use that word about."

"Ah, but you *are* lustful!" said Disenchantment. "In principle, of course, all lust is the same. But the word has many different meanings. For example, the typically lustful man in the common sense of the word is a man who likes a pretty face, who is fond of singing and dancing, who is inordinately given to flirtation; one who makes love in season and out of season, and who, if he could, would like to have every pretty girl in the world at his disposal, to gratify his desires whenever he felt like it. Such a person is a mere brute. His is a shallow, promiscuous kind of lust.

"But your kind of lust is different. That blind, defenceless love with which nature has filled your being is what we call here 'lust of the mind.' 'Lust of the mind' cannot be explained in words, nor, if it could, would you be able to grasp their meaning. Either you know what it means or you don't.

"Because of this 'lust of the mind' women will find you a kind and understanding friend; but in the eyes of the world I am afraid it is going to make you seem unpractical and eccentric. It is going to earn you the jeers of many and the angry looks of many more.

"Today I received a most touching request on your behalf from your ancestors the Duke of Ning-guo and the Duke of Rong-guo. And as I cannot bear the idea of your being rejected by the world for the greater glory of us women, I have brought you here. I have made you drunk with fairy wine. I have drenched you with fairy tea. I have admonished you with fairy songs. And now I am going to give you my little sister Two-in-one—'Ke-qing' to her friends—to be your bride.

"The time is propitious. You may consummate the marriage this very night. My motive in arranging this is to help you grasp the fact that, since even in these immortal precincts love is an illusion, the love of your dust-stained, mortal world must be doubly an illusion. It is my earnest hope that, knowing this, you will henceforth be able to shake yourself free of its entanglements and change your previous way of thinking, devoting your mind seriously to the teachings of Confucius and Mencius[20] and your person wholeheartedly to the betterment of society."

Disenchantment then proceeded to give him secret instructions in the art of love; then, pushing him gently inside the room, she closed the door after him and went away.

Dazed and confused, Bao-yu nevertheless proceeded to follow out the instructions that Disenchantment had given him, which led him by predictable stages to that act which boys and girls perform together—and which it is not my intention to give a full account of here.

Next morning he lay for a long time locked in blissful tenderness with Ke-qing,[21] murmuring sweet endearments in her ear and unable to tear himself away from her. Eventually they emerged from the bedroom hand in hand to walk together out-of-doors.

Their walk seemed to take them quite suddenly to a place where only thorn-trees grew and wolves and tigers prowled around in pairs. Ahead of them the road ended at the edge of a dark ravine. No bridge connected it with the other side. As they hesitated, wondering what to do, they suddenly became aware that Disenchantment was running up behind them.

"Stop! Stop!" she was shouting. "Turn back at once! Turn back!"

Bao-yu stood still in alarm and asked her what place this was.

"This is the Ford of Error," said Disenchantment. "It is ten thousand fathoms deep and extends hundreds of miles in either direction. No boat can ever cross it; only a raft manned by a lay-brother called Numb and an acolyte called Dumb. Numb holds the steering-paddle and Dumb wields the pole. They won't ferry any-one across for money, but only take those who are fated to cross over.

"If you had gone on walking just now and had fallen in, all the good advice I was at such pains to give you would have been wasted!"

Even as she spoke there was a rumbling like thunder from inside the abyss and a multitude of demons and water monsters reached up and clutched at Bao-yu to drag him down into its depths. In his terror the sweat broke out over his body like rain and a great cry burst from his lips,

"Ke-qing! Save me!"

Aroma and his other maids rushed upstairs in alarm and clung to him.

"Don't be frightened, Bao-yu! We are here!"

But Qin-shi, who was out in the courtyard telling the maids to be sure that the cats and dogs didn't fight, marvelled to hear him call her name out in his sleep.

---

[20] **Mencius:** Confucian scholar and philosopher from the fourth century B.C.E.; the second most important Confucian writer after Confucius himself. Mencius's writings form one of the Four Books, texts used in Confucian education in China.

[21] **Ke-qing:** Means "combining the best of both"; Ke-qing is a composite of Dai-yu and Bao-chai, who represent distinctive but complementary aspects of the ideal woman.

"'Ke-qing' was the name they called me back at home when I was a little girl. Nobody here knows it. I wonder how he could have found it out?"

If you have not yet fathomed the answer to her question, you must read the next chapter.

From Chapter 6

[Jia Bao-yu's First Experiment in the Art of Love]

Qin-shi was surprised to hear Bao-yu call out her childhood name in his sleep, but did not like to pursue the matter. As she stood wondering, Bao-yu, who was still bemused after his dream and not yet in full possession of his faculties, got out of bed and began to stretch himself and to adjust his clothes, assisted by Aroma. As she was doing up his trousers, her hand, chancing to stray over his thigh, came into contact with something cold and sticky which caused her to draw it back in alarm and ask him if he was all right. Instead of answering, he merely reddened and gave the hand a squeeze.

Aroma had always been an intelligent girl. She was, in any case, a year or two older than Bao-yu and had recently begun to have some understanding of the facts of life. Observing the condition that Bao-yu was in, she therefore had more than an inkling of what had happened. Abandoning her question, she busied herself with his clothes, her cheeks suffused by a crimson blush of embarrassment. When he was properly dressed, they went to rejoin Grandmother Jia and the rest. There they bolted a hurried supper and then slipped back to the other house, where Aroma profited from the absence of the nurses and the other maids to take out a clean undergarment for Bao-yu to change into.

"Please, Aroma," Bao-yu shamefacedly entreated as she helped him change, "*please* don't tell anyone!"

Equally ill at ease, Aroma giggled softly.

"Why did you . . . ?" she began to ask. Then, after glancing cautiously around, began again.

"Where did that stuff come from?"

Bao-yu blushed furiously and said nothing. Aroma stared at him curiously and continued to giggle. After much hesitation he proceeded to give her a detailed account of his dream. But when he came to the part of it in which he made love to Two-in-one, Aroma threw herself forward with a shriek of laughter and buried her face in her hands.

Bao-yu had long been attracted by Aroma's somewhat coquettish charms and tugged at her purposefully, anxious to share with her the lesson he had learned from Disenchantment. Aroma knew that when Grandmother Jia gave her to Bao-yu she had intended her to belong to him in the fullest possible sense, and so, having no good reason for refusing him, she allowed him, after a certain amount of coy resistance, to have his way with her.

From then on Bao-yu treated Aroma with even greater consideration than before, whilst Aroma for her part redoubled the devotion with which she served him. But of this, for the time being, no more. [. . .]

FROM CHAPTER 8

[Jia Bao-yu and Xue Bao-chai Discover Corresponding Inscriptions]

When Bao-yu and Xi-feng were back and had seen the others, Bao-yu told Grandmother Jia of his wish to have Qin Zhong[22] admitted to the clan school. He pointed out that a congenial study-companion would stimulate him to greater effort and gave her a glowing account of Qin Zhong's amiable qualities. Xi-feng was at hand to lend her support. She told Grandmother Jia that Qin Zhong would be calling on her within a day or two to pay his respects. Their infectious enthusiasm put the old lady in a high good humour, which Xi-feng took advantage of to ask if she would accompany her to the dramatic entertainment which her opponents had promised in two days' time.

In spite of her years Grandmother Jia loved any kind of excitement and when, two days later, You-shi came to fetch Xi-feng, the old lady did in fact accompany them, taking Lady Wang, Dai-yu, and Bao-yu as well. By about noon, however, she was ready to go back and rest, and Lady Wang, who disliked noise and excitement, took the opportunity to leave with her. This left Xi-feng as principal guest, and she moved into the place of honour and stayed there for the rest of the day, enjoying herself immensely and not returning until late in the evening.

After accompanying Grandmother Jia back to her apartment and seeing her safely settled down for her nap, Bao-yu would have liked to go back and watch some more plays but was afraid that his presence would be an inconvenience to Qin-shi and his other "juniors." Remembering that Bao-chai had been at home unwell during the past few days and that he had still not been to see her, he thought he would go there instead and pay her a call, but fearing that if he went the quickest way through the corner gate behind the main hall he might meet with some entanglement on the way or, worse, run into his father, he decided to go by a more circuitous route.

The maids and nurses who attended him had been expecting him to change into his everyday clothes, but seeing him go out of the inner gate again without doing so, followed after him assuming that he was going back to the other mansion to watch the plays. To their surprise, however, he turned left when he reached the covered passage-way instead of going straight on, and made off in a north-easterly direction.

But he was out of luck, for as he did so he found himself facing Zhan Guang and Shan Ping-ren, two of the literary gentlemen patronized by his father, who were walking towards him from the opposite direction. They descended on him gleefully, one of them clasping him round the waist, the other taking him by a hand.

"Angelic boy! How seldom one has the pleasure! Is it really you, or is this some delightful dream?"

They prattled on for what seemed an age before finally releasing him. As they were going, one of the old nurses detained them a moment longer.

"Have you two gentlemen just come from the Master's?"

---

[22] **Qin Zhong:** The younger brother of Qin-shi; Qin Zhong is Bao-yu's best friend.

The two gentlemen nodded and smiled conspiratorially:

"Sir Zheng is in his little study in the Su Dong-po Rooms, having his afternoon nap. All is well!"

They hurried off. Bao-yu smiled too, relieved that his father was safely out of the way. Turning once again, this time north-wards, he made his way swiftly towards Pear Tree Court.

Once more he was unlucky. The Clerk of Stores Wu Xin-deng, a man called Dai Liang who was foreman at the granary, and five other foremen were just at that moment coming out of the counting-house together and, catching sight of Bao-yu, at once stood respectfully to attention. One of their number, a buyer called Qian Hua who had not seen Bao-yu for some considerable time, hurried forward, dropped on his right knee, and touched his hand to the ground in the Manchu salute. Bao-yu smilingly extended a hand to raise him up. The men all relaxed in smiles.

"I saw some of your calligraphy in town the other day, Master Bao," said one of them. "It's getting really good! When are you going to give us a few sheets for our-selves, to put up on the wall?"

"Where did you see it?" Bao-yu asked.

"Any number of places," the men told him. "Everyone has been praising it no end. They even come to us asking for specimens."

"You can have some easily enough if you really want to," Bao-yu said. "You have only to ask one of my boys."

He hurried on. The men waited for him to pass before dispersing about their business.

To omit further details of his progress, Bao-yu came at last to Pear Tree Court, and going first into Aunt Xue's room, found her giving instructions to her maids about some embroidery. Her response to his greeting was to draw him towards her and clasp him to her bosom in an affectionate embrace.

"What a nice, kind boy to think of us on a cold day like this! Come up on the kang and get warm!"

She ordered a maid to bring him some "boiling hot tea."

Bao-yu inquired whether Cousin Pan was at home. Aunt Xue sighed.

"Pan is like a riderless horse: always off enjoying himself somewhere or other. He won't spend a single day at home if he can help it."

"What about Bao-chai? Is she quite better?"

"Ah yes, of course!" said Aunt Xue. "You sent someone to ask about her the other day, didn't you? That was very thoughtful of you. I think she's inside. Go in and have a look! It's warmer in there than here. You go in and sit down, and I'll be with you in a moment when I've finished tidying up."

Bao-yu got down from the kang and going to the doorway of the inner room, lifted up the rather worn-looking red silk curtain which covered it. Bao-chai was sitting on the kang inside, sewing. Her lustrous black hair was done up in a simple bun without any kind of ornament. She was wearing a honey-coloured padded gown, a mulberry-coloured sleeveless jacket with a pattern in gold and silver thread, and a greenish-yellow padded skirt. All her clothing had the same sensible, rather well-worn look about it.

He saw no hint of luxury or show,
only a chaste, refined sobriety;

to some her studied taciturnity
might seem to savour of duplicity;
but she herself saw in conformity
the means of guarding her simplicity.

"Have you quite recovered, cousin?" Bao-yu asked.

Raising her head, Bao-chai saw Bao-yu enter the room. She rose quickly to her feet and smiled at him.

"I am quite better now. It was nice of you to think of me."

She made him sit on the edge of the kang and ordered Oriole to pour him some tea. Then she proceeded to ask him first about Grandmother Jia, then about Lady Wang, and then about the girls, while her eye took in the details of his dress.

He had a little jewel-encrusted coronet of gold filigree on the top of his head and a circlet in the form of two dragons supporting a pearl round his brow. He was dressed in a narrow-sleeved, full-skirted robe of russet-green material covered with a pattern of writhing dragons and lined and trimmed with white fox-fur. A butterfly-embroidered sash with fringed ends was fastened round his waist, and from his neck hung a padlock-shaped amulet, a lucky charm, and the famous jade said to have been inside his mouth when he was born.

Bao-chai's eye came to rest on the jade.

"I am always hearing about this famous stone of yours," she said smilingly, "but I have never yet had a chance of examining it really closely. Today I think I should like to have a look."

She moved forward as she spoke, and Bao-yu too leaned towards her, and taking the stone from his neck, put it into her hand.

Looking at it as it lay on her palm, she saw a stone about the size of a sparrow's egg, glowing with the suppressed, milky radiance of a sunlit cloud and veined with iridescent streaks of colour.

Reader, you will, of course, remember that this jade was a transformation of that same great stone block which once lay at the foot of Greensickness Peak in the Great Fable Mountains. A certain *jesting poet* has written these verses about it:

> Nü-wa's stone-smelting is a tale unfounded:
> On such weak fancies our Great Fable's grounded.
> Lost now, alack! and gone *my* heavenly stone—
> Transformed to this vile bag of flesh and bone.
> For, in misfortune, gold no longer gleams;
> And bright jade, when fate frowns, lack-lustre seems.
> Heaped charnel-bones none can identify
> Were golden girls and boys in days gone by.

The words which the scabby-headed monk had incised on the stone when he found it lying in its diminished shape under Greensickness Peak were as follows.

(On the front side)

MAGIC JADE

Mislay me not, forget me not,
And hale old age shall be your lot.

(On the reverse side)

1. Dispels the harms of witchcraft.
2. Cures melancholic distempers.
3. Foretells good and evil fortune.

When Bao-chai had looked at the stone all over, she turned back to the inscription on the front and repeated it a couple of times to herself out loud:

Mislay me not, forget me not,
And hale old age shall be your lot.

"Why aren't you pouring the tea?" she asked Oriole. "What are you standing there gawping for?"

Oriole laughed.

"Because those words sounded like a perfect match to the ones on your necklace."

"So you have an inscription, too?" said Bao-yu pricking up his ears. "I must have a look."

"Don't take any notice of her!" said Bao-chai. "There is no inscription."

"Cousin, cousin," said Bao-yu entreatingly, "*you've* had a look at *mine*. Be fair!"

Bao-chai could not escape the logic of this entreaty.

"There is a motto on it which someone gave us once for luck and which we had engraved on it," she admitted. "That's the only reason I always wear it; otherwise it would be too tiresome to have a heavy thing like this hanging round one's neck all the time."

As she was speaking she undid the top buttons of her jacket and gown and extracted the necklace that she was wearing over the dark red shift beneath. Its pendant was a locket of shining solid gold, bordered with sparkling gems. There was a line of writing engraved on either side of it which together made up the words of a charm:

Ne'er leave me, ne'er abandon me:
And years of health shall be your fee.

He recited them a couple of times and then recited the words of his own inscription a couple of times.

"Why, yes!" he cried delightedly. "The two inscriptions are a perfect match!"

"A scabby-headed old monk gave Miss Bao-chai the words," said Oriole. "He said they must be engraved on something made of gold . . ."

Bao-chai angrily cut her short, telling her to mind her business and pour the tea. To change the subject she asked Bao-yu where he had just come from.

Bao-yu was now sitting almost shoulder to shoulder with her and as he did so became aware of a penetrating fragrance that seemed to emanate from her person.

"What incense do you use to scent your clothes with, cousin?" he asked. "I have never smelt such a delicious perfume."

"I can't stand incense perfumes," said Bao-chai. "I could never see the point of smoking perfectly good, clean clothes over an incense-pot."

"In that case, what *is* this perfume I can smell?"

Bao-chai thought for a moment.

"I know! It must be the Cold Fragrance Pill I took this morning."

"What's a Cold Fragrance Pill?" said Bao-yu with a laugh. "Won't you give me one to try?"

"Now you're being silly again. Medicine isn't something to be taken for amusement."

Just at that moment the servants outside announced "Miss Lin" and almost simultaneously Dai-yu came flouncing into the room. Catching sight of Bao-yu she let out a wail of mock dismay.

"Oh dear! I *have* chosen a bad time to come!"

The others rose and invited her to be seated.

"Why did you say that?" Bao-chai asked her.

"If I had known *he* was coming, I shouldn't have come myself."

"What exactly do you mean by that?"

"What do I mean by that?" said Dai-yu. "I mean that if I only come when he does, then when I don't come you won't have any visitors. Whereas if we space our-selves out so that he comes one day and I come the next, it will never get either too lonely or too noisy for you. I shouldn't have thought that needed much explaining."

Observing that Dai-yu was wearing a greatcoat of red camlet over her dress, Bao-yu asked whether it was snowing outside.

"It's been snowing for some time," said one of the old women standing below the kang.

Bao-yu asked someone to go and fetch his winter cape.

"You see!" said Dai-yu. "When I come, he has to go!"

"Who said anything about going?" said Bao-yu. "I just want them to have it ready for me."

"It's no time to go now, while it's still snowing," said Bao-yu's old nurse, Nannie Li. "Much better stay here and play with your cousins. In any case, I think your Aunt Xue is getting tea ready for you. I'll send a maid to fetch your cape. Shall I tell the boys outside they can go?"

Bao-yu nodded, and Nannie Li went outside and dismissed the pages. [. . .]

FROM CHAPTER 32

*[Jia Bao-yu and Lin Dai-yu
Have an Awkward Encounter]*

[Between Rong-guo and Ning-guo estates, Jia Zheng and Lady Wang have ordered the construction of Prospect Garden, an expansive and lush garden with elegant quarters, to receive Bao-yu's older sister, the Imperial Concubine Jia Yuan-chun. After her visit, Jia Yuan-chun decides that the new garden should be used as a residence for the girls of the family as well as for Bao-yu. Bao-chai moves into All-Spice Court; Dai-yu, into the Naiad's House; and Bao-yu, into the House of Green Delights. Thereafter, Bao-yu and his cousins spend their days reading, writing verses, playing Go, practicing calligraphy, and further developing and complicating their triangular relationship. The peaceful existence in the gardens is often disrupted by quarreling, hurt feelings, and jealousy between Dai-yu and Bao-chai. While he has affection for both cousins, Bao-yu shows in various subtle ways that he favors Dai-yu, but through miscommunication, misunderstanding, and sheer evasiveness Dai-yu is kept guessing about Bao-yu's inclinations. Chapter 32 shows an example of

Dai-yu's jealousy, as she reads too much significance into the fact that Bao-yu had just received a gold kylin—one that he had recently lost—from Shi Xiang-yun, an orphaned niece of Grandmother Jia, who is visiting the Jia compound. The chapter also illustrates here how Bao-yu and Dai-yu have difficulty expressing their true feelings for each other.]

. . . Dai-yu rightly surmised that now Xiang-yun had arrived, Bao-yu would lose no time in telling her about his newly acquired kylin.[23]

Now Dai-yu had observed that in the romances which Bao-yu smuggled in to her and of which she was nowadays an avid consumer, it was always some trinket or small object of clothing or jewellery—a pair of lovebirds, a male and female phoenix, a jade ring, a gold buckle, a silken handkerchief, an embroidered belt, or what not—that brought the heroes and heroines together. And since the fate and future happiness of those fortunate beings seemed to depend wholly on the instrumentality of such trifling objects, it was natural for her to suppose that Bao-yu's acquisition of the gold kylin would become the occasion of a dramatic rupture with *her* and the beginning of an association with Xiang-yun in which he and Xiang-yun would do together all those delightful things that she had read about in the romances.

It was with such apprehensions that she made her way stealthily towards Green Delights, her intention being to observe how the two of them were behaving and shape her own actions accordingly. Imagine her surprise when, just as she was about to enter, she heard Xiang-yun lecturing Bao-yu on his social obligations and Bao-yu telling Xiang-yun that "Cousin Lin never talked that sort of rubbish" and that if she did he would have "fallen out with her long ago." Mingled emotions of happiness, alarm, sorrow, and regret assailed her.

Happiness:

Because after all (she thought) I wasn't mistaken in my judgement of you. I always thought of you as a true friend, and I was right.

Alarm:

Because if you praise me so unreservedly in front of other people, your warmth and affection are sure, sooner or later, to excite suspicion and be misunderstood.

Regret:

Because if you are my true friend, then I am yours and the two of us are a perfect match. But in that case why did there have to be all this talk of "the gold and the jade"? Alternatively, if there had to be all this talk of gold and jade, why weren't we the two to have them? Why did there have to be a Bao-chai with her golden locket?

Sorrow:

Because though there are things of burning importance to be said, without a father or a mother I have no one to say them for me. And besides, I feel so muzzy lately and I know that my illness is gradually gaining a hold on me. (The doctors say that the weakness and anaemia I suffer from may be the beginnings of a consumption.) So even if I *am* your true-love, I fear I may not be able to wait for you. And even though you are mine, you can do nothing to alter my fate.

---

[23] Xiang-yun . . . kylin: Xiang-yun is the great-niece of Grandmother Jia. A kylin is a unicorn-like mythological creature, combining the forces of the yin and yang, with the head of a dragon, deerlike hooves, and a horselike body; said to appear only at the birth of a sage, the creature is a symbol of longevity, wisdom, and good luck.

At that point in her reflections she began to weep; and feeling in no fit state to be seen, she turned away from the door and began to make her way back again.

Bao-yu had finished his hasty dressing and now came out of the house. He saw Dai-yu slowly walking on ahead of him and, judging by her appearance from behind, wiping her eyes. He hurried forward to catch up with her.

"Where are you off to, coz? Are you crying again? Who has upset you this time?"

Dai-yu turned and saw that it was Bao-yu.

"I'm perfectly all right," she said, forcing a smile. "What would I be crying for?"

"Look at you! The tears are still wet on your face. How can you tell such fibs?"

Impulsively he stretched out his hand to wipe them. Dai-yu recoiled several paces:

"You'll get your head chopped off!" she said. "You really *must* keep your hands to yourself."

"I'm sorry. My feelings got the better of me. I'm afraid I wasn't thinking about my head."

"No, I forgot," said Dai-yu. "Losing your head is nothing, is it? It's losing your kylin—the famous *gold* kylin—that is really serious!"

Her words immediately put Bao-yu in a passion. He came up to her and held his face close to hers.

"Do you say these things to put a curse on me? or is it merely to make me angry that you say them?"

Remembering their recent quarrel, Dai-yu regretted her careless reintroduction of its theme and hastened to make amends:

"Now don't get excited. I shouldn't have said that—oh come now, it really isn't *that* important! Look at you! The veins are standing out on your forehead and your face is all covered with sweat."

She moved forward and wiped the perspiration from his brow. For some moments he stood there motionless, staring at her. Then he said:

"*Don't worry!*"

Hearing this, Dai-yu herself was silent for some moments.

"Why *should* I worry?" she said eventually. "I don't understand you. Would you mind telling me what you are talking about?"

Bao-yu sighed.

"Do you really not understand? Can I really have been all this time mistaken in my feelings towards you? If you don't even know your *own* mind, it's small wonder that you're always getting angry on *my* account."

"I really don't understand what you mean about not worrying," said Dai-yu.

Bao-yu sighed again and shook his head.

"My dear coz, don't think you can fool me. If you don't understand what I've just said, then not only have *my* feelings towards *you* been all along mistaken, but all that *you* have ever felt for *me* has been wasted, too. It's because you worry so much that you've made yourself ill. If only you could take things a bit easier, your illness wouldn't go on getting more and more serious all the time."

Dai-yu was thunderstruck. He had read her mind—had seen inside her more clearly than if she had plucked out her entrails and held them out for his inspection.

And now there were a thousand things that she wanted to tell him; yet though she was dying to speak, she was unable to utter a single syllable and stood there like a simpleton, gazing at him in silence.

Bao-yu, too, had a thousand things to say, but he, too, stood mutely gazing at her, not knowing where to begin.

After the two of them had stared at each other for some considerable time in silence, Dai-yu heaved a deep sigh. The tears gushed from her eyes and she turned and walked away. Bao-yu hurried after her and caught at her dress.

"Coz dear, stop a moment! Just let me say one word."

As she wiped her eyes with one hand, Dai-yu pushed him away from her with the other.

"There's nothing to say. I already know what you want to tell me."

She said this without turning back her head, and having said it, passed swiftly on her way. Bao-yu remained where he was standing, gazing after her in silent stupefaction.

Now Bao-yu had left the apartment in such haste that he had forgotten to take his fan with him. Fearing that he would be very hot without it, Aroma hurried outside to give it to him, but when she noticed him standing some way ahead of her talking to Dai-yu, she halted. After a little while she saw Dai-yu walk away and Bao-yu continue standing motionless where he was. She chose this moment to go up and speak to him.

"You've gone out without your fan," she said. "It's a good job I noticed. Here you are. I ran out to give it to you."

Bao-yu, still in a muse, saw Aroma there talking to him, yet without clearly perceiving who it was. With the same glazed look in his eyes, he began to speak.

"Dearest coz! I've never before dared to tell you what I felt for you. Now at last I'm going to pluck up courage and tell you, and after that I don't care what becomes of me. Because of you I, too, have made myself ill—only I haven't dared tell anyone about it and have had to bear it all in silence. And the day that your illness is cured, I do believe that mine, too, will get better. Night and day, coz, sleeping and dreaming, you are never out of my mind."

Aroma listened to this declaration aghast.

"Holy saints preserve us!" she exclaimed. "He'll be the death of me."

She gave him a shake.

"What are you talking about? Are you bewitched? You'd better hurry."

Bao-yu seemed suddenly to waken from his trance and recognized the person he had been speaking to as Aroma. His face turned a deep red with embarrassment and he snatched the fan from her and fled.

After he had gone, Aroma began thinking about the words he had just said and realized that they must have been intended for Dai-yu. She reflected with some alarm that if things between them were as his words seemed to indicate, there was every likelihood of an ugly scandal developing, and wondered how she could arrange matters to prevent it. Preoccupied with these reflections, she stood as motionless and unseeing as her master had done a few moments before. [. . .]

From Chapter 89

[Lin Dai-yu Vows to Waste Away after Hearing of Jia Bao-yu's Engagement]

[The remaining chapters of Volumes 2 and 3 show Bao-yu facing increasing pressure as he grows up and is forced to come to terms with marriage and his Civil Service examinations. Like his frail cousin Dai-yu, for whom his affection has increased, Bao-yu becomes prone to fits and ailing health, exacerbated by conflict with his father, Jia Zheng, whose disappointment in his intelligent but insouciant son grows ever stronger. Meanwhile the heyday of the Jia family has passed, and mismanagement, corruption, and misfortune lead to one crisis after another. As the narrative resumes, Jia Zheng has been called away to the ministry and Bao-yu has again slackened in his studies, though he keeps up appearances by attending school. Having been reminded of one of his maids, Skybright, who died earlier, Bao-yu in a melancholy mood has written an ode to her memory. Chapter 89 offers another example of Dai-yu's sensitivity and of the pastimes of the cousins living in their separate rooms in Prospect Garden.]

[. . .] When he had finished writing, Bao-yu took a burning joss-stick, held the paper to it, and set the ode alight. He sat in silence until the bundle of incense-sticks had burned to the end, then opened the door and walked out.

"Why are you coming out again so soon?" inquired Aroma. "Are you feeling low again?"

He feigned a laugh.

"I was rather depressed earlier on. I needed to be on my own for a bit in a quiet place. I feel better now. I think I shall take a stroll."

He walked straight out into the Garden. When he reached the Naiad's House, he called from the courtyard:

"Is Cousin Lin at home?"

"Who's that?" replied Nightingale.

She raised the door-curtain and saw him standing there.

"Oh it's you, Master Bao," she said with a smile. "Miss Lin is inside. Please come in and sit down."

As Bao-yu went in with her, Dai-yu's voice could be heard from the inner room:

"Nightingale, please ask Master Bao to come in and wait a moment."

Bao-yu, walking towards the inner room, stopped to admire the pair of calligraphic scrolls that hung one on either side of the doorway. The calligraphy looked recent and had been done on strips of dark purple paper, splashed with gold and decorated with a pattern of clouds and dragons. The two lines ran:

> Through casement green the moon shines brightly still;
> In bamboo chronicles the ancients are but empty words.

Bao-yu read them with an appreciative smile and passed through into the inner room.

"What are you doing, coz?" he inquired with a smile.

Dai-yu stood up, took a couple of steps towards him, smiled, and said:

"Please sit down. I'm copying out part of this sutra. I only have two lines left to do. I'll just finish and then we can sit and chat."

She told Snowgoose to pour him some tea.

"Please carry on writing," said Bao-yu. "Don't take any notice of me."

His attention had been caught by a painting hanging on the centre wall of the room. It was a vertical scroll showing Chang E, the Moon Goddess, with one of her attendants, and another fairy, also with an attendant who was carrying what seemed to be a long bag containing clothes. Apart from the clouds that surrounded the figures, there were no background details of any kind. The linear style of the picture was reminiscent of the Song master Li Long-mian. It bore the title "The Contest in the Cold," written in the antique *ba-fen* style.[24]

"Have you hung this picture of the Contest in the Cold here recently, coz?" asked Bao-yu.

"Yes. I remembered it yesterday while they were tidying the room, and so I brought it out and told them to hang it up."

"What's the allusion in the title?"

Dai-yu laughed.

"Surely you know! It's such a well-known poem . . ."

"I can't quite recall it at present," confessed Bao-yu, smiling rather sheepishly. "Please tell me."

"Don't you remember Li Shang-yin's[25] lines:

Braving the cold,
Fairy Frost and Lady Moon
Parade their rival charms . . . ?"

"Of course!" exclaimed Bao-yu. "How exquisite! And what an unusual subject! This is the perfect time of year to have it up too."

He continued to amble round the room, inspecting it in a leisurely fashion, and Snowgoose brought him a cup of tea. He drank his tea, and in a few minutes Dai-yu finished the section of the sutra she was copying, and stood up.

"Forgive me," she said.

"You know you don't have to stand on ceremony with me," he replied with a smile.

He observed that she was wearing a little pale blue fur-lined dress embroidered with flowers, and an ermine-lined sleeveless jacket, while her hair was coiled up in her everyday style and had no flowers in it but only a flat hairpin of purest gold. Her padded underskirt was pink, and embroidered with flowers. How graceful she seemed, as a jade tree leaning in the wind; how gentle, as a fragrant lotus whose petals are moist with dew!

"Have you been playing your Qin[26] at all these last few days?" he inquired.

"Not for a day or two. This sutra-copying makes my hands too cold."

---

[24] *ba-fen* style: Or *pa fen*; a relatively symmetrical style of Chinese calligraphy.

[25] Li Shang-yin (c. 813–858): A highly influential poet of the Tang dynasty (618–907), known for his passionate intensity as well as his innovative use of irony.

[26] Qin: A seven-stringed zither; one of the oldest and so most distinguished of Chinese musical instruments, classed among the Four Treasures of the Chinese literati.

"Maybe it's just as well," said Bao-yu. "I know the Qin is a fine thing in its way, but I can't see that it does any real good. I have never heard of it bringing prosperity or long life; it only seems to cause sorrow and distress. And it must be such a labour to memorize those tablatures. I think, coz, that with your delicate constitution you should avoid anything so strenuous."

Dai-yu smiled somewhat scornfully.

"Is that the Qin you play?" Bao-yu went on, pointing to one hanging on the wall. "Isn't it rather short?"

"Not really," explained Dai-yu. "When I was a little girl and first started learning, I couldn't reach on an ordinary Qin, so we had this one specially made. It's not a collector's piece of course, made with wood 'saved from the flames'—but it has a Crane Fairy and a Phoenix Tail, and the Dragon's Pool sound-hole and Goose Foot tuning-pegs are all in the correct proportions. And look at the crackling on the varnish. Doesn't that look just like Cow Hair crackle to you? The fine workmanship gives it a beautiful tone."

"Have you been writing any poetry recently, coz?" Bao-yu went on to inquire.

"Not much, not since the last meeting of the club."

He laughed. "You can't fool me. I heard you chanting. How did it go now?

Why grieve to watch
The wheel of Karma turn?
A moonlike purity remains
My constant goal . . .

I found your setting very striking. You did write it, didn't you?"

Dai-yu: "How did you come to hear it?"

Bao-yu: "I heard you playing when I was walking back from Smartweed Loggia a few days ago. The music was so lovely and I didn't want to interrupt you, so I just listened quietly for a while and then went on my way. There is one thing I've been meaning to ask you. I noticed that in the first part you use a level-tone rhyme, but suddenly change to an oblique tone at the end. Why is that?"

Dai-yu: "That is free composition. One doesn't have to abide by any rules. One just goes wherever the inspiration takes one."

Bao-yu: "I see! I'm afraid such subtleties were lost on my untrained ears."

Dai-yu: "True lovers of music have always been few."

Bao-yu realized that without meaning to he had said the wrong thing, and was afraid that he had alienated Dai-yu. He sat there for a while. There was so much he wanted to say, but he was now too nervous to open his mouth again. Dai-yu had also spoken without thinking, and on reflection she wished that she had not been so scathing, and withdrew silently into her shell. Her silence only increased Bao-yu's own misgivings, and finally in some embarrassment he stood up and said:

"I must be on my way to see Tan. Please don't get up."

"Give her my regards when you see her, will you?" said Dai-yu.

"I will," he replied, and departed. Dai-yu saw him to the door, then returned to her chair and sat brooding to herself.

"Bao-yu's been so odd recently. He doesn't seem to say what he's thinking. He's friendly one minute and distant the next. I wonder what it means?"

Nightingale came in.

"Have you finished copying for today, Miss? Shall I put your writing things away now?"

"I shan't be doing any more," replied Dai-yu. "You can clear them away."

Dai-yu went into the inner room and lay down on her bed, slowly turning all these things over in her mind. Nightingale came in to ask if she would like some tea.

"No, thank you. I just want to be alone and lie down for a bit."

"Very well, Miss."

Nightingale went out, to find Snowgoose standing in the doorway, staring oddly in front of her. She went up to her and said:

"What's the matter with you?"

Snowgoose was lost in thought, and the question gave her quite a turn.

"Sh! Don't say a word! I've heard something very strange. If I tell you, you must promise not to breathe a word to anyone."

As she said this Snowgoose shot her lips out in the direction of Dai-yu's bedroom, then began walking away, nodding to Nightingale to follow her. They reached the foot of the terrace and she began again in a whisper:

"Have you heard that Bao-yu's engaged to be married?"

Nightingale gave a start.

"I don't believe you! It can't be true!"

"It is! Nearly everyone knows except us."

"Who told you?"

"Scribe. His fiancée is a prefect's daughter. She's very good-looking and comes from a wealthy family."

As Snowgoose was speaking, Nightingale heard Dai-yu cough and thought she could hear her getting up again. Worried that she might come out and overhear them, she took Snowgoose by the hand and motioned to her to be silent. She looked inside, but all seemed quiet. She asked Snowgoose in a low whisper:

"What exactly did Scribe say?"

"Do you remember," replied Snowgoose, "a day or two ago you sent me to Miss Tan's to thank her for something? Well, she wasn't home, but Scribe was. We started chatting, and one of us happened to mention Master Bao and his naughty ways. Scribe said: 'When will Master Bao ever grow up? He doesn't take anything seriously. And to think that he's engaged to be married now—and still as silly as ever!' I asked her if the engagement had been settled, and she said that it had and that the go-between was a Mr. Wang, a close relation on the Ning-guo side, so the whole thing was a foregone conclusion."

Nightingale put her head thoughtfully to one side. "How very strange!" she thought to herself.

"Why has no one in the family mentioned it?" she asked Snowgoose.

"That's Her Old Ladyship's idea—so Scribe said. It's in case Bao-yu finds out and is distracted from his studies. She made me promise not to tell a soul, and said she would blame *me* if word got around."

Snowgoose pointed towards the house.

"That's why I haven't mentioned it in front of *her*. But today when you asked, I thought I could tell you the truth."

As she was speaking there was a loud squawk from the parrot:

"Miss Lin's back! Put the kettle on!"

The two maids had the fright of their lives and turned round expecting to see Dai-yu. But seeing no one, and realizing their mistake, they scolded the bird and went inside. They found Dai-yu at her chair. She was out of breath and had clearly only just sat down. Nightingale asked rather awkwardly if she wanted any tea or water.

"Where have you two been all this time?" asked Dai-yu. "No one came when I called."

She walked back to the kang and lay down once more facing the wall, telling them to let down the bed-curtains. They did so and left the room, each secretly thinking to herself that she had overheard them, but neither daring to say so.

Dai-yu, brooding on her bed, *had* heard them whispering outside and had crept to the door to eavesdrop. Details of their conversation eluded her but the main substance was clear. She felt as though plunged into a great ocean. The prophecy contained in her nightmare was to be fulfilled after all. Bitterness and grief overwhelmed her. There was only one way of escape left. She must die. She must not live to see this dreaded thing take place. Without Bao-yu what would life be worth anyway? She had no parents of her own to turn to. Surely if she neglected herself daily from now on, in a few months she would be able to undermine her health and leave this world and all its troubles behind her?

Having formed this resolution, without bothering to pull up her quilt or put on any extra clothes she closed her eyes and pretended to be asleep. Nightingale and Snowgoose came in several times to wait on her, but seeing no sign of movement did not dare disturb her, even for dinner. Later, when the lamps were lit, Nightingale peeped through the curtains and saw that she had fallen asleep with her covers in a crumpled heap at her feet. Afraid she might catch cold, Nightingale gently pulled them over her. Dai-yu lay still until she had gone, then pushed them back again.

Meanwhile Nightingale questioned Snowgoose again:

"Are you sure you weren't making it up?"

"Of course I wasn't!" replied Snowgoose rather indignantly.

Nightingale: "But how did Scribe come to know?"

Snowgoose: "It was Crimson that heard it first at Mrs. Lian's."

Nightingale: "I think Miss Lin must have overheard us. I can tell that something has upset her greatly. We must be careful never to mention it again."

The two maids tidied up and made themselves ready for bed. Nightingale went in to see how Dai-yu was and found the quilt in the same crumpled heap as before. She pulled it lightly back. That night passed without further event.

The next morning Dai-yu rose early without waking either of the maids, and sat up on her own, lost in thought. Nightingale awoke to find her already up and said in surprise:

"You're up very early this morning, Miss!"

"I know I am," replied Dai-yu rather curtly. "It's because I went to sleep so early last night."

Nightingale quickly dressed and woke Snowgoose, and the two of them waited on Dai-yu at her toilet. She sat staring into the mirror. Tears began to stream down her face, and her silk scarf was soon wet through. In the poet's words:

> A wasted face
>   reflected in the spring stream;
> And pity flows
>   from face to mirror'd face
>   and back again.

Nightingale stood by, not daring to utter a single comforting word, for fear that she would say the wrong thing and cause further anguish. Dai-yu sat motionless for a considerable while, then finally began her morning toilet, negligently, her eyes still brimming with tears. When it was done, she remained sitting where she was for a few minutes, then asked Nightingale to light some of the Tibetan incense.

"But Miss," protested Nightingale, "you've hardly had any sleep. What do you want to go lighting incense for? You're surely not going to start copying the sutra again are you?"

Dai-yu nodded.

"But you woke so early, Miss. If you start writing now you'll exhaust yourself."

"What does that matter? The sooner it's finished the better. I only want to do it to keep myself occupied anyway. And in days to come you will have my writing to remember me by."

As she said this tears began to pour down her cheeks, and Nightingale was no longer able to offer consolation but burst into tears herself.

Dai-yu was resolved that from this day forward she would deliberately destroy her health. She soon lost her appetite, and gradually began to waste away. Bao-yu visited her whenever he could after school, but although there were a million things she wanted to tell him, her consciousness that they were no longer children inhibited her from showing her affection by teasing him in the old way, and rendered her powerless to express what was preying on her mind. Bao-yu for his part would have liked to talk with her sincerely and offer her some genuine comfort; but he was afraid of aggravating her illness by offending her in some way, and so when he did see her, he merely inquired politely how she was feeling and added a few words of encouragement. Theirs was a true case of estrangement in the very extremity of love.

Grandmother Jia and Lady Wang showed a motherly concern for Dai-yu, which however went no further than calling in the doctor. Not knowing the inner source of her illness, they put it down to her sickly constitution, and Nightingale and Snowgoose were much too afraid to tell them the truth. Dai-yu weakened day by day. After a fortnight her stomach had shrunk to the point where she could no longer bring herself to eat even gruel. Every conversation she overheard during the day seemed to her to be connected in some way with Bao-yu's marriage. Every servant she saw from Green Delights seemed to be involved in the preparations. When Aunt Xue came to visit her, Bao-chai's absence confirmed her suspicions. She began to hope that no one would come to see her. She refused to take her medicine. Her only remaining wish was to be left alone, and to die as quickly as possible. In her dreams she constantly heard people addressing the new "Mrs. Bao," and her mind grew totally obsessed with the idea, like the proverbial drinker who, seeing a curved bow reflected in his cup, is convinced that he has swallowed a snake.

A few weeks of this self-imposed starvation and it seemed as if she must soon die. Even the thinnest of gruels was now an impossibility. Her breathing was scarcely perceptible. She was hanging on by the slenderest thread. To learn whether she was to survive this crisis or not, please turn to the next chapter.

From Chapter 90

[Lin Dai-yu Hears Good News and Begins to Recover;
Grandmother Jia Determines Jia Bao-yu's Fate]

During the first week or so of Dai-yu's decline, when Grandmother Jia and her aunts had taken it in turns to visit her, she had still possessed strength enough to make an occasional response to their inquiries. But now she would eat nothing whatsoever, and for several days had hardly said a word. The strange thing was that although at times she seemed unconscious, there were periods when she was perfectly lucid. They began to suspect something, and interrogated Nightingale and Snowgoose more than once. But the maids were too scared to say what they knew. Nightingale for her part, while she would have liked to discover the latest news from Scribe, feared that the truth would only provide a further shock and hasten the hour of Dai-yu's death, and so when she saw Scribe, she avoided the subject completely. Snowgoose, as the transmitter of the news, felt responsible for Dai-yu's condition and longed for a hundred tongues to cry out "I never said a word!" She too, when questioned, maintained a close silence.

Nightingale, seeing that Dai-yu would eat nothing, and judging that all hope was now gone, stood by her bedside crying for a while, then went outside and whispered to Snowgoose:

"Go in and watch her carefully. I'm going straight over to tell Her Old Ladyship, Her Ladyship and Mrs. Lian. She has definitely taken a turn for the worse today."

She departed, and Snowgoose went in to take her place. She found Dai-yu lying very still, as if in a deep sleep. Being only a child with no experience of such things, she took this state for death itself, and began to feel both tearful and frightened. If only Nightingale would hurry up and come back! At that very moment she heard footsteps outside the window. That must be Nightingale now! Breathing a sigh of relief, she stood up at once and went to the doorway of the inner chamber, lifting the door-curtain in expectation. She heard the swish of the outer door-curtain, and in came not Nightingale but Scribe, sent by Tan-chun to inquire how Dai-yu was. Seeing Snowgoose standing in the inner doorway, she asked:

"How is Miss Lin?"

Snowgoose nodded to her to come in and Scribe entered the inner room with her. She noticed that Nightingale was not there, and when she looked at Dai-yu and saw how feebly she was breathing, a look of horror came over her face.

"Where's Nightingale gone?" she asked.

"To tell their Ladyships," replied Snowgoose.

Certain that Dai-yu, if not actually dead, was by this time at any rate "dead to the world," Snowgoose decided to take advantage of Nightingale's absence to question Scribe. Taking her by the hand, she asked in a whisper:

"Did you really mean what you said the other day—about Mr. Wang, and Master Bao's betrothal?"

"Of course I did!" replied Scribe.

"When was it settled?"

"I never said it was! What I told you was just what I'd heard from Crimson. Later I was at Mrs. Lian's myself, and heard her say to Patience that the whole thing was something the Master's literary gentlemen had thought up, to please him and provide themselves with a connection. As it happened Lady Xing didn't even think it a good match. But even if she had approved, everyone knows how unreliable her judgement is. Besides, Her Old Ladyship already has someone else in mind for Master Bao, someone here in the Garden. Lady Xing had no idea of that, of course, and Her Old Ladyship only allowed them to go ahead with the normal inquiries for the Master's sake. Mrs. Lian said Her Old Ladyship wants Bao-yu to marry one of his cousins, and her mind is quite made up, so any other proposals are a waste of time."

Snowgoose was beside herself.

"Then our mistress is dying for nothing!" she exclaimed.

"What *do* you mean?" asked Scribe.

"Don't you know? The other day Miss Lin overheard me telling Nightingale about the betrothal—that's why she has brought herself to this terrible state now."

"Sh!" whispered Scribe. "She might hear you!"

"She's completely dead to the world," replied Snowgoose. "Look—she can't last more than a day or two now."

As she was speaking, the door-curtain was drawn aside and in came Nightingale.

"For goodness' sake!" she exclaimed. "Can't you two do your gossiping somewhere else? You might as well *drive* her to her death!"

"I simply cannot believe such strange goings-on," muttered Scribe.

"My dear Scribe," retorted Nightingale, "don't misunderstand me please. I didn't mean to offend you, but you must be so stupid to gossip like that."

The three of them were interrupted by a sudden cough from Dai-yu's bed on the kang. Nightingale hurried to the bedside, while Snowgoose and Scribe stood in silence. Nightingale bent down and whispered to Dai-yu, who was lying with her face to the wall:

"Would you like some water, Miss?"

There was a barely audible "yes" and Snowgoose promptly filled a cup half-full with hot water and handed it to Nightingale, who held it in the palm of her hand. Scribe meanwhile had moved towards the kang and was about to speak to Dai-yu when Nightingale motioned to her not to say anything and she checked herself. They stood waiting. After a short interval Dai-yu coughed again and Nightingale inquired at once:

"Would you like the water now, Miss?"

There was another faint "yes" and Dai-yu seemed to want to lift her head, but was too feeble to do so. Nightingale climbed up onto the kang by her side and, holding the cup in her hand, first tested the water to make sure it was not too hot, then raised it to Dai-yu's mouth, supporting her head until the rim of the cup reached her lips. Dai-yu took a sip, and Nightingale was about to remove the cup when she saw that Dai-yu wanted some more. She held the cup where it was. Dai-yu drank again, shook her head to show that it was enough, took a deep breath and lay down once more. After a pause she opened her eyes a fraction and asked:

"Was that Scribe I heard talking just now?"

"Yes, Miss," replied Nightingale.

Scribe was still in the room and came up to the kang at once to convey Tan-chun's message. Dai-yu stared at her for a minute and nodded. After a pause she said:

"When you go home, give Miss Tan my regards will you?"

Scribe took this to mean that Dai-yu wanted her to leave and made her way quietly out of the room.

Now although Dai-yu's condition was extremely grave, her power of reason was unimpaired. She was aware of Scribe's arrival and vaguely heard the first words she exchanged with Snowgoose. She felt too exhausted to cope with a visitor, and so pretended to be asleep. But as the conversation progressed, it became clear to her that what she had taken to be a fact had never been more than a proposal. And then she heard Scribe repeat Xi-feng's words, that Grandmother Jia intended to marry Bao-yu to one of his cousins, to one that lived in the Garden; and who could that be but herself? Just as at the winter solstice Yin gives birth to Yang, so now in her mind darkness gave way to light. She suddenly felt much clearer within herself, decided to drink some water, and even spoke to Scribe.

It was at this moment that Grandmother Jia, Lady Wang, Li Wan, and Xi-feng arrived on the scene, in response to Nightingale's urgent summons. Now that Dai-yu's inner doubts had been so dramatically dissipated, she no longer presented the spectacle of the dying maiden that Nightingale had led them to expect. She was still weak and low in spirits, but was able with an effort to say a few words in reply to their inquiries. Xi-feng called Nightingale over and questioned her:

"Miss Lin is not nearly as ill as you made out. Why did you exaggerate so? We were most alarmed."

"Honestly, ma'am," replied Nightingale, "only a while ago she was in a bad way. That's why I came over. I would never have dared to bother you otherwise. She does seem a lot better now. It's most strange."

Grandmother Jia said to Xi-feng with a smile:

"You shouldn't take what she says so seriously, my dear. She doesn't understand such things. Mind you she was quite right to speak up if she noticed anything the matter. I've no time for young people who never say a word or do anything for fear of appearing foolish."

The ladies stayed for a few minutes chatting, then, deciding that all was well, returned to their apartments.

Truly:

No remedy but love
Can make the lovesick well;
Only the hand that tied the knot
Can loose the tiger's bell.

After this Dai-yu's condition continued to improve steadily, and Snowgoose and Nightingale offered many a secret prayer of thanks to the Lord Buddha.

"Thank goodness she's better!" said Snowgoose to Nightingale. "But what an odd illness! And what an odd way to get better!"

"We know what caused it," said Nightingale. "It's this sudden recovery that's puzzling. I think Bao-yu and Miss Lin must be destined to be married after all. 'The course of true love never did run smooth,' but 'Marriages made in heaven can never be broken' either! You can tell they are destined to be together. That's what they both want in their hearts, and that must be what Heaven has decreed for them. Remember what happened to Bao-yu last year, when I told him Miss Lin was going home to the South? He nearly died of shock, and made the most terrible scene. And now that one remark of ours has nearly been the death of her. Theirs must be a bond from some previous life, made a century ago at the Rock of Rebirth!"

They exchanged a secret smile at this romantic theory, and Snowgoose exclaimed: "Thank goodness she's better anyway! We must never mention it again! Even if Bao-yu were to marry another lady and I witnessed the wedding with my own eyes, I swear I wouldn't breathe a word of it to anyone."

Nightingale laughed.

"Well said!"

Theirs were not the only secret discussions on this subject. Dai-yu's strange illness and stranger recovery gave rise to a great deal of whispering and speculation in the household, which soon reached the ears of Xi-feng. Lady Wang and Lady Xing vaguely suspected something, and Grandmother Jia herself had a shrewd idea what was at the bottom of it all. The four ladies were gathered one day in Grandmother Jia's apartment, and in the course of their conversation the subject of Dai-yu's illness came up.

"There is something I want to say to you all," said Grandmother Jia. "Bao-yu and Miss Lin have been together ever since they were little, and this has never troubled me, as I have always thought of them as children. But of late I have noticed how frequent these illnesses of hers are becoming—how suddenly they come, and how suddenly they go—a sure sign that she is growing up. It really won't do to allow them to stay together indefinitely. What do you all think?"

After a thoughtful silence Lady Wang replied, choosing her words with care:

"Miss Lin reads such a lot into things. And Bao-yu's childish manner is deceptive: He can be extremely stupid and tactless. If we remove either one of them from the Garden, won't it be too obvious? It has always been said that every boy becomes a groom and every girl becomes a bride. Don't you think, Mother, that a better solution would be to go ahead as quickly as possible and get them both married?"

Grandmother Jia frowned.

"I know that Miss Lin's peculiar temperament is in some ways attractive. But I don't think we could possibly have her as a wife for Bao-yu. Besides, I'm afraid that with such a delicate constitution she is unlikely to live to any age. I'm sure Bao-chai is in every respect the more suitable choice."

"Of course we all agree with you there, Mother," said Lady Wang. "But we must find a husband for Miss Lin too. If we do not, and if she has taken a fancy to Bao-yu—after all, it is only natural for a girl to have such feelings as she grows up—it might make things very difficult if she were then to discover that he was already betrothed to Bao-chai."

"There can be no question," replied Grandmother Jia, "of marrying an outsider before one of the family. The order must be: first to marry Bao-yu, then to have Miss Lin betrothed. Besides Miss Lin is two years younger than Bao-yu anyway. If I understand you correctly, we shall have to conceal Bao-yu's betrothal from her . . ."

Xi-feng turned at once to the various maids present:

"Is that clear? Not a *word* of Master Bao's betrothal to anyone! If I catch one of you talking about it I shall show no mercy."

"Feng dear," continued Grandmother Jia, "I have noticed that since your illness you have taken less interest in what happens in the Garden. You really must give it more of your attention. It's not just the sort of thing we have been talking about. Any repetition of that disgraceful drinking and gambling that was discovered among the servants last year must be prevented at all costs. Be rather more particular, will you, and keep a watchful eye on what goes on. They need to be disciplined, and you seem to be the one they respect most."

"Yes, Grannie," said Xi-feng.

The ladies sat talking for a while longer, then left to go their separate ways. [. . .]

FROM CHAPTER 96

[Lin Dai-yu Learns That Jia Bao-yu
Will Marry Xue Bao-chai]

[In the chapters omitted here, the family's declining fortunes increasingly worry Jia Zheng and Xi-Feng, who has become chronically ill. Several minor incidents show that the moral authority within the household has broken down further. Two ominous events lead to speculation about the future of the family: Crab trees are struck by the blight blossom out of season, and, more important, Bao-yu loses the jade stone that came into the world with him at his birth. With the jade stone missing, Bao-yu begins to lose his wits and falls into a state of mental lethargy from which, according to a fortune teller, he can be rescued only by marriage to a "lady with a destiny of gold." Meanwhile Jia Zheng has been appointed to an official post that will take him away from his home. These factors lead Jia Zheng and Lady Wang to determine that the marriage between Bao-yu and Bao-chai must take place immediately, though the reader knows that the "lady with a destiny of gold" can only be Dai-yu. After Grandmother Jia learns from the maid Aroma that Bao-yu is in love with Dai-yu, Xi-Feng comes up with a plan to trick Bao-yu into marrying Bao-chai by making him believe that his bride is Dai-yu. As Chapter 96 begins, Dai-yu knows nothing of these arrangements.]

[. . .] A day or two after these events, Dai-yu, having eaten her breakfast, decided to take Nightingale with her to visit Grandmother Jia. She wanted to pay her respects, and also thought the visit might provide some sort of distraction for herself. She had hardly left the Naiad's House, when she remembered that she had left her handker-chief at home, and sent Nightingale back to fetch it, saying that she would walk ahead slowly and wait for her to catch up. She had just reached the corner behind the rockery at Drenched Blossoms Bridge — the very spot where she had once buried the flowers with Bao-yu — when all of a sudden she heard the sound of sobbing. She stopped at once and listened. She could not tell whose voice it was, nor could she dis-tinguish what it was that the voice was complaining of, so tearfully and at such length. It really was most puzzling. She moved forward again cautiously and as she turned the corner, saw before her the source of the sobbing, a maid with large eyes and thick-set eyebrows.

Before setting eyes on this girl, Dai-yu had guessed that one of the many maids in the Jia household must have had an unhappy love-affair, and had come here to cry her heart out in secret. But now she laughed at the very idea. "How could such an ungainly creature as this know the meaning of love?" she thought to herself. "This must be one of the odd-job girls, who has probably been scolded by one of the senior maids." She looked more closely, but still could not place the girl. Seeing Dai-yu, the maid ceased her weeping, wiped her cheeks, and rose to her feet.

"Come now, what are you so upset about?" inquired Dai-yu.

"Oh Miss Lin!" replied the maid, amid fresh tears. "Tell me if you think it fair. *They* were talking about it, and how was I to know better? Just because I say one thing wrong, is that a reason for sister to start hitting me?"

Dai-yu did not know what she was talking about. She smiled, and asked again: "Who is your sister?"

"Pearl," answered the maid.

From this, Dai-yu concluded that she must work in Grandmother Jia's apartment. "And what is your name?"

"Simple."

Dai-yu laughed. Then:

"Why did she hit you? What did you say that was so wrong?"

"That's what I'd like to know! It was only to do with Master Bao marrying Miss Chai!"

The words struck Dai-yu's ears like a clap of thunder. Her heart started thump-ing fiercely. She tried to calm herself for a moment, and told the maid to come with her. The maid followed her to the secluded corner of the garden, where the Flower Burial Mound was situated. Here Dai-yu asked her:

"Why should she hit you for mentioning Master Bao's marriage to Miss Chai?"

"Her Old Ladyship, Her Ladyship, and Mrs. Lian," replied Simple, "have decided that as the Master is leaving soon, they are going to arrange with Mrs. Xue to marry Master Bao and Miss Chai as quickly as possible. They want the wedding to turn his luck, and then . . ."

Her voice tailed off. She stared at Dai-yu, laughed, and continued:

"Then, as soon as those two are married, they are going to find a husband for you, Miss Lin."

Dai-yu was speechless with horror. The maid went on regardless:

"But how was I to know that they'd decided to keep it quiet, for fear of embarrassing Miss Chai? All I did was say to Aroma, that serves in Master Bao's room: 'Won't it be a fine to-do here soon, when Miss Chai comes over, or Mrs. Bao . . . what *will* we have to call her?' That's all I said. What was there in that to hurt sister Pearl? Can *you* see, Miss Lin? She came across and hit me straight in the face and said I was talking rubbish and disobeying orders, and would be dismissed from service! How was I to know their Ladyships didn't want us to mention it? Nobody told me, and she just hit me!"

She started sobbing again. Dai-yu's heart felt as though oil, soy-sauce, sugar, and vinegar had all been poured into it at once. She could not tell which flavour predominated, the sweet, the sour, the bitter, or the salty. After a few moments' silence, she said in a trembling voice:

"Don't talk such rubbish. Any more of that, and you'll be beaten again. Off you go!"

She herself turned back in the direction of the Naiad's House. Her body felt as though it weighed a hundred tons, her feet were as wobbly as if she were walking on cotton-floss. She could only manage one step at a time. After an age, she still had not reached the bank by Drenched Blossoms Bridge. She was going so slowly, with her feet about to collapse beneath her, and in her giddiness and confusion had wandered off course and increased the distance by about a hundred yards. She reached Drenched Blossoms Bridge only to start drifting back again along the bank in the direction she had just come from, quite unaware of what she was doing.

Nightingale had by now returned with the handkerchief, but could not find Dai-yu anywhere. She finally saw her, pale as snow, tottering along, her eyes staring straight in front of her, meandering in circles. Nightingale also caught sight of a maid disappearing in the distance beyond Dai-yu, but could not make out who it was. She was most bewildered, and quickened her step.

"Why are you turning back again, Miss?" she asked softly. "Where are you heading for?"

Dai-yu only heard the blurred outline of this question. She replied:

"I want to ask Bao-yu something."

Nightingale could not fathom what was going on, and could only try to guide her on her way to Grandmother Jia's apartment. When they came to the entrance, Dai-yu seemed to feel clearer in mind. She turned, saw Nightingale supporting her, stopped for a moment, and asked:

"What are you doing here?"

"I went to fetch your handkerchief," replied Nightingale, smiling anxiously. "I saw you over by the bridge and hurried across. I asked you where you were going, but you took no notice."

"Oh!" said Dai-yu with a smile. "I thought you had come to see Bao-yu. What else did we come here for?"

Nightingale could see that her mind was utterly confused. She guessed that it was something that the maid had said in the garden, and only nodded with a faint smile in reply to Dai-yu's question. But to herself she was trying to imagine what sort of an encounter this was going to be, between the young master who had already lost his wits, and her young mistress who was now herself a little touched. Despite her apprehensions, she dared not prevent the meeting, and helped Dai-yu into the room. The funny thing was that Dai-yu now seemed to have recovered her strength. She did not wait for Nightingale but raised the portière herself, and walked into the room. It was very quiet inside. Grandmother Jia had retired for her afternoon nap. Some of the maids had sneaked off to play, some were having forty winks themselves, and others had gone to wait on Grandmother Jia in her bedroom. It was Aroma who came out to see who was there, when she heard the swish of the portière. Seeing that it was Dai-yu, she greeted her politely:

"Please come in and sit down, Miss."

"Is Master Bao at home?" asked Dai-yu with a smile.

Aroma did not know that anything was amiss, and was about to answer, when she saw Nightingale make an urgent movement with her lips from behind Dai-yu's back, pointing to her mistress and making a warning gesture with her hand. Aroma had no idea what she meant and dared not ask. Undeterred, Dai-yu walked on into Bao-yu's room. He was sitting up in bed, and when she came in made no move to get up or welcome her, but remained where he was, staring at her and giving a series of silly laughs. Dai-yu sat down uninvited, and she too began to smile and stare back at Bao-yu. There were no greetings exchanged, no courtesies, in fact no words of any kind. They just sat there staring into each other's faces and smiling like a pair of half-wits. Aroma stood watching, completely at a loss.

Suddenly Dai-yu said:

"Bao-yu, why are you sick?"

Bao-yu laughed.

"I'm sick because of Miss Lin."

Aroma and Nightingale grew pale with fright. They tried to change the subject, but their efforts only met with silence and more senseless smiles. By now it was clear to Aroma that Dai-yu's mind was as disturbed as Bao-yu's.

"Miss Lin has only just recovered from her illness," she whispered to Nightingale. "I'll ask Ripple to help you take her back. She should go home and lie down." Turning to Ripple, she said: "Go with Nightingale and accompany Miss Lin home. And no stupid chattering on the way, mind."

Ripple smiled, and without a word came over to help Nightingale. The two of them began to help Dai-yu to her feet. Dai-yu stood up at once, unassisted, still staring fixedly at Bao-yu, smiling and nodding her head.

"Come on, Miss!" urged Nightingale. "It's time to go home and rest."

"Of course!" exclaimed Dai-yu. "It's time!"

She turned to go. Still smiling and refusing any assistance from the maids, she strode out at twice her normal speed. Ripple and Nightingale hurried after her. On leaving Grandmother Jia's apartment, Dai-yu kept on walking, in quite the wrong direction. Nightingale hurried up to her and took her by the hand.

"This is the way, Miss."

Still smiling, Dai-yu allowed herself to be led, and followed Nightingale towards the Naiad's House. When they were nearly there, Nightingale exclaimed:

"Lord Buddha be praised! Home at last!"

She had no sooner uttered these words when she saw Dai-yu stumble forwards onto the ground, and give a loud cry. A stream of blood came gushing from her mouth.

To learn if she survived this crisis, please read the next chapter.

Chapter 97

Lin Dai-yu Burns Her Poems
to Signal the End of Her Heart's Folly
And Xue Bao-chai Leaves Home
to Take Part in a Solemn Rite

We have seen how Dai-yu, on reaching the entrance of the Naiad's House, and on hearing Nightingale's cry of relief, slumped forward, vomited blood, and almost fainted. Luckily Nightingale and Ripple were both at hand to assist her into the house. When Ripple left, Nightingale and Snowgoose stood by Dai-yu's bedside and watched her gradually come round.

"Why are you two standing round me crying?" asked Dai-yu, and Nightingale, greatly reassured to hear her talking sense again, replied:

"On your way back from Her Old Ladyship's, Miss, you had quite a nasty turn. We were scared and did not know what to do. That's why we were crying."

"I am not going to die yet!" said Dai-yu, with a bitter smile. But before she could even finish this sentence, she was doubled up and gasping for breath once more.

When she had learned earlier that day that Bao-yu and Bao-chai were to be married, the shock of knowing that what she had feared for so long was now about to come true, had thrown her into such a turmoil that at first she had quite taken leave of her senses. Now that she had brought up the blood, her mind gradually became clearer. Though at first she could remember nothing, when she saw Nightingale crying, Simple's words slowly came back to her. This time she did not succumb to her emotions, but set her heart instead on a speedy death and final settlement of her debt with fate.

Nightingale and Snowgoose could only stand by helplessly. They would have gone to inform the ladies, but were afraid of a repetition of the last occasion, when Xi-feng had rebuked them for creating a false alarm. Ripple had already given all away, however, by the look of horror on her face when she returned to Grandmother Jia's apartment. The old lady, who had just risen from her midday nap, asked her what the matter was, and in her shocked state Ripple told her all that she had just witnessed.

"What a terrible thing!" exclaimed Grandmother Jia, aghast. She sent for Lady Wang and Xi-feng at once, and told them both the news.

"But I gave instructions to everyone to observe strict secrecy," said Xi-feng. "Who can have betrayed us? Now we have another problem on our hands."

"Never mind that for the moment," said Grandmother Jia. "We must first find out how she is."

She took Lady Wang and Xi-feng with her to visit Dai-yu, and they arrived to find her barely conscious, breathing in faint little gasps, her face bloodless and white as snow. After a while she coughed again. A maid brought the spittoon and they watched with horror as she spat out a mouthful of blood and phlegm. Dai-yu faintly opened her eyes, and seeing Grandmother Jia standing at her bedside, struggled to find breath to speak.

"Grandmother! Your love for me has been in vain."

Grandmother Jia was most distraught.

"There now, my dear, you must rest. There is nothing to fear."

Dai-yu smiled faintly and closed her eyes again. A maid came in to tell Xi-feng that the doctor had arrived. The ladies withdrew, and Doctor Wang came in with Jia Lian. He took Dai-yu's pulses, and said:

"As yet, there is no cause for alarm. An obstruction of morbid humours has affected the liver, which is unable to store the blood, and as a consequence her spirit has been disturbed. I shall prescribe a medicine to check the Yin, and to halt the flow of blood. I think all will be well."

Doctor Wang left the room, accompanied by Jia Lian, to write out his prescription.

Grandmother Jia could tell that this time Dai-yu was seriously ill, and as they left the room, she said to Lady Wang and Xi-feng:

"I do not wish to sound gloomy or bring her bad luck, but I fear she has small hope of recovery, poor child. You must make ready her grave-clothes and coffin. Who knows, such preparations may even turn her luck. She may recover, which will be a mercy for us all. But it would be sensible anyway to be prepared for the worst, and not be taken unawares. We shall be so busy over the next few days."

Xi-feng said she would make the necessary arrangements. Grandmother Jia then questioned Nightingale, but she had no idea who it was that had upset Dai-yu. The more she thought about it, the more it puzzled Grandmother Jia, and she said to Xi-feng and Lady Wang:

"I can understand that the two of them should have grown rather fond of one another, after growing up together and playing together as children. But now that they are older and more mature, the time has come for them to observe a certain distance. She must behave properly, if she is to earn my love. It's quite wrong of her to think she can disregard such things. Then all my love *will* have been in vain! What you have told me troubles me."

She returned to her apartment and sent for Aroma again. Aroma repeated to her all that she had told Lady Wang on the previous occasion, and in addition described the scene earlier that day between Dai-yu and Bao-yu.

"And yet, when I saw her just now," said Grandmother Jia, "she still seemed able to talk sense. I simply cannot understand it. Ours is a decent family. We do not tolerate unseemly goings-on. And that applies to foolish romantic attachments. If her illness is of a respectable nature, I do not mind how much we have to spend to get her better. But if she is suffering from some form of lovesickness, no amount of medicine will cure it and she can expect no further sympathy from me either."

"You really shouldn't worry about Cousin Lin, Grandmother," said Xi-feng. "Lian will be visiting her regularly with the doctor. We must concentrate on the wedding arrangements. Early this morning I heard that the finishing touches were being put to the bridal courtyard. You and Aunt Wang and I should go over to Aunt Xue's for a final consultation. There is one thing that occurs to me, however: with Bao-chai there, it will be rather awkward for us to discuss the wedding. Maybe we should ask Aunt Xue to come over here tomorrow evening, and then we can settle everything at once."

Grandmother Jia and Lady Wang agreed that her proposal was a good one, and said:

"It is too late today. Tomorrow after lunch, let us all go over together."

Grandmother Jia's dinner was now served, and Xi-feng and Lady Wang returned to their apartments.

Next day, Xi-feng came over after breakfast. Wishing to sound out Bao-yu according to her plan, she advanced into his room and said:

"Congratulations, Cousin Bao! Uncle Zheng has already chosen a lucky day for your wedding! Isn't that good news?"

Bao-yu stared at her with a blank smile, and nodded his head faintly.

"He is marrying you," went on Xi-feng, with a studied smile, "to your cousin Lin. Are you happy?"

Bao-yu burst out laughing. Xi-feng watched him carefully, but could not make out whether he had understood her, or was simply raving. She went on:

"Uncle Zheng says, you are to marry Miss Lin, *if* you get better. But not if you carry on behaving like a half-wit."

Bao-yu's expression suddenly changed to one of utter seriousness, as he said:

"I'm not a half-wit. You're the half-wit."

He stood up.

"I am going to see Cousin Lin, to set her mind at rest."

Xi-feng quickly put out a hand to stop him.

"She knows already. And, as your bride-to-be, she would be much too embarrassed to receive you now."

"What about when we're married? Will she see me then?"

Xi-feng found this both comic and somewhat disturbing.

"Aroma was right," she thought to herself. "Mention Dai-yu, and while he still talks like an idiot, he at least seems to understand what's going on. I can see we shall be in real trouble, if he sees through our scheme and finds out that his bride is not to be Dai-yu after all."

In reply to his question, she said, suppressing a smile:

"If you behave, she will see you. But not if you continue to act like an imbecile."

To which Bao-yu replied:

"I have given my heart to Cousin Lin. If she marries me, she will bring it with her and put it back in its proper place."

Now this was madman's talk if ever, thought Xi-feng. She left him, and walked back into the outer room, glancing with a smile in Grandmother Jia's direction. The old lady too found Bao-yu's words both funny and distressing.

"I heard you both myself," she said to Xi-feng. "For the present, we must ignore it. Tell Aroma to do her best to calm him down. Come, let us go."

Lady Wang joined them, and the three ladies went across to Aunt Xue's. On arrival there, they pretended to be concerned about the course of Xue Pan's affair. Aunt Xue expressed her profound gratitude for this concern, and gave them the latest news. After they had all taken tea, Aunt Xue was about to send for Bao-chai, when Xi-feng stopped her, saying:

"There is no need to tell Cousin Chai that we are here, Auntie."

With a diplomatic smile, she continued:

"Grandmother's visit today is not purely a social one. She has something of importance to say, and would like you to come over later so that we can all discuss it together."

Aunt Xue nodded.

"Of course."

After a little more chat, the three ladies returned.

That evening Aunt Xue came over as arranged, and after paying her respects to Grandmother Jia, went to her sister's apartment. First there was the inevitable scene of sisterly commiseration over Wang Zi-teng's death. Then Aunt Xue said:

"Just now when I was at Lady Jia's, young Bao came out to greet me and seemed quite well. A little thin perhaps, but certainly not as ill as I had been led to expect from your description and Xi-feng's."

"No, it is really not that serious," said Xi-feng. "It's only Grandmother who will worry so. Her idea is that it would be reassuring for Sir Zheng to see Bao-yu married before he leaves, as who knows when he will be able to come home from his new posting. And then from Bao-yu's own point of view, it might be just the thing to turn his luck. With Cousin Chia's golden locket to counteract the evil influence, he should make a good recovery."

Aunt Xue was willing enough to go along with the idea, but was concerned that Bao-chai might feel rather hard done by.

"I see nothing against it," she said. "But I think we should all take time to think it over properly."

In accordance with Xi-feng's plan, Lady Wang went on:

"As you have no head of family present, we should like you to dispense with the usual trousseau. Tomorrow you should send Ke to let Pan know that while we proceed with the wedding, we shall continue to do our utmost to settle his court-case."

She made no mention of Bao-yu's feelings for Dai-yu, but continued:

"Since you have given your consent, the sooner they are married, the sooner things will look up for everyone."

At this point, Faithful came in to take back a report to Grandmother Jia. Though Aunt Xue was still concerned about Bao-chai's feelings, she saw that in the circumstances she had no choice, and agreed to everything they had suggested. Faithful reported this to Grandmother Jia, who was delighted and sent her back again to ask Mrs. Xue to explain to Bao-chai why it was that things were being done in this way, so that she would not feel unfairly treated. Aunt Xue agreed to do this, and it was settled that Xi-feng and Jia Lian would act as official go-betweens. Xi-feng retired to her apartment, while Aunt Xue and Lady Wang stayed up talking together well into the night.

Next day, Aunt Xue returned to her apartment and told Bao-chai the details of the proposal, adding:

"I have already given my consent."

At first Bao-chai hung her head in silence. Then she began to cry. Aunt Xue said all that she could to comfort her, and went to great lengths to explain the reasoning behind the decision. Bao-chai retired to her room, and Bao-qin went in to keep her company and cheer her up. Aunt Xue also spoke to Ke, instructing him as follows:

"You must leave tomorrow. Find out the latest news of Pan's judgement, and then convey this message to him. Return as soon as you possibly can."

Xue Ke was away for four days, at the end of which time he returned to report to Aunt Xue.

"The Circuit Judge has ratified the verdict of manslaughter, and after the next hearing his final memorial will be presented to the Provincial Supreme Court for confirmation. We should have the commutation money ready. As for Cousin Chai's affair, Cousin Pan approves entirely of your decision, Aunt. And he says that curtailing the formalities will save us a lot of money too. You are not to wait for him, but should do whatever you think best."

Aunt Xue's mind was greatly eased by the knowledge that Xue Pan would soon be free to come home, and that there were now no further obstacles to the marriage. She could see that Bao-chai was unwilling to be married in this way, but reasoned with herself: "Even if this is not what she ideally wants, she is my daughter and has always been obedient and well-bred. She knows I have agreed to it, and will not go against my wishes."

She instructed Xue Ke:

"We must prepare the betrothal-card. Take some fine gold-splash paper and write on it the Stems and Branches of Bao-chai's birth. Then take it to Cousin Lian. Find out which day has been fixed for the exchange of presents, and make all the necessary preparations for sending ours. We shall not be inviting any friends or relatives to the wedding. Pan's friends are a worthless lot, as you yourself said, while our relations consist mainly of the Jias and the Wangs. The Jias are groom's family, and there are no Wangs in the capital at present. When Xiang-yun was engaged, the Shis did not invite us, so we need not get in touch with them. The only person I think we should invite is our business manager, Zhang De-hui. He is an older man and experienced in such things, and will be a help to us."

Xue Ke carried out these instructions, and sent a servant over with the betrothal-card. Next day, Jia Lian came to visit Aunt Xue. After paying his respects, he said:

"I have consulted the almanac, and tomorrow is a most propitious day. I have come here today to propose that our two families exchange presents tomorrow. And please, Aunt Xue, do not be too critical about the arrangements."

He presented the groom's notice, which bore the date of the wedding. Aunt Xue said a few polite words of acceptance and nodded her assent. Jia Lian returned at once and reported to Jia Zheng.

"Report to your Grandmother," said Jia Zheng, "and say that as we are not inviting anybody, the wedding should be kept very simple. She can exercise her discretion over the presents. There is no need to consult me any further."

Jia Lian bowed, and went in to convey this message to Grandmother Jia. Meanwhile Lady Wang had told Xi-feng to bring in the presents that were being given on Bao-yu's behalf, for Grandmother Jia's inspection. She also told Aroma to bring Bao-yu in to see them. He seemed highly amused by the whole business, and said:

"It seems such a waste of everyone's time, to send all these things from here to the Garden, and then have them brought all the way back, when it's all in the family anyway!"

This seemed to Lady Wang and Grandmother Jia sufficient proof that, whatever anyone might have said to the contrary, Bao-yu still had his wits about him, and they said as much to each other in tones of some satisfaction. Faithful and the other maids could not help but smile too. They brought the presents in and displayed them one by one, describing them as they went along:

"A gold necklace and other jewellery in gold and precious stones — altogether eighty pieces; forty bolts of dragon-brocade for formal wear and one hundred and twenty bolts of silks and satins in various colours; one hundred and twenty costumes for the four seasons of the year. They have not had time in the kitchen to prepare the sheep and wine, so this is money in lieu."

Grandmother Jia expressed her approval, and said softly to Xi-feng:

"You must tell Mrs. Xue not to think of this as an empty formality. In due course, when Pan is back and she has that weight off her mind, she can have these made up into dresses for Chai. In the meantime, we shall take care of all the bedcovers for the wedding-day."

"Yes Grandmother," replied Xi-feng, and returned to her apartment. She sent Jia Lian over first to Aunt Xue's, then summoned Zhou Rui and Brightie to receive their instructions.

"When delivering the presents," she said, "you are not to use the main gate. Use the little side-gate in the garden, that used to be kept open. I shall be going over myself shortly. The side-gate has the advantage of being a long way from the Naiad's House. If anyone from any other apartment notices you, you are to tell them on no account to mention it at the Naiad's House."

"Yes ma'am."

The two men departed for Aunt Xue's apartment at the head of a contingent of servants bearing the presents.

Bao-yu was quite taken in by all this. His new feeling of happy anticipation had caused a general improvement in his health, though his manner of speech remained rather eccentric at times. When the present-bearers returned, the whole thing was accomplished without a single name being mentioned. The family and all the staff knew, but were under orders from Xi-feng to maintain absolute secrecy, and no one dared disobey.

Dai-yu meanwhile, for all the medicine she took, continued to grow iller with every day that passed. Nightingale did her utmost to raise her spirits. Our story finds her standing once more by Dai-yu's bedside, earnestly beseeching her:

"Miss, now that things have come to this pass, I simply must speak my mind. We know what it is that's eating your heart out. But can't you see that your fears are groundless? Why, look at the state Bao-yu is in! How can he possibly get married, when he's so ill? You must ignore these silly rumours, stop fretting, and let yourself get better."

Dai-yu gave a wraithlike smile, but said nothing. She started coughing again and brought up a lot more blood. Nightingale and Snowgoose came closer and watched her feebly struggling for breath. They knew that any further attempt to rally her would be to no avail, and could do nothing but stand there watching and weeping. Each day Nightingale went over three or four times to tell Grandmother Jia, but Faithful, judging the old lady's attitude towards Dai-yu to have hardened of late, intercepted her reports and hardly mentioned Dai-yu to her mistress. Grandmother Jia was preoccupied with the wedding arrangements, and in the absence of any particular news of Dai-yu, did not show a great deal of interest in the girl's fate, considering it sufficient that she should be receiving medical attention.

Previously, when she had been ill, Dai-yu had always received frequent visits from everyone in the household, from Grandmother Jia down to the humblest maidservant. But now not a single person came to see her. The only face she saw looking down at her was that of Nightingale. She began to feel her end drawing near, and struggled to say a few words to her:

"Dear Nightingale! Dear sister! Closest friend! Though you were Grandmother's maid before you came to serve me, over the years you have become as a sister to me . . ."

She had to stop for breath. Nightingale felt a pang of pity, was reduced to tears, and could say nothing. After a long silence, Dai-yu began to speak again, searching for breath between words:

"Dear sister! I am so uncomfortable lying down like this. Please help me up and sit next to me."

"I don't think you should sit up, Miss, in your condition. You might get cold in the draught."

Dai-yu closed her eyes in silence. A little later she asked to sit up again. Nightingale and Snowgoose felt they could no longer deny her request. They propped her up on both sides with soft pillows, while Nightingale sat by her on the bed to give further support. Dai-yu was not equal to the effort. The bed where she sat on it seemed to dig into her, and she struggled with all her remaining strength to lift herself up and ease the pain. She told Snowgoose to come closer.

"My poems . . ."

Her voice failed, and she fought for breath again. Snowgoose guessed that she meant the manuscripts she had been revising a few days previously, went to fetch them and laid them on Dai-yu's lap. Dai-yu nodded, then raised her eyes and gazed in the direction of a chest that stood on a stand close by. Snowgoose did not know how to interpret this and stood there at a loss. Dai-yu stared at her now with feverish impatience. She began to cough again and brought up another mouthful of blood. Snowgoose went to fetch some water, and Dai-yu rinsed her mouth and spat into the spittoon. Nightingale wiped her lips with a handkerchief. Dai-yu took the handkerchief from her and pointed to the chest. She tried to speak, but was again seized with an attack of breathlessness and closed her eyes.

"Lie down, Miss," said Nightingale. Dai-yu shook her head. Nightingale thought she must want one of her handkerchiefs, and told Snowgoose to open the chest and bring her a plain white silk one. Dai-yu looked at it, and dropped it on the bed. Making a supreme effort, she gasped out:

"The ones with the writing on . . ."

Nightingale finally realized that she meant the handkerchiefs Bao-yu had sent her, the ones she had inscribed with her own poems. She told Snowgoose to fetch them, and herself handed them to Dai-yu, with these words of advice:

"You must lie down and rest, Miss. Don't start wearing yourself out. You can look at these another time, when you are feeling better."

Dai-yu took the handkerchiefs in one hand and without even looking at them, brought round her other hand (which cost her a great effort) and tried with all her might to tear them in two. But she was so weak that all she could achieve was a pathetic trembling motion. Nightingale knew that Bao-yu was the object of all this bitterness but dared not mention his name, saying instead:

"Miss, there is no sense in working yourself up again."

Dai-yu nodded faintly, and slipped the handkerchiefs into her sleeve.

"Light the lamp," she ordered.

Snowgoose promptly obeyed. Dai-yu looked into the lamp, then closed her eyes and sat in silence. Another fit of breathlessness. Then:

"Make up the fire in the brazier."

Thinking she wanted it for the extra warmth, Nightingale protested:

"You should lie down, Miss, and have another cover on. And the fumes from the brazier might be bad for you."

Dai-yu shook her head, and Snowgoose reluctantly made up the brazier, placing it on its stand on the floor. Dai-yu made a motion with her hand, indicating that she wanted it moved up onto the kang. Snowgoose lifted it and placed it there, temporarily using the floor-stand, while she went out to fetch the special stand they used on the kang. Dai-yu, far from resting back in the warmth, now inclined her body slightly forward—Nightingale had to support her with both hands as she did so. Dai-yu took the handkerchiefs in one hand. Staring into the flames and nodding thoughtfully to herself, she dropped them into the brazier. Nightingale was horrified, but much as she would have liked to snatch them from the flames, she did not dare move her hands and leave Dai-yu unsupported. Snowgoose was out of the room, fetching the brazier-stand, and by now the handkerchiefs were all ablaze.

"Miss!" cried Nightingale. "What are you doing?"

As if she had not heard, Dai-yu reached over for her manuscripts, glanced at them and let them fall again onto the kang. Nightingale, anxious lest she burn these too, leaned up against Dai-yu and freeing one hand, reached out with it to take hold of them. But before she could do so, Dai-yu had picked them up again and dropped them in the flames. The brazier was out of Nightingale's reach, and there was nothing she could do but look on helplessly.

Just at that moment Snowgoose came in with the stand. She saw Dai-yu drop something into the fire, and without knowing what it was, rushed forward to try and save it. The manuscripts had caught at once and were already ablaze. Heedless of the danger to her hands, Snowgoose reached into the flames and pulled out what she could, throwing the paper on the floor and stamping frantically on it. But the fire had done its work, and only a few charred fragments remained.

Dai-yu closed her eyes and slumped back, almost causing Nightingale to topple over with her. Nightingale, her heart thumping in great agitation, called Snowgoose over to help her settle Dai-yu down again. It was too late now to send for anyone. And yet, what if Dai-yu should die during the night, and the only people there were Snowgoose, herself, and the one or two other junior maids in the Naiad's House? They passed a restless night. Morning came at last, and Dai-yu seemed a little more comfortable. But after breakfast she suddenly began coughing and vomiting, and became tense and feverish again. Nightingale could see that she had reached a crisis. She called Snowgoose and the other juniors in and told them to mount watch, while she went to report to Grandmother Jia. But when she reached Grandmother Jia's apartment, she found it almost deserted. Only a few old nannies and charladies were there, keeping an eye.

"Where is Her Old Ladyship?" asked Nightingale.

"We don't know," came the reply in chorus.

That was very odd, thought Nightingale. She went into Bao-yu's room and found that too quite empty, save for a single maid who answered with the same "Don't know." By now Nightingale had more or less guessed the truth. How could they be so heartless and so cruel? And to think that not a soul had come to visit Dai-yu during the past few days! As the bitterness of it struck her with full force, she felt a great wave of resentment break out within her, and turned abruptly to go.

"I shall go and find Bao-yu, and see how *he* is faring! I wonder how he will manage to brazen it out in front of me! I remember last year, when I made up that story about Miss Lin going back to the South, he fell sick with despair. To think that now he should be openly doing a thing like this! Men must have hearts as cold as ice or snow. What hateful creatures they are!"

She was already at Green Delights, and found the courtyard gate ajar. All was quiet within. Suddenly she realized:

"Of course! If he is getting married, he will have a new apartment. But where?"

She was looking around her in uncertainty, when she saw Bao-yu's page boy Inky rush past, and called to him to stop. He came over, and with a broad smile asked:

"What are you doing here, Miss Nightingale?"

"I heard that Master Bao was getting married," replied Nightingale, "and I wanted to watch some of the fun. But I can see I've come to the wrong place. And I don't know when the wedding is taking place, either."

"If I tell you," said Inky in a confidential tone, "you must promise not to tell Snowgoose. We've been given orders not to let any of you know. The wedding's to be tonight. Of course it's not being held here. The Master told Mr. Lian to set aside another apartment."

"What's the matter?" continued Inky, after a pause.

"Nothing," replied Nightingale. "You can go now."

Inky rushed off again. Nightingale stood there for a while, lost in thought. Suddenly she remembered Dai-yu. She might already be dead! Her eyes filled with tears, and clenching her teeth, she said fiercely:

"Bao-yu! If she dies, you may think you can wash your hands of her in this callous way: but when you are happily married, and have your heart's desire, you needn't think you can look *me* in the face again!"

As she walked, she began to weep. She made her way, sobbing pitifully, across the Garden. She was not far from the Naiad's House, when she saw two junior maids standing at the gate, peeping out nervously. They saw her coming, and one of them cried out:

"There's Miss Nightingale! At last!"

Nightingale could see that all was not well. Gesturing to them anxiously to be silent, she hurried in, to find Dai-yu red in the face, the fire from her liver having risen upwards and inflamed her cheeks. This was a dangerous sign, and Nightingale called Dai-yu's old wet-nurse, Nannie Wang, to come and take a look. One glance was enough to reduce this old woman to tears. Nightingale had turned to Nannie Wang as an older person, who could be expected to lend them some courage in this extremity. But she turned out to be quite helpless, and only made Nightingale more distraught than before. Suddenly she thought of someone else she could turn to, and sent one of the younger maids to fetch her with all speed. Her choice might seem a strange one; but Nightingale reasoned that as a widow, Li Wan would certainly be excluded from Bao-yu's wedding festivities. Besides she was in general charge of affairs in the Garden, and it would be in order to ask her to come.

Li Wan was at home correcting some of Jia Lan's poems, when the maid came rushing frantically in and cried:

"Mrs. Zhu! Miss Lin's dying! Everyone over there is in tears!"

Li Wan rose startled to her feet and without a word set off at once for the Naiad's House, followed by her maids Candida and Casta. As she walked, she wept and lamented to herself:

"When I think of all the times we have spent together—oh my poor cousin! So lovely, so gifted! There is hardly another like her. Only Frost Maiden and the Goddess of the Moon could rival her. How can she be leaving us at such a tender age, for that distant land from whence no travellers return . . . And to think that because of Xi-feng's deceitful scheme, I have not been able to show myself at the Naiad's House and have done nothing to show my sisterly affection! Oh the poor, dear girl!"

She was already at the gate of the Naiad's House. There was no sound from within. She began to fret.

"I must be too late! She must have died already and they are resting between their lamentations. I wonder if her grave-clothes and coverlet are ready?"

She quickened her step and hurried on into the room. A young maid standing at the inner doorway had already seen her, and called out:

"Mrs. Zhu is here!"

Nightingale hurried out to meet her.

"How is she?" asked Li Wan.

Nightingale tried to answer but all she could muster was a choked sob. Tears poured down her cheeks like pearls from a broken necklace, as she pointed silently to where Dai-yu lay. Realizing with a pang what Nightingale's pitiable condition must portend, Li Wan asked no more, but went over at once to see for herself. Dai-yu no longer had the strength to speak. When Li Wan said her name a few times, her eyes opened a slit as if in recognition of the voice. But her eyelids and lips could only make a trembling suggestion of a movement. Although she still breathed, it was now more than she could manage to utter a single word, or shed a single tear.

Li Wan turned around and saw that Nightingale was no longer in the room. She asked Snowgoose where she was, and Snowgoose replied:

"In the outer room."

Li Wan hurried out, to find Nightingale lying on the empty bed, her face a ghastly green, her eyes closed, tears streaming down her cheeks. Where her head lay on the embroidered pillow, with its border of fine brocade, was a patch the size of a small plate, wet with her tears and the copious effusions of her nose. When Li Wan called to her, she opened her eyes slowly, and raised herself slightly on the bed.

"Silly girl!" Li Wan upbraided her. "Is this a time for tears? Fetch Miss Lin's grave-clothes and dress her in them. Are you going to leave it till it is too late? Would you have her go naked from the world? Would you ruin her honour?"

This released a fresh flood of tears on Nightingale's part. Li Wan wept herself, fretfully wiping her eyes and patting Nightingale on the shoulder.

"Dear girl! Look how you are upsetting me now, and making me cry. Hurry and get her things ready. If we delay much longer, it will all be over."

They were in this state of trepidation, when they heard footsteps outside, and someone came running into the room in a great flurry, causing Li Wan to start back in alarm. It was Patience. When she saw their tear-stained faces, she stopped abruptly and stared at them aghast for a while.

"Why aren't you over there?" asked Li Wan. "What do you want here?"

As she spoke, Steward Lin's wife also came into the room. Patience answered:

"Mrs. Lian was worried, and sent me to see how things were. As you are here, Mrs. Zhu, I can tell her to set her mind at rest."

Li Wan nodded. Patience went on:

"I should like to see Miss Lin myself." So saying, she walked into Dai-yu's bedchamber, with tears on her cheeks. Li Wan turned to Steward Lin's wife and said:

"You have come just in time. Go and find your husband, and tell him to prepare Miss Lin's coffin and whatever else is necessary. When everything has been satisfactorily arranged, he is to let me know. There is no need to go over to the house."

"Yes, ma'am," replied Lin's wife, but made no move to go.

"Well? Is there something else?" asked Li Wan.

"Mrs. Lian and Her Old Ladyship," replied the steward's wife, "have decided that they need Miss Nightingale in attendance over there."

Before Li Wan could say anything, Nightingale spoke up for herself:

"Mrs. Lin, will you be so kind as to leave now? Can't you even wait until she is dead? We will leave her then, you need not fear. How can you be so . . ."

She stopped short, thinking it inadvisible to be so rude, and changing her tone somewhat, said:

"Besides, after waiting on a sick person, I fear we would not be fit for such an occasion. And while Miss Lin is still alive, she may ask for me at any time."

Li Wan tried to make the peace between them.

"The truth is," she said, "that this maid and Miss Lin have an affinity from a past life. Snowgoose, I know, was Miss Lin's original maid from home, but even she is not so indispensable as Nightingale. We really cannot separate them just now."

Lin's wife, who had been considerably put out by Nightingale's outspoken response, was obliged to contain herself when Li Wan came to the maid's defence. Seeing Nightingale reduced to floods of tears, she eyed her with a hostile smile and said:

"I shall ignore Miss Nightingale's rudeness. But am I to report what you have just said to Her Old Ladyship? And am I to tell Mrs. Lian?"

As she was speaking, Patience came out of Dai-yu's bedchamber, wiping her eyes.

"Tell Mrs. Lian what?" she asked.

Lin's wife told her the substance of their conversation. Patience lowered her head in thought. After a moment, she said:

"Why can't you take Snowgoose?"

"Would she do?" asked Li Wan. Patience went up to her and whispered a few words in her ear. Li Wan nodded, and said:

"Well in that case, it will be just as good if we send Snowgoose."

"Will Miss Snowgoose do?" Lin's wife asked Patience.

"Yes," replied Patience. "She will do just as well."

"Then will you please tell her to come with me straight away," said Lin's wife. "I shall report to Her Old Ladyship and Mrs. Lian. I shall say that you are both responsible for the arrangement, mind. And later you can tell Mrs. Lian yourself, Miss Patience."

"Of course," replied Li Wan curtly. "Do you mean to say that someone as old and experienced as you cannot even take the responsibility for a small thing like this?"

Lin's wife smiled.

"It is not that I can't take the responsibility. It is just that Her Old Ladyship and Mrs. Lian have arranged everything and the likes of us don't really know what's going on. In the circumstances, it seems only right to mention you and Miss Patience."

Patience had already told Snowgoose to come out. Over the past few days Snowgoose had fallen rather into disfavour with Dai-yu, who had called her a "silly, ignorant child," and her feelings of loyalty towards her mistress had as a consequence been rather blunted. Besides there was no question of her disobeying an order from Her Old Ladyship and Mrs. Lian. She therefore tidied her hair quickly and made ready to go. Patience told her to change into her smartest clothes and to go with Mrs. Lin. Patience herself stayed on and spoke for a short while with Li Wan. Before she left, Li Wan instructed her to call in on Lin's wife on her way and tell her that her husband should make the necessary preparations for Dai-yu with all possible speed. This Patience agreed to do and went on her way. As she turned a corner in the Garden, she caught sight of Lin's wife walking ahead of her with Snowgoose and called to her to wait.

"I will take Snowgoose with me. You go and tell your husband to prepare Miss Lin's things. I will report to Mrs. Lian for you."

"Yes, Miss Patience," said Lin's wife, and went on her errand.

Patience then took Snowgoose to the bridal apartment, and reported there herself before going to see to her own affairs.

When Snowgoose saw the wedding preparations in full swing and thought of Dai-yu lying at death's door, she felt a pang of grief. But she dared not show her feelings in the presence of Grandmother Jia and Xi-feng. "What can they want me for?" she wondered. "I must see what is going on. I know Bao-yu used to be head over heels in love with Miss Lin. And yet now he seems to have deserted her. I begin to wonder if this illness of his is genuine or just a pretence. He may have made the whole thing up so as to avoid upsetting Miss Lin. By pretending to lose his jade and acting like an idiot, perhaps he thinks he can put her off, and marry Miss Chai with a clear conscience? I must watch him closely, and see if he acts the fool when he sees me. Surely he won't keep up the pretence on his wedding-day?" She slipped in and stood spying at the inner doorway.

Now, though Bao-yu's mind was still clouded from the loss of his jade, his sense of joy at the prospect of marrying Dai-yu—in his eyes the most blessed, the most wonderful thing that had happened in heaven or earth since time began—had caused a temporary resurgence of physical well-being, if not a full restoration of his mental faculties. Xi-feng's ingenious plan had had exactly the intended effect, and he was now counting the minutes till he should see Dai-yu. Today was the day when all his dreams were to come true, and he was filled with a feeling of ecstasy. He still occasionally let slip some tell-tale imbecile remark, but in other respects gave the appearance of having completely recovered. All this Snowgoose observed, and was filled with hatred for him and grief for her mistress. She knew nothing of the true cause of his joy.

While Snowgoose slipped away unobserved, Bao-yu told Aroma to hurry and dress him in his bridegroom's finery. He sat in Lady Wang's chamber, watching Xi-feng and You-shi bustling about their preparations, himself bursting with impatience for the great moment.

"If Cousin Lin is coming from the Garden," he asked Aroma, "why all this fuss? Why isn't she here yet?"

Suppressing a smile, Aroma replied:

"She has to wait for the propitious moment."

Xi-feng turned to Lady Wang and said:

"Because we are in mourning, we cannot have music in the street. But the traditional ceremony would seem so drab without any music at all, so I have told some of the women-servants with a bit of musical knowledge, the ones who used to look after the actresses, to come and play a little, to add a bit of a festive touch."

Lady Wang nodded, and said she thought this a good idea. Presently the great bridal palanquin was borne in through the main gate. The little ensemble of women-servants played, as it entered down an avenue of twelve pairs of palace-lanterns, creating a passably stylish impression. The Master of Ceremonies requested the bride to step out of her palanquin, and Bao-yu saw the Matron of Honour, all in red, lead out his bride, her face concealed by the bridal veil. There was a maid in attendance, and Bao-yu saw to his surprise that it was Snowgoose. This puzzled him for a moment.

"Why Snowgoose, and not Nightingale?" he asked himself. Then: "Of course. Snowgoose is Dai-yu's original maid from the South, whereas Nightingale was one of our maids, which would never do."

And so, when he saw Snowgoose, it was as if he had seen the face of Dai-yu herself beneath the veil.

The Master of Ceremonies chanted the liturgy, and the bride and groom knelt before Heaven and Earth. Grandmother Jia was called forth to receive their obeisances, as were Sir Zheng, Lady Wang, and other elders of the family, after which they escorted the couple into the hall and thence to the bridal chamber. Here they were made to sit on the bridal bed, were showered with dried fruit, and subjected to the various other practices customary in old Nanking families such as the Jias, which we need not describe in detail here.

Jia Zheng, it will be remembered, had gone along with the plan grudgingly, in deference to Grandmother Jia's wishes, retaining grave though unspoken doubts himself as to her theory of "turning Bao-yu's luck." But today, seeing Bao-yu bear himself with a semblance of dignity, he could not help but be pleased.

The bride was now sitting alone on the bridal bed, and the moment had come for the groom to remove her veil. Xi-feng had made her preparations for this event, and now asked Grandmother Jia, Lady Wang, and others of the ladies present to step forward into the bridal chamber to assist her. The sense of climax seemed to cause Bao-yu to revert somewhat to his imbecile ways, for as he approached his bride he said:

"Are you better now, coz? It's such a long time since we last saw each other. What do you want to go wrapping yourself up in that silly thing for?"

He was about to raise the veil. Grandmother Jia broke into a cold sweat. But he hesitated, thinking to himself:

"I know how sensitive Cousin Lin is. I must be very careful not to offend her."

He waited a little longer. But soon the suspense became unbearable, and he walked up to her and lifted the veil. The Matron of Honour took it from him, while Snowgoose melted into the background and Oriole came forward to take her place. Bao-yu stared at his bride. Surely this was Bao-chai? Incredulous, with one hand holding the lantern, he rubbed his eyes with the other and looked again. It *was* Bao-chai. How pretty she looked, in her wedding-gown! He gazed at her soft skin, the full curve of her shoulders, and her hair done up in tresses that hung from her temples! Her eyes were moist, her lips quivered slightly. Her whole appearance had the simple elegance of a white lily, wet with pendant dew; the maidenly blush on her cheeks resembled apricot-blossom wreathed in mist. For a moment he stared at her in utter astonishment. Then he noticed that Oriole was standing at her side, while Snowgoose had quite vanished. A feeling of helpless bewilderment seized him, and thinking he must be dreaming, he stood there in a motionless daze. The maids took the lamp from him and helped him to a chair, where he sat with his eyes fixed in front of him, still without uttering a single word. Grandmother Jia was anxious lest this might signal the approach of another of his fits, and herself came over to rally him, while Xi-feng and You-shi escorted Bao-chai to a chair in the inner part of the room. Bao-chai held her head bowed and said nothing.

After a while, Bao-yu had composed himself sufficiently to think. He saw Grandmother Jia and Lady Wang sitting opposite him, and asked Aroma in a whisper:

"Where am I? This must all be a dream."

"A dream? Why, it's the happiest day of your life!" said Aroma. "How can you be so silly? Take care: Sir Zheng is outside."

Pointing now to where Bao-chai sat, and still whispering, Bao-yu asked again:

"Who is that beautiful lady sitting over there?"

Aroma found this so comical that for a while she could say nothing, but held her hand to her face to conceal her mirth. Finally she replied:

"That is your bride, the new Mrs. Bao-yu."

The other maids also turned away, unable to contain their laughter.

Bao-yu: "Don't be so silly! What do you mean, 'Mrs. Bao-yu'? Who *is* Mrs. Bao-yu?"

Aroma: "Miss Chai."

Bao-yu: "But what about Miss Lin?"

Aroma: "The Master decided you should marry Miss Chai. What's Miss Lin got to do with it?"

Bao-yu: "But I saw her just a moment ago, and Snowgoose too. They couldn't have just vanished! What sort of trick is this that you're all playing on me?"

Xi-feng came up and whispered in his ear:

"Miss Chai is sitting over there, so please stop talking like this. If you offend her, Grannie will be very cross with you."

Bao-yu was now more hopelessly confused than ever. The mysterious goings-on of that night, coming on top of his already precarious mental state, had wrought him up to such a pitch of despair that all he could do was cry—"I must find Cousin Lin!"—again and again. Grandmother Jia and the other ladies tried to comfort him but he was impervious to their efforts. Furthermore, with Bao-chai in the room, they had to be careful what they said. Bao-yu was clearly suffering from a severe relapse, and they now abandoned their attempts to rally him and instead helped him to bed, while ordering several sticks of gum benzoin incense to be lit, the heavy, sedative fumes of which soon filled the room. They all stood in awesome hush. After a short while, the incense began to take effect and Bao-yu sank into a heavy slumber, much to the relief of the ladies, who sat down again to await the dawn. Grandmother Jia told Xi-feng to ask Bao-chai to lie down and rest, which she did, fully dressed as she was, behaving as though she had heard nothing.

Jia Zheng had remained in an outer room during all of this, and so had seen nothing to disillusion him of the reassuring impression he had received earlier on. The following day, as it happened, was the day selected according to the almanac for his departure to his new post. After a short rest, he took formal leave of the festivities and returned to his apartment. Grandmother Jia, too, left Bao-yu sound asleep and returned to her apartment for a brief rest.

The next morning, Jia Zheng took leave of the ancestors in the family shrine and came to bid his mother farewell. He bowed before her and said:

"I, your unworthy son, am about to depart for afar. My only wish is that you should keep warm in the cold weather and take good care of yourself. As soon as I arrive at my post, I shall write to ask how you are. You are not to worry on my account. Bao-yu's marriage has now been celebrated in accordance with your wishes, and it only remains for me to beg you to instruct him, and impart to him the wisdom of your years."

Grandmother Jia, for fear that Jia Zheng would worry on his journey, made no mention of Bao-yu's relapse but merely said:

"There is one thing I should tell you. Although the rites were performed last night, Bao-yu's marriage was not properly consummated. His health would not allow it. Custom, I know, decrees that he should see you off today. But in view of all the circumstances, his earlier illness, the luck turning, his still fragile state of convalescence and yesterday's exertions, I am worried that by going out he might catch a chill. So I put it to you: If you wish him to fulfil his filial obligations by seeing you off, then send for him at once and instruct him accordingly; but if you love him, then spare him and let him say goodbye and make his kowtow to you here."

"Why should I want him to see me off?" returned Jia Zheng. "All I want is that from now on he should study in earnest. That would bring me greater pleasure by far."

Grandmother Jia was most relieved to hear this. She told Jia Zheng to be seated and sent Faithful, after imparting to her various secret instructions, to fetch Bao-yu and to bring Aroma with him. Faithful had not been away many minutes, when Bao-yu came in and with the usual promptings, performed his duty to his father. Luckily the sight of his father brought him, for a few moments, sufficient clarity to get through the formalities without any gross lapses. Jia Zheng delivered himself of a few exhortatory words, to all of which his son gave the correct replies. Then Jia Zheng told Aroma to escort him back to his room, while he himself went to Lady Wang's apartment. There he earnestly enjoined Lady Wang to take charge of Bao-yu's moral welfare during his absence.

"There must be none of his previous unruliness," he added. "He must now prepare himself to enter for next year's provincial examination."

Lady Wang assured him that she would do her utmost, and without mentioning anything else, at once sent a maid to escort Bao-chai into the room. Bao-chai performed the rite proper to a newly married bride seeing off her father-in-law, and then remained in the room when Jia Zheng left. The other women-folk accompanied him as far as the inner gate before turning back. Cousin Zhen and the other young male Jias received a few words of exhortation, drank a farewell toast, and, together with a crowd of other friends and relatives, accompanied him as far as the Hostelry of the Tearful Parting, some three or four miles beyond the city walls, where they bid their final farewell.

But of Jia Zheng's departure no more. Let us return to Bao-yu, who on leaving his father, had suffered an immediate relapse. His mind became more and more clouded, and he could swallow neither food nor drink. Whether or not he was to emerge from this crisis alive will be revealed in the next chapter.

FROM CHAPTER 98

Crimson Pearl's Suffering Spirit Returns
to the Realm of Separation
And the Convalescent Stone-in-Waiting Weeps
at the Scene of Past Affection

On his return from seeing his father, Bao-yu, as we have seen, regressed into a worse state of stupor and depression than ever. He was too lacking in energy to move, and could eat nothing, but fell straight into a heavy slumber. Once more the doctor was called, once more he took Bao-yu's pulses and made out a prescription, which was administered to no effect. He could not even recognize the people around him. And yet, if helped into a sitting position, he could still pass for someone in normal health. Provided he was not called upon to do anything, there were no external symptoms to indicate how seriously ill he was. He continued like this for several days, to the increasing anxiety of the family, until the Ninth Day after the wedding, when according to tradition the newly married couple should visit the bride's family. If they did not go, Aunt Xue would be most offended. But if they went with Bao-yu in his present state, whatever were they to say? Knowing that his illness was caused by his attachment to Dai-yu, Grandmother Jia would have liked to make a clean breast of it and tell Aunt Xue. But she feared that this too might cause offence and ill-feeling. It was also difficult for her to be of any comfort to Bao-chai, who was in a delicate position as a new member of the Jia family. Such comfort could only be rendered by a visit from the girl's mother, which would be difficult if they had already offended her by not celebrating the Ninth Day. It must be gone through with. Grandmother Jia imparted her views on the matter to Lady Wang and Xi-feng:

"It is only Bao-yu's mind that has been temporarily affected. I don't think a little excursion would do him any harm. We must prepare two small sedan-chairs, and send a maid to support him. They can go through the Garden. Once the Ninth Day has been properly celebrated, we can ask Mrs. Xue to come over and comfort Bao-chai, while we do our utmost to restore Bao-yu to health. They will both benefit."

Lady Wang agreed and immediately began making the necessary preparations. Bao-chai acquiesced in the charade out of a sense of conjugal duty, while Bao-yu in his moronic state was easily manipulated. Bao-chai now knew the full truth, and in her own mind blamed her mother for making a foolish decision. But now that things had gone this far she said nothing. Aunt Xue herself, when she witnessed Bao-yu's pitiful condition, began to regret having ever given her consent, and could only bring herself to play a perfunctory part in the proceedings.

When they returned home, Bao-yu's condition seemed to grow worse. By the next day he could not even sit up in bed. This deterioration continued daily, until he could no longer swallow medicine or water. Aunt Xue was there, and she and the other ladies in their frantic despair scoured the city for eminent physicians, without finding one that could diagnose the illness. Finally they discovered, lodging in a broken-down temple outside the city, a down-and-out practitioner by the name of Bi Zhi-an, who diagnosed it as a case of severe emotional shock, aggravated by a failure to dress in accordance with the seasons and by irregular eating habits, with consequent accumulation of choler and obstruction of the humours. In short, an internal disorder made worse by external factors. He made out a prescription in accordance with this diagnosis, which was administered that evening. At about ten o'clock it began to take effect. Bao-yu began to show signs of consciousness and asked for water to drink. Grandmother Jia, Lady Wang, and all the other ladies congregated round the sick-bed felt that they could at last have a brief respite from their vigil, and Aunt Xue was invited to bring Bao-chai with her to Grandmother Jia's apartment to rest for a while.

His brief access of clarity enabled Bao-yu to understand the gravity of his illness. When the others had gone and he was left alone with Aroma, he called her over to his side and taking her by the hand said tearfully:

"Please tell me how Cousin Chai came to be here? I remember Father marrying me to Cousin Lin. Why has *she* been made to go? Why has Cousin Chai taken her place? She has no right to be here! I'd like to tell her so, but I don't want to offend her. How has Cousin Lin taken it? Is she very upset?"

Aroma did not dare tell him the truth, but merely said:

"Miss Lin is ill."

"I must go and see her," insisted Bao-yu. He wanted to get up, but days of going without food and drink had so sapped his strength that he could no longer move, but could only weep bitterly and say:

"I know I am going to die! There's something on my mind, something very important, that I want you to tell Grannie for me. Cousin Lin and I are both ill. We are both dying. It will be too late to help us when we are dead; but if they prepare a room for us now and if we are taken there before it is too late, we can at least be cared for together while we are still alive, and be laid out together when we die. Do this for me, for friendship's sake!"

Aroma found this plea at once disturbing, comical, and moving. Bao-chai, who happened to be passing with Oriole, heard every word and took him to task straight away.

"Instead of resting and trying to get well, you make yourself iller with all this gloomy talk! Grandmother has scarcely stopped worrying about you for a moment, and here you are causing more trouble for her. She is over eighty now and may not live to acquire a title because of your achievements; but at least, by leading a good life, you can repay her a little for all that she has suffered for your sake. And I hardly need mention the agonies Mother has endured in bringing you up. You are the only son she has left. If you were to die, think how she would suffer! As for me, I am wretched enough as it is; you don't need to make a widow of me. Three good reasons why even if you want to die, the powers above will not let you and you will not be able to. After four or five days of proper rest and care, your illness will pass, your strength will be restored, and you will be yourself again."

For a while Bao-yu could think of no reply to this homily. Finally he gave a silly laugh and said:

"After not speaking to me for so long, here you are lecturing me. You are wasting your breath."

Encouraged by this response to go a step further, Bao-chai said:

"Let me tell you the plain truth, then. Some days ago, while you were unconscious, Cousin Lin passed away."

With a sudden movement, Bao-yu sat up and cried out in horror:

"It can't be true!"

"It is. Would I lie about such a thing? Grandmother and Mother knew how fond you were of each other, and wouldn't tell you because they were afraid that if they did, you would die too."

Bao-yu began howling unrestrainedly and slumped back in his bed. Suddenly all was pitch black before his eyes. He could not tell where he was and was beginning to feel very lost, when he thought he saw a man walking towards him and asked in a bewildered tone of voice:

"Would you be so kind as to tell me where I am?"

"This," replied the stranger, "is the road to the Springs of the Nether World. Your time is not yet come. What brings you here?"

"I have just learned of the death of a friend and have come to find her. But I seem to have lost my way."

"Who is this friend of yours?"

"Lin Dai-yu of Soochow."

The man gave a chilling smile:

"In life Lin Dai-yu was no ordinary mortal, and in death she has become no ordinary shade. An ordinary mortal has two souls which coalesce at birth to vitalize the physical frame, and disperse at death to rejoin the cosmic flux. If you consider the impossibility of tracing even such ordinary human entities in the Nether World, you will realize what a futile task it is to look for Lin Dai-yu. You had better return at once."

After standing for a moment lost in thought, Bao-yu asked again:

"But if as you say, death is a dispersion, how can there be such a place as the Nether World?"

"There is," replied the man with a superior smile, "and yet there is not, such a place. It is a teaching, devised to warn mankind in its blind attachment to the idea of life and death. The Supreme Wrath is aroused by human folly in all forms—whether it be excessive ambition, premature death self-sought, or futile self-destruction through debauchery and a life of overweening violence. Hell is the place where souls such as these are imprisoned and made to suffer countless torments in expiation of their sins. This search of yours for Lin Dai-yu is a case of futile self-delusion. Dai-yu has already returned to the Land of Illusion and if you really want to find her you must cultivate your mind and strengthen your spiritual nature. Then one day you will see her again. But if you throw your life away, you will be guilty of premature death self-sought and will be confined to Hell. And then, although you may be allowed to see your parents, you will certainly never see Dai-yu again."

When he had finished speaking, the man took a stone from within his sleeve and threw it at Bao-yu's chest. The words he had spoken and the impact of the stone as it landed on his chest combined to give Bao-yu such a fright that he would have returned home at once, if he had only known which way to turn. In his confusion he suddenly heard a voice, and turning, saw the figures of Grandmother Jia, Lady Wang, Bao-chai, Aroma, and his other maids standing in a circle around him, weeping and calling his name. He was lying on his own bed. The red lamp was on the table. The moon was shining brilliantly through the window. He was back among the elegant comforts of his own home. A moment's reflection told him that what he had just experienced had been a dream. He was in a cold sweat. Though his mind felt strangely lucid, thinking only intensified his feeling of helpless desolation, and he uttered several profound sighs.

Bao-chai had known of Dai-yu's death for several days. While Grandmother Jia had forbidden the maids to tell him for fear of further complicating his illness, she felt she knew better. Aware that it was Dai-yu who lay at the root of his illness and that the loss of his jade was only a secondary factor, she took the opportunity of breaking the news of her death to him in this abrupt manner, hoping that by severing his attachment once and for all she would enable his sanity and health to be restored. Grandmother Jia, Lady Wang, and company were not aware of her intentions and at first reproached her for her lack of caution. But when they saw Bao-yu regain consciousness, they were all greatly relieved and went at once to the library to ask Doctor Bi to come in and examine his patient again. The doctor carefully took his pulses.

"How odd!" he exclaimed. "His pulses are deep and still, his spirit calm, the oppression quite dispersed. Tomorrow he must take a regulative draught, which I shall prescribe, and he should make a prompt and complete recovery."

The doctor left and the ladies all returned to their apartments in much improved spirits.

Although at first Aroma greatly resented the way in which Bao-chai had broken the news, she did not dare say so. Oriole, on the other hand, reproved her mistress in private for having been, as she put it, too hasty.

"What do you know about such things?" retorted Bao-chai. "Leave this to me. I take full responsibility."

Bao-chai ignored the opinions and criticisms of those around her and continued to keep a close watch on Bao-yu's progress, probing him judiciously, like an acupuncturist with a needle.

A day or two later, he began to feel a slight improvement in himself, though his mental equilibrium was still easily disturbed by the least thought of Dai-yu. Aroma was constantly at his side, with such words of consolation as:

"The Master chose Miss Chai as your bride for her more dependable nature. He thought Miss Lin too difficult and temperamental for you, and besides there was always the fear that she would not live long. Then later Her Old Ladyship thought you were not in a fit state to know what was best for you and would only be upset and make yourself iller if you knew the truth, so she made Snowgoose come over, to try and make things easier for you."

This did nothing to lessen his grief, and he often wept inconsolably. But each time he thought of putting an end to his life, he remembered the words of the stranger in his dream; and then he thought of the distress his death would cause his mother and grandmother and knew that he could not tear himself away from them. He also reflected that Dai-yu was dead, and that Bao-chai was a fine lady in her own right; there must after all have been some truth in the bond of gold and jade. This thought eased his mind a little. Bao-chai could see that things were improving, and herself felt calmer as a result. Every day she scrupulously performed her duties towards Grandmother Jia and Lady Wang, and when these were completed, did all she could to cure Bao-yu of his grief. He was still not able to sit up for long periods, but often when he saw her sitting by his bedside he would succumb to his old weakness for the fairer sex. She tried to rally him in an earnest manner, saying:

"The important thing is to take care of your health. Now that we are married, we have a whole lifetime ahead of us."

He was reluctant to listen to her advice. But since his grandmother, his mother, Aunt Xue, and all the others took it in turns to watch over him during the day, and since Bao-chai slept on her own in an adjoining room, and he was waited on at night by one or two maids of Grandmother Jia's, he found himself left with little choice but to rest and get well again. And as time went by and Bao-chai proved herself a gentle and devoted companion, he found that a small part of his love for Dai-yu began to transfer itself to her. But this belongs to a later part of our story.

Let us return to the wedding-day. Dai-yu, it will be remembered, had lost consciousness while it was still light, and was holding onto life by the slenderest thread. Her weak breathing and precarious heart-beat caused Li Wan and Nightingale to weep in despair. By evening however, she seemed easier again. She feebly opened her eyes, and seemed to be asking for water or medicine. Snowgoose had already left, and only Li Wan and Nightingale were at her bedside. Nightingale brought her a little cup of pear-juice blended with a decoction of longans, and with a small silver spoon fed her two or three spoonfuls of it. Dai-yu closed her eyes and rested for a while. Consciousness would flicker momentarily within her, then fade away again. Li Wan recognized this peaceful state as the last transient revival of the dying, but thinking that the end would not come for a few hours, she returned briefly to Sweet-rice Village to see to her own affairs.

Dai-yu opened her eyes again. Seeing no one in the room but Nightingale and her old wet-nurse and a few other junior maids, she clutched Nightingale's hand and said with a great effort:

"I am finished! After the years you have spent seeing to my every need, I had hoped the two of us could always be together. But now . . ."

She broke off, panting for breath, closed her eyes and lay still, gripping Nightingale's hand tightly. Nightingale did not dare to move. She had thought that Dai-yu seemed so much better, had even hoped she might pull through after all; but these words sent a chill down her spine. After a long pause, Dai-yu spoke again:

"Sister Nightingale! I have no family of my own here. My body is pure: promise me you'll ask them to bury me at home!"

She closed her eyes again and was silent. Her grip tightened still further around Nightingale's hand, and she was seized with another paroxysm of breathlessness. When she could breathe again, her outward breaths became longer, her inward breaths shorter and more feeble. They quickened at a rate that caused Nightingale great alarm, and she sent at once for Li Wan. Tan-chun happened to arrive at that very moment. Nightingale said to her in an urgent whisper:

"Miss! Come and look at Miss Lin!" As she spoke, her tears fell like drops of rain. Tan-chun came over and felt Dai-yu's hand. It was already cold, and her eyes were glazed and lifeless. Tan-chun and Nightingale wept as they gave orders for water to be brought and for Dai-yu to be washed. Now Li Wan came hurrying in. She, Tan-chun, and Nightingale looked at each other, but were too shocked to say a word. They began wiping Dai-yu's face with a flannel, when suddenly she cried out in a loud voice:

"Bao-yu! Bao-yu! How could you . . ."

Her whole body broke into a cold sweat and she could say no more. They tried to calm her down and support her. She sweated more and more profusely and her body became colder by degrees. Tan-chun and Li Wan told the maids to put up her hair and dress her in her grave-clothes, and to be quick about it. Her eyes rolled upwards. Alas!

> Her fragrant soul disperses, wafted on the breeze;
> Her sorrows now a dream, drifting into the night.

The moment Dai-yu breathed her last was the very moment that Bao-yu took Bao-chai to be his wife. Nightingale and Dai-yu's other maids began to wail and lament. Li Wan and Tan-chun recalled all their past affection for her, a memory made the more poignant by the lonely circumstances of her death, and they too shed many bitter and heartfelt tears. The wedding chamber was a long way off, and the guests heard nothing of the weeping, but from the Naiad's House, in a brief interval of silence between their lamentations, they heard a faint snatch of music in the distance. They strained their ears to catch it, but it was gone. Tan-chun and Li Wan went out into the garden to listen again, but all they could hear was the rustling of the bamboos in the wind. The moonlight cast a wavering shadow on the wall. It was an eerie, desolate night. [. . .]

FROM CHAPTER 119

[Jia Bao-yu Takes the Provincial Examinations and Then Renounces All Worldly Ties]

[After the marriage of Bao-yu and Bao-chai, the Jia family continues to decline precipitously. Prospect Garden, abandoned by almost all but the caretakers, falls into disrepair, and several of the Jia family members—including Jia Lian and Xi-feng—are implicated in various schemes of corruption. Jia Zheng himself is impeached for failure to control his subordinates, though the emperor intervenes and reassigns him to the Board of Works. Grandmother Jia, who along with Jia Zheng has been holding the households together, eventually dies, as does Xi-feng. In the meantime, Bao-yu's condition fluctuates, but after a long convalescence he begins to improve and he finally consummates his marriage with Bao-chai. Eventually, a monk comes to the door bringing the lost jade. Bao-yu immediately recognizes it as his own and falls into a deep reverie during which he visits the underworld. After his sudden recovery from the reverie, Bao-yu's condition rapidly improves and he agrees to take his examinations, although he has secretly resolved to give up his worldly ties.]

[. . .] The time drew near for the examination. All the family were full of eager anticipation, hoping that the two boys would write creditable compositions and bring the family honour. All except for Bao-chai; while it was true that Bao-yu had prepared well, she had also on occasions noticed a strange indifference in his behaviour. Her first concern was that the two boys, for both of whom this was the first venture of its kind, might get hurt or have some accident in the crush of men and vehicles around the examination halls. She was more particularly worried for Bao-yu, who had not been out at all since his encounter with the monk. His delight in studying seemed to her the result of a somewhat too hasty and not altogether convincing conversion, and she had a premonition that something untoward was going to happen. So, on the day before the big event, she despatched Aroma and a few of the junior maids to go with Candida and her helpers and make sure that the candidates were both properly prepared. She herself inspected their things and put them out in readiness, and then went over with Li Wan to Lady Wang's apartment, where she selected a few of the more trusty family retainers to accompany them the next day, for fear they might be jolted or trampled on in the crowds.

The big day finally arrived, and Bao-yu and Jia Lan changed into smart but unostentatious clothes. They came over in high spirits to bid farewell to Lady Wang, who gave them a few parting words of advice:

"This is the first examination for both of you, and although you are such big boys now, it will still be the first time either of you has been away from me for a whole day. You may have gone out in the past, but you were always surrounded by your maids and nurses. You have never spent the night away on your own like this. Today, when you both go into the examination, you are bound to feel rather lonely with none of the family by you. You must take special care. Finish your papers and come out as early as possible, and then be sure to find one of the family servants and come home as soon as you can. We shall be worrying about you."

As she spoke, Lady Wang herself was greatly moved by the occasion. Jia Lan made all the appropriate responses, but Bao-yu remained silent until his mother had quite finished speaking. Then he walked up to her, knelt at her feet, and with tears streaming down his cheeks kowtowed to her three times and said:

"I could never repay you adequately for all you have done for me, Mother. But if I can do this one thing successfully, if I can do my very best and pass this examination, then perhaps I can bring you a little pleasure. Then my worldly duty will be accomplished and I will at least have made some small return for all the trouble I have caused you."

Lady Wang was still more deeply moved by this:

"It is a very fine thing, what you are setting out to do. It is only a shame that your grandmother couldn't be here to witness it."

She wept as she spoke and put her arms around him to draw him to her. Bao-yu remained kneeling however and would not rise.

"Even though Grandmother is not here," he said, "I am sure she knows about it and is happy. So really it is just as if she were present. What separates us is only matter. We are together in spirit."

Li Wan feared that this scene might provoke Bao-yu to one of his fits. Besides, she sensed something inauspicious. She hurried forward:

"Mother, today we should be filled with joy. You mustn't upset yourself like this. Think how sensible and dutiful and hard-working Bao-yu has been of late. All he needs to do now is to sit the examinations with Lan, write his papers properly, and come home early. Then he can show copies of what he has written to some scholars connected with the family, and we'll just wait for the good news."

She told one of the maids to help Bao-yu to his feet. Bao-yu turned and bowed to her:

"Sister-in-law, you are not to worry. Lan and I are sure to pass. What is more, Lan has a brilliant future ahead of him, while you yourself will one day become a lady of noble rank and dress in the finest robes."

Li Wan smiled:

"If all this were ever to come true, it would at least be some compensation . . ."

She stopped short, fearing to cause Lady Wang further distress. Bao-yu felt no such inhibition:

"If Lan does well and upholds our family tradition, my late brother may not have lived to witness it, but you will at least see his dearest wishes fulfilled."

It was getting late, and since Li Wan did not wish to prolong this exchange any further, she contented herself with a brief nod. Bao-chai had already perceived the strangeness of the conversation. Not only were Bao-yu's remarks ominous in themselves, but every word uttered by Lady Wang and Li Wan seemed laden with inauspicious meaning as well. Not daring to express this presentiment of hers openly, Bao-chai held back her tears and remained silent. Bao-yu came up to her and made her a deep bow. It seemed to them all such an eccentric way to behave, and no one could imagine what it was supposed to mean; nor did anyone dare to laugh. The general amazement increased when Bao-chai burst into floods of tears, and Bao-yu bade her farewell:

"Coz! I'm going now. Stay here with Mother and wait for the good news!"

"It is time for you to go," replied Bao-chai. "There is no need to embark on another of your long speeches."

"Strange that you should be urging me on my way," said Bao-yu. "I know it is time to go."

He glanced around him and saw that Xi-chun and Nightingale were absent.

"Say goodbye to Xi-chun and Nightingale for me," he said. "I shall certainly be meeting them again."

Everyone was forcibly struck by the strange blend of sense and nonsense in Bao-yu's words. They thought him momentarily confused, in part by the unprecedented nature of the occasion, in part by Lady Wang's injunctions. To all of them the best course of action in the circumstances seemed to be to speed him on his way and get the thing over with.

"They're waiting for you outside. No more dilly-dallying now, or you'll be late."

Bao-yu raised his head and laughed.

"Off I go! Enough of this foolery! It's over!"

"Well—off you go then!" they all cried, laughing nervously. Only Lady Wang and Bao-chai were sobbing inconsolably, as if they were parting from him forever. Finally Bao-yu walked out through the door and on his way, giggling like a half-wit.

> Entering the lists of worldly renown,
> He breaks the first bar of his earthly cage.

. . . At last came the day when the examinations were due to be concluded and the students released from their cells. Lady Wang was eagerly awaiting the return of Bao-yu and Jia Lan, and when midday came and there was still no sign of either of them, she, Li Wan, and Bao-chai all began to worry and sent one servant after another to find out what had become of them. The servants could obtain no news, and not one of them dared to return empty-handed. Later another batch was despatched on the same mission, with the same result. The three ladies were beside themselves with anxiety.

When evening came, someone returned at last: it was Jia Lan. They were delighted to see him, and immediately asked:

"Where is Bao-yu?"

He did not even greet them but burst into tears.

"Lost!" he sobbed.

For several minutes Lady Wang was struck dumb. Then she collapsed senseless onto her couch. Luckily Suncloud and one or two other maids were at hand to support her, and they brought her round, themselves sobbing hysterically the while. Bao-chai stared in front of her with a glazed expression in her eyes, while Aroma sobbed her heart out. The only thing they could find time to do between their fits of sobbing was to scold Jia Lan:

"Fool! You were with Bao-yu—how could he get lost?"

"Before the examinations we stayed in the same room, we ate together and slept together. Even when we went in we were never far apart, we were always within sight of each other. This morning Uncle Bao finished his paper early and waited for me. We handed in our papers at the same time and left together. When we reached the Dragon Gate outside there was a big crowd and I lost sight of him. The servants who had come to fetch us asked me where he was and Li Gui told them: "One minute he was just over there clear as daylight, the next minute he was gone. How can he have disappeared so suddenly in the crowd?" I told Li Gui and the others to split up into search parties, while I took some men and looked in all the cubicles. But there was no sign of him. That's why I'm so late back."

Lady Wang had been sobbing throughout this, without saying a word. Bao-chai had already more or less guessed the truth. Aroma continued to weep inconsolably. Jia Qiang and the other men needed no further orders but set off immediately in several directions to join in the search. It was a sad sight, with everyone in the lowest of spirits and the welcome-home party prepared in vain. Jia Lan forgot his own exhaustion and wanted to go out with the others. But Lady Wang kept him back:

"My child! Your uncle is lost; if we lost you as well, it would be more than we could bear! You have a rest now, there's a good boy!"

He was reluctant to stay behind, but acquiesced when You-shi added her entreaties to Lady Wang's.

The only person present who seemed unsurprised was Xi-chun. She did not feel free to express her thoughts, but instead enquired of Bao-chai:

"Did Bao-yu have his jade with him when he left?"

"Of course he did," she replied. "He never goes anywhere without it."

Xi-chun was silent. Aroma remembered how they had had to waylay Bao-yu and snatch the jade from his hands, and she had an overwhelming suspicion that today's mishap was that monk's doing too. Her heart ached with grief, tears poured down her cheeks, and she began wailing despondently. Memories flooded back of the affection Bao-yu had shown her. "I annoyed him sometimes, I know, and then he'd be cross. But he always had a way of making it up. He was so kind to me, and so thoughtful. In heated moments he often would vow to become a monk. I never believed him. And now he's gone!"

It was two o'clock in the morning by now, and still there was no sign of Bao-yu. Li Wan, afraid that Lady Wang would injure herself through excess of grief, did her best to console her and advised her to retire to bed. The rest of the family accompanied her to her room, except for Lady Xing who returned to her own apartment, and Jia Huan who was still lying low and had not dared to make an appearance at all. Lady Wang told Jia Lan to go back to his room, and herself spent a sleepless night. Next day at dawn some of the servants despatched the previous day returned, to report that they had searched everywhere and failed to find the slightest trace of Bao-yu. During the morning a stream of relations including Aunt Xue, Xue Ke, Shi Xiang-yun, Bao-qin, and old Mrs. Li came to enquire after Lady Wang's health and to ask for news of Bao-yu. . . .

The entire household, masters and servants alike, still waited anxiously day and night for news of Bao-yu. Very late one night, during the fifth watch, some servants came as far as the inner gate, announcing that they had indeed wonderful news to report, and a couple of the junior maids hurried in to the inner apartments, without stopping to inform the senior maids.

"Ma'am, ladies!" they announced. "Wonderful news!"

Lady Wang thought that Bao-yu must at last have been found and rising from her bed she exclaimed with delight:

"Where did they find him? Send him in at once to see me!"

"He has been placed seventh on the roll of successful candidates!" the maid cried.

"But has he been *found*?"

The maid was silent. Lady Wang sat down again.

"*Who* came seventh?" asked Tan-chun.

"Mr. Bao."

As they were talking they heard a voice outside shouting:

"Master Lan has passed too!"

A servant went hurrying out to receive the official notice, on which it was written that Jia Lan had been placed one hundred and thirtieth on the roll.

Since there was still no news of Bao-yu's whereabouts, Li Wan did not feel free to express her feelings of pride and joy; and Lady Wang, delighted as she was that Jia Lan had passed, could not help thinking to herself:

"If only Bao-yu were here too, what a happy celebration it would be!"

Bao-chai alone was still plunged in gloom, though she felt it inappropriate to weep. The others were busy offering their congratulations and trying to look on the cheerful side:

"Since it was Bao-yu's fate to pass, he cannot remain lost for long. In a day or two he is sure to be found."

This plausible suggestion brought a momentary smile to Lady Wang's cheeks, and the family seized on this opportunity to persuade her to eat and drink a little. A moment later Tealeaf's voice could be heard calling excitedly from the inner gate:

"Now that Mr. Bao has passed, he is sure to be found soon!"

"What makes you so sure of that?" they asked him.

"There's a saying: 'If a man once passes the examination, the whole world learns his name.' Now everyone will know Mr. Bao's name wherever he goes, and someone will be sure to bring him home."

"That Tealeaf may be a cheeky little devil, but there's something in what he says," agreed the maids.

Xi-chun differed:

"How could a grown man like Bao-yu be lost? If you ask me, he has deliberately severed his ties with the world and chosen the life of a monk. And in that case he *will* be hard to find."

This set the ladies weeping all over again.

"It is certainly true," said Li Wan, "that since ancient times many men have renounced worldly rank and riches to become Buddhas or Saints."

"But if he rejects his own mother and father," sobbed Lady Wang, "then he's failing in his duty as a son. And in that case how can he ever hope to become a Saint or a Buddha?"

"It is best to be ordinary," commented Tan-chun. "Bao-yu was always different. He had that jade of his ever since he was born, and everyone always thought it lucky. But looking back, I can see that it's brought him nothing but bad luck. If a few more days go by and we still cannot find him—I don't want to upset you, Mother—but I think in that case we must resign ourselves to the fact that this is something decreed by fate and beyond our understanding. It would be better not to think of him as having ever been born from your womb. His destiny is after all the fruit of karma, the result of your accumulated merit in several lifetimes."

Bao-chai listened to this in silence. Aroma could bear it no longer; her heart ached, she felt dizzy and sank to the ground in a faint. Lady Wang seemed most concerned for her, and told one of the maids to help her up. . . .

The next day Jia Lan had to attend court to give thanks for his successful graduation. There he met Zhen Bao-yu[27] and discovered that he too had passed. So now all three of them belonged to the same "class." When Lan mentioned Bao-yu's strange disappearance, Zhen Bao-yu sighed and offered a few words of consolation.

The Chief Examiner presented the successful candidates' compositions to the throne, and His Majesty read them through one by one and found them all to be well balanced and cogent, displaying both breadth of learning and soundness of judgement. When he noticed two Nanking Jias in seventh and one hundred and thirtieth place, he asked if they were any relation of the late Jia Concubine. One of his ministers went to summon Jia Bao-yu and Jia Lan for questioning on this matter. Jia Lan, on arrival, explained the circumstances of his uncle's disappearance and gave a full account of the three preceding generations of the family, all of which was transmitted to the throne by the minister. His Majesty, as a consequence of this information, being a monarch of exceptional enlightenment and compassion, instructed his minister, in consideration of the family's distinguished record of service, to submit a full report on their case. This the minister did and drafted a detailed memorial on the subject. His Majesty's concern was such that on reading this memorial he ordered the minister to re-examine the facts that had led to Jia She's conviction. Subsequently the Imperial eye lighted upon yet another memorial describing the success of the recent campaign to quell the coastal disturbances, "causing the seas to be at peace and the rivers to be cleansed, and leaving the honest citizenry free to pursue their livelihood unmolested once more." His Majesty was overjoyed at this good news and ordered his council of ministers to deliberate on suitable rewards and also to pronounce a general amnesty throughout the Empire.

When Jia Lan had left court and had gone to pay his respects to his examiner, he learned of the amnesty and hurried home to tell Lady Wang and the rest of the family. They all seemed delighted, though their pleasure was marred by Bao-yu's continued absence. Aunt Xue was particularly happy at the news, and set about making preparations for the payment of Xue Pan's fine, since his death sentence would now be commuted as part of the amnesty.

A few days later it was announced that Zhen Bao-yu and his father had called to offer their congratulations, and Lady Wang sent Jia Lan out to receive them. Shortly afterwards Jia Lan returned with a broad smile on his face:

"Good news, Grandmother! Uncle Zhen Bao-yu's father has heard at court of an edict pardoning both Great-uncle She and Uncle Zhen[28] from Ning-guo House, and restoring the hereditary Ning-guo rank to Uncle Zhen. Grandfather is to keep the

---

[27] **Zhen Bao-yu:**   The son of one of Jia Zheng's friends; he bears a physical resemblance to Jia Bao-yu and appears late in the novel as a kind of foil to Jia Bao-yu, who thinks of him as an obsequious "career worm."

[28] **Uncle Zhen:**   Both Jia She (Jia Zheng's older brother) and Zhen had been involved in scandals and stripped of their titles. In part due to Bao-yu's composition in the examinations, the Jia family is once again in the emperor's favor.

hereditary Rong-guo rank and after his period of mourning will be reinstated as a Permanent Secretary in the Board of Works. All the family's confiscated property is to be restored. His Majesty has read Uncle Bao's composition and was extremely struck by it. When he discovered that the candidate concerned was Her Late Grace's younger brother, and when the Prince of Bei-jing added a few words of commendation, His Majesty expressed a desire to summon him to court for an audience. The ministers then told him that Uncle Bao had disappeared after the examination (it was I who informed them of this in the first place), and that he was at present being looked for everywhere, without success, whereupon His Majesty issued another edict, ordering all the garrisons in the capital to make a thorough search for him. You can set your mind at rest now, Grandmother. With His Majesty taking a personal interest in the matter, Uncle Bao is sure to be found!"

Lady Wang and the rest of the family were delighted and congratulated each other on this new turn of events. [. . .]

FROM CHAPTER 120

[Zhen Shi-yin Expounds the Nature
of Passion and Illusion;
and Jia Yu-cun Concludes the Dream of Golden Days]

Jia Zheng had arrived in Nanking with Grandmother Jia's coffin, accompanied by Jia Rong and the coffins of Qin-shi, Xi-feng, Dai-yu, and Faithful. They made arrangements for the Jia family members to be interred, and then Jia Rong took Dai-yu's coffin to her own family graveyard to be buried there, while Jia Zheng saw to the construction of the tombs. Then one day a letter arrived from home, in which he read of the success achieved by Bao-yu and Jia Lan in their examinations—which gave him great pleasure—and of Bao-yu's disappearance, which disturbed him greatly and made him decide to cut short his stay and hurry home. On his return journey he learned of the amnesty decreed by the emperor, and received another letter from home telling him that Jia She and Cousin Zhen had been pardoned, and their titles restored. Much cheered by this news, he pressed on towards home, travelling by day and night.

On the day when his boat reached the post-station at Piling, there was a sudden cold turn in the weather and it began to snow. He moored in a quiet, lonely stretch of the canal and sent his servants ashore to deliver a few visiting-cards and to apologize to his friends in the locality, saying that since his boat was due to set off again at any moment he would not be able to call on them in person or entertain them aboard. Only one page-boy remained to wait on him while he sat in the cabin writing a letter home (to be sent on ahead by land). When he came to write about Bao-yu, he paused for a moment and looked up. There, up on deck, standing in the very entrance to his cabin and silhouetted dimly against the snow, was the figure of a man with shaven head and bare feet, wrapped in a large cape made of crimson felt. The figure knelt down and bowed to Jia Zheng, who did not recognize the features and hurried out on deck, intending to raise him up and ask him his name. The man bowed four times, and now stood upright, pressing his palms together in monkish greeting. Jia Zheng was about to reciprocate with a respectful bow of the head when he looked into the man's eyes and with a sudden shock recognized him as Bao-yu.

"Are you not my son?" he asked.

The man was silent and an expression that seemed to contain both joy and sorrow played on his face. Jia Zheng asked again:

"If you are Bao-yu, why are you dressed like this? And what brings you to this place?"

Before Bao-yu could reply two other men appeared on the deck, a Buddhist monk and a Taoist, and holding him between them they said:

"Come, your earthly karma is complete. Tarry no longer."

The three of them mounted the bank and strode off into the snow. Jia Zheng went chasing after them along the slippery track, but although he could spy them ahead of him, somehow they always remained just out of reach. He could hear all three of them singing some sort of a song:

> On Greensickness Peak
> I dwell;
> In the Cosmic Void
> I roam.
> Who will pass over,
> Who will go with me,
> Who will explore
> The supremely ineffable
> Vastly mysterious
> Wilderness
> To which I return!

Jia Zheng listened to the song and continued to follow them until they rounded the slope of a small hill and suddenly vanished from sight. He was weak and out of breath by now with the exertion of the chase, and greatly mystified by what he had seen. Looking back he saw his page-boy, hurrying up behind him.

"Did you see those three men just now?" he questioned him.

"Yes, sir, I did," replied the page. "I saw you following them, so I came too. Then they disappeared and I could see no one but you."

Jia Zheng wanted to continue, but all he could see before him was a vast expanse of white, with not a soul anywhere. He knew there was more to this strange occurrence than he could understand, and reluctantly he turned back and began to retrace his steps.

The other servants had returned to their master's boat to find the cabin empty and were told by the boatman that Jia Zheng had gone on shore in pursuit of two monks and a Taoist. They followed his footsteps through the snow and when they saw him coming towards them in the distance hurried forward to meet him, and then all returned to the boat together. Jia Zheng sat down to regain his breath and told them what had happened. They sought his authority to mount a search for Bao-yu in the area, but Jia Zheng dismissed the idea.

"You do not understand," he said with a sigh. "This was indeed no supernatural apparition; I saw these men with my own eyes. I heard them singing, and the words of their song held a most profound and mysterious meaning. Bao-yu came into the world with his jade, and there was always something strange about it. I knew it for an ill omen. But because his grandmother doted on him so, we nurtured him and brought him up until now. That monk and that Taoist I have seen before, three times altogether. The first time was when they came to extol the virtues of the jade; the second was when Bao-yu was seriously ill and the monk came and said a prayer over the jade, which seemed to cure Bao-yu at once; the third time was when he restored the jade to us after it had been lost. He was sitting in the hall one minute, and the next he had vanished completely. I thought it strange at the time and could only conclude that perhaps Bao-yu was in some way blessed and that these two holy men had come to protect him. But the truth of the matter must be that he himself is a being from a higher realm who has descended into the world to experience the trials of this human life. For these past nineteen years he has been doted on in vain by his poor grandmother! Now at last I understand!"

As he said these words, tears came to his eyes.

"But surely," protested one of the servants, "if Mr. Bao was really a Buddhist Immortal, what need was there for him to bother with passing his exams before disappearing?"

"How can you ever hope to understand these things?" replied Jia Zheng with a sigh. "The constellations in the heavens, the hermits in their hills, the spirits in their caves, each has a particular configuration, a unique temperament. When did you ever see Bao-yu willingly work at his books? And yet if once he applied himself, nothing was beyond his reach. His temperament was certainly unique."

In an effort to restore his spirits, the servants turned the conversation to Jia Lan's success in the exams and the revival of the family fortunes. Then Jia Zheng completed and sealed his letter, in which he related his encounter with Bao-yu and instructed the family not to brood over their loss too much, and despatched one of the servants to deliver it to Rong-guo House while he himself continued his journey by boat. But of this no more. [. . .]

GLOSSARY OF LITERARY AND CRITICAL TERMS

Absurd Literary movement that evolved in France in the 1950s. The Absurdists saw the universe as irrational and meaningless. They rejected conventional PLOT and DIALOGUE in their work, emphasizing the incoherence of the world.

Accent The emphasis, or stress, given to a syllable or word in pronunciation. Accents can be used to emphasize a particular word in a sentence: *Is* she con*tent* with the *con*tents of the *yel*low *pack*age?

Acmeists A group of twentieth-century Russian poets, most notably Anna Akhmatova (1889–1966), who rejected Symbolism in favor of linguistic clarity.

Acropolis The most fortified part of a Greek city, located on a hill; the most famous acropolis is in Athens and is the site of the Parthenon.

Act A major division in the action of a play. In many full-length plays, acts are further divided into SCENES, which often mark a point in the action when the location changes or when a new character arrives.

Age of Pericles The golden age of Athens in the fifth century B.C.E. when Pericles (c. 495–429 B.C.E.) was the head of the Athenian government. During this period, Athenian democ-racy reached its height; the Parthenon was constructed and drama and music flourished.

Agnosticism The belief that the existence of God or anything beyond material phenomena can be neither proved nor disproved. The French ENLIGHTENMENT philosopher François Voltaire (1694–1778) is considered by many to be the father of agnosticism. The term *agnostic,* however, was first used by the English biologist Thomas Huxley (1825–1895) in 1869.

Ahasuarus, the Wandering Jew A legendary figure during ancient times who was said to have mocked Jesus en route to the crucifixion and was therefore doomed to wander the earth in penance until Judgment Day.

Allegory A narrative in which the characters, settings, and episodes stand for something else. Traditionally, most allegories come in the form of stories that correlate to spiritual concepts; examples of these can be found in Dante's *Divine Comedy* (1321). Some later allegories allude to political, historical, and sociological ideas.

Alliteration The repetition of the same consonant sound or sounds in a sequence of words, usually at the beginning of a word or stressed syllable: "*descending dew drops*"; "*luscious lemons.*" The repetition is based on the sounds of the letters, not the spelling of the words; for example, "*keen*" and "*car*" alliterate, but "*car*" and "*cite*" do not, even though both begin with *c*. Used sparingly, alliteration can intensify ideas by emphasizing key words.

Allusion A brief reference to a person, place, thing, event, or idea in history or literature. These references can be to a scene from one of Shakespeare's plays, a historic figure, a war, a great love story, a biblical authority, or anything else that might enrich an author's work. Allusions imply that the writer and the reader share similar knowledge and function as a kind of shorthand.

Ambiguity Allows for two or more simultaneous interpretations of a word, phrase, action, or situation, all of whose meanings are supported by the work. Deliberate ambiguity can contribute to the effectiveness and richness of a piece of writing; unintentional ambiguity obscures meaning and may confuse readers.

Anagram A word or phrase made up of the same letters as another word or phrase; *heart* is an anagram of *earth*. Often considered merely an exercise of one's ingenuity, anagrams are sometimes used by writers to conceal proper names, veil messages, or suggest important connections between words, such as between *hated* and *death*.

Antagonist The character, force, or collection of forces in fiction or drama that opposes the PROTAGONIST and gives rise to the conflict in the story; an opponent of the protagonist, such as Caliban in Shakespeare's play *The Tempest*.

Antihero A PROTAGONIST who has the opposite of most of the traditional attributes of a hero. He or she may be bewildered, ineffectual, deluded, or merely pathetic. Often what antiheroes learn, if they learn anything at all, is that they are isolated in an existence devoid of God or any absolute value.

Apartheid The South African system of official racial segregation, which was established in 1948 and lasted until the early 1990s. The term *apartheid* means "state of being separate." Apartheid divided people into racial categories—colored, or Indian, as well as black and white—and severely limited the movements and activities of the colored and black groups, giving particular privilege to people of European heritage. After intense international pressure, the resistance movement leader, Nelson Mandela (b. 1918), was released from prison in 1990. One year later he became the country's first black president.

Apostrophe A statement or address made either to an implied interlocutor, sometimes a nonhuman figure or PERSONIFICATION. Apostrophes often provide a speaker with the opportunity to reveal his or her internal thoughts.

Archetype A universal symbol that evokes deep and sometimes unconscious responses in a reader. In literature, characters, images, and themes that symbolize universal meanings and basic human experiences are considered archetypes. Common literary archetypes include quests, initiations, scapegoats, descents to the underworld, and ascents to heaven.

Aryans A people who settled in Iran (Persia) and northern India in prehistoric times. Their language was also called Aryan, and it gave rise to the Indo-European languages of South Asia. Linguists now use the term *Aryan* to refer to Indo-Aryan languages. In the nineteenth and twentieth century the term was appropriated (most infamously by Adolf Hitler and the Nazi government) to define a "pure" race of people responsible for the progress of the modern world and superior to non-Aryans.

Aside In drama, a speech directed to the audience that supposedly is not audible to the other characters onstage.

Associationism A British eighteenth- and nineteenth-century school of philosophy that derived its ideas from, among others, philosophers John Locke (1632–1704) and David Hume (1711–1776). Associationists believed that one's view of reality is formed from bits and pieces of sensations that join together through patterns of association.

Assonance The repetition of vowel sounds in nearby words, as in "asl*ee*p under a tr*ee*" or "*ea*ch *e*vening." When the words also share similar endings, as in "asl*eep* in the d*eep*," rhyme occurs. Assonance is an effective means of emphasizing important words.

Atheism The belief that God does not exist and that the Earth evolved naturally.

Avant-garde Writers, artists, filmmakers, and musicians whose work is innovative, experimental, or unconventional.

Bataan Death March The forced march of 10,000 American and 65,000 Filipino soldiers who were captured in 1942 by the Japanese on the Bataan Peninsula of the Philippines during World War II; the prisoners of war, many of whom were suffering from exhaustion, malaria, and other ailments, were compelled to march 55 miles from Marivales to San Fernando. They were then packed into railroad cars and taken to Capas, where they were made to march another 8 miles to a prison camp. Up to 650 Americans and some 10,000 Filipinos died before reaching the camp, where still many others died.

Ballad An uncomplicated verse originally meant to be sung; it generally tells a dramatic tale or simple story. Ballads are associated with the oral traditions or folklore of common people. The folk ballad stanza usually consists of four lines of alternating tetrameter (four accented syllables) and trimeter (three accented syllables) following a rhyme scheme of *abab* or *abcb*.

Ballad stanza A four-line stanza, known as a QUATRAIN, consisting of alternating eight- and six-syllable lines. Usually, only the second and fourth lines rhyme (an *abcb* pattern). Samuel Taylor Coleridge adapted the ballad stanza in *The Rime of the Ancient Mariner* (1798).

Battle of Dresden A battle in 1813 outside the capital of Saxony, where Napoleon defeated an allied army of 400,000 men. It was Napoleon's last great victory before his final defeat one year later.

Battle of Plassey Plassey was the village in West Bengal, India, where the British defeated the Bengal army in 1757, which led to Britain's domination of northeast India.

Bengali Traditional language of Bengal in eastern India, now the national language of Bangladesh and the official language of the West Bengal region of India; also, someone who comes from Bangladesh or West Bengal.

Bengali literary renaissance A movement in the second half of the nineteenth century to develop literature in the Bengali language that would describe the everyday life of contemporary Bengal. Rabindranath Tagore, Madhusudan Dutta, and Bankim Chandra Chatterjee were important writers of the movement.

Bhagavad Gita An ancient text of Hindu wisdom from the first century B.C.E. or first century C.E. inserted into the epic poem *The Mahabharata.*

Bible-based calendar Calendar based on Scripture that dates the creation of the earth at 4004 B.C.E. Archbishop James Ussher constructed it in the mid seventeenth century.

Bildungsroman A novel that traces the PROTAGONIST's development, generally from birth or childhood into maturity. An early prototype is Goethe's *Wilhelm Meister's Apprenticeship* (1795–96). The form has flourished in the ensuing two centuries and includes such modern masterpieces as James Joyce's *Portrait of the Artist as a Young Man* (1916).

Bill of Rights A document that spells out the rights of a citizen in either England or the United States of America. The American Bill of Rights, the first ten amendments to the Constitution, was ratified in 1791 and guarantees freedom of religion, press, assembly, and petition; the right to bear arms; protection under the law; and the right to a speedy trial. See also ENGLISH BILL OF RIGHTS.

Biographical criticism An approach to literature that maintains that knowledge of an author's life experiences can aid in the understanding of his or her work. Although biographical information can sometimes complicate one's interpretation of a work and some FORMALIST CRITICS, such as the NEW

CRITICS, disparage the use of an author's biography as a tool for textual interpretation, learning about the life of an author can often enrich a reader's appreciation for that author's work.

Blank verse Unrhymed IAMBIC PENTAMETER. Blank verse is the form closest to the natural rhythms of English speech and is therefore the most common pattern found in traditional English narrative and dramatic poetry, from Shakespeare to the writers of the early twentieth century.

Bolshevik Revolution The revolution in Russia in 1917 in which the government of the hereditary tsar was overthrown and replaced by a Communist regime under the leadership of Vladimir Lenin. After the Bolshevik Revolution, the Russian empire became the Union of Soviet Socialist Republics, or USSR.

Bourgeoisie Prosperous urban middle class that emerged in the wake of the INDUSTRIAL REVOLUTION and gained wealth and power in the nineteenth century. In MARXIST theory, the bourgeoisie is identified as the owners and operators of industry, as opposed to the PROLETARIAT, who live by the sale of their labor.

Brahman In the UPANISHADS—sacred Hindu texts—Brahman is the ultimate reality that transcends all names and descriptions and is the single unifying essence of the universe. A brahman, or brahmin, is also a Hindu priest and thus of the highest caste in the traditional Hindu caste system.

Brahmanism A religion that recognizes the creator, Brahma, and the priestly class of brahmans who administer Hindu rituals.

Buddhism A religion founded in India in the sixth century B.C.E. by Siddhartha Gautama, the Buddha. While Buddhism has taken different forms in the many areas of the world to which it has spread, its central tenet is that life is suffering caused by desire. In order to obtain salvation, or nirvana, one must transcend desire through following an eightfold path that includes the practice of right action and right mindfulness.

Bunraku New name for JORURI, traditional Japanese puppet theater.

Bushido The code of honor and conduct of the Japanese SAMURAI class. *Bushido* emphasizes self-discipline and bravery.

Byronic hero A character based on the heroes in the poems of Lord Byron (1788–1824), such as Childe Harold, Manfred, and Cain. The Byronic hero is an outsider, even an outlaw—proud, defiant, and moody—who seems burdened by an undefined sense of guilt or misery.

Cacophony In literature, language that is discordant and difficult to pronounce, such as the line "never my numb plunker fumbles" from John Updike's "Player Piano." Cacophony (from the Greek for "bad sound") may be unintentional, or it may be used for deliberate dramatic effect; also refers to the combination of loud, jarring sounds.

Caesura A pause within a line of poetry that contributes to the line's RHYTHM. A caesura can occur anywhere within a line and need not be indicated by punctuation. In SCANSION, caesuras are indicated by a double vertical line.

Canon The works generally considered by scholars, critics, and teachers to be the most important to read and study and that collectively constitute the masterpieces of literature. Since the 1960s, the traditional English and American literary canons, consisting mostly of works by white male writers, have been expanding to include many female writers and writers of varying ethnic backgrounds.

Captivity narratives Autobiographical accounts detailing American colonists' experiences as prisoners of Native Americans; extremely popular from the late seventeenth century through the nineteenth century. Often written to illustrate spiritual or moral growth through trials, these narratives typically describe a dramatic capture and lengthy travels and ordeals, culminating in escape or release. Much was made of the divide between "savage" and "civilized" society, of fear of assimilation into an alien culture, and of the promise of salvation for the chosen few.

Carpe diem Latin phrase meaning "seize the day." This is a common literary theme, especially in lyric poetry, conveying that life is short, time is fleeting, and one should make the most of present pleasures. Andrew Marvell's poem "To His Coy Mistress" is a good example.

Catharsis Meaning "purgation," or the release of the emotions of pity and fear by the audience at the end of a tragedy. In *Poetics,* Aristotle discusses the importance of catharsis. The audience faces the misfortunes of the PROTAGONIST, which elicit pity and compassion. Simultaneously, the audience confronts the protagonist's failure, thus receiving a frightening reminder of human limitations and frailties.

Character, characterization A character is a person presented in a dramatic or narrative work; characterization is the process by which a writer makes a character seem real to the reader.

Chivalric romances Idealized stories from the medieval period that espoused the values of a sophisticated courtly society. These tales centered around the lives of knights who were faithful to God, king, and country and willing to sacrifice themselves for these causes and for the love and protection of women. Chivalric romances were highly moral and fanciful, often pitting knights against dark or supernatural forces.

Chorus In Greek tragedies, a group of people who serve mainly as commentators on the play's characters and events, adding to the audience's understanding of a play by expressing traditional moral, religious, and social attitudes. The role of the chorus is occasionally used by modern playwrights.

Cliché An idea or expression that has become tired and trite from overuse. Clichés often anesthetize readers and are usually signs of weak writing.

Closet drama A play that is to be read rather than performed onstage. In closet dramas, literary art outweighs all other considerations.

Colloquial Informal diction that reflects casual, conversational language and often includes slang expressions.

Comedy A work intended to interest, involve, and amuse readers or an audience, in which no terrible disaster occurs and which ends happily for the main characters.

Comic epic One of the earliest English novelists, Henry Fielding (1707–1754) characterized the kind of literature he was creating in his novel *Joseph Andrews* (1742) as "a comic epic in prose," thus distinguishing it from serious or tragic epic poems that treated noble characters and elevated subjects. His novel was about common people and everyday events.

Comic relief A humorous scene or incident that alleviates tension in an otherwise serious work. Often these moments enhance the thematic significance of a story in addition to providing humor.

Communist A supporter of the political system in which all property and wealth is owned collectively by and shared equally among all members of society. Communism derived largely from the theories of Karl Marx and Friedrich Engels, as presented in *The Communist Manifesto* (1848).

Conflict In a literary work, the struggle within the PLOT between opposing forces. The PROTAGONIST is engaged in a conflict with the ANTAGONIST.

Confucianism A religion/philosophy that has influenced Chinese and East Asian spirituality and culture for over two thousand years. Based on the writings of Confucius (Kongfuzi; 551–479 B.C.E.), Confucianism asserts that humans can improve and even perfect themselves through education and moral reform. In its various manifestations, Confucianism has affected the social and political evolution of China and East Asia while providing a spiritual and moral template.

Connotation Implications going beyond the literal meaning of a word that derive from how the word has been commonly used and from ideas or things associated with it. For example, the word *eagle* in the United States connotes ideas of liberty and freedom that have little to do with the term's literal meaning.

ConsonanceA common type of near-rhyme or half rhyme that consists of identical consonant sounds preceded by different vowel sounds: *home, same; worth, breath.*

Continental Congress Assembly of delegates representing the thirteen British colonies in North America. The First Continental Congress convened in 1774 and drafted a petition to King George III; the Second Continental Congress met in 1775, organized an army under the leadership of George Washington, and adopted the Declaration of Independence on July 4, 1776.

ConventionA characteristic of a literary GENRE that is understood and accepted by readers and audiences because it has become familiar. For example, the division of a play into acts and scenes is a dramatic convention, as are SOLILOQUIES and ASIDES.

CosmogonyA theory that explains the origins of the universe.

Council of Areopagus Council in Athens — named after the place where it held its meetings — that was the political forum prior to the establishment of the COUNCIL OF FOUR HUNDRED. Areopagus later remained active as a criminal court.

Council of Four HundredA council established by Solon in Athens in 594 B.C.E. as a rival to the COUNCIL OF AREOPAGUS, which, according to Solon, had become too corrupt. Solon granted each of Athens's social classes equal representation in the senate. Each class was represented by one hundred men.

CoupletA two-line, rhymed stanza. Pope is the master of the HEROIC COUPLET, a two-line, rhymed, iambic-pentameter stanza that completes its thought within the closed two-line form.

CreoleThe culture and language of some of the Spanish and French settlers of South and North America. Many Creoles speak a mixed form of French, Spanish, and English.

Crimean War(1853–1856) A war fought on the Crimean peninsula in the Black Sea between the Russians and the allied forces of the British, the French, and the Ottoman Turks. The war arose from religious conflicts in the Middle East. When Austria threatened to enter the war, Russia agreed to peace terms resulting in the Treaty of Paris (1856), but the shift in power had long-lasting effects, notably the unification of Germany and Italy.

CrisisThe moment in a work of drama or fiction where the elements of the conflict reach the point of maximum tension. The crisis is part of the work's structure but is not necessarily the emotional crescendo, or climax.

Critical realism Politically driven, early-twentieth-century school of Chinese literature pioneered by Lu Xun (1881–1936); examines societal tendencies through the actions of realistic characters.

CubismAn early-twentieth-century movement centered in France, primarily in painting and collage, that attempted to show objects from several perspectives at once; proponents included the artists Pablo Picasso (1881–1973) and Georges Braque (1882–1963).

Cultural criticism An approach to literature that focuses on the historical as well as the social, political, and economic contexts of a work. Popular culture — mass-produced and mass-consumed cultural artifacts ranging from advertising to popular fiction to television to rock music — is seen on equal footing with "high culture." Cultural critics use widely eclectic strategies, such as NEW HISTORICISM, psychology, gender studies, and DECONSTRUCTION, to analyze not only literary texts but everything from radio talk shows to comic strips, calendar art, commercials, travel guides, and baseball cards.

DadaismAn early-twentieth-century AVANT-GARDE movement inaugurated by French poets Tristan Tzara (1896–1963) and Hans Arp (1887–1966) and German poet Hugo Ball (1886–1927), all living in Zurich during World War I. Stressing irrationality and the absurdity of life in an era of mechanized mass-destruction, dadaism is often seen as nihilistic; in its emphasis on free association and instinctive composition, it can be viewed as a precursor to surrealism. The French painter Marcel Duchamp (1887–1968) may be dadaism's most renowned practitioner.

Daoism (Taoism) A religion / philosophy based on the *Dao De Jing* of Laozi (Lao-tzu) that emphasizes individual freedom, spontaneity, mystical experience, and self-transformation, and is the antithesis of CONFUCIANISM. In pursuit of the *dao,* or the Way—the eternal creative reality that is the essence of all things—practitioners embrace simplicity and reject learned wisdom. The Daoist tradition has flourished in China and East Asia for two thousand years.

Decembrist Revolt After the death of Tsar Alexander I (r. 1801–25), a group of liberal officers, many of whom had served in the Napoleonic Wars, attempted in December 1825 to depose his heir, Nicholas I (r. 1825–55), in the hope of bringing to power a ruler who would guarantee them a constitutional monarchy. The officers were crushed by Nicholas, who punished them severely to discourage other reform-minded Russians.

Deconstructionism An approach to literature that suggests that literary works do not yield single fixed meanings because language can never say exactly what one intends it to mean. Deconstructionism seeks to destabilize meaning by examining the gaps in and ambiguities of a text's language. Deconstructionists pay close attention to language in order to discover and describe how a variety of close readings can be generated.

Deism An unorthodox religious philosophy prominent in the seventeenth and eighteenth centuries in northern Europe and America. Deists believe that religious knowledge can be arrived at through reason rather than through revelation or formal religious instruction. Deism constructs God as a rational architect of an orderly world; the deist God creates the world and sets it in motion but does not become directly involved in human affairs.

Denouement French term meaning "unraveling" or "unknotting" used to describe the resolution of a PLOT following the climax.

Dialect A type of informal DICTION. Dialects are spoken by definable groups of people from a particular geographic region, economic group, or social class. Writers use dialect to express and contrast the education, class, and social and regional backgrounds of their characters.

Dialogue Verbal exchange between CHARACTERS. Dialogue reveals firsthand characters' thoughts, responses, and emotional states, and thus makes the characters real to readers or the audience.

Diaspora The wide dispersion of a people or a culture that was formerly located in one place. Two historical diasporas of note are the diaspora of the Jews from Palestine following the Roman destruction of the Second Temple in 70 C.E. and the African diaspora caused by the slave trade. Both the Jews and the Africans were dispersed across many continents.

Diction A writer's choice of words, phrases, sentence structure, and figurative language, which combine to help create meaning.

Didactic poetry Poetry designed to teach an ethical, moral, or religious lesson.

Dionysus The god of wine in Greek mythology, whose cult originated in Thrace and Phrygia—north and east of the Greek peninsula. Dionysus was often blamed for people's irrational behavior and for chaotic situations. However, many Greeks also believed that Dionysus taught them good farming skills, especially those related to wine production. Greek tragedy evolved from a ceremony that honored Dionysus, and the theater in Athens was dedicated to him.

Doggerel A derogatory term for poetry whose subject is trite and whose rhythm and sounds are monotonously heavy-handed.

Drama Derived from the Greek word *dram,* meaning "to do" or "to perform," the term *drama* may refer to a single play, a group of plays, or to plays in general. Drama is designed to be performed in a theater: Actors take on the roles of its characters, perform indicated actions, and deliver the script's DIALOGUE.

Dramatic monologue A type of lyric or narrative poem in which a speaker addresses an imagined and distinct but silent audience in such a way as to reveal a dramatic situation and, often unintentionally, some aspect of the speaker's temperament or personality.

Dualistic tradition Religious and philosophical doctrine dating from ancient times in which the antagonistic forces of good and evil determine the course of events.

Early Modern era Period extending from about 1500 to 1800, marked by the advent of colonialism and capitalism.

Edenic New World Early European immigrants to the New World often described it as a new Eden, a Garden of Paradise.

Edo The ancient name for Tokyo. During the TOKUGAWA period (1600–1868), Edo became the imperial capital of Japan.

Eight-legged essay The *ba-gu wen,* an essay of eight parts written on a Confucian theme and developed during the MING DYNASTY in China (1368–1644) as a requirement for the civil service examinations.

Electra complex The female version of the Oedipus complex as theorized by Sigmund Freud to describe a daughter's unconscious rivalry with her mother for her father's attention. The name comes from the Greek legend of Electra, who avenged the death of her father by plotting the death of her mother.

Elegiac couplets The conventional strophic form of Latin elegiac love poetry, consisting of one dactylic hexameter line followed by one dactylic pentameter line. A dactylic hexameter line is composed of six feet, each foot comprising one long, or accented, and two short, or unaccented, syllables; the sixth foot may be shortened by one or two syllables; the pentameter line consists of five such feet. The elegiac couplet is also known as a "distich."

Elegy A mournful, contemplative lyric poem often ending in consolation, written to commemorate someone who has died. *Elegy* may also refer to a serious, meditative poem that expresses the speaker's melancholy thoughts.

Elysian land In Greek mythology, some fortunate mortals spend their afterlife in the bliss of the Elysian Fields, or Islands of the Blest, rather than in Hades, the underworld.

End-stopped line A line in a poem after which a pause occurs. End-stopped lines reflect normal speech patterns and are often marked by punctuation.

English Bill of Rights Formally known as "An Act declaring the Rights and Liberties of the Subject, and settling the Succession of the Crown," the English Bill of Rights was passed in December 1689. It conferred the crown upon William and Mary, who succeeded the ousted James II; it stated that no Catholic would ever be king or queen of England, extended civil rights and liberties to the people of England, and confirmed Parliament's power in a constitutional government. See also BILL OF RIGHTS.

Enjambment In poetry, a line continuing without a pause into the next line for its meaning; also called a run-on line.

Enlightenment Refers to a period of time in Europe from the late seventeenth through the eighteenth century, also called the Age of Reason, in which reason, human progress, and order were venerated. The Enlightenment intensified the process of secularization that had begun during the Renaissance and favored the use of empirical science to resolve social problems. Enlightenment philosophers questioned the existing forms of education and politics and fought tyranny and social injustice. Enlightenment ideas led to the American and French Revolutions in the late 1700s. Leading philosophers also questioned the Bible and gave rise to a new movement of freethinkers—people who rejected the church's dogma and encouraged rational inquiry and speculation.

Ennui French for boredom or lack of interest; the term is associated with a widespread discontent with the pleasures of the modern world.

Eos The Greek goddess of the dawn who loved the young men Cleitus, Cephalus, and Orion, the hunter.

Epic A long narrative poem told in a formal, elevated style that focuses on a serious subject and chronicles heroic deeds and events important to a culture or nation.

Epigram A brief, pointed, and witty poem that usually makes a satiric or humorous point. Epigrams are most often written in couplets but can be written in any form.

Epiphany In fiction, when a character suddenly experiences a deep realization about himself or herself; a truth which is grasped in an ordinary rather than a melodramatic moment.

Eros The Greek god of love, associated with both passion and fertility. Freud used the term *Eros* in modern times to signify the human life-drive (desire) at war with THANATOS, the death-drive.

Euphony From the Greek for "good sound"; refers to language that is smooth and musically pleasant to the ear.

Existentialism A school of modern philosophy associated with Jean-Paul Sartre (1905–1980) and Albert Camus (1913–1960) that dominated European thought in the years following World War II. Existentialists are interested in the nature of consciousness and emphasize the role of individual will in shaping existence. Existentialism holds that discrete, willful acts of choice create the only meaning that exists in an otherwise meaningless universe.

Exposition A narrative device often used at the beginning of a work that provides necessary background information about characters and their circumstances. Exposition explains such matters as what has gone on before, the relationships between characters, theme, and conflict.

Expressionism An artistic and literary movement that originated in Germany in the early twentieth century. Expressionism departs from the conventions of realism to focus on the inner impressions or moods of a character or of the artist. Influenced by the increased mechanization of the modern world and by MARXISM, expressionism often reveals the alienation of the individual.

Fabliau Although the *fabliau* originated in France as a comic or satiric tale in verse, by the time of Giovanni Boccaccio (1313–1375) and Geoffrey Chaucer (1340–1400) the term also stood for bawdy and ribald prose tales like "The Miller's Tale" in Chaucer's *Canterbury Tales* or Boccaccio's "Rustico and Alibech."

Farce A form of humor based on exaggerated, improbable incongruities. Farce involves rapid shifts in action and emotion as well as slapstick comedy and extravagant dialogue.

Fascism An ideology that combines dictatorial government, militarism, control of the personal freedom of a people, extreme nationalism, and government control of business. Fascism peaked between the 1920s and '40s, when Adolf Hitler, Benito Mussolini, and Francisco Franco gained power in Germany, Italy, and Spain respectively.

Feminism A school of thought that examines the oppression, subjugation, or inequality of women. Feminism has flourished since the middle of the twentieth century and has taken different forms, focusing variously on language, the meaning of power, and the institutions that perpetuate sexism.

Feminist criticism An approach to literature that seeks to correct or supplement a predominantly male-dominated critical perspective with a feminist consciousness. Feminist criticism places literature in a social context and uses a broad range of disciplines, including history, sociology, psychology, and linguistics, to provide interpretations that are sensitive to feminist issues.

Fenian Society A secret organization of Irish nationalists founded in 1858 promoting Irish independence from England by means of violent revolution. The organization was named after the Fenians, professional soldiers who served Irish kings in third-century Ireland. With support from cells among Irish emigrants in America, South Africa, and Australia, the Fenian Society, led by James Stephens, launched a rebellion in 1867 that, although it failed, helped to galvanize political opposition to English rule and call attention to the problems in Ireland.

Feudal aristocracy A system of government that existed in Europe in the Middle Ages. The feudal system refers to a mode of agricultural production in which peasants worked for landowners, or lords, in return for debt forgiveness, food, and governmental responsibilities such as military protection. The lords or landowners constitute the upper class, or aristocracy, but at the top of the hierarchy was the monarch who controlled the government and the granting of fiefs, or tracts of land.

Figures of speech Ways of using language that deviate from the literal, denotative meanings of words in order to suggest additional meanings or effects. Figures of speech say one thing in terms of something else, such as when an eager funeral director is described as a vulture.

Fin de siècle French for "end of the century"; generally refers to the final years of the nineteenth century, a time characterized by decadence and ENNUI. Artists of this era romanticized drug addiction and prostitution; open sexuality, including homosexuality, also marked the period. In Paris and Vienna, the Art Nouveau movement in the fine arts flourished and was informed by the blossoming of radical ideas in the wake of the Paris Commune of 1871. Notable fin-de-siècle figures include artists such as Aubrey Beardsley and writers such as Oscar Wilde.

Fixed form A poem characterized by a fixed pattern of lines, syllables, or meter. A SONNET is a fixed form of poetry because it must have fourteen lines.

Flashback A literary or dramatic device that allows a past occurrence to be inserted into the chronological order of a narrative.

Floating World (*ukiyo-e*) A Japanese artistic movement that flourished in the seventeenth, eighteenth, and nineteenth centuries in Tokyo. Ukiyo-e depicts the floating or sorrowful world; its most frequent media are woodblock prints, books, and drawings. Originally considered a popular rather than a high art, ukiyo-e treated literary, classic, and historical themes within a contemporary context, and it was particularly appealing to the emerging merchant classes.

Flying Dutchman The legend of a ghostly ship doomed to sail for eternity. If a vision of it appears to sailors, it signals imminent disaster. Most versions of the story have the captain of the ship playing dice or gambling with the Devil.

Foil A character in a literary work or drama whose behavior or values contrast with those of another character, typically the PROTAGONIST.

Foot A poetic foot is a poem's unit of measurement and decides the rhythm. In English, the iambic, or ascending, foot is the most common.

Foreshadowing Providing hints of what is to happen next in order to build suspense.

Formalist A type of criticism dominant in the early twentieth century that emphasizes the form of an artwork. Two of its prominent schools are Russian formalism, which favors the form of an artwork over its content and argues for the necessity of literature to defamiliarize the ordinary objects of the world, and American NEW CRITICISM, which treats a work of art as an object and seeks to understand it through close, careful analysis.

Formula literature Literature that fulfills a reader's expectations. In detective novels, for instance, the plot may vary among different works, but in the end the detective solves the case in all of them. Science fiction, romance, and Westerns are other examples of formula literature.

Found poem An ordinary collection of words that can be understood differently when arranged or labeled as a poem. A found poem could be something as banal as a "to do" list or personal advertisement, but the poet who "finds" it argues that it has special, unintentional value when presented as a poem.

Founding myth A story that explains how a particular nation or culture came to be, such as Virgil's *Aeneid,* which describes the founding of Rome. Many epic poems, sometimes called national epics, are founding myths.

Four classes In Hindu tradition, humans are created as one of four classes, or *varna:* in descending order, the BRAHMANS (priests), the *Ksatriya* (warriors), the *Vaisya* (merchants and farmers), and the *Sudra* (laborers and servants).

Framed narration Also called *framed tale*. A story within a story. In Chaucer's *Canterbury Tales,* each pilgrim's story is framed by the story of the pilgrimage itself. This device, used by writers from ancient times to the present, enjoyed particular popularity during the thirteenth, fourteenth, and fifteenth centuries and was most fully developed in *The Arabian Nights,* a work in which the framing is multilayered.

Free association A Freudian exercise wherein a patient relates to an analyst anything that comes to his or her mind, no matter how illogical or apparently trivial, without any attempt to censor, shape, or otherwise organize the material. In literature, the term refers to a free flow of the mind's thoughts; it is an important element of stream-of-consciousness writing.

Free verse Highly irregular poetry; typically, free verse does not rhyme.

French Revolution The first of four major revolutions in France in the late eighteenth and nineteenth centuries; it began with the storming of the Bastille in 1789 and ended in the coup of the Eighteenth Brumaire, on November 9–10, 1799, when Napoleon overthrew the revolutionary government. The original goal of the revolution had been to establish a constitutional monarchy that would transfer power from the nobility, headed by King Louis XVI, and the clergy to the middle classes. That aim was abandoned, however, when the king and queen were beheaded in 1793 and a republic was created.

French Symbolists Symbolism was an AVANT-GARDE movement in France in the late nineteenth century that arose from revolutionary experiments with language, verse form, and the use of symbols in the poetry of Stéphane Mallarmé (1842–1898) and Paul Verlaine (1844–1896); according to the Symbolists, poetic language should not delineate ideas but rather evoke feeling and moods, insinuate impressions and connections. French Symbolism, which often is extended to include the poetry of Charles Baudelaire (1821–1867) and Arthur Rimbaud (1854–1891), who anticipated some of its principles, exerted a profound influence on modernist poetry in Russia as well as throughout Europe and the United States.

Freudian criticism A method of literary criticism associated with Freud's theories of psychoanalysis. Early Freudian critics sought to illustrate how literature is shaped by the unconscious desires of the author, but the term has developed and become more broadly defined to encompass many schools of thought that link psychoanalysis to the interpretation of literature.

Gay and lesbian criticism School of literary criticism that focuses on the representation of homosexuality in literature; also interested in how homosexuals read literature and to what extent sexuality and gender is culturally constructed.

Gender criticism Literary school that analyzes how an author's or a reader's sex affects the writing and reading experiences.

Genre A category of artistic works or literary compositions that have a distinctive style or content. Poetry, fiction, and drama are genres. Different genres have dominated at various times and places: In eighteenth-century Europe, the dramatic comedy was the preferred form of theater; in the nineteenth century, the novel was the dominant genre.

Genroku period (1688–1703) A Japanese cultural period during the EDO era when a growing number of affluent *chonin,* or townsmen, sought diversion in the FLOATING WORLD, or *ukiyo-e*—city districts where courtesans, along with theater, dance, song, and the arts, flourished.

German Romanticism A German form of nineteenth-century Romanticism. In addition to German Romantic poets like Friedrich Holderlin (1770–1843), Novalis (1772–1801), and Heinrich Heine (1797–1856), Germany produced the Romantic theorists Friedrich Schlegel (1772–1829), F. W. J. Schelling (1775–1854), and August Wilhelm Schlegel (1767–1845), who believed that the Christian myth needed to be replaced with a modern one.

Ghazal A form of lyric poetry composed of three to seven couplets, called *sh'ir*, that follow the strict rhyme scheme of *aa ba ca da*, and so on, known as the *qafiyah*. Strict adherence to the form requires the use of the *radif*, a word that is repeated in a pattern dictated by the first couplet, throughout the poem. Literally meaning "dialogue with the beloved," the *ghazal*, as practiced in Arabia, Persia, Turkey, and India beginning around 1200, became the predominant form for love poetry.

Giri Japanese term for social duty and responsibility.

Glorious Revolution of 1688 The forced abdication of the Catholic king James II of England, whose attempts to exercise royal authority over Parliament galvanized the largely Protestant English nation against him. Although largely a bloodless revolution, some fighting between Catholics and Protestants took place in Ireland and Scotland.

Gnostics Members of an ancient sect in the Middle East who believed that hidden knowledge held the key to the universe. Throughout history there have been Gnostics who have formed secret societies with secret scriptures and who have believed they understood the workings of the cosmos.

Gokan A book combining pictures and text; often adapted from classic Chinese or Japanese stories.

Gothic A style of literature (especially novels) in the late eighteenth and early nineteenth centuries that reacted against the mannered decorum of earlier literature. Gothic novels explore the darker side of human experience; they are often set in the past and in foreign countries, and they employ elements of horror, mystery, and the supernatural.

Gothic novel A subgenre of the novel whose works concentrate on mystery, magic, and horror. Especially popular during the late eighteenth and early nineteenth centuries, gothic novels are often set in castles or mansions whose dungeons or secret rooms contribute to the atmosphere of mystery.

Greater Dionysia In ancient Greece, dramas were performed at festivals that honored the god Dionysus: the Lenaea during January and February and the Greater Dionysia in March and April. The best tragedies and comedies were awarded prizes by an Athenian jury.

Hadith Islamic source of religious law and moral guidance. According to tradition, the Hadith were passed down orally to the prophet Muhammad, and today they are critical to the study of the early development of Islam.

Haikai A form of Japanese linked verse that flourished from the sixteenth through the nineteenth centuries, *haikai* is a sequence of alternating stanzas usually composed by two or more writers. The sequence opens with a *hokku*, a three-line stanza of seventeen syllables that alternate 5, 7, 5; the hokku is followed by alternating three- and two-line stanzas of seventeen and fourteen syllables, respectively. Bashō, the greatest of the haikai masters, preferred a sequence of thirty-six stanzas. Haikai is distinguished from RENGA, an earlier form of Japanese linked verse, primarily by diction and tone; whereas renga, with its origins in court poetry, uses elevated diction and reflects a cultivated seriousness, haikai introduces more colloquial diction, is more lighthearted, and treats common aspects of human experience. The hokku eventually became a separate form, now known as HAIKU.

Haiku Unrhymed Japanese poetic form that consists of seventeen syllables arranged in three lines. Although its origins can be traced to the seventeenth century, it is the most popular poetic form in Japan today. See HAIKAI.

Hamartia Error or flaw. In ancient Greek tragedies, the hero falls through his own *hamartia*.

Hellene Greek.

Heroic couplet A rhymed, iambic-pentameter stanza of two lines that completes its thought within the two-line form. Alexander Pope

(1688–1744), the most accomplished practitioner of the form in English, included this couplet in his *Essay on Criticism:* "True wit is nature to advantage dressed, / What oft was thought, but ne'er so well expressed."

Hexameter couplets The conventional strophic form of Greek and Latin epic poetry consisting of two dactylic hexameter lines; each line is composed of six feet and each foot comprises one long (accented) and two short (unaccented) syllables. The final foot is known as a catalectic foot, for it is generally shortened by one or two syllables.

Hieros gamos Literally, "sacred marriage"; a fertility ritual in which the god-king or priest-king is united with the goddess or priestess-queen in order to provide a model for the kingdom and establish the king's right to rule.

Hinduism The major religion of India, based upon the ancient doctrines found in the SANSKRIT texts known as the VEDAS and the UPANISHADS, dating from 1000 B.C.E.

Historical criticism An approach to literature that uses history as a means of understanding a literary work. Such criticism moves beyond both the facts of an author's life and the text itself to examine the social and intellectual contexts in which the author composed the work.

Homeric Hymns At one time attributed to Homer, the *Homeric Hymns* (seventh–sixth centuries B.C.E.) are now believed to have been created by poets from a Homeric school or simply in the style of Homer. Five of the longer hymns contain important stories about gods such as Demeter, DIONYSUS, Apollo, Aphrodite, and Hermes.

Hubris Exaggerated pride or arrogance; in Greek tragedies, hubris always causes fatal errors.

Huguenots French Protestant members of the Reformed Church established in France by John Calvin in about 1555. Due to religious persecution, many fled to other countries in the sixteenth and seventeenth centuries.

Hyperbole An exaggerated figure of speech; for example, "I nearly died laughing."

Iambic pentameter A poetic line made up of five feet, or iambs, or a ten-syllable line.

Ibsenism After the plays of Norwegian dramatist Henrik Ibsen (1828–1906): a concern in drama with social problems treated realistically rather than romantically.

Idealism Philosophical Idealism in its various forms holds that objects of perception are in reality mental constructs and not the material objects themselves.

Image The two types of images are literal and figurative. Literal images are very detailed, almost photographic; figurative images are more abstract and often use symbols, such as this image of the night in T. S. Eliot's "The Love Song of J. Alfred Prufrock" (1917):

> Let us go then, you and I,
> When the evening is spread out
> against the sky
> Like a patient etherized upon a table

Industrial Revolution Advancements in mechanization beginning in the mid eighteenth century that transformed manufacturing, transportation, and agriculture over the next century and a half. Most historians regard the Industrial Revolution as the phenomenon that has had the largest impact on the present, changing the Western world from a rural to an urban society and moving the workplace from the fields to the factories. Because of it, the economy changed rapidly, and the production of goods increased exponentially, raising the West's standard of living. The new working class, however, lived in horrible conditions in the cities.

Industrialization The process of building factories and mass producing goods; typically, also part of urbanization.

Inquisition A medieval institution set up by the Roman Catholic pope to judge and convict anyone who might constitute a threat to papal power. The threats took various forms, including heresy, witchcraft, alchemy, and sorcery. The Inquisition held a great amount of power in medieval Europe, especially in southern European countries. The most powerful was the Spanish Inquisition, authorized in 1478, which executed thousands of victims, among them Jews, Muslims, and heretics, through public burning.

Irish Literary Renaissance A movement of the late nineteenth century of Irish writers, including William Butler Yeats (1865–1939), Lady Gregory (1852–1932), and J. M. Synge (1871–1909), who aimed to revitalize Irish literature and to renew interest in and revaluate Irish myth, legend, folklore, history, and literature. The literary renaissance was part of a broader cultural effervescence in Ireland in the late 1890s that included the founding of the Gaelic League, which promoted the use of the Irish language, and the startup of the Gaelic Athletic Association, which restored Irish sports.

Irony A device used in writing and speech to deliberately express ideas so they can be understood in two ways. In drama, irony occurs when a character does not know something that the other characters or the audience knows.

Jainism A religion founded in India in the sixth century B.C.E. by Vardhaman, who is known as Mahavira, or the "great hero." Formed in direct opposition to the rigid ritualism and hierarchical structure of traditional Hinduism, Jainism espoused asceticism, renunciation of the world, nonviolence, and the sanctity of all living beings.

Jewish mysticism Like all forms of mysticism, Jewish mysticism focuses on learning and practices that lead to unity with the creator; its teachings are referred to as the Cabala, or Kabala.

Joruri The form of puppet theater that developed in Japan in the seventeenth and eighteenth centuries in which expert puppeteers manipulate lifelike dolls while a master chanter, accompanied by the SAMISEN, sings and chants the story, speaks for the characters, and describes the scenes. The term derives from *ningyo,* meaning puppet or doll, and *joruri,* which alludes to the often-told story of Lady Joruri, the main character of a popular story dating back to the fifteenth century who was the subject of the first puppet play. Today joruri is known as BUNRAKU,

after the great puppeteer Bunraku-ken Uemura (d. 1810), and Bunraku-ken Uemura II (1813–1873), who established a puppet theater in Osaka in 1842 after interest in joruri declined.

Judgment of Paris In Greek legend, Paris (Alexandros) was selected by the god Zeus to judge which of three goddesses was the most beautiful. He chose Aphrodite, who bribed him by agreeing to help him seduce Helen, the most beautiful woman alive. His stealing of Helen and refusal to return her was the cause of the Trojan War.

Julian calendar Calendar used from the time of Julius Caesar, c. 46 B.C.E., until 1582, when it was generally replaced by the Gregorian calendar, which is still in wide use today.

Kabuki A popular form of Japanese theater primarily about and aimed at the middle classes and that uses only male actors; Kabuki developed in the sixteenth and seventeenth centuries, parallel to *JORURI,* or puppet theater, which often shares the same plots and stories and even the same plays.

Kibyoshi Literally, "yellow back"; a simple illustrated book usually concerned with life in the licensed quarters.

Laissez-faire A French phrase meaning "let them do"; a doctrine in classical economics that asserts the economy should operate on its own, without interference from the government.

Leatherstocking Tales Novels by James Fenimore Cooper (1789–1851), including *The Pioneers* (1823), *The Last of the Mohicans* (1826), *The Prairie* (1827), *The Pathfinder* (1840), and *The Deerslayer* (1841). All featured a PROTAGONIST nicknamed "Leatherstocking."

Leitmotifs Themes, brief passages, or single words repeated within a work.

Leviathan A dragon or sea monster mentioned in the Hebrew Scriptures, suggesting an ancient combat myth. See Isaiah 51:9–10, Isaiah 27:1, Psalm 74:12–14, Psalm 89:10, and Job 26:12–13. See also RAHAB.

Liberalism An ideology that rejects authoritarian government and defends freedom of speech, association, and religion as well as the right to own property. Liberalism evolved during the ENLIGHTENMENT and became the dominant political idea of the nineteenth century. Both the American and French Revolutions were based on liberal thought.

Limerick A humorous, sometimes nonsensical poem of five lines, with a strict scheme of meter and rhyme.

Line A sequence of words. In poetry, lines are typically measured by the number of feet they contain.

Literary epic A literary epic—as distinguished from folk epics such as the *Mahabharata* or *The Iliad*—that are made up of somewhat loosely linked episodes and closely follow oral conventions—is written with self-conscious artistry, has a tightly knit organic unity, and is stylistically rooted in a written, literate culture. In actuality, great epics often blur the distinction between the oral or folk epic and the literary epic.

Local-color tales Stories that seek to portray the people and way of life of a particular region by describing the speech, dress, and customs of its inhabitants.

Lyric A brief poem that reflects the imagination and emotion of the speaker. With its etymology in the word *lyre,* a lyric poem was originally meant to be sung to the accompaniment of a lyre, a medieval stringed instrument that is associated with poetic inspiration. Although modern lyric poetry is not necessarily meant to be sung, it does retain its melodic quality. Lyric poetry is highly subjective and informed by the speaker's imagination; it has flourished throughout literary history.

Magical realism A movement in fiction in which REALIST technique is used to narrate stories that combine mundane and miraculous events, everyday realities and the supernatural. The term is most often used to describe the work of Colombian novelist Gabriel García Márquez (b. 1928), Mexican author Carlos Fuentes (b. 1928), Peruvian novelist Mario Vargas Llosa (b. 1936), and Argentine author Julio Cortázar (1914–1984).

Manchu Also known as the Jurchen, a people who lived northeast of the Great Wall of China, in the area now known as Manchuria; when civil disturbances weakened the authority of the Ming emperor, the Manchu, with the assistance of some from inside China, took control of Beijing and founded a new empire. Their dynasty, known as the QING or Manchu dynasty, lasted from 1644 to 1911.

Manifest Destiny Term coined in 1845 for the American belief that the United States was not only destined but obligated to expand its territory westward to the Pacific Ocean.

Marxism A school of thought based on the writings of German Socialist thinker Karl Marx. Among its main tenets are the ideas that class struggle is the central element of Western culture, that a capitalist class thrives by exploiting the labor of a working class, and that workers must struggle to overcome their capitalist exploiters through revolution and thereafter establish a socialist society in which private property does not exist and all people have collective control of the means of production and distribution.

Marxist criticism Literary criticism that evolved from Karl Marx's political and economic theories. Marxist critics believe that texts must be understood in terms of the social class and the economic and political positions of their characters and plot.

Masque Developed in the Renaissance, masques are highly stylized and structured performances with an often mythological or allegorical plot, combining drama, music, song, and dance in an elaborate display.

Materialism A worldview that explains the nature of reality in terms of physical matter and material conditions rather than by way of ideas, emotions, or the supernatural.

Mathnavi Persian poetic form used for romantic, epic, didactic, and other types of poems whose subjects demand a lengthy treatment; its verse structure is similar to that of the Western heroic couplet, but with two rhyming halves in a single line.

Meiji Restoration After years of feudal reign in Japan, the emperor was restored to his position in 1868. He adopted *Meiji*, meaning "enlightened rule," as the name of his era. In this period, massive INDUSTRIALIZATION took place in Japan, which became a significant competitor for world power. The military was also strengthened to combat European and American imperialism.

Melodrama A dramatic genre characterized by suspense, romance, and sensation. Melodramas typically have a happy ending.

Mestizos Peoples in the Americas of mixed ethnic or cultural heritage, usually a combination of Spanish and Native American.

Metaphor A comparison of two things that does not use the words *like* or *as.* For example, "love is a rose."

Meter The rhythm of a poem based on the number of syllables in each line and which syllables are accented. See also FOOT.

Michiyuki A conventional form in Japanese drama (and also in fiction) wherein a character's thoughts and feelings are evoked through the places he or she visits on a journey; often, by means of symbolism and allusion, the journey suggests a spiritual transformation.

Middle Passage The transatlantic journey from West Africa to the Caribbean or the Americas of slave ships transporting their human cargo during the time of the slave trade (sixteenth–nineteenth centuries).

Millenarianism A utopian belief that the end of time is imminent, after which there will be a thousand-year era of perfect peace on earth.

Ming dynasty (1368–1644) Founded by Zhu Yuan-zhang, who restored native Chinese rule from the Mongols who had ruled China during the previous Yuan dynasty (1271–1368) established by Kubla Khan. The Ming dynasty saw a flourishing of Chinese culture, the restoration of Confucianism, and the rise of the arts, including porcelain, architecture, drama, and the novel.

Mock epic A form that parodies the EPIC by treating a trivial subject in the elevated style of the epic, employing such conventions as an invocation to the muse, an extended simile, and a heroic epithet that burlesques its subject.

Modernism In its broadest sense, this term refers to European writing and art from approximately 1914, the beginning of World War I, to about 1945, the end of World War II. Although many writers of this time continued to work with the forms of fiction and poetry that had been in place since the nineteenth century, others such as James Joyce (1882–1941), Virginia Woolf (1882–1941), William Faulkner (1897–1962), Rainer Maria Rilke (1875–1926), and Thomas Mann (1875–1955) broke with the past, introducing experimentation and innovation in structure, style, and language. *Modernism* can also refer to a spirit of innovation and experimentation, or the break with nineteenth-century aesthetic and literary thinking and forms, or the exploration of psychological states of mind, alienation, and social rupture that characterized the era between the two world wars.

Monologue A speech of significant length delivered by one person; in drama, a CHARACTER talks to himself or reveals personal secrets without addressing another character.

Mystery religions Mystery cults were very popular in ancient Greece and Rome for at least one thousand years, beginning around 1000 B.C.E. The details of each cult were kept a secret, but all cults shared a rigorous rite of initiation, a concern about death, and a hope for immortality centered on a deity who had personal knowledge of the afterlife. The most popular Greek versions were the Orphic and Eleusinian mysteries. The mysteries of Isis and Mithra were favored in the Roman world.

Mythological criticism A type of literary criticism that focuses on the archetypal stories common to all cultures. Initiated by Carl Jung in the early twentieth century, mythological criticism seeks to reveal how the structures lodged deep in the human consciousness take the form of archetypal stories and are the basis for literature. Jung identified four principal ARCHETYPES that together constitute the Self: Shadow (rejected evil), Anima (feminine side of male self), Animus (masculine side of female self), and Spirit (wise old man or woman).

Narrative poem   A poem with only one basic rule: It must tell a story. Ballads, epics, and romances are typically narrative poems.

Narrator   The voice that in fiction describes the PLOT or action of a story. The narrator can speak in the first or the third person and, depending on the effect the author wishes to create, can be very visible or almost invisible (an explicit or an implicit narrator); he or she can be involved in the plot or be more distant. See also POINT OF VIEW and SPEAKER.

Naturalism   A late-nineteenth-century literary school that sought to apply scientific objectivity to the novel. Led by Émile Zola (1840–1902) and influenced by Darwinism, Naturalists created characters who were ordinary people, whose lives were shaped by the forces of heredity and the environment.

Nawab   The title given to a local Muslim ruler in India during the Mughal empire (1526–1857).

Négritude   A literary movement founded in the early 1930s by three Black Francophone writers in Paris: Léopold Sédar Senghor (1906–2001), Aimé Césaire (b. 1913), and Léon Damas (1912–1978). In their work, these Négritude writers protested French colonial rule and the European assumption of superiority. They wanted their writings, which honored the traditions and special qualities of the African and Caribbean peoples, to inspire independence movements in the colonies.

Neoclassicism   A style of art and architecture that was characterized by the simple, symmetrical forms of classical Greek and Roman art. It originated as a reaction to the Rococo and Baroque styles and was the result of a revival of classical thought in Europe and America. Neoclassical writing characterized the Augustan Age, a period comprising roughly the first half of the eighteenth century. Its name suggests an analogy to the reign of Emperor Augustus in the Roman Empire (63 B.C.E.–14 C.E.), when many of the great Latin poets, especially Virgil, were writing.

Neo-Confucianism   Refers generally to the philosophical tradition in China and Japan based on the thought of Confucius (551–479 B.C.E.) and his commentators, particularly Mencius (370–290 B.C.E.) and Zhu Xi (1130–1200). Neo-Confucianism, which arose during the Sung dynasty (960–1279), asserts that the understanding of things must be based on an understanding of their underlying principles; in moral and political philosophy, it emphasizes the study of history, loyalty to family and nation, and order.

Neo-Sensualism   Also known as the New Sensibilities or New Perceptionist school, this approach was founded by Kawabata Yasunari and other AVANT-GARDE writers, including Yokomitsu Riichi (1898–1947), and headquartered at the University of Tokyo in the 1920s. In 1924 these writers founded a magazine called *The Literary Age.* Influenced by European writers as well as by Japanese poetic traditions and *Nō* drama, neo-Sensualists sought to break with the confessional style of REALIST and NATURALIST writers and aimed for a more purely aesthetic, nonlinear style of fiction writing.

Neo-Shintoism   *Shinto* is a term given to indigenous Japanese beliefs as distinguished from Buddhism, which was introduced to Japan in the sixth century C.E. In the seventeenth century, Shinto and Confucianist ideals came into contact with one another and produced an ideology that emphasized political philosophy and valued the virtues of wisdom, benevolence, and courage.

New Criticism   A type of formalist literary criticism that completely disregards historical and biographical information to focus on the actual text. The New Critics perform a close reading of a work and give special attention to technical devices such as symbols and images and, in poetry, rhythm.

New Historicism   A literary school developed as a reaction to NEW CRITICISM in the 1980s; presently, it is one of the leading schools of literary criticism. Like the nineteenth-century historicists, the New Historicists argue that historical and other external contexts must be part of textual analysis.

Nigerian-Biafran War Nigerian civil war that started when the Igbo people declared the eastern region of Nigeria an independent state named the Republic of Biafra. Recognized by only three countries, Biafra was almost immediately attacked by Nigerian troops. After a bloody fight resulting in close to three million casualties, the Biafran government surrendered in January 1970.

Ninjo Japanese term that denotes human feelings or passion, drives that often come into conflict with *GIRI,* or social duty and responsibility.

Nō The highly elaborate and ritualistic classical theater of Japan, known for its minimalist approach to plot, scenery, and stage effects and the stately performance and Zen-like mastery of its actors; *nō* means "talent" or "accomplishment." The great master and theorist of *Nō* drama is Zeami Motokiyo (1363–1443), who wrote several of the most famous *Nō* plays, including *Atsumori* and *The Lady Aoi.*

Novel An extended work of fictional prose narrative. The novel is a modern outgrowth of earlier genres such as the romance. There is considerable debate as to the origins of the novel; some critics trace it to Cervantes's *Don Quixote* in 1605. In England, the novel came into being in the beginning of the eighteenth century and has since developed far beyond its original realistic and moralistic aims, making it one of the most flexible of literary genres.

Octave A STANZA of eight lines in poetry.

Ode An elevated form of LYRIC generally written on a single theme, using varied metric and rhyme patterns. With the ode, poets working within classical schemes can introduce considerable innovation. There are three major types of odes in English: the Pindaric, or Regular; the Horatian; and the Irregular. The Pindaric ode is structured by three-strophe divisions, modulating between the strophe, antistrophe, and epode, which vary in tone. The Horatian ode uses only one STANZA type with variation introduced within each stanza. The Irregular ode, sometimes called the English ode, allows wide variety among stanza forms, rhyme schemes, and metrical patterns.

Oedipus complex A term from Freudian psychoanalysis that refers to the unconscious male desire to kill one's own father and to sleep with one's own mother. The term derives from the Greek myth of Oedipus, who unknowingly murdered his father and married his mother; his self-inflicted punishment was to blind himself. FREUDIAN CRITICS do not take the complex or the story literally, but frequently use it to examine in literature the guilt associated with sexual desire and competition with or hostility toward one's father.

Onomatopoeia A word that sounds like the thing it refers to: for example, the *buzz* of bees.

Open form Also known as FREE VERSE. A type of poetry that does not follow established conventions of METER, RHYME, and STANZA.

Organic form The concept that the structure of a literary work develops according to an internal logic. The literary work grows and becomes an organic whole that follows the principles of nature, not mechanics. The created work of art is akin to a growing plant that relies on all of its parts working together.

Orientalism The academic study and knowledge of the Middle East and Asia that developed during the imperialism of the nineteenth century. Orientalism is a Western approach to understanding the cultures, languages, and religions of the East. Especially in the early studies, the Orient was seen as exotic and romantic, but its inhabitants were regarded as uncivilized and inferior. Although by now these views have been challenged and changed, they are arguably still prevalent.

Oxymoron A rhetorical figure of speech in which contradictory terms are combined, such as "jumbo shrimp" and "deafening silence."

Parable A short narrative designed to teach a lesson about life in which the moral isn't directly stated; a form popular during biblical times.

Paradox An argument or opinion that is contradictory but true. For instance, "You have to be cruel to be kind."

Paraphrase To rewrite or say the same thing using different words.

Parian White marble from the Greek island of Paros.

Parody A humorous imitation of another, usually serious, work. Parody can be a form of literary criticism that exposes defects in a work, or it can function as an acknowledgement of a work's cultural and literary importance.

Patois A regional dialect of a language.

Peloponnesian War (431–404 B.C.E.) War between the Athenian and Spartan alliance systems that encompassed most of the Greek world. The war set new standards for warfare—Athens used the navy to support the land offensive, for instance—but the new tactics also prolonged the fight; instead of there being one decisive battle, the war dragged on for three decades. Eventually, Athens was defeated, and Sparta took over the defeated power's overseas empire.

Persian Wars A series of wars between a coalition of Greek city-states and the Persian empire fought between 500 and 449 B.C.E.; the Greek victory set the stage for the flourishing of Greek culture.

Persona Literally, a persona is a mask. In literature, a persona is a speaker created by a writer to tell a story or to speak in a poem. A persona is not a character in a story or narrative, nor does a persona necessarily directly reflect the author's personal voice. A persona is a separate self, created by and distinct from the author, through which he or she speaks.

Personification A figure of speech in which abstractions or inanimate objects are given human qualities or form.

Picaresque Term used to describe a novel that is loosely structured around a succession of episodes that focus on a rather thinly drawn *picaro,* or hero. The hero's adventures generally provide a sweeping and detailed view of a society and its customs, which are often satirized by the writer. Examples include Cervantes's *Don Quixote* and Voltaire's *Candide.*

Picture poem A poem whose lines form the image of the object it describes.

Plot The pattern of events or the story told in a narrative or drama.

Point of view The perspective from which the author, SPEAKER, or NARRATOR presents a story. A point of view might be localized within a CHARACTER, in which case the story is told from a first-person point of view. There is a range of possibilities between first-person point of view and omniscience, wherein the story is told from a perspective unlimited by time, place, or character.

Polis Greek term meaning "city"; designates the Greek city-states, such as Athens and Sparta, that arose in the sixth century B.C.E.

Postcolonial criticism Literary analysis of works produced in countries such as India, Africa, and the Caribbean that were once under the control of a colonial power. In some cases the term refers to the analysis of works about the colony written by authors who have been heavily influenced by the colonizing culture.

Postcolonialism The social, political, cultural, and economic practices that arose in response and resistance to colonialism and imperialism. This term also refers to the historical period following the colonial era, corresponding roughly to the second half of the twentieth century.

Postmodernism A literary and artistic movement that flourished in the late twentieth century as both a departure from and a development of MODERNISM. Postmodernism is frequently characterized by self-consciousness and self-reflexiveness: Postmodern literature is aware of the way it operates in a long literary tradition and responds to this awareness by revealing or referring to itself. Postmodern literature differs from modern literature in its emphasis on surface rather than depth, humor rather than psychological anguish, and space rather than time.

Pragmatism A philosophical approach that explains meaning and truth in terms of the application of ideas and beliefs to practical action.

Pre-Raphaelites A group of artists and writers, including John Everett Millais (1829–1896),

Dante Gabriel Rossetti (1828–1882), and William Holman Hunt (1827–1910), who rebelled against convention in poetry and painting by means of a strict adherence to details of nature; they aimed to capture what they perceived to be the truth, simplicity, and clarity of medieval painting—its pure colors, spiritual or mystical ambience, and sensuousness.

Problem play A drama in which the conflict arises from contemporary social problems. Bernard Shaw's *Mrs. Warren's Profession* (1893) and Shakespeare's *All's Well That Ends Well* (1602–04) are problem plays.

Proletariat The modern industrial working class, which, as defined by Karl Marx, lives solely by the sale of its labor. See also BOURGEOISIE.

Prologue Text that typically is placed prior to an introduction or that replaces a traditional introduction; often discusses events of importance for the general understanding of the narrative.

Prose poem A poem printed as prose without attention to line breaks. The prose poem argues for the flexibility of poetry by eschewing strict attention to METER and even RHYTHM, yet the language of a prose poem is frequently figurative and characterized by other poetic conventions such as ALLITERATION or internal rhyme.

Protagonist A leading figure or the main character in a drama or other literary work.

Protestant work ethic German sociologist Max Weber (1864–1920) first linked Protestantism to the habits of diligence and hard work that contributed to the rise of capitalism. The Puritans, whose form of Protestantism influenced early American life, interpreted prosperity resulting from work as a sign of God's favor.

Psychological criticism An approach to literature that draws on psychoanalytic theories, especially those of Sigmund Freud (1856–1939) and Jacques Lacan (1901–1981), to understand more fully the text, the writer, and the reader.

Pun A play on words that relies on a word's having more than one meaning or sounding like another word.

Purdah Practice adopted by some Muslims and Hindus that obscures women from public sight by mandating that they wear concealing clothing, especially veils. The custom originated in the seventh century C.E. and is still common in Islamic countries, though it has largely disappeared in Hinduism.

Qing dynasty (1644–1911) Also known as the Manchu dynasty, named after the MANCHU, a people from the north of China who took over China in 1644 with the help of rebel Chinese; the last dynasty in Chinese history, the Qing saw an increase in the influence of foreign interests and trade.

Quatrain A stanza of four lines in a poem.

Qur'an Or Koran; the sacred scriptures of Islam.

Rahab A term appearing several times in the Hebrew Scriptures; literally means "stormer," an allusion to the ancient monster of chaos in earlier Semitic creation myths. See also LEVIATHAN.

Rastafarianism An African-influenced religion that originated in the Caribbean in the twentieth century; venerates the former emperor of Ethiopia, Haile Selassie, forbids the cutting of hair, and embraces black culture and identity.

Rationalist Utilitarianism Revolutionary way of thinking established by, among others, Leon Trotsky (1879–1940). The Rationalist Utilitarians adopted the ethical theory proposed by John Stuart Mill (1806–1873) that all political actions should be directed toward achieving the greatest good for the greatest number of people. Mill, however, believed that decisions based on direct observation should determine action, while the Rationalist Utilitarians held that logical reasoning should play that role.

Reader-response criticism A critical approach to literature in which the primary focus falls on the reader, or the process of reading, not on the author. Reader-response critics believe that a literary work does not possess a fixed idea or meaning; meaning is a function of the perspective of the reader.

Realism Most broadly defined, realism is the attempt to represent the world accurately in literature. As a literary movement, Realism flourished in Russia, France, England, and America in the latter half of the nineteenth century. It emphasized not only accurate representation but the "truth," usually expressed as the consequence of a moral choice. Realist writers deemphasized the shaping power of the imagination and concerned themselves with the experiences of ordinary, middle-class subjects and the dilemmas they faced.

Recognition Based on the Greek concept of tragedy, recognition, or *anagnorisis,* is the point in a story when the PROTAGONIST discovers the truth about his or her situation. Usually this results in a drastic change in the course of the plot.

Reformation Also known as the Protestant Reformation, this sixteenth-century challenge to the authority of the Catholic Church caused a permanent rift in the Christian world, with those loyal to the pope remaining Catholic and those rejecting papal authority forming new Protestant faiths such as the Anglican, Lutheran, Calvinist, Anabaptist, and Presbyterian. The Reformation originated — and was most successful — in Northern Europe, especially Germany; its notable leaders include Martin Luther and John Calvin.

Renaissance man A term used to describe someone accomplished in many disciplines, especially in both science and the arts, like Leonardo da Vinci and other figures from the European Renaissance who were talented in many fields.

Renaissance sonneteers Poets of the European Renaissance who wrote fourteen-line love poems, often addressed to lovers who resisted or ignored their entreaties. Two types of Renaissance sonnets are commonly identified, the Italian and the English. These are alternatively known as the Petrarchan, after the Italian poet Petrarch who originated the form, and the Shakespearean, after the form's preeminent English practitioner. The major difference between the two types is that the Italian usually has five rhymes and the English seven.

Renga A form of traditional Japanese court poetry that uses elevated diction and links a number of haiku-like poems. Usually written by two or more poets who alternate verses, the traditional *renga* is a succession of three- and two-line compositions that evokes a particular season in each verse.

Resolution The point in the plot of a narrative work or drama that occurs after the climax and generally establishes a new understanding; also known as *falling action.*

Reversal The point in the plot of a story or drama when the fortunes of the PROTAGONIST change unexpectedly; also known as the *peripiteia.*

Revolution of 1830 In July 1830, the opponents of King Charles X (r. 1818–24) took to the streets of Paris to protest his corruption and the undermining of liberal reforms. Charles abdicated the throne, and bankers and industrialists brought in King Louis-Philippe (r. 1830–48), who promised to uphold the reforms Charles had tried to dissolve.

Revolution of 1848 Often called the February Revolution, when French king Louis-Philippe (r. 1830–48) was overthrown and the Second Republic was established. This revolution inspired uprisings in many European countries.

Rhyme The repetition of identical or similar-sounding words or syllables, usually accented, in lines of poetry. Rhymes may be at the end of lines or internal to the lines.

Rhythm The pattern of stressed and unstressed syllables in prose and especially in poetry that can lend emphasis, reinforce a sound association, or suggest regularity or recurrence. The rhythm of a literary work can affect the emotional response of the reader or listener.

Romantic hero The PROTAGONIST of a romance, novel, or poem who is shaped by experiences that frequently take the form of combat, love, or adventure. The romantic hero is judged by his actions more than his thoughts, and he is often on a journey that will affect his moral development.

Romanticism A literary and artistic movement that swept through Europe in the early nineteenth century; its defiance of neoclassical principles and rationalism roughly parallels the political upheaval of the French Revolution, with which it is often associated. Romanticism in its simplest form exalts nature, the innocence of children and rustics, private emotion and experience, and the pursuit of political freedom and spiritual transcendence.

Rosetta stone A slab of basalt inscribed with texts in hieroglyphic, demotic, and Greek. Found by Napoleon's troops in Northern Egypt in 1799, it enabled Egyptologist J.-F. Champollion (1790–1832) to decipher Egyptian hieroglyphics for the first time (1821).

Russo-Japanese War (1904–1905) Russia's aggressive Far-Eastern policy following the SINO-JAPANESE WAR (1894–95) and the Russian construction of a railway across Manchuria resulted in increasing animosity between the two nations. Russia twice violated the treaty with China and lost the year-long war with Japan, destabilizing Russian power in the region.

Salamis Site of an important naval battle where the Greek fleet defeated the Persians in 480 B.C.E.

Samian War The Samian War (441–439 B.C.E.) was fought to bring the island of Samos—which had broken off from the league of Greek states led by Athens—back into the alliance and into compliance with Athenian hegemony.

Samisen A three-stringed instrument with a long fretless neck and a nearly square sound box introduced in Japan in the late sixteenth century; the samisen became the preferred instrument for accompanying the narration of JORURI.

Samsara A HINDU term for the cycle of birth, life, and death, and rebirth; many Hindu practices aimed at obtaining release, *moksa*, from the otherwise endless repetition of life and death.

Samurai Japanese feudal aristocrat and member of the hereditary warrior class. Denied recognition in the MEIJI RESTORATION (1867).

Sanskrit The classical language of ancient India, in which many of the major HINDU religious and literary texts were written.

Satire A literary or dramatic genre whose works, such as Jonathan Swift's (1667–1745) *Gulliver's Travels,* attack and ridicule human behavior.

Scansion A system of poetic analysis that involves dividing lines into feet and examining patterns of stressed and unstressed syllables. Scansion is a mechanical way of breaking down verse in order to understand the regularities and irregularities of its METER.

Scene In drama, a subdivision of an ACT.

Script The written version or text of a play or movie that is used by the actors.

Sentimentality Extravagant emotion; T. S. Eliot defined this as "emotion in excess of the facts."

Sepoy The name given to Indians serving in the British army.

Sepoy Mutiny A rebellion in southern India in 1857 started by local Sepoys in reaction to regulations that violated their religion. The rebellion ended in 1858 after the British army intervened.

Sestet A STANZA of six lines; the last stanza of a Petrarchan SONNET is a sestet.

Setting The time, place, and social environment that frame the characters in a story.

Shinju play A play culminating in suicide; one of three major types of JORURI plays. The others are the *jidaimono,* or history play, and the *sewamono,* a play about contemporary domestic life. Some critics see the *shinju* play as a type of *sewamono.*

Shogun A military ruler of feudal Japan between 1192 and 1867. The shogunate was an inherited position in the military that operated under the nominal control of the emperor.

Simile A figure of speech, introduced by *like* or *as,* in which two things are compared as equals.

Sino-Japanese War (1894–1895) A conflict between Japan and China that revealed the weakness of the declining Chinese empire and the emerging strength of Japan. The war, which developed from a conflict over the control of Korea, culminated in Japan's victory: China recognized the independence of Korea, ceded Taiwan, and lifted trade restrictions with Japan.

Slave narrative Autobiographical narrative by a former slave describing his or her life and mistreatment under slavery, attempts to escape, and ultimate liberation. The narratives, which employed many devices from popular fiction, were accompanied by testimonials to their authenticity.

Slavophile Literally, someone who admires Slavs, a people of Eastern Europe. In nineteenth-century Russia, the term referred to someone who believed in the national traditions of Russia, who felt that Russia had the true religion, and who believed he or she was destined to export Russian teachings and establish the kingdom of God on earth.

Social Realism A type of realism that concentrates on the unpleasant realities of the modern world and attempts to expose injustice and to encourage political reaction.

Socialist Realism A standard for art and literature developed in the Soviet Union in the 1930s; it demanded that art depict the life of the people realistically and celebrate the ideals of the revolution. Mao Zedong (1893–1976) enforced similar standards in China after the People's Republic was established in 1949.

Sociological criticism School of literary criticism that seeks to place a work of art in its social context and define the relationship between the two. Like Marxist critics, sociological critics are oriented toward social class, political ideology, gender roles, and economic conditions in their analyses.

Soliloquy A literary or dramatic discourse in which a character speaks without addressing a listener.

Sonnet A fourteen-line LYRIC poem. The first basic sonnet form is the Italian or Petrarchan sonnet, which is divided into an eight-line octet and a six-line SESTET, each with a specific but varied rhyme pattern. The English or Shakespearean sonnet is divided into three four-line QUATRAINS followed by a two-line COUPLET; the quatrains are rhymed *abab cdcd efef* and the couplet is also end rhymed, *gg*.

Sophists Literally, wise men. Greek teachers who provided instruction in logic and rhetoric to pupils who could afford their expensive fees. Rhetoric was a new discipline whose study was observed to provide an advantage in politics and in the courts. Soon *Sophist* came to mean one who used methods of argumentation that undermined traditional beliefs and manipulated reality. When Socrates (c. 470–399 B.C.E.) challenged the authority of the Sophists, he was brought to trial and executed.

Spanish civil war (1936–39) War between the Falange Fascist Party led by General Francisco Franco and liberal republican loyalist forces; often seen as the staging ground for World War II. The war ended with republican defeat and the establishment of a right-wing dictatorship.

Speaker The person or PERSONA who speaks in a poem—often a created identity who cannot be equated with the poet.

Spiritual autobiography An autobiography that gives special importance to self-examination, interpretation of Scripture, and belief in predestination. St. Augustine's *Confessions* (c. 400), detailing a life of sin, conversion, and spiritual rebirth, is generally regarded as the archetypal spiritual autobiography.

St. Augustine (354–430) Influential Catholic theologian from North Africa whose *Confessions* (c. 400) tells the story of his conversion to Christianity.

St. Francis (c. 1181–1226) Founder of the Franciscan religious order; known for his kindness.

Stage directions Written directions explaining how actors are to move onstage. See also SCRIPT.

Stanza A poetic verse of two or more lines, sometimes characterized by a common pattern of RHYME and METER.

Stock responses Predictable responses to language and symbols. See also CLICHÉ.

Stream of consciousness A term first used by the American philosopher and psychologist William James (1842–1910) to denote the often disjointed and even incoherent flow of ideas, sensations, thoughts, and images running through the conscious mind at any given moment. In literature, "stream of consciousness" generally refers to novels or short stories that attempt to achieve psychological realism by depicting the raw, unedited contents of a character's mind. Such depictions may involve "interior monologues" wherein an author presents a character's thoughts either with (indirect) or without (direct) any commentary, ordering, or editing. This device, associated with high modernism, reached its height in the work of James Joyce.

Stress A syllable receiving emphasis in accordance with a metrical pattern.

Sturm und Drang Literally, "storm and stress." Refers to a period of intense literary activity in the late eighteenth century associated with Idealism and the revolt against stale convention. The movement was named after a play about the American Revolution, and its leading participants included Goethe (1749–1832) and Schiller (1759–1805).

Style The distinctive manner in which an author writes and thus makes his or her work unique. A style provides a kind of literary signature for the writer.

Subplot A PLOT subordinate to the main plot of a literary work or drama.

Superman Also called "overman," or *Übermensch* in German. A term introduced by the German philosopher Friedrich Nietzsche (1844–1900) to denote a superior man who would exercise creative power and live at a level of experience beyond the standards of good and evil and thus represent the goal of human evolution.

Surrealism An aesthetic movement centered in twentieth-century France that extolled the direct and free expression of the unconscious as understood by Freudian psychology; proponents of surrealism include the writer André Breton (1896–1966), who wrote *Manifesto of Surrealism* in 1924; the filmmaker Jean Cocteau (1889–1963); and the painters Salvador Dalí (1904–1989) from France and Joan Miró (1893–1983) from Spain. A combination of precise, realistic detail and dreamlike fantasy characterizes surrealism.

Suspense The anxious emotion of the audience or reader anticipating the outcome of a story or drama, typically having to do with the fate of the PROTAGONIST or another character with whom a sympathetic attachment has been formed.

Symbol A representative of something by association. Though a symbol is often confused with a metaphor, a metaphor compares two dissimilar things while a symbol associates two things. For example, the *word* "tree" is a symbol for an *actual* tree. Some symbols have values that are accepted by most people. A flag, for instance, is for many a symbol of national pride, just as a cross is widely seen as a symbol of Christianity. Knowledge of a symbol's cultural context is sometimes necessary to understand its meaning; an apple pie is an American symbol of innocence that a Japanese person, for example, would not necessarily recognize.

Symbolism As the French writer Paul Valéry (1871–1945) notes in *The Existence of Symbolism* (1939), Symbolism "was not a school. On the contrary, it included many schools of the most divergent types." Symbolism generally refers to a movement among poets in France anticipated in the work of Charles Baudelaire (1821–1867) and Arthur Rimbaud (1854–1891) but practiced as a self-conscious movement by Stéphane Mallarmé (1842–1898), Paul Verlaine (1844–1896), and Jules Laforgue (1860–1887). Symbolists sought to convey the fluidity and evocative harmony of music in their work, and to capture tones, fragrances, sensations, and intuitions rather than concrete images or rational ideas.

Syncretism The attempt to combine differing beliefs, such as philosophy and religion, or two religious systems, such as Christianity and a native African tradition.

Syntax The way parts of speech are arranged in a sentence.

Tantrism A minor HINDU tradition written down in scriptures called Tantras. Tantrism holds the supreme deity to be feminine and teaches that spiritual liberation can be won through erotic practices.

Terza rima A verse form composed of iambic three-line STANZAS. The triplets have ten- or eleven-syllable lines. Terza rima is used to perhaps its most brilliant end in Dante's (1265–1321) *Divine Comedy.*

Tetragrammaton The four consonants of the Hebrew alphabet YHWH used to approximate God's secret name; this name and its utterances are believed to contain special powers.

Thanatos "Death" in Greek. According to Sigmund Freud, our two primary drives are EROS (love) and Thanatos (death).

Theater of the absurd A school of modernist, non-realistic drama especially influential from the 1950s to the '70s. Italian playwright Eugene Ionesco described its subject matter as "man . . . lost in the world, [so] all his actions become senseless, absurd, useless."

Theme A topic of discussion or a point of view embodied in a work of art.

Theosophical Society Founded in 1875 in London by Helena Petrovna Blavatsky in order to promote the reconciliation of Eastern religious doctrines with Western mysticism. Blavatsky, who wrote *Isis Unveiled* (1877) and faced charges of charlatanism, believed in the spiritual nature of things, the reincarnation of the soul, and the power of grasping one's spiritual essence, particularly by means of mystical experience.

Thesis The presentation of a purpose or hypothetical proposition, or a dissertation with an original point based on research.

Tokugawa era (1600–1868) Period of Japanese history named after Tokugawa Ieyasu (1542–1616), who was named shogun in 1603; also known as the EDO era because Tokugawa made Edo (now Tokyo) the capital. The early Tokugawa was a period of international isolation, political stability, nation building, and prosperity for the middle classes; it was also a time of great literary and cultural growth, particularly in the popular cultural forms such as KABUKI and JORURI (puppet) theater, the popular novel, and colored woodblock art, all aimed at the flourishing middle classes.

The Tokugawa era ended in 1867 when a group of disaffected SAMURAI restored imperial rule under the teenage emperor Meiji (r. 1867–1912) in the MEIJI RESTORATION and opened Japan's doors to Western trade and cultural exchange.

Tone A manner of expression in writing that indicates a certain attitude toward the subject or the implied audience.

Totalitarianism A system of centralized government in which a single unopposed party exerts total and repressive control over a country's political, social, economic, and cultural life.

Tragedy A dramatic or literary form originating in Greece that deals with serious human actions and issues. The actions must create feelings of fear and compassion in the spectator that are later released (CATHARSIS). Typically, the main character is of a high stature or rank, so his or her fall is substantial. Even though tragedies are sad, they seem both just and believable. The tragedy raises serious moral and philosophical questions about the meaning of life and fate.

Tragicomedy A drama that combines tragedy and comedy and in which moral values are particularly questioned or ridiculed.

Transcendentalism A philosophy derived from ROMANTICISM that flourished in the United States in the early nineteenth century. American writers Ralph Waldo Emerson and Henry David Thoreau championed and articulated the philosophy, which contends that the individual mind has the capability to transcend the human institutions that seek to fetter it. The transcendentalists believed that the most valuable pursuit was to experience, reflect upon, and study nature and its relation to the individual.

Travel narratives A form of narrative that recounts the incidents that occur and the people and things that the narrator meets and sees while visiting a place with which she or he is typically unfamiliar. Prose and poetic accounts about exploration and adventure in unfamiliar lands and places as well as in more or less familiar locations are considered travel narratives. Such narratives typically are told episodically and chronologically, engage in elaborate strategies to validate their authenticity, and raise important and complex questions about the representation of the "other" — that is, the ability of the traveler to depict accurately the people, places, and cultures he or she is describing.

Triplet In poetry, a group of three lines of verse.

Ukiyo-e A school of Japanese woodblock printing arising in the EDO period that captured images of everyday life in the FLOATING WORLD (*ukiyo*). The greatest *ukiyo-e* artists include Moronobu (c. 1618–c. 1694), Harunobu (1725–1770), and Hiroshige (1797–1858).

Ukiyo-zoshi "Stories of the FLOATING WORLD" or "tales of the floating world"; a Japanese style of fiction associated with the hundred-year period from about 1683 to 1783 that took as its subject matter the everyday lives of *chonin*, or townspeople, and was written in colloquial language. Ihara Saikaku is said to be the originator of *ukiyo-zoshi*; many authors in this tradition not only imitated his style but plagiarized his works.

Ultraists A group of Spanish writers who influenced Jorge Luis Borges. The Ultraists rejected middle-class materialism and sought refuge in the artifice of poetry and in exotic images and metaphors.

Understatement A figure of speech that says less than what is intended.

Upanishads A body of sacred texts dating from the seventh century B.C.E. that provide a mystical development of and commentary on earlier Vedic texts.

Urdu An Indo-European language closely related to Hindi. Urdu is the official language of Pakistan and is also spoken in India and Bangladesh.

Utilitarianism An ethical tradition dating from the late eighteenth century that assumes an action is right if it promotes happiness of both the agent and those affected by the act. Judgments of right and wrong depend upon the consequence of an action rather than strictly on motives.

Vedas The earliest Indian sacred texts, written in SANSKRIT, dating from sometime between 1000 and 500 B.C.E.; they contain hymns and ritual lore considered to be revelation, or *sruti*.

Verisimo Italian school of literary Realism influenced by Gustave Flaubert and Émile Zola.

Vernacular fiction Fiction that attempts to capture accurately the typical speech, mannerisms, or dialect of region. *The Satyricon* of the Roman author Petronius is often considered the first work of vernacular fiction.

Verse Poetic writing arranged according to a metrical pattern and composed of a varied number of lines.

Victorian In English history, *Victorian* refers to the age of Queen Victoria (1837–1901) and the values of respectability, social conservatism, and sexual repression characteristic of that time.

Villanelle Originally a complicated French verse form that appeared in English in the 1800s. The villanelle is a nineteen-line poem of five tercets (three-line STANZAS) and a final two-rhyme QUATRAIN. The first and third line of the first tercet repeat alternately, closing the succeeding stanzas.

Wampanoag One of several Algonquin peoples residing in New England in the seventeenth century. Their territory extended from Narragansett Bay to Cape Cod.

Well-made play The plays of Augustin Eugène Scribe (1791–1861) and those of his followers, whose popular comedies were especially in vogue during the second half of the nineteenth century, established the rules for the "well-made play." The well-made play was carefully constructed around a single situation that built scene by scene to a climactic revelation. The situation usually involved a misunderstanding, a secret, or a suppressed document that, when discovered, prompted a REVERSAL and a DENOUEMENT. The dialogue was colloquial and realistic, and the subject matter commonplace and trivial. The well-made play was intended to amuse, not instruct.

Weltliteratur Term coined by Goethe for works of literature that transcend local and national concerns to treat universal human themes.

Yin and yang A pair of opposites derived from a dualistic system of ancient Chinese philosophy; symbolically representing the sun and the moon, *yang* is positive, active, and strong, while *yin* is negative, passive, and weak. All things in the universe are formed from the dynamic interaction of these forces.

Yomihon A serious, often didactic "reading book," as opposed to a picture book. This GENRE, popular in the early nineteenth century, often presented historical romances influenced by classic Chinese fiction.

Zen A prominent school of Buddhism that seeks to reveal the essence of the enlightened mind. Zen teaches that everyone has the potential to attain enlightenment but that most are unaware of this potential because they are ignorant. The way to attain enlightenment is through transcending the boundaries of common thought, and the method of study is most frequently the intense, personal instruction of a student by a Zen master.

Acknowledgments (continued from p. iv)

Baien Miura, excerpt from "Reply to Taga Bokkei," from *Deep Words: Miura Baien's System of Natural Philosophy,* translated by Rosemary Mercer. Reprinted with the permission of E. J. Brill Publishers, Leiden, The Netherlands.

Cao Xueqin and Gao E, excerpts from *The Story of the Stone,* translated by David Hawkes and John Minford. Copyright © 1973 by David Hawkes. Reprinted with the permission of Penguin Books, Ltd.

Chikamatsu Monzaemon, "The Love Suicides at Amijima," from *Major Plays of Chikamatsu,* translated by Donald Keene. Copyright © 1961 Columbia University Press. Reprinted with the permission of the publisher.

René Descartes, excerpt from *Discourse on Method,* from *The Philosophical Works of Descartes, Volume 1,* translated by Elizabeth S. Haldane and G. R. T. Ross. Reprinted with the permission of Cambridge University Press.

Denis Diderot, "Supplement to Bougainville's Voyage," from *Diderot: Interpreter of Nature,* Second Edition, translated by Jean Stewart and Jonathan Kemp (New York: International Publishers, 1963). Reprinted with the permission of International Publishers.

Olympe de Gouges, Declaration of the Rights of Woman, from *Women in Revolutionary Paris, 1789–1795,* translated with notes and commentary by Darlene Gay Levy, Harriet Branson Applewhite, and Mary Durham Johnson. Copyright © 1979 by the Board of Trustees of the University of Illinois. Reprinted with the permission of the editors and the University of Illinois Press.

Marie le Jars de Gournay, "On the Equality of Men and Women," translated by Patricia Clark Smith. Reprinted with the permission of the translator.

Ihara Saikaku, "What the Seasons Brought to the Almanac Maker," from *Five Women Who Loved Love,* translated by William Theodore de Bary. Reprinted with the permission of Charles E. Tuttle Co., Inc., Boston and Tokyo.

Gottfried Wilhelm Leibniz, "Supplement to Theodicy," from *Leibniz Selections,* translated by George M. Duncan, with revisions by Philip P. Wiener. Copyright 1951 and renewed © 1979 by Charles Scribner's Sons. Reprinted with the permission of Pearson Education, Inc., Upper Saddle River, NJ.

Jean-Baptiste Poquelin Molière, *"Tartuffe" by Molière,* translated by Richard Wilbur. Copyright © 1961, 1962, 1963 and renewed 1989, 1990, 1991 by Richard Wilbur. Reprinted with the permission of Harcourt, Inc. CAUTION: Professionals and amateurs are hereby warned that this translation, being fully protected under the laws of the United States of America, the British Commonwealth, including the Dominion of Canada, and all other countries which are signatories to the Universal Copyright Convention and the International Copyright Union, is subject to royalty. All rights, including professional, amateur, motion picture, recitation, lecturing, public reading, radio broadcasting, and television, are strictly reserved. Particular emphasis is laid on the question of readings, permission for which must be secured from the author's agent in writing. Inquiries on professional rights (except for amateur rights) should be addressed to Curtis Brown, Ltd., 10 Astor Place, New York, NY 10003; inquiries on translation rights should be addressed to Harcourt Inc., Permissions Department, Orlando, FL 32887. The amateur acting rights of *Tartuffe* are controlled exclusively by the Dramatists Play Service, Inc., 440 Park Avenue South, New York, NY 10016. No amateur performance of the play may be given without obtaining in advance the written permission of the Dramatists Play Service Inc. and paying the requisite fee.

Sir Isaac Newton, "Preface to the First Edition," from *Mathematical Principles of Natural Philosophy,* edited by Florian Cajori, translated from the Latin by Andrew Motte. Copyright 1934, ©1962 by the Regents of the University of California. Reprinted with the permission of University of California Press.

Pu Song-Ling, "The Mural," translated by Denis C. Mair and Victor H. Mair, from *The Columbia Anthology of Traditional Chinese Literature,* edited by Victor H. Mair. Copyright © 1994 by Columbia University Press. Reprinted with the permission of the publisher. "The Wise Neighbor," from *The Golden Casket: Chinese Novellas of the Two Millennia,* translated by Christopher Levenson. Copyright © 1964, renewed 1992 by Harcourt, Inc. Reprinted with the permission of the publisher.

Ramprasad, selections from *Grace and Mercy in Her Wild Hair: Selected Poems to the Mother Goddess,* translated by Leonard Nathan and Clinton Seely. Reprinted with the permission of Hohn Press.

Jean-Jacques Rousseau, excerpt from *The Social Contract,* translated by G. D. H. Cole. Copyright 1950 by G. D. H. Cole. Excerpt from *Émile,* translated by Barbara Foxley. Copyright 1933 by Barbara Foxley. Both reprinted with the permission of Dent.

Shen Fu, "The Joys of the Wedding Chamber," from *Six Chapters of a Floating Life,* translated by Leonard Pratt and Chiang Su-hui. Copyright © 1983 by Leonard Pratt and Chiang Su-hui. Reprinted with the permission of Penguin Books, Ltd.

François-Marie Arouet de Voltaire, *Candide, or Optimism,* translated and edited by Daniel Gordon. Copyright ©

1998 by St. Martin's Press. Reprinted with the permission of Bedford / St. Martin's Press.

Image Credits

Page 1: The Art Archive / Dagli Orti
Page 13: The Courtauld Institute Gallery, Somerset House, London
Page 16: (c) Kathleen Cohen
Page 17: Giraudon / Art Resource, NY
Page 23: Snark / Art Resource, NY
Page 88: The Huntington Library / Superstock
Page 92: The Huntington Library / Superstock
Page 144: Courtesy of the Trustees of the Boston Public Library
Page 150: Courtesy of the Trustees of the Boston Public Library
Page 153: Courtesy of the Trustees of the Boston Public Library
Page 200: Yale Center for British Art, Paul Mellon Collection
Page 204: Private Collection / The Stapleton Collection / Bridgeman Art Library
Page 219: Courtesy of the Trustees of the Boston Public Library
Page 236: Courtesy of the Trustees of the Boston Public Library
Page 269: Réunion de Musées Nationaux / Art Resource, NY
Page 271: The Metropolitan Museum of Art, The Jules Bache Collection, 1949. All Rights Reserved, The Metropolitan Museum of Art
Page 340: Private Collection / Bridgeman Art Library
Page 341: Private Collection / Bridgeman Art Library
Page 342: Musée de l'Air et de l'Espace, Le Bourget, France / Lauros-Giraudon-Bridgeman Art Library
Page 343: Mary Evans Picture Library
Page 345: Freer Gallery of Art, Smithsonian Institution, Washington, D.C.: Purchase F1981.30
Page 347: Copyright Image Select / Art Resource, NY
Page 353: Tate Gallery, London / Art Resource, NY
Page 367: Giraudon / Art Resource, NY
Page 401: Courtesy of the American Antiquarian Society, Worcester, MA
Page 402: Courtesy of the American Antiquarian Society, Worcester, MA

Page 474: The Art Archive
Page 476: Courtesy of the American Antiquarian Society, Worcester, MA
Page 478: Courtesy of the American Antiquarian Society, Worcester, MA
Page 481: Courtesy of the Trustees of the Boston Public Library
Page 517: National Portrait Gallery, Smithsonian Institution / Art Resource, NY
Page 518: Courtesy of the American Antiquarian Society, Worcester, MA
Page 557: The Pierpont Morgan Library / Art Resource, NY
Page 561: Courtesy of the National Archives
Page 565: Musée de la Ville de Paris, Musée Carnavalet, Paris, France, Giraudon / Art Resource, NY
Page 569: Art Resource, NY
Page 603: Musée de la Ville de Paris, Musée Carnavalet, Paris, Giraudon / Art Resource, NY
Page 608: The Art Archive
Page 610: Courtesy of the British Museum
Page 611: Courtesy of the British Museum
Page 613: Courtesy of the British Museum
Page 627: The Art Institute of Chicago
Page 629: The Art Archive / Eileen Tweedy
Page 650: Itsuo Museum, Osaka
Page 687: Freer Gallery of Art, Smithsonian Institution, Washington, D.C.: Gift of Victor and Takako Hauge
Page 720: The Art Archive / Marco Polo Gallery Paris / Dagli Orti (A)
Page 721: Erich Lessing / Art Resource, NY
Page 723: Claydon House, Buckinghamshire, UK / National Trust Photographic Library / John Hammond / Bridgeman Art Library
Page 725: The Japan Ukiyoe Museum
Page 729: Photograph (c) Copyright Fitzwilliam Museum, University of Cambridge
Page 746: Tate Gallery, London / Art Resource
Page 767: Courtesy of the Museum of Fine Arts, Boston. Reproduced with permission. © Museum of Fine Arts, Boston. All Rights Reserved.
Page 768: Laurie Platt Winfrey
Page 771: The Art Archive / Bibliothèque Nationale, Paris
Page 773: University of Wisconsin–Madison / Library